The Ideological Condition

Historical Materialism Book Series

The Historical Materialism Book Series is a major publishing initiative of the radical left. The capitalist crisis of the twenty-first century has been met by a resurgence of interest in critical Marxist theory. At the same time, the publishing institutions committed to Marxism have contracted markedly since the high point of the 1970s. The Historical Materialism Book Series is dedicated to addressing this situation by making available important works of Marxist theory. The aim of the series is to publish important theoretical contributions as the basis for vigorous intellectual debate and exchange on the left.

The peer-reviewed series publishes original monographs, translated texts, and reprints of classics across the bounds of academic disciplinary agendas and across the divisions of the left. The series is particularly concerned to encourage the internationalization of Marxist debate and aims to translate significant studies from beyond the English-speaking world.

For a full list of titles in the Historical Materialism Book Series
available in paperback from Haymarket Books, visit:
https://www.haymarketbooks.org/series_collections/1-historical-materialism

The Ideological Condition

Selected Essays on History, Race and Gender

Himani Bannerji

Haymarket Books
Chicago, IL

First published in 2020 by Brill Academic Publishers, The Netherlands
© 2020 Koninklijke Brill NV, Leiden, The Netherlands

Published in paperback in 2021 by
Haymarket Books
P.O. Box 180165
Chicago, IL 60618
773-583-7884
www.haymarketbooks.org

ISBN: 978-1-64259-593-2

Distributed to the trade in the US through Consortium Book Sales and
Distribution (www.cbsd.com) and internationally through Ingram
Publisher Services International (www.ingramcontent.com).

This book was published with the generous support of Lannan
Foundation and Wallace Action Fund.

Special discounts are available for bulk purchases by organizations and
institutions. Please call 773-583-7884 or email info@haymarketbooks.org
for more information.

Cover art and design by David Mabb. Cover art is a detail of *Long Live
the New! no. 22*, Kazimir Malevich drawing on Morris & Co. design, paint
and wallpaper on canvas (2016).

Printed in the United States.

10 9 8 7 6 5 4 3 2 1

Library of Congress Cataloging-in-Publication data is available.

for Michael Kuttner
who has been with me for the entire period of writing these essays
and living the life from which they came

Contents

PART 2
The Making of a Subject: Gender, 'Race' and Class

PART 3
Nation, Multiculturalism, Identity and Community

PART 4
Ideology, Nationalism, Gender and Politics

PART 5
Class, Culture and Representation

PART 6
Decolonisation

Foreword

David McNally

Influence comes in a variety of ways. Some of these can make one a 'big name', even if the intellectual effect involved is a mile wide and an inch deep. For several decades, Himani Bannerji has been closer to the opposite end of this spectrum. Her intellectual influence is nowhere near so wide as her theoretical work is deep. But because it eschews superficiality and probes the multidimensionality of experience in capitalist society with exceptional clarity, Bannerji's influence on her readers is profound and sustained. Whatever one thinks of claims for depth psychology, Bannerji's work can be described as a *deep Marxism*.[1]

At the core of Bannerji's project is the development of what she calls an 'anti-racist feminist Marxism'. This is no promotional slogan meant to placate contending intellectual and political constituencies. It is instead a critical programme. Across her books and essays, Bannerji fires off challenges to dominant approaches to feminism and anti-racism, as well as to positivistic Marxism. She has been busy exploding their theoretical categories from the inside in order to reconstruct their objects of study as complex and dynamic relations, each co-constitutive of the other. As she writes in *Thinking Through: Essays on Feminism, Marxism, and Anti-Racism*, critical social theory conducts 'a relational and integrative analysis which needs a deconstructive method to display the process of mediation. It can both take apart and put back together (in a non-aggregative fashion) an event or an experience within a wider context by using a materialist theory of consciousness, culture and politics'.[2] Note two things here.

First, Bannerji opposes aggregative social theory – something which troubles her about intersectional analysis too. Race and class, for example, do not need to be added together because they are already co-constituting relations, each inseparable from the other. Bannerji seeks to disclose the complex ways in which social relations and events are *internally* related. ' "Race"', she writes in a telling formulation, 'cannot be disarticulated from "class" any more than milk

---

1 In this Foreword, I do not provide a biographical sketch of Himani Bannerji's life and intellectual work. For something along these lines, see 'A Conversation between Himani Bannerji and Somdatta Mandal,' published as an appendix to this volume.

2 Himani Bannerji, *Thinking Through: Essays on Feminism, Marxism, and Anti-Racism* (Toronto: Women's Press, 1995), p. 67.

can be separated from coffee once they are mixed, or the body separated from consciousness in a living person'.[3] It follows that there is no class relation that is not simultaneously raced and gendered.

Note, secondly, Bannerji's insistence on the inseparability of 'consciousness, culture and politics'. Politics does not occur in some rarefied sphere of state apparatuses, however much these are part of the field of the political. All politics is lived, reproduced through relations of everyday life. To explore social domination, therefore, is to interrogate how it is formed in a network of social practices. The latter, of course, have cultural registers – and Bannerji is profoundly interested in these. But her orientation eschews *culturalism*, as she calls it – which is preoccupied with signs and discourses unto themselves – in order to ground cultural *production* in the force-fields of domination and resistance. In an approach that has clear affinities with Gramsci, Bannerji reads cultural phenomena as *fields of practice*, implicating the body, language, ideology, identity. And because practical fields are integral systems, multiple relations are lived *together* in an irreducible unity. This is why distinct social relations do not have to combine; they were never disconnected to begin with.

'Non-white and white people living in Canada or the West know', she writes, 'that this social experience is not, as lived, a matter of intersectionality. Their sense of being in the world, textured through myriad social relations and cultural forms, is lived or felt or perceived as being all together and all at once'.[4] It follows that, 'We need to venture into a more complex reading of the social, where every aspect can be shown to reflect others, where every little piece of it contains the macrocosm in the microcosm'.[5] And so, we are operating simultaneously at the 'levels' of 'consciousness, culture and politics', which are, needless to say, not really levels at all, but registers of social experience. I would call this a deeply *dialectical* approach – although this is a term Bannerji tends to avoid – and it is one of the things that accounts for the deep influence she has had on so many of her readers.

As should now be apparent, the concept of depth I deploy here is not archaeological. Bannerji does not subscribe to notions of layered strata, one resting above or below others. Hers is not a theory of levels, but of process and relations. Rather than temporally discrete strata, she shows us churning, volcanic depths where past and future intermingle in dazzlingly complex ways. How else to understand the title of her essay 'Nostalgia for the Future', in which she

---

3   Himani Bannerji, 'Building from Marx: Reflections on Class and Race,' *Social Justice*, 32:4 (2005), p. 149.
4   Bannerji, "Building from Marx," p. 144.
5   Bannerji, "Building from Marx," p. 146.

reflects on the poetry of Ernesto Cardenal. Henri Lefebvre famously insisted that space is hyper-complex. What Bannerji does is to extend this insight to the entire range of human experience.

One of the strikingly innovative things about Bannerji's work is her concern with ideology as *formation*, rather than form; with its *objectification*, as much (or more) than its object. In this respect, her ideology-critique bears resemblances to the ways in which Barbara Fields and Karen Fields have focused on *racecraft* – the actual process of making and reproducing 'race' – over the analysis of a thing called 'racism'.[6] It follows that there is for her nothing merely 'superstructural' about the social relations in which race, gender and class are lived, or in which nationalism and patriarchy are mobilised. It also follows that contexts must be attended to with great care. Bannerji is deeply suspicious of false universalisms that evade the specific textures differentiating life and experience in distinctive locations within global capitalism. Her essays on culture and nation in India and Canada – the two primary nation-state sites of her life and labours – overflow with insights into the particular. This, however, is in the service of a new kind of universalism – one which cannot yet be born – of the sort adumbrated by Frantz Fanon in the concluding chapter of *The Wretched of the Earth*, and which she finds lurking in the poems and writings of Rabindranath Tagore, to which she turns in the essays below. Thus, while attending closely to difference and specificity, Bannerji refuses to join any cults of particularity. The project of human emancipation – at whose heart resides that of decolonisation – remains a universalising one. Yet, universal emancipation cannot be achieved by passing over the differences of race, empire, sexuality, and gender. It involves working through the differences, not past them.

Himani Bannerji has thus placed herself at the centre of attempts to renew historical materialism in ways that might be adequate to our times. Her compelling interventions on nationalism, racism, fascism, and fundamentalism remind us that this is no merely theoretical project, necessary as theoretical analysis and clarification remain. There is an urgency to her essays on genocide and violence against women; there is a commitment to join understanding to the necessity to act. Bannerji's writings in these areas shake up all forms of naturalisation. Like the epic theatre of Bertolt Brecht, to whom she has always been drawn (as readers of her essays on political theatre in West Bengal will recognise), Bannerji de-familiarises. She shows us the making of violence – through patriarchy, cultural nationalism, and empire – in startling new ways.

---

6   Karen E. Fields and Barbara J. Fields, *Racecraft: The Soul of Inequality in American Life* (New York: Verso Books, 2012).

Indeed, whoever seriously engages Bannerji's work finds that they never again think about culture, race, ideology, gender, class, and capitalism in quite the same ways. They discover that their *way of seeing* has subtly shifted. I count myself among this privileged group.

Any reference to ways of seeing surely invokes the work of John Berger, very much a kindred spirit of Bannerji. It also alludes to the enduring influence of feminist 'sociologist' Dorothy Smith on her thinking. Smith was Bannerji's teacher and doctoral supervisor at the University of Toronto from 1980 to 1988, and it is clear that Bannerji's project owes much to her engagement with Smith's research on 'the conceptual practices of power', especially where gender is concerned.[7] From Smith she also absorbed a commitment to developing concepts from practical experience, a sort of allergy to theory as end-in-itself. But from the start of her work with Smith, Bannerji was also interrogating race and its constitution in and through capital and class, while reworking these notions in the process. Bannerji deployed central insights from Smith to develop a more robust historical materialist account of the *production* of ideology. Smith emphasized 'experience' as the ground of all theorising – something she shares with a historian like E.P. Thompson, however much she would have been critical of his inattentiveness to gender – and Bannerji takes this as a point of departure for thinking about ideology. In her work, ideological formations like nationalism and patriarchy are elucidated as social practices, organising relations of ruling *and* laying grounds for resistance.

In the essays collected in this volume, we are treated to a dazzling array of studies on 'the ideological condition' – essays ranging from class subjectivity in nineteenth-century Bengal to official (government-designed) multiculturalism in Canada today, from the critique of sociology to building from Marx an adequate account of race and racial formation. The breadth of these essays is stunning. Even more striking, as I have hinted, is their depth.

As for the title of this volume, *The Ideological Condition: Selected Essays on History, Race and Gender*, Bannerji has written this:

> ... I named the book that because all the texts are engaged in defining 'ideology' in both senses that Marx used the notion. I have stayed close to Marx because I find his way of engaging with ideology in terms of how it is actually produced, his attempt to disclose the very method through

---

7   See especially, Dorothy Smith, *Texts, Facts, and Femininity: Exploring the Relations of Ruling* (London: Routledge, 1990), Smith, *The Conceptual Practices of Power: A Feminist Sociology of Knowledge* (Boston: Northeastern University Press, 1990); and Smith, *Writing the Social: Critique, Theory, and Investigations* (Toronto: University of Toronto Press, 1999).

which just about any common noun or adjective can become ideology – I
mean the three tricks. To my mind this technique of ideology production
has been under-attended.

The other aspect of ideology, namely the content, the specific ruling ideas and their discursive forms, has been mainly how ideology has
been understood. While that is obviously important, I try to figure out
how these ideas came to attain the ideological status and the result their
deployment produced. Their political nature for me includes the notion
of ideology as used by many critics as any set of political ideas and their
relations. I have tried to work out through some critical excursions as well
as applications how to deepen our understanding of what ideology is in
Marx's sense and what it does to our social and political understanding of
the historical and the immediate world we live in and what we could do
about that.[8]

This is, needless to say, no small project. But the attentive reader will soon see
that Bannerji is equal to the task. Bannerji's is a Marxism for our times, one that
deeply engages issues of identity, oppression and decolonisation in terms of
'a materialist theory of consciousness, culture and politics'. Bannerji socialises
elusive concepts like identity, probing their multi-dimensionality, and engaging them from the standpoint of a universalising emancipation. In all these
ways, the essays collected here constitute a major contribution to the renewal
of critical Marxism. I do not exaggerate when I say these essays display intellectual fireworks coupled to what Martin Luther King called 'the fierce urgency of
now'. They are the gifts of a rare critical thinker – guides to undoing our ideological condition the better to remake our world.

---

8   Personal correspondence with this writer, July 2018.

Acknowledgements

These essays cover a long period of time, during which much has happened historically, politically and in critical theorisation. They are moments of my participation in the intellectual struggles, debates and discussions. They amount to crossing disciplinary boundaries to create an adequate historical materialist critique of the socio-political and cultural conjuncture of modes of capital's production and reproduction.

Acknowledgements are not merely a matter of thanking a number of people and institutions. Of course they involve that, but they also have tucked into them relationships, intellectual interchanges, political solidarities and emotional support. A retrospective collection such as this, which ranges through most of my life of growing critical and political awareness, codes a development, aspects of which may even be unknown to me. It involves surprises, as I realise that seeds of my present concerns, modes of query and theoretical frameworks were planted along the way, beginning a long time ago.

To begin with I would like to thank David McNally for making this book possible. His belief in my critical thinking, his sharing of my politics, his unflagging encouragement to bring forward my work into public space, have been the strongest gestures of loving comradery that I have known. I must here also acknowledge my deep gratitude to Dorothy E. Smith, whose feminist reading of Marx, in particular her understanding of his critique of ideology, continues to guide my work to date. Her affectionate encouragement and engagement with the development of my ideas/critical framework has continued to sustain me. The feminist marxism that I embarked on with my reading of Smith deepened with my interest in applying her critique to understanding the role of gender/patriarchy in ideological and social formations in colonial Bengal. In terms of signal influences I must also acknowledge the comradely intellectual exchanges with Philip Corrigan in several areas of my interest, but especially in those of historical sociology and the relations between culture and politics. In this regard I must also remember Ioan Davies (late), who inspired me to delve into the works of Antonio Gramsci and Walter Benjamin.

Because I have lived my adult life in India and Canada, both organised politics of communist parties as well as social movements have provided the content and direction of my critical/political awareness. In India the extensive presence of communist parties and explicitly socialist/communist cultural theorisation and production have honed my understanding, while in Canada and the anglophone world I was more exposed to social movements. I was forced to be cognisant of the constitutive relations of class struggle, feminist and anti-racist movements without prioritising one over the other.

This preamble was necessary because there are far too many people who have nourished me to name them all. But some stand out for their prominent presence in the particular writings that I have produced. In the Indian context, for my PhD research I remain deeply thankful to (the late) Shobha Sen, incontestably the most important woman actor on the stage of twentieth-century Bengali theatre, and (the late) Utpal Dutta, the greatest among theatre personalities in Bengal as playwright, actor, director and theatre critic from the same era. Without their incredible generosity in giving time, providing supporting documents and invitations to rehearsals, I could not have deepened my understanding of the relationship between politics and culture. My strong appreciation must be extended to Arun Mukherjee, the founder, director, dramatist and major actor of Chetana, with whom I spent many exciting hours in rehearsals and discussion on various aspects of political theatre, particularly regarding the question of representation of class. The entire group of Chetana actors at that time must be acknowledged, particularly (the late) Biplabketan Chakrabarty, an inimitable comic actor. Among those who provided me with great insight into the relation between culture and politics, my thanks also go to Manabendra Bandyopadhyay, Shivaji Bandyopadhyay, Mihir and Malini Bhattacharya, Ratnabali and Tirthankar Chattopadhyay, and Suchetana Chattopahdyay, all of whom to this day continue to enliven and enlighten me. Without the indispensable support of (the late) Jasodhara Bagchi, the founder-director of Jadavpur University School of Women's Studies, I would not have critiqued patriarchy and the situation of women in colonial Bengal in the way I do. Amiya Kumar Bagchi, the founder and former director of the Institute of Development Studies Kolkata, with brotherly solidarity and his great scholarship, helped me to cross the boundaries of my literary-aesthetic studies and learn to range in the fields of political economy and economic history. I also want to thank Nirmala Bannerji, of the Indian Centre for Social Sciences Research, a pioneer of feminist development studies. My gratefulness extends to *Sachetana*, one of the earliest feminist activist organisations in India, in which we mutually developed our ways of analysing and challenging patriarchy. I also acknowledge the many intellectual and social interactions with Tanika and Sumit Sarkar, Aijaz Ahmad, and (the late) Jayati Gupta, who provided me with great critical resources and insights in reading marxist and feminist critical theory. They have prominently contributed to my own version of historical materialism. Special thanks are due to Kirti Singh, a leading feminist lawyer and head of the legal cell of the All India Democratic Women's Association, not just for her help in making clear the situation pertaining to Indian women and law, but for generously giving me a space in her family and home.

I deepened my exploration in the making of the consciousness of middle-class women (*bhadramahila*) in bourgeois colonial Bengal by my association with Anna Davin, Sheila Rowbotham and Catherine Hall, among other members of The History Workshop Journal in London. Their writings in women's/feminist history helped me to further define my own feminist historical sociology. I would especially like to acknowledge my debt to (the late) Swasti Mitter, a prominent figure in feminist political economy of gender and labour and women and development, who hosted me and engaged in numerous discussions on women's labour in India.

In Canada I especially want to thank Shahrzad Mojab and Judith Whitehead for their collaborative approach with me and for their friendship. I must also extend heartfelt thanks to Pamela and Keith McCallum, Ato Sekyi-Otu, Nahla Abdo, Ena Dua, Ananya Mukherjee-Reed, Tania Dasgupta, Radhika Mongia, Kanishka Gunewardena, Stefan Kipfer, Brenna Bhandar, Sue Ferguson, Peter Kulchisky, Leslie Roman, Patricia Vertinsky, Raju Das and Robert Latham for their friendship and critical engagement with my work, as well as for providing me with a space to speak from. I must also remember (the late) Howard Buchbinder and (the late) Amir Hassanpour, with whom I enjoyed so many hours in great discussion, and whose thoughts have been part of my consciousness. Outside of academia, in the wide area of social movements and resistance, I would like to acknowledge the solidarity, inspiration and fun provided by Punam Khosla, Krishanta Sri Bhaggiyadatta, May Yee, Prabha Khosla, Dionne Brand, Winnie Ng, John Greyson, Richard Fung, Tim McCaskell, Makeda Silvera, Stephanie Martin, Yola Grant, Constance Nakatsu, Arun Prabha and Alok Mukherjee, and Aminur Rahim and Iqbal Hasnu.

Last but not least, I must acknowledge my debt to my undergraduate and especially graduate students. Their own political and critical engagement, their innovative and refreshing readings of texts which could be otherwise stale and uninspiring with use, their sustained support of my concerns and critical framework, my take on historical materialism and forms of political resistance, are all present in my writings. They were and are wonderful interlocutors and listeners. Without them I could not have explored and organised the ideas in these essays. Many of my former students are present-day colleagues. Our conversation continues beyond the classroom into the present time. I cannot name them all, but I would like to mention a few: Sourayan Mookerjea, Gail Faurschou, Davina Bhandar, Michael Ma, Donna Harrison, Andrew K. Thompson, Alex Levant, Katherine Nastovsky, and my last and present graduate student, Gökbörü Sarp Tanyildiz. In these politically and intellectually difficult times they have kept alive my hope and a sense of future in scholarship that breaks the boundaries between academia and the realities of the world that we live in. I am confident that the struggle that I joined a long time ago for revolutionary social change will continue with them. Surely we will move towards a better world and avoid the mistakes of the past, because we cannot step into the same river twice.

Overview of Previously Published Articles

The chapters in this reader were first published as articles or book chapters in the following publications.

Building from Marx: Reflections on 'Race', Gender and Class, in *Educating from Marx: Race, Gender and Writing*, edited by S. Carpenter and S. Mojab, New York: Palgrave 2011; Ideology, in *Marxism and Feminism*, edited by S. Mojab, London: Zed Books 2015; But Who Speaks for Us? Experience and Agency in Conventional Feminist Paradigms, in H. Bannerji et al, *Unsettling Relations: The University as a Site of Feminist Struggles*, Toronto: Toronto Women's Press 1991; Politics and the Writing of History, in *Nation, Empire, Colony*, edited by R. Pearson and N. Chaudhury, Bloomington: Indiana University Press 1998; Ideology, Anti-colonialism and Marxism, in *The Bullet*, http://socialistproject .ca/bullet/1341.php 2016; Tradition of Sociology and Sociology of Tradition, in *International Journal of Qualitative Studies in Education* 16, No. 2, 2003; Beyond the Ruling Category to What Actually Happens: Notes on James Mill's Historiography in *The History of British India*, in H. Bannerji, *Knowledge, Experience and Ruling Relations*, edited by M. Campbell and A. Manicom, Toronto: University of Toronto Press 1995; Pygmalion Nation: Critique of Subaltern Studies' Resolution of the Women Question, in *Economic and Political Weekly*, No. 11 2000; Introducing Racism: Notes towards an Antiracist Feminism, in *Resources for Feminist Research/Documentation sur la Researche Féministe* 16. No. 1, 1987; In the Matter of X: Building 'Race' into Sexual Harassment, in *Thinking Through: Essays on Feminism, Marxism and Anti-Racism* Toronto: Women's Press 1995; Attired in Virtue: Discourse on Shame (*Lajja*) and Clothing of the Gentlewoman (*Bhadramahila*) in Colonial Bengal, in *From the Seams of History*, edited by Bharati Ray, New Delhi: Oxford University Press 1994; Fashioning a Self: Educational Proposals for and by Women in Popular Magazines in Colonial Bengal, in *Economic and Political Weekly*, Vol. 16, No. 43, 1991; Age of Consent and Hegemonic Social Reform, in *Gender and Imperialism*, edited by C. Midgley, Manchester: Manchester University Press 1998; The Paradox of Diversity: The Construction of a Multicultural Canada and 'Women of Colour', in H. Bannerji, *The Dark Side of the Nation: Essays on Multiculturalism, Nationalism, and Gender*, Toronto: Canadian Scholars Press 2000; On the Dark Side of the Nation: Politics of Multiculturalism and the State of 'Canada', in *Journal of Canadian Studies* 31, No. 3, 1996; A Question of Silence: Reflections on Violence Against Women in Communities of Colour, in *Scratching the Surface: Canadian Anti-Racist Feminist Thought*, Toronto: Toronto Women's Press 1999; The Passion of Naming: Identity, Difference and Politics of Class, in H. Bannerji, *Thinking Through: Essays on Feminism, Marxism and Anti-Racism*, Toronto: Women's Press 1995; Truant in Time, *Destination: Film, Video and Installation by South Asian Artists*, Iron Gallery exhibition catalogue 1993; Making India Hindu and Male: Cultural Nationalism and the Emergence of the Ethnic Citizen in Contemporary India, in *Ethnicities* 6, No. 3, 2006; Writing 'India', Doing 'Ideology': William Jones' Construction of India as an Ideological Category, in *Left History*, Vol. 2 No. 2, 1994; Demography and Democracy: Reflections on Violence Against Women in Genocide or Ethnic Cleansing, in *Resources for Feminist Research/Documentation sur la Researche Féministe* 30, Nos. 3–4, 2004; Cultural Nationalism and Woman as the Subject of the Nation, in H. Bannerji, *Demography and Democracy: Essays on Nationalism, Gender and Ideology*, Toronto: Canadian Scholars Press 2011; Patriarchy in the Era of Neoliberalism: The Case of India, in *Social Scientist* 44, Vol. 3–4, 2016; The Mirror of Class: Class Subjectivity and Politics in Nineteenth Century Bengal, in *Economic and Political Weekly* Vol. 4, No. 19, 1989; Language and Liberation: A Study of Political Theatre in West Bengal, in *Ariel* October, 1984; Nation and Class in Communist Aesthetics and the Theatre of Utpal Dutt, in H. Bannerji, *The Mirror of Class: Essays of Bengali Theatre*, Calcutta: Papyrus 1998; Nostalgia for the Future: The Poetry of Ernesto Cardinal, in H. Bannerji, *The Writing on the Wall: Essays on Culture and Politics*, Toronto: TSAR 1993; A Transformational Pedagogy: Reflections on Rabindranath's Project of Decolonisation, in *Tagore: The World as His Nest*, edited by S.R. Dasgupta and S. Datta, Kolkata: Jadavpur University Press 2016; Beyond the Binaries: Notes on Karl Marx's and Rabindranath Tagore's Ideas on Human Capacities and Alienation, in *Marxism With and Beyond Marx*, edited by A.K. Bagchi and A. Chakrabarty, New York: Routledge 2014.

PART 1

Methods

∴

SECTION 1

Ideology and the Social

••

CHAPTER 1

Building from Marx: Reflections on 'Race', Gender and Class

I know I am not alone. There must be hundreds of other women, maybe thousands, who feel as I do. There may be hundreds of men who want the same drastic things to happen. But how do you hook up with them? How can you interlink your own struggle and goals with these myriad, hypothetical people who are hidden entirely or else concealed by stereotypes and/or generalities of 'platform' such as any movement seems to spawn? I don't know. I don't like it, this being alone when it is clear that there will have to be multitudes working together, around the world, if radical and positive change can be forced upon the heinous status quo I despise in all its overwhelming power.[1]

∙∙
∙

It is conventional in academic and political circles by now to speak of 'race' in the same breath as gender and class. It is more or less recognised that 'race' can be combined with other social relations of power and that they can mediate and intensify each other.[2] This combination of 'race', gender, and class is often expressed through the concept of 'intersectionality', in which three particular strands of social relations and ideological practices of difference and power are seen as arising in their own specific social terrain, and then crisscrossing each other 'inter-sectionally' or aggregatively.[3] It is a coming together of social issues to create a moment of social experience.

Yet, speaking of experience, both nonwhite and white people living in Canada/the West know that this social experience is not, as lived, a matter of inter-

---

1 Jordan 1989, p. 115.
2 For the beginning of theorisation on the relationship between 'race,' gender, and class, which forms the departure point for this essay, see Bannerji 1993, 1995; Davis 1983; Smith, Hull, and Bell-Scott 1982.
3 The notion of 'intersectionality' is the most common one used in critical race theories as well as in legal theories. See, for example, Crenshaw 1989, and Collins 1989.

sectionality. Their sense of being in the world, textured through myriad social relations and cultural forms, is lived or felt or perceived as being all together and all at once. A working-class non-white woman's (black, South Asian, Chinese, etc.) presence in the usual racialised environment is not divisible separately and serially. The fact of her blackness, her sex, and gender-neutral personhood of being working class blend into something of an identity simultaneously and instantaneously.[4] This identification is both in the eye of the beholder and her own sense of social presence captured by this gaze. The same goes for a white woman, yet when confronted with this question of 'being' and experience we are hard put to theorise them in terms of a social ontology. What could be the reason for this inadequacy of conceptualisation that fails to capture such formative experientiality? If it is lived, then how can it be thought, and how can we overcome our conceptual shortcomings? It is my intent here to suggest a possible theorisation that can address these questions, or at least to grasp the reasons for why we need to ask them in the first place. This is not a matter of responding simply to a theoretical challenge, but rather to a political one as well. This is a basic piece of the puzzle for the making of social democracy.

If democracy is to be more than a mere form consisting of political rituals that only serve to entrench the rule of capital and sprinkle holy water on existing social inequalities, it must have a popular and actually participatory content. This content should be of social and cultural demands concentrating in social movements and organisations working through political processes that aim at popular entitlement at all levels. Such politics needs a social understanding that conceives social formations as complex, contradictory, and inclusive phenomena of social interactions. It cannot be a simple arithmetical exercise of adding or intersecting 'race', gender, and class in a stratificatory mode. It cannot posit 'race' as a cultural phenomenon and gender and class as social and economic. It needs to overcome the overall segmentation of the social into such elementary aspects of its composition. For example, a trade union cannot properly be said to be an organisation for class struggle if it only thinks of class in economic terms without broadening the concept of class to include 'race' and gender in its intrinsic formative definition. Furthermore, it has to make its understanding actionable on this socially composite ground of class.[5]

---

4 See Terkel 1982. See also Bannerji 1995, pp. 121–58.
5 There needs to be an examination of Canadian labour history or texts of labour studies to see how 'race' in its various forms has been incorporated in theorising class, labour, or class politics. It would be interesting to see if, in that domain, there are texts comparable to Roediger 1992 or Bolaria and Li 1988. This is an invitation to further research. Black feminist historians have started the project, but it needs to go deeper.

Outside of the trade unions, which are explicitly 'class' organisations, the usual practice in current social-justice movements is to adopt what is called 'coalition' politics without discriminating among the platforms on which these organisations have been put together.[6] This coalitionist activism is not only a tactical matter, but also reflects the same pluralist aggregative logic of social understanding. Organisations that are class based and those that are not come together because of their shared interest in certain issues. But in what would be called 'new social movements', the very issues of class and capital would be considered unnecessary, if at all.[7] So popular demands on grounds of gender, 'race', sexuality, identity, and so on have to be primarily formulated outside of class and capital and in cultural terms. In this political framework, 'anti-racism' becomes more a question of multiculturalism and ethnicity, as the socially relational aspects of racialisation embedded in the former are converted into a cultural demand. It is not surprising that, of late, there has been a sharp decline in work on 'race' that combines hegemonic/cultural common sense with the workings of class and state.[8] The turn to postmodernism and the turn away from marxism and class analysis have resulted in increasing valorisation of cultural norms and forms and made theories of discourse into vehicles for 'radical' politics. If, in the past, we had to deal with the economism and class reductionism of positivist marxists, now our battle is with 'cultural reductionism'. Neither of these readings of social ontology allows us to do justice to politics for social justice. Our theoretical journey must begin somewhere else to reach another destination.

1   Theorising the Social

The theorisation and politics I suggest are not exercises in abstraction. They do not eschew thinking or organising on specific issues relating to economy, culture, or politics. They can be highly specific or local in their scope – about neighbourhoods or homelessness in Toronto, for example – or speak to cultural problems. But, using these different entry points into the social, they have to analyse and formulate their problems in terms of political problematics that show how these particular or local issues only arise in a wider or extra-local context of socio-economic and cultural relations. If they are 'spe-

---

6 Consider, e.g., the Metro Network for Social Justice.
7 For a classic example of this formulation, see Laclau and Mouffe 2001.
8 By this I mean anthologies such as the Birmingham Centre for Contemporary Cultural Studies 1982.

cific' issues, we have to realise that it is because they are 'specific' to a general, larger set of social, structural, and institutional relations.[9] Can, for example, the type of homelessness experienced in Toronto be possible outside of the way capitalist economic and social development have proceeded in Canada as a whole? Redressing the wrongs in this case, one has to think and ask on grounds beyond the immediate situation; one has to go above and behind it. It would not do either to think of 'poverty' as an issue or problem by itself (only to be added to 'race', class, or gender) or to conceive of these outside of capital.

In spite of frequent lip service paid to reflexive social theorisation, or even some excellent works on class, slavery, colonialism, and imperialism, especially by historians, we need to venture, therefore, into a more complex reading of the social, where every aspect or moment of it can be shown as reflecting others; where each little piece of it contains the macrocosm in its microcosm – what Blake called 'the world in a grain of sand'. What we have instead is a thriving theory industry that ruptures the integrity of the social and joyously valorises 'fragments', preferring to posit a nonrelational inchoateness, or to add them whenever necessary. By such accounts, as I said before, the social amounts to an ordering of regulatory parts – the old utilitarian arithmetic – and, properly speaking, is inconceivable. Marxists and neo-marxists have also succumbed to a ceaseless debate on modernism and postmodernism, allowing the aesthetic, moral category of the 'modern' to distract them. Seeking to bypass the terms of this debate, I would like to come back to Marx's own formulation of 'the social', the ontological or the existential, in different terms or concepts. Here, I assume 'the social' to mean a complex socio-economic and cultural formation, brought to life through myriad finite and specific social and historical relations, organisations, and institutions. It involves living and conscious human agents and what Marx called their 'sensuous, practical human activity'.[10] Here, culture and society are not in a mechanical relation of an economic base and a cultural superstructure. All activities of and in the social are relational and are mediated and articulated with their expressive as well as embedded forms of consciousness. Here, signifying and communicative practices are intrinsic moments of

---

9   For an understanding of my use of the term 'specific', see Bannerji 1995, pp. 41–54.
10   Marx and Engels 1970, p. 121. Additionally, my use of the notion of 'the social' needs a note, an acknowledgment of the debt I owe not only to Marx's work but also to that of Dorothy E. Smith, who in all her works, but primarily in *Writing the Social*, has offered a relational and constitutive view of it. In essays such as 'Ideological practices of sociology,' in *Conceptual Practices of Power*, Smith has also elaborated on Marx's and her own 'reflexive' method. See also Bannerji 1999, pp. 55–98.

social being. Using such a formulation of the social, here it is my primary concern to perform a marxist critique of what 'race' in particular means to 'class' and gender. In other words, I am trying to socialise the notion of 'race'.

Before articulating my theory of the social, I would like to pause over the habit of fragmentive or stratified thinking so prevalent among us, which ends up by erasing *the social* from the conception of ontology. This same habit can also produce an evaluative gesture whereby 'the cultural', for example, becomes secondary, apparent, or illusory, and 'class', understood as a function of 'economy', becomes the 'real' or the fundamental creative force of society. Culture as superstructure 'reflects' or 'corresponds to' the economic base. Alternatively, we have the reverse conceptual habit, whereby the formative power of discourse determines the social. By becoming primarily discursive, the social becomes a thought object. Epistemologies reach a proportion of exclusivity, which is of course not new and about which Marx speaks in his first *Thesis on Feuerbach*.[11] Through both of these reductive modes, class politics can ignore 'race' or gender, or politics based on any of these others can ignore class. Positivist marxism can also rank the importance of social issues of struggle by relegating gender relations to the status of 'secondary contradictions', while 'race' or caste are seen as mere 'cultural' forms of inequality. Currently, the mainstream Western labour movements often dismiss issues of 'race' as politics of discourse or ethnic/cultural identity. Conversely, 'race' activists may dismiss class or anti-imperialist politics as 'white' politics. Gender or patriarchy may be considered as entirely redundant by both groups, while feminists who can theorise community on grounds of being women may find 'race' and class both redundant or of no intrinsic significance.[12] Furthermore, all groups might find what they do not consider important to be also divisive and detrimental for the advancement of their movements. My primary concern, on the other hand, is to bypass these conceptual positions and to offer an inclusive marxist critique with a social interpretation of difference, especially in regard to what 'race' means to class and gender. In other words, how class can be transformed from an economic to a social concept, which constitutively implicates both social relations and forms of consciousness. What I intend is best presaged by Edward P. Thompson

---

11   In his 'First thesis,' Marx says, 'The chief defect of all hitherto existing materialism ... is that the thing, reality, sensuousness is conceived only in the form of *the object or contemplation*, but not as *sensuous human activity, practice*, not subjectively ... [and] the active side was developed abstractly by idealism – which, of course, does not know real, sensuous activity as such' (1972, p. 121. Italics in the original).

12   Two interesting formulations of this exclusionary method are to be found in now classic texts: Spelman 1998, and Smith, Hull, and Bell-Scott 1982.

in *The Making of the English Working Class*, when he discusses class and class consciousness as active creations of social individuals.[13]

It is not news to hear that the culture of positivist thinking that pervaded the nineteenth-century European (especially English) intellectual world and the prestige accorded to a measuring scientifism changed the tenor of social thought from the earlier philosophical tone. Notions such as 'knowledge' and 'science' took on a definitely technological and quantitative aspect, and to this were added strict notions of causality as well as the idea of social 'laws' parallel to 'natural laws' – an offshoot of the study of human evolution. If we look at the later work of Engels, for example, we can see how later marxism absorbed this culture of utilitarian positivism and scientifism.[14] As economics emerged as a science, since it could lend itself most fully to quantification, marxism changed from being a 'critique' of political economy as attempted by Marx to becoming political economy. The notion of economy came to substitute for notions of the social. As such, social organisation and society became enunciations or functions of the economy. Lived social relations and experiencing subjects became subjected to one-dimensional views of the social; that is, of economic relations or structures. This habit of scientifism has endured, erupting in Louis Althusser's claim, for example, regarding an 'epistemological break' in Marx's opus – periodising it into philosophical and scientific.[15] The concept and practice of 'scientific' marxism or socialism became a credo of communist parties throughout the world.

This scientific or positivist marxism, with its truncated and reified understanding of the social, interestingly relied much more on some characteristics of eighteenth-century liberal thought rather than on Marx's own writings. Not the least of these is a compartmentalising way of thinking that ruptures the formative, complex integrity of the social whole and creates segments or spheres of 'the economic', 'the political', and 'the cultural', which are in reality ontologically inseparable. This separation of social spheres was essential for the rising bourgeois state and society. In bourgeois or liberal democracy,

---

13   In this book, Thompson *socialises* the concept of class, thus retrieving it from economism. He introduces into the social-relational aspect the element of conscious subjectivity. 'Class' for him is an 'active process which owes as much to agency as to conditioning. The working class did not rise like the sun at an appointed time. It was present in its own making' (1974, p. 9). Also, I concur with his statement that class is 'a historical phenomenon, unifying a number of disparate and seemingly unconnected events, both in the raw material of experience and in consciousness' (Ibid.)

14   Engels 1969.

15   See Althusser and Balibar 1973, especially Althusser's considerations on science and theory, in part 1, 'From capital to Marx's philosophy,' (1973, pp. 48–70).

in spite of its universalist claims, equality could only be formal, and thus the notions of 'liberality' and 'democracy' could not be actually realised. But this way of thinking in self-contained spheres has become hegemonic or naturalised enough such that programmatic, political marxism can, unconsciously perhaps, fall back upon the same separation of spheres. Broadly speaking, 'class' thus becomes an overarching economic category, gender/patriarchy a social one, and 'race', 'caste', and 'ethnicity' categories of the cultural. It is not hard to see then how class struggle or class consciousness can be theorised and acted on minus 'race' and gender, or vice versa. But not all marxists submitted to this liberal/bourgeois fragmentary and economistic reading of the social. So called for their difference from others, 'cultural marxists' such as, for example, Georg Lukács, Walter Benjamin, and Raymond Williams actively explored the formative relations between culture and society in their broadest sense, while Antonio Gramsci theorised on relations between these and the institutions of the state and civil society.[16]

2   Socialising 'Race'

At the outset, I need to state that the social phenomenon that I refer to as 'race' is not a biological distinction actually inhering in people themselves. It is a way, and a power-inscribed way, of reading or establishing difference, and finding long-lasting ways to reproduce such readings, organisation, and practice. Roughly, this is what people signal when they say that 'race' is a construct. The nonexistence of 'race' as a physical entity has been remarked on by critical Darwinians, such as Stephen J. Gould,[17] for example. This accounts for my use of quotation marks, hedging the term from the danger of becoming considered as an actual fact of nature. 'Race', therefore, is neither more nor less than an active social organisation, a constellation of practices motivated, consciously and unconsciously, by political or power imperatives with implied cultural forms – images, symbols, metaphors, and norms, which range from the quotidian to the institutional. This is the view that I wish to sustain through my theorisation here.

If we consider 'race' as a connotative, expressionist cluster of social relations in the terrain of certain historical and economic relations, and class as an ensemble of property-oriented social relations with signifying practices, it

---

16   See Gramsci 1971. Especially attend to his treatment of the relationship between the state and civil society in the different essays.

17   Gould 1981.

is easy to see how they are formatively implicated. From this standpoint, one could say that modern 'race' is a social culture of colonialist and imperialist capitalism. 'Race', therefore, is a collection of discourses of colonialism and slavery, but firmly rooted in capitalism in its different aspects through time. As it stands, 'race' cannot be disarticulated from 'class' any more than milk can be separated from coffee once they are mixed, or the body divorced from consciousness in a living person. This inseparability, this formative or figurative relation is as true for the process of extraction of surplus value in capitalism as it is a common-sense practice at the level of social life. Economic participation, the value of labour, social and political participation and entitlement, and cultural margin-alisation or inclusion are all part of this overall social formation.

This integrity of 'race' and class cannot be independent of the fundamental social organisation of gender; that is, the sex-specific social division of labour, with mediating norms and cultural forms. Various proprietorial relations, in-cluding of bodies, productive and reproductive labour, normative institutional and commonsensical cultural, are thus in a reflexive and constitutional rela-tion.[18] It is this that multinational corporations fall back on in the third world when they hire an overwhelmingly female labour force to raise their profit mar-gin. In every social space, there is a normalised and experiential as well as ideological knowledge about whose labour counts the least. The actual real-isation process of capital cannot be outside a given social and cultural form or mode. There is no capital that is a universal abstraction. Capital is always a practice, a determinate set of social relations – and a cultural one at that. Thus, 'race', gender, and patriarchy are inseparable from class, as any social organisa-tion rests on intersubjective relations of bodies and minds marked with socially constructed difference on the terrain of private property and capital.

3   Going Back to Marx

In all modes of society there is one specific kind of production which pre-dominates over the rest, whose relations thus assign rank and influence to others. It is a general illumination which bathes all the other colours

---

18   For the implication of 'proprietorial' or moral notions, as well as familial relations, and for a reflexive/constitutional view of the social, see classic statements by Marx and Engels 1970, pp. 26, 44, 49, 52. There, discussing the family as a moment of property, they say, e.g., that it is 'the first form ... where wife and children are the slaves of the husband' (52). See also Marx and Engels 1972a or Engels 1972. Later theorisations retain the core of their insight. In the North American context, see Davis 1983.

and modifies their particularity. It is a particular ether which determines the specific gravity of every being which has materialised within it.[19]

To perform a reflexive theorisation of the social, it helps to go back to some key concepts used by Marx himself. Of the many he used, I will primarily concentrate on three: the 'concrete' (in *Grundrisse*), 'civil society' (in *The German Ideology*, *The Communist Manifesto*), and 'ideology' (in *The German Ideology*, *The Holy Family*, and *The Jewish Question*). On a related note, we could use notions such as 'mediation', 'reification', and 'fetishism', which, though only partially articulated by Marx himself, were developed by marxists. It is interesting that of these marxists, such as Lukács, Benjamin, Althusser, Dorothy E. Smith, and Fredric Jameson, to name a few, none were political economists. As critical social and cultural theorists they sought to break free from an economistic or class-reductionist as well as cultural-reductionist understanding of the social as elaborated in particular by capital.

Marx adapted the Hegelian concept of 'the concrete' in his notes on *Capital* compiled as *Grundrisse*. It seems to me that his treatment of this concept holds the correlates of reflexive epistemology earlier outlined as historical materialism in *The German Ideology*. About this notion he makes the following remarks:

> The concrete is concrete because it is the concentration of many determinations hence the unity of the diverse. It appears in the process of thinking, therefore, *as a process of concentration, as a result, not as a point of departure, even though it is the point of departure in reality*, and hence also the point of departure for observation [*Anschauung*] and conception.[20]

The 'concrete' as the social, we can see, has a dual character for Marx. It is, on the one hand, a mental or conceptual category and, on the other, an existing specific social formation. Thus, it is both 'a point of departure' (as the social) and 'a point of arrival' (as theory). Something that is 'concrete' is not like an 'object' that is visible, such as a table or a chair, but nonetheless its 'concreteness' is a determinate form of social existence. It is concretised by specific social relations with mediating and expressive as well as reproductive forms of consciousness and practices. In fact, this 'concrete' social form is to be seen in contrast to a fact or an 'object', because it is not reified/fixed, hypostatised. It is a fluid, dynamic, meaningful formation created by living subjects in actual lived

---

19   Marx 1973.
20   Ibid., 101; italics mine.

time and space, yet with particular discernible features that both implicate it in other social formations and render it specific. From this perspective, then, 'race', as I said before, is a connotative cluster of social relations, implicated in others coded as 'economic' and 'social', that is, class and gender. If one were to broaden 'class' into a sociological category, thus making it stand for an entire ensemble of social relations, signifying practices and organisations, it could not be articulated within specific sociohistoric formations such as ours without 'race'. For this reason, one could say that 'race' is the ideological discourse as well as cultural common sense of a patriarchal, colonial, and imperialist capitalism. In such an existential historical terrain, disarticulating 'race' from 'class' is impossible. Denuded of its metaphysical trapping, the notion of the 'concrete', then, in Marx's usage, becomes one of social formation signalling a constitutive complexity. Social relations and organisation, both complementary and contradictory, with historical accretion and inflection, go into the making of the social ontology of the subject-agent. But it also has a capacity for conceptualising these in a non-mechanical, non-serialised way.

It is sensible to move from the concepts 'concrete' and 'the social' to the notion of 'civil society', which is crucial to Marx's critical epistemology,[21] and to note its intimate connection with the notion of 'mode of production'. Marx's emphasis here is on the *mode*, the organisational and social ground for production as well as reproduction and their entailed politics, administration, and cultures. *The German Ideology*, where he presents his ideas on the making of the social and social change, is a rich source for understanding the complexity of modes of production as articulated by Marx. Breaking free of the qualitative and ontological separation between civil society and the state, economy, and culture, and between the political and public sphere and the private and familial, he presents in this text an integrated, constantly elaborating historical/social space. It is the theatre of class struggle and revolution. This historical and social movement is not presented as evolutionist and teleological, and it is shot through with both resisting and dominating forms of consciousness. Here are some examples of what he has to say about the civil society, the ground for 'the mode' or the style and the fashion for organising an everyday life for the production of private property and related moral and cultural propriety. For

---

21   For an expanded discussion of 'civil society', see Marx and Engels 1970, pp. 57–60, as well as the section 'History: Fundamental conditions,' pp. 48–52, in the same volume. Both involve discussions of the construction of the social, where the organisation of social relations involves all basic aspects of life, including that of consciousness. Here, production and consumption are unthinkable in separation and without an intrinsic, active, and material form of consciousness.

Marx, 'civil society is the true source and theatre of all history, and how absurd is the conception of history held hitherto, which neglects the real relationship and confines itself to high-sounding dramas of princes and states'.[22] He also treats civil society as 'social organisation ... which in all ages forms the basis of the state and of the rest of the idealistic superstructure'.[23]

If we scrutinise Marx's statements, two issues primarily grab our attention. First, that the 'mode' of the social is a dynamic and integral one. In its character as a formative process, it cannot be an aggregative one. This processual nature requires both temporal and spatial aspects, where it is here and now a specific form, which, however, will move on to something else in the future. But some aspects of this formation which lie in the now will, therefore, be in the past as well. You cannot tear this live social way of being and its formational journey into component parts and yet expect it to live and move. Just as a dismembered and dissected human body does not yield up the secret of a conscious evolving life, neither does a 'mode' of production reveal its live social being when considered as segregated, though 'intersecting', social relations and forms of consciousness. It is this that is precisely wrong with what is called 'the intersectional method'. In this, one has to agree with those romantics of the nineteenth century with whom Marx shared much of his *Weltanschauung* or worldview – that the whole is more than the sum of its parts.

The second issue of note is that of culture and consciousness. It is clear from explicit statements that consciousness is not an afterthought of existence. All activities are 'sensuous practical human' ones and, as such, of conscious agents and subjects. Hence Marx's need to put forward the notion of 'practical consciousness'[24] as a fundamental moment of all aspects of 'concrete' form of existence. In this learning, changing, and transmitting process, life goes on, history moves on and is made – both consciously and subconsciously. The gesture of forging a primitive tool, rubbing two sticks together, judging the seasons by the stars, becomes the science and technology of our present times. In this schema, no apple falls out of sight of a conscious eye. It is not surprising, then, that private-property-based ways of establishing propriety and reproducing difference would be a basic part of social existence involving consciousness

---

22   Ibid., p. 57.

23   Ibid., p. 57.

24   Along with discussing 'primary historical relationships', Marx speaks of 'consciousness ... which here makes its appearance in the form of agitated layers of air, sounds, in short, of language. Language is as old as consciousness, language is practical consciousness that exists also for other men, and for that reason alone it really exists for me personally as well; language, like consciousness, only arises from the need, the necessity, of intercourse with other men' (Marx and Engels 1970, p. 51; italics in the original).

and institutionalisation. Viewed thus, 'race' is no more or less than a form of difference, creating a *mode* of production through practical and cultural acts of *racialisation*. 'Race' is such a difference and it cannot stand alone.[25]

If this formative integrity or 'unity' of the social is 'ruptured' (to use another of Marx's phrases in *Grundrisse*), then we have phenomenal object forms or thought objects that are fetishised. The work of marxist theorists is to deconstruct this object form and return it to its concrete diverse social determinations. As Lukács puts it, an ontology of social being can only be appropriately understood with an epistemology that connects thought to its material sociohistorical ground.[26] As such, empiricist or positivist versions of marxism will not do because they tend to depict the concrete as no more than a 'thing' or an 'object' – as a dead 'fact'.

Attempts to rupture mutually constitutive and diverse determinations to present this as reality lead to the kind of problem that bedevils social movements, which for their effectiveness ought to integrate 'race', gender, and class. Unintentionally, we produce reified thought objects that defy social understanding and are occlusive or truncated. We confuse the specificity of social forms or figurations with disconnected particularities. Thus, culture becomes nonmaterial, asocial, solely discursive, while economy or polity lack mediatory forms of consciousness. As pointed out earlier, this fractured reading results in ideology, in bourgeois democracy's claim to offer equality of citizenship or rights while legally preserving and enhancing actual social relations of inequality and ruling. It is in the criticism of this bourgeois political economy that Marx repeatedly elaborates his theory of a mode (as style, fashion, ensemble) of production. In opposition to liberal/bourgeois thought, he shows how each specific social form serves as the microcosm of the social macrocosm, just as each physical cell of the body holds the entire genetic code. Such a mode of understanding is antidualist and antipositivist. The mode of production, as he puts it in the *Grundrisse*, is not 'linearly, causally organised'.[27] By employing the notion of mediation, between social relations and forms of consciousness, both practical and ideological, he shows how an entire significatory/communicative and expressive social ensemble must obtain for any specific economy and polity to operate and be effective. Seen thus 'socially', class cannot be genderless or cultureless, nor can culture be genderless and classless.

---

25   For a clear understanding of the concept of difference, see Gates 1985. Though the authors of the essays are not marxist, they provide examples of cultural materialism with a strong basis in cultural history.

26   See Lukács 1980.

27   Marx 1973, p. 97.

It is obvious that capital is a social practice, not just a theoretical abstraction. As such, its reproductive and realisation processes are rooted in civil society, in its cultural/social ground. Class in this sense, for Marx and others, is a category of civil society.[28] The exploitation of labour is not simply an arithmetical ratio of labour to technology in the terrain of means of production. Social and cultural factors, for example, of gender and 'race', enter into it and with their implied norms and forms organise the social space that comprehends capitalism as a *mode* of production, an organisation of civil society. We enter a realm of extensive and subtle mediations that determine forms, values, processes, and objects of production.[29] Therefore, 'class', when seen concretely, both relies upon and exceeds what we call economy. The once vocal debates on the household labour of women, wages for housework, and the relationship of slavery to capitalism revealed the far-flung sociocultural roots of economy. Thus, we might identify 'race' and patriarchy/gender with the so-called extra-economic or cultural/discursive, nonetheless social, moments of the overall mode of capitalist production, which has its own social ontology. It is to this formative relation between production and reproduction that Marx signals when he speaks of mediation as 'the act through which the whole process again runs its course'.[30] As modes of mediation, gender or 'race' therefore not only help to produce the constant devaluation of certain social groups' embodiment and labour power, but also create a 'colour coded' cultural common sense for the state and the society as a whole.[31]

The epistemology that ruptures the integrity of the socially concrete at a conceptual level and posits this as a property of the social is identified by Marx in *The German Ideology* as 'ideology'. In contrast to much marxism familiar to us, he does not consider ideology only in terms of its thought content, but rather considers the very form of knowledge production that generates such content that de-socialises, de-politicises, and de-historicises our social understanding. Though Marx's primary concern is with the precise method that produces ideology, he is also deeply concerned with the thought content or ideas that are generated. As they are ideas of ruling, they need to be specifically addressed by our political organisations. As such, racialising discourses need to be considered in these terms. In a section entitled 'Ruling class and ruling ideas', Marx states:

---

28   See, e.g., Hegel's view of 'civil society' in C.J. Arthur's introduction to Marx and Engels 1970, p. 5.

29   On the importance of the concept of mediation, see Marx 1973, pp. 331–3.

30   Ibid., p. 94.

31   See Backhouse 1999, and Razack 2002.

> The ideas of the ruling class are in every epoch the ruling ideas, i.e., the class which is the ruling *material* force of society, is at the same time its ruling *intellectual* force. The class which has the means of material production at its disposal, has control at the same time over the means of mental production, so that thereby, generally speaking, the ideas of those who lack the means of mental production are subject to it.[32]

After offering this cryptic, though highly suggestive, view of the creation of a 'cultural commonsense' that legitimates and reproduces the overall relations and institutions of ruling, Marx states categorically that 'ruling ideas', or what we call generally prevalent ideas, 'are nothing more than the ideal [i.e., cultural/formal] expression of the dominant material relationships, the dominant material relationships grasped as ideas; hence of the relationships which make the one class the ruling one, therefore, the ideas of its dominance'.[33] It is not surprising that the dominant relations of patriarchal colonial capitalism would produce racist patriarchal discourses of physical, social, and cultural differences. This is exactly what happens when the discourses or ideological categories of 'race' or 'human nature' are employed to 'explain' social behaviour or cultural characteristics, while in actuality no more than interpreting them.

But, most importantly, the question is of how such occlusive, substitutive, or displacing discourses of ideological categories are generated. In *The German Ideology*, Marx outlines this epistemological practice, connecting it with the social division of manual and mental labour. He exposes the disciplinary practices of metaphysicians whereby everyday ideas, events, and experiences are decontextualised, overgeneralised, or overparticularised from their originating social relations and interests. Then, these empirical bits of de-grounded ideas are reconfigured into discursive systems or interpretive devices, which take on a semblance of independence and substantiveness. It is helpful to actually both paraphrase and quote Marx here. Considering ideology to be an epistemological device employed in decontextualisation and extrapolation, Marx offers us a disclosure of the method. His disclosure reveals what he calls 'tricks', and there are three of them. We can begin by 'considering the course of history' by 'detach[ing] the ideas of the ruling class from the ruling class itself and attribut[ing] to them an independent existence'.[34] Having detached them from their specific social and historical locations, we now 'confine ourselves to

---

32   Marx and Engels 1970, p. 64. Emphasis in the original.
33   Ibid., p. 64.
34   Ibid., p. 65.

saying that these or those ideas were dominant at a given time, without bothering ourselves about the condition of production and the producers of these
ideas'.[35] Now we have a set of ideas or discourses independent of their social
ontology. They appear to generate each other, appear even *sui generis*, but are
claimed to be shaping, even creating, the very social realities that gave rise to
them in the first place. Thus, consciousness gives rise to existence, rather than
existence to consciousness, understood as conscious existence. Life imitates or
illustrates theory. Only 'if we ignore the individuals and world conditions which
are the source of these ideas', says Marx, then we truly produce 'ideology'.[36] We
can blithely forget that notions such as honour and loyalty came to being in the
time of aristocracy and the dominance of the bourgeoisie produced concepts
of freedom or equality.[37] So 'increasingly abstract ideas hold sway, i.e., ideas
which increasingly take on the form of universality'.[38] Hiding behind abstract
universality and time-honoured metaphysicality, ideas of ruling, for example,
those of 'race' or gender, represent their interests 'as the common interest of all
members of society'.[39]

Intellectuals or ideologues organic to a system of ruling, guardians of property relations, then take upon themselves the task of development and sys-
temisation of these decontextualising concepts. We know well the amount of
philosophical, 'scientific', and cultural labour that has gone into the production
of 'race', and of the practices that have gone into racialisation of whole legal systems and polities.[40] Needless to say, diverting attention from power-organised
differences in everyday life, history, and social relations can only be useful for
the purpose of ruling, of hegemony, not of resistance.

Ideological forms masquerade as knowledge. They simply produce discursivities incorporating bits of decontextualised ideas, events, or experiences with
material consciousness of a practical kind. The modus operandi of these 'ruling knowledges' relies on epistemologies creating essentialisation, homogenisation (i.e., de-specification), and an aspatial and atemporal universalisation.
Given that ideology's one most powerful trick is to cut off a concept from its
originating and mediating social relations, even critical and resisting concepts,
such as 'class' or the feminist category of 'woman', when used in such a way, can

---

35   Ibid., p. 65.
36   Ibid., p. 65.
37   Ibid., p. 65.
38   Ibid., p. 65.
39   Ibid., p. 65.
40   This ideological process that Marx talks about is addressed in different ways by, e.g., Hard-
      ing 1993 or Dua and Robertson 1999.

become occlusive and serve the interests of ruling relations through exclusion and the invisibility of power in relations of difference. The world of feminist theory has been riven by struggles in which it became evident that the category of 'woman' in its desocialised (class/'race') and dehistoricised (colonialism and imperialism) deployment has helped to smuggle in middle-class white women's political agendas and has hidden the relationship of dominance that some social groups of women hold with regard to other social groups.[41]

4   Conclusion

> Men [sic] make their own history, but they do not make it just as they please; they do not make it under circumstances chosen by themselves, but under circumstances directly found, given and transmitted from the past.[42]

What, we might ask, are the consequences of the ideological practice of the dissociation of 'race', class, and gender, which both marxists and non-marxists have engaged in? As far as social movements are concerned, this has made them largely ignore the task of fashioning a fully socially informed politics. For marxists, their ideological/ economistic reading of class, the habit of separating class from culture and social relations of gender/patriarchy, has succeeded in creating at best compromised petty bourgeois politics. By dubbing the issue of 'race' as a non- or anticlass one, they have marginalised those sections of the people who are the most dispossessed and who provide the fodder for capital both in the West and elsewhere. Thus, issues of 'race' and gender have become mainly identified with liberal politics, with those of rights and citizenship, not of socialist struggles. Labour movements and whatever is left of the women's movement are thus unrepresentative and incomplete social or anticapitalist movements, and as such participate in replicating the organisation of capital and bourgeois rule.

Another consequence has been a promiscuous mixture or coalition of class-, gender-, and 'race'-based politics whose lack of common understanding and of internal constructive grounds have created only tenuous possibilities of association and acrimonious relations. Furthermore, an inability to create socialised

---

41   This issue has been also addressed in postcolonial feminist writings. See Midgley 1999, and McClintock 1995.

42   Marx 1972d, p. 437.

class or anticapitalist movements has given room for the development of cul-turalist 'race' groups, which, with the help of *official* multiculturalism, have held social movements hostage to 'identity' and fundamentalist politics. The oppres-sions created by unequal, dominating social relations do not disappear through being rendered invisible as such. They do not disappear in actuality. Denuded of their full sociohistorical concreteness or reality at both the civil society and state levels, they surface in ideological forms of reified 'race' and ethnic nation-alist identities or in acts of basic despair and desperation.

The best way to understand this destructive politics of ideology is to remem-ber Marx in *The Eighteenth Brumaire of Louis Bonaparte*, where he speaks of displaced, substituted cultural identities that accomplish the work of class rule on the stage of hegemony. The masks of god that are worn by current fundamentalist political agencies can only serve to remind us of the Roman masks worn by successive protagonists of the French revolution – until the excluded, unintegrated, class-based sociocultural forms/identities terminated in a fascism instead of social emancipation. Present-day nationalism, imperi-alism, and official multiculturalism have all resorted to 'identity' politics and unleashed wars, genocides, and general social oppression and surveillance. Bush and Blair's civilisational or christian utterances, their capitalist and milit-aristic ambitions masquerading in the masks of democracy and freedom, and their co-opting feminist discourses of rescuing Muslim women are devastating ideological identity projects. It is only by practising a 'concrete' social analysis that these legitimating, unificatory sleights of hand, which have drawn a large section of North Americans (mostly white) to identify with various myths of domination, can be challenged.

The marxists in the West, in particular because they call for a *social* polit-ics, need to take heed of their own implication in undercutting class struggle by furthering 'identity' politics through their defensiveness or 'tolerant' liberal-ism with regard to 'race'. Being quick to dismiss much popular anger at social injustice as peripheral to anticapitalist or class struggle, they have adopted a path that cannot bring any 'real' social transformation. An inability to regard colonial capitalist and imperialist politics as racist, combined with the colo-nialist 'identity' politics of the last five hundred years, have rendered western marxists politically ineffectual. If anti-racist feminist movements challenging hegemony have in them an element of recuperation of erased cultural identity, this is not necessarily disastrous in and of itself. The major point is to assess from what standpoint this so-called identity is elaborated, and what cultures, histories, and social relations it evokes. Whose identity are we talking about – that of the oppressors or of the oppressed? Theorists of the left or marxists have no reason to fear 'identity', because there is enough ground in the works of Marx himself to create social movements that do not have to choose between culture, economy and society or 'race', class, and gender in order to organise politics of social revolution. Going beyond gestures of intersectionality, coalition, and social cohesion, marxists have recourse to a nonfragmentary understanding of the social, which could change the world as we know it.

CHAPTER 2

Marxism and Antiracism in Theory and Practice

[This chapter is based on an interview-style conversation between Himani Bannerji and the editors of *Theorising Anti-Racism: Linkages in Marxism and Critical Race Theories*]

Enakshi Dua (ED) and Abigail B. Bakan (AB): You have said that you have three *political* and intellectual commitments: as a marxist, a feminist, and an antiracist. And you have commented that these political and analytical commitments are stated separately due to a lack of integrative language in the intellectual and political terrains in which we live. Could you describe the intellectual and political processes that have contributed to such theoretical separations, and how you see their linkages?

Himani Bannerji (HB): I will answer by reflecting on the framework I use to understand the complex world that I feel, see, experience and act in around me. I see social relations and organisations of our world as pivotal – they are unequal social relations and institutions of power and exploitation of labour regarding survival and the enjoyment of life's amenities. These relations simultaneously extend to a sense of social entitlement or the lack of it, and influence our participation in the production of our political and cultural life. We have referred to these ensembles of unequal social relations as the concepts of class, patriarchy, and racialisation which interconstitute each other.

Though appearing to be highly specific, the social relations are not standalone structures or forms, like buildings that are connected through roads – they are complexly involved social formations. If the building metaphor can be sustained, these social relations are like the ingredients in each brick that make up the house. They are embedded in the design of the whole society that we live in. They in-form the overall social formation, what Marx called 'the mode of production', shaping and modifying specific life forms – in other words our social habitat. While we live in this habitat, it also lives in us, expressing the dominant ethos. People and their social life are both internal and external to each other, they cannot be separated out as self-contained relations and forms. By extending my analogy, think of the colours of these bricks. Once we mix the colours, for example yellow with blue, we produce green. Once they are mixed, however, once it is green, one cannot pull out the blue from the yellow – thus patriarchy or gender from race and class. This fusion can only be 'known' through a critical epistemology, but it cannot be experienced or inhabited as segmented realities of class, patriarchy, and racialisation. Instead they are the formative and expressive modes of how we accomplish or carry on our 'social' being. They are inseparable in our consciousness and actions as existential modes unless they are critically and analytically scrutinised in the examination of the social organisations, local and extra-local, of which we are a part.

To characterise our social being in a fragmentary fashion, independent of the overall social organisation, and to try to identify with only one set of relations and their mediating devices of consciousness is wrong in my view. That is what we do when we take one set of social relations and fix or reify them as our primary identifier. This is a synecdochical attempt to make an independent whole out of a part of our social existence, daily practices and consciousness. It is a kind of freezing, a rigidification of our consciousness and a false representation of our daily life or culture and politics. It is a reification which is implied in the conventional usage of what we call 'identity'.

Words are used in such different ways that I want to clarify what I mean by a 'fixed identity'. What is commonly meant by identity, as in 'identity politics', has typifying features, as in Weber's notion of the 'ideal type'. It is a reified and rarefied notion, a contra-dynamic notion. People's actual lived experiences are very different qualitatively. To grasp the actuality of our social being and experiences we need to move away from this type of fixed identity. In the widest sense an 'identity' should encompass not only what I am at any point in time in terms of my cultural self-naming, but also what I do. What I *am* is not a fixed thing – it lies in a historic social time, it changes depending on the changing reality.

My being, or anyone's being, is bound up with this overall being in and of the social in which we live. Whatever helps me to understand that complexity of being, which is a 'social' and not an empty being, in continuous and dynamic relations, in responsive and creative relations and actions, in grasping the varied ways of thinking, of knowing and explaining, is what matters. These methods and modes of knowledge and inquiry – and their transmission to others – have to take place within a language of analytic theory. In theoretical terms we have called them marxism, feminism and anti-racism. They are not my identity, or fixed properties of my being in the world, but rather my ways of understanding the social relations that build our world. I live in that world and it lives inside me and it shaped my consciousness, which is in a communicative relation with others.

Of course after many years definite ways of knowing, of analysis or critique, become an essential part of what John Berger calls our 'ways of seeing'. You may loosely bring in these critical epistemological and political features in identifying me for convenience, but these identities so-called exceed any originary group belonging of whatever kind. And these so-called identities of being feminist, marxist and anti-racist are mutually constitutive and dynamic. They are not ways of being in a static ahistorical and asocial way, but rather defined by collectivity. Depending on how we understand them, they indicate ways of acting in the world and changing it in the process. If they are identities, then, they are identities of 'becoming' involving active participation and critique. I have spoken about this identity of becoming in my essays in *The Writing on the Wall* and *Thinking Through*.[1]

You have asked me how this fragmented perception of the social comes about which breaks up the social whole into distinct strands of social relations and forms of consciousness, such as 'race' or 'gender' or 'class'. They are then made to 'intersect' or added to each other. This amounts to putting up walls in the social space, thus creating separate, self-contained spheres and then artificially joining them. This is the essence of liberal thought, which is based on atomistic and positivist premises which provide aggregative plurality. The reason for such separations lies in the failure to go beyond phenomenal appearances – in empiricism, which should be distinguished from empirical inquiries. This empiricism is connected with taxonomic and fixating impulses consisting of details which are accommodative or responsive to history and social organisation. They are disparate facts, and as such they do not help us to grasp the nature of the overall social formation and accompanying forms of consciousness. My approach is not one of rejection of the empirical reality or science. By 'science' I mean the activities of the enquiring spirit that promote critical insight. In that sense history, for example, is a scientific endeavour. I am alluding instead to a method of reification based on natural sciences motivated by an urge for unchanging laws and 'facts' about a dynamic entity called 'society'. This is how 'laws' of nature were promulgated from the seventeenth and eighteenth centuries onwards to serve as a methodological template for social understanding. Seeking the dynamism and the fluidity of social reality was considered a metaphysical and non-scientific pursuit, seen as romanticism acceptable in poetic writing. But we see how in Marx's historical materialist epistemology, in his critique of ideology in *The German Ideology* (Part I),[2] for example, the organisation of a society with its historical, social and cultural realities is not understandable through crude quantification and methods of accounting, such as those favoured by empiricism and liberal thought.

---

1 Bannerji 1993. See especially the 'Introduction', in Bannerji 1995. Especially the chapter 'The Passion of Naming'.

2 Marx and Engels 1970.

So, understanding the source of fragmentation as outlined above, there is little difficulty in putting together a theoretical framework of marxist anti-racist feminism. In other words, I do not experience difficulty in finding a common ground in the social relational anti-ideological epistemology articulated by marxism which incorporates class, gender and racialisation. The point of departure for my critique is not any 'ism', any creed of thought, but from a method of enquiry and analysis, namely, historical materialism, which provides a comprehensive understanding of the social with all its contradictions and of its protean and prolific nature. The social in its overall determinations and mediations – both understood here in the sense they are discussed by Raymond Williams, involving social relations, institutions, organisations, and forms of consciousness[3] – compels us to seek methods of inquiry and critique that can grasp these components in their constitutive formations. At the level of their formation there are no rigid boundaries possible between forms of consciousness, both immediate and historical, social organisation, relations and practices. The world we live in is a creative and dynamic composition of all these elements, all at once. So, beginning with a project of enquiry, we look to all of the resources of the social we can draw upon to get a larger picture, and this has to be a picture that does not swallow up all particularities of formation and complexities of determination and mediation in a general abstraction. Rather, the particular relations provide the concrete and formative aspects of the reality we explore. Otherwise how, for example, do we understand the differences and similarities of patriarchy as it is experienced by women of different social groups and classes all over the world and in history?

1   On the Contributions of Dorothy Smith

ED and AB: You were of course a student of Dorothy Smith, and you have often indicated how influential she has been in your own work. Can you elaborate how you see Dorothy Smith's contribution specifically to understanding race and racism?

HB: There is much in my work that I can trace to Dorothy's writings, but I will focus on two key concepts that helped me to understand the concept of race and the processes and practices of racialisation: her formulations of the every-

---

3   Williams 1977, especially the Introduction and chapter on ideology.

day world as problematic,[4] and her reading of Marx's epistemological method or critique of ideology as particularly found in *The German Ideology*.[5]

The notion of the everyday world as problematic is very important. And by 'problematic' I see Dorothy meaning two things. There can be a word-play on the notion of 'problematic' as applied in a critique related to social movements. In an ordinary colloquial sense our everyday world is problematic, but also the everyday world is not just a descriptive expression but is itself a sociological 'problematic' in the sense that it presents us a field of investigation, comprises a space of inquiry. I find Dorothy's way of understanding how each little bit of the everyday is constituted through multiple social relations and textual mediations to be very helpful. This expands my point of entry into the social as there are many doors to begin the journey of our thinking about reality. For me, her entry into the social organisation of knowledge and institutions through women's experience and broadening out to the ruling apparatus and its textual mediations is very useful. Dorothy's understanding of what we call 'experience' is very important here, because what she is telling us is that experiences are felt and named moments of life, of social interaction, by exploring and analysing which we enter into a more comprehensive understanding about social reality. What is immediate, what is around us, what we are going through, provide a concrete entry point through which we can get a formative view of patriarchy, racism and class. When you enter through any one of the doors of experience with its specificity you embark on an understanding that a seemingly bounded form is actually a congealed form of social reality. You enter the path of exploring social organisations and relations and possible forms of consciousness, modes of mediation found in any felt and named social moment. If racism is the entry point, why should this method not be useful for investigating and historicising it? Dorothy's sociological method is not saying to us that where we enter our investigation is where we stay – indefinitely and at the level of description or impact alone. It is by coming in through the passage or the door of an experience and taking it apart and then re-locating it in the social that we learn to figure out what went into the making of that experience. It unlocks the door to history and material practices. There is every reason to find this method crucial for understanding 'race' and racism. At least that is how I use it.

Dorothy herself developed this critical and investigative method in the context of patriarchy and class, but this means that she undertook a task of inquiry,

---

4   Smith 1987.
5   Smith 1990.

a social analysis, not just a critique of others' theorisation or providing a 'theory'. Her method is rooted in Marx's critique of ideology as found in *The German Ideology* and *The Holy Family*, among other of his texts. She discovered in Marx how concepts and their deployment can lead to an occlusion, a foreclosure, of understanding 'what actually happens'. The use of the word 'woman' as a conceptual category, for example, provides a case in point. The word 'woman' can be deployed so that it has a kind of general and abstract or a highly selective meaning, depending how this word is placed in capturing social relations. The notion of 'woman' could then either conceal the social relations, if employed abstractly, or reveal them in specific uses. Dorothy moved beyond simple abstraction by historicising and specifying the notion of woman, by socialising it so that the notion of patriarchy came into play in conjunction with prevailing social relations. As such, patriarchy could be both present at all social levels but also implicated in other social relations, for example, of class or racialisation. This refusal to use language in an undifferentiated, desocialised way is something that I have learned from her. This enables me and others to use concepts critically, not ideologically for the purpose of concealing or erasing.

Dorothy's work has helped me to understand 'race' and racism by bringing attention to the complex relationship between discourses, texts and social relations in syntactical terms, as a kind of grammar of thought involving practice. Thus the form of thought, not just its content, becomes important for us by understanding not just the word but its placement in speech or writing. Her grasp of Marx's 'three tricks' for producing ideology in elaborating how ideology is created through certain technologies of mental labour – as ways of displacing words and their meaning through de-socialising, de-historicising, and de-politicising, becomes the focal point of her reading of institutional ethnography and social organisation of knowledge. These ideological abstractions then are used as reality while the actual sociality is treated as their illustrations or evidences of truth. This reading of Marx's critique of ideology has been the most important part of my use of Dorothy's works.

Ideological forms of knowing that have been explained by Marx and elaborated by Dorothy deserve a thorough reading by anyone interested in the use of concepts in their critical work. Nothing is too small – any instance or event, such as a newspaper story, can exemplify ideology. You can perform ideology by picking up certain bits of details or ideas in a story and instead of situating the bits in a historical social context and content you attach them to a fictitious set of assumptions, making what Marx called 'mystical connections'. For Marx and for Dorothy this is the central trick of ideology.

The empirical details when attached to assumptions of universality or essence give them an ahistorical, asocial aspect of verity. So instead of making a historical social enquiry about an event, you lift it to the level of an enduring significance. The outcome of all this is that the thought object thus composed becomes a kind of a theory – a template, a lens – for perceiving the social. This inverted relationship between theory and social reality provides an ideological epistemological mode which is not accountable to what the reality actually is or was, around which developed a disinformation. The concept of 'race', cobbled together and fitted into moral and physical discourses of difference in the service of oppressive social relations, offers us a prime example of ideology.

To make my point a little clearer, let us take a common event – an incident at a bus stop where a stranger calls you a racist name. You say to yourself, how is this naming possible, why is she or he doing this, in what society or country is it being done? This is your entry point – when you are violated, you're upset, you're angry and even confused. This is the moment of experience – your concrete 'object' of exploration and inquiry. So you say, let's enter into this moment and see how this could have happened as a practice as well as a concept – a descriptive stereotype and a social judgment of inferiority. And then you try to look at what name you were called, where else you have heard it or seen it in written form, who called you this name, and all the surrounding circumstances. The dynamics of relations in a particular locale are now placed in a context, at the bus stop, in a city, in a nation state with a colonial history and familiar to practices of slavery, indenture and conquest of the aboriginal peoples. From this spatial location and moment in time you start summoning prevalent knowledges and an analytical framework that incorporates history, the very formation of a settler colonial country and state and the cultural common sense rooted in the idea of race. With these things in mind you realise that without them already available this racist naming, this violent moment, would not have been possible.

We should return at this point to the notion of experience, and to the everyday world which is both our problem and problematic. This experience of the everyday is of course individually felt, but it is not individualistic as it is something we share with others who are targets of racist slurs. And in fact we share this moment also with those who do the name-calling. This is a strange kind of sharing, because it involves an antagonism born of a history – it signifies two kinds of presences. There is the man or the woman who calls you the racist name, and there is 'I', the person who gets called that name. Both are parts of the story that constitutes my experience. So the story and the experience turn out to be complicated. This experience anti-ideologically considered opens a door to an exit through the possibility of an anti-racist response.[6]

---

6 For more on experience, see the chapter, 'But who speaks for us?' in my collection *Thinking Through*.

This discussion, I hope, shows that the notion of 'race' can be treated as an ideology. It is a word that has been evolved and used in the context of social relations of domination in order to manage difference based on power as well as to obscure and obfuscate them with the help of reified categories or ideas. The idea of 'race', therefore, is an ideological instrument produced in relations of ruling and justification. The stereotypes give them a substantive quality – an illusion of truth.

How does 'race' solidify as an accepted form of knowledge, as a 'scientific truth', even in our time? The reason for that is the implantation of an idea of difference involving value judgment in the human body. 'Race', situated in the idea of 'science', is seen to inhere in the body and biology, rather than in being a product of social relations and history. This 'race' is incorporated in practices, discourses or texts that are considered as credible knowledge. Another way to think of it is that 'race' conceived as a scientific truth does not signal us to read beyond the abstraction. When seen in terms of biology with a substance of its own, 'race' takes on a life that separates it from everything social. It signals to a quality in people themselves. But if you put a question mark after it, or quotation marks around it, as I do, you can begin to see it as an exploitative and violent use of language.

To emphasise further, some uses of language are definitely ideological. Take the example of the concept of 'human nature'. When you ask in a classroom, do you think racism will continue, or how did it begin, a large number of students will say that it is human nature to be racist. Now, that sort of treatment of language which naturalises a social construction and its ramified practices is evident in all relations of oppression and is reproduced through what Dorothy calls 'textual mediation', as well as what Gramsci calls 'common sense'. They are of course not the same thing. From Dorothy's work on language and social relations in *Writing the Social*,[7] we know that concepts or language are forms of sociality. It is not the lexical but the use aspect of language that we need to focus on. It is the social use or the manipulation of language that create systems of meaning. We have to deny the substantiveness or independence of these ideological notions from social reality, and Dorothy's reading of Marx, Bakhtin and Mead can help us in this.

While speaking of Dorothy's use or reading of Marx's critique of ideology I should point out that her reading of this is quite unique. To consider ideology in terms of the *form* or a method of knowledge production rather than only as a body of content of ideas is still a novel move. Many important theorists, more

---

7 Smith 1999.

important than me, have ignored the fact that ideology is not merely content – only a set of ideas generated through relations of power. The production of this body of content or ideology is actually a form of thinking, which can make all kinds of ideas move from their own social location in language into becoming this obscuring anti-social content. For example, Edward Said has shown us that 'orientalism' is a discursive mode originating from a colonial mindset born of relations of power between Europe and Asia, and here I completely agree with him. But what exactly happens to make the orientalist discourse come into being as a form of thought? What conceptual grammar is at work in its production? Speaking of misrepresentation of the East/Orient in Western colonial discourse, Said does not tell us if it is at all possible to 'represent' the Arab, to 'represent' the Orient, or if the very project of representation itself contains the seeds of such discursive uses. This is because there is no 'the' Arab, no 'the' Orient, or 'the' Oriental. The capital letters themselves create an illusion of homogeneity. No one can for all time give the characteristics of a people. They cannot be singularised or essentialised by either the Arabs themselves or the Europeans. And Said misses uttering that fact explicitly, even when he may imply it.

In fact, that is the problem with trying to singularise and homogenise, to particularise and essentialise. That can lead us to a stereotypical or racialised use of language. I think that Dorothy's work, her reading of Marx and its use, challenges this taken-for-grantedness, this silence about the use of language. Her epistemology extends to the query regarding the textually mediated nature of practices of power, the production of relations of ruling. She understands how texts feed into texts as living mental labour feeds on dead mental labour, and the content in this closed circuit becomes a kind of fetish. We do need to know the *content* of ideology in order to actually organise specific resistances, because for this the details are needed. But we also have to realise that these are details in a context, for a purpose and only for now. We cannot just sit on a standard truth about peoples and societies forever. We need to locate language in its ideological use, in the social relations and technologies of linguistic and knowledge production, and refer to history and politics – to reality – in order for us to create and participate in resistances of our time.

And so I have my own contribution to understanding 'race' and racialisation, but Dorothy is someone whom I consider as my teacher. She facilitated critical thinking in me, so I found her to be a pathfinder for my own work.

2   On Marxism, Colonialism and Nationalism

ED and AB: There is significant debate regarding marxism in terms of its relevance to colonialism and nationalism. Can you elaborate on how you understand these connections?

HB: I find in Marx a reflexive and critical methodology to question Marx himself. I don't find this reflexivity in liberal thought, for example, in John Stuart Mill's writings. You cannot question liberalism from within liberalism, but you can question Marx from within marxism and say that his work has limits. This you do by applying his own critical method to his own writings. Take for example Marx's writing on India – this work, as pointed out by many, such as Edward Said in *Orientalism*,[8] is at times racist and as such ideological. But in the course of criticism of Marx you can see the usefulness of his historical materialist method for the purpose of critique and analysis in general.

The question of colonialism generally entails that of nationalism. As we know, nationalism has come up for extensive criticism in feminist and transnational feminist critique. In the way these critiques are posed 'nationalism' has only one meaning and thus has been singularised. This broad rejection and denunciation of 'nationalism' poses important questions for us. Can we speak of a decontextualised nationalism, an all-purpose, one size fits all type of politics? Am I then to condemn Palestinian nationalism? This is after all the case of a nation without a state aspiring to a nation state. And am I to condemn Canadian Aboriginal peoples for their 'national' self-identification and aspirations? Am I to say that their quest for and fulfilment of the conditions for nationhood is something that should not have any demanding and positive role in the Canadian state formation? So even though nationalism may be critiqued, we cannot answer every question related to it with a single answer. We need to take apart these different situations for nationalist struggles and note that they stand concretely for different kinds of social projects and politics. I understand nationalism as a plural notion, and think that the nationalisms of the colonised and the coloniser are qualitatively different.

From the point of view of the colonised we can see nationalism as a response to an outside conquest and rule with an absolutist power which takes over the country and encompasses the entire lives of the conquered peoples. This is the nationalism of colonial powers – a nationalism of the aggressive, the conquering and the colonising. The colonising powers/countries have a hegemonic

---

8   Said 1979.

intention consisting of both force and production of consent, and they also possess a colonial common sense. As they go about their colonising missions many in them probably believe these missions to be good for the colonised, as indicated by Rudyard Kipling in his idea of the white man's burden. I make a distinction between the nationalism of that kind and the nationalism of the colonised people who are defending themselves and seek their independence. We need to consider Frantz Fanon here, who has been important for my work and has influenced my reading of Marx.[9]

The resistance to colonisation is often expressed by nationalism and creates a national imaginary which consists of a resisting identity and aims to create a state. But not all such resistances are typically nationalist in either content or form. The word 'nationalism' signifies resistance with the political aim of structuring a state while also defining a cultural identity. But not all responses to colonialism are geared towards a state formation. And even within the nationalisms of the colonised there are differences.

To give an example, there is a mistake in thinking that everything that happened in India in the nineteenth or twentieth centuries in relation or response to British colonialism was 'nationalist'. Much of the resistance to colonisation was simply people responding to different forces – ideas and practices that came into their world with a sudden force and violence. Before these responses developed an ideologically clear and articulated position which nationalism properly requires, Indian people had *ad hoc* and spontaneous responses that were diversely cultural and social and inchoately political. Much of the poetry, literature, and other forms of social and economic expressions of the first half of nineteenth century India can be seen in this way, and they cannot simply be reduced to nationalism. Indians also picked and chose, especially in cultural matters. Before then we only had verse narratives, but the presence of European literature gave rise to novels in the vernaculars, and out of that came brilliant Indian writers and their prose novels, and they were not written with an eye to Western popularity as they were not in English.

People took what they were ready for and needed to take. They learned a language, through which they read all kinds of works – including Karl Marx, Tom Paine or William Godwin, and so on – and fashioned a new vocabulary and politics. From these kinds of chaotic cultural and political formations only some parts were selectively, carefully, put together as different kinds of nationalist ideologies, for example, as the ideology of the Indian National Congress and related movements. But these articulated nationalisms did not spread into

---

9 Fanon 1963.

everything else, and not everything social or cultural was done in the name of the nation or to achieve a nation state.

Speaking of the diversity of nationalisms in the Indian context we can pinpoint one form of nationalism as liberal democratic. These nationalists do not reject capitalism; they just want national control over capitalism in India. They are not challenging class relations, profit or private property, but they would like to do something about poverty. The amount of poverty that dawned on India thanks to British rule, they might like to reverse some of it. They consider the existing class relations as natural reality of sorts and accept the organisation of capitalist society from which class relations emanate. Though the Indian constitution rejects the caste system it continues as a social practice and feudal relations that existed prior to capitalism become partly integrated in the political structure – a situation similar to Western liberal democracies where 'race' and class are foundational. They declare that people live in an unjust world, and adopt a constitution which will admit to that. And so the Indian governments begin their first five-year plan after independence in 1947 and conceive of a rights-based constitution. Formally, irrespective of gender, race, creed, etc., some social goods are considered to be the basic rights of Indian citizens. However, capitalism continues, as do all kinds of relations of ruling, such as patriarchy and class, with attempts at legal redress. In other words, this Indian nationalism is bourgeois democratic in character.

Another form of Indian nationalism is that of the Hindu fundamentalists or the Hindu right, with a high degree of cultural essentialisation. These Hindu nationalists also espouse capital, class and, of course, caste. They consider themselves as anti-Western and anti-modernists in ideology and cultural practices, but make economic and military deals with the u.s., Israel and so on. But at the same time they are authoritarian in their politics, reject the equality of citizenship and eject minority citizens from the sphere of rights. In social terms, therefore, you will be clubbed with your 'own' religious group, subjected to religious personal laws, and that will be your only recourse in family matters and issues of inheritance. Now this too is nationalism. But while they talk about the evils of Western culture and claim to speak in the name of the Indian people or previously of all the colonised, they want to give to the people of India a fully developed imperialist capitalism, a neo-liberalism replete with an essentialised cultural identity.

But there is still another form of the nationalism of the colonised, that I would call national liberation, which Frantz Fanon and other anti-colonial leftists of the third world talked about. This is a nationalism that calls for a de-colonisation – true de-colonisation, not a false one. Fanon speaks about this phenomenon of 'false decolonisation' in his critique of the politics of the national bourgeoisie in *The Wretched of the Earth*. What is involved in this? In reality, one might say in response, all these anti-colonial liberation projects, even when they are socialist, have reproduced oppressive relations and rely on forms of other nationalisms. And they have. But it is not because they are socialist that these unequal relations and ideas have been reproduced, but because they are not yet wholly socialist. At least in theory their politics is based on a provision to fight inequality, and to do so at all levels and, therefore, leave room for real betterment.

These templates of nationalism that I offer here, and particularly my idea of national liberation, would not have been possible without Marx's critique of bourgeois politics of his time, without his development of the idea and politics of communism. Nor would I have believed in the possibility of self and social emancipation. Nor would national liberation thrive without Marx's idea of people actually making their history, and in reality, in society and, therefore, struggling against circumstances not of their choosing.

As you describe me, I do remain an unashamed and unrepentant marxist and a small 'c' communist. I do not think we do anybody any good if we fail to offer them a dignified life, an enabling 'wherewithalness', and not just survival. And what would it take to create that dignified 'wherewithalness', for the poorest of the poor? It would involve a politics of everybody, of white and non-white men and women together, and seek to create a community of equals in the nation's space.

Among some marxists who are economic determinists there is a separation of culture from everything else in life and society, as in the notion that the superstructure is 'less important' than the base, or gender inequality as a form of secondary contradiction. There is not much of this base-superstructure separation in Marx's own work, but there is in some of that of Engels. But on the other hand Engels' consciousness was distinctly against gender inequality. So we need a marxist method, but we also need to consider the question of a full counter-hegemony, as well as the limits to hegemony. This will help us in devising our critique of and organisation against racist patriarchal capitalism.

While we are about it, we need to ask why it is that some critical and political ideas and practices stick, and some do not. We need to consider why some ideas are challenged from within the very space where they originate. All that is really important. Just as Marx's epistemology is important, so is it important to read others, such as Gramsci.[10] Gramsci's notion of hegemony, and his understanding of popular common sense, and the facilitation of the 'good sense' through

---

10   Gramsci 1971.

the work of the political organiser – are significant for our politics. I think it would be good to do something that uses the possibilities inherent in Gramsci's political thought and its relationship to, as well as departures from, Marx's work. With these tools at our disposal, we can challenge the iniquities of patriarchy, racism and practices of class.

Ideology

1 A General Introduction

The notion of ideology is frequently found in many academic disciplines. It has also become present in the media and speeches of politicians as well as in common parlance. Though its pervasive presence indicates its importance, the meaning of the term is often vague. This diverse and indeterminate use requires a close scrutiny.

Ideology is most often associated with ideas and beliefs related to power and politics, and the use of ideology assigns culture or forms of consciousness a central role in the creation or assertion of power relations. Ideology also refers diffusely to interpretive frameworks, conscious or common sensical, which John Berger called 'ways of seeing'.[1] These usages show a creation and internalisation of world views by social subjects and the nature of their agency. They are reminiscent of Antonio Gramsci's ideas of 'commonsense' and 'hegemony'.[2] The present entry focuses on marxist feminist uses of the notion of ideology, particularly with regard to social transformation and socialist politics and revolution. At the outset we need a general introduction to ideology as a concept and to bring to the fore its epistemological dimensions. We will examine the method of its production and the content or the type of thought objects this process produces, as well as their socio-political effects.

The concept of ideology has a history prior to the advent of Marx and marxism. Its different uses, however, consistently connected it from its inception to forms of consciousness pertaining to power and politics, combining in its conceptual import its social context and the development of its content. Any study of ideology explores the nature of certain ideas and beliefs and their organisation into systems of meaning, thus creating a 'science' of ideas. The term 'ideology' was first used by Destutt de Tracey in eighteenth-century France[3] and implied a secular origin of ideas (a shift noted in the writings of Hegel and Young Hegelians).[4] Ideology could be seen as a branch of philosophy, with a secular understanding born of the 'enlightenment'. The notion of ideo-

---

1 Berger 1972.
2 See Gramsci 1971.
3 Williams 1977, p. 56.
4 See Marx's introduction in Marx and Engels 1970.

logy achieved an important role during and after the French revolution, serving as social enquiry which enables consciously transformative politics. The view that ideas had social origins, could be studied, systematised and manipulated for social and political purposes, was indeed novel. This 'science of ideas' was developed at a time when monarchic and feudal forces and the absolutist role of the church were eroding. It was claimed that a system of socio-political ideas was itself a social force. It is in this context that Marx and Engels saw the importance of ideology and launched their critique.

2   Marx and Ideology

Marx's critique of ideology, especially in *The German Ideology*, is one of the key components of historical materialism, his method of social inquiry and historiography. His understanding of the past as 'history', and not just as memorial narratives or a miscellany of events or facts, showing the connection between the writing and the making of history, relied on the critique of ideology. Marx's interest in this indicates that he placed the greatest importance on consciousness and its socio-historical and political role. This cardinal role he attributed to consciousness and epistemology, however, did not make him an idealist or cultural determinist, just as his emphasis on the economy did not render him an economic determinist. His understanding of different forms of consciousness is to be considered in relation to a material grounding of ideas in socio-historical processes. For Marx the production of ideas is as much 'real sensuous activity' as any other form of labour.[5]

Raymond Williams provides a summary of conventional views of Marx's understanding of ideology. In this context ideology is seen as: 1) 'a system of beliefs characteristic of a particular class or group; 2) a system of illusory beliefs – false ideas or false consciousness – which can be contrasted with true and scientific consciousness; 3) the general process of the production of meanings and ideas'.[6] But as Williams points out, one needs to go beyond these simplifications to an in-depth account of Marx's critique of ideology. The point of departure for such an account lies in Marx's 11th thesis on Feuerbach, which states that '[p]hilosophers have so far only *interpreted* the world in various ways; the point is to *change* it'.[7] Notably, Marx does not set up an antithesis between 'interpreting' and 'changing' the world, rather he emphasises the word

---

5   Marx and Engels 1970, p. 121.
6   Williams 1977, p. 55; see also pp. 75–82.
7   Marx and Engels 1970, p. 123. Original emphasis.

'only'. For him interpretation must provide a knowledge which is capable of directing a social change which heralds socialist/communist revolution, thus enabling a conscious making of history. This requires a critical method for producing knowledge for accessing the real bases of history. Marx not only criticises the 'ruling' ideas which oppress people, but discloses through his critique their very process or grammar of generation.

The pathway to a 'true' form of knowledge or an inquiry or a 'science' of society starts from the life activities of embodied, conscious socio-historical subjects as they produce and reproduce themselves. Any other starting point of social inquiry is ideological. Theory must therefore be rooted in concrete reality of lives of people and their society, which they create through material forms of labour. As Marx puts it, consciousness or ideas cannot make history, but living, active people do – it is *their* history, their society and ideas, their life lived in determined time and space/place, that are the objects of social transformation. Even the stance of ideology which proclaims the 'independence' of ideas can only exist because the social and intellectual conditions implying a separation of mental and manual labour are present. In *The German Ideology* Marx points out that production of ideology does not exhaust all the activities of consciousness. We must keep in mind that *while all ideology is a form of thought, not all forms of thought are ideological.* The production of ideology is thus a very specific form of mental activity towards a particular result.

Consciousness, according to Marx, has two main forms: practical and ideological, both subject to refinement and high specialisation of labour. It is this highly specialised ramification that creates the appearance of disconnection and qualitative difference between mental and manual labour and the impression of autonomy and predominance of concepts/ideas over reality. Marx's critique of ideology is built on the axiom that human existence has never been un-conscious. From its inception humanity is conscious. It is a 'practical consciousness'[8] which we continue to generate. Beginning with evolution of language to the creation of concepts and categories, in creating relations to others for communication and skill transmission, as well as in transforming nature, consciousness is involved as shaping and being shaped by people. It is only through this involvement that ontology becomes *social*. Human consciousness is thus both a physical and a mental capacity in an indivisible way. Marx debunks the attribution of an exalted *sui-generis* nature to ideas and situates them in cumulative social-historical formations and products of consciousness.

---

8   Ibid., p. 50.

The production of ideology requires experts in the technology of generation of ideas. These professionals are called 'philosophers' or 'metaphysicians' by Marx. They form an important part of the social organisation and the legitimation of capitalist relations of accumulation and ruling. Intellectual specialisation or 'disciplines' are the domains of these experts. A pervasive market begins to appear for ideas as commodities, and ideology is diffused in the upper and lower strata of society. Only then does it become possible to say that ideology or the ruling ideas of any age are those of its ruling class.[9] Belief in the autonomy of knowledge, in its transcendent or objective status, is itself an ideology which conceals the actuality of social organisation and relations and the situated nature of knowledge. Marx offers a *social* ontology of epistemology. For him '[c]onsciousness is, therefore, from the very beginning a social product, and remains so long as men exist at all'.[10] Using the example of language, he categorises most forms of consciousness as *practical consciousness*. Language, he says, is as old as human consciousness and it 'exists also for other men, and for that reason alone, it really exists for me personally as well'.[11] It is intrinsically social. '... [A]s well language, like consciousness, only arises from the need, the necessity, of intercourse with other men'.[12]

But the historical context of the creation of ideology and the social nature of its content notwithstanding, the question that confronts us is – how is ideology produced? What, according to Marx, is its epistemological grammar? In *The German Ideology* he presents us with the 'secret' of its production process, its syllogism. He speaks of 'three tricks' for producing ideology.[13] It begins with an idea, a theory, or 'discourse', with the belief in the precedence and primacy of an idea over material/social conditions, in its transcendence from history. Marx shows that the first task for producing ideology is to separate ideas from their producers, that is, separate ideas from their social and individual origin. Thus 'ruling ideas' (ideas that are dominant in society) are separated from 'rul-

---

9   Ibid., 'The ideas of the ruling class are in every epoch the ruling ideas, i.e. the class which is the ruling *material* force of society, is at the same time its ruling *intellectual* force. The class which has the means of material production at its disposal, has control at the same time over the means of mental production, so that thereby, generally speaking, the ideas of those who lack the means of mental production are subject to it. The ruling ideas are nothing more than the ideal expression of the dominant material relationships, the dominant material relationships grasped as ideas; hence of the relationships which make the one class the ruling one, therefore, the ideas of its dominance' (p. 64. Original emphases).

10   Ibid., p. 51.

11   Ibid., p. 51.

12   Ibid., p. 51.

13   Ibid., p. 65.

ing individuals' (intellectuals who are bourgeois or at their service) who help to produce justifications for the 'ruling relations'. An epistemological act of de-contextualisation leading to extrapolation of ideas from their original situation evacuates their socio-historical content or concrete materiality. 'If now in considering the course of history we detach the ideas of the ruling class from the ruling class itself and attribute them an independent existence ...', they become general propositions.[14] Marx also says, '... if we confine ourselves to saying that these or those ideas were dominant at a given time, without bothering ourselves about the conditions of their production and the producers of these ideas, if we thus ignore the individuals and world conditions which are the source of the ideas', we can do little except to produce ideology in the guise of knowledge.[15] This process can be exemplified in notions such as 'honour' and 'loyalty' in feudal times and those such as 'freedom', 'equality' and 'individual' in capitalist times. In its fully separated state the process of production of ideas increasingly depends on dislocation, displacement and abstract formulation.

Once the evacuation of reality takes place a substitute or 'mythical' connection has to be provided between these extrapolated bits of empirical reality. This second 'trick' of the production of ideology can be done by using metaphysical empty universalism or rational abstractions such as the ideas of 'essence', 'natural', 'human nature', 'homogeneity', and so on. The fabricated autonomy and human-like agency of ideas asserts that an 'age' or an 'epoch' is moulded by certain ideals rather than by people. This homogenises diverse and contradictory ideas and activities into stereotypes and predictabilities. The paradigmatic uses of 'modernity' and 'tradition' are good examples, as are racist and sexist stereotypes. A homogeneity indicating a-historicity erases the contradictory relations of an actual social formation and cultural complexities. Certain constellations of ideas are then posited as dominant ideas (for example, 'race') and offer pseudo-explanatory and descriptive services. Marx disarticulates this constellation of ideas or a code into its components through historicisation and socialisation. In doing this he refuses the ideological concepts their status as forms of determination *in* and *as* history.

The third 'trick' in Marx's formulation of the production of ideology occurs as the appearance of reality that ideological notions or usages convey occludes their origin in 'metaphysics', erasing an *overtly* idealistic appearance to make it seem *secular* – for example, the movement from God to 'Man' is more suited to 'modern' times (Feuerbach). There are other ideological sleights of hand, such

---

14   Ibid., p. 65.
15   Ibid., p. 65.

as that of making a person out of a concept, for example, by personalising many ideas into *the Idea* and making it the prime mover of history.[16] Common nouns or adjectives can be similarly treated, such as the ideas of 'whiteness' or 'blackness' as used in a racialised discourse. Thus concepts are treated as people with agencies, while actual people are seen as their mere bearers.

3   Feminism and Ideology

Marx's critique of ideology could be an indispensable part of feminist analyses and political projects. Patriarchy and gender could then be treated as ideological categories in certain usages and as social categories which name particular types of social formations. The time-honoured equation of women with nature, the naturalisation of gender and sexual division of labour or the institution of the family provide examples of ideology. For that matter, the construction of a singular and fixed category called 'woman' which is extrapolated from actual women's historical and social relations can itself be seen as an ideological practice. Marx's critique also helps to explode conventional binary paradigms encoded in notions such as masculine and feminine, which in this usage become reified and reifying conceptual devices only tenuously or contingently connected with biological differences. Likewise, binary categories such as nature and culture or civilisation, emotion or imagination and reason or rationality, the home and the private sphere and the world or the public sphere, should be treated as ideological formulations when they go beyond a descriptive function. These concepts and the spatialisations they elaborate match a private-property-based, patriarchal, ideological social organisation scored with numerous ruling relations. When scrutinised through the historical materialist method, antithetical masculine-feminine categories reveal their imbrication in sexual and social divisions of labour as developed in history. The moral construction and regulation and economic and legal aspects of the state and society are frozen in these static categories. Marx's anti-ideological method chal-

---

16   See ibid.: 'Once the ruling ideas have been separated from the ruling individuals and, above all, from the relationships which result from a given stage of the mode of production, and in this way the conclusion has been reached that history is always under the sway of ideas, it is very easy to abstract from these various ideas '*the* idea', the notion, etc. as the dominant force in history, and thus to understand all these separate ideas and concepts as 'forms of self-determination' on the part of *the* concept developing in history. It follows then, naturally, that all the relationships of men can be derived from the concept of man, man as conceived, the essence of man, *Man*'. (pp. 66–7, original emphases.)

lenges the conventional practice of attributing men and women with exclusive social ontologies and their 'natural' habitats.

We can see, therefore, that an effective and socially actionable understanding of patriarchy as a historically concrete social formation can be uncovered by anti-ideological historical materialism. This realisation is essential if feminism is going to be a force for social change. The question why this insight is so frequently lacking calls for a scrutiny of the epistemological positions which underlie different types of feminist theorisations, the most dominant stream of which arises from liberal perspectives. Liberalism is not a reflexive and historically grounded epistemological position, and can offer no account of social relations and ideas that inspire its own and other social thought. Liberal thought is empiricist and thus has no concept of an overall constitutive social whole. The integrity of the social is perceived by liberal thinkers as discrete issues or spheres which are to be aggregated for different purposes. Liberal approaches to social formation and transformation tie feminists who rely on them to conceptualising social problems in terms of relational and intellectual dysfunctions, and thus to seeking only social reform. This treatment of gender or patriarchy creates a one-dimensional view of its hegemony and leaves the overall social organisation and relations that form them invisible and unaddressed. It makes no distinction between the reality and the ideology of patriarchy and gender. 'Race' and 'class' are similarly understood, forcing us to rely on manipulation of concepts such as 'difference', 'intersectionality' or 'co-constitution' without accounting for their historical and social formation.[17]

The discomfort of trying to bring class, 'race' and gender together into a meaningful and formative relation with each other can be attributed to an ideological way of thinking which prevents us from seeing the social as a concrete formation.[18] This concreteness extends even to the most miniscule aspect of society. The different aspects of society are not static. They are simultaneously

---

17   In this context see Bakan 2008, an interesting way of conceptualising the social as a 'dialectical totality' relying on reconceptualising 'the politics of difference', claiming that major forms of difference are categorised 'by human suffering identified in [Marx's] work' (p. 239). The main forms of human suffering are exploitation, alienation and oppression. 'Race', gender and class are seen as 'categories' of difference. However, it is important to note that from our point of view Bakan does not move the critique of ideology any further than connecting the notion of difference with that of categories.

18   Marx says in *The Grundrisse*, 'The concrete is concrete because it is the concentration of many determinations, hence the unity of the diverse. It *appears* in the process of thinking, therefore, *as a process of concentration, as a result, not as a point of departure, even though it is the point of departure in reality*, and hence also the point of departure for observation (Anschauung) and conception'. Quoted from Bannerji 2011, p. 48.

conscious, practical and evolving. They are what Marx calls sensuous practical human activity. The necessity of capturing formational moments involved in the production and reproduction of the social as a concrete consequence of different determinations forces us to name them and specify their categorical function. As I have written elsewhere in this context:

> The 'concrete' as the social, we can see, has a dual character for Marx. It is, on the one hand, a mental or conceptual category and, on the other, an existing specific social formation. Thus, it is both 'a point of departure' (as the social) and 'a point of arrival' (as theory). Something that is 'concrete' is not like an 'object' that is visible, such as a table or a chair, but nonetheless its 'concreteness' is a determinate form of social existence. It is concretised by specific social relations with mediating and expressive as well as reproductive forms of consciousness and practices. In fact, this 'concrete' social form is to be seen in contrast to a fact or an 'object', because it is not reified/fixed, hypostatised. It is fluid, dynamic, meaningful formation created by living subjects in actual lived time and space, yet with particular discernible features that both implicate it in other social formations and render it specific.[19]

These names for our present times and the global northern context are 'class', 'gender' and 'race' – but these categorical names are not 'things' in themselves. They are congelations of historical social relations with conscious social subjects and agents securely in their formational centre. The ideological gesture has been to consider these names or categories as substantive 'things', as separate realities which then come into 'co-constitutive' or 'intersectional' relations. In this ideological practice, which asserts appearances or phenomenal forms as stable social ontologies, they substitute the ever-forming concrete social realities. Reality then takes on a secondary life, as illustrative of this category 'things'. This is the inversion that Marx critiques throughout his opus, in one form or another. Anti-ideological critique reverses this ideological practice where ideas/categories are ideas or categories of a socio-historical, practical and intellectual formation. If we did not consider class, gender and 'race', for example, as determining realities, but as determined social formations, we could use them as names for certain formative relations.

Marxist feminism generally uses his critique of ideology, especially the process of its production, rather cursorily, conventionally downgrading his interest

---

19   Bannerji 2011, pp. 48–9.

in consciousness. This under-use of Marx's interest in consciousness results in ideology being treated as a neutral organisation of ideas. Thus in common with non-marxists, marxist feminists also employ ideology as a synonym or a vehicle for political ideas.[20] The primary use of Marx's critical social analyses has been made by feminist political economy. There his analysis of the capitalist mode of production in its intricate complexity has provided a fertile ground for understanding the formation of capital, forms of social production and the labour theory of value, among other things. The feminist political economists have contributed to an expansion of Marx's method of analysis and pointed out his own ideological blinders through their critique of his gender unconsciousness and under-theorisation of social reproduction. But feminist historical sociologists, while using the category of class for a nuanced understanding of gender and patriarchy, moral regulation and sexist stereotypes as patriarchal 'ruling ideas', have not paid much attention to how ideology is created, and more to how it is deployed. The most notable exception is in the sociological writings of feminist marxist sociologist Dorothy E. Smith, for whom Marx's anti-ideological epistemology has played a crucial role. In her sociological methods of inquiry, consisting of 'social organisation of knowledge' and 'institutional ethnography', Marx's critique of ideology has been pivotal.

Feminist critiques of mainstream epistemology have been generally performed by non-marxist theorists, such as Catherine MacKinnon, Sandra Harding, Lorrain Code and Nancy Fraser, among others. They have addressed women's lives, experiences and the marginalisation of their knowledges, as well as their invisibility created through patriarchal omissions and commissions. But not even the anti-capitalist materialist marxists, including Maria Mies or Silvia Federici, have paid the notion of ideology any sustained attention as important for theorising. Of the two, Mies, who is more explicitly a marxist thinker and engaged with patriarchal capitalist accumulation on a global scale, has productively drawn upon Marx's concept of social division of labour and the devaluation of women's labour. She emphasised the importance of ideological forms of consciousness in producing and reproducing women's subor-

---

20   See Barrett 1988. For Barrett the interest is in ideology as content, a body of connected ideas, discourses and stereotypes. As summarised in a piece on the blog Survivingbaenglish, '... Barrett develops a detailed account of what she identified as the four key mechanisms by which textual representation reproduced ideology: stereotyping; compensation by the discourse of the supposed moral value of femininity; collusion i.e. manipulation of consent; and recuperation – the negation of challenges to the dominant gender ideology'. While all these mechanisms are valuable points of inquiry for reproduction of patriarchy as ideological content, no use is made by Barrett of ideology's process of production that Marx considers so important.

dination. Her critique of the conventional women-nature equation is a version of an anti-ideological critique from a materialist viewpoint, as she offers an in-depth disclosure of patriarchy's relationship to property relations, extending to women being social property. Mies' feminist critique of 'development' operates both at the levels of political economy and critical epistemology.

Smith considers prevailing patriarchal ideas as 'ruling ideas' which mediate and textualise the ruling relations of capitalism. Her specific use of Marx's epistemological critique of ideology is pioneering not only for women's studies but for sociology as a field of social inquiry. Through the application of Marx's method Smith discovers the 'social organisation' of knowledge and the constitutive role of ideological knowledge in developing bourgeois institutions or ruling apparatuses. Her critical sociology, including her innovation of 'institutional ethnography', allow for an anti-racist feminist extension for both marxist and feminist thinking. The wide scope of Smith's contribution in critical sociology extends from her initial stage of writing a 'sociology for women' to one for 'people'. Confining the challenge of patriarchal ideology to the realm of consciousness alone, the linguistic or discursive approach to social relations endangers the very project of feminism. It itself becomes an ideological venture and attributes to consciousness the power of self and social reproduction. Concrete realities of daily lives, experiences, activities and social interrelations are thus linguistically/discursively overdetermined. Articulated discursively, the project of feminism mainly becomes a pedagogic one trying to change consciousness without changing the world. Feminist politics framed within this schema begins and ends with antithetical discursivities recommending 'educational' empowerment for women, especially through the education of 'rights'.[21] This is the understanding of patriarchy from which national and international women's non-governmental organisations and advocacy based social movements are predominantly organised. The agenda of the 'development' agencies for women are concerned with the 'issues' rather than the social organisation that gives rise to them. Thus feminism is incorporated in patriarchal corporate agencies and managerial bureaucracies of the state, which creates

---

21   Catherine MacKinnon, who has read Marx and understood some aspects of materialist critique, provides us with the most interesting version of the liberal feminist account of difference between marxism and feminism. An interesting but deeply dualistic reading of both marxism and feminism, this essay illustrates both the useful and the misleading sides of liberal feminist thinking. 'As marxist method is dialectical materialism, feminist method is consciousness raising ...' (1982, p. 543). It sees feminism as an essence of collective subjectivity of women, while marxism 'refers to a reality outside thought which it considers to have been an objective – that is, truly non-socially perspectival – content' (p. 543). It is this version of marxism and feminism that I critique in this essay.

a class of women experts who hold power over other women. In their role as technical/administrative policy makers or service providers they help build the ruling apparatuses that oppress the very women they want to 'empower'. In this way, even unintentionally, feminists can become ideologues for patriarchal capitalism's reproduction and for constructing an ideological feminism for its legitimation. Such a feminism is a competing ideology within patriarchal social relations and consciousness. Feminist political struggles are reduced to struggles between two sets of antithetical ideologies.

4   Ideology, Feminist Theory and Women's Standpoint

If liberal feminism with its emphasis on the socially and materially ungrounded primacy of consciousness is a subjectivist reductionism, its opposite, a dominantly structuralist viewpoint, is an objectivist materialism. It would be absurd to argue that any form of knowing is unconnected to either the knower's experiences and activities, her location and participation in society or her subjective apprehension of them. The idea of a humanly uncreated social or economic 'structure', a system with its own 'laws' which affect people foundationally, is patently fabulous, as is the notion of an absolute subjectivism which can create the world as it pleases. Experience, social location, relations and history serve as the standpoint of knowledge for a materialist understanding of the world. Thus the ideology of an objectivist knowledge created from the 'outside' has to be counter-posed by knowledge produced from the 'inside' by social insiders. This ushers in the question of the standpoint of knowledge being treated differently by different schools of feminist thought. Investigating the issue of 'standpoint' of knowledge prompts us to compare non-marxist and marxist feminist approaches. Non-marxist women's standpoint theorists emphasise the direct nature of knowledge which arises from women's experience, thus removing the role played by epistemological mediation. It assumes a single axis of standpoint produced by lived patriarchy as the overall social determinant. This location of the woman subject is claimed as the clearest vantage point for knowing social reality. The woman subject seen as situated at the greatest distance from the 'centre' of power thus becomes the ideal knower. This version of standpoint theory puts us in a quandary because it posits an unmediated existential experience as being both the problem to be understood as well as the endpoint for the search for truth. If we challenge this presupposition of an unmediated truth born of direct experience, then within this schema we are left with multiple and relative competing truths. Such an epistemological position cannot provide a solid ground for any project of social transformation. The different locations and relations of women across the society with their different experiences do not add up to an overall character of social organisation.

The feminist marxist version of standpoint theory, however, can be the best epistemological choice because it takes into account not only direct, non-mediated experiences but also social relations and forms of mediation that enter into the process of knowledge production. Dorothy E. Smith's 'A Sociology for Women'[22] provides us with this position. Using Marx's anti-ideological/materialist method of beginning our social inquiry from the everyday lives and experiences of women (people), Smith accords a crucial role to women's experiences in the creation of a transformative knowledge. But these experiences are not left as 'individual' but are socialised instead, thus integrating finite forms of social organisation and relations with their diversities and contradictions as components of an individual's experience. Smith clarifies how specificity of women's experiences arises as she shows that they inhabit a social organisation of which patriarchy is a vital organising component. It is this complex and contradictory social organisation which accounts for actual and ideological unevennesses and ruptures that women experience. Women's feeling of being at odds with what is around them comes from the social relations and ideas which are both implicated in and at odds with each other. This practical consciousness of contradiction between what women live and what they are told creates what Smith calls a 'fissure' integral to women's (people's) consciousness. This 'fissure' or 'the line of fault'[23] is markedly evident among all social groups who are oppressed and marginalised, but among others as well. There is a daily experience of a double message between actual social relations, practical consciousness and ideology. The situation is further complicated by the fact that an 'outsider' of one group could be the 'insider' of others. The challenging question that arises in this context is what is ideological and what is actual in our lives? How can we grasp what conceals the ongoing organisational relations and ideas and instead presents us with a seamless account of our lives? These questions do not arise in liberal standpoint theory but are indispensable to a marxist anti-ideological feminism because the actual and concrete social relations are considered in this approach both contradictory and convergent.

Generally speaking, women and patriarchy and social and biological reproduction entered relatively late in marxist theorisation. Early socialists/communists considered patriarchy lower in the scale of their revolutionary agenda. Thus self and social emancipation are by default seen as masculine prerog-

---

22   Smith 1987.
23   Ibid.

atives and, therefore, more fundamental to the revolutionary project. Here certain versions of marxism evince an ideological occlusiveness because an ideological perception of production has disconnected it from reproduction. The naturalisation of this division has continued to hide constitutive relations between production and reproduction, of different kinds of labour as well as public and private spaces. Though practically experienced as integrated, their integrity remained theoretically invisible. The social forms of class and class struggle were consequently set apart and even at variance in forging a revolutionary project based on a dynamic constitutive conception of the social. To think non-ideologically would be to note that pre-existing sexual and social division of labour bequeathed by patriarchy to capitalism. Capitalism with its re-spatialisation of women and reproduction to 'private' life, redefining labour as wage labour, became common sense, an internalisation of ideology in daily life. Yet a reflexive and critical reading of Marx also provided the basis for focusing on patriarchy as a major social problematic. The self-reflexivity of his method and his search beyond bourgeois conceptual axioms offered the possibility of fresh epistemological critiques and analyses. Social analysis grounded in comprehensive notions such as the mode of production, social formation and their accompanying forms of consciousness all provided a historical materialist understanding. It was evident that patriarchy could not be understood on its own without being placed within the social formation as a whole, nor could social practices or ideas and norms be conceived without a socio-sexual division of labour, enabling 'gender' with masculine and feminine imperatives. Feminist political economy disclosed how patriarchal sexual division of labour is indispensable in the realisation of surplus value.

It is important to note that feminist political economy holds a tension in trying to reconcile the structural imperatives of political economy with the subjective and agentic dimensions of the concept of the 'woman' found in feminist theorisation. It is this tension that was expressed by Heidi Hartmann in her formulation of the problem as an 'unhappy marriage' of feminism and marxism. As I have noted elsewhere, '[i]f we assess marxist/socialist feminism in terms of agency or representation, we find little interest in either. We are clearly pitted in the midst of an unresolved relationship between two social projects premised on different grounds'.[24] Until recently marxist feminist uses of class analysis have been economistic, structure based, with an assumption of a male working class. But in their feminist incarnation, marxist feminists have had to rely on women's experiences and responses, where their subjectivities and

---

24   Bannerji 1995, p. 75.

agencies provide the central theoretical focus. Much of the influence in the area of non-subjectivism and displacement and introjection of ideology into the social structures comes from the work of Louis Althusser.[25] The point is to go beyond the binary formulation of structure and subjectivity, which cannot be done 'through either a subsumption of feminism in marxism or through arithmetic exercise which constructs a social whole by adding together qualitatively different epistemological stances'.[26] To get over this binary formulation we need to have a theory of consciousness in which experience is grounded in concrete forms of social being and knowing. Experience or the subjective moment arising in daily lives of people must be our point of entry but not the endpoint. We must extend our understanding of an individual's experience, intention and location into social and historical levels. Then it will become evident that the local and immediate experiences are specific forms of a general larger social organisation and relations. It is by reading my experience in these historical, social terms that the standpoint of my knowledge would allow for deeper social understanding. The objective and subjective moments will come together through a progressive revelation of how the larger social organisation and forms of consciousness contain and shape our lives. Our experiences in the local can become truly comprehensible within that framework. The we would go beyond self-referentiality and connect with others in time and space.

It should be obvious how feminists and marxists could both benefit enormously from using Marx's own version of the critique of ideology, as it is possible to deploy categories such as 'woman' or 'class' in critical, expository or in ideological and occlusive ways. Eschewing ideology, we could step out of the various false perceptions of 'women' and socialise the 'woman question'. Marx's critique of ideology could offer the richest method for apprehending the social. We could see how the social, reduced to the market economy, disconnected the economic aspect of society from all others. Extrapolating ideas from their social contexts and content is the essence of ideology. Substituting a part of the social for the whole, or an a-historical whole which denies specificity of the constitutive parts, are both ideological enterprises. Formulation of the social whole in terms of the base (the 'economic' infrastructure) and the superstructure (the socio-cultural forms), or a 'corresponding' or 'reflect-

---

25   See Althusser 1977a. On close examination Althusser's understanding of ideology and
       Marx's are not the same. Whereas for Marx ideology is only one aspect of forms of con-
       sciousness, Althusser's concept of ideology occupies the entire mental space, thus making
       it impossible to develop a qualitatively different set of critiques and concepts that lead to
       socialist/communist revolution.
26   Bannerji 1995, p. 79.

ive' relation between society and culture, all arise from such an epistemology. The hierarchic ranking of class and gender cannot capture the nature of social formation. The answer to this dualist problem does not lie in appending the 'woman question' to the 'class question'. An ideological view of society which breaks the social into fragments without constitutive relations, or homogenises or essentialises social reality, makes both social analysis and revolutionary social transformation inconceivable. It is interesting to note how non-marxist feminists and economistic marxists both suffer from this dualist ideological approach.

The process of development of ideology lies in the division of mental and manual labour at its most developed. The thought products – the intellectual objects that mental labour produces – enter as 'things' into relations with each other. They achieve a status similar to commodities in their circulation. They also have their dead labour and living labour dimensions and create an ever growing edifice of self-serving conceptual products. As such, it is no surprise, especially in their alienated and intellectual forms, that thoughts become reified realities. Keeping this in mind might lead us to use categories in an investigative manner, exploring the concrete nature of social formations.

This is of course a very difficult thing to do. As Marx puts it in the Afterword to the second German edition of *Capital*, Volume I, the mode of presentation has the danger of obscuring the mode of production.[27] The category or concept 'capital' is thus in need of analysis so that its formational complexities correct the ideological vision of seeing capital as a 'thing' rather than a particular social relation and concomitant formation. The same can be said of 'commodity', 'money', 'wage-labour' and so on.[28] If concepts are not 'things' or ground level realities, they are ways of talking about something. It is this 'something'

---

27   To put it in Marx's words: 'Of course the method of presentation must differ in form from that of inquiry. The latter has to appropriate the material in detail, to analyse its different forms of development, to trace out their inner connexion [sic]. Only after this work is done, can the actual movement be adequately described. If this is done successfully, if the life of the subject-matter is ideally reflected as in a mirror, then it may appear as if we had before us a mere a priori construction' (Marx 1971a, p. 28. See also pp. 26–9.).

28   To understand this process of reification of ideas and their circulation through mutual exchanges it would be useful to read section 4 of *Capital*, Vol. I, chapter 1: 'The Fetishism of Commodities and the Secret thereof'. In the production of ideology, as in the production of commodities, 'the social character of men's labour appears to them as an objective character stamped upon the product of that labour; because the relation of the producers to the sum total of their own labour is presented to them as a social labour, existing not between themselves but between the products of their labour' (Marx 1971a, p. 77). This could be said of ideology as well, as there is an independent relationship conceived between the reified ideas.

that we need to address in discussing a raced, patriarchal class formation. Critique of ideology also needs ideas, but these ideas send us out of the category into a lived, socio-historical world. They must point outward rather than deeper into themselves – they are, after all, names burdened with the content of reality.

CHAPTER 4

But Who Speaks for Us? Experience and Agency in Conventional Feminist Paradigms

1 The Personal and the Political: Beginning from Our 'Selves'

One always learns better with blood.[1]

It has been difficult to write about being a student and a teacher in Canada. I would rather not have learnt or taught all the lessons that I did in these classrooms which mirror our everyday world. But there is no better point of entry into a critique or a reflection than one's own experience. It is not the end point, but the beginning of an exploration of the relationship between the personal and the social and therefore the political. And this connecting process, which is also a discovery, is the real pedagogic process, the 'science' of social science.

First – there are colonial memories and memories of underdevelopment and neocolonialism. I grew up in Pakistan and India. Both countries were liberated through a long struggle for independence. The white man finally had left us, the states were ours, but inscriptions and fossils of colonialism lay everywhere, though often unrecognisable as such because they were so effectively internalised. I went to a 'good' school, where everything was taught in English, and which served the children of the ruling class. Here Bengali, my mother tongue, the main language of nationalist culture of my region, with its hundreds of years of script and literature, was subordinated to Shakespeare. And later, sitting in the library of Presidency College under the portrait of Professor Richardson,[2] I did not know that I was a part of Macaulay's design for creating a special class.[3] Great literature or culture were universal, we learnt. They transcend space and history. English literature and language seemed ours by the

---

1 An old Columbian proverb.
2 Presidency College was one of the earliest colleges established by the British in India (Calcutta) during the colonial era, early in the nineteenth century. Richardson was a renowned professor of English literature at this college.
3 Macaulay, in a now famous Minute to the British Parliament in 1835, urged: 'We must do our best to form a class who may be interpreters between us and the millions whom we govern ... a class of persons, Indian in blood and colour but English in taste, in opinions, in morals and in intellect'. Quoted in Chatterjee 1976, p. 58.

same logic. They surpassed the little historical local England and embodied a state of cultural perfection. So we never quite thought that Charles Dickens, for example, had a particular local home and a daily social belonging.

My alienation from this 'universal culture' began in England. That 'our' Dickens might have looked at me in the streets of London, as others did, with a thinly veiled hostility – and not seen our common ground in the 'universality of a refined literary sensibility' – became apparent to me many years ago in Portobello Road. In that poor district, lying in a damp room, reflecting on my days at art galleries, book stores and landmarks such as John Keats' house, I was faced with a reality for which I was unprepared. I felt small and bewildered, and put up a struggle to keep something of myself from vanishing and to maintain a little sense of significance. Though I did not know it then, I was being produced as 'the other', as 'different', but not neutrally different, not just as a cultural variation on the theme 'human', but as 'different and inferior'. But at this time I only suffered from this at the level of feelings – feelings that had not yet been named, interpreted and become my experience. As yet I had no shared world or any social/political analysis, nor points of comparison. My alienation was produced everywhere – by everything – and it inverted itself to a thought of pure oneness with one's social environment, of belonging, to a longing for 'home'.

That great classroom of the Western world into which I was thrown headfirst in England remains with me, as does the institutional classroom. When I came to study as a non-white 'foreign student' in Canada – in streets, personal interactions, and in the classrooms and halls of the University of Toronto – my learning continued. I was a student in the English department, where my self and interests were rendered more silent than I would have thought possible. I remember feeling confused and a growing sense of frustration and rage. Nothing that was relevant to me seemed to count. I realised the degree to which I was a marginal member of the discipline, whose 'universality' by this time had given way in my mind to being highly local and particular, whose historicity and ideological character became daily more visible. Deprived of a general sense of social belonging, of being a comfortable user of the local cultural grammar, divided by my gender, race and marxism, I was an 'outsider' in and to my discipline and the classrooms that I inhabited. Often I was the only non-white student in these classes. Other students would talk among themselves with ease and were willingly responded to by the professors even when there were disagreements. I looked for reasons for their sense of a shared reality. It was not in their reading or thinking ability – because I had both – but in their 'whiteness' together (middle-class Anglo/ European cultural heritage and white skin) and their political commonality. They carried on discussions as though I was not there, or if I made a comment which interjected, conversation would resume and the waters close above my head. I was an outsider and not much by the way of intellectual performance was expected of me. In fact, no one thought of me – for or against – in any real way. I repeated my M.A., kept very good grades, took my comprehensives and sometimes got asked by eminent English professors whether I felt cold in *saris*, ate beef or was comfortable in English. Wading through trivia, fluent in English, but not in aestheticised colonialese, I searched for ways to understand what was happening to me and whether and how it also happened to others. In this way I wanted to create my own experience by understanding in social and political terms these events and interactions which frustrated and thwarted me. To make a long story short – I found Frantz Fanon, George Jackson, Angela Davis and the Black Panthers, Karl Marx, Che Guevara and African liberation movements, Vietnam. And redeemed academia by discovering Raymond Williams, C.B. MacPherson, Frederic Jameson, and finally and irrevocably found feminist literature. By the time I discovered them all I had become rather useless to English, and English to me, as practised by the University of Toronto, the Harvard of the North. Having explained at length the title of my doctoral dissertation – 'Conservative Ideology and the Educational Ideas of S. T. Coleridge' – making a distinction for my teachers between 'thought' and 'ideology' – I finally left the department with a half-finished thesis. As a marxist and a feminist, conscious of racism and imperialism, I dropped out of the department as does a leaf from a branch when its stem has dried. Upon leaving the classroom I experienced relief. Now there was the crude harassment of everyday life, sexist racism,[4] but not the subtle, refined cruelty of intellectual racism and colonialism.

I concentrated on writing poetry, political-cultural criticism and on articulating myself somehow to the women's movement that existed in Toronto. But there, in the place I least expected, a naive believer at this point in 'sisterhood is powerful', eager to add my voice, to speak from my own experience as an active participant in the revolution of half of the world's population, I experienced my deepest disappointment. With a change of rhetoric, my English classroom was there all over again, in fact the dramatis personae often overlapped. Once when young I was let down by my bourgeois belief in the universality of 'culture'. In my mid-thirties I went through a similar but worse experience. I realised painfully, to paraphrase Orwell, that 'all are women, but some are more women than others'. Controversies over International Women's

---

4 The notion of 'sexist racism' first attracted my attention in two essays in Birmingham Centre for Contemporary Cultural Studies 1982. See Carby 1986, pp. 212–35; and Pratibha Parmar 1982, pp. 236–75. See also Bannerji 1986a.

Day, which I celebrated with fervour, conveyed to me the astounding revelation that imperialism was not a 'women's issue'. Readings informed me that class and gender struggles were to be separately conceived and waged, that women were 'class-less', a 'caste' perhaps, and patriarchy was an 'autonomous' power system. And a growing essentialism as well as a perverse biologism persisted through all this. Racism was not even mentioned as a real issue by the 'Canadian women's movement'.[5] Our lives, our labour remained unmentioned, and intellectual/cultural production unsolicited, in the annals of publications of the (Canadian) Women's Press. We were at best a separate category of sub-women – 'immigrant', 'visible minority', 'ethnic', 'black', later 'women of colour'. All were labels – except 'black' – with no political history of militancy behind them. Here in relation to feminism and the women's movement my otherisation was even more overtly accomplished than in the university – and in the context of an assumed 'sisterhood', the damage was much deeper. The greatest gain however, was meeting with young black women, whose experience and politics matched with mine, whose poetry along with mine named our world. Affirmed by them in a fundamental way in my reality, I felt the legitimacy of my anger as a 'black' woman. In those days we thought that whoever was 'not white' in a racist society was a part of the great political metaphor – 'black'. The British use of this term in *Race and Class*, for example, or in anti-racist organising, legitimised our choice of political self-description. We had not yet become ethnically or culturally territorial about our political identities.

And – resenting entrepreneurialism, lacking a space for developed intellectual work and with a smouldering anger about being indirectly 'pushed out' – I returned to school. This time in sociology, at the Ontario Institute for Studies in Education – where the feminist marxism of Dorothy Smith, the generally more permissive attitude towards political, intellectual work and that I was working on my three interests – India, communism and political theatre – mitigated to some extent the institutional and social forms of alienation, namely racism, otherisation and 'feminist' aggression in the monopoly of definition of the term carried out by white Anglo/European women.

All this while, however, like Shente of Brecht's *Good Person of Szechwan*, I wore another hat as another persona. From 1970 to 1974, I was teaching at Victoria College as a part-time lecturer in the English department and from 1974 to 1989 I was a temporary, contractual, part-time, piece-work teacher of part-time students at Atkinson College, York University. In the last year I have, at this late

---

5   For a discussion on the politics of International Women's Day and the March 8th Coalition, see Egan, Gardner and Persad 1987, pp. 20–47.

stage of my life, finally found favour in the eye of the establishment and become an assistant, non-tenured (but possible) professor. Once, a long time ago, I was a tenured faculty in India – from 1965 to 1969. I came to Canada on leave from my job – and it took twenty years to find myself comparable employment.

But as a teacher in social science and sociology my difficulties are of equal magnitude – and of the same kind – as those experienced as a student of English. Of the many problematic aspects of my teaching relations I will speak of a few key ones – and conceptualise them in terms of who I am and who the students are, what I teach and how.

Once again I must begin from myself. From my body as a political signifier. The gendered perception of my sex receives a further negative (and also a latently violent) reference from a prevailing racist common sense. This perception of the students is not neutral – it calls for responses from them and even decisions. I am an exception in the universities, not the rule. As a body type I am meant for another kind of work – but nonetheless I am in the classroom. And what is more, I am authority. I grade and therefore am a gatekeeper of an institution which only marginally tolerates people like us in scarcity rather than in plenty. What I speak, even when not addressing gender, race and class, does not easily produce suspension of disbelief. Working in a course on 'Male-Female Relations' which I co-designed and co-taught for six years with a colleague – who is male, white, older, taller, bigger, and a full-time faculty member – I saw the specificity of student response towards me, where I had continuously to work against my subordination. Whenever expertise or administration was at issue, my status as an equal worker had to be forcefully underlined. It was rarely, except technically, seen as my course as well. The overall attitude of the students towards me in this course was not exceptional. It fits with other courses which I taught or teach by myself. It is not surprising that this combination of racist social practices, media presentations and cultural common sense all made it initially hard for us to settle into a stable professor-student relationship.

I have written elsewhere about this experience of teaching.[6] Suffice it here to say that there were also 'other' students, as I was the 'other' teacher, and together we found that neither sociology (not even the conventional marxist variety) nor feminism (not even marxist feminism) spoke to our lives, our experiences, histories and knowledges of the world. The existing literature, the conventional paradigms – of both left and 'bourgeois' sociology/feminism, or radical ones – had little or tangential application for us. Neither in the sociology of the family as presented by Eli Zaretsky (male marxist), nor in the

---

6   See Himani Bannerji 1987.

political economy of the marxist/socialist feminists, nor in the books on 'our repression/oppression' in terms of sexuality, did we find much that spoke of our lives – either as lived by us in the West or in those parts of the world homogenised from a metropolitan perspective as 'the third world'. Racism was and is considered a separate problem from sexism, and seen as a 'black' problem. Making themselves 'white' by the same stroke of the pen which gave and gives us this special/peculiar status – these women construct(ed) their separate world, which purportedly did not come into being through the same social relations that ours did. The absence, the gap, the silence regarding the presence of 'others' or 'their issues', did not bother the theoretical and investigative minds of these white feminists of all varieties.

This physical non-representation in special/textual politics was not problematised. It was not remarked that non-white women were and are not seen as a real part of 'feminist' textual production. The fact that this 'exclusion' is organised by the very same principles that generate 'inclusion' for white women still remains invisible to white feminists by and large.

Unvalidated in our bodies, experiences and theorisation, we daily learnt and taught a literature, theoretical paradigms and methods that alienated us from our lives. Thus we were and are offered the possibility of a political or an intellectual agency on grounds and terms that are inauthentic to our lives and not created by us. This was and is quintessential alienation. The more we participate(d) in these processes, the more a giant edifice of knowledge augments the power of others over and against us. Where are we to turn? Where can we find interpretive frameworks and methods that are more than 'alternative' and would go beyond 'inclusion'? How can we gain an insight into the social relations and culture of advanced capitalism which allows for direct representation and a revolutionary political agency?

2   **Beginning from the 'Other' End: A Critique of 'Otherising' Social Relations and Intellectual Modes**

> Have you read the grievances some of our sisters express on being among the few women chosen for a 'Special Third World Women's Issue' or on being the only Third World woman at readings, workshops, and meetings? It is as if everywhere we go, we become Someone's private zoo.[7]

---

7   Minh-Ha 1989.

So far then, we get a glimpse of how it is that what Foucault called 'know-ledge/power' relations are inscribed all over my academic experience. It is obvi-ous that the production of knowledge is a part of social production as a whole, and as much attention must be paid to the social relations of 'knowledge' as to its content. Teacher-student relations in the classroom, relations among the students themselves, and the world outside the class which we enter in the pur-suit of 'objective', 'positive' knowledge, all influence the form and content of our learning. All social and cultural relations and forms, both of oppression and privilege, directly and indirectly shape what and how we learn, or even whether – as exemplified by my 'drop-out' behaviour – we wish to continue 'learning' at all. Even if we can no longer speak in such quaint nineteenth-century ways as 'education educes the whole soul of man' (sic), we do know that knowledge comes in two types – a producer's knowledge and a consumer's knowledge. In the former we participate in our learning as creators and in the latter as mere functionaries and hoarders of information or 'facts'. The overall social relations that construct(ed) my classrooms demonstrate the disincent-ives to learning and teaching as non-white women.

If the social relations of production of knowledge in institutional settings constitute a silent but powerful set of learning imperatives, the content itself – texts, literature, analytic/interpretive frameworks, methods or paradigms (in short what we call curriculum) – presents us with the other half of our prob-lem. They not only teach 'facts' or supply 'information', but actually create what John Berger calls 'ways of seeing': perspectives and interpretive modes which encompass systematic ideological stances, but also go beyond them in form-ing an overall cultural social vision and praxis.[8] This textual mediation also does not inhabit a separate social sphere. It actually draws on and systemat-ises, and often uncritically, cultural common sense and everyday practices and invests them with the status of knowledge (as social facts, norms, etc.) as well as knowledge-creating procedures (theories and methods). These textual omis-sions and commissions confer a normalcy to reificatory textual devices and can, for example, naturalise orientalism and sexist racism. When practised by ourselves they develop into grotesque forms of self-alienation. Sometimes an even more unusual situation results. A text which is coherent with my experi-ence as a non-white woman, for example, when inserted into the tentacles of an alienating interpretive device, loses its original reference points and meaning, and becomes inert and inverted. Thus, *The Wretched of the Earth* in the light of O. Manoni's *Prospero and Caliban* (1956) becomes an example of Oedipal

---

8 Berger 1972. An essential reading on cultural commonsense, especially the essay on 'The Nude'.

counterphobia of the colonised, or Angela Davis' *Women, Race and Class* (1983) an example of 'black feminism', no more than just a 'different' perspective in feminism.

These problems of generating the content or the curriculum point to fundamental aspects of knowledge production that affect us all positively or adversely. If the purpose of learning/teaching determines the type of knowledge produced, implicit in this knowledge is always a notion of political agency. The agency, whether it is active or passive, of a producer or of a consumer, varies according to the goal – which may either be social change or the continuation of the status quo. If knowledge is to be 'active', that is, oriented to radical social change, then it must be a critical practice of direct producers, whose lives and experiences must be the basis for their own knowledge-making endeavour. What Paolo Freire called the 'banking method' – treating the student as a storehouse of 'facts' of a fixed content – is then out of the question.[9] This critical/active knowledge then is a basic form and part of a general political process – which relies on the subjectivity of the student and the teacher – and consciousness (both its products and forms) is seen as socially grounded.

The educational process consists of establishing transformative connections between how people live or act and how they think. The usefulness of this knowledge lies in its ability to give a reliable understanding of the world and to impact or change lives rather than simply to 'function efficiently'. Thus an 'active' education begins from experience (the immediate and the local) through an understanding of the increasingly complex mediations which structure it and culminates into political effectiveness. The intellectual project of feminism is par excellence one example of such 'active' knowledge.

Feminism ideally rests on a transformative cognitive approach, which validates subjectivity and direct agency.[10] It is disinterested in 'expertise', which reduces women to outsiders and operators of the machinery of the status quo knowledge. Thus beginning from ourselves, with a project of self and social transformation (encoded in the slogan 'the personal is political'), does not require an apology but, on the contrary, becomes a basic imperative. If this is the fundamental stance of feminist politics and pedagogy, then we are left with a puzzling situation for non-white women. What, we must ask, accounts for the reificatory or exclusionary textual and social practices which we, non-white women, encounter even in the context of feminist pedagogy? By what

---

9   See Freire 1970.
10   See Smith 1987, 'A Sociology for Women', 'Institutional Ethnography: A Feminist Research', and other essays.

magic do we become textually invisible, or at best segregated into our special status, denied real agency and our lives constructed as peripheral to the everyday workings of society?

The answers to these questions do not lie in individual ill-will and racist conspiracies (though they may exist) but rather in the theories, methods and epistemologies used by feminists, and the cultural common sense within which they arise. In this, feminist theory is no different from any other theory which serves different class and ideological interests (even when it does so unselfconsciously – in the name of 'women').

My project is to consider the basic epistemological standpoints of some of the major feminist approaches, ignoring their apparent political differences and labels. The organising concepts for this assessment are central to any study of epistemology. They are generally presented in a binary relationship to each other and arranged in the following pair patterns: general/universal and particular, essential/abstract and concrete, local/immediate and extralocal/mediated, part and whole, experience/consciousness and the mode of production, and finally, subjectivity and material conditions. As we might notice, some of these pairs express the same content as the others. The efficacy of any social theory is determined by its ability to demonstrate and theorise adequately the formational (i.e., non-oppositional) interplay between these different moments of social cognition. The explanatory, analytical and descriptive/ethnographic task of social theory requires that it be able to dis-cover the mediations[11] of different social moments in non-polar terms, and bring out the 'specificity' of any fragment of experience by providing it with a general name as well as with a particular authenticity at the same time. That is, it must show how any situation/experience is distinctively, particularly, locally itself and yet/also constituted by and exemplary of social forces which lie in, around and beyond it. The most 'trivial' incident, understood in this way, can reveal certain basic and necessary relations intrinsic to the social organisation and forms of consciousness as a whole. At its best it is a relational and an integrative analysis which needs a deconstructive method to display the process of mediation. It can both take apart and put back together (in a non-aggregative fashion) an event or an experience within a wider context by using a materialist theory of consciousness, culture and politics. I characterise different feminist theories according to their ability to comprehend and represent conceptually

---

11 For the concept of mediation, understood in a marxist sense, see Williams 1977, 1983 and, Marx 1973. This has been a key concept in marxist cultural theory, but increasingly important in social theory.

a mediational and formational view of social practice. Their ability to accomplish a less one-sided social analysis and interpretation, I claim, depends on their understanding and handling of mediation.

Of the available feminist frameworks, I will begin with the one which is most common – and which we learnt as our first feminism. For this we have to turn to the type of sex/gender/power relation in the works of Kate Millet, Betty Friedan or Germaine Greer, for example, and their essentialist interpretation of an earlier anthropological concept of patriarchy.[12] Patriarchy was denuded of its content as a general social organisation and division of labour (for example, of hierarchical kinship relations among men or between elder female kin and younger male kin) or as an overall organisation of the mode of production (a regulator of production, consumption, distribution and exchange). The concept of 'patriarchy' (originally meant for the study of pre-capitalist social formations) was read as an unmediated form of power relations between men and women. The feminist interpretation of patriarchy distilled from it a universal theory of power – direct, interpersonal domination by (any) man over (any) woman.[13] Male need and power to dominate was seen as both intrinsic and original (biological/quintessential), and as socially manifested through 'gender' relations. Patriarchy was found in its purest form (as original impulse or even instinct) in the domination of women in the area of sexuality, and relatedly in maternity. All other social relations and contradictions manifest this domination and are subsumed in the primary antagonism expressed in male-female gender relations. Man and woman face each other in opposition – their subjectivities in 'essential' otherness and confrontation. This antagonistic otherness originates outside of history and social organisation but provides their foundational ground.[14] The authentic ground of woman's subjectivity is pre-

---

12   Though Simone de Beauvoir's *The Second Sex* (1974) has been lumped together with the work of other essentialist feminists, it is not quite of the same philosophical and political persuasion. Marxist phenomenological feminism of de Beauvoir with a historicised notion of 'patriarchy' is a far cry from Millett, Friedan, etc.

13   For a clear view of 'patriarchy' as re-interpreted by liberal and radical feminists, see Millet 1971 or Dworkin 1980.

14   See Miles 1985. Her full statement on this issue sums up the stand of many others, and particularly rests on the theory of 'essentially' different male/female consciousnesses propounded by O'Brien 1981, based on 'their materially different experience of the process of reproduction' (quoted by Miles, 1985, p. 21). Miles' own statement is worth quoting: '… unless one accepts *the sociobiological or liberal notion of innately aggressive and competitive, acquisitive man* it must remain problematic why the existence of surplus and other resources for domination are actually used by some to dominate others' (18. Emphasis added). Miles' and O'Brien's ahistorical use of the concept of materialism to develop an essentialist perspective based on a biological or other *innate human nature* argument is

sumed to rest on her unitary woman-self and otherness to man (two single and singular subjects with ontologically antithetical consciousnesses), assuming a global sameness for all women, trans-historically and socially, as well as trans-personally.

Feminist theory of this kind exposes, challenges and subverts its own version of patriarchy. This it does by positing a synthetic category called 'woman' as a unified consciousness and a universal subject. The category is still based on otherness to man, but this otherness when undominated exists freely for itself as subject in the world. Feminist essentialism, with its hypothetical/synthetic woman subject, cannot situate women in history and society. As such, it eradicates real contradictions among women themselves and creates a myth ('woman') and an abstraction, by isolating gender from all other social relations. This transcendence from history and from actual lives of people as inessential or accidental is entirely based on an idealist epistemology.

Gender and patriarchy, seen thus, become ideological constructs and lose their power as concepts for social analysis and, even as constructs, they are fundamentally paradoxical. The theorisation rests on the assumption that what is 'real' or universal is 'essential' (supra-social/historical), while at the same time deducing this 'essence' and universality from historical and social particularities. The complex and constitutive mediation of an entire social organisation is thus 'ruptured' by disarticulating one relation – 'gender' – and conferring on it an autonomous status and transcendent universality. This paradoxical theory is made credible less by any essential truth about women that it reveals than by relying on details of relations of power which are pervasively present in most societies we know about. Social history is thus portrayed as an endless repetition of an interpersonal patriarchal drama with a constant ratio of power and powerlessness held by the two protagonists.

Decontexting 'patriarchy' or gender from history and social organisation – which is structured by both cooperative and antagonistic social relations – obscures the real ways in which power works. Using this framework, we cannot

---

different from the use of the concept in marxist terms, as in the anthology edited by Kuhn and Wolpe 1980, but is used earlier by Firestone 1970. Whereas the Kuhn and Wolpe collection has little historical perspective, it interprets the notion of the 'material' to mean a 'social' perspective rather than a biological/physical one. An interesting, though quite erroneous, reading of materialism and marxism in an essentialist context comes out in Nancy Hartsock's *Money, Sex and Power – Toward a Feminist Historical Materialism*. She claims that '[Women's] experience and relation with others, with the natural world, of mind and body – *provide an ontological base for developing a nonproblematic social synthesis ...*' (Hartsock 1984, p. 246. Emphasis mine). For a critique of Hartsock's essentialism see Kline 1989.

conceptualise a reality in which women are complicit and 'gender' is implicated in, both creating and maintaining class and racist domination. Nor can we
see the cooperative engendering of the social space of classes, or the simultaneity of this cooperation with the necessary subordination of women within the
dominant and subordinate classes. Through this theorisation we cannot speak
of women's experiences in relation to class and race (in the West). This pre-
interpretation of reality valorises all women as *woman* and at the same time
denies their actual lived relations. That 'race' (as a category for organising ruling relations) or class become invisible in this essentialism is only logical.

This invisibility adds to the status quo of oppression. Working-class white
and non-white women do not have reasons to feel 'equal' to the essentialist theorists. They are drowned rather than empowered by this generality. All notions
of 'sisterhood' break down in front of actual experience which resists this false
universality according to which *all women* have identical subjectivities and are
equally oppressed and certainly not by each other.[15] Feminist essentialism, in
the end, becomes a cloak for smuggling in the interests of privileged women.
As Elizabeth Spelman puts it, ' "Woman" as an essentialist/universal category is
a Trojan horse – the more universal the claim, the more likely it is to be false'.[16]
Feminist theory provides a friendly home for white middle-class privilege and
concerns.

Many white feminist theorists in recent years have become aware of the pitfalls of essentialism. Interest in the essential 'other' of man (and its negation)
has shifted to 'other women'.[17] Not entirely a spontaneous gesture of reflexivity,
this is also a response to the vigorous dissatisfaction and anger of non-white
women[18] and white and non-white lesbians. In the new theorisation, experi-

---

15   See Tania Das Gupta's introduction to *Race, Class, Gender* (1989) on 'white middle-class
       women pretending to speak for all women'.
16   Spelman 1988, p. 13.
17   'Paradoxically, in feminist theory it is a *refusal* to take differences among women seriously
       that lies at the heart of feminism's implicit politics of domination' (Spelman 1989, p. 11). For
       an example of such 'a refusal' to see real differences among women, especially white and
       non-white women, see particularly the introduction of *The Politics of Diversity* (Hamilton
       and Barrett 1986). On different approaches to the question of difference see also Harding
       and Hintikka 1983 and Eisentein and Jardine 1985, among many other anthologies (some
       included in the bibliography). The politics of 'difference' ranges from neo-pluralism of
       'diversity' to a more radical insistence on relations of power, of which good examples are
       writings by bell hooks, Trinh T. Minh-ha, or even the philosopher Spelman, or the literary
       critic Toril Moi. Sandra Harding, however, would fall within the 'diversity' tradition.
18   For powerful examples of Black and Asian women's protest see *The Empire Strikes Back*
       (Birmingham Centre, 1982) and many others in the U.S. and U.K. The theoretical range
       lies between marxism (Angela Davis) and radicalism (bell hooks).

ence, subjectivity and political agency have been at the centre of the debate. Here the particularity and immediacy of experiences of oppression by different groups of women have been theorised and politicised under the concept of 'difference'. Emphasising diversity, particularity, multiple and changing subject positions and self-representation, the politics of difference has rejected the universalist position.

The admission of 'experience' to theory has moved feminist theory into speaking of the concrete and the tangible. In Britain and the U.S., for example, it has been most forcefully brought to attention that racism is a central determinant of women's experience in advanced capitalism, as are, relatedly, poverty, discrimination and dispossession.[19] As non-white women have spoken up for themselves, so they have been valorised as 'different' and granted, in theory, the right to equal access to a representational voice. A large section of the feminist mainstream accepts that only we can speak for ourselves, and that women's varied experiences provide the ground for multiple types of politics.[20]

This politics of 'difference' is, however, not as unmixed a blessing as it appears to be. If the paradigm of feminist essentialism played up the general/universal at the cost of the socio-cultural and historical particulars, this politics of difference errs on the side of the particulars, often making it impossible to see the forest for the trees. It invents multiple political personalities within one subject and invests expressions of these and other different subject positions with an equal and real value. This creates the possibility of a positive coexistence among them, without any regard for either experiential coherence or the genuinely antagonistic social relations that underlie the speech act or expression and thus provide the context of and the reasons for the 'difference'. This emphasis on experience and expression as the main form of political activity equates politics primarily with free speech/cultural expression within a general format of civil liberties. Often in the feminist context it means that so long as a white woman (middle-class) does not speak for me, but gives me equal time (since she controls the space prior to my arrival), all is well. But being 'equal' to white women who themselves are unequal on class and other grounds does

---

19   See Moi 1985, where she critiques a 'humanist, totalizing aesthetics' and politics and
      speaks for changing subject positions and related politics both among and within sub-
      jects. For her and others, we need to 'radically undermine the notion of the unitary self'
      and give up 'the search for a unifed individual identity (or gender identity) or indeed a "tex-
      tual identity"'. 'Any other approach is "highly reductive and selective"' (pp. 137–9). Also in
      this context of de-centring see McCallum 1985.
20   A good case in point is Minh-ha 1989, which carefully outlines the objectification of Third
      World women through colonial discourse, but considers this domination at the level of
      discourse alone.

not reflect on or bring into question the societies of fundamental inequality in which we live. Through this framework we can't 'see' the overall social relations and common sense which organise the sexist racist experiences of non-white women, making their colour a socio-cultural signifier of a deeper and exploitative 'difference'. Furthermore, while concentrating mainly on the expression of our own oppression, it becomes difficult to keep other oppressions in sight, or to think beyond our own advancement. The task of overall change, that of re-organising social relations of inequality as a whole, becomes peripheral to the main project.

The concept of 'difference', therefore, clearly needs to be problematised. Where does such 'difference' reside? Who are we 'different' from? Upon reflection it becomes clear that the 'difference' which is politically significant is not a benign cultural form. The 'difference' which is making us 'different' is not something inherent or intrinsic to us but is constructed on the basis of our divergence from the norm. Since non-white women vary enormously from each other, as do different groups of whites from each other and from us, it remains a question as to why white middle-class heterosexual feminists do not need to use the 'difference' argument for their own theory or politics? When questioned thus, 'difference' becomes a matter of our *similarity* to each other as non-white women in a racist social organisation which 'otherises' us, ascribing a self-ness/sovereignty to white women. It is only these racist modes which create political signifiers out of our skin colour, physiognomy, culture, etc., and produce oppressive experiences. Our 'difference' then is not simply a matter of 'diversities', which are being suppressed arbitrarily, but a way of noting and muting at the same time fundamental social contradictions and antagonisms. The concept of 'difference', with its emphasis on expression/textual/linguistic view of social reality, obscures these antagonisms at the level of everyday life and overall (national or international) social and economic organisation.[21] It prevents us from seeing that racism is not solely a 'cultural'/ideological prob-

---

21   This is so pervasive that it defies listing. However, a few representative texts of political economy of Canadian women will indicate the absence that I notice. Acton 1974; FitzGerald 1982; Maroney and Luxton 1987 will give an idea of the narrow concept of race I speak of, and how simplistically class and gender are conceived when understood outside of the practices of colonialism, imperialism and Canadian capitalism and their attendant racist discourse and common sense. Also see Mitchell and Oakley 1986, throughout the introduction of which everything is spoken of but racism or the particularities of the lives of non-white women in the U.K., U.S. and Canada. Any talk of 'working-class women,' failing this contextualisation, is mere empty rhetoric. In the Canadian context, see the separate and marginal role of 'women of colour' in *Feminist Organising for Change* (Adamson et al 1988).

lem and that the ground of our racist oppression is the same as the ground of white privilege. In the name of 'difference' we tend not to go beyond a rich and direct description of personal experience to a social analysis which will reveal the sameness of social relations that construct the experience of 'white' privilege and 'black' oppression.

The politics of 'difference' hides in its radical posture a neo-liberal pluralist stance, even when power and brutality are stressed as 'differential' factors. Generally it amounts to advancing a metatheory of competing interests built on the concept of a free market. The political sphere is modelled on the market place and freedom amounts to the liberty of all political vendors to display their goods equally in a competition. But this view of society as an aggregate of competing individuals, or at best as fragmented groups or communities, makes the notion of an overall social organisation theoretically inconceivable and thus unnameable. All such attempts are dismissed as totalising and detrimental to individuality, uniqueness of experience and expression. Concepts such as capital, class, imperialism, etc., are thus considered as totalising, abstract 'master narratives', and untenable bases for political subjectivity since they are arrived at rationally and analytically, moving beyond the concreteness of immediate experience. And the master narrative of 'patriarchy' (which the 'difference/diversity' feminists do conform to – since they identify themselves as 'feminists'), fractured through experience and locked into identity circles, also cannot offer a general basis for common action for social change, without sinking into a fear of 'essentialism' or 'totalisation'.

Obviously a situation of equal representation is better than that of monopoly. And speaking in their own voice does 'empower' people. Failing all else, even the speech act itself can become liberatory. If the classrooms I inhabit(ed) had a discourse of 'difference', we would not be so frustrated, outraged or silent. We would be the direct producers within the discourse. But what would we speak about? How would we communicate our particular ways of being and seeing to others who do not share our experiences? And what finally would be the objective of our speaking?

The refined particularism and individualism of the politics of 'difference' not only avoids naming and mapping out the general organisation of social relations, it also reduces the concept of experience from an interpreted, dynamic process of subjective appropriation of the social into a far more static notion of 'identity'. De-emphasising the social and the historical in the interest of individual uniqueness, expanding at most as similarity of detail, the concept focuses on a content rather than a process and creates knowledge enclosures. Thus the stories we tell from our immediate life become the end of our political destination, rather than serving as the first steps to an active/interpretive definition of self, which bears a constitutive relation to our social world. That subjectivity arises in a shared 'social' and mental space, is obscured.

That this social space is riven with genuine antagonisms and contradictions, where the privilege of some women directly militates against the rights of many others, does not however prevent it from being 'shared'. It is a common social terrain inhabited by all. Occupying different parts of the social topography and allowing for differential access to social, economic and cultural resources and political power does not exempt anyone from the possibility or the responsibility of naming what constitutes the social whole. Beginning and ending in 'difference', i.e., a fragmented presentation of subjectivity, merely hinders us from facing/uttering the fact that a whole social organisation is needed to create each unique experience, and what constitutes someone's power is precisely another's powerlessness. A rich description of an immediate experience is an indispensable point of beginning, but it must expand into a complex analysis of forms of social mediation.

The concept of 'difference' opens and closes simultaneously some very basic epistemological and social questions. Opening the door to many experiences and possibilities, it closes out, in its fear of generalisation and equation of subjectivity with immediate feelings and experience, any 'social' explanation for these very same things. If it establishes anything larger and in common, it is by the simple principle of matching of detail. With each change in the configuration of details reality itself differs or changes. This empiricism equates each decontextualised variation of detail – what immediately seems to be – with what actually happens. It is this empiricism which makes 'difference' theories unusable beyond a politically or a discursively expressive gesture. At its widest, it expands into 'issues' and 'communities' which remain as discrete, self-enclosed ontological entities (with equal rights, however). Lacking an analysis of forms of consciousness and social relations, theories of 'difference' lack the potential for a revolutionary politics. Colonialism, imperialism, class or 'race' – all concepts which require a broad historical and social scope – exist primarily as discursive practices, defying any systematic existence or naming outside of the individual's interaction with them. In the end they are converted into metaphors of 'power' whose sources and reasons for continuation remain undefinable.

Even this best aspect of the liberal tradition cannot provide a social analysis which uncovers or explains how it is that white and black women (in a racist society) arrive at opposite results/effects by sharing the same social relations. And for that social analysis I turned to 'marxist/socialist feminism', considering it a doubly revolutionary social project involving class and gender/patriarchy. But here the situation is even more complicated, in so far as representation/

direct agency as well as issues of 'race' are not the focus or basis of this social analysis. 'Racism' and 'race', as well as non-white women as producers of theory or politics, are generally absent from the textual world of 'marxist/socialist feminism'.[22] This absence is not only a matter of disappointment and acrimony for non-white women, but even more fundamentally it throws the whole theoretical and political project of marxist feminism into question.

If we assess marxist/socialist feminism in terms of its theory of agency and representation, we find little interest in either. We are clearly pitted in the midst of an unresolved relationship between two social projects premised on different grounds. The 'marxism' or class analysis of marxist feminism is mainly a certain version of Marx's idea of 'political economy'. Sharing with their male counterparts the agenda of a 'scientific' social analysis, feminist political economy is largely an attempt to situate women and the sexual division of labour in capitalist production. Feminists also equate marxism mainly with political economy and use the same positivist method for reading *Capital*, though in retaliation against the sexism and gender-blindness of male practitioners. The major marxist feminist achievement consists of annexing the home to capital, as a site for and, function of, its reproduction.[23] That is, it makes public and economic the 'private' form of capital-labour relations, as though by stripping it bare to its true economic functions. This economistic and productionist emphasis continues right through feminist political economy. The absence of women is rectified, and as the domestic labour and 'wages for housework' debates indicate, women can now be seen as fully contributory to capital, producing 'value' at home, 'reproducing' to augment surplus value indirectly. In this attempt to make 'the private' public, lived social relations and forms of con-

---

22   See Luxton 1980 for a humane example of this approach. Speaking of nuclear households and seeing them primarily as sites of 'domestic labour', she formulates the everyday life at home in terms of 'labour process'. As she puts it, a household is '... a *production process* that is conducted between two arenas of economic exchange – the labour or job market and the consumer goods market' (1980, p. 16). See also Fox 1980, for 'value' production at home and a discussion on 'domestic labour'.

23   Books such as *Double Ghetto* (Armstrong 1978), for example, would call for such an overview and specificity, from the logic of the text itself, which calls for a materialist (i.e., historical and social) analysis of organisation of labour by Canadian capital. The inability of political economy to come to terms with racism, for example, is noticed by Dorothy Smith in her comment on feminism's uncritical acceptance of its conventional reifying discourse. 'The contours of the discursive barriers are perhaps most strikingly displayed in our failure as feminists working within the political economic tradition of racism implicit in our practices and arising less from attitudes we hold as individuals as from just the ways that we participate in and practice the discursive assumptions and the structuring of the 'main business' within the relations of ruling' (Smith 1989, p. 53).

sciousness that constitute a personal, cultural, home life – all dubbed 'subject-ive' and therefore phenomenal – remain outside of the purview of an analysis of 'class' and capitalism. An abstract and economistic reading of *Capital*, which ignores use value and the social and reduces the whole mode of production into 'economy' (i.e., solely a sphere of exchange value and circulation), disat-tends Marx's analysis of capital as a *social relation* rather than a 'thing'. It is not surprising, therefore, that this economistic reading of *Capital* did not lead to a general appreciation of seemingly ideological-cultural factors such as 'race' and ethnicity. That racism and sexism are necessary social relations for the organ-isation of colonial or modern imperialist capitalism in the West seems to figure as an afterthought in recent writings.[24]

But even as an 'economistic' understanding of our world, feminist polit-ical economy needs to extend itself beyond its present state. In the Canadian case we need work that gives us a world of commodity production with pro-ducers as living, conscious agents rather than as functional assumptions of the production process, and that also presents the Canadian economy in its organisational and structural complexity. When delinked from its history as a white settler colony and its present as an imperialist capitalist state which continues to import labour on the basis of ethnicity, race and class – creat-ing 'class' in its own terrain – the Canadian economy becomes an abstraction. The erasure of the factors of 'race', racism and continual immigration prevents an adequate understanding of the Canadian economy. The construction of the Canadian labour market (its segmentation) and capital accumulation in rela-tion to uneven development or concrete forms of the exploitation of surplus value are important examples. Yet we know that an accurate economic char-acterisation of the political economies of Britain, Canada and the u.s., for example, or of France and West Germany, cannot be made without showing how fundamental a role 'ethnicity' and 'race' have played as organisational and administrative categories of both the economy and the state. The conscious-ness which marxist feminists acquired of 'gender' and of women's contributory role in capital did not open their eyes to the social specificity of differential exploitation that actually exists in an economic organisation.[25] Not even *func-*

---

24   The fact that capital needs to reproduce itself and does so through class makes class more
      than an economic function and category. Class as an assemblage of social relations with
      specific forms of consciousness is examined in two later essays of mine. See Chapter 1 of
      this volume and Bannerji 2019.
25   See Armstrong and Connelly 1989. 'In our view, class has to be reconceptualised through
      race and gender within regional, national and international contexts. The static categoriz-
      ing of class that has been used in so much of class analysis does not capture the experience
      of gender, race/ethnicity or class' (p. 5). This statement draws our attention to the same

tionally did they apply the categories of 'race' and ethnicity and attend to practices of racism to augment their understanding of capital. Only very recently, as a result of protest and analysis by non-white women themselves, do we hear the litany of 'gender, race and class' recited in the introductions to essays/books on political economy.[26] But why is racism still at the level of being named rather than an integral part of the economic analysis?

The source of this failure in the political economy of marxist feminists lies in the abstraction characterising their original positivist reading of marxism. This was further modernised with a sophisticated reading of capital and its state and ideology under the influence of Louis Althusser. As an antidote to the earlier positivist 'economism' we received new theories of self-contained and self-reproducing but interlocking 'structures' of society (determined by the economy in the *last* rather than the *first* instance), at which we arrived 'scientifically' (ascending the steps of 'generalities'). Experience, the self, the social and the cultural, that is, anything subjective, was abandoned as an ideologically contaminated form of unreality. The subjective dimension of class and class struggle, involving theorisation of political agency and direct representation, became redundant to the consideration of revolution. In the name of 'scientific' analysis, all bases for political subjectivities were erased and with them the complexities of different kinds of social contradictions.

The social space was then conceived as a chain of linked 'structures' which somehow 'reproduced' themselves and spun off into others by using human agents to fulfil their will and purpose.[27] The revolutionary thrust of Marx's writing on self-emancipation and the making of history, the relationship between

---

lack that I speak about, to be found throughout feminist political economy. See also the introduction to *The Politics of Diversity* (Hamilton and Barrett 1986) and its view of Canada as an entity of two nations, Anglo-French, even though a token 'politically correct' gesture is made to the plight of the Native Peoples of Canada. Roxana Ng, in her essay 'Sexism, Racism, Nationalism' comments on the racist character of this type of historiography.

26 An interesting example of this *structural* understanding comes out in the domestic labour formulations. Meg Luxton's *More Than a Labour of Love* begins by stating: 'Housewives make up one of the largest occupational groups in Canada' (p. 11) and goes on to speak of the four structures or 'distinct work processes' of a household, '*each* composed of a variety of tasks and *each having its own history*, its own internal rhythms and pressures and its own particular patterns of change' (1980, p. 19. Emphases added).

27 See Sargent 1981. In her introductory piece, 'New Left Women and Men: The Honeymoon is Over', Sargent speaks in terms of 'the problem of day to day work (who cleans the office ... etc.)' and 'the problem of theory (who leads the revolution ... etc.)', outlining the dilemma for women of the left of 'going or staying' as experientially determined. In Sargent's analysis, 'who' or the agency and experience are central but not thought out, and nowhere does she question the type of marxism practised by the male left. Instead we only hear 'who leads the revolution,' etc.

politics and class consciousness, were irrelevant to the project. The subjective dimension of the revolutionary project was dismissed as 'humanist' and 'idealist', belonging to the pre-scientific revolution stage ('epistemological break') in Marx's development. Marxists with theories of political subjectivity involving experience and agency, such as Sartre, for example, theorists of different liberation movements, such as Fanon, or marxist writers of cultural and historical theories, such as Williams or Thompson, were hardly drawn upon (Sheila Rowbotham and a few others remain exceptional). Not only for non-white women, but for anyone interested in creating a revolutionary social movement at all, there is no *active*, conscious and creative, no fully subjective ground for direct political agency within the framework of Althusserian marxism. And since 'racism' in these terms is considered a cultural/ideological – a superstructural – phenomenon, it can thus be dismissed, or relegated to the status of a superficial attitudinal problem.

This objective, structural abstraction in the political economy of socialist/marxist feminists – which provides the theoretical groundwork for their overall social project – sits very uneasily with the utterly subjective position that they advance as 'feminists' in their gender revolution. Marxist feminists themselves have commented at length on this dilemma, and phrased it in terms of an 'unhappy marriage between marxism and feminism'.[28] Latterly, 'socialist feminists' have sought to question further as well as seek to reconcile this unhappy union. But they seem to have shunted aside an in-depth consideration of the dilemma and decided that quantity can change quality even when the epistemological and analytical premises are antithetical. That is, they have added to the economic structural analysis another set of structures immediately out of the range of wage labour. The 'private' realm of the family as a 'social structure' and the 'ideological structure' of patriarchy were added onto each other in the realms of public and domestic production. This economistic analysis has been supplemented by its counterpart in the radical feminist analysis of the 'personal sphere', but without an effective integration in marxist theory. Topics such as motherhood and sexuality, picked up from radical feminism, have been included in texts on women's oppression as indicators of this merger, but have either been economistically interpreted or have found their place, though subordinate, alongside economic factors as 'cultural/personal' aspects of the mode of production.

This 'unhappy marriage of marxism and feminism' cannot be dealt with, as Heidi Hartman has noticed, through either a subsumption of feminism in

---

28   Smith 1989, p. 53.

marxism or through an arithmetical exercise which constructs a social whole by adding together qualitatively different epistemological stances.[29] As Marx pointed out in the first thesis on Feuerbach, an objectivist ('materialist') standpoint is fundamentally opposed to a subjectivist ('idealist') one, and both stand in equal antithesis to a reflexive, historical materialist standpoint which conceives of the social in terms of 'sensuous, practical human activity'.[30] Lacking a concept of a cultural social formation and narrowing the social to mean the economic, marxist feminists create an unbridgeable gap between self, culture and experience and the world in which they arise, and have little to say about political subjectivity.

No real and coherent ground can be found in the work of marxist feminists for constructing a directly revolutionary agency. It is only in so far as they are feminists that they can legitimately rely on a subjective dimension (but which they make exclusively 'idealist'). It is not as 'marxists' (i.e., scientific social analysts) that they can draw upon their experience in the male world or political organisations. It is only their 'feeling/experiencing' selves as feminists that dictate that they should directly do their own politics and oust men (even great male theorists) from the role of representation. But this legitimation on the basis of 'feeling/ experience' never comes together with their 'scientific' and objective economic analysis.[31]

Without a materialist and historical view of consciousness, without a theory of a *conscious* and transformative relation between labour, self and society, the notion of self or subjectivity remains unconnected to social organisation or history in any formative and fundamental sense. The 'feminist' component of marxist feminism is an uncritical adoption of an essentialist or idealist subjectivist position, just as much as the 'marxist' component is an objective idealism. In present-day socialist feminism this dilemma is silenced rather than resolved. And in this diffusion or contradiction between two irreducibly different epistemological positions feminists are seeking – and aided in their compromise by – theories of 'difference'.

29   See Hartman 1979. 'The marriage of Marxism and feminism has been like the marriage of husband and wife depicted in English common law, Marxism and feminism are one, and that one is Marxism. Recent attempts to integrate Marxism and feminism are unsatisfactory to us as feminists because they subsume the feminist struggle into the "larger" struggle against capital' (p. 2).

30   Marx and Engels 1970.

31   Hartman 1981 or Eisenstein 1979, are powerful examples of this divided intellect and self as marxists and feminists, and concomitantly of separate conceptions of gender and class as two separate social categories to be added up together. See the remarks on this separation in Joseph 1981.

The theory of 'difference', and a plea to 'diversity' or a tolerant co-existence, has liberated socialist/marxist feminists from the earlier worry about an integrative analysis or theoretical consistency. A text such as *What is Feminism?* edited by Mitchell and Oakley (1986), both old-time marxists, displays this compromise most effectively in its selection of topics, authors and analysis. 'Together we are women', once the trademark of liberal feminists, has appeared in marxist feminism as well – but interestingly enough, throughout the text the concept 'women' (with its diversity) signals mainly to white skin as its boundary and displays the insidiousness of a common sense racism.

3   Beyond 'The Other(s)', 'Identities' and 'Structures'

> [People] make their own history, but they do not make it just as they please; they do not make it under circumstances chosen by themselves, but under circumstances directly found, given and transmitted from the past.[32]

These theories of 'other(s)', 'identities' and 'structures' – all of which contain some truth, and much that is false in them – obviously cannot explain my world or meet the pedagogic needs with which my paper started. Subsuming concrete contradictions in an abstraction of essentialism or structuralism, or simultaneously creating multiple subjectivities while enclosing them into static 'identities', does not, in the end, create a knowledge that allows us an authenticity of being and politics.

For that, we need to go beyond gestures, signals and constructs, into producing an actively revolutionary knowledge. Here I agree with Marx that we cannot be satisfied with simply 'interpreting' or presenting different versions (or sub-versions) of the world, we need to change it. It is not enough for us to have the ability, right or space to express ourselves and to describe our experiences. We have to end the oppressive conditions, the social organisations, ultimately not of our own making, which give rise to our experience. We must be simultaneously aware of the cognitive, practical and transformative relation between our consciousness and the world we inhabit. We need to remember that this world into which we are born, or migrate (voluntarily, yet at the pull of capital, or driven by political exigencies), has existed prior to our entry into it and goes way beyond the local and the immediate. Needless to say it exerts a formative pressure – an objective determination – on us. We

---

32   Marx 1972d, p. 595.

are the active-while-acted-upon agents without whom history would be simply reduced to a self-reproducing Hegelian category. So we non-white women, who seek not only to express but to end our oppression, need reliable knowledge which allows us to be actors in history. This knowledge cannot be produced in the context of ruling but only in conscious resistance to it. It must retain the integrity of our concrete subject positions within its very project and its present-day method of investigation, in so far as it searches the history and social relations to trace the reasons for and the forms of our oppression.

This new theorisation must challenge binary or oppositional relations of concepts such as general and particular, subject and object, and display a mediational, integrative, formative or constitutive relation between them which negates such polarisation. This could be done by further developing Marx's concept of mediation, displayed and discussed in *Capital* as well as in *Grundrisse*. The sole purpose of the concept is to capture the dynamic, showing how social relations and forms come into being in and through each other, to show how a mode of production is an historically and socially concrete formation. This approach ensures that the integrative actuality of social existence is neither conceptually ruptured and presented fragmentarily nor abstracted into an empty universalism. Neither is there an extrapolation of a single aspect – a part standing in for the whole – nor the whole erasing the parts. Within this framework the knowledge of the social arises in the deconstruction of the concrete into its multiple mediations of social relations and forms which displays 'the convergence of many determinations'.[33]

This allows us to create a knowledge which provides an approximation between our internal (mental/conceptual) and external reality. Then we can show, through a formative interplay between the subjective and the objective moments – i.e., the particulars of different social relations – how the social and the historical always exist *as* and *in* 'concrete' forms of social being and knowing. Our selves and worlds express, embody, encompass and yet extend beyond individual experience, intention and location. Everything that is local, immediate and concrete is thus to be considered as 'specific' rather than 'particular' – a single entity reveals both its uniqueness and its species nature, that is, its homology with, or typification of, the general. Spacio-temporally it exists here and now, while also acquiring its being in history and the social organisation which surrounds it.

I have indicated throughout that we need a reflexive and relational social analysis which incorporates in it a theory of agency and direct representa-

---

33   Marx 1973, p. 93.

tion based on our experience. As such I can directly express what happens to me. But my experience would only be the starting point of my politics. For a further politicisation my experience must be recounted within a broader socio-historical and cultural framework that signals the larger social organisation and forms which contain and shape our lives. My expressive attempt at description can hold in itself the seeds of an explanation and analysis. We need to go beyond expressive self-referentiality and connect with others in time and space. For this reason, an adequate description of the smallest racist incident leaves room for reference or contextualisation to slavery, colonisation, imperialism; exploitation of surplus value and construction of the labour market through gender, 'race' and ethnicity; nation states to organise and facilitate these processes and practices; and concomitant reifying forms of consciousness.

At this point we must ask the question whether the issue of racism, since we (non-white women) suffer from it, is a so-called 'black' issue. The right to express and demand direct representation and to act on racism, and the legitimacy of the different women's groups to be active on this issue, have been the centre of much acrimony and caused divisions. The options are mostly phrased in terms of substitution (white women speak for us) and silence (ours), or direct expression (by us – 'White women listen!') and silence (theirs). 'You can't speak my reality' has been a strong demand of ours. But in real political terms, are these the only options that face us – those of mutually exclusive agencies? Or must we begin to use my previously suggested integrative and reflexive analysis to work out a political position which allows anyone to speak for/from the experience of individuals and groups while leaving room to speak 'socially' from other locations, along the lines of the relations that (in)form our/my own experience?

My emphasis is on the concept 'social', which allows many or all to speak about the same problem or reality without saying the same thing. The 'social' of course does not always signal empathy, sympathy, agreement and positive cooperation. It includes not only existential similarities but profound contradictions as well. Friends and enemies are constructed by the same ground rules. The social signifiers of an oppressive experience can be 'shared' by others who inhabit the same social relations of ruling but benefit from them. Those ruling relations and categories of administration based on imputations of inferiority (physical or cultural) characteristic of racism pervade the whole social space of advanced capitalism. It is as familiar a set of practices and ideas to white people as to non-whites – to the doer and the done unto. As such there is no reason as to why 'racism' is solely a 'black' experience, though there are different moments and entry points into it, since different aspects of the same social relations are visible at different intersections, from different social locations.

This still does not take away a participant role (willing or unwilling) from either the white or the non-white members of the society. There is always a social and an intellectual possibility for anyone to follow this Ariadne's thread of a relational and reflexive analysis, and thus to go beyond the immediate, through the labyrinth of the mediation and organisation of social relations and consciousness to the Minotaur of a post-colonial imperialist capitalism. If that is her issue, then any woman, white or black, can speak to 'racism' as 'her experience' without substitution, guilt or condescension. Indeed, there are many stories to tell.

In the context of this relational/reflexive social analysis, how must we understand the experience and subjectivity of the knower who is also a political actor? This can only happen if we cut through the false polarity posited between the personal/the private/the individual and the mental, and the social/collective/the public and the political, and find a formative mediation between the two. This calls for a move to revise in marxist terms what 'materialism' has crudely meant to some feminist thinking. Defining it in machines and biology, but also valorising the historical and the social, we can display 'being' as 'social' being and display the social organisation as a subject's creation – as 'sensuous, practical, human activities', though not often for herself.

In *The German Ideology* Marx speaks of such a historical-cultural materialism which posits an interconstitutive relation between the mental and the social, implying thought and expression in and as social relations between people, as well as creativity, through the concept of conscious labour. The social is fundamentally communicative and formative and it negates solipsism. That meaning is always implicated in organisation and practice as 'practical consciousness' becomes evident for Marx through the very existence of language, which is both a result and the condition of being 'social'. Everything that is 'social' then, has a conscious producer or an agent who stands between creating and mediating thought and practice, as simultaneously a bridge between and a source for both the personal and the social.

For an individual, her knowledge, in the immediate sense (which we call 'experience') is local and partial. But, nonetheless it is neither 'false' nor fantastic. It is more than the raw data of physical reflexes and feelings. It is the originating point of knowledge, an interpretation, a relational sense-making, which incorporates social meaning. This 'experience' creates and transforms. It is a continuous process of relating with the world as 'our world' (not a 'good' world, necessarily). To cut through the conventional dualisms of gender-organised mental and manual labour and their philosophical forms we would have to recognise and validate our own ability to experience, and the experiences themselves, as the moments of creativity and the embodiment of formative, rather than dualist, relations. Experience, therefore, is that crucible in which the self and the world enter into a creative union called 'social subjectivity'.

The role of experience and subjectivity in the production of 'scientific' knowledge and revolutionary politics has been controversial among academics and orthodox marxists. Even the socialist or marxist feminists have not given centrality to the experiencing subject (outside of her/his economic functions). The major tendency has been to rely on 'scientific' political economy and to dismiss experience and subjectivity as an outgrowth of bourgeois individualism and psychologism. It is mainly in marxist cultural theory, preoccupied with problems of representation and materialism in culture, and in marxist phenomenology and work based on that of Antonio Gramsci, that we find theorisations validating experience/subjectivity. In these traditions, a concept of direct and creative agency is built into the process and content of knowledge. Here experience acts as a fulcrum or a hinge from which we can turn both inward and outward.

A very significant use of 'experience' (perhaps the most extended attempt) in the marxist feminist tradition is in the work of Dorothy E. Smith. Here it is less theorised in terms of *what experience is*, but more methodologically used for what it does in organising a social inquiry.[34] It is not treated by her as world view or a body of content as much as a set of social relations, and disjunctive relations at that, within the social organisation for ruling (us). Thus it serves as the point of departure for investigation, and is deconstructively employed. It is a (woman) subject's immediate and lived (as interpreted) experience of herself and the world she happens to be in, which simultaneously positions her as a knower-subject and a social-object of research. Entitled 'social organisation of knowledge', Smith's method provides us with a critique of the discourse of Cartesian rationalism and of the mental and manual division of labour as social (institutional) and conceptual practices of power. Disclosing the bourgeois ideological and patriarchal character of this discourse by entering it from the woman's standpoint, Smith establishes the validity of beginning from the local and the immediate – namely, our experience – in order to explore the larger social organisation.

This historical materialist understanding of experience, which treats it as an interpretive relation rather than valorising any person's or group's experience as a repository of 'truth', provides a possible active knowledge apparatus.[35] We

---

34   See Smith 1987.
35   See Thompson 1978.

retain through this combination both our direct agency and our representation as knowers and practitioners but also can achieve a validated status for our experience which contains the potential for revolutionary knowledge.

In this theorisation experience is not understood as a body of content indicative of a seamless subjectivity or psychological totalisation, but rather as a subject's attempt at sense-making. Using it, we, non-white women, can begin to use our alienating experiences in classrooms as the point of departure or a set of references for a comprehensive social analysis. Any such experience of alienation holds in it the double awareness of being 'self' and the 'other', our personal and public modes of being. From this vantage point the social relations and discursive practices of our classrooms become visible as practices and discourses of domination, otherisation and objectification. We see how conventional social theories, for example, have, without malice or intention, built into them alienating forms and ideas which distance us from ourselves as social subjects.

The social analysis we need, therefore, must begin from subjectivity, which asserts dynamic, contradictory and unresolved dimensions of experience and consequently does not reify itself into a fixed psychological category called identity which rigidifies an individual's relationship with her social environment and history. Subjectivity and experience, understood in this way, argue for a coherence of feeling and being without forcing either a homogeneity on or a fragmentation of subjectivity, as advocated by post-modernism. Since political agency, experience and knowledge are transformatively connected, where but in ourselves and lives can we begin our explanatory and analytical activities? On what but our authentic subjectivity can we lay the foundations of a revolutionary politics? This renders the talk of 'false consciousness' redundant and rather signals a beginning in what Gramsci called 'the twilight zone of commonsense'.

A socialist revolution is obviously not to the taste of everybody nor a matter of civil rights, but if the fundamental need for a just, equitable and humane society is to be granted any legitimacy at all, we cannot but seek the eradication of the social organisation that produces alienation and domination. This eradication cannot be truly achieved through spontaneous insurrections, visions and uncensored expressions. We need a social analysis whose theory and practice involve political actors who both produce this knowledge and make it organisationally actionable. Its task in the Canadian context is to uncover the norms and forms of imperialist capitalism which organise our social space and individual experiences. Such a revolutionary knowledge cannot but be anti-racist/anti-imperialist, and cannot be created outside of the experiences and representation of non-white women. This does not mean an ontological privileging of any individual non-white woman's personal experiences and views as 'the truth' about society, but rather using these many truths, descriptions of differences, as the widest point of entry into a social analysis of mediation of those social relations – encoded as gender, race and class. This allows us a convergence of existence with theory and method and of experience with politics. And it is toward this ideal that I grope, both as a student and a teacher – a praxis born out of our humble lives as nonwhite women living in the jungle of an advanced capitalist society.

Politics and the Writing of History

The writing of history is not a transparent affair. In common with other forms of writing, the writing of history entails issues of representation, which in their own turn entail issues of epistemology and ideology. As an integral part of the project of writing history, 'representation' presents us with a great deal of complexity. It has, virtually, a double edge to it. By claiming to represent someone, some moment in time, some situation – in fact all three, all at once – through our reporting, recording, or narration, 'representation' implies both epistemological and (re)constructive responsibilities. It occupies both the terrains of the formal aesthetic and the ideological political. This it does simultaneously through the same inscriptional act. On the one hand, it brings the absent to the present, the invisible into visibility – readers hear or overhear voices, see the worlds of social subjects or moments, who and which can mainly be seen, heard, or known of through representational inscriptional gestures. Distanced through time and space, subjects and moments can mainly enter into our knowledge through the historian/writer's work – her attempts at representation. Thus, representation both marks moments of absence and offers us a presence – obviously at the second level of construction.

Works of history, then, are not immediate forms and entities. As represented, constructed, narrated existences they are only too obviously discursive and perspectival. They involve epistemologies, ideologies, and aesthetics, all of which make the project of representation a political matter. This is the moment of 'on the other hand' – representation as recovery, narrating, and construction. But the necessary modes of mediation, forms of construction, are after all not uniform, automatic, and all inclusive. Without any negative intention on the historian/writer's part, her ideological knowledge frameworks, her chosen forms of representation, may or may not permit certain presences or visibilities.[1] Thus projects of recovery, of rendering visible, may continue, produce, and reinforce conceptual practices of power. It is this phenomenon that is challenged by feminist historians' thematic of 'hidden in/from history'.[2] It accompanies the

---

1 Smith 1990.
2 Sheila Rowbotham is one of the first historians to have pointed to this in her two early women's history books, *Hidden from History* and *Women, Resistance and Revolution*. See also an early collection of feminist and women's history (Mitchell and Oakley 1976).

endeavour to be present or visible in 'history' by forcing the level of representation to correspond to that of lives and events at the level of the everyday world.

To substantiate what I mean, I need only to signal to women, colonised peoples, working classes, gays and lesbians, and nonwhites in 'race'-organised societies to make the fact of their representational absence visible. Even in the hands of major historians, one or the other group has often been rendered invisible through the historians' adoption of dominant discourses and epistemologies.[3] This puts them outside of the privileged purview of those whose interests and imaginations constitute powerful and effective communities, nations, and their states – both in their making and writing. In short, I am speaking about the relationship of history writing and history making to 'relations of ruling' and their institutional/cultural discursivities and ideologies.[4] These relations of ruling and their forms of consciousness, which can be coded as gender, class, or 'race' and as regulation of sexuality, are constitutively implicated in the works of the historian/writer and they forbid as well as resist 'other' voices and presences – the 'other' subjects of power.[5]

The chapters in this volume (Chaudhuri and Pierson 1998) testify to the politics of historical representation. They speak to these very prohibitions and occlusions, to exclusions and absences, and to negative, distorted constructions or representations of presences. They question in diverse ways the dominant practices of representation, of established ways of writing history, and in that process rewrite it. Interrogations, investigations, and criticisms are extended to not only what is conventional to critique, namely narrations and constructions rooted in patriarchal colonialism and imperialism, but also to nationalisms – to the forms and ideologies in which resistances have been imagined and projected. This is worth noting since we, in the West, have become rather accustomed to a non-marxist, that is, classlessly cultural binary version of critique of colonial discourse.[6] Unidimensional and essentialising, what Frantz Fanon has

---

3   The historians I have in mind are Eric Hobsbawm, E.P. Thompsom, Christopher Hill, Rodney Hilton, and Perry Anderson, to name a few, who have been particularly empty on gender, 'race', or sexuality issues, even when they have been left or progressive and written histories of class and state formation and class struggle.

4   See Smith 1987 for this concept, and for its feminist sociohistorical use, see Mohanty 1991a.

5   This epistemological critique regarding erasures and distortions is made by antiracist and feminist scholars. See Bannerji 1995, pp. 55–99, for this process of silencing and construction of the reified other. See also Mohanty 1991b, for a searching critique of methodologies of representation as applied to third world women, mainly with regard to 'western feminist writers'.

6   See Said 1979 and Alloula 1986, for examples of this, for both original theorisation and one of the earliest sustained applications. See also Ahmad 1992, critique of Said.

called 'Manichean', forms of antagonisms have long dominated the critical stage.[7] This essentialised formulation, with its unified blocks of opposition, constructs undifferentiated social subjects and political agents. These seamless narratives abstract the social subjects from their sociohistorical specificities and project through default masculinist fables. These are about masculine and elite protagonists, and they suppress the exposure of social relations of power, of deeply antagonistic contradictions that create 'differences'.

The chapters of this book are written from perspectives of difference, and they submit both colonial and nationalist discourses to queries and critiques. They introduce the much wider and deeper question of hegemony and show how both of these types of discourses, though apparently opposed, actually perform the work of ruling. They deconstruct discursivities productive of reification and show how women, for example, become object sites for hegemonic contestations between the patriarchal male elites of the coloniser and the colonised.[8] They become 'objects' through and of power struggles. By bringing women back into history, or more importantly, by performing a methodological critique that exposes their erasure, their reification, and (mis)construction, feminist historians the world over are engaging in a crucial intellectual and political task. In particular, I would like to draw attention to Indian feminist women historians, political scientists, and cultural theorists who have produced an impressive body of work in this direction. A few examples should suffice. Anthologies such as *Recasting Women, Women Writing in India* (vols. 1 and 2), and *Forging Identities* are important to name.[9] Historians such as Tanika Sarkar bring to the issue of nationalism, especially as manifested in Hindu fundamentalism, a trenchant feminist critique.[10] Cultural theorists such as Lata Mani and Gayatri Chakravorty Spivak extend an equally necessary feminist critique toward the critique of colonial discourse.[11] Thus, not only alternative but oppositional ways of questioning and framing representations of women are put forward. These critical enterprises bring us to the substantive nature of social and political agencies of women of both the colonies and the ex-colonies.

---

7   For a critique of a reductionist binary view, phrased as 'Manichean,' see Frantz Fanon 1963.
8   For a discussion about women and the familial domain as sites for hegemonic contestation, see the introduction to Sangari and Vaid 1990. See also Sarkar 1993a; Bannerji 1992 and 1994a. Also see the anthology by Hendricks and Parker 1994, which offers the same critique from the standpoint of feminist anthropology regarding colonisation and racialisation of women in the colonies.
9   Sangari and Vaid 1990; Hasan 1994.
10 Sarkar 1992a and 1992b.
11 Mani 1990; Spivak 1988b.

They, the 'objects' of colonial patriarchal representation, now as 'subjects' of history question these former representations and represent themselves.

For this new critical representational work, we do need to forge categories of difference. But this 'difference' cannot be constituted in simple or ontological identity terms. Rather, difference should be understood in terms of social relations of power and ruling, not as what people intrinsically are, but what they are ascribed as in the context of domination. We need also to expose and question the role played by the social location of the knower in the production process of knowledge, including in the notion of 'location' as not only a spatio-temporal but a politico-linguistic dimension.[12] If a feminist historian, for example, doing a critique of colonial discourse could summon to her aid the importance of understanding the effect of class and other social locations on the possible representational apparatuses of the knower and a fluency in the vernacular of the region, be culturally literate in the vernacular, how different would her work be from that produced solely within the parameter of neglect of the question of location and the colonised's history, language, and culture? If research can go beyond the written word to that of the spoken, sung, and/or otherwise signified representations, how much fuller becomes its contribution to understanding the world of African diasporic women, for example, and other migrant 'others'.[13]

The writing of history then is not only not a transparent affair, but it is not innocent either. Since at all times it is an epistemological and intellectual project, it also has an ideological-political dimension to it. And this is above and beyond intentionality. Fundamental questions arise, not only about representational efforts to make the past accessible to the present, about aesthetic problems of representation and realism, but also, and crucially, about the relationship between the discursive (as forms of consciousness in the broadest sense) and the social.[14] To raise these questions is to put squarely in the middle of what appears to be a purely intellectual-academic enterprise the question of power and its object, of what Michel Foucault has called 'power/knowledge'.[15] It shades off into the existence of marginal knowledges, and raises the exciting or alarming, depending on our stakes, possibility of emergence of unsettling knowledge practices and forms from these very marginalised spaces. The work of Edward Said, for example, in *Orientalism*, offered us an anticolonial adapta-

---

12   For the importance of 'location' as a defining element of knowledge and representation, see Smith 1987.

13   Pratt 1992.

14   Mohammad 1986.

15   Foucault 1980a.

tion of this Foucauldian frame. But this critical exercise, so effective in exposing 'the Orient' as an imperial knowledge construction, itself enters another circle of seamless ideological closure. When held up to the critique of gender and class, Said's version of critique of colonial discourse proves to be susceptible to a type of nationalism whose ideological space occludes a view of internal social relations of power.[16]

This example, only one of many, which simultaneously contains critical acuteness and ideological occlusion, makes us ask how such absences and erasures come about? What epistemological, discursive procedures have become so naturalised that even in recuperative, critical tasks there are such absences and unawarenesses? What, again, creates in many or most western feminist works such utter silence about 'other women', who are constantly present in their world?[17] How do the lives and works of Black women and women of colour existing beside them in North America assume an invisible status? And when and how, one might ask rhetorically, and through whose agency, does this silence break? Who enters through the fissures of hegemonic discourse, from the 'outside', to make their absence visible, their silence audible? The answer is only too obvious – the excluded themselves, in their own social substantiveness and agency, in the course of their struggles, create this epistemological corrective and change, not just expose, the politics of discourse. It should also be noted that these erasures, silences, and oversights are most often not a matter of actual, purposive acts of antagonism. In fact, if they were so, the situation would be far simpler and easier to deal with. It is much more interesting to explore why these obvious omissions or badly theorised problematics did not attract the attention of well-known progressive historians, feminists, marxists, and nationalists.

Can we begin by asking, then, about the question of location, of the relationship between social ontology and epistemology? Is there a connection between an author's historical project, knowledge framework and the author's sex, class,

---

16   My criticism of Said is on the grounds of leaving out the issues of gender and class in his critique of colonial representation of the 'other'. This undifferentiated reading leaves us with a homogenised view of both the coloniser and the colonised, without offering any ground for assessing or criticising nationalism, for example. See Emberly 1993; see also Ahmad 1992, for a searching critique of Said on the grounds of history and class formation. For a critique of nationalism on gender and class grounds, see authors such as Chatterjee 1990, Sarkar 1992a, as well as Bagchi 1995.

17   This is discussed extensively in Spelman 1988, and hooks 1981. See also Gunew 1991, and Collins 1990. We have to consider that feminist history of class formation in England, for example, largely ignores themes of 'race' and/or the empire. Examples of these might be otherwise excellent feminist histories.

and 'race' privileges? Is it automatically 'always already' the case that a knower's language and knowledge framework are unrelated to who she/he is? And even where that is the case, for example, when a working-class historian produces elite history, do we not have to examine those modes and conventions of the discipline itself through which this becomes possible? Do not academic disciplines, irrespective of an individual's choice, identify themselves through self-markings of discursivities and common senses, which themselves possess a social ontology? Is there, then, a shared set of routine intellectual practices, ideologies, and languages designating what is meant by doing or writing of history?

A notion of a 'discipline', with its boundaries, its recognisable lineaments, seems to settle in place, articulating the practitioners in the field. Before we know, we are interpellated by it, and we replicate it through our own activities, for example through the notion and practice of 'scholarship', occlusive and exclusive epistemologies.[18] Within these disciplinarian boundaries, objects and subjects of inquiry, the meaning and modes of what 'inquiry' could mean, fall into place. Not that 'history', for example, as a field of discipline, does not expand in topics through time. From the days of 'decline and fall', through 'world history' or 'universal history' of the world historical spirit, 'history' has moved on to other concerns and terrains. It has ramified into areas of state formation, military and naval actions and exploits, and trade and economics. With the development of organised class struggles, social history began to be written, while anticolonial struggles consolidating national cultural identities also created their new histories. But in spite of this expansion, many peoples are, or until relatively recently were, left out of 'history'. Black people, indigenous peoples, women, and gay men and lesbians, for example, did not feature in histories of working classes or national struggles.[19] Certain psychological and sociological domains that were demarcated as the realm of the 'private', for example, did not, for the longest time, qualify as material for either the writing or the making of 'history'. Sex and sexuality, family lives, the body and morality, socialisation of children, to name a few topics, fall or fell outside of history writ-

---

18   For these occlusive and exclusive properties of 'discipline,' see Dorothy E. Smith, 'Ideological Practices of Sociology', in *Conceptual Practices of Power*. One could substitute 'history' for 'sociology' without any violation of her argument and see how the common practice of qualifying as a member of the 'discipline' brings one into a positivist and an abstract, essentialising frame. See also Bannerji 1994b.

19   I use the category 'Black' to code peoples of African origin living in diaspora. Others, formerly colonised, indigenous peoples, or those coming from the third world, have been named with their countries of origin – for example, Turkish women.

ing's disciplinarian purview.[20] Thus, invisibility and exclusion, sporadic presences through distortions, remain as endemic dangers in the disciplinarian mode. In the conventions of academic history writing, there appears to be a sublime indifference to issues of power, while in practice the discipline relies on social relations produced through power, which it must do to qualify as an academic discipline in a world so severely divided in classes, on mental and manual divisions of labour.

This naturalisation of power/knowledge brings us to the notion of hegemony functioning as disciplinarian common sense. Here an ideological mode has been arrived at, thereby creating a sort of a practitioners' consensus. This mode has become so pervasive as to have been naturalised through grand metanarratives of history. In this mode of history writing, even critical categories such as nation, class, or gender, which may have initially challenged ideological bases of colonialism, bourgeois class power, or patriarchy, can end up in closures of solipsism or self-referentiality. Sociohistorical or economic-cultural relations of power that constitute historical concreteness of class, for example, may become not only subsumed but submerged in seamless, self-validating narratives. Specificities of all kinds are thus reduced to symptoms of each one of these governing categories or are overlooked and erased as immaterial to the plot lines of the main story. What is represented in and as history and how, then, become contingent to these foundational metanarrative urges. Joan Scott's critique of E.P. Thompson's otherwise wonderful book *The Making of the English Working Class* reminds us of the pitfalls of this symptomatic metahistory of genderless class.[21] Needless to say, we find an equal emptiness when we scrutinise the text from an anti-imperialist, antiracist stance. But interestingly enough, Scott's own critique does not pay attention to this absence, and does not consider the importance of 'race' or the empire for class formation in England.[22] The chapters in this volume about appearances and disappearances of

20   France has produced historians of moralities or 'mentalities' or private lives, such as Aries and Duby 1992, and Copely 1989. Histories of childhood, such as Steedman 1996, and of sexuality and the body, such as Lacqueur and Gallagher 1987 or Walkowitz 1992, are some examples of new types of history writing.

21   Thompson 1974; see also Hall 1992, for a critique of genderless history.

22   Scott 1988. See also Riley 1988. This lacuna in feminist history is present even in texts that otherwise devote themselves to unsettling such fundamental notions as 'women'. There is a remarkable absence of nuancing this notion with difference in a book such as Riley's, which otherwise raises such interesting issues. The same absence of the colonial enterprise or slavery, or the roles that they play in defining the rising bourgeoisie's sense of themselves, in their notions and practices of 'family', marks such an otherwise influential text as Davidoff and Hall 1987. The same could be said of Levine 1987. These are two

Black people in European or in North American history books speak to many
perils of occlusive or hegemonic nationalist historiography. Eric Hobsbawm's
history of capital's development, of industry and empire, with its indifference
to women, gender, peasants, and issues of 'race' and racism, provides us another
classic example of writing history where the governing typology of 'class' can
exist independently of gender and 'race'.[23]

In this story of thematised continuity, theoretical impulses from Foucault
and Foucauldians have been influential in introducing new spaces through
breaks and ruptures. Specificities and particular histories, disruptive of the
grand marches of metanarratives, have been introduced. Microhistories, which
privilege the local sites of temporalities and bounded spatialities, have brought
in other narratives that challenge the linear constructions of established academic history. Stories of empires, nations, and capital and class have been traversed by stories of women, colonised and displaced peoples, and marginally
located 'others', such as gays and lesbians. This sensitivity to power/knowledge
and specificities, this lens of difference, has been strengthened by techniques of
deconstruction. Together, as cultural and political critique, they have undone
the fabric of metahistory. At this time, both the writing of history and the
making of it have taken on the look of incomplete projects that approximate
more closely the actual state of affairs – both epistemologically and politically.
One such critical sweep that challenges 'elite history' might be mentioned here
since it has assumed much currency. This project is known as 'subaltern history'.[24] It was initiated by Indian diasporic historian Ranajit Guha and carried
on mainly by Indian historians and the odd Indian political scientist. This was
an attempt to dismantle two metahistorical frameworks at once. Both marxist
historiography and nationalist historiography were discredited as elite, teleological, and colonial, and thus repressive and unrepresentative of popular
projects of history writing. But it is at this point, when we are most critical, that
we have to be most careful. We need to be vigilant that our critical histories do
not themselves end up by creating reified subjects and narratival closures.

With regard to 'subaltern history', two absences are glaringly evident – namely, the absence of women as either subjects or agents of making or writing

---

examples out of many where awareness of one oppression, or the attempt to put back in
an erased population, does not open the authors' eyes to others belonging to the same
category, nor do they see how influential the empire, colonies, and racialisation were in
creating the European subject, both male and female, of all classes. Ann Laura Stoler
makes the point very strongly in *Race and the Education of Desire: Foucault's History of
Sexuality and the Colonial Order of Things*.

23   Hobsbawm 1974; 1979 and 1962.
24   See Ranajit Guha 1982b, 1985. For a critique of 'subaltern studies', see O'Hanlon 1988.

of history and, of course, of any gender analysis. As far as writing history is concerned, in the course of the almost fifteen years of the existence of *Subaltern Studies*, only two or three women have been published sporadically in the volumes. Once there was an appearance of a woman historian, Tanika Sarkar, and from time to time we caught a glimpse of Gayatri Chakravorty Spivak, who popularised the *Subaltern Studies* group in the West. Any interest in 'the woman question' so-called is totally superadded, one essay by a political scientist of the group notwithstanding, particularly since the same essay has reappeared in slightly altered versions in a few places with no response to critiques offered by feminist historians and cultural theorists working in the same area of women and nationalism. But what is even more astonishing is that the subaltern named 'woman', whom even the old marxist Engels was pleased to recognise as 'the proletariat of the proletariat', has no definitional space within the subaltern project. Furthermore, those who reject the metanarrative of 'class' in their resistance to a marxist teleological reading and representation of history are content with an abstract, homogenised, and undifferentiated notion of 'the community'. The ethnicising, racialising, communalising, and patriarchal possibilities and political uses of this notion are generally overlooked.[25] Class and gender in particular disappear in the black hole of 'subaltern' theorisation. Needless to say, the one subject, author, and agent of 'history', both in the sense of writing and doing, that emerges from this historiographic venture in combatting marxist history is male by default. Furthermore, the postulation of a cultural or political consciousness that is 'subaltern' and yet independent of class, 'race', and gender and removed from 'elite consciousness', introduces into this subaltern project and politics an ahistorical and asocial form of political consciousness and unconscious. This stance elevates the subaltern consciousness in rebellion or upsurge as above society and criticism. The spontaneous sociopolitical expressions of subaltern males are not supposed to be tainted by dominant ideologies or characterised by practices of power internal to the 'subaltern' group.[26] This makes it difficult to criticise male violence against women, such as that of rapes during communal riots, or the particular ways religious fundamentalists place women on their agendas. The theoretical framework of this project is such that subaltern males as heroes in and of history, as peasants, tribals, minorities, and so forth cannot be perceived as doing wrong.

---

25   Gyan Pandey's *Construction of Communalism in Colonial North India* (1990) shows some of the problems of reading 'communities' without specificities of class formation in a consistent and analysed manner. This makes critiques of nationalism and identity politics largely solipsistic.

26   See Guha 1983.

To say this is not to make merely a theoretical critique of this historiography. It is especially important to state this now for an urgent political reason in the current environment of Indian politics when a violent, fascist, Hindu fundamentalist strand of nationalism is on the path of ascendency.[27] Its objects of violence are Muslims, women (both Hindu and Muslim), and the Left in any shape or form. It is dangerous to project this 'nationalist' upsurge, marked by the demolition of the Babri Mosque in December 1992 and subsequent riots that spread all over the country, as 'subaltern' and liberatory just because it is seemingly spontaneist in its violence. It is even more dangerous to shore up this spontaneist and fascistic version of history-making by writing essays on 'Indian tradition' and 'Indian psyche'.[28] The notion of 'Indian', when formulated through this lens of 'tradition', not only invents these traditions and their compound called 'India', but hinduises India and dehistoricises it by the same stroke. This neo-orientalism of traditional essentialism, in tandem with its opposite but equally pernicious spontaneism, ends up by supporting all forms of social and 'epistemological violence', not the least of which is against women.

If these are some of the pitfalls of anti-elite 'subaltern' history writing, we need to watch out also for the dangers of 'microhistory'. It too began with the intuition of challenging the erasures of metahistory. As we concentrate on the local, the particular, and the immediate in resistance to metanarratives, we need to be wary of the epistemological traps peculiar to empiricism. This may result in work that centres on single issues, localities, or groups to the exclusion of complexities that go into their making, which cannot locate where they lie in socio-historical-political topography. Thus it is possible to work on single issues, for example on 'gender' or 'class', as though they do not hold a mediating, constituting relationship with each other, or were not formal 'congelations' of multiple social relations and forms of consciousness. In the same vein, the study on a locality or a community can become an enclosed sociohistorical venture, what Marshall Sahlins has called an 'island of history'. Even when a work is anti-essentialist and thus attentive to difference, the value of

---

27   Hindu fundamentalism becomes an issue in Indian history, not as a passing political deviation or attitude, but actually as the party forming the government following the 1996 national elections. This rule lasted only thirteen days, but does give us a glimpse into things to come. For feminist and progressive critiques of hindu fundamentalism and nationalism inscribed in it, see Dutta, Agnes, and Adarkar 1996.

28   Ashish Nandi's work in this direction of reworking the concept of tradition is highly problematic. See Nandi 1988. See also Chakravarty 1993, for a neoconservative view of gender and women's roles.

the work as a representational endeavour lies in the way 'difference' is understood and deployed as a notion. If difference is understood solely as an ontological and descriptive category, it is bound to end up in an ahistorical enclosure
of identity. Historicisation and socialisation of 'difference' take us away from
empiricism or foundationalism, and mark difference as a signifier for relations
of power and a cultural and political form of domination. Read in this way,
'difference' or its related category 'identity' ceases to create the dangerous possibility of becoming an ideological-political prison of the self. It is through
such a segregated and reified reading that much work based on difference or
identity becomes as static and empty of dynamism as that based on essentialism. This empiricism ends up by creating micro-metahistory, in which the very
historicity of the formation of subject, self as a being in history, is lost. It is
in this way that histories of different oppressions are written as though they
have never heard of each other or know of the long chains that bind them.
Thus, we can write of memories and experiences of Jewish or African-American
women and not connect racism with antisemitism. This is not to say that each
book must write everything, but it is possible to be alert to the fact that the
theoretical framework of the work could admit of a complex social organisation and multiple relations and constructive semiologies of power. What, for
example, is one to say about books in recent-day Germany that can speak about
the oppression of the Jewish woman without casting the theoretical net wide
enough to make possible, in theoretical terms, the oppression of her Turkish
sisters?[29]

I can only hope in conclusion that I have brought forward, even if minimally and superficially, problems of representation (political) and representation
(aesthetic-epistemological) as particularly connected with history. But we are
still left with having to puzzle out how, in the process of criticising, we create more and other closures, how a set of ideological concentric circles comes
into being as we run out of our disciplinarian, regulating intellectual regimes.
Some corrective speculations are in order here, and I will attempt some suggestions. One way of overcoming closures might be to ground the topics, issues,
problems, and so on with which we are immediately engaged into the broader
sociohistorical relations that constitute and extend behind and before them.
This is to place and deconstruct an event, an experience, a moment – in short,
a phenomenon – in the purview within which it arises. It is as though we were

---

29   See Chaudhuri and Strobel 1992. This collection, and the framework discussed in the intro-
      duction, allows for much more inclusive, critical, and interesting possibilities of writing
      feminist history where white and nonwhite women can take part in discussing agency
      without erasures or 'appropriation'.

to study a wave as a stable form, as an arc of water, and yet be attentive to the vast mass of liquid from which it formed and into which it will decompose. This would mean not only studying the formative discourses themselves but the world that needs, gives rise to, and mediates its moments through those discourses. I suggest also studying and comparing discourses, their rise and fall – the birth and death of discourses. There is a need to compare accounts, to read one through another.

This proposal necessarily brings me to the edge of disciplines, to the point when boundaries must be broken. Feminist historians, among 'other' historians, have long realised the impossibility, and absurdity, of 'writing representation' without attending to the social and the cultural. Sociologists and anthropologists who are similarly engaged in 'social research' realise the ludicrous nature of studying the social without history and culture and simply reducing it to demographics. The notion of 'graphic' (as in ethnography) has shifted from the graph of applied statistics to that of graphic art, of images. Memories, experiences, daily practices, and oral histories now jostle with conventions of disciplines, allowing for recreations never seen before. Disciplinarian purity has finally and happily yielded to hybridities such as 'historical sociology'. But underlying these practitioners' art and choices is the deepest question of methodology – not simply as an instrument of digging and measuring – but in the sense in which Marx, for example, speaks of it in the preface of *Das Kapital*. This is a question of epistemology – that very conceptual framework of inquiry – within which any knowing takes place. This is where being and doing in time, in life, and in death, must be understood as socially organised moments and experiences that are structured on multiple, contradictory warps and wefts. Any conceptual device that allows us to frame or address that and helps us to inquire deeply into a social formation may be called our desirable method.

Ultimately, the note on which I want to end is political. This should not be an abrupt gesture, since from the very beginning I have kept politics in our peripheral vision. What I have tried to say so far is that in the end – in the 'last instance', should I say? – the issue of critical and intellectual work (I do not only say 'academic') is a political issue. Keeping in mind the possibilities of change and criticism, breaks and fissures that exist even within the scope of our disciplinarian hermeneutics, we have to face the fact that the impetus for radical intellectual criticism comes from the struggles in our lives, from the world in which we live. Our being in the world and the struggles that surround us mirror each other. From social movements that create both history and possibilities of critical knowledge from memories and experiences politicised as organisations and identities of people come our inspiration to write new histories. So our last and most important source for writing in oppositional ways comes from the political, and this politics, I insist, has to be deeper than skin or sex if it has to work for transformation of knowledge and society at once.

CHAPTER 6

Ideology, Anti-colonialism and Marxism

[An interview with Mahdi Ganjavi]

Mahdi Ganjavi (MG): You are among the philosophers and social critics who have written extensively on the concept of ideology. In your article 'Ideology',[1] by means of a close reading of Marx and Engels' *The German Ideology*, you argue that while all ideology is a form of thought, not all forms of thought are ideological. You assert that any 'true' social inquiry should start from the concrete reality of people's lives and their society, i.e. life activities of conscious socio-historical subjects as they produce and reproduce themselves. Furthermore, you argue against the assertion that knowledge can be 'objective' or 'autonomous'. Similar to Dorothy Smith in her piece *Reinterpretation of Marx's Epistemology*,[2] you maintain that any knowledge is by nature a situated one.

How can an argument in favour of situated knowledge distance itself from necessarily resulting in spatialising epistemologies? Theoretically speaking, can we think of any true social inquiry that has not situated itself in terms of the class struggle?

Himani Bannerji (HB): I should begin by saying that I am not a philosopher, but a historical materialist sociologist who is interested in actual social organisations, their forms of relations, and modes of inquiry into them. Unlike philosophers, I do not offer universal metaphysical speculations between subject and object – the nature of Reality and the nature of universal categories, such as that of 'absolute being', 'man', 'nature' and so on. Historical materialist sociology, which can also be called historical sociology, is less concerned with the content, and certainly the eternal validity of any social content articulated for the purpose of understanding a specific social problem, but rather is a method of inquiry which examines a set of procedures which claim to arrive at an objective truth. In this, I am a practitioner of 'social organisation of knowledge' and 'critical ethnography' as well as inquiries into the nature of ruling institutions – all of which are developments of the marxist feminist methods of Dorothy E. Smith. To assess my work it is not only important to refer

---

1 Bannerji 2015b.
2 Smith 2015.

back to Marx, but also to a feminist application of his critique of ideology as found in Smith's *The Conceptual Practices of Power*[3] and *Writing the Social*.[4] This distinction I make between philosophy and critical sociology is crucial for understanding the distinction Marx makes between a transformative 'science' of society and metaphysics/ideology produced by philosophers (see *The German Ideology*).

In my work a critique of ideology provides the central principle through which I inquire into the rise of social phenomena and their experience by individuals. The notion of 'the social' involves an interconstitutive relationship between lived social relations and forms of consciousness centred mainly on relations of power and oppression, which provide for the rise of property and concomitant relations of propriety or morality. The feminist anti-racist critique that I provide is at its basic level a critique of ideology. You are right to point out the distinction I make between ideology and different forms of thought, such as use of concepts and categories, empirical research, etc., which are not always already ideological in nature. As Marx says, practical consciousness, empirical consciousness, scientific social analysis and production of ideology are not to be confused with each other. Though they are permeable forms of thought with possibilities of influence from each other, their distinctions/specificities must be maintained. Thus all ideology is a form of thought, but not all forms of thought are ideological. This is the point missed by Louis Althusser in his article on ideological apparatuses of the state,[5] and it continues to bedevil much critical social analysis of our time. Furthermore, my use of the notion 'social' is a materialist version, with all the contradictions, complexities and dynamism involved in all modes of production and their social formations and cultures. This is an attempt to eschew the use of the philosophical notion of 'totality' put forward by Lukács, Fredric Jameson and others. My interest is on an internal set of relations necessary for pressing on with a revolutionary project rather than a seamless, unbroken circle or totality. The social, therefore, is constantly changing constitutive relations between different social moments, such as social, economic, cultural and so on. Seen from this point of view, capital is an evolving and fracturing social reality, and cannot be understood as being wholly determined by one of its moments, such as the economic.

The issues you raise regarding subjective and objective forms of knowledge need to be further scrutinised. When a piece of knowledge is seen as starting

---

3 Smith 1990.
4 Smith 1999.
5 Althusser 1970.

from any situated locale, in an individually inhabited social space, the end-point of that knowledge production is not that of another contiguous, restricted knowledge space. Situated knowledge signifies a connection between local and extra-local possible spaces of knowledge. To give an example, a racist slur is both a concrete immediate phenomenon and one that needs to be traced back to historical and current social relations and cultural practices. Thus a political movement such as Black Lives Matter, arising out of racist police killing of African Americans in the U.S., has to be referred back to the days of slavery as well as systemic and social racism that mark the lives of African Americans today. This is what I mean by situating knowledge, not simply a narrow particular standpoint of an individual unregistered in any social map. This knowledge is not 'subjective' in the sense of being an immediate state of feeling, a kind of opinion, as held by one isolated individual or a restricted social group. If it is so, then it is an experience that itself needs to be understood through a historical, sociological analysis. This analysis is not a matter of opinion, a random set of claims, but rather a method of inquiry that breaks up the unity and immediacy of that experience, for example of racism, sexism or homophobia, into a social inquiry of socio-economic organisation and relations and historical-cultural setting. This form of 'objectivity' makes a truth claim regarding what is actually happening (Smith) and permits no relativism regarding the reality we inhabit. Racist patriarchal capitalism can thus be shown as actually existing, rather than as my personal opinion that it does so. The kind of partisanship that this knowledge holds is not a subjective one but a social one based on the unequal relations of power and property that we seek to understand.

This may seem like an unnecessarily long beginning, but I cannot even begin to answer the rest of your questions without this clarity regarding what I am actually trying to do.

MG: Language plays a crucial role in the creation of forms of thought. According to Dorothy Smith, categories are the forms of thought in which the social relations come to consciousness. However, language is also very powerful in terms of masking the actual social existence that has created its materiality. Thus, in many cases an ideological inquiry would take shape, simply by means of a referential practice of reading from category to phenomenon. This is developed historically and theoretically in your article 'The Tradition of Sociology and the Sociology of Tradition'.[6]

---

6   Bannerji 2003.

It can be argued that the sensuous experience of living an alienated life has resulted in an alienated relation to language itself. You are a poet and literary critic as well. In what sense can poetry assist us in our struggle against ideological forms of expression?

HB: Yes, language, by which I mean forms of common signification and expression, not just words, is the most vital element of being human. From written and spoken words to musical notations, conventions of art, scientific research to learning and transmission of practical skills, all fall within the general definition of language. They are all modes of communication involving experiences, social relations, the activation of all our capacities, what Marx calls 'sensuous, human practice'. In this sense we can speak of structures and conventions and denotative functions of language as much as associative and connotative uses of language. As such, though the structural aspects of language which are generally available to all are individualised and socialised by popular usage, we could say that languages do not speak us, but we speak them, in a manner which Mikhail Bakhtin calls 'dialogical'. Categories, to speak of them especially, which are used by us to code and transmit knowledges, are contexted by and referential to the reasons for their usage as well as to the relations between the speaker and the listener in the broadest sense of these terms. Thus categories are embedded codes of knowledge which are part of and create social spaces of knowledge and expression. The particular usages and the general structures of language are both socially determined and determining. The sociality of human 'being' is expressed in language, and begins with what Marx calls forms of 'practical consciousness'. To define and refine these usages, forms and genres are created, developed over a historic period of complex and contradictory social relations and individual experiences. This process has been and is always at work, something without which being human would not be possible.

Uses of language are varied and range from poetic, to ideological and scientific. So the occluding use of language that Marx calls ideology and Dorothy Smith defines as the way ideology works to hide reality from us, is itself a social phenomenon. It would not be possible for us to create ideology if the social possibilities for doing that were not present. Mental and manual division of labour at their highest point of separation, which can deny social origins of ideological thought, depends wholly on social organisation in which production of practical objects and thought objects actually took two different paths of production relations. This point of bifurcation is reliant upon and reproduces class relations. The intelligentsia, who are producers of thought objects, become an elite group which is an extension of the bourgeoisie, while the manual or practical workers form another class, their interests at odds with the elite. Ideological uses of terms and expressions prevent us from seeing this connection and erase the fundamental connection between forms of art, knowledge, etc. and everyday life and work of others whose production of surplus is used to maintain the elite. Thus ideology's claim to absolute sovereignty of ideas is in reality absurd and impossible, as is the disconnection it asserts between philosophy, art and society.

This brings us to the consideration of poetry in its social origin and role. However much we may call art, including poetry, a realm independent of the social, we see that communication itself is impossible outside of the social, dialogical mode. Poetry or art in general achieve their character as such because they share a common space of meaning between the speaker/writer and the listener/reader. But of course poetry can be an ideological practice if it signals its interlocutor away from its content and only toward its structural form. But ultimately such formalisation still abides by certain usages of shared understanding. Ultra-modernist art forms in cryptic poetry or completely abstract painting still depend on sense making, and therefore on the evocation of some feelings and experiences within the audience or the onlookers. The effectiveness of poetry depends on evoking resonances that are uncountable, and connotation of words and images is also without boundaries. This does not mean any contradiction between socialised and individualised practices and reception of poetry/art. Poetry can serve an anti-ideological purpose through these evocations which connect us to the image or the poem and all that it draws from within ourselves and the world that we inhabit. The anti-ideological role that poetry plays is evident in the fact that it is poetry, meaning that it is not a private, non-intelligible utterance. Reliant upon this dialogic imagination, which is practically experienced without words by both the creator and those who enjoy the creation, poetry is born in a social habitat, and good critics point out the connections and resonances between individual experiences of art as content and the established genres of form which have accumulated historically. The death of ideology is caused by our practical consciousness itself lying at the foundation of language of any kind.

However distancing and distorted our existence may be in a world of commodity fetishism, in the end there is nothing 'alien' about anything that is social. It is a matter of not just writing proclamative poetry which urges us on to take up activities of resistance, but also understanding the very nature of any experience which cannot be possible outside of our social existence. Just as in other forms of critical awareness and struggle, we have to trace our way back to the very social relations that produce alienation. So in reading literature and looking at art, etc., we must perform the same act of unravelling. This unravelling is not only at the level of consciousness, and we must notice the direct experiential element that lies at the bottom of our mind – our feelings and perceptions – which ultimately makes it possible to dis-alienate ourselves. At all cost we must avoid thinking about social life and culture as two separate realities, or culture as a mere reflection of what is really real, namely our socio-economic existence. This division apparent in certain kinds of marxist art and cultural theories, that conceives the social whole as being qualitatively differentiated and ranks them in terms of their reality content, is itself an ideological/alienating way of thinking. The perception of a separation between art and life must be rejected.

MG: You argue against the Eurocentric assertion that enlightenment values such as reason, secularism, etc. were Western, but instead call for a move beyond the essentialised binary of West and the rest in order to also historically inquire into the development of enlightenment ideas in both modern and medieval Eastern cultures. You have simultaneously devoted your scholarly life to Marx and Tagore. In 'Marx's and Tagore's Ideas on Human Capacities and Alienation',[7] you have argued that bringing together the philosophic, social and political thought of these two can assist us in examining and renewing our understanding of socialism, a much needed scholarship in the current crisis of socialism. In what sense, other than the particularities of Indian society, can the ideal radicalism of Tagore – a man believing in a highly sophisticated Hindu spirituality – contribute to the historical materialist understanding of the social?

HB: Your question has several parts to it. To answer your assertion that I conflate European enlightenment with simple Eurocentrism and use the discourse of the West and the East or West and the rest, I consider that type of discourse to be a-sociological and a-historical. The notion of reason and its various applications, in my opinion, is not only to be found in Europe, but in India, China, the Middle East, in the Perso-Arabic and Moorish traditions. The notion of enlightenment is not applied to them, nor do we find secular social/materialist standpoint or universal abstraction in them. In this way philosophy/metaphysics become the property of Europe – 'the west' – while non-European spaces are essentially invested with notions such as religion and tradition. It is this that I find problematic and a derivative of Eurocentrism/colonial discourse. So what is enlightenment? The intellectual constellation that we call 'enlightenment' comprises worldviews and conceptions that arose in parts of Western Europe

---

7   Bannerji 2014.

with the rise of capitalism within the Hellenist/humanist background of the Renaissance. Its authors were anti-feudal and pro-bourgeois development, and enlightenment was the notion that they offered in contrast to the 'dark ages' of centuries of medieval Europe. This 'enlightenment' then was turned into a hegemonic justification in the historical context of capitalist colonialism and transformed into a legitimation device for the purpose of expansion of capitalism in all its brutalities. This is the 'white man's burden' that Rudyard Kipling talks about in his poetry and his novels, such as *Kim*. Rationalist thought is therefore not a monopoly of bourgeois appropriation of the discourse of universalism and secular social thought. This is what I had in mind when I critiqued the colonial and bourgeois aspect of European critical thought. Scientific developments and rudimentary forms of demands from below existed both in Europe and in other countries of the world, as depicted in the history of uprisings by the peasants, farmers and landholders exemplified in the Magna Carta. Enlightenment in relation to its contribution to democracy appropriated the social thought produced by rebellions of lower social classes, evidenced again in the Thirty Years War in Europe. The rise and fall depicted in the history of empires are as dependent on the Spartacuses of this world as they are on the elite philosophical abstract thinking found in stages and spaces prior to the European enlightenment. The problem for me, then, is the occidentalism imputed to my views. Neither 'orientalism' nor 'occidentalism' serve the interest of the critique of ideology. They need to be deconstructed through the method of historical materialism.

In reply to statements and questions regarding my studies in Marx and Tagore, I have the following to say. To begin with, I make no artificial effort to bring these two authors together, in the sense of conflating one with the other. What interests me in both is their critique of dehumanisation brought about by capitalism's greed and colonisation as much as techno-mechanical rationality/mentality, which the critical theorists have called 'instrumental reason'. Adorno and Horkheimer's *Dialectic of Enlightenment*[8] or Herbert Marcuse's *Reason and Revolution*,[9] or Bertel Ollman's work on alienation,[10] or even István Mészáros book *Marx's Theory of Alienation*,[11] all point out the creative, imaginative, wholly social dimension of labour and production that can be read into Marx's critique of alienation in the *Economic & Philosophic Manuscripts*

---

8   Adorno and Horkheimer 2002.
9   Marcuse 1970.
10   Ollman 1971.
11   Mészáros 1970.

of 1844. Marx's concept of labour, written large, emphasises the transformative relations that human capacities bring to people, nature and sense of beauty. In the section on consumption and production in the *Grundrisse* Marx talks about the beauty and refinement that highly evolved human capacities in social, technical, aesthetic and formal modifications can achieve over a period of time. Crude needs are succeeded by the need for beauty, as for example he offers in the same section, in the contrast between eating raw meat, bloody and torn to pieces, and a beautifully laid out dinner table in an elite European household of his time, laid out with well-cooked and well-garnished meat with silver forks and knives. The ideas of creativity or imagination are perfectly coherent with the act of production and modes of consumption enjoyed by a society at any given stage. In this sense Tagore would stand to Marx in the relation of Schiller and Goethe to Marx, both authors whom Marx admired.

Whereas Tagore is not a systematic thinker who at all points knows how to connect capitalism with forms of consciousness, yet as his novels, such as *Gora* or *Home and the World*, and his innumerable poems, essays and letters show, he was a social critic of considerable depth engaged with the question of decolonisation as social transformation. The reputation of Tagore as a 'spiritual' writer is an invention of his readers, particularly in the European world, where he is racialised through the concept of 'the oriental', a man of the East. Whereas a larger dimension of human capacity to feel wholeness and the principle of joy in being in the world cannot be measured in positivist terms, it can nonetheless be rooted in the profound relationships between the self and others, between self and nature, and in the relationship between the different parts of one's own self. A recognition of this fact and of lives of people lived under relations of private property of people's labour and its products enjoyed by the few, are what Marx talks about in his critique of alienation. When Marx compares the worst human architect with the best of bees in designing their hive and finds the former superior, it is to this creative, reflective aspect of the human mind that he signals. There is no danger of contamination from Tagore's creativity, social critique and love for the other to those engaged in the task of furthering the development of historical materialism. Marx's own love for literature, ranging from Aeschylus and other Greek dramatists to the Romantic poets of his own time, and his own attempts of writing poetry, fuelled his socialism. So I think we are safe.

MG: Gandhi is increasingly discussed in the media and by numerous authors as an anti-violence political leader. In such de-grounded articulations of Gandhi, the notion of class struggle in the Indian independence movement is eliminated in favour of emphasising its anti-violence characteristics. What are your thoughts on such articulations of the history of the Indian anti-colonial movement?

HB: The Indian freedom struggle contained different political tendencies. There were some attempts at armed struggle with no particular discernible class consciousness. Colonialism and poverty, forced underdevelopment and hegemonic influences of the English colonial power were evident for all to see. But the country was too large and broken into different provinces, linguistic groups, and regional economic practices to have provided a strong unifying base for sustained armed struggles that could challenge the organised army of the British authorities. The Communist Party of India, which was established in 1924 and remained at a rudimentary stage, yet suffering repression by the British-Indian state, manifested itself in great trade union struggles in the textile and jute factories. Its presence was dispersed in the main industrial centres, in the port areas and relatively small industrial enterprises. Whereas some anti-colonial groups were influenced by communist principles or class struggle, they were unable to exert a very large influence and create the necessary huge mass base needed for freeing India from colonial capitalism. The dominant particular party that emerged from the late nineteenth century was the Indian National Congress (INC). The influence of the INC in the early twentieth century, until the arrival of M.K. Gandhi, was largely middle class and urban. A strand of economic nationalism, also developed in the late nineteenth century, did not expand and take deep roots.

Gandhi's arrival in 1915 from South Africa was a major turning point for the beginning of the development of a mass base in small towns and rural areas. It was not the charisma of Gandhi alone, but actually the theoretical principles of his political organisation that helped the Congress to develop a hugely powerful organisation which accommodated all the different classes. This class cohesion created against the British was both a gift and a problem for development of class struggle. The INC accommodated varieties of nationalism in a complex set of political ideologies which at once had place for economic nationalism (supporting a growing national bourgeoisie), landlords, peasants and the middle class. Significantly, the interests of the working class, the notion of proletarian leadership, was completely absent from the Congress platform. The tactics of the INC included mass boycotts of British goods, rejecting the colonial education system, civil disobedience performed by hundreds of thousands of people across the country, and principled courting of arrest which overflowed the British jails. With a great constitutional knowledge, a strategy of supporting the nascent Indian bourgeoisie, promoting an alternative form of textile production through mass use of spinning wheels, creation of cooperatives in the agricultural sector, and a general refusal to comply with British administrative needs and demands, the INC became the largest mass-based political movement of the world at that time. Its social and moral character held a strong hegemonic sway and equally appealed to tradition and modernity. In terms of tradition it created a paradoxical situation in rejecting caste divides and communal hatred between Hindus and Muslims. Yet its very validation of religion as a viable part of political subjectivity left the door open for a Hindu cultural nationalism to become one of the strands of the Congress. Equally important was its aspiration to a liberal democratic state which would separate the church and the state, create a citizenship on the ground of individual personhood and embrace secularism not on the ground of rejecting religion but of the constitutional right of coexistence among all the religions.

Gandhi guided the INC through all these tactics with the strategic goal of winning Indian independence. The moral appeal of his doctrine of non-violence was strong, as it relied on notions of compassion and sympathy. However, simultaneously with non-violence, such massive situations of boycott, the great scope of the Quit India movement, road and railway line blocks by masses of people, were hardly free from violent practices of the colonial state and powerful responses from Indians themselves. Two books, *Modern India* by Sumit Sarkar[12] and *The Ascendency of the Congress in U.P.* by Gyan Pandey,[13] among others, give a good idea of the complex development of the time and the different voices in which Gandhi and the INC spoke to different sections of the Indian population. The moral tenets of Gandhi, compelling as they are, were only an element of the huge organisational capacity for the creation of a mass base across the country. It is not surprising that the practices of civil disobedience, including currently those of the Palestinian movement for Boycott, Divestment, Sanctions (BDS), straddle both non-military operations on the one hand, and on the other may hit a point where armed struggle would become a necessity. A proper understanding of Gandhi's moral and political philosophy must be supported by a knowledge of the actual workings of the Indian National Congress in undivided India. Congress' competence in creating innumerable cell organisations became the vector for Gandhi's philosophy of non-violence, coded in the notion of *satyagraha*, which means 'a quest for the truth'.

One important idea that Gandhian Indian National Congress held up for all to see can also be found in the works of Antonio Gramsci. Gramsci's insistence

---

12   Sarkar 1988.
13   Pandey 1978.

on the necessity of vitalising the civil society and creating a historic bloc of protest through the creation of 'passive revolution' signals to Gandhi's idea of politicising. What Gramsci calls the necessary work of the organiser, which is to sift through popular commonsense, or what we might call the political unconscious, is also to be found in Gandhi's writings, though they came from different political positions, and Gandhi certainly was not aware of the work of Antonio Gramsci. The news of the Indian freedom struggle was so prominent in the European media that Gramsci might have been aware of Gandhi's ideas. The interest in Gandhi is not new. He has been researched and used by political theorists of many parts of the world.

MG: Tagore is famous for his arguments against the pitfalls of nationalism. You too, in *Cultural Nationalism and Woman as the Subject of the Nation*,[14] support a non-nationalist feminist liberation, which is simultaneously anti-capitalist, anti-feudal as well as anti-imperialist. The same line of argument can be seen in your critique of subaltern studies in *Pygmalion Nation*.[15] Can you elaborate on such a project of liberation? In what sense can Tagore assist us in developing our understanding of a non-nationalist anti-colonial/imperial struggle?

HB: Taking your cue from Frantz Fanon's statement regarding 'the pitfalls of nationalism' (*The Wretched of the Earth*),[16] you seem to be asking me to suggest how Tagore may be useful for putting forward a project of not only a non-nationalist but an anti-nationalist form of decolonisation. Before I proceed to directly comment upon Tagore, I would like to pause on the topic of the relationship between social movements and class struggle. In responding to the previous question I indicated Gandhi's idea of using popular political consciousness and integrating it with an anti-colonial struggle, and Gramsci's idea of war of position to be moved to the notion of war of manoeuvre led by a communist party ('The Modern Prince'), quite different from that of Gandhi. We need to move on to a way of bringing class struggle and social movements together. This is a proposal which is more in keeping with Gramsci's political direction than with Gandhi's. Within Gramsci's theoretical framework speculated upon during his prison years we can find a far more complex and nuanced version of communism/socialism which would create the kind of national liberation whose emergence I would like to see. Such a communism would match

---

14   Bannerji 2011a.
15   Bannerji 2011b.
16   Fanon 1963.

social and economic transformation with a polity and a state based on a participatory as opposed to a bourgeois democracy. This would allow us to move away from a reactive type of politics which simply reverses the terms of power, and changes the ruling classes from foreign to native. A real decolonisation needs a concrete notion of the social, which cannot be taken up piecemeal and only changed partially. Thus social relations and ideologies of patriarchy, caste and racialisation must be seen as integral to class relations and state formation. Lenin, for example, raised questions regarding such a necessity in *State and Revolution* when he prompted us to ask whether a wholly new state formation is necessary for creating a communist society, polity and economy. This question has not yet been answered, especially in practice, anywhere yet. Brief glimpses of a truly popular participatory democracy have been sighted in the interstices of political formation, such as very briefly in the organisation of the Paris Commune, in the earliest phases of the Bolshevik and Cuban Revolutions, for a brief period in liberated Nicaragua and the abruptly truncated socialist programme of Hugo Chaves' Bolivarianism. One might see in these moments the possibilities and concrete practices of what we could call truly communism – they are all elaborated upon a deep faith in and an actual exposition of human capacities.

It is here that Tagore's contribution should be appreciated, both in revealing deformations and dangers of societies saturated with violence, greed, military and capitalist industrial complexes, and in moving toward the notion of universal humanism which is socially and historically grounded. Here the idea of the 'human', a core of oneness, loses its trans-historical status and becomes a socially experienced, sensuous, practical human activity which Marx talked about. In asserting creativity, beauty and mutual human compassion Tagore offers us a worldview wholly compatible with a communist project.

MG: De-linking the questions of race, gender and ethnicity from the question of capitalism, most contemporary social movements are detached from anti-capitalist movements and also from each other, not only in terms of historical analysis, but also structure, political aspirations, and methods of resistance. How can an emancipatory theory emerge in the contemporary world which results in the structural incorporation of these movements?

HB: This question is largely answered by what I have said so far. What I would stress is the need for a convergence of all social movements against oppression, with a clear view of forming a socio-political reality which preserves the ideal of participatory democracy. Though my ideas are widely shared, I have not seen a stable form of such a convergence, which would not erase the specificity of particular experiences of oppression and yet be able to create a politics in which the political and the social would be seen as interconstituting each other.

MG: Would you elaborate on your contribution to a critique of intersectionality? In your view, how do class, race and gender constitute each other under the condition of capitalist imperialism?

HB: I can see the convenience of using the concept of intersectionality in talking about social oppressions, such as gender, race and class. As this formulation brings together three themes which have been generally left as discrete social issues, it allows us to introduce the two other issues while talking about each one of them. But as I will show later there is a problem in the very concept of intersectionality while describing or analysing social phenomena or experiences. Before I move on to pointing out the difficulties, I would like to give a brief context to the rise of the concept of intersectionality.

Until the 1980s or so, the notion of intersectionality was more or less limited to the field of mathematics such as intersection of two lines, overlapping intersections by two spheres or in description of topography such as a place where two or more roads cut across each other. But in the '80s an attempt on the part of Afro-American women in particular to be critical of what passed as feminist thought led to the application of 'intersectionality' for describing multiple oppressions or the convergence of multiple oppressions. This is in particular a strong response to the fact that black women suffered not only from patriarchy but also racism. In this account the patriarchal experiences of black women could not be isolatedly feminist or isolatedly racist. Two particular Afro-American feminist theorists, Kimberle Crenshaw and Patricia Hill Collins, both in the very last years of the 1980s coined and circulated this notion. It became the most prized conceptual device in feminist theory, signalling to single subjects under multiple dominations. In the area of theory as much as in everyday life contestations in feminist theory between what is called white and feminist theorisations of black women and women of colour found the notion of intersectionality indispensable.[17]

However, while I do not have any particular or any principled reason to reject this term, as I understand its intention of capturing different aspects of domination within a single subjective identity, I still find it somewhat misleading. It is not misleading in that it asserts the complexities of domination that we experience in a racialised society, but it still speaks to categories or discourses

17   Interviewer note: To read more on intersectionality see: Aguilar 2015.

about something rather than the social relations that are coded under the terms or categories such as gender, race or class. The intersectionality approach does not address the social relations which are foundationally present in any mode of production, it rather begins with the codes and applies them to the social relations that are their points of origin.

The intersectional approach in my view is still an aggregative one because it assumes or does not speak to any social ground which each category seems to represent. Thus three discursive systems named as gender, race and class arise it seems on three separate grounds and then are brought together to signify the simultaneity of their presence. In other words, they take an approach that is issue-based while at the same time struggling to give them a systemic appearance. While intersectionality signals expansion and inclusion and introduces into liberal feminism of the previous era a new plurality, it still functions within a liberal plural scheme in which instead of running parallel, gender, race and class systems cut across each other. The liberal paradigm within which Crenshaw and others seek to address the oppression of women on a ground of negative differences does not tell us why and how the social relations and forms of consciousness that arise happen at all. Adding to the notion of intersectionality another notion of co-constitution does not help matters. An intersectionality approach leads us to better laws, removing injustice in terms of liberal democracy, but not to a socialist revolution which challenges the very organisation of racialised and patriarchal capital and class.

What then is my suggestion? The point of departure of my critique? Simply speaking I think that any social explanation must begin from the actualities of social organisation, social relations and their attendant forms of consciousness. We must therefore speak to an entire complex of social whole, which are constituted in and through a diversity and contradictions of social relations, and their verbal articulations. The idea of the social provides us with an existential productive and reproductive base, forms of acquisition and production of surplus, their justifications and conceptual transmissions, the division of labour in various types, all must be prior to the categories through which we name them. As the social relations constitute each other, so do their forms of thought, their moral regulations and hierarchy. This way of thinking about society gives us a concreteness which cannot be found in aggregating different categories and using aspects of reality as their illustrations. Therefore, it is my belief that one must begin from actual social relations and their lived concrete experiences and conceptions to arrive at some understanding of what is actually happening. The methodological approach described above is that of historical materialism. In such an approach, reality is always created and mediated through practical consciousness represented in various articulations and intellectual systems. It is not a matter of discursivity alone. To adopt such a discursive position would be what Marx calls ideological, that is when categories produced in the context of separation of mental and manual labour serve to conceal rather than reveal social processes and the differentiated topography inhabited by people who are producing the surplus and those who have the right to their accumulation and actual possession. Any marxist feminist treatment of race, gender and class therefore must take into account the historical social relations within which the dominant and the dominated inhabit.

SECTION 2

Ideology and History

∵

Tradition of Sociology and Sociology of Tradition: The Terms of Our Knowledge and the Knowledge Produced

> Knowing is always a relationship between knower and known. The knower cannot be collapsed into the known, cannot be eliminated; the knower's presence is always presupposed. To know is to always know on some terms, and the paradox of knowing is that we discover in its object the lineaments of what we already know.[1]

∴

1   Introduction

These lines from Dorothy Smith's essay 'The Ideological Practices of Sociology' provide the starting point of my inquiry into the tradition of sociology, particularly into the construction of and roles played by the concept of 'tradition' within sociology, with regard to the kind of knowledge it offers of non-European societies which fall into the orbit of colonialism and imperialism. For this we need to attend to the key point in Smith's statement that the knower is distinct from what is known and that her immediate subjectivity is less material in the process of knowledge production than the common generally shared terms of this process. This is so, because 'to know is always to know on some terms' – the knower is a participant only within these 'terms', and these 'terms' are not her personal invention.

My concern is with these 'terms' of knowledge through which the knower participates, knowingly or unknowingly, in the process of knowledge production. Indeed, there are the terms, beyond any individualisation of knowledge making, within and through which knowledge is named as such and is articulated. What becomes apparent is that 'discoveries' or knowledges are more a recognition and an expansion of an already existing apparatus, through not

---

1   Smith 1990, p. 33.

necessarily noted as such. In this sense, what we 'discover' or know has 'the lineaments of what we already know'.

It is within this framework of what Smith calls 'social organisation' (as opposed to sociology) 'of knowledge' that I want to consider the discipline or tradition of sociology and its branch – sociology of tradition and traditional societies. The word 'tradition' here functions as a 'term', as a constellation of concepts and epistemological practices of knowledge. I would like to demonstrate that the knowledge produced by sociology of tradition is tautological – it illustrates, or provides a representative construction of, 'tradition', the 'terms' that the sociologist went in with in her task of inquiry. Of course, 'the sociologist' may not agree with this description of her vocation or profession. She would be surprised to be told that the 'tradition(s)' she 'discovered' in societies characterised as 'traditional' have little to do with them, or that the very notion of 'tradition' is a disciplinarian baggage or marker of the sociologist's own chosen discipline.

The sociologist's denial, I would claim, is enunciated on the 'terms' of positivist objectivism characteristic of the type of traditional or mainstream sociology, an approach to be distinguished from science – a project of reflexive and critical inquiry. The sociologist is blind to the terms of her knowledge because positivism, a kind of empiricist idealism inherent in traditional sociology, confuses social knowledge with object fetishism. As Smith says in 'Toward a Sociology for Women' (1987), a long habit of such objectivist procedural expertise blinds us – just as we get used to the roads that we travel every day. But perhaps a better analogy lies in the use of a coin which has changed many hands, the image and inscription mostly rubbed off because of its status as currency. We don't often think that its validation as currency derives from a formal or abstract system or structure of exchange value. So it is with the sociological invention of the terms of 'tradition', with a constellation of concepts imbricated within it, as a mode of production of social knowledge. These can be categories of cultural interpretation, classification, value judgement and ultimately political ideology.

What Smith says, and I support, regarding ideological practices of sociology derives from Marx in The *German Ideology*[2] and other texts, where he offered an epistemological critique of ideological forms of consciousness in terms of analysing and representing the socio-historical. He spoke to terms of knowledge. Thomas Kuhn in *The Structure of Scientific Revolutions*[3] also spoke of conceptual paradigms which organise whole fields of inquiry and create an

---

2   Marx and Engels 1970.
3   Kuhn 1970.

ethos within which possibilities of knowledge are formulated. He pointed out that these paradigms are often not visible to their practitioners. Foucault spoke about 'discourse' in a similar vein, showing its constructive as well as interpretive properties. The effective presence of terms of knowledge has ranged from social analyses to forms of representation and narration. What we want to know is what are the conceptual bases and environments within which traditional or mainstream sociology arose – and specifically what kinds of paradigmatic, discursive or ideological practices were possible in that conjuncture in regards to non-European societies with which Western Europe came into a colonial encounter since 1492. Among these non-European societies, we are primarily interested in those about which the epithet 'traditional' is freely applied – around which sociology of tradition moulds itself. These are Asian societies about which Europeans were aware from pre-colonial times. The Middle East or West Africa, Egypt, India and China fall within this category of being 'traditional', interchangeably with 'the East' or 'the Orient'.

Sociology of tradition, which simultaneously constructs and rests on the notion of the 'traditional' society, develops, as do the traditions of sociology and anthropology, in the historical juncture of colonialism. As such, it is a discipline with a colonial context and a colonial content. Its organising assumptions centre around the concept of cultural difference between the colonising and colonised societies. This difference is articulated through forms of cultural essentialism within socio-economic relations of ruling. Edward Said in *Orientalism* describes how this ruling discourse of cultural/civilisational difference is congealed within the category called 'the Orient' and develops through successive stages of Europe's relations with the Middle East.[4] In its character as an essential difference, the 'Orient' serves as a binary concept to whatever is perceived as the occident or the cultural essence of Europe. This orient, when transposed through British colonial incursion in India, and partially into China, developed the fullness of its cultural connotation – and was also called 'the East' or 'Far East' and contrasted with the 'West'. These categories emerged and were consolidated between the seventeenth and nineteenth centuries.

From then various world historiographical attempts were made, of constructing and ascribing cultural and historical essences of spaces, ages and stages. The universal history of Hegel is the prime example. Early bourgeois Europe became the focal point, a state of achieved civilisation, in relation to which non-European societies were codified and judged. Thus 'other' – that is, non-Western European – societies were considered as unrealised or imperfect

---

4 Said 1979.

forms of Idea in its various historical materialisation ventures. Hegel's description of India is influential in this respect.

> This Idealism, then, is found in India, but only as an Idealism of imagination, without distinct conceptions; one which indeed does free existence from Beginning and Matter ... but changes everything into the merely Imaginative ... since, however, it is the abstract and absolute Thought itself that enters into these dreams as their material, we may say that Absolute Being is presented here as in the ecstatic state of a dreaming condition.[5]

The subsequent contribution of colonial historians, such as James Mill or Lord Elphinstone, etc., is also crucial in this project of constructing tradition and traditional societies. Written at the behest of mapping out social territories to be subjected to colonial ruling, administration and exploitation, this body of knowledge creates fixed civilisational characteristics of the traditional East in exclusive relations with the modernist, progressive West. The contribution of orientalist scholar administrators, such as William Jones, the first chief justice of the East India Company in Bengal, should also not be neglected. They actively invented traditions out of Hindu and Muslim scriptures and gave them legal status in matters of inheritance of property and personal law. This civilisational construct of 'India' put forward by the orientalist administrators such as Colebrook, Halhead or Wilson show transparently the relationship between the discourse of tradition and ruling. The terms of these types of knowledges are the terms of colonisation, and they arise both outside and within the discourses themselves.[6]

The conceptual and representational efforts of traditional sociology and sociology of tradition are both a critical and a political project. Anticolonial, anti-imperialist political theorists as well as anti-racist feminists have treated this body of knowledge as a repository of constructed content, as an accretion of concepts and images, enunciated through and for relations of domination. A pattern of circulation is detected within this knowledge or representational content which travels through arteries of various discursivities and intertextualities. As the quotation from Hegel shows, this circulation allows a problematic and questionable content to take on the status of a stable and a transcendental (or 'objective') form of social knowledge. Tejaswini

---

5 Hegel 1956, p. 139.
6 See Bannerji 2001a.

Niranjana, an Indian feminist critic, in her *Siting Translation* has commented on how this process has developed into 'a conceptual economy' which provides a silent foundation for further knowledge projects.[7] This 'conceptual economy' may be read as what Smith has called 'terms' of knowing. It amounts to positing an unproblematic assertion of correspondence between social reality and its representation. Jacques Derrida also critiques a similar formation when he speaks of a 'logocentric metaphysics' which erases the foundational dependence of putatively transcendental or objective disciplines (such as philosophy or sociology) on mundane, historical/temporal power-informed representational concepts, practices and forms. These epistemes or base concepts for creating knowledge are not bound by or produced solely within the 'field' of the academic discipline, for example of sociology. Rather they are an intrinsic part of historical, socio-economic and political relations. They create 'a conceptual network in which the discipline itself has been constituted'.[8]

2   Traditional Sociology and Colonial Discourse

Traditional sociology was born after the mid-nineteenth century, in a world engaged in developing capitalism, in colonising, in slavery, in empires. Its 'conceptual economy', its 'epistemes', 'congealed base units' or terms of knowledge, are in and of that world. This knowledge apparatus is marked by its capitalist and colonial origin or context and content, and engaged in knowledge endeavours, representational constructions and administration – both at 'home' and 'abroad'.

Though it is true that the impulse of sociology can be traced back to humanist scholars, such as Giambattista Vico, who proposed secular inquiries into the nature of emerging bourgeois societies of Western Europe, it could not escape the imperatives of class and colonial domination. It defined its disciplinarian profile in the late nineteenth century, and until then overlapped with history, philosophy and anthropology, which it lost in the period leading up to the Second World War. Sociology shared with these knowledge projects the urge to study 'otherness', especially as exemplified by non-European civilisations existing from antiquity. The point was to emphasise difference between these and Western ones, to endow them with strangeness, and oth-

---

7   Niranjana 1992, p. 73.
8   Niranjana 1990, p. 2.

erness – rather than apply to them principles of universality and similarities otherwise so respected by European intellectuals. The pivot of difference was expressed in two opposed and essential fixed social types – the West and the East. These were pseudo-historical cultural stereotypes, only vaguely connected to geography, repeated or refracted in the colonial relational spaces. These stereotypes entered into particular projects of social theorists, for example of Karl Marx on colonialism, or of Max Weber in his essays on religion or in the studies of Islam, China and India.

Judging by its terms of knowledge production, a large part of mainstream or traditional sociology can be identified as colonial 'discourse', its epistemological devices as an exercise in ideology. While I will comment on the difference and similarity between the notions of 'discourse' and 'ideology', I should now concentrate on how sociology becomes colonial discourse not in this or that detail, but paradigmatically, and primarily through the binary interpretive concepts of tradition versus modernity. It is a complex constellation of this paradigm, with all its ideological content and claims serving as a sort of force field of knowledge – particularly expressed as the orient – that mutates sociology into colonial discourse. The discourse of the orient and tradition is also connected with one of civilisation and savagery.

We shall begin our discussion of the notion of tradition, a word in ordinary usage whose paradigmatic implications are largely lost, with what Raymond Williams has to say about it in *Keywords*.[9] His entry on 'tradition' traces the long journey of this word, in the course of which it transforms through historical and cultural changes. It retains from its earliest known meanings and as it evolves a rural/non-urban, ritualistic, religious and handed-down quality, but in the context of the rise of industrial capitalism and rationalism acquires the connotation of the anti-rational or even irrational. The French Revolution and its libertarian principles might have had something to do with this change as well – since its stand against feudalism, aristocracy, and the Catholic Church or the organising role of religion as such may have also contributed to the connotation and practice of what may be called tradition.

A decline of tradition is lamented by romantic conservatives in England, for example. Poets and critics such as Burke, Coleridge, Carlyle, T.H. Green or Matthew Arnold wrote out their nostalgia and regret for an organic, non-alienating society of community and 'tradition'. Some, such as Burke or Carlyle, even advocated a return to the past, to a 'golden age' or 'organic communities' of the middle ages. Myths proliferated about these themes of loss and return. Atti-

---

9   Williams 1983.

tudes towards tradition polarised European intellectuals and middle classes. Need for tradition and search for the past were reflected in Abbé Du Bois' departure for India and his praise for its caste society, or showed in the orientalist administrators of the East India Company and founders of the Royal Asiatic Society.

Whatever the attitude towards 'tradition', the identification of tradition with the past and with Europe as it once was, was a key issue. Schlegel, for example, found (this) past of Europe in contemporary non-European societies, which held for him (still) intact 'the internal organisation and primitive bases of human thought'.[10]

The second point to be made in this context is that tradition is a modernist notion and had come to stay – as had its counterpart, modernity. If contemporary Europe were to be modern, non-Europe was perforce to be traditional. Defined economically as pre- or non-capitalist, culturally bound by iron rules of religion, ritual and hierarchy, politically under despots and warlords, locked in isolated village communities, resisting urbanisation and revelling in particularist consciousness – a grand discourse expanding into a paradigmatic form of the East or traditional society became hegemonic. So much so that this paradigm shaped the understanding of cultures, societies and politics of both the West and the East. Its diffusion and currency outside of fields of academic expertise – of humanities and social sciences – both signal and eclipse its nature as a paradigm. Yet when we pause to think, we realise that this interpretive schema, this problematic for organisation of knowledge, was not always already there.

It is time now to return to the topic of 'terms' of knowledge from the point of view of epistemology. We must now point out the connections and distinctions between different components of these terms. Though paradigm, discourse, and ideology have overlapping dimensions, they are also distinct knowledge practices. It is their distinctness, as well as their complementarity, that provides us with the necessary apparatus for producing knowledge, for modes of representation.

The concept of the paradigm is similar to what has come to be called the problematic. A paradigm, like a problematic, is an organisation of a field of knowledge which accommodates a multiple set of ideas organised into discourses. Nor need these discourses or ideas be without contradiction, as long as they are held in place by overarching categories or concepts. For example, an orientalist or racialised discourse of ethnicity may depict 'the Oriental', typ-

---

10   Said 1981, p. 128.

ically male, as essentially effeminate, while portraying him also as 'cunning', 'cruel', and 'dangerous'. The image of a fine-featured, long-fingered, dark-eyed Arab in Richard Burton's description of Arabia or in numerous eighteenth- or nineteenth-century paintings can hold both these suggestions in a patterned coherence or ambiguity, because in the end they are suspended in the complex 'otherness' implied in the paradigm of the East and the West.

If the notion of the paradigm is close to that of the problematic, the notion of discourse is more focused. It is more about actual conceptual content, about details organised in a systematic constellation of ideas, producing a defined schema of cultural interpretation. It is this content orientation which defines the notion of discourse for me. It provides the constructive characterising ground of representation. It is in this sense that Edward Said defines 'Orientalism' as a particular discourse filling in Foucault's more general notion of 'power/knowledge'. He contextualises and historicises a body of content, showing how European knowledge of the Middle East is immanent in the position or situation of colonialism. Representational details, such as cultural stereotypes, are elements of this discourse.

What then, we have to ask, is ideology? My reading of this concept goes beyond the conventional one of an organised body of related ideas with a political over- or undertone. Ideology, for me, following Marx's critique in *The German Ideology* and other texts, is the process of creating a dehistoricised and dehistoricising body of content – of representation of social reality. It is also simultaneously a way of erasing and distorting it. The production and functioning of the notion of 'race' or the 'Orient' – as types of fixating, second level cultural forms – can serve as examples of 'ideology'. The paradigm of 'othering' that underlies and contains the distorted particularities of 'race' through sociobiology and eugenics are examples of ideology. They may be called pieces of 'false knowledges' or anti-knowledges from the point of view of social inquiry. They are produced and inscribed within relations of power as a mode of its continuance. It is in this sense that Marx chose to describe them as 'ruling ideas' and stated that 'the ruling ideas in any age are the ideas of the ruling class'.[11]

But in defining ideology we cannot simply rest on content, on 'what' the particularly distorting, falsifying accounts, stereotypes or othering images, representations or ideas are. We cannot only take to task what 'the Orient' means in this sense or what people from the Middle East are represented as or not. We need to do more. We have to tackle this issue epistemologically – as a particular

---

11   Marx 1973, p. 64.

mode of production of knowledge, which inevitably produces a degrounded, a dehistoricising set of concepts, categories and meanings which erase, occlude, reify, distance or displace the historical and the social. These are the practices that Marx talks about in *The German Ideology* as the three tricks for producing ideology rather than social knowledge.

This ideological nature of the paradigm of tradition and modernity is bared with regard to its relationship with time and history. Their ideological image erases lived time, with its complex, contradictory, multiple and historically specific social relations. The notion of tradition, for example, signals to a unifying, uniform and originary past which, however, continues to exist as such into the present. This is what marks 'tradition', its unchangeable nature as an enduring bit of the past, not susceptible to history. Its status as a conceptual construct for the production and interpretation of cultural constructs should be evident from this. The same can be said about its antithesis – 'modern' – which also cuts loose from lived time and social relations, from contemporaneity. As such there is much which is here and now which is not 'modern', while 'tradition' is a fixed cultural body of ideas and images travelling through time. It is the conceptualisation of a past that is immutable, arrested and yet dynamic, present in our time, exerting pressure on it. Time in this ideological schema of tradition is circular time, its movement an eternal repetition, while the notion of 'modern', equally freed from historical time, is on its unstoppable linear journey of progress. Thus, the paradigm of tradition and modernity is not only an ahistorical and asocial form of knowledge, but an anti-historical and antisocial one as well. It is a method for disarticulating the different social moments – the cultural, the historical, the economic or political – from each other, and making Idea in the Hegelian sense the prime mover of history. Most often this Idea, in connection with tradition, we will see, is closely tied with religion.

As conceptual categories, then, tradition and modernity are cultural and not social or historical. In fact they are value categories, categories of moral/cultural/aesthetic judgement. This is what implicates them – as categories or a composite of paradigm – into relations of ruling, of capital, class, colonialism and imperialism. Depending on the political standpoint, 'tradition' or 'modernity' becomes the value of choice. Neither reveals their historicity as concepts, and both rest on the social relations and principles of property, class, colonialism and imperialism.

The Tory conservatism of traditionalist political theorists such as Burke or German romanticism of cultural theorists like Fichte tells the story. An example of a political practice involving both is that of British rule in India – evolving from the East India Company rule of Tory, orientalist and monopolistic administrators to that of the Whig, utilitarian and free-trading colonial state. The former espoused tradition, making India Hindu, even Aryan, depicting it as an antique traditional civilisation in decay; the latter condemned the same traditionality from the standpoint of modernity, that is, of instrumental rationality and industrial capitalism. The orientalists legitimised colonialism as a means of returning India to its glorious past, and maintained an analogy with ancient European civilisation, though arrested, while the modernist legitimation of colonisation consisted of introducing civilisational and social improvement through progress.

In this process of cultural essentialism, a cultural and actual occupational politics of space, the East and the West both signified a state of mind, myths of blood and belonging, of Aryan past and racial purity, of village societies and Muslim despots. This also proliferated and spilled out into Indian politics. A mirror image of colonialism evolved in certain types of nationalism reliant on a transvaluation of the paradigm of tradition and modernity. Herodotus' fantastic account of the Indus valley civilisation, rife with gold-digging ants and the anthropophagi (men with mouths and eyes in their stomachs) passed into European 'knowledge' of India.

3   Tradition of Sociology: Enter the Colonial Administrator, Scholar and the Academic

A product of modern European civilisation studying any problem of universal history, is bound to ask himself to what combination of circumstances the fact should be attributed that in Western civilisation, and in Western civilisation only, cultural phenomena have appeared which ... lie in a line of development having universal significance and value.[12]

It is certain that the few features of which we have any description from the Greeks, bear no inaccurate resemblance to those which are found to distinguish this people at the present day. From this resemblance, from the state of improvement in which the Indians remain, and the stationary condition in which their institutions first, and then their manners and character, have a tendency to fix them, it is no unreasonable supposition, that they have presented a very uniform appearance during the long

---

12   Weber 2002, p. 13.

interval from the visit of the Greeks to that of the English. Their annals, however, from that era till the period of Mahomedan conquests, are a blank.[13]

These two quotations, from a great European sociologist and a British colonial administrator turned historian whose book provided the template of Western histories of India, show such a remarkable similarity because they are articulated within the same paradigm of tradition and modernity, the colonial discourse of otherness. And they are ideological statements, in the marxist sense, as they arise in an epistemology of social occlusion and dehistoricisation. They direct us not to social investigations about what Smith calls 'what actually happens' in contradictory social relations, practices or forms of consciousness which mark these societies and their history, but to European self-referential ideological constructs or colonial discourse.[14] Yet for more than a century these ideological knowledge templates have stood in for and guided the path of institutionally accredited social knowledge.

This is most probably not what Vico had in mind when he proposed a science of the social from a standpoint of secular humanism. Yet, the historicity as well as the ideological nature of this particular type of sociology has hidden behind the metaphysics of a universal, abstract notion of knowledge and history. Often we have not seriously questioned the 'terms' of this knowledge as ideology or power/knowledge.

But it should be obvious that these 'terms' came into the conceptual realm, into academic disciplines, from social relations, histories and exigencies of ruling. The traditional sociologist, of course, will refuse to acknowledge this – especially as he, like Max Weber, has advanced himself as an acolyte of a real, objective and value-free knowledge. He harks back to the Weberian notion of neutrality of science, hoping for a procedure of decontamination, of emptying out to save him. But the 'terms' of power don't go away for all that, they persist, as Freud would have said, as a 'return of the repressed', or as what Fredric Jameson has called 'the political unconscious', or Gramsci, hegemony.

An examination of some aspects of Max Weber's sociology (or history) shows that they rest on conquerors' accounts, on their intertextualities. After all, Weber's hinduisation of India and exclusion of Islam did not originate with him. Nor did James Mill's *History of British India* produce 'British India' through honest historical research. As I mentioned before, they relied on eighteenth-

---

13   Mill 1975, p. 2.

14   Smith 1990.

and early nineteenth-century colonial administrators' writings and on common sense and practices of colonial knowledge. Ramila Thapar, writing on Weber's and Durkheim's views of India, and their influence on future scholars, has remarked on these issues and prevalent methods of knowledge production. As she puts it: 'The exclusion of Islam [from India's civilisational ethos] stemmed from the nineteenth century tendency to identify religions with their places of origin and therefore Islam was limited to West Asia'.[15] Though this leaves us wondering about the Eastern roots of Christianity, we also learn that Weber's anachronistic search for the roots of capitalism in antiquity – resulting in his sifting through the religious ethic of India during the first millennium BC rather than a comparable period when capitalism appeared in Europe – is also not peculiar to him. As Thapar says: 'So strong was the preconception of the unchanging nature of Indian society [read 'the East'], that generalisations based on the sources of the Vedic period (1000 B.C.) were considered adequate for the precolonial period up to the eighteenth century'.[16]

In this context of building on others' knowledge, we should remember Edward Said on 'Orientalism' regarding the contribution of English and French administrators, literary elites, travellers, and colonial officers in India, such as A.C. Lyall in *Asiatic Studies: Religious and Social*[17] or Henry J.S. Maine in *Village Communities in the East and West*,[18] who also helped in the shaping of the nineteenth-century civilisational problematic constructing India. The emergence of pure scholars – philologists or indologists, such as Max Müller – would be impossible without this administrative scholarly aid. Marx's reliance on these colonial knowledge sources for the notion of the Asiatic mode of production is common knowledge. Bryan Turner in *Marx and the End of Orientalism*,[19] and before him others, such as Talal Asad or Said, also discussed this. Though Marx himself, unlike Weber or Durkheim, was not a pure academic, his influence on future scholars or political thinkers about non-European political economy and history veered them towards orientalism.

But it is Max Weber who put in place the most well-developed paradigm or problematic of tradition and modernity – imbricating in it interpretive schemas, issues and approaches which became enormously influential for sociological research and sociological and cultural common sense. No sociologist single-handedly did as much to entrench and elaborate the discourse of the

---

15   Thapar 1993a, p. 54.
16   Ibid.
17   Lyall 1884.
18   Maine 1876.
19   Turner 1978.

orient/the East and the occident/the West, or to implant into future history, sociology and politics notions such as oriental or Asiatic despotism, the isolated village community, or generalisations on Islam and Islamic societies.

Scholars have remarked on terms set by orientalism for Weber's so-called knowledge of Islam and his study of India and China, all of which he represented as closed and inescapably traditional, that is, religious societies and cultures. His work on India or China is based on limited secondary sources and unquestioning acceptance of accumulated orientalist discourses. The same is true for his work on Islam. Why, we might ask, did Weber study India or Islam at all, when he was not really or primarily interested in them, knew none of the relevant languages and societies, and had no access to tools of assessment for adequate and relevant sources? And what did he add to the body of knowledge regarding these areas that pre-existed him or to the prevalent judgement and knowledge?

To answer these questions with an unqualified negative may be shocking to some, but useful. We need to recognise that Weber's Eastern sociology was entirely undertaken to clarify his real interest in the spiritual/cultural roots of capitalism in the West. His aim was to establish an unqualified, essential difference between these antithetical spaces of the West and the East – zones of irreducible otherness. Speaking from the standpoint of a critical methodology, we need to note that Weber approached history and the development of social systems from what Marx called an idealist and ideological standpoint. As with Hegel, the Idea, variously named, became the prime mover or engine of history. This is revealed in Weber's titling the first chapter of *The Protestant Ethic* as 'the spirit of capitalism'. Thus, he chose to explore the development of capitalism not in terms of historical and social relations and changes, as did Marx, but consciously contra-Marx, in terms of religious consciousness, understood in monolithic terms. It is this ideological method that distinguishes Weber's work from that of Marx, in their historiographies and sociologies, in spite of their common dependence on orientalism.

As is usual with the ideological method, Weber relied heavily on abstraction, essentialisation, homogenisation and cultural reductionism, as well as on positing stereotypes or reified notions. Social spaces became uniform cultural spaces, designated by 'ideal types', which he posed as heuristic devices for classifying societies, with their appropriate stereotypical cultural and character types. Even though these types were supposed to be helpful devices rather than representations in the historical and social objective of his work, they took on a concreteness thanks to his ideological method. They became icons of colonial/civilisational otherness and consolidated the difference between the West and the East.

These Ideal types of Weber, his orientalist social characterisations, discouraged historical inquiry and found their content from pre-existing cultural ascriptions. In this way India continued to be a land of tradition, in a state of cultural or social arrestation, ideally embodying casteist or brahminical Hinduism. As arrested, enclosed societies, outside of history, these oriental societies would never achieve a culture of rationalism, individualism, private property and capitalism. These things were not in their cultural/spiritual essences. An inner-worldly protestant ethic with its vocational asceticism, typical to the essence of the West, which was rationalist and historically dynamic, was to be sharply distinguished from this. Tradition, a prebendalist economy, was the 'fate' of India, a 'mosaic society' for the 'Islamic' world, while capitalism was of the West.

Of all the myths, ideal types and otherised ethnicities put in place by Weber and others, the complex known as oriental despotism deserves a consideration in detail. It has been summarised as follows: 'Its main postulates were the existence of isolated, self-sufficient village communities, superimposed by the despotic ruler and his court who creamed off the surplus from the peasantry through bureaucracy of revenue collectors'.[20] The control of land supposedly rested with the ruler while private property was non-existent, and the irrigation system was controlled by a centralised imperial bureaucracy. To this was added the notion of the divine origin of kings. No social differentiation or social classes were supposed to exist in these Eastern spaces, as Weber did not concede any intermediary groups between kings and peasants. As such, no political struggles or institutions developed here. The village communities, according to Weber and his sources, were autonomous from political superstructures, their social life organic, unchanging and integral to religion of a brahminical, casteist and racialised Hinduism. Religion was the only and the real cohesive factor in this fragmented collection of isolated localities.

Weber's myth of oriental despotism, though also attributed to India, is rooted in what he says about Islam and Islamic society, where the ideal types of the oriental despot and his subject the Muslim can be found. According to Bryan Turner, 'Weber's view of Islamic society comes very near to being a comprehensive summation and condensation of all the streams of analysis – history, economics, religious studies, sociology – which constitute the Orientalist conception of the Middle East'.[21] It is his contention that Weber's theory of Islamic society as a mosaic society provided the template for future work

---

20   Thapar 1993a, p. 33.
21   Turner 1978, p. 44.

on the Middle East. Myths and mystifications flowed from it. Weber's Islamic society, like his Hindu society, is a fragmented, localised set of social entities, but instead of being made up of isolated and passive village communities, it is 'a mosaic or patchwork of tribes, religious minorities, social groups and associations. This massive diversity ... is a major weakness ... a flaw within the social structure'.[22] This made it difficult to 'organise consistent, coherent opposition to the authoritarian rule of the imperial household', and though internecine strife and intrigues abounded, a general politics could not emerge from it.[23]

Islam, then, is projected by Weber as simultaneously divisive, diverse and monolithic – with its centre of power in religion and priests, as with Weber's perception of Hinduism brought into cohesion by brahmans and the caste system as a rigid, racially modified endogamous ideological system. The Islamic society is thus seen as held together 'through such mechanisms as the Sufi brotherhoods, the 'Ulema' and the 'Sha'ria'.[24] This paradox of complete ideological unity and social diversity does not provide a reliable framework for writing histories and sociologies of the Middle East. As Turner puts it:

> The mosaic model for 'Islamic Society' is not, therefore, especially convincing since it requires us to believe that this social system was both completely integrated around Islamic values and totally divided in terms of ethnicity, stratification and association. The mosaic world also requires an acceptance of the assumption that this patchwork society experienced occasional revolts but never underwent any real revolutionary restructuring of the social system.[25]

Just as with the study of India, Weber relied on limited secondary sources and translated high classical texts about the Middle East. He was not only not in any position to assess them, but also never queried them or their underlying assumptions. With regard to India, he did not dispute the eighteenth-century orientalist theory that India was based on an Aryan civilisation, which in the nineteenth century became a racial theory with ideological sanctions from Comte along with Max Müller's studies, Gobineau and the socio-biology of Thomas Huxley and other so-called Darwinists. Weber's perception of caste society as based on racial segregation, with the Aryans forming higher castes, had important consequences for the study of caste in India. That he was not

---

22   Ibid., pp. 39–40.
23   Ibid., pp. 39–40.
24   Ibid., p. 40.
25   Ibid., pp. 40–1.

averse to racialisation is clear in his views on the Poles in the context of German culture and society. The ideological nature of the 'terms' of his knowledge prevented him from creating an apparatus of social analysis which begins from peoples, societies and histories instead of from essentialising governing ideas. But this was hardly unique. As an Indian scholar puts it:

> By this time the Indian pre-colonial past had been interpreted by a large number of sophisticated ideologues who, under the guise of the newly found objectivity of the nineteenth century, were supporting a variety of preconceptions or what they believed were definitive models or ideal types. In most cases the interpretations were highly coloured by the intellectual preconceptions current in Europe at the time.[26]

Weber's method of studying India as well as his views on it and non-European societies became extremely influential in further studies of India or the Middle East. For example, Louis Dumont's *Homo Hierarchicus* portrays India in terms of caste and religion all the way into the 1960s, in spite of its liberal democratic and left polity, secular cultural activities and thoughts, and considerable communist movements.[27] John Barrington Moore's *Democracy and Dictatorship*, also Weberian in perspective, casts over the region the old ethos of Asiatic despotism, village communities and mosaic society.[28] It was not 'authentic' for the East – near, middle or far – to be a secular society and/or to develop class politics. Whereas these Western scholars deplored the anti-democratic impulses which they noted in Asia, an ethos in which they included communism as an irrational collectivist or totalitarian formation, they also depreciated and erased social and political movements that contradicted their paradigm and myths of the East and the West, of modernity and tradition. Conversely, they did not read Christianity into the ethos of the West in the context of the holocaust, nor noted the political discourse in which the Middle East is/was represented through cultural myths dating back perhaps even to the crusades. Even in the writings of marxist political theorists as noteworthy as Perry Anderson's *Lineages of the Absolutist State*, the section on the 'House of Islam' continues the same sort of essentialising myth.[29]

If Weberian or orientalist sociology and historiography had this occlusive, mythical impact on the Western knowledge of the other, what impact did

---

26   Thapar 1993a, p. 27.
27   Dumont 1970.
28   Moore 1967.
29   Anderson 1974.

it have on the East? A study of early Indian nationalism, involving Hindu cultural revivalism or supremacy, will show that this same body of colonial knowledge and cultural identities was the basic formative material for them. The Aryan myth complete with the swastika, the sense of superiority of caste society, a close feeling towards the British and the German 'race' and even actual support of nazism by some, the exclusion of Muslims as 'foreigners' and definition of Islam as a violent, belligerent, sensualist religion – a whole paraphernalia of illiberalism and fascism arose within the terrain of that knowledge.

Weber's orientalist, hinduised, casteist India is also the India of today's Hindu fundamentalists. The only difference is in the positive valuation of this symbolic cultural constitution. The fact that this Hindu nationalism has to still struggle so hard to create credibility in India, still loses elections and launches into massacres of 'others', such as Muslims, Christians, low-caste Hindus and Dalits, to bring the polity into its fascist orbit – this may not be either visible or believable to those in the West growing up in Weber's tradition. Certainly not those who believe in an essentially non-secular, 'traditional' character of these Eastern cultures/societies, proclaimed as still feudal or cultures without civil society. Democracy, as successful or unsuccessful in India, is seen as antithetical to the typically Indian essence. It is not surprising that the United States has found in the current BJP Hindu nationalist regime in India, in the military dictatorship of Pakistan, and the islamised Bangladesh of Khaleda Zia, the right kinds of allies who support local and foreign capitalism in the name of god.

4   From the Sublime to the Vulgar: The Mass Mediation of Tradition
        and Modernity

It isn't necessary to understand something in order to destroy it.[30]

When we step down from the high halls of academia, from the exalted expressions of colonial discourse, into the everyday grind and grunge of news reporting and opinion pages of newspapers, we find the same ideological procedures, the same or derivative images/icons/modes of representation at work. From at least the eighteenth century to now, they have been transmitted as ways of understanding or representing the West and the East. They constitute the

---

30   Brecht 1979, p. 64.

hegemonic cultural common sense of racist cultures with their formerly colonial and now imperialist relations and histories. But did Max Weber, and other
scholars, in any sense cause this?

Of course we cannot speak of Max Weber's knowledge practices and resulting ideas as 'causes' of everyday Western orientalism or racism, but can we
ignore their convergence with the legitimation of and contribution to them?
Weber here himself stands as an ideal type of scholar – a type that defines
institutional knowledge both as content and form. He and the crude journalists of the Canadian media, for example Margaret Wente, Celine Gallipeu or
Marcus Gee, all of the Toronto *Globe and Mail*, share the same paradigms, discourses and ideological practices that make history, society and politics of the
third world countries magically disappear. But it isn't just that. Scholars such as
Weber contributed to a mass dissemination of the mythologies of 'the Orient',
'the East', 'Asia', and their Western binaries – providing them with seemingly
historical and sociological content. The problematic of tradition versus modernity has become an invisible but incontestable way of conceptualising world
societies and cultures. And certainly the ghosts of Weber's ideal types, with
their paradox of essentialisation and pseudo-concreteness, haunt the world
of popular representation. Many who saw and read the media production of
u.s. and Canadian responses to 11 September – 'the u.s. under attack' – or the
representation of the war on Afghanistan and its legitimation, saw also the
working up of anxieties and racial stereotypes which manufactured the consent of the u.s. and Canadian citizenry in the passing of anti-terror legislation
or the Patriot Act. The media representation of the situation in Israel, the depiction of Palestinians' struggles, are wholly encompassable within Weber's ideal
type of Islamic societies. It is difficult not to notice the similarity of method
and content between the high and the low forms of knowledge and attempts
at sense-making.

No matter how nobly motivated and well-read Weber was, his ideal types
allowed him to mask in the cloak of learning a cultural essentialism born of
relations and histories of colonial domination. However laudable his method of
abstraction may be for science, in their social deployment these abstract types
became a systematisation and categorisation of orientalist/racist cultural perceptions and value judgments. As with racist or any other stereotypes, they can
give us no real knowledge of societies and peoples. There is little to be learnt
except prejudice and mythology from Weber's view of Islam, for example. As
with him, so with modern-day Canadian and u.s. reporters, no matter how
much detail they pile up about Iraq, Afghanistan or Pakistan; they are neutralised by a uniformly otherising stance and the content of a Weberian, colonial
discourse.

The mass media continues to proliferate racist representations which are also those employed by the u.s. and Canadian authorities in racial profiling. In this epic theatre of war, Huntington's cliché of a 'clash of civilisations' (another bit of the East/West, tradition/modernity paradigm), the *dramatis personae* directly descend from the ideal type of oriental despotism. The Occident, its binary, is typified as an emissary of civilisation, of rationalism, a veritable white knight of freedom and democracy. This image is made in teflon. It is never dented, from Hiroshima to now, by nuclear bombs, napalm, smart bombs, cluster bombs, land mines, or death of civilians, by infliction of mutilation, madness and destruction of nature. The rational way of seeing all this is as 'collateral damage', as the 'other' in this discourse is not human but a type. The West as the 'self' is. There is no twin in death in the East for those who died in the twin towers of New York.

These ideal types, which are wrapped into the discourse of the orient, we have met many times, until they have become real for us. We have met them in the high scholarship of Weber and others, and we have met them in Hollywood melodramas and commercials. We have met them in everyday invectives against Arabs, Muslims or Islam, and on brands of condoms named Sheik, signalling the unbridled lust of the Eastern despot or moor. I am speaking about, reminding us, of the Oriental Potentate, the author of Asiatic despotism, who looks at us through Rudolph Valentino's mascara-darkened eyes, through the rugged faces of the arabs of Richard Burton or Lawrence of Arabia. Without this stereotype, this discourse of the orient in place, could the world of Western politics and news create the Asian/oriental/Islamic leaders that they present us with? Even though these leaders differ vastly from each other politically, are even at loggerheads with each other, as for example with Gamal Abdel Nasser, Saddam Hussein or Yassar Arafat – they are represented as being cast in the same mould. They are the living ideal types of the autocratic or despotic/absolute Eastern rulers. That they should be capable of tolerating dissent, or that democracy or secularism may be a desired politics for any of them or in their societies, is impermissible within the framework of the East.

In media reporting and Western perceptions of Israel and Palestine in these representations, Weber's West and East cohabit the same space in a warring deadlock. The positive modernity of a Westernised Israel rarely seems to be compromised, no matter how dreadful its theocracy, the state terror or the devastation and encirclement of Palestine grows. The display and use of the latest in weaponry by Israel is portrayed as a beleaguered response to primitive Palestinian aggression born out of the fanaticism of Islam and the barbaric intransigence of Islamic societies. The discourse of violence of Islam in this all-encompassing political framework covers not only the Hamas, but the secular PLO as well. The same ideal type of oriental despotism and the violence of Islam covers Syria or Lebanon, Saddam Hussein or the secular Ba'ath Party, while carefully keeping Saudi Arabia, a U.S. ally, temporarily out of the picture.

Both modernist or traditionalist Muslim leaders of the Middle East, Central or South Asia are drawn on the same template. As an interesting aside, the taint of being an Asiatic went some way in the portrayal of Stalin, from Georgia. Trotsky described him as ruthless, cunning and slant-eyed. Perry Anderson's formulation of Western and Eastern marxism holds a similar tone of orientalism.[31] It would appear that the stereotypes, icons, and representational paraphernalia of the reporters of the newspapers do not require originality and innovation. What they do is to tap into the collective unconscious of racist/colonial discourse of the reader through phrases or images – that is, connect with the terms of knowledge that have become deeply lodged. The cartoons carried by the newspapers are another – a visual – representation of this conceptual racism, of its diversified stereotypes. The nose, for example, has been a very significant body part in this respect – there is an ironic and uncanny similarity in the caricatured nose of the Arab and that of Jews in Nazi cartoons, Jews in the 1930s having been the representatives of the East living in the West.

The other ideal types in the complex of the orient are the fanatic Islamic fighters – coming down to us from the days of the crusades. The descriptions of Al Qaeda are not dissimilar to those of Islamic tribal warriors with their relentless ferocity and religious fanaticism, written during the crusades and in the colonial period. Then there are the Islamic assassins and villains, stock characters of European melodramas starting with Othello, and those of Hollywood, personified by Osama bin Laden or Mohammed Atta in the current context. The Muslim priest, a cruel and cunning fanatic, is another member in this cast of ideal types. Women figure here as passive victims of the Islamic tradition, a veiled damsel in distress to be rescued by the Western white knight from the clutches of a cruel priest and a sensualist oriental despot.[32] Occasional glimpses of love slaves are also caught, particularly from Western women's writings about the orient. Mary Wollstonecraft to modern-day Western tourists or writers of the East, as well as feminists, have spoken of both. The stereotypes of 'the terrorist', 'the Arab', the 'jihadi' that have deluged our consciousness in the last few months, in whose elusive footsteps we still move, seeking to level the Hindukush mountains in his search, is the same 'fanatic Muslim' whom the immigration and airport authorities invent and deter, or Hollywood por-

---

31   Anderson 1974.
32   See Spivak 1988a.

trays as The Terrorist. Often he is attributed an otherworldly and unrelenting asceticism which Weber found to be peculiar to Eastern religions.

We cannot end this section without commenting on the notion of 'terror' – which has justified the sacrifice and death of political and civil liberties in the West – as a feature of the paradigm of tradition and modernity. What qualifies as 'terror' in the current Western context is a traditional form marked by religion and collectivities – either as a collective conduct of faith and irrationality, or anti-capitalist irrationality. The deployed technology here is primitive, of direct presence in bodies and action, and involves the irrational, a basic characteristic of the East. The self-harming of the suicide bomber falls within this paradigm, while the massive machinery of state terror run with an organised bureaucracy and army does not. And, most importantly, all is containable within Weber's ideal construction of the East. The opposite to this 'terror' is the non-terror or 'democracy' of the state of Israel or the United States, modern nations marked by 'freedom and democracy' which can only be achieved in a Western bourgeois society, and an apotheosis, or as Weber would have said, 'the fate' of capitalism. This non-terror is comprised of the armies of the modern state, which kill with a rational, Weberian accounting goal in mind. These forces of modernity reveal their faces, they fear no recognition or reprisal upon being seen. They do not fight for a collectivity of faith, but rather for a world where each individual is, as Weber considered right, a free entrepreneur – a world of efficient mercenaries. Though it must be noted that this world of capitalist rationality, which Weber saw as an 'iron cage', 'the fate' of the occident, subsumed within 'the spirit of capitalism', was not a happy world for him, it was his only possible world. It was inevitable, a Faustian bargain with the devil, which he hoped could be avoided by a neutral, objective, scientific knowledge and an efficient bureaucracy. Its ideal types eventually came out as Hitler, Nazi capitalism, storm troopers, a civilisation of gas chambers.

Under the circumstances of massacres of Muslim minorities by Hindu supremacists or fundamentalists in India since 27 March 2002, it would be wrong not mention the contribution of orientalism – popular and academic – in this. This carnage in Gujarat and the attacks against Muslims in Punjab, both governed by the same Hindu supremacist party, the BJP, that is the central government of India, holds the same orientalist perceptions of Muslims that I have talked about, and uses them to the same end of legitimation of violence. The rhetoric of terror and the terrorist which resounds here does the same in India and with U.S. support of this Hindu fundamentalist government. As in the U.S. and Canada, the Indian government is simultaneously spinning the orientalist rhetoric of violence of Islam while asking for religious tolerance, or its officials visiting mosques. This perception, as we know, dates back to the same texts and authors that mark the Weberian tradition, and this dual governing tactic is equally old. The orientalist constructions of a Hindu India, foreignness of Islam and Muslims, are essential to the ideology of the BJP, RSS, VHP and paramilitary youth groups – as a group self-identifying as 'a holy or monastic family'.

It is important to note that the Canadian media has for the most part unquestioningly offered to us the orientalist/Hindu supremacist view of Hindus as a dedicated religious group who are fighting for their religious identities and rights. Why hasn't this media asked how Muslims, approximately 12 per cent of the Indian population, could threaten the vast majority of a billion people? Why does the Western media not note the struggle in India over secularism and democracy, but only speak of Hindus and Muslims? Could it be that the same blinding terms of knowledge, the same myths that I outlined, are the influences? How can they not see that the language of riot that they apply to situations in India or Palestine dehistoricises their presentation of the conflicts and gives them a false moral calculus with which they invest the killers and their victims with the same power and responsibility?

The popular imagination has been so deeply inscribed with the images of Islamic fundamentalism and violence that Hindu fundamentalism or Christian fundamentalism do not easily show as possibilities for terror and persecution. In the case of India this is an old story – from the days of the East India Company to Weber and after – that Hindus and Hindu society are invested with a passive and spiritual otherworldliness punctuated by revolting caste practices and brutalities towards Hindu women. But this violence has been considered to be inwardly focused. To this common sense is added the myth of Hindu vegetarianism, cow-loving sanctity of life and nature. It is not known that this non-violent image relies on Buddhism – a non-Hindu religion and movement now wholly marginalised in India. This mythic Hindu image, with its aura of peace, meditation and nirvana, which makes India into a giant yoga camp, cannot accommodate the image of petty bourgeois Hindu fanatics who kill for gain, blood lust and misogyny in the name of god and come to national political power. This myth of Indian non-violence may have gained a concreteness due to the life and politics of Mahatma Gandhi, himself felled by the bullet of a Hindu fundamentalist assassin in a moment of prayer. This assassin was an RSS associate – that is, an associate of the current authors of carnage in the Indian state of Gujarat. If the Western media could see beyond its ideological orientalist blinkers, they could ask why are not the RSS, VHP or the youth groups of the BJP not being banned as terrorist groups, or why white supremacist and Christian militia groups in the U.S. are not similarly considered. After all, Musharraf Pervez had to do this with regard to Muslim fundamentalists in Pakistan, though with little effect.

The struggle continues. Capitalist rationality, as critical theorists such as Marcuse, Adorno and Horkheimer remarked, turns out to be a gigantic irrationality. George W. Bush also calls for a crusade, for an operation Infinite Justice, and crucifies the world on an Axis of Evil. The sacred and the profane, the East and the West, tradition and modernity dissolve in the imperatives of history and capitalist interest, and sociology must rise to the task of going beyond the paradigm and against ideology.

Beyond the Ruling Category to What Actually Happens: Notes on James Mill's Historiography in *The History of British India*

> Knowing is always a *relation* between knower and known. The knower cannot be collapsed into the known, cannot be eliminated; the knower's presence is always presupposed. To know is to always know on some terms, and the paradox of knowing is that we discover in its object the lineaments of what we know already.[1]

∴

1 Introduction

The concept of tradition is always with us, even though, and perhaps because, we live in North America or Europe, coded as the West. Associated with certain parts of the world, their peoples and cultures, characterising them as 'others' not 'us', tradition and its conceptual satellites appear in an automatic gesture of comprehending and creating difference. Tradition serves as an interpretive and constructive device, providing a discursive staple for newspapers and television shows, scholarly texts, feminism and fashion magazines, development policies and UN sanctioned bombing of Iraq. Sections of the world, variously called 'the East', 'the South', or 'the third world', contrasted to 'the West', 'the North' or 'the first/developed world', have been designated as domains of tradition.

Edward Said, very early in a long line of critics of colonial discourse, noted a historical knowledge-power relation encoded in the category 'the east' or 'the Orient'.[2] He drew our attention to an essentialist, homogenising representational apparatus which levelled with its imperial gaze diverse non-European

---

1 Smith 1990, p. 33.
2 See Said 1979, regarding cultural-colonial construction of 'the Orient' or 'the East' as a knowledge/power category, and the implication of 'the West's' cultural-political identity and politics.

regions into imaginary geographies and vast historic-cultural blocs. One of the interpretive devices that helped to accomplish this task was 'tradition'. The adjective 'traditional' (relatedly underdeveloped, backward, as opposed to 'modern', progressive, advanced or developed) seems to synthesise disparate cultural characteristics to the satisfaction of the West.[3] Associated with stereotypes of mysticism and spirituality, dowry, wife-burning, female infanticide, overpopulation, primitive technology, peasants and villages, India in particular has been projected as a 'traditional' society. It has long held a binary relationship to the West's self-representation, ramified through its package of science and rationality, technological-economic development, 'open society' and political freedom.[4]

Deconstructing this traditional 'India' as an ideologically representational category by unpacking the constituent social relations and epistemological method of its production, implies an examination of the notion of tradition as a mode of reification. Furthermore, to return this 'imagined India' to the realm of history necessitates its disarticulation from the notion of tradition which dehistoricises the cultures of Indian peoples.[5] This chapter attempts a part of that task by examining the epistemological mechanism, the social relations embedded within that notion, and the resulting representational character of 'India' as produced by James Mill in *The History of British India* (first published 1817). The importance of this book in terms of representing India in the West, and also to India itself, is difficult to exaggerate.

2   Text, Rule and Ideology

We could, I imagine, be easily asked, why ascribe a single text such importance, and what power can conceptual practices have in the creation of hegemony? What in short, is a written text or epistemology to ruling?

The answer to these questions lies in a Gramscian understanding of the concept of hegemony. According to this, even though force is the fundamental content of hegemony, it does not reside only in physical brutality or a machinery for direct coercion. The initial moment of conquest has to be translated or mediated into an administration of power. The work of intellectuals who inter-

---

3   See Williams 1983, pp. 318–20, for an evolution and application of this concept.
4   See the discussion of modernisation theorists of the MIT school in the context of 'development', such as Kuznets 1966 and Rostow 1985, for an overall grasp of this position.
5   See Inden 1990, for an extended discussion of this colonial cultural-political construction of India, which attempts a project partially similar to Said's *Orientalism*.

pret the reality to be ruled and inscribe this into suitable categories provides the administrative basis for a sustained, reproducible rule.[6] In the case of India, Orientalist scholar-administrators of the East India Company, along with those of the colonial state, provide this conceptual or categorical framework.

On this basis an 'India' is constructed from the standpoint of European colonial rule. It consists of a set of 'virtual realities vested in texts and accomplished in the distinctive practices of reading and writing'.[7] The ruling nature of this construction is evident from the fact that it tells us less about that country than about the social imperatives of the producers of that knowledge.[8] The importance of texts which transmit knowledge, especially about 'distant amorphous' places, to the West from whence also colonialism and imperialism spring, must always be kept in mind. They provide the building blocks for cultural and ideological representation of these areas.[9] Socio-cultural relationships between these spaces are conducted mainly through what Smith calls 'the textual mode'.[10] Furthermore, these constructed 'objects of knowledge' claim authority for neutral or unbiased representation. No allowance is made for the possibility that the knower's, for example Mill's, intention or location in relations of ruling are implicated in the types of discourse deployed and developed.[11]

This epistemological erasure of the social, through the adoption of a metaphysical mode entailing occlusiveness, displacement and objectification, is named as ideology by Marx in *The German Ideology*. Here ideology is not solely the *content* or a collection of particular ideas and stereotypes, but also, and mainly, *an epistemological method*. A close reading of *The German Ideology* shows that not only are the 'ruling ideas of any age ... the ideas of the ruling class', but also how these ideas are implicated forms and products of social relations necessary for ruling.[12] We begin to see constructive and reflexive relations between the apparatuses of ruling and knowledge.

This ideological method which degrounds and obscures the historical/material dimension of ideas naturally postulates a superordinate and separate

---

6   Said 1979. See also Smith 1987, pp. 181–5 on the notion of 'standpoint' of knowledge, and Smith 1990, pp. 31–57, on the ideological (i.e., ruling) role of intellectuals (sociologists and others) in the construction and maintenance of the ruling apparatus.
7   Smith 1990, p. 62.
8   Said 1979, pp. 4–9.
9   Said 1979, p. 9.
10   Smith 1990, pp. 61–5 and 83–8.
11   Smith 1990, pp. 14–18. See also Smith 1987, pp. 49–69, on the implications of knower's location in the production of knowledge.
12   Marx and Engels 1970, p. 5.

realm for them. In *Ideological Practices of Sociology*, Smith transposes Marx's critique of philosophy to the standard knowledge procedures of conventional (bourgeois) sociology and insists that they are neither 'objective' (except reificatory) nor 'pure'.[13] The productive tools and impacts of these procedures, when queried on the ground of everyday life, amount to a categorical and segregated organisation of relations of ruling, involving specific semiotic systems. They are, for her, 'isomorphic with relations of ruling' and necessarily invert the actual lived subject/object relations. They write over subjectivities, experiences and agencies of peoples in history.[14]

Smith's marxist critique of sociology as ideology can be extended to historiography of colonial history. I have chosen James Mill's *The History of British India* for an exploration of its epistemological processes with the intention of uncovering how Mill's 'India' is an ideological constellation, what Ronald Inden calls an 'imagined India'.[15]

3   Making India British: James Mill and Colonial Historiography

> It is certain that the few features of which we have any description from the Greeks, bear no inaccurate resemblance to those which are found to distinguish this people at the present day. From this resemblance, from the state of improvement in which the Indians remain, and the stationary condition in which their institutions first, and then their manners and character, have a tendency to fix them, it is no unreasonable supposition, that they have presented a very uniform appearance during the long interval from the visit of the Greeks to that of the English. Their annals, however, from that era till the period of Mahomedan conquests, are a blank.[16]

Mill's *The History of British India* has stood in for 'Indian history', even though Mill encapsulates his real project in the very title of his study. The title holds, as does the book, an actuality and an ambition within one cover. India at the time of his writing (1805–17) was not fully under British control, either in terms of occupation of territories or in terms of knowledge. A comprehensive task of

---

13   See Smith 1990, pp. 14–16 and 66–70.
14   Smith 1990, pp. 83–8.
15   Inden 1990.
16   Mill 1968, pp, 118–19.

creating knowledge for ruling had been already undertaken by the orientalists in the eighteenth century, but an 'India' equal to the task of colonial rule had not yet been fully formulated. Besides, both in England and India there were many turns and reversals in political philosophy of governing and practical politics. The notion of 'British India', therefore, projects both a partial actuality and a desire of full domination, as well as their conceptual bases.[17] Mill's India is thus an ingested and aspired to social space for colonial rule. The book's towering status as a colonial text is evinced in securing Mill the job of the Chief Examiner of India House, the highest post in England of the most lucrative instrument of colonial rule. Administrators, legislators, missionaries and businessmen engaged with India, among others, read this book as a compulsory text. An important footnote is John Kenneth Galbraith's preface to the 1968 edition.[18] Galbraith read Mill before venturing out as American Ambassador to India. His preface abounds in admiration of Mill for giving the modern reader a fundamental grasp on Indian reality.

This preface supports Mill's claim that *The History of British India* would stand as an enduring representation of India for the West. An assessment, thus, of this crucial text as ideology should be conducted along the following lines:

1.   The epistemological method and historical context, including the social positionality of the author;
2.   The particular content with regard to ascriptive stereotypes of concepts and images;
3.   The overall political implications of these textual and conceptual practices with regard to the type of social subjectivity or historical agency ascribed to the Indian people.

Speaking of context, James Mill is primarily known as the apostle of Bentham's utilitarian philosophy and its application to matters of government. It is less known that in earlier life Mill was an evangelical preacher, and he remained close to Wilberforce and the Clapham sect. He was admired by William Bentnick, the governor general of Bengal, and by important parliamentarians such as Thomas Babbington Macauley. For his formulation of 'British India' he relied on the archival compilations of the East India Company and translated resources of the Orientalists. But his particular interest, unlike theirs, did not lie in the antiquities and their revival, and he successfully ejected parts of the earlier approach which combined a negative cultural-moral judgement of the contemporary Indian society with a respect for India's ancient civilisation.

---

17   Ibid.
18   Ibid.

Mill's history project, and thus his historiography, obviously stems from the standpoint of a colonial empire. It is not in 'discovering' India as an historical entity, but in vindicating the moment of colonial rule that he found his intellectual motive force. His purpose was to unfold the implications of events which marked the 'commencement of the British Intercourse with India; and the Circumstances of its Progress, till the Establishment of the Company on a durable basis of Act of Sixth of Queen Anne'.[19] The scope of the three-volume project consists of:

> [R]ecording the train of events, unfolding the Constitution of the Body, half political, half commercial, through which the business has been ostensibly performed; describing the nature, the progress and effects of its commercial operations, exhibiting the legislative proceedings, the discussions and speculations, to which the connexion of Great Britain with India has given birth, analyzing the schemes of government which she has adopted for her Indian dominions, and attempting to discover the character and species of relation to one another in which the mother country and her eastern dependencies are placed.[20]

The attempt consisted of situating and legitimising British colonial rule in a pattern of ruling successions in India. Emphasising force and repeated invasions by foreigners, characterising the Mughal empire in particular as foreign rule, and portraying the Mughals as despotic and a degenerative influence on the Hindus, Mill argued for the necessity of an English empire in India. It was as a rule of reason and a civilising mission that he justified this rule. Throughout his first chapter, on the English mercantile companies and the foundation of the colonial empire in Bengal, Mill presents an innocent commercial history. All European atrocities of conquest and commerce, including slave trade, are erased while presenting English achievements and superiority in 'the spirit of commerce'. The only moral judgement is levelled at the Dutch for executing nine Englishmen in the 'massacre at Amboyna'. The Mahomedans, however, attract heavy condemnation on the ground of savagery and ruthlessness, while 'that brilliant empire, established by the English' was entirely legitimated in India.[21] It was even portrayed as sanctioned succession, as in the following statement:

---

19   Mill 1968, p. 1.
20   Ibid., p. 2.
21   Ibid., p. 33.

A firman and decree of the Emperor, conferring [these] privileges was received on the 11th of January, 1643; and authorised the first establishment of the English on the continent of India, at that time the seat of most extensive and splendid monarchies on the surface of the globe.[22]

The 'recording of train of events' was thus no neutral narrative venture for Mill. *The History of British India* had but one main objective, to project and promote British rule in India.

This objective required a representational characterisation of the object of rule – namely, Indian peoples. The remainder of the three volumes is dedicated to this enterprise, the construction of a definitive socio-moral version of India, beginning with the most extensive chapter on 'manners, morals and customs of the hindoos'. This is followed by a temporal history, also laced with moral and cultural judgements. Together they contained both justification and direction for the development of the colonial state.

Mill's history consciously eschews any archival or empirical research, including the knowledge of local classical or vernacular languages and texts. Thus it is not impeded by or accountable to information that may not fit in the introjected ideological schema. This colonial historiography is distinct from that of writing European history where the historian attempts a direct familiarity with the sources and records events in time. In colonial historiography, however, the historian, according to Mill, plays the role of a judge who is faced with a crime and a set of circumstances and testimonies of witnesses. These he must construe as 'evidences' of a typical event, as well as decide on the credibility of the witnesses.[23] He must then read or hear the testimonies, etc., with the legal provisions pertaining to this crime. Whether something is an 'evidence' at all will depend on what it is an 'evidence' of, that is, on the pre-existing legal construction of that crime. Mill's legal discourse contains explicit epistemological principles and statements. Beginning with the premise that he 'knows' 'India' (the crime) even before he undertakes his task, he employs a principle of relevance and logic in selecting and sorting evidences for this pre-conceived knowledge which originates outside his research. Thus the text is a fully fleshed version of his presuppositions, details of which are to be read as illustrations of his preconceptions of Indian history and society. The attempt results into a seamless 'imagining' or construction of 'India', unaccommodating of complexities which might have problematised this construction.

---

22   Ibid., p. 21.

23   See Mill's 'Preface' to Volume I for the full exposition of his method of history writing and his conception of what properly constitutes 'history'.

Mill's proudly stated historiography, which adopts a metaphysical mode as a tool of social research, could be termed an idealist rationalism. This method was critiqued by Marx as the epistemological method of ideology. Discrediting the need for a material basis or actual research, etc. for writing history, Mill starts with an essentialist version of a 'real India' as opposed to the phenomenal one, which is qualitatively different from and unaccountable to the empirical and social. Logical deductions and interpretations rely, thus, on this pre-historical and empirical essentialist notion of the 'real'. Merging the formality of logic with the universal claims of metaphysics, Mill purports to provide his readers with the 'real truth' about India. He never questions his presumptions about India, their sources, or the existing social relations between a colonial investigator and a colonised reality. Totally unselfconscious, he characterises his method as that of 'positive science', resting on notions of 'true' and 'false' causes, 'witnesses' and 'evidences' in order to come to the right sociomoral judgements about India.[24] However, in this process Mill not only creates moral judgements; they also became 'facts' about India which function as metaphysical and foundational categories for classifying, judging and administering Indian peoples and societies. Thus, the writing of history becomes a production of ideology, content and epistemology matching each other, occluding constructive relationships between consciousness and society. Unlike the sciences, Mill's method dispenses with verification, with the obligation to test preconceptions and so forth against the archival, empirical sources, both vernacular and European. He discourages new research, since he considers that a 'sufficient stock of knowledge was already there'.[25]

The standpoint of domination is also implicit in the fact that Mill never considers the ability or the right of Indians to define and represent themselves. His text as a whole is both a device and a justification for that silencing. The only voice and image permitted to 'the native' would be those she/he would acquire in the course of the colonial narrative.

The ideological character of Mill's enterprise, which fears any threat to his ideal type, emerges in his complex intertextual relationship with the English Orientalists.[26] Since no narrative even remotely resembling a history could have been written without previous records and translations, Mill was highly dependent on the Orientalist archive. Though he did not in all points share their view of India, the 'lineaments of what they already knew' provided the

---

24 Mill 1968, pp. 6–7.
25 Ibid., p. 5.
26 Throughout Volume I, Book II, Mill disputes with the orientalist historians and translators just as much as he disputes the fact of India having a history.

pedestal for his project. But he resorted to a strategy of abstraction to decontextualise and incorporate previous research and interpretations, and manipulated stereotypes and attitudes as he needed them.

Mill's major debt to the Orientalists for an ideological version of India lay in the polyvalent concept of 'tradition'. It is this grab-bag category of cultural interpretation and representation which provided Mill's staple or modality for constructing 'difference'. It created a ground for essentialism and thus generalisation, since everything found in or about India could be read in light of this pre-established concept. The peculiar relationship held by this concept to time and social agency, bespeaking an arrested time, fixity and repetition, allowed any reading of India through the lens of tradition as both chaotically mobile and rigidly fixed. This imputed changeless, passive lack of agency was then put forward as an intrinsic characteristic of Indian peoples and their histories. Caught in the conceptual grip of 'tradition', events and changes of a few thousand years could then be seen as 'blank annals' or an eternal repetition.[27]

The deployment of the concept of 'tradition', which did not originate in the colonial encounter or in Mill but pre-existed in Europe for other and similar sense-making purposes, became a major device for constructing both the 'crime' and the evidence for Mill the historian-judge. Orientalist scholar-administrators such as William Jones had already established traditionality as an essence of Indian society, and of the 'Hindoos' in particular. In fact, from the era of Warren Hastings in the 1770s to the time when Mill was writing his book, colonial civil legislation in India continually assumed and constructed 'tradition' through translation of Hindu and Muslim scriptures and a selective compilation of their personal laws.[28]

The concept of 'tradition', when deployed in the otherisation of India, entailed the related notions of 'civilisation' and 'antiquity'. While concepts such as 'tradition', 'antiquity' and 'civilisation' were invested with positive connotations for the colonial conservatives of the eighteenth century, they also served as conduits for varying moral judgements about colonised societies at each stage. What was meant by 'civilisation' or its importance at each stage decided whether a country with an old history and complex sociocultural organisations could be called civilised. Thus, the attitude toward civilisation and traditionality, as well as the ascribed types of traditions, decided whether a country was 'civilised' or 'barbaric' or 'savage'. And those who had power and the need to define the 'truth about India', claiming self-transcendence, had decided that

---

27   Mill 1968, pp. 118–21.
28   For Hastings and personal law, see the introduction, Sangari and Vaid 1990.

it was a traditional country. Thus, it was at once in and out of time and history, replete with peculiar 'barbaric' traditions. Mill also went by categorical formulations of 'India' as accomplished by the India Office, but unlike the Orientalists, denied either the value or the existence of an ancient civilisation in India. As a utilitarian and Malthusian economic liberal he not only had little interest in traditional societies or ancient civilisations, but even less in Eastern ones.

Mill's book therefore begins by disputing the Orientalist ascriptions of antiquity and civilisation to India. His version of this country is projected in no uncertain terms at the very outset: 'Rude nations seem to derive a peculiar gratification from pretensions to a remote antiquity. As a boastful and turgid vanity distinguishes remarkably the oriental nations, they have in most instances carried their claims extravagantly high'.[29] He goes on to criticise Orientalist accounts of Hindu creation stories and the Hindu methods of record-keeping and chronicle writing. Dubbing the Orientalist acknowledgement of Hindu claims to antiquity as duped submission to the 'national pride of barbarians', he dismisses indigenous records, literature, and other archival sources as worthless for writing 'history'.[30] 'Judging' the sources and 'witnesses' in this peremptory way, Mill simultaneously displays his power location as a reader of Indian reality and manipulates, controls and constructs sociocultural 'facts' about India according to his own discursive organisation.

This disregard for matters indigenous to India, echoed later by Macaulay in his influential 'Minute on Education for India'[31] as 'monstrous fables' of barbarians, often pits Mill against the Orientalists. He is particularly dismissive of their impartiality and accuracy, since they knew Indian languages, lived there and enjoyed the literature that they found. Thus, they lacked the necessary detachment which Mill considered essential for a judge-historian, and he found himself eminently suitable for this task on the very grounds of his lack of knowledge of languages, direct connections with or experiences of India.

H.H. Wilson, on the other hand, an Orientalist scholar-administrator who went on to become Boden Professor of Sanskrit at Oxford, subsequently edited *The History of British India* and provided extensive footnotes correcting Mill's 'errors' in representing Indian culture or history. Asserting that Europeans cannot 'know' India without learning its ancient and modern languages and read-

---

29   Mill 1968, p. 107.
30   Ibid., pp. 118–19.
31   Curtin 1971.

ing extensively to develop a cultural literacy to be complemented by life experiences and discussions with Indians, Wilson offered in his 'corrections' a text parallel to Mill's.

Wilson's footnotes and commentaries highlight Mill's enormous ignorance of India and his even greater arrogance that his very ignorance was a prerequisite for knowledge. Mill was one of the earliest propagators of the notion that India did not have a 'history', a notion that was to be found from William Jones to Marx though to modern times. For Mill, India lacked 'history' both in terms of an intellectual discipline and in terms of a social progression or evolution in time, expressive of agency and originality. Presenting Hindus both as infantile liars as well as the real 'natives' of India, caught in fantasy and blind to the difference between fact and fiction, and Indian Muslims as foreign invaders who only kept minimal records, Mill regarded European historians such as himself as the real historians of India.

Mill's view of himself as the definitive historian of India, while denying India any history, creates crude inconsistencies in his text. On the one hand, his own lack of willingness and ability to do primary research on India makes him reliant on early Greek and later European sources. He is thus constrained to say that Orientalists 'had studied the Indian languages' and 'acquired the means of full and accurate information'.[32] On the other hand, they were seduced by that very knowledge into a positive view of India, especially of the Hindus. Mill draws instead upon the Greeks for denigrating social features which 'bear no inaccurate resemblance to those which are found to distinguish this people at the present day'. Consequently, he states in the same breath that 'we have no reason to suppose that their knowledge of the Hindus was valuable'.[33] Mill's double project is to degrade and deny Indians any worthwhile historical and cultural agency and thus any history of its expression. His ultimate aim seems to have been the establishment of an empty historico-cultural slate for India inscribed with barbaric traditions. He shares with the evangelical missionaries the conviction that Indians (mainly Hindus) are essentially degenerate and full of 'insincerity, mendacity, venality and perfidy'.[34]

Mill's pathological dislike of Indians, and the colonial context and the content of his book, are secured by his manipulation of categories such as 'tradition', 'civilisation', 'barbarism' and 'savagery'. He constructs simultaneously a social space which is rigidly ordered and enclosed and yet formless and

---

32   Mill 1968, p. 118.

33   Ibid.

34   Niranjana 1990, pp. 776–7. See also Hyam 1992, for a reworked version of masculinity and personality of colonised males.

primeval. A telling example of this is to be found in his reading of the caste system, which he sees both as atavistic or irrational and forged with 'iron laws'.[35] Wilson's extensive footnote on this topic, however, not only shows up Mill's scanty reading and reliance on rumour, but also illustrates the complexity of caste as a form of fast mutating social practices and organisation rather than a mere discourse of tradition.[36] Mill's ascriptive confidence actually rests on the a priori notion of European social superiority over conquered 'others'.

What also becomes evident from the struggle between the text and the footnotes is that the modalities of colonial rule vary in historically specific moments. The goals and practices of a mercantile monopoly (East India Company) differ substantially from ideological aspirations of the rising colonial state. Thus, Mill's dismissal of the need to research Indian history can be contrasted to Wilson's view that research on India was in 'the veriest of infancy', or that Mill's opinions of Indian society, 'to say the least of them', were 'premature'.[37] Wilson's view of India as 'traditional' was coherent with a positive ascription of 'civilisation', qualifying its decline. But for Mill a steep decline follows the Aryans, whom he erroneously sees as 'aboriginal' to India. After the Aryan 'golden age' India becomes a static yet chaotic society. Further degenerating under Muslim invasions and rule, it remains stagnant and decadent until the arrival of the British.[38] Thus, Mill creates his own 'Robinsonade' through this teleology of European and Indian history moving towards capital and colonisation, using enlightenment notions of civilisation and humanism together with the moral lens of evangelicalism.[39] That is to say, he creates a history of India as a part of an overall current political and ideological project.

As such, Mill denies or distorts all political developments within India, particularly that of a state formation and the development of social government and legislation. He invents a nomadic stage of Aryan pastoralism which he inlays with an English nuclear family form.[40] This happy pastoral stage, according to Mill, is followed by a tortuous route of decline. But Orientalist and other European insistences force him to impute to India a highly qualified form of barbaric 'civilisation'. 'The first rude form of a national polity' is to be found in 'fully as early a period as any portion of the race'.[41] But he also adds that the

---

35   Mill 1968, p. 153.
36   Ibid., p. 125n1.
37   See Wilson's footnotes (Mill 1968) on issues of caste and other social practices in Chapter II, and on government laws in Chapter III, especially pp. 126–40.
38   Mill 1968, p. 113.
39   On 'Robinsonade' see Marx 1973, pp. 83–5.
40   Mill 1968, p. 122.
41   Ibid.

'cautious inquirer will not probably be inclined to carry this era very far back'.[42]
The legislative texts of the earlier periods, such as Manu's *Dharmashastra* as
translated by the Orientalists, are seen by Mill as exceptional achievements of
'superior spirits' rather than as the result of a general development of political
and social government.[43] According to him:

> The first legislator of the Hindus, whose name it is impossible to trace,
> appears to have represented himself as the republisher of the will of God.
> He informed his countrymen that, at the beginning of the world, the cre-
> ator revealed his duties to man, in four sacred books, entitled Vedas; that
> during the first age, of immense duration, mankind obeyed them, and
> were happy; that during the second and third they only partially obeyed,
> and their happiness was proportionately diminished; that since the com-
> mencement of the fourth age disobedience and misery had totally pre-
> vailed, till the Vedas were forgotten and lost; that now, however, he was
> commissioned to reveal them anew to his countrymen, and to claim their
> obedience.[44]

Wilson's comment on this is telling: 'The whole of this is imaginary; there is
no such legislation, there are no such assertions in Hindu tradition'.[45] Flying
in the face of all available evidence encoded in *Dayabhaga* property laws, Mill
also claimed that there was no private property, revenue or justice system in
India, nor a system of public finance and public works, nor a knowledge of the
art of war. For this lack he resorted to explanations based on the 'laziness of
the hindus'.[46] Wilson's comments, therefore, establishing his difference from
Mill, allow for variant readings of a colonised society from within the very precincts of colonial rule. These debates from within also expose at their clearest
the articulation between knowledge and social relations of power, and their
historical specificities.

   All disagreements notwithstanding, the overall colonial project comes out
loud and clear when we see that Mill develops as a key in his history one Orientalist theme to its fullest – that of Asiatic Despotism, which should be distinguished from European Enlightened Despostism. In this formulation converged negative perceptions of the 'two peoples' of India. The sources of this

---

42   Ibid., p. 122n1.
43   Ibid., p. 124.
44   Ibid., 125.
45   Ibid., 125n1.
46   Ibid., p. 133n1.

despotism were traced to both caste-bound, 'traditional' Hindus (with their self-enclosed village societies) and Muslims, already renowned in post-crusade Europe as absolute despots, with racial and religious propensities in this direction.[47] Unlike Europe, 'Asiatic' political institutions and economies are claimed to be sustained by brute force, superstition, authoritarianism and tradition.[48] Mill projected this stance through the conflation of the typology or the iconography of the Monarch and the actual or practical system of government in different historical stages. Taking statements from Manu literally, oblivious to similar European iconography of the monarch (for example in Hobbes' *Leviathan*), Mill posited a monstrously totalitarian system of government for India as an intrinsic expression and requirement of the peoples.[49]

The Eurocentrism or racism inherent in the concept of Asiatic Despotism is a manipulation of the concept of 'traditional society'. This is exposed through Mill's and Wilson's contradictions with each other, as well as through the contradictions within Mill's text. For example, the rigidity of this notion and Mill's ascribed chaos and formlessness of Indian cultures and polity are both accommodated by 'tradition', and as a whole play condemnatory roles. Wilson's copious footnotes also signal to the complexity of actual political practices, in sharp contrast to Mill's construction of symbolic fixities. Wilson questions both Mill's claims that the government which 'almost universally prevailed in the monarchies of Asia ... was contrivance extremely simple and rude',[50] and that the Hindu king/sovereign combined all functions of the state in himself.[51] Instead he draws attention to the similarities between European and Indian governing systems, remarking that:

> In the more skillful governments of Europe, officers were appointed for the discharge of particular duties in the different provinces of the empire ... [and] ... all together act as connected and subordinate wheels in one complicated artful machine.[52]

The notion of Asiatic Despotism in India should therefore be seen as less descriptive than ascriptive, as a conceptual artefact for colonial legitimation. It allowed Mill and others to justify and advocate despotic rule for India by mar-

---

47   Said 1981.
48   Mill 1968, p. 141.
49   Ibid.
50   Ibid., p. 142.
51   Ibid., p. 143.
52   Ibid., p. 145.

shalling the concept of tradition and locating it as India's cultural essence. It is through this device that India was judged as fundamentally unsuited to democracy, and positively responsive to authoritarianism. This same sentiment was expressed by James Mill in his *Essay on Government*, while his son John Stuart Mill in *On Liberty* justified a despotic, though enlightening rule of India on the same grounds.[53] Later Indian demands for a constitutional rule could be thus dismissed on this very ground. Marx's essays on colonialism and India, along with the thesis of lack of history, contains the same credo of Asiatic Despotism.

Developing further the colonial project of ethnicisation, Mill constructed Hindus and Muslims into separate and self-enclosed cultural categories and organised Indian history into three periods of rule, namely Hindu, Muslim and British, with a particular social ethos ascribed to the rulers. This process of fragmentation and categorisation, commencing in the eighteenth century, became a developed historiography in *The History of British India*. It lent itself to a periodisation pattern of European cultural and social history. The 'golden age of the Aryans' thus declined into the 'dark middle ages' of Muslim conquests and rule, followed by the enlightened rule of Britain. Contrary to all evidence, Muslims were projected as foreigners or outsiders, and the composite or hybrid culture of North and East India were ignored. All this provided a distortion of Indian history while providing the bases for a colonialist strategy of divide and rule. While the British presence was legitimated by trade permissions and land grants given by the Muslim emperors and lesser Muslim rulers, the Muslims themselves were portrayed as usurpers. Indeed, the fear that they were seen by Indians as invaders and usurpers was never allayed for the British even by their massive military might. The equation therefore of themselves with the Mughals as equally and a better type of outsider, as well as the negative depiction of the Muslims, gave the English a moral prerogative to rule. It is therefore not surprising that Mill's claim for Europeans as better rulers rests upon negative stereotypes of Muslims as warlike and full of 'saracenic' fanaticism with an inbuilt tendency towards sensuality, cruelty and luxury. The fact that the Muslims made a self-conscious historical effort by writing biographies and descriptions or keeping state records, or produced great art, architecture, mathematics and philosophy, did not redeem them in Mill's eyes. Nor was he able to see Indian Islam as a specifically Indian and syncretic formation, or Muslims as Indians in diverse groups in their regional cultural varieties.

---

53 'Despotism is a legitimate mode of government in dealings with barbarians, provided the end be their improvement, and the means justified by actually effecting that end' (Mill 1972, p. 73).

By reinforcing the Orientalist notion of the Hindus as the (ab)original sons of the soil, Mill 'hinduised' India in a highly effective way, while taking away from 'Hindu India' the attributes of a progressive or significant civilisation. Thus the 'Hindus' were greatly in need of being civilised – a feat which the Muslim rulers, who were themselves barbaric, and unlike the English had succumbed to the 'Hindu' culture, could not accomplish. Distancing himself from the seduced Orientalists, Mill had no project for restoring India to its pristine ancient glory. The ancient venerable India of the Orientalists is for Mill mainly a moment of civilisational immaturity, 'the dawn of childhood of human kind'. As a patri- archal and patrician stern ruler and judge, rather than an indological scholar, Mill advocates discipline and punishment for the good of this 'wild, barbaric, savage and rude' people.[54] As far as he was concerned, Indians were 'a people over whom the love of repose exerts the greatest sway, and in whose character aversion to danger forms a principal ingredient'.[55]

It is interesting to note how Mill slides between binary notions, such as age and childhood, order and chaos, nature and culture, barbarism and tradition, in his ideological construction of 'India'. He resolves the contradiction between tradition and savagery or barbarism by positing that their traditionality is itself an indication of savagery. It is this elision between tradition and savagery, or culture and nature, or better still, culture as nature,[56] which allows Mill the maximum leverage to accommodate diverse cultural features without himself suffering from any sense of contradiction.[57] It also allows him to systematically introject inferiority into the difference between Europeans and their Indian colonised subjects. This silences the Indian prerogative of self-representation and justifies colonial rule as an expression of progress or improvement.

Mill completed his project in 1817, but his historiographical method, which produces ideology, separating forms of knowing from ways of being both in his- tory and in present day social organisation, continues. The project of inventing cultural categories to accomplish the task of ruling continues unabated. The attribution of 'tradition' to any society is still a legitimation for domination, and an excuse to modernise, that is, to recolonise.

---

54   Mill 1968, p. 123.
55   Ibid., p. 153.
56   See Dirks 1992, pp. 1–3.
57   Niranjana 1990, p. 776.

Pygmalion Nation: Towards a Critique of Subaltern Studies and the 'Resolution of the Women Question'

Men make their own history, but they do not make it just as they please; they do not make it under circumstances chosen by themselves, but under circumstances directly found, given and transmitted from the past. The tradition of all the dead generations weighs like a nightmare on the brain of the living. And just when they seem engaged in revolutionising themselves and things, in creating something entirely new, precisely in such epochs of revolutionary crisis they anxiously conjure up the spirits of the past to their service and borrow from them names, battle slogans and costumes in order to present the new scene of world history in this time-honoured disguise and this borrowed language.[1]

∙ ∙ ∙

It is in consciousness, let us remember, that people make sense of the world in which they live; it is in consciousness again that they make their judgements on how to change it.[2]

∙ ∙
∙

1   Introduction

Any discussion of nationalism in countries that were colonised by European powers must begin with the problem of decolonisation and how it has been politically addressed.[3] In this regard we may speak broadly of three major ways

---

1   Marx 1972d, p. 437.
2   Chatterjee 1989b, p. 178.
3   Any discussion of decolonisation and nationalism must remember Fanon 1963, who alerted us to both its liberatory and dominating potentials. Though he introduced us to the notion of 'false decolonisation' as part of the 'pitfalls of national consciousness' of the colonial petty

in which the politics of decolonisation has been undertaken, all of which have an element of nationalism, insofar as they seek to achieve a sovereign state within some social and cultural definition of a nation. But in spite of these common elements, we can still speak of multiple nationalisms, as does Aijaz Ahmad in his *Lineages of the Present*. Refusing a single ideological articulation for all nationalisms, or their outright rejection, Ahmad reminds us of nationalism's 'diverse histories' and its 'pluralities' in terms of 'typologies'.[4]

Speaking 'typologically' then, I would like to point out that of these three types of nationalism, two consist of anti-colonial ideological articulations and politics which accept private property and class society both nationally and internationally, while differing in polity towards cultural/social forms of power and moral regulations that emanate from such proprietal social organisations. Thus practices and ideologies of caste, patriarchy, or gender and 'race' are viewed differently by them, and this difference gives rise to governments which are either liberal democracies or illiberal authoritarian national states. The third type of nationalism, whose primary class base, unlike the first two, extends beyond the petty bourgeoisie into the working class and/or the peasantry, is anti-imperialist in the marxist sense. It views colonialism as an integral aspect of international, specifically European, capitalism. Its reading of 'the nation' is marked by a critique of private property, of capital and class. Its politics, therefore, is based on a more complex social analysis and ideological formulation than demanded by a univocal anti-colonialism. We may call this type of nationalism 'national liberation'.[5] Beginning with a premise of socio-

---

bourgeoisie, he did not consider this to be the fate of *all* nationalisms or decolonisation efforts. See also Sekyi-Otu 1996.

4 See Ahmad 1996, especially the essays 'Class, Nation and State: Intermediate Classes in Peripheral Societies' and 'Culture, Nationalism, Intellectuals'. As he puts it: 'The word "nationalism" refers to such diverse histories and practices that it might be better to speak of it in the plural, or to speak at least in terms of *typologies* of nationalism' (1996, p. 403). See also Ahmad 1992.

5 See Ahmad 1996, where he writes: 'I don't think that there is a particular ideology to which all nationalisms are invariably articulated. A famous Stalinist definition has it that all nationalisms are bourgeois. I don't think so. There are also nationalisms of the poor, the defeated, the beleaguered. Cuban nationalism or Sandinista nationalism is manifestly not bourgeois. I would even say that virtually all revolutions that took place in the Third World had a strong component of anti-imperialist nationalism in them, sometimes under bourgeois hegemony, sometimes not' (1996, p. 403). It is this last type of nationalism, one not under bourgeois hegemony, that I mean when I speak of 'national liberation' movements. See also the essay on 'Nation and Class in Communist Aesthetics and the Theatre of Utpal Dutt' in Bannerji 1998b. This notion of pluralities of nationalism contrasts with the view of Edward Said (Eagleton 1990), for example, who in his 'Yeats and Decolonization' says: 'Instead of liberation after decolonization one simply gets the old colonial structures replicated in new national terms. That is one problem with nationalism. Its results are written across the formerly colonised

economic equality, it can logically include struggles against patriarchy/gender, caste, 'race', and other sociocultural inequalities.

These different national projects imply different ideological and epistemological premises which entail their own particular organisational processes and political consequences. Currently, as national liberation projects are in a state of disarray, and even liberal democracies of the Third World are being dismantled, an illiberal or authoritarian nationalism is increasingly gaining ground.[6] As noted above, its polity obliterates liberal democratic provisions for constitutionally enshrined formal equality manifested in individual rights as entailed by secular citizenship. It accepts the economic dictates of local and global capitalism, while seeking to dismantle existing left and secular progressive organisations. It speaks in the name of a singular national tradition or culture, and of an authentic national identity based on this cultural essence. By reducing national culture to religion and fixed traditions it naturalises inegalitarian or hierarchical socio-moral injunctions.[7] Thus this illiberal nationalism manipulates the project of anti-colonialism by promising an identification with a pre- or an anti-modernist and antihumanist national identity which confuses simple inversions of modernist cultural forms with anti-colonialism. This gives rise to a right-wing cultural nationalism which is constructed with a content of reworked colonial discourse, including orientalism.[8] The epistemology of this cultural nationalism relies upon anti-marxist, anti-democratic, and generally anti-egalitarian (including anti-feminist) conceptual frameworks. Sumit Sarkar, in *Writing Social History*,[9] while discussing the dependence of current historiography on non-materialist cultural theories and its political implications, remarks on this phenomenon in the Indian context. Commenting on the

---

world, usually in the fabrics of newly independent states whose pathologies of power, as Eqbal Ahmad has called them, bedevil political life even as we speak. The other problem is that the cultural horizons of nationalism are fatally limited by the common history of coloniser and colonised assumed by the nationalist movement itself. Imperialism after all is a cooperative venture' (1990, p. 75).

6 For a discussion of 'illiberal nationalism' and its citizenship projects, see Basu 1993; and Lele 1995.

7 See, for example, Butalia and Sarkar 1995.

8 This political phenomenon is not only to be found in the 'fundamentalist' regimes in Iran, Afghanistan, or Pakistan, but has become a prominent force in India as well. With the destruction of a fifteenth-century mosque in Ayodhya in 1992, followed by pogroms against Muslims, Christians, and Dalits, a Hindu cultural nationalism, in the making since the nineteenth century, has overtaken the Indian political stage. For details on the politics of demolition of the mosque in Ayodhya, see Mandal 1993. 'Dalit' is the term adopted by people formerly known as 'untouchables' in the caste system.

9 Sarkar 1997b.

historiography of the subaltern studies group, Sarkar notices in their writings a theoretically engineered separation between class and culture, history and social organisation, leading to a cultural overdetermination. This amounts to dehistoricisation or a mythicisation of history.[10]

Sarkar's observations on subaltern studies are coherent with critics who have spoken to the influence of post-structuralism and postmodernism in social sciences and history. They have noted the use of interpretive philosophies, anti-materialist cultural theories, and relativist cultural anthropology in accomplishing the task of dehistoricisation and culturalisation of politics.[11] This theoretical practice has reduced power to a discursive phenomenon, and anti-colonialism to cultural nationalism. An exploration of post-colonial studies provides us with examples of this type of theorisation.[12] Sarkar refers to this when he critiques the theoretical 'stimulation' provided by Edward Said and Michel Foucault in South Asian historiography.[13] He points to the swing from economic reductionism to cultural reductionism through a process that starts with a critique. Speaking of the historiography of subaltern studies, he says:

---

10   For Sarkar's view on dehistoricisation and mythicisation of history, resulting from seeing colonialism, for example, as 'abstracted from histories of production and social relationships', see Sarkar 1997b, p. 4. Regarding this anti-materialist and ahistorical stance of subaltern studies, see Alam 1983.

11   Many scholars and critics have written on the effects of post-structuralism and postmodernism on social sciences and history. For history, see Sarkar 1997a; for social sciences see Harvey 1989 and Norris 1993. As Norris puts it, the aim of these is 'to undermine every last category of socialist thought while claiming to offer a new kind of "strategy", a politics of multiple, decentred "discourses" which allows no appeal to such old-fashioned notions as experience, class-interest, ideology, forces and relations of production, etc., replacing them with talk of "subject-positions", constructed in and through the play of various (often conflicting) discursive alignments' (1993, p. 290). See also, on the ideological practices of postmodernism, Smith 1999, especially the essay 'Telling the Truth after Postmodernism'.

12   It has so overwhelmed the world of current theory that many marxists have recanted or adopted an embarrassed vigilance regarding marxism as a form of 'orthodoxy' and 'economic reductionism'. On retreat from marxist theorisation and politics, see Wood 1986. For an example of what this new non- or anti-marxist social thought and politics might look like, see Laclau and Mouffe 2001. For an Indian version of this radicalism, see Omvedt 1993. For a more nuanced, non-polemicist view from a historian's standpoint, see Sarkar 1990. As Sarkar puts it: 'I remain more convinced than ever about the relevance of many ideas flowing from Marxian modes of historical analysis, indeed their superiority over other approaches to history and society. At the same time, the history and historiography of Indian nationalism bear ample witness to the stultifying effects of other aspects of what was considered to be true or orthodox Marxism' (1990, p. 6).

13   Sarkar 1997b, p. 4.

What had started as an understandable dissatisfaction with the economistic reductionism of much 'official' marxism is now contributing
to another kind of narrowing of horizons, one that conflates colonial
exploitation with western cultural domination. Colonial discourse analysis abstracts itself, except in the most general terms, from histories of
production and social relationships. A 'culturalism' now further atten-
uated into readings of isolable texts has become, after the presumed
demise of marxism, extremely nervous of all 'material' histories: the
spectre of economic reductionism looms everywhere.[14]

What Sarkar says of subaltern studies' theoretical manoeuvres is consistent
with the simple cultural critique of post-colonial studies. From this epistemological position, social organisation, relations, and institutions are either erased
or deeply subordinated, while the culture of the colonised is periodised as
pre-colonial, colonial, and postcolonial in a parody of history.[15] This cultural
interpretation relies on the paradigm of tradition and modernity, attributing
tradition or premodernity as a cultural characteristic to the colonised. Anti-
colonial politics, therefore, becomes one of recovery of the premodern or the
traditional. It is the necessary step for 'imagining' the nation. In the case of
India, this premodern traditional culture translates into one of brahmanical
Hinduism, thus presenting us with the proprieties implied in a patriarchal,
casteist national identity securely resting on practices of private property and
class. The curious thing about subaltern studies is that this is done in the guise
of radical politics by implanting the Gramscian language of subalternity within
the nationalist project of Hindu Bengali middle classes.[16]

My critique of Chatterjee will focus on his culturalist presentation of both
colonial hegemony and the counter-hegemonic task of nationalism. I will con-

---

14   Sarkar 1997a, p. 4.
15   For an extended presentation of both colonialism and nationalism as cultural enterprise,
      as discursive forms of domination, see Chatterjee 1986a.
16   See Chatterjee 1986a, chapter 2, section III. In this context, it needs to be noted that since
      women had not been included in the category 'subaltern', there was not a great deal of
      writing about them. Nor were they initially members of the collective of *Subaltern Stud-
      ies*. In the last issues of the journal more women joined the group, Gayatri Spivak, Susie
      Tharu, and Tejaswini Niranjana among them. More writing has also appeared on women
      and gender. Among the original members who are the theoretical directors of this group,
      Partha Chatterjee has shown an extensive interest. But Dipesh Chakrabarty has also been
      influential, especially through the article, 'The Difference-Deferral of (A) Colonial Mod-
      ernity: Public Debates on Domesticity in British Bengal'. Sudipta Kaviraj comments on
      women in nationalism in his book (1995). Though not a member of the group, Julie Steph-
      ens wrote an anti-feminist piece (1989).

centrate primarily on his formulation of culture or moral propriety as divorced from relations of property by focusing on certain topics which are persistently present in his theorisation. This should enable us to get a clearer view of his (and the subaltern studies group's) version of subalternity and its politics. As such I will explore the topics of subjectivity and agency of Bengali Hindu middle-class women as reflected in Chatterjee's mirror of nineteenth-century Bengali nationalist thought.[17] Chatterjee has phrased these themes in an essay in *Recasting Women: Essays in Colonial History* in terms of what he has called 'the nationalist resolution of the women's question' (the title of his essay).[18] This so-called women's question, current in the language of various types of male social reformers, including the reforming colonial state in search of legitimacy and hegemony, refers to the socio-economic and cultural status of women and the issue of substantiveness of women's legal and political personhood. Even though this question signalled different understandings of social mores and politics coming from different standpoints, Chatterjee makes no distinction between colonial and indigenous social reformers. The notion of 'resolution' refers, according to Chatterjee, to a successful solution found by the nationalist thinkers of his choice, thereafter rendering the social content relating to 'the question' unimportant.

That Chatterjee introduces the question of women in a study of hegemony is quite pertinent. Students of social reform, culture, and nationalism in Bengal have long known of its importance.[19] Its status in Chatterjee's work becomes an entry point for a general assessment of the social and political theorisation of subaltern studies. This issue of women, of cultural projections or moral constructions and regulations pertaining to them, is just as important for assessing these present-day theorists of nationalism and decolonisation as it is for understanding the character of social and nationalist thought of the nineteenth-century Bengali male elite. Chatterjee needs the help of a constellation of topics associated with women – such as family, motherhood, conjugality, and sexuality – to provide a theory of hegemony regarding Bengali/Indian nationalism. Thus his interest in women is not in any way incidental and descriptive, but

---

17   See Chatterjee 1990. This essay was published in an edition of the same name in 1989 by Kali for Women in New Delhi, as well as in *American Ethnologist*, with a modified introduction. It also is incorporated with slight modifications as chapter 6 of Chatterjee 1993a.

18   Sangari and Vaid 1990.

19   Some students of social reform and nationalism interested in women: Tanika Sarkar, Uma Chakravarty, Jasodhara Bagchi, Himani Bannerji, Kumari Jayawardena, Gulam Murshid, Indira Raychoudhury. One of the earliest discussions pertaining to women in nationalist discourse and the absence of reform for women in the later part of nineteenth century Bengal, is in Sarkar 1985.

rather provides a vehicle for developing a theory of hegemony, and for assessing the successes and failures of Bengali/Indian nationalist thought. His assumptions regarding this matter are shared by the theoretical collective to which he belongs.[20]

My proposed mode of entry into the historiography of subaltern studies is rather uncommon. Though various criticisms of the group's epistemological and political positions have appeared over time, the importance of 'the women's question' for a fuller assessment of their historiography and politics has not been sufficiently emphasised.[21] Other than an essay by Kamala Viswesaran, itself a critical extension of the subaltern theoretical framework, no sustained exploration of their general framework has been made through their treatment of these themes.[22] The treatment of women and patriarchy has featured also in some episodic critical rejoinders by Roslin O'Hanlan and other feminists.[23] But Chatterjee's views on women have generally had a wide and positive reception among feminists, historians, and cultural theorists themselves, perhaps because he came into the discussion of gender and nationalism early and was included in *Recasting Women*, an early and highly influential Indian feminist anthology.[24] There are frequent citations of his essay in articles on women in India, whose writers, even when feminist, have glossed over his essentially conservative cultural nationalist stance on women. This relative lack of interest in critiquing Chatterjee's or the subaltern approach to women and patriarchy may also be a consequence of these issues being seen as topics of special interest, as special material for feminist critique. As a result, the general theoretical or political critique of Chatterjee's works, almost wholly done by men, has not been properly subjected to a gender analysis, even when critiqued from a marxist standpoint. Kumkum Sangari's essay 'Politics of Diversity – Religious Communities and Multiple Patriarchies',[25] which is a response to Chatterjee's article on 'Secularism and Toleration',[26] is the only substantial attempt to integrate a marxist critique of subaltern studies with a feminist one. The intention of this paper is precisely to do so, and thus to situate Chatterjee's

---

20   See for example, Kaviraj 1995 or Chakrabarty 1992; 1998.

21   For example, Alam 1983; Sarkar 1997c.

22   Visweseran 1996.

23   For feminist or women's criticism of *Subaltern Studies* see O'Hanlon 1988; O'Hanlon and Washbrook 1992. In the writings of Uma Chakravarty and Jasodhara Bagchi, for example, there are critical references to the subaltern claim of 'resolution of the women's question', but not a critique per se.

24   Sangari and Vaid 1990.

25   Sangari 1995.

26   Chatterjee 1994.

acclaimed 'resolution of the women's question' in a discussion on property and propriety within a historical materialist reading of hegemony. In view of the growing transnational popularity of subaltern studies among feminists and post-colonialists, it is important to explore this problematic 'resolution' and to offer an integrative critique from a feminist-marxist standpoint. This method helps us to understand basic aspects of cultural nationalism, both new and old, not only in India, but elsewhere as well.

It is well known that the consciousness of the bourgeoisie or petty bour-geoisie, colonial or otherwise, has expressed itself everywhere through class-inflected patriarchal constructions and practices, and also that the nation-state in the colonial context has often reinvented itself in the same mould, though in the name of anti-colonial national culture.[27] Moral constructions and regu-lations, especially regarding middle-class women's conduct, mark these aspira-tions to a 'national' gender morality. Such nationalist cultural patriarchal exer-cises, speaking in the language of identity, collectivity, and community, have helped to deflect critical attention from structural relations of property and class. These enunciated nationalist moralities encapsulate both a particular-ising and an essentialist move. The current Hindu right in India has further developed the patriarchal cultural configurations evolved by the Hindu reviv-alists of the nineteenth century as a national imaginary. The consequences of this move in terms of secularism, individual rights, and democratic citizenship, especially with regard to the disenfranchisement of women and minorities, make it imperative that we understand this type of cultural nationalist the-orisation. For it not only describes but prescribes anti-modernist conservative cultural collectivities with inherently repressive subjectivities and agencies.

This patriarchal and upper class/caste imaginary of the Hindu revivalists, claimed to be a successful attempt at nationalist hegemony by their present-day supporters, brings to mind the well-known Graeco-Roman myth of Pyg-malion and Galatea. It involves Pygmalion, an artist, who falls in love with one of his own sculptures. It is an idealised feminine form that he names 'Galatea' and courts. In his delusion, his own aesthetic and moral construct becomes an actual woman, a living being who is supposedly endowed with a substantive subjectivity and agency, though in reality she is wholly encompassed within his vision and has no existence apart from it. This myth crystallises for us what Chatterjee means when he calls a construct of feminine morality resulting from a Hindu brahmanical and upper-class patriarchy a 'resolution' of 'the women's

---

27   Thus mini-nationalisms flourish in the West in new multicultural modes (Bannerji 1998a), while European ethnic nationalism or Eurocentrism has always masqueraded as 'national' culture (Hall 1992).

question'. We also see the same process of mythmaking at work in the creation of this Bengali Galatea who is a moral and aesthetic projection of the patriarchal and narcissistic Bengali Hindu male elite imagination current in the late nineteenth century and which has continued to the present. As we shall see, Chatterjee, though aware of possibilities of critical response towards this patriarchal imaginary, discovers a way to vindicate this female construction and find a present-day relevance for it. He cannot but do so, since he is caught within his own post-colonial, cultural nationalist theoretical framework, and, therefore, must eschew any gesture of criticality. To do so would amount to an admission of patriarchal and class oppression, and a legitimation of a modernist demand for women's substantive individuality and political agency. A post-colonial commitment to classlessness, cultural overdetermination, and anti-modernity brings in its wake an automatic legitimation of patriarchy. In the next section I will explore the theoretical trajectory which brings Partha Chatterjee and the subaltern studies historiography to this stance.

2   Mapping the Subaltern Discursive Territory

I have one central objection to Anderson's argument in his [*Imagined Communities*]. If nationalisms in the rest of the world have to choose their imagined community from certain 'modular' forms already made available to them by Europe and the Americas, what do they have left to imagine? History, it would seem, has decreed that we in the postcolonial world shall only be perpetual consumers of modernity. Europe and the Americas, the only true subjects of history, have thought out on our behalf not only the script of colonial enlightenment and exploitation, but also that of our anticolonial resistance and postcolonial misery. Even our imaginations must remain forever colonised.

I object to this argument not for any sentimental reason. I object because I cannot reconcile it with the evidence on anticolonial nationalism. The most powerful as well as the most creative results of the nationalist imagination in Asia and Africa are posited not on an identity but rather on a difference with the 'modular' forms of the national society propagated by the modern West. How can we ignore this without reducing the experience of anticolonial nationalism to a caricature of itself?[28]

---

28   Chatterjee 1993a, p. 5.

A more fundamental methodological problem is the abandonment in practice of any quest for immanent critique through the elision of possibilities of mutually conflicting groups taking over and using in diverse, partially-autonomous ways, elements from dominant structures and discourses. What is ignored, in other words, is precisely that which had been central to Marxist analysis: the dialectical search for contradictions within structures. If modern power is total and irresistible within its own domain, autonomy or resistance can be located only in grounds outside its reach: in a 'community-consciousness' that is pre-colonial or somehow untainted by post-Enlightenment power-knowledge, or in fleeting, random moments of fragmentary resistance. These become the only valid counterpoints against the ultimate repository of that power-knowledge – the colonial or postcolonial 'nation state'. We have moved, then, from perspectives in which relationships between capitalist imperialism and multiple strands within anti-colonial movements had constituted the basic framework, to one where the post-Enlightenment modern state is counterposed to community. Questions of exploitation and power have been collapsed into a unitary vision of the modern bureaucratic state as the sole source of oppression.[29]

A feminist historical materialist critique of 'subaltern thought' requires that we map out the overall discursive trajectory of its theorists. For this reason we need to explore Partha Chatterjee's approach to patriarchal political culture encoded as the nationalist 'resolution of the women's question' in his books, *Nationalist Thought*[30] and *The Nation and Its Fragments*,[31] as well as his essays in *Subaltern Studies*. But his treatment of patriarchy and women needs to be put into context by Ranajit Guha's introduction to the first volume of *Subaltern Studies*, which provided the theoretical and political manifesto for the project of this group.[32] Chatterjee's theoretical journey has to be measured in relation to this declarative document.

---

29 Sarkar 1997a, p. 5.
30 Chatterjee 1986a.
31 Chatterjee 1993a.
32 See Guha 1982b. This journal to date has published nine volumes. Editorship has been shared by Partha Chatterjee, Dipesh Chakrabarty, David Hardiman, Gyanendra Pandey and Gautam Bhadra, but the majority of the volumes have been edited by Ranajit Guha, who served in a directive capacity in a theoretico-political sense. As Sumit Sarkar puts it: '*Subaltern Studies* emerged in the early 1980s in a dissident-Left milieu, where sharp criticism of orthodox Marxist practice and theory was still combined with the retention of a broad socialist and Marxian horizon' (1997c, p. 83). But 'things have changed

Ranajit Guha's introduction, among other things, criticised Indian nationalism (seen as a single ideological formulation) for its comprador character, its compromise with colonial, that is, modernist, discourse. This view is also reflected in Chatterjee's *Nationalist Thought*, but there is here, as in his other texts, a difference of tone from that introduction. The earlier unqualified critique of Indian nationalism is now modified by an ambivalence regarding its overall character and achievement. Though strengthening Guha's emphasis on politics as primarily a phenomenon of consciousness, Chatterjee is no longer categorical in his condemnation of nationalist thought's inability to imagine the nation in a substantive manner. Taking issue with Benedict Anderson's *Imagined Communities*,[33] he presents moments of both success and failure in nationalist thought's hegemonic venture for decolonisation of India.[34] Presenting the Indian/Bengali case as a template for nationalism everywhere in the colonised world, Chatterjee locates the moment of success in the Hindu Bengali elite's ability to evolve a cultural nationalism based on pre- and anti-modernist collective identities encoding the difference between a colonial and a national culture. These identities rely on traditional/religious moral regulations pertaining especially to the domestic life of the colonised, thus making the 'private' lives of the Hindu Bengali elite an uncontaminated aspect of an otherwise colonially inflected civil society.

> Another area in that inner domain of national culture was the family. The assertion here of autonomy and difference was perhaps the most dramatic. The European criticism of Indian 'tradition' as barbaric has focused to a large extent on religious beliefs and practices, especially those relating to the treatment of women. The early phase of 'social reform' through the agency of the colonial power had also concentrated on the same issues ... [U]nlike the early reformers, nationalists were not prepared to allow the colonial state to legislate the reform of 'traditional' society. They asserted that only the nation itself could have the right to intervene in such an essential aspect of its cultural identity.[35]

---

much since then, and today a transformed *Subaltern Studies* owes much of its prestige to the acclaim it is receiving from that part of the Western academic postmodernistic counter-establishment which is interested in colonial and postcolonial matters' (84). To date, Sarkar's essay is the best, fairest critique of *Subaltern Studies* historiography.

33   Anderson 1991.
34   Chatterjee 1993a.
35   Ibid., p. 9.

The hegemonic failure of nationalist thought, however, is detected in the 'public' aspect of the same civil society, where it cannot develop a proposal for a truly national state and polity. In *The Nation and Its Fragments*, Chatterjee discusses how the Indian elite cannot create authentically national public institutions for education, for example, or for publishing, based on identities of difference.[36] Seen thus, the alleged 'resolution of the women's question' by nationalist thought rescues this flawed hegemonic venture and expresses what Chatterjee considers to be their subaltern consciousness and political agency. To understand this shift of emphasis in Chatterjee's writings, and also those of other collective members, from an unqualified rejection of colonial elite politics to its partial redemption, we need a deeper discussion of subaltern theorisation.

The current theoretical approach of subaltern studies was not born as was Athena, fully armed from Jove's brow. It began by asking some basic questions regarding both bourgeois and communist revolutionary politics in India, especially with regard to agency and forms of consciousness. Asked in the light of the perceived failure of communist parties in India and the debacles of Indian liberal democracy in bringing about a real social and economic transformation, these questions were quite crucial. They drew Ranajit Guha and others to the political theories of Antonio Gramsci and the use of his concept of subalternity to name their own politico-epistemological enterprise. Though the concept 'subaltern' is not indexed in the first volume of *Subaltern Studies*, the preface by Ranajit Guha refers both to the *Concise Oxford Dictionary* and to Antonio Gramsci's six-point programme for subaltern politics and history in 'Notes on Italian History'.[37] Guha outlines the collective's politico-theoretical critique in the following way:

It is the study of this historic failure of the nation to come to its own, a failure due to the inadequacy of the bourgeoisie as well as the working class to lead it into a decisive victory over colonialism and a bourgeois democratic revolution of either the classic nineteenth century type under the

---

36   For Chatterjee, submission to modernity, which compromises the nationalist project as outlined in *Nationalist Thought*, is most prominent in state formation and the creation of public institutions, such as schools. As he puts it: 'Through the nineteenth century and into the twentieth, accompanied by the spread of the institutions of capitalist production and exchange, these legal and administrative institutions of the modern state penetrated deeper and deeper into colonial society and touched upon the lives of greater and greater sections of the people. In this aspect of the political domain, therefore, the project of nationalist hegemony was, and in its postcolonial phase, continues to be, to institute and ramify the characteristically modern forms of disciplinary power' (1986, p. 74).

37   Gramsci 1971.

hegemony of the bourgeoisie or a more modern type under the hegemony of workers and peasants, that is, a 'new democracy' – it is the study of this failure which constitutes the central problematic of the historiography of colonial India.[38]

This critique regarding questions of class agency and hegemonic failure gradually changed into critiques solely about culture and consciousness. This process also converted Gramsci into a cultural politician. This theoretical position, as outlined in Chatterjee's *Nationalist Thought*, was consolidated by drawing on Anwar Abdel Malek and Edward Said, and to some extent on Michel Foucault, insofar as political power came to be seen as a discursive phenomenon.[39] This change accompanied Chatterjee's (and others') deepening criticism of marxist theorisation and ultimately resulted in the anti-marxism referred to earlier. Concepts such as subalternity or hegemony, designed by Gramsci in his prison years to speak of class formation, class consciousness, and class struggle in an Aesopian language, were voided of their content of historical and social relations. A marxian structural analysis of power and critique of ideology, replaced by a Foucauldian notion of domination, marked the moment of post-colonialism in subaltern studies. It was then that political and symbolic economies fully parted company.

Thus, the theoretical picture at the very beginning of subaltern studies is unclear, since it straddles premises of cultural overdetermination and the class basis of popular political agency. Its language at this stage is a mixture of class and populism and a power/knowledge type of discourse analysis. This is evident in Ranajit Guha's use of the concept of 'the people' in both a cultural and a class sense when he indicates their absence from India's revolutionary projects.[40] 'The people' are variously termed by him. Sometimes they feature as 'subalterns' presented in Weberian terms of stratification, as lower layers of deprived social groups, and sometimes they evoke a marxian concept of class, especially when Guha refers to the weak development of capitalism and social differentiation in India, and relates the inarticulate nature of elite and popular political consciousness to these structural facts. But the cultural thrust of the group's query is noticeable from the beginning. They speak of politics and history extensively in terms of values – of cultural norms and forms – and thus

---

38   Guha 1982b, p. 7. See also Sarkar 1984.

39   See Chatterjee 1986a, but also Chatterjee 1995, p. 8, which speaks to the 'connections between colonial power and colonial knowledge'.

40   Ranajit Guha's notion of 'the people' and its alternation with 'the subaltern' needs to be noted with regard to the 'autonomy' of their consciousness, its detachment from class. See Guha 1982b, p. 4.

of power as coded and deployed in symbolic terms. They also read transformative politics in terms of insurrections of rural underclasses, later expanded to
include small town and urban riots. These rural insurrections are studied for
clues to both the success and failure of revolutionary enterprises. They are valorised as authentic for being non- and anti-modernist expressions of power as
consciousness, as opposed to the organised movements of peasants and the
proletariat led by the communist party or the trade unions. Revolutionary history, it appears, has to be written solely in 'annals of blood and fire' to be true
to the essence of Indian polity.[41]

Ranajit Guha's criticism of modernism and organised politics of the national
elite, though mainly directed at the Nehruvian strand of the Congress Party and
its elite historians and ideologues, has a comprehensive quality to it. But it is
this rejection of elite nationalism which is qualified and partially rehabilitated
by Chatterjee due to his detection and validation of a non-Nehruvian, non-
modernist strand within the Bengali/Indian nationalist tradition. The historiography and textual productions of this type of nationalism, even though elite
enterprises, are considered as containing genuinely anti-colonial elements. An
interest in politics of consciousness, present from the beginning, now in combination with a heavy reliance on cultural texts and an elimination of class
analysis, creates a full-fledged culturalism, considering power in terms of cultural or ideological primordialities. While Chatterjee conducts this theoretical
operation in the context of Bengali elite nationalism, Ranajit Guha, in *Elementary Aspects of Peasant Insurgency*, does the same with regard to 'tribes' and
other rural 'subalterns'.[42] Chatterjee ends up in a wholly non-marxist theoretical apparatus, but not without an initial marxist aura.[43] Until he builds enough
theoretical stepping stones away from marxism to disarticulate politics and culture from class and other social relations of property, he is reliant on a marxist
language and body of theoretical literature.

These theoretical manoeuvres of Chatterjee deserve closer examination
because they both necessitate and elaborate the schema through which the
'resolutionary' reading of nineteenth-century Bengali revivalists' writings on

---

41 For a general picture of the topics of interest to *Subaltern Studies*, see Sarkar 1997c. This
    overview shows a decline of interest in the rural subalterns and a growth of interest in
    the urban elite, their ideological inventions and politics, and displays a defence of their
    anti-colonial nationalism. Though Sarkar wants to rescue the earlier 'history from below'
    impetus of *Subaltern Studies*, we trace a romanticisation in their view of history-making,
    since their primary interest lies in insurrections and normative positions. See, for example,
    an exposition along these lines by Bhadra 1989.

42 Guha 1983.

43 Chatterjee 1982; 1983.

women comes about. He begins from the debates on transition from pre-capitalism to capitalism and also from debates on modes of production then current (in the 1960s and 1970s) in marxist social and political theories.[44] He recapitulates in his essay the debate between Maurice Dobb and Paul Sweezy regarding the causes and modalities of the emergence of capitalism. Dubbing the class formulations of these two economists as 'techno-economic', Chatterjee seeks to create a specifically political theory which can address issues of power and domination without reference to 'techno-economic' entities such as class. For this theoretical necessity he turns not to Foucault or Said initially, but to Robert Brenner, another marxist who intervened in the Dobb-Sweezey debate from a non-economistic perspective and raised 'the political question of the transition problem'. Chatterjee says:

> But what Brenner's contribution brings out above all is the theoretical importance of locating the element of 'indeterminacy' in the transition problem in the *political* form of the class struggle. Brenner has been able to demonstrate convincingly that the path of transition is not uniquely determined by the techno-economic terms of evolution of a certain mode of production. The problem now is to define the theoretical terms in which this *political* question of the transition problem can be attacked.[45]

Though for Brenner 'the political question' entailed the question of class politics, with class understood as a sociological category arising from but going beyond the productive forces, and thereby not reduced to, but of the economy as well, Chatterjee reads his emphasis on politics differently. For him, the 'political form of the class struggle' involved in the transition, entailing, as Ernesto Laclau would say, the specificity of the political, takes a cultural character.[46] Thereby, political ideologies are to be articulated 'indeterminately' and generally independently of class understood as a techno-economic or structural category.

To create, then, a theory of politics which could jettison class and yet retain the notion of power (the core of politics), Chatterjee turned to other marxists whom he also adapted to his need (though less so than Brenner), namely, Etienne Balibar and Louis Althusser, the latter at the peak of his popularity in the 1970s. Chatterjee, making his move to Althusser using a derivative position provided by Etienne Balibar, whom he footnotes, gives as his point of departure the following: 'The task [of defining theoretical terms for questions of

---

44   Chatterjee 1983.
45   Chatterjee 1983, p. 315. Author's emphasis.
46   Laclau 1979.

power] requires new theoretical categories. It is now widely accepted that the political structures of society ... are not mere reflections of its "economic" structures built around the activities of social production'.[47] His move to Althusser – though nowhere does he mention Althusser outright – is in the following terms:

> There are institutions, and instituted processes, of power and of ideology, which intervene and give the political structures a certain relative autonomy. But merely to state this is to stop short of posing a crucial problematic: What precisely constitutes 'relative autonomy'? Where is it located? How are we to identify and describe it in the domain of our theoretical concept? Put in other words, what are the theoretical concepts and analytical relations which are specific to the world of the political?[48]

Althusser's concept of the relative autonomy of the superstructure, his view of ideology as ubiquitous and 'material', provided Chatterjee with the theoretical angle he needed to establish the rule of ideas in politics. He erased in totality determinations exerted by social class and economy on politics, which for Althusser himself lay in the limbo of the deferred 'last instance'. This move enabled Chatterjee to establish the primacy of consciousness as the 'specific' feature of politics, and he searched further for particular 'concepts and analytical relations' for a political theory of 'peasant struggles, feudal domination and the contribution of the absolutist state'.[49] In short, he wanted to create a theory of politics as well as a political theory which would be adequate for understanding India as a particular political entity with a specific character resulting from a mixture of communitarian and feudal-absolutist forms. He also included in the purview of feudal absolutism the mode of governance practised by the British colonial state as bourgeois absolutism.

It is with this Althusserian, and only subordinately Balibarian, mediation that Chatterjee separated 'modes of production' from 'modes of power' and turned to the appropriation of Gramsci for the validation of his theoretical enterprise. This also allowed him to be hospitable to Foucault's discursive theories of power and his equation of enlightenment or modernity with domination, and to do so with the help of Edward Said's theory of representation in the context of colonial discourse as a cultural apparatus for domination. Seemingly responsive to the then-prevailing marxist belief that politics is connected to property relations, Chatterjee, in 'More on Modes of Power', conceded to use

---

47   Chatterjee 1983, p. 315.
48   Ibid., pp. 315–16.
49   Ibid., 316.

the notion of property, but read it in non-economic or discursive terms. For him, property was not a fact of the mode of production, but rather of political power in which class is not an essential element, and as such has to be understood as involving 'the question of rights or entitlements in society, of the resultant power relationships, of law and politics, of the process of legitimation of power relations'.[50] Thus Chatterjee conflated property with legal and cultural propriety, and, freed of the burden of class and economy, depicted consciousness as a self-originating and self-reproductive force and as the key source and site of politics. Particularly for societies imbued with strong non-bourgeois elements, culture was to be the basic ground of politics and category of theorisation.

Althusser's help notwithstanding, Chatterjee's theoretical perspective would not have been possible without Weberian sociology and colonial anthropology.[51] Through them he reinterpreted Marx's *Precapitalist Economic Formations* by reading Marx's views on political organisation of three social stages as shorn of all economically and socially proprietorial relations.[52] Instead, Chatterjee adopted a Weberian paradigm of tradition and modernity in order to substitute the marxian notion of 'mode of production'. According to this schema, he placed India at the traditional end of the spectrum, and this helped him to consider class as an unimportant factor in Indian politics. He characterised India in the Weberian style as primarily a communal-feudal or traditional society with a defined singular non-urban tradition, where political power resides in the collectivity of the community consciousness and is experienced politically as a relationship of hierarchy with features of domination expressed in physical force, rather than through a legal machinery of state power and administration.[53] Only in the fully developed bourgeois mode, found in the West, could Chatterjee conceive of power as having an element of class relations. Class would not be a politically material factor unless complete social control were secured over the labour process by establishing rights of property in the means of production and in the product by the impersonal operations of the market. Politics in this bourgeois stage broke the ideological unity and form of the two other modes of power, namely those of the communal and the

---

50   Ibid., p. 316.

51   For Chatterjee's debt to Weberian sociology and cultural anthropology and their general influence on Indian, especially 'subaltern,' historiography, see Thapar 1993a, and especially the essays Thapar 1993b and 1993c. Chatterjee 1983, pp. 316–23, serves as a precise example of this Weberian and colonial cultural anthropological reading, as does the entire theoretical framework for Guha 1983.

52   Marx 1964a.

53   Chatterjee 1983, p. 318.

feudal stage. The precondition to this bourgeois politics was the emergence of a clearly articulated civil society, with its division into public and private spheres, and the emergence of individual and legal rights of citizenship. Representative government of the modern state was nothing other than 'the fundamental institution for wielding power'.[54] This type of politics and mode of governance, however, could not apply to India, since Chatterjee saw India as an essentially pre-bourgeois society.

Thus, according to Chatterjee's Weberian sociology, any claim of modernity and bourgeois social relations was inauthentic to the Indian ethos. Any exploration of Indian polity and society in terms of class relations and/or secular-rationalist thought, therefore, was tantamount to adopting an inappropriate colonial or modernist discourse. Legitimate sources and practices of authority and power relations in India had to lie in the traditions of the community and feudalism, and thus an authentic politics would always entail a predetermination by consciousness, of spontaneity, physical force, and moral injunctions. For an analogue to clarify Indian politics, Chatterjee refers to what Marshall Sahlins has to say about 'tribal' forms of power in Africa, where the superstructure itself is to be seen as 'a political arrangement' and 'the economic [i.e., property relations or class] is only a side factor. The issue is instituted authority'.[55] For India, as well as Africa, this 'political arrangement' encompasses everything else, including the economy.

In order to put Chatterjee's characterisation of India in its proper perspective we should also remember the social or non-academic context of the emergence of subaltern studies. This refers to the maoist politics common in India from the mid-1960s through the 1970s, towards the end of which period the journal *Subaltern Studies* emerged. Maoist politics in India at this time characterised Indian society and history as being semi-feudal and semi-colonial. This resonates with the subsequent 'subaltern' formulation of India by Chatterjee, Guha, and others as described above. But there is an important difference in that the maoist emphasis on class and class struggle and, in particular, on the peasantry as a revolutionary class disappears, binding the notion of subalternity only to a pre-modernist content and form of community or feudal politics with an extra-parliamentary, extra-party, and insurrectionary bent. It is to this type of politics that Partha Chatterjee signals when he speaks of 'the subordinate forces' which 'battle ... to assert (perhaps to reassert) an alternative mode of power and authority based on the notion of the community'.[56] In his essay

---

54   Ibid.
55   Sahlins 1968, p. 322.
56   Chatterjee 1983, p. 334.

'Caste and Subaltern Consciousness', he speaks further in favour of caste politics over politics of class or individual rights.[57] It is clear that, for the subaltern theorists, Indian decolonisation can be brought about neither by nationalist liberal democratic politics nor by national liberationist politics of class against capital and imperialism.

This legitimation of a classless politics of nationalism, articulated by a section of the colonial Bengali elite in premodern, feudal-communitarian, or traditional terms, cannot but project Hindu revivalists of Bengal as 'subaltern' agents of nationalism, while excluding their social critics. Since the notion of the 'subaltern', though emptied of its class content, had retained its nuance of forced subordination (since it denoted persons of 'inferior rank'), it was now expanded to fit the Hindu elite, who held an inferior rank in the colonial hierarchy and aspired to a higher one of control. This fitted Guha's definition of subalternity as a 'general attribute of subordination',[58] and Sumit Sarkar's description of it as an 'omnibus term' which, presumably, could include 'the exploiters and the exploited'.[59] Sarkar included all Indian classes in this subalternity except the urban gentry and intellectuals, while Chatterjee also included them, since he considered them agents of decolonisation, both 'false' and 'true'. Neither Chatterjee nor Sarkar, at this stage, saw any need for a class analysis, or the relevance of property relations, for exploring politics or power relations in 'largely pre-industrial societies'.[60] Equating class with industrial societies and class consciousness, Sarkar spoke of the difficulty of asserting class as a relevant category and opted for subalternity.[61] Ranajit Guha saw this 'subaltern' consciousness disarticulated from social relations as autonomous, not originating from elite politics, nor dependent upon it.[62] It is traditional, as its 'roots can be traced to the precolonial times', and still relevant, as it is 'by no means archaic in the sense of being outmoded' for the purpose of current politics.[63] Though this 'subaltern' consciousness is not to be found in the same degree of purity among the colonial elite as among the 'tribals' and poor peasantry, since their 'traditional' politics has often been 'rendered ineffective by the intrusion of colonialism', they have not lost all connection to the pre-colonial, traditional culture.[64] As such, they may also be accorded with a certain degree of this

---

57   Chatterjee 1989b.
58   Guha 1982b, p. vii.
59   Sarkar 1984, p. 273.
60   Sarkar 1984 and Chatterjee 1989b.
61   Ibid.
62   Guha 1982b, p. 4.
63   Ibid.
64   Ibid.

'subaltern autonomy' of consciousness. Chatterjee's definition of nationalist thought relies on what Sarkar calls the 'relatively autonomous political domain ... with [its] specific features and collective mentality'.[65]

The source for partial rehabilitation of the colonised elite, or ruling classes, lies in their subalternity to the colonial power, which results in a Janus-like double-headed consciousness[66] 'characterised by an amalgam of loyalty and opposition to foreign rule'.[67] It is this, their stratified middle condition of being a 'middle term' between the foreign elite and local lower classes, which gives content to their ontology of 'subalternity'. This is the epistemological standpoint of their ideological efforts of mediation, through which they link or order pre-colonial religious and modernist secular forms of consciousness. This, claims Chatterjee, sets up a tension and revolutionary moments in their ideological enterprise, and he considers a nineteenth-century Bengali holy man, Ramakrishna, in light of this partial subaltern or 'national' consciousness, which is constructed with continued or reinvented tradition or religion. As religion is seen by Chatterjee as 'a constitutive force in a subaltern consciousness',[68] the closer the elite to religion – through what Sumit Sarkar considers to be Ramakrishna's petty bourgeois brahmanical Hinduism – the more 'subaltern' they are.[69] The elite, with both an autonomous and a borrowed part to their consciousness, embody for Chatterjee 'the struggle by the subordinated to resist the dominating implications [of] a universalist code [meant] for society as a whole'.[70] The resistance consists of defying universal codes of justice and relying on the culture and authority of a religious-ideological community in order to have differential forms of conduct.[71]

This assertion of the local elite's difference from the European colonisers extends to other local 'foreigners', such as Muslims, who are considered foreign since Islam originated outside India, even though the converts were indigen-

---

65   Sarkar 1984, p. 273.

66   On the Janus-headed nature of the middle class, see Chatterjee 1993b. This paper also appeared as chapter 3 of Chatterjee's book (1993a) under the title 'The Nationalist Elite,' with two introductory paragraphs added.

67   Asok Sen 1987, p. 207, ultimately holds a more negative view of the elite and their politics than Chatterjee. For Sen, what obtained was 'the experience of a historical process where the dominant classes, foreign and indigenous, had neither will nor initiative to bring about any coherent social transformation' (p. 206), and that 'their scramble for power and privilege prevailed over national consideration' (p. 207).

68   Chatterjee 1989b, p. 169.

69   Sarkar 1997d, pp. 283, 288.

70   Chatterjee 1989b, p. 174.

71   Ibid., p. 176.

ous. In his essay, 'Gandhi and the Critique of Civil Society', Chatterjee asserts Gandhi's success as a 'subaltern' leader to the extent that he pursued a religious or traditional form of conduct which was integral to his social thought.[72] Gandhi's rejection of the very idea of a civil society, his communitarianism emanating from his religiosity, and his equation of values of tradition with truth, are all held up by Chatterjee as the 'subaltern' path to a true decolonisation. Gandhi's failure as a genuine 'subaltern' leader is considered to lie in his inability to escape modernity's constructional and ideological imperatives in terms of political parties, state formation, and modes of governance. This modernist failure of the Indian National Congress is embodied by the politics and social thought of Jawaharlal Nehru. Thus, for Chatterjee, the Gandhian project of an authentic subaltern decolonisation is hijacked by the annexation of his traditionalist ideology and politics by the Indian industrial bourgeoisie and secular intelligentsia. As he sees it:

> It still remains a principal task of modern Indian historiography to explain the specific historical process by which these political possibilities that were inherent in the Gandhian ideology became the ideological weapons in the hands of the Indian bourgeoisie in its attempt to create a viable state structure within a process of class struggle in which its dominance was constantly under challenge and its moral leadership constantly fragmented.[73]

The uncompromised 'subaltern' sentiment for an authentic decolonisation is best expressed in Chatterjee's own words: 'For countries like India the concepts of bourgeois equality and freedom, *owing to their externality to the immanent forms of social consciousness,* cannot even claim the same degree of effectiveness as expression of the unity of society, despite their formal enshrinement in the political constitution'.[74] This statement makes it obvious that subaltern historiography espouses an epistemology and politics that assume what Sumit Sarkar now sees as a 'total rupture' in (Indian) history and social organisation, promulgating two watertight phases, the pre-colonial and the colonial. This artificial separation, he says, can result in a 'temptation' which makes 'the former a world of attractive ur-traditions of innocence confronting Western power-knowledge', thereby removing the past and tradition from critical purview.[75] It is not surprising that such a traditionally-based and essentialist

---

72   Chatterjee 1984.
73   Ibid., p. 194.
74   Chatterjee 1989b, p. 178. Emphasis added.
75   Sarkar 1997b, p. 5.

nationalist ideology of a unifying yet hierarchical nature would render not only issues of class but of patriarchy or gender irrelevant for both the colonial and pre-colonial times.

Along the axis of this historical rupture there proliferates a series of binary cultural essences which obey the tradition-modernity paradigm of Weberian sociology and cultural anthropology. The pre-colonial and the colonial cultural essences are thus paired in two columns, marking the community in opposition to the individual, home to the world, and tradition to modernity. A nation imagined within this dualist framework needs a gesture of transcendence in order to function as a unifying form. This transcendence or unity of hierarchy is supplied by the religious traditional mode which can both overcome the dualities as well as encompass or annex whatever modernity that comes in its way. All local social relations of difference and their cultures are erased, while those between essentialised and unified versions of stages of the premodern, and the modern, and between the colonial and nationalist discourse are retained. The traditional/religious national community is projected as benign and protective, while the colonial or modern state becomes the main source of oppression.[76] This ideological stance converts the issue of class patriarchy or the question of social reform for women, for example, into a colonial imperative or imposition, thus disallowing any critique of women's oppression conducted by the national community. This makes any legal reform or notions of citizenship based on individual rights or personhood of women into colonial gestures, even after India became independent. All regimes of domination are thus seen as derivatives of European enlightenment, and rationalism is considered the instrument and ethics of domination.[77] The codes for this domination are textual, and they wear the mask of knowledge. Accordingly, science is 'the instrument of colonisation', part and parcel of the discourse of power which underpins Western culture, which establishes its colonising hegemony through the concept of universality.[78] Obviously, within this framework there is no room for integrating

---

76   Ibid., p. 6.
77   For Chatterjee, modernity is undifferentiated and a unified essence, and serves as an ethics of domination. This domination is accomplished by technology, the idea of progress, and rationalist and scientific thought. The heart and vitality of colonisation is provided for Chatterjee by modernist thought, whose actual political modality is 'an epistemic foundation of universality' (Chatterjee 1986a, pp. 7–11 and 14–17). Chatterjee moves the episteme of domination (by science, rationality, etc.) from conquest of nature to conquest of people. In the context of 'social stratification,' domination is 'by man of man' [sic]. 'Rational conceptions of society ... subtly transfer' this domination (p. 14). Chatterjee 1995 further develops these notions. The same theoretico-political stance is to be found in diasporic South Asian postcolonialists and subalternists, for example, in the writings of Arjun Appadurai, Gyan Prakash, and others.
78   Chatterjee 1986a, pp. 14–16.

decolonisation as a specific historical project of a particular society with a universal project of social justice.

Decolonisation as a culture and discourse of (counter-) power aims to replace the modernist/universalist/scientific/secular and rationalist colonial discourse with its opposite representational and narrative forms. This, it is presumed, would end the epistemic and moral domination by an alien culture. Based on the principles of difference and inversion of modernity, the nationalist or decolonising discourse would aim at the construction of non-colonial subjectivities or identities. Chatterjee tries, therefore, to separate out the discursive elaborations of nineteenth-century Bengal into three cultural-ideological strands – one of a partially authentic nationalism, another which is a Western and colonial derivative, and a third which is fragmentary, local, and inarticulate. The last is identified with local marginal groups, for example with low-caste groups or women 'fallen' from their middle-class social positions into a demimondaine world, about whom Chatterjee writes in *The Nation and Its Fragments*.[79] Nationalist thought is then by definition a pre- and anti-modernist, univocal and particularist enterprise. As Chatterjee puts it, if we miss out on seeing this, then we 'miss out on the fascinating story of the encounter between a world conquering western thought and the intellectual modes of non-western cultures ... It also results in a crucial misunderstanding of the true historical effectivity of nationalism itself'.[80] Nationalist thought thus 'demarcates itself relentlessly from colonial discourse', and 'its politics impels it to open up that frame-work of knowledge which presumes to dominate it, to dispel the frame-work, to subvert its authority, to challenge its morality'.[81] But, as already noted, as the discourse of a colonially contaminated elite, nationalist thought cannot free itself wholly from the liberal rationalist dilemma. Though the national imaginary produced by the Hindu elite communitarians is much more substantive than Western theorists of nationalism, such as Kedourie or Anderson, would have us believe, it still falls prey to modernism. This, Chatterjee noted, supporting Kedourie, happens in the public sphere, in the very

---

79   On the idea of 'fragments' of the nation, see Chatterjee 1993a. In the section entitled 'The Women Left Out', based on the autobiography of Binodini, a nineteenth-century actress, Chatterjee outlines what he means by 'fragment' (1993a, pp. 151–5). Speaking about 'narrative of the nationalist transition,' he mentions those whom the nation 'betrays' or leaves out, for 'it could define a cultural identity for the nation only by excluding many from its fold' (p. 155). But this fragment status is blamed on modernist compromise more than anything else, which includes 'the political history of the postcolonial state seeking to replicate the modular forms of the modern nation-state' (p. 156).

80   Chatterjee 1986a, p. 41.

81   Ibid., p. 42.

conception of its national project as one of modern state formation and its political apparatus – 'it remains a prisoner of the prevalent European intellectual fashion'.[82]

As European 'intellectual fashion' in politics rests on the division between state and civil society, nationalist thought, in order to be authentically hegemonic, must negate or suppress this separation and a politics of a secular civil society. Chatterjee counterposes the notion of 'community', an appropriate Indian social form, to that of the colonial imposition of a discourse of 'civil society'. When suppression becomes impossible, then nationalist thought has to adapt this discourse of civil society to its own communitarian needs. As Chatterjee sees it: 'The trouble was that the moral-intellectual leadership of the nationalist elite operated in a field constituted by a very different set of distinctions – those between the spiritual and the material, the inner and the outer, the essential and the inessential. That contested field over which nationalism had proclaimed its sovereignty and where it had its true community was neither coextensive with nor coincidental to the field constituted by the public/private distinction'.[83] But the nationalist elite of Bengal have not been successful in constituting this 'true community'. Instead, according to Chatterjee, they have partially accepted civil society and modernist modes of politics and state formation, and thus engaged in what Gramsci called 'transformism', leading to 'a passive revolution'.[84] But they still have a partial achievement to their credit – that of the creation of a hegemonic moral and cultural discourse which constructs and regulates their private life and can, therefore, assert itself against their public life of colonial submission to modernity. It is here, in their homes, that the Bengali Hindu elite proclaim their limited but still effective cultural hegemony, turning the private/public divide to their own benefit. And the crux of this enterprise lies in fashioning a subjectivity and agency for women and a general domestic conduct which are commensurable with this religious-traditional ideological stance. That in this process they have drawn upon and reinforced brahmanical patriarchy is considered a minor detail and a negligible problem. What Chatterjee applauds in his chosen nationalist thinkers is their success in partially subordinating modernity through the imperatives of tradition or religious communitarianism, the crucial factor for an anti-colonialism of 'subalternity'.

---

82   Ibid., pp. 10–11.
83   Chatterjee 1993a, p. 10.
84   For Chatterjee's use of Gramsci's concepts, including those of 'transformism' and 'revolution', see Chatterjee 1986a, chapter 2.

3   Woman: The Sign of the Nation

Colonial critics invariably repeated a long list of atrocities perpetrated
on Indian women, not so much by men or certain classes of men, as by
an entire body of scriptural canons and ritual practices which, they said,
by rationalising such atrocities within a complex framework of religious
doctrine, made them appear to perpetrators and sufferers alike as the
necessary marks of right conduct. By assuming a position of sympathy
with the unfree and oppressed womanhood of India, the colonial mind
was able to transform this figure of the Indian woman to the sign of the
inherently oppressive and unfree nature of the entire cultural tradition of
the country.[85]

To be sure, the project of bourgeois individuality was a strong factor in
... modernity, the idea of the autonomous individual existing for her own
ends was something that animated this modern. But Kula, Grihalakshmi
etc., for all their undeniable phallocentrism, were also ways of talking
about formations and pleasure, emotions and ideas of good life that associated themselves with models of non-autonomous, non-bourgeois and
non-secular personhood.[86]

These two passages contain key 'subaltern' positions regarding the issue of
women's status in India with respect to their personhood, social subjectivity,
and agency. Beneath the seeming distinctness of these two statements there is
an underlying commonality of approach regarding the placement of women in
the project of nationalist hegemony. Let us examine them closely.

In Chatterjee's statement, the reader's attention is quickly shifted from 'atrocities' perpetrated on Indian women to the 'colonial critics' of these atrocities.
They have a single 'colonial mind' and a 'long list' of ills of women. We are
not invited to discuss whether their list is true or false, but rather to question
who they are and what their critical motivation might be. They complain about
'Indian culture' itself, against the 'complex religious doctrines' of Hindus, with
their 'scriptural canons and ritual practices' for 'rationalising such atrocities'.
But these 'necessary marks of right [Hindu] conduct', presumed to be inegalitarian by the critics, are not queried by Chatterjee. Instead, we are directed
to be suspicious of any 'position of sympathy with ... this figure of the Indian

---

85   Chatterjee 1989a, p. 622.
86   Chakrabarty 1998, p. 84.

woman'. It is as though there were no actual patriarchal oppression of women in India, but rather only a colonial fiction of such oppression, a tendentious critique of the culture of the colonised with a view to legitimate colonisation. The question of Indian women's oppression is, at best, bracketed in favour of criticising colonial discourse, by implication vindicating nationalist thought. From this standpoint, to adopt a critical posture towards Indian society and a sympathetic one towards Indian women would be tantamount to taking the side of the coloniser.[87] The issue of brahmanical patriarchy, therefore, becomes unimportant, or even non-existent, because colonisers draw our attention to it. Instead of finding other criteria than the European civilisational one for querying Indian patriarchy, the reader is drawn into a fight between the coloniser and the implied nationalist position. Patriarchies on both sides are ignored, as they convert women of colonised societies into their ideological signs of hegemony. Under such circumstances, any social criticism or demand for reform for Indian women would spell submission to colonial discourse. Chatterjee's own decolonisation proposal does not permit any critique of Indian patriarchy.

Dipesh Chakrabarty's position is similar to that of Chatterjee and reliant upon the same premises. He also criticises the modernist or colonial perspective which is necessary for a critique of patriarchy and for demands of social reform.[88] On the same ground of authentic anti-colonialism, it would be wrong for him to demand that women should be autonomous individuals. Therefore, the patriarchal mores that would be seen as oppressive by feminist and modernist critics are defended by Chakrabarty. For him the Hindu constructions of Grihalakshmi, the goddess of the home, and Kulalakshmi, the preserver of the purity of lineage and traditions, though 'undeniably phallocentric', are considered less problematic than the advocacy of individual rights or personhood for women. Thus, the 'idea of the autonomous individual existing for her *own* ends' (emphasis added) would be a colonial design, though the same autonomy for males would be no such thing. Possibilities for women's autonomy as social subjects and agents are subordinated to the guardianship privileges of the male elite of the community, however patriarchal. Women are thus advised or presumed to be contented with their status of 'non-autonomous, non-bourgeois, non-secular personhood'. This is the nationally permitted social space within which women must look for their social 'formations and pleasure, emotions and ideas of good life'. To disagree with this goal of a happy subordination to

---

87   A very similar argument seems to be at work in Mani 1990; 1998, but there is a difference
      here: Mani's commitment is to women and feminism, and not to cultural nationalism in
      any shape or form.
88   Chakrabarty 1995; 1998.

brahmanical patriarchy would be construed as joining up with those 'colonial minds' criticised by Chatterjee.[89]

Chatterjee and Chakrabarty's statements, which are coherent with the general 'subaltern' theorisation, provide the backdrop for understanding the claimed 'resolution of the women's question' accomplished by nationalist thought. Both authors depend on 'subaltern' characterisation of India as a semi-feudal and semi-colonial society, and thus support cultural markers that would be authentic to this definition. Both authors signal to the colonial 'mode of power' and its anticolonial/nationalist response, and thus cannot accommodate a critique of a class-based gender/patriarchy. To do otherwise would transgress their view of what constitutes politics in an essentially pre- and non-modern social space. Dipesh Chakrabarty's two versions of the woman subject, the colonial/modern and the national/pre-modern, are examples of required political identities, seen as a part of the creation of a non-secular nationalist discourse.

In his essay on Ramakrishna and the middle class of Calcutta, Chatterjee speaks to such a creation of 'the dominant forms of nationalist culture and social institutions'. They are 'new forms of public discourse', 'new forms of public criteria of social respectability, new aesthetic moral standards ... suffused with the spirit of nationalism'. They provide the bases for 'new forms of political mobilisation'.[90] Thus the Hindu revivalist faction of the Bengali middle class becomes the voice of anti-colonialism, and the teachings of their sage Ramakrishna reflect the ethics of nationalism. Making no distinction between what Sumit Sarkar has shown to be a petty bourgeois form of religious consciousness and nationalism as such, Chatterjee treats his teachings in the *kath-amrta* as a 'text that reveals to us the subalternity of the elite'.[91]

This 'subalternity' of the elite, a necessary subject position for the creation of nationalist thought, with its domination-subordination dialectic, is presented as textured with (masculine) fears and anxieties. It fixes upon upper class/caste women as symbolic signs and sites of hegemonic content and contest.[92] These male fears and anxieties are presumed by Chatterjee to be unrelated to and unexpressed in actual situations of domestic violence, but are imbricated as symptoms of colonial subordination, and thus constitute a legitimate part of nationalist thought. It is a part of the process of inversion of values through

---

89 See, in this context, Sarkar 1992, for a very different discussion of women's subjectivity, agency, and their representation.

90 Chatterjee 1993b, p. 41.

91 Ibid., p. 42.

92 On male anxieties in the colonial context, see Sinha 1995.

which the colonial sign of oppressed Indian women now becomes the positive sign of the difference of the nation. As such, brahmanical patriarchy itself
could serve as a sign of 'our' freedom, making social organisation through caste,
class, and gender an indicator of 'our' culture. The masculinist nature of this
discourse and the 'subaltern' theorists' uncritical acceptance of it have been
noted by Kamala Viswesaran.[93] For her, it 'would not be unfair to say that while
the praxis of subaltern studies has originated in the central assumption of subaltern agency, it has been less successful in demonstrating how such agency
is constituted by gender'. She also notes that the 'occasional subaltern theorist
when he has ventured to comment on the role gender has played in nationalist
ideology, has been strangely content to point to the absence from nationalist registers'.[94] She concludes by asking: 'Is then the silence on the subject of
women within the parameter of subaltern studies somehow related to the simultaneous creation of nation and (counter) narration?'[95]

Viswesaran's criticism supports mine, though ultimately we diverge. She
mainly expands and corrects rather than rejects the 'subaltern' historiography,
and notes less the nature of their utterances than their 'silence on the subject
of women'. I, however, find both their omissions and commissions problematic. Overall, however, she corroborates my stance that their particular historiographical slant on women is integral to how they themselves, and not just the
nineteenth-century nationalists, 'narrate' the nation. As things stand, we are
left with the problematic conversion of Indian/Bengali women into a figure of
speech for both nationalism's and 'subaltern' theorists' declarative discourse
of anti-colonialism. After all, from their standpoint, fashioning women into
a sign of the nation or a representative metaphor of colonial oppression features as the success story of nationalist hegemony.[96] Chatterjee outlines this
premise thus: 'The world was where the European power had challenged the
non-European peoples and, by virtue of its superior material culture, had sub-
jugated them. But it had failed to colonise the inner, essential identity of the
East which lay in its distinctive, and superior, spiritual culture'.[97] As this 'inner'

---

93   Viswesaran 1996. In her project Viswesaran agrees with Gayatri Spivak that 'all repres-
      entation is overdetermined by a structure of interests', but she has to know *how* it is
      so. So she asks, 'What are the places subaltern speech is denied; the ways in which it is
      contained; the moments when an act of speech might puncture, even rupture, official
      discourse?' (Viswesaran 1996, p. 84). Her subalterns are, obviously, women, and women of
      lower classes.
94   Viswesaran 1996, p. 85.
95   Ibid.
96   On this issue of women as 'signs' of the nation, see Jasodhara Bagchi (1985, 1990).
97   Chatterjee 1990, p. 239.

realm was spatially translated into 'home' – the family life of the colonised – women become the sign of an autonomy and are subjected to a commensurate moral construction.[98] Chatterjee speaks at length about this woman sign in his essay 'A Religion of Urban Domesticity':

> We know that the figure of woman often acts as a sign in discursive form-ations, standing for concepts or entities, that have little to do with women in actuality. Each signification of this kind also implies a corresponding sign in which the figure of man is made to stand for other concepts or entities, opposed to and contrasted with the first. However, we also know that signs can be operated upon – connected to, transposed with, differ-entiated from other signs in a semantic field where new meanings are produced.[99]

Viswesaran points out astutely that 'it is the failure of the subaltern studies his-torian to break from the discourse he analyses, which results in an inability to adequately theorise a gendered subaltern subject'.[100]

This failure is all the more glaring since the patriarchal obsession of nine-teenth-century Hindu revivalists and cultural nationalists has been much dis-cussed. Advocates of social reform at the time or the later proponents of 'Bengal Renaissance'[101] as well as feminist historians and cultural theorists in the last decades, have all spoken to it.[102] As the editors of *Embodied Violence* say in their introduction:

---

98   Ibid., pp. 242, 245.
99   Chatterjee 1993b, p. 60.
100   Viswesaran 1996, p. 86.
101   On 'Bengal Renaissance' and social reform, see Susobhan Sarkar (1985). Sarkar character-ises the 'Bengal Renaissance' in the following way: 'The impact of British rule, bourgeois economy and modern Western culture was felt first in Bengal and produced an awakening known usually as the Bengal Renaissance. For about a century, Bengal's conscious aware-ness of the changing modern world was more developed than and ahead of that of the rest of India. The role played by Bengal in the modern awakening of India is thus com-patible to the position occupied by Italy in the story of the European Renaissance' (13). A main feature of this modernist thought was an insistence on social reform, especially for women. For Sarkar this renaissance is seen as a positive phenomenon and the basis for a modernist nationalism and society for India.
102   This dangerous phenomenon of religious and communalist revivalism underpinning a certain type of nationalism, especially the Hinduisation of upper class/caste women's con-duct, has been written about by Uma Chakravarty, Tanika Sarkar, and Jasodhara Bagchi, among others.

The ideological base of identity politics and exclusionism is not new, it goes back a hundred years or so to a period of nationalist upsurge ... During colonialism, religious revivalism was a powerful opposition movement ... This revivalism involved an assertion of a national identity and a cultural linguistic consciousness that was constructed in opposition to the identity and culture imposed on colonised peoples by their European rulers. The revivalism of the majority communities had adverse effects on minorities and women.[103]

Uma Chakravarty's book on Pandita Ramabai, *Rewriting History*, for example, or her other writings on the brahmanical oppression of Hindu widows, articulate a thoroughgoing criticism of religious revivalism.[104] They take us well beyond the facile equation of Hindu revivalism with nationalism, and social reformism with colonial complicity. Sumit Sarkar also articulates a critique of this stance and shows the difference between the anti-reformist woman-blaming of the Hindu revivalists and nationalists and Vidyasagar's perception of women as victims of brahmanical Hinduism.[105] The asymmetry between Hindu revivalism and nationalism that Sarkar exposes makes the question of anti-colonialism much more complicated than the simple post-colonial theorisation of Chatterjee.

Partha Chatterjee and his fellow 'subalterns' cannot part company with the Hindu cultural nationalists due to their own theoretical constraints. The anti-modernism of their post-colonial stance, along with their cultural interpretation of politics which disconnects property from propriety and forbids them to discuss women as properties of the nation, direct them otherwise. They cannot avoid seeing the Hindu revivalist elite as the political agent of decolonisation, since decolonisation for a society such as India implies for them a communitarian moral construction and regulation. They also cannot include women among nationalist agents because the simplicity of their anti-colonial identities, the rupture of Bengal's (or Indian) history into premodern and modern phases, along with an essentialised and demonised view of modernity which complements their Weberian reading of Indian society, all make it impossible for them to do so. In order for women to be seen as 'subaltern' political subjects and agents rather than the property of the nation, these theorists would have to embrace an egalitarian view of gender relations, which would be unac-

---

103   Jayawardena 1996, pp. ix–x.
104   Chakravarty 1998; 1995.
105   Sarkar 1997a, pp. 260–81.

ceptably modernist.[106] It would amount to seeing women as 'subalterns' of the 'male' subalterns, and calling for an autonomous subjecthood based on universal notions of social justice. But as this could not be done, they settled for what they considered to be the best option for women. This consisted of seeing a regulated female identity in which certain external features of modernity were instrumentalised at the behest of the male elite of the community as a 'resolution of the women's question'.

Chatterjee's dualist moral characterisation of the nineteenth-century Bengali elite was given a historical facelift in a schematic division of their cultural and political consciousness into two time periods.[107] This binary moral schema is produced and serialised by reducing the multiple and competing ideological strands prevalent among them into a single essentialised form of consciousness. This reduced consciousness is solely constructed in its relationship to colonial discourse or modernism. The first stage, exemplified by social reformers such as Rammohan Roy or Vidyasagar, represents a total capitulation to colonialism or modernity which is opposed by fully traditionalist anti-reformers such as Radhakanto Deb. This latter strand of Hindu opposition is seen by Chatterjee as evolving into a representational nationalist discourse and thus assumes a political legitimacy during the later part of the nineteenth century. This new ideological stance instrumentalises modernity and contains it within the requirements of Hindu religious tradition, seeking to prevent social reforms. This approach is exemplified by the resistance to the Age of Consent Act in 1891 and by the reasons for their opposition.[108]

The annexation of modernity to augment tradition or the community mode of power has been seen as an excellent political move, not only by Chatterjee and other subaltern theorists, but by some feminists as well. Shahnaz Rouse, for example, in an otherwise feminist essay, praises Chatterjee for what she considers his overcoming a tradition-modernity dichotomy for women by showing the mechanism of a 'resolution' of their opposition.[109] She states: 'For unlike the commonly held separation between "tradition" and "modernism", this [Chatterjee's formulation of 'the resolution'] suggests the maintenance of a balance – constantly shifting and reformulated – between the two, where "modernisation" occurs in the spiritual/inner/private/home'.[110] For Rouse this 'manner of

---

106 On the theme of Indian women's agency in the context of nationalism, see Viswesaran 1996, but also Nair 1994 and Thapar 1993.
107 Chatterjee 1990; 1993a, pp. 116–34.
108 For the Age of Consent Act, see Bannerji 1998c. For details of the debate surrounding it, see Kosambi 1991.
109 Rouse 1996.
110 Ibid., p. 44.

understanding nationalist constructions is enormously useful not only for the context in which Chatterjee evokes it – that of Bengali social reformism – but, as significantly in the context of Muslim nationalism leading eventually to the creation of Pakistan'.[111] There is, however, a contradiction in Rouse's reading of Chatterjee. If there were truly any 'modernisation' of the 'inner' sphere, a qualitative overcoming of the binary rather than an annexation of the 'modern' by 'tradition' and as such the traditionalisation of the public sphere itself, then one could not have the threat of theocracy which has dogged Pakistan.

Partha Chatterjee and Dipesh Chakrabarty are both aware of the quandary they face by the project of constructing 'national' identities, which must on the one hand forge a unifying discourse of nationality and authenticity, while on the other cope with modernity and internal differences. As Chakrabarty puts it, nationalist thought must 'subsume the question of difference within a search for essences, origins, authenticities which, however, have to be amenable to global European construction of modernity so that the quintessentially nationalist claims of being "different but modern" can be validated'.[112] This is a large part of the 'resolutionary' process of identity construction for women spoken of by Chatterjee. He notes in these constructions the gesture of recuperation of Orientalism, of 'classicisation of tradition', whereby anti-modernist moral regulations appeal to antique lineages and ethnicise difference, while tactically responding to modernising pressures.[113] Meredith Borthwick's work on Bengali women's education supplies him with examples of this process, as does the struggle over women's education described by her and Dagmar Engels.[114] Chatterjee sees in Bengali nationalist women figures a 'resolved', ideological synthesis. But the authors that he cites upon closer reading tell us a different story. Their texts are replete with stories of struggles and unresolved attempts at compromise regarding formal schooling of women or the content of their education.

Chatterjee, however, can create a fiction of nationalist resolution from them because he has erased debates and differences that are etched in Bengali soci-

---

111   Ibid.
112   Chakrabarty 1998, p. 51.
113   Chatterjee 1990, p. 244.
114   See Borthwick 1984 and Engels 1996. Engels writes: 'After 1900 many Hindu girls were sent to school for the first time. The idea of social progress had become acceptable and was no longer identified with giving up Hindu religion and becoming a Brahmo. In the second half of the nineteenth century the debate over the curriculum had become increasingly critical of "male" education for women. Gradually a compromise was struck between "male" and "female" curricula, between an academic education for boys and a domestic education for girls' (Engels 1996, p. 167).

ety by seeing it strictly in terms of a colonial/derivative and nationalist discourse. His stance postulates a single and synthesised traditionalist consciousness for the middle classes as a whole by the later part of the nineteenth
century. We are invited to forget the outpouring of complexities and contradictions to be found in the social consciousness of the time, especially in the
role played by gender in class formation. The introduction to *Recasting Women*,
for example, discusses the asymmetrical and changing relations between class
formation and patriarchy in culture during the colonial period.[115] As Kumkum
Sangari and Sudesh Vaid put it, the 'relation between classes and patriarchies
is complex and variable. Not only are patriarchal systems class differentiated,
open to constant and consistent reformulation, but defining gender seems to
be crucial to the formation of classes and dominant ideologies'.[116]

The fact that many Hindu girls went to school without their families giving
up Hinduism, or that intermittent compromises were struck between academic
and domestic education for women, cannot obliterate the struggles that underpinned women's education both at home and in the public world.[117] Issues of
women's economic status and legal and political personhood which continue
to this day were forged at that time. It is an unresolved state of affairs, or a state
of ideological disharmonies, rather than one of a resolutionary synthesis.[118] The
same conflicts and daily life of patriarchal oppression in the cause of class are
also depicted by Bengali writers, both male and female (such as Ashapurna
Devi or Manik Bandyopadhyay) well into our present time. These dimensions
of 'the women's question', however, are sacrificed by Chatterjee in order to
attribute successful accommodational strategies to Hindu cultural nationalism. The Galatea-like persona of a good Hindu wife-mother eclipses the realities of social formation and the frictions between domesticity and profession for
women. In spite of all the talk of resolution and accommodation, the discourse
of Hindu *bhadramahila* (an educated modernist 'lady' persona) and *grihalakshmi* (figure of the goddess of home/hearth, not primarily signified by modernity) did not come to any happy fusion. But this situation is neither noted nor
regretted by Partha Chatterjee or Dipesh Chakrabarty, and their sentiment of
approval for the claimed 'resolution' is captured by Chakrabarty when he says:

> The highest form of personhood [for women] was one constituted by the
> idea of self-sacrifice, the idea of living for others, not in the spirit of civic
> virtue that Rousseau would have applauded, but in a spirit of subordin-

---

115   Sangari and Vaid 1990, pp. 1–26.
116   Ibid., p. 5.
117   See Bannerji 1997a.
118   Bagchi 1985.

ation to non-secular and parochial principle of dharma. The idea ... was not at all innocent of power, domination and even cruelty but, whatever else it may have been, it was never merely a ruse for staging the secular-historicist project of the citizen-subject.[119]

This indifference to women as political agents or social subjects is directly related to their theoretical anti-modernist rejection of 'the secular-historicist project of the citizen-subject'. Even an awareness of 'power', 'domination', and 'cruelty' towards women in this nationalist discourse cannot overcome their dislike for modernity. This explains Chatterjee's 'strange contentment' with the nationalist figure of the 'new woman' achieved through a 'new' patriarchy, which manages to retain much of the brahmanical nature of the 'old patri-archy', though now modified and elevated to the level of both nationalist con-duct and a general spirituality. This religiosity which is attributed to domest-icity, embodied in the woman as a central signifier of the nationalist imagin-ary, serves as a major political icon in both literature and art.[120] It presents us with the paradox of the private serving as a public sign, as nationalism's bid to subvert the 'civil society' by annexing the discourse of modernity. This 'new woman' construct exemplifies the basis of the polity for a proposal of the new nation-state. Here a traditionally inscribed civil society was to solve the prob-lem of social order. The 'new woman' figure is thus meant to disrupt and subvert the main enemy, modernity, though it would have to be continually readjusted to resist modernist pressures.

The logistics of creating this non-modernist woman figure lay, as Chatterjee noted, in adapting the discourse of civil society and state, the public and the private, by introducing a retreat of one part of the civil society, 'the world', into the other, the 'home'.[121] The public or outer sphere, however, does not refer to the 'techno-economic' reality of class, but rather to the realm of public cultural institutions. As such, the world of writing and publishing are seen by Chat-terjee, following Benedict Anderson, as examples of the public sphere, and as unconnected to home and domesticity. The latter were to be protected from the modernity of not just the state, but of public culture, and from the encroaching influences of modernist morality of social reform.

---

119   Chakrabarty 1998, p. 85.
120   See Bagchi 1985.
121   On 'home and the world', see Chatterjee 1990, pp. 239–43: 'But the crucial requirement was to retain the inner spirituality of indigenous social life. The home was the principal site for expressing the spiritual quality of the national culture, and women must take the main responsibility of protecting and nurturing this quality' (p. 243). These same ideas are discussed in Chatterjee 1993a. In this context see also Dirks 1993 and Nandy 1983.

The conceptual fortification of the domestic space and its primary deniz-
ens, women, entailed the definition and inversion of essential characteristics of Europe and India in civilisational terms. As Chatterjee notes, European
civilisation was morally signified for the nationalists by its modernist traits of
materialism, individualism, legalism, and representative government. Indian
civilisation was contrasted with it through a premodernist attribution of religi-
osity/spirituality, communal or collective social conduct, and political power.
A liberal democratic discourse of rights-bearing individual-citizens and legislative social reforms was antithetical to its ethos. Since Europe and India were
two essentially different civilisations, colonialism meant the imposition of an
alien culture through the successful creation of a secular, rationalist culture in
India. But, as Chatterjee points out, in this same cultural difference, otherness,
or alienness lay the nationalist escape route. Since only like can really influence
like, and materialism and spiritualism are qualitatively antithetical, modernist colonial discourse could be seen as external to the essence of India and
incapable of influencing its spiritual inner self. Since the colonial conquest of
the superstructure was thus external and non-essential, though Indian/Bengali
economy, public institutions, and governing forms became susceptible to it,
Indian/Bengali morality and home life remained relatively free. This freedom
was articulated in its pure form in the ideology of feminine conduct, through
typologies for an ideal national womanhood.

Nationalists claimed, and 'subaltern' theorists saw, this cultural logistics to
be an effective strategy for decolonisation. The home was considered a base
from which to attempt sovereignty in the national space as a whole. The home,
the spiritual-moral domain guarded by the *grihalakshmi* woman, thus became
a highly politically charged environment. It was presented as the only free zone,
with a continuation of indigenous sovereignty that antedated colonial rule.
Under these circumstances legislation for social reform, or any public attempt
to influence the private, amounted to home invasions by an alien force. As
such these public reform enterprises had to be defeated outright, or at least
silenced and contained. It is no surprise, therefore, that references to women's
oppression, by either the colonial government or indigenous social reformers,
were treated as colonial lies and treachery. The situation for local reformers, as
Uma Chakravarty notes, was precarious, and expressed in the language of 'patriots and traitors'.[122] Both male reformers, such as Vidyasagar with his crusade
for widow remarriage, and women engaged in social reform, such as Pandita
Ramabai or Krishna Bhabini Das, became victims of more than verbal viol-

---

122   Chakravarty 1996; 1998.

ence.[123] Dissolving rather than 'resolving' the women's question, one should say, became imperative for this type of nationalist thought and its construction of the 'new woman' trope.

What is obvious to any careful reader is that 'subaltern' theorists, including Chatterjee, cannot disentangle their own thesis of successful decolonisation from that of Hindu revivalist nationalism, and are thus forced to '(counter) narrate' their own position on the nation through a patriarchal imaginary. For Viswesaran, this neo-orientalist Said- and Foucault-influenced post-colonial theorisation, with a leftover trace of Althusser's notion of ideological overdetermination, displays the same blindness to 'difference' of which they accuse modernist universalists. In the end they create a more essentialist, though sophisticated, version of Hindu revivalism.

As we noted, this cultural essentialism and anti-modernism, postulated on a separation between class and politics, is theorised by Chatterjee very early in his career. It is an ideological gesture which averts our attention from women's oppression, as well as their debates regarding their own subjectivities and agencies when they entered the arena of public discourse in the last quarter of the nineteenth century.[124] In fact, 'the women's question' is considered 'resolved' by Chatterjee when men lose the status of guardians and sole representatives of women. Male and female critics who still continue to call for social reforms for women are dubbed Westernised and unrepresentative. Others, who are called the 'fragments' of the nation by Chatterjee, fall below nationalist agency since they have little power of articulation and nothing substantive to say in terms of promulgating a full discourse.[125] The utterances of 'fallen' women, such as the actress Binodini, are marked by a sense of loss of belonging rather than by criticism.[126] As reform and rights-seeking women voice their demands for economic and social independence and their aspirations for full citizenship, they emerge as the enemy of the nation.

We note that the persona of this 'new woman', created by a male subaltern elite in a mode of seeming deification, is doubly subjected. She is subjected both to the patriarchal colonial state and to the patriarchal nation.[127] This means personal subjection to the patriarchal Brahmanism of male family authorities as guardians of the national community and their anticipated

---

123   For documented evidence of violence against Vidyasagar, see Sarkar 1997e.
124   Chatterjee 1983.
125   Chatterjee 1993a.
126   See Chatterjee 1993a, chapter 7, which relies largely on Binodini's memoir *Amar Katha* [My Story]. This was recently translated into English and published by Kali for Women, translated by Rimli Bhattacharya.
127   On the topic of women's double subjection by the male patriarchal community and the

national government. Thus, women are treated as political and economic social minors, as dependents of their male kin. This subjection, which continues from the home to the community and the nation, is the actual lived content of the proposed 'non-secular, non-autonomous personhood' that Chakrabarty applauds. It is through this mode that women are to imagine and live an emotionally satisfying and nationally contributing life. Such a proposal holds a profound double standard for men and women, and demands for men the modernity of a legal individual personhood, the modern status of citizenship and state power, while leaving women without agency in a minoritised subjecthood. Within the scope of this type of proprietorial cultural nationalism, men are members of the (Hindu) community without compromise to their economic, legal and individual rights, and political power, while women are not. Even in the colonial period, Hindu elite men proved their nationalism by demanding their rights from the colonial state, as for example, by agitating in support of the Ilbert Bill for equal participation in the colonial administration,[128] or by demanding 'home rule'.[129] While male social and political identity can straddle both communitarian and modernist lines and advance to the stage of national freedom, it becomes primarily women's responsibility to remain faithful to the discourse of cultural nationalism, and thus to remain as an immanent existence in antimodernist terms. To maintain their status as vessels of national and family honour, they must be removed not only from the juridical outreach of the colonial state, but also from the deliberative sphere and influence of indigenous female and male reformers. In other words, even before the nation becomes the state, they are the true and first subjects of the emerging nation. This construction of female proprieties and their legal and political implications provides us with a model for understanding what it might mean to hold a minority status within a nation-state which correlates citizenship with gendered ethnicity.

We cannot complete this discussion without some comment regarding the male nationalist sense of danger and anxiety mentioned by Chatterjee. It

---

colonial state, see Chakravarty 1996. She speaks of 'dual structures of authority' of local caste patriarchy and the 'new statutory laws' of the colonial state: 'Both structures upheld the authority of the patriarchal family, and its property forms even though they were apparently dissimilar and at times in conflict with each other' (1996, p. 206). Also on the issue of control of women, see ibid. For Balgangadhar Tilak, the famous nationalist leader of Maharashtra, and many others, 'it was the husband and the traditional hindu community who were to decide how to manage the sexuality of the wife; neither the state, nor the liberal reformers, nor even the women themselves, had the right to do so' (p. 213).

128   On Ilbert Bill details, see Sinha 1995.

129   On 'home rule' see Sarkar 1988.

needs to be asked why it is that only some men who are constituted as agents within a cultural nationalist discourse experience these feelings, while other males, 'reformers' for example, find women's social and political personhood and political agency uplifting. We should also point out that this discourse of threatened masculinity is in no real way different from other colonial or master discourses regarding populations who are sought to be ruled. The fear and anxiety of Bengali elite males regarding women, resulting even in cruelty and violence towards them, derive partially from the fact that anti-colonial difference is displaced, through the subjection of women rather than through direct confrontation with the actual rulers. The fear of the possibility of women's resistance to this fixed role of both subordination and mythicisation or idealisation obviously can intensify this male anxiety and invest it with a violent intent which rulers often project upon the ruled. This mirrors the actual violence they themselves perpetrate. As with any ruling discourse, this discourse is structured through moral purity and moral panic. A steady stream of this type of discourse regarding the social and moral anarchy of women and other 'natural subordinates' marks much of the cultural production of Hindu revivalists and nationalists. Sumit Sarkar, in his essay 'Renaissance and Kali Yuga', speaks to this phenomenon.[130] Chatterjee himself, however, describes this misogyny of Hindu nationalism quite complacently, while speaking sympathetically of male anxiety in his essay on middle-class domesticity and spirituality as well as in his other writings. Nowhere does he question the use of colonial subjection as an alibi for violence against women, and instead presents us Ramakrishna's description of women at its face value: 'The female body is here a representation of the prison of worldly interests, in which the family man is trapped, only to lead to a daily existence of subordination, anxiety, pain and humiliation, whose only culmination is decay and destruction'.[131] Or we get this quotation from Ramakrishna's *Kathamrta*: 'Master: What is there in the body of a woman? Blood, flesh, fat, gut, worms, urine, salt, shit, all this. Why do you feel attached to a body like this?'[132] Chatterjee sees no reason to look further than the elite male's subjection by colonialism to discover and criticise the sources and influences of such statements. Instead, he normalises this violence against women as an ordinary colonial syndrome. Males who do not experience this misogyny when subjected to colonialism, and in fact feel sympathy or empathy for socially subjected women, are dubbed anti-nationalists. Chatterjee also leaves unquestioned Ramakrishna's attempts to appropriate phys-

---

130   Sarkar 1997f.
131   Chatterjee 1993b, p. 55.
132   Ibid.

ical and psychic femininity despite his hatred for actual women, especially as sexual beings. Lastly, he fails to note that by making women's sexuality (as *kamini*), seeking *artha* (wealth) and *kama* (sexual pleasure), the root cause of man's destruction and travail, thus converting woman into incarnate promiscuity and lust for gold, the nationalist male in fact could achieve a degree of peace with colonialism.[133]

This nationalist spirituality, marking its difference from modernity, has neither an ethic of compassion nor of social justice, but operates on a highly particularised Hindu/brahmanical communitarian discourse. The heart of moral purity in this context is the sacrifice of the woman for the family, the (religious) community, and the nation. For a woman to be otherwise is to be the *alakshmi*, the bad or Westernised woman, who is the wicked spirit or the demoness, rather than *grihalakshmi*, the goddess of the home/hearth. Thus, to quote Chatterjee, signs are 'operated upon – connected to, transposed with, differentiated from other signs in a semantic field where new meanings are produced'.[134] The hatred for female sexuality depends on the recognition that, in the search for pleasure, women (or people in general) can become self-oriented. Even more than their search for knowledge and formal education, this sexual impulse or desire can propel them to break the boundaries of the religious communitarian prescription, to find a safer space in the realm of modernity.

Thus, patriarchal nationalism brings with it, as does patriarchy in general, more than an epistemic violence. It equates women's sexuality with promiscuity and prostitution, and its hatred for women's sexuality and for prostitutes encourages many forms of violence. Women of the nation are thus permitted to be sexed beings only as property, as owned beings to serve their husbands and patriarchal lineage by being mothers of the nation and national heroes. The Hindu notion of *patidevata*, the husband god, equates serving god with serving the husband in bed or elsewhere, making it a woman's primary religious or spiritual conduct and asserting that there is no other scripture that she needs to know. The critical or modernist woman, by contrast, is seen as an incarnate inversion of this ideal conduct, and is subjected to much violent visual and verbal satire. Hindu revivalist dystopia has her as a central sign of a 'fallen' age, expressed through these images of inversion. This dystopic woman sign includes not only the sexual woman, but also other aspects of the 'modern woman' in her other incarnations, 'allegedly ill-treating her mother-in-law, enslaving the husband, neglecting household duties, to read novels, and wast-

---

133   Ibid., p. 60.
134   Ibid., p. 55.

ing money on luxuries for herself'.[135] Though the Western-educated 'modern women', as distinguished from the 'new woman', were the main targets, their unlettered sisters were not spared from criticisms of immorality either. Such women could also embody unrestrained lust and wilfulness, as could their educated and sophisticated counterparts. But it is for the Westernised women that the strongest condemnations were reserved because they were considered 'arrogant, immodest, defiant of authority and neglected domestic duties'.[136]

The educational initiatives of nationalism, both in home and formal schooling, tried to devise an educational curriculum to counteract modernist influences. A vast number of tracts and pamphlets were written to instil this new traditional Hindu morality, and girls' schools were created to dispense it. Thus there were competing ideological strains and curricula regarding women's education which went far beyond the issues of literacy, information, and skills. Chatterjee devalues or erases these competing ideological strands or differences by a selective reading of men's writings in the late nineteenth and early twentieth century, as well as of women's autobiographies and reflections. His reading and presentation have the advantage of manufacturing consent by attempting to show women's active role in their interpellated subjectivity. He claims that women saw this surrender as their contribution to the national cause and as 'the honour of a new social responsibility', and the 'new patriarchy' as 'a new and entirely legitimate sign of subordination'.[137] The moral lineage of mythic Aryan womanhood, critically discussed by Uma Chakravarty, or that of the epic women figures of the Ramayana and Mahabharata, such as Sita, Sati, and Savitri, were offered as positive options for their obedience to patriarchy rather than for their moments of excess and transgression.[138] This version is different from how Sarala Debi Choudhurani put tradition to assertive use by drawing upon the Hindu pantheon and myths through the notion of Shakti (deified female power) for direct personal agency in nationalist armed struggle.[139]

4   Conclusion

We should return now to the question of decolonisation with which this essay began. Throughout I have tried to show how what I have called an illiberal

---

135   Sarkar 1997f, p. 205.
136   Chakrabarty 1998, p. 61.
137   Chatterjee 1990, p. 244.
138   Chakravarty 1990.
139   On Sarala Debi Choudhurani, see Kumar 1993.

form of nationalism is in essence a right-wing cultural nationalism which arrogates to itself the ideology and agency for a genuine decolonisation, despite its demonstrably anti-emancipatory politics. By separating culture and discourse from economy and social organisation, and constructing a national community upon a unifying cultural essence, this type of nationalism erases history, social relations and ideologies of radical difference, such as class, caste, 'race' and patriarchy. This creates a condition of domination and subalternity for large numbers of people who live within the space of such a national imaginary and its actual manifestation as the state. The epistemologies involved in such an anti-liberatory ideological and political operation consist of a profound repudiation of historical materialism and critical sociology.

As this essay shows, a major political consequence of such a theorisation of hegemony and subalternity is manifested in the derivative character of social subjectivity and agency for women. Their subalternity is rendered invisible or unimportant. The domination of women implicit in Hindu, or any other, cultural nationalism is not simply described by theorists such as Chatterjee and Chakrabarty, but given a prescriptive status. But large numbers of Indian/Bengali women since the nineteenth century do not agree with their secondary and objectified status as subjects rather than citizens of the nation. Their house has been divided for over a century. As people who have actually suffered the tyranny of this patriarchal nationalism, their understanding of and relationship to modernity is not only more complex than the 'subaltern' theorists would have us believe, but ultimately positive. Current struggles by and for women in India against patriarchy, regarding *sati*, dowry, female infanticide, and the bill for Muslim women's personal law, all indicate this attitude of critical modernity. Women's awareness of the imperfections of the modern nation-state has not prompted most of them to fetishise cultural nationalism and Indian tradition in the name of anti- or post-colonialism. Much of Bengali literature, by writers of both sexes, speaks simultaneously to colonial and familial oppression. Even in the nineteenth-century literature, words such as *paradhin* (under the control of someone else) and *swadhin* (free or self-owning) are loaded with meanings which encompass colonisation and the oppressive character of the indigenous societies.[140] As books such as *The History of Doing*[141] show, when women became actors in the anti-colonial struggle they were dynamically active in many directions regarding social justice. Their writings brought together the trope of freedom from the gilded cages of their family homes and the freedom of their country from colonial domination.

---

140   On *swadhin* and *paradhin*, and the general implication of women's language of freedom
          and domination, see Tharu and Lalata 1993.
141   Kumar 1993.

Women's difference from men in their approach to nation-building ranges from demands for property or economic self-sufficiency to entitlement of political agency and citizenship. These demands often are connected to a resistance to patriarchal proprieties of women's sexuality and motherhood. Tanika Sarkar shows us how women's autobiographies reflect a desire for much more than the roles of chaste wives, good mothers, or good daughters.[142] Chatterjee or Chakrabarty do not seem to register this, for if they did they could not continue to valorise the 'new patriarchy' of nationalism despite women's problems connected with early and arranged marriages, marital rapes, early and numerous childbirths, and high mortality and morbidity. After all, what they consider as women's acquiescence to nationalist patriarchy may also be seen as women's desexualisation. Their religiosity or espousal of celibacy upon widowhood may be seen as rational responses to the forced and onerous role of Hindu wife and mother, which also entails unwelcome pregnancy. Thus, the choice of women to become maiden educationists may contain elements of resistance to their subordination. Even a cursory reading of women's writings will show that they displayed a much stronger passion for reason, education, and politics than for romantic love. It is not the home, the passion of nationalist thought, but the public sphere, resonating with a discourse of reason, which attracted women inexorably.

Considered in this light, the typological barriers in consciousness erected by the nineteenth-century Hindu elite are not secure ones, and for reasons not found in Partha Chatterjee. We often see 'Westernised' and 'nationalist' constructs coming close to each other for reasons far different from Chatterjee's thesis of 'resolution'. Here modernity is not simply instrumentalised, stripped of its criticality, and annexed by tradition. More often tradition recedes, leaving grounds for a nonpatriarchal subjecthood and agency for women. Nor are the female 'fragments' of the nation such pathetic typecasts in the fringe of Bengali middle-class respectability. Reading between the lines of middle-class male editing and representation of actresses such as Binodini as pathetic creatures, we find traces of strident women who are satirised by farces of the nineteenth century. These women show a distinct propensity to flout both 'new' and 'old' patriarchy. This 'subaltern' agency for resistance among middle-class women, their counter-discourse, is invisible in subaltern studies' schema of 'resolution'. This claim to 'resolution', incidentally, was not made by nineteenth-century nationalists themselves, but rather by theorists such as Chatterjee. The nationalists themselves recognised the unresolved nature of 'the women's question',

---

142   Sarkar 1993b.

which prompted them to maintain a vigilance over the discursive field regarding women and moral education.[143] It is Partha Chatterjee and Dipesh Chakrabarty and their fellow post-colonialists who project such a seamless image of social hegemony of cultural nationalism. What is more, by doing so they contribute to the legitimation of violence against women. When they legitimate a traditional social discourse in the name of anti-colonialism, they validate a masculinist discourse of community. They are trapped in this stance by their ideological, that is, socially occlusive, theoretical formulation. Indeed, decolonisation, in the sense of a broader view of social justice, is not conceivable within this schema. This occlusion of the social and over-valorisation of the premodern cultural in its most benevolent form allows for a false empowerment of women – the creation of the myth of the Devi, woman as a goddess figure. The violence against women latent in this figure shows in the actualities of repression in women's lives.

In conclusion, we need to remember that the monolithic character of Indian/Bengali nationalist thought as projected by Partha Chatterjee and others of the subaltern group is his/their own ideological construction within the epistemology and politics of post-structuralist post-colonialism. It is primarily Chatterjee who creates this synthetic ideological entity and invents the 'resolutionary' claim in its support. No history of nationalism or of women in India would support either his monolithic construction or this claim. Through a discursive organisation of a slippage between life and ideological constructions, Chatterjee reduces all forms of consciousness during the colonial era to the status of nationalism and anti-nationalism or colonial discourse. This gesture restricts his readers to a small set of selected anti-modernist texts and a binary politics. His selection obeys his theoretical schema and forces all ideas or cultural forms to be absorbed or arrayed in two columns of cultural essences – the colonial/modern and the anti-colonial/pre- and anti-modern. It is through this ideological strategy that the story of women's containment and betrayal by property-owning cultural nationalism becomes the story of their contentment and valorisation. This is the fusion of patriarchal brahmanical de-scription with pre-scription which upholds Chatterjee's slim claim to the hegemony of nationalist thought. But it should be obvious that any project of decolonisation which separates property and power from moral proprieties, avoids the issue of social justice, and subsumes differences within an essentialist rhetoric of cultural nationalism, can only lead to new and internal forms of colonisation.

---

143   These issues, particularly regarding morality, are discussed at length in Choudhury 1988.

PART 2

The Making of a Subject: Gender, 'Race' and Class

··

CHAPTER 10

Introducing Racism: Notes towards an Anti-racist Feminism

From its very early phase the word 'silence' has been important in the vocabulary of feminist writing. It spoke of being silent or having been silenced – of two distinct but related themes. In a cluster with 'silence' there are other words speaking of gaps, absences, being 'hidden in history', of being organised out of social space or discourse, or into apathy, and of 'a problem without a name'. Not exceptionally, therefore, there also appeared other expressions – signifying women's struggles about gaining or giving a voice, a direct assumption of our subjectivity, creating a version of the world from 'our' own standpoint, and thus speaking from our own 'self' or 'centre' or experience.

For many years now I have read and taught this literature. I have spoken of it as combatting sexism internally within ourselves and externally in relation to a sexist world. I did this for years and in a way it had a resonance for me, and gave me the feeling that finally I had a way of interpreting what I felt since my early childhood. But very soon I began to develop a discomfort and sometimes even a feeling of antagonism towards this type of feminist writing, for reasons initially unclear to me. Of course, this was accompanied by feelings of guilt and worries that perhaps my politics were not feminist after all. Needless to say, I did not encounter feminists in the university who experienced any basic and fundamental sense of insufficiency with this feminism, which passes as *the* feminism. I had heard of old struggles between feminists on the ground of class, but when I came into the scene the talk of class, if it ever existed in Canada, had ceased to have any serious content. With the exception of isolated instances, class was paid mere lip-service, and the discourse of gender, professionalism and mobility had asserted itself in the university. Lacking colleagues, I spoke to my students and other women in the city who, like me, also happened to be non-white, or so-called 'immigrants' from the less industrialised parts of Europe and Latin America. It was speaking with these women that saved my sanity, because this feeling of discomfort that I had with feminist currency or discourse seemed to be something other than paranoia or reactive politics on my part. In editing 'Women of Colour', Issue 16 of the feminist magazine *Fireweed*, some of us tried to grope towards a formulation of what felt wrong and of some of the reasons for our entry at a wrong angle into the feminist world of Toronto.

In time I began to understand better what was going on in my classroom. The truth was that neither I nor many of my students with a Third World or southern European background were participating in our own capacities as 'persons' in that classroom; rather we were 'personas', characters called 'students' and 'teacher' in a Canadian university, learning the 'feminist framework' which in the end turned out to be the story of the European bourgeois family. At the end of some of the books we used, a section on 'women of colour' was included, but this topic was not integrated into the book's overall perspective. Similarly, in some of the university's courses a section or two was taught on the topic of 'women of colour' or 'immigrant women', but again the issues were not integrated into the course material as a whole. I began to toy with the idea of designing a course on 'Women of Colour' or 'Immigrant Women ... and racism!'

So this was the issue – that once more there were gaps or silences, that people like us were never present in what we taught and read. In volumes of material produced in the West on women, with all the talk of 'herland' and 'herstory', our absences have not ceased; our voices, if we have any, are very small ones. I have rarely, while doing work in Women's Studies proper, come across a framework or methodology which addresses or legitimises the existence and concerns of women like us, or helps give our voices strength and authenticity. How then can we speak of 'gaining voices', 'shattering silences', of sharing experiences, being empowered, and so on? The great bulk of Canadian literature on women and what passes for Women's Studies curricula leaves the reader with the impression that women from the Third World and southern Europe are a very negligible part of the living and labouring population in Canada. Furthermore, the silences in this literature would seem to imply that nothing much is to be learned about the nature of economic, social and political organisation of Canada by studying the lives or concerns of women of colour. Not even most of the works of feminist women writers claiming to be interested in 'class' in Canada contain full-length chapters on such a population. One might ask what produces this phenomenon which simultaneously expresses a lack of consciousness as well as a false consciousness? And this happens in a country with the history of a settler colonial state and economy, where 'reserves' exist in large numbers for the Indigenous peoples, where a working class is still being created through racist immigration policies and segmentation of the labour market, and where a u.s. dependent capitalism has long ago entered an imperialist phase?

The full answer to my question of how we got here is complex and not fully visible to me. But I do have these notes towards an answer which offer us a possibility of explanation as well as a basis for moving towards an anti-racist feminism. It is this possibility rather than the urge for sharing experiences which impels me to this writing. The answer begins in the history of colonial and imperialist economic, social and political practices which have in the past and now continue to construct Canada. It also lies in certain habits or ways of thinking and seeing that have emerged in the course of history, as well as clearly developed ideologies and methods for constructing social and political discourse – feminist or any other.

For my exploration I will rely to some extent on Antonio Gramsci's notion of common sense, which, put simply, might be seen as the submerged part of the iceberg which is visible to us as ideology. Writers such as Fredric Jameson have phrased it in terms of the political unconscious. Its efficacy for understanding the situation of non-white people living in the West is clearly demonstrated by a volume produced in Britain about race and racism in the 1970s, entitled *The Empire Strikes Back*. In this volume Errol Lawrence paraphrases Gramsci in a way which is useful for me. He writes:

> The term 'common sense' is generally used to denote a down-to-earth 'good sense'. It is thought to represent the distilled truths of centuries of practical experience; so much so that to say of an idea or practice that it is only common sense, is to appeal over the logic and argumentation of intellectuals to what all reasonable people have known in their 'heart of hearts' to be right and proper. Such an appeal can act at one and the same time to foreclose any discussion about certain ideas and practices and to legitimate them.[1]

What is more, common sense is accretional, and being unthought out it leaves plenty of room for contradictions, myths, guesses and rumours. It is therefore by no means a unified body of knowledge, and as a form of our everyday way of being it is deeply practical in nature. The general direction of its movement as such comes from common socio-economic and cultural practices which, in turn, common sense helps to organise. From this point of view the history, ontology, and ongoing practice of an imperialist capitalist society appears to me to find its epistemology in the common sense of racism. Whereas clearly stated racism definitely exists, the more problematic aspect for us is this common sense racism which holds the norms and forms thrown up by a few hundred years of pillage, extermination, slavery, colonisation and neo-colonisation. It is in these diffused normalised sets of assumptions, knowledge,

---

1   Lawrence 1982, p. 48.

and so-called cultural practices that we come across racism in its most power-ful, because pervasive, form.

These norms and forms are so much a daily currency, they have been around for so long in different incarnations, that they are not mostly (even for an anti-racist person) objects of investigation, for they are not even visible. They produce silences or absences, creating gaps and fissures through which non-white women, for example, disappear from the social surface. Racism becomes an everyday life and 'normal' way of seeing. Its banality and invisibility is such that it is quite likely that there may be entirely 'politically correct' white indi-viduals who have a deeply racist perception of the world. It is entirely possible to be critical of racism at the level of ideology, politics and institutions – do Southern Africa solidarity work, or work with 'women of colour' for example – and yet possess a great quantity of common sense racism. This may coexist, for example, with a passively racist aesthetic. Outside of the area which is con-sidered to be 'political' or workplace – i.e. public life – this same white activist (feminist or solidarity worker) probably associates mainly or solely with white, middle-class people. That fine line which divides pleasure and comfort from politics is constituted with the desire of being with 'people like us'.

While white obviously racist individuals are avoided, the elements of every-day life – family forms, food, sport, etc. – are shot through with racism. Non-white people associating with them will/do feel oppressed by their very way of 'being' rather than by what they say or do 'politically'. These white progress-ive activists may have dealt with the overtly political, ideological dimension of their own racism, but not with their common sense racism. It is perhaps for this reason that the racism of the left feminists is almost always of omission rather than that of commission. They probably truly cannot see us or why it is that racism and 'ethnicity' are integral to the study of women in Canada – even when they study the area of labour/capital relations, i.e. class. And those feminists who do see us or that racism is an issue very often deal with it in the spirit of Christian humanism, on the ground of morality and doing good, or in the spirit of bourgeois democracy, which 'includes' or adds on representatives from the 'minority' communities.

The fact of the matter is that it is almost impossible for European societies as they are to eliminate racism in a thoroughgoing way. Racism is not simply a set of attitudes and practices that they level towards us, their socially constructed 'other', but it is the very principle of self-definition of European/Western soci-eties. It could be said that what is otherwise known as European civilisation – as manifested in the realm of arts and ideas and in daily life – is a sublimated, formalised, or simply a practised version of racism. In his book *Orientalism*, Edward Said draws our attention to this as he points out that the 'Orient was almost a European invention' and 'one of its deepest and most recurring images of the other' – but additionally '… the Orient has helped to define Europe (or the West) as its contrasting image, ideal, personality and experience'.[2] What he says of 'orientalism' can be said of racism as well, that it is '… a style of thought based upon an ontological and epistemological distinction made between "the Orient", and (most of the time) "the Occident"'.[3]

If we substitute the two terms with Black and white, or better still with a comprehensive binary of white and non-white, European (including the u.s. and Canada) and non-European – we get the picture. Europe or America created (and continues to create) myths of imperialism, of barbarism/savagery, a general inferiority of the conquered, enslaved and colonised peoples and also created myths of exoticism at the same instant as it defined itself also as an 'other' of these. The negative determinations of Europe's or America's/Canada's racism manifest themselves everywhere. Some of the humblest to the most cerebral/aesthetic dimensions of white people's life are informed with racism. Its notion of female beauty, for example, which is so inextricably meshed with eroticism (sexuality) is fundamentally racist – not only sexist – not to mention some of the obviously 'social' practices, such as mothering, 'good housekeeping', etc. The racist assumptions about 'the black family' as manifested in the works of u.s. sociologists such as Daniel Moynahan, constitute the negative dialectic of a 'good American (white) home (family)'. This is taken up very clearly in the essays of Pratibha Parmar, Hazel Carby, Errol Lawrence, et al. in *The Empire Strikes Back*, where the racism of British, middle-class social assumptions are fully bared by being put next to the white/European 'civilised' ideals of the family. As many Black writers point out – most importantly Franz Fanon in *The Wretched of the Earth* and Aimé Césaire in *Discourse on Colonialism* – the coloniser (slaver or imperialist or whatever) not only reorganised the identity and social space of the colonised, but also at the same instant, through the same process, his own. Europe was not only substantively itself, but also non-Africa, non-India.

It is not surprising then that both in its omissions and commissions racism is an essential organising device of European (white) feminist discourse – as much as of any other type of discourse. If this were to be effectively challenged it would need the turning of every stone of imperialism. White feminists would have to re-examine the very ground of their historical-social identity, their own subjectivity, their ways of being and seeing every bit of what passes for 'cul-

---

2 Said, 1978, pp. 1–2.

3 Ibid., p. 2.

ture' or art. In short, it would be a process of re-making themselves, and their society, in totality. This would of course have to take place in the world, not in their heads, since common sense, as I said before, is a very practical matter. In the world, as practices, it would have to be a kind of anti-imperialist, anti-capitalism that tries not only to undo ideologies, institutions, economies and state powers as they presently exist, but also to reconstruct the most mundane aspects of social life, and to re-think class – that well-spring of struggles and changes.

So we have a sense now of what may be some of the reasons for the fact that in the annals of feminist history, or 'herstory', in Canada, there are only fleeting glimpses of us. A few allusions to 'slavery', a few numbers indicating a statistical state of being in the records of government agencies, some reference to an entity called the 'immigrant woman' or the 'visible minority' woman, are what we have so far. The result is that for a few years I stood next to a blackboard and in the name of women – all women – taught a one-dimensional theory of gender and patriarchy, which primarily reveals the concerns and preoccupations of white, middle-class women. And I sensed among many of my women students a disinterest, a withdrawal and a patient resignation to the irrelevancies of an institutional education. Now I no longer do that kind of teaching, and instead try to raise the issues I raised in the paragraphs above to question those methods of social analysis current among us, which are by and large liberal-empiricist or idealist (ideological) ones. I also try to show how these methods, in the end, serve the interest of the status quo – a white imperialist hegemonic discourse. This cannot but serve the interests of white, middle-class women.

While reading feminist writing, a reader cannot but be aware of the particular connotation the word 'woman' takes on, which extends way beyond description into the realm of power and politics. Gendered divisions of labour and accompanying relations of power are connotatively inseparable from this word nowadays. But as it gains a political nuance, so it also takes on a quality of universality and an overridingness. As the word becomes in some ways political/ actionable on one ground – that of gender and patriarchy – so it also becomes an abstraction. How does this happen? And what does it have to do with not attending to racism?

In this method of operating, the abstraction is created when the different social moments which constitute the 'concrete' being of any social organisation and existence are pulled apart, and each part assumed to have a substantive, self-regulating structure. This becomes apparent when we see gender, race and class each considered as a separate issue – as ground for separate oppressions. The social whole – albeit fraught with contradictions – is then constructed by an aggregative exercise. According to this, I, as a South Asian woman, then have a double oppression to deal with, first on the count of gender, and second on the count of race. I am thus segmented into different social moments, made a victim of discrete determinations. So it is willing the moment of gender, when it is seen as a piece by itself, rupturing its constitutive relationship with race and class. Needless to say, race and class could also be meted the same treatment. What this does is to empty out gender relations of their general social context, content and dynamism. This, along with the primacy that gender gains (since the primary social determinant is perceived as patriarchy), subsumes all other social relations, indeed renders them often invisible. The particular – i.e. one moment – begins to stand in for the whole.

This process is fully at work in the method and social analysis of much of the feminist literature we read. What seems to happen is that the word 'woman' takes on a conceptual/categorical status encoding patriarchal social relations which are viewed as substantive structures. So issues pertaining to 'women' would be discussed largely without locating them in a historical, social organisation context, such as that of race and class (in the case of Canada). In fact, the notion 'women' in plurality is substituted with that of *Woman* – a singular yet universal entity. So it becomes possible for a feminist journal to call itself *Canadian Woman Studies*. The assumption is, of course, that all women are one, and this is inescapable since the logic of such a method of decontextualising, or dehistoricising, can only lead to this conclusion since the aspect of gender is not constitutively related to other social and formative relations.

Having established this pseudo-universality which confers a legitimacy and an interpretive and organising status to this notion of 'woman' – the actual pieces of writing, however, go on to speak of some very concrete existing problems and experiences of particular groups of women, and not to do philosophy. They are in fact specific problems and experiences of the woman who is writing, or of people like herself, that are peculiarly oppressive for her. There is, of course, nothing wrong with that – as long as we know it and are not presented with it as 'Everywoman's problems' and concerns. This is of course not done, since to speak in the name of all confers a legitimacy without which such a stand of authority could not have been constructed. Nor are problems of race and class emphasised or seen as related to gender issues, because such a thing would break down the homogeneity and even reveal the class location of the theorist/writer. The result of course is that with which I started at the very beginning – my/our experience – a new political and academic field in which we are marked by absence, subsumption and, if we are noticed at all, we are given an interpreted status by those who are in a position to control and generate forms of discourse. As at the level of method, one moment stands in for others in a controlling, hegemonic relation to the rest, so that in the actual writing, one group of women's interests (however valid for them) is smuggled in, masquerading as the interests of all women.

Both the method and the politics implied in it are old. It is the fact that they are employed in an oppositional political context – namely feminism – that makes it initially hard to recognise them. In *The German Ideology*, Marx talked about this very method of extrapolation, universalisation, establishing 'mystical' connections and eventually interpretive schemes, 'theories'. This is his critique of ideology. In his 'Introduction' to what has come to be called *The Grundrisse*, he further critiques this ideological method, when he makes an attempt to create a method of social analysis in which the different social moments can retain both their specificity and reveal their implication and constitutive relation to all other specific social relations.

The advantage of this ideological procedure is well brought out in the context of the bourgeoisie's assumption of political power. We see in several texts – beginning with the most explicit *Communist Manifesto* to *The Eighteenth Brumaire of Louis Bonaparte* – Marx speaks of how it benefits a particular class to speak of itself/its interests, etc. as the universal class/interests. It is a way to gaining power and keeping power. As Gramsci put it years later in the context of Italy, to gain and keep leadership one must exert a moral and social hegemony. If the middle-class women's interests are those of all of us, then we must drown ourselves in their version of the world and their politics. This gives them a solid base to wage their own hegemonic fractional conflict with bourgeois males, while we intensify our own oppression. If we were actually to advance our own position, we could not but show that organisation by race (or racism) is a fundamental way of forming class in Canada, and that this formation of class is a fully gendered one. Far from being our 'sisters', these middle-class women are complicit in our domination. Being class members of a middle class created on the terrain of imperialism and capitalism – hiding it (even from themselves perhaps) behind ideological methods constructed for ruling – they cannot but be part of our problem, not the solution.

This version that I have offered of the mainstream feminist theories, or even of those socialist feminists who are colour-blind or leave out the determinations of class, is also arrived at by being sensitised by the work of Dorothy E. Smith. In her work on Marx's method, attempts at creating a sociology from a woman's standpoint, and enquiry into how the work of sociologists (academics in general) in the process of ruling holds an exploitive system in place – Smith gives us an extremely valuable insight into the production and practice of ideology. Also valuable has been the work of Michel Foucault, who bared for us the role of power in constructing/defining what constitutes knowledge and thus in constituting the 'other' in the course of, or for the purpose of, domination. It must also be mentioned that the liberal empiricist method of thinking in terms of single issues, so current in North American academia and politics, is also particularly favourable to this ideological way of thinking about (and subsequently acting in) the world. And all this fits right in with the racist common sense of a people whose self-definition and social organisation, not to mention economic organisation, has been fundamentally based on racism and imperialism.

The ground of discourse as much as the ground of everyday living are contested grounds. Class struggle in Canada goes on – even in the name of extending a helping hand. Class rule solidifies itself in an oppositional guise, where bourgeois men and women wrestle for power but form a solid body vis-a-vis us. Maybe one should re-read Mao tse Tung – and figure out where the contradictions lie – and where they are genuinely antagonistic or non-antagonistic. The poor in the French Revolution did get to storm the Bastille, but Napoleon came to power. Here we – the other women – haven't even stormed the Bastille, but a Napoleon is already in the wings.

In the Matter of 'X': Building 'Race' into Sexual Harassment

In the summer of 1992, I received a call from a law firm to work as an expert witness for a complaint of sexual harassment of a woman. There was a problem, however, to consider and to accommodate. She was not just a 'woman' undergoing the usual sexual harassment common in workplaces, but she was a 'black woman'. How could we build that fact of blackness into the case so that we could say that racism was an integral part of the sexual harassment which she underwent? We knew that there were three oppressions (among others) at work in Canadian society – namely, racism, sexism and classism – and that X's experience included all; but how were we to think of these oppressions in such a way that we could show her harassment as a composite or a crystallised form of both?

I decided to work on the case because X's oppression enraged me, and also offered a political and an analytical challenge. How to think of gender, 'race' and class in terms of what is called 'intersectionality', that is, in terms of their interactiveness, their ways of mutually constructing or reinforcing each other, is a project that is still in the process of being worked out. Somehow, we know almost instinctively that these oppressions, separately named as sexism, racism and class exploitation, are intimately connected. But when it comes to showing how, it is always difficult, and strains the capacity of our conventional ways of speaking on such matters. And, if abstract theorisation is partially possible, the concrete uncovering of how they actually work continues to have an elusive quality to it. The case of X is one of innumerable experiences of its kind, in varying degrees of intensity and complexity, which mark lives of black women in the West. Here the West means the u.s. and Canada, but it includes Britain and other European countries as well. For that reason also, it was a challenge to think through a problem which exists within such a wide scope.

1   A Brief Outline of the Case (Outline Provided by the Firm of Cornish and Roland)

It is useful at the outset to specify who X is, though very briefly and mainly in terms of her work trajectory. But this offers some of the particulars with regard to which I tried to understand how she was specifically sexually harassed as a black woman. The following are some of the facts put forward as a part of the submissions of the claimant X.

Job Progression:

1.   X is a 45-year-old black woman and sole-support mother.
2.   X began working for Y company in 1980 on the assembly lines, first as a packer for detergent, then shampoo, then toothpaste, and finally soap. These jobs were classified as 'light' and were predominantly female.
3.   The work force at Y was predominantly white; also, to the best of X's knowledge, she was one of only two black female employees in the production area of the factory.
4.   Towards the end of 1983 or the beginning of 1984, X applied for and was promoted to the position of packer 'heavy-duty' in the soap department. 'Heavy' jobs were historically performed exclusively by men and were performed in an area that was physically separated from the area in which X had previously been working. X was the only woman employed in that area. She was also one of very few visible minority employees in the area.
5.   In mid-1984, X was again promoted – this time to 'utility', a job demanding greater skill. She was required to learn how to trouble-shoot on the line and to drive a forklift, to obtain supplies for the line and replace the operator for breaks and lunch. This job was also within the 'heavy' tasks area and had been exclusively performed by men; X was the only woman employed in this capacity.
6.   X was next transferred to 'mills' as a prerequisite for promotion to the 'operator' position within the heavy tasks area. In this area she mainly worked alone mixing soap for the assembly lines.
7.   As an operator, X was responsible for overseeing a packing line operation. This included the requirement to work in a 'lead hand' type of relationship with the utility and packer. The position required her to follow written instructions, document mechanical problems and master the new vocabulary specific to the job. In addition, X was required to have a more in-depth knowledge of the operation and equipment on the line in order to adjust and trouble-shoot its operation. Her performance would essentially be judged by the rate at which her line could maintain production; to do so, X required a high level of cooperation from her male co-workers who filled the packer and utility positions on her line.[1]

---

1   Submissions of the Claimant 'X,' nos. 1–7.

X's experience of harassment at the workplace was extensive and ranged from job sabotages to being subjected to various obscenities. They may be summed up as:

a.   active sabotage of the work for which she was responsible,
b.   discriminatory treatment with respect to training and work assistance by senior co-workers,
c.   forced exposure to hostile material which denigrated both her race and sex, placed at and near her work station,
d.   social isolation and ostracism by co-workers,
e.   public pejorative name-calling and sexually and racially derogatory remarks.[2]

Particular details of this conduct, randomly selected by me, include the following:

11.   ... X was subjected to adverse treatment: the white female lead hands would run the line she was packing at an unusually high speed, would damage her locker and referred to her publicly as 'a fucking bitch'.

12.   Although X complained to management, the behavior was allowed to continue. Further, when her co-workers threatened to have her fired and complained about her to the foreman, she was transferred out of the area to the soap department.

19.   Co-workers created an environment that was hostile to her gender and race. Pictures of 'Sunshine Girls' [barely-clothed women consistently featured on the third page of *The Toronto Sun*] were displayed in her work area. When X complained, the co-workers were told to remove them, but they refused. Despite the workers' insubordination, no action was taken against them. Note, however, that when white women walked through the area, the posters were taken down and hidden. X also heard racially derogatory comments directed at a Filipino male worker. She herself was repeatedly referred to as a 'bitch'.

21.   ... Obscene pictures were left at her work station and in her toolbox. One was a hand drawn sketch in which a black woman was giving a 'blow job' to a white man. Another was a picture also hand drawn of a black woman giving a white man a 'hand job' while a gang of white men stood in line for their turn. X was repeatedly referred to as 'a fucking bitch' and 'cunt'. One worker went so far as to throw a bar of soap at her which hit her on her head; though her foreman was nearby, he did nothing. On one occasion, she went out to lunch with a male co-worker, the co-worker was asked on his return whether X had 'fucked' him in the parking lot.[3]

---

2   Submissions, p. 2.
3   Submissions, nos. 11, 12, 19, 21.

Though X remains anonymous in terms of her personal identity, these details allow us to imagine her more concretely.

2   Reflexive Perspective

Upon some reflection it became clear to me that we have to develop a critical understanding of how 'sexual harassment' is constructed with regard to women. By this I mean the need to consider two key issues, one being the conceptualisation of the term 'sexual', the other the category 'woman' or 'women' that is consistently, if contingently, linked to the complaint. The latter is perhaps the best starting point for beginning to examine the former. So let us start with the categories 'woman'/'black woman'. For after all, it is the need to make a transition from 'woman' to 'black woman' that needed my expertise.

Why is there a problem in making this shift? What changes if we do? If we keep these questions in mind and reflect on the category 'woman' as conventionally used in Canada (or in other Western countries) in legal or ordinary parlance, we come to feel the fact that this category is simultaneously empty and full of social content. It both erases *and* asserts the society's history, social organisation and prevalent ideologies, values and symbolic cultures. It both validates and denies powered relations of difference. What I mean by these statements is that when we use this term 'woman' non-adjectivally in any given situation, we don't actually mean an *abstract*, a *general* or an *essential* entity. What we mean or refer to is a woman whose life conditions are most in keeping with the prevailing social, legal and cultural structures, institutions and beliefs. That is, it is a woman whose life lies squarely in the middle of the dominant social organisation of the masculine and the feminine, or is most normalised within its gender organisation. It is so normalised as to have become a sort of a code – this 'woman' needs no specifying adjective or adjunct signifier. In societies based on class and 'race', she is neither classed nor 'raced'. Who on earth could this woman be?

In answering this question while sitting in Canada or the U.S., conducting a relatively uncomplicated case of sexual harassment, the actual subject emerges. The 'woman' in question, serving as the base type for sexual harassment complaints, is a *white* woman. She demands *this* specific adjective, if we are to stretch the law beyond her to other women. Otherwise, though we can deal with her case, we cannot even begin to address the wrongs of her sister, the *black* woman, specifically here an Afro-Canadian woman, whose difference enters into the peculiar type of sexual harassment meted out to her. And yet, *normally*, daily, why is this category 'woman' non-adjectivised for a white woman, while all others have their differences 'raced' or 'coloured?'

The erasure of the fact of a white woman's whiteness which elevates her into a universal category is proof of the racist nature of Canadian/Western social organisation, moral regulation and cultural practices. Silence or absence does not always, or here, mean powerlessness. Here the silence or erasure amounts to a reference to the fact of an all-pervasive presence. About this we say – 'it goes without saying ...'. When a subject becomes so central as to be an icon or a typology for what goes on everyday, situating devices such as adjectives become unnecessary.

So the racism that X encounters during her sexual harassment begins in this undifferentiated notion of the 'woman'. In the Canadian context, it is an unspoken example of a social organisation based on 'race', where some are typologically 'woman' and 'others' are its variants, such as, black woman or woman of colour. What this abstraction both encodes and conceals is that no one is spared. The whole of the socio-legal apparatus and environment are, in practice, in social relations and values, 'raced'. It is *because* white women are implicitly but fundamentally 'raced' as white and thus as members of the 'master race', that they don't need to be named as such. This leaves us with a dilemma of either naming them in terms of the overall racist social organisation to get some actual insight into inequality, or of not naming them while 'other' named women suffer injustices based on their difference. These are the options before us, and it is not a surprise then that the shift is hard to make from sexual harassment of 'women' to that of 'black women'. It pulls at deep roots, and calls for a shift at other levels of perception and politics.

Now, if we can accept that women are differently 'sexed' in a 'raced' society, we can then begin to combine sexism with racism. Others before us have done so – Pratibha Parmar, for example, uses the term 'sexist racism', which can be easily reversed into 'racist sexism'. This composite concept codes a gender-'race' organisation of the Western societies in general and the society X lives in, and this society is historically connected to colonialism and slavery, and presently to an imperialist form of capital. So the central sociological issue which arises out of the case of X is that of 'racist sexism' and its various ramifications, which have had an overwhelmingly negative impact on her economic and personal life. These are the issues which need to be understood and through which the notion of 'sexual harassment' needs to be considered. They involve a broader analysis of Canadian society in terms of history, political economy, culture which are structured through social organisation of gender, 'race' and class.

I see X's life as an existential whole which is constituted by a diverse set of social relations which cannot be separated out in actuality. Racism is after all a concrete social formation. It cannot be independent of other social relations of power and ruling which organise the society, such as those of gender and class. Similarly, gender and class, in a society organised through practices and ideologies of 'race' and ethnicity, are structurally and ideologically inseparable from them. As such, one can only think of racism, sexism and class as interconstitutive social relations of organised and administered domination. It is their constantly mediating totality which shapes people's perception of each other, and as such, X's co-workers cannot see her as three separate social entities – 'raced', gendered and classed. They see her as a *black woman*, in the entirety of that construction, about whom there are existing social practices and cultural stereotypes, with which they are all familiar. One can see how gender matters within the 'raced' groups and between them. Both black men and black women are subject to racism, but there is a distinct gender-appropriate difference in 'raced' stereotypes regarding them. Similarly, though white and black women both suffer from sexism, there is a 'raced' difference in the cultural common sense regarding how they are to be gendered. Stereotypes regarding all Canadian women share a common element of patriarchal or gender organisation, but this patriarchy operates through radically different significations and expectations of their social presences and functions.

I shall also use the term 'racist sexualism' to convey the female/male or heterosexual dynamic of racist sexism, as I shall also claim that racist sexism is wholly possible between white and black women (or women of colour) not just between white men and black women. I shall endeavour to show in my reading of the case that racist sexism is the foundation on which racist sexual harassment is erected and that this occurs in the case of X and all other women who are non-white. I hope that by pointing out this simultaneous, formative and dynamic interrelation between racism, sexism and implicitly of class, since race and class coincide in North America, I shall help to avoid a pointless and time-consuming debate about which is primary.

3   Reading X's Case

When the packer and utility finally returned, X attempted, for the second time, to start up the line. When she moved around in position to see whether the packer and utility were at work, she saw a group of white male employees standing around the line looking toward her. At that point she noticed that someone had placed a twelve inch long, bright green, *Irish Spring* soap carving of a penis with white foam at its tip, on the assembly line where X would be forced to see it.

The carving remained on the line for 30–45 minutes in full view of X
and the group of white male co-workers who hovered around jeering and
staring at X ... X recognised the incident to be not only humiliating and
isolating, but a threat.[4]

My reading of the case of X begins with this incident of the carved penis. In a
history of incidents all of which amounted to small or big acts of harassment,
this marks the culmination point. This event and her reaction to it must be seen
as both a personal experience and a social moment, neither of which can be
understood without an examination of her workplace. Her workplace, similar
to others, cannot be seen only as a place of economic production, but must also
be understood as a coherent social and cultural environment which is organised through known and predictable social relations, practices, cultural norms
and expectations. What happens in this environment, which is daily and highly
regulated, cannot just be treated as random or unpredictable behaviour. As we
shall see from the general pattern of her harassment (as submitted in X's complaint) there was nothing random about the carved penis incident.

This incident marked the moment of X's ultimate humiliation, where not
only was she forced to see this repugnant object, but also to provide a spectacle for others in doing so. As we see from the submissions, X felt this to be
not a joke, but rather an act of violence against her and a threat. In a manner
of speaking it is in its intensity and singularity an archetypal experience, and
it highlights for the reader the real quality of her six-year work life in this company. The perspective which I have introduced in the beginning of this paper
is the lens through which we can now view X's work life and her workplace.

Let us begin with the organisation and 'race' composition of her workplace.
It is significant for our purpose that X worked in an almost all-white workplace. When she worked in the women's section there was, to the best of her
knowledge, only one other non-white woman working on the same floor with
her. There were approximately fifty white women working with her. When she
moved into the men's section not only were there no women there, but the
one or two non-white men who existed, appeared and disappeared among a
male white work force of about a dozen. This workplace (as in other industrial
concerns) was divided into men's and women's, 'heavy' and 'light' labour sections, respectively. As a whole, then, the 'normal' atmosphere was white, where
the absence or exclusion of non-white people was nothing out of the ordinary.

---

4 *Submissions, nos.* 29, 30.

This recognition of the 'normal' character of her workplace allows us to treat her experience there as a piece of everyday life, which then needs to be broken down, or deconstructed to reveal a whole range of socio-cultural forces which play themselves out through forms of behavior which can be called 'harassment' (sexual or not). This deconstructive analytical method which takes daily incidents apart, at the same time helps to situate or locate an event within its social space, within a matrix of social relations. Feminist sociology has often taken recourse to it. The work of Dorothy E. Smith, for example, may be especially looked into for a clear idea of how such a situating critique might be put together. In this framework, a worker's or any person's experience is not seen just as her own, but as a possible experience with particular variations of all similar workers or persons within that setting and context. Similarly, the social and cultural relations of any particular workplace can be assessed as ongoing and unfolding social and cultural processes, practices and values present in the society as a whole. This is to treat 'power' as a 'concrete' social form and relation with a specific history and locale – not as an abstract concept, and this is the only way to point out the systemic socio-structural and historical aspects of sexism or racism. This moves our understanding of oppression from intentionality (good/bad people story) to a more fundamental notion of social organisation, where such experiences are routinely possible because they are intrinsic to the properties of certain organisations.

This helps us to take the next step, to locate the characteristics of the workplace within the broader Canadian society. We need to show that the workplace displays characteristics which exist in the everyday Canadian world. Therefore, *individual* behaviour, workplace relations, daily life within its precincts all come within the purview of *social behaviour* and greater social and economic forces. Thus, X's work life, for example, cannot be fully understood outside of the general pattern of Canadian labour importation, labour market, labour process and workplace. We have to consider which community works where, how, at what and the reasons for doing so. A comparative study of work and workplaces brings this out clearly, as do cases brought to the labour and management mediating bodies, of peer behaviour brought to the personnel offices or the unions.

The socialisation and organisation of behaviour and social pattern and organisation of workplaces and so on in terms of 'race', gender and class, require an understanding of Canadian history. Issues of colonialism, indentured labour and ethnicised immigration history need to be brought into view. Numerous studies in state or class formation in Canada provide an understanding for who become the working class, who is allowed to work here, at what jobs and wages, and what are the general socio-economic expectations from non-white immigrants. This chapter will refer to this historical dimension only in so far as it speaks to this particular case and the present time in Canadian labour organisation and economy. This means a broad overview of non-white, especially non-white women's, labour in Canada, and a study of the role played by the Canadian state (immigration policies and so on), which has constructed and manipulated notions such as 'race' and ethnicity through its policy-making and administrative procedures. Sometimes, more than others, the state has been explicit about this.

Finally, we must address daily cultural practices and everyday common sense perceptions of groups of people living in Canada regarding each other. They are connected with a historical popular consciousness and the creation of social meanings regarding different types of people. This extends to both their physical and cultural characteristics, giving rise to normative conventions and stereotypes which have powerful and daily socio-economic and political consequences. These stereotypes indicate something about the expected physical presences and absences of certain groups of people within any given social space. Sexual division of labour or gender roles express precisely this meaningful location of bodies and their physical functions within assigned social spaces or boundaries. Thus, for example, the female body is stereotypically conceived within a so-called private space (home) and the male in a public one (workplace). The former (supposedly) belongs to the world of reproduction (social and biological), the latter to that of production (economic and intellectual). The factual and actual presences of women in the public sphere has always been undercut by this ideological construction of the 'two spheres' and cultural and moral assumptions and behavior appropriate to that division. This has had dire personal and economic consequences for all women and has been the centre of debates regarding women in 'non-traditional' jobs, or the value of housework.

Similar to this binary organisation, and in fact grounded in it, there has been a stereotypical, though often contradictory set of spatial perceptions and 'normal' expectations of the presence of black bodies in gender and class terms. Thus a society which is historically founded on colonialism, slavery, or the formation of class and culture on the ground of 'race' and ethnicity, provides a further crucial twist to the social meanings of bodies and their appropriate location within the social space. There is not only a general administration of social space, including work space, which is so-called gender divided, but it is organised through silent practices of 'race' and its attendant stereotypes. This is evident in the social map of occupations and workplaces, where men and women in general are expected to hold to two spheres, but within that, that is, within the public sphere or workplace with their own internal gender organisation, black men and black women are expected to hold subordinate and inferior and further segregated positions.

An examination of Canadian immigration policy and economic history will show that certain jobs are reserved areas of the minority communities. We can practically predict that the lowest-paying, possibly piece-working, most unhealthy and unclean jobs will be the preserves of the non-white communities, and within that the women of those communities will hold the most dead-end, vulnerable, worst-paid positions. The expected and permissible presences and absences of black people in general, and black women in particular, will be drastically different and marginalised as compared to whites. Stereotypically, a black male or female will not be expected to fill the professional social space, but that of manual and industrial labour or the lower levels of white collar jobs. The world of high culture and intellect will neither expect them nor will they be found there in significant numbers. Thus, in a society based on the ethics of upward mobility, the non-white population will be mainly expected to reproduce the working class, making class formation a 'raced' affair. In keeping with that dominant culture, including the media, cultural and educational administration, and other aspects of the state, such as welfare, all participate in creating and maintaining the appropriate socio-economic and cultural boundaries. The presence of black women in unexpected areas, i.e. in places which are contrary to ongoing conventional practices and expectations of both all women or black men, will signal a major *transgression*, and call for responses which will enforce prohibition and segregation. Racist or sexist or racist-sexist responses in the workplace can thus be interpreted also as attempts to re-establish the so called 'norm' – whereby norms of gender and 'race' and 'raced' gender are, perhaps unconsciously even, sought to be reasserted. From this standpoint, X's story can be read as a copybook case of reassertion of racist/sexist social norms through an exercise of common sense racism.

A further note regarding the concept of 'common sense racism'. This term is useful for expanding the meaning of racism from something that is articulate, aggressive and blatant, or a clearly thought out ideological position (for example, of the Ku Klux Klan, or that of an 'apartheid' government) to the level of everyday life and popular culture. Here racism takes on a seemingly benign form of what 'we' 'know' about 'them', meaning a collection of conventional treatment, decorum and common cultural stereotypes, myths, regarding certain social groups. For example, we can refer to the apparently harmless notion of 'blacks have an innate sense of rhythm', or the myth propagated by Philip Rushton and others that some 'races' are more civilised or modern and intellectual than others due to having better genes. Furthermore, these 'race'-based stereotypes commonly inform our daily life, though they originate from a long history of and presently organised racist practices which imply white suprem-acy. In sociological texts produced in Britain such as *The Empire Strikes Back*, Peter Freyer's *Staying Power, Not In Our Genes*, edited by Steven Rose and oth-ers, or Sandra Harding's edited collection *The Racial Economy of Science*, we find excellent analyses of this seemingly harmless everyday racism, which also reveal racism to be an intrinsic aspect of Western economies and culture. Given this, common sense racism in conjunction with a more organised, practical and ideologically violent version can together provide a better explanation for understanding X's experiences. The staging of the penis incident shortly before her departure from the workplace would have certainly done credit to even the KKK.

4   A Breakdown and a Breaking Down – A Deconstructive Description

When asked to describe her multiple experiences of harassment, including that of the carved penis, X said:

> Everybody apparently denied everything that I said or seen and that noth-ing was going to be done about it. And I don't – like I said, I started at my feet this here shaking and all of a sudden I started hollering and the guys were standing behind the union steward as he was telling me that it was all in my head, nobody seen anything and these guys were standing behind him laughing and all of a sudden the body just started going out of con-trol, and that's when I had to eventually leave my line because it moved up to my knees. I never experienced anything like this before.[5]

What is striking about this description is how personal and social it is simul-taneously. In fact its traumatic character, which is intensely individually exper-ienced, is essentially dependent upon the social environment of the workplace, a particularly organised and motivated presence of other workers, who are both male and white, and intent upon producing a humiliation and terror in a black woman who has strayed into their work domain. Her presence, it seems, has disturbed their sense of territory and violated the pre-established convention of the 'normalcy' of their workplace. After all the 'normal' atmosphere of this place as in many industrial concerns is 'white', i.e. exclusive of blacks or non-white people whose physical presences therefore would be exceptions rather

---

5   Submissions, nos. 29, 30.

than a rule. The social relations of 'race' and gender here express or contain a 'normalcy' which cannot be anticipatory or positive toward the presence of non-whites, especially of a female black worker. This silent organisation of labour on the grounds of 'race' and gender has an implicit racist-sexism embedded in it, though presumably no one has explicitly instructed these white male (and female) workers in an ideology and explicit administration of racism, as in apartheid South Africa or in certain southern states of the U.S. The norm has been diffused in the place, among other things, through a convention in hiring, through a systematic physical absence, which has incrementally created the white workers' sense of their 'normal' space or territory. The question that confronts us then is how these white workers, who are used to their white 'normalcy', cope or deal with this abnormal or unusual presence of non-white (and female) co-workers in their midst? What appears from X's testimony is that a general atmosphere of exceptionality regarding her presence pervades right through the workplace. X herself states that she had the option of adjusting to this very hostile environment, to the degraded demands and expectations that white men and women had of her, or to be expelled from it. Therefore, if we do not understand that her troubles began much earlier than that of working in the men's section and while among white women, we will not get a clear view of her experiences in the workplace. It is here that the analytical category of racist-sexism provides us with the basis for the later phase of 'sexual harassment' that she undergoes.

'Sexual harassment', which conventionally implies a heterosexist male/female dynamic, becomes a limited concept for understanding the fundamental nature of X's experience, unless we expand it to include racist-sexism, which also exists between white and black or non-white women. This racist-sexism is endemic to the everyday world of her workplace, and to miss this by seeing her as 'just another woman among women' is to gloss over the actual social relations of her workplace. It is important to note that these other women among whom X worked were white and thus brought up in a general culture of racism. We should also note that women internalise patriarchy as much as men do, and can be profoundly sexist towards themselves and others. In X's case, though they could not or did not assault her 'sexually', they assaulted her by calling her names, ordering her around and in general by levelling against her stereotypes common in the dominant (Anglo Canadian) culture about black women and women of colour. They had the power and numerical strength to do so as they were never prevented by the union or personnel management. The specificity of details of X's work life indicate one important truth, that though a white woman worker could have been harassed by her female or male co-workers, she would not have undergone this precise type of aggression, this intensity of humiliation and surplus domination which is expressive of racist-sexist practices and attitudes towards black women.

As I began by saying, there is a danger of reproducing racism in treating X's blackness as a given and therefore of omitting the words 'black' and 'white' as adjectives or indicators of meaningful social presences. Through the omission of these adjectives the concrete nature of the workplace becomes invisible to us. If we want to uncover the actual social relations present from the very beginning of her work life, we have to show how the organisation of the workplace holds the same ongoing racist relations which are strengthened by the overall lack of a non-white presence. The details of the submission show how 'white' assumptions, meaning racist notions regarding her 'black womanness', came out in a persistent aggression upon her consistent refusal to comply to illegitimate orders and expectations. Strong, hardworking, often unresponsive to their insults, persistent, she seems to have violated a whole set of norms that the white women workers, for example, held as basic to 'women'. And her very moral and physical strength and persistence when under adversity became a negative quality, some sort of an 'uppity nigger' syndrome. The condition under which she would have been seen as 'normal' or tolerated, was that of subservience. When she refused to do this and excelled at her job, she was not only considered a misfit but as downright intolerable. They complained about her frequently, and finally forced her out of the women's section. As she was a 'good worker' she was promoted, but also segregated from the (white) 'women's world'. She was in relative isolation in different stages of her work, both pushed into and choosing isolation for reasons of self-protection. Both white women and white men may have seen her as 'unfeminine', but she also fell squarely within the stereotype of black women as hard labourers, beasts of burden – a construction of common-sense racism dating all the way back to slavery.

It has to be noted that though white men's 'sexual harassment' is what ostensibly drove her out of her job, both white women and men united in creating a situation that forced X out of this workplace. The extent, persistence and scope of this is so large and long-lasting that it cannot at all be explained in terms of an interpersonal dynamic, her personal temperament or psychological problems. It is clear that the subsequent 'sexual harassment' itself had a wide basis of social, i.e. environmental support. She did not fit a 'woman's place' in the workplace in terms of the ideology of the feminine, and even less so a black woman's place. An aura of 'masculinity' was attributed to her. After all, she was not demoted to more menial jobs, but instead promoted to eventually handle that male symbol, industrial technology. This earned her more pay, at a higher risk, and a greater isolation.

X with her ability to stand up to pressures, and to persist in her work and her goal of working for a better life, violated stereotypes of femininity that white women may have had about themselves, and certainly regarding the competence of black women. This display of her strength may have unified them against her, as she did not cry, appeal or withdraw ('feminine' behaviour) upon persecution but kept to herself and did her job efficiently. White men also might have found her ability to surmount obstacles and improve her skills equally intolerable and wanted her 'out'. In the end, after six long years of struggle, she 'broke down'. That is, they succeeded in 'breaking her down'. This occasion was therefore much less an outcome of her own psychological predisposition, than an achievement of her co-workers in keeping with social relations of power which intrinsically structured her workplace. It is this fact that gets obscured when we attempt to understand her experience solely in terms of a 'race'-gender neutral notion of 'core' workers versus 'others', or in terms of personal psychological problems. Even 'sexual harassment' obscures more than it reveals.

It is interesting that white women's view of her as 'unwomanly' is echoed by the psychiatrist's report which portrays X's behaviour as 'unfeminine', relying on a model of gendered behaviour. When female patients display what they call more than a 'normal' amount of (for women) persistence and independence they are masculinised or become denatured women. How internalised must sexism be among women to have become so transparently mixed with professional assessment, whereby perseverance, independence, hard work etc. are seen as typically 'male' behaviour and dependence, and weakness 'female'. Thus it was 'male' or 'unnatural' of X to have kept going on so long in the face of adversity. She disproved the assumption of the white women on the shop floor that X would quit if pressure were kept up. In fact, X presented them with both an anomaly and a challenge, and both the white women and white men tested out the full range of their sense of normalcy regarding how much she could tolerate. The situation was obviously unequal, with no supporters on her side since anyone who was sympathetic to her was intimidated. Her expulsion then was a question of time. She had challenged too many stereotypes, too much of the established forms of 'race'/gender labour organisation of workplaces in Canada, by being a persistent black female worker in a 'non-traditional' job, among white females and males.

If these white women wished to make sure that she did not stay where she did not belong, X felt the full weight of this state of not belonging and unwantedness. But she needed the job and, moreover, desired an improvement in her job situation. She also recognised that in her 'light' job among women she would have to put up with all kinds of harassment without any more money to provide compensation. So if she were going to have to work hard in an unpleas-ant workplace, she wanted to be elsewhere, where she could actually make more money and possibly be left alone. Here no interaction would be expec-ted of her either because she was alone or because she was a woman among men. What she wanted basically was to learn more about machinery and to advance in her career.

These are, according to X, the reasons for which she left behind a so-called woman's job to go into a so-called man's job. There was a period in 'the mill' where she worked by herself, between her transition from 'light' job to 'heavy'. That was a period when she re-organised herself for a new phase in her work life. This was a phase of isolation both in terms of work and environment. She was not quite anywhere, neither in a 'man's job' nor in a 'woman's job'. But soon an opportunity came for a promotion and she was chosen to become an operator as her work had been considered extremely good by the foreman. He decided to give her a try. It is possible that he did not know where else to send her with her good work record and the continuous complaints of the white women. In a manner of speaking he neutralised her in gender terms and treated her as an abstraction, as a production facility, as 'a hand'. And it is through this neutralisation of her gender, brought about by her anomalous status, a de-feminisation, that X was put into men's work.

By the same characteristic which de-feminised X she created another threat or a challenge to male workers. She was a 'superworker'. She worked too hard and capably, and workplace studies show that there has always been resent-ment of superworkers both among time and piece workers. Superworkers provide an object of resentment and threat for two reasons. One, by being an unbeatable competition for others, which calls for this worker's elimination. The competition and intolerance become even more intense if this worker is of an undesirable 'race' or gender, for example, a black woman who makes a substantial wage in overtime. As we know X was working even harder during her breaks, partly because she feared being harassed, and partly because she wanted to make money. This produced an animosity that is typical to organ-isation of class, which in actuality is neither 'race' nor gender neutral. Class is after all a competitive phenomenon, and this competition provided the reasons for resenting her, as both a superworker and a black woman superworker in a white workplace. It was intolerable that she should show up others as compar-atively lazy or unenterprising. She was never seen as somebody who deserved the money she made. Everything that X did was seen as a transgression on her part and thus was utterly unacceptable to the working community which sur-rounded her.

So if somebody who should not be there in the first place is seen as the cause of so many 'problems', why should the other workers not try to get rid of her? This is precisely what they did. At this point all the norms and forms of racism, patriarchy and class came to work and were levelled towards this woman who violated the whole working community's sense of what is owing to a black woman and the conduct required of her. A sense of outrage and non-acceptance accounts largely for the passion and intensity, which is otherwise inexplicable, with which for six years they pursued her until they drove her out. By breaking her down they reasserted on the shop floor all the norms of a racist-sexist and class-bound society.

The expectations from X obviously were that she should fit some common notion of her 'natural' inferiority as a black woman and should also 'know her place'. Her ascribed role was to serve (in all senses), both in social and sexual terms, the white women and men, i.e. members of the dominant culture, and this is what she failed to do.

X's presence in the 'heavy' task area or the men's section received much legal attention because the language of 'sexual harassment', which relies essentially on heterosexuality as the offending motive, can easily attach itself to what is found within that domain. Since this area involves a direct male/female inter-action, 'sexual harassment' becomes obviously more actionable here. The viol-ations here are also the most gross and blatant. I would like to point out that 'sexual harassment' here has to be read as 'racist sexual harassment'. The fact of her 'race' provides the differential, the specificity of both the type of sexism and sexual harassment which she encounters. This section of the shop floor is not only a separate section physically removed from the women's area but also a section which is the sole preserve of white male workers. We have to imagine a group of white males, with the spattering of one or two non-white males among them, who are getting progressively frustrated with a black woman's ability to learn technological skills and withstand pressures. We also heard that there was the odd non-white person who wanted to help X, but were intimidated or pos-sibly fired, for doing this.

Here, in this social space of the men's section, the racist sexism which pre-vailed generally in the workplace became 'racist (hetero)sexualism'. It becomes obvious quite early in the stage of her transfer that these men want her out of their world and they use various racist (hetero)sexual strategies to drive her out of their space. This is substantiated in terms of the pornographic pictures placed in her tool box, frequent name calling such as 'cunt', or 'bitch', displays of 'Sunshine Girls' in her work area, frequent work sabotage and uncooperative behaviour and finally the display of the green penis with its tip of foam on it. This penis and all other incidents encode not only the sexual but the overall social relations of power, in the shape of assumptions and stereotypes which structure the workplace. X is put at all times in the most problematic situation.

Everywhere she goes she is unwanted, everywhere she is expected to fail. She is promoted and simultaneously set up to fail by lack of co-operation from others. The job of an operator, as we see from the submission, entails cooperation with co-workers, but they refuse to provide it. They not only use the verbal threats and insults but also stage repeated and extensive sabotage of the machinery, work process and her training. Her punishment for the transgression is to be situated at the intersection of winning and losing. This persistent sabotage and hostility of fellow workers indicate that X violated some basic norms of the environment, not the least of which was that blacks are not supposed to command whites and are mostly not in positions to do so. Furthermore, a woman is not supposed to tell a man what to do. Nor is a woman supposed to be working with heavy machinery and a man is not supposed to be a woman's cleaner or her helper in a technological work process even where 'race' is not at issue. The problem is further compounded in the case of a woman who is black, who demands these facilities as a routine part of her job, which in the first place should have been a white man's prerogative. What 'self-respecting' white man would take orders from a black woman? Or help her to rise above himself in the hierarchy of either the workplace or society at large?

Studies have shown that white women are harassed by white men in a comparable situation on gender grounds, because a white man will not take orders from a white woman. In a workplace as elsewhere there is a continuum of set gender expectations or cultural norms. In this case, sexist harassment is doubly compounded and intensified with racist modulations. There is a difference in the nature of sexual harassment that X undergoes. Sexual harassment of white women by white men often involves an element of direct personal body contact or direct sexual solicitations, which is pornographic but not always or immediately brutal. That is, sexual overtures are directly made – for example, bottoms and breasts are pinched, various simultaneously lucrative and degrading offers and innuendos are directly made. In short, there is a personal harassment that points to the particular signification of white women's bodies for white men. This signification, which is implicitly 'raced', takes on a very specific racist sense in the case of a black woman's body as perceived by white men. It is important to note that none of X's recorded harassments actually involves direct personal sexual contact or conventional sexual innuendos. Her oppressors do not seek sexual favours from her, or offer career related favours, such as a promotion for sexual bribes. Her sexual harassment is mediated through pornographic images of black women *servicing* white males by performing oral sex. The degradation and the objectification essential to this type of image involving black women have a tone of racist sexual violence. They compound elements of rape and evoke threats of gang rape, as well as inflicting public humiliation in a grotesque form. Studies on pornography and sexual representation of black women show similar forms which are degrading, servile and objectifying. In these images of racist sexual servitude, various racist representations of black women, including of animality, coalesce into one synthetic image.

These images of sexual servitude and animality depicting black women are old, they are historical. They hold memories of slavery and a long history of racism in the context of class domination. Indentured labour, degrading immigration practices and immigrant labour fuse with practices of rape of black women on the plantations, their present-day humiliation in domestic labour and welfare offices and their association with supersexed behaviour. In short, everything that we can attach racism to as a social and historical phenomenon. They represent a woman compositely, as a woman and a black woman, who is a member of a sub-working class or a sub-serving class from which subservience can be demanded by whites. This specificity of 'raced' gender involves a development of an everyday racist-sexism into a stage of racial (hetero)sexual harassment.

Finally, we have to make sense of the green soap carving of a penis with its tip of white foam. This image and its display to a captive X marks a violation of any woman's sense of self and symbolises a gross male sexual aggression, though not performed directly on X's body. Though the word 'rape' has not been used in the submission, that this is a symbolic or a ritual reenactment of a gang-rape should not escape any sensitive observer. However, to say this is not to say enough. The character of this symbolic gang rape needs to be con-textualised. In X's case it encodes centuries of master-slave relations which may have been limited as economic practice to certain countries but were culturally and socially generalised throughout the West. The practice of lynching black men and some black women is conveyed by the same gesture, in the associative contextualisation of its meaning. I would like to combine the violence of both lynching and rape and call it a 'lynch rape'. The symbolic enactment of a gang rape is also infused here with the spirit of a spectacle which lynching entails because of its collective and public nature. Unlike the pornographic pictures that her co-workers put in her tool box, which X could see privately, by display-ing the soap penis in the public space and having a number of men view her viewing the penis, there is an enactment of a ritual. It then becomes a spectac-ular symbolic action signifying a ritual degradation and a sort of a punishment. The moment marks X's progression – from the women's section in 'light' work, to the men's section in the workplace which she left shortly after this incid-ent. The time in between was one of a continuous struggle for self respect, survival and self-improvement. It is this struggle, unequal as it was, which cul-minated in this horrifying spectacle of a symbolic/ritualised gang rape which was tantamount to lynching in being an exemplary form of punishment. This is the trajectory of the work life of X at Y company. And not any moment of it is explicable without an account of the dominant social relations and forms of consciousness which structured her workplace and the society in which it existed.

In order to understand the systemic or structural dimension of this racist sexism, we must examine the behavior of the company's administrators and its union. First, we should look at the union's response. X complained to the union on various occasions. On what ground, we may ask, did the union as workers' organ of self-representation not defend its own member? Throughout the six years, not a single action was taken by the union against the harassing peer group. Only towards the end of her stay the union responds minimally to the pressure of the personnel office to secure an apology from one of the workers. While this indicates a basic acknowledgement of X's situation, on most occasions the union representatives ignored her complaints and tore and threw them away. So we cannot but infer from this that the union had no room for any redress especially regarding racist peer behaviour. The executive members and shop staff of the union were all white males and the general membership was mostly white. As the union did not concede X's accusations of racism and sexism it is obvious that they had no interest in restructuring the workplace, so that it would become a safe workplace for X or other non-whites or white women workers, for that matter.

If broken machinery in the workplace creates accidents and therefore must be changed, then a bad set of social relations in a workplace are equally dangerous and productive of injury. It must also be the responsibility of the workplace to change them. This is a question of both emotional and physical safety. The kind of mechanical problem that the white male workers created through their uncooperative behaviour resulted in the lack of X's physical safety, it also resulted in reducing her productivity. But the company and the workers were so fully acculturated to sexism and racism and worker harassment that they refused to recognise these as legitimate grounds for initiating changes or redress. In spite of the fact that their job was to facilitate management at all levels of the factory, the employers took no responsibility, notwithstanding the presence of due process which exists in all workplaces. One of these officials even went so far as to threaten her, by saying 'If you think this is bad, wait 'til you come back and see what happens to you'. It is important to note that threats are directed at the very person who is the victim rather than at the aggressors. All this not only shows poor management, but most of all, structured and normalised racist sexism within the workplace, of which I have spoken before. It is evident that the workplace takes for granted what they may call a 'normal' amount of abuse on these grounds. It is not until after the penis incident that the foreman actually noted a complaint of X in his log book. There is no written record of sabotages by X's co-workers, who did not show up to put the bins under the soap shoot, for example, or did not help with her machine breakdowns and even actively damaged them. Not only was nothing ever noted by the union or recognised by the management, but X was continuously denied the truth of her own work experience. She was always silenced and ignored. This can only be seen both as an intentional attempt to confuse and debilitate her as well as an unconscious attitude of contempt and hostility towards her. The frustration produced by this situation created a deep disturbance within X which resulted in a nervous collapse.

It is interesting that the physical symptoms of her 'nervous breakdown' came precisely when they disacknowledged the reality of her experiences. Obviously this conduct of negligence and silencing on the part of the workplace is indicative of normalisation of daily abuse. This notion of an acceptable amount of abuse or racism and sexism in the workplace is similar to discussions of an acceptable degree of radiation. It ignores what any radiation at all does to a human body, but arbitrarily decides that it is acceptable to expose humans to this or that degree of it. Similarly this normalisation of sexism and racism poisons the whole work environment and serves as a kind of encouragement rather than a disincentive to those who are racist-sexist. It provides a signal for workers to continue the harassment. It seems that in this normalisation of sexism and racism male workers and male management overcome the traditional division between them and unite in their racism and sexism and share the same fund of stereotypes about 'others'.

We have already talked about assumptions and expectations existing in countries such as Canada about non-white people which are racist-sexist. These notions and images are cultural codes of common sense in the everyday life of Canada. They are not self-conscious projections and practices of people. Nobody needs to read a book to learn them. They are handed down or are absorbed from daily living in the general social environment. Among these we have to look at specific stereotypes and see how they fit with the way X was treated by her co-workers. The conventional racist wisdom in North America is that black women will put up with a large amount of abuse, or that black working-class women are particularly without a claim to social respect. Other representations or stereotypes involve an equation between black people and physicality. A racist discourse denies black women any intellect or rationality but, instead, attributes to them merely a body for sex, reproduction and labour. It is considered her 'natural' role in life to meet the white society's needs for physical services. This 'beast of burden' image of black women is prevalent from the times of slavery to now, and it has repeatedly provided the common sense basis for how she is to be seen or treated. The other image, which in a way contrasts with the above, is that of a superwoman, of a dominant, abrasive and castrating woman and mother. This myth claims that black women are so strong that they can endure any hardship. Michelle Wallace in her book *Black Macho and the Myth of the Superwoman* talks about how this mythic black woman figure is constructed. This myth, even if it seemingly aggrandises the black woman, is essentially dehumanising and debilitating. Reading between the lines, we find the presence of all of the above assumptions or stereotypes at work regarding X in her workplace.

It should be mentioned in this context that black women's sexuality as depicted in the West, from advertisements to the music industry to pornography, has been degrading and often portrayed in animal terms. This is consistent with the pornographic racialised sexualisation which confronted X. The photographs which were put in her tool box are consistent with the degraded idea that a black woman can mainly serve an organ or a part of a white male, and with the inference that she is herself no more than a sexual organ (e.g. a 'cunt').

It has been pointed out in literature on pornography that sexual violence against women reduces all women to mere genitalia and secondary sexual characteristics – to objects. But in X's case, the use of a dildo or the carved penis expresses more sharply the profound violence of pornography when racism is mixed with sexism. Racist-sexist pornographic stereotypes are common and powerful. In softer forms they exist in advertisements, for example, which frequently depict a black woman as an exotic body comparable to a powerful horse or a panther. A more social and mundane version of this is to be found in Daniel Moynihan's study of the black family where black women as mothers and wives are shown as matriarchs who castrate black men. Moynihan's report, criticised as being racist, has still been extremely influential in subsequent reports and research dealing with poor black women and black families. The other related but inverse image is one of servitude and physical nurture. Aunt Jemima, for example, is a popular version of this servant mother, where the black woman is reduced to a single physical and social function intended mainly for white consumption. This total mother figure denotes nothing but a serving, physical motherhood. There is no intellectual, moral or even sentimental dimension to it. Nowhere, either in the luxurious, ebony images in the advertisements, or in this supermother figure, or in the notion of a super woman rising above all adversity, do we ever find an association of black women with mind, soul, heart, emotion, intelligence and creativity. What we know about X's work experience makes everything fit like a copybook exercise to all this literature on black women and racist-sexism.

Now that we have looked at X's case with regard to racist-sexist cultural common sense and internal social organisation and relations of her workplace, we need to locate this workplace within today's greater Canadian society. We need to ask who works where and at what jobs, in what conditions and at what wages in Canada? Studies show that Canadian immigration and labour history and labour management patterns consist of different stages, at each of which immigrants were brought in for the precise purpose of creating the working class. Immigrant groups were and are to fit into certain slots of labour requirement and those slots were/are not in the area of developing professions. Often they are not even in highly skilled trades but rather in the most menial services and unskilled manufacturing. There is an overwhelming presence of immigrant women within these sectors, for example, in the textile industry or in service sectors, such as office or domestic work. In other skilled industrial sectors which are non-textile, very few white women drift in, and almost no black women. X was a rare exception. We saw through her case the predictable difficulties of an untypical worker in an environment of skilled work. Women both black and white are typically to be found in the less skilled or manual areas of the work world, and black women even more so. Research on women, work and technology has told us that technology drives women out of work both in the first world and the Third World.

In the general spectrum of labour very particular kinds of work are performed by black women or by women of colour. If one wants to find out where women of colour work within the industries, one does not go to the front of the factory, which is its public profile, but rather into its basement, into the least ventilated, the darkest and the most oppressive areas in the workplace. Even in the non-industrial sector they work in areas which are always unpleasant and risky. It can be farm work, for example – growing mushrooms or picking strawberries while living in barracks or being bussed in with their children from cities. There are many cases of children falling into pits and dying. They can also be at home 'homeworking' for the garment industry in oppressive conditions and underpaid, as Laura Johnson describes in *Seam Allowance*, where Chinese women sit inside closets all day with sewing machines. In the factories these women inhabit segmented corners where they endlessly swallow lint or other pollutants from the air and perform the task of sewing on half a thousand buttons a day or perform some other mindless and repetitive work.

This situation is expected, not an exception. It is the norm of organisation of labour and labour market in Canada with the active help of Immigration Canada. The state is the main agency through which such labour has been sought, brought in and employed in this country. Immigration histories point out how, with other imported workers, the immigrant non-white worker was brought to Canada in order to fill certain productive requirements. The worse the job, the more the so-called 'open door' policy is adopted towards Third World countries, giving rise to the existing local black communities. They are also blamed, once they have come, for all the economic problems that pre-existed their arrival. Canadian companies in Latin America, for example, put up advertisements promising a good life upon arrival to Canada. They project many incentives, and once the immigrants are in Canada they provide a vulnerable labour force and are often considered undesirable by the white population. This produces a captive body of extremely insecure workers who can neither go back or go forward and which can be kept as a 'flexible labour force' for when the labour is needed and pushed out when not. This labour has to be continuously kept in reserve. Most of all, it is to be understood that this part of the labour force is meant to be unskilled and kept as lower status members of the working class. They are called 'newcomers' or 'immigrants' even after they acquire citizenship and are made to feel like 'guest workers', eternally labelled and marginalised as 'migrants', 'aliens', and 'outsiders'. This is evident in what the white workers think of X, even though she, unlike many of them, is a many-generations Canadian. The prevailing racist attitude creates the feeling that non-white immigrants in particular are always on sufferance. They are often in jobs and sectors which are non-unionised. Canadian labour is as a whole under-unionised, and to attempt to create a union is a 'kiss of death' because the involved workers face the possibility of being fired and are usually never reemployed either by the firm that fired them or by most other firms. And where there is a union, as we saw with X, it does not necessarily protect these workers as they are not seen as equal members (with whites) within the union. X knew all of this, so she decided to learn to live with it all, to rise above it and to fight it as best she could. That is why she did not quit her job. The next place she would go to, as she told me, would be no better necessarily, in this company at least she was making $16.00 an hour. It was worth the trouble of learning to live with the problems, she told me, rather than being at a place which pays the minimum wage and offers the same harassments.

So when we examine these social relations and stereotypes which structure Canadian society and work, we can see how non-white people form sub-groups within the Canadian working class as a whole. The black community thus belongs to the lower part of the ladder and within that community, women hold a place which is even lower. This is systemic racism since the economy pervasively organises a labour market on the basis of 'race' and ethnicity, and it is systemically impossible to profit without having workers who can be paid little and made to work much. After all, the less it puts out for production costs, including the wage of the worker, the more profit the company makes. Judging by this, women's work, and especially the work of non-white women, is the cheapest to purchase. We should remember that the wage differential between men and women in Canada has increased rather than decreased in the last decades. This is not an atmosphere of challenging discrimination.

The problem of racist-sexist organisation of labour is not only that of Canada and the United States. Writers such as Pratibha Parmar or Errol Lawrence from England have pointed out the power or pre-existing stereotypes for determining the nature of employment that non-white women or men hold in Western countries. Ranging from Turkish and other 'guest workers' in Europe, to Bangladeshi women 'homeworking' in Britain, to black women such as X, all non-white, immigrant workers fall within pre-existing gender-'race' slots of work and stereotypes which define the dominant culture's expectations and views of them.

These images and stereotypes of inferiority of black or non-white women are obviously economically profitable to the business community. If the worth of women's labour is low, then non-white women's labour value is even lower. Racist-sexism propagates these stereotypes and keeps this value low, and the workers vulnerable. That is why we have to relate the present situation of X to the economy of Canada, while pointing out the complicity of the Canadian state in her domination. In studies on domestic labour in Canada (for example, *Silenced* by Makeda Silvera) we see how the state is engaged in procuring domestic workers for the upper-middle class, who are almost invariably white. This workforce is mostly non-white, consisting mainly of Filipinos (currently) and women from the Caribbean. We can see the material basis of racist-sexist stereotypes when we go, for example, to the airports in Britain or Canada, where South Asian women provide the cleaning workforce.

Racist-sexist cultural representations are integral to the organisation of the economy. Much has been written on images of South Asian women as submissive, docile and unresisting to patriarchal abuse. In Canada, books such as *Seam Allowance*, speaking to the myth of Chinese women's 'nimble fingers', and *Silenced*, about superexploitation of Black and South Asian women as domestic workers, often bring into play certain stereotypes of sexual laxity and affinity with gross physical labour. bell hooks in *Ain't I a Woman?* or Angela Davis in *Women, Race and Class*, among many others, discuss the racist-sexist perception of black women in North America from slavery to 'free labour'. One only needs a periodic look at the *Toronto Sun*, for example, or the television, to see what images and assumptions are circulated by the popular media among masses of people, both black and white. Stereotypes range from 'yellow peril' to 'black (now Asian) criminality', and are cultural lenses through which communities are viewed and introduced to each other literally via media. Mis- or disinformation crowd the news and other television programmes, while the fashion industry, sports and music equate black people with the body and a natural gift for rhythm, and the Chinese with an innate propensity to do well in mathematics. The quintessence of all this was in the geneticist theories of social scientists such as Phillip Rushton, which have found a lethal expression in Murray and Hernstein's current work.

5   Conclusion

Far removed as these themes may seem from the case of X, upon deeper reflection it should become clear from the above that they are intimately related. These greater social forces in their interaction fundamentally construct X's experience, where she and her co-workers become actors in a social drama of sexist-racism and sexual harassment. This drama however is not restricted to this company, and selected 'bad' individuals. Culture to education, child socialisation to the greater workings of the economy, media and the state, all combine openly and insidiously to acculturate members of society in racist-sexism. Jokes about 'Pakis', nursery rhymes about 'catching a nigger by the toe', to serious physical assaults, sexual and otherwise (including regular police shootings of male black youth and of Sophia Cook – a black woman shot in Toronto by a police officer while she sat in a parked car), all constitute our present day social environment and its 'normalcy'. In such a situation, what befell X cannot be seen in any way as her own doing. Millions of white women, and black and non-white women (and men), living in the West, have to deal with different types of sexual harassment, or racist-sexual harassment. It is not X who needs to change, as her employers suggested, but the society in which she lives. She should not be paying economic and emotional prices for wrongs that have been historically and are presently being done to her people, on the grounds of being a black working-class woman. Just as the women engineering students killed in Montreal by Marc Lepine had a right to be where they were and learning subjects hitherto kept at a distance from women in most countries, so did X have a right to her dignity and her presence in the industrial section of this multinational pharmaceutical company operating in Canada.

CHAPTER 12

Attired in Virtue: Discourse on Shame (*Lajja*) and Clothing of the Gentlewoman (*Bhadramahila*) in Colonial Bengal

In those days there was a particular rule for women. Whoever became a *bou* (bride/daughter-in-law) was to veil herself for an arm's length or so, and not speak to anybody. That's what made a good *bou*. Clothes then, unlike now, were not made of such fine fabric, but were rather coarse and heavy. I used to wear that piece of heavy cloth, and veil myself down to my chest, and do all those chores. And I never talked to anyone. My eyes never looked out from within that cloth enclosure, as though [I was] blindfolded like the bullocks of the oil presser. Sight did not travel further than [my] feet.[1]

• • •

The starting point of these reflections was usually a feeling of impatience at the sight of the naturalness with which newspapers, art and common-sense constantly dresses up a reality which even though it is the one we live in, is undoubtedly determined by history. I resented seeing Nature and History confused at every turn, and I wanted to track down, in the decor-ative display of what-goes-without-saying, the ideological abuse which, in my view, is hidden there.[2]

• •
•

1   Introduction

Judging by the moral and legal preoccupations of the colonial state and the indigenous intellectual elite (wholly male), the nineteenth century of Bengal

---

1   Dasi 1868.
2   Barthes 1973, p. 11.

could be called the Age of Social Reform.[3] The rapid process of colonisation, the type of colonialism brought into India by the English and new class formations in Bengal gave rise to a radical sense of disjunction and changes in existing social relations and values, precipitating a sense of social and moral crisis.[4] Questions ranging from religious to everyday life, inclusive of sexuality, gender relations and the family, erupted in endless public discussions, debates and disclosures. Persistent and vigorous attempts at social legislation and institutionalisation, for example of education, accompanied these intellectual efforts at reorganising and reconceptualising the new social relations, values and their practical demands. These moral utterances and social projects of the Bengali middle class intelligentsia did not form a monolithic whole, but rather consisted of ideological-discursive strands which converged, competed and contradicted with each other.[5]

Interestingly enough, the largest bulk of these reforms and discussions were aimed at women and gender relations prevailing in the family, thereby seeking to reorganise much of the existing social forms and functions. The heart of the social project was 'the degradation and the decadence' of society, typified by the state in which Bengali women and families of the propertied classes existed.[6] Tanika Sarkar, for example, has commented that the Bengali male

---

3 Themes of social reform and social change in various ways dominate studies on nineteenth-century social and cultural history of Bengal. Books as diverse as Borthwick 1984; Joshi 1975; Raychaudhury 1988; Sarkar 1979; 1985a; Sen 1977, among numerous others, speak of these topics with different social analyses and interpretations.

4 See the preface to Raychaudhuri 1988, pp. ix–xvi and note: 'But whether the change was introduced by self-conscious effort or impersonal influences, one notes an all-pervasive concern, almost obsessive, in their social and intellectual life – an anxiety to assess European culture in the widest sense of the term as something to be emulated or rejected' (p. xi). The terms and forms of this assessment are considered in their complexities and contradictions by Sarkar 1985a; see also Bagchi 1985 and Forbes 1975.

5 Bannerji 2001a, 'Fashioning a Self: Educational Proposals for and by Women in Popular Magazines in Colonial Bengal': 'The social location of the significational aspects of ideology supplies the multiplicity of meanings, fissures, the openings and closures (always semiotically signalling out), which even the most thought out ideological formulation can not escape' (p. 142). It should also be noted that 'writers on ideological formations in nineteenth century Bengal are, not surprisingly, preoccupied therefore in dealing with "shifts and slides", "liminality" and so on – pointing to a multidimensionality within one ideological position or its class articulation' (p. 143).

6 The assessment of the state of Bengali society and 'civilisation' by judging the condition of women from a European/Christian standpoint is pervasive in missionary literature, for example. Also Sinha 1989 speaks of the overall English colonial disposition to 'Victorian sexual ideology' and 'specific gender identities' and their imposition on an 'alien culture inextricably linked to the pursuit of colonial economic and political power ...' (Sinha 1989, pp. 2–3). This ruling and condemnatory design is also spoken of by Ballhatchet 1980.

intelligentsia's interest in women's 'improvement' bordered on the obsessive.[7] But to ameliorate the living conditions of Bengali (middle class) women, to improve their minds and morality, to regulate their conjugal and household roles, signified a concern for the upliftment of Bengali society as a whole. The 'natural' constitution of the female mind, it was felt, along with women's social condition, needed a serious 'recasting'.[8]

Constructed through the colonial discourse of 'civilisation' (later 'improvement' or 'progress'), used both by the 'enlightened' or westernised middle-class Hindus and their reformed, non-idolatrous counterparts, the Brahmos, 'the woman question' emerged as a highly controversial one. The idea was to bring the women members of the propertied classes within the purview of 'civilisation', 'progress' and utility. Tracts, plays, farces, novels and even poetry on domesticity, conjugality, and moral and practical education for women swamped the printing presses. This process, however, was not a unilinear move of submission to colonisation or 'westernisation'. Attempts at understanding what is 'civilisation' and how to achieve it contained thorough searches of and reflections on both indigenous and European practices and values. Ambiguity and criticism regarding both marked most of the attempts at synthesising and imitating.[9]

In any case, a strand of the Bengali male intelligentsia, whose consciousness had a formative and positive relationship with European thought, took on the role of Pygmalion and sought to fashion for themselves a Galatea. This

---

7 T. Sarkar writes: 'subjection for most sections of the [male] intelligentsia meant loss, albeit with some potential for progress. Against this fundamental and all-encompassing loss of selfhood, the only sphere of autonomy, of free will, was located within the Hindu family: to be more precise, with the Hindu woman, her position within an authentic Hindu marriage system and the ritual surrounding the deployment of her body ... [T]here was a thorough examination of every aspect of the problem' (1989, p. 1).

8 The criteria for social reform, though not strictly an expression of or an agenda for colonising the Bengali mind, are evolved in the colonial context and in relation to colonial content as well. The *Autobiography* of Shibnath Shastri, for example, provides an excellent sense of what is entailed in such social reform, while a book such as *Re-casting Women: Essays in Colonial History* (1989) offers a feminist reading for such attempts at 're-forming' or 're-casting'. See the Introduction to that anthology, which takes its name from Koilashchandra Bose's statement 'On the Education of Hindu Females' (1846): 'She must be refined, reorganised, recast, regenerated'.

9 See Bannerji: 'The project of the creation of a new social identity or a new common sense is only partially a planned one. Its complex nature is not accounted for by the correspondence theory of base and superstructure, but rather it is various, disparate and *ad hoc*, and often in the colonial case, one of an acute and quick response. Imitation, reaction absorption and recreation were all ingredients in this social response' (1989, p. 1042). See also Chatterjee 1986a, and Addy and Azzad 1973.

was to be a moral or discursive portrait of the ideal feminine, otherwise known as *bhadramahila* (the gentlewoman). The moral-cultural configuration of this discursive image or sign was embedded in, and endowed with, duties, pleasures and graces appropriate to the cultural commonsense of the 'westernised' sections of the middle classes. No aspect of this construct was beyond (male) utterance, both in formulation of character (moral-domestic) and in appearance (moral-erotic/aesthetic). Men sought to become experts in all matters pertaining to women, flouting existing social proprieties deeply grounded in a sexual/cultural division of labour.[10]

A signal example of this ideological-aesthetic meddlesomeness was the attempt by 'enlightened' Hindu and Brahmo men to 're-dress' the women of their own classes. The image was to simultaneously express and construct their overall class culture, that is, also their morality. Sartorial experiments on captive household females provided a concretisation of reform aspirations, as we see in Swarnakumari Debi's *Sekele Katha* (Story of Old Times), the scope of which entailed a basic change within the everyday life of the household.[11] The need for a sartorial change was initially contexted to the entry of non-kin males within the 'inner quarters' of the household. The move came in several steps, building the sartorial project into the social-moral life of women and the household:

> At the time of this new improvement of our household/home, Keshab babu became a disciple of my esteemed father. Into the inner quarters, impenetrable to the rays of the sun [a hyperbolic metaphor to signify its aristocratic honour], he was the first unrelated man, who was greeted like a close relative and welcomed to enter. Many people marvelled at this great act of courage. But that my venerable, sage-like father, who forsook friends and relatives for the sake of the right religious conduct [*dharma*], who did not hesitate to give up all earthly comforts, would receive Keshab babu (who was an outcaste of his home for converting to the true religion, seeking refuge with his wife, as a disciple) into his own home with a father's affection, was not a matter of surprise.[12]

---

10 See the Introduction to Sangari and Vaid for a discussion of the class agenda of social reform: 'Middle class reforms undertaken on behalf of women are tied up with the self-definition of the class, with a new division of the public from the private sphere, and of course with a cultural nationalism' (1989, p. 9). See also H. Bannerji 1992.

11 Debi 1916.

12 Ibid., p. 3.

Next came another male, both a teacher for the girls and women, and a disciple of her father, Debendranath Tagore, the founder of Brahmo Samaj, a form of ecumenical reformed Hinduism: 'My esteemed father was disappointed in the education supplied [to the women of the household] by 'mems' [white governesses]. The new preacher of the Adi Brahmo Samaj Strijukta Ayodhyanath Pakrashi was employed to teach in the inner quarters'.[13] Several women and girls were to study with him. Both events occasioned an 'improvement' in clothing appropriate to the notion of feminine civility:

> On this occasion clothes of the denizens of the women's quarters were reformed, [due to the fact] that it was impossible to appear in front of men [non-kin] in the Bengali women's usual garb of only a *sari*. My older sister, maternal aunt and sisters-in-law used to come to the study in a kind of civil and refined outfit of a *peshawaj* [outfit of aristocratic Muslim women] and a shawl. My esteemed father always had a distaste for the clothing of Bengali women, and deeply desired to reform it. He did not stint in effort to realise this wish, at times on my *Didis* [older sisters], but tirelessly on the infant daughters. In those days, the youngest children in our household wore clothes similar to the girls and boys of muslim aristocratic families. After we grew up a little, we wore a new type of clothing every day. My father looked through a large number of paintings and ordered new designs. The tailor attended him every day and so did we.[14]

Even though the vagaries of styles and the moral dimensions of these 'reforming' experiments elicited ridicule from the anti-reformist middle-class Hindu male faction, the situation as a whole revealed the general male preoccupation with the question of an appropriate social subjectivity for women.[15] They all postulated a relationship between the inner and outer self of women and saw her clothing as a moral signifier of her social role and thus of what they saw as the culture of their *samaj* (society) or class. The covering and uncovering of her body, the particular parts which were to be hidden or disclosed, and the

---

13   Ibid., p. 5.
14   Ibid., pp. 30–1.
15   The plethora of literature on women's social subjectivity and the family is too large for selective citation, but from Bankim Chandra Chattopadhyay, the conservative thinker on women, to Rabindranath Tagore, a liberal, the same preoccupation is shared. The names of a few 'improving' texts are cited below: Basu 1892 and 1901; Basu I., 1884; Basu M., 1887 and 1884; Biswas 1886; Raychoudhury, 1884.

style/manner in which this was done, were contested grounds for moral and aesthetic visions among males.[16]

This male monopoly on the aesthetic form and moral content of ideal femininity came to an end in the last decades of the century. Even though the social context remained the same, and patriarchy provided the basic philosophy for the appropriate investiture of the female body, educated middle class women of 'enlightened' homes themselves had much to do and say regarding both the discursive-ideological and actualisation processes. Summoned into education and cultural activities by the hegemonic agenda of their classes, informed by the moral and intellectual atmosphere generated by male reformers, middle-class women stepped into the world of public utterance approximately from the 1870s and added to the existing discourse of 'reform'. Through various journals and magazines, this rudimentary female intelligentsia participated actively in fashioning their own subjectivities as expressed in the sign called *bhadramahila* or the gentlewoman. One has to remember that Debendranath Tagore's moral-sartorial dream was finally fulfilled by a woman, his daughter-in-law, Gyanada Nandini Debi. As his daughter Swarnakumari Debi puts it:

> But he could not settle on a costume/attire after so much experimentation. His dissatisfaction came to an end when [my] middle sister-in-law returned from Bombay, dressed in a civil and elegant attire in imitation of Gujrati women. This attire, an integral combination of indigenousness, decorum and modesty, was just what he had wanted. It suited what he desired and removed a fundamental deprivation of the daughters of Bengal.[17]

Malabika Karlekar, in her book *Voices from Within*, remarks on this negotiated self-making, showing how women both compromised with and pushed the boundaries of the class-patriarchy of the Bengali middle class.[18]

A long discussion ensued among educated middle-class women through magazines such as *Bamabodhini, Bharati, Sahitya, Pradip, Mukul,* and *Sakha*.[19]

---

16   This is also noted in the European colonial racist-sexist context. For example, Sander Gilman's essay, 'Black Bodies, White Bodies: Toward an Iconography of Female Sexuality in Late Nineteenth Century Art, Medicine and Literature' (1985, pp. 223–61) remarks on the nature of the body – both female and black – as a signifier for colonial and other forms of domination and an ideological repository or re-presentation, as well as a site of moral hegemony.

17   Debi 1916, pp. 31–2.

18   Karlekar 1991.

19   Borthwick 1984, gives us an overview of the world of middle-class Bengali women, espe-

The discussion was a serious attempt to think through what an 'appropriate reformed female' subjectivity, coded as *bhadramahila*, should be, and how that should be projected as a visual-moral sign. The notion of 'appropriateness' was conceived with reference to gender and family relations in the new context of the colonially inflected, respectable middle classes. Appearance, in the sense of body-self presentation through clothing, was a particularly important theme. The morality of the *bhadramahila* was to be translucent in the self-composition through clothes, and this theme of self-composition, along with that of the body, provided the discursive organisation for the women's texts. In spite of the fact that the women reformers came into a pre-organised moral-discursive space, their own discourse on women, femininity and clothing was tempered with a recognition of the power of gender roles. Even though they did not fashion it in its entirety, they substantially inflected the sign of *bhadramahila* – the moral/aesthetic/erotic configuration of women of propertied classes in Bengal.

This paper examines the discursive organisation of sartorial morality as put forward by some of the women writers of major Bengali magazines, especially with respect to forms of class subjectivities they propose for Bengali women. The concentration here is minimally on fashions or styles, but rather on the emergence of a social morality which seeks to serve, to some extent does serve, as an unofficial form of moral regulation created by the civil society. This demarcates at the level of proposals or ideology social spaces, personal interactions between men and women, and the kind of moral personality a *bhadramahila* should have. Attitudes towards the female body and sexuality are all a part of this insignia of virtue and vice. The clothes are meant to propose a definitive relationship between the women and their class/social status.

Significations of the moral and the immoral, the sexual and the social (posed as asexual and therefore virtuous) are never kept out of sight. In fact, the position that the sexual and the social are in some ways antithetical captures a process and a project of profound privatisation of sexuality which in reality is publicly and discursively constructed. Here we need to remember Michel Foucault's response to S. Marcus' *The Other Victorians* where he challenges Marcus' 'Repressive Hypothesis' and points out the public, discursive nature of the very project of privatisation of sexuality in nineteenth-century western Europe. Hearing the bubble/babble of voices on morality and the notion of the appropriately 'feminine' (an euphemism for female sexual conduct), we can-

cially with regard to their educational project, as put forward in women's magazines of the time. She lists the women's magazines and approximates their circulation, claiming a large readership in Dhaka, in Calcutta and its suburbs, in small towns and even villages, both among men and women.

not but ask Foucault's questions with regard to the projects of social reform in nineteenth-century Bengal:

> Why has sexuality been so widely discussed, and what has been said about it? What were the effects of power generated by what was said? What are the links between these discourses, these effects of power, and the pleasures that were invested by them? What knowledge was formed as a result of this linkage? The object in short is to define the regime of power-knowledge-pleasure that sustains the discourse on human sexuality [in our parts of the world].[20]

The negative revelation of the female body as an absent signifier through explicit forms of prohibition, and thus the covert allusion to its sexual potentialities, is publicised and made central to the sartorial project for the gentlewoman. These essays by the women writers, full of rich descriptions, critical comments and exhortations, allow us to provide a semiology and ideology of culture and class in a concretely embodied and engendered fashion. And we can begin, as Foucault suggests, to question and situate our sources and voices,

> to account for the fact that [sexuality in various names] is spoken about, to discover who does the speaking, the positions and viewpoints from which they speak, the institutions which prompt people to speak about it and which store and distribute the things that are said. What is at issue, briefly, is the 'over-all discursive fact', the way in which sex is 'put into discourse'.[21]

2   Clothing as Embodiment or Sign

> Are there objects which are *inevitably* a source of suggestiveness as Baudelaire suggested about Woman? Certainly not ... *for it is human history which converts reality into speech*, and it alone rules the life and the death of mythical language. Ancient or not, *mythology can only have an historical foundation, for mythology is a type of speech chosen by history: it cannot possibly evolve from the 'nature' of things.*

---

20   Foucault 1980a, p. 11.
21   Ibid., p. 11.

Speech of this kind is a message. It is therefore by no means confined to oral speech. It can consist of modes of writing or of representations.[22]

In order to treat proposals and images for women's clothing as historical and ideological constructs or signs, we should explore the particular relationship displayed in them between bodies of women (of the middle classes) and their clothes, thus aiming towards the spatio-social meaning of the location of these bodies. Thus clothes are to be seen as forms of moral investiture. As the editor of the magazine *Antahpur*, Hemantakumari Choudhury, remarks, clothes are to be seen as a sign of progress, marking moments in moral/cultural advancement from primitivity to civilisation:

> What are clothes and why are they necessary? Only those are clothes, wearing which the body may be fully covered, and which cover/prevent shame. It is known from reading the history of the most primitive stage of humanity that human kind then had no clothes to wear. Tree barks, leaves, animal fur or leather covered the bodies of different groups/peoples. The proof of this is to be found today among savage deep-forest or mountain dwellers. The ancient aryans, when they first arrived in India, dwelt in the forests near the Himalaya mountains. Initially they felt the need of clothes in order to prevent themselves from feeling the cold ... But as humans became more civilised they used their intelligence to fashion material fit for covering their bodies ... and God has always given to women a love of beauty and a sense of modesty.[23]

This version of the evolution of clothes claims that the human body itself has to be always understood as a vehicle which is capable of signifying a moral and historical stage (of civilisation), and the case of women as special within that.

The essays on clothing in the magazines and other supporting texts[24] support a similar evaluative perspective on human and female bodies. This perspective, however, makes little sense unless contexted to the notion of class, understood in its broadest and originary sense of social relations between mental and manual division of labour, inclusive of the sexual division and thus extending 'class' into both areas of social production and reproduction. These magazines and tracts make it clear that the female body of the propertied

---

22   Barthes 1973, p. 110 (my emphasis, excluding the first one).
23   Choudhury 1901, p. 137.
24   For example, autobiographies of women printed in the last century or reprinted more recently such as Dasi 1868.

classes is not to be seen directly in terms of its potentialities for reproduction or social labour (as befitting for non-labouring classes as a whole). The kind of social reproductive activity or labour which involves middle-class women is primarily viewed through the lens of morality, of the ideologically class-gendered notions of appropriate behaviour or decorum such as *sabhyata* (civility), *shobhanata* (decorum/propriety/decency), and *lajja* (shame/modesty). Of the three, the first two, understood as civilised behaviour or refinement, are applicable for both males and females of the middle classes, though inflected in an appropriately patriarchal way, implying an overall moral unity of the civilising project with gendered differentiation. But the concept of *lajja*, which is also a morally judgmental term and should translate more as 'shame' than 'shyness' or modesty, governs or underlies all references to civilised 'proper' behaviour when applied to girls and women. This is so central a notion that Kumari Soudamini, among others, writes in *Bamabodhini Patrika* a small treatise on *lajja*. In tackling this topic she instantly applies it to women in a manner which straddles both the realms of manners and morals:

> Shame is of two types. Of these one prevents human beings from sinful deeds, the other is peculiar to women. This essay is about the kind pertinent to women. There is no race/peoples on earth that deny that 'women should have a sense of shame'. Shame resides in the hearts of women in every country. There is only one difference, that some have more of it in their hearts than others. According to social customs, it is expressed differently in different countries. Whatever is regarded as a sign of shame in one country, in another may be considered a sign of shamelessness ... Another name for real sense of shame is modesty, and those women who are really possessed of a sense of shame, are also 'modest' ... [O]ne can not be truly modest (possess a sense of shame) simply by veiling one's face and not speaking to anyone. In fact not speaking to people might express pride. Those who are truly modest can not have hearts which contain pride or insolence, they are adorned by gentleness, politeness, good manners, tranquility, etc.[25]

It is to be noted that Kumari Soudamini repeatedly speaks of shame as an internal quality, links it with innocence along with refinement, unlinks it from hypocrisy and distinguishes it from 'savage', that is, uncivil or impolite behaviour:

---

25   Soudamini 1872, pp. 99–100.

Those who are truly possessed of modesty/sense of shame can never be hypocritical. Their hearts are adorned with the virtue of innocence, and their behaviour/manners express this sense of true modesty/sense of shame ... One should not behave like an uncivilised person to show modesty/sense of shame. That gives it a grotesque look. Many women of Bengal are in the thrall of this grotesque type of shame/modesty.[26]

She firmly establishes this sense of shame as a behaviour particularly appropriate to male-female relations and as a way of undercutting female provocation of male sexuality and of initiation of sexual response on her own part. The following passage shows the link she establishes between shame, exposure and covering of the female body and passionate enactments and utterances, and further clarifies the sexual theme, though the writer's own sense of shame/modesty prevents her from blatantly stating any of that:

They [upper class women] wear very fine [transparent] clothing and appear at ease in front of their male and female servants. Some women veil themselves but scream ugly things and carry on a fight with someone. That person who has never seen her face can [however] hear the crude words which emit from her mouth.[27]

Her concern about the sexual implication of the exposed female body and uncensored behaviour becomes explicit when she offers a 'civilising' suggestion to counteract women's current bathing practices.

Bathing, rubbing down of bodies [of women], etc., are done in places which can be seen. Therefore there should be a rule that male or female servants won't enter anywhere without permission, and bathing etc. will take place in privacy or secrecy.[28]

Sexuality permeates every corner of the social atmosphere she creates where possibilities of 'indecencies' are always present. From clothes to conversation, all must be ruled by 'shame': 'However one should converse in such a way that it does not give rise to any untoward [bad/sexual] thoughts in the minds of [the male] interlocutors'.[29] Thus the colonial notion of civilisation, with pro-

---

26   Ibid.
27   Ibid.
28   Ibid.
29   Ibid.

priety, gentility and refinement as corollaries, to which only the new propertied classes aspired, can be always extended to sexuality, to which can also be
associated the custom of enclosure for feudal, pre-British aristocracy. To be civilised is to have a sense of shame, and it is the antithesis of sexual provocation
brought on by explicit sexual display or seduction which is indicated in terms
of clothing by the degree of exposure of the female body. Revealing and hiding
it selectively thus works both as a lure and a deterrent to male lust, and confers on it the status of a significant and fetish object in the context of the social
morality of the new propertied classes.

The overall discourse on/of shame or *lajja* is a curious blend of indigenous and colonial values regarding women, nature and the body. Here misogyny
blends with a rejection of the natural or physical in any form. The female body
and sexuality are read through the notions of the primitive and the savage. In
essays such as 'Sindur' (Vermillion), all ornaments and colour decorations on
the body are despised as savage and sexual, and women are portrayed as savages within 'civilisation.'

> With the improvement in education and growth of civilisation bad popu-
> lar customs slowly disappear. Savages do not pay attention to the beauty
> of [their] mind, but rather adopt ways to enhance their physical beauty.
> They draw designs on their bodies, use vermillion in their hair, and pierce
> their ears and noses to wear ornaments. Since these bad popular cus-
> toms of this country are associated with religion, their persistence is more
> severe. Piercing ears, nose and wearing vermillion by women of Bengal
> are the foremost among these. The Hindu scriptures enjoin: 'only those
> may be considered as good wives who colour their bodies with turmeric
> powder, use antimony or mascara and vermillion'. But among our women
> readers, whose minds have been minimally enlightened by knowledge,
> there has developed a profound disgust for female customs and supersti-
> tions.[30]

Certain behaviours, therefore, are classified as 'lower types' of body-behaviour,
and contrasted to higher, intellectual-moral, or civilised ones of Europe. 'Exposure' and physicality also provide the hinge on which turn the themes of 'civilisation' and 'savagery' or 'barbarism'. Hiranmayee Debi's essay 'Sutikagrihey
Banaratwa' (Apishness in the Nursery) further builds into it the relevant element of social Darwinism.[31]

---

30   Anonymous 1869, pp. 121–3.
31   Debi 1891a. In this essay the idea of animality is securely linked by Debi with children

Hemantakumari Choudhury, in her essay on women's clothing, 'Striloker Paricchad' (Women's Attire), states: 'The more civilised humans became, the more clothes they made', marking the stages of civilisation from body to mind, paralleled by going from nakedness to wearing clothes, valorising the mental over the manual and the physically reproductive.[32] The civilised man or woman is well covered and plain, unadorned by ornaments, which she considers, as do the christian missionaries, clearly as fetishes. The plainly clothed English gentlewoman or the low church preacher, for example, as ideal female and male images, are contrasted to the well-adorned florid Bengali *Babu* who is 'effeminate', and his female sexually provocative counterpart, the *Bibi*, who is pagan hedonism/decadence incarnate.[33]

The project of essays on shame or decency, as characteristic traits of the *bhadramahila*, is to render upper class/caste women's body and physical life invisible, attempting to rarefy and ideologise as far as possible the actual everyday life of women and all their bodily functions. The *bhadramahila*, which is no more or no less than the sign of genteel womanhood, is thus the interpellating device for middle class women whose lives must illustrate particular gender-class relations of their time. Thus shame is 'an adornment of women', an especially commendable feminine virtue which both displaces the upper class/caste woman from her body as well as identifies her with it. Going beyond the sense of common social decency, *lajja*, as applied to women, also incorporates within it a keen awareness of sexual possibilities, infusing elements of denial, forbiddenness and guilt within female sexuality. As a concept it subsumes all kinds of physical and social needs and functions within a sexual discourse, enclosed in a general imperative of self-censorship. Essays such as Krishabhabini Das' 'Strilok O Purush' (Women and Men), or articles in *Bamabodhini*, situate shame as a central concept in 'femininity' and expli-

---

and savages and associated with any kind of physicality among adult men and women. It marks stages in the development of civilization through social stages and life stages, the goals of both being the suppression of the physical or the 'natural/emotional,' and elevation of the non-physical/rational. Social Darwinism's 'scientific' support for misogyny remains a field to be explored in the Bengali colonial context.

32   Choudhury 1901, pp. 137–40.

33   For the notion of the effeminate Babu and his female counterpart, see Bannerjee 1988 or 1989, and nineteenth-century satirical journalism such as Sinha 1856 or Thakur 1841. See also Sinha, where she states: 'The suspicion against the Bengali middle class found expression in the popularity of the racial and cultural stereotype of the "effeminate Bengali Babu"' (1995, p. 6) and 'The Victorian Anglo-Indian generally considered Bengali society to be steeped in sensuality. They were constantly appalled by open discussion of sexual matters in the Hindu household. The *Pioneer* found the talk of sex "too odious for description in a newspaper read in respectable households"' (p. 21).

citly connect it with 'civilisation', which implies both a de-sexualisation and a de-physicalisation. Opinions vary as to whether as an emotion it is learned or innate, but all the writers agree on creating a social ethics of denial and repression.

A transparent homology is established between the body, sexuality and savagery or primitivity. Discounting both the long existence of public and common bathing as a daily practice in villages, or of ritual occasions, the writers emphasise sexual possibilities inherent in it. The women bathers are seen as 'whores', though this word is carefully avoided as a 'bad' or 'indecent' expression. The adjective *jaghanya* (repulsive/abhorrent) is endlessly repeated through the text, particularly with regard to visibility of the female body. Accepting that civilisation means the denial of the body and the female body in particular, the theme of shame becomes a way of defining and institutionalising virtue and vice. Virtue is unphysical and thus unfemale, and also not the prerogative of those who engage in physical production. It is not connected with anything biological or manual in nature. It is non-reproductive and intellectual,[34] and proposes a new type of segregation which is maintained by self-surveillance.

The female body is invested in different ways in private and public spaces and in terms of the onlooker. Her clothes and presence thus possess a set of architectural and social correlates coded as *andarmahal* (inner quarters) and *griha* (home/hearth) and as 'home' and 'the world'. This spatial organisation is imbued with moral-cultural imperatives which are embedded in a specific social reproduction entailing its own sexual division of labour. With the proposal for change (only partially actualised) in the organisation of social reproduction, where the 'inner quarters' give space to the notion of 'home/hearth', in which the household is a joint enterprise of men and women with 'free mixing', there arises the idea of women's 'emergence' from the inner quarters to the presence of non-kin males. The necessity and the origin of the sartorial innovations and renovations are always referred back to this notion of 'emergence' and the presence of male company, connected in turn to 'civilisation:'

> The kind of clothing women wear here [in Bengal] is not considered reprehensible because it is customary. But upon even a slight consideration

---

34   This makes us rethink the whole notion of motherhood as found in Bengal, which seems to function as an antidote to women's sexual being. This may have been a way to redeem the physical and the reproductive without any overt or implied reference to sexuality – all allusions to motherhood are posed antithetically to female sexuality. See Bagchi 1990 and Krishnaraj 1995.

it will become apparent that it is slightly better than remaining naked by throwing a piece of cloth [over the body].

How perfunctory clothing may be, can be seen among women of this place. This may indicate a lack of show/pride, but it cannot protect one from the winter's wind or allow one to maintain civility, both major criteria of clothing. In no civilised country is there a custom of this kind of clothing, many laugh upon seeing it ...

Any civilised nation is against the kind of clothing in use in the present time among women [literally, 'weak ones'] of our country. Indeed it is a sign of shamelessness. Educated men [literally, 'those who have mastered knowledge'] have been greatly agitated about it, almost everyone wishes for another kind of civilised clothing.

There is a custom here of [women] wearing fine and transparent clothing, which reveals the whole body. Such shameless attire in no way allows one to frequent civilised company. If it happens that there is wise counsel being offered about religion/proper conduct, it may so happen that we can not attend to those wise words because of the clothes around. This shows how such clothes can stand in the way of our [moral] improvement.[35]

The phenomenon of 'emergence' is noted by Swarnakumari Debi in the context of her own sister-in-law's experience:

My middle older brother returned from England in 1864, and his service began in 1865. In those days the enclosure [of women] in the inner quarters was fully alive. Then women had to go in covered palanquin, with a guard running beside it, even to go from one house to the next within the same compound. If mother got permission to bathe in the Ganges after much pleading, they plunged her in the river along with the palanquin. When middle older brother was taking his wife to Bombay, even then he could not make her walk through the front yard. It was such a shameful deed for the daughter-in-law [of a good family] that everyone expressed particular disapproval. Therefore she had to get into the ship in a palanquin.[36]

But times moved inexorably:

---

35   Khastagiri 1872, pp. 148–52.
36   Debi 1916, p. 37.

Two years later when middle older brother came home with his wife, then no one could ask the daughter-in-law/bride to come into the house in a palanquin. But the tragedy that was enacted by witnessing the bride of the family descend from the carriage in front of the house [in public] like a white woman, is indescribably.[37]

Hemantakumari Choudhury expands on the theme of Bengali women's clothes by speaking of a need for change in the attitudes of women towards their own bodies:

Indian women, imitating the Begams [wives] of the Nawabs, started using very fine or transparent clothes. As a result of this, wives of Bengali homes felt no shame in going to bathe in the Ganges, or attending invitations. But finally many have begun to realise the bad taste involved in the custom of wearing one transparent/fine piece of cloth.[38]

These statements imply a basic change both in reality to some extent, and certainly ideologically, in the social context of female presence in Bengal. Reproductive labour carried on primarily by women within the household, outside of male participation, in large joint family structures, gives place to a reorganised emotional-moral space approximating the model of a nuclear family, at least conceptually and morally. Women writers such as Nagendrabala Mustafi decried the old arrangement, calling it an 'enclosure' and speaking of the horrible degeneracy among women as a result: 'We are trapped like birds in a cage of enclosure, our mental capacities are gradually becoming sluggish, our hearts are not able to blossom in the light of knowledge'.[39]

The 'emergence', then, contrasted to 'enclosure' or 'seclusion', came to be seen as *stri swadhinata* (women's freedom), a goal of social reform and an indicator of social 'progress'. But depending on the ideological stance of social critics, this could also mean an inversion of the desirable social/moral order (noted as *ghor kali*, or a fallen age).

The discursive organisation of physical exposure, including veiling or leaving bare the face, is created by the usual mixture of colonial and pre-colonial moral categories for social reform applicable to all aspects of social life. They are posed as moral binary terms: civilisation/barbarism, modern/traditional,

---

37   Ibid., p. 37.
38   Choudhury 1901, p. 139.
39   Mustafi 1896, pp. 30–1.

spiritual/physical, rational/irrational, decent/indecent, virtuous/sexual or sensual.[40] These form a moral and interpretive cluster and pose a constitutive relation between sexuality and society. They inscribe the (female) body with distinct sexual-social meanings. Accordingly, this body and its sexuality enter the realm of morality, both at the level of action and of desire. This creates a basis for both an everyday and institutional administration of sexuality in general and female sexuality in particular. The formal/sartorial presentation of the female body in particular becomes a powerful signifier of the success and failure of a moral regulation and offers a scope of controlled sexual expression as much as of suppression. It maps out the moral boundaries of the propertied classes, and subsumes within them the question of the practicalisation of desire.

This regulatory construction of sexuality, with a manipulation, fear and negation of the body, expresses the upper classes' notion of sexuality. It reveals at the same moment the social relations between, and ideological positions on, mental and manual labour. The relationship of the body or 'nakedness' to 'civilisation', expressed as sexuality versus rationality, and visualised as clothing, encodes the evaluation of, and power relations between, mental and manual labour. It typically valorises the mind (and its functions) over the body or nakedness (and its functions). *Lajja* or physical shame (this does and does not approximate the christian notion of guilt) becomes a pro-rationalist moral measuring concept which establishes the criteria for 'civilisation'. It calls for privileging the domination of nature, body and passion or 'irrationality' by various 'higher' mental capacities. The control of the female body through the moral mechanism of *lajja* or 'shame' becomes an expression of contempt, control and fear of female sexuality and the body as being quintessentially physical or 'natural'.

This misogynistic and controlling attitude is most blatantly expressed in an anonymous piece on women's public bathing. 'Civilisation' provides the focal point of judgement from which the bathers are viewed. The unsigned piece deserves to be quoted at length:

> Education helps to change many disgusting/revolting habits. As people become more civilised, they engage in civilised customs and practices, as befitting of the times. But habit has such an overwhelming power that people continue to nurture many disgusting practices because of it.

---

40   On this theme, see Sayer 1991, and also Inden 1990 where he traces the emergence of these concepts and applies them to the European construction of India.

Women's bathing customs in this country are one of these highly disgusting matters ... How it is that civilised and educated people engage to this day in this disgusting/revolting custom I can not tell! No doubt habit is the cause. But if they are not vigilant about such disgusting/revolting things they will become obstacles for women's improvement.

Genteel/civilised, as well as uncivilised women of villages bathe without any reservation together with men. This is not a matter of little disgust! And bathing [here] does not simply mean returning home after a dip. If only that were the case, even that would be no small matter of disgust. But [instead] women, eschewing all shame, stand next to men and clean their body parts in a most revolting manner ... On top of that, the kind of fine [clothing] material they wear is not fit to go out in society, and when that material becomes wet and clings to the body, then there is no difference between being naked and dressed. Many a time a decent man hesitates to get out of the pond in such clothes, but women, displaying remarkable ease, get out of the pond and walk home in their wet clothes.

Finally, it is respectfully submitted to women that they do not engage in such a disgusting activity. It is far better to go for a week without a bath, or even to go to the pond at dawn. Yet it is never reasonable to wash the body or clothes that are on, in front of men. I don't know when you will learn the real use of shame![41]

It is evident that this discourse and the actual principle at work in the designing of the attire are both obsessively centred on control through the segregation, obscuration and obstruction of movement of the female body.

3   Woman's Body: Enclosure and Exposure

The sense of crisis that we have mentioned before came to be crystallised in the theme of women's 'emergence' into the public/male domain and also the entrance of men into the household. Ideological consideration on the social crisis pivoted on the theme of women's transgression and the permissiveness of progressive men. The conservative literature of the time echoed with fear and anger about women's public presence. But scrutiny reveals that it is not the presence of women in the public space as such, which created this fear

---

41   Anon. 1871, pp. 71–3.

and anger, but rather the type and context of the space and presence.[42] The earlier public activities by women did not challenge the established sexual division of labour and the relatively stable and segregated domains of social reproduction. Therefore, it is not just the spatial transgression which upset the anti-reformists.[43] It is rather the 'unnaturalness' of their social presence in the capacity of intellectual interlocutors of men, as students, and as actual and potential professionals, such as teachers or doctors, which produced an ideological/moral response of managing the crisis.[44]

If this was the 'conservative' concern, the male reformers' concerns were no less anxious and acute. The female body and its moral-social-functional implications in the context of changing social reproduction overwhelmed them just as much. While advocating an education for women, and their 'emergence' from the 'inner' domain, they sought just as anxiously to curb any possibility of gender destabilisation or any real autonomy for women. Thus the attempts to re-dress them in 'civilised attire' may have had less to do with the fact that they wore a single piece of unstitched cloth in the women's quarters than with the fact that they were feared to be found where they should not have been, doing 'what men do'. This is not to say that there was no resistance to a regular form of exposure, or an advancement of the inner quarters or the *andarmahal* as a woman's 'natural' place. Even a writer like Krishnabhabini Das, who felt that economic independence was a positive gain or at times a necessity for women, in her essay 'Striloker Kaj ar Purusher Kaj' (Woman's Work and Man's Work) put forward this division of labour normatively. This 'natural' labour was as much about appropriate activities as about the placement of the female body or where such activities should take place. She should 'naturally' be found at 'home', keeping out of men's way, not competing with them and leaving the public space at their disposal. The sartorial re-casting, therefore, meant much more than an introduction of women's fashion or style in clothing, but rather

---

42 Articles in the magazines allude to the common presence of large numbers of upper and lower class women in public spaces for reasons of pilgrimage and other religious activities as well as social rituals, or for practical reasons such as that of bathing, washing clothes or fetching water, long before the 'emergence'.

43 It is not an accident that much of the satire against 'modern women' was levelled at 'educated' women, who were very well covered in an asexual and virtuous manner. These women as 'disguised prostitutes' and home-breaking 'masculine' viragoes attracted more ridicule and venom from the satirists than prostitutes.

44 See satires against 'educated' women, who are seen as 'masculine,' and their husbands as 'feminine'. This 'unnatural' social presence was caricatured and castigated in images and written texts. The thesis about this inversion indicating the end of an aeon, going through a fallen stage, is expressed in the notion of *Kali Yuga*, the age of Kali.

a proposal to re-cast both at an ideological/moral and a social/practical level a prevalent social organisation. Anxiety, signified by new experiments at dressing, reflected an anxiety over the loss of patriarchal power in a new form of social organisation. Articulating in diverse ideological propositions the actual and possible shift in social relations created by colonialism, the male reformers also sought to shape or direct these changes. Thus women 'emerged' in a new moral and social regalia which sought to counteract any threat to patriarchy. The clothing project meant the investiture of the female body in a new enclosure – a sartorial enclosure.[45]

This problem posed by the female body and its relative exposure was curious since Bengali men lived with both in life and art until well into the British rule.[46] Suddenly we are reminded of the 'uncivilised' appearance of women in their 'traditional' garment of an 'unstitched' piece of cloth, lacking undergarments to conceal their breasts and lower bodies. This new awareness could only have been due to the recognition that the prevailing patriarchal social organisation would undergo a shock in the new context. The possibilities of male-female relations no longer regulated through appropriate kinship conduct and established modes of biological-social reproduction occasioned much speculation and articulation of moral strategies. Tanika Sarkar addresses this very issue when she says:

> When we look at the nineteenth century household manuals and contrast them with the ancient ... we find that the real point of departure in our material relates not so much to the strategies of control but to unprecedented possibilities in the conditions of the women's existence.[47]

But Tanika Sarkar makes a mistake in not seeing the reform project as building in control in the very texture of how possibilities are conceived. The situation contained a special problem of signification in continuing and reorgan-

---

45   Regarding *griha*, see Bannerji 1992.

46   It is obvious that Bengali men and women lived with each other with the kind of clothing that they later repudiated as 'savage' or 'uncivilised' without any violation of ethics and aesthetics. In her popular journalism about Indian women's clothes and ornaments, Chitra Deb, for example, brings out a basic change in erotic aesthetics and ethics between pre- and early colonial times and the later nineteenth century among the propertied classes; see Deb 1989. Two English women visitors in India, Eliza Fay and Fanny Burney, also leave us with descriptions which do not show any negativity among the Bengali households as to what women or men wore. Bannerjee 1989.

47   Sarkar 1989, p. 3.

ising patriarchy. A discourse on shame and attempts to practicalise it through clothes and other moral imperatives restrained and incorporated 'possibilities' of women's fuller subjectivities within a patriarchal class project.

The attempted reconstruction was therefore a re-construction through both older and newer ideological and social norms and forms. The 'emergence' was also a continuation of the 'enclosure', a continuation of control of women's bodies, labour and sexuality into the new phase of colonial middle class formation. As such, in the matter of appearance, which provides us, as do all visual signs, with a more flexible and spacious signifier, the enclosure/emergence opposition undergoes a formal and moral elision. Even though the icon/sign signals to what may be called *new* possibilities, it also signals *new* restraints. The new image incorporates much of the old enclosure through a formal and an ideological reshaping. The attempt is re-presented as 'virtue', as a consciously designed textile-moral contraption. The woman of the 'enlightened' middle class Bengali home was to present herself as the sign called *bhadramahila*, attired in virtue.

4   *Lajja*, National Culture and Women's Clothing

The social meaning of the body goes beyond what is functionally understood by sexual reproduction. It relates to the social organisation as a whole, and involves a general morality and politics not exclusive of sexuality. The importance of physical appearance with appropriate signifiers for cultural representations is obvious in the context of Bengal's nationalism. This national culture implies and aspires to a certain kind of morality and constructs the Bengali women's ideal sexuality, and projects this as the sign of *bhadramahila*. *Lajja*, or a sense of shame, is integral to this construct of femininity, in nationalist terms, and the sartorial project consists of designing a 'national' visual form. As cultural nationalism gained momentum from the 1860s onward, European women's clothes were not seen as just 'alien' or 'foreign' but actually 'shameful' in the national context. The question of direct imitation always gave place to attempts of construction. A minuscule section among the elite wore gowns while saris were being experimented with. But it is interesting to note that saris won the day. The reason for this outcome is the elision between feminine shame/modesty and *deshiata*, or 'nationalist' cultural authenticity, which includes a restrained female sexuality. Writer after writer in the women's magazines creates a transparency between a proper female sexual morality and a national apparel. As Soudamini Khastagiri puts it:

Relatively speaking [relative to wearing one piece cloth] clothes of nations such as those of the English may be better. But in some aspects they are a thousand times worse than ours. Therefore, if we seek to imitate them, we get rid of some faults only to embrace their deficiencies.[48]

She states that such clothes are a betrayal of national identity and what is culturally appropriate femininity for 'us'. It is hypocritical and artificial for Indians to wear western clothes, and by so doing, they become marginalised in both societies. An anonymous writer quotes approvingly from another woman, Rajlaxmi Sen: 'Therefore whatever preserves national culture, and enables all to identify [one] as a woman of Bengali homes and covers the body thoroughly, and is appropriate for both the rich and the poor, allowing at the same a free movement of the body, should be worn'.[49]

An essay by Jyotirmayee Gangopadhyay written many years later echoes exactly the same sentiment: 'There was a time when the new promoters of women's emancipation, both male and female, adorned themselves in western clothes ... They adopted these clothes as an expression or symbol of their views'.[50] But she also stated:

We have many proofs of the fact that educated men and women did not wish to wear western clothes, since they conveyed an anti-nationalist mentality. Most educated women, and it is not an exaggeration to claim about 99%, do not consider gowns as tasteful as saris.[51]

The same sentiment is echoed by Soudamini Khastagiri:

It is never as enjoyable to imitate clothes of other nations, as to create one from one's imagination, and which is suited to both *national characteristics* and is also *civilised*. And besides, there is a sense of artificiality if Bengalis wear the clothing of English or any other nation. They are considered of that culture and are treated as such. If a Bengali person dresses like the English and frequents their society, they engage in reviling the Bengalis in front of him, which he has to listen to with patience. Such clothes also deprive one of full acceptance among one's own people.[52]

---

48   Khastagiri 1872.
49   Anon. 1872, p. 2.
50   Gangopadhyay 1924, p. 1055.
51   Ibid., 1056.
52   Khastagiri 1872.

Or further:

> It is a duty to keep characteristics/signs of one's nation/culture in people's clothing or manners. Therefore it is not fit to imitate other nations wholly, this expresses lowness in status. We will accept the good things about religion and conduct [moral character] of other countries, but there is no need to imitate them in matters of appearance. Even when the [female] attires of the English, or Northern or Western Indians, or Muslims or the Chinese may be beautiful, Bengali women should not wear them. The duty consists of wearing clothing which shows one's national culture, covers one's body fully and which indicates instantly that one is a woman of Bengal.[53]

As we saw in Swarnakumari Debi's description of her reformer father Debendranath's sartorial experiments, a combination of 'shame/modesty' and a patriarchal nationalist aesthetic have always provided the bases of new designs. Sarala Debi's essay 'Swadeshi Poshak' (Nationalist Clothing) is also a good example of what is meant by a national cultural identity. Concepts such as *shobhanata* (appropriateness/decorum), *shabinata* (decency) or *shilata* (courtesy) are shown to be the moral underpinnings of the fashion design of nationalism. This 'national' and sexually moral apparel also marks out the good from the bad woman, and advocates a complete sexual repression and sartorial segregation for widows. This is also the opinion of Soudamini Khastagiri, who states:

> Nowadays some women wear *kamij* [a type of long shirt with long sleeves], jacket, sari and shoes. That is fine, but even some bad/loose women of this country wear them. For this reason one should use a shawl covering from head to toe, which especially hides the upper body. This will indicate a daughter of a respectable family ... And one should also adopt a way of distinguishing married women from widows.[54]

She and others suggest a recipe for dressing in ways signifying respectability (class, national culture and shame/modesty). For wearing at home, an *ijar* (bloomers or drawers), *piran* (a short-sleeved shirt) and a sari, or a long *piran* and a sari. For going out an *ijar*, a *piran*, a sari, pyjamas, shoes and socks, though

---

53 Khastagiri 1872.
54 Khastagiri 1872.

the latter are optional, female 'shame' not residing in the feet. The experiment is obviously never complete and always on the verge of a collapse under scrutiny, and even this figure of modesty, national culture and 'good' class is not considered 'authentically national' or modest by a large section of Hindu conservative society. It is still considered 'anglicised' and 'masculine' both in morality and form, and ridiculed in the caricatures of the street painters of Kalighat.

Lajja, put forward as a major female ethic, projecting a high social status and an indication of national authenticity, serves as a subjective regulator of female physicality or sexuality. As an internalised censor, uplifted to virtue, it becomes the most personal, therefore moral, way of controlling women. A good example is the portrait of Krishnabhabini Das in a Hindu widow's garb, after her rejection of Western clothes. It is an act and an image through which she redeems herself in the eyes of her previous critics, through her acceptance of a garb of purity signifying sexual self-effacement and self-sacrifice.

> Almost every day at the mall I saw a woman well-dressed in European clothes. It surprised me a little, because even though she was dressed in European clothes, the expression on her face was sweet and gentle ...
>
> Where was that woman dressed in English costume now? This was a widow of Hindu homes in front of me! She was worth being worshipped. She knew of no good qualities to boast of in herself, nor had she any temptation in that direction. She never wanted to be famous. Becoming one with the very earth in humility, she carried on her tasks. Her white and pure attire of a widow created such a sense of respect and awe [towards her].[55]

In keeping with her image of white purity is her personal morality: 'After becoming a widow she gave up all kinds of comfort. She never slept in a bedstead anymore, but rather made a bed on the floor. Never ate anything good, such as fruits or sweets. She gave up everything'.[56] By discarding the European garb of her former married state and the definition of herself as an individual, with limited self-interests, she enters simultaneously into the orbit of shame and cultural national authenticity. Her portrait serves as a radiant icon of female purity, which reaches its climax with widowhood. Sexuality can now be erased completely both in the name of virtue and national culture.

---

55   Debi 1923, p. 742.
56   Ibid., p. 742.

An obsessive concern for well-coveredness of the female body and the visual projection of purity are the negative signifiers for female sexuality – a perpetual reminder of what lies within and what a woman must not disclose – except at the risk of being outcast both personally and politically. A passive sexuality is thus established for middle- or upper-class women, where lacking the volition of exposure or disclosure, she becomes a contained but persistent zone for activating male sexuality. The cover of clothing is presented as the future promise of un-covering by an outside agent. Unveiling her, or 'freeing' her from a fabricated encasement, becomes a male prerogative and pleasure. The passivity of the construct called *bhadramahila* is ensured by the fact that her *bhadra*ness (gentility or modesty or class status) is dependent upon her desexualisation. She must be constantly aware of the male gaze and avoid being or doing anything sexually provocative. From this point of view 'shame' becomes the ideological construct on which pornography (not the same as erotic literature) is hinged. Nineteenth-century male reforming literature is full of indirect allusions or moralising on what is forbidden or hidden. Thus shame, or decency, while considering female clothing, supersedes discussions on beauty, or is equated with it.

Sartorial moral philosophy of Bengal, whether produced by women or men, implies an invisible and constant male gaze at women. The purpose of this gaze, or rather its origin/occasion, is domination, to create an ideological object, a sexually circumscribed 'other'. Women themselves, through their own subscription to the same discourse of 'shame and civilisation', participated in the same enterprise. Their construct of femininity is thus not only opposed to the masculine, through sharing the premise of gentility, but also self-divided and self-censoring. It consists of the moral notion of appropriately gendered 'goodness', 'otherising' her own sexuality from herself through patriarchal prescriptions. The antithesis of this female goodness is the bad woman, epitomised in the notion of the prostitute.[57] This self-division is reflected in the divide

---

57   In an unpublished paper, Ratnabali Chattopadhyay discusses the iconography of the 'bad woman' or the prostitute and the referential relationship between this construct and that of *sati*, the chaste good woman, or the *bhadramahila* with her refined moral purity: 'In a number of moral tracts the chaste wife (*patibrata stree*) and the prostitute (*beshya*) are constructed into visible signs' (1992, p. 29). Chattopadhyay also quotes a few lines from an anonymous tract entitled 'Stridiger Prati Upadesh' (Advice to Women): 'The good wife, *patibrata*, is shy, silent, does her duty and is totally undemanding, stays away from men, keeps her whole body covered and does not wear flashy clothes,' while the '*beshya* is loud-mouthed, always restless, bares special parts of her body, falls on men, demands jewelry and continuously wears revealing clothes' (1874, p. 29). This distinction was so widely touted, and morally organised, that it is not surprising that it formed a part of the con-

among women themselves, towards other women, and regarding the attitude towards their own body and eroticism. And it should be noted that the ideology of 'proper clothes' designed for women of the urban propertied classes is held out as a typology to all others, and is a part of a general hegemonic design. Its 'naturalisation' as appropriate aspiration for gentility creates a mythology, a system of signs, which encodes a reconstructed morality of a nationalist but anglicised section of the urban propertied classes.

The nature of this new morality as indicated by *lajja* for women cannot be understood outside of Bengal's colonial context. The sense of crisis that filled the air manifested itself as much in idealising/ideologising the collapse of the older organisation of social spaces, as in attempts of reprivatisation and in directing the course of change, particularly as regards women and the family. It contains a colonial response, both in an anger towards and a submission to European judgement on the decadence/savagery of Indians both male and female.[58] The prescription for female sexuality, constructed within a colonial context, shifts from being direct to that of a repressed Victorian christian ladyhood. This becomes clear if a contrast is established between the icon of the de-sexualised gentlewoman and the pre-anglicised version of female sexuality in eighteenth-century Bengal, when a woman's sexual initiative is portrayed with respect and frankness by male poets such as Bharatchandra. In this epic poetry from the eighteenth century, the woman is not an 'object' of male desire, as is to happen later, when this very male desire is circumscribed by a general ideology of de-sexualisation of the human body through a narrative of vice.[59] The much advocated serene, unsexual moral female image, which is only nuanced

---

sciousness of middle class educated women who were particularly sensitive regarding their respectability or *bhadrata* and wanted no confusion between their own project of emancipation and the 'freeness' of 'bad/loose' *itar* women.

58   Many authors, both Indian and Western, have commented on the British preoccupation with Indian moral degeneracy and savagery, particularly with regard to sexual morality and women. For example, Major C.A. McMohan writes: 'Native public opinion would not go with us in an attempt to put a stop to professional prostitution. The mind of a native is no more shocked at the thought that a girl should be born to prostitute than that a man should be born to be blacksmiths and carpenters. Prostitution is an institution the history of which in India at all events is lost in the mist of ages. Prostitutes danced before Yudishthir and Rama and in the guise of dancing girls and singers. They are a necessary part of most domestic ceremonies today' (Home Judicial File No. 48.p.1143, 7th June 1872, to C.M. Riwarzi Esq., Officiating Undersecretary to the Government of Punjab). See also Niranjana 1990 as well as Bandyopadhyay 1991.

59   See Ballhatchet 1980 and also Chattopadhyay 1992, p. 17: 'The main focus of the missionary narrative rested on recreating the atmosphere of vice. This was done to show the exact division of space that existed between the rulers and the ruled'.

by indirect and repressed physicality, is a sign of 'femininity' rather than of womanhood or femaleness. It also desexualises or contains male sexuality, or rather is an expression of its containment, since it is at its most 'feminine' in a passive form, and does not solicit a directly sexual male attention.

The colonially inflected patriarchal world view of the middle classes of Bengal, however, should be understood as being both local and foreign. The sign of the *bhadramahila* is a great example of this reconstruction of consciousness. It is in a sense a re-worked or anglicised version of the older Bengali *sati* (the chaste woman-wife). In its current phase of a gentlewoman the direct physical control and violence of patriarchy has been domesticised and substituted by an ideological encirclement of clothing and other forms or morality which mix chastity and sacrifice with the moral code of a utilitarian Christian lady.

After the first half of the nineteenth century, 'the feminine' emerges as a notion among the western educated population in Bengal. It is found everywhere – from education to clothes. It is not surprising, therefore, that many women, in search of a direct agency and strength, turned to the colonial-nationalist myth of the Aryan Woman or notions of the mother goddess. If we compare women's and men's use of the construct of the Aryan Woman we find that women are attracted to the myth in search of notions such as dynamism and clothing designed for public and open spaces, while men to the Aryan Woman's moral qualities which are passive, such as constancy, chastity and sacrifice:

> The clothes worn by Aryan women in ancient times bear no resemblance with the present time. In those days women had freedom. Women frequented war zones and courts freely. In many cases wives or sisters had to ride on horses with their husbands or brothers. This is why it was not suitable for them to wear just beautiful clothes. There was a great similarity between male and female clothing.[60]

The same may be said of the typology of English and American women used by Krishna Bhabani Das, Hiranmayee Debi and others who represent freedom, agency and self-sufficiency, without fully displacing women from the private or domestic sphere.

---

60   Choudhury 1991, p. 138.

5   Conclusion

These essays by women on civilisation, shame, the body and clothing both organise and express the consciousness of a significant strand of the developing 'westernised', reforming middle classes of Bengal. They display the commonsense of classes created on a colonial terrain which also contain competitive 'national' aspirations. In the case of the garb of the *bhadramahila*, however, much more so than in the area of education, for example, the colonial context and content overdetermine the hegemonic forms of these classes. This sartorial-moral enterprise is profoundly English nineteenth century in its ethos. Fundamentally distinct from pre-colonial, feudal notions of grandeur or status, this attire is an intrinsic response to and an absorption within a colonial influence. The ideology of Victorian femininity provides the lens through which is perceived and configured the indigenous dominant ideology about womanhood.

The *bhadramahila*, both in form and content, is the Bengali males' response to European accusations of their barbarism. The configuration here depends on a particular set of social relations which express the gender organisation of the propertied classes. Here we have multiple but coherent discourses of patriarchy in so far as local and colonial elements of gender and class ideologies converge into an overall misogyny and a general rejection of the physical. As we noted before, class, in the sense of division and valorisation of mental over manual labour, extends into a positive hatred of the body and sexuality as embodied by women as 'nature' and 'the primitive'. Racism itself is concretised with patriarchy and classism in the European stereotypes of animality and sensuality of Bengali/pagan women in particular, but also men.[61]

If this seems like an exaggerated way of stating the colonial ideological design, we need to only look at Kenneth Ballhatchet's book on racism and sex in the Raj which gave the 'Hindoos' and their women in particular a savage, evil and corrupting role with regard to Europeans. Accusations of barbaric sensuality and primitivity fill the pages of Mill's *History of British India*, mission-

---

61   See the account of Rev. James Ward, excerpted by Sumanta Bannerjee: 'Before two o'clock
        the place was cleared ... when the doors of the area were thrown open, and a vast crowd of
        natives rushed in, almost treading one upon another, among whom were the vocal singers
        ... who entertained their guests with filthy songs and danced in indecent attitudes before
        the goddess, holding up their hands, turning around, putting forward their heads towards
        the image, every now and then bending their bodies and almost tearing their throats with
        their vociferations' (1989, p. 54).

ary tracts, letters, travelogues and drawings of Europeans in India/Bengal.[62] Rationality, or access to reason, is seen as a far away dream for Indians, so close are they supposed to be in religion and everyday life to sensuality and nature. Their spirituality or literary creation itself is seen at best as a product of a sensual, distorted imagination, rather than of spiritual transcendence.[63] And if the Indian/Bengali society as a whole, characterised in terms of its males, is such a natural excrescence, then how much more so the Bengali women, whose identity with nature has not been ruptured by any rational interruption. The European enlightenment's moral-social schema, which rests on 'civilisation vs. barbarism/moral decay' of Indian males, or an ambivalence towards 'tradition', expresses itself in a man-to-man condemnation of Indian males (as sensualists and females manque) as oppressors of 'their women', and confers on the colonial (male) rulers the role of protectors or reformers of Indian women. For Indian males, vying for the same status of reformer-protector, this means a combination of self-hatred (for being 'female/effete') acquired in the colonial context, and a hatred of women (for being natural, uncivilised, etc.) which is both colonial and pre-colonial.

The project of social reform for women therefore allows for externalising or displacing their views of the self and self-hatred onto society at large and women in particular. It also calls for curbing 'naturality' (femaleness) in themselves. In the same sexually repressive configurated design aimed at women, morally-sartorially, the project of self-improvement is collapsed with self-repression for men. Thus domination of nature as embodied by women could be projected as social reform, offering examples of rationality (therefore true masculinity a la old Brahmanism and European enlightenment/utilitarianism) on the part of Bengali male intelligentsia. Indians such as Rajnarayan Bose (and many others) expressed just this conjuncture when their reforming zeal was expressed in terms of 'she must be refined, reorganised, recast and regenerated'. This introjected colonial judgement, along with a reorganised older patriarchy, provided much of the middle classes' hegemonic self-definition. It could therefore be said that the clothes designed for the *bhadramahila* inscribed on women's body the moral-political agenda of the same classes. Krishnabhabini Das and Swarnakumari Debi, describing changes in the social organisation of a household, speak of growing male control over all aspects of women's lives. Much of their own writing aims to establish a relative autonomy for women while maintaining a somewhat differentiated social domain.

---

62   See, among numerous sources, Das Gupta 1959; Martin 1837; Long 1974; Marshman 1864; Carpenter 1868.

63   See Inden 1990.

The virtuous attire designed for the gentlewoman of Bengal is a reworking of existing and incoming social and cultural forms. This convergence, negotiation and fusion on grounds of cultural commonsense and ideology between colonial and indigenous patriarchal class values can only happen because the European forms and norms are not dissimilar to those prevailing in Bengal. The intelligibility of colonial, foreign notions actually rests on prior social organisation in Bengal or India. A highly evolved division of labour as expressed in the caste system and forms of class, valorisation of mental production by placing Brahmins (priest-scholars) at the head of the society, the deprivation of women (even of the Brahmin caste) and low caste physical-manual producers of intellectual prerogatives, all contain a basic similarity to European social organisation in terms of gender and class organisation. The pre-existing social organisation thus provides enough ground for weaving in or re-working colonial misogyny, elitism and racism. Fundamentally patriarchal, Brahminical rationalism and asceticism is also characterised by a basic hatred and contempt towards women (as natural, physical entities) and the lower castes/classes as unreconstructed body or nature, and thus collapses the woman and the *sudra* (low caste).[64]

This predisposition could not have been inimical to colonial-capitalist class distinctions, protestant christianity, utilitarianism and Cartesian rationalism, all of which were fundamentally anti-woman, anti-physical/manual producer and racist. Frantz Fanon has written about the colonial discourse as a discourse of Cartesian masculinity in which the coloniser/conqueror is the sole male or intellectual subject and the colonised is an object, a body, an animality and by extension a femaleness.[65] The equation of women with nature, with the reproduction of physical life, womb and instinct, and by extension with feelings and primitivity, was equally well-known to both India and Britain. This is why the

---

64   Sukumari Bhattacharji, a scholar on ancient India, as well as Uma Chakravarty have done much work on the status of women in ancient India, challenging the Aryan myth. The physical status of women is evident, according to Bhattacharji, from the settled agricultural period by her deprivation of education and control over her body (and its fruits) by men: 'The wife had no property rights, nor had she any right over her body (*Satapatha Brahmana* IV 4: 2: 13). If she refused to oblige the husband sexually she should first be coaxed and cajoled, then bribed and "brought over" (cf. *avakriniyat*) with gifts; if she still refused, he should beat her with his palm or with a rod into submission (*Brhadaranyaka Upanishad* VI 4: 7)' (Battacharji 1989, p. 30).

65   Fanon 1963, pp. 35–43. Fanon points out the physicality/body status attributed to the colonised and the rationalist essentialism of the European coloniser's 'self'. This shares the same ground with patriarchy insofar as women are seen as 'nature' or 'body' and equated with a reproductive self, qualitatively a different consciousness, and incapable of rationality.

woman of India and the savage, and the Indian/Bengali woman as the quint-essentially savage, must be reformed and clothed or re-clothed. This is not to say that the European attitude towards European women was any different or better. European contempt (and hatred) for females of the conquered species was disguised as paternalistic charity. This charity, mediated through notions of civilisation and progress, offered both an indictment of Indian society and a legitimacy for colonial rule.

The women writers of the magazines share to a great extent, in spite of their nationalism, the colonial view of themselves and their society. They adopt the same trajectory of historiography originating from James Mill, starting with the golden age of the Aryans, moving through the dark ages of Muslim rule to the present moral and intellectual decay, to the English era of enlightenment which calls for social reform.[66] These sartorial innovations therefore represent a recovering of a higher, intellectual-moral self, a disguising and a muting of the 'natural', through consciously eliminating sensuality/sexuality signalled by hiding of the female body. If nothing else, through the reform attempts the basically reproductive natural femaleness is tempered with virtue, taming sexuality and animality into sweet sentimentality and mothering. The colonially proffered image of the Victorian, Christian middle-class woman which overshadows this sartorial project, less the grand lady than the helpmate of missionaries and social reformers, represents the icon of a civilised society, while holding forth the possibility of moral improvement to a section of Bengali women.

Much more so than in education, where the feminist thrust of the women's self-improvement project is strident in spite of subscription to norms of a class-patriarchy, it is in the area of clothing and the body that a guilt-ridden, shameful, indigenous-cum-colonial patriarchy holds women in thrall. While the same women are unashamedly demanding in acquisition of intellect and reason, they are held in place by 'shame' in the matter of their body, sensuality and sexuality. It is with 'shame' that middle-class women are most inexorably riveted to patriarchy. The life of Krishnabhabini Das is a prime example of this situation. It shows what suspicions she had to allay for going to England, being educated and independent, what she traded off, in order to gain a morally correct image. That white-robed icon of the Hindu widow which hides her femaleness in a heavy garb of coarse cloth, which mutes all expressions and potentiality of sexuality, which tempts no male, is her uniform of legitimacy

---

66   For the myth of the aryan woman and its implications for nationalism, and nationalism's
      influence on social reform for women, see Chakravarty 1989.

for being a 'modern' woman and advocating women's emancipation and education. Only attired in virtue can she fully expiate her past of transgressions.
So even she, critical and strident as she is, a tireless promoter of reason and
knowledge, subscribes to the same discourse of shame, to the triumph of male
brahminical-colonial rationality over the female mind and body.

If we are to consider the issues of subjectivity and agency of women in
nineteenth century Bengal, it becomes apparent through this sartorial-moral
project that middle-class women are held hostage between colonialism and
nationalism, patriarchal class subjectivity and their resistance to it.[67] In helping to create an icon/sign for the emerging aspirations of a Bengali culture and
Bengali nationalism, women capitulated far more to a patriarchal fashioning
of themselves than in any other area of social change and development. The
values they represent sartorially are in no way contrary to those of men, and
in fact the more 'enlightened' they are, the more they compensate by sacrificing their social-sexual agency, for their encroachment in the male domain of
reason and public service.

In the end, we might say that though middle class women 'come out' or
'emerge' by overstepping the boundaries of an earlier 'inner quarters' in terms
of location in space and an earlier division of labour, their sartorial morality
indicates an object-subject ideological status which they themselves are active
in bringing forth. As relegated agents of an objectified subjectivity, they enter
a textile prison, fashioned by male tailors and fathers of Bengal's social reform.
This prison is constructed from lace, linen, cotton and silk, and from the sober
and sombre tints of shame and guilt adding up to virtue.

---

67   On this notion of divided subjectivity of women caught in the interpellation of class and
      patriarchy, see Bannerji 1997a, pp. 138–9: '[I]t can be said that women class members were
      "summoned" both by Bengal's urban propertied classes' formative agenda and Bengali
      nationalism's "emancipatory" calls to become "social actors", and hence their presence
      in the stage of education. This amounts to "dominant ideology" interpellating women to
      function as class subjects, while that subjectivity itself is sought to be contained, man-
      aged, truncated and inauthenticated by the repression of their full social being through
      patriarchy'.

Fashioning a Self: Educational Proposals for and by Women in Popular Magazines in Colonial Bengal

Woman was not created to be the ignorant slave or the plaything of man. As it is the purpose of a woman's life to do good to others, and to live for them, so does a woman live for herself. And the serious responsibilities that are entrusted to her demand not only a sympathetic heart, but also a cultivated head.[1]

• • •

We call this *moral regulation*: a project of normalising, rendering natural, taken for granted, in a word 'obvious' what are in fact ontological and epistemological premises of a particular and historical form of social order.[2]

• •
•

1   Introduction

Nineteenth-century Bengal is characterised by its preoccupation with social reform, much of which concentrated on women. Immediately meant for bettering the lot of women, it also aimed at reorganising fundamental social relations and forms of consciousness structuring the family and lives of women among the middle classes.[3] A reconstructive contestation resulted between the colonial state and the Bengali male intelligentsia whose object was 'the new Bengali woman'. But from the last decades of the century women themselves sought to contribute to this formative process of their social subjectivities and agencies. The issue of education attracted much attention, being the most well-

---

1 Das 1891c.
2 Corrigan and Sayer 1985, p. 4.
3 Sangari and Vaid say something similar: 'Middle class reforms undertaken on behalf of women are tied up with the self-definition of class, with a new division of the public from the private sphere and of course with a cultural nationalism' (1990, p. 9).

articulated and definitively ideological area within the scope of social reform. Controversies raging around women's education, and 'the educated woman', alias *bhadramahila* (the gentlewoman), signalled far beyond the immediate social problems of women and served as a complex signifier of the composition of social subjectivities (that is, 'common sense') of the middle classes.[4] Seen thus, the various social reform projects of the century could be interpreted as marking moments in a battle for hegemony, in which a class, or a class fraction, elaborates an ideological stance in its bid to become morally, culturally and politically, a dominant force within the civil society or everyday life. That is, it is a stage in what Gramsci has called 'the passive revolution',[5] amounting to attempts at transforming the common sense of classes prior by persons within the ruling relations to, or concurrently with, assuming a directly political role. The important question for us, then, while dealing with social reform, is what role women themselves, of their own volition, play in this 'passive revolution', which involves being drawn into the hegemonic fold, and of women themselves as agents in this hegemonic process.[6] We need to know, as with all studies in the subjective-cultural dimensions of class formation and politics, how women fared in the 'self-making' of their classes, and of themselves, and what modes they adopted in this necessary task of fashioning selves and society.

Although most public facilities were not available to women in their self-defining project, the print media, creating a bridge between the public and the private, offered them a wide communicative space. These women were already 'educated', far beyond the literacy stage, the older ones mostly at home, and many of the younger ones in girls' schools. Magazines such as *Bamabodhini* established by the male reforming intelligentsia held space for women writers under the heading of *Bama Racana* ('Women's Writings'). But there were also other magazines, such as *Bharati* (edited by such eminent women as Swarnakumari Debi), along with *Antahpur, Sahitya, Mukul, Sakha, Pradip* and others,

---

4   Here the term 'common sense' is used in the sense in which Antonio Gramsci formulates it in *The Prison Notebooks*; see, e.g., his use in 'The Study of Philosophy' (1971, pp. 323–3). Gramsci considers this as the general state of consciousness in the everyday sense – pre-scientific, pre-ideological. It is a kind of 'political unconscious'.

5   Gramsci 1971, pp. 105–20. This speaks to the development of what Gramsci calls 'the equilibrium of political forces' where the ground is moving towards a readiness for a politico-military hegemony by transforming the cultural-social domain.

6   Ibid. This concept is ubiquitous in Gramsci's work. The whole of *The Prison Notebooks* may be read in terms of the definition, refinement, complication and assumption of hegemony. Gramsci's use of this Machiavellian (and older) concept is marked by his understanding of ruling or power that lies in building 'consent' which provides 'legitimation' at a moral and social level.

all of which created an extensive sphere of social influence and a field of participation for the rudimentary women intelligentsia of the time.[7] It is through an exploration of the content and quality of this influence and participation that we can arrive at some understanding of the type of social subjectivity and agency that these women created for themselves. This does not require an extensive media study, but more an exercise in historical sociology using representative material.

In the pages of these magazines, the women writers and their women readers build up an extensive network and a general fund of communicative competence. They work up 'women's issues', 'women's approaches', and invite pieces on new themes or hold essay competitions from among the readers. Thus it is difficult to see them as solely male-identified and as an isolated mimic intelligentsia, as Sumanta Banerji seems to suggest in his book *The Parlour and the Street*.[8] Even though the loss of an *andar mahal* (inner/women's quarters) makes for a substantial change and losses in a certain type of popular and women's culture, as he claims, what follows cannot simply be seen as a destruction of a 'women's culture and community' and the emergence of a class of women thoroughly absorbed in the male moral-intellectual space with women isolated from one another. Rather, the attempt seems to be to introduce new communicative modes, availing of a certain kind of facility such as the journal or magazine, with the purpose of creating another social, moral and cultural space for and by women, with different mediations and signifiers. Thus the situation is not one of complete co-option by sexism of their male counterparts, as women of the *andar mahal* also were not fully co-opted by the general patriarchal social organisation within which they lived. Obviously both the society of women in the *andar mahal* culture and that of the magazine culture shared forms of patriarchal consciousness with their male counterparts, but what is interesting is that beyond, and through, their particular educational 'women's agenda' they sought a guidance role within society as a whole, as 'women' members of propertied classes. As Krishnabhabini Das put it, 'It is unjust to say that only men should cultivate that intelligence, that God has given both men and women. God could never have imparted such a great gift without a noble end in view'.[9] From this step of universality she deduces the 'noble end in view':

---

7   See Borthwick 1984, pp. 60–108, on women's education and the role of magazines in this process. Borthwick gives statistics and tables showing the extensive spread of female education (1984, pp. 76–80).

8   Bannerji, S. 1989, pp. 147–8.

9   Das, 1891c.

Especially, since the education of male kind (*purush jati*) depends essentially on women's education and sense of morality, and since we can directly see how a man's character depends on his home life, especially on his mother's example, then who can deny that higher and quality education for women, lies at the root of national progress and morality?[10]

This sentiment and argument, expanding in concentric circles, from the mother, the home, to the nation – from the self-improvement of the woman, through her son, to the nation – are found consistently and centrally in the works of all the women writers who provide material for this essay. They are Swarnakumari Debi, Gyanadanandini Debi, Sarala Debi, Hironmoyee Debi, and Krishnabhabini Das. In order to explore the ideological dimensions of their thought, I seek to locate their educational proposals within a larger problematic of mediatory and constitutive relations between the social relations and cultural forms of gender, class and colonialism. The ideological dimension is particularly explored with regard to the nature of social subjectivity and agency, assumed and recommended by these articles, and their implications for the hegemonic aspirations for their class or class fraction. In this process, it is hoped that it will become clear how 'cultural', in the broadest sense, 'class' is, and how deeply gendered is the agenda of 'class', and how 'classified' is the construction of gender relations within it.

The special type of subjectivity that women have within a class topography can be captured conceptually by adapting Louis Althusser's notion of ideological interpellation.[11] This allows for the conception of a social agency for a divided and yet a unified purpose. That is, it allows for problematising women's relationship to the patriarchal and gendered norms and forms of their own class. This has to be thought through as a situation for women of all classes, but especially for women of propertied classes who are simultaneously empowered by their social location and subordinated to the class's patriarchal, gendered organisation. From this perspective it can be said that women class members were 'summoned' both by the Bengali's urban propertied classes' formative agenda and Bengali nationalism's 'emancipatory' calls[12] to become 'social

---

10   Das 1891c. This and all subsequent translations from Bengali are mine.
11   Althusser 1984, pp. 44–51. While presenting how ideology interpellates individuals as subjects, Althusser states: 'I shall then suggest that ideology 'acts' or 'functions' in such a way that it 'recruits' subjects among individuals (it recruits them all), or transforms the individuals into subjects (it transforms them all) by that very precise operation I have called interpellation or hailing and which can be imagined along the lines of the most commonplace everyday police (or other) hailing, 'Hey, you there!'' (1984, p. 48).
12   See Chatterjee 1990.

actors', and hence their presence on the stage of education. This amounts to the 'dominant ideology' interpellating women to function as class subjects while that subjectivity itself is sought to be contained, managed, truncated and unauthenticated by the repression of their full social being through patriarchy. The women intelligentsia of the time are themselves not unaware of this double-edged situation. Their texts are therefore structured through complicity and antagonism, convergence and contradiction, making them simultaneously objects and subjects of their own discourse.[13]

Studying an ideological process so woven with complex mediations of unequal relations of power, we need to be specially attentive to the processes of conceptual negotiation and moral syncretism which involve various adaptive, co-optive, exclusive and innovative strategies. We have to note traces of 'collaboration' which are highlighted by the very marks of 'resistance'. We need to look both for values and symbols, interpretive devices and epistemologies, which share gendered patriarchal (local and colonial) class terms, and for those which they fashion through an 'inner struggle' against patriarchy within the same class space.

Finally, at the end of this introduction, we must stress what has been noted by many scholars of hegemonic formation and alluded to by myself, that the ideological agenda, or the hegemonic agenda, is invariably an agenda of morality, of values expressed through both ideas and practices. This is to say, as do Philip Corrigan and Derek Sayer,[14] or Judith Walkowitz[15] and others studying Victorian reformation, that the hegemonic agenda, among other things, is a *moral agenda*. It is through the creation, re-creation and the diffusion of a set of norms and forms that the necessary 'consent' can be built which is essential for hegemony's fullest expression. Gauri Visvanathan uncovers the hegemonic (moral) design, the shaping force of values and worldviews in something seemingly so innocuous as the teaching of 'English Literature' in India.[16] In our case we do not examine the doings of a colonial state, but rather those of a social group who hold a subordinate and/or collaborative position within classes which are ruled (by English colonialism) and ruling (of the indigenous productive classes) and who wish to throw off the yoke of colonial subjection. One of their main moral ideological tools, as with colonialism, is also 'education',

---

13   See Corrigan and Sayer 1985. This book offers an extremely useful demonstration of the moral dimension to the study of state formation. This same approach is also very useful for aspirations to hegemony as well.

14   Corrigan and Sayer 1985.

15   Walkowitz 1980.

16   Visvanathan 1989, pp. 8–9.

and we look at the informal aspect of education in examining non-institutional ideas and content for and by women in these magazines.

2   Framing a Method

As noted by scholars of women's education such as Meredith Borthwick,[17] women's education in the nineteenth century and well into the twentieth had little to do with economic functions, needs, or development of professional expertise among women: 'Whereas education for males was directly related to the pursuit of employment, female education had no economic function'.[18] In the period that the present study covers, from about 1880 to 1910, the magazines make it clear that the main public use of women's education lies in its very nature as a private acquirement. Its ability to meet social needs to create appropriate personalities, familial-social relations and households, and to offer a moral basis for the everyday life of the *bhadralok* or the gentry, provide the ground for its justification. Women's educational projects are thus always phrased in terms of both social and moral 'betterment', and the totality of this 'betterment' is consistently expressed as the welfare of the family. 'Proper' child-raising, character building and conjugality is the core of the familial life, supplying the occasion and the legitimation for a non-institutional, home-based education among the women of urban propertied households, especially in the households of the professionals and the bureaucrats.[19] Even when 'schooling' is considered later it is not in terms of acquisition of knowledge, profitable or otherwise, but rather in terms of attitudes of family members or the life-style of the family. The general sentiment is phrased by Krishnabhabini Das herself:

> There are some who raise objection to women's education on the ground that women lose their womanly virtues through the influence of education. They compete in everything with men and pay no attention to housework, etc. But if they [those who object] were to open their eyes they could see that this belief is wholly erroneous. In spite of the great amount of progress made in women's education in America, women there are neither inattentive to their homes, nor ignorant of child-care. In fact

---

17   Borthwick 1984.
18   Visvanathan 1989, p. 61.
19   Ibid., p. 68.

they are able to do both child-care and housework with great regulation and discipline, thus increasing happiness within the home, and facilitating the progress of their nation. Of course a few women, wearing men's clothing, abuse their independence and higher education, but does it make any sense to be outraged about women's education and independence in general by the examples of a few?[20]

Even though her own examples of ideal results of education come from America, it is clear that she uses these to make a point supporting her demand in the Bengali context. In her essay on 'Life of the Nation and the Hindu Woman', Krishnabhabini Das reiterates the nation's dependence for its future improvement on women and their organisation of family life.[21]

The cluster of women, education and the family around which the social reform agenda is organised point to fundamental ways in which to rethink social and cultural dimensions of 'class'. The centrality of the family as a site for social construction becomes explicit when we realise that norms and forms, the moral and cultural life of this institution, are not static, ahistorical and 'natural'. Writers such as Philip Ariès in *Centuries of Childhood* or Eli Zaretsky in *Capitalism, The Family and Personal Life* bring home to us the fact that the word 'family' signifies a dynamic organisation of social reproduction which is both grounded in and mediates the general social relations of production.

It is important to realise that the concern for educational social reform which alters family mores indicates the need to devise new forms of social reproduction. If a society needs to develop new forms of 'class consciousness', subjectivities, ways of being and seeing, this can only be done in its most fundamental form by reworking the family form. The family is after all an institution which is equally grounded in the unregulated life of the civil society and the institutional life of polity, law etc. The sexual-social division of labour that characterises the family at different stages, or of different social classes, are of a piece with gender organisation and division of labour that mediate the mode of production as a whole. Therefore, what we concretely understand as 'class', its subjective, cultural moment, is vitally expressed and constructed through familial gender relations, for example, socialisation to masculinity and femininity, mothering, and so on. It is not surprising that these form the very topics for the new educational project outlined by the women intelligentsia.

---

20   Das 1891a.
21   Das 1891a, pp. 286–91.

Education is always a moral proposal and the concept of morality allows us to be social and personal at the same time. It is only fitting that the educational proposals for and by women are primarily conceptualised in moral terms – of 'educing' or cultivating moral sentiments of the woman and her family. This agenda is not simply a spontaneous expression of common sense, but rather of a well thought-out ideological position which has substantially reconstructed and rearticulated its prior elements. This elaborates 'appropriate' social norms and forms for inhabitants of a particular section of the social space and creates 'social' individuals, identities and subjectivities within historically constructed relations.[22]

Before we can proceed to an examination of the material at hand we must also note that this two-way relationship between common sense – the everyday world – and ideology is central to hegemony. Ideology (as a conscious, unified and organised system of ideas)[23] results from attempts at a conscious and coherent discursive construction, through selectively interpreting and putting together elements from common sense and articulating it to ontological and epistemological premises of a particular and historical form of social order and social class or classes. But its articulated unity is continuously fractured in the process of social circulation among other relations of everyday life, and crumbles or diffuses back into common sense. This fracturing itself is provided by the multiple significational nature of common sense and prevailing contradictions in social relations. The social location of the significational aspect of ideology supplies the multiplicity of meanings, fissures, the openings and closures (always somatically signalling out) which even the most thought-out ideological formulation cannot escape. This process of continuous widening (drawing into common sense) and narrowing (being 'shaped' into 'ideology') has been remarked upon by all scholars dealing with history of consciousness. Partha Chatterjee, for example, in his *Nationalist Thought: A Derivative Discourse?* phrases it in terms of a wider 'problematic' and a narrower 'thematic', one as a realm of possibilities, and the other as a narrower zone of 'intentionality' marked by a 'subject matter'.[24]

An examination of the women's texts must be attentive to this two-way relation between common sense and ideology. While we trace the determinate direction of the ideological proposal, we have to remember the continuous process of negotiation that is involved in an ideological effort – between differ-

---

22   Corrigan and Sayer 1985, p. 4.
23   See the chapter on ideology in Williams 1977.
24   See chapter 2, 'The Thematic and the Problematic,' in Chatterjee 1986a.

ent aspects of common sense – and the tension between and within ideology (fractured or whole) and lived experience. In fact it is the ability to mediate, manage and contain these divergent elements which makes or mars the success of an ideology and charts the direction and the political cultural form of hegemony. This fluidity in ideological formation clearly indicates the difficulty of demarcating forms of consciousness 'residual, dominant and emergent' with any precision, and exposes the fallacy in a 'reflective' view of culture. Writers on ideological formations in nineteenth century Bengal are, not surprisingly, therefore preoccupied in dealing with 'shifts and slides', 'liminality' and so on – pointing to a multidimensionality within one ideological position or its class articulation.[25]

In the middle of such fluidity what we can speak of, however, is only a claim, a contested claim at that, by certain ideological positions as candidates for hegemonic ascendancy. The ephemeral (non-classic) texts that we are concerned with, no less than others with well-defined and developed ideological positions, must also be read within this same analytical framework which has usually been advanced for such macro-formulations, such as the ideology of 'nationalism'. The enterprise put forward by these women reformers advances claims on two levels: at that of ethics – implying an epistemology; and that of practical management – purporting to create a 'better social life' both in the realm of ideas and practically at that of social reproduction. These 'claims' all rest on the legitimacy of a universal good but do not actually transcend the particularities of class and gender interests; they are an essentialist way of speaking about the 'is' and 'oughts' of the social life of women and men of propertied classes. The generalisations on what women 'are', their nature and so forth, build on or reflect an empirical knowledge of experiences and material conditions of those who are producers of the ideology. It is with this proviso in mind that we can appreciate the thesis of this paper, that by studying the educational writings of the women reformers/intelligentsia at the turn of the century we can come to an understanding of the advocated gender relations (within urban propertied classes in Bengal) in terms of one of the hegemonic agendas advanced by competing agents for their roles and places within nationalist politics. Within the purview of this ideological formation, to quote Corrigan and Sayer: 'Certain forms of activities are given the official seal of approval,

---

25   'It is in the shifts, slides, discontinuities, and unintended moves, what is suppressed as much as what is asserted, that one can get a glimpse of this complex movement, not as so many accidental disturbing factors but as constitutive of the very historical rationality of its [nationalism's] process' (Chatterjee 1986a, p. viii). See also S. Kaviraj's discussion on 'liminality' in the works of Bankim Chandra Chattopadhyay.

others are situated beyond the pale. This has cumulative, and enormous, cultural consequences for how people identify ... themselves and their place in the world'.[26]

3 The Matter at Hand

The language of social reform in nineteenth century, and the early years of the twentieth, is inscribed with the discourse of 'crisis'. Allusions to 'continuity and change', 'tradition and modernity', all involve the management of gender roles and division of labour outside and within the family in terms of the needs of the new times. For example, Tapan Ray Chaudhury, in *Europe Reconsidered: Perceptions of the West in Nineteenth Century Bengal*, makes this idea of 'new times' and 'encounter' between 'the East' and 'the West', the point of departure for his whole interpretive and historical exercise. The 'encounter' he points out, means 'a change'. 'It is a part of modernisation', 'the revolution in their world view'. He also notes that the 'changes occurred' – not just through 'influence' – not just through the 'adoption of cultural artefacts, like specific elements in western life habits and belief systems ... The contact was a catalyst ... It induced mutations in inherited ways'.[27]

Though not in terms of 'the catalyst' and 'mutation', the same emphasis on 'change' (rather than on continuity) comes out in the works of many scholars in the area, for example, that of Tanika Sarkar. In her essay on 'Hindu Conjugality and Nationalism in Late nineteenth Century Bengal', she remarks on the extreme and unprecedented nature of this 'change' brought about by the colonial encounter in the following terms: 'For the first time, since Manu perhaps, and in a very different sense from him, family life and womanhood directly and explicitly emerges as a central area of problematisation'.[28] A few pages later she points out 'a compulsive, almost obsessive probing of tension spots ... all the traumas of a woman's life were brought out and examined, nothing was taken for granted'.[29]

Whereas Tanika Sarkar puts her finger on the concrete as well as the ideational nature of the change in historical-sociological terms, Tapan Ray Chaudhury, in spite of the suggestive notions of 'the catalyst' and 'mutation' of 'inher-

---

26   Chatterjee 1986a, p. 6.
27   Chaudhury 1988, pp. ix–x.
28   Sarkar 1989, p. 1.
29   Sarkar 1989.

ited ways', leaves us solely at the level of history of ideas.[30] The ideas, such as they were, are left unproblematised in terms of actual social relations and politics, whereas Tanika Sarkar's essay, though not speaking exactly in these terms, can be drawn upon to explore the meaning of this change in terms of social reproduction or in terms of forming political ideologies.[31] Chaudhury does not connect the 'ideal constructs' with anything as concrete as social reproduction or formation. Contentions between different conceptual or symbolic forms in terms of hegemonic contradictions within the complex parameters of gender, class and colonialism are not reflected in his pool of history of ideas.

But if we were to read between the lines in all this talk of 'change and continuity', 'tradition and modernity', 'crisis' and 'the new times', watch the prolific world of ideas in its frantic exuberance of proposals searching eclectically, adapting and innovating the past and the present, the local and foreign forms and norms of consciousness – we might come to the conclusion that most fundamental social formations, involving social identity and political subjectivity, lay at stake in this change. We would also realise that the fact that 'education' is both practical and a conceptual and a moral aspect makes it a wide entry point into social re-formation and creation of ideology. Understandably, the century reverberates with thoughts on education, especially with women's education. This search for the right conduct, right epistemology fitted to, produced from, a particular social ontology does not, unlike Sumit Sarkar's or Partha Chatterjee's or Gulam Murshid's[32] observation (though otherwise they vastly differ from each other), decline with the rise and consolidation of nationalism and Hindu revivalism,[33] nor does it come to a contained and a managed stage through the same nationalist development.[34] The 'crisis of Bengal Renaissance' (of values and projects represented by Rammohan Roy, Vidyasagar, Derozio and the Young Bengal, etc.) did not really put a halt to the urge for social reform, including a search for the solution of 'the woman question'. 'Reform' and 'revival',

---

30   Choudhury 1988.

31   Sarkar 1989.

32   Murshid 1983.

33   'Hindu revivalism' should be considered as another orientalist inflexion of nationalism, another construct, which means something very particular by the word 'Hindu,' and certainly the concept of 'revivalism' screens the fact that this is an 'invention of tradition' (Hobsbawm and Ranger 1983). With this awareness in mind, I use this expression simply as a conventional code word signifying the selective use of 'Hinduism' as a part of the nationalist ideology.

34   See Chatterjee 1990. The abeyance of the women's question is not a failure of liberal thought for this author, but 'nationalism had in fact resolved "the women's question" in complete accordance with its preferred goals' (Chatterjee 1990, p. 237).

enlightenment and nationalism, sought exclusive or negotiatory paths with each other, and sometimes, especially in the voices of women such as Krishnabhabini Das, utilitarianism spoke with a 'difference' from the vantage point of gender inhabited by middle-class women.

By the later part of the last century there was a fuller development of the middle classes, of new modes of mediation and culture, a clearer political agenda, and new negotiatory terms leading to divergent formulations of the relations between nationalism (male, upper class/caste) and class formation on the one hand and the needs of women on the other. Positive and negative valorisations of women's active role in society and concern with the symbolically feminine and feminised symbols co-existed with furious or calmly reflective thoughts and projects on women's education, for example, or the family. It is true that the more exalted (male) writers did not feel positive about 'the educated woman' in all her dimensions (though some agreed about the need of some education for women), but less exalted ones, more pervasive because of being writers of magazine and occasional literature, both men and women, wrote a vast number of pamphlets, books and articles on women, family and education.

The educational content of the magazines under investigation assumes a miscellaneous air unless we thematise them to establish a focus. This thematisation revolves around the family, involving a desire for reconstruction of forms and relations of social reproduction embodied by it. This is inclusive not only of a sexual division of labour but also of a cultural-moral dimension. The two central themes in this context are the familial social space designated as *andarmahal/antahpur* (inner quarters) and *griha* (home/household); the main creator-organiser of this space is named in the latter half of the century as *grihini* (the mistress of the home/home-maker), especially in her incarnation of *bhadramahila* as the mother. This typology of 'sentimental, morally-educative motherhood' subsumes social relations peculiar to the ideal social space of the *griha*. These two notions, of *griha* and the *bhadramahila* mother-homemaker, an educator and a nurturer, involve much more than a domestic labourer or a biological reproducer and a physical dwelling space. The aim of education, as propounded in the magazines, is to enunciate and elaborate on these concepts, to construct the typologies and to socialise them through various practical advices and know-hows.

The model of the ideal home or *griha* which emerges from the magazines pages, and to which the concept of the *bhadramahila* is integral, offers a critical insight into the changes in conceptual and actual organisation of the social space in nineteenth century Bengal. The usual use of the words *andar/antahpur* and *griha* is non-discursive, that is, descriptive, and interchangeable.

They are used to designate a 'private' social space as opposed to the 'public' one and to neutrally demarcate a physical, architectural and social inferiority with no indication of their 'essential' difference. But as women reflect in these magazines on the changes in their social space, and construct the ideal home, the newness of the concept of *griha* (now) and its difference from *andar* (then) stare us in the face. Sharing many of the social functions, they yet mark or represent different moments of social reproduction and ways of thinking about society. They also indicate a very different relationship to *bahir* (the public/the outside world). This *andar/antahpur*, which indicates a social domain in women's care and which is the constant habitat of women, children, domestic servants and the nocturnal habitat of adult males, can only be understood in its specificity when contrasted to *griha*, 'the home' which forms the central project of thoughts on women's education.

The main difference between *andar* and *griha*, treated discursively, consists of the fact that while the former indicates a separate physical domain for women, appropriate to a more differentiated type of sexual division of labour with very little indication of any direct normativeness or emotionality inscribed in the concept, the latter is a concept of morality and affect. It speaks less articulately to a strongly differentiated division of labour, and more to the moral, emotional social relations appropriate to a distinctly narrower social space presided over, created by, a central female figure. It is conceived more in terms of an emotional and moral privatisation than of a physical privatisation. Lacking an architectural correlate (which forbids adult kin-males much participation, and non-kin males [non-servants] of any), *griha* represents a state of mind, an ideological venture propounding a conscious moral and social being, rather than a functional place on earth. It is here that self-consciously advanced moral (and social) projects of 'mothering' and 'conjugality' bloom, and it has to be 'achieved' through a process of ideological clarifications, and conscious, practical socialisation. *Griha* encapsulates the ideal type of moral harmony imbedded in the life style of the *bhadralok* (the western educated urban gentry).

What these magazines bring out is the fact that this master concept of the home, implying familial life surrounded by ideological clusters of a new social design and moral imperatives, provides the main destination of women's education. In Swarnakumari Debi's reminiscences in 'Sekele Katha' ('The Story of Yesterday' or 'Old Times'), for example, we find a description of a gradually vanishing *antahpur* being replaced by a more 'modern' form.[35] Concerned with

---

35   Debi 1916.

women's education in pre-modern days, Swarnakumari Debi offers us a view
of life in the women's quarters where even the selective nature of the topic
does not shut out a sense of everyday life. We catch a glimpse of a whole social
domain when she says:

> In our *Antahpur*, in those days, reading and writing, like eating, resting
> and worshiping, were daily rituals among women. Just as every morning
> the milkmaid brought the milk, the flowerwomen supplied the flowers,
> and Deben Thakur came with his almanac and rolls of astrological charts,
> to foretell the daily auspicious and inauspicious details, just so a bathed
> and purified, white-robed and fair skinned Baishnabi Thakurani appeared
> within the interior of the household radiant with the light of knowledge.
> She was no mean scholar.[36]

Or:

> I remember the days when the flower woman came to sell books – what
> a commotion it created in the women's quarter! She brought a few new
> books published in *Battala* – poetry, novels, tales of fantasy – and in-
> creased the size of sister's library. As in every room there were dolls, other
> toys, clothes, so there were books in trunks. When I grew up I thumbed
> through them.[37]

This *andar* or *antahpur* simultaneously expanded and contracted and was
focused through the moral design of social reform whose object was women.
Swarnakumari Debi herself describes this transition and links it to the return
of her father Debendranath Thakur, from the foot of the hills of the Himalayas.
Both the narrowing, the centralisation of the household from a social domain
to a moral design, as well as its expansion in breaking the segregation of the
inner/the outer, male and female world, become clear from her following statements. She begins by drawing the reader's attention to Debendranath's stature
as a 'social reformer', not to be encompassed within the conventional view of
him as a 'religious reformer:'

> We can testify to the fact that it is through him that women's higher edu-
> cation received its foundation [in Bengal]. He was the first to reform the

---

36   Debi 1916, pp. 1114–1124.
37   Ibid.

custom of child marriage, and carefully attended to the project of creating civilised clothing for women.[38]

Not content with that, he discarded the stone *shalagram* and initiated everyone into the Brahmo religion, and:

> He also removed mean female-rituals, prevalent through India, one by one from women's quarters. He invented a mature age of marriage ... and put together a marriage ritual. From my middle sister on all weddings in this household are performed in that way. When his infant daughters reached the proper age he started their education by using an improved method. He hired a *pandit* for us. After completing the second primer we began to learn Sanskrit. 'Mems' [white women] started coming into the women's quarter.
>
> At the time when our household was being thus improved, Keshab Babu became my father's disciple. For the first time, a non-kin male entered from the outside world, into the women's quarter, unpenetrated by even the rays of the sun.[39]

It is evident that this evolution in the ideological-moral dimension of the familial social space, as described by Swarnakumari Debi in its pre- and post-social reform phase, serves to illustrate the difference put forward above between *andar* and *griha*. It also spells out a new social division of labour, for example, in the male reformer's involvement with women's daily lives and rituals, and an equally new relationship to *bahir*, which comes into the house as adult kin and non-kin family members and white women.

It is in a piece by Gyanadanandini Debi, entitled 'Stri Shiksha' (Women's Education), written in 1882, that we get the manifesto for women's education.[40] This advocates and displays the good results of the desegregation of the sexes, that is, of a rigid sexual division of labour, and shows how education is both the cause and the result of this process. It elaborates an educational content which incorporates affective-moral functions into women's household tasks. Like Krishnabhabini Das, she also redefines and recodes the conventions of

---

38   Ibid.

39   Ibid.

40   See also Debi 1882. 'If the purpose of education is to discharge duties enjoined by one's condition, then we have to examine the situation of women in our country [she supplies a list of household and social tasks] ... In this modern condition these duties cannot be discharged without a thorough education for women'.

gender. In the extreme practicality of Gyanadanandini's itemisation of education we see the construction of the home of the *bhadramahila* linen by linen, and relation by relation. The principle of organisation of the text, which may seem rather eccentric because household chores and conjugality are put on the same plane, becomes evident if we see these chores also as moral/sentimental codes. Thus it is that she can speak of the necessary companionship of the husband and wife, of pleasing the husband with musical skills and child-rearing in one breath with tailoring, recipes, clothing and ornaments, nursing and healthcare involving a knowledge of anatomy, physiology, hygiene, chemistry, accounting and so on. This goes with Krishnabhabini's previously quoted statement that women will not be worse home-makers, mothers and wives, but rather much better, if they are educated.

This construct of the *griha*, 'the home' (practically 'the hearth'), is centred around, or radiates from, the construct of the sentimental, educative mother who is one of the mother figures thrown up at this time. Her traits are those of the *bhadramahila*. She is not the *bibi*, the caricature of the educated/modern woman, but rather her reversal; a self-consciously fashioned figure from all the benefits of an education and cultural exposure available in the new social context. Not diabolic or inverted, an image of the leaden times of *kali yuga*, masculinised through overstepping her 'women's domain' as depicted, for example, by Kalighat painters, she is instead sweet, moral, capable of reason and learning – a creator rather than a destroyer of homes. Through the new mode advocated by women themselves rises, in conjunction with their reforming male counterparts, an individual nurturer of the body and the sentiments. She builds 'character' on postulates of personal morality and psychology, rather than, for example, a directly collective conduct of caste and class. In this scheme of motherhood, physical reproduction is socialised in a particular way, through a philosophy compounded of notions of sentimental education from England and Europe, theories of the German kindergarten education of Froebel, utilitarianism, social Darwinism, compounded by indigenous and foreign notions of the innate motherhood of women.

Along with this sentimental-educator mother is born 'the sentimental child' which subsequently becomes the basis of a whole literary genre of reminiscences, for example, Rabindranath Tagore's *Chhelebela* (Childhood). This construct of the child, individually nurtured by mother and mother nature, provides the basis of personal *bildungsroman*, of autobiographies. This child construct is male, and every female child is typed on 'the mother'. The required educational content for women (and girls) is directed at *his* developmental process. Krishnabhabini Das' essay on 'Kindergarten' captures the essence of this mother-child relation, and its educative content and mode. As she puts it, 'mothers are the natural teachers' of (male) children, the real education of children begins at her knee.[41] The process begins from birth, and the distinction between education and socialisation is obliterated:

> A child has an inkling of his mother's love or her nature through his senses, and this love slowly enters into the child's half asleep soul as mother holds him to her bosom or puts him into his cradle with great care, and breast feeds him as soon as he wakes. In this way a mother's selfless love, joy and gratitude enters the child's soul and lays the foundation for a sacred, noble and exalted human nature. It is through this affectionate interchange of mother and son that a sense of the spiritual first awakens in the human [male] heart.[42]

Both Krishnabhabini and Gyanadanandini speak of the mother's educational role in terms of teaching to play, to sing and so on:

> In mother's sweet and simple songs and games of house keeping are spent the child's three years. At four the child should go to a kindergarten. But of course where boys learn from their mother all of what the kindergarten could teach, for them their home is their school, they need not go any where else.[43]

The above passages should be explored with regard to changes in the mode of physical and social reproduction as conceived in *griha* and its contrast with the ways of *antahpur* or *andar malal*. To begin with, it speaks to a single female nurturing figure, a biological parent, personally, daily, engaged full-time in child raising. This individually-based duo of mother and child is remote from child raising in the context of a joint family where the care of children is done by different female kin figures – grandmothers and aunts, older female siblings and cousins of various sorts. It is interesting that no allusion is made here to these sources of nurture and socialisation which actually existed in everyday life. They also do not refer to the fact that childhood in Bengali upper class/caste homes is also highly dependent on female and male servants. The construct does not have any space for these extra actors on its ideological stage. It is the triad of mother, father (that is, wife and husband) and the child that is the icon of this 'holy family'. And of course all interactions are individualised.

---

41   Das 1891b.
42   Das 1891b.
43   Das 1891b.

In Sarala Debi's short autobiographical sketch of her childhood, we find this same approach to childhood, a time of growth read through the construction of individual nurturing and sentimental care, all embodied in the presence or absence, of the mother.[44] Rabindranath speaks of a childhood spent in the domination of male servants and other male mentors as though it was his personal fate. But the text gives evidence of an ordinary daily life where not just he but all male children routinely grew up being fed, bathed and clothed in the inner quarters, returning there at night to sleep, while being inducted into a male life and conduct by older men. It would appear from his account of sufferings that there were other male co-sufferers. But Rabindranath, like Sarala Debi, read the workings of the division of labour between *antahpur* and *bahir* through the ideological lens of *griha*, a sentimental small unit, where a woman, the very same woman, is always involved in caring for (male) children. The interesting thing about Sarala Debi's account is that she also read her life among her siblings, the joint family nurture that she was provided with, through the same frame of missing a 'sentimental mother-care'. And she was unusual in that she demanded this care, the realisation of the ideal type of nurture, which was put in place to raise boys. She, in that sense, was not the nurturer of the model, but the nurtured. And the most important thing from the point of view of social reproduction is precisely the fact that what these authors wanted and missed, and their actual experiences, indicate the difference between *andar/antahpur* and *griha*, both in terms of ideology and practice. In fact, the concept of *griha* might have anticipated an embryonic form of nuclearisation of urban middle class families and its moral regulation and captured a tendency of change in the pattern of social reproduction among the urban propertied classes. The *andarmahal/antahpur*, on the other hand, has no particular reference to the individual, in terms of his/her psychic, moral life. Rather, it comes across mainly as a 'domain', a physical/architectural correlate of women's social location within a general patriarchal mansion.

Since the organisation of *andarmahal* and *griha* are both gendered and patriarchal, it is not surprising that the women writers display an ambivalence, bordering sometimes on antagonism, regarding both. On the one hand they deplore the segregation and what they consider to be the social unimportance of women in the former; on the other, they resent the Pygmalion-like role that men play in shaping the *griha* and its regulatory form, *garhastha*. In Gyanadanandini's 'Stri Shiksha', Swarnakumari Debi's 'Strishiksha O Bethune School',[45] and 'Sekele Katha',[46] Krishnabhabini Das' 'Striloker Kaj O Kajer

44   Debi 1906.
45   Debi 1888.
46   Debi 1916.

Mahatya' ('Women's Work and its Value Greatness'),[47] and articles submitted for essay competitions by women for *Bamabodhini* under the title of 'What Advantages may Accrue should Women's Education become Common in this Country and What Disadvantages Result from Its Absence',[48] we find much evidence of this ambivalence regarding this segregated social space of the older division of labour and the new relatively fused one. In their constant reflection on 'then' (as *andarmahal* social organisation seems a vanishing form) and 'now' (the '*griha*' of the new *bhadramahila*) they are at times nostalgic, or down-right angry, about the loss of a domain for women which, they felt, held a relative autonomy of male non-interference. In an essay entitled 'Amader Hobe Ki?' ('What will Happen to Us?') Krishnabhabini Das projects such a resentment when she says:

> Even in terms of freedom our mothers and grandmothers lived in a bet-ter state. As everyone knows, Hindu women were in enclosure for a long time, but even so they had a full right to pilgrimages, worshipping at holy sites, and other religious rituals of religion, and travelling. But on account of this 'little or half education' we are about to lose this pleasure of our distinct [or separate] lives. Now Bengali young men are furious at the very mention of women's pilgrimages, they don't believe in worshipping 'dolls'. Well then, explain to them [women] why such things are bad, and what religion really means, and take them elsewhere and show them nature's beauty, and you will see in what a short space of time they rid themselves of superstition.[49]

Her essay on 'Swadhin o Paradhin Nari Jiban' ('Independent and Subjected Life of Woman'), Krishnabhabini Das[50] repeats her accusations about male encroachments in all areas of 'modern' life as instructors and judges of women. Swarnakumari Debi's 'Shekele Katha', while hailing the reforms introduced by her father in the woman's quarters, actually evokes a nostalgia about the happy bustling women's world in her description of the by-gone days.

But the other pole of this ambivalence is the forward-looking overall thrust of their work. Upon scrutiny it begins to become clear that this ambivalence

47   Das 1892.
48   See *Bamaracana Competition*, 'Edeshe Stri Shiksha Samyak Prachalit Na Howatai ba kiki apakar haitechhe?' *Bamabodhini* 1866.
49   Das 1890a.
50   Das 1888.

comes from holding a subordinate location within both social/familial forms and regrets, not the loss of the segregation, but the loss of control/power women may have over their own lives. In fact, the underlying standpoint of women, along with an evolving class social/moral agenda, is that of a quest for influence and power. In the final analysis they are not positive about the little special power that women had in their *antahpur* lives. Having once broken the older barriers, they do not wish to be put back into a new form of male control. Thus education becomes the rallying cry – which coincides with the reforming male demand – but women go beyond the prescribed male agenda in demanding for women the full right to higher education, not just the 'little learning' to serve the male purpose which is handed out to women. Noticing the threat of the loss of 'self' that the new reorganisation of social reproduction holds in the context of a steady male redefinition of woman's life and work, Krishnabhabini wrote about how a male-defined or patriarchal morality is being 'normalised' and how women had to be content with the little learning that they were permitted and faced continuous male criticism of their unwitting ignorance. She pleaded for a higher, 'useful' education that would end women's *paranirbharata* (dependence on others) and spoke thus about the male judges, censors and experts:

> Lately Bengali men have become completely puffed up in the arrogance of their education and civilisation. They lecture everywhere about *Swatantrata* (independence/freedom/self-distinction), but, even in their dreams, they cannot conceive of the fact that the bud of national independence and civilisation must first quicken in characters of that nation's individuals. How each parent treats his/her children, or young men their mothers, sisters and wives, tells us about that nation's civilisation and progress. But if any other nation looks into our lives what will it say about the shameful things that exist in Hindu families, such as quarrels between fathers and sons, between brothers, the general degradation of wives, all sorts of tensions within families? What will happen to the young men's arrogance about their civilisation and education?[51]

She echoes the sentiment of many of her peers when she says:

> Whenever there is the talk of righting the wrongs of Hindu women, and establishing their equality with men, many [men] refer to the scriptures

---

51   Das 1890b.

and speak of their status as the goddess [Devi]. But where do we see any respect for this goddess?

No other young male of India show such hatred (contempt), neglect, distrust, towards mothers, wives or sisters, as does the Bengali.[52]

This ambivalence about emancipation, about women 'coming out' and men 'coming in', is not from our point of view a case of the 'reluctant debutante'. As mentioned before, not only Krishnabhabini, in the essays mentioned above, or in 'Karjya Mulak Shiksha O Jatya Unnati' ('Useful Education and National Progress'), but also Hiranmoyee Debi in her various social scientific articles and observations of Newnham College where she studied, put forward a strong stress on making women's education a 'real' social and personal achievement, not simply an expression of the new gentry's life style – the aim being 'real emancipation', that is, a degree of self-definition and social-familial control. Even Swarnakumari Debi, while describing 'those days' so nostalgically, in the end falls on the side of 'serious education', of philosophy, spiritual thought, literature of the classic kind and so forth, which came in with the new social mode and women's education. Women such as these repeatedly stressed the need to go further, rather than to retreat. But within their general class position, the gender struggle continued.

All the women writers agree that this loss of domain is to be recouped by extending to women 'real educational' facilities which would provide them with the required information, morality and cultural practices to create an informed self, a good son and a good home. The loss of the previous domain was to be counteracted by women taking on some of what was considered the male part in the division of labour, as mental producers. Neither *jenana* education nor *jenana* living are advocated as solutions for women's lack of viability. It is also their genuine concern for women's intellect, morality and authority which make them deplore these customs, not just a submission to the patriarchal mode. And finally, not only do women feel that they should have the right to 'come out' and live in 'mixed company', but they also do not wish to do so in the older feminine terms; rather, they set new terms and conditions for their emergence and emancipation. The hearth-centric education therefore contained in itself this double-edge of containment and emancipation of women, typified by the mother figure, which contains in itself simultaneously the sternness of moral authority and sweet sentimentality.

52   Das 1890b.

These contrary dimensions of power and submission, of sentimentality and moral education, intuition and rational investigation into the laws of nature (senses) are revealed at their best in the essays on child education and child-rearing They contain an injunction for unqualified dedication to and love for the child, but also forms of guidance and discipline. Texts such as Gyanadanandini's 'Kindergarten' or Krishnabhabini Das' essay by the same name, or her essay 'Sansare Shishu' ('Child in the Family'), for example, are organised around the apt metaphor of the gardener and her garden. Plant imageries, imageries of natural growth are accompanied by the image of a gardener that knows and loves the nature of the plan, and co-operates with it intelligently 'for its own good' by pruning and otherwise gently directing it. The mother is thus the first teacher to the child – who must know better than the child what his real emotional and moral nature is, and thus produce the finally desired result.

These essays on mother's role in child raising and education, while stressing sentiments, are materialist in their emphasis. Discussing principles of human nature and reason, with the help of Rousseau, Froebel, Helvetins and others, they posit a clear relationship between body and mind, senses and intellect, thus connecting physical reproduction with social, moral and intellectual education. They discuss how knowledge arises in the first instance from sensory impressions. Putting forward the proposition that 'whatever enters the mind is through the senses', they go into details of toys, 'to suspend a coloured ball or rattle over the child's cradle', to a series of games observed in detail which teach children while they delight and express the needs of the senses.[53] Throughout, of course, the mother learns about the child and can trace in his developing lineaments the physiognomy of adulthood. Science combines with the intuition of sentimental education, and we find statements such as the following to that effect:

> As the embryo of a fully grown tree lies hidden in the seed, which in time becomes a huge tree with roots, as the seed of life within an egg matures into a bird with wonderful limbs and wings in the due course of time, so in the child or the infant lies the possibility of a whole human being.[54]

Though no one can go against this natural law and all that it implies, and here we see why social Darwinism attracts the highly educated Hironmoyee Debi,

---

53   Das 1893.
54   Das 1893.

these laws of emotions, morality and intellect (of the whole human nature and the individual nature of the child) can be learnt about. Kindergarten philosophy and social Darwinism are both attractive because both theoretically and practically they offer the mother instructions in knowledge for child-rearing. Here, in the notion of instruction to the mother, we see a super addition to the theme of maternal love and intuition. Though her 'natural' predisposition makes her the best teacher, she herself needs to be educated in moral philosophy and practical sciences for her precise job. While discussing kindergarten education at home, it is thought that 'A woman can effortlessly learn [Froebel's philosophy] and use this knowledge in a short time, and show great results. A child is the dearest treasure of the mother, who will be more attentive to and successful in his education?'[55] And, the thought continues in a peculiar blend of a naturalist and practical argument, it is in fact better to teach it all to her, because she shows a greater proficiency than 'a most learned man'. And 'for a woman to be simultaneously a nurturer and an educator, she absolutely needs to acquire knowledge, which is produced by the type of mental cultivation, that give her strength and help in this matter'.[56] This kind of logic that connects the natural with the moral/intellectual, and places women centrally in the realm of social construction, is stated succinctly (and repeatedly) in the following statement:

> Nature has vested in women the responsibility for people's health, and their moral and mental health lie hidden within their physical condition. Therefore, it is only by understanding the laws or dictates of nature and following them that one can devise a design for children's physical, moral and mental health.[57]

In this construct of motherhood, intuitional mothering combines with the attributes of a teacher, thus reworking a patriarchal service ideology into a still gendered but relatively autonomous and stern form. If loving is the attribute of a mother, then moral authority and discipline marks the teacher. This implies a permission for emotionality for both the mother and the child, as well as the practice of emotional discipline, which lies at the heart of morality. The pruning process of the gardener curbs excesses, develops the emotional life of the duo with discretion and judgment. The new education deplores corporal punishment, harshness and so forth, but achieves a restraining effect through a sus-

---

55   Das 1893.
56   Das 1893.
57   Das 1893.

tained and reasoned appeal to conscience and personal love. Gyanadanandini in 'Stri Shiksha' offers an example of how to discipline a child, and points out in her discussion about 'children's games' (devised as a part of the educational plan by the instructors) the end in view, namely, social adjustment/norm induction (i.e., control) and discipline. The randomness of play is undercut by the fact that it is the parent or the school who decides when a game begins and ends, or what rules to follow: 'Children must have much joy in these games, but they must obey the rules of the game and the school'.[58] Thus, 'No one can join or break the game at will'. Through this training process they are inducted into a 'gentleman's conduct'. Good manners, politeness, obedience, rule maintenance, thrift, and so on, all fall within this province of the 'feminine' method of schooling. And of course this ideological venture of personal-moral education itself rests on another new ideological notion, that of the 'individual'. It presupposes a private realm of conscience, though in harmony with a social or a collective conduct.

The novelty and daring implied in this type of motherhood (where women both consent to a gendered/patriarchal service role, and turn it around to gain social control) and its attempt to recoup and expand a lost domain, while seeking to embody a moral authority, does not become fully evident unless we examine accounts of actual lives of women presented by various reformers as the point of departure for reform. Rammohan Roy's description of women as a physically abused household drudge,[59] Vidkyasagar's portrayal of women's lives of continuous male repression, Rasasundari Dasi's description of her daily life and secret attempts at education, among many, show how radical an emphasis this insistence upon a teaching role provided.[60]

But, of course, as with all ideologically interpellated agents, it was a *radical*, not a *revolutionary*, proposal. The women intelligentsia undercut their submission through reform, but the same gestures of reform further entrenched the conditions for their submission. This becomes clear when we remember that not only do women gain power by being delegated agents of class socialisation as a whole, but are engaged in a more ambiguous scheme in gender terms. While the mother-child figure can be expanded to include all men and women

---

58   Das 1893.

59   'At marriage the wife is recognised as half of her husband, but in after-conduct they are treated worse than inferior animals. For the woman is employed to do the work of a slave in the house, such as, in her turn, to clean the place very early in the morning, whether cold or wet, to scour the dishes, to wash the floor, to cook night and day, to prepare and serve food for her husband, father, mother-in-law, sister-in-law, and friends and connections' (Roy 1820, p. 126).

60   Dasi 1987.

in an affective and educative relation, thus conferring onto the woman an adulthood and the man an infantilisation, it is in the long run not as empowering to women as it may initially appear. Insofar as such an ideology calls for women to be active participants, they gain an agency and a degree of self-definition of a socially regulatory role. But the tyranny of being governed by the needs of the child to be educated and moral to nurture the *bhadralok*, or heroic in order to nurture the heroic sons of Indian nationalism, all go to show the double-edged nature of such an ideologically interpellated form of subjectivity. In this connection, Sarala Debi's essays on women's conduct in the political context of nationalism provide the best examples of such heroic subordinated selves of women. Gender controversies put forward by 'less political' women writers offer a far more radical stand than she, who accepts the male typologies of Bengali cultural nationalism (and of other Indian provinces), and seriously sets about promoting the myth of aryan Hindu heroism, inventing and advocating hero-creating rituals for women. The ritual of *Virashtami* was mainly a support and morale boosting for males rather than for women to be 'heroes' in their own right. But again, as with the educative role of women, this was also partially empowering to women, since a direct gesture to power is partly a gesture of power. This dilemma is emphasised in a negative form in an essay by Jasodhara Bagchi entitled 'Representing Nationalism: Ideology of Motherhood in Colonial Bengal'.[61] In it, speaking of the construct of the mother goddess and the feminised ideology of Bengali nationalism, and their impact on the status of women in Bengal, she is forced to come to the conclusion that 'it was ultimately a way of reinforcing of a social philosophy of deprivation for women. It was a signal for women to sacrifice everything for their menfolks'.[62] She goes on to say:

> The nationalist ideology, therefore, simply appropriated this orthodox bind on women's lives by glorifying it. This renewed ideological legitimacy made it even more difficult for women to exercise their choice or autonomy in the matter.[63]

Though the construct of the sentimental educative mother, unlike the goddess *Devi* or *Bangamata* typology, has more of an agency space for women in offering them a critical and active role of reason and moral authority, this statement holds some truth for it as well. Though the self-improvement and dedication

---

61   Baghci 1990.
62   Ibid., p. 70.
63   Ibid., p. 70.

of a highly-educated mother does not call for self-sacrificing in any direct and explicit manner (which is why this is probably the most favourite typology for middle-class women), the boundaries between dedication and sacrifice are blurry in many cases.

Where these boundaries are most clearly drawn, among the women writers I explore, is in the works of Krishnabhabini Das. Sharing with others, male and female, a general urbanity and emphasis on the practical, daily dimension of this motherhood and mothercraft, her ideological position leaves room for an ego for women, a right to develop a 'self'. In this, she makes an efficient use of the openings that are to be found in the concept of a moral, educative mother, to escape from the first circle of patriarchal containment. In fact, it is the morality of complete self-abnegation preached to women, and the consequent male exploitation, that she deplores in the essay 'Amader Hobe Ki?' ('What will Happen to Us?'). Discussing *matrittwa* and *satittwa* (motherhood and wifehood) and their destructive use by the contemporary middle-class Bengali young men, she comments: 'But as the beautiful flower when put into a child's hand lies immediately torn in the dust, as jewels are grounded to dust in the hands of a mad man, so does that great virtue [woman's selflessness] lie trodden underfoot when put into 'unworthy [man's] care'.[64] She notes a growing misogyny among the males of urban propertied classes, and a great hypocrisy among male reformers who preach various virtues to Bengali women, including the fortitude and courage of Roman mothers. But she notes with sarcasm: 'Many Roman mothers such as Cornelia, pass in front of our eyes among Hindu women, but how many Caiuses, or Tiberiuses, appear in the midst of Bengali families?'.[65] She attributes women's selflessness to a forced submission to patriarchal ideology and economic dependence, and mentions the ease with which men gain control over, or the possession of, women in Bengali society. After all:

> She [the wife] knows that the husband is the only recourse for a Hindu woman. Whether that husband is honest or dishonest, kind or cruel, he remains the object of a Hindu wife's worship. Following him is the foremost religious conduct enjoined to her. Probably just for that very reason ignorant, churlish young men return that bottomless love, devotion and faith, with such cruel arbitrariness.[66]

---

64   Das 1890a.
65   Das 1890a.
66   Das 1890a.

She turns the patriarchal notion of women as 'natural mothers' on its head and uses it as the reason for the upliftment of women's education: 'That nature has given women the higher role of being the 'mother of the world' is a notion that has to be understood in its real meaning. To make it come true, so they truly live up to that high calling, requires an equally advanced education'.[67]

This slide between self-sacrifice, self-dedication and self-improvement is the range within which the various constructs of nineteenth-century motherhood can be situated. Arguments, such as those of the women educators and reformers (in tandem with their male counterparts) or their antagonists, for or against a greater incorporation into a patriarchal mode, lean more towards one pole than the other. But underlying this controversy is a basic difference, or manipulation, of an epistemology. We are confronted in this with the classic mode of arguing by nature and reason, and secondarily, with arguments relatedly based on the 'nature of women' and 'women as nature'. Educational philosophy for women was constructed on the basis of these initial epistemological convictions. The notion of the self-sacrificing mother rests on the premise of the 'natural motherhood' of women and an intrinsic, essentially feminine nature of the female psyche. This equation between women and nature, women as creatures of instincts, emotions and intuitions – rather than of rationality – was both positively and negatively valorised.[68] This created an ambivalence about women as both weak (frail and feminine) and strong (primal power). What kind of feelings or instincts women actually have, what their 'femininity' essentially consists of, and other related speculations filled the world of social thought. But what is apparent on the whole is that both pro- and anti-reform schools shared much in common by subscribing to some sort of a notion of argument by nature and the innateness of a gender-coded consciousness. Thus, reform and reaction shared a similar epistemology, though their different manipulation of the nature-reason binary determined their views on women's education. The special view of the 'feminine', with its core of motherhood, overdetermined whether women were educable or otherwise. Wherever the 'feminine' indicated the entire absence of the rational intellect, any principle of enlightenment was not superadded to emotions in order to create educational possibilities. But much of the argument for education of

---

67   Das 1890a.

68   A discussion of these different aspects of 'motherhood' and their ideological implications is presented in Bagchi's article (1990). She notices an invention and continuity in this tradition of symbolization through constructs of motherhood of different kinds. She also points out something which is equally tenable for the construct I deal with, namely, that these are 'public' politico-symbolic enterprises, not 'private' existing realities.

women came from simultaneously assuming their potential for reason and the notion of the instinctually feminine. It advocated a 'knowledge' which would both augment and correct the traits of femininity, namely, 'educe' their basic nurturing instincts. Often, there was a belief in a gender differential in the content and purpose of women's education, which, however, was not universally or wholly accepted by all women educationists. Their social subjectivity took on here a double-agency whereby they criticised and accepted, re-interpreted and added to a patriarchal epistemology.

The women reformers' epistemological participation in the themes of reason and nature shows that even though they share the basic premise of an essential femininity or the naturalness of women, they strongly hark back to the principle of reason as an attribute of their general humanity. In fact, they perform a reconciliatory gesture by implanting reason in nature, the intellect in the senses, as is evident in the way they conceptualise the educational growth of the child. They claim that women are 'natural' but that 'reason' is a sex-neutral 'natural' gift for both men and women. Krishnabhabini Das, for example, develops this approach in her polemic with an anonymous male critic who wrote in *Sadhana* against her essay 'Shikshita Nari' ('The Educated Woman'). In 'Shikshita Nari' she begins by addressing a pseudo-scientific a-biological argument for barring women from education, namely, that women have a smaller brain. While her complicity with 'scientific education' makes her unable to challenge the initial thesis, she introduces a critical dimension from her interest in social psychology. She believes that social and mental activities have an effect on the body:

> The smaller brain size among women is caused by the absence of education from primitive times to now. There is no doubt that if women received the same education as men, from the time of the creation to the present time, then their brains would have developed equally with men.[69]

She claims that the same would have happened to men had they undergone the same experience.

In her reply to her critic she introduces the theme of nature in a way that is advantageous to women, succeeding in denaturalising the arguments against women's education by giving once more a critical social dimension to the position. She concedes the value of 'feminine virtues' advocated by her male critic but goes on to make her point:

---

69   Das 1891c.

No thinking person can deny that woman's gentleness, innocence, modesty, etc. are admired everywhere. But no one respects a woman's ignorance. For this reason, a true education can only improve these virtues of women, rather than degrade them ... Therefore, when the critic of *Sadhana* says that nature has particularly vested woman with a special function, an instinct and a drive, and made her 'a denizen of home' – who would disagree with him? But, on the other hand, who would deny that though nature has made woman a home-dweller, she has not endowed her with the instincts of a cage-dweller, or made her a creature who is permanently incarcerated? Therefore, when everywhere in the world, using this excuse of natural weakness, men wholly rob and control women, and continue to argue whenever the topic of women's education and independence is raised, then it does not require much intelligence to recognise the male selfishness and tyranny that lie at the bottom of women's incarceration. Since it is possible to torture people by inflicting on them both starvation or physical force, by preventing the natural exercise of their physical faculties or by repressing their emotional needs, a powerful group or a race can oppress another in both ways.[70]

From this position that she representatively held along with other women, Krishnabhabini wrote other essays, such as 'Strilok O Purush' ('Women and Men'), 'Karyamulak Shiksha O Jatya Unnati', 'Sansare Shishu', and so on, wherein she claimed that whereas there are some special additions to be made for women, the fundamental educational basis for both sexes should be the same. She claims that: 'Education is equally healthy for both sexes. Knowledge, and its pursuit, which fill a man's mind with good thoughts and intentions, is equally healthy for women'.[71] Swarnakumari Debi's positive view of the educational changes introduced by her father corroborates Krishnabhabini's position. She points out the fact that Baishnabi Thakurani 'was no mean scholar', and that:

> She even excelled in Sanskrit, and needless to say, knew excellent Bengali. Above all, she had a wonderful ability to describe, and charmed everyone by her recitations ... Young, newly weds, married daughters learnt from the Baishnabi, but the unmarried girls went together to the gurumahashay's *pathshala*. It may not have done much else, but laid the foundations for learning for girls and boys on the same principle.[72]

---

70   Das 1891c.
71   Das 1891c.
72   Debi 1916.

She speaks with great admiration of one of her mother's aunt, for her interest in serious, philosophical and classical education (along with readings in lighter literature – novels and fantasies), and that education introduced by her 'esteemed' father, who brought male and classical education into their *antah-pur*, and, not content with *jenana* education imparted by *pandits* and white governesses, sent his daughters to Bethune School. She particularly prised the fact that he 'enriched his family's store of learning, especially by polishing the intelligence, knowledge, and religiosity, of the inhabitants of the women's quarters, by advising them on 'true' religion, spirituality, conduct, and at times by speaking about science in a simple language'.[73]

These details argue for a reliance on the universality of reason while showing how women can use reason for self-development and definition, and use it, as in the following quotation, to make a practical, domestic contribution. This passage argues that an education meant for males and economic viability is also needed for the home. The formulation pushes motherhood and the home to the border of the public domain.

> Many are unwilling for women to learn affairs of administration. According to them, habits of work are needed only for shop-keeping and running offices. There is [supposedly] no need for that kind of education in the little lives of women in their little homes. But if we pause a while, we see that management, habits of accounting, etc., are indispensable in smaller and larger affairs of life ... In this there is no difference between running a home or an office or shop. This cannot be done with little knowledge and intelligence. Like all other serious responsibilities – running a home requires controlling family affairs, maintaining order and accuracy – hardwork, thrift, frugality, skill and judgement.[74]

This reinterpretative enterprise concerning the concepts of motherhood and the home, in the first place, expands women's work of humanising (*manush kara*) their children to themselves on a basis of universalism. Then it is pushed by Krishnabhabini, for example, to introduce the concept of 'women's freedom' (*shri swadhinata*) and economic freedom as integral to humanisation. Though, as mentioned at the outset, the great injunction of the Bengali primer which warns that only 'Those who study will ride in carriages or horses [or 'horse drawn carriages']' does not wholly apply to middle class women, writers such

---

73   Debi 1916.

74   Das 1891c.

as Krishnabhabini deem it important for a woman's and a mother's dignity to be self-supportive in times of penury. Economic viability is recommended in the name of a moral and social independence and as a display of women's capacity rather than of poverty. Thus Hiranmayee Debi in 'Newnham College'[75] and Krishnabhabini in 'Ingraj Mahilar Shiksha O Swadhinatar Gati' ('English Women's Progress in Education and Independence')[76] speak about women's career development. Of course, they are careful to link this achievement with a better motherhood and better home.

It is easy to see, then, in their negotiatory and adaptive ideological strategies, why the women educators or reformers did not find much of use in even the powerful figure of the mother goddess. Since their project was both practically ethical and social, they could not look to this symbolism of an asocial, unpractical, mythic nature for any direction in concrete terms of social reproduction. Nor is this 'mother figure' a 'mothering' one in terms of her association with weapons and war rather than with a child in arms. It is understandable that a writer such as Sarala Debi, with her concern about national politics rather than the politics of reproduction, found the heroic, aryan version of the 'mother goddess' congenial, while the others in these magazines hardly allude to her in any important way. This abstinence cannot be read so simply in terms of a Brahmo influence, as it is the convention to do, since women of non-Brahmo background refrained from using it, while Sarala Debi, who used it herself, came from one of the oldest Brahmo families in Bengal. It is the fact that their central concern is the family, the home and motherhood, in a daily practical or reproductional rather than a symbolic or metaphoric way, which should be looked into for a credible explanation of the non-occurrence of this phenomenon which swept the world of male cultural nationalism. The domesticated, quasi-Hindu, aestheticised version of this mother goddess, in the figure of *Bharatmata* (mother India) did not fare any better in the negotiatory scheme. It is perhaps the urban-folk symbol of the *Bangamata* (mother Bengal) that to some extent shared the affect base with the new Bengali mother. But the critical educative and practical elements introduced by the typology of the sentimental educative mother only allow for a partial convergence. The basic construct of womanhood that underlies this notion of motherhood is, therefore, non-mythical, non-aestheticised or non-symbolic. It is, rather, a signifier, a configuration of a set of mundane, secular, urban and domestic social codes. The ideal woman type, the mother, is of the same world as the creator of

75   Debi 1891b.
76   Das 1891a.

the typology. The typology combines in one construct the woman, 'feminine' intuitions or insights, and principles of utilitarianism in her pursuit of practicality, with shadows of universal reason or enlightenment. She is 'feminine' but with a difference.

Looking for reasons that make this difference between a fully patriarchal view of motherhood and the view of writers such as Krishnabhabini Das, we cannot avoid realising the presence of a gendered Victorian femininity and an equally Victorian utilitarian reform tradition which I have alluded to before. The cultural inflexions of Victorian England in the world of consciousness of the middle classes of Bengal is too expected and obvious a reality to deserve much attention. Many of the themes mentioned so far – 'the individual', 'the child', 'sentimental education', 'mother educator' and so on – are to be commonly found in English literature and social thought beginning from the late eighteenth century through the Victorian era; various developments of romanticism are expressed as continuous but unsettled relations between reason or rationality and emotions or intuition. Dicken's *Hard Times* is a powerful statement of this, while Mill expatiated on his total ethics by adding Coleridge (emotion/intuition/imagination) to Bentham (rationality/utility/practicality). To what extent these modes of thought influenced or created new thoughts among the colonial intelligentsia cannot be precisely indicated, but Gauri Visvanathan's *Masks of Conquest*, for example, or readings from contemporary literature, official documents, and the growth of publishing, all indicate a diffusion and absorption of romantic and Victorian sentimental discourse and forms in Bengal. So, perhaps it is not an overstatement to say that educational projects in Bengal at this time were promulgated on the terrain of colonial discourse. 'The gestures of enlightenment and reform', to quote Gauri Visvanathan, 'co-existed or existed through colonial forms'. As Bengali women expressed themselves often through the patriarchal Bengali mode, so they relied on certain 'colonial' concepts as well: their ethos at times was Victorian.[77]

But to simply brand these women as colonial or creatures of patriarchy reveals neither the real complexities and contradictions implied in their ideological position nor indicates clearly the nature of class formation in Bengal. It is after all the case that class consciousness anywhere forms from available cultural symbolic presences in the environment and the social relations that they mediate. It is hard to think what else it could be if consciousness is socially produced and materially organised. Thus it is far more interesting to sidestep the notion of colonial discourse which works so well to read the administrator

---

77   Visvanathan 1989, pp. 66–93.

but not the administered, and to instead show it as a common cultural element to which the women intelligentsia also hold an interpellative relation. As we found in the case of their relation to the male-stream social thought of the local male intelligentsia, so are they ambivalent with regard to the wisdom of the patriarchal Victorian world view: they are both moulded by and resisting it.

The figures of the Victorian lady and that of the Victorian woman reformer, the successful, economically viable, good homemaker American woman, the female intelligentsia of different colleges in prestigious English centres of learning, scores of emerging women white collar workers and professionals, all these work as examples and mobilising signifiers in the writings of these educationists. They allow for imaging the woman face of the new social relations of production. These images concretise the women intelligentsia's own role as both active agents and colonised interpreters. Their use of these as reference points and as inspiring anecdotes of the freedom of other women elsewhere is both a venue of expression of their own freedom and desire as women as well as being an acknowledgment of 'our' inferiority, of being organised as the 'other' while the frame is searching for the 'self'.

Thus, Victorian womanhood was adapted and absorbed with a double-edge to it. There was that 'feminine' sensibility combined with refinement and sentimental predilections, but this was simultaneously undercut, most vigorously by women themselves with utilitarian reformism – through the practical homemaker and the figure of an asexual, moral, forthright female educator for whom conjugality or mothering is less a pleasure than a duty. It is in fact in this depreciation of female sexuality, the insistence on constructing a manageable conjugal form which serves mainly men and male children and 'the home', in trading off intensity or passion as a woman for a sweet sexless and moral motherhood that the Victorian influence is most effective. This sentimental utilitarian familial mode does not allow for any excess, especially for women, so deprived it is of any passionate or 'heroic' gesture and so full of emotional/sexual repression for both men and women. Domesticity, the hallmark of the little affective home, is its typical social form with which the women intelligentsia seem to be in a constant struggle, creating it as an extension of themselves while seeking to go beyond it in their arguments for women's independence and reason. In this matter, they use the utilitarian/enlightenment discourse and pick up their western examples less as a colonial self-castigation, but more as ways in which to undercut both local and colonial forms of patriarchy. In essays on the progress of European women there is no hint of any inherent inferiority or disability of Bengali or Indian women. The Western educated woman stands as realised examples of the capabilities of all women.

Where women are criticised for being dependent on colonialism for their concept of 'freedom' as women, that is, by being seen to function as an anti-nationalist force, one can only point out the basically orientalist and coloni-ally patriarchal nature of Bengali cultural nationalism. Though it engaged in various transferences and inversions, it grounded itself discursively in colonial discourse. Historians such as Uma Chakravarty and Sumit Sarkar remark on various aspects of this phenomenon, for example, the Hinduisation and Ary-anisation of this nationalism.[78] And yet the colonial nature and orientalism of this discursive space does not create much trouble for men, whereas the use of European ideas and attitudes by women earn the epithets 'anti-national', 'anti-patriotic' and 'imitators of the west' for women. It is here that nationalism cannot wholly contain the implications of social reform for women even where it supports some formal education for them. The point of conflict rages not around the fact that women 'come out', or that they are literate, and so on, but against the very terms and conditions for their own emancipation that women such as Krishnabhabini present. The fragile masculinity of Bengali middle-class males, 'feminised' by the colonial relations and discourse, felt fundamentally threatened by the epistemologies, social views and demands of such women, and saw them as emasculators.[79]

This threatened response is in the end quite predictable, given that women use European material with a principle of selection and, as such, chose anti-patriarchal ideas and practices and as often as not point out the gender struggle in the coloniser's society. Their admiration for the Victorian code of chivalry and social refinement never constitutes the very core of their adaptation of utilitarian or enlightenment ideas of education, self-improvement and home-making. The resentment against the misogyny and private gender malpractices of male nationalist figures or reformers is not only a proof of admiration of a colonised nation for customs of their foreign masters and mistresses.

One cannot end a discussion about the relationship between women's emancipation, education and nationalism without pointing out the same am-bivalent relation here as in other areas of social subjectivity of women. Here

---

78   Here we need to look at Chakravarty's essay where she speaks about identity formation for 'the nationalist cause,' and the difficulty of constructing an 'alternative identity' for women 'given the need for a different kind of regeneration that was necessary in her case' (1990, p. 50). There was no 'single or coherent model', hence the 'Spiritual Maitryee', 'Super-woman' Aryan construct.

79   See Sarkar 1989 on this threat to masculinity. Sarkar shows how Hindu men perceived the Hindu marriage (and by extension the family) as the 'last unconquered space' and also how 'sensitive and fragile this structure was' (1989, p. 1).

too there is a tension between becoming a subject in and through an ideology which is both inspirational and circumscribing. *Stri swadhinata* (women's emancipation) is an accompanying part of the call for national emancipation, for the conceptual space of the discourse of *swadhinata-paradhinata* (freedom-subjection) underlies the women's gender struggle as well. To respond to the call of the nation [male], to be socially and nationally useful, to be the 'mother of the hero', the 'mother of the race', coincides with the need for women's need for an active social agency. And yet as the word 'freedom' is increasingly foregrounded, it becomes apparent to women how concepts such as *satittwa* and *matrittwa* can bring women back into the patriarchal fold. There remains always a tension between achieving full subjectivity as women and as class members. Nationalism, with its gender codes and patriarchal relations, though newly configured, activates the moral-cultural code of class hegemony.

4   Conclusion

From the twists and turns of adaptive and negotiatory strategies sketched above, it should be obvious that we can come to no conclusion regarding the ideological position of the writers explored without stating, first and last, the impossibility of establishing one, single, unified-monolithic consciousness for each class. Not only is it impossible because mental spaces are constructed from invisible but powerful, uncountable sources, recreated and created in such various forms and contents, but also because a class itself is never, even objectively speaking, a solid, one-piece entity. It is a fragmented entity from within. Whereas each fraction within the class may hold the same relation to the means of production, or a place in the ruling apparatus, its subjective and objective social existence is fractionalised and fractured. Antonio Gramsci's 'Notes on Italian History', for example, outlines one possible political formation on the basis of such fractionalised existence, and shows some of the ways and needs for homogenisation or unification in the course of Italian bourgeois development. Marx's discussion in *The Eighteenth Brumaire*[80] also speaks to fragmentation, fissures, ruptures and attempts to eliminate and/or negotiate them, which is the sum of a political process. As pointed out by writers such as Asok Sen, Partha Chatterjee and others, Bengali nationalism shows numerous fragmentations and negotiatory containment and formative strategies.[81] It

---

80   Marx 1972d.

81   See Sen 1977 on class formation and forms of consciousness and ideology, and also Joshi 1975.

is worth remembering that the same or similar relations to the means of production, and the same or similar existence in the terrain of colonial capitalism did not produce an invariant, solid ideological position. The ideological range extends from secular economic and utilitarian liberalism to Hindu revivalism, wherein secularists can coexist with or participate in religious cultural forms and the Hindu revivalists can support economic liberalism and use positivism for their argument's presentation.

The difficulty of pinning down the elements of any ideological mode is further complicated for Bengal because of the type of class formation, or lack of clear differentiation, which colonialism dictated. In the world of post-1793 (Permanent Settlement) Bengal, class fusion, their general retardation, the fusion and distinction between the country and the city, the colonial and local, popular and elite, the cultural interface, all go towards the making of the most divergent class subjectivities within which there are formations that compete and seek to dominate each other. As a corollary to this indeterminacy there is the peculiar nature of the propertied classes in Bengal which are, like Janus, two faced – ruled and ruling. Whereas the coercive aspect of the colonial discourse is remarked upon, one should also note that in a society with such a highly developed hierarchy in mental and manual labour, the local elite discourse also *voluntarily* took to a foreign elite discourse. There was a convergence of aims and views which were not simply 'imposed' on the colonised. A society that was hierarchical (caste/class), patriarchal and familiar to empires and the military, with developed forms of commercial capital, with an organised elite (both Hindu and Muslim), did not exactly need to be inducted into 'the command of language and the language of command'.

These notes about the general formation of ideology or the Bengali colonial context are important for us in our assessment of the position of the women writers. Their consciousness is elaborated in the same terrain and shares the same common sense of both absorption, submission, resistance and subversion. We see in the above discussion how they share a base with both reformers and revivalists, working within a colonial, and a local, patriarchal social mode. But what is significant about them is this added double-edged dimension of resistance to patriarchy while sharing at the same time a colonised space with their male counterparts and putting the middle class's homes in order. It is the 'difference' that marks their acceptance of 'motherhood' and 'femininity' while their experience as colonised people marks the way they manipulate colonial cultural elements. This double relation stamps their social agency and textures the organisation of their thought. There is obviously no denying the 'westernisation' of their consciousness. It may also be remarked that the strand of thought we have examined here is peculiar to a Brahmo-Victorian combined ethos. And it is also inferred, as it was by members of the male nationalist intelligentsia of the time, that it is wholly anti-nationalist. But again Gyanadanandini in 'Ingraj Ninda' (Blaming the English) or Krishnabhabini in 'Bilat Bhelki' (The English Trick) perform an interesting feat when they point out that there is no need to blacken all of Western civilisation and to valorise all aspects of ours, but rather to search eclectically for what we can take from 'them' in order to develop our own culture and economy and get on with the main business of moving towards a 'genuine independence'. This is an example of the adaptive strategy which is to be found in the case of the main theorists of Bengal's cultural nationalism as well. Such an attitude is a product of, and holds a project for, the here and now, allowing for an over-all 'modernity' along with a reinterpreted 'tradition' and a reworking of English and European rationalist thought.

In the cases of both the male and female intelligentsia we see the birth of social subjectivities which have absorbed into their own making many indigenous cultural forms as cultural lineaments of the colonisers. Of course, the values, symbols and epistemologies that are thus culled and reorganised do not fuse perfectly. Signifiers continue to have their lives in the domain from which they were culled unless undercut and mixed thoroughly in the new project. They can, and do, often pull away into unintended directions. The Victorian woman, at times, can and does overdetermine the construct of the Bengali *bhadramahila*. But what is of greater importance to us is the general direction through (not to) which this educational ideological venture moves. It keeps a balance, a fine tension between speaking as and for a (gendered) class, as well as 'women'. It seeks to re-define gender codes, expressing new relations of social reproduction while striving towards a relative autonomy by using the concept of 'individual freedom' as a subset of 'national freedom'. Finally it appeals to the notion of 'humanity' as a form of legitimation and destination for the whole project.

In this interpellated ideological form neither patriarchy nor the gender division of labour are discarded but are rather redefined and displaced in such ways as to mediate the emerging new social relations and to form a new ideological cluster. As class agents, the summoned subjects, the women intelligentsia are active 'modernisers' and inventors of 'tradition'. Their domain however, is social reproduction rather than social production, and they help to crystallise an ideology of 'home', womanhood and a type of motherhood, all of which serve as complex social and emotional signifiers working with desire and practical needs. Even to this day, and especially now, it is this cultural-symbolic cluster to which domestic capital and consumer advertising cater in a promise to make a dream come true. Both the exhortatory and practical articles testify to this concern and the ability of women to transform and organise social mediation through the family form. The transformation of the *andarmahal/antahpur* into *griha*, the emergence of the *bhadramahila* as a mother and a conjugal partner, even when captured at a conceptual level through an organisation of the common sense of the propertied classes into an ideology, both anticipate and mark the moment of advent of a 'modern' society where women and men can overstep the older sexual division of labour. In this new construct and proposed mediation women can 'come out' and be 'public' and men can 'go in', and yet the psyches and social relations become increasingly more individualised – that is, privatised and personal.

Lest we substitute history of ideas and glimpses of social life for the real history of how people actually live, and forget how grey is 'the twilight zone' of their common sense, we can only remind ourselves that what we are dealing with is a *construct*, a *category* for interpreting reality, 'trimming off an epoch in history'. We have attempted to merely highlight an aspect of class formation in terms of consciousness and social reproduction, with an emphasis on the hegemonic. We have tried to show the formation of a normative agenda put together selectively from the common sense of urban propertied classes of colonial Bengal, and sought to illustrate how they are cathected to their social ontologies, concretely put forward as reform projects.

Marx in *The Communist Manifesto* introduced a notion that he did not elaborate upon. It is that of the 'hidden struggle' of classes.[82] In *The Civil War in France* or *The Eighteenth Brumaire* we see its elaboration and historicisation through the depiction of class struggle that happens 'within' and not just 'between' classes. In the language of Gramsci and the Gramscians this could be understood as hegemonic fractionalism. This fractionalism is as much an 'objective' aspect of class formation (for example, different stages or aspects of capital) as it is the subjective foundation for how people make their history. In this sense the realms of ideology or common sense, that is, the cultural dimension of social reproduction, are as much a site for class politics as is the world of social-economic production. The conquest of civil society, as Gramsci points out, is the conquest of the hearts and minds of the people. This is the formation of consensus on which ruling rests. It is this that provides the 'moral regulation' that is institutionally and daily elaborated and sought to be implemented. Social agencies arise from within this 'moral regulation' and work with and against it. If we reconsider what the women's magazines have to say in this light, then what we have to say about the social subjectivity and agency of women in

---

82   Marx and Engels 1984, p. 15.

the context of education (social reform) points to a whole range of possibilities of cooperation and antagonism. Possibilities open and close at the same time. In fact, the dynamic is such that one might say that often they open in order to close, to take in seemingly disparate elements, whose absorption offers bonding possibilities with others of different positions. They are the communicative competence of the central ideological position – as, for example, the different typologies of motherhood, their submissive and subversive elements, signal to each other. But it is equally impossible to see this ideological enterprise as fully intentional, with a blue-print from its birth. All we can say is that in their ventures of self-creation, which involves discovery and compromise, writers such as Swarnakumari Debi, Gynanadanandini Debi and Krishnabhabini Das, in particular, bring to the fore social topics structured in such current symbolic, conceptual terms that wider and wider circles of women can speak to each other in at least partially meaningful ways. An example of this is surely the overlapping discursive worlds of the middle-class Hindu and Muslim women. Writers such as Begam Rokeya, for example, in the magazine *Nabanur*, speak to the same topics, though with a specific concern for the realities of Muslim women's lives, and share a very similar discursive space.

The ideological success that this social reform enterprise initiated a long time ago, in terms of hegemonising the consciousness of present-day Bengali middle-class women, can perhaps be guessed if we look at the current epistemological and ideological substructure of welfare policies and practices regarding women. Much of what structures even today the paraphernalia and attitudes towards education, social work, and even some aspects of feminist politics and thought, derives from the typology, subjectivity and form of agency constructed in the pages of these eminently perishable magazines a long time ago.

This paper, at the beginning stage of my research, is a search for an exploratory and analytical framework for a long term project that I have undertaken in order to display the gender organisation of class, and the ideological construction of subjectivities and agencies of/for women put forward by social reform projects in colonial Bengal.

This project has been very kindly sponsored by the School of Women's Studies, Jadavpur University, Calcutta, which has offered me the most vital necessities for research, namely encouragement and an access to original material. The latter has come from Abhijit Sen of The School, who has most painstakingly and discerningly copied out articles from magazines which are literally on the verge of extinction – they are mostly in an unxeroxable condition. These articles, until Abhijit rescued them, hardly saw a reader since their first appearance. Abhijit's collection is towards the publication of volumes of an anthology with an introduction by himself. This project is also to be sponsored by The School of Women's Studies. I should take the opportunity here of thanking Professor Jasodhara Bagchi, the Director of the School, herself a scholar in the area, for the discussions we had which have helped me to move towards a formulation of an analytical perspective, and for her willingness for a long term involvement, and her continued support for my work for a time long prior to this stage of my scholarship.

Age of Consent and Hegemonic Social Reform

Until recently colonialism in general and British colonial hegemony in India in particular has been largely considered in terms of economic exploitation, military repression and direct political administration. This view of hegemony as unequivocally coercive omits to consider its legitimation-producing aspects. This subtle and complex dimension of hegemony amounts to a reorganisation of the civil society of the colonised which is accomplished through a diffusion of cultural-ideological constructions and moral regulations.[1] Though this legitimation aspect of hegemony is present in most colonial enterprises in varying degrees depending on the nature of the enterprise, it is the case with India that British colonialism sought to legitimise itself through self-characterisation as rule of law and social reform.[2]

Significant legislation pertaining to social reform which sought to penetrate deeply into the everyday life and culture of Indians (in particular of Bengal) marked the passage of British rule in India. This legislation involved such intimate and private aspects of life as marriage, motherhood, women's relationship to their bodies, sex and sexuality and, less intimately, property laws and education. The processes leading up to the enactment of reform legislation entailed the elaboration of colonial cultural constructions and modes of moral regulation. They accomplished the process of colonial state formation in India by ascribing cultural-moral identities to the indigenous population which served in the capacity of ideology for ruling.[3]

In this enterprise patriarchy and the reorganisation of gender relations provided the most crucial elements. Patriarchal colonial moral imperatives came into nineteenth-century Bengal deeply inflected with British/European ideas of 'race' and difference. The laws therefore actually far exceeded their stated legal purpose and in effect provided a set of norms and forms for the society to adhere to.[4] This was particularly effective with the rising Bengali middle classes, who were formed in the terrain of colonial rule. One such law, perhaps the most hegemonically charged, is the Age of Consent Act of 1891.

---

1 See Corrigan and Sayer 1985 and also Corrigan 1981.
2 See Cohn 1983; also Cohn 1985, pp. 276–329.
3 See Bannerji 2001, pp. 54–72; also Bannerji 1994b.
4 On the role played by the creation of difference and 'race' in the course of ruling, see Sinha 1995, pp. 33–68.

This paper explores this Act's ideologically hegemonic dimensions with respect to the production of identities for Bengali Hindu middle-class women. Since these female identities are conceived with reference to their male counterparts, a discussion about them is necessary. These hegemonic identities were not restrained within the boundaries of the Act and they continue to texture all manner of social legislation and discussion which surrounded them.

On 9 January 1891, the Viceroy of India, Lord Lansdowne, introduced before the Supreme Legislative Council a Bill to amend Section 376 of the Indian Penal Code, which would affect an amendment of Schedule II to the code of criminal procedure of 1882. Drafted and presented at length before the Council by the Honourable Andrew Scobble, circulated for opinion to a large number of colonial administrators, both Indian and British, medical and legal practitioners, including notables among the Muslim and Hindu communities, the Bill was passed with unprecedented speed on 19 March 1891. Entitled 'The Age of Consent', raising the age of legally permissible sex for girls from ten years (the limit set in 1860) to twelve years, this act became the most controversial of reforms legislated by the colonial state.

The objective of this Bill, soon to become an Act, was a final definition and settlement of the age at which any female of the Indian communities could become the object of male sexual penetration. The violation of this age limit would constitute a criminal offence irrespective of the marital status of the female or the relationship between the female and the male offender in question. This Act was crucial in the state's attempt to regulate sex and forms of sexuality among the Indian subjects. It defined legal sex as being heterosexual and penetrative, while equating sexual transactions both within and outside of marriage, including prostitution. The same legal provisions would thus hold for rape, statutory rape and illegal solicitation, and implicitly impact on the population growth of the country.[5] This state regulation of the private lives of the colonial subjects also had a profound moral dimension, on the basis of which the reform was proposed and justified. That entailed a negative cultural-moral construction of the local population which was perceived by the colonial authorities to be in dire need of reform.

The Bill created an overwhelming reaction among the indigenous male population at its consultation stage. Huge rallies were organised in protest, especially in Calcutta and Bombay, as well as petitions and signature campaigns.

---

5   A Malthusian way of viewing both 'home' and colonial society in terms of 'population growth' was in place by the time the Age of Consent Act is passed. It forms an active part of governance in both spaces, and is also connected with this interest in reproductive biology, eugenics, women and motherhood. See Whitehead 1995; see also Arnold 1993.

Though some support for the Act was also forthcoming, in the main the state faced the accusation of a highhanded imposition.[6] Anticipating this, the colonial state performed various exercises of legitimation. It not only went through motions of public consultation, but also created a Viceroy's Council which minimally took care of the issue of representation. Of the fifteen members, four were Indians, two each from the Hindu and Muslim communities. In addition a Select Committee was appointed to review the objections raised about the Bill, and a few minor changes suggested by it were incorporated into the Act. Of the two Hindu Council members, one voted negatively, despite being a loyal legal practitioner. The Act in its final state made compromises. A husband's offence, considered non-cognisable, removed for him the penalty of transportation for life,[7] as well as made provision for the case to be tried by the district magistrate (a post reserved for the British), rather than being arrested and investigated by the police.

This large controversy surrounding the age of consent in its Bill stage was not a struggle between two homogeneous groups, namely the coloniser and the colonised, embodying the principles of modernity and tradition, respectively.[8] As research has shown, preoccupation with social reform and modernity, or social order and tradition, is in no consistent way the project of the British or Indians ranged in oppositional relation. During different phases of colonialism British attention shifted from 'tradition' to 'modernity' or vice versa. The British sought to create a colonial ideological apparatus for ruling just as much on one basis as on the other. Lata Mani, for example, has shown this effectively in terms of the invention of tradition in her work on *sati* and colonial representation of Indian women.[9] Colonial rule in nineteenth-century India meandered along a tortuous path between the traditionalism of the orientalists and the modernising drive of the utilitarians, all in search of developing a technology for legitimation and social control which would elaborate a hegemonic reorganisation of the indigenous civil society.

The same hegemonic aspirations marked the indigenous male elite, who were also preoccupied with the same issues of social reform and social control.[10] They took opposing stances to proposed colonial legislation, and in

6   See Kosambi 1991.

7   A 'non-cognisable' offence was bailable; 'transportation' for life meant a life sentence.

8   See Sinha 1995, pp. 1–32, for an extended discussion of this position. See also Stoler 1989.

9   See Mani 1990 for a discussion of *sati* and the deployment of the categories 'tradition' and 'modernity' in the service of patriarchal 'race'-inscribed colonial hegemony. Also see Spivak 1988b, pp. 271–313.

10   See Bannerji 1997a and 1994a.

some cases constructed other reasons than those of the states for proposing or demanding laws. Being pro- or anti-reform cannot therefore be read as
simple signs of being pro- or anti-colonial, that is, of being a colonial loyalist
or a nationalist. There were many instances when loyal British subjects dis-
agreed with the proposed Age of Consent Act or the legislation against *sati*.[11]
Boundaries to intervention seemed to be drawn by loyalists and nationalists
alike, mainly in the matter of domestic life consisting of legislations regarding
women, the control of their bodies and sexuality, marriage and family.[12]

Since neither the issues involved nor the project of social reform as such
were unknown and unacceptable to the local male elite, we are left with having
to answer why this particular Act called for such reaction, rather than the Act of
1860 which fixed the age of marriage and sex for girls at ten years. Not even the
banning of *satidaha* (1829) nor the introduction of widow remarriage created
such an organised protest. Though more research needs to be done in this area,
some speculation might be in order. One could begin from the shadow cast over
the 1891 Act by the death of a ten-year-old girl, Phulmoni Dasi, in 1889. Many,
even colonial officials, blamed not only her husband but also the British government for allowing the act of sex with a ten-year-old girl. Reformers of all types
found this reprehensible and the state responded to their criticism by raising
the age of consent to twelve. This change was considered insufficient by some,
while others thought the decision should be left to family members and other
guardians. All of these responses were catalysed at the consultation stage of
the 1891 Bill, probably because it was the second such act of social legislation[13]
to regulate the social morality of the 'natives' related to the issue of control of
marriage and sexuality. The state was again posing as the guardian of 'native'
morality, claiming to be the protector of Bengali/Indian women, and making
charges of immaturity, brutality and incompetence against local males.

This attempt at social and moral interference into the private sphere of
Bengali homes and sex lives seems to have unsettled the unofficial trade-off
between the local male elite and the state. The 'home and the world split'
which has been identified as the base of the national(ist) identity,[14] was certainly severely challenged by such a reform proposal, precipitating moral contestation and political turmoil. Interpreted as a virtual assault on indigenous

---

11   See Sarkar 1985, pp. 1–17. Sarkar speaks of loyal British subjects, such as Radhakanto Deb,
      who did not support the anti-*satidaha* stance.
12   See Sarkar 1987; 1992a; 1992b.
13   The first regulation of marriage and consummation was the Act of 1860.
14   Chatterjee 1989a. See also Chatterjee 1994.

rights to self-definition, objections came not only from *shastric*[15] individuals but also from others asserting the principle of non-interference. If the Act of 1860 marked the threshold of local tolerance, then that of 1891, following thirty years of deepening anti-colonial politics, created a massive upsurge. To this was added a sense of betrayal since this Act reneged on Queen Victoria's 1858 proclamation of non-interference in indigenous social or private life which she made after the onset of the Great Rebellion in 1857.[16]

It is obvious that debate over the 1891 Act involved an extensive dramatis personae as the project of hegemony involved colonial rulers and their champions and diverse opponents. This chapter, however, does not attempt to cover the full spread. Instead it focuses on one selected group of protagonists and examines their representational discursivities with respect to hegemonic colonial social reform. It is the ideological and cultural premises of the state's proposals and their creation of a body of representation or a 'symbolic cultural constitution' of indigenous women, and relatedly of men, which are under scrutiny here.[17] This focus can be justified on two important grounds. I concentrate on the dominant or the governing group which sets in place a political-cultural agenda which provides the terms for hegemonic contestation. In this agenda patriarchy, organised through a colonial racist perception, projects a site of contestation, a specific and concrete object of rule – namely women, their bodies and familial and sexual conduct.[18] This war of moral and cultural attribution, identity and self-definition is centred on or carried through reform projects that seek to define and organise the lives of local women. This means the regulation of the conduct of families where the control of the conduct of women was to take place. The moot issues are therefore the moral construction and regulation of a 'Hindu' culture and a 'Hindu' woman, which are equally at stake for the colonial and the local male elite.[19] This is an indelibly patriarchal project for both. But what is central for us is that the cultural-normative terms and regulatory boundaries are initiated by the colonial state: others respond to these even when they create overlapping or oppositional ideological spaces. This chapter concentrates on the discursive-ideological forms arising from the state's proposals and considers them as moments of evolution in the 'ruling discourse'

---

15   *Shastric* refers to individuals who subscribe to the *shastras* or religious/scriptural injunctions of the hindus.

16   The Great Rebellion, or *Mahabidroh*, refers to the armed resistance against British colonialism in 1857. It is also known as the Sepoy Mutiny.

17   Inden 1990.

18   Sangari and Vaid 1990, pp. 1–26.

19   See Chakravarti 1990; also Carroll 1983; Burton 1994; and Sarkar 1992a.

of colonial India. The representations of Bengali/Indian Hindu women, their male counterparts and society need to be read in the wider context of British colonial rule as a global project for social/cultural hegemony. My purpose is to focus on these identities and their role as forms of moral regulation and mediation within the textual apparatus for ruling.

1   **Whose Consent? At What Age? Discursive Constructions, Ideological Interpellations and the Colonial State**

The reforming impulse of the British colonial state in India had little to do with the protection of women and girls, though initiated in their names. This becomes evident from the fact that the issue of the woman's or the girl's own consent is hardly discussed in the official documents. Nowhere is there a provision in the Bill for a direct role to be played by the very people whose bodies are to be the discursive battleground between indigenous men and a patriarchal colonial state. Texts of submissions by and to the state make it apparent that the notion of 'consent' is only a nominal gesture towards women and girls as objects of a legal and social transaction.[20] In actuality they provide the legal guardian (father or custodian) with permission to alienate his (or her) daughter's or ward's body to a male user as husband, client or sexual keeper and also to initiate her pregnancy. Legal penetration and impregnation thus crucially depend on the determination or definition of 'the age' which would provide the state with a fixed and justifiable criterion for 'consenting' to the guardian's 'consent'. It is this definition which was to confer 'womanhood' upon a 'child' or a 'girl', with or without individual onset of puberty, and thus prevent charges of rape and violent assault against the sexual (ab)user, sparing him, the parents, guardians and pimps the danger of legal prosecution.

     The determination of the criterion for 'the age', however, lay with legal, scientific and religious experts as well as community leaders mobilised by the state and aimed beyond questions of violence against women or children, to an overall definition of an acceptable moral and social order. As this moral order was to be the core of the reform attempted by the state, it needed contrasting points of reference to both an ideal and a degraded type of morality. Thus, through a complexly woven set of legal, scientific/medical and moral

---

20   See Government of India, Legislative Department, *Papers (Nos. 4, 11, 12) Relative to The Bill to Amend the Indian Penal Code and the Code of Criminal Procedure, 1882* (Indian Office Library and Records [IOLR]), London, for a full file of the submissions.

discourses, marked with inflexions of christianity and humanism, the state created legislative proposals which served as a social terrain for ruling through
the imperatives and models of reform. These legislative practices and their
discursive-ideological presentations are simultaneously forms of state regulation and cultural moralisation. At once instruments of legitimation and a penal
apparatus, they projected an 'enlightened' self-identity of the colonial power
which then sought to rule and reform the colonised 'other' for its own good.

Ascribed identities, put forward as 'difference' produced in a colonial context, have little substantiveness to them, but are rather ideological projections
articulated from within the relations of ruling. This type of difference, therefore, is not initially articulated by the population under rule, and as such are not
socio-historically 'intrinsic' to their society. Thus, the characterisation of India
as an essentially religious/traditional society has less to do with India itself than
with being a marker which is invented to differentiate it from England/Europe
as rational and secular spaces. This difference is a reforming design which contains a perceived degradation of the 'other' and the 'enlightened' benevolence
of the colonial reformer.

The reforming desire of the self-proclaimed moral and rational colonial
ruler, the ascribed degraded nature of the object of reform, and the tropes of
Indian women's abuse at the hands of Indian men and white men rescuing
brown women, in short the entire baggage of the colonial project, stand out
in the following quotation from the Honorary Secretary, Public Health Society
of Calcutta, summarising reports and submissions from medical practitioners.
He reports on the opinion of Dr. K. McLeod, Brigade-Surgeon and professor of
medicine at Calcutta Medical College. This helps us get a sense of the power-
driven and complex meaning of reform as encoded in the Age of Consent Act.

> The desired reform is one which will serve to remove a blot from our
> Indian codes, which will *ameliorate and elevate in a wide and deep reach-*
> *ing manner the condition of the women of India.* It seems to the Coun-
> cil that *it is to the improvement of that condition that the attention of all*
> *who seek for well-founded and permanent reform in India should mainly*
> *be directed* ... [The] evidence of history goes to show the high status [of
> women] attained in European countries has proceeded slowly, it may
> be, but necessarily and surely, ever since the period when the status of
> women was first elevated, and when she first began to be regarded not
> as the mere toy and slave of her husband, but as his equal and fellow
> worker. *Here again the legislature can give a right direction to popular opin-*
> *ion in this country, and can serve an educational purpose, the value of which*
> *is almost impossible to overestimate. The evils dealt with in this letter sap*

national vigour and morality; and the reform which the Council of the Health Society seek to press on the attention of the Supreme Govt., seems to be the natural and necessary corollary of all those beneficent schemes for raising the physical, moral and mental status of the native, and of which the noble institution founded by the Countess of Dufferin is one phase.[21]

This submission from one of the most important members of the colonial medical administration in India attests to an attitude of White Man's Burden endemic to reform projects of this kind. This responsibility for reform encodes the colonial/European self-identity and the 'difference' between them and the constructed 'native other'. Through this reforming gesture the colonising country posed as the universal standard of perfection, as a pre-scribed social model, upon which to base the moral improvement of the colony. The condition of women is evidently used as an index of both societies, of the perfection of one, and the baseness of the other.[22] The superior agent for change, the colonial state, claims to deserve, and reserves the right of, interpretation and implementation at all times. In keeping with this exalted role, Dr McLeod invests the colonial legislature with the legitimate task of providing the 'right direction to popular opinion in [India]' and thereby serving 'an educational purpose' for uplifting the 'native's' morals. This moral legislator and educator was to eradicate 'evil' practices, particularly so when associated with sexuality, among an uncivilised subject population which is yet to reach a proper adulthood or maturity. The 'native' (always male) was allegedly indulging in sexual activities which 'sap national vigour, and national morality', in particular by co-habiting with 'underage' girls, which spelt 'the degeneration of the Indian race'.[23]

---

21   Government of India 1882, pp. 419–20, pt. 15.

22   The colonial reformers here write within the discursive tradition of using the social status or the 'condition' of women as an index for 'civilisation'. This European enlightenment measure of self-identity and difference from 'others' is to be found in Mary Wollstonecraft, John Stuart Mill, and Frederick Engels, among others.

23   Government of India 1882, p. 424, pt. 2. This construction of the 'native' is complex. It ranges through depictions of an infantile, immature, weak, hyper-sexed, undersexed, animalistic, decadent and brutal sexuality – leaving no consistent stereotype in view. The element that is consistently present is objectification and denigration, expressing a relation of dominance and its terms, rather than an unvarying body of content. This is clearly brought out in Pratt 1992. Hyam 1992 describes this phenomenon, though uncritically. Sinha 1995 is another critical and rich exposition on this construction of the 'native' (male) as a sexual colonial subject.

'Native' sexual practices are categorically considered by Dr McLeod as the most important issue before the government which 'has a wide bearing in a social point of view as regards the native community, and also with reference to the importance of the race'.[24] These references to 'the race', 'the nation', and 'the native community' signal to a perception of the collective perverse and infantile sexual identity of the other, 'Bengalis in particular', who are 'enervated by this unnatural custom'. The unnatural practice is seen as being pervasive enough to wear away 'the stamina to withstand the baneful effects of malaria and cholera germ'.[25]

In striking contrast to this degenerated 'native' is the morally superior, sexually contained, thus more physically robust European. A submission provided by a Bengali doctor, himself using colonial discourse and working for the medical administration, states: 'After years of observation of the worst epidemic diseases of Bengal the conclusion is reached that placed in an equally unhealthy environment, the European may be said to enjoy an immunity to which the Indian is an utter stranger'.[26] This same European model of socio-sexual morality, consisting of restraint as health, is used by the British administrator who seeks to interpose himself between the 'native' man and 'his' woman, as her rescuer from the 'native's' unnatural sexual appetite. For this he has to legislate against the 'native', but by doing so he accomplishes 'beneficent schemes for raising the physical, moral and mental state' for the whole of the 'native' society. The Age of Consent Act is thus considered the most 'important step towards improvement of the race'. The lofty character of the colonial reform/civilising mission thus expands out into ever widening circles of responsibility and achievement. Thus 'reform is demanded in the interests of the state, of native society, of the Indian peoples, and of humanity ...'[27] And in this grand scheme of civilisation the European/British man is an embodiment of civilisation, posing as both a teacher and a judge.

The construction of the 'native' as a microcosm of a degraded society is a general colonial practice with a common epistemology, but it is also culturally

---

24   Government of India 1882, p. 424, pt. 2.
25   Government of India 1882, p. 426, pt. 5.
26   Government of India 1882: 426, pt. 5.
27   Government of India 1882: 420, pt. 16. Dr McLeod and his medical colleagues' sentiments are entirely shared by C.C. Stevens, Chief Secretary to Sir Stewart Bayley, Lieutenant Governor of Bengal, as well as all the other administrators whose opinions he compiles in his file of submissions to the highest colonial authorities. These documents are copy-book exercises of the integrity of discourses on social reform and colonial rule. Their foremost accomplishment is the degraded characterisation of the colonised society in totality, particularity as microcosmically reflected in the character of the 'native'.

specific to each colonial situation. In the case of India, the social space itself was declared to be 'traditional' (read 'backward', 'superstitious', 'pagan' and so on), while its inhabitants were religiously identified as 'Hindu' or 'Musulman'. 'The Hindu' and its counterpart were then ascribed certain moral and cultural characteristics which were also differentiated in terms of gender. Within the colonial semiotic range 'the Hindu' had a special feature – it was an ideological category that allowed an articulation between the colonial project and the local population. Its ideological status is evinced by its homogenising and essentialist character, and its morally regulative function was best displayed by its sexual and reproductive ascriptions to the subject population.[28]

Reform, it was felt by the state, can only come to 'the Hindu' from the outside, from the civilised Europeans.[29] In the first instance, 'it is not supposed that a reform of a deep seated custom in the domestic life can be carried out without a persistent opposition'. The state, therefore, must legislate this and

---

28   See Bannerji 1994b. This 'seamlessness', a result of an essentialising epistemology, has been noted by many critics as a characteristic feature of power/knowledge. For the most influential critique of this, see Said 1979. For India, see Bannerji 1994b and Niranjana 1990. The emergence of this category 'Hindu', and its identification with 'India', with its own peculiar ideological and cultural baggage, extended over a long period. It was in the making beginning in the era of the Orientalists, of the East India Company's accession to the status of government of Bengal and of the post-mutiny (1857) inclusion of India into the Empire (1865). Every stage of legislated social reform, from *satidaha* (burning of widows on their husband's pyre) to widow remarriage and to the Age of Consent added to the formulation of the notion of 'the Hindu' and to the typification of its content. The last in particular was the widest in its scope of debates and discussions and the culminating step in this process of construction and ascription of a national identity to the ruled, thus finalising the most comprehensive 'difference' between Europeans and Indians. The ideological nature of the category 'Hindu,' its essentialist, de-historicised and homogenised character, becomes obvious from the way in which the texts produced by colonial administrators and medical and legal experts exorcise from that category all of its cultural and historical particularities.

29   Thus, in the interests of colonial hegemony at different levels, colonial administrators and experts, both foreign and local, either suppress facts or contradictions among them, or leave them unaddressed in the text. They adopt a strategy of refusal to draw any logical conclusion from them. Interpreted in this fashion, indigenous reformers are referred to as Europeanised supporters of the state, but ignored as a substantive body of social agents and critical thinkers. At best there is an ambivalence towards them. But even this ambivalent relationship to 'educated men' and to 'a strong and a very intelligent body of public opinion' does not destabilise the ascribed typicality of the notion of 'the Hindu'. In fact, these local 'reformers' are depicted as exceptions which prove the rule of orthodoxy and tradition in 'the Hindu way of life'. What remains underlined is Stevens' assertion that this 'practice [*garvadhan*] is favoured and enforced by the educated men of the community' (Government of India 1882, p. 416).

'should not leave it to the growth of improved public opinion'.[30] After all, was not India, as translated and represented by Jones, Colebrook, Wilson and others, a land of traditions? Even if reform, introduced by the British, 'for at least a generation engaged the thoughts of the best men of all of the native communities', 'the Hindu' could not be trusted to come through on his own.[31] The state could not, therefore, 'pursue a gentle course of non-interference, especially with regard to something so fundamental yet sensitive, the matter of sexual consummation'.[32] As stated in one submission: 'It [the age of consent] is a question extremely difficult to deal with, because there gather about it the silent but coercive force of traditions, the sanctions of immemorial customs, and the misunderstood [by the Hindus, not the British] injunctions of religion ...'.[33] In fact some of the administrators regretted that there was a certain softness shown by the erstwhile colonial state to the 'Indian tradition' as regards the social life.[34] Nonetheless, the civilising responsibility had to be discharged by any means necessary: 'Reforms introduced from the outside require force as a factor, in their acceptance by the people or communities they may concern, and it may be doubted if they are ever thoroughly assimilated'.[35]

---

30   Government of India 1882, p. 416.

31   Ibid., p. 417.

32   Ibid., p. 417.

33   Ibid., p. 417.

34   There was for example that proclamation made by Queen Victoria in 1858 which promised non-interference in religious and daily life, made in fear in the period of the Sepoy Mutiny. As an anti-traditional member of the Council of the Health Society of Calcutta put it, 'the history of British rule and the working of the British courts in India manifest a distinct leaning towards, and non-interference with, the customs and religious observances of the Indian people' (Government of India 1892: 417). The rulers largely agreed that such a stance was obviously no longer needed with the final eradication of armed resistance to British rule and the solidification of the Empire. Besides, as science and civilisation were considered to have progressed apace in Britain and Europe in the meanwhile, the contrast between these enlightened societies and those of the traditional, benighted 'natives' was deemed much sharper than earlier in the century. The earlier Orientalist perception of an ancient Indian civilisation was to be replaced by that of James Mill and his intellectual successors, in tandem with that of the Christian missionaries. Assertions of Indian 'savagery', 'rudeness' and 'the perfidy, venality and mendacity' of 'the Hindus' abounded in official textual spaces. Now science, medical expertise and medical jurisprudence could be summoned to impose a civilising order upon a barbaric traditional society. Since much of India had been thoroughly colonised economically and militarily by the 1870s, the annexation of the civil society had to be stepped up. The hazards of doing this were also recognised, particularly as 'the Hindu' might not be able to morally assimilate this enlightenment, even if he did intellectually comprehend it.

35   Government of India 1892, p. 417.

However, the rulers had to be circumspect about this use of force, and seek hegemonic consent from local sources. The Age of Consent Act should not only 'commend itself solely to the Anglo-Indian community', though it would provide the model. The sympathy of the people in England, 'and especially of [English] women', was crucial, but the colonial state would need to draw on all of that surreptitiously. It would be 'an evil if the impressions were to get abroad that the Government of India in a matter of this sort found the springs of its actions in the sentiments and wishes of the people of England'.[36] One would have to make a show of seeking local assistance, and the loyal part of the Hindu subjects, the Westernised 'reformers', could perhaps be of some assistance. There was, after all, 'a stir, attention in public press in India' brought on by the case of 'the unhappy child Phulmoni Dossee'.[37] The death of a ten year old girl, produced legally through marital rape, became an occasion for legitimation, that is expansion of hegemony, of the colonial state.

2   Discursive Construction of 'Hindu' Sexuality and Reproduction

The colonial discourse of racial identity and inferiority which characterised the 'Hindu' as a construct was intrinsically patriarchal, with regard to both the men and women of Bengal. To begin with, subjectivity and agency were accorded only to the male, as the 'native' was a masculine construct, and the 'native society' under reform was 'his' and seen as suffused with his cultural characteristics. The British (also referred to by a masculine singular noun) could only conduct businesses with the male members of 'other' societies. The 'native females' were rendered invisible through a double move of possession and objectification. As 'Hindu women' they were seen as the subject of male governance in their own community, and claimed as objects of reform by the British state. At least that much was tacitly agreed upon by both male parties in this hegemonic contestation. But social reform purporting to 'improve' or reorganise the colonial society threatened this equilibrium of power relations. With the Age of Consent Act matters reached a head. As far as the Hindus were concerned the colonial state sought now to usurp the authority of the 'native' or 'Hindu' male, since he was claimed to be an unfit, brutal governor of women of his community.

---

36   Ibid.
37   Ibid.

The British state argued that 'Hindu' women and girls were also to be treated with some consideration as Her Majesty's subjects, since they lived under men full of 'moral abominations'.[38] Their situation was an index of the fundamentally degenerate state of the society and the Hindu men they lived with were to be seen as no more than child rapists. The official documents claimed that they were 'subjected to more or less frequent acts of connexion with their husbands', even when below the legal age.[39] Unique to the 'Hindu' character was the fact that 'legalised love of child-wives in marriage' was 'represented by lust for female children outside of marriage'.[40] This perversity, if tolerable with prostitutes, when manifested within marriage was to be considered criminal rape, and punishable by life imprisonment and transportation.

This condemnation of the 'Hindu' male would have been more than a mere ideological stance had any regard been manifested for actual variations in social practices, and had any consideration been displayed by the state for Indian/Bengali women and girls as legal and social persons by providing them with a real role in debates around the Age of Consent Act. Instead, we find in these colonial legal constructions a deep contempt towards the women themselves. The colonial administrator saw the 'Hindu' woman as a partner in the degeneration of 'Hindu' society, and she was even more of a degraded object for him than the 'Hindu' male. Preoccupation with 'the age' rather than consent made the girl/woman little more than a body and a reproductive system to be regulated and investigated. In fact the moralistic stance towards the 'Hindu' male and his society hid the instrumental use of the theme of violence against women for the purpose of condemnation of local societies and provided the legitimation of colonial domination. It created for the state a space for conducting research in the areas of sex and reproduction in the name of science and civilisation. The practices and objectives of the colonial medical establishment leading to this Act converts the body of the 'native/Hindu' woman or girl into an object of scientific penetration and vivisection.[41] The construction and publicisation of the private life of 'Hindu society' tore to pieces both the 'Hindu' male and the female. The white man condemned the 'Hindu' as both weak or effeminate and predatory or brutal, and posed as the ultimate guardian-patriarch who could legally and medically control the 'Hindu' woman's sexual and reproductive life.

---

38   Ibid., p. 416.
39   Ibid.
40   Ibid., p. 423.
41   See Whitehead 1995; Forbes 1975, pp. 407–19.

To appropriate legal control and moral definition of a whole society's sexual and reproductive life, and particularly to create a valid atmosphere of objectification, it had to be proved that the terrible lot of 'Hindu' women and girls was due to a moral failure of her own society which sprung from its own intrinsic nature.[42] This essential quality, which distinguished 'Hindus' from Europeans, was that of 'tradition' and an identification between being a 'Hindu' and being 'traditional'. Everything about 'Hindus', according to this view, signalled iron laws of orthodoxy, as opposed to the European rationality and progressivism as well as the morality of Christianity. An example offered of this 'traditionality', presumably peculiar to 'Hindus', was their attitude toward marriage. The writer of *Hindu Law*, and an 'expert' on Hindu society, Sir Thomas Strange, is quoted by the administrators in order to characterise the 'Hindus' and to justify the need to reform. According to Strange:

> Marriage, from a Hindu point of view, is a religious duty in the nature of a sacrament invested with sanctions of the highest character, which retain their hold upon the sympathies and customs of the people, because they can be traced back with exceptional freedom from modifications to very early times. Wherever there are Hindus there marriage holds a place it is difficult for other nations to comprehend.[43]

This definition obliterates the Christian or any other religion's approach to marriage as a sacrament and a commitment for life, and provides a directive of difference through the concept of 'tradition'. This relegates 'Hindu' society outside of history and time, and confers on it an opacity or density which puts it outside of European comprehension. In being beyond European comprehension this 'traditional' 'Hindu' society becomes the ultimate other of Europe/Britain and beyond the pale of reason or change. The unchanging quality of this society is further reinforced by drawing upon statements of indigenous colonial administrators:

> Girls in our climate could not be left unmarried up to fourteen years, nor would a girl of that age submit to the present system of marriage ... Unlike *sultanism* [concubinage], marriage is interwoven with the whole texture of our society, especially the Hindu society. You cannot seriously alter the marriage system without altering the whole fabric.[44]

---

42   See Levin 1994, which draws on connections with other critiques of moral and social purity stances, on social histories of ruling as implying moral regulation.

43   Government of India 1882, p. 421.

44   Ibid., p. 421.

The Age of Consent Bill was a peculiar concession to traditionality insofar as the colonial authorities consulted local scriptural experts and claimed to continue non-interference with the age of marriage if not of consummation. Since wives were supposedly 'indispensable' to Hindus for religious observances, they would be allowed to marry any time they wanted, and to a girl of any age. Colonial administrators spoke on this matter with the authority and tone of Brahmins when they commented on the 'four orders' [caste] which in 'the Hindu view of life ... distinguish the different periods of human life'.[45] They were willing to concede to the 'Hindu' belief that marriage 'completes the expiatory ceremonies of sinful taint contracted in the parent's womb', and for women and *sudras* (low caste) this was the only expiatory rite allowed.[46] British men argued, with scriptural quotations, that marriage provided the only important 'obligations to women' and they were equal to 'the ordinances of the vedas'. There were cautionary remarks on 'the difficulty and delicacy of tasks before the government', and how reform must thus 'be moderate in extent and must be as far as possible a return from a deteriorated custom and compliance ...'[47] A 'return' to what, one might ask, and the answer, curiously, refers to an earlier state of civilisation of the 'Hindus' themselves, of being 'Aryans'. For Bengalis in particular, reform would consist of becoming equal to more 'manly races' in India at the present time.[48] Aryans, it seemed, waited to consummate their marriages, or even married at a later age than was the present practice in Bengal. It is noted that marriage 'takes place earlier in Bengal than in the Hindustan provinces, where it may be supported that among a more purely Aryan population the custom approaches more nearly to the ancient practices ...'[49]

This concession to 'traditions of Hinduism', both as constructed by the British, and especially those regarding marriage, meant little more than a contemptuous tolerance of 'degenerate' practices in keeping with the perceived negative moral characterisation of this Bengali/Indian society. In fact it is this very concession, with its ascriptions of depravity, which gave the state the reason or excuse to extend its jurisdiction over the sex life of its subjects as a whole and over women's lives in particular. While marriage must be allowed, it was felt that 'the consummatory homebringing of the wife stands upon no such special and peculiar ground; and may be considered in the interest of the people and

---

45   Ibid., p. 417.
46   Ibid.
47   Ibid.
48   Ibid.
49   Ibid.

in these interests be regulated and defined'.[50] This consummatory homebringing, referring to 'the age' at which a girl could be sexually used, brought the British authorities directly into contact with the bodies of Indian/Bengali girls and women. They were perceived as a biological organisation of a certain type of human species, rather than as substantive human beings, or even as objects with any sexual connotation for the white male. Throughout these submissions, the female of the Hindu species, unlike the male, was credited with no personality, subjectivity or agency, no matter of what distorted variety. She could only be perceived as a vehicle for 'Hindu' (male) sexual perversity and as a breeder for that society. This status as 'the native female' or 'tropical girl/female' determined the ideological discursivities revolving around her.

It is important to note that this pathologisation, in addition to presenting Bengali/Indian women as passive bodies, also has a degraded sexual connotation which is informed by the prevailing racism of European medicine and social anthropology.[51] These disciplines experimented or speculated upon black or dark-skinned people, the inhabitants of the tropics. They were invested with dangerous disease-carrying potential and degraded sexual stereotypes.[52] Whether deployed by a local or a British doctor, the discursive composite of 'the native female' or 'tropical woman/girl' contained a passive yet oversexualised connotation. The geographical and sexological homologies between females of the tropics and its warm climate and lush vegetation fantasise an early puberty for the tropical woman (as fruits/vegetation mature quickly in the heat) and an eager sexual readiness.[53] This conflation gave the European Enlightenment's generally patriarchal equation between women and nature a profoundly racist twist. This discourse explains the curious fact in the Age of Consent documents that the doctors, who do not subscribe to the Hindu *shastras*, at the end of their medical-rationalist arguments against them accept the age of twelve as 'the age of consent'. Though they often state the 'medical fact' that puberty does not arrive properly before the ages of fourteen to sixteen either in India or in England, they end by concluding that 'in this country' twelve could be acceptable as 'the age'. This racist patriarchal discursive

---

50   Ibid.

51   Other than sources already cited in this context, see Gilman 1985a; also Harding 1993 for a comprehensive context to the colonial scientific/medical construction of the colonial subject in India.

52   See Levin 1994 on disease carrying potentials as well as on a basically 'abnormal,' diseased view of the subject population.

53   For an introjection of climate and geography in creating negative and reifying views of 'others,' and in creating racialised forms of difference as an area of critique of colonial and neocolonial discourse, see Lutz and Collins 1993.

apparatus of difference modifies in the last instance the scientific, charitable or humanitarian concern of the medical man and the scientist.[54]

The central point of these discussions or representations was the girl's or woman's body.[55] There is almost no mention of any personality, volition or moral agency of the girl or the woman. Physicality, paralleled with passivity, is the core of this discursive construction of 'the tropical woman/girl', especially where 'good' women or girls, deserving of protection and charity, are mentioned. A hint of female sexual agency, always conceived as perverse, comes through when older female relatives or older prostitutes are mentioned as engaging in unnatural activities of manipulation of the girl's genitalia in order to facilitate premature coitus. Often this 'evil practice' of child marriage and premature consummation is blamed on older female relatives in the context of the family.[56] A positive female sexuality is utterly inconceivable within this discursive framework. The 'Hindu' woman is invariably seen as a sexual object of 'Hindu' males, an instrument for his use and a vessel for biological reproduction. It is through this view, either as a wife or a child prostitute, that she constitutes a site for the extension of the state apparatus of criminal and medical jurisprudence and also provides an avenue for the expansion of European/British scientific/medical knowledge.[57]

This degraded identity of the 'Hindu' girl or woman is essential to an overarching moral condemnation of the subject. If the colonised male is portrayed

---

54 For a complex view of the medical/scientific experts' approach to the questions of 'the age' (a question which consumes them with a need for facts), a generally committed relationship to the colonial project, and their Hippocratic and humanitarian concerns, the entire set of submissions by Drs Harvey, McLeod, Webb (author of *Pathologica India*), Chandra, Gupta, Chevers, etc., in the Indian Office Library and Records file has to be read and carefully scrutinised. Government of India 1882, pp. 420–6. Their stance becomes clearer when we keep an eye on how they speak of girl brides/wives and prostitutes.

55 The archetypal medical description of 'the girl's' body necessary for ascertaining 'the age' comes from a Bengali doctor, Major B. Gupta, whose expertise is developed on the same grounds as that of the British doctors. An M.B. officiating as a Civil Surgeon in Hooghly, he gives us the clear clinical view. See Government of India 1882, p. 426.

56 Allusions to female relatives as evil influences and sadistic participants in 'the girl's' life are made frequently by different functionaries of the state, both British and Bengali. These allusions to older women, who 'prepared' 'the girls' for their use by husbands and male clients, need further research.

57 The formative conjunction of science and the legal apparatus of the colonial state emerges and evolves as medical jurisprudence. Much of the scientific endeavour is at the service of the development of a legal apparatus. This extends on the one hand into comparative statistics (Government of India 1882, p. 426), close physiological and anatomical studies of 'the girl' (1882, pp. 422, 425), and on the other hand into acrimonious, resentful reports of 'secrets' of native child births, closely guarded by midwives and female relatives.

as brutal and infantile, with a perverse will and a tradition-enclosed mentality, then the female is the physical substrate of this society. As such, the search for 'the age' operationalises that degrading construction and ascription. It begins with an imperative and assumption of the following kind:

> [I]t is necessary to ascertain the minimum age at which a girl acquires her capacity for sexual intercourse, and the minimum age at which she attains to full maturity for maternity. Such minimum age is, as a rule, lower in a warm country like the plains of India, compared to countries in cold latitudes.[58]

Though some medical practitioners sometimes doubt the geographical dictation of female puberty, more or less the same sentiment extends through the dossier of C.C. Stevens. Scientific experts who are concerned about the effects of climate on 'race' determine in the main the way in which the 'native female' is perceived.

The language of medical submission is an active discursive process of objectification – through physicalisation and pathologisation – of women and girls. The texts are a curious and even macabre mixture of scientific interest and a kind of pity which is generally shown towards an animal. Women and girls are constantly described in terms of their sex and reproductive organs and events of rape, childbirth, mortality and autopsy. Though a protective attitude is put forward regarding them, this is done in terms of moralistic, victim-creating pronouncements, never attributing any active, intelligent, feeling humanity to them. Not only do these women/girls not speak in the texts, they very rarely even appear with a face or a personality, except as anatomical-biological organs or pathology and a doctor's probe on a dissection table. Except in one or two memos in a large body of submissions, women/girls remain non-humanised, without an outward body or appearance and even those texts display features of objectification. The following is an example:

> Premature sexual intercourse tells also by its remote effects on Indian wives. Mechanical dilation of the hymen, conical dilation of the vagina, displacements of the uterus, and peculiar hyper-tropical condition of the labiae are its local effects. With an undeveloped pelvis pregnancy entails very often serious consequences, viz. difficult labour, puerperal complications and heavy infantile mortality. Among its constitutional effects I

---

58   Government of India 1882, p. 424.

may note down the arrested development of body and mind. A victim of this atrocious practice is known by her girl-like face, hands and feet, with the body and figure of an old woman, a description that applies to most Indian women. A mechanical submission to domestic drudgery and tyranny is a sufficient test of her intelligence.[59]

Written by a Bengali doctor, this description, with also its brief reference to the fears and tears of a young girl visiting her husband's home, is the only vaguely humanising reference to women and girls as sentient beings. This may be joined with that of a British doctor who compares the fate of a young girl unfavourably with that of an animal, stating that a female animal has more freedom from sexual and reproductive tyranny than a child wife/mother in Bengal.[60]

The submissions supporting the Act, and many against a merely legislative or the present legislative solution, testify to a horrible cruelty against women and girls. Allusions to injuries, rape, pain and blood fill the pages. However, only a few of the submissions partly call into question the mythology of the early sexual maturity of girls in the tropics. Some experts are ready to say that the age of twelve is not satisfactory: 'It is absolutely no test whatever that maturity for the purpose of maternity [for that matter, for the act of sex] has been attained'.[61] Some make a distinction between 'puberty' and 'nubility', and deplore the 1860/61 penal code.[62] One states that the law 'instead, almost seems to sanction the infliction of injuries which in many instances prove fatal, and in still more numerous cases seriously affect the future health and well-being of native women'.[63] One doctor speaks of 'the terrible strain of premature maternity' and points out that 'at least in 20% of marriages children were born to child wives', between twelve and thirteen years. The injuries are repeatedly detailed: 'difficult and delayed labour, laceration and sloughing of the passage, death of the child, exhaustion, fever, abscesses, contractions, and fistula'.[64] 'Minority', 'maternity' and 'mortality' are inseparably joined in the reader's mind as s/he progresses through the dossier.

This fleeting awareness of cruelty does not mitigate, but in fact deepens, the pathologisation marked by the typicalities of 'race'. This 'raced' female has

---

59   Ibid., p. 426.
60   Ibid., p. 425.
61   Ibid., p. 418.
62   Ibid.
63   Ibid., pp. 418–19.
64   Ibid., p. 419.

no possibility of going beyond matter and nature; she is even more of a physical entity than the European woman.[65] Her pathology then has the anthropology of 'inferior races', and is mainly considered in terms of breeding or reproduction. The life-cycle of this 'Hindu/tropical female' falls into two periods: the earlier, briefest period called childhood, which is pre-sexual and prereproductive; and most of her life, in which she serves as a male's sex object and reproduces. These two aspects are uniformly collapsed into one. The dividing line between two parts of life – of childhood and womanhood – is the blood line of menstruation, and the only question worth asking about her is 'the aptitude of [her] sexual organs for intercourse with an adult man'.[66] This simultaneously translates out in concerns for her ability to conceive and have a healthy pregnancy, and these are the features which supply the legal formula for 'the age'.

Bodies of women and girls, therefore, were studied in great detail. The entire working apparatus of an extensive colonial medical establishment also featuring 'native' doctors launched forth into an in-depth exploration. 'Unanimous in their abhorrence of the present custom' (Government of India 1882: 422), they debated with each other, speculated upon and penetrated these bodies with scalpels in hand, bodies which would show them the secrets of human reproduction in general, but also that of a 'tropical species'. Social statistics, medical and scientific literature from Europe, general studies in anatomy and physiology, all converged on this project. Brigade-Surgeon McLeod and others refer to long standing research on Indian girls/women and reproduction. He cites 30–35 years of research contained in Dr Allen Webb's *Pathologica Indica* (1850s), Dr Harvey's work, which analyses 127 cases, journals such as *Indian Medical Gazette*, and others, and extensively cites his own work, 'Child-wives', in the *Gazette*.[67] As a responsible medical scientist and doctor he discharged his duties solemnly: 'I have brought the whole subject before the Calcutta medical society with a view to eliciting additional facts and ascertaining the opinions of native medical men'.[68] Piece by piece from autopsy reports, surgical dissections, hospital and private cases, police reports and records, a sizable body of information emerges. Bengal in particular, the seat of the Empire, but also

---

65   Lloyd 1984 and, Pateman and Shanley 1991, in their Introduction show how establishing a transposable relation between European women and nature contraindicates women's assumption of citizenship. This connection becomes an absolute equation when used towards women of the colonised spaces. See Gilman 1985a and Alloula 1986.

66   Government of India 1882, p. 425.

67   *Indian Medical Gazette* 1982, p. 423.

68   Ibid., p. 423.

other parts of India, become a vast laboratory of research on reproduction, on the mechanism of copulation, on population and maternal and infant mortality. But along with this incremental increase in scientific knowledge there is an equally incremental solidification of an ideological moral stance towards both this population under rule and 'tropical' others in general. This creates an extension of the medical notion of pathology into moral spheres and a social anthropology, a *Pathologica Indica*, which becomes the colonial perception of India. The old Orientalist discursivities constellated around 'tradition and civilisation' are fed into medical science and jurisprudence and further amplify otherisation and negative difference by connecting with pathology. The 'native' is not only 'traditional' and 'savage', as Jones and Mill would claim respectively, but by the same token pathological and perverted. These traits constitute the essence of 'his' society. The 'Hindu female' is not very much more than a cow or any other animal, to be probed into, to be construed as an index of the degradation of the society of which she forms a part, to be an open book on sex and reproduction in the tropics.

Indeed there is an overweening curiosity among various types of experts, bordering on indecency, regarding the gynaecological and obstetrics life of the 'native female'. Documents which otherwise exude the coldness of morgues and the precision of autopsies resonate with a righteous scientific wrath at being prevented access into the deepest recesses of their objects' homes, functions and bodies. 'Native' customs of midwifery, as well as gynaecology, are deeply resented and discredited by these experts, as are the practices of 'Hindu medicine' or the *ayurveda*. At this point, diverse interpretations of the *shastras* (scriptures) become useful as a tool for discrediting any Indian claim to science and medicine. Not only are 'Hindu' medical practices, either of popular or elite variety, condemned, but so also the 'Hindu' household which prevents the outsider, especially male (white and indigenous) doctors, from entering into it. *Purdah*, the *zenana* or the *andarmahal* are railed against as obstructions in the way of saving lives, and worse still, for obstructing science.[69] An atmosphere of rumours is created around these homes and what happens within them, including sexual and gynaecological knowledges of older women and midwives that the medical establishment is not privy to. It is also stated that rapes and deaths of women frequently occur there, particularly connected with premature sex and motherhood. As one writer put it:

---

69   See footnote 31 on the resentment against midwives and female relatives and native family
       relations and daily social life.

The death of Phulmoni has only brought before the public an evil the existence of which is no new development of recent years, and which is far from being co-extensive with the limits of the experience of medical officers, coroners and juries sitting in Presidency towns.[70]

The concept of 'race', which is ubiquitously present in this otherising-identifying discourse, dovetails neatly with European scientific and moral concern with motherhood and breeding which is present both in and out of colonial discourse. In the case of Bengali/Indian (read as 'native/tropical' women), notions of motherhood and breeding are collapsed into the broader discourse of physicality and animality. Fertility, fecundity and population growth, rather than lofty and sentimental notions and images, dominate any consideration of motherhood. If there is any genuine concern for the health of women and girls in the Indian context, it is mainly in terms of eugenics.

The central question here is of regulating copulation and reproduction, and in the proper propagation of the 'race'. In fact 'race' and motherhood became functions of each other in this discourse as they constitute each other as signifiers in this situation. Women and girls are to be seen primarily as a race of mothers and as mothers of races. The official concern with the weak masculinity of Bengali males finds its cause in the weakness of the 'race', that is, in premature, overactive sex life and unregulated breeding. Motherhood within this discursive framework is not connected to the socially active verb of 'mothering', but rather to that of breeding. The importance of this discourse lies in the fact that this approach is shared equally by the 'native' and the European/British doctors, and provides the basic theme which echoes in different ways in different aspects of the controversy surrounding the Age of Consent Act.

3   Conclusion

This exercise in decoding what the colonial authorities meant by 'Hindu' women, men or society makes it evident that the discursive specificity of British colonial cultural politics in India has a global context. 'Colonial discourse' holds a generic sort of quality to it, showing up in other European countries' textual/inscriptional forms of colonial ruling. Though our task here has been to explore a single strand in that repertory, we find similar ascriptions containing comparable forms of moral regulations elaborating from a ground plan of

---

70   Government of India 1882, p. 425.

domination.[71] The 'Hindu' woman/girl of these documents marks a moment in the overall 'symbolic cultural constitution', not only of a colonial 'India' but of a global European identity politics, where we see projected binary identities of inferior 'others' *and* of the 'enlightened self' of Europe.

These cultural and moral identities, as the 'Hindu' woman/girl for example, were both static and pejorative. As a contrast to European idealised identities, this is a form of difference, but of an exclusive and negative nature. The real subject, the European/British male ruler, is however hidden, or spread ubiquitously through the pages of the documents without any necessity for self-naming.[72] The entire discussion emanates from the 'I/eye' of the colonial administrator, his values and relevances produced in the cause and course of rule.

No matter what is its content, colonial discourse is reifying and concretised by social relations and cultural forms of power, coded as gender, 'race' and class. In spite of a wide and complex range of constructions, it is ultimately a 'master/slave', 'black/white', 'patriarch/woman' binary discourse. The importance of studying this undiluted form of colonial discourse, baring its raw edges, is essential for understanding how totalising power of any kind develops and operates beyond a simple functional project. If there is a colonialism it must have a discourse which is coherent with it and characteristic of it. One cannot help but notice the autonomy and strength of colonial discourse. A worldview, a cultural grammar, and a political ideology having a tenacious and unvarying direction have come into being. This does not make it a rigid or monolithic template of concepts and images. It develops at different levels and stages, opposing images and notions constitute its body; but at any given moment, in any shape or form, it remains reificatory – an instance of power/knowledge. It is strong enough to enter not only into middle class nationalist discourse, but also into discursivities of both European and third world socialist/communist revolutionary and feminist politics.

We should also insist here that all of the European/British political-ideological world is not to be seen as monolithic in discourse and intention. Just as in the colony, the metropole was also divided by ideological and factional disagreements. By the late nineteenth century some British feminists, doctors and missionaries had their disagreements with or evinced some criticism of colonial India. But the purpose of this chapter is not to explore these

---

71   For an interesting reading of colonial identities as sites of domination and resistance, where stereotypically ascribed colonial women subjects take up the project of shaping themselves through lived forms and fantasies, see Sears 1996.

72   Bannerji 1995, pp. 17–40.

'other' discourses of England, and perhaps it is worth stressing that these 'other' discourses cannot be wholly disarticulated from colonial discourse, and is often underwritten by colonial Christianity – a discourse of charity and civilisation, or a discourse of horror. These critics did not necessarily contradict the state's language and attitude of hegemonic reform and rescue. We cannot therefore either decentre or minimise attempts at negative otherisation such as the one examined here. While similar otherisations were at work at 'home', that is, in England, objectifications there took other turns, consequences and contestations. In the case of India, it is still imperative to see what became of these ruling forms of consciousness and modes of reification as they played out their identity games in the heart of the Empire, mobilising 'race' to the purpose of patriarchal class rule.

PART 3

Nation, Multiculturalism, Identity and Community

∴

The Paradox of Diversity: The Construction of a Multicultural Canada and 'Women of Colour'

> Multiculturalism has acquired a quality akin to spectacle. The metaphor that has displaced the melting pot is the salad. A salad consists of many ingredients, is colorful and beautiful, and it is to be consumed by someone. Who consumes multiculturalism is a question begging to be asked.[1]

∴

1   Introduction: Comparing Multiculturalisms[2]

Women of colour, diversity, difference and multiculturalism – concepts and discourses explored in this essay – are now so familiar that we are startled when reminded about their relatively recent appearance on the stage of politics and theory. Current political theorisation in the West happens very often about and through them, especially when we speak of representational subjectivities and identities and political agencies. My acquaintance with the use of multicultural discourse, which implicates concepts such as women of colour, diversity and difference, among others, is restricted to anglophone western countries. And even among these I am most familiar with Canada and the United States, and reality. This essay particularly explores and critiques the uses of multicultural discourse, especially as it rests on the notion of diversity, in Canada, where I have lived long enough to study its emergence, and experienced the effects of its deployment in politics and our everyday life. I hope that my concentration on Canada, which has its own particular history and polity, will still help

---

1   Davis 1996, p. 45.

2   This is a reworked version of a paper given at Southeastern Women's Studies Association Annual Conference, Athens, Georgia, April 1997. Thanks are due to the Faculty of Educational Studies, University of British Columbia, for the time given to do research for my work as a visiting scholar. I would especially like to thank Professors Leslie Roman and Patricia Vertinsky for their encouragement and support.

to throw light on discourses and practices of multiculturalism in the U.S., Britain, and even Australia, especially as an ideology for governing, as a source for organising communities on the basis of racialised ethnicities. This offers a source of internal social differentiation and legitimation for various mainstream and official practices which extend from education at home to foreign policy for bombing Iraq. As well, comparison is always a revealing activity for exploring politics everywhere. I should mention at the outset that, whereas the discourse of multiculturalism with its core concepts of diversity or difference have a general cross-border or transnational appeal, the related agentic expression 'women of colour' is primarily North American. Its use is not common in British feminist vocabulary, for example, where 'black women' or 'black and Asian women' are terms of choice. Also, women with African or aboriginal backgrounds do not readily respond to this name, as they consider themselves to have highly substantive cultural histories and special claims to the politicised notions of blackness and aboriginality.

But before we explore Canada specifically, we should begin by noting that the discourse of multiculturalism as used in Canada and the U.S. needs to be differentiated in one major respect. Whereas multiculturalism is a state initiated enterprise in Canada, with a legal and a governing apparatus consisting of legislation and official policies with appropriate administrative bureaus, in the U.S. that is not the case. This is not surprising because the historical and political conjunctures in Canada, with regard to state formation and national identity and its post-1950s image of itself as a 'mosaic' society, are coherent with such an ideological elaboration by the state.[3] The United States, on the other hand, with its war of independence from Britain, has been known for its longstanding and strong nationalism, its assimilationist or melting pot political culture, with a general drive to Americanise the cultures within its national boundary while also actively seeking an international cultural hegemony. This imperative directing ethnic cultures inside and outside of the U.S. to succumb to American culture, together with the fact that construction of 'race' more than (racialised) ethnicity has directed class formation in the U.S. from the eras of slavery and industrialisation until recently, when ethnicity of the Hispanic or Asian population is much in view, give multiculturalism in the U.S. a much more complex and ambiguous character than in Canada. There one can speak of multiculturalism from above or from below, whereas in Canada the case is somewhat different, since it is state initiated.

---

3 Porter 1965.

My impressions regarding multiculturalism in the u.s. come from read-ing both critical and creative literature, from anthologies such as *Mapping Multiculturalism*,[4] *Multiculturalism: A Critical Reader*[5] and *Revolutionary Mul-ticulturalism: Pedagogies of Dissent in the New Millennium*,[6] to name some of the more important ones. These representative collections, along with others, point to an increasing use of a culturalist/ethnicist discourse (often racial-ised) by the u.s. corporate and governmental sectors, while also indicating the lack of state-sponsored and centralised legal forms of multiculturalism. The anthologies speak to a basic contradiction. They disclose how governing in the u.s. continues to use an assimilationist universalism deployed through a language of liberal pluralism and citizenship, while also proliferating and rely-ing on a language of racialised ethnicity of social and cultural alienness. Both at the level of common sense and administration this double-edged politics and the discourse of the alien and the illegal are so active that they man-age to reduce affirmative action from an attempt at social justice into a 'race' advantage question. Both this tendency of homogenisation and the exclusion-ary use of cultural difference by government and economy, with a not-so-latent racialisation, have been questioned from the populist left or left liberal per-spectives. Many of the essays in these anthologies also seek to evolve a politics of radical pluralism or of radical democracy. They sometimes stretch the con-ceptual boundaries of multiculturalism from below to speak of not just radical democratic or social democratic, but revolutionary changes. For this last group the discourse of multiculturalism has meant an entry point into an opposi-tional, or at least an alternative, way of contesting the dominant culture and making participatory space for the nation's others. This other in the multicul-tural context referred less to African Americans, who are linked more directly with the issue of 'race', than to Hispanic or Asian American and white rad-ical democrats, though of late increasingly it turned to African Americans as well.

To go from these general observations to more specific ones which sup-port my claims, we need only to look at Gordon and Newfield's introduction to *Mapping Multiculturalism*. Dating the arrival of multicultural discourse to the very early 1990s, they carefully weigh out its pros and cons. They point out the discourse's potential (under certain circumstances) for providing 'a major framework for analysing intergroup relations in the United States', and its abil-ity to confront racism and connect to 'race relations' which are in need of major

---

4 Gordon and Newfield 1996.
5 Goldberg 1994.
6 McLaren 1997.

changes.[7] Seen thus, multiculturalism becomes the heir to the deceased civil rights movement, and helps to disclose what Omi and Winnant call 'dispersed projects' of racism.[8] But the perceived downside to multiculturalism was that in the 1980s it 'replaced the emphasis on race and racism with an emphasis on cultural diversity … and allowed the aura of free play to suggest a creative power to racial groups that lacked political and economic power'.[9] What Gordon and Newfield do not mention, but imply, is that this 'aura of free play', this culturalisation of politics, hides the hard realities of profit and class making in the u.s., and also establishes the centrality of an American culture by simultaneously designating other cultures as both autonomous and subcultures. A scathing criticism of multiculturalism as a tool for corporate America, both in terms of its internal diversity management and international capitalism or globalisation, features in the essays. One of the strongest of these is the piece by Angela Davis.

Angela Davis' attempt to link social and economic relations of a racialised u.s. (international) capitalism to a critique of multiculturalism is partially offset by those who seek to use it for the creation of a coalitional subject, especially in the feminine. Here the concept of cultural hybridity, construed as integral to multiculturalism, gives it a populist or a radical face, as for example, in Norma Alarcon's conjugated subjects.[10] For Alarcon, and others such as Chela Sandoval or Michelle Wallace, multiculturalism with its possibilities for cultural hybridity becomes a freeing discourse for subject construction which goes beyond the masculinised rhetoric of cultural nationalism or the fixity of a national identity.[11] For Michelle Wallace,[12] as for Hazel Carby[13] in *Race Men*, this is a conscious politics signalling a paradigm of multiple determinations and incommensurability.[14] This is where notions such as 'border' identity, a new public sphere and so on become central.[15] For Peter McLaren multiculturalism can be revolutionary by giving him 'a sense of atopy, indeterminacy, liminalities,

---

7   Gordon and Newfield 1996, p. 1.

8   Ibid., p. 3.

9   Ibid.

10   Alarcon 1996.

11   Sandoval 1991.

12   Wallace 1994.

13   Carby 1998.

14   Wallace is aware of the problems associated with multiculturalism, but supports it in general from a psychoanalytic perspective involving many aspects of self-formation.

15   See in this context Peter McLaren's introduction to *Revolutionary Multiculturalism* (1997), but also Connolly 1995.

out of overlapping cultural identifications and social practices',[16] while Anzaldua speaks to a multicultural subject and the importance of 'making face' and 'making soul'.[17]

It is interesting to note the relative absence of enthusiasm for multiculturalism among those critics who hold a political economic perspective and see it as an ideology for local and global capitalism and cross-border domination by the u.s. economy. Gomez-Pena, speaking about Mexican immigrants to the u.s. rendered into 'illegal aliens', illustrates how neo-liberalism 'under the banner of diversity',[18] and thus of multiculturalism, renders 'service to capitalist accumulation'.[19] Michael Parenti,[20] in the same critical vein, characterises the u.s. as fascist, and speaks to the use of a multicultural discourse to create identities which McLaren terms as forms of 'ideological trafficking between nationality and ethnicity',[21] while Jon Cruz speaks of multiculturalism's role in negotiating between global capitalism and the fiscal crisis of the state.[22] This radical political economy perspective emphasising exploitation, dispossession and survival takes the issues of multiculturalism and diversity beyond questions of conscious identity such as culture and ideology, or of a paradigm of homogeneity and heterogeneity as used by D.T. Goldberg, or of ethical imperatives with respect to the 'other'.[23]

The use of the discourse of multiculturalism in Britain is, as in the u.s., a complicated and voluntary affair. Unlike Canada, the British state has not put forward definitive legislation on this basis. Modes of governance regarding 'race' relations or adjudication of racism do not seem to be conducted through a discourse of multiculturalism. Nor has multiculturalism or diversity management yet become an active instrument for the u.k.'s corporate culture in regulating or handling class or labour-capital relations. There may be some symptoms of multiculturalism emerging in the state and economy for management or containment of racialised class relations and exploitation, but they are far from being prominent.

As regards speaking from below, British antiracism is not primarily culturalist. It appears to have its roots in direct political organisation against the British state and the economy – particularly regarding importation of labour through

---

16   McLaren 1997, pp. 13–14.
17   Anzaldua 1990.
18   Gomez-Pena 1996, p. 66.
19   McLaren 1997, p. 8.
20   Parenti 1996.
21   McLaren 1997, p. 8.
22   Cruz 1996.
23   Goldberg 1994.

immigration and refugee laws and policies, as well as in the tradition of British labour politics.[24] The struggle in Britain, it seems, has been much more structural than cultural, some cultural issues around the Bangladeshi and Pakistani Muslim immigrants and citizens notwithstanding. The centrality of the dominant English culture, with its colonial self-importance dating back from the days of the empire, has not yielded to any talk of adjustment under the pressure of 'other' cultures, though the large presence of immigrants from South Asia and the Caribbean has made some difference in literary and everyday cultural life – in novels, cinema, music or food habits, for example. In an official sense the state of Britain and its political ideology do not respond to diversity by gestures of inclusivity, but rather continue the 'Englishness' that the era of the empire has created. Stuart Hall, Erol Lawrence or Paul Gilroy have all spoken extensively to this phenomenon, stressing the racist practices and cultural commonsense of the English national imaginary in books such as *The Empire Strikes Back*, while the journal *Race and Class*, edited from London by A. Sivanandan, or his book *A Different Hunger*, speak to the racist imperialist capitalism of Britain and its highly racialised class formation.[25]

Speaking of political subjectivities and identities, antiracist politics in Britain has largely developed under the umbrella of black and class politics. The notion 'black', disarticulated from a biologistic connotation, has codified an oppositional political stance, and this is what Julia Sudbury, for example in *Other Kinds of Dreams*, speaks to as she develops her thesis on black womanist politics of coalition in Britain.[26] She tells us that, avoiding the British government's divisive naming of local non-white population as 'black' and 'Asian', women of the third world in Britain – i.e. non-white women – have called themselves 'black'. The term 'black', therefore, is not a correlate of being African in this usage.[27] But Sudbury also points out that there have been and are contestations around this term, and we see that recently there are some direct allusions to U.S. popular multiculturalism by black British intellectuals. In this connection they speak positively of multiculturalism regarding possible alliances and coalitions among women and men of different ethnic groups living in Britain.[28] A similar left liberal stance on the question of political identity and agency has emerged in the works of Stuart Hall, for example 'New Ethnicities'

---

24   See Centre for Cultural Studies 1982; Gilroy 1987.
25   Sivanandan 1982.
26   Sudbury 1998.
27   Regarding the term 'black women' in political usage, see Sudbury 1998, p. 20, fn 1.
28   Sudbury outlines in her introduction the history of these different bids at political identities and their shifts.

in *'Race', Culture and Difference*.[29] Hall's antiracist multiculturalism has drawn attention to 'a self-representation, a conscious and strategic doubling of oneself and each other, a way of affecting not only the content but also the relations and politics of representation'.[30] Similarly, Kobena Mercer spoke of 'Thatcherite tillering through the shoals of minority demands', in contrast to the U.S. in the 1980s, where multicultural discourse had arisen, suggesting 'a breakdown in the management of ethnic pluralism'.[31] Likewise Paul Gilroy, in *Black Atlantic*,[32] has been careful to move away from what Cedric Robinson, denying 'specular imagining[s]' of black and white, has called the Manichaeism of black and white fixed identities.[33] This emphasis on changing, opening and hybridised identities of black enlightenment thought, which in Gilroy's case also speaks to modernism among black intellectuals, has probably also been evolved to keep a distance from black cultural nationalism, such as that of Louis Farrakhan, or even the growing Afrocentric perspective of black American intellectuals such as Molefi Asante.

Whatever these complex reasons for different positions on multiculturalism may be, it is evident that black British use of multiculturalism, which has been both anticolonial and cultural in terms of political identities and agencies, generally came out of an antiracist and anti-empire struggle mounted from a class perspective. We will be hard put to find in it much of a statist multiculturalism. Instead we may find what we have called multiculturalism from below or popular multiculturalism. It is through the door of the notions of hybridity, openness and fluidity of identities, rather than strong state or ethnic nationalism, that a multiculturalist approach has marked 'black' politics in Britain.

This same situation is evident in non-white women's politics in Britain. It encompasses intergroup politics, for example between African, Caribbean, Indian and Bangladeshi women, as well as politics between them, the white women's movement and the state. Here too we have the dialectic of universalism or sameness and particularism or difference as in the U.S., and sometimes this is left as an insoluble contradiction. New black women's politics, more womanist than feminist, moved away from the earlier, mainly white, women's liberation movement, to one where there was sought, if not always realised, a cohesion of different women. But the politics of grassroots non-white women's activism which Julia Sudbury records and analyses has a strong antiracist com-

29   Hall 1992.
30   Ibid., p. 270.
31   Gordon and Newfield 1996, p. 5.
32   Gilroy 1993.
33   Robinson 1996, p. 116.

ponent, and also a greater attachment to prevalent politics and political culture of the third world countries from which the women come.

This seems to have created a few important responses speaking to problems and divisiveness among non-white women themselves. Amina Mama[34] has seen this type of womanist black women's politics as a facade for identity/authenticity politics, while Pratibha Parmar[35] and Floya Anthias[36] have spoken to both the divisiveness and points of identity among women. Others have spoken to the resentment among Asian women, who seem to feel that in spite of politicisation of the term 'black', it has meant African leadership in antiracist women's struggles.[37] On the other side, there has been also a resentment among Afrocentric women who question the move away from Africa as a point of departure for antiracist politics, and resent the extension of this term to include others.[38] A very different take on all of this has been put forward by those who, excited by the notion of a post-modern, hybrid (feminine) subject of multiple and shifting subject positions, have approached questions of political subjectivity and agency from a radical multicultural position, similar to those in the United States. I shall mention two anthologies and a book in this respect, which try to go away from the language of blackness/whiteness: Floya Anthias, N. Yuval-Davis and H. Cain, *Racialised Boundaries*, K. Bhabnani and A. Phoenix, *Shifting Identities, Shifting Racisms*,[39] and A. Brah, *Cartographies of Diaspora: Contesting Identities*.[40]

This discussion on the variations of the themes of multiculturalism and women of colour should make it evident to what extent they are dependent on context and location in terms of whether they serve the status quo or the opposition. Particularly in the United States, feminists have variously named themselves as women of colour, black women or third world women – often interchangeably – and wrote and organised towards the forging of a social politics in connection with coalition building towards social democracy, radical democracy and a multiculturalist, anti-imperialist feminism. I would like to draw attention especially to women of colour politics with regard to fashioning selves, social subjectivities and agencies, all of which touch the boundaries of identity. The two influential anthologies edited by Chandra Mohanty,

---

34   Anthias et al. 1992.
35   Parmar 1990.
36   Anthias et al. 1992.
37   Modood 1990.
38   see Sudbury 1998, pp. 129–31.
39   Bhabnani and Phoenix 1994.
40   Brah 1996.

Ann Russo and Lourdes Torres[41] and Jacquie Alexander and Mohanty[42] give us powerful versions of a radical, or even revolutionary, use of this term. Not unlike Britain, where feminist organising has sought to create a space 'by offering a form of affiliation that has shifted from sameness and commonality [with white or generic women] to the recognition of distinct social histories', non-white U.S. feminists have also used the notion of women of colour interchangeably with that of black women.[43] Angela Davis, in her preface to Sudbury's book, does so quite unselfconsciously, indicating a routine practice.

Such unselfconsciousness is possible because of the radicalisation of this term, women of colour, by anthologies such as *Third World Women and the Politics of Feminism*. The introduction of this book directly signals the radical political use of this term by equating women of colour with third-world women as a mode for creating a 'viable oppositional alliance'.[44] The authors claim that this 'is a common context of struggle rather than color and racial identification'.[45] This 'common context' is the same as 'relations of inequality' which mark the entry of women of colour into the U.S. labour force, for example.[46] Mohanty, in her essay 'Under Western Eyes', also makes it clear that 'woman' is not a found meaning, but is a social subject and agent, a constructed category, and this construction takes place 'in a variety of political contexts'.[47] This same oppositional antiracist position is clarified in Ann Russo's 'Race, Identity and Feminist Struggles: We Cannot Live without Our Lives'.[48] She too does not problematise the category women of colour, but contexts it to antiracist feminist organising. As she puts it: 'Simply adding women of colour to a list of women's issues, I would agree, actually leads to guilt and condescension, as well as to a partial and limiting politics and vision'.[49] The result of such add-ons is not an oppositional antiracist subjectivity for women of colour, but one of being constructed as 'problems', 'victims' and 'special cases'.[50]

The same oppositional use is further developed in *Feminist Genealogies, Colonial Legacies, Democratic Futures*. Here the woman subject-agent is again called woman of colour or third world woman, with 'aim(s) to provide a com-

---

41   Mohanty, Russo and Torres 1991.
42   Alexander and Mohanty 1997.
43   Sudbury 1998, p. 11.
44   Mohanty et al. 1991, p. 7.
45   Ibid., p. 7.
46   Ibid., p. 24.
47   Ibid., p. 65.
48   Mohanty et al. 1991.
49   Ibid., p. 301.
50   Ibid. p. 301.

parative, relational and historically based conception of feminism, one that differs markedly from the liberal pluralist understanding of feminism …'[51] This political-theoretical position which redeems the term woman of colour from liberal pluralism is expressed by Paula M.L. Moya in explicating and building on Cherrie Moraga's stance in *This Bridge Called My Back*.[52] Moya (with Moraga) rids the notion of its cultural pluralism by associating it with non-white, third world women's 'flesh and blood experiences' in the U.S., and by extension other western capitalist democracies.[53] She quotes Moraga about this 'theory in the flesh' which 'emphasises the materiality of the body by conceptualising "flesh" as the site on or with which the woman of color experiences the painful material effects of living in a particular social location'.[54] Thus Moya builds out of Moraga a realist theory of identity, distinct from identity as projected by cultural nationalism, under the name of women of colour. Moya reveals the nature of political identity advocated by Alexander and Mohanty and the opposition against which it is advanced. It needs to be quoted at some length to show her and their take on identity as both a socially grounded and a multifaceted affair:

> The problem posed by postmodernism is particularly acute for U.S. feminist scholars and activists of color, for whom 'experience' and 'identity' continue to be primary organising principles around which they theorise and mobilise. Even women of color who readily acknowledge the nonessentialist nature of their political or theoretical commitments persist in referring to themselves as, for instance, 'Chicana' or 'Black' feminists … For example, Moraga acknowledges that women of color are not 'a 'natural' affinity group' even as she works to build a movement around and for people who identify as women of color. She can do this, without contradiction, because her understanding of the identity 'women of color' reconceptualises the notion of 'identity' itself. Unlike postmodernist feminists who understand the concept of 'identity' as inherently and perniciously 'foundational', Moraga understands 'identity' as relational and grounded in the historically produced social facts which constitute social locations.[55]

---

51   Alexander and Mohanty 1997, p. xvi.
52   Anzaldua and Moraga 1983.
53   Alexander and Mohanty 1997, p. 23.
54   Ibid., p. 23.
55   Ibid., p. 127.

This radical/oppositional take on the issue of identity obviously stems from what I have earlier called multiculturalism from below. It speaks to the forging of an oppositional/coalitional identity, to becoming rather than being born as a woman of colour as a process of an anti-imperialist political conscientisation takes place among feminists. Alexander and Mohanty and the writers of the *Genealogies* anthology are explicitly critical of any subscription to racist-imperialist social relations and forms of consciousness, especially by feminists who claim to engage in counter-hegemonic politics.

This discussion of women of colour is incomplete without a reference to Patricia Hill Collins, who in her two books *Black Feminist Thought*[56] and *Fighting Words: Black Women and the Search for Justice*,[57] has tried to create an epistemology of resistance, while also speaking of black or Afrocentric identities. Since the second book is a further development of the first, we will look at both her epistemological and agency theorising projects. Her theorisation of black feminist thought is one of specialised knowledge created in rejection of and opposition to the claim to universality of standard European academic knowledge. This universality actually turns out to be nothing other than the 'interests of their creators'.[58] The issue of social ontology or who produces any thought, then, is material for Collins, and she says: 'At the core of Black feminist thought lie theories created by African-American women which clarify a Black women's standpoint – in essence an interpretation of Black women's experiences and ideas by those who participate in them'.[59] This position vindicates non-academic knowledge as experts' knowledge, thus reclaiming black women's intellectual tradition, generated from their everyday ideas. In this way black women – 'mothers, teachers, church members and cultural creators' – become intellectuals.[60] Not just written sources but spoken word, oral traditions, and interactions of the community produce knowledge, and this knowledge, infused with 'Afrocentric feminist sensibility' becomes the heart and body of black feminist thought.[61] At this point we might ask the questions about identity and political agency that Collins brings to us. It seems to be different from a coalitional approach in the use of women of colour or third world women, especially as Afro-American social ontologies or experiences are

---

56   Collins 1990.
57   Collins 1998.
58   Collins 1990, p. 15.
59   Ibid.
60   Ibid.
61   Ibid., p. 16.

sources for black feminist thought.[62] As Collins says, not anyone can produce black feminist thought. Can women from non-African descents be producers of black feminist thought? Interestingly Collins comes up with an inclusive and positive answer. She tries to disarticulate this notion from biology or even possibly from African history in the United States. 'Separation of biology from ideology', she says, 'must be made'.[63] You don't have to be African American to be a black feminist and produce that type of knowledge. By nature, Collins says, black feminist thought is deconstructive. Its task is 'exposing a concept as ideological and culturally constructed rather than as natural or a simple rejection of reality'.[64] In this she signals to Linda Alcoff's position of 1988; her example of deconstructive knowledge is Sojourner Truth's problematisation of the category 'woman' in her 'Ain't I a woman' speech. Collins continues her work of resistance epistemology in *Fighting Words*, and in this book explicitly speaks to black feminist thought's contribution to critical social theory.[65] In this text, written particularly to create an ethical-political agency for activists looking for social rather than sectarian justice, Collins does not resort to the category women of colour. To a large extent her radicalisation of the term 'black women' signals to the strand of British antiracist activism written about by Sudbury. Though still interested in Afro-centrism, Collins seeks to void that notion of its cultural nationalist and particularist context, thus leaving us with an interesting text full of tensions between a general ethical politics and a strong emphasis on the African diaspora's history of domination and resistance.

One could go on much longer on antiracist, anti-imperialist feminism in the U.S. One could also speak at length of the slide of multiculturalist discourse, with its core terms of diversity, difference and women of colour, into liberal culturalism, into its co-optation as a tool for what Angela Davis calls 'diversity management', that salad bowl corporate view of difference.[66] But I will stop here, using this introduction as a broadly sketched background for my more limited project, consisting of an exploration of the term 'women of colour' as a part of a constellation of ideological agentic and identity terms constituting multiculturalism in the Canadian context. The most salient aspect of this context is that multiculturalism is a state sanctioned, state organised ideological affair in Canada. Not just in Orwell's ideologically constructed communist dystopia, but in actual mundane granting/funding, in electoral policies

---

62   Alexander and Mohanty, 1997; Mohanty et al., 1990.
63   Collins 1990, p. 20.
64   Collins 1990, p. 14.
65   Collins 1998, p. xviii.
66   Davis 1996, p. 41.

and outcomes, in ethnic cultural fairs and religious celebrations, in court legal defences, this particular variant of multiculturalism organises the socio-cultural, legal-economic space of Canada. This paper attempts to critically examine the particular meaning such a conjuncture provides to the notion of women of colour and its home space of the discourse of diversity and multi-culturalism. In this, radical potentials spoken of above are substantially dimin-ished.

2   Canada: Constructing 'The Woman of Colour' through Multiculturalism and Diversity

People who are not familiar with North American political and cultural, espe-cially feminist, language are both puzzled and repelled by the expression 'woman of colour'. I know this because this expression has become a part of my ordinary vocabulary in recent years, and often when I have used it in India my interlocutors, even feminist ones, looked puzzled or annoyed. Most remarked on what a strange expression that was, and others reminded me that I had reverted to a racist, segregational language of apartheid and the Amer-ican South – a 'coloured woman'. Even when I tried to insist on the difference between these two expressions, these women were reluctant to relinquish this association. Their reaction reminded me of a time, during my early years in Canada in the early seventies, when I learned and evolved my antiracist fem-inist politics without this word anywhere in sight. At some point it travelled to us from below the 49th parallel, and found a congenial home on our tongue.

The Indian women's response was similar to my own long years of reluct-ance to use this notion for any purpose of social analysis and critique. I speak of this in my introduction to the anthology *Returning the Gaze*[67] and in my essays in *Thinking Through*.[68] There I use the notion 'non-white' for the purpose of creating an antiracist critique, maintaining that in the context of analyzing racialised social organisation and relations, what needs to be stressed is the non-whiteness of this woman social subject of oppression. After all, it is on this basis that she is being oppressed or discriminated against, and others (white women) comparatively privileged. Every other particularity about this subject is built on this binary conceptualisation and politics. But having said this, I have to admit that of late the expression woman of colour has crept up on me, espe-

---

67   Bannerji 1993, pp. ix–xv.
68   Bannerji 1995.

cially when I am speaking in common language in my daily interchange with other non-white women who are doing antiracist work. They use it, as do their U.S. counterparts, as a term of alterity, or even of opposition to the status quo in spite of the statist nature of this concept in Canada, and so do I. The question is, how or why did this happen? What necessities or circumstances drew me into this orbit?

To answer this question, I have to move back in time. I remember that one of the earliest occasions when I heard this expression was when I was invited to read poetry in a cultural festival. It was called something like Rainbow Women: Multicultural Women in Concert. It was organised by Faith Nolan, now a well-known black Canadian singer. I was struck by the notion of rainbow women, which, I was told, had to do with my being a woman of colour and bringing this colour to join others in a rainbow combination. I was not taken by this exercise. I found woman of colour to be both a coy and an offensive notion and, like many others, thought of the expression 'coloured'. I did not want to call myself this. Nor did I feel convinced of the capacity for resistance attributed to this notion, which encoded a multicultural unity, cherishing diversity, through promulgating a generic or homogenising term which would cover all non-white others, mostly those who were not black. So there I had it, two groups of non-white women – black and of colour – arranged in a gradually paling hierarchy, with one end of the spectrum touching the darkest shade of colour. This colour hierarchy struck me then, as it does now, as an offensive way of creating social subjects and political agents. It falls back, even if unconsciously, on the hegemonic common sense of social culture and politics of slavery and apartheid. What colour are you, it asks: are you black, white, yellow, or brown? Shades of negative differences, of being considered mulatto, quadroons, octoroons (ideologies and social relations of plantation societies) lie behind this formulation. They are presumably promulgated in good faith, to fight racist-sexism and white privilege. It is also significant that most of the time this term does not refer to black women, or those of the First Nations. I was quite determined not to use it, but as the '80s rolled by woman of colour was Canadianised. She had, as they say in Canada about immigrants, 'landed'. And here I am using it every once in a while, for the purpose of intelligibility, to keep in step with my fellow antiracist feminists!

So what discursive revolution, paradigm shift, occurred in Canada during the '80s and the '90s which could have been hospitable to, or indeed embraced, this woman of colour? In my view, there are two broad political areas which need to be problematised. One could be called, following Louis Althusser,[69] the

---

69   Althusser 1971.

ideological apparatuses of the state, including its political and civil administration; and the other, the civil society,[70] the everyday world of common social
relations, values and practices of culture and power. We may begin first by
speaking of the state, not because it was the first to name us as political agents
in terms of being women of colour. It did not, as the term had a U.S. origin. But
it provided the political culture for accepting, using and naturalising a colour-
based notion of subjectivity and agency, which in continuity with Canada's
colonial formation came to dominate the cultural politics of Canada's other
women. Canadians have been living in an historical and current environment
of political colour coding, even, or mainly, when forging a liberal democratic
politics for the country as a whole.

My claim may be more clear if I were to draw attention to the entry of
official multiculturalism onto the Canadian political stage. The open door
policy of immigration, especially attributed to the Liberal party and its cha-
rismatic leader, Pierre Trudeau, throughout the 1960s and '70s, had brought
many people of colour, other 'races', into the country.[71] The reason for this
was the expectation of capitalist industrial growth in Canada and the aspiration to the creation of a liberal democratic nationhood. The former British
colonies in particular provided cheap labour, both skilled and un-skilled, as
well as the democratic grounds for converging otherness. Thus colour, the cognate of race, refracted into indirect notions of multiculture and ethnicity, was
much on the mind of the Canadian state, just as much as in the nineteenth
or early twentieth centuries.[72] Unlike the radical alternative political-cultural
activists, the Canadian state was careful not to directly use the notion of colour in the way it designated the newcomers. But colour was translated into
the language of visibility. The new Canadian social and political subject was
appellated 'visible minority', stressing both the features of being non-white and
therefore visible in a way whites are not, and of being politically minor players.
It is at this time, at the urging of the National Directorate of Women and the
Secretary of State, that non-white women made a niche for themselves in the
mainstream politics by creating a representational organisation, the National
Coalition of Visible Minority Women.[73] This status of visible minority was not
felt by a large number of women to be problematic or compromising, since

---

70   Gramsci 1971.

71   For a history of immigration in Canada, see Law Union of Ontario 1981.

72   On 'race,' colour and the Canadian state's immigration policies in the late nineteenth/early
      twentieth century, see Government of Canada 1974; 1986.

73   See Carty and Brand 1993; also Ng 1993. For an uncritical liberal view, see Government of
      Canada 1986.

they shared political values with the mainstream. Minor as their part was, set apart by their visibility, which was also the only ground of their political eligibility, they were content. Until then they were covered under the umbrella of immigrant women, a category that included and expanded beyond non-white women, who were also called third world women. All these expressions have remained in our political-cultural language, but visible minority women has become the strongest. A categorical child of the state, cradled by the Ministry of Multiculturalism and the Secretary of State, this expression underpins and is the mainstream counterpart of the more grassroots notion of the woman of colour. This popular feminist term actually relied for its political meaning and vitality upon the mainstream analogue and the same discourse of multiculturalism pertaining to visible minority women embedded in both state and society for its existential environment. With no interest in class politics, and no real analysis of or resistance to racialisation or ethnicisation, chiefly preoccupied with bureaucratic representation or inclusion for a very limited power sharing within the status quo, these political terminologies became current usages. The multi-ethnic, multinational state, with its history of racialised class formation and political ideology, discovering multiculturalism as a way of both hiding and enshrining power relations, provided a naturalised political language even to the others of the Canadian society. Not surprisingly, these expressions found their way into general feminist academic and activist discourse and into NGOs for women and into the political discourse of International Women's Day. In particular, visible minority women translated well into women of colour and that became the name chosen by alternative politics of Canada. This practice followed the United States, and it solved the problem of finding a name for building coalition among all women. It vaguely and pleasantly gestured to race as colour and, of course, to gender/patriarchy by evoking woman. But the concept of race lost its hard edges of criticality, class disappeared entirely, and colour gave a feeling of brightness, brilliance or vividness, of a celebration of a difference which was disconnected from social relations of power, but instead perceived as diversity, as existing socio-cultural ontologies or facts.

The suitability of woman of colour for Canadian political culture was such that no one did then, or does now, speak about the absurdity of calling white women colourless or invisible. As for the degeneration of powered difference into diversity, class analysis was, after all, not the main interest of the North American women's movement, while race was accepted by most as an existential, cultural fact, if not always a biological one. This political stance has led to the seeking for better race relations, in which feminists aspiring to diversity have participated. So the term unproblematically combined within itself both the common sense of race and the antidote of liberal pluralism. The apartheid notion of coloured woman stood behind and cast a long shadow over her modern sister, since it was the subliminal principle of intelligibility of this recent coinage, no matter how radically aimed.

Common sense of skin and colour, particularly in the colonial context, is old. Bodies – skin, facial features, height, build, and so forth – had been morally and politically signified for centuries in North America and Europe (see Gillman 1985). Reducing Africans to 'negroes' was an ideological and semantic normalcy for centuries in European and English languages. The 'yellow peril' had resulted in the dispersion of the Japanese people into concentration camps. Colour, ethnicity and bodies had long been conflated with moral/cultural ontologies. It is not an exaggeration to say that it was within the context and content of these practices, meanings and political possibilities that the liberal multicultural construction of woman of colour took place. Its epistemological pivot rests on the seemingly benign concept of diversity, a re-named version of plurality, so central to the concept and politics of liberalism. This positivity which is implied in the ideology of diversity mitigates the revulsion that women might feel towards calling themselves or others women of colour. A colour-coded self-perception, an identity declared on the semiological basis of one's skin colour, was rendered palatable through this ideology of diversity. Our colour provided the sovereign mark, significant enough to be used as a counter in the political discourse of liberalism. As with all liberal pluralist projects, this constituent element of political identities of others did not come up for scrutiny or a critique, but rather became a given, commonsensical category of representation, as though always already there. Moreover, the word 'colour' became an associational and connotative path to diverse histories and cultures of the nations of other women. They themselves summoned it to convey their colourfulness through it, thereby quickly slipping into the cultural discourse of tradition versus modernity. Their colour signalled traditional cultures, in a constellation of invented traditions.[74] Culturally integrated colour was thus seemingly divested of its racist undertones, and lost its location in power relations. This erasure indicates the epistemological possibilities of the notion of multicultural diversity. If this desocialised and ahistorical notion of diversity were not a naturalised form of political culture and discourse in Canada, and in the West as a whole, such a coinage or neologism would not have been so easily adopted by women who see themselves as practitioners of politics of

---

74   On invention of tradition see Hobsbawm and Ranger 1983; also Mani 1989, and Ismail and
      Jeganathan 1995.

opposition. The formal equality of liberal pluralism encoded by diversity also helped to allay anxieties and suspicions.

It may be objected that I am making a mountain out of a mole hill by focusing so much on one single political and cultural expression. Does a name, it may be asked, make so much difference? Would not a rose by any other name smell as sweet? If we had instead called ourselves non-white women, for example, what different political task would we have accomplished? My answer to these anticipated objections or questions would be that the language with which we build or express our political agency has to be taken very seriously. An expression in that context, even when it seems innocuous and solitary, has to be treated as a bit of ideology, and as a part of a broader ideological semantics called discourse. Thus we have to treat woman of colour as a name for a particular type of political agency and examine its ability to disclose our lives and experiences as lived within an organisation of social relations of power. It is only then that we can attend to the political direction to which this agency points us. Treated thus, we can safely say that the notion woman of colour does not direct us to examine crucial social relations within which we live, to histories and forms of consciousness of power that mark our presence in the u.s. or Canada. Instead this, as a naturalised reworking of coloured woman, performs an ideological accommodation of 'race', while erasing class. Also, in thus equating our political identities with a racialised cultural construction, a second level of reality is created which is far from the actualities of our lives. Yet these social actualities are the realities that need to be daily addressed and changed through our politics. If, at least in the course of our antiracist feminist politics, we call ourselves non-white women, we can gesture towards white privilege. The use of a negative prefix automatically raises issues and questions. But a substitution through the language of diversity and colour distracts us from what actually happens to us in our raced and gendered class existence and culturalises our politics. In other words, it depoliticises us.[75]

Since the responsibility for this depoliticisation falls upon the epistemology and ideology of diversity, the cornerstone of a pluralist liberal politics and its legitimation, we need to explore extensively and critically the workings of the concept of diversity. Official multiculturalism, which has also become the politics of Canadian civil society, our daily political commonsense, cannot be challenged otherwise. The political culture generated by the state in its reflexive dependence on everyday social culture cannot be kept insulated from the

---

75   On culturalising politics, see Benjamin 1969b.

ongoing life of the civil society. If resistance politics develops from below, from the civil society, and if that realm itself is saturated with an historical and official political culture of domination, then that politics of resistance itself can become a part of the state's ideological apparatus. The dangers inherent in constructing a multicultural Canada, with a reified and racialised political agency called woman of colour, calls for a critique of the epistemology and ideology of diversity. The next section of this chapter, therefore, engages in this critique, and takes up diversity which endows its discursive affiliates, such as woman of colour, with the power to erase or empty out actual social relations and forms of power – 'race', gender and class – while creating an aura of concreteness or meaning whose actual relevances or coordinates are located within the state's discourse of ruling.

3   The Name of the Rose, or What Difference Does It Make What I Call It

Diversity has become a commonplace word in our political and cultural world. This seems to have happened in the last decade or so – it has sort of crept up on us. So much so that even businesses have adapted their talk about profit and productivity to the language of diversity, while governments and public institutions set up bureaucracies in its name. On our side, that is, on the side of the people, from below, organisations have been created merging notions of community with diversity – speaking to ethno-cultural pluralities and collective cultural identities. We have versions of this in our everyday language, and in that of scholarship. We have critical feminist anthologies of the politics of diversity,[76] while political theorists have used the term in their communitarian and liberal ways.[77]

So it seems that the time has come to take this rather banal notion of diversity and explore its current popularity in terms of what it does for us politically. To begin with, this word has been used to signify a multiplicity of socio-cultural presences, as a cornucopia of differences of all sorts, that mark the Canadian social space. But this purely descriptive use of the term, signalling heterogeneity without implied power relations, ulterior aim or use, is not the only, or the main, use that has been made of it. This simple descriptive, at most

---

76   For an example of feminist anthologies using 'diversity' in the title, see Hamilton 1986, especially the introduction.
77   See Eliott & Fleras 1992; Kymlicka 1995; Taylor 1992, 1993; Trudeau 1968.

designatory use has been a device for constructing an ideological cultural language or discourse that allows for an instant jump from description to political meanings and practices.

This discourse of diversity is a fusion of a cultural classification, or an empirical/descriptive gesture, with politics. That is, our empirically being from various countries, with our particular looks, languages and cultures, has become an occasion for interpreting, constructing and ascribing differences with connotations of power relations. This process and its conceptual products combine into a political discourse and related ideological practices. In this political deployment the notion of diversity escapes from its denotative function and dictionary meaning and emerges as a value-free, power neutral indicator of difference and multiplicity. But this very character and claim of neutrality allows it to become the governing concept of a complex discourse of social power with its own and related webs of concepts. There is a process of surpassing as well as of subsumption involved in this creation of an ideology from the notion of diversity. Conceived as discourse diversity is not a simple descriptive affair. As a centrepiece of a discourse of power and as a device for social management of inequality, it is simultaneously interpretive or meaning-making and actively practical. It creates and mediates practices, both conceptual and actual, of power – of ruling or governing.[78] In this discursive mode the concept of diversity entails two functions, which together allow it to be articulated or bonded with other political notions and practices already in place. Together with them, such as with feminism or antiracism, they form a conceptual network and signal to ideological practices of socio-political administration which are certainly not value neutral.

The two ways in which the neutral appearance of the notion of diversity becomes a useful ideology to practices of power are quite simple. On the one hand, the use of such a concept with a reference to simple multiplicity allows the reading of all social and cultural forms or differences in terms of descriptive plurality. On the other, in its relationship to description it introduces the need to put in or retain a concrete, particular content for each of these seemingly neutral differences. The social relations of power that create the difference implied in sexist-racism, for example, just drop out of sight, and social being becomes a matter of a cultural essence.[79] This is its paradox – that the concept of diversity simultaneously allows for an emptying out of actual social relations and suggests a concreteness of cultural description, and through this

---

78   On ideological categories and conceptual practices of power and relations of ruling, see the first two chapters of Smith 1990.

79   Bannerji 1991.

process obscures any understanding of difference as a construction of power. Thus there is a construction of a collective cultural essence and a conflation of this, or what we are culturally supposed to be, and what we are ascribed with, in the context of social organisation of inequality. We cannot then make a distinction between racist stereotypes and ordinary historical/cultural differences of everyday life and practices of people from different parts of the world. Cultural traits that come, let us say, from different parts of the third world are used to both create and eclipse racism, and we are discouraged from reading them in terms of relations and symbolic forms of power. The result is also an erasure of class and patriarchy among the immigrant multi-cultures of others, as they too fall within this paradox of essentialisation and multiplicity signified by cultural diversity of official multiculturalism. In fact, it is this uncritical, de-materialised, seemingly de-politicised reading of culture through which culture becomes a political tool, an ideology of power which is expressed in racist-sexist or heterosexist differences. One can only conclude from all this that the discourse of diversity, as a complex systemically interpretive language of governing, cannot be read as an innocent pluralism.[80]

The ideological nature of this language of diversity is evident from its frequent use and efficacy in the public and official, that is, institutional realms. In these contexts its function has been to provide a conceptual apparatus in keeping with needs which the presence of heterogeneous peoples and cultures has created in the Canadian state and public sphere. This has both offset and, thus, stabilised the Canadian national imaginary[81] and its manifestation as the state apparatus, which is built on core assumptions of cultural and political homogeneity of a Canadianness. This language of diversity is a coping mechanism for dealing with an actually conflicting heterogeneity, seeking to incorporate it into an ideological binary which is predicated upon the existence of a homogeneous national, that is, a Canadian cultural self with its multiple and different others.[82] These multiple other cultural presences in Canada, interpreted as a threat to national culture which called for a coping, and therefore for an incorporating and interpretive mechanism, produced the situation summed up as the challenge of multiculturalism. This has compelled administrative, political and ideological innovations which will help to maintain the status quo. This is where the discourse of diversity has been of crucial importance because this new language of ruling and administration protects ideologies and practices

---

80   For the ground of a theoretical critique of diversity, see Roman 1993.
81   On the Canadian national imaginary see Bannerji 1998a.
82   See Bannerji 1997b.

already in place. It is postulated upon pluralist premises of a liberal democratic state, which Canada aspires to be, but also adds specific dimensions of legitimation to particular administrative functions.[83]

The usefulness of the discourse of diversity as a device for managing public or social relations and spaces, of serving as a form of moral regulation of happy co-existence, is obvious. The Canadian government and other public institutions, the media, and the ideological projection of the Canadian nation (and its unity) are marked by this discourse. In the universities, both in pedagogic and administrative spheres, this language is prominent. It is the staple discourse of arts and community projects, conditioning their working agendas as well as the politics of the funding bodies. In workplaces diversity sensitisation or training has largely displaced talk about and/or resistance to racism and sexism. Even law appeals to diversity in using cultural and religious defences, suppressing contradictions and violences of patriarchy, for example, while fulfilling the state's pluralist obligations.[84] In the context of making the Canadian nation, unity is posited in terms of diversity, with pictures of many facial types, languages and cultures – 'together we are …'[85] It is not surprising that Benetton produces a diversity slogan of 'united colours' to capture its multicultural markets.

The discourse of diversity has also inscribed our social movements – the women's movement or the trade union movement, for example – where again it helps to obscure deeper/structural relations of power, such as of racism and sexism or racist heterosexism,[86] both among women and the working class, and reduces the problem of social justice into questions of curry and turban. Thus social movements share crucial ideological assumptions of those whom they seek to fight and supposedly have political differences with. In this regard it is important to do a brief retrospective on the issue of difference within feminist theorisation and the women's movement. The issue of 'race' in particular became one issue of contention.

---

83   For diversity language in administration, see Davis 1996 on the language of corporate multiculturalism.

84   See Volpp, 1994.

85   Common slogan of several government advertising campaigns, to be filled in with 'Ontario' or 'Canada'.

86   For homophobia and racist heterosexism in cultural nationalism or ethnic communitarianism, see, in the U.S. context, Collins 1998 and Carby 1998, to name two texts. In the Canadian context very little has been written about this phenomenon, probably due to the deeply social and economic involvement of the so-called communities in the state's policies of multiculturalism. See Dua and Robertson 1999, especially my paper Bannerji 1999.

Many years ago Elizabeth Spelman[87] wrote a book criticising North American liberal/bourgeois feminism for its Eurocentrism. Her book, entitled *Inessential Woman: Problems of Exclusion in Feminist Thought*, created disturbing resonances in the world of North American anglophone feminist theories, and many of us used her critique to get a clarity on our own dissatisfaction about mainstream feminism. This critique of essentialism and Eurocentrism, which I addressed in 'But Who Speaks for Us',[88] developed into a critique of an ideological and identity stance known as whiteness. The most well-known form of this notion is in Ruth Frankenberg's *White Women, Race Matters: The Social Construction of Whiteness*.[89] Though various critiques and adjustments were made of Spelman's and Frankenberg's theorisations and politics, their articulations remain powerful even as they, as white women, confront other white women and speak as insiders to that social ontology. Many others, including Ann Laura Stoler,[90] wrote on various ideological and political aspects of whiteness. However, as Leslie Roman says:

> [T]o say that white is a color does not rescue the concept of 'race' from similar forms of empty pluralism and dangerous relativism invoked by the larger essentialist discourse of 'race'. Try as I might to recognise whiteness as a structural power relation that confers cultural and economic privileges, the phrase, spoken declaratively by the racially privileged, can also become a form of white defensiveness.[91]

But of more immediate importance for us are the critiques made by black and third world feminists, such as Collins, Mohanty and Alexander, regarding the politically exclusionary, debilitating and epistemologically occlusive effects of such theorisation as conducted within the academy. In their anthology Alexander and Mohanty especially take to task women's studies within U.S. academies. Even among those who claim oppositional knowledge and practices, they declared, 'the color of our gender mattered'.[92] They were, they stated, neither 'the right colour' nor gender, nor nationality in terms of self-definition of the U.S. academy, and by extension of the women's studies estab-

---

87   Spelman 1988.
88   Bannerji 1991.
89   Frankenberg 1993.
90   Stoler 1995.
91   Roman 1993 p. 72.
92   Alexander and Mohanty 1997, p. xiv.

lishment.[93] Alexander and Mohanty broaden their critical outreach and compare this outsider status in institutions of learning to the citizenship machinery and ideology deployed in the u.s. The outsider or the alien is born both within the u.s. and outside of its national territories. As they put it: 'Our experience makes sense only in analogy to African-American women'.[94] The authors in this anthology also question the political and epistemological impact that postmodernism is having within women's studies. As Mohanty and Alexander see it, '... in its haste to dissociate itself from all forms of essentialism, [this impact] has generated a series of epistemological confusions regarding the interconnections between location, identity and construction of knowledge'.[95] This refusal of experience, history, and identity in its broadest sense of self-recovery, often found in the curricula of women's studies, has delegitimised the type of grounded social knowledge spoken of by Collins in her two books. The organic intellectuals of the oppressed become invalid by definition if they cannot claim their lives as sources for learning and theorising, as exemplars for the unjust relations within which they live. As Mohanty and Alexander put it: '... localised questions of experience, identity, culture and history, which enable us to understand specific processes of domination and subordination, are often dismissed by postmodern theories as reiteration of cultural "essences", or unified stable identity'.[96] These current critiques were anticipated as early as 1982 by Hazel Carby.[97]

This discourse of diversity in its comprehensive ideological and political form is materialised and extended as the discourse of multiculturalism, with its linguistic constellation of visible minority, women of colour and so on. Cultural sensitivity towards and tolerance of others (to the core/national culture and agency) are two behavioural imperatives of this multicultural politics, both at the level of state and society. The all-pervasive presence of diversity in our public discourse has created a situation where even those who are not entirely comfortable with its discursive constellation use it in its various guises in an unconscious submission to what is around, and for reasons of intelligibility. Being effective with funding proposals means translating our needs and concerns into the discourses of multiculturalism. This means speaking in the language of cultural communities and their diversities, of ethnicities and women of colour and visible minorities – both male and female. Otherwise our funders or the state do not hear us.

---

93   Ibid., p. xiv.
94   Ibid., p. xiv.
95   Ibid., p. xvii.
96   Ibid., p. xvii.
97   Carby 1986.

So, it would seem that there is much invested in the fact of naming, in the words we use to express our socio-political understandings, because they are more than just words, they are ideological concepts. They imply intentions and political and organisational practices. Calling people by different names, in different political contexts, has always produced significantly different results. These names are, after all, not just names to call people by, but rather codes for political subjectivities and agencies. Naming ourselves in terms of class, for example as the proletariat, assuming class as the basis of our political identity, would imply a different political ideology, practice and goal, than if we constructed our political agency with names such as women/people of colour or visible minorities. Contrary to Shakespeare's assertion that a rose by any other name would smell as sweet, we see that not to be the case in political-ideological matters. In politics the essence of the flower lies in the name by which it is called. In fact it is the naming that decides what flower we have at hand. To say this is to say explicitly that discourse is more than a linguistic manoeuvre. It is a matter of putting in words, mediating and organising social relations of ruling, of meanings organised through power. It is best to remind ourselves of the title of Dionne Brand's poetry book, *No Language is Neutral*.[98]

4   The Essence of the Name, or What Is To Be Gained by Calling Something Diversity

In order to understand how the concept of diversity works ideologically, we have to feed into it the notion of difference constructed through social relations of power and read it in terms of the binaries of homogeneity and heterogeneity already referred to in our discussion on multiculturalism. It does not require much effort to realise that diversity is not equal to multiplied sameness, rather it presumes a distinct difference in each instance. But this makes us ask, distinctly different from what? The answer is, obviously, from each other and from whatever it is that is homogeneous – which is an identified and multiplied sameness, serving as the distinguishing element at the core in relation to which difference is primarily measured. The difference that produces heterogeneity suggests otherness in relation to that core, and in social politics this otherness is more than an existential, ontological fact. It is a socially constructed otherness or heterogeneity, its difference signifying both social value and power. It is not just another cultural self floating non-relationally in a socio-historical vacuum.

---

98   Brand 1990.

In the historical context of the creation of Canada, of its growth into an uneasy amalgam of a white settler colony with liberal democracy, with its internally colonised or peripheral economies, the definitions and relations between a national self and its other, between homogeneity and heterogeneity, sameness and diversity, become deeply power ridden.[99] From the days of colonial capitalism to the present-day global imperialism, there has emerged an ideologically homogeneous identity dubbed Canadian whose nation and state Canada is supposed to be.

This core community is synthesised into a national we, and it decides on the terms of multiculturalism and the degree to which multicultural others should be tolerated or accommodated. This 'we' is an essentialised version of a colonial European turned into Canadian and the subject or the agent of Canadian nationalism. It is this essence, extended to the notion of a community, that provides the point of departure for the ideological deployment of diversity. The practice is clearly exclusive, not only of third world or nonwhite ethnic immigrants, but also of the aboriginal population.[100] Though often described in cultural linguistic terms as the two nations of anglophones and francophones, the two nations theory does not include non-whites of these same language groups. So the identity of the Canadian 'we' does not reside in language, religion or other aspects of culture, but rather in the European/North American physical origin – in the body and the colour of skin. Colour of skin is elevated here beyond its contingent status and becomes an essential quality called whiteness, and this becomes the ideological signifier of a unified non-diversity.[101] The others outside of this moral and cultural whiteness are targets for either assimilation or toleration. These diverse or multicultural elements, who are also called newcomers, introducing notions of territoriality and politicised time, create accommodational difficulties for white economy, and also for the ruling practices of the state. An ideological coping mechanism becomes urgent in view of a substantial third world immigration allowed by Canada through the 1960s up to recent years.[102] This new practical and discursive/ideological

99   On the racialised nature of Canada's political economy as a white settler colony, and its
      attempts to retain features of this while installing itself as a liberal democracy, see Bolaria
      and Li 1988.
100   It is redundant really to speak of the exclusion/marginalisation of the aboriginal people
      in Canada, both in terms of their claim to land and livelihood as well as culture, but the
      following books are interesting as examples of discussions on these issues. See Kulchyski
      1994 and Monture-Angus 1995.
101   On reading the skin as whiteness, as an ideological/political construction, see Franken-
      burg 1993.
102   See Eliott and Fleras 1992.

venture, or an extension of what Althusser has called an ideological state apparatus, indicates both the crisis and its management. After all, the importation of Chinese or South Asian indentured labour, or the legally restricted presence of the Japanese since the last century, did not pose the same problems which the newly arrived immigrants do.[103] As landed residents or apprentice citizens, or as actual citizens of Canada, they cannot be left in the same limbo of legal and political non-personhood as their predecessors were until the 1950s. Yet they are not authentic Canadians in the ideological sense, in their physical identity and culture. What is more, so-called authentic Canadians are unhappy with their presence, even though they enhance Canada's economic growth. Blue ribbon Hong Kong immigrants, for example, bring investments which may be needed for the growth of British Columbia, but they themselves are not wanted.[104] But they, among other third world immigrants, are here, and this calls for the creation of an ideology and apparatus of multiculturalism (with its discourse of a special kind of plurality called diversity) as strategies of containment and management.

If this statement seems to be unfounded, we need only note the time around which multiculturalism and the diversity discourse is invented in Canada. Multi-ethnic European immigrations of the past did not inspire it, nor are the present-day European immigrants the targets of this discourse, even though cultural, religious, and linguistic differences are very high between them and the two nations of anglophone and francophone communities. An unspoken but active melting pot stance pretty much seems to have been in place. We began to hear of the notion of diversity from the time of allowing citizenship to the previously indentured Chinese and South Asians, from the time of Canada's open door policy in relation to its plans for capitalist growth. The metaphor of Canadian society as the vertical mosaic is an early intimation of the complexities of evolution of a political ideology involving otherness in a liberal democratic context. The open door policy not only allowed but actively pursued immigration from ex-colonised third world countries. Along with that came political refugees. This is when diversity came to be seen as really diverse, in spite of the fact that many came from French and English speaking countries, many were Christians, and a large number had more than a passing acquaintance with cultures of Europe and North America. But as they were not indentured workers, or for the most part not illegals, their presence as workers, taxpayers and electoral constituencies was a force to be reckoned

---

103   See Bolaria and Li 1988.

104   On immigration to Canada from Hong Kong, and recent Chinese immigration, see Wong 1997, Li 1993; also Skeldon 1995.

with and a problem to be managed. The multicultural policy had to be evolved and put in place for them.

The Canadian state had to deal with a labour importation policy which was primarily meant to create a working class, but not guest workers as in Germany. This involved resistance from white Canadians, from the so-called Canadian worker. It also had to contain the mobility drives of immigrants who were otherwise compliant, but wanted to get a secure economic niche in the country's labour and consumer markets. In the very early 1980s Prime Minister Pierre Trudeau enunciated his multicultural policy, and a discourse of nation, community and diversity began to be cobbled together. There were no strong multicultural demands on the part of third world immigrants themselves to force such a policy. The issues raised by them were about racism, legal discrimination involving immigration and family reunification, about job discrimination on the basis of Canadian experience, and various adjustment difficulties, mainly of child care and language. In short, they were difficulties that are endemic to migration, and especially that of people coming in to low income jobs or with few assets. Immigrant demands were not then, or even now, primarily cultural, nor was multiculturalism initially their formulation of the solution to their problems. It began as a state or an official/institutional discourse, and it involved the translation of issues of social and economic injustice into issues of culture.[105] Often it was immigrant questions and quandaries *vis a vis* the response of the so-called Canadians that prompted justificatory gestures by the state. These legitimation gestures were more directed at the discontented Canadians than the discriminated others. Multiculturalism was therefore not a demand from below, but an ideological elaboration from above in which the third world immigrants found themselves. This was an apparatus which rearranged questions of social justice, of unemployment and racism, into issues of cultural diversity and focused on symbols of religion, on so-called tradition. Thus immigrants were ethnicised, culturalised and mapped into traditional/ethnic communities. Gradually a political and administrative framework came into being where structural inequalities could be less and less seen or spoken about. Antiracism and class politics could not keep pace with constantly proliferating ideological state or institutional apparatuses which identified people in terms of their cultural identity, and converted or conflated racist ascriptions of difference within the Canadian space into the power neutral notion of diversity. An increase in threats against third world immigrants, the rise of neo-Nazi white supremacist groups and ultra conservative politics, along

---

105   See Kymlicka 1995.

with a systemic or structural racism and anti-immigration and anti-immigrant stances of political parties, could now be buried or displaced as the immigrants' own cultural problem. Politics in Canada were reshaped and routed through this culturalisation or ethnicisation, and a politics of identity was constructed which the immigrants themselves embraced as the only venue for social and political agency.

Now it was projected to the world at large that what the incoming third world population of Canada primarily wanted was the same religious, linguistic and cultural life they had in their countries of origin. They were frozen into being seen as traditional cultures and thus socially conservative in entirety. They were bringing down the standards of Canadian modernity and criminalising the country. The problem for the Canadian state and society then became one of considering what or how much they could retain in Canada of their previous cultures without compromising the national character. The fact that their demands came in many types, and the most important ones pertained to discrimination by the state and the economy which threatened worthwhile employment possibilities, family re-unification for refugees, facilities for women, and so forth, became political non-issues. This emphasis on culture, on immigrants' ethnic self-definition and fundamentalist cultural survivalism, deflected proper publicisation and criticism of police violence or general safety issues for non-white people, especially for black youth.[106] In almost every case of police shooting, the police were given immunity, and immigration laws became tighter while deportations increasingly became a threat. De-skilling, not just through underemployment or unemployment, but through state/institutional decertification of professionals, is also a basic fact of third world immigrant lives.[107] No third world immigrant is left in doubt that he/she is in Canada on public and official sufferance and is to be grateful for being allowed into the country. They are made to feel that otherness is of an antagonistic variety to Canadians, and they also know that this otherness is not in them, but in how they are perceived, what ascriptions pre-exist their arrival into the country, how racialisation and ethnicisation have already put a white Canada in place. They come to know that they are seen as virtually invading this Canada. It becomes quickly evident that in a society that preaches the gospel of wealth, they would not and are not expected to go very far. They judge by their presences and absences in the social and economic spaces that they are here to primarily reproduce the under classes.

---

106   Between 1988 and 1992 three unarmed black young men were killed by police in Toronto and one in Montreal, and one young woman permanently paralysed in a police shooting.
107   See Bolaria and Li, 1988, p. 18; Government of Canada 1986; Government of Canada 1984.

Through the decades from the 1960s political developments took place in Canada which show the twists and turns in the relationship between third world immigrants and the state.[108] With the disarray of left politics in the country and growth of multicultural ideology, all political consciousness regarding third world immigrants has been multiculturalised. These cultural/ethnicised formulations were like chemical probes into a test tube of solution around which dissatisfactions and mobility drives of the others began to coalesce. Wearing or not wearing of turbans, publicly funded heritage language classes, state supported Islamic schools modelled on the existence and patterns of catholic schools, for example, provided the profile of their politics. They themselves often forgot how much less important these were than their full citizenship rights, their demand for jobs, non-discriminatory schools and work places, and a generally non-racist society. Differentiated second- or third-class citizenships evolved, as a non-white sub-working class continued to develop. Their initial willingness to work twice as hard to get around their lack of success, which spoke of their shifty, lazy work habits and their scamming and unscrupulous use of the welfare system. This is especially ironic since they often came from countries, such as those in the West Indies, from which Canada continues to bring substantial profits. But this story of neo-colonialism, of exploitation, racism, discrimination and hierarchical citizenship never gains much credibility or publicity with the Canadian state, the public or the media. This reality is what the cultural language and politics of diversity obscures, displaces and erases. It is obvious that the third world or non-white immigrants are not the beneficiaries of the discourse of diversity.

The state of Canada wants its differentiated inferior citizens to speak in the state's own language of multicultural identity, of ethnicity and community. This is mainly the language of representation permitted to them. Ethnic or racialised cultural community, not political community organised on the basis of class, gender and racialisation, is what the state is willing to acknowledge in their case. Continuous struggles involving issues of 'race' and class have created something called 'race' relations in some institutions, which, if it becomes antiracist in any real way, is descaled or defunded. Human Rights Commissions, treating cases individually, with no proper powers of enforcement, often act as pawns of the state and capital, adjudicate very few cases and rule rarely in favour of the complainant. Ritualistic non-discrimination clauses that are at times present in state documents to mediate 'race' relations often create

---

108   For example, the change in immigration policy from the 'family reunification' programme to a primarily skills based one shifts the demography of Canada. It brings a kind of immigrant, perhaps from Eastern Europe, who does not pose the problem of 'race'.

the impression that 'races' actually exist as biological social entities determining behaviour and culture, and only need to relate better. There is not even a language within the state's redress apparatus to capture or describe the racist sexism towards third world or non-white women or men. By simultaneously blocking the politico-social process of racialisation from view while organising people as raced ethnicities, the state of multiculturalism seeks to obscure issues of class and patriarchy as actionable, and therefore the possibility of discovering intercommunity commonalities – for example between third world immigrants and aboriginal peoples, or among the different strands of working classes – diminishes considerably.

Multiculturalism as an official practice and discourse has worked actively to create the notion and practices of insulated communities. Under its political guidance and funding a political-social space was organised. Politically constructed homogenised communities, with their increasingly fundamentalist boundaries of cultures, traditions and religions, emerged from where there were immigrants from different parts of the world with different cultures and values. They developed leaders or spokespersons, usually men, who liaised with the state on their behalf, and their organisational behaviour fulfilled the expectations of the Canadian state. New political agents and constituencies thus came to life, as people sought to be politically active in these new cultural identity terms. So they became interpellated by the state under certain religious and ethnically named agencies. Hard-headed businessmen, who had never thought of culture in their lives before, now, upon entering Canada, began using this notion and spoke to the powers that be in terms of culture and welfare of their community. But this was the new and only political playing field for 'others' in Canada, a slim opportunity of mobility, so they were/are willing to run through the multicultural maze. What is more, this new cultural politics, leaving out problems of class and patriarchy, appealed to the conservative elements in the immigrant population, since religion could be made to overdetermine these uncomfortable actualities, and concentrated on the so-called culture and morality of the community. Official multiculturalism, which gave the conservative male self-styled representatives *carte blanche* to do this, also empowered the same male leaders as patriarchs and enhanced their sexism and masculinism. In the name of culture and god, within the high walls of community and ethnicity, women and children could be dominated and acted against violently because the religions or culture and tradition of others supposedly sanctioned this oppression and brutality. And as politically and ideologically constituted homogenised cultural essences which are typed as traditional, such as Muslim or Sikh or Hindu communities, violence against women could go on without any significant or effective state intervention.

For these newly constructed communities, which came to life from scattered populations of the world and based their tenuous cohesion on a minimal doctrinaire affiliation (such as the Hindu religion, for example), a heterosexist world view and mistrust of class politics, the multicultural dispensations of the state were a fortunate intervention. Their ethnic self-appellations, born of their long familiarity with colonial and imperialist discourse, were perfectly in keeping with colonial-racist stereotypes used by the Canadian state and culture. It was and is not noted either by the multicultural state or its clients, the so-called communities, that back in their so-called home countries, in whose names their multiculture is fabricated, the contestation that is going on bears little resemblance to these monolithic identities that they project in Canada. Being real countries, lived historical political spaces, these countries were and are going through many political and social struggles, changing their forms, none of which were in a position to be petrified into immutable cultural identities.[109] The genealogies of these reified cultural identities which are mobilised in Canada are entirely colonial, though they are being constantly re-worked in the modern context of state formation and capital's transformation. In fact the earlier European orientalist racist perceptions of India, for example, perfectly tally with the Canadian state's and the media's perception of the Indian communities in Canada.[110] The concept of tradition is the principle of continuity and serves as the interpretive and constructive category in both cases. A simple binary of cultural stereotyping of tradition and modernity stands for India and Canada, respectively. The problem of multiculturalism, then, is how much tradition can be accommodated by Canadian modernity without affecting in any real way the overall political and cultural hegemony of Europeans. It is also assumed by both the state and the media, as well as the male representatives of the communities, that Indians or South Asians are essentially traditional and as such patriarchy is congenial to their cultural identity, while class conflict is a modern or non-traditional aberration.

The result of this convergence between the Canadian state and conservative male representatives or community agents has been very distressing for women in particular. Between the multicultural paradigm and the actuality of a migrant citizen's life in Canada, the gap is immense. Among multiculturalists of both the communitarian and the liberal persuasion Canada is a

---

109   See Butalia and Sarkar 1997. The essays in this anthology show the intensity of the political struggle between secular, left feminist forces and the Hindu right.

110   An India or South Asia has been invented, with befitting identities or cultural stereotypes for people of the subcontinent living in the diaspora. A production of orientalism and a more forthright racism, these stereotypes rest on the use of the concept of tradition.

nation space which contains different 'races' and ethnicities, and this presence demands either a 'politics of recognition' or a modified set of individual and group rights.[111] But for both groups this diversity of others or difference between Canadian self and other has no political dimension. It speaks to nothing like class formation or class struggle, of the existence of active and deep racism, or of a social organisation entailing racialised class production of gender. The history of colonisation is also not brought to bear on the notions of diversity and difference. So, the answer to my original question – what is to be gained from a discourse of diversity and its politics of multiculturalism? – lies in just what has actually happened in Canadian politics and its theorisation, what I have been describing so far, namely in the erasure and occlusion of social relations of power and ruling. This diversified reification of cultures and culturalisation of politics allows for both the practice and occlusion of heterosexism and racism of a narrow bourgeois nationalism. This means the maintenance of a status quo of domination. Many hard socio-political questions and basic structural changes may now be avoided. People can be blamed for bringing on their own misfortunes, while rule of capital and class can continue their violence of racism, sexism and homophobia.

5 Conclusion

It should be obvious by now that diversity discourse portrays society as a horizontal space, in which there is no theoretical or analytical room for social relations of power and ruling, of socioeconomic contradictions that construct and regulate Canadian political economy and its ideological culture. Yet the very need to formulate notions of multiculturalism and diversity, and their introjection into politics and state formation, into the very modes of governance, indicates that all is not as harmonious as it should be. The presence of certain peoples in the Canadian socio-economic and cultural spaces has obviously been considered exceptional, unusual or irregular. Yet their presence has also called into question much of what has been considered usual or regular. This has meant initiating a degree of adjustment for the majority communities and their state which, while sidestepping existing ideological practices, has meant the invention of this ideological state apparatus and cultural language of multiculturalism.

But the discourse of diversity is not new or *sui generis*. As I mentioned before, it is derived from and is in keeping with a language of plurality that has existed

---

111   Taylor 1992.

in liberal democracy. It relies, as we saw, on reading the notion of difference in a socially abstract manner, which also wipes away its location in history, thus obscuring colonialism, capital and slavery. It displaces these political and historical readings by presenting a complex interpretive code which encapsulates a few particularities of people's cultures, adding a touch of reality, and averts our gaze from power relations or differences which continue to organise the Canadian public life and culture. They assert themselves as perceptions of otherness encoding a hegemonic European-Canadianness.

As I have shown above, by obscuring or deflecting from historical and present power relations, perceptions and systematised ideologies, the deployment of diversity reduces to and manages difference as ethnic cultural issues. It then becomes a matter of coexistence of value-free, power-neutral plurality, of cultural differences where modernity and tradition, so-called white and black cultures, supposedly hold the same value. That is, diversity discourse tries to set up a sphere which claims to be outside of hegemony. It does so uncritically, unreflexively, and yet cannot escape the role of being an instrument of designation of some cultures as *real* culture, while others fall into the category of subculture and multiculture, cultures of the peripheries. This is not dissonant with colonial anthropology's way of assigning non-European cultures a special, hyphenated and bracketed status.[112] This way of thinking accomplishes depoliticisation at deeply complex conceptual and political levels. Simultaneously as it disarticulates culture from hegemony, it reduces all political issues into cultural ones and converts culture into a private matter. This removes the civil society – its politically charged expressions, ways of being and seeing, what Gramsci called social common sense – from being considered as the soil and the material for political formations and articulation. This process in effect transforms the category culture into a practical device which both erases and stands in for the social. Any materialist dialectic of culture is dispensed with.[113]

This conceptual feat of emptying out difference of its actual political and cultural content, and thus presenting it as neutral diversity, can only be done by relying on the wholly artificial separation of the public and the private – as parallels of the political and the personal. It is possible because the concept of diversity is much more hospitable to an abstract notion of plurality than that of difference, which instantly summons questions of comparison to others with regard to whom any difference is postulated. A socialisation, and therefore

---

112   For examples of colonial anthropology, see Radcliffe-Brown 1965 or Evans-Pritchard 1965; also for its more postmodernist, radical versions, see Geertz 1988 or Comaroff and Comaroff 1991.

113   For a materialist view of culture, see Williams 1980.

politicisation, of this concept of difference is far more likely than diversity to lend itself to content saturated with social relations of class, gender, 'race', sexuality and so on. This makes difference a much better heuristic device, if not exactly an analytical concept, for understanding situations which both imply and call for politics. We might at this point ask, how we should name ourselves, or what would be an effective name for capturing the oppositional thrust of our political agency? Though it is not possible for me to provide an answer which would satisfy all feminists, nor is it my intention to do so, this topic of named agency and its subjectivity demands a greater clarification. I am content to call myself an antiracist and marxist feminist. It is a distinctly political and socially grounded cultural identity. It does not rely solely on the culture of community at birth, but also speaks to what we have become as political subjects and agents in our own adult political and cultural efforts. This striving for a political self-definition, a self-conscious anti-oppression task of historical recovery, is not a matter of essentialised cultural diversities, but rather, as Paula Moya says, it involves an act of 'deconstruction of difference'.[114] With class, 'race' and gender and sexuality seen as components of this difference, we admit of both solidarities and relations of opposition. We can unite, as coalition is a basic prerequisite of organising for change, with others inhabiting similar socio-cultural locations, and see that unity in political terms. This seeing of common social conditions produced through oppressive relations, rather than an essentialised version of cultures, is an act and task of political conscientisation. This admits of asymmetrical social and cultural locations and power relations (for example, between straight and lesbian non-white women in North America), while also moving toward a new level of political consciousness and a culture of resistance. This culture also exists historically with us, as our legacy.

This same question of political naming, or agency, has been discussed by many feminists, white and non-white. For Mohanty and Alexander, the answer lies in democracy, but not of the capitalist liberal type. They evolve the notion of feminist democracy, but feminist distinct from radical feminism. They speak to a 'transborder, transnational participatory democracy' which resists hegemonic democracy of our times, and to 'universal citizenship', to 'anticapitalist, anticolonial feminist democracy' in a very similar way to my proposal.[115] This is not radical democracy without class, class struggle or anti-imperialism. Thus it is different from the projects for new social movements as enunciated by Ernesto Laclau and Chantal Mouffe and their followers, who believe that they can

114   Alexander and Mohanty 1997, p. 141.

115   Ibid., pp. xxix–xi.

make democracy real without fighting racialised gendered, local, national and global capitalism. Alexander and Mohanty eschew cultural relativism encouraged by multiculturalism from above, and seek a redefinition of justice. They want to see a 'critical application of feminist praxis in global contexts' which insists on 'responsibility, accountability, engagement and solidarity', and advance in their anthology 'a paradigm of decolonisation which stresses power, history, memory, relational analysis, justice (not just representation), and ethics as the issues central to [their] analysis of globalisation'.[116] I would say this is a proposal which we should support as the most extensively liberatory one.

But as things are at present, people are not doing a politics consistent with my proposal. We continue to subscribe to the discourse of diversity or liberal plurality, forgetting both its depoliticising capacity and its ability to perform a most powerful political function. We might remind ourselves what the political cognates of diversity are. We might ask what is its home discourse, for concepts do have homes in a general discursive constellation, and what are their ideological-political imports? The discursive home and political cognates of diversity lie in liberal democracy, whose particular ways of constructing a self-enclosed, self-sustaining polity through the mechanism of installing a separation between the state and the civil society, and the reduction of equality into a formal gesture, have long been noted.[117] This is the meaning of the concept of citizenship in liberal or bourgeois democracy, which rests on divesting the political from the social, the equality of citizenship from the inequality of class and other power relations. The so-called diverse cultural or ethnic communities are also constructed on this model as equal to each other and to the dominant Canadian culture of Euro-Americans. Diversity relies on the postulation of an abstracted, non-social ground zero.

Diversity as discourse, with its constellation of concepts such as multiculturalism, ethnicity, community, and so forth, becomes an important way in which the abstract or formal equality of liberal democracy, its empty pluralism, can gain a concreteness or an embodiment. Through it the concept of citizenship rids itself of its emptiness and takes on signals of a particularised social being or a cultural personhood. The sameness implied in the liberal notion citizenship is then stencilled onto a so-called diverse culture, and offers a sense of concrete specificity. This purported plurality with pseudo-concreteness rescues class democracy, and does not let the question of power relations get out of hand. Differences or diversities are then seen as inherent, as ontological or cul-

---

116   Ibid., p. xix.
117   See MacPherson 1977.

tural traits of the individuals of particular cultural communities, rather than as racist ascriptions or stereotypes. This helps the cause of the status quo and maintains ascribed and invented ethnicities, or their displaced and intensified communal forms. The discourse of diversity makes it impossible to understand or name systemic and cultural racism, and its implication in gender and class.

When concreteness or embodiment is thus ideologically depoliticised and dehistoricised by its articulation to the discourse of diversity, we are presented with many ontological cultural particularities which serve as markers of ethnicity and group boundaries. Since these ethnic communities are conceived as discrete entities, and there is no recognition of a core cultural-power group, a dispersion effect is introduced through the discourse of diversity which occludes its own presumption of otherness, of being diverse, and which is predicated upon a homogeneous Canadian identity. It is with regard to this that diversity is measured, and hides its assumptions of homogeneity under the cover of a value and power neutral heterogeneity. Thus it banishes from view a process of homogenisation or essentialisation which underpins the project of liberal pluralism.

Ultimately then, the discourse of diversity is an ideology. It has its own political imperatives in what is called multiculturalism elaborated within the precincts of the state. It translates out into different political possibilities within the framework of capitalism and bourgeois democracy, and both communitarian liberals and liberals for individual rights may find it congenial to their own goals. Politics of recognition, an ideology of tolerance, advocacy of limited group rights, may all result from adopting the discourse of diversity, but what difference they would actually make to those people's lives which are objects of multicultural politics, is another story.

CHAPTER 16

On the Dark Side of the Nation: Politics of Multiculturalism and the State of 'Canada'

This chapter is primarily concerned with the construction of 'Canada' as a social and cultural form of national identity, and various challenges and interruptions offered to this identity by literature produced by writers from non-white communities. The first part of the paper examines both literary and political-theoretical formulations of a 'two-nation', 'two solitudes' thesis and their implications for various cultural accommodations offered to 'others', especially through the mechanism of 'multiculturalism'. The second part concentrates on the experiences and standpoint of people of colour, or non-white people, especially since the 1960s, and the cultural and political formulating derivable from them.

> I am from the country
> Columbus dreamt of.
> You, the country
> Columbus conquered.
> Now in your land
> My words are circling
> blue Oka sky
> they come back to us
> alight on tongue.
> Protect me with your brazen passion
> for history is my truth,
> Earth, my witness
> my home,
> this native land.[1]

1 The Personal and the Political: A Chorus and a Problematic

When the women's movement came along and we were coming to our political consciousness, one of its slogans took us by surprise and thrilled and activated

---

1 K. Bannerji 1993, p. 20.

us: 'the personal is political!' Since then years have gone by, and in the meanwhile I have found myself in Canada, swearing an oath of allegiance to the Queen of England, giving up the passport of a long-fought-for independence, and being assigned into the category of 'visible minority'. These years have produced their own consciousness in me, and I have learnt that also the reverse is true: the political is personal.

The way this consciousness was engendered was not ideological, but daily, practical and personal. It came from having to live within an all-pervasive presence of the state in our everyday life. It began with the Canadian High Commission's rejection of my two-year-old daughter's visa and continued with my airport appearance in Montreal, where I was interrogated at length. What shook me was not the fact that they interviewed me, but rather their tone of suspicion about my somehow having stolen my way 'in'.

As the years progressed, I realised that in my life, and in the lives of other non-white people around me, this pervasive presence of the state meant everything – allowing my daughter and husband to come into the country; permitting me to continue my studies or to work, to cross the border into the u.s.a. and back; allowing me the custody of my daughter, although I had a low income; 'landing' me so I could put some sort of life together with some predictability. Fear, anxiety, humiliation, anger and frustration became the wire mesh that knit bits of my life into a pattern. The quality of this life may be symbolised by an incident with which my final immigration interview culminated after many queries about a missing 'wife' and the 'head of the family'. I was facing an elderly, bald, white man, moustached and blue-eyed – who said he had been to India. I made some polite rejoinder and he asked me – 'Do you speak Hindi?' I replied that I understood it very well and spoke it with mistakes. 'Can you translate this sentence for me?' he asked, and proceeded to say in Hindi what in English amounts to 'Do you want to fuck with me?' A wave of heat rose from my toes to my hair roots. I gripped the edge of my chair and stared at him – silently. His hand was on my passport, the pink slip of my 'landing' document lay next to it. Steadying my voice I said 'I don't know Hindi that well'. 'So you're a PhD student?' My interview continued. I sat rigid and concluded it with a schizophrenic intensity. On Bloor Street in Toronto, sitting on the steps of a church – I vomited. I was a landed immigrant.

Throughout these twenty-five years I have met many non-white and Third World legal and illegal 'immigrants' and 'new Canadians' who feel that the machinery of the state has us impaled against its spikes. In beds, in workplaces, in suicides committed over deportations, the state silently, steadily rules our lives with 'regulations'. How much more intimate could we be – this state and we? It has almost become a person – this machinery – growing with and into our lives, fattened with our miseries and needs, and the curbing of our resistance and anger.

But simultaneously with the growth of the state we grew too, both in numbers and protest, and became a substantial voting population in Canada. We demanded some genuine reforms, some changes – some among us even demanded the end of racist capitalism – and instead we got 'multiculturalism'. 'Communities' and their leaders or representatives were created by and through the state, and they called for funding and promised 'essential services' for their 'communities', such as the preservation of their identities. There were advisory bodies, positions, and even arts funding created on the basis of ethnicity and community. A problem of naming arose, and hyphenated cultural and political identities proliferated. Officially constructed identities came into being and we had new names – immigrant, visible minority, new Canadian and ethnic. In the mansion of the state small back rooms were accorded to these new political players on the scene. Manoeuvring for more began. As the state came deeper into our lives – extending its political, economic and moral regulation, its police violence and surveillance – we simultaneously officialised ourselves. It is as though we asked for bread and were given stones, and could not tell the difference between the two.

2   In or of the Nation? The Problem of Belonging

> Face it there's an illegal
> Immigrant
> Hiding in your house
> Hiding in you
> Trying to get out!
> * * * *
>
> Businessmen Custom's officials
> Dark Glasses Industrial Aviation
> Policemen Illegal Bachelorettes
> Sweatshop-Keepers Information Canada
> Says
> 'You can't get their smell off
> the walls'.[2]

---

2 Bhaggiyadatta 1981, p. 23.

The state and the 'visible minorities' (the non-white people living in Canada) have a complex relationship with each other. There is a fundamental unease with how our difference is construed and constructed by the state, how our otherness in relation to Canada is projected and objectified. We cannot be successfully ingested, or assimilated, or made to vanish from where we are not wanted. We remain an ambiguous presence, our existence a question mark in the side of the nation, with the potential to disclose much about the political unconscious and consciousness of Canada as an 'imagined community'.[3] Disclosures accumulate slowly, while we continue to live here as outsider-insiders of the nation which offers a proudly multicultural profile to the international community.

We have the awareness that we have arrived into somebody's state, but what kind of state; whose imagined community or community of imagination does it embody? And what are the terms and conditions of our 'belonging' to this state of a nation? Answers to these questions are often indirect and not found in the news highway of Canadian media. But travelling through the side-roads of political discursivities and practices we come across markers for social terrains and political establishments that allow us to map the political geography of this nation-land where we have 'landed'.

We locate our explorations of Canada mainly in that part where compulsorily English-speaking visible minorities reside, a part renamed by Charles Taylor and others as 'Canada outside of Quebec' (COQ).[4] But we will call it 'English Canada' as in common parlance. This reflects the binary cultural identity of the country to whose discourse, through the notions of the two solitudes, survival and bilingualism, 'new comers' are subjected.[5] Conceptualising Canada within this discourse is a bleak and grim task: since 'solitude' and 'survival' (with their Hobbesian and Darwinist aura) are hardly the language of communitarian joy in nation-making.

What, I asked when I first heard of these solitudes, are they? And why survival, when Canada's self-advertisement is one of a wealthy industrial nation? Upon my immigrant inquiries these two solitudes turned out to be two invading European nations – the French and the English – which might have produced two colonial-nation states in this part of North America. But history did not quite work out that way. Instead of producing two settler colonial countries like Zimbabwe (Rhodesia) and South Africa, they held a relation-

---

3 Anderson 1991.
4 This division of Canada into Quebec and Canada outside of Quebec (COQ) is used as more than a territorial expression by Taylor 1993.
5 For an exposition of the notions of 'solitude' and 'survival,' see Atwood 1972.

ship of conquest and domination with each other. After the battle at the Plains of Abraham one conquered nation/nationality, the French, continued in an uneasy and subjected relation to a state of 'Canada', which they saw as 'English', a perception ratified by this state's rootedness in the English Crown. The colonial French then came to a hyphenated identity of 'franco-something' or declared themselves (at least within one province) as plain 'Quebecois'. They have been existing ever since in an unhappy state, their promised status as a 'distinct society' notwithstanding. Periodically, and at times critically, Quebec challenges 'Canadian' politics of 'unity' and gives this politics its own 'distinct' character. These then are the two solitudes, the protagonists who, to a great extent, shape the ideological parameters of Canadian constitutional debates, and whose 'survival' and relations are continually deliberated. And this preoccupation is such a 'natural' of Canadian politics that all other inhabitants are only a minor part of the problematic of 'national' identity. This is particularly evident in the role, or lack thereof, accorded to the First Nations of Canada in the nation-forming project. Even after Elijah Harper's intervention in the Meech Lake Accord, the deployment of the Canadian Army against the Mohawk peoples and the long stand-off that followed, constant land claims and demands for self-government/self-determination, there is a remarkable and a determined political marginalisation of the First Nations. And yet their presence as the absent signifiers within Canadian national politics works at all times as a bedrock of its national definitional project, giving it a very particular contour through the same absences, silences, exclusions and marginalisations. In this there is no distinction between 'coq' or English Canada and Quebec. One needs only to look at the siege at Oka to realise that as far as these 'others' are concerned, Europeans continue the same solidarity of ruling and repression, blended with competitive manipulations, that they practised from the dawn of their conquests and state formations.

The Anglo-French rivalry therefore needs to be read through the lens of colonialism. If we want to understand the relationship between visible minorities and the state of Canada/English Canada/ coq, colonialism is the context or entry point that allows us to begin exploring the social relations and cultural forms which characterise these relations. The construction of visible minorities as a social imaginary and the architecture of the 'nation' built with engravings of conquests, wars and exclusions. It is the nationhood of this Canada, with its two solitudes and their survival anxieties and aggressions against 'native others', that provides the epic painting in whose dark corners we must look for the later 'others'. We have to get past and through these dual monoculturalist assumptions or paradigms in order to speak about 'visible minorities', a category produced by the multiculturalist policy of the state. This paper repeats, in its conceptual and deconstructive movements, the motions of the people themselves who, 'appellated' as refugees, immigrants or visible minorities, have to file past immigration officers, refugee boards, sundry ministries and posters of multi-featured/coloured faces that blandly proclaim 'Together we are Ontario' – lest we or they forget!

We will examine the assumptions of 'Canada' from the conventional problematic and thematic of Canadian nationhood, that of 'Fragmentation or Integration?' currently resounding in post-referendum times. I look for my place within this conceptual topography and find myself in a designated space for 'visible minorities in the multicultural society and state of Canada'. This is existence in a zone somewhere between economy and culture. It strikes me then that this discursive mode in which Canada is topicalised does not anywhere feature the concept of class. Class does not function as a potential source for the theorisation of Canada, any more than does race as an expression for basic social relations of contradiction. Instead the discursivities rely on hegemonic cultural categories such as English or French Canada, or on notions such as national institutions, and conceive of differences and transcendences, fragmentation and integration, with regard to an ideological notion of unity that is perpetually in crisis. This influential problematic is displayed in a *Globe and Mail* editorial of 29 March 1994. It is typically pre-occupied with themes of unity and integration or fragmentation, and delivers a lecture on these to Lucien Bouchard of the Bloc Quebecois:

> It has been an educational field trip for Lucien Bouchard. On his first venture into 'English Canada' (as he insists on calling it) since becoming leader of Her Majesty's Loyal Opposition, Mr. Bouchard learned, among other things, there is such a thing as Canadian Nationalism: not just patriotism, nor yet that self-serving little prejudice that parades around as Canadian Nationalism – mix equal parts elitism, statism and Anti-Americanism – but a genuine fellow-feeling that binds Canadians to one another across this country – and includes Quebec.

Lest this statement appear to the people of Quebec as passing off 'English Canada' disguised as 'the nation' and locking Quebec in a vice grip of 'unity' without consent or consultation, the editor repeats multiculturalist platitudes meant to mitigate the old antagonisms leading to 'separatism'. The demand for a French Canada is equated with 'self-serving little prejudice' and 'patriotism' and promptly absorbed into the notion of a culturally and socially transcendent Canada, which is supposedly not only non-French, but non-English as well. How can this non-partisan, transcendent Canada be articulated except in the discourse of multiculturalism? Multiculturalism, then, can save the day for English Canada, conferring upon it a transcendence, even though the same transcendent state is signalled through the figure of Her Majesty the Queen of England and the English language. The unassimilable 'others' who, in their distance from English Canada, need to be boxed into this catch-all phrase now become the moral cudgel with which to beat Quebec's separatist aspirations. The same editorial continues:

> Canada is dedicated to the ideal that people of different languages and cultures may, without surrendering their identity, yet embrace the human values they have in common: the 'two solitudes' of which the poet wrote, 'that protect and touch and greet each other', were a definition of love, not division.

But this poetic interpretation of solitudes, like the moral carrot of multicultural love, is quickly followed by a stick. Should Quebec not recognise this obligation to love, but rather see it as a barrier to self-determination, Canada will not tolerate this. We are then confronted with other competing self-determinations in one breath, some of which ordinarily would not find their advocate in *Globe and Mail* editorials. What of the self-determination of the Cree, of the anglophones, of federalists of every stripe? What of the self-determination of the Canadian nation? Should Mr. Bouchard and his kind not recognise this national interest, it is argued, then the province's uncertainties are only beginning. In the context of the editorial's discourse, these uncertainties amount to the threat of a federalist anglophone war. The 'self-determination of the Cree' is no more than an opportunistic legitimation of Canada in the name of all others who are routinely left out of its construction and governance. These 'different (from the French) others', through the device of a state-sponsored multiculturalism, create the basis for transcendence necessary for the creation of a universalist liberal democratic statehood. They are interpellated or bound into the ideological state apparatus through their employment of tongues which must be compulsorily, officially unilingual – namely, under the sign of English.[6]

'Canada', with its primary inscriptions of 'French' or 'English', its colonialist and essentialist identity markers, cannot escape a fragmentary framework. Its imagined political geography simplifies into two primary and confrontational possessions, cultural typologies and dominant ideologies. Under the circumstances, all appeal to multiculturalism on the part of 'Canada Outside Quebec'

---

6   For an elaboration of these concepts, see Althusser 1977a.

becomes no more than an extra weight on the 'English' side. Its 'difference-studded unity', its 'multicultural mosaic', becomes an ideological sleight of hand pitted against Quebec's presumably greater cultural homogeneity. The two solitudes glare at each other from the barricades in an ongoing colonial war. But what do either of these solitudes and their reigning essences have to do with those whom the state has named 'visible minorities' and who are meant to provide the ideological basis for the Canadian state's liberal/ universal status? How does their very 'difference', inscribed with inferiority and negativity – their otherwise troublesome particularity – offer the very particularist state of 'English Canada' the legitimating device of transcendence through multiculturalism? Are we not still being used in the war between the English and the French?

It may seem strange to 'Canadians' that the presence of the First Nations, the 'visible minorities' and the ideology of multiculturalism are being suggested as the core of the state's claim to universality or transcendence. Not only in multiplying pawns in the old Anglo-French rivalry but in other ways as well, multiculturalism may be seen less as a gift of the state of 'Canada' to the 'others' of this society, than as a central pillar in its own ideological state apparatus.[7] This is because the very discourse of nationhood in the context of 'Canada', given its evolution as a capitalist state derived from a white settler colony with aspirations to liberal democracy,[8] needs an ideology that can mediate fissures and ruptures more deep and profound than those of the usual capitalist nation-state.[9] That is why usually undesirable others, consisting of non-white peoples with their ethnic or traditional or underdeveloped cultures, are discursively inserted in the middle of a dialogue on hegemonic rivalry. The discourse of multiculturalism, as distinct from its administrative, practical relations and forms of ruling, serves as a culmination for the ideological construction of 'Canada'. This places us, on whose actual lives the ideology is evoked, in a peculiar situation. On the one hand, by our sheer presence we provide a central part of the distinct pluralist unity of Canadian nationhood; on the other hand, this centrality is dependent on our 'difference', which denotes the power of definition that 'Canadians' have over 'others'. In the ideology of multicultural nationhood, however, this difference is read in a power-neutral manner rather than as organised through class, gender and race. Thus at the same moment that difference

---

7 On multiculturalism, its definition and history, see Fleras and Elliot 1992.
8 On the emergence of a liberal state from the basis of a white settler colony, see Bolaria and Li 1988. Also see Kulchyski 1994, and Tester and Kulchyski 1994. For a 'race'/gender inscription into a semi-colonial Canadian state, see Monture-Angus 1995.
9 For an in-depth discussion of mediatory and unificatory ideologies needed by a liberal democratic, i.e. capitalist state, see Miliband 1984, chs. 7 & 8.

is ideologically evoked it is also neutralised, as though the issue of difference were the same as that of diversity of cultures and identities, rather than that of racism and colonial ethnocentrism – as though our different cultures were on a par or could negotiate with the two dominant ones! The hollowness of such a pluralist stance is exposed in the shrill indignation of anglophones when rendered a 'minority' in Quebec, or the angry desperation of francophones in Ontario. The issue of the First Nations – their land claims, languages and cultures – provides another dimension entirely, so violent and deep that the state of Canada dare not even name it in the placid language of multiculturalism.

The importance of the discourse of multiculturalism to that of nation-making becomes clearer if we remember that 'nation' needs an ideology of unification and legitimation.[10] As Benedict Anderson points out, nations need to imagine a principle of 'com-unity', or community even where there is little there to postulate any.[11] A nation, ideologically, cannot posit itself on the principle of hate, according to Anderson, and must therefore speak to the sacrificing of individual, particularist interests for the sake of 'the common good'.[12] This task of 'imagining community' becomes especially difficult in Canada – not only because of class, gender and capital, which ubiquitously provide contentious grounds in the most culturally homogeneous of societies – but because its sociopolitical space is saturated by elements of surplus domination due to its Eurocentric/racist/colonial context. Ours is not a situation of co-existence of cultural nationalities or tribes within a given geographical space. Speaking here of culture without addressing power relations displaces and trivialises deep contradictions. It is a reductionism that hides the social relations of domination that continually create 'difference' as inferior and thus signifies continuing relations of antagonism. The legacy of a white settler colonial economy and state and the current aspirations to imperialist capitalism mark Canada's struggle to become a liberal democratic state. Here a cultural pluralist interpretive discourse hides more than it reveals. It serves as a fantastic evocation of 'unity', which in any case becomes a reminder of the divisions. Thus to imagine 'com-unity' means to imagine a common-project of valuing difference that would hold good for both Canadians and others, while also

---

10   For a clarification of my use of this concept, see Habermas 1975. This use of 'legitimacy' is different from Charles Taylor's Weberian use of it in *Reconciling the Solitudes*.

11   See Anderson 1991, Introduction and ch. 2. Anderson says, 'I ... propose the following definition of the nation: it is an imagined political community – and imagined as both inherently limited and sovereign. It is *imagined* because the members of even the smallest nation will never know most of their fellow members, meet them, or even hear of them, yet in the minds of each lives the image of their communion' (p. 6).

12   Anderson 1991, ch. 2.

claiming that the sources of these otherising differences are merely cultural. As that is impossible, we consequently have a situation where no escape is possible from divisive social relations. The nation state's need for an ideology that can avert a complete rupture becomes desperate, and gives rise to a multicultural ideology which both needs and creates 'others' while subverting demands for anti-racism and political equality.

Let me illustrate my argument by means of Charles Taylor's thoughts on the Canadian project of nation-making. Taylor is comparable to Benedict Anderson insofar as he sees 'nation' primarily as an expression of civil society, as a collective form of self-determination and definition. He therefore sees that culture, community, tradition and imagination are crucial for this process. His somewhat romantic organicist approach is pitted against neoliberal projects of market ideologies misnamed as 'reform'.[13] Taylor draws his inspiration, among many sources, from an earlier European romantic tradition that cherishes cultural specificities, local traditions and imaginations.[14] This presents Taylor with the difficult task of 'reconciling solitudes' with some form of a state while retaining traditional cultural identities in an overall ideological circle of 'Canadian' nationhood. This is a difficult task at all times, but especially in the Canadian context of Anglo-French rivalry and the threat of separatism. Thus Taylor, in spite of his philosophical refinement, is like others also forced into the recourse of 'multiculturalism as a discourse', characterised by its reliance on diversity. The constitution then becomes a federal Mosaic tablet for encoding and enshrining this very moral/political mandate. But Taylor is caught in a further bind, because Canada is more than a dual monocultural entity. Underneath the 'two solitudes', as he knows well, Canada has 'different differences', a whole range of cultural identities which cannot (and he feels should not) be given equal status with the 'constituent elements' of 'the nation', namely, the English and the French. At this point Taylor has to juggle with the contending claims of these dominant or 'constituent' communities and their traditions, with the formal equality of citizenship in liberal democracy, and with other 'others' with their contentious political claims and 'different cultures'. This juggling, of course, happens best in a multicultural language, qualifying the claim

---

13   In *Reconciling* (ch. 4) on 'Alternative Futures' for Canada, Taylor fleshes out his desirable and undesirable options for Canada. This is also found in Taylor 1992.

14   Taylor is quite direct about his German romantic intellectual heritage. In *Reconciling*, in an essay entitled 'Institutions in National Life,' he states, 'In Herder I found inspiration, ideas that were very fruitful for me, precisely because I was from here, I was able to understand him from the situation I had experienced outside school, outside university, and I was able to engage with his thought, internalise it, and (I hope) make something interesting out of it' (p. 136).

of the socio-economic equality of 'others' with the language of culture and tolerance, converting difference into diversity in order to mitigate the power relations underlying it. Thus Taylor, in spite of his organicist, communitarian-moral view of the nation and the state, depends on a modified liberal pluralist discourse which he otherwise finds 'American', abstract, empty and unpalatable.[15]

Reconciling the Solitudes and *Multiculturalism and the Politics of Recognition* are important texts for understanding the need for the construction of the category of visible minorities to manage contentions in the nationhood of Canada. Even though Taylor spends little time actually discussing either the visible minorities or the First Nations, their importance for the creation of a national ideology is brought out by his discussion of Anglo-French contestation. Their visceral anxieties about loss of culture are offset by 'other' cultural presences that are minoritised with respect to both, while the commonality of Anglo-French culture emerges in contrast. Taylor discovers that the cultural essences of COQ have something in common with Quebec – their Europeanness – in spite of the surface of diversity. This surface diversity, he feels, is not insurmountable within the European-Anglo framework, whose members' political imagination holds enough ground for some sort of commonality.

> What is enshrined here is what one might call *first level diversity*. There are great differences in culture and outlook and background in a population that nevertheless shares the same idea of what it is to belong to Canada. Their patriotism and manner of belonging is uniform, whatever their differences, and this is felt to be necessary if the country is to hold together.[16]

Taylor must be speaking of those who are 'Canadians' and not 'others': the difference of visible minorities and First Nations peoples is obviously not containable in this 'first level diversity' category. As far as these 'others' are concerned the Anglo-European (COQ) and French elements have much in common in both 'othering' and partially 'tolerating' them. Time and time again, especially around the so-called Oka crisis, it became clear that liberal pluralism rapidly yields to a fascist 'sons of the soil' approach as expressed by both the Quebec state and its populace, oblivious to the irony of such a claim. It is inconsistent of Taylor to use this notion of 'first level diversity' while also emphasising

---

15   For an exposition of this idea, and Taylor's rejection of an 'American' solution for 'Canadian' identity, see 'Shared and Divergent' in *Reconciling*.

16   Taylor 1993, p. 182.

the irreducible cultural ontology of Quebec as signalled by the concept of a 'deep diversity'.[17] But more importantly, this inconsistency accords an owner-ship of nationhood to the Anglo-French elements. He wrestles, therefore, to accommodate an Anglo-French nationality, while the 'deep diversities' of 'oth-ers', though nominally cited, are erased from the political map just as easily as the similarity of the 'two nations' *vis-a-vis* those 'others'. Of course, these manip-ulations are essential for Taylor and others if the European (colonial) character of 'Canada' is to be held *status quo*. This is a Trudeau-like stance of dual unifica-tion in which non-European 'others' are made to lend support to the enterprise by their existence as a tolerated managed difference.

This multicultural take on liberal democracy, called the 'politics of recogni-tion' by Taylor, is informed by his awareness that an across-the-board use of the notion of equality would reduce the French element from the status of 'nation' to that of just another minority. This of course must not be allowed to happen, since the French are, by virtue of being European co-conquerors, one of the 'founding nations'. At this point Taylor adopts the further qualified notion of visible minorities as integral to his two-in-one nation-state schema. For him as for other majority ideologues they constitute a minority of minorities. They are, in the scheme of things, peripheral to the essence of Canada, which is captured by 'Trudeau's remarkable achievement in extending bilingualism' to reflect the 'Canadian' character of 'duality'.[18] This duality Taylor considers as currently under a threat of irrelevancy, not from anglo monoculturism, but from the ever-growing presence of 'other' cultures. 'Already one hears West-erners saying ... that their experience of Canada is of a multicultural mosaic'.[19] This challenge of the presence of 'others' is, for Taylor, the main problem for French Canadians in retaining their equality with English Canadians. But it is also a problem for Taylor himself, who sees in this an unsettling possibil-ity for the paradigm of 'two solitudes' or 'two nations' to which he ultimately concedes. In order to project and protect the irreducible claims of the two dominant and similar cultures, he refers fleetingly and analogically, though fre-quently, to aboriginal communities: 'visible minorities' also enter his discourse, but both are terms serving to install a 'national' conversation between French and English, embroidering the dialogue of the main speakers. His placement of these 'other' social groups is evident when he says: 'Something analogous [to the French situation] holds for aboriginal communities in this country; their

17   Ibid., p. 183.
18   Ibid., p. 164.
19   Ibid., p. 182.

way of being Canadian is not accommodated by first level diversity'.[20] Anyone outside of the national framework adopted by Taylor would feel puzzled by the analogical status of the First Nations brought in to negotiate power sharing between the two European nations. Taylor's approach is in keeping with texts on nationalism, culture and identity that relegate the issues of colonialism, racism and continued oppression of the Aboriginal peoples and the oppression visited upon 'visible minorities' to the status of footnotes in Canadian politics.

Yet multiculturalism as an ideological device both enhances and erodes Taylor's project. Multiculturalism, he recognises at one level, is plain realism – an effect of the realisation that many (perhaps too many) 'others' have been allowed in, stretching the skin of tolerance and 'first level diversity' tightly across the body of the nation. Their 'deep diversity' cannot be accommodated simply within the Anglo-French duality. The situation is so murky that, 'more fundamentally we face a challenge to our very conception of diversity'.[21] 'Difference', he feels, has to be more 'fundamentally' read into the 'nation': 'In a way, accommodating difference is what Canada is all about. Many Canadians would concur in this'.[22] 'Many of the people who rallied around the Charter and multiculturalism to reject the distinct society are proud of their acceptance of diversity – and in some respects rightly so'.[23]

But this necessary situational multiculturalism acknowledged by Taylor not only creates the transcendence of a nation built on difference, it also introduces the claims of 'deep diversities' on all sides. Unable to formulate a way out of this impasse Taylor proposes an ideological Utopia of 'difference' (devoid of the issue of power) embodied in a constitutional state, a kind of cultural federalism:

> To build a country for everyone, Canada would have to allow for second-level or 'deep' diversity in which a plurality of ways of belonging would also be acknowledged and accepted. Someone of, say, Italian extraction in Toronto or Ukrainian extraction in Edmonton might indeed feel Canadian as a bearer of individual rights in a multicultural mosaic. His or her belonging would not 'pass through' some other community, although the ethnic identity might be important to him or her in various ways. But this person might nevertheless accept that a Quebecois or a Cree or a Dene might belong in a very different way, that these persons were Cana-

---

20   Ibid., p. 182.
21   Ibid., p. 182.
22   Ibid., p. 181.
23   Ibid., p. 182.

dian through being members of their national communities. Reciprocally, the Quebecois, Cree, or Dene would accept the perfect legitimacy of the 'mosaic' identity.[24]

This Utopian state formation of Taylor founders, as do those of others, on the rocky shores of the reality of how different 'differences' are produced, or are not just forms of diversity. For all of Taylor's pleas for recognising two kinds of diversity, he does not ever probe into the social relations of power that create the different differences. It is perhaps significant from this point of view that he speaks of the 'deep diversities' of Italians or Ukrainians but does not mention those of the blacks, South Asians or the Chinese. In other words, he cannot raise the spectre of real politics, of real social, cultural and economic relations of white supremacy and racism. Thus he leaves out of sight the relations and ideologies of ruling that are intrinsic to the creation of a racist civil society and a racialising colonial-liberal state. It is this foundational evasion that makes Taylor's proposal so problematic for those whose 'differences' in the Canadian context are not culturally intrinsic but constructed through 'race', class, gender and other relations of power. This is what makes us sceptical about Taylor's retooling of multicultural liberal democracy by introducing the concept of 'deep diversity' as a differentiated citizenship into the bone marrow of the polity, while leaving the Anglo-French European 'national' (colonial and racist) core intact. He disagrees with those for whom

> ... [the] model of citizenship has to be uniform, or [they think] people would have no sense of belonging to the same polity. Those who say so tend to take the United States as their paradigm, which has indeed been hostile to deep diversity and has sometimes tried to stamp it out as 'un-American'.[25]

This, for Taylor, amounts to the creation of a truly Canadian polity that needs a 'united federal Canada' and is able to deliver 'law and order, collective provision, regional equality and mutual self help ...'[26] None of these categories – for example, that of 'law and order' – is characteristically problematised by Taylor. His model 'Canada' is not to be built on the idea of a melting pot or of a uniform citizenship based on a rationalist and functional view of polity. That would, according to him, 'straight-jacket' deep diversity. Instead,

---

24   Ibid., p. 183.
25   Ibid., p. 183.
26   Ibid., p. 183.

The world needs other models to be legitimated in order to allow for more humane and less constraining modes of political cohabitation. Instead of pushing ourselves to the point of break up in the name of a uniform model, we would do our own and some other peoples a favour by exploring the space of deep diversity.[27]

What would this differentiated citizenship look like in concrete example, we ask? Taylor throws in a few lines about Basques, Catalans and Bretons. But those few lines are not answer enough for us. Though this seems to be an open invitation to join the project of state- and nation-making, the realities of a colonial capitalist history – indentures, reserves, First Nations without a state, immigrants and citizens, illegals, refugees and 'Canadians' – make it impossible. They throw us against the inscription of power-based 'differences' that construct the self-definition of the Canadian state and its citizenship. We realise that class, 'race', gender, sexual orientation, colonialism and capital cannot be made to vanish by the magic of Taylor's multiculturalism, managed and graduated around a core of dualism. His inability to address current and historical organisations of power, his inability to see that this sort of abstract and empty invitation to 'difference' has always enhanced the existing 'difference' unless real social equality and historical redress can be possible – these erasures make his proposal a touch frightening for us. This is why I shudder to 'take the deep road of diversity together' with Charles Taylor.[28] Concentration and labour camps, Japanese internment, the Indian Act and reserves, apartheid and ethnic 'homelands' extend their long shadows over the project of my triumphal march into the federal Utopia of a multiculturally differentiated citizenship. But what becomes clear from Taylor's writings is the importance of a discourse of difference and multiculturalism for the creation of a legitimate nation space for Canada. Multiculturalism becomes a mandate of moral regulation as an antidote to any, and especially Quebec's, separatism.

3 On the Dark Side of the Nation: Considering 'English Canada'

If one stands on the dark side of the nation in Canada everything looks different. The transcendent, universal and unifying claims of its multiculturally legitimated ideological state apparatus become susceptible to questions. The

---

27   Ibid., p. 184.
28   Ibid., p. 184.

particularised and partisan nature of this nation-state becomes visible through the same ideological and working apparatus that simultaneously produces its national 'Canadian' essence and the 'other' – its non-white population (minus the First Nations) as 'visible minorities'. It is obvious that both Canada and its adjectivised correlates English or French Canada are themselves certain forms of constructions. What do these constructions represent or encode? With regard to whom or what are we etherised and categorised as visible minorities? What lies on the dark side of this state project, its national ethos?

Official multiculturalism, mainstream political thought and the news media in Canada all rely comfortably on the notion of a nation and its state both called Canada, with legitimate subjects called Canadians, in order to construct us as categorical forms of difference. There is an assumption that this Canada is a singular entity, a moral, cultural and political essence, neutral of power, both in terms of antecedents and consequences. The assumption is that we can recognise this beast, if and when we see it. So we can then speak of a 'Pan-Canadian nationalism', of a Canada which will not tolerate more Third World immigrants or separatism, or of what Canada needs or allows us to do. And yet, when we scrutinise this Canada, what is it that we see? The answer to this question depends on which side of the nation we inhabit. For those who see it as a homogeneous cultural/political entity, resting on a legitimately possessed territory, with an exclusive right to legislation over diverse groups of peoples, Canada is unproblematic. For others, who are on the receiving end of the power of Canada and its multiculturalism, who have been dispossessed in one sense or another, the answer is quite different. For them the issues of legitimacy of territorial possession, or the right to create regulations and the very axis of domination on which its status as a nation state rests, are all too central to be pushed aside. To them the same Canada appears as a post-conquest capitalist state, economically dependent on an imperialist United States and politically implicated in English and u.s. imperialist enterprises, with some designs of its own. From this perspective 'Pan-Canadianism' loses its transcendent inclusivity and emerges instead as a device and a legitimation for a highly particularised ideological form of domination. Canada then becomes mainly an English Canada, historicised into particularities of its actual conquerors and their social and state formations. Colonialism remains as a vital formational and definitional issue. Canada, after all, could not be English or French in the same sense in which England and France are English and French.

Seen thus, the essence of Canada is destabilised. It becomes a politico-military ideological construction and constitution, elevating aggressive acts of acquisition and instituting them into a formal stabilisation. But this stability is tenuous, always threatening to fall apart. The adjective 'English' stamped into

'Canada' bares this reality, both past and present. It shows us who stands on the other side of the 'Pan-Canadian' project. Quebeckers know it well, and so their colonial rivalry continues. And we, the 'visible minorities' – multiculturalism notwithstanding – know our equidistance from both of these conquering essences. The issue at stake, in the end, is felt by all sides to be much more than cultural. It is felt to be about the power to define what is Canada or Canadian culture. This power can only come through the actual possession of a geographical territory and the economy of a nation-state. It is this which confers the legal imprimatur to define what is Canadian or French Canadian, or what are 'sub'- or 'multi'-cultures. Bilingualism, multiculturalism, tolerance of diversity and difference and slogans of unity cannot solve this problem of unequal power and exchange – except to entrench even further the social relations of power and their ideological and legal forms, which emanate from an unproblematised Canadian state and essence. What discursive magic can vanish a continuously proliferating process of domination and thus of marginalisation and oppression? What can make it a truly multicultural state when all the power relations and the signifiers of Anglo-French white supremacy are barely concealed behind a straining liberal democratic facade?

The expression 'white supremacist',[29] harsh and shocking as it may sound to many, encodes the painful underpinnings of the category visible minorities. The ideological imperatives of other categories – such as immigrants, aliens, foreigners, ethnic communities or New Canadians – constellate around the same binary code. There is a direct connection between this and the ideological spin-off of Englishness or Frenchness. After all, if nations are 'imagined communities', can the content of this national imagination called Canada be free of its history and current social relations of power? Does not the context inflect the content here and now?

At this point we need to remind ourselves that there are different kinds of nationalisms – some aggressive and others assertive. Benedict Anderson makes a useful distinction between an 'official nationalism' of imperialism, and the 'popular nationalism' of lived relations of a settled society and its shared historical/cultural relations.[30] The former, Anderson claims, is about hate and aggression; the latter, about love and sacrifice of a people for a shared culture, ancestral history and a shared physical space. This 'popular nationalism' in my view is clearly not possible for Canada, whose context is the colonisation and continued marginalisation of the First Nations while seeking to build a liberal

---

29   On the development of active white supremacist groups in Canada, and their 'Englishness,' see Robb 1992. Also Ward 1978.

30   Anderson 1991, p. 86. But see also the chapter on 'Official Nationalism and Imperialism'.

democratic state. In Canada, such 'popular nationalism' contains legal/coercive strategies and the means of containment and suppression of all 'others'. The kinship or blood-ties of which Anderson speaks as elements of a nation are ranged along two contending sides.[31] On the side of Canada there is a history and kinship of European/English colonial and subsequently American complicity in domination, of bad faith and broken promises and at best, of guilt. On the other side is the labour-migration kinship of all who stand in the underside of this Canada, roped in by relations of colonialism and imperialism with their race, gender and cultural discrimination. This European domination is coded as 'civilised' and 'modernising' and signified through 'white',[32] while global resistance or acquiescence to them are carried on by 'others' who are colour coded as 'visible', meaning nonwhite, black or dark.

The case of Canada and its nationalism, when considered in this light, is not very different from the 'official nationalism' of South Africa, erstwhile Rhodesia, or of Australia. These are cases of colonial 'community' in which nation and state formations were created through the conquering imagination of white supremacy.[33] An anxiety about 'them' – the aboriginals, pre-existing people – provides the core of a fantasy which inverts the colonised into aggressors, resolving the problem through extermination, suppression and containment.[34] Dominant cultural language in every one of these countries resounds with an 'us' and 'them' as expressed through discursivities of 'minority/sub/multi-culture'. A thinly veiled, older colonial discourse of civilisation and savagery peeps out from the modern versions. Here difference is not a simple marker of cultural diversity, but rather measured or constructed in terms of distance from civilising European cultures. Difference here is branded always with inferiority or negativity. This is displayed most interestingly in the reading of the non-white or dark body which is labelled as a visible and minority body.[35] The colour of the skin, facial and bodily features – all become signifiers of inferiority, composed of an inversion and a projection of what is considered evil by the colonising society. Implied in these cultural

---

31   Ibid., p. 19.

32   On the construction of 'whiteness' as an ideological, political and sociohistorical category see Allen 1994, and Roediger 1992; also Frankenberg 1993.

33   On the use of 'whiteness'/Europeanness as an ideology for ruling, including its formative impact on sexuality of the ruling, colonial nations, see Stoller 1995.

34   On this theme see Joseph Conrad's *Heart of Darkness*, E.M. Forster's *A Passage to India* and Said 1993.

35   On the reading of the black, dark or 'visible minority' body, see the collection of essays in Gates 1985, especially Gilman 1985.

constructions is a literal denigration, extending into a valorised expression of European racist-patriarchy coded as white.

This inscription of whiteness underwrites whatever may be called Englishness, Frenchness, and finally Europeanness. These national characteristics become moral ones and they spin off or spill over into each other. Thus whiteness extends into moral qualities of masculinity, possessive individualism and an ideology of capital and market.[36] They are treated as indicators of civilisation, freedom and modernity. The inherent aggressiveness and asociality of this moral category 'whiteness' derives its main communitarian aspect from an animosity towards 'others', signalling the militaristic, elite and otherising bond shared by conquerors. The notion of Englishness serves as a metaphor for whiteness, as do all other European national essences. Whiteness, as many have noted, thus works as an ideology of a nation-state. It can work most efficiently with an other/enemy in its midst, constantly inventing new signifiers of 'us' and 'them'. In the case of Canada the others, the First Nations, have been there from the very inception, modulating the very formation of its state and official culture, constantly presenting them with doubts about their legitimacy. Subsequently, indentured workers, immigrants, refugees and other 'others' have only deepened this legitimation crisis, though they also helped to forge the course of the state and the 'nation'.[37] 'English', as an official language, has served to create a hegemonic front, but it is not a powerful enough antidote as an ideological device to undermine antagonisms that are continually created through processes of ruling; it is the ideology of 'whiteness/ Europeanness' that serves as the key bonding element. Even though the shame of being an Italian, that is, non-English, in Canada outweighs the glory of the Italian renaissance, 'Italian' can still form a part of the community of 'whiteness' as distinct from nonwhite 'others'. It is not surprising, therefore, to see that one key element of white supremacy in Canada was an 'Orange' mentality connecting Englishness with whiteness and both with racial purity. Books such as *Shades of Right*,[38] for example, speak precisely to this, as does the present day right-wing nationalism of 'English'-based groups. Quebec's 'French' nationalism has precisely the same agenda, with a smaller territorial outreach. In fact, racialisation and ethnicisation are the commonest forms of cultural or identity parlance in Canada. This is not only the case with 'whites' or 'the English' but also with 'others' after they

---

36   See Stoller 1995, but also Sinha 1995.
37   The history of immigration and refugee laws in Canada, and of the immigrants, indentured workers and refugees themselves, must be read to comprehend fully what I am attempting to say. See The Law Union of Ontario 1981. Also Canada 1974, and Canada 1986.
38   Robb 1992.

spend some time in the country. A language of colour, even self-appellations such as 'women of colour' (remember 'coloured women'?), echo right through the cultural/political world. An unofficial apartheid, of culture and identity, organises the social space of 'Canada', first between whites and non-whites, and then within the non-whites themselves.

4   A Rose by Any Other Name: Naming the 'Others'

The transcendence or legitimation value of the official/state discourse of multiculturalism – which cherishes difference while erasing real antagonisms – breaks down, therefore, at different levels of competing ideologies and ruling practices. A threat of rupture or crisis is felt to be always already there, a fact expressed by the ubiquity of the integration-fragmentation paradigm in texts on Canada. Instead of a discourse of homogeneity or universality, the paradigm of multiculturalism stands more for the pressure of conflict of interests and dynamics of power relations at work. This language is useful for Canada since imagining a nation is a difficult task even when the society is more homogeneously based on historic and cultural sharing or hegemony. Issues of class, industry and capital constantly destabilise the national project even in its non-colonial context. Gramsci for example, in 'Notes on Italian History', discusses the problem of unification inherent in the formation of a nation-state in the European bourgeois context.[39] Unificatory ideologies and institutions, emanating from the elite, posturing as a class-transcendent polity and implanted on top of a class society reveal as much as they hide. These attempts at unification forge an identifiable ideological core, a national identity, around which other cultural elements may be arranged hierarchically. It transpires that the ability and the right to interpret and name the nation's others forms a major task of national intellectuals, who are organic to the nation-state project.[40]

If this difficulty dogs European bourgeois nationalism, then it is a much more complicated task for Canada to imagine a *unificatory* national ideology, as recognised by members of the 'white' ideological bloc espousing non-liberal perspectives. Ultraconservatives in general have foresworn any pretence to the use of 'multi-cultural' ideology. They view multiculturalism as an added burden to a society already divided, and accord no political or cultural importance

---

39   Gramsci 1971.
40   On organic intellectuals as intellectuals who are integral to any ideological and class project, see Gramsci, 'The Intellectuals,' in Gramsci 1971.

to groups other than the French. The political grammar of 'national' life and culture, as far as the near and far right are concerned, is common-sensically acknowledged as 'English'. According importance to multiculturalism has the possibility of calling into question the 'English' presence in this space, by creating an atmosphere of cultural relativism signalling some sort of usurpation. This signal, it is felt, is altogether best removed. English/Europeanness, that is, whiteness, emerges as the hegemonic Canadian identity. This white, Canadian and English equation becomes hegemonic enough to be shared even by progressive Canadians or the left.[41] This ideological Englishness/whiteness is central to the programme of multiculturalism. It provides the content of Canadian culture, the point of departure for 'multiculture'. This same gesture creates 'others' with power-organised 'differences', and the material basis of this power lies both below and along the linguistic-semiotic level. Multiculturalism as the 'other' of assimilation brings out the irreducible core of what is called the real Canadian culture.

So the meaning of Canada really depends on who is doing the imagining – whether it is Margaret Atwood or Charles Taylor or Northrop Frye or the 'visible minorities' who organise conferences such as 'Writing Thru "Race"'. Depending on one's social location, the same snow and Canadian landscape, like Nellie McClung and other foremothers of Canadian feminism, can seem near or far, disturbing, threatening or benign. A search through the literature of the 'visible minorities' reveals a terror of incarceration in the Canadian landscape.[42] In their Canada there is always winter and an equally cold and deathly cultural topography, filled with the RCMP, the Western Guard, the Heritage Front and the *Toronto Sun*, slain Native peoples and Sitting Bull in a circus tent, white-faced church fathers, trigger-happy impassive police, the flight and plight of illegals, and many other images of fear and active oppression. To integrate with this Canada would mean a futile attempt at integrating with a humiliation and an impossibility. Names of our otherness proliferate endlessly, weaving margins around 'Canada/ English/French Canada'. To speak of pan-Canadian nationalism and show a faith in 'our' national institutions is only possible for those who can imagine it and already are 'Canada'. For 'others', Canada can

---

41   This becomes evident when we follow the controversies which are generated by writers' conferences, such as 'Writing thru "Race"', or the black communities' response and resistance to the Royal Ontario Museum's exhibition on African art and culture, 'Out of the Heart of Africa'.

42   See, for example, Brand 1983, Sri Bhaggiyadatta 1993, Bannerji 1986b, and collections such as McGifford and Kearn 1990.

mean the actuality of skinhead attacks, the mediated fascism of the Reform Party, and the hard-fist of Rahowa.[43]

It is time to reflect on the nomenclature extended by multiculturalism to the 'others' of 'Canada'. Its discourse is concocted through ruling relations and the practical administration of a supposed reconciliation of 'difference'. The term visible minorities is a great example: one is instantly struck by its reductive character, in which peoples from many histories, languages, cultures and politics are reduced to a distilled abstraction. Other appellations follow suit – immigrants, ethnics, new Canadians and so on. Functional, invested with a legal social status, these terms capture the 'difference' from 'Canada/English/French Canada' and often signify a newness of arrival into 'Canada'. Unlike a rose which by any other name would smell as sweet, these names are not names in the sense of classification. They are in their inception and coding official categories. They are identifying devices, like a badge, and they identify those who hold no legitimate or possessive relationship to 'Canada'. Though these are often identity categories produced by the state, the role played by the state in identity politics remains unnoticed, just as the whiteness in the 'self' of 'Canada's' state and nationhood remains unnamed. This transparency or invisibility can only be achieved through a constellation of power relations that advances a particular group's identity as universal, as a measuring rod for others, making them 'visible' and 'minorities'.

An expression such as visible minorities strikes the uninitiated as both absurd and abstract. 'Minority', we know from J.S. Mill onwards, is a symptom of liberal democracy, but 'visible?' We realise upon reflection that the adjective visible attached to minority makes the scope of identity and power even more restricted. We also know that it is mainly the Canadian state and politics which are instrumental in this categorising process and confers this 'visibility' upon us. I have remarked on its meaning and use elsewhere:

> Some people, it implies, are more visible than others; if this were not the case, then its triviality would make it useless as a descriptive category. There must be something 'peculiar' about some people which draws attention to them. This something is the point to which the Canadian state wishes to draw our attention. Such a project of the state needed a point of departure which has to function as a norm, as the social average of appearance. The well-blended, 'average', 'normal' way of looking becomes the base line, or 'us' (which is the vantage point of the state),

---

43   The acronym for Racial Holy War, a neo-nazi rock band.

to which those others marked as 'different' must be referred ... and in relation to which 'peculiarity' [and thus, visibility] is constructed. The 'invisibility' ... depends on the state's view of [some] as normal, and therefore, their institution as dominant types. They are true Canadians, and others, no matter what citizenship they hold [and how many generations have they lived here?] are to be considered as deviations ...[44]

Such 'visibility' indicates not only 'difference' and inferiority, but is also a preamble to 'special treatment'. The yellow Star of David, the red star, the pink triangle, have all done their fair share in creating visibility along the same lines – if we care to remember. Everything that can be used is used as fodder for visibility, pinning cultural and political symbols to bodies and reading them in particular ways. Thus for non-whites in Canada,

their own bodies are used to construct for them some sort of social zone or prison, since they can not crawl out of their skins, and this signals what life has to offer them in Canada. This special type of visibility is a social construction as well as a political statement.[45]

Expressions such as 'ethnics' and 'immigrants' and 'new Canadians' are no less problematic. They also encode the 'us' and 'them' with regard to political and social claims, signifying uprootedness and the pressure of assimilation or core cultural-apprenticeship. The irony compounds when one discovers that all white people, no matter when they immigrate to Canada or as carriers of which European ethnicity, become invisible and hold a dual membership in Canada, while others remain immigrants generations later.

The issue of ethnicity, again, poses a further complexity. It becomes apparent that currently it is mainly applied to the nonwhite population living in Canada. Once, however, it stringently marked out white 'others' to the Anglo-French language and ethos; while today the great 'white' construction has assimilated them. In the presence of contrasting 'others', whiteness as an ideological-political category has superseded and subsumed different cultural ethos among Europeans. If the Ukrainians now seek to be ethnics it is because the price to be paid is no longer there. Now, in general, they are white vis-a-vis 'others', as is denoted by the vigorous participation of East Europeans in white supremacist politics. They have been ingested by a 'white-Anglo' ethos, which

---

44   Bannerji 1993, p. 148. On this theme of social construction of a racialised 'minority' subject and it inherent patriarchy, see Carty and Brand 1993 and Ng 1993.
45   Bannerji 1993, p. 149.

has left behind only the debris of self-consciously resurrected folklores as special effects in 'ethnic' shows. The ethnicities of the English, the Scottish, the Irish, etc. are not visible or highlighted, but rather displaced by a general Englishness, which means less a particular culture than an official ideology and a standardised official language signifying the right to rule. 'Ethnicity' is, therefore, what is classifiable as a non-dominant, sub or marginal culture. English language and Canadian culture then cannot fall within the ministry of multiculturalism's purview, but rather within that of the ministry of education, while racism makes sure that the possession of this language as a mother tongue does not make a non-white person non ethnic. Marginalising the ethnicity of black people from the Caribbean or Britain is evident not only in the Caribana Festival but in their being forced to take English as a second language. They speak dialects, it is said – but it might be pointed out that the white Irish, the white Scots, or the white people from Yorkshire, or white Cockney speakers are not classified as ESL/ESD clients. The lack of fuss with which 'Canadians' live with the current influx of Eastern European immigrants strikes a profound note of contrast to their approach to the Somalis, for example, and other 'others'.

The intimate relation between the Canadian state and racism also becomes apparent if one complements a discussion on multiculturalism with one on political economy. One could perhaps give a finer name than racism to the way the state organises labour importation and segmentation of the labour market in Canada, but the basic point would remain the same. Capitalist development in Canada, its class formation and its struggles, predominantly have been organised by the Canadian state. From the days of indenture to the present, when the Ministry of 'Manpower' has been transformed into that of 'Human Resources', decisions about who should come into Canada to do what work, definitions of skill and accreditation, licensing and certification, have been influenced by 'race' and ethnicity.[46] This type of racism cannot be grasped in its real character solely as a cultural/attitudinal problem or an issue of prejudice. It needs to be understood in systemic terms of political economy and the Gramscian concepts of hegemony and common sense that encompass all aspects of life – from the everyday and cultural ones to those of national institutions. This is apparent if one studies the state's role in the importation of domestic workers into Canada from the Philippines or the Caribbean. Makeda Silvera, in *Silenced*, her oral history of Caribbean domestic workers, shows the bonds of servitude imposed on these women by the state through the inherently racist

---

46   See Avery 1995. Much work still needs to be done in this area, in which class formation is considered in terms of both 'race' and gender, but a beginning is made in Brand 1991, and Brand and Sri Bhaggiyadatta 1985.

laws pertaining to hiring of domestic workers.[47] The middle-man/procurer role played by the state on behalf of the 'Canadian' bourgeoisie is glaringly evident. Joyce Fraser's *Cry of the Illegal Immigrant* is another testimonial to this.[48] The issue of refugees is another, where we can see the colonial/racist as well as anti-communist nature of the Canadian state. Refugees fleeing ex-Soviet bloc countries, for example, received a no-questions acceptance, while the Vietnamese boat people, though fleeing communism, spent many years proving their claim of persecution. The racism of the state was so profound that even cold-war politics or general anti-communism did not make Vietnamese refugees into a 'favoured' community. The story of racism is further exposed by the onerous and lengthy torture-proving rituals imposed on Latin Americans and others fleeing fascist dictatorships in the Third World. In spite of Canada's self-proclaimed commitment to human rights, numerous NGOs, both local and international, for years have needed to persuade the Canadian state and intervene as advocates of Third World refugees. Thus the state of 'Canada', when viewed through the lens of racism/difference, presents us with a hegemony compounded of a racialised common sense and institutional structures. The situation is one where racism in all its cultural and institutional variants has become so naturalised, so pervasive that it has become invisible or transparent to those who are not adversely impacted by them. This is why terms such as visible minority can generate so spontaneously within the bureaucracy, and are not considered disturbing by most people acculturated to 'Canada'.

Erol Lawrence, in his Gramscian critique 'Just Plain Common Sense: The "Roots" of Racism', uses the notion of common-sense racism to explain the relationship between the British blacks and the state.[49] He displays how common sense of 'race' marks every move of the state, including official nomenclatures and their implementation in social and political culture. Lawrence remarks on how hegemony works through common sense or expresses itself as such:

> The term common sense is generally used to denote a down-to-earth 'good sense'. It is thought to represent the distilled truths of centuries of practical experience; so much so that to say of an idea or practice that it is only common sense, is to appeal over the logic and argumentation of intellectuals to what all reasonable people know in their 'heart of hearts' to be right and proper. Such an appeal can all at once and at the same

---

47   This is powerfully brought forth through the issue of the importation of domestic workers to Toronto from the Caribbean in Silvera 1989.

48   Fraser 1980.

49   Lawrence 1982.

time (serve) to foreclose any discussion about certain ideas and practices and to legitimate them.[50]

The point of this statement becomes clearer when we see how the Canadian state, the media and political parties are using 'visible minorities', 'immigrants', 'refugees' and 'illegals' as scapegoats for various economic and political problems entirely unrelated to them. For this they rely on common sense racism: they offer pseudo-explanations to justify crises of capitalism and erosion of public spending and social welfare in terms of the presence of 'others'. Unemployment, endemic to capital's 'structural adjustment', is squarely blamed on 'these people'. This explanation/legitimation easily sticks because it replicates cultural-political values and practices that pre-exist on the ground. These labelling categories with racialised underpinnings spin-off into notions such as unskilled, illiterate and traditional, thus making the presence of Third World peoples undesirable and unworthy of real citizenship. Englishness and whiteness are the hidden positive poles of these degrading categories. They contain the imperative of exclusion and restriction that neatly fits the white supremacist demand to 'keep Canada white'. The multiculturalist stance may support a degree of tolerance, but beyond a certain point, on the far edge of equality, it asserts 'Canadianness' and warns off 'others' from making claims on 'Canada'. Through the same scale of values East European immigrants are seen as desirable because they can be included in the ideology of whiteness.

'Difference' read through 'race', then, produces a threat of racist violence. The creation of a 'minority' rather than of full-fledged adult citizens – the existence of levels of citizenship – adds a structural/legal dimension to this violence. Inequality within the social fabric of Canada historically has been strengthened by the creation of reserves, the Department of Indian Affairs, the exclusion of Jews, and the ongoing political inequalities meted out to the Chinese, the Japanese and South Asians. These and more add up to the tenuousness of the right and means to existence, jobs and politics of the 'visible minorities'. Being designated a minority signals tutelage. It creates at best a patron-client relationship between the state and 'others' who are to be rewarded as children on the basis of 'good conduct'. Social behaviour historically created through class, 'race' and gender oppression is blamed on the very people who have been the victims. Their problems are seen as self-constructed. The problem of crime in Toronto, for example, is mainly blamed on the black communities. Black young males are automatically labelled as criminals and frequently shot by the police.

---

50   Ibid., 1986, p. 48.

It is also characteristic that an individual act of violence performed by any black person is seen as a representative act for the whole black community, thus labelling them as criminal, while crime statistics among the white population remain non-representative of whiteness.

Visible minorities, because they are lesser or inauthentic political subjects, can enter politics mainly on the ground of multiculturalism. They can redress any social injustice only limitedly, if at all. No significant political effectiveness on a national scale is expected from them. This is why Elijah Harper's astute use of the tools of liberal democracy during the Meech Lake Accord was both unexpected and shocking for 'Canadians'. Other than administering 'difference' differentially, among the 'minority communities' multiculturalism bares the political processes of co-optation or interpellation. The 'naming' of a political subject in an ideological context amounts to the creation of a political agent interpellating or extending an ideological net around her/him, which confers agency only within a certain discursive-political framework. At once minimising the importance and administering the problem of racism at a symptomatic level, the notion of visible minority does not allow room for political manoeuvre among those for whose supposed benefit it is instituted. This is unavoidably accompanied by the ethnicisation and communalisation of politics, shifting the focus from unemployment due to high profit margins, or flight of capital, to 'problems' presented by the immigrants own culture and tradition. Violence against women among the 'ethnics' is thought to be the result of their indigenous 'traditions' rather than of patriarchy and its exacerbation, caused by the absolute power entrusted by the Canadian state into the hands of the male 'head of the family'. The sponsorship system through which women and children enter into the country seems calculated to create violence. Food, clothes and so-called family values are continually centre staged, while erasing the fundamental political and economic demands and aspirations of the communities through multicultural gestures of reconciling 'difference'. The agent of multiculturalism must learn to disarticulate from his or her real-life needs and struggles, and thus from creating or joining organisations for antiracism, feminism and class struggle. The agencies (wo)manned by the 'ethnic' elements – within terms and conditions of the state – become managers on behalf of the state. In fact, organising multiculturalism among and by the non-white communities amounts to extending the state into their everyday life, and making basic social contradictions to disappear or be deflected. Considering the state's multicultural move therefore allows a look into the state's interpellative functions and how it works as an ideological apparatus. These administrative and ideological categories create *objects* out of the people they impact upon and produce mainstream agencies in their name. In this way a little niche is created within the state for those who are otherwise undesirable, unassimilable and deeply different. Whole communities have begun to be renamed on the basis of these conferred cultural administrative identities that objectify and divide them. Unrelated to each other, they become clients and creatures of the multicultural state. Entire areas of problems connected to 'race', class, gender and sexual orientation are brought under the state's management, definition and control, and possibilities for the construction of political struggles are displaced and erased in the name of 'ethnic culture'. The politics of identity among 'ethnic communities', that so distresses the 'whites' and is seen as an excessive permissiveness on the part of the state, is in no small measure the creation of this very culturalist managerial/legitimation drive of the state.

What, then, is to be done? Are we to join forces with the Reform Party or the small 'c' conservative 'Canadians' and advocate that the agenda of multiculturalism be dropped summarily? Should we be hoping for a deeper legitimation crisis through unemployment and rampant cultural racism, which may bring down the state? In theory that is an option, except that in the current political situation it also would strengthen the ultra-right. But strategically speaking, at this stage of Canadian politics, with the withdrawal and disarray of the left and an extremely vulnerable labour force, the answer cannot be so categorical. The political potential of the civil society even when (mis)named as ethnic communities and reshaped by multiculturalism is not a negligible force. This view is validated by the fact that all shades of the right are uneasy with multiculturalism even though it is a co-opted form of popular, non-white political and cultural participation. The official, limited and co-optative nature of this discourse could be re-interpreted in more materialist historical and political terms. It could then be re-articulated to the social relations of power governing our lives, thus minimising, or even ending, our derivative, peripheral object agent status. The basic nature of our 'difference', as constructed in the Canadian context, must be rethought and the notion of culture once more embedded into society, into everyday life. Nor need it be forgotten that what multiculturalism (as with social welfare) gives us was not 'given' voluntarily but 'taken' by our continual demands and struggles. We must remember that it is our own socio-cultural and economic resources which are thus minimally publicly redistributed, creating in the process a major legitimation gesture for the state. Multiculturalism as a form of bounty or state patronage is a managed version of our antiracist politics.

We must then bite the hand that feeds us, because what it feeds us is neither enough nor for our good. But we must wage a contestation on this terrain with the state and the needs of a racist/imperialist capital. At this point of the new world order, short of risking an out-and-out fascism, the twisted ideological evolution of multiculturalism has to be forced into a minimum scope of social politics. Until we have developed a wider political space, and perhaps with it keeping a balance of 'difference', using the avenues of liberal democracy may be necessary. Informed with a critique, multiculturalism is a small opening for making the state minimally accountable to those on whose lives and labour it erects itself. We must also remember that liberalism, no matter who practices it, does not answer our real needs. Real social relations of power – of 'race', class, gender and sexuality – provide the content for our 'difference' and oppression. Our problem is not the value or the validity of the cultures in which we or our parents originated – these 'home' cultures will, as living cultures do in history, undergo a sea-change when subjected to migration. Our problem is class oppression, and that of objectifying sexist-racism. Thinking in terms of culture alone, in terms of a single community, a single issue, or a single oppression will not do. If we do so our ideological servitude to the state and its patronage and funding traps will never end. Instead we need to put together a strategy of articulation that reverses the direction of our political understanding and affiliation – against the interpellating strategies of the ideological state apparatus. We need not forget that the very same social relations that disempower or minoritise us are present not only for us but in the very bones of class formation and oppression in Canada. They are not only devices for cultural discrimination and attitudinal distortion of the white population, or only a mode of co-optation for 'visible minorities'. They show themselves inscribed into the very formation of the nation and the state of 'Canada'. Thus the politics of class struggle, of struggle against poverty or heterosexism or violence against women, are politically more relevant for us than being elected into the labyrinth of the state. The 'visible minorities' of Canada cannot attain political adulthood and full stature of citizenship without struggling, both conceptually and organisationally, against the icons and regulations of an overall subordination and exploitation.

In conclusion, then, to answer the questions 'How are we to relate to multiculturalism?' and 'Are we for it or against it?' we have to come to an Aesopian response of 'ye, ye' and 'nay, nay'. After all, multiculturalism, as Marx said of capital, is not a 'thing'. It is not a cultural object, all inert, waiting on the shelf to be bought or not. It is a mode of the workings of the state, an expression of an interaction of social relations in dynamic tension with each other, losing and gaining its political form with fluidity. It is thus a site for struggle, as is 'Canada' for contestation, for a kind of tug-of war of social forces. The problem is that no matter who we are – black or white – our liberal acculturation and single-issue oriented politics, our hegemonic 'subsumption' into a racist common sense, combined with capital's crisis, continually draw us into the belly of the beast. This can only be prevented by creating counter-hegemonic interpretive and organisational frameworks that reach down into the real histories and relations of our social life, rather than extending tendrils of upward mobility on the concrete walls of the state. Our politics must sidestep the paradigm of 'unity' based on 'fragmentation or integration' and instead engage in struggles based on the genuine contradictions of our society.

A Question of Silence: Reflections on Violence against Women in Communities of Colour

Calcutta, 15 November 1997

Dear Ena and Angela,

Breaking with scholarly protocols, I am writing this piece as a letter to you because what I want to say needs an embodied reader. The topic is too close to our every-day life and politics to come wrapped in a package of academic or theoretical abstractions. Thank you for asking me to write, and for accepting a piece that is more reflection than definitive research. Thank you also for being my ideal readers through whom I can speak to others.

1

Issues of patriarchy and violence against women are disturbing in general, but they become even more so when considered in relation to our so-called own communities. I am speaking of South Asian communities about which I know most, but what I have to say may apply to 'other' Canadian communities which are non-white.[1] I know that violence against women is a pervasively present phenomenon among us, in spite of much talk about honour and respect for women, including deification of the feminine principle as claimed by the Hindus. I also know that not only I, but large numbers of women, have been in a position to know of instances of violence of various degrees, and have not known what to do or where to speak about it. We have often spoken among ourselves in a private or personal capacity, and sometimes we have expressed

---

1 I am aware that calling people 'non-white' is a debatable practice. I would not do so if I were to use it as a term denoting identity – namely, as a signification for *who we are.* I use this term here as a political signifier, not an ontological one, to point out the hegemonic cause of our woes, namely racism. In this matter where we come from, our national cultures, are less significant than the fact that whoever is not 'white' will fall within the purview of racialisation and discrimination. For this purpose I prefer to use the expression 'non-white,' since the conventional terms 'woman of colour,' 'immigrants,' etc. do not always do the job at hand.

our concerns publicly. I have been haunted by the story of a Sri Lankan woman who killed her two daughters and attempted suicide. These events are not, as far as I can understand, a matter of personal pathology – they have to be informed with a consideration of her migration, her isolation, her lack of economic and social support, an extremely abusive marriage, and a sexist and racist host society, where hospitals continue to neglect signs of violence against women. On a lesser scale, we worry about women who leave the temporary refuge of the shelters for their 'homes', returning to the same partners whose violence drove them out in the first place. But in spite of our general concern and common knowledge, I have not read anything extensive or substantial on the phenomenon of violence against women within their so-called communities – communities which are constituted by outside forces with (rather than by) 'people of colour'. Perhaps there is writing coming out of the United Kingdom or United States, but it has not gained enough prominence to attract public attention.

So, as things stand now, a direct critical assessment, social analysis, or political project on this issue has not been undertaken. We seem to have left this task mainly to poets and fiction writers, whose business we think it is to deal with experience. And as you know, as social scientists we have been taught to regard experience with extreme suspicion as a source for reliable social knowledge. Even though certain types of feminist theorists have sought to valorise experience, the current discursivism of feminist theories has put a big question mark against experience, against actual lives as they are lived by women. But rendered into literary or cultural artefacts and relegated to the borderlands of fact and fiction, what we know and say about community violence against women does not create the same pressure for address or redress as it would if we had to admit that this violence is a direct part of our diasporic reality. We would then have to speak to and act on patriarchal violence within our homes, within the moral or social regulation of the very modalities of constituting 'the community'. As things are, we maintain a public silence, even if we know it only rebounds on us negatively. We need to explore this silence, to ask what our investment in it might be. This is precisely what I am trying to do in this letter, as well as to speak to the nature of patriarchal violence within the terrain of our domestic lives.

We cannot even begin to plumb the depth of this silence unless we recognise its complex character. As you know, silence is highly telling – it can mean anything from complicity to resistance. Its presence, in the shape of an absence in public discourse about violence against women in South Asian or other nonwhite communities, speaks volumes about our political and socio-cultural organisation and stance. And even though this silence creates large holes in the fabric of our public political culture, that which we have not addressed directly seeps out, is displaced or slips into other concerns or issues. The repressed returns, as it were, in court cases, in refugee and immigration hearings, in women's shelters, changing individual and private instances into examples of public and collective lives.

One of the reasons for this paradoxical silence may be that public utterance puts us in a situation of responsibility – it makes us accountable to and for others and ourselves. After all, what we say in print, in any public medium, is fixed in form, content, and time. It becomes part of an acknowledged, even official reality, liable to be seen as a distinct political position. We are no longer just overheard or peeped into. The doors of the community open as we speak 'out'. So, obviously, we are wary, not only about what we say in public, but where and how we say it. We want to assess the location and reception of our public statements, our disclosures and discussions in the arena of social communication. We are, if anything, overly sensitive towards the ideological strands or networks into which they will be woven, how our statements will be received by those who are not 'us', particularly those 'others' who consider us not as people, but as 'ethnic communities'. These are not unimportant considerations for those who hold not only 'minority', but 'visible minority', status in a white and Christian majoritarian nation-state. But then we are in a situation of double jeopardy, since speaking and not speaking both entail problems. In fact, we may be better off breaking this silence, since this articulation itself is a political act giving rise to other political possibilities. But going public in this matter requires that we are able to expose and critique the patriarchal constitution of our communities, which is the same as all other communities, without too much squeamishness about our dirty laundry.

2

To put forward our critique regarding violence against women in our communities, we cannot begin by taking the concept of 'community' for granted. We need to remember that it is a political and cultural-ideological formation reliant upon social relations which are the bases of social life, and not a spontaneous or natural association of people. This constructed and contingent nature of the concept of community is important to keep in mind, since it is becoming increasingly common in social sciences to treat this concept, along with a definite article or an adjective, as a natural, almost an instinctive, form of social and cultural association. Cultural anthropology, with its various types of relativism, seems to have been an important source for this practice of considering 'community' as a self-contained and natural formation, a social given, which may be interchangeable with the concept of civil society.

But if, instead of naturalising 'community', we see it as a formation, an ideological, that is, cultural and political practice, it becomes possible for us to develop a critique of the social organisation, social relations, and moral regulations which go into the making of it. We can then begin to see that a group of people with a language, a religion, or an interest in common may only become an identifiable and stable social and political structure – in spite of the presence of power relations among them – through a combination of internal and external factors. It is in their interaction of contradiction and convergence that a so-called community is formed. This community, as in the case of women and on issues of gender and patriarchy, can only hold itself together by maintaining a silence about issues of power. A community is also formed both on grounds of difference and commonness. The difference is obviously from those who lack features in common, and therefore are 'others' to the collective 'self' of the community, usually a smaller group marked out as different by the majority. This makes the community into a minoritarian concept, one whose political and social roots lie in being collectively marked out as different from the hegemonic group. It is not difficult to understand this process of community formation when we see the different ways in which the Canadian state and hegemonic common sense mark out their social 'others'. This othering implies racism, ethnicisation (with a 'race' component), and homogenisation. People who are thus 'othered' also bond together *vis à vis* these designatory processes in a defensive move, while being penned within a political and cultural boundary. Silence regarding malpractices within these stereotypically constructed and defensively self-constituted communities is therefore not unexpected.

Inscribed and instituted politically from the outside, the communities themselves also suppress internal sources of division and seek to present themselves, at least in their representational endeavours, as seamless realities. Silence, therefore, regarding class, gender, and other power relations, characterises this voluntary aspect of community-making as well. And as we shall see later, the technology for constructing difference relies on the concept of tradition, which is implicated in both aspects of community formation. This is what characterises these communities as traditional, in contradistinction to the 'modernity' of the 'Canadians', the second half of this binary paradigm. This construction of traditionality is then fleshed out with the invention of particular traditions – relevant for different nationalities and cultural groups. Needless to say the notion of a traditional community rests explicitly on patriarchy and on severely gendered social organisation and ideology. These are legitimated as an essence of the identity of these communities. This traditional (patriarchal) identity, then, is equally the result of an othering from powerful outside forces and an internalised Orientalism and a gendered class organisation.

Keeping these processes of community formation in view – disputing its natural and synonymous status as and with civil society – we can begin our critique by invoking our general membership as women of these communities. We need to remember that we are the 'others' of white women in the Canadian national imaginary, and this is connected with the fact that we are an integral part of the peoples who were brought as indentured workers, or migrated to Canada from former colonies under severe economic conditions created by post-colonial imperialism. Unlike European or white women, we present 'Canada' with the problem of inassimilation. We are simultaneously essentialised into homogenised yet racialised and ethnicised subjects, whose actual differences are drowned in the multicultural discourse of diversity. We are worried, understandably, to speak of 'our' brutalities and shortcomings, because of not being even minimally in control of the public and political domains of speech or ideological construction. The pre-existence of a colonial/racist/Orientalist perception and stereotypes of us, embedded in official and everyday structural and cultural practices and meanings, have been powerful sources of distortion and misrepresentation of our subjectivities and politics. This, of course, is not only true of Canada but of elsewhere in the West as well. This sexist-racist common sense, with its pervasive presence in the political economy and dominant culture of Canada, is rooted in a history of colonial conquests, genocides and ongoing projects of profit and rule. This is productive of an ethos of European or white supremacy which provides the political conscious or unconscious of Canada's nation state and political-cultural space. We are simultaneously present and absent in these spaces, and in the apparatus of the state. It is this paradox of presence and absence, of difference and sameness (as some sort of members of this Canadian nation), that multiculturalism both constructs and augments. Our political and social identities are contingent upon this. We might say that the reasons both for our presence in Canada and for the official discourse of multiculturalism are connected to our actual absence in and abdication of public space and speech regarding ourselves and our communities' horrendous treatment of women.

The situation is complicated. But how can it be any different, when we come from colonial and imperialist histories and presents and find ourselves in the midst of a white settler colony struggling to transform itself into a liberal democracy? Canada's participation in imperialism on the coat tails of the United States is not hidden from public view. Inhabiting this terrain, our refugee and immigrant statuses mark us as second-class citizens, if citizens at all. We stand, both men and women, uncertainly at the edge of 'Canada', the nation. Comprehended in this political economy, a racialised class organisation which is as much about whiteness as blackness, we step back in time. We are recolonised, directly – and that isn't just speaking metaphorically. Coming from countries which have seen anti-colonial struggles in one form or another and shaken off direct colonial rule, we put ourselves back into socio-political spaces closely resembling a colony – at least where we are concerned. Here we are marked by a difference which has less to say about us – our histories and cultures – than about a mode of sociopolitical interpretation within a pre-established symbolic and practical schema of a racialised or ethnicised colonial and slave-owning discourse.

It is at the receiving end of this proliferation of denigrating differences and homogenisation that the incoming 'others' go through their community formation. Of course, at the same time they are going through a process of class formation as well, which is creating a difference among themselves, as much as between them and 'Canadians'. But the discourse of community cannot and is not meant to express or accommodate that. In the ideological discourse of 'the community' it was made to appear that when people migrated, they did so as communities, not as responses to national and international political economy.

We can say, therefore, that there is nothing natural about communities. In fact they are contested grounds of socio-cultural definitions and political agencies. Contradictory processes of creating 'us' and 'them' are at work in them, and we have here a situation of mini-hegemonies confronting and conforming to a national ideological hegemony. Form and content of communities reflect this, and we continue to be constructed and excluded by the same overarching hegemony. This becomes evident when we look at the discourse and workings of official multiculturalism, in which where we are from, as nationalities and cultures – Jamaica, Vietnam, or India – matters very little when we are being distinguished from 'Canadians', while our specific differences provide the stepping stones for this general difference. We know very quickly that we are not 'them' or 'Canadians', while our 'us' can cross national boundaries, and sometimes it does. Racism, Eurocentrism, or ethnocentrism, which impacts on all non-whites in this way, generates a space for a broader community among us, creating a ground for anti-racism. But this again is not a given or a foregone conclusion, since internalised racism or community boundaries generally help create a closed in socio-cultural space and a highly fragmented political agency. So while there is in this mechanism of mass exclusion, called multicultural community, room for the excluded to unite irrespective of their different regional and individual histories, languages, and religions, the unity in actuality has not been more than that of region, religion, and perhaps language.

In fact, regional and linguistic communities seem to be in the process of fast alternation on the ground of religion – thus being 'Hindus' and 'Muslims' has currently become alarmingly relevant. This deepening of traditionality has not boded well for women among these communities.

So, possibilities for a community of the excluded notwithstanding, we have been docile with regard to the political economy of Canada. We have by and large uncritically inhabited the socio-economic zones, grids, or boxes created for us by Manpower and Immigration or Employment and Immigration Canada. We have been legally bonded and bounded. This boundary, invisible though inexorable, is the outer wall of the community – whatever that may be – and it not only keeps others 'out', but us 'in'. From this point of view community is not only an ideological and social category, but also a category of the state. This becomes evident if we reflect on the role of this category in the mode of administering the civil society, for example, in electoral politics, in organising the labour market, in social assistance or cultural funding.

You might at this point object to this non-cultural way of reading the socio-genetics of the concept of community, which goes against the grain of conventional use of the term. You might refer to the role that our own ethnocultural varieties and differences play in the making of communities. You might want to speak of religions, languages, social customs – the semiotic and moral constructions and regulations that we identify ourselves by. Are we not marked as communities in these terms, making 'us' distinct from others? These would be, or should be, our questions if we were to read the 'community' as an equivalent for the civil society. But as I have pointed out, communities are formed through the pressure of external forces far more than for reasons of cultural expression. There is no reason for the inhabitants of any region to engage in an exercise of collective self-identification unless there is the presence of a dominant group which is ascribing certain definitions and identity markers onto them. This process of complex and contradictory interactions between external and internal forces, which I have already spoken to, makes it evident that 'community' is a very specific way of politicising and organising cultural particularities of social groups. In this it is no different from the use of the concept of caste or religion with which the colonial powers created administrative and ruling regimes in the colonies.

Questioning the status of the community as a natural, social formation does not automatically imply a dismissal of points of commonality among peoples of different regions, cultural habits, nationalities, and histories, or, for that matter, among religious groups from those regions. It is true that such people often tend to seek each other out, to speak the same language, eat the same food, or display fashions. Very often in the earlier part of their existence in Canada it is a survival necessity for learning the ropes in the new country, getting employment or business contacts, and so on. But if the Canadian society into which they come were non-threatening and non-exclusive, if racism were not a daily reality, this stage of cultural bonding would be short, and more fluid than it is at present. In that case cultural practices would not harden into 'identities' or ethnic typologies, but temporary stages of social becoming, both at individual and collective levels. Such elective affinities or cultural associations cannot be called communities, which imply organisation and institutionalisation – a mechanism for a rigid cultural reproduction. Voluntary cultural associations are both temporary and much less organised, and often a very small part of the existence of people. This is evident if we observe the European or white immigrants who may live in ethnic networks, for example the Italians or Ukrainians, but who did not ossify into permanent communities with fixed and branded identities.

Things are different with us, that is, non-white immigrants – even if we are conversant in English or French, which people from South Asia, Africa, and the Caribbean generally are. With them the process is reversed, since they come as individual migrants and slowly harden into the institutional form of the community. The reason for this, I am afraid, is not what is inside of them, but rather in their skin. Their skin is written upon with colonial discourse – which is orientalist and racist. Thus memories, experiences, customs, languages, and religions of such peoples become interpreted into reificatory and often negative cultural types or identities. The political process of minoritisation accompanies this interpretive exercise, and together they lead to the formation of communities. When we speak of 'diversity' it is this set of reified and politicised differences that we are invoking, and they provide the basis for ethnocultural identity and politics of representation.

That communities are not simple self-projections of cultural groups, but rather, inherently political formations, is something we need to keep in mind. This is particularly important in the last two decades, when a discourse of community and cultural diversity has been engraved into the Canadian body politic. This is not just at the level of society at large, but in the official formulation and implementation of multiculturalism. Though it may strike one as curious that any 'ism' can be made out of culture (we don't, after all, talk of 'culturalism' as state policy), we do live in an era when political and ideological stances are created and institutionalised out of features of everyday life or cultures (especially of non-white people). Entire administrative apparatuses are alerted to cultural characteristics of non-white/non-European 'others', extending from law and policing to mental health and labour. Such cultural 'isms' and their practicalisation in the context of ruling and administration cannot but need and create essentialist characteristics in the interests of stability and predictability. If the groups were not to be seen as homogeneous in terms of possessing these essential traits, no administration could be put in place. Difference and diversity would not then be effective categories for deployment in ruling, but indeed contrary to it.

We might ask at this point a question or two regarding the content of these putative differences and diversities. Is this content entirely invented? Are they simply baseless, imagined essentialities? The answer to this question points us towards the epistemology implied in the creation of all ideological categories, as elaborated by Marx, and best discussed in *The German Ideology*. It is not that ideology invents particular socio-cultural features, found among many, but rather it centres some and erases others which might contradict the centrality of the selected ones. These selected features do not exist as discrete or floating pieces, but rather assume a categorical status by an extraneous connection which is established among them, often in a causal or positive mode. In other words, a discursive mode is established which creates falsehood, we might say, by a particular arrangement of existing characteristics. It is the whole discursive organisation that is distortive or untrue, not particular features as such, and it is in their establishment as 'essential' that the harm is most palpable. This ideological activity of consciousness has been called power/knowledge when particularly annexed to the project of ruling. Critique of colonial discourse, now so frequently practised, provides us with more than ample examples of this. It is there we see that paradigms, such as that of civilisation and savagery or tradition and modernity, offer the discursive terrain or interpretive schema for understanding or representing cultural traits of colonised or enslaved peoples. It is from this source that the content of difference and diversity of official multiculturalism evolves. This reduces non-Europeans the world over into pre-modern, traditional, or even downright savage peoples, while equating Europeans with modernity, progress, and civilisation. The social ethos and cultural identities of the 'others' of Europe are presumed to be religious, their conduct ritualistic, and their temperament emotional and unruly. They are at once civilisationally ancient (and therefore in decay) and primitive (therefore undeveloped). These are the ideological underpinnings of the not so benign discourse of multicultural diversity. This is difference and representation as constructed through historical and social relations of power, and it leads to the making of a selective constellation of cultural attributes and ideological packages which contour and control the multicultural community.

This, then, is the ascriptive or normative process through which multicultural communities come to life and into political play in relation to state repression and conditional or limited rewards. Furthermore, we have a situation here of double reification, which combines communitisation from above (state and dominant ideology or hegemonic commonsense) and from below (from the subject populations themselves). These reified collectivities of difference create a situation of unofficial apartheid, a general culture of apartheid in the overall sociocultural terrain of the country. Essentialised cultural identities already in place are rigidly maintained, while the general culture of apartheid proliferates fragmented and enclosed cultural territories which are both officially and voluntarily maintained. Political participation of non-white immigrants or their political subjectivities or agencies are increasingly conceived and conducted on these bases. The concept of community and its organisation, then, provides the articulating basis between people and the state.[2]

3

These complexities of community formation provide us the problematic within which patriarchal violence, in its various manifestations, has to be grounded. We must remind ourselves here of the pervasive presence of patriarchy and specific forms of gender organisation in all societies of our present day world, and of their long historical presence. Both general social organisation and specific forms of ruling, of creating hegemonies, require this gendering and patriarchy as ideological and moral regulation. Whether this patriarchy is intrinsic and biologically based or contingent need not detain us here. What is important is that they have been historically in place for a very long time. The incoming peoples about whom we have been speaking come from spaces as deeply patriarchal and gender organised as the social space they enter into in Canada. They do not learn patriarchal violence after coming here. They also come from a social organisation and politics of class, from national hegemonic systems, all of which are organised by gender and patriarchy. Class and gender, seemingly two distinct systems of oppression, are only so in theory – in practice they constitute and mediate each other in a network of overall social relations of power. White or not, immigrants and 'Canadians' all live in this gendered and classed social reality. So violence against women, latent or blatant, is not surprising among communities which have, like all other social groups, all the social con-

---

2   Here we might, following Althusser, speak of being interpellated by the ideological apparatuses of the state, the state being understood as both an institution and a general political body. The political subjectivities and agencies of communities constructed through these processes are both conditional and subcontracted to current hegemonies.

ditions for this and other patriarchal forms of violence, such as homophobia. Misogyny, an extreme form of patriarchy, cannot be discussed here in detail – but it should suffice to point out that the homosexual male has long been feminised, and the lesbian seen as a masculinist, female aberration. The hatred for both contains, on the one hand a displaced hatred for women, and on the other an anger or even hatred for those who invert the patriarchal social norm of heterosexuality. Unlike the artificial divide instituted between the West and the rest, there is in fact a deep commonality between them in matters pertaining to these hegemonic norms, and regarding practices and ideologies of property and class. What, then, is the specificity of violence against women within the confines of the community?

The answer to this question refers us back to the point I made about recolonisation, which occurs when people of former colonies return to direct white rule by coming to the West. Class and gender organisation and normative behavior undergo a peculiar twist in this situation. On the one hand the process of internalisation of colonial values, such as of racism, is intensified and projected through self-hatred and anti-Black racism; on the other hand, this submission gesture is refuted or compensated by gestures of resistance. They revive and develop further a certain kind of nationalism, with some features in common with the nationalism of formerly colonised countries. This can happen very easily as these non-white, non-European communities function like mini-cultural nationalities in this recolonising context. They seize upon the mainstream's and the state's tendencies and rules to differentiate them, and adopt these cultural differences. They proclaim these differences to be substantive and inherent, and proclaim their cultural autonomy in the face of an ethics of assimilationism while seeking to become political agents within the same framework of ideologies and institutions. Their resistance, what there is of it, is mostly cultural, and typically minority politics, which cannot and does not aspire to state formation, unlike anticolonial nationalisms. In this surrender-submission dialectic they rely mainly on colonial discourse, especially as they are from 'the East'. The main idea that they carry over with themselves and deepen on the Western soil is their self-characterisation as 'traditional'. From this stance they engage in self-reification as a collective group, and develop logically their self-projection as religious, anti- and pre-modern peoples. They evoke mythical pasts or histories to support their current ideological stances, and create a politics internal to their definition of community which relies extensively on patriarchal moral regulations. This invention of tradition legitimises and institutionalises them as clients of the state, while the essentialist logic of community formation homogenises all into one, and a few can represent the rest to the state and the world at large.

The community, as we can see, is a very modern formation, as is cultural nationalism. Its appeal to tradition, i.e. religion and antiquity, are its passwords into some limited space in the realms of power. To speak authoritatively in a representational capacity it is therefore imperative to speak in moral terms. This is most effectively done through a religious discourse and related practices of moral regulation. It requires in particular an absolute subscription to feudal or semi-feudal patriarchies, as well as the erasure of class, as this leads to social conflicts. All this provides a situation of surplus repression for women, sexual 'others', as well as for people of lower class standing – all in the way of creating communities. Hierarchy and patriarchy as natural or divinely ordained conduct allows for a peculiar situation where class and gender power are both vindicated and occluded at once. Domination of women, of sexual 'others', and subordination of children take on here the character of duties that each male head of the family and the male leaders of the community, who may also be religious heads, must perform. Patriarchal social violence is thus daily and spiritually normalised in these walled towns of communities or religious and cultural ghettoes.

What is put forward by the communities as assertion of difference, as resistance, often turns out to be colonial discourse with reversed valuations. In this context, tradition is considered in a highly positive light, while modernity, rationalism, and social criticism are negatively valorised. Religious fundamentalism is considered a particularly authentic sign of our Easternness. This is mini-cultural nationalism writ small, within a larger national imaginary, putting up its barricades and political signs with a neo-colonial inflection. This situation is not new. In the context of development of one strand of nationalism in India, among the Hindu petty bourgeoisie, we have already seen this situation on a much larger scale. Many scholars and critics, feminists and others, have remarked on the peculiar importance of the sign of woman, as mother in particular, and of the feminisation of the land or country as mother-goddess. These ideological manoeuvres have little to do with women, except to indicate their property or service role to the nation. The same could be said of the use of women and familial regulations pertaining to the ideological positioning of the community.

4

The vested interests of upwardly mobile males, with religious patriarchal power in their hands, either in these types of communities or in nationalist projects, makes it difficult to question the imputed homogeneity or unity of the community. 'Divisive' issues of gender and class, or for that matter of internalised colonial discourse or racism, cannot therefore be broached without enormous resistance and silencing from within. In formulating the interest of women and the causes of their oppression, no matter how aware of and informed with other social relations of power, we thus need to step back from the ideological and political schema of the community. Furthermore, we need to speak about patriarchy in inter- and intra-class terms, even at the risk of being misunderstood as separatist feminists, because it involves being 'disloyal' to our so-called civilisations or national cultures.

If we do take this 'disloyal' stance, which is the only real critical stance we can take, we can see that a cognisance of patriarchy and gender is also a cognisance of class and property relations in general. It is this that patriarchal or male perception cannot see or tolerate. Their resistance to colonial or national domination has never been questioning of either property or patriarchy. This is where their male and petty bourgeois or bourgeois class character is fully visible. This does not mean that mini-cultural nationalities or political collectives do not engage in class politics, but they do so, fully though implicitly, with the purpose of upward mobility rather than in the interest of social and economic equality. They are part of the phenomenon of class formation, and display the same characteristics as did the bourgeoisie in their earliest years of state formation, when they spoke in the name of all. It is then that they created theories of democracy and liberalism, which they were unable to actualise due to their class interests. In this commitment to an ethics of possession and politics of property, where property includes labour power and physical or reproductive capacities, the 'others' of metropolitan capitalist democracies are in no way different from the mainstream, though their operational modalities may be highly situation specific.

In this erasure of class and gender, in protecting property and its proprieties, the 'traditional' communities and the 'modern' Canadian state show a remarkable similarity and practical convergence. Through the state's need to create an apparatus of political interpellation of 'others', official multiculturalism came into being. This could then create political agencies through the various modalities of development of multiculturalism, whose ideology is refracted in the language and practices of diversity and implementation of institutional projects. Neither class nor gender, which are differences created through social relations of power, nor 'race', another of these excruciating constructs of power, could be raised as issues within this discourse of diversity and redressed. In fact, what counted as difference were so-called cultural differences, and the project was aimed at preaching 'tolerance' to the majority while leaving relations of power unchallenged either among them or among the objects of their tolerance. An intensification of class, gender, and patriarchy was encouraged through multicultural identifications, since the 'others' were deemed 'traditional' (i.e. patriarchal, hierarchical, and religious) and thus 'natural' practitioners of these inequalities. Criticisms of abuse of women in the community, even when brought into the court, fell prey to 'cultural' or 'religious' legal arguments.

This continues to be the case. Definitional boundaries which are vital for legal and social jurisdiction of the Canadian state, which is as thoroughly 'traditional' in these matters as the immigrants, rest on these essentialisation gestures. It suits the Canadian state just as much as it suits the elite in the communities to leave intact these traditions and rituals of power. That the community is a political-ideological construct, particular to history and a politics, and therefore ignores the real diversities among people migrating from 'other' countries, can have no place in this scheme of things. Progressive and critical people among these immigrants are thus dubbed atypical, Westernised, and inauthentic to their culture, both by the leading conservative elements among them and by their progenitor protector, the Canadian state. Violence against women or sexual 'others', aggressive and hateful attitudes towards the religion of others, especially towards Islam, become the bedrock of normal community identity. Oppression of women and feudal (rather than bourgeois) patriarchy thus become 'our' social being, and such behaviour earns or maintains a colonial or racist contempt for us, while being treated permissively by the state. This deprives women of legal and political recourse and social assistance. On the other hand, the same type of characterisation also deprives Muslim males in Canada, particularly from Arab countries, of legal justice, since the community as a whole is tarred with the brush of fanaticism.

Communities, or the elite of these mini-nationalities, of course play their card of cultural difference according to dictates. They too, in spite of their anti-liberal stance, separate culture from all other social moments, such as that of economy. Equating 'culture' with religion, and making a particularly elite brand of that religion the fountainhead of all ethical and customary values, they too assert the master script and make no fundamental socio-economic demands. Through the mask of pre-modernity and anti-materialism they participate most effectively in a capitalist state of a highly modern nature. In return for proclaiming a primordial traditionality they are left alone as rulers of their own communities, to rule over women, sexual 'others', the economically dispossessed, and children. The social space of countries they migrate from or flee as refugees becomes a state of mind rather than a place in history. The political and cultural conflicts raging in South Asia, in Egypt or Algeria or Latin America, for example, where secularism and religious fundamentalism are in struggle, are altogether erased. A totalising myth of tradition engrosses entire land masses, in fact two-thirds of the world, which foundationally rests on pat-riarchy. This is the imputed and self-proclaimed organic unity or wholeness of communities!

When we look at the status of women in the communities, we find it to be one of 'property', of belonging to individual male heads of families as well as to the institutions called the family and the community. The morality of a collect-ive organic nature seems to apply to them, whereas males are encouraged to individualism and entrepreneurialism in their very definition of masculinity. This control over women as a community's property, the object of patriarchal command, is not only traditional or god-given, but this sacred authority is actu-alised and reinforced by the secular construction and sanction of the Canadian state. The legal category of 'the head of the family', with all the prerogatives and responsibilities pertaining to it, is entirely a category of state-delegated power to men. It is a category that extends from 'immigrants' to 'Canadians', and offers men who hold this position practically a life-and-death power over women and children. This has been discussed especially with regard to 'sponsored immig-rants', generally wives, who are held at the mercy of their husbands since they have no legal rights in Canada independent of their relationship with their husbands. The threat of deportation that hangs over their head – the loss of livelihood, displacement, separation from children, and social disgrace that might result from a breakdown of sponsorship – is a violent and volatile one. This is what makes innumerable women stay with their husbands in dangerous and humiliating situations, or to return to their so-called homes. Any challenge to the cultural identity of being 'traditional', which means questioning religious and patriarchal injunctions, cannot be very effectively mounted from such a vulnerable socio-economic location. If this law were to have been amended, and wives of immigrating husbands could be seen as independent political and legal adults, not as their dependents, we might have seen something quite different from 'traditional' behaviour. It is then that we would have known whether Muslim women veil themselves because they want to, or because they are made to under conditions of subtle and overt duress. As it is we have no way of knowing their real will, since they are subject to what is called 'multiple' but also converging patriarchies of the community male elite and the Cana-dian state. Facile anti-racism or cultural nationalism simply offers a window-dressing of legitimation.

To return to a theme introduced earlier, we might say that women's status as a 'sign' or even a symbol for 'our' cultural autonomy amounts to no more than being handmaidens of god, priest, and husband. This subordination or domination is mediated and regulated through the patriarchal family code, and anchored to the moral regulations of honour and shame. Any deviance from the domestic patriarchy of family (extended into wider kinship networks), from strict heterosexist codes, is a pathway to shame and punishment. This may range from censure to physical violence and social ostracism by the community. Women, and involved men, who help to bring about sexual disgrace may even be killed. The cases of killings of 'deviant' women in Vancouver – for example, a woman who left her community by developing an emotional and sexual attachment outside of it – may be extreme, but not out of line with this moral regulation. The irony, therefore, of a situation where the most powerless member of the community is exalted to the status of goddess or an embodiment of honour of the community, should not be lost on anyone. In fact, if she were not powerless, she could not have been pushed into the mould of a symbol or disembodied into a metaphor. This metaphoric or symbolic exaltation is simultaneously an objectification of women and of 'our' difference from 'the West'. Disembodiment and objectification are the foundation of violence against women, which cannot happen without a material or social base of domination. It is not an accident that the honour of this symbolic investiture is not conferred upon men, and that women have no choice about being chosen as symbolic or significatory objects.

The dehumanisation involved in converting a person, an embodied sociohistorical being, into a sign or symbol implies much more than an epistemological violence. It is based on the same principles that enabled a physical, social, and symbolic violence to be visited upon Jews in pogroms and the holocaust, on various indigenous peoples in colonial genocides, and on Africans in slavery. Thus patriarchy, anti-Semitism, or racism, with or without fusing into each other, provide an overall social organisation of relations of domination which extends from everyday-life repressions to extermination. The symbol is a formalisation of actual violent, social relations which organise the society as a whole. It is a way of encoding, naming, and perpetuating them. This reality is evident in widow immolations in India, stoning of adulterous women in Pakistan, or female genital mutilation among some groups in Africa, to give a few examples. Discursivities entailed in these symbolic expressions mediate and stabilise violent social relations through various forms of textualisation. They make room for elite males to be exonerated from responsibility as perpetrators of such social violence.

The significational figurations of women have been used as objects of hegemony by colonisers, nationalist elites and their analogues in Canada – the communities of non-white immigrants, and by the state. Women have become objects for creating history, but are given no role of their own to play in the making of it, except as victims of wars. The organisation of societies in terms of gender has identified women with the private sphere, except at a symbolic level. This means an identification with 'home', domesticity, and the family, which come into being through their activities and end up by being their enclosures.

The most prominent of the women signs in the contexts of nations and communities is that of the mother, the ultimate incarnation of the 'good woman'. The 'goodness' of women in this extreme patriarchal incarnation, but in others as well, is manifested in a nurturing and sacrificing conduct at the service of the patriarchal family and equally patriarchal causes of larger collectivities, such as the nation or the community. Fear of disruption of this normative design comes chiefly from a fear of women's sexuality, which is, therefore, demonised and punished. The somewhat lesser disruptive source is the life of reason, which would put women in public spaces. Any move made by women in these directions is therefore considered to be 'Western', 'white', or 'colonial', that is, treasonable to the greater 'national' or community causes. But it is also 'abnormal', as it would upset the sign of difference with which 'our' co-opted male elite make political deals in multicultural terms or create attempts at cultural national resistance. It is important to note that both female sexuality and interest in rationality or education become threatening because they confer on women active roles which transgress the normative public-private divide. Containment and control of women through the normative mechanism of femininity underpin both proscriptions. In situations where such fully religious fundamentalist conduct cannot be enjoined, the prescriptive moral regulations still hold in a somewhat compromised or 'modernised' manner. But it is not an exaggeration to say that the more women belonging to the community could be forced into its organising religio-patriarchal norms and forms, the more the community could proclaim its definitively authentic status. Straying from these laid-down paths would call for censures of betrayal of a nature similar to those extended towards white women by white supremacist groups for betraying the empire, the 'race', or the nation through miscegenation.

When we examine issues of patriarchal violence against women, it becomes apparent that the traditional community's social organisation does not serve the greater good of the collectivity. Neither women nor less privileged men have their interests represented in it. The real benefit that it confers on males of all classes is great power over women and children, even men who are excluded or marginalised by the host society. This is not unlike national governments which cannot face up to international financial powers, but rule as dictators within national boundaries. In fact, the international or the multicultural national state's approval of them is dependent upon how well they can control these internal forces and their potential for opposition.

By a perverted extension of this logic the men of these communities are excused, even by anti-racist or otherwise feminist activists, for their generally sexist or even violent misconduct against women. Racism and class discrimination are held responsible for the rage that men vent on women, children, or homosexual members of their communities. This tolerance can extend up to severe abuse or even murder. Locking up women without their clothes, severe beating, mutilation or burning them with cigarette stubs, are some of the violences we have heard of. It is extraordinary how infrequently it is noted, if at all, that women too are subjects of colonialism and racism, and these oppressions are intensified by sexism or gross forms of patriarchy. It is a known fact that non-white women mostly work at worse paying and more menial jobs than their husbands, keep a double day of work inside and outside the home, and suffer from particularly humiliating forms of sexual harassment. In spite of all this, a woman does not often take out her frustration on her husband and children, as a man does. And certainly her mistreatment of them is never explained in the same terms, nor extenuated by the community and others for the same reasons, with which even the Canadian justice system credits abusive men. Whereas compromised and reduced masculinity of such men is noted sympathetically by scholars of colonialism and slavery, the compromised humanity of women, their punishment through hyper-femininity, rarely draws equal attention. If anything, a woman who wants to go beyond such roles and ascriptions, who is critical of patriarchy within the community, is often blamed for aiding and abetting in the colonial project of emasculation. Meanwhile, police and other forms of state and daily racist, social violence are directed against non-white women. The police murder of the sons of black women (and men) is as much a violence against their mothers (and fathers) as is the shooting of Sophia Cook or the strip search of Audrey Smith.

5

I have outlined so far, and quite extensively, some salient aspects of the social problematic and certain specificities regarding violence against women in the community. Obviously a lot more remains to be said. But this is an attempt to break the silence I referred to at the beginning of my letter. I have tried to point towards a politics which, I hope, addresses the multiple social relations of power which organise our society. I have tried to show that a simplistic binary politics of self and other, of essentialist identities pitted against each other in a politics of cultural nationalism, is not a viable option for women. This reflection of cultural nationalism, of so-called multicultural community politics, does not erase racism or colonial oppression. In fact, a real struggle against the socially hegemonic forces and their expression in the Canadian state requires the perspective that I have offered. We cannot allow ourselves to be blackmailed in the name of cultural authenticity, identity, and community, any more than we can be duped by the mythologies of social democracy proffered by a racist and imperialist bourgeois state.

What awaits us is the political task of forging a real anti-racist feminism informed by a class analysis, with a critique of imperialism exposing the hoax of globalisation. This politics cannot be brought to life if we stop only at a critique of patriarchal and gendered social organisation. Such a critique, without an awareness and theorisation of women as historical and social agents, would fall into the trap of showing women as victims of men and society. We must remember, then, that because women are also subjects of colonialism, racism, and class organisation, because they also inhabit the same social relations as men, they too are part of the dynamics of resistance and domination. They have the same political needs, rights, and potentials as men – to be full citizens or members of nation states and to become agents in revolutionary politics.

It will not serve women to look for enclosed and co-opted identities in the name of family, god, nation, or the multicultural state – to live for their approbation. Our politics will have to be indifferent to special pleadings of arguments of spurious difference, but concentrate instead on the workings of the construction of difference through social relations of power, on the instruments of ruling. Developing a critical perception of sexist-racist social and cultural common sense and of the apparatus of the state, questioning laws that position 'immigrants' in vulnerable roles within the political economy, questioning 'multiculturalism' which co-opts and distorts popular political agency – these are our immediate tasks. Obviously they are not easy tasks, nor are results to be achieved instantly. Nor can they be carried on within the locked doors of community or identity politics. We, non-white women, women of 'communities', must claim various political movements in Canada as our own. This means the women's movement and movements of resistance against state and class power, against pervasive and insidious racism and homophobia. Though it may sound like a tall order, it is possible to enter our politics through the door of particular 'women's issues', for example, and come into the arena of a general political resistance. It is only in doing this that one can shape one's politics in ways that are nuanced by other struggles, where what comes out is the convergence of various politics against oppression, and not their separate directions. I don't think we need to fear a loss of specificity, of our selves, in a vast sea of abstraction or generalities controlled by others. If we can frame our critique and create organisations that challenge patriarchy, heterosexism, class, and 'race' with even a semblance of integrity, we will create the bases for an embodied, social revolution. Needless to say, in this process we will have to redefine our friends and enemies, our notions of insiders and outsiders, and to whom, when, how, and about what we can talk. This open letter about our silence is only a very small experiment at that talk.

With love and solidarity,
Himani

CHAPTER 18

The Passion of Naming: Identity, Difference and Politics of Class

> When I left the house of bondage, I left everything behind. I wasn't going to keep nothing of Egypt on me, and so I went to the lord, and asked him to give me a new name. And the lord gave Sojourner, because I was to travel up and down the land, showing the people their sins, and being a sign unto them. Afterward I told the lord, I wanted another name, 'cause everybody has two names; and the lord gave me Truth, because I was to declare the truth to the people'.[1]

∴

'Identity' has recently become a common word in our political vocabulary. Once a preserve of Romantic poets and philosophers, this word has now become a coin in many hands. Serving as an adjective for diverse political projects ranging from nationalism to liberal democracy, this word has put the ideas of 'being' or subjectivity and experience in the centre stage of politics. This has been mainly done with the notion of representation, in both political and cultural senses, speaking to distribution of power and claims for political agency. Some have considered this shift as a positive development in politics, others as a distraction and a disaster. Most marxists, feminists or otherwise, have considered this to be a regressive, divisive and individualistic, in general a troublesome, move.[2] The use of related notions of difference and representation have fared only a little better. Thus working with notions of subjectivity, experience, agency and representation have been mostly left to

---

1 Sojourner Truth, 'Nothing out of Egypt,' in Dionne Brand's *Bread out of Stone*, pp. 140–1.

2 Issues of identity and difference and their political implications have preoccupied feminist theorists and organisers extensively. Substitution of political agents, problems in building coalitions in the women's movement in the West, as well as various epistemological critiques of essentialism have been advanced. For marxist feminists the stumbling block in 'identity politics' seems to have been the difficulties that surround the concept of experience. Among many, the following marxist feminist critiques give some idea of problems encountered with 'identity politics': Adams 1989; Haris 1989; Briskin 1990; Hartmann 1979; Seagal 1987.

the post-modernists or post-structuralists, cultural theorists of all sorts – to make of them what they will. If the word 'identity' can be used as a code for an involvement with all these issues then we can say that we have now arrived at the slogan of 'identity or class' as two mutually exclusive forms of politics.

This situation is reminiscent of the problematic formulated by Marx in the 'First Thesis on Feuerbach' in *The German Ideology* on the false separation between a sense of self or being, and the world that being inhabits. To paraphrase Marx, the idealists have captured the theorisation of consciousness, of the sense of self and imaginative cultural being, while the materialists have mastered an understanding of organisation or structure of the world. Both insist on their unconnected and autonomous natures, and for Marx, both are wrong. For him the project consists of an introjective and constitutive theorising of the two moments – of the self or consciousness as being in and of the world, and of the world as history and structures made by the self with forms of consciousness.[3] This approach he felt would develop a knowledge adequate for changing the world, with a centrally situated agent or subject without whom no transformative politics would be possible. If we as marxists take this to be our stance as well (coded as dialectical or historical materialism) then our task consists of providing a reflexive or dialectical understanding of 'identity' and its associated concepts such as 'difference', 'subjectivity' and 'agency'. This can only be done in relation to our world, namely, to the history and social organisation of capital and class – inclusive of colonialism, slavery and imperialism. In so doing we bring together the Gramscian use of the concept of hegemony – particularly speaking to everyday life, experience and culture, with the marxist concepts of class and ideology, and Marx's historical and organisational understanding of capital. We can then get out of the narrow compass of 'culture or class', 'politics of identity or class struggle'. We can also enrich ourselves by reading from Marx's *Eighteenth Brumaire* those lines about how people as historical subjects or agents make their own history – though not under conditions of their own choosing – and how they need names or a specified agency to make this history. This cultural-political identity or named agency is central to their historical subjectivity. The issue of a named representation thus remains central to Marx's historical and political project, irrespective of what Marx has to say about peasants and representation.[4] We don't need to accept his negative view of the peasantry in order to appreciate his interest in specified cultural-political

---

3   Marx and Engels 1970.
4   Marx 1972d.

identities as integral to any political project. The Roman costume drama played out by the petty bourgeoisie in the French revolution is, for Marx, a must for studying the context or content of class politics and the nature of the French revolution. What emerges from all this is that there could be much that is politically significant in a name – in an ascribed or assumed identity. 'A Rose by any other name', therefore, 'would not smell as sweet!'

If we were not to understand identity produced of difference as antithetical to class, we would begin by unsettling our categorical approach to both those concepts, and that of representation as well. After all, we don't always already know what identity and difference mean in their configurations with history, capital and class, in the hands of diverse historical agents who are located in specific historical moments and social relations of power. We need to explore particular instances of identity projects in order to put some different interpretations on these notions than the usual culturalist or marxist ones.

To begin with, we need to get a clear impression of who is supposedly engaging in this type of quest for a named agency, in what many have almost dismissively come to call as 'identity politics'. Who experiences this gesture as positive, as that of creation of a community, and who as an exclusion, and why? What are the different versions of 'identity', their distinctions and slippages in actual historical moments? And, most importantly, why is there such a craving for an identity, and the presence of languages of experience, subjectivity, difference and an insistence upon representation in certain kinds of politics?

It will not take much insight to recognise that people who are most exercised about the issue of identity in terms of political and personal power relations are all people who have been repressed and marginalised. They range from nationalities and religious groups to those who have been constituted as subaltern cultural and political subjects or agents, or minoritised on grounds of sex, sexual orientation and/or various interpretations of the body in the construction of 'race'. People who inhabit these sites, produced through multiple relations of ruling, are at present the most active in this quest for an identity and politics based on it. They are, to borrow a phrase of Eric Wolf, people without history,[5] and thus people without names of their own choosing. The way they are non-named is not the same as how elite European males remain non-named in humanist texts of literature or philosophy, for example.[6] Their

---

5   Wolf 1982.
6   The unnamed centrality of the male (elite) self in the European world of what Aijaz Ahmad calls 'high Humanities' is discussed in many feminist writings. Two interesting examples are Simone de Beauvoir's very early treatment of it in *The Second Sex* and Genevieve Lloyd's *The Man of Reason*.

politics does not centre in issues of agency and representation, or disclose who the real political subject might be, which if it did, would reveal the actual particularism of their knowledge and political projects. Relying on their centrality in actual relations of ruling and thus on their status as the universal representative of all humans, projected in their appropriation of the term 'mankind', they are not aware of being engaged in any form of identity politics through their very humanist universalism. They do not see their deployment of that 'human' identity as a device of control. Similarly, though on a much smaller scale or a lower plane, white bourgeois feminists have not seen their feminist theories and politics as those of identity, even though their own point of departure was their own ascribed and self-perceived difference from white men. They also did not position themselves with regard to non-white women – whom they rendered invisible by both ascribing difference and by practically and theoretically neglecting that very difference. 'Identity politics', they claimed, is what those 'others' do – namely Black, First Nations, Chicano and other 'women of colour', while the word 'feminism' remains a universal world view as their preserve and entirely white identified. In fact to my knowledge the somewhat derogatory term 'identity politics' does not originate among those 'others' who are seen as practising it, but rather in more central and sovereign political spaces.

Whatever the state of their particular political self-consciousness it appears that whole groups of people, suffering from denials, erasures, dis- or misidentification, evince a passion for naming themselves. This naming or identity, for them, extends beyond the individual to a historical and a collective one. In fact writing history becomes their key project. Women's, gay and Black history projects daily proliferate, and titles such as *Hidden in History, Am I that Name?*, and so on, point to conscious attempts at recovery, exploration and naming, or renaming in politically actionable terms. They consider these representative acts based on their subjective content as crucially political, which is why they are phrased in terms of gaining a voice and in languages of silence and speaking, of writing and reading, and of volition and freedom. Even though politically, intellectually and aesthetically their formulations move to diverse directions, articulating themselves to political positions which may be antithetical to each other, they share this common concern for an identity or a named representation. This is how separatist cultural nationalism, liberal pluralism (for example, as multiculturalism), or commoditisation and consumption of ethnicity, may share a common and initial recognition with Black workers movements, anti-racist feminism and national anti-imperialist liberation projects. Political possibilities and subjects or actors are therefore many, but here, in this chapter, I will concentrate on identity, difference and representation as they concern colonial and post-colonial and post-slavery subjects who live in the metropolis of North America. I will attempt to overcome the either/or relationship of subjectivity and class politics outlined earlier, and to situate identity-related issues within a larger historical and political scope.

1   Part 1: Identity, Difference and Violence

'Look, a Negro!' It was an external stimulus that flickered over me as I passed by. I made a tight smile. 'Look, a Negro!' It was true. It amused me. 'Look, a Negro!' The circles were drawing a bit tighter. I made no secret of my own amusement. 'Mama, see the Negro! I am frightened!' Frightened! Frightened! Now they were beginning to be afraid of me. I made up my mind to laugh myself to tears, but laughter had become impossible.

I could no longer laugh, because I already knew that there were legends, stories, history, and above all historicity ... Then, assailed at various points, the corporeal schema crumbles, its place taken by a racial epidermal schema.[7]

I cannot speak of the need for an identity, the loss of one, of being marked out as 'different' or the meaning of that difference, as experienced by non-white people in either the metropole or far corners of the earth, without remembering Franz Fanon, without naming violence as non-naming, misnaming and the need for collective self-naming. Aimé Césaire long ago drew our attention to the violence of Prospero's naming of Caliban and his island, and daily we hear of 'criminal blacks', of 'Pakis', 'Coons', 'Chinks' and 'niggers'. In the scholar's world colonially signified expressions such as the Orient, the traditional society, underdeveloped countries, or stereotypes or essentialised moral and cultural entities such as the native, the Muslim, the Arab, the African, and the Indian, continually assail us. In the realm of social science we hear of genes and IQ, especially of Black genes and IQ, and these 'scholarly findings' are matched by state practices of strip-searching a Jamaican woman in public, or conducting an internal examination of a Guyanese woman in Pearson airport, while handcuffed and tied to a chair.[8] Police violence swarms around the Black community. 1492 to 1994 – the movie reel keeps unwinding ... We can go on about this endless 'now' of colonial, imperialist history, about violence and identity, the makers of difference and the identification tags they create. All this directly

---

7   Fanon 1990.
8   Incidents reported in Toronto newspapers in 1994.

relates to the need and search for a new identity which keeps nothing of Egypt, of bondage about it. This is not a matter of mythologies or poetic metaphors, though that also, but rather of wars in the long moments of history, of contestations for meanings and their daily practices.

There has been throughout colonisation, slavery and after, an identity politics already in place – though not acknowledged as such. Political and cultural critics such as Fanon or Said and other anti-colonial, anti-imperialist writers have drawn our attention to colonial culture or discourse, to cultural imperialism and reified or distorted representation. Criticism and condemnation of European humanism or enlightenment mark a recognition of its hand-in-glove involvement with a capitalism elaborated through colonialism and slavery. What cultural theorists such as Gayatri Chakravorty Spivak have called 'epistemic violence'[9] has its expression and roots in everyday life and state practices. Expressions such as 'immigrant', 'alien', 'foreigner', 'visible minorities', 'illegal' and so on, denoting certain types of lesser or negative identities, are in actuality congealed practices and forms of violence or relations of domination. These identities are 'othered' not only from Europe's 'enlightened self' with its discourse of civilisation and savagery, but fraught with possibilities of self-division, if not active self-hatred or mimicry. This violence and its constructive or representative attempts have become so successful or hegemonic that they have become transparent – holding in place the ruler's claimed superior self, named or identified in myriad ways, and the inadequacy and inferiority of those who are ruled. This is so pervasive and naturalised that when spoken about it takes on a hollow ring or the rhetorical quality of a political rant. And yet this hegemony does exist, not just as forms of consciousness, but as organic and mediatory to structures and institutions, to legalities and moralities, to semiotics of cultural life. And as the names proliferate they provide legitimation, informing relations of ruling or of doing capital, class and imperialism – and thus provide the ground for the experience of being non-white in Europe or North America.[10]

This whole process involves a constant set of constructing difference, as markers for identities of both the rulers and the ruled. It is against this identity politics that the identity/difference projects of the marginalised/colonised people must be understood or judged. The hegemonic identities are so crucial to every aspect of life that they modulate or inflect everything from street culture to electoral politics and arts funding. Produced on the terrain of exclu-

---

9   Spivak 1988b.
10   See Bannerji 1991.

sion and violence, embodying negative forms of difference, as these hegemonic identities or stereotypes are, their reversals or replacements involve angry rejections and exclusivity. These demands for exclusivity on both sides touch base with each other, and this is why conferences such as 'Writing through Race' throw the Canadian arts world into a frenzy. But Fanon did say that both colonisation and decolonisation are violent processes. There is after all no escape from history, from violence, in a society that still recycles 'slave-names' and all that went with them. So a Tamil man lies in a coma from what a neo-Nazi youth understands to be his identity. The Ministry of Immigration and the neo-Nazi youth in their different ways 'Keep Canada White', as vigilantes and California Proposition 187 ('Save Our State') crush Mexican labour's migration there as illegal, while legalising u.s. capital's robbery of Mexico.

2   Part 2: Identity, Difference and History

> Thus the figure of Sarah Bartman [a Hottentot Woman] was reduced to her sexual parts. The audience which had paid to see her buttocks and had fantasised about the uniqueness of her genitalia could, after her death and dissection, examine both ...
>
> The polygenetic argument is the ideological basis for all the dissections of these women. If their sexual parts could be shown to be inherently different, this would be a sufficient sign that the blacks were a separate (and, needless to say, lower) race, as different from the European as the proverbial orangutan.[11]

> Two of the Negro's most prominent characteristics are the utter lack of chastity and complete ignorance of veracity. The Negro's sexual laxity, considered so immoral or even criminal in the white man's civilisation, may have been all but a virtue in the habitat of his origin. There, nature developed in him intense sexual passion to offset his high death rate.[12]

Identity, in the sense of historical and social subjectivity and agency, is produced from and susceptible to divergent political-cultural notions of difference. Depending on how that notion of difference is understood, its meaning and use shade off into different political directions. Resting on the core of a

---

11   Gilman 1985a, pp. 232–5.
12   Collins 1983, pp. 180–1.

recognition of the self and its individuation with regard to others, the concept of identity in the context of capitalist development and international division of labour and power takes on a peculiar convolution in this basic self-other relation. For the colonised or 'raced' subjects the notion of identity involves a loss of pre-colonial, relatively substantive forms of subjectivities through a colonising reductionist gesture towards their historicity, multiplicity and dynamism. They become essentialised, unified or totalised as cultural entities, i.e. they undergo a reification, with specifically ascribed meanings produced through the colonial negative definitions of the other. These imposed stereotypes encode at once the identity of the subject population and those who subjugate and rule them. As such these stereotypes are inversions of colonial capitalist European enlightenment and humanism, of the acclaimed European ideal rational self and their negative moral (Christian) configurations. For example, if the coloniser is typified as a rational man, then 'the native' is inversely the type of an irrational animal. This is why in Shakespeare's *The Tempest* Prospero cannot reach his full definition of a civilised man without the ascription of savagery and monstrosity to Caliban and his mother Sycorax.

These stereotypes or negative identities are, however, clearly in conflict with experiences, histories, and cultures of the colonised or enslaved and currently of minoritised peoples. How Sarah Bartman of Africa was being identified as Hottentot Venus was clearly based on a colonial European perception of her 'difference' from them, and comparatively valued with the European woman's body in its equally ideological and idealised sense. It is also compared at the lowest end of the scale to animals. At no point does this definition or identification of Sarah Bartman have anything to say of her substantive and historical self, or of her experience of herself as a woman or a human in her self or society. This phenomenon of the colonial construction of the subject as 'the native', 'the Negro', 'the African', and so on, has been remarked on by Fanon, Ngugi wa Thiong'o and others. We could provide unending instances of these dominating constructs. Imposed from the outside or above as they are, they are nonetheless forms of social, cultural and political subjectivities which imply a lack of an authentic set of agencies and yet produce real psychological and political consequences.

This distortion or erosion of subjectivity is produced from a divided sense of the self, or even its erasure, which obtains in the colonial, social and cultural space. Fanon and many others theorising ideological or psychological formations of agency in the context of anti-colonial and anti-imperialist struggles speak of the creation of political subjectivities among the colonised which are positively rooted into mental and ideological structures of their own oppression. They come up, therefore, with notions of the comprador bourgeoisie, of 'mimic men', of 'interpreters', or collaborators as central figures to their explorations of political subjectivity, agency and history. This hegemonic dimension remains crucial to the process of revolutionary politics, and is integral to the process of identity formation in a deeper sense than implied by the notion of conscious co-optation or betrayal. It becomes a matter of understanding the construction of difference and the content of this difference, and in being able to think through how these differences are implicated in social organisation and relations of ruling and resistance. The problem before us then ceases to be the overthrow of a simple regime of clearly articulated and unmediated forms of domination – of people, resources and cultures, of bodies and labour – but rather becomes one of a study of construction of identities in a history and social organisation of ruling and their deconstruction and reconstruction in an oppositional context. This is why critics such as Edward Said, David Theo Goldberg, Henry Gates Jr., or Angela Y. Davis do not have a simple answer to the questions of identity and representation. Certainly there is no pure source or essence or origin to return to, nor any escape to a subjectivity which is ahistorical – no matter how brutal or degrading that history may be.

So we might say that both the need for an identity which negates the imposed one, as well as the character of the emerging forms, depend on the specific history of domination and dispossession. The questioning and reconstructing of identities have to take place in the context of this hegemonic history – and involves situating them within their particular social, cultural and ideological relations and forms. It is also important to remember that the task is always more than one of simple negation, and that such tasks are always threatened by the danger of falling into a simple inversion ('their good is our evil' syndrome), and thus continuing with the older schema. It involves avoiding the creation of mythologies rather than a search through and for history. Mythologies are often liable to be created or resorted to in a need to escape oppressive histories past and present. This is particularly important for those who live in the diaspora, and as such are more circumscribed in their political agencies than those who can engage numerically in a critical mass in full-scale anti-colonial or national struggles.

But fortunately history is longer than colonisation, than Anno Domino, and textured with a host of contradictory social formations and forms of consciousness. And also the everyday life of people is larger than the scope of any discourse, and is structured not only with complex social relations but also with multiple and competing discursivities. History, we could say therefore, is as much about ruptures as continuities, and about contradictions as homogeneities. As such it is certain that this stereotypically identified and differentiated 'colonial subject', 'the native', 'the negro', 'the coolie', 'the oriental', and so on –

to mention a few ideological constructs – are never fully produced or articulated as finished and formed identities. As Fanon points out, the colonised person always contains the dual persona of 'the native' and the people. When understood and critiqued in terms of resistance, then, these projected identities reveal what Dorothy Smith calls a 'line of fault' or contradiction running through them.[13] It is from this 'line of fault' of a disjunction, or fissures in the selves and subjects, that possibilities of new identities and of struggle and revolution emerge. This process of construction of identities and resistance begs a return to actual social relations of history, to more than discursively constructed socially similar groups. Communities of resistance, therefore, are or need to be much more than imagined.

3   Part 3: Identities, Difference and Politics of Class

> The chief defect of all previous materialism – that of Feuerbach included – is that things [Gegenstand], reality, sensuousness are conceived only in the form of the object, or of contemplation, but not as human sensuous activity, practice, not subjectively. Hence it happened that the active side, in contradistinction to materialism, was set forth by idealism – but only abstractly, since, of course, idealism does not know real, sensuous activity as such.[14]

It is curious how many times in history we have come to face an utterly false dichotomy, a superficial view of the situation in our politics. As Marx pointed out – it is absurd to choose between consciousness and the world, subjectivity and social organisation, personal or collective will and historical or structural determination. It is equally absurd then to see identity and difference as historical forms of consciousness unconnected to class formation, development of capital and class politics. The mutually formative nature of identity, difference and class becomes apparent if we begin by taking a practical approach to this issue, or their relation of 'intersection'. If 'difference' implies more than classificatory diversity, and encodes social and moral-cultural relations and forms of ruling, and establishes identities by measuring the distance between the ruler and the ruled, all the while constructing knowledge through power – then let us try to imagine 'class' or class politics without these forms and content. This

---

13   Smith 1987.
14   Marx 1972d, p. 143.

would amount to understanding class solely as an abstraction, without the con-stricting particularities of differences of gender and 'race'. One could also fall into the danger of treating it as a cultural phenomenon, as an essential form of identity separate from gender and 'race'. This is done by Stanley Aronow-itz in *The Politics of Identity*, when he treats class, 'race' and gender as three culturally significant categories and puts them in some kind of relation to one another.[15]

In the former case, class as an abstraction would cease to refer to the social, being gutted of its practical, everyday relations and content of consciousness. In the latter case, it would become a cultural essence that exists independently, though in an additive relation to other cultural essentialities. But a concrete organisation of class is impossible minus historical, cultural, sexual and polit-ical relations. Without these social mediations, formative moments, or con-verging determinations, the concrete organisation of class as a historical and social form would not be possible. Marx points this out in *Grundrisse* when he speaks of the concrete as the convergence of many determinations. Not even the crudest form of economic reductionism would be possible without these social relations and cultural forms, since economies exist as conscious moments and practical organisation of societies.

Let us, for example, look at the process of actual exploitation and accumula-tion of surplus value. If it is to be seen as a state of constant manipulation and realisation process of concrete labour in actual labour time – within a given cost-production system and a labour market – then we cannot dispense with existing social and sexual division of labour and their moral (cultural) valu-ation. Difference is thus encapsulated not only within production/reproduc-tion dialectic of capital, in its labour process and organisation, but also in the way labour is valued and remunerated. There is a direct connection between lower value of the labour of women in general all over the world, and of non-white women in particular, and the profit margin. Gender and 'race' in the post-Fordist era of capital, as Swasti Mitter shows in her book *Common Fate, Common Bond* on women's international division of labour,[16] are crucial to the workings, movements and profit levels of multinational corporations.

We should also note that the type of difference encoded by 'race' adds a pecu-liar twist to gender. In societies such as ours in Canada not only is all labour gendered and 'ghettoised', as Pat and Hugh Armstrong state in their book *The Double Ghetto*,[17] but all forms of gendered labour are 'raced'. This even becomes

---

15   See the introduction and first chapter of Aronowitz 1992.
16   Mitter 1986.
17   Armstrong 1978.

a cultural phenomenon, as stated for example, in D.T. Goldberg's *Racist Culture*,[18] and includes both whites and non-whites. 'Race' in that sense, or difference, is a totalising identification or difference. If we go further, we could say that European capitalism has been 'raced' right through its history. If we look at Marx's chapter on 'the genesis of Capital' (*Capital*, vol. 1) we can see the substantive, historical importance of force, crude conquest, pillage and plunder in capital's stage of primitive accumulation. Subsequently capital develops more mediated aspects of force or violence in the notion of 'race' as deployed in the procurement of unfree – slave or indentured – labour, and the organisation and valuation of this and eventually of wage labour. Historians such as Eric Williams or Herbert Gutman, along with political economists such as Walter Rodney, have shown us the integrity of 'race', class and capital. Marx himself in *Capital* and elsewhere has pointed out the roles played by state-mediated, morally and legally regulated forms of force in exploitation. This is evident from religious debates on lack of soul in Black and Indigenous peoples to scientific debates on mono- and polygenesis, as well as laws based on 'race' in all colonies. The enlightenment dualism of body and mind, civilisation and savagery, latterly the modern and the primitive, have geographies, populations, forms and values of labour commensurate with them. Black labour/white labour are not only opposed social and moral values, they are also dialectically constitutive value of capital as we have historically known it. Crudely speaking, once they could enslave Black labour, making money also in the process of exchange in direct commoditisation, today they can pay less for it. Once they colonised Mexico with no compunction, today they can have NAFTA with a seeming consensus process. Post-colonial, imperialist relations ensure the necessary economic and politico-military relations for this while hegemonic common sense gives it a concrete form and legitimacy. Meanwhile, in the metropolitan countries the white working class resents the non-white working class, while capital benefits as a whole from this manipulation. Labour histories of Canada, a white settler colony struggling to become a liberal democracy, testify to the truth outlined here. Forms of property and labour enshrined in Canada, from the first land grabbing and occupation to now, have been wholly organised by and inscribed with the difference of 'race' and ethnicity. There is no 'class' here without 'race'.

If identity projects which I am speaking about are related to oppressions organised on the basis of 'race' and gender, then the integration of the two calls for a special comment. We have a peculiar situation here, where gender

---

18   Goldberg 1993.

difference as integral to the valuation of women's labour comes out in power-ful asymmetrical complexities when 'raced'. If mental and manual division of labour entail gender distinction, and they in turn reflect the enlightenment reason vs. nature dichotomy, then 'racing' of peoples amounts to identifying whole populations with mainly the body or animality. This illuminates the identification of the Black woman with an intensified naturality or animality. In *Women, Race and Class*, Angela Davis discusses the representation or 'race'-ascribed identity of the Afro-American woman, and the peculiar character of the description of her womanhood and her labour. According to Davis, Black women, being treated by slave masters as equally productive workers as men on the ground of their 'race' and slave status, were 'sexed' rather than gendered. Thus they fell outside of the purview of 'gender' in the sense of the Southern slave owner's ideology of the feminine or notions of chivalry and protection. Instead, they worked equal number of hours with men, were put in stocks, flogged during pregnancy, and were seen and treated as 'breeders' rather than mothers, and as labour and commodities rather than as members of families.[19]

Davis' presentation of gender, 'race' and class makes it impossible to think of an identity for Afro-American women which does not integrate the three, and does not relate to history – the history of slavery. This integration would be necessary for all social groups of women in North America, both Black and white. Black people's struggles in North America cannot then be without an assertion or a construction of an identity (or a named subjectivity) denoting a historical demand for self-determination. If class as an analytical and political concept is not going to be used as merely a tool of abstraction or an ideolo-gical trick to perform erasure of the social and the historical, then it cannot be understood independently of concrete social relations which specify the con-cretising forms of difference.

4   Conclusion

> The philosophers have only *interpreted* the world, in various ways; the point, however, is to *change* it.[20]

At the end I want to return to various forms of politics which operate with and within the notion of identity at a level of collectively political intelligibility,

19   Davis 1983.
20   Marx and Engels 1970, 11th Thesis on Feuerbach (author's emphasis).

because the concept after all posits sameness along with or as a factor of difference. This also implies not only a semiotic dimension but one of desire, of volition and creativity, in the context of history and memory, and of effectiveness in power relations. It can signal to not only who one is historically and at present, but at its best it can speak to who one can become – it can speak of agencies and political possibilities. I say possibilities and not any predetermined politics. It is here that it becomes evident that there are radically different ways of politicising a project which may have an originary compulsion in common with other politics.

Since political subjectivities are articulated within a given political and ideological environment, and self-identities are fraught with contradictory possibilities, as mentioned earlier, then there is no guarantee that there is only one form of politics of identity which will emerge, or that it will avoid the formulation of 'identity and community versus structures and class'. Victims and subjects of capital do not automatically become socialists. Misery does not automatically produce communism, and desire for change born of suffering does not spontaneously know 'what is to be done?' to end oppression. The class- or culture-reductionist stance is as prevalent among those who have been oppressed as those who do not fall within that category. Here we might speak of cultural reductionism of those 'identity politicians' who, ignoring questions of class and capital, have either ended up with separatist cultural nationalism or multiculturalism. In this they have also dehistoricised and decontextualised, de-validated their own project of deconstruction and reconstruction. Evading contradictions in their own lives and world, which have old and ramified roots and implications, especially obscuring questions of class and gender, they have encouraged political projects which are as riddled with inscriptions of power, from which they wish to escape.

Creating mythological histories and imagining communities on the ground of religion, for example, or 'traditional values', they have only secured avenues of class formation and mobility among themselves. Consequences of this for women, and of male/female relations in these imagined communities, in the name of culture, tradition and religion, have been the reinforcement of patriarchy and class. Overall political consequences have not fared better, and these culturalist interpretations have bonded at best with liberal democracy or at worst with forms of cultural and social fascism. The main problem here is not that this type of identity-based politics relies on a recovery of history, culture and experience and excludes whites or challenges them on cultural appropriation. Nor is it wrong in speaking in local or particular rather than universal, all-inclusive terms, as for example does liberal democracy in propounding equality in utterly formal terms. The problem lies in the fact that this limits the nature of the struggle that non-white people themselves engage in, which stays within the terms of already existing politics. The danger is either of a compromise and an upward mobility, or of a separatist nationalism of culture, while instrumentalising culture to a stance of acceptance of property and propriety relations of capital and class. This is hardly what Ngugi has called 'decolonising the mind' or Fanon's 'true decolonisation'.

This cultural reductionism or a relativist multiculturalism is not only to be found among those who have been labelled as practitioners of 'identity politics', those who wave banners of experience and cultural membership as a precondition for speaking. If the political implications of post-modernist/post-structuralist forms of thought were to be fully spelled out, we would get the same cultural reductionism, ahistorical imaging of communities or liberal individualism.[21] Aijaz Ahmad's introduction in *In Theory* puts forward this fact forcefully,[22] which is also supported by the simple, though not simplistic, view of Christopher Norris' *The Truth About Postmodernism*.[23]

So here we are as marxists faced with the unhappy options of an agent or subjectless marxist structuralism, always already interpellated by capital and ideology, or a triumph of the will of the desiring, ever-changing subject, who is not placed in social relations and history. Or we might even have the 'radical' option of measuring our discursive prisons inch by inch, but no social ground or theorising to elaborate a historical subjectivity in all its social relations of contradiction. This is the dualism of the aesthetic and the economic. Once we saw colonisation as destruction of economies and drain of wealth, now we see its crimes as being those of robberies of representation. But each position leaves something wanting. How do we get out of this stance of cultural capital versus economic capital, or in other words, discourse or forms of consciousness versus political economy?

Though I have no definite answer to this question, interpreting identity as I have done, by integrating difference and class with it, historicising it, helps to a large extent. One has to cast the net wide, and saturate the notion of being with becoming – 'political possibilities' being the key theme. Having an open-ended notion of social-self-definition helps, over one which is self-enclosed, static and essentialised. It helps to situate the notion of identity into history, rather than using it as a conjuring stick for creating mythologies. Identities can-

---

21   See the introduction to my *Returning the Gaze: Essays on Racism, Feminism and Politics*,
      where the problematic political possibilities of 'identity politics' and its articulation with
      multiculturalism are spelled out in more detail.
22   Ahmad 1992.
23   Norris 1993.

not be any more of the past, the very history along whose paths we look back for our origins dictates the logic of being contemporary to our own historically situated present. Identities need to be signs and signals of the future – they must speak to individuals as collectivities of resistance, summoning and inter-pellating them in their names of resistance, beyond the 'house of bondage'. As signs they should hold clues to what was and what will be. Sojourner moving at free will is a condition and a sign against the prison of slavery, of dynamism as opposed to fixity; and Truth as a denial of distortion, of silence and lies, is con-nected to this dynamism, since unfreedom provides the conditions of untruth.

A child that grows up hating or being ashamed of her own looks, body, lan-guage and people can be traumatised and self-destructive. This situation has the possibility of creating angry, submissive and disempowered people because they lack the possibilities of making their own history. This is what racism or sexist/heterosexist racism can theoretically produce. Any class politics which denies this and cannot see itself in this light betrays itself. Socialism then ceases to be a social politics. In this light, for reasons of personal empower-ment, cultural projects with a political nuance – such as Black History month, for example, or heritage language training – are precious to us. If these simple assertions or acts of representation threaten white people it is their own task to think through why they feel so. Their fury at not being central to every project – a furious feeling of exclusion when they never noticed the absence of others in their world unless forced by others to notice it – is also their own political business. Quick charges of 'reverse racism' and sneering about 'political cor-rectness' regarding minimum, forced concessions such as multiculturalism or Human Rights – are not wounds in which we have to apply a salve. These angers and complaints come from being dislodged from centrality – from white fem-inists, for example, at being shaken in their claims of victimisation, or from a collective guilt and anger of those resting on white privilege who resent having to feel guilty.[24]

I have, then, no problem about many aspects of what is called 'identity polit-ics' so quickly, so dismissively, as long as the notion of identity does not become another way of erasing history and its constructive social relations. The notion of 'identity' also, similar to many other useful notions, can become an ideolo-gical tool – and perform the same function that ideology has to, namely, make the connections invisible. The other danger in an overreliance on this power-ful concept is that it can become merely a mental phenomenon and highly

---

24 On the theme of 'whiteness', its social and ideological construction, see Frankenberg 1993, and Spelman 1988.

individualistic when considered only culturally. This approach lends itself to a very limited notion of experience – where distinctions are obliterated between immediate responses, and unconsidered feeling impacts politicised interpretive efforts of agents who are conscious of an event's social and historical situation and meaning and who link forms of consciousness with the economy, the state and history. It is this linking or reflexivity which can create actionable names for a people which are capable of being transformed into a political-cultural identity.

CHAPTER 19

Truant in Time

London. Huge streets. Buildings in a gigantic outline of constructed mountains, foothills and passes. Endless streams of travellers. Labyrinths unfold under my feet. I recognise that the English are a nation of miners as I move, stage by stage, walking, running, stumbling, hurtling down passages, escalators which work or don't, towards a destination that steadily diminishes in the face of my extensive journey. I am nameless. This anonymity yet the endless oneness with an outpouring humanity, with stranded islands of green in their midst, are both a relief and a dread, a being and a disappearance. *How small can an 'I', a consciousness be?* I ask myself, shrinking like a pupil in a strong sun, gripped by a dread.

I hold myself like a child by the hand, remember linguistics, cultural literacy, the ways I have been created by a long habitation in the West. Walking in the evening through a cobalt blue into which the street is sinking, there is an ache inside me. The blue jar of this evening holds everything and nothing – namely it holds me, temporarily anonymous, yet concretely and historically within space and time. It is the same me who came to this 'other' world a long time ago, came with an apparatus for making sense which was adequate to the task. But the task changed with choices made in time, and knowledge increased and changed as well. The difference between what I found myself in and what I grew up with was immeasurable. All my familiarity with European art and culture had not prepared me for the everyday life and interactions that I encountered. For one thing, I did not know the internal workings, the constructions and relations between whiteness and blackness. I did not know that colonisation went way beyond the Indian Independence of 1947. While substantive lives went on in these national territories, here in Canada, the u.s., England and Europe, I was recolonised. And not just I, but all of those others who had gathered in these metropolitan centres of the West. Then began a contestation, of making and being made over. I was myself and myself refracted in unrecognisable pieces.

1   Being and Becoming

Walking through certain neighbourhoods in London I was surprised by the number of women and girls wearing head coverings of some sort. They are mostly Bengalis, I am told, and also that some years ago they would not have done this either here or in Bangladesh. But this is not unique to Bengalis. Black people are Africanising, Hindus have found their Hinduness, Sikhs the essence of Sikhism ... All relegate patriarchal injunctions of obedience upon women, and rely upon cultural insignias to indicate their difference. A piece of cloth draped around the head or the body, hairdos, certain colours and designs – trivia assembled into constellations of meaning, revealing difference. They impose their moral regulations, attempt an immutable conduct in a world governed by relativism and consumption. Their rigidity serves only to indicate this basic fragility. These people who are so insistently ethnic, fundamentally religious or traditional are not just of the older generation – the expected conservatives harking back to tradition. They are young, and not necessarily or consistently religious. The traditions are not of a whole cloth, they are invented from bits and pieces, from parental cultural baggage now tarnished by the salt water of voyages, colours fading in the grey drizzles or the cold winds of the West. They come from music listened to on cassettes, and from Bombay films, which have gained among the expatriate youth an iconic dimension uncluttered by mutations created by the realities of life in India. Not much comes from reading, since written material lacks the perfect emptiness and malleability of the visual image or of echoed sound. This India of the mind says little about that country as an historical reality, but reveals much about us who live in the West. Reorganising Orientalist constructions and expectations, these symbols of our Indian identity speak instead to our peculiar kind of 'Englishness', 'Canadianness' and so on. They are variants of that multicultural invention called an 'ethnic community', trapped in a lyrical catchall word, 'the diaspora'.

But why do we do this? Why has a huge anguish currently seized these inhabitants of the West, who are somehow connected to ex-colonies, to histories of slavery and conquest, forcing them to proclaim their identities and claims of authenticity? It was not always so. Peoples have migrated far in remote history. Studies reveal conquering armies, nomadic journeys and new settlements. New languages such as Urdu have arisen, attires and jewelleries, music and poetry, and sensibilities have extended and insinuated themselves with the suppleness of vines in places where they did not originate. But the slow, rather organic nature of that development is different from that of relatively recent history. It is since colonisation, and now recolonisation, under a siege of cultural imperialism and racism, that we find an intense upsurge of cultural politics. This politics of being, essentialising or fixing who we are, is in actuality often an inversion or continuation of ascribed colonial identities, though stated as 'difference'. The stereotypical contents of Africanness or Indianness, for example, are in the end colonial constructs, harbouring the coloniser's gaze. We look at ourselves with his eyes and find ourselves both adorned and wanting.

Why do we want to be 'authentic' so badly? What makes us think that an existence at any given moment is anything but authentic? Being always has a content, a form, a room and a reason in history, in daily life and in desire. Yet this simple truth is so often overridden by pervasive racism organising our world, a racism with constructive relations with patriarchy and class oppression. Our discomfort is with why we came at all, and why in this way – the 'why' referring to colonisation, pulled along by the long chains of imperialism. It is not a 'free choice', even when we are not refugees. This is a dance of power, if not always a dance of death. We enter preorganised terrains, the same terms hold here as in trade and financial relations between Western capitalism and the Third World.

Racism casts a long shadow over our lives. The imaginary geographies of colonialism swamp us in this new space. Inconsistent identities, reversible but all negative, are levelled at us. Alternately or simultaneously we are savage/over refined, primitive/decadent, squalid/exotic, ascetic/animalistic, barbarians and traditional. It is not simply a video game played out on a TV screen; everything from the schooling of children to UN legitimation of invasions of the Third World depends on these constructions. We are covered with a new thin film of discursive skin, physiognomies and gestures are typified, costumes fabricated. We resist this process and are dubbed aliens, immigrants, foreigners. And so we change, both in anger and by seduction. Our consciousness is, after all, in and of our history. But anger, anguish and a rush of lostness is overpowering when we realise that our migrations did not take us where they should have, that our refuges have betrayed us.

2   Home, Heart and History

Then begins our antiquarian, nostalgic search for a 'home', for belonging in the most ideal sense, as the child belongs oceanically in the body of the mother. We invent a 'home', our paradise lost, our story of the Fall. We begin to wear, display, eat 'home'. 'Home' becomes a magic installation, a multimedia production, and we, both creators and creatures of that production, run through a hall of mirrors projecting and losing a fatuous authenticity, proclaiming an ascribed difference. This difference does not rest on what we *are* socially, culturally or visually, but rather on what we *are not*, namely, not white. Its criterion of identification, whiteness, with its package of signifiers, is impossible for us to attain. Thus we re-enter colonisation. The issue then is not that we are 'different', but that we hold a kind of 'difference' which signals to 'homelands' or multicultural ethnic reservations. It is then that a mythical 'home' arises in the ghettos of Brick Lane or Harlem. 'Home' becomes a symbolically constructed fort from which we wage wars, while retreating within it in a deepening isolation. This is true of even those who want to join the ranks of the masters, who wish to leap over the chasm of bodies interpreted through history. But prevented by social ontology and appearance, they become vendors of identity, alienation and authenticity. A new art comes into life, a new skin trade, fundamentally different from one aimed at self-knowledge and self-expression. The very notion of identity is rendered stereotypical, thus static and useless. This art or cultural production never grapples or comes to terms with the fundamental issues of displacement that migration creates, rendering adults into groping children, backs bending under the extra burden of racism. It never seeks out the real meaning of a remembered 'home', which serves in exile as a painted back-drop without perspective, against which our lives are lived – continuing as fine filaments of nuance. On the contrary, the ethnic art that so desperately parades identities often ends up purveying exotic otherness, some with more skill than others, but all in a kind of second-hand, magic realism.

But beyond metaphors and cultural mythologies, we are here, where we live. We live in a shared social organisation, in situations of unemployment, taxation and social welfare. The second generation grows up on cultural languages which are not foreign to them, though they are still designated as foreigners. Forms of sexuality, private and public conduct are real to them in ways that may be distant or displaced for their parents. This life is as real as any other and there is not much point in saying one does not belong. The problem lies in thinking that belonging only means a happy positivity. This, strangely, after tasting the distances and pains enclosed within the four walls of the family!

Belonging is often long and painful, but it is belonging nonetheless. How else can it be anything but painful in a society that is built on one's subordination? The vivid sense we have of being outsider-insiders is clearly a sign of belonging. Our existence, like that of others, does not need to be validated like a stamped passport issued by a national authority. Existential and cultural possibilities lying within our social being are numerous. The emigre condition is in no way better or worse than living at 'home' within nation states. Living is simply what it is. It is here and now, protean, elusive and dynamic. It spills over fixed definitions and forms. In this journey we continue and change, are alone and accompanied; taking ourselves by the hand we turn corners, always to become and to be.

PART 4

Ideology, Nationalism, Gender and Politics

∴

Making India Hindu and Male: Cultural Nationalism and the Emergence of the Ethnic Citizen in Contemporary India

A social group can, and indeed must, already exercise 'leadership' before winning governmental power (this indeed is one of the principal conditions for the winning of such power); it subsequently becomes dominant when it exercises power, but even if it holds it firmly in its grasp, it must continue to lead as well.[1]

∵

1   Introduction[2]

The last decades of the twentieth century have been marked with great political turmoil and turnarounds. I speak of the imperialist assaults against and the disarray of communism and socialism, and think of Nicaragua, Mozambique or Cuba. We are faced with the death of all national liberation projects, or even of liberal democracy, to be replaced, or already replaced, by petty bourgeois ethnic-religious nationalisms driven by neo-liberal economic goals and related imperialist agendas of globalisation spearheaded by the u.s. and multinational corporations.

I want to clarify at the outset the distinction I make here between different types of nationalisms, between what I call 'national liberation' and liberal democratic and ethnic/religious nationalisms. My distinction primarily revolves around property and class relations and related proprietorial or moral-cultural differences, including that of gender, all involving social power and inequality. Anti-colonial and anti-imperialist national liberation movements aim at eliminating these socio-economic inequalities of property relations and their mediatory moral constructions and regulations. They also bring culture

---

1 Gramsci 1971, p. 59.
2 This paper grew out of the annual lecture in Political Science, University of Alberta, Edmonton, November 2000.

into the political arena, as do the other nationalisms, but national liberation movements do so by creating possibilities for the politicising of culture in terms of the reversal of unequal property relations, and so moving towards the creation of an egalitarian society. Petty bourgeois or even bourgeois nationalisms, on the other hand, do not address property, class, gender and cultural relations of inequality in any substantial way. Instead, they stand for private property at all levels and accept class, gender and other inequalities in varying degrees and use culture to either displace or subsume differences resulting from social power relations. They create national ideologies which underpin the constitution of the state and deflect attention from actual social and cultural relations of power and their histories and organisation. Thus, there are differences between nationalisms that aspire to liberal democracy and ethnic-nationalist demographic states.[3]

This difference primarily consists in their general polity and state forms. These may be illiberal and authoritarian, or democratic. Liberal/bourgeois democratic nationalism rests on a doctrine of individual political rights enshrined in a constitution for limitedly addressing the wrongs of a society where inequality is otherwise normalised. The notions of a rights-bearing individual citizen, along with those of universal citizenship, are invested with formal legal equality, irrespective of the citizen's class, gender, caste, 'race', religion and ethnic community. But nationalism and a nation state can also lack these political and legal means of redress, substituting, therefore, the rights-bearing citizen-individual persona with a culturally articulated and authoritarian collective one. This illiberal polity is constituted by a hierarchical, subordinating scale of ethnic racialised communities or collectivities, suspending the limited political provisions which exist in liberal democracies. Often religion, such as in Israel or Saudi Arabia, or belonging to cultural/ethnic communities and tribes, as in some African countries, including former South Africa, serve as ground for this type of ethnic-national imaginary and citizenship, but, as with the emergence of Bangladesh and Sri Lanka, language and other notions of tradition can serve as well.

A few of these ethnic/cultural nationalisms have recently succeeded in attaining state power, often by dismantling liberal democratic states. And others, such as Israel, have succeeded in colonial occupations. Though sanctified by appeals to origin, tradition and god, such nationalisms or states are by no means 'traditional' in the sense of being derived from feudal, ancient or monarchic ones. They are modern capitalist states, mostly formerly colonial and

---

3   See Ahmad 1992, 1996 and Bannerji et al. 2001b.

part of the nexus of imperialism. They have combined the unfreedom of a class society with that of the 'free market', a neo-liberal stance with an authoritarian form of governing and ideologies which are often connected with institutional religions and their ancillary cultural practices. Some, such as the Bharatiya Janata Party (BJP, Indian People's Party), have manipulated the dual voices of political democracy and of a civil society scarred with Hindu communalism,[4] and have used organised authoritarianism to achieve their anti-democratic end. Such political projects are strategically and ideologically sophisticated and simultaneously speak of participation and exclusion, of consent and force, of faith in democratic laws which are undercut by carefully orchestrated civil society violence. The national imaginary and a polity thus constructed elaborate cultural-political ideologies which necessarily invent an enemy – the Jew for the Nazis, the Arab for the Zionists, the Muslim for the Hindu right, and the secular person for religious supremacists or fundamentalists. Principles for the creation of a national community and animosity towards such enemy 'others' are located in a univocal, monopolitical interpretation of religion, culture, tradition and community, and are articulated to the morality and identity of a constructed, unified and collective subject. For this purpose, ethnic nationalists rewrite or invent histories, substituting history and actual social relations with 'traditions' and scriptural injunctions which emphasise only certain texts and their interpretations. They proliferate myths of blood, belonging and prior occupation of land. There is always, in these totalitarian political projects, appeals to antiquity, to the past, in a retrievalist fashion, and to myths of origin, for the purpose of mediation and legitimation.[5] This ideological articulation justifies expulsions of peoples, their displacements, armed occupations, pogroms, concentration camps and state terrorism. Notions of organicity, of community, of holy histories, ancient genealogies and god's promises to his chosen people are all deployed to these ends. There are also myths propagating the right of return, and all of these ideological and justifying political positions are infused with ideas of the racial-cultural superiority of the dominant group. Discourses are brought into play which smuggle in selected and invented tra-

---

4   The notion of communalism is used in India to indicate religious chauvinism, a fundamentalist religious community active in social and political relations of power. It has none of the positive connotations that might be expected by Western readers who have become used to seeing the term 'community' and its cognates in highly valorised terms. In Indian usage a rigid form of group identity is considered as a narrow sense of belonging, contra-universal.

5   On the role of 'invention' and legitimation in nationalist struggles, see Hobsbawm and Ranger 1984. The view of nationalism and cultural politics outlined here negates the possibility of any originary, authentic cultural presence in national/political imaginary. It shows how the past is invoked to legitimise present-day politics or is outright 'invented' as 'tradition'.

ditions with moral and religious – and therefore binding – injunctions for the group members. Thus, culture takes on the quality of the sacred. The ethnicities which are in power and those which are subordinated are by no means 'natural cultural communities', but rather they have been subjected to ideological constellations of 'found' and reworked cultural elements existing within the competing hegemonies of the civil society.

Let us now attend to the situation in India in the light of this perspective. Here, for the last two decades in particular, there has been a significant increase in right-wing Hindu movements. A Hindu supremacist political tendency dating back to the colonial period has formed a coalition comprised of the Bharatiya Janata Party (BJP) and its right-wing allies and has risen to the highest level of state power through various stages of socio-cultural and electoral manipulations. The BJP's third foray as the central government of India just ended in May of 2004. What is special about the BJP is its relatively new history as a political party and its sudden and rapid upsurge. This success cannot be explained without reference to its long historical roots or base in civil society cultural organisations, such as the *Rashtriya Swayam Sevak Sangha* (RSS). Founded in 1925 by K.B. Hedgewar and other Hindu cultural militants, the RSS has encoded in its name the notions of 'voluntarism' and social work, as the name means 'national volunteers organisation'. Its cultural reformational work from that time on has been dedicated to creating an essentialised version of Hinduism – *hindutva* ('Hinduness') – for inventing or constructing an authentically 'Hindu' culture and identity. Its present expression as a political party, the BJP, provides evidence of its success in operationalising the moral imperatives, cultural inventions and mandates of this *hindutva* with a neo-liberal agenda. This is not dissimilar to attempts at Islamicist capitalism as conducted in Iran or Pakistan. Speaking in the discourse of a culture and tradition in which the notion of the 'national' is equal to 'Hindu', articulated to jargons of authenticity, foreignness and 'sons of the soil' criteria of citizenship, the BJP and its base community of the Hindu right hope to hegemonise the entire Indian political terrain. Its religious-cultural drives are spearheaded by the political machinery of the provincial governments where the BJP is in power and fronted by the civil society or non-governmental organisations and decentred agents of the RSS and *hindutva*. The primary agenda is to ethnicise the polity as a whole while setting terms of reference for Hindu political domination, thus shifting previous discourses of political subjectivity and agency based on universal citizenship, class, caste, patriarchy and region. Within this purview, projects of social justice are unutterable and discredited while putting in place collectivities of animosities and exclusion based primarily on religion. Furthermore, the BJP and the Hindu right have arrogated unto themselves the mantle of anti-colonialism and nationalism, seeking to obscure in the process their pro-colonial policy of co-existence with British rule during the long independence struggle.[6]

The BJP and the Hindu right's rapid rise to state power in India after a period of relative passivity begs questions and theorisation. We need to rethink the concepts of citizenship, subjectivity, agency and democracy, the politics of rights and class and the relationship between formal politics and the supposedly non-political spaces and practices of society. Thus, we need to think about civil society and its relationship to the state, class and governance. To do this we should revisit Marx and Gramsci, attending to their use of the idea of the civil society, their critiques of ideology and cultural common sense, their thoughts on class consciousness and class struggle and to their understanding regarding the roles that religion or culture play in social transformation. In short, we need to explore the complex project of hegemony. We have to situate our discussion on the politics of ethnic nationalism and find out how national imaginaries, political subjectivities and agencies emerge, and how the new ones dislodge the old. This challenges the claim of primordiality, spontaneity and naturalness of ethnicist imaginaries and ideologies and shows how any political subjectivity or agency is not always already there, but needs to be fashioned through organisation for politicising culture.

2   Marx, Gramsci and the Civil Society: Politicising Culture

Marx introduced the notion of civil society into the consideration of politics and historical transformation both for practice and theorisation. Expanding the political beyond its limited sphere into the social world of economic and other social relations of everyday life, he found the resolution of his search for the 'real' chains of humanity.[7] In Marx, the civil society is an inflected use of Hegel's, for whom it signified a qualitative and categorical distance from the state and politics. Unlike Hegel, Marx did not accept the commonplace of bourgeois thought which saw society as intrinsically, ontologically, divided into the public and the private. Hegel's identification of politics with the public sphere left the civil society as an unregulated sphere of 'natural' activities of living, of production, reproduction, of common sense and daily culture. In this Hegelian mode, civil society was the netherworld of women, workers and work, of popular beliefs, and it had no historical role – in fact, it lay out-

---

6   See Noorani 2000, pp. 42–7.
7   Marx and Engels 1970, p. 36.

side of what he would call the historical domain. The realm of the political, of history-making, through which the Idea looked for its self-realisation, was in that of thought.[8] It is Marx who valorised the realm of the everyday, of civil society, and brought it right within the centre of politics. The civil society came to be the 'reality' from which he drew his arsenal for change, and civil society itself had to be changed for social revolutions to occur. For Marx, a whole ensemble of social relations, division of labour beyond the point of production, along with forms of consciousness, both practical and ideological, entered into political discourse and conscious organisation of politics. The state rose out of this ensemble and mediated, reflected and maintained the organisation of social relations coded as 'class'. The state was only phenomenally 'transcendental', its character wholly social, implying also cultural. It is this overall space that Marx meant when he spoke of civil society as being the theatre of history.

This question of making of history, the heart of the *Manifesto of the Communist Party*[9] and the first part of *The German Ideology*[10] including his 'Theses on Feuerbach', to name only a few texts, clearly shows how important conscious human agency and critical and resisting subjectivity were for him. This clearly involved consciousness, its cultural manifestations, intrinsically in the project of what Gramsci was to speak of as 'hegemony'. Thus, any political effort was also a 'cultural' effort. The role played by communists in that sense is one of interpreters and interpellators of culture, in which diverse worldviews, social understandings, were tested in the crucible of the practice of organising. The 'proletarian consciousness' as proposed by Marx cannot simply amount to talk about reification and false consciousness. His complex understanding of culture, in providing obstacles and inspirations for revolutionary transformation, is signalled in his understanding of religion, for example, both as 'the opium' of the people but also as an expression of their suffering, their 'sigh'. Thus, religion encoded for him a deeply felt experience of the social and an immediate way of acting on it. The great importance of ideology, an instance of cultivated consciousness, in producing 'ruling ideas for the ruling class' which occlude and erase history and social relations of power indicates Marx's concern with cul-

---

8   In his 'Introduction' to Marx and Engels' *German Ideology*, C.J. Arthur says of Hegel's use of the concept of civil society the following: 'In Hegel's philosophy civil society has a prominent role as that sphere in which man is constituted as a separate individual. His interests are civil and economic, not political. He does not feel himself a participant in public affairs, but views the state as an external necessity ...' (1970, p. 5).

9   Marx and Engels 1972a.

10   Marx and Engels 1970.

ture and consciousness.[11] His texts *The Civil War in France*[12] and *The Eighteenth Brumaire of Louis Bonaparte*[13] work out culture's role in shaping politics, and its implication in the relationship between state and civil society.

For Marx, political issues cannot be isolated or worked upon outside of the formative ground of the civil society. His comments on bourgeois democracy and its difference from social democracy rest entirely on how state formation accommodates the civil society, to what extent its oppressive relations are eliminated or maintained. The state, for Marx, is not even a relatively autonomous institution, though it has its specific administrative and ruling apparatus which functions differently from the way everyday life is organised and lived. Nonetheless, the state and civil society are mutually formative. Thus, the technology of democracy could not be properly understood without an exploration of civil society existence, including culture. Presumably then, political projects and processes could not be independent of both acting and reshaping that seemingly non-political realm of everyday life.

Marx's insights can be further elaborated from Antonio Gramsci's prison writings, which take into account both the Bolshevik revolution and the rise of fascism in Europe. Incarcerated in Mussolini's prison as the leader of the Italian Communist Party, Gramsci asked questions pertaining to what was *not* done, so that the Italian experiment with class struggle produced fascism rather than a communist revolution. His attention also was drawn to the separation of the political from civil society, onto the realm of everyday life and culture. It is in exploring cultural common sense, relating it to structural issues and political modalities – the state – that Gramsci unravelled the great puzzle of hegemony.

The point of departure for all of the texts in *Selections from the Prison Notebooks*[14] is the topic of hegemony. They emphasise the absolute importance of hegemony and consider how this can be won or lost. Whatever the political position of any group, its success lays in becoming hegemonic. It is important to note that Gramsci's understanding of civil society does not quite follow that of Marx. He leaves the economy somewhat out of his definition, and as such the structural notion of class provides the container and the context of civil society. But the political forms an intrinsic dimension of it, as do all instituted and otherwise cultural norms and forms. In his essay 'Intellectuals', civil society moves from the realm of the economic 'base' to that of 'superstructure'. As he sees it, the immediate theoretical task of the intellectual is 'to fix *two* major *super-*

---

11   Marx and Engels 1970.
12   Marx 1972d.
13   Marx 1972c.
14   Gramsci 1971.

structural "levels", the one that can be called "civil society", that is the ensemble of organisms commonly called "private", and that of "political society" or "the State".[15] But he also says:

> [T]he distinction between [civil society and political society] is not an 'organic' but a 'methodological' one. Thus it is asserted that economic activity belongs to civil society, and that the state must not intervene to regulate it. But since in actual reality civil society and the state are one and the same, it must be made clear that laissez faire too is a form of state 'regulation', introduced and maintained by legislative and coercive means.[16]

As is clear from this passage, state and civil society are one and the same. These are the key moments for hegemony, which 'the dominant group exercises throughout society'. This is done both through 'direct domination', that is, 'command exercised by the state [and] the juridical government', and through cultural projects of education and religion. Hegemonic functions working through these spaces 'are *purely* organisational and connective'.[17]

In 'State and Civil Society', Gramsci detects in the state cultural characteristics. Here he adds to the coercive dimensions of the state an 'ethical' aspect. He speaks of a 'cultural state', thus ensuring a continuity between everyday living and organised ruling: 'every state is ethical in as much as one of its most important functions is to raise the great mass of population to a particular cultural and moral level, a level (or type) which corresponds to the needs of the productive forces for development, and hence to the interest of the ruling class'.[18] While his comments are especially directed to public education, they extend in scope to 'a multitude of other so-called private initiatives and activities which form the apparatus of the political and cultural hegemony'.[19] The results of these activities are expressed in the conclusion that the state has no autonomy.

Once we have established this intimacy between state and civil society, we cannot trivialise culture or cultural politics and attribute separate realms to organising for state-forming politics and to creating cultural organisations. This

---

15   Ibid., p. 12. My emphasis.
16   Ibid., p. 160.
17   Ibid., p. 12. Emphasis mine.
18   Ibid., p. 258. On the ethical state, see Corrigan and Sayer 1985 and Birmingham School of Cultural Studies 1982. The latter collection connects the institutional racism of the British state to racist cultural common sense.
19   Gramsci 1971, p. 257.

is so even where these cultural organisations are not interested in achieving or abetting state power in the first instance, because they may have a tendency towards a long period of political incubation. Gramsci fully takes this into account when he compounds his notion of hegemony, which, according to his translators and editors, involves a fusion between '*direzioni*' (leadership) and '*egemonia*' (hegemony).[20] Thus hegemony is both 'supremacy manifesting as domination' and 'intellectual moral leadership' of society.[21] It becomes not an achieved static state of domination (both for good and bad politics) but a process of reproduction which reorganises culture and society unceasingly. As Gramsci comments in 'Notes on Italian History', the hegemonic process is one of 'gradual and continuous absorption, the absorption of the enemies' elite' with the aim of a 'passive revolution', signalling an ever readiness for a 'war of position'.[22]

The question of 'who', of which political agency, puts forward this self-conscious hegemonic process is crucial here. This is where the problem of hegemonic contestation arises. In 'State and Civil Society' Gramsci suggests that the 'class claiming to be capable of assimilating the whole society, and which was really able to express such a process' could do this.[23] And it would do this through its idea of social, moral and political order projected as 'state and law'.[24] This state would be both a political and social state, and its law both moral and conveniently phrased as juridical. This is possibly done with a relative ease through religious canons which already have a juridical-moral form and authority. This could end the liberal democratic separation between religion/church and the state, allow the agents to 'conceive the end of state and law, [now] rendered useless since they have exhausted their function'.[25] In this situation, which is not domination in ordinary parlance, there will be a totalisation created through a fusion between the state and civil society, but it will still have a ruling character to it. The political and the cultural will together form a fused discourse and practice of power – making religious injunctions the law of the land. The rights-bearing individual citizen subject will disappear and entitlements derive from membership in the hegemonic collectivity; the non-hegemonic will live on the margin and rely on tolerance of the members of the religious majority. The state itself, says Gramsci,

---

20   Ibid., p. 55.
21   Ibid., p. 57.
22   Ibid., p. 59.
23   Ibid., p. 260.
24   Ibid., p. 260.
25   Ibid., p. 260.

would be the 'private' apparatus of 'hegemony and civil society' because it will belong to a particular ethnic group.[26]

The initiators and conductors of this hegemonic drive for Gramsci are civil society 'intellectuals', both traditional and organic to the specific project. They may, rarely, come as independent individuals, but more commonly as members of cultural groups and political parties. Thus this hegemonic cultural effort has nothing spontaneous about it. It is a worked-over set of discourses, constructions or representations, deeply embedded in an overall political project. It is not, for example, religion in its diversity practiced particularly by groups or individuals, but rather a collated, synthesised and propagandised version of it. It is a cultural form whose energy is harnessed to the cause of power and eventual state-formation. Outside of the context of religious parties of the Catholic right, Gramsci also speaks of the Communist Party of Italy (PCI), in his 'The Modern Prince', in the context of a hegemonic contender against the former. Against the parties of the right, Gramsci here explores popular common sense in relation to oppositional consciousness, symbols and signifiers at a mass level of discontent, and resistance to the status quo, and fashions out of this a revolutionary agenda. As a facilitator and consolidator of hegemony the PCI with its affiliate mass and class organisations tries to create a passage through culture (in its broadest sense) from the civil society, the realm of daily life and private experiences, to the public and overtly political sphere. Here spontaneity, as with other cultural experiences and expressions, is subsumed in the process of organisation through which previously formed inchoate, disparate common sense 'germinates' into ideology reaching from 'the structure to the sphere of superstructure'.[27] The idea is for each hegemonic contestant to fight 'to prevail ... to propagate itself through society – bring about not only a unison of economic and political aims, but also intellectual moral unity ...'[28] This proposal is presented on a 'universal plane', signifying a development of all the 'national energies'.[29]

The work for hegemony consists in large part of working with common sense and ideologies found in the civil society. This is explicit in Gramsci's essay 'The Study of Philosophy'. His particular treatment of the notion of 'common sense' confers on it the status of a critical tool for cultural-political study. It actively introduces into social and political analysis the realm of normalisation, of taken-for-granted views, values, symbolic and signifying practices.

---

26   Ibid., p. 261.
27   Ibid., p. 181.
28   Ibid., p. 181.
29   Ibid., p. 182.

This is the type of 'philosophy' that is imbibed by people in a daily sense, providing them with a moral and political unconscious. But it is a passive form of the unconscious which comes from the surroundings of a person, 'from language itself, which is a totality of determined notions and concepts and not just of words grammatically devoid of content'.[30] Again Gramsci uses the examples of religion and folklore: 'popular religion and therefore ... the entire system of beliefs, superstitions, opinions, ways of seeing things and of acting ... collectively bundled together under the name of "folklore"'.[31] So common sense becomes a state of consciousness which, in a basic sense, is internalised from what one lives in, giving rise to 'a conception of the world mechanically imposed by external environment'.[32] Gramsci expands on this view by saying: 'common sense is a collective noun, like religion; there is not just one common sense, for that too is a product of history, and a part of the historical process'.[33]

For this complex contradictory common sense to become an ideological form requires what Gramsci calls a 'reduction', the destruction of its spontaneity, randomness and diversity – 'they cannot be so reduced "freely"', but generally by employing 'authoritarian means'.[34] In fact, again speaking of religion, he says that this politicisation of religion/culture, this reduction, is achieved by the evacuation of the 'confessional (spiritual) sense' from religion. Religion, thus devoid of religiosity, becomes a 'secular' force. It is to be taken in 'the secular sense of a unity of faith between a conception of the world and a corresponding norm of conduct. But why call this unity of faith "religion" and not ideology, or even *frankly* "politics"'?[35]

It should be obvious from this discussion why Gramsci is so important for an understanding of the hegemonic/political project of the Hindu right in India. With the help of his theorisation, particularly in this era of intense use of religion in politics, we can see, not only in India but elsewhere as well, how religion can serve as an instrument and alibi for hegemony. Perhaps Gramsci's insider's knowledge of the implication of the Italian Catholic church in the project of fascism gives him a special clarity which is useful for us. It resonates with all students of politics and religion/culture when he says: 'The principle elements of common sense are provided by religion, and consequently the relationship

---

30   Ibid., p. 323.
31   Ibid., p. 323.
32   Ibid., p. 323.
33   Ibid., p. 326.
34   Ibid., p. 326.
35   Ibid., p. 326. Emphasis mine.

between common sense and religion is much more intimate than that between common sense and the philosophical systems of intellectuals'.[36]

Needless to say, organic and traditional intellectuals of the right know how to reconstruct and manipulate this common sense, to shape a sword out of the cross. The *Sangh Parivar*, the composite body or family of the Hindu right, started with the intention of becoming hegemonic by elaborating cultural and then political arms of their organisation. The centrality of religion for this right-wing political project is explained by Gramsci as source for both ideology and legitimation found ready to hand as common sense. But equally, as he would agree, it would be wrong to see this role of religion as only an 'instrument', because it is through the 'reduction' of religion, in and through it, that Hindu ethnic cultural nationalism could find the ground or social and moral content for a totalising politics.

3   Duality and Dialectic of Hegemony: The Case of the *Sangh Parivar*

This detailed review of Marx and Gramsci puts in perspective the discussion thus far on nationalism and the cultural politics of the Hindu right and will continue to illuminate the rest of this chapter. This nuanced critical framework allows for a materialist analysis for the general problematic of hegemony and the politics of the Hindu right in India.

The centrality of the civil society in Marx's political analysis puts not only class or social relations but also forms of consciousness or culture squarely within projects of ruling and making of history. This overcame the bourgeois convention of separating the private aspect of the social from the public. Marx afforded no autonomy, transcendence and superiority to either culture or class, but rather displayed them in a mediatory and constitutive relationship which did not permit isolated analysis of either. The other crucial element lies in Marx's concept of 'ideology' as distinct from 'practical', everyday forms of consciousness. In this he provided a critical epistemology for understanding the implication of culture/consciousness in relations of ruling, of developing hegemony. We see how 'ideology' is an essential device for producing ways of thinking, conceptual categories which produce occlusion, dehistoricisation and depoliticisation in our understanding of the social. The notions of *hindutva*, Hindu nation, culture and identity, and even the national entity called 'India' by the *Sangh Parivar* or the Hindu right, are such ideological cat-

---

36   Ibid., p. 420.

egories. To emphasise the point we need to note that this mode of thought relies on methods of essentialisation, homogenisation, abstraction and overgeneralisation. A metonymic or synechdochal conceptual relationship is always at work, all performed by removing content from context, thus an isolation of the content substituting a part for the whole or the whole for a part. In such a schema what appears and what is are qualitatively different. We can see in the propaganda of the Hindu right how through their common sense politics, the history of India is transformed into a myth by becoming a 'Hindu India', while myth becomes history in fabricated historicity and use of literary and scriptural texts as grounds for 'Hindu identity' and 'Hindu pride'.

What Gramsci says about cultural politics is entirely congruent with Marx. For Gramsci also common sense and culture are immanent aspects of the civil society. Mediating, expressing and constituting social relations, culture and common sense are intrinsic to social ontology. It is this which makes Gramsci say that everyone is a kind of philosopher. It is this view which presents state formation as a cultural state and makes the state an 'ethical state'.

Gramsci maintains a distinction similar to Marx's between daily practical haphazard consciousness and ideology, while for Gramsci the difference is between common sense as a passive form of internalisation and its active form as a social and political subjectivity. So hegemony might consist of unreflexive and externally imposed ideas, or of active, critical ones which galvanise the civil society to resistance and revolution. Hegemony can thus be towards a revelatory knowledge, or towards a reductive one, ahistorical, asocial, a dematerialised synthetic form. As we have seen above, he discusses this issue frequently in relation to the manipulation of religion towards a political ideology. This is well illustrated by the Indian case.

The *Sangh Parivar* has a two-headed appearance because it simultaneously uses a liberal democratic form of electoral political party and grass roots organisations as cultural/civil society activists. Though itself thoroughly anti-democratic, the *Sangh Parivar* has made good use of liberal democratic tenets of freedoms of speech, association and assembly in order to create a large and public scope for its organisations and their ideological consolidation. This, of course, is what they would prevent if they could solidify their presence in mainstream political and state power. In this context, it is useful to remember that the Nazis came to power in Germany openly, legally, democratically. Critics have noted this and tried to explore the phenomenon in different ways. The question before us is, does this signal a dualism within the *Sangh Parivar* or faith combine, or do we see a dialectical relationship between the two faces, voices, stances and modes of operation? On scrutiny, it appears that the dualism thesis can be dismissed as mere appearance, situational, or even an opportunistic behaviour. The seeming duality has the advantage of appealing to Hindu aggression and anger, on the one hand, and soothing general social fears and anxieties on the other. The two features come from two operational sources – from the difference between the use of familiar, politically reassuring liberal democracy which has mainstreamed the Hindu right's politics, and the extreme and sustained social politics of *hindutva*, of exclusion and hatred, maintained by the so-called cultural organisations.

The RSS's old history of communal violence has deterred many practicing Hindus from supporting it. Since the 1980s, the riots and pogroms against Muslims, Christians and *dalits*[37] has further created terror among a substantial portion of Indians, while elating some. This fear has, on the one hand, presented the Hindu right as a powerful political force to reckon with, but on the other, deterred their credibility for representing the nation of India as a multi-religious society. Their political ambition has needed to manipulate both the fear factor and its antidote. Presenting *hindutva* politics as reasonable and accommodative through the BJP has been a gesture signalling that they are capable of playing the game of politics by rules of liberal democracy. Riots created by the RSS are thus presented as spontaneous gestures of the Hindu community/majority, while the BJP seems to speak only to a general representational national politics. Even within the *hindutva* project itself, opposite tendencies have been noted. The authors of the excellent book *Khaki Shorts, Saffron Flags*,[38] written mainly to explore the *Sangh Parivar*'s cultural politics, note the two faces of the Parivar: a) an aggressive masculinity and appeal to Hindu manhood symbolised by the epic war hero, Ram; and b) a smiling, benevolent hinduness, also symbolised by Ram, only this time calling on Hindu nurturance as a sweet baby. Together they widen the scope of *hindutva*.

The *Sangh Parivar*'s organised violence, which claims spontaneity, was toned down by the BJP, especially as it emerged for a period as the party in national state power, aided by its right-wing allies (the National Democratic Alliance, NDA). Each riot or pogrom against Muslims or Christians was followed by mild utterances from the prime minister, Atal Behari Vajpayee, seeking to distance the party from these so-called popular outbursts. However, delaying

---

37   The word *dalit* literally means something that has been ground down. Meant as 'the oppressed', it was adopted as a political protest by a part of the Indian population who were called 'untouchables' or *harijans* (God's children), a construction of Gandhi. The notion of untouchability is connected to the Indian caste system within the dictate of which people outside or at the lowest end of the hierarchy of hindu caste were considered not touchable by the upper and middle castes.

38   Basu et al. 1993.

tactics of various kinds were employed against holding enquiries into the violence and the preparation of reports. Investigative committees were stacked with RSS and BJP supporters, and the judiciary itself was manipulated, giving an appearance of justice created through favourable rulings by BJP-appointed judges. But these tactics have not blinded the many critics of *hindutva* politics. A.G. Noorani,[39] one of the foremost political analysts of India, has written a book entitled *The RSS and the BJP: A Division of Labour*, in which he has shown their collusive relations.

But of course it is not the first time in history that democratic discourse and practices have been employed to achieve anti-democracy. So let us begin by noting the way in which the BJP deploys democratic discourse and electoral apparatuses to this end. The manipulations of classical democratic notions of 'majority' and 'minority' are worth scrutiny. In this the BJP is not unique or innovative, but carries to a logical conclusion practices and meanings put in place by its colonial and postcolonial predecessors in state power, predecessors who identified ethnicity with political agency in both overt and covert fashion. However, the thoroughness is what is new, and the shifting of the notions of political majority and minority to an ethnic definition and identifying the notion of community as a religious community.[40] Ethnicised/religious identities become the ground for political subjectivities and agencies. As such, 'majority' begins to mean Hindus (85 percent) and 'minority' Muslims (12 percent), with 'others' (3 percent) who are marginal minorities – and it needs to be noted that the majority Hindu category includes many groups who do not wish to be identified as Hindus.[41] This ethnic categorisation of the country's population, when translated into a political equation, demonstrates a gradation in citizenship by establishing religious/ethnic terms for claims on the resources of the nation. In so far as 'others', or non-Hindus who are also non-Muslims, are numerically fewer, the substantial minority, that is, the Muslims, are the direct antithesis of the powerful Hindu majority.

Hindus, therefore, would become the natural constituents and authentic citizens of the nation state. The last two decades of *Sangh Parivar* political machinations that replaced secular citizenship with a religious/ethnic one laid bare the ideological nature of the so-called primordial dimensions of national subjectivity. Thus, the process exposes contingencies that are involved in polit-

39   Noorani 2000.

40   See Basu et al. 1993. The authors speak specifically to this altering of meaning of democratic discourse. The entire Introduction explores the perversion of democracy introduced in the Indian polity by the Hindu right.

41   See Iliah 1998.

ical representation. There was even a plan under the BJP-led government to inscribe religion into the Indian constitution itself and render all other differences other than religion as subordinate. If successful, this would reverse measures undertaken by the Indian state to redress multiple oppressions historically suffered by social groups at the hands of brahminical or casteist Hinduism.[42] This would also end the 'positive discrimination' legislated by the state for historically disadvantaged groups. As such, provisions for 'reservation' or quotas meant to mitigate conditions of deprivation and marginalisation, themselves highly inadequate as a solution, were to come onto the chopping block.

The BJP's anti-secular, anti-modernist political agenda has necessitated the instatement of a discourse of 'tradition', and, as for all such projects, has led to the invention of traditions which are commensurate with their goal. They have either innovated traditions or drawn upon prior or existing ones and then proceeded to collage them reductively and deploy them in the sphere of civil society or make legal interventions based on them. These invented traditions of ethnicity and religion have tones of racialisation and employ caste modalities which are useful for their reproduction, diffusion and stability. Though this synthesis of tradition – the creation of homogeneous religious cultures – is difficult to elaborate and sustain in a country like India with its wide ranging diversities, a relentless effort is being made through governing and cultural/ideological practices of the Hindu right. This relies on a pre-existing discourse of 'foreigners' and 'foreignness' created by both the colonisers and nationalist resistance. Islam and Christianity – practised for over a millennium and indigenised to India – have become regular targets of the Hindu right, and their practitioners targeted for the stripping of their full citizenship status. This new equation of ethnicity with any entitlement is replete with the jargon of authenticity, origin and genealogy. Ironically, these inventions or myths have an overwhelming reliance on European Indology and orientalism and employ a colonial discourse extending from William Jones to Max Mueller, among others.[43]

This tradition of Hinduised cultural nationalism has been so naturalised that it has often come to stand in for 'Indian' culture. And it must be emphasised that this *hindutva*-based 'Indian' culture and identity developed its accent of difference not contra-British but, significantly, contra-Muslim. In fact, the cultural foreignness of Europeans posed no threat because the myth of aryanness, of shared origins between Hindus and Europeans, had become pervasive.[44]

---

42   See Hassan 2000; Omvedt 1993.
43   See Bannerji 2001a, pp. 18–71.
44   The Hindu right and *Sangh Parivar*'s penchant for embracing the ayran myth is well discussed in Basu et al. 1993 as well as in Noorani 2000. Another text that discusses this

This Hindu cultural nationalism was underwritten or augmented by a doctrine of racial purity (as was the Nazis' nationalism) derived in equal parts from casteist, brahminical Hinduism, orientalist Indology and social Darwinism.[45] A form of Western eugenics converged with casteist/brahminical notions pertaining to physical and ritual purity and pollution and created a murky admixture. This is demonstrated by Golwalkar's admiration for the Nazi agenda:

> To keep up the purity of the Race and its culture, Germany shocked the world by her [sic] purging the country of the Semitic Races – the Jews. Race pride at its highest has been manifest here. Germany has also shown how well nigh impossible it is for Races and cultures, having differences going to the root, to be assimilated into one united whole, a good lesson for us in Hindustan to learn and profit by.[46]

Major social thinkers of the BJP and Hindu right political tradition, such as Dayanand Saraswati, Veer Savarkar and K.B. Hedgewar, all subscribed to notions of racial purity, and particularly designated the Muslims as impure. It must also be mentioned that the Indian nationalist movement, with its multiple ideological strands, had a large amount of Hindu revivalism woven through it.[47] Even when it proved weaker and lost to secularism and liberal democracy in the formation of the independent state in 1947, this revivalism had seeped into the broader political arena. The bloodbath of religious communalism heralding the partition and the independence of India pushed forth a secular constitution, but a shadow of religious communalism and casteism darkened it. This culminated in the assassination of Mahatma Gandhi and overdetermined the last few decades' turn to ethnic/Hindu politics.

The BJP's political strength comes not from a history of party politics, as did that of the Indian National Congress, but from a long tradition of cultural

---

issue from a feminist and anti-caste standpoint is Uma Chakravarti 1990, whose article comments on the indological colonial discourse's contribution to the social and political thought of the Hindu right in terms of 'national Aryan/Hindu' civilization and ideals of Hindu Aryan masculinity and femininity. All of these Aryan constructs emphasised vigour, courage, discipline, and martial traits in men and chastity in women. This Aryan myth, formed for example in the cultural/social characterisation of Hindus by the indologists, though in decline, encouraged the Hindu right to seek a fraternal bond with Europeans.

45 See Thapar 1993a. Her work has been the most important source of contestation of the mythic Hindu history that has been constructed. She scrutinises both the reactionary constructions and the incompetence of this revisionist history.

46 Quoted in Noorani 2000, p. 20.

47 Sarkar 1973 and 2002.

politics practised through child and youth recreational cells, social work and religious rituals among Hindus. The RSS, the parent organisation of the BJP, made a crucial distinction between 'cultural' and 'territorial' nationalism, and considered that this cultural nationalism and identity could well exist within British political rule.[48] Its playing field was, thus, the civil society itself, as the ambition of state power lay outside of its domain. This hegemonic political heritage is what the present-day BJP is drawing on. The major enemy for the RSS were, as mentioned above, the Muslims of India. The virulence of this identity politics becomes obvious when we learn that Gandhi's assassin, Nathuram Godse, sought to avenge what the Hindu right saw as the former's pro-Muslim politics. This right cultural nationalism at no point in time submitted to tenets of Gandhi's pacifism and liberal democracy, and considered marxists and communists as secular and inciters of class politics with a passionate hatred. Secularism, class struggle or individual and human rights were, and are, all deemed antithetical to Hindu character and culture.

Along with its features of liberal democracy, the secular Indian state in general held an ambiguity in its heart. Its claims of universal citizenship were compromised by often conducting its parliamentary politics in ethnic terms as well as by conducting legal matters pertaining to family and inheritance through personal, that is, religious or traditional injunctions and customs.[49] This reflects both the ethnicised social relations within the civil society and their inscription in the state. This is a continuum as well as an outcome of ethnicising the politics of pre-independence India. After all, India and Pakistan were mutilated at birth by ethnic strife through unprecedented carnage, violence against women and transfer of populations. Popular memories of these events and experiences were and continue to be manipulated by interpretations and interventions of political parties and of social and religious groups. This too deeply scarred bodies and minds within civil society, and continues to provide ground for mobilisation by the BJP and other right-wing Hindu parties in India. All this serves to remind us that the BJP's political agenda

---

48   The notions of cultural and political nationalism were already in use by the end of the nineteenth century in Bengal. Rabindranath Tagore used them in his novels, and connected cultural nationalism to what he called 'constructive *swadeshi*' (nationalism) intended for cultural and social reform (see Chapter 6, this volume). But his usage was secular and had no antimuslim connotations. In the RSS context in Maharashtra, U.P. and M.P., the notion of cultural nationalism took on a virulent anti-muslim and communal character and 'political' nationalism was degraded to mere 'territorial' nationalism, thus showing a distance from the Indian National Congress and Gandhi – both in terms of desire for forming a national state and having an all-India and inclusive view of the nation.

49   Desai 2002.

is not *sui generis*. It collates and constructs political ideologies and organisational practices from aspects of the Indian civil society and the state which are congenial to their interests. It then tries to create a political apparatus wide and flexible enough to encompass both the civil and the political society. Ethnicisation of the Indian polity and society gained momentum during the 1980s and the decades following. The impetus came not only from the Hindu right and ethnic electoral practices of the Indian state but also from the Khalistan upsurge to create an independent Sikh homeland. The struggle was armed and the Indian army entered the holiest Sikh shrine at Amritsar by force. Violent events and counter-events followed, including a massacre of Sikhs in Delhi in 1984. Swift construction and deployment of ethnicised communities, identities and national imaginaries became the political game in the country. The existing pluralism of liberal democracy was treated as an accommodating device for this. But relatedly, these contesting hegemonies sharpened the high-caste Hindu male as the typological Indian citizen – in effect if not in law. The rise of this caste-and faith-based politics reorganised and depressed class politics to a large extent in many parts of India, redrawing boundaries of involvement and belonging. Though a few provinces, such as West Bengal, Tripura and Kerala, continued with strong communist movements and governments, new growth in left-wing politics was stalled. The birth of new ideologies which cut across class lines and mobilised difference to the cause of communalist and caste collectivities simultaneously occluded class and secularism. The Mandal Commission Report, which expanded on legislation pertaining to the redress of caste oppression, both challenged and entrenched caste as a crucial political factor.[50] The violent anti-Muslim movements and *hindutva* upsurge that occurred at this time had connections with the Report.[51]

This political environment reveals the basic truth about the relationship between the state and the civil society that Marx and Gramsci noted. Though they do have different and specific modes of operation, the dual plane ascribed to them is only apparent. In the scheme of an overall social ontology, their disconnection is phenomenal. Their actual relationship is one of a dialectical constitutiveness. The BJP is, after all, rooted in conventional Hindu brahminical religious practices and beliefs constellated by the RSS, and Muslims came to be

---

50 In 1979 the Indian government established the 'Second Backward Class Commission', known as the Mandal Commission after the name of its chair. For a comprehensive discussion of this and its fall-out effects see Seth 2000.

51 With regard to the BJP's relationship with various caste groups, see Shah 2002, especially Shah's own essay in the volume.

scapegoated for independent India's various ills. The long-existing sentiments against Pakistan also fed into the agenda of the BJP, with the BJP creating an expectation among Hindus of the takeover of the economic space occupied by Muslims and also promised a cultural purification. Pogroms against Muslims followed one another and rioters and arsonists obeyed the Hindu land speculators' and real estate developers' direct and indirect incitements. Competition for business, big and small, and for jobs was also drawn into the Hindu right-wing agenda. All this eventually resulted in 1992 in a bid for state power by the BJP with the strength of its civil society base through the spectacular gesture of destroying a fifteenth-century mosque built in Ayodhya by the Mughal emperor Babur, popularly known as the Babri Masjid. This attack ritualised the Hindu supremacist view of Muslims as invaders and foreigners, the illegitimate occupants of the Indian soil, and it signified a move towards their suppression and possible expulsion. Thousands of Hindu *karsevaks* (volunteers) crawled out of the woodwork of the civil society and they came armed. More interestingly, they were not effectively deterred by the ruling apparatus of the Indian state not yet in the grasp of the BJP. This grand symbolic gesture signalled a nation-wide drive of terror against Muslims but also against Christians, who could not, unlike the Sikhs and Buddhists, be compressed within the definitional container of *hindutva*.

4   Hindu Masculinity and the Hindu Family: *Hindutva* Moral Regulations

These violent forms of grass-roots cultural politics became a template for future Indian politics, which culminated in a massive onslaught against Muslims in Gujarat in 2002. Muslims, and increasingly *dalits* and Christians, have lost lives and property, and violence against women of these communities has become a regular occurrence.[52] A few lines of testimony from a witness and survivor of mass rape in February 2002 should be enough to expose the nature of Hindu masculinity:

> The mob started chasing us with burning tyres after we were forced to leave Gangotri society. It was then that they raped many girls. We saw about 8–10 rapes. We saw them strip 16-year-old Mehrunissa. They were

---

52   On violence against muslim women, see Dutt 2002; on police complicity in this 'civil society'-based violence, see Setalvad 2002.

stripping themselves and beckoning to the girls. Then they raped them, there right there on the road. We saw a girl's vagina slit open. Then they were burnt.[53]

With all these activities, parts of India entered into a phase of power relations which can only be called social and political fascism.[54] The dynamic of this dialectic between the state and civil society is still unfolding. The naturalisation of this ethnic exclusion is evidenced in an Indian Army recruitment advertisement in Jammu which states openly: 'Muslims and traders [who are mostly Muslims] not wanted'.[55] But in the usual manipulative mode, the prime minister of the BJP-led government offered at the same time to sit at the table with *all* Kashmiri groups to facilitate the peace process between Hindus and Muslims, Pakistan and India. Apparently the right hand of the state, its democratic one, does not know what its left hand, the coercive apparatus of the police and the army, is doing. As a whole, the state both constructs and feeds from the same volatile communalised ground as its civil society groups. It is clear that Indian liberal democracy provides the opportunity for an authoritarian state and uses the democratic form to orchestrate social violence. This creative contradiction is manifest, for example, in the incident of Canadian film director Deepa Mehta's inability to shoot *Water* in India. In this case, she had permission from the Indian government authorities for making a film critical of orthodox Hinduism, while Hindu youth groups led by the RSS and its sympathisers attacked the film crew and destroyed the sets. Nobody involved in this rampage was ever criminally charged. But the outreach of ethnicisation (Hinduisation) of the polity grew larger as a result. It is obvious that this creative manipulation of democratic and civil society politics is a far more effective hegemonic device than a unidimensional party politics which has only an

---

53   Cited in Engineer 2003, p. 297.
54   There are extensive discussions regarding the naming of the BJP and the *Sangh Parivar*'s politics. But there is a general consensus that it would be quite apt to call it fascism. Noorani 2000, for example, has no hesitation in identifying it as a fascist combine. Aijaz Ahmad refuses to call it 'Hindu nationalism'. It is important to quote him here at some length to avoid deflecting our attention from the fascist politics of the BJP because it is not a replica of the classical fascism produced in Mussolini's Italy. For Ahmad, the BJP/Sangh Parivar has to be investigated regarding what kind of nationalism it is. He states that 'ideologies and movements of the fascist type have been a punctual feature of the imperialist period and they have arisen ... in the advanced as well as the backward countries, the colonizing European ones as well as the colonies ... Indeed, Indian communal fascism should be studied in relation as much to other fascist movements of the Third World as to the European ones ...' (2002, pp. xiv–xv)
55   In *Asian Age* of 7 April 2001.

electoral machinery and agenda. This creates an optical illusion through which the BJP prime minister, as the head of a democratic state, obedient to representational politics, appears moderate and even benevolent, while the party's cultural affiliates appear as Hindu hardliners. It is an orchestrated obfuscation meant to delude the public. It has both generated and relied upon a myth of spontaneity about *hindutva* politics.

Contrary to this myth of spontaneity that fills much of the literature current on politics of community, civil society and culture,[56] there is a careful and long process of ideological and organisational work behind this aspiration to hegemony. As Gramsci said, this hegemonic directive status can only be achieved through a constant attempt to stimulate and reorganise civil society both passively (for example, through sports and cultural education) and actively (for example, through destruction of mosques and their replacement with temples). The RSS, VHP (*Visva Hindu Parishad* or World Hindu Council), and *Bajrang Dal* (Storm Brigade) provide the sources for these activities. These organisations have a history involving adept cultural activists who define 'national' identity and morality. Working at a level that is simple and apprehensible to the common people, drawing on religious and conservative moral common sense, the RSS or the VHP do not speak of politics in the electoral sense. Rather, they constantly construct themes of religious and cultural difference and power at both national and international levels. This manufacturing of consent is underpinned always by the threat of brute force. The frontline activists are the youth cadres of the *Bajrang Dal*, though other recruits and sympathisers prove also highly active. Here the regular 'self-defence' training in martial arts involving indigenous weapons, such as sticks, swords, javelins and tridents, comes in handy. Marches with weapons, training camps for body building and after-school sports and cultural programmes, are all meant to develop Hindu male identity and provide resources for what Gramsci called

---

56   This literature is discussed critically and in detail by Vanaik 1997. He shows with much
      evidence (with more in Basu et al. 1993) how much work went into the production of the
      ideology of *hindutva* and its social dissemination, and how this political version of religion
      has nothing everyday and popular about it. He does not see either the BJP or the *Sangh
      Parivar* as expressions of faith in its spiritual and common sense. This evidence challenges
      the myth of spontaneity expressed, for example, in Bharucha 1993, which identifies the
      hindutva upsurge with a popular identification of religion. The question of spontaneity
      also becomes prominent in discussions of the Hindu right's vehement rejection of secularism as antithetical to the spirit of Indian (Hindu) civilisation. Religion and traditionalism
      are seen as an ineluctable part of Indian (Hindu) consciousness, and critics of secularism, such as T.N. Madan 1998, express such a view with little more finesse than the *Sangh
      Parivar*'s intellectuals. This is also the case with Ashis Nandy 1998.

'the war of position'. This projected Hindu identity, a *hindutva* culture, is seen in a positive light by a part of the middle and lower-middle classes, for example, by traders, office and other white-collar workers, and by college and school teachers and students. Unemployed youth, hoodlums and known criminals all become part of this army of hegemony, combining consent with force.

On the level of conduct of daily life, this violence becomes an authoritarian code and is mediated and expressed through the ideals of the high-caste patriarchal family. The *hindutva* family code inculcates hierarchical familial relations, with father at the head and filial as well as wifely obedience and caste proprieties. It resonates with a cult of powerful leaders and unquestioning obedience to superiors and group loyalty. The family is the training ground for *hindutva* masculinity deployed in riots and pogroms which destroys the families of 'others', unleashes rapes and foeticide of Muslims, and kills Christian missionaries and rapes nuns.[57] The ideology of the patriarchal family also provides the model for the organisational structure of the *hindutva* civil society organisations and their relationship to each other and their representative political parties. A hierarchical unity or organicity is achieved through the familial model and is signalled by their self-styled appellation as the *Sangh Parivar* (the family association). This practice is not unlike that of the Mafia, who adopted their organisational model from feudal Catholic patriarchy. This family simultaneously partakes of democratic party politics operating in India as the BJP and as an international ideological and mobilisation front (VHP), especially in the United States, United Kingdom and Canada. The youth group for men and boys (BD) and a group for women, the *Durga Vahini*, complete the picture. The RSS's own familial structure has persisted from the 1920s, continuing traditions of leadership and hierarchy initiated by M.S. Hedgewar and entrenched by a long line of *pracharaks* (proselytisers or propagandists).

A word about the leaders and the preachers would not be out of place here. The family form of the *Sangh Parivar* is headed by a father figure known as the *sarsanghchalak* (the ultimate director) of the RSS. He has incontrovertible authority over all the organisations. Under him are the *chalaks* or directors of provincial branches, who in turn control the pracharaks or the propagandists/preachers. This tightly knit body has both a military discipline and a monastic touch to it. These men are all high-caste unmarried celibates (*brahmacharis*), and the RSS is mainly a male organisation. They are the interpreters of Hindu scriptures and preceptors of the right Hindu moral conduct.

---

57   On sexual assault and violence against women of minority communities, especially Muslims and Christians, see Agarwal 1995, Sarkar 2002, and Engineer 2003, especially pages 296–331.

They engage in a discourse of moral purity and crisis centred on an anxiety about Hindu 'degeneracy' due to secularism and Muslim influence. The Hindus belonging to progressive, left and communist organisations are tainted with these vices. This anxiety at times borders on an enraged hysteria and erupts in attacks or rituals of violence. Chastity and physical strength are the key concerns, leading to absurd notions regarding the saving of vital body fluids, that is, avoiding the wasting of semen. Texts such as Savarkar's *Hindutva! Who is a hindu?*[58] expand on these themes, as do later texts such as Golwalkar's *A Bunch of Thoughts*[59] and *We, or, Our Nationhood Defined.*[60]

This ethos of male anxiety regarding virility and chastity (see Sinha 1995; Bannerji 2001a) is displayed in attacks on 'foreigners' as well as in the domination of women and their sexuality. The theatre of some of these activities is the home or the family, and that space is marked by the presence of the 'good' maternal and the 'bad' sexual woman. Women's chastity and maternity are particularly important for their reproductive capacity as vessels for the nurturing of the Hindu race and its purity. This is the key moral/religious conduct for women, who, unlike men, need no scriptural education. Non-procreative sex, though overlooked as masculine need, is frowned upon for women. In fact, there are whole groups of women who are encoded as sexual by nature, as Muslim women are, and so are considered to be legitimate targets for Hindu sexual violence. In this suspicion of women's sexuality in general there is an anxiety about bastardy. Muslims are routinely addressed as a bastard or impure nation and stereotyped as sexually lax, as signified by the koranic permission for divorce and the taking of four wives. Needless to say that the age-old Hindu caste practices of polygamy and discarding of wives is never spoken about.

The RSS's familial morality regarding women's identification with chastity, wifehood and motherhood is also prevalent in Indian nationalist discourse, especially of the Hindu revivalist or Gandhian variety. The same ideological pedestal accorded to women as 'mothers of the nation' and as mother goddesses is found in the RSS, including permitting women to bear arms in protection of the nation as her (male) children. As such, the RSS has allowed women to become supporting members since the 1930s in the capacity of *rashtra sevikas* or the tenders of the nation/state. Their eventual emergence as a body of organised women under the name of *Durga Vahini*, the Brigade of Durga (a power goddess), extended active militant roles to them within the purview of casteist

58   Savarkar 1923.
59   Golwalkar 1963.
60   Golwalkar 1939.

patriarchy. The present-day *Sangh Parivar* takes pains to teach girls right conduct as women and considers them to be a vibrant part of the Hindu cause. The two iconic RSS female figures, Uma Bharati and Swadhi Ritambhara, are important in BJP politics.[61] The former became the Chief Minister of an Indian province. The spokesperson for the BJP who also held the position of federal Minister of Culture and Broadcasting is a woman, Sushma Swaraj. As was the case with German National Socialist women, the women of the Hindu right can be highly active as long as they obey the general patriarchal dictates of *hindutva*. Finally, the typology of the high-caste Hindu family encodes a model for both society and the polity. This form and its morality expand from the so-called private civil society space to the public one in a two-way movement. The male leaders of the nation are supposed to hold homologous relationships to fathers and husbands in the national family, while women are its mothers and daughters.[62]

The other major task of the Hindu male seems to be to repress, and if possible erase, Muslims from the national space they call 'India'. This has a connection with the domination of low-caste women and men. If women in general as well as Muslims, low castes and 'untouchables' are considered prone to violations of chastity, then a Hindu male, and *any* Hindu male, could be their guardians and punish any act they see as a violation of morality. This automatically brings in physical and sexual violence against women.

As Hinduism is an amorphous religious formation which is polytheistic, animistic, man-god ridden, sect divided and generally chaotic, unbounded by a central church, text or core myth, to engage in what Gramsci called 'reduction', or Marx the making of ideology, is urgent. If a political consciousness is to be forged from it, there needs to be an organicity, a synthetic unity. This was felt from the nineteenth century onwards by modernist social reformers and traditional Hindu revivalists alike. Taking off from two such late nineteenth- and early twentieth-century efforts propagated by organisations such as the *Aray Samaj* (Aryan Society) and the *Santana Hindu Dharma Sangsta* (Assembly of Ancient Hindu Religion), Dr. Hedgewar tried to initiate such an essentialising process. In forging *hindutva*, he reached out to the Hindu epic *Ramayana*

---

61   An article by T. Sarkar 2001a, based on an interview with the prominent RSS woman figure
      Ritambhara, gives us an insight into the type of female empowerment the hindu right can
      confer.

62   The history and cultural environment for the type of Hindu masculinity idealised by the
      RSS and the Hindu right up to the present moment are to be found in Hindu reformist and
      revivalist culture and cultural nationalism in India, especially in Bengal and Maharashtra.
      Two explorations of these themes are Chowdhury 2001 and Basu 2003.

(Tale of Rama) as written in the sixteenth century by Tulsidas and held dear by Hindus in India's Hindi-speaking areas. In establishing this epic as a literal and historical narrative and source material for a Hindu nation, Indian history was made into Hindu history, thus laying claim to antiquity and origin for legitimation of a political project. The epic's hero, Rama, was developed into the ideal high-caste Hindu morality, and his masculinity enhanced. In the mid-1980s Ramanand Sagar, the director and producer of a television serial of the epic, rearranged Tulsidas' version and marketed it, recalling Gandhi's love for this epic and his use of Ram's reign, *Rama Rajja*, as his concept for utopia. Sagar, however, changed Gandhi's version of Ram, a model of justice and compassion, into a vengeful Hindu war hero in tune with the Indian Army's ideals.

5   Politics of Civil Society: Hegemony and Media

The *Sangh Parivar*'s use of the *Ramayana* TV serial is an example of the use of spectacle for the purpose of hegemony, and it spun off into various media productions. Through myths and their politicising potentials, force was fused with cultural common sense to provide a constructive moment in state formation. The myth of Rama provided the holy water to be sprinkled on a fascist project and fabricated a unified Hindu society. This evacuation of internal contradictions within communities in terms of class, caste and gender is an ideological sleight of hand which aids the Hindu right manipulations towards state power. The fact that the so-called civil society is not actually a 'civil' space, but one textured with fundamental unequal relations that are connected to all aspects of the economy and polity, also gave them an upper hand. Thus they could simultaneously posit homogenous oppositional groups within it, while erasing these groups' internal power relations.

From this wider political angle we can see how the *Sangh Parivar* drank from the same watering hole of ethnicised aspects of Indian nationalism and how it benefited from the official, so-called secular but implicitly Hindu culture of Indian state and governing practices. A good example can be found in Indian national radio programmes, which took a major role in shaping the ideals of national and moral culture. This was more effectively popularised after the arrival of the television, and continues to date through state and private channels. This media did and does market an essentialised Hindu ethos that the state-run television epic *Ramayana* relied on. Throughout the 1980s, Ramanand Sagar produced this long epic serial in keeping with the state's mandate to make the media the educator of Indian heritage and history. Sagar used state-of-the-art television technology and presented this narrative of ideal familial, moral and political conduct culminating in the birth of an ideal (Hindu) state. The trajectory of this series encompasses the prince Rama's banishment from the kingdom of Ayodhya by his father, Dasharath. His patrimonial dispossession was caused by the king's unmanly submission to a woman's ploys and malice. Rama left the kingdom and went into a forest retreat accompanied by his chaste and obedient wife, Sita, who then is abducted by Ravana, the lustful demon king of Sri Lanka. The rest, like Homer's *Iliad*, is a story of revenge and retrieval of Sita and the destruction of the island. Rama returns victorious to his kingdom and puts the final touches to the assertion of Hindu masculine conduct by banishing Sita on the basis of rumours of unchastity. This *Ramayana* is solely a high-caste Hindu narration of nation which is a composite of patriarchy replete with misogyny, casteism, militarism and xenophobic patriotism – a moral nourishment for the Indian army. The serial's appeal was intense, aided by popular familiarity with the story and its high-end though simplistic production. The moral constructions of this show and its iconic figures, both male and female, embodied the Hindu right's ideals and made the Rama myth the central cultural-political myth of modern India. It pushed aside other Hindu epics, such as the *Mahabharata*, even in regions where it was previously not so important.

Armed with these nationally broadcast configurations of *hindutva*, the RSS found an everyday cultural-religious discourse for interpellating many ordinary Hindu believers. An important and militant member of both the BJP and the RSS, L.K. Advani, went on an all-India *hindutva* campaign to bring together 'Ram's children', in a Toyota truck decked up as Ram's chariot, complete with a huge cardboard cut-out figure of Ram and his general, the monkey god Hanuman. In his speeches he invoked a Hindu crisis, a deviation from the path of high-caste conduct, and lavishly used the language of purity in order to save India from Muslim degeneracy. He offered this anti-Muslim fervour as an antidote to regenerate India to its ancient and pristine past. Though not all Indian provincial governments allowed free passage to this *yatra* (march) of Ram's chariot, many did. Everywhere in its path there followed Hindu hatred and violence against Muslims. They were the demon Ravana to Hindu Ram's godly heroism. To this depiction of Muslims and ethnic 'others' as aberrations of Indian culture were added communists, feminists and secularists in general. The Hindu right began to aggrandise itself as an anti- or post-colonial cultural force, and some noted Hindu intellectuals lent them a hand in this direction.[63]

---

63   These intellectuals rarely identified themselves forthrightly as supporters of *hindutva*, but accomplished this through a postmodernist stance on anti-colonialism by sophisticatedly reworking the orientalist paradigm of the binary of tradition and modernity, where

Secularism or modernism of any kind began to come under heavy theoretical fire from post-modernists. The VHP also did much in garnering common
support from Hindus outside of India, especially through hefty donations. The
Sangh Parivar has also shown a sustained and skilled use of advertisement and
all forms of media currently available in India. They have a bent towards the
spectacular, as did the German National Socialists. They have manufactured
audiotapes and videotapes of music, lectures, stories of the glorious Hindu
past, and saints' lives. They also published comics, chapbooks and pamphlets.
A new feature of major Indian railway stations is stalls for these cassettes and
their favoured religious texts. Interestingly, Hitler's *Mein Kampf* (translated
into English and vernacular languages) is often on sale as well. The *Parivar*
organises fairs, processions and marches celebrating Hindu holidays and Hindu
pride. These cultural-political efforts were accompanied by the Indian media's
growing overall Hinduisation and an increase in religious identity politics. In
the name of a national cultural identity, using modern reproductive technology, a reactionary modernity claiming 'tradition' for self-affirmation sought to
hide from view the workings of a vicious neo-liberal and fascist political economy.[64] This 'invention of tradition' marks the most significant turn in modern
Indian politics.

The stereotypes of Muslims circulated by the Hindu right are a combination of representations originating from the crusades and discourses of later
orientalism.[65] They are not indigenous to India from pre-British times and
they gained currency through European orientalists or indologists and colonial administrators. A look through Max Mueller's *India: What It Can Teach Us*[66]
will show us how India becomes a Hindu civilisation through indologists, well
known as linguists and philologists, who prepared British civil servants to come
to India. For Max Mueller as well as others, Indian history goes into a decline
after the arrival of Muslim kings and chieftains with their Islamic, Turkish
and Perso-Arabic cultures. The fusion between these and indigenous cultures
and religions and the cultural effervescence that results from it are absent in
their annals of Indian history. The orientalist representations of Muslims, on
the contrary, are those of a cunning, rapacious, intemperate and anti-spiritual

---

modernity is homogenised into knowledge for colonisers and tradition offers a site of resistance. See Desai 2002, pp. 56–137. The two authors who belong to this group and are well
known in the West are Ashis Nandy and Dipesh Chakrabarty. Desai argues that Nandy
treads theoretical grounds of a kind of fascism.

64   Herf 1986.
65   See Said 1981; 1994. Both texts explore the origins and character of stereotypes disseminated the world over through European colonialism about Islam and Muslims.
66   Mueller 2000.

people. Myths of uncontrollable Muslim sensuality and amorality were spread wide and far. These contrast with the aura of wisdom, spirituality and fairness with which Hindus/Aryans are invested. The middle eastern origin of Islam prompted the theorists of the Hindu right to call Muslims traitors to India because their *janmabhumi* (birthplace) was not the same as their *punyabhumi* (holy land). This is the sentiment expressed by Golwalkar in the following statement:

> We repeat: in Hindusthan, the land of the Hindus, where lives and should live the Hindu Nation – satisfying all the five essential requirements of the scientific nation concept of the modern world, consequently only those movements are truly 'National' as aim at re-building, revitalising and emancipating from its present stupor, the Hindu Nation. All others are traitors and enemies to the National Cause, or ... idiots.[67]

It should be evident by now how the Hindu right has forged a formidable hegemonic device. Those who consider cultural politics as unimportant or secondary to what they deem 'real' politics do not have the capacity to either understand or resist this fascist hegemony. Nor do those liberals who separate the social from the cultural or the political. Secularism can provide a common platform to unite liberal democratic and left parties and win an electoral victory over the BJP and the *Sangh Parivar*, as happened in 2004, but this is not enough to hold back the re-emergence of *hindutva* fascism. As in other epochs of its history, the *Parivar* has gone into a temporary recession to work at the social base and will probably reappear in the interstices of class and caste struggles in India. Its victory over the last decades has been to ethnicise the Indian polity and to religiocise the conception of community and citizenship. There is an urgent need to create modalities for other hegemonies, other 'wars of position'.

It is not possible to conclude a consideration of this dialectics of hegemony without referring to Marx's essay *The Eighteenth Brumaire of Louis Bonaparte*.[68] Here Marx addresses simultaneously the problem of hegemony and the emergence of petty bourgeois authoritarianism and police state in the context of the crisis of class formation and class struggle. The politics he speaks of would be called fascism today. In particular, he refers to the use of the past and cultural traditions by the aspiring petty bourgeoisie under the guise of monarchism. He shows how class struggle can be disguised under cultural masks that divert

---

67   Quoted in Noorani 2000, p. 20.
68   Marx 1972c.

attention from the politics at hand. In the case of the Sangh Parivar, as with other religious ideological politics, a fascist politics has stepped up to the stage in the name of Ram, wearing the masks of gods and goddesses. The Indian past too has been drawn upon in the most ahistorical manner, Hindu 'traditions' and myths having materialised as nightmares for Muslims, Christians, dalits and Indian society as a whole. It is, as Marx says, as if

> [T]he tradition of all the dead generations weighs like a nightmare on the brain of the living. And just when they seem engaged in revolutionising themselves and things, in creating something entirely new, they anxiously conjure up the spirits of the past to their service and borrow from them battle slogans and costumes in order to present the new scene of world history, in this time-honoured disguise and this borrowed language.[69]

In the *Communist Manifesto* Marx and Engels spoke about 'open' and 'hidden' struggles of classes, and the possibility of their victory over each other or 'a common ruin of contending classes'.[70] In India we have had a long moment of a fascist manoeuvre of hidden forms of class struggle. Our task is to go behind these ideological disguises and discover the real faces of the aspirants for hegemony and avoid a common ruin.

---

69   Marx 1972c, p. 15.
70   Marx 1972d, p. 595.

Writing 'India', Doing 'Ideology': William Jones' Construction of India as an Ideological Category

Our knowledge of [contemporary] society is to a large extent mediated to us by texts of various kinds. The result, an objectified world-in-common vested in texts, coordinates the acts, decisions, policies, and plans of actual subjects as the acts, decisions, policies, plans of large-scale organisations.[1]

∴

1 Introduction: A New Historiography as a Critique

The objectives and representational efforts of European history have come up for interrogation from some quarters in the last two decades. The reasons for this lie in a wide recognition of a constructive relationship between knowledge and power. This critical impetus seems to have come more from Foucault's 'power/knowledge' formulation and other associated attempts than from an extension of Marx's theory of ideology which was until then the primary critical tool for establishing relations between ideas and exercises of class power with class understood mainly as an economic form. Interest in Marx's notion of ideology dropped considerably in the Anglo-American academic world after the entrance of Michel Foucault's and Antonio Gramsci's works in translation, while social movements with no direct connection with class as defined by Laclau and Mouffe gained momentum. Political economy receded into the background and cultural theories became highly prominent in studying politics. Whereas attempts at working in Marx with Foucault and Gramsci were rarer, there was a greater success in blending Foucault with Gramsci. This was achieved particularly through a manipulation of the categories 'hegemony' and 'common sense' in culturalist terms. An important moment of this success, at least in the English-speaking world, was Edward Said's *Orientalism*.[2] But

---

1 Smith 1990, p. 61.
2 Said 1979.

Orientalism was only the tip of the iceberg of critiques which addressed the power/knowledge relations of the conventional academic disciplines. History writing in particular came in for a trenchant criticism from those who sought to create new interdisciplinary histories, epistemologies and new forms of narratives – sensitive to discursive inscriptions of power or power as discourse. Other disciplines were also affected; Philip Abrams' *Historical Sociology*[3] and the writings of Philip Corrigan, Derek Sayer and Joan Scott, among others, may be remembered in this context. These were radical, marxist or even anti-marxist efforts, drawing upon classical European philosophy, literary and cultural theories. Criticisms of metaphysics and foundationalism offered by Jacques Derrida or Richard Rorty, for example, provided the theoretical bases for many, in combination with Foucault's discursive structuralism.

The new schools produced important critiques, especially thematised around 'difference' and 'representation'. They uncovered significational forms of domination in culture, showing how culture was textured with colonialism, racism, sexism and heterosexism. Of these attempts a very important one was the critique of colonial discourse (popularised by Edward Said) which centred on the relationship between reification and domination in the colonial representation (i.e., construction) of Europe's 'others'. Among the representation of these colonised 'others', cultural construction of India became a central area of critique. Perhaps the most extensive of these is Ronald Inden's *Imagining India*.[4] Here Inden takes history (his own discipline) to task for 'imagining' (i.e., representing cum constructing) India through the epistemological lens of colonialism:

> I criticise the knowledge of 'Others' that Europeans and Americans have created during the periods of their world ascendancy. The specific object of my critique is the Indological branch of 'orientalist discourse' and the accounts of India that it has produced since the Enlightenment, but it also takes on the other disciplines that have had a major part in making these constructs of India – the history of religions, anthropology, economics and political philosophy.[5]

It does not take much perspicacity to realise that Inden's orientation is sensitised by Said's *Orientalism*, though his critique of Indology, mainly based on the

---

3 Abrams 1982.
4 Inden 1990.
5 Ibid., p. 1.

philosophy of R.G. Collingwood (1889–1943), takes him to a somewhat different political conclusion than Said's critique of orientalism.

While we need not detain ourselves with an examination of *Imagining India*, it is clear that this re-reading of Indian history derives from a general attempt to establish *representation* as a key theme in historiography. It expands 'history' to include various narrative forms, among them translation. Interpretive deconstruction becomes the current method of history writing and replaces more conventional tasks of archival retrieval, documentation and so on, with their explanatory or 'truth' claims.[6] As a representational effort history becomes a cultural-political project. It is read as a repository of constructed content, of an accretional body of concepts and images, regarding and standing in for the object/subject under representation. This representational content is read as a gesture of power/knowledge, with embedded moral regulations and political imperatives, for all of which the word ideology, albeit in a non-marxist sense, is sometimes loosely used. A pattern of circulation is also detected within this representational content traveling through the arteries of discursivities and intertextualities. A gathering body of themes, images, icons and narrative forms, such as travelogues or translations for example, are explored to determine what the representational terms are and how they constellate as discursive apparatuses decisive for constructing the 'other'.[7]

This discursive generation and movement of content has come to be considered problematic in that it allows an historically specific content to take on the status of a stable, and even an essential and transcendental, form of knowledge. It has been noted that through this process there developed, over a period of time, a 'conceptual economy' which has provided a foundation for the proliferation of power/knowledge projects.[8] In an essay on *Translation, Colonialism and the Rise of English*, Tejaswini Niranjana points out crucial aspects of this incremental, circulatory and ideologically informing nature of colonial knowledge production in the orientalist context of translation of Indian texts. According to her:

> In the colonial context, a certain conceptual economy is created by the set of related questions which is the problematic of translation. Conventionally, translation depends on the Western philosophical notions of reality,

---

6 For different approaches to history writing and historiography, see Carr 1964; Thompson 1974; Abrams 1982; Scott 1988; and the introduction to Guha and Spivak 1988.

7 There are numerous examples of this. To name a few we can cite Said 1979; Gates 1985, and Pratt 1992.

8 Niranjana 1990, p. 773.

representation and knowledge. Reality is seen as something unproblematic, 'out there'; knowledge involves a representation of this reality; and representation provides direct, unmediated access to a transparent reality. These concepts render invisible what Jacques Derrida calls the logocentric metaphysics by which they are constituted.[9]

For Niranjana, the problem with this 'conceptual economy' is its unproblematic assertion of correspondence between reality and its re-presentation. This transparency and an 'out-thereness' of the representational content allows it to stand-in for reality. Following Jacques Derrida, she connects this 'conceptual economy' to a 'logocentric metaphysics' which erases the foundational dependence of putatively transcendental disciplines (such as philosophy) on mundane, historical/temporal power-informed representational practices and forms.

Assuming Derrida's critique of metaphysics as her point of departure, Niranjana phrases this problem of power/knowledge in philosophy, history and translation in the following way:

> Here I should point out that classical philosophical discourse does not merely engender a practice of translation that is then employed for the purposes of colonial domination; I contend that, simultaneously, translation in the colonial context creates and supports a conceptual economy which works into Western philosophy to function as a philosopheme, a congealed base unit which does not require further breaking down through analysis. As Derrida suggests, the concepts of 'Western metaphysics' are not bound by or produced solely within the 'field' of philosophy. Rather, they come out of and circulate through various discourses at different levels and in different ways, providing thereby 'a conceptual network in which philosophy *itself* has been constituted'.[10]

If we adopt this idea of a conceptual economy of knowledge, then an inter-conceptual and inter-textual nature of knowledge production becomes visible. In addition, it becomes difficult to speak in isolated disciplinarian terms, or solely in terms of synchronicity of representational content or modes. We can and need to speak of a whole intellectual culture, containing a foundational body of 'philosophemes' as 'conceptual naturals' which are unexamined as

9   Ibid., p. 773.
10   Ibid., p. 773.

such. But these 'philosophemes' regularly serve as epistemes which are axiomatic as interpretive devices for further knowledge. Attention is drawn to this by Dorothy E. Smith, for example, in the epigram to this paper, who calls them our 'terms of knowledge', or 'the lineaments of what we already know' in our new knowledge. They provide the anchor or meaning connection between our old and new learning.[11] Niranjana's article shows how such a 'conceptual economy' with its elementary 'epistemes' is provided by the orientalist William Jones' translations of classical Indian texts, and how it structures representation of India for the west. She demonstrates how this content persists through this process of intertextual naturalisation underwriting a diverse body of European writings on India. She convincingly argues that this content functions as a sort of code of power or ideology, embodying the political hermeneutics of colonialism.

Niranjana equates ideology with the representational *content* captured in their distorted and reified forms. This is also Inden's or Said's position, as well as that of others writing on colonial discourse. Their work uncovers the existence of ideological-representational epistemes and their 'economy'. Stereotypes or hypostatised negative and otherising differences, captured in images and concepts, are deconstructively uncovered, disclosing patterns of connected discursivities. But there seems to be little attention given to the fact that in understanding mis-representations which are constructions of power, there is an equally urgent need to inquire into the epistemological method of their production. It is only through a combination of criticism of ideology as content along with an inquiry into its method of production that we could offer a fuller critique of domination with regard to representation and ideology. It is only then that we could properly historicise or contextualise, and deconstruct the social relations which structure these congealed discursive/cultural forms of power – which Said calls 'Orientalism' or Inden 'the symbolic cultural constitution' of an imagined India. What is missing therefore in this alternative (to marxist analysis) critical deconstruction of representation is a sustained inquiry into epistemology which results in the production of otherising forms of knowledge.

Expanding the equation of ideology as content into an enquiry of an epistemological method is possible only in terms of Marx's own conception and criticism of ideology as explicitly stated in *The German Ideology* and implied and referred to in his other texts. This is elaborately discussed by D.E. Smith

---

11   See Smith 1990, chapter 2, 'The Ideological Practice of Sociology' in its entirety for the reading of ideology I have evolved for this paper.

whose own feminist theorisation treats ideology as fundamentally a problem of epistemological method rather than as a body of 'false' or distorted ideas (concepts, categories or images).[12] This type of marxist critique of ideology shows how a critique of culture primarily based on the content of representation suffers from the danger of degenerating into a descriptive compendium rather than a critical enquiry into a problem of meaning and knowledge in the context of social relations of power. Thus the possibility of developing a non-reifying, truly deconstructive analytical, that is, altogether non-ideological knowledge, remains inarticulate.

A thoroughgoing critical suggestion, therefore, consists of a proposal for a critique which has two distinct yet ineluctably constitutive aspects: one of *content*, identified as a body of particular conceptual/imagistic re-presentations, and the other, the 'conceptual practice' or an epistemological *method of generation* of this content. This entails not only the task of replacing a 'false' content with a 'true' one, or casting a general suspicion upon it, but also of shifting our gaze to the social relations of its production, until knowledge itself can be seen as a form of social relation. This amounts to devising a critical method which reveals any form of representation to be an imaged or coded, interpreted and conceptualised formal-cultural articulation of a definite set of socio-historical relations.

This inquiry, which attempts to situate the representational content, rests on reflexivity. It involves a query into how visibilities and invisibilities, silences and occlusions, inclusions and exclusions are intrinsic to certain modes of knowing, and how these modes or 'conceptual practices' are encoded in substantive representational forms. This reflexivity is essential for disclosing the implicit social relations which are embedded in representations, since a decontextualised knowledge-object behaves pretty much like any independent objectified construction, for example a car, which does not exhibit in its bounded being the social relations of its production; or that of capital – particularly as it enters into a relation of circulation and consumption, away from the process of its production.

This comparison between a car and a reified cultural form, such as an orientalist one, is not so unusual. It can be understood by paying heed to the unproblematised and transparent representation of the colonial creators who supply the conceptual-imagistic content regarding the colonised 'others', particularly aimed at a Western audience and readers. The 'philosophemes' or

---

12   For Smith's notion of ideology, especially as a discursive/epistemological form of 'relations of ruling,' see chapters 2 and 3 in Smith 1990.

social assumptions that vitiate this body of knowledge are, after all, not generated within the content which they inform or structure. Any criticism of this discourse needs to situate its content into its historical-social relations and uncover its epistemological method whereby it incorporates particular social relations into a cultural form and concepts. The very characteristics of this knowledge form must thus be accounted for. Otherwise we can only critique this or that construction/representational content with regard to its truth claim, or its stand-in effect for the moments of the social. A simple cultural critique locks us, in the last instance, into a series of representational recursivities. There is actually no exit from these mirroring representational constructs, since one is always expecting to come up with one which is 'true', forgetting that the social (that is, 'reality' in a non-metaphysical sense) is always more intensive and extensive than its re-presentation or discursive form even in the most nuanced form of telling.

So far, the cultural critiques of various forms of othering, difference and so on have treated the problem of relation between the social and its re-presentation more or less as one of content. Less sophisticated talk about 'stereotypes' and more complex or refined talk about 'inscriptions', 'discursivities' and 'differences' have this same accent in common. Even when the critics name history, it remains as an assumption, somewhere out there, as a frame to the text under consideration. Since history is mainly entered into the production of consciousness as an accretion of images and ideas, we cannot, therefore, see it as an organisation and mediation of social relations as forms of thought. Thus orientalism or Indology is treated by Said or Inden mainly as a problem of cultural hegemony cradled within history or a temporal space marked by power. In promising a thoroughgoing critique of hegemony, or 'ideology', cultural critique of colonial discourse has mostly remained at the level of collections of cultural constructs. Criticism has revealed highly sensitive aspects of the content and of hermeneutic relations among them, displaying instability and unreliability on the basis of gaps, fissures and inconsistencies. As such, they decode an attribution of meanings to India or West Asia, revealing imagined geographies of power. This also translates into presentations of peoples of these regions as passive and reified subjects and-agents. Lata Mani's acute observations on English representation of *sati* as a nodule of patriarchal-colonial imagination, and thus a form of displaced violence, help to throw light on this:

> Within the discourse on *sati*, women are represented in two mutually exclusive ways: either as heroines able to withstand the raging blaze of the funeral pyre, or else as pathetic victims coerced against their will into the flames. These poles preclude the possibility of a female subjectivity that

is shifting, contradictory, inconsistent. Such a constrained and reductive notion of agency discursively positions women as objects to be saved – never as subjects who act, even if within extremely constraining social conditions. This representation of Indian women has been fertile ground for the elaboration of discourses of salvation, in context of colonialism, nationalism, and, more recently, Western feminism. For the most part, all three have constructed the Indian woman not as someone who acts, but as someone to be acted upon.[13]

There cannot be any doubt about the political nature of these constructions and the value of having a cultural critique of them. The direction of the predicative role of the cultural-moral construction of 'India' as a category for ruling can never be underestimated, especially with regard to mediating knowledge relationships between the knower and the known.

But to go beyond the ideological circle and the politics of representation in ways that offer other epistemological possibilities needs an anti-ideological 'conceptual practice' of power[14] which entails criticising particular established representations with regard to a theory of reification. In other words, the cultural critique of knowledge as content must also rest upon an epistemological critique of the method of production of knowledge. My suggestion, therefore, is not to abandon a cultural critique of content, leaving Foucault and others behind, but to augment this critique with Marx's own methodological critique. This calls for a different reading of Marx than that provided by many western marxists or by the Soviet Academy of Social Sciences through a slogan-like use of sentences from *The German Ideology*, such as the 'ruling ideas of any age are the ideas of the ruling class'. Displaying a cruder form of content orientation than cultural criticism, this approach obscures the fact that Marx's debate with Feuerbach hardly centred itself in a demand for a content substitution, for 'true' or 'authentic' as opposed to 'false' ideas about social reality.

In fact, what disturbs Marx is what Feuerbach *had* done in that direction by substituting Hegel's notion of the Idea (or Christian notion of 'God') with that of 'Man' and 'human essence'. This was considered by Feuerbach and the Young Hegelians (early Marx included) as a paradigm shift. However, Marx subsequently disputed this revolutionary claim in *The German Ideology*, where he argued against the very epistemology at work in Feuerbach and Hegel, rather than the content that resulted from it. He elaborated a counter-method to the

---

13   Mani 1992, p. 397.
14   This is borrowed from the title of Smith's book, *The Conceptual Practices of Power*. It is a
       code name for the *doing* of ideology as social relations of ruling.

'speculative rationalism' of Hegel and other more disguised speculative philosophers (metaphysicians) such as Feuerbach. Focusing on the central problematic of a constructive relationship between particular and general, concrete
and abstract, experience and analysis, Marx went on to formulate a reflexive critical method. His foremost concern is thus not content or closed, discursive structures, what he calls 'interpretive categories' to 'trim off epochs
of history' with.[15] In its place he formulates an exercise in practical philosophy by discerning the main epistemological procedures or 'three tricks' of
'speculative philosophy' (or metaphysics). This he claims to be the working
apparatus of ideology. Equating 'philosophy' (metaphysics) with ideology, he
calls for a materialist knowledge or a form of knowing which allows for social
change. Ideology, on the other hand, is marked out by Marx as the characteristic job of intellectual disciplinarians – whose specialisation and expertise
consist of practices, relations and discursivities of a mental labour, decapit-
ated from manual and physical labour. Intellect thus severed and spherised,
not surprisingly, seeks 'transcendence' from the mundane, from history and
everyday life, aspiring to a claim of absolute, universal, essential, once-for-all
knowledge.

Marx's critical method is something of a back calculation which picks up a
construction or a reified content – a 'ruling idea', so to speak – and regrounds
it in actual social relations. Considering knowledge as a form of social organisation (as forms of intelligibility, mediation and expression), identifying the
relationship between manual and mental division of labour with property and
class (as an organisational rather than a solely brutal control over labour of others), he challenges the universalist/essential claims of 'ruling ideas' of the ruling
classes represented as the single rational, universally valid ones.[16] Ideology is
put forward as not only what is believed in but as a form of *doing* a certain
kind of thought or belief, an active epistemological gesture, whose method of
production is uncovered by the 'three tricks:'

Trick 1:   Separate what people say they think from the actual circumstances
           in which it is said, from the actual empirical conditions of their lives,
           and from the actual individuals who said it.
Trick 2:   Having detached the ideas, arrange them to demonstrate an order
           among them that accounts for what is observed. (Marx and Engels
           describe this as making 'mystical connections'.)

---

15   Marx and Engels 1970.
16   Ibid.

Trick 3:   Then change the ideas into a 'person'; that is, set them up as dis-
           tinct entities (for example, a value pattern, norm, belief system and
           so forth) to which agency (or possible causal efficacy) may be attrib-
           uted. And redistribute them to 'reality' by attributing them to actors
           who can now be treated as representing the ideas.[17]

Marx's critique of ideology puts forward the methodology for a practical knowledge or 'praxis'. It consists of uncovering *systematically* how a dissociation is
produced between history/society and forms of consciousness. It directs us to
look out from a representational construct, rather than look at it. Concrete
social relations congealed within the constructed form are treated as a formalised mutuality of consciousness and the social.

Accepting the position that reifying forms of knowing which privilege *any*
content as universal and essential will result in a reified content stops us from
searching for a more 'authentic' content. When candidates for this 'authenticity' are paced through the anti-ideological critique it becomes a non-issue
to discuss what an Arab or a Hindu actually 'is'. Our attempts go beyond any
homogenisation or essentialising, and we recognise the diversity, the historicity
and social nature of the content. We treat content as formalised and conceptualised expressions of their constitutive social relations of power, situated
within forms of ruling and certain ways of knowing and representing. Thus
knowledge exceeds the cultural end product – either of concepts or images –
to be stored eventually in textual hold-alls. The issue of 'truth' is expanded from
content, or *what* is produced, to that of its process and relations, to the *how* and
why of its production. This marxist anti-ideological knowledge, conventionally
known as historical materialism, provides a grounded critique of idealism, or
metaphysics, reaching deeper than the Derridean counter-discursivity, a particular spin-off from his version of criticism of metaphysics.[18] A fuller critique
of colonial discourse cannot be achieved solely through Derrida or other cultural critiques which have not been able to move out into a social and historical
space outside the labyrinth of language and conceptualisation.

So an anti-ideological analysis, rather than a cultural critique of representation, involves a thorough criticism of the two-fold dimension of ideology – as a
'conceptual practice' and a particular content. The concreteness of the content
is crucial for determining the specificity of the ideological excursion under consideration. To challenge any domination, for example, the resistance must be

---

17   This is Smith's version of Marx's formulation (1990, p. 43).
18   See Derrida 1978, especially the essay 'Violence and Metaphysics: An Essay on the Thought
     of Emmanuele Levinas'.

addressed practically and specifically. This implies definite references to terms, of time, space and cultural forms. It is this which points out how abstraction or erasures of these elements are basic to any relations of ruling – for example, of colonialism. Attention to content also allows us to make distinctions between different moments of ruling. Thus content, understood as intertextuality, or a 'conceptual economy' based on 'philosophemes', creates not only the recognised veins of intellectual disciplines, but also crumbles into a cultural commonsense which subsists as the political unconscious of any society. But having said so, one has to be equally mindful of ruling as an epistemological procedure which organises social relations of domination. This procedure, involving how thinking is done at all, is also implied in all situations of domination without partiality to this or that project. As the content of ideology travels through various transcriptive modes through time and space, so does its method as *the method* for producing knowledge, and elaborates itself in finer and finer forms of rationalisation, or technology, of production of ideas and images. Thus the relationship between content and form, between the social and the cultural, the intellectual and the political, can never be torn apart into separate realities. Niranjana's quotation of Derrida's remark about the circularity of 'logocentric metaphysics' expresses partially what Marx meant by ideology.[19] In a manner of speaking, a critique of ideology is a critique of metaphysics. It also reveals a constructive relationship between empiricism and metaphysics. A stereotype, or an otherising cultural construct, can thus be seen as a particularist essentialism or universalisation – whereby this or that feature of the empirical is fuelled with a transcending idealist drive which sends it out of the orbit of time as lived history. Thus constructs of power, even of Indology or orientalism, are not necessarily 'inventions' or 'lies' within their own scope of telling, but rather an illicit expansion and universalisation of lived and observed particulars. Thus the idealist/essentialising method of metaphysics dignifies an empirical bit of the concrete into a timeless verity.

According to the version of anti-ideological critique, the question of cultural representation of India has a wider problematic than offered by critics such as Inden. A methodological critique now integrates with a cultural critique. The empirical fact that colonial history and thus the representation of India were in the main produced by Europeans of a certain political and moral persuasion, at a certain juncture in history, is here combined with an epistemological critique. While recognising that idealist or metaphysical epistemology – that is, ideological method – that produces reified knowledge is not a European monopoly,

---

19   See also Smith's notion of the circularity of ideology in 1990, pp. 93–100.

we also attend to the European colonial context of the texts so produced, which hold a content appropriate to the time and design of that colonialism. We recognise that an 'imagined', 'translated', orientalist 'India' was born through an intellectual process which was implicated in a particular set of socio-cultural relations existing at that time. This content, or an attribution to India, produced through and as ruling independently of Indian agency, entered into European circulation both transcendentally as 'knowledge' and practically as categories for administration.[20] Just as 'the Orient', 'Africa', 'the dark continent' contributed to the colonial significational and administrative-exploitive system, so did this 'India'.[21] This 'India' is therefore more than 'imagined', but is rather both an epistemic and a practical form of exploitation and violence.[22]

We can now begin to explore certain representative colonial texts to make our understanding more concrete. Keeping an eye on particular knowledge procedures, their inscriptions and transcriptions, their intertextual travelling paths and 'conceptual economy', we can go beyond Said and other critics of colonial discourse. We integrate a marxist theory of ideology with specific semiotic content. More than gesturing towards a power/knowledge relation as always already there, we concentrate on the historical dimension and its social organisation and relations of knowledge. This allows for more than an exhaustive study of the metamorphosis of cultural content. We become alert to the dangers of reified knowledge *per se* which is not provided by a simpler cultural critique of representation. It becomes apparent that not only in the context of colonialism, but in creating *all* negative 'others' (internal and external to *any* society), fixed, transcendental, homogeneous and essential verities are crafted by welding together bits of empirical observables with the method of metaphysics. The fuller critique thus advances beyond the relatively well-mapped realm of images, categories or constructs of power, and begins to consider knowledge in terms of *social relations* and modes of mediation also between the knower and the known. If 'knowing' consists of 'a *relation* between the knower and the known',[23] then it follows that the *content* of that knowing is deeply informed by that relation which also dictates and reflects the 'terms' of understanding which are embedded in it. They constitute the knower's historical and social knowledge apparatus.

Clear distinctions therefore have to be made between ideology, which erases and occludes by degrounding ideas from history and society, and knowledge

---

20   Smith 1990, pp. 61–5 and 83–8.
21   Dirks 1992, pp. 1–25. See also Mohamed 1995.
22   See Spivak 1988b for 'epistemic violence'.
23   On knowing as a relation and ideology as ruling, see the 'Introduction' in Smith 1987.

procedures which allow for relational disclosures. The acknowledgment that some forms of knowing contain disclosive dimensions, and others block them, renders spurious any questions regarding the fallible nature of perception, while retaining the knowledge relevance of history. If we concentrate on the methodological critique, we can implicate the knower and 'what' she comes up with (as content) in that very method which is employed in producing knowledge. We cannot only 'show' the content as facts, description or information, but also unravel the knowledge-organising social relation and cultural practices of the knower impacting on the known. Thus, rather than being only an end product, knowledge becomes material to, and a form of, social, conceptual and finally political relations and organisation. This approach to knowledge spells an open-endedness of content in that it is always dynamic and incomplete, but persistently reflexive. It should be contrasted to an ideological approach which produces seamless conceptual or image objects that bind loose ends, erase contradictions which are a part and parcel of social relations and locations of the knower and the known. Fixed facts, concepts and images of India or of Europe, whose claim to verity relies on metaphysical notions such as 'essential', 'typical', 'objective' and 'universal', are seen in the end to be ideology.

What then are some of the particular knowledge-producing procedures and content which constructed 'India' for the west? How are we to understand this 'India' from an anti-ideological perspective? What follows is my example of a fuller exploration of the work of one of the earliest English writers on India, who is a scholar in his own right as well as an administrator. He represented India to the West from his vantage point within colonial relations, and these representations took root and branched out as 'philosophemes' of further European knowledge of India and provided the categorical bases for forms of ruling. The writer in question is William Jones, Chief Justice of the Supreme Court of Bengal, and a co-founder with Warren Hastings of the Royal Asiatic Society (1784), a scholar of classical European and Indian languages and a translator of Sanskrit legal texts. I chose to study this author and his authoritative text rather than an overall cultural compendium of images, opinions and descriptions as the basic element of 'India' because 'India' as constructed by him occupies foundational textual and administrative spaces. His 'India' is truly a 'ruling' category in so far as it directs other texts both in terms of knowledge production and in the work of administering the East India Company and the colonial empire. His texts thus hold an inscriptional status and confer the seal of truth upon others which were reproduced through their ideological pre-scriptions. This author, in short, is crucial in leaving an imprimatur on what Europe and the west came to know as India.

2   Contexting the Text

> When I was at sea last August, on my voyage to this country [India], which
> I had so long and ardently desired to visit, I found one evening, on inspect-
> ing the observations of the day, that *India* lay before us, and *Persia* on our
> left, whilst a breeze from *Arabia* blew nearly on our stern ... It gave me
> inexpressible pleasure to find myself in the midst of so noble an amphi-
> theatre, almost encircled by the vast regions of *Asia*, which has ever been
> esteemed the nurse of sciences, the inventress of delightful and useful
> arts, the scene of glorious actions, fertile in the production of human
> genius, abounding in natural wonders, and infinitely diversified in the
> forms of religion and government, in the laws, manners, customs and lan-
> guages, as well as in features and complexions of men. I could not help
> remarking, how important and extensive a field was yet unexplored, and
> how many solid advantages unimproved ...[24]

The ideological concerns and construction of 'India' as produced by William
Jones and other orientalists requires a simultaneous probing of method and
content in order to determine its ideological status. This means situating the
knower, William Jones, on the deck of a ship, arriving at Calcutta not just as a
visitor, but as the head of the colonial justice system and an aspiring explorer of
India bent on 'improving solid advantages'. It also means observing how India
the known becomes Jones' 'India', a knowledge object for colonial ruling. Thus
the knower and the known are contexted to history, politics and society, rather
than being entities of a timeless zone of metaphysics. This situating attempt
reveals the nature of European necessity for 'understanding' and 'improving'
India. The timing of Jones' knowledge enterprise makes it evident that his construction of 'India' happens at a very particular juncture of European history,
when discursive practices rather than sole brutalities of conquest are becoming
material to forms of ruling. Institutions of knowledge such as The Asiatic Society (1784) straddle at this period the double and integrated realms of reflection
and ruling, thereby mediating brute force with 'facts' and 'truths'. English colonisation of India becomes both a knowledge enterprise and an administration
of socio-political and economic domination.[25] Even though Jones is mainly a

---

24   Jones 1799.
25   These knowledge activities brought about by the occasion of colonisation involve putting
     together a stable mode of textualisation, of inscription and transcription, which encode
     and organise administrative forms and relations of ruling in concretely ideological terms.
     See Guha 1982a; Stokes 1969; Visvanathan 1989.

humanist – a translator, linguist and a cultural essayist – an examination of his method and content of knowledge regarding India discloses an epistemology for a specific social ontology of power.

Jones' purpose is to re-present India, that is, to create a stock of knowledge about its history, culture and society with an aim to stabilising these representations so that they can be seen as generally valid. For this Jones establishes a truth claim with regard to his formulations as 'essential' equivalencies for Indian reality contexted to ruling. In this the differences between orientalists such as Jones and Utilitarians such as James Mill become subordinated to their overall colonial hegemonic projects.[26] Though Jones' discourse of the sublime, of 'Drawing Orient knowledge from its fountains/pure, through caves obstructed long, and paths/too long obscure',[27] may seem an antithesis of the cold Benthamite sneering prose of Mill, yet the claim of 'discovering' an 'authentic India' dominates the colonial texts in general.[28]

The outgrowth of this discovery of 'India', culminating in a sort of mythology, provides the interpretive and interpellative framework for the orientalisation of India, or what Inden calls the 'symbolic cultural constitution' of the indological construct. The content, or the resulting stereotypes, are either exotic (as with Jones) and/or negative towards India (for both Jones and Mill).[29] Jones' opinions in particular are often ambiguous or contradictory, swinging between respect for and distrust of Indians and India. The sentiments expressed regarding 'Asiatick civilisations' in the epigram above, or throughout the first volume of his *Works*, clash remarkably with his opinion of the people of the region expressed as a negatively differentiated cultural category which he calls 'the Indian'. His dislike for Indians is evident in the following lines, where he re-

---

26   For similarities and differences among orientalists and utilitarians, see Majeed 1992.

27   William Jones, 'A Hymn to Surya,' as quoted by Niranjana 1990, p. 775.

28   This language of exploration and discovery is pervasive in the European colonial enterprise. From Columbus to William Jones to Henry Morton Stanley and beyond, this discourse helps to obscure the dimension of force, brutalities and denigrations integral to colonisation. Within this overarching discursivity, the notion of authenticity and exposure of the real, the true, the original, etc., find their place. The metaphor or trope of 'caves' or hidden and lost knowledge is present equally ubiquitously. A modern example of this is the complex use of the cave in E.M. Forster's novel *A Passage to India*, charting the journey of the colonial English psyche into the cave of 'India' and beyond. The aesthetic of the sublime that is found in these metaphoric discursivities present, in overabundance in William Jones' poetry, is a major genre of visual depiction of India to Europe. For an excellent example, Archer and Falk 1989.

29   See the chapter on 'Manners, Morals and Customs' of Hindus in Mill (1968 [1]) for examples of negative stereotypes, also partly shared by Jones (for example, in Jones 1970 [11], p. 712).

quests his friend not to be 'like the deluded, besotted Indians, among whom I live, who would *receive liberty* as a curse instead of a blessing, if it were possible *to give it them*, and would reject, as a vase of poison, that, which, if they could taste and digest it, would be water of life'.[30]

An aspiration of 'mastery' over a land and its people, as well as their forms of knowledge, inspires and infuses Jones' *Works*. This becomes explicit in Sir John Shore's (Lord Teignmoutt's) 'Introduction' to Jones' *Collected Works*. Jones, as Shore puts it, was no mere linguist and translator. Though he 'eagerly embrace[d] ... the opportunity of making himself master of the *Sanskrit*', he 'would have despised the reputation of a mere linguist'.[31] His real motive, according to Shore, was the pursuit of 'Knowledge and Truth' regarding Indian culture and society in service to his own country, as he aimed to create a just and benevolent rule over India in keeping with its own nature. Since this was not manifest, according to Jones, it needed to be exposed or re-presented:

> Such were the motives that induced him to propose to the government of this country [colonial Bengal], what he justly denominated a work of national utility and importance, the compilation of a copious digest of *Hindu* and *Mahomedan* Law, from *Sanskrit* and *Arabick* originals, with an offer of his services to supervise the compilation and with a promise to translate it. He had foreseen, previous to his departure from Europe, that without the aid of such a work, the wise and benevolent intentions of the legislature of *Great Britain*, in leaving, to a certain extent, the natives of these provinces in possession of their own laws, could not completely be fulfilled; and his experience, after a short residence in India, confirmed what his sagacity had anticipated, that without principles to refer to, in a language familiar to the judges of the courts, adjudications amongst natives must too often be subject to an uncertain and erroneous exposition, or wilful misinterpretation of their laws.[32]

Such statements go to show that the act of territorial possession of India was at the same time an act of construction of authoritative knowledge, particularly 'compiled' and 'selected' as Indian Law, by the rulers. This imputation of authority and appeal to a 'real' knowledge hides the interested and immediate (as opposed to 'pure' and transcendental) nature of Jones' version of India,

---

30   Jones 1970 [II], p. 847.
31   Jones 1799 [I], p. v.
32   Ibid., pp. v–vi.

which both encodes and administers domination by an active supersession of 'native knowledge' of their own laws.

Thus Jones' translations or cultural essays, as with any ideological excursion, are structured with and motivated by extraneous knowledge imperatives, their legitimating appeal lying in a metaphysical (universalist/essentialist) mode. This epistemology, which hides the reified and tendentious nature of this knowledge, performs an inversion of subject-object relations. The erasure of history and everyday lives of colonised Indians, the very fact of domination itself, are obscured and written over. The distortion or deformation of content which this results in is part and parcel of the ideological method discussed above. As pointed out above, it functions on a double level: of abstraction or emptying out of historicity and agency, and of filling in these abstractions with empirical illustrations of their 'truth'. Performing metonymic or synechdochal gestures, that is, generalising a part for the whole or vice versa, this epistemology lays the ground for a power/knowledge exercise which, when articulated to conquest and colonial rule, becomes 'colonial discourse'. A good example of this procedure is Jones' construction of the 'submissive Indian' based on personal contempt for the colonised and individual instances of submission or obsequiousness, while ignoring instances of resistance to British rule or his own fear of their subversiveness.[33] The application to Indian society and governments of the notion of 'Oriental/Asiatic despotism', learned during his Persian studies, is another instance of this colonial discourse.[34] The purpose of legitimation is only ambiguously served through the irony that Jones, the Chief Justice of a colonial rule, should berate Indians for a debased and slavish mentality while using this assumption about their nature to justify colonialism. In the 'Tenth Annual Discourse to Asiatic Society', for example, Jones felt that he 'could not but remark the constant effect of despotism in benumb-

---

33   On this projected evil, and fear of the colonised other in their various forms, see the classic text by Joseph Conrad, *The Heart of Darkness*, and its critique in Fanon 1963. It is brought out eloquently by Taussig 1992, p. 139: 'Hated and feared, objects to be despised, yet also objects of awe, the reified essence of evil in the very being of their bodies, these figures of the Jew, the Black, the Indian, and woman herself, are clearly objects of cultural construction, the leaden keel of evil and mystery stabilising the ship and course that is Western History'.

34   The discursive legacy of this has been discussed by Said 1981. The notion of Oriental/Asiatic despotism and assumptions about Asiatic society embedded in it develop through Mill 1968, Lyall's *Asiatic Society*, Marx's and Weber's essays on colonialism in India and Indian society, among others, enter into the later sociological and historico-political assumptions of Barrington Moore, Perry Anderson and many others. 'Despotism' becomes synonymous with the 'East', providing in both early and later periods of history a legitimation for colonial rule and other dominations.

ing and debasing all those faculties which distinguish men from the herd that grazes; and to that cause he would impute the decided inferiority of most Asiatic nations, ancient and modern ...'[35]

The ideological method of erasure and categorical construction in Jones' *Works* is connected with his pursuit of metaphysics. Thus, the vindication of his knowledge of India lies in 'purity' and transcendence from history, social relations and other perceived accidentalities. This immutability provides the solid basis or authority for ruling, to be held as valid by both Europeans and Indians, and is central to Jones' project of colonial rule in India. As Niranjana remarks:

> The most significant nodes of William Jones' work are (a) the need for translation by the Europeans, since the natives are unreliable interpreters of their own laws and cultures; (b) the desire to be a law-giver, to give the Indians their 'own' laws; and (c) the desire to 'purify' Indian culture and speak on its behalf. The interconnectedness between these obsessions are extremely complicated. They can be seen, however, as feeding into a larger discourse [of Improvement and Education] that interpellates the colonial subject.[36]

As a representative of the system, Jones felt that India belonged to England, and in transference, to him. He imagined an India through his own interpretive schema and symbolic organisation, omitting 'unnecessary', that is, unfitting details. Thus the 'purification' or 'sanskritisation' which he performed is itself an act of colonisation.[37] Helped by a metaphysical method and artistic/linguistic skills, the special forte of Jones, this self-interested, particularist project of ruling achieves a transcendent and universal glow. Good examples are to be found in his emulation of Vedic hymns, in which his adoption of the persona of a brahmin-truth seeker keeps the crudities of the ruling project safely out of sight.:

> And if they [the gods] ask, 'What mortal pours the strain?' ...
> Say: 'from the bosom of you Silver Isle [England],
> Where skies more softly smile,

---

35   Niranjana 1990, p. 774.
36   Ibid.
37   'Sanskritization' literally means purification, and 'Sanskrit,' the language, literally means that which has been purified. Sanskrit, interestingly, has never been a spoken language, i.e., a vernacular, for any particular social group.

He came; and, lisping our celestial tongue,
Though not from Brahma sprung,
Draws Orient knowledge from its fountains pure,
Through caves obstructed long, and paths too long obscure'.[38]

These Indian conceits and the pastoralism, compounded with the image of
the truth seeker, add up to a richly textured colonial discourse. They allow the
romantic paganism of Jones to coalesce with that of a universal knower. Yet
this knower is also a European to the west, a Man of Reason, with a mission to
reveal the 'real India'.[39] This ideal knower represents the truly 'human' knower,
as opposed to 'the native' or 'the debased Indian' who can never aspire to such
a status. Thus Jones' quest for knowledge and 'discovery' of India is both an
allegory of 'Man's discovery of Truth' and a medium for colonisation. The mask
of the poet and metaphysician (the truth-seeker) hides the brutalities of conquest and the historical particularities and conditionalities of this so-called
universal knowledge and representation.

From the point of view of the production of ideology as method, this dual
disappearance of the social actualities of both knower and the known is crucial,
as also is their reappearance on a secondary plane of metaphysics as the universal knower and the known object, securely attached to the platform of ruling.
Through this transmutation the empirical moments of what is known, that is,
what is seen, read or heard in or about India/Indians, are textually re-figured
and discursively aligned. Pre-existing discourses of power provide what Marx
called 'mystical connections' – that is, a coherent 'interpretive schema' – for
which the empirical becomes but an embodiment or illustration of an idea
previously held. The main interpretive schema or discourse within which Jones
writes 'India' is one of 'civilisation' and 'tradition', with implicit and explicit binaries of 'improvement', 'native savagery' or 'Oriental barbarism'. The notion of
'tradition' plays a powerful and ambiguous role, switching from one pole of
meaning to the other. It must be noted that these discourses are already in
place and used in Europe prior to colonisation of India. Traditionality and savagery are alternately, or in conjunction, considered the 'essential' character of
India, while reason, rationality, improvement and civilisation are seen as the
attributes of Europe. The metaphysical dimension of this discursivity allows
for atemporality, unchangingness and repetition to be built into the concept

---

38   'A Hymn to Surya' [the Sun], quoted in Niranjana 1990, p. 775.
39   See in this context a short but useful discussion in Majeed 1992, pp. 31–40, regarding Jones'
      reading of Indian history and its expression in his poetry. Majeed and others, for example
      V. de Sola Pinto, have situated Jones within the tradition of English romantic poetry.

of knowledge. Thus immovable stereotypes mark the passage of the history of India, and Europe/England and India face each other in an essential ontology of difference. An example can be found in the common practice of equating India with ritual violence and sacrifices.[40] This is then opposed to European civilisation or rule of law. Europe therefore is never equated with witch burning or other frequently held *auto da fé* or brutalities of punishment.[41] These are never considered 'essential' or characteristic to European civilisation, while the sporadic occurrence of *satidaha* (burning of women on their husband's pyre) in India is seized upon as the 'essence' of Indian civilisation and worked into the colonial justice system and the moral regulation of Indian society.

Thus, we can see that an ideological formulation of content is not necessarily 'a lie', or 'wholly arbitrary' in any ordinary sense, but rather an illicit and essential extension of the empirical or the particular into a universal. As noted earlier, this is a matter of fuelling an empirical moment with a metaphysical conceptual dynamic which interpellates the empirical into conceptual frames which are far wider than their immediate scope. The reading of India, therefore, takes place in a European discourse of knowledge belonging to early bourgeois society. Indian colonisation as a knowledge project for ruling is thus situated within the European renaissance and enlightenment notions of reason and humanism which are introjected into the construction of India in the shape of metaphors, allegories and images as well as morally regulatory views. Details of Indian life, history and culture are fitted into an over-arching elite code of European 'civilisation', marked by a deep sense of superiority over 'others'. This epistemological manoeuvre implies interpellative and interpretive processes which render invisible and unnameable actual social relations, values and contradictions in existence in India. In this colonial knowledge universe we are, as D.E. Smith points out, in a blind alley of 'phenomena the only practical universe of exploration, or substrate of which is the social organisation and relation of sociological [read: colonial/ideological] discourse itself'.[42] However, we need to explore this formative and knowledge phenomena in greater detail if we want to understand more concretely how the full scope of ideology embraces both form and content.

---

40 This view of India as a land of ritual violence is as old as Herodotus. Rich examples can be drawn from British writings on *satidaha*. See Mani 1992 or Bannerjee 1989.

41 As, for example, outlined by Michel Foucault 1979, numerous studies on the evolution of European criminal laws, or studies on the European counter-reformation and the Inquisition, especially historical works on the treatment of witches and heretics.

42 Smith 1990, p. 33.

3   'India:' A Knowledge of Power

> By India ... I mean that whole extent of country, in which the primitive
> religion and that language of the *Hindus* prevail, at this day with more or
> less their ancient priority, and in which the *Nagari* letters are still used
> with more or less deviation from their original forms.[43]

Anyone familiar with the *Works* of William Jones will recognise in the above
lines some key words in his vocabulary which serve as governing categories for
his voluminous opus on India. As stated above, these keywords constellate into
a quasi-knowledge paradigm, a discursive organisation and interpretation of
culture and language. They also ambiguously shade off into value judgement
while also speaking of languages. Again the keywords, predictably, are 'purity'/'original forms'/'ancientness'. They are paired with notions such as 'prim-
itiveness' of religion (inclusive of language and culture) and 'deviation' from
their 'original forms'. This discursivity is in keeping with Jones' preoccupation
with the ancientness of India and of retrieving or rescuing it from history and
re-presenting it in its essential form. This is how he attempts 'to know India
better than any other European ever knew it', and to represent it for others,
implicitly, Europeans.[44] There is also an assumption here of a transparent relationship between reality and its representation as displayed by all aspects of
Jones' construction of India.

Emphasis on this discourse of purity and its perversion (read as corruption produced through socio-historical changes), helps us to read Jones' *Works*
in terms of value judgements regarding what Jones thought India once was
and what it had degenerated into in his time. This cultural-moral judgement
entailed an assessment of what Jones called 'the manners', and James Mill, the
'Cultures, Morals and Customs' of 'the Hindoos'. Jones contrasted these changing 'manners' to the immutable 'moral' truths enshrined in scriptural-legal
texts, such as Manu's *Dharmashastra*. His struggles could be seen as a way to
control the chaos of 'manners' and to keep out history with the fence of edited
and anthologised texts. He states as much in his prefaces to the legal digests of
Muslim and Hindu law – *Al Sirajyyah* and *Institutes of Hindu Law*.

Jones' intense awareness of the destabilising effects of history and changing social/cultural relations and forms is best displayed in his legal project.
A self-conscious decision to textually fix the law is taken in face of the recog-

---

43   Jones 1799 [1], p. 23.
44   Majeed 1992, p. 24.

nition of the power of changing manners and customs. As he puts it in the preface to *Institutes of Hindu Law*:

> It is a maxim in the science of legislation and government, that laws are of no avail without manners, or, to explain the sentence more fully, that the best intended legislative provisions would have no beneficial effect even at first, and none at all in a short course of time, unless they were congenial to the disposition and habits, to the religious prejudices, and approved immemorial usages, of the people, for whom they were enacted ...[45]

And because he is so aware of these customs and prejudices, the fixation of pieces of texts of Hindu ancient law becomes a fetish object for him. In fact Jones learns Sanskrit only to assure himself that the *real law* from the texts was being instituted by the Company and crown courts. His fears of corruption and deviation are enhanced by his perception of deceitfulness in 'the natives', showing the chronic insecurity of a ruler who is dependent on local experts for gaining access to knowledge necessary for ruling. His vehemence against 'the imposition' by pandits and maulavis is matched by his rhetoric of moral 'purity' in the exigencies of ruling. As he puts it: 'It is of utmost importance that the stream of Hindu Law should be pure; for we are entirely at the power of the native lawyers, through our ignorance of *Sanscrit*'.[46] This also made him argue for the learning of Persian by the servants of the Company – Persian had been the court or official language in northern and eastern India since pre-colonial times, and ignorance of it formed a barrier to their trade and advancement activities, as they could not make any local transactions in writing:

> [T]he servants of the company received letters which they could not read, and were ambitious of gaining titles of which they could not comprehend the meaning; it was found highly dangerous to employ the natives as interpreters, upon whose fidelity they could not depend; and it was at last discovered, that they must apply themselves to the study of the Persian language ...[47]

If this need for languages was present among the English traders even in pre-colonial days, it became more acute, according to Jones, in the era when the

---

45   Jones 1799 [III], p. 53.
46   Jones 1970 [II], p. 666.
47   Jones 1799 [II], pp. 126–7.

East India company assumed the task of ruling India and evolving a justice system. Jones' metaphysical and moral drive for 'purity' was concretised through a 'fixed text', a core of legal references intended for English judges and administrators, in order to discipline the natives.

Texts and facts, representation and reality, were mediated and constructed through anthologisation and inscription of moral codes, of legal and social conduct. This was a totalising enterprise, as ruling discourse has to be, and it covered all aspects of 'native' realities. Even the essays on botany written by Jones exemplify a homology to his ruling project. In 'Plants of India', for instance, he emphasised the same inscriptive injunctions which we find in his works of law and culture. Here too he valorised ancient languages on account of their purity and transcendental hold on 'truth'. His suspicion regarding the vulgar and the vernacular, about fluctuations in popular cultural idioms, organise his essays on plants. An example of this is the following advice to botanists on Indian flora:

> Now the first step, in compiling a treatise on the plants of *India*, should be to write their names in *Roman* letters, according to the most accurate orthography, and in *Sanscrit* preferably to any vulgar dialect; because a learned language is fixed in books, while popular idioms are in constant fluctuation, and will not, perhaps be understood a century hence by the inhabitants of these Indian territories, whom future botanists may consult on the common appellations of trees and flowers ...[48]

The same ambitions characterise his taxonomy of India's plants as of its scriptural laws, and create a template of ideal reality against which all actuality is to be measured.

Rejection of history and social change marks Jones' political conservatism. The creation of transcendental verities through recovering the 'original' India amount to no more than that. These constructs seemingly militate against his actual experience of living there, but are in fact motivated by what he perceives as the 'debasedness' of Indians in his time. This 'degeneration' of the people is comparable to the vernacular corruption of the original and pure Sanskrit. In this respect Jones shared much with James Mill, both dispensing with experience as a source of 'truth', while constructing their 'truth about India' against the backdrop of their unstated experience or view of contemporary Indian society.

---

48   Jones 1799 [II], p. 2.

Jones was close to the conservative thinker Edmund Burke in recognising the importance of 'prejudices'. He supported the establishment of a supreme court in India to protect the British subjects and rule the 'natives', with the provision 'that the natives of the more important provinces be indulged in their own prejudices, civil and religious, and supported to enjoy their own customs unmolested'.[49] But this indulgence had its limit, in his canonical version of elite Hindu and Muslim laws. Through these compilations, colonial rule could claim a legitimacy in local terms even when the actuality was composed of social relations of colonialism and in reality supported prejudices of the Europeans. This legal attempt was meant to remove shadows of usurpation and force from the colonial rule.

Javed Majeed, in *Ungoverned Imaginings: James Mill's The History of British India and Orientalism*, also speaks of Jones' literary and legal works in terms of creating a legitimating indigenous idiom for ruling.[50] He shows how Jones' translations and compilations of *Digests* of Hindu and Muslim laws gradually led to appropriation of power over the local societies and to the supersession of indigenous agencies for self-rule. According to Majeed:

> [F]or Jones the apparent monopoly of a form of indigenous knowledge by certain classes could only be broken through translation. This would mean that *the British would be as conversant in their traditions as they were*, and that their idioms would be *desacralised* through the very act of translation.[51]

The power/knowledge character of the orientalist construction of India produced a seeming paradoxical relation of repression and dependence between the colonial elite and 'the authority of the sacerdotal classes'.[52] But actually the project had two stages. Initially indispensable, Indian scholars were slated for elimination once the English translations and compilations were concluded. As Majeed puts it:

> The position of Muslim law officers remained intact until 1817 [when regulation 17], empowered Nizamat Adalat, the central criminal court of Calcutta, to overrule the fatwas of the law officers in all cases. With this Muslim Law lost its status as the criminal law of the land, although it was

---

49   Jones 1799 [III], p. 5.
50   Majeed 1992.
51   Majeed 1992, p. 20. Emphasis added.
52   Ibid.

not until 1864, after the Indian Penal Code was promulgated in 1862, that the institution of law officers and their fatwas was abolished.[53]

Thus, legitimating colonial rule in an Indian idiom did nothing to undercut power relations between England and India. If anything, this peculiar form secured legitimation much more effectively in the first stages of English rule than an imposition of British law could have done. The self-assigned creators and keepers of 'truth' about India were doing the work of ruling effectively. What Majeed has forgotten to add with regard to English appropriation of Indian traditions, and Lata Mani and Bernard Cohn remind us, is that these same 'desacralisation' procedures which translated Indian texts also conferred on the colonial authorities the power to decide and name what these so-called 'native traditions' were.[54] They 'invented' traditions as they needed.[55]

The results of these inventions were deeply consequential for the Indian society. Majeed himself refers to this in an undeveloped fashion when he remarks on Jones' 'mistaken attempts' to compile *one* uniform code of Hindu and Muslim law. This one 'true' version of social morality for each community, he feels, 'reinforced conservatism', leading to centralisation of legal power in the name of an ideal order, distinct from actual practice:[56] 'In fact, the insistence on certainty and uniformity, and the attempt to codify traditions, actually meant that sometimes Anglo-Hindu law was more orthodox than the Shastras'.[57] Majeed's perception is similar to Charles Bayly's, who in *Indian Society and the Making of the British Empire* speaks of rigidification of caste through colonial modes of standardisation of knowledge of Indian societies into 'rank and grade Indian social orders'.[58] This colonialist knowledge project increased the social importance of local elite, brahmin pandits and Muslim maulavis on whom the rulers depended, and '[the] scene was set for the emergence of a more stratified and rigid system of caste, and a more homogeneous religious practice *within all the main communities*'.[59] This natural fit between the administrative requirements and standardisation of social knowledge which was produced through the mechanism of an ideological epistemology is hard to ignore.

---

53   Ibid.
54   See Hobsbawm and Ranger 1983, especially the Introduction.
55   Cohn 1983.
56   Majeed 1992, p. 28.
57   Ibid., p. 27.
58   Ibid., p. 28.
59   Ibid., p. 28. Emphasis added.

Jones' own location as a knower within relations of ruling, of Britain over India and Asia, is evident in the following example from 'The Second Anniversary Discourse (1785) for the Asiatic Society'. Here the relative variations of Europe and Asia in the scale of power and culture are clearly marked out. For Jones,

> Whoever travels in Asia, especially if he be conversant with the literature of the countries through which he passes, must naturally remark the superiority of European talent; the observation indeed is as old as Alexander; and, though, we can not agree with the sage preceptor of the ambitious prince, that 'the Asiaticks were born to be slaves', yet the Athenian poet seems to be perfectly in the right, when he represents Europe as a sovereign princess and Asia as her handmaid.[60]

This statement provides a visual icon encoding a relationship of dominance and servitude between Europe and Asia (Britannia and India), made seductive by an ambience of grandeur and beauty supplied by Jones' romanticism. It is then qualified and underscored by his position as the representative of the region: 'but, if the mistress be transcendentally majestic, it cannot be denied that the attendant has many beauties, and some advantages peculiar to itself [sic]'.[61]

These sentiments and images are not, of course, unique to Jones. They are an intrinsic part of a representational apparatus created in the process of European colonisation. English patriotic poems or songs such as James Thompson's 'Rule, Britannia' and innumerable engravings and etchings of the time show the trinity of Europe or Britannia, a bejewelled white upper-class woman, often a Queen, and her two dark and dusky attendants – Africa and Asia. This colonial iconography is the result of a mediation between written political allegories and a convention in art.[62] This patronising though romantic attitude is paraphrased by Jones in a more prosaic fashion when he reminds the all-European members of the Asiatic Society not to be too arrogant and dismissive towards Indians or Asians: 'although we must be conscious of our superior advancement in kinds of useful knowledge, yet we aught not therefore to contemn the people of Asia ...'[63]

---

60   Jones 1799 [I], p. 10.
61   Ibid.
62   Much, for example, has been written on Manet's Olympia attended by a black maid, onto whom the European male gaze has shifted the white woman's burden of an unregulated sexuality.
63   Jones 1799 [I], p. 10.

The general style of colonial discourse adopted by William Jones (and other orientalists) deserves a specific discussion. It possesses a peculiarly complex character which expresses domination through classical and orientalist scholarship, Burkean conservative politics, and a romantic aesthetic. Thus Jones is not to be confused with a 'liberal imperialist' like Mill and other Utilitarians.[64] Though he served the interest of the British empire he did this differently in his style or discourse. Majeed draws our attention to this aspect of Jones' works:

> What has been ignored is the fact that Jones' attempt to define an idiom in which cultures could be compared and contrasted was in part a response to the need for such an idiom that the cultures of the heterogeneous British empire could be compared, the nature of the British rule overseas determined, and the empire unified by the same ethos. For Jeremy Bentham and James Mill, the comparison and contrast of cultures was essential for their formulation of a programme of reform which would be relevant to both Indian and British society, but their approach to this issue was to be very different from Jones'.[65]

If Jones was not interested in 'improving' India and Indians in ways utterly alien, how did he carry out the task of construction of a cultural identity for the country and its peoples? How did he construct the necessary difference between Europe and India? The 'difference' (between Europeans and Indian 'others') was produced through a mixture of arrogance and fascination rooted in an organicist conservative and romantic imagination. He surmised that debased Indians had the possibility of a cultural/moral rejuvenation if, and only if, led by enlightened European guides and rulers like himself.

In order to do this Jones played the insider, and manipulated some of the significational systems from classical Sanskrit literature. He therefore donned the exotic mask of an Indian. As Lawrence of Arabia played an Arab, Jones of India played 'Brahmin' and 'pagan' to claim a representational status. Thus his poetic persona embodies cultural essences that were fabricated by Jones himself. His reforms, unlike those of the Utilitarians, do not use the discourse of 'rationality' as much as that of purification and retrieval. Many of his poems are hymns to Vedic deities, where the benevolent character and intention of the British rule speak an Indian idiom to authentically represent India to the West (at this point Indians were not widely trained in English).[66] The poems

---

64   Majeed 1992, pp. 40–3.
65   Ibid., p. 16.
66   Ibid., p. 22.

accomplish the moral imperatives of British rule in India, and it becomes the ideal condition within which 'the Hindu' or 'India' can return to their pristine glory. This 'Hymn to Laxmi', for example, shows such a view:

> Oh! bid the patient Hindu rise and live
> His erring mind, that Wizard lore beguiles
> Clouded by priestly wiles,
> To senseless nature bows for nature's God.
> Now, stretch'd o'er ocean's vast from happier isles
> He sees the wand of empire, not the rod;
> Ah, may those beauties, that western skies illume,
> Disperse the unhappy gloom![67]

Another poem, the 'Hymn to Ganga', is a perfect act of cultural appropriation. It indicates a ruler's right to arrogate the culture of the colonised unto himself. Here Jones represents 'India' as an 'ideal Indian', in accordance to a cultural synthesis that he has put together. The poem is 'feigned to have been the work of a BRAHMEN, in an early age of HINDU antiquity, who, by a prophetical spirit, discerns the equity of BRITISH government, and concludes with a prayer for its peaceful duration under good laws well administered'.[68] This naturalised Indian Jones, or the imagined 'Brahmen', ends by pronouncing a benediction for British rule in India and prays for its long life:

> Nor frown, dread Goddess, on a peerless race,
> With lib'ral heart of material grace,
> Wafted from colder isles remote:
> As they preserve our laws, and bid our terror cease,
> So be their darling laws preserved in wealth, in joy, in peace![69]

This indigenous idiom and the persona adopted by Jones are not to be confused with an act of surrender by the Europeans to Indian culture, but rather understood as a gesture of incorporation. Jones and his colleagues felt the same right to Indian cultural goods as to commercial goods and revenue while simultaneously forging a tool of legitimation. This allowed a control over the colonised in what appeared to be in their own moral and cultural terms. This

---

67   Jones 1799 [II], p. 365.
68   Jones 1799 [VI], p. 383.
69   Jones 1799 [VI], p. 392.

model of ruling, as noticed by many scholars, came from the English perception of the cultural modalities of the Mughal empire. It minimised the fact of
the colonial nature of British rule and made it appear organic to the local societies.[70] And most significantly, the conceptual-imagistic concreteness called
'India' that emerged through these interpretive-constitutive processes of multiple relations of ruling came to be accepted by the west (and in a certain sense,
even by Indians themselves) as the 'real India'.[71]

This totalising aspiration of orientalist knowledge of India is necessarily
dependent on flexibility, in as much as it has to deal with a non-unified actuality. Thus it resorts to notions of typicality as well as exceptionality and diversity
in order to maintain its typologies and essentialist stance. From this point of
view, it has been served well by the concept of tradition, which automatically
entails the notion of its violation. Through this reading device contemporary
indigenous discussions and debates on social conduct and laws of inheritance, property and family could be read and pushed aside as deviation from
'tradition', thereby rendering indigenous discursivities static and un-Indian.
Through this process colonial rule became the saviour of India and the orientalists its spokespersons, while representations created by them re-presented
Indian reality. This gave a historical agency to the rulers themselves, who, like
Jones, saw the restoration of the 'original India' as their historic task. Thus the
rulers stole from the 'natives' their history, and interposed themselves between
a people and their cultural-political past and future, making decisions as to how
to rule them, supposedly, in their own idiom.

The enormous power involved in this definitive, antiquarian textualisation
for contemporary ruling becomes evident in its gigantic proportions if we
hypothetically put Europe in India's place. The arrogance and absurdity of ruling a country on the basis of scriptural/legal texts produced hundreds of years

---

70   Majeed 1992, p. 25; Cohn 1983.
71   Making India 'traditional', while reifying or inventing traditions, put in place an interpret-
      ive frame-work which has lasted from orientalism to the current phase of international
      development. It should be obvious by now that Jones considered the colonial project as
      one of ruling India for her own good, as a gesture of rescuing and restoring. Thus, he con-
      sidered the task of the East India Company's servants to be twofold: intellectual-moral,
      and legal/administrative. He was not alone in this understanding, but his predecessors
      and colleagues, such as Warren Hastings, Halhed, C.T. Colebrook, and H.H. Wilson, all
      conformed to this vision and task. Learning languages, translating, selecting, compiling
      and canonising texts, fixing and constructing characteristic traditions – in short, project-
      ing the real 'genius' of the country – were their full-time occupation. The purpose was to
      create a representational apparatus of India which would provide a controlled and pre-
      dictable (for the colonisers) ground for ruling.

ago becomes evident if we propose that Europe be conquered by India or China, and it rules present-day Europe on the basis of an archivally researched, selected and canonised version of Greek laws from the days of Plato and Aristotle. Furthermore, this renders the interim period of development in European thought, between antiquity and now, as accidental and inessential excrescences with regard to Europe's true essence. This is precisely what Jones and others tried to do in India, with a considerable degree of success by constructing mythologies which were also ideologies of 'India', Hinduism and Islam.

Politically speaking, the orientalist conservatism has to be contexted to the French revolution. It has much of the romantic, organicist conservatism of Edmund Burke. Jones befriended Burke until the impeachment of Bengal's governor general, Warren Hastings, who was Jones' administrative superior, patron and collaborator in Asiatic research in India. Orientalists were also the heirs of the European renaissance and enlightenment. They were humanist scholars, educated in European classics and classical languages, and admirers of Greco-Roman antiquities. This expertise and orientation was combined with a mercantalist and physiocratic view of India's economic 'improvement'.[72] All this underpinned their political vision, and many, including Jones, advocated 'enlightened despotism' for India and contrasted it to 'Asiatic despotism'. In short, these men inherited and developed personal and political history and an intellectual framework before coming to India. These interpretative devices and frameworks are what they built on both in terms of the form and content of their ideological projects when they sought to 'know' and represent India. As such, they relied on a common content for constructing 'Asiatic others' prevalent in Europe throughout the post-crusade era, but there were also other stereotypes or perceptions applicable to groups which lent themselves to use in the colonial situation. Constructions or stereotypes of the peasant and rural societies within Europe, the Arab or the Moor, European women and lower classes, for example, have much in common, both in method and content, with those of the later 'Asiatic', 'Oriental' or 'Indian'. Geopolitical mythologies regarding the East, used liberally in literature, for example in Christopher Marlowe's *Dr Faustus* or Dr Samuel Johnson's *Rasselas, The Prince of Abyssinia*, in the plays of Dryden or Aphra Behn, traveller's narratives, and so on, had existed for a long time before Company rule in India. Upon scrutiny it becomes clear that the orientalist 'symbolic, cultural constitution' of India draws on these pre-existing conceptual contents and cultural forms rather than fully inventing brand new ones.

---

72   Guha 1982a.

If renaissance humanism, the values of the enlightenment, along with classical antiquarianism, are left unexplored as sources for cultural construction and ideology in the colonial context, the value-laden nature of the term 'civilisation' as applied to India would make no sense. The invention of Greece and Rome and the classical past which went with it, along with the invention of 'traditions' which are signifiers of 'European civilisation', must all be examined as sources for constructing 'India' and its 'traditions'. The concept of 'civilisation', for example, becomes a heavy burden, not only because it ceases to signal a process of becoming, an ideal for all societies, but instead provides a typological standard already arrived at by Europeans by which 'others' must be measured.[73] This led to India being evaluated through European, especially Greco-Roman, icons and standards, and occupying an ambiguous position of antiquity on the one hand, and being classed as inferior (to Europe) on the other. This ambiguity of 'India' resonates with the shifting horizon of 'European civilisation' and its continued bifurcation into Apollonian Greece and Dionysian Asia.

A shifting boundary between Greece and Asia, indicated for example by the status of Egypt, Turkey or Macedonia, contains the elements of orientalism or Eurocentrism.[74] The humanist fabrication of the 'Apollonian Greece' stands face to face with changing perceptions of Asia Minor and Egypt, characterised alternately as sources of rational, universal thought and of mystery religions or occultism and Dionysian irrationalism. The same ambiguity and shift between admiration and denigration is also to be found in the orientalist perception of India. The same historiography as found in Europe, with its notions of ages and stages, is applied to it. A history of decline is also perceived here, evolving to decay, from the golden age to the contemporary era. In Europe itself this historiography had invented time and traditions which went into the construction of the European 'middle ages' (the middle of what?) or the 'dark ages' (contrasted to 'enlightened'), of 'renaissance' and 'enlightenment'. The same perspective, with its curious mixture of romanticism and rationalism, of neo-classical aesthetic and the sublime, was brought to bear on India and produced representational images and knowledge. European paintings, etchings or verbal descriptions of the time produce 'India' through these same modalities.

73   See Williams 1983.
74   See Bernal 1993.

4   Conclusion

This chapter considers the issue of representation specifically in the colonial context, with regard to a fuller understanding of the concept of ideology, encompassing both the content and the form or method of production of knowledge. The elaborated theorisation is then sought to be made apprehensible through a discussion of William Jones' *Works* in terms of production of ideology. No doubt more could be said of them, as his opus is voluminous, but the paper concentrates instead on uncovering how historical and social relations of his ruling enterprise informed the (ac)claimed metaphysical disinterestedness of his work. This essay should also go a little way toward understanding how ideological knowledges arise which are not only current in their own time, but persist through time into further stages and modes of power. The method of metaphysics, constructively applied to historical moments, as Jones does to his encounter with India in the last years of the eighteenth century, flies the produced 'knowledge' way beyond the confines of its locale and its time, and settles into the status of truth and fact. So it is that Jones' 'India' becomes the lens through which not only his contemporary colonising Europeans but many future nationalist Indians saw their country and themselves.

CHAPTER 22

Demography and Democracy: Reflections on Violence against Women in Genocide or Ethnic Cleansing

Even before the current conflict, Israelis were beginning to worry about what some of them term the demographic dilemma. Because the birth-rate is higher among Palestinian Arabs than among Israeli Jews, within as little as a decade Jews could be outnumbered 'between the Jordan River and the [Mediterranean] Sea'. At that point, some fear that Israel could either lose its Jewish character or its democratic system, becoming in effect an apartheid state.[1]

• • •

I heard girls screaming. I saw a naked girl running with twenty-five men chasing her. The sweet shop owner was distributing sweets to rioters. The police fired on the muslims rather than the mob.[2]

• •
•

1 Introduction

On 28 February 2002, Hindu fundamentalists in political and social power in the Indian state of Gujarat went on a rampage against Muslims living in the state. More Muslims were killed there than people in the terrorist attack on the World Trade Centre in New York on September 11, 2001. This was accompanied by massive violence against women as well as a thoroughgoing dispossession and displacement of Muslims. We encounter here a situation where terrible crimes against humanity have been perpetrated, and they face us with profound questions about justice and its interface with law and the state. It is

---

1   Adams 2003.
2   Bano 2002.

imperative for us to ask these questions, to discuss them and their possible answers. The issues they raise involve us and have profound implications beyond their geographical-national territories. Though the media in Canada or the United States have paid only lip service to this massacre of Muslims, we cannot ignore it. So I have written this piece to raise issues and questions, to provoke discussion on violence against women in genocide or ethnic cleansing, framing them within the larger theme of the relationship between demography and democracy. We will begin with a brief outline of the scope of the carnage in Gujarat.

2   The Scope of the Carnage

The information presented here is based on five reports prepared by Indian civil liberties groups, one report prepared by the All India Democratic Women's Association, the mass organisation of the Communist Party of India (Marxist), as well as on excerpts from documents of the National Human Rights Commission of India and articles published in *Frontline*, a bi-weekly Indian news magazine.

The carnage was wholly directed against the Muslims living in Gujarat, and sixteen out of the twenty-four districts of the state were severely affected. Muslims constitute approximately 12.5 percent of the total Indian population and their socio-economic situation was the best in Gujarat.

To begin with, the number of people killed ranges from 850 to 1,000 by government count, while the non-official estimate is around 2,000. About 2,500 people have 'disappeared', many of whom have died. Regarding property, approximately 10,204 dwellings were burnt, as well as 10,429 shops. Some 1,278 shops were ransacked and 2,623 vending carts destroyed. More than 150,000 people were displaced. Officially there were 103 relief camps holding 113,697 people, though unofficial figures for the number of camps is 121. It is claimed that the relief camps were closed sooner than they should have been as the Gujarat government considered it safe for the victims to return to the devastated areas still seething with tension. After their return, murders and other forms of victimisation of Muslims continued and are continuing. Many continue to live in the abandoned camps without amenities or relief.

Importantly for us, the reports all spoke to gang rape of women, of objects inserted into vaginas and wombs, uteruses slashed, foetuses extracted and burnt. Many of the rape victims were cut into pieces and charred. Exact numbers are not available as the police refused to take First Information Reports (FIRS). As for cultural genocide, hundreds of mosques, tombs and other holy sites, including those of major Muslim singers and poets, as well as schools (madrasas), were destroyed. Most notable among these destructions is the razing of the tomb of a sixteenth-century Sufi poet, Vali Gujarati, which was paved over overnight to form part of a road.

3   The Context and a Short Description

On 27 February 2002, a train bringing back volunteers of Hindu fundamentalist groups from Ayodhya, where they had gone to agitate for the building of a Ram temple on the site of a sixteenth-century mosque razed by the same groups in 1992 and now under legal dispute, was torched. This resulted in the deaths of 58 Hindu persons, including 26 women and 12 children. Though the results of a government inquiry were released recently stating that this fire started inside the train, rather than being set from outside, Muslims were immediately blamed for carrying out a preplanned attack. Twenty-six hours later, on 28 February, a huge carnage, orchestrated by the Hindu nationalist party BJP and the above-mentioned groups, started against Muslims and continued into late March with greater intensity and thereafter at a lower intensity. Total terror and mayhem resulting in the figures mentioned above happened at a cyclonic speed – hunting Muslims in a free-for-all for all Hindus who cared to join in. To quote the editorial of *Communalism Combat*:

> Dead bodies no longer resembled human beings: they were reduced – whenever they have not been burnt to ashes – to a grotesque and pathetic sight that was a haunting reminder of the depth of hatred and intense dehumanisation that the politics of inherent superiority and exclusiveness generates.

According to eyewitnesses and survivors, attacking mobs numbered from 2,000 to about 15,000 Hindus. They were armed with deadly agricultural implements, swords, trishuls/tridents, pistols and rifles. Some carried mobile phones to co-ordinate the attacks. As mentioned above, rape and foeticide were significant instruments for the subjugation of the Muslim community. There was a further chilling aspect to this, as most of the victims were hacked and burned, barring a few.

By all local and international accounts the state government of Gujarat and its ruling party the BJP, as well as the central government of India, at different levels all contributed to this violence. Both the chief minister of Gujarat, Narendra Modi, and the prime minister of India, Atal Behari Vajpayee, the leader of the BJP at the Centre, condoned and justified it. Modi called it a 'natural reaction' against Muslim terrorism, while Vajpayee said in a BJP convention in Goa in April: 'If there was no Godhra there would have been no Gujarat'. BJP top brass in the central government and their allies all had a thesis of pre-planned attacks by Muslims and immediately alleged the evil hand of Pakistan in the train episode, though Gujarat intelligence had no prior hint of such a thing. Encouraged and orchestrated by the state of Gujarat, armed squads launched their *Kristallnacht*. Both Hindu and Muslim eyewitness and surviv-ors and enquiries conducted by civil liberty groups, NGOs and government commissions have named BJP ministers, MLAs, councillors and politicians as mob leaders and perpetrators. Also, various police officers have been cited and condemned for having taken active part in the carnage, with condemnation extending to police conduct in general. By all accounts, the BJP state members have flaunted the Indian constitution, Indian criminal code and the Arms Act. It has been felt by many that 'should they be allowed to go scot-free, the very nature of Indian democracy would be in peril'.

Left parties, women's groups, civil liberty groups and investigative journ-alists have concurred that the BJP and its Hindu fundamentalist base groups had been planning this carnage since they came to power in 1998, when they declared Gujarat to be a laboratory of *hindutva* (the essence of Hinduism). A few activities of the state, as found in the Reports, should be noted: that chief minister Modi let 72 hours elapse before he made attempts to control the mobs; in the few areas where police stopped the carnage, those officers were trans-ferred immediately to other posts; the size of the mobs and the similarity in their types of weapons and attacks all point to co-ordinated, trained cadres; BJP ministers, councillors and MLAs were in the police control room directing police and instructing them not to take action; it has been noted that officials of the BJP and its cultural groups, especially the RSS and Visva Hindu Parishad (VHP, World Hindu Congress), had a meeting on the evening of 27 February to orchestrate this; and to make matters utterly volatile, the BJP called a province wide *bandh* (work, market and transportation stoppage) on 28 February which they had planned before, to start the provincial election campaign.

The conduct of Gujarat police especially has brought deep condemnation. Their conduct has been one of complicity with the Hindu attackers, of perpet-ration of crime as well as criminal negligence to protect the life, dignity, prop-erty and livelihood of Muslims. Examples recorded in the Reports are watching attacks idly, shooting at victims, taking part in rapes and looting, turning off their mobile phones, to refuse help and refusal to take reports of crimes or not-ing non-specific perpetrators, such as the mob. Furthermore, there are reports that, beginning from 16 March, police conducted search and destroy operations of Muslim homes, arresting Muslim males indiscriminately, including under-age boys, and liberally employed the Prevention of Terrorism Ordinance (POTO) to detain and torture them.

4   Issues and Analysis

Our reflection on genocide or ethnic cleansing of the Muslims of Gujarat needs to begin with a consideration of a set of general aspects as well as of certain particular ones pertaining especially to violence against women in the Indian cultural context. But we cannot get to these specific aspects without a consideration of the general ones. Thus we have to query the conventional wisdom of various international human rights bodies that consider genocide or ethnocide as an exceptional moment in the life of nation states, when the power of the state runs amuck against a certain part of the population living within its jurisdiction and/or as moments of episodic violence due to struggles between groups which fight either to gain or retain state power. These situations, as in Liberia, Rwanda, the Congo or Bosnia, provide examples of the above and the bases for formulation of charges of 'crimes against humanity'. There is of course truth to this formulation, and this truth provides for us a direction of intervention from an international standpoint, but just to say this is not to say enough. There are gaps or omissions which in fact make this view blind to certain genocides while prosecuting participants of others. It makes it imperative to punish Slobodan Milošević but not George W. Bush for 'crimes against humanity', or Charles Taylor of Liberia but not Ariel Sharon of Israel. The blindness comes from not recognising two truths: firstly, the nationalist nature of Western imperialism, which has a deeply inscribed ethnocentric mode of mediation and deployment (for example, Bush's civilisation discourse regarding the legitimation of invasion of Afghanistan); and secondly, that some state formations and their ideologies are inherently and intrinsically genocidal/ethnocidal while others are not. The basic reason of existence for some states, such as the state of Israel – as the passage quoted at the beginning of this paper shows – is ethnicist. Though there may be certain features of democracy within it, the current apartheid nature of this state is not unclear to anyone who observes the socio-economic condition, rights and duties of Israeli Arabs. The issue of ethnicity, both culturally and numerically – that is, demographically, provides the ground for Israel's state formation and ideology of its nationhood. Since Israel, until the very recent days of the second intifada, was considered by the Western media to be an oasis of democracy in the deserts of the Arabian Peninsula, its obvious ethno-nationalism escaped most of the conventional human rights bodies. It is this rumour of democracy which prompted the removal of the United Nations' long-held position that Zionism is racism.

Genocide/ethnocide has been generally spatialised by the Western, that is, mainstream, political discourse as a third-world phenomenon or a phenomenon of 'backward', formerly communist, European states, as has also been the ideology of ethnic nationalism. Without lingering here on some obviously ethnocentric aspects of the Western democracies, we can safely say that in spite of this there are differences between state formations, and some more straightforwardly liberal democratic states (we are bracketing the question of socialist states here) have more than ethnocentrism as their constitutive ideological component. Ethnicity, or monoculturalism, is after all not the only way to imagine a nation. We need, therefore, to distinguish between different national imaginaries and their expression into a state and other political machineries. It needs to be noted that ethnic nationalism, which is no less rooted in class, capital, imperialism or neo-colonialism than the liberal state of bourgeois nationalism, is a special kind of state. It has genocide/ ethnocide inscribed into its very being. Bourgeois nationalism has none of the correctives at juridico-political levels that are instituted in the rights-based polity of liberal democracy.

If these distinctions between national imaginaries/ideologies and states are not kept in mind, we only render invisible the imperatives of genocide/ethnocide of ethnic nationalism and simply spatialise our political understanding framed by the imperial knowledge paradigm of tradition versus modernity which is paralleled with the discourse of East versus West. We can then join the international human rights administrators in considering genocide/ethnocide as exceptional moments in history and seek to provide 'stable' states, whose definition consists of accountability to international bodies. Such states are seen to stand for 'normalcy'. The job of the international rights bodies is to produce this very 'normalcy'. It should also be pointed out that they read genocide/ ethnocide mainly as phenomena of great physical violence understood in the light of the Nazi holocaust unleashed on Jews. Though cultural genocide, for example as perpetrated in Canada, the United States and Australia against indigenous peoples, is recognised within an extended definition of genocide, it is subordinated to the more dominant holocaust reading. In focusing on a discourse of the exceptional and the excessive, the horror of carnage and so on, this conventional rights approach has somewhat erased the 'normal' or hegemonic nature of genocide. Though the stench of slaughter is unavoidable with this notion, we need to connect that stench to the everyday character, to the 'normal' existence of an ethnic nationalist hegemony. We need to recognise this normalcy as the working and ideological apparatus of this kind of political culture and its state. They integrally hold an element of genocide or ethnocide both in a diffused cultural and a hard-fisted physical manner. The pogrom against Muslims in Gujarat and the plans and projects of the Hindu right all over India should be situated within these general considerations of genocide.

To speak specifically about the case of India, we need to know that the political imaginary of the nation and its active practices are constructed and conducted by Hindu fundamentalist groups (known as the *Sangh Parivar* or the holy family) and their representative political party, the Bharatiya Janata Party (BJP, Indian Peoples Party). This party holds an absolute majority at the state level in Gujarat, while it holds power in the central government of India with the help of a right-wing coalition. Its goal is to have a *hindu rashtra* (Hindu state) articulated within an essentialised and right-wing religio-political ideology of *hindutva* (Hinduness). The massacre of Muslims on 28 February 2002 and after has to be situated within the chain of violent events against them since the demolition of the mosque in Ayodhya in 1992. The scale of carnage in Gujarat, of course, is much larger, but the actions themselves are by no means an aberration, exceptional or abnormal, indicating a temporary lapse of social/political sanity to be set on the right course by the intervention of national and international human rights organisations. Genocide or ethnocide is the very ideological core of this kind of Hindu nationalist project. In the very definition of how the notion of 'Hindu' and Hinduism are constructed as a type of ethnicity there is a compulsion for ethnocide, or what has come to be called ethnic cleansing. Even when this Hindu ethno-nationalism is not actively genocidal, even when it 'tolerates' Muslim and Christian 'minorities', genocidal or eliminationist premises underwrite it. As with all other ethno-nationalist projects, it constructs a hierarchical set of differences between people living within a national/political territory on grounds of racialised ethnicities, including religion, thus calling for their erasure from and subordination in the main frame of society, culture and history.

We should note in this context how the conventional categories of 'majority' and 'minority' found in the discourse of democracy have been appropriated by Hindu nationalists in India. They are not descriptions of neutral numerical groupings based on varying stands on political issues, as for example presented by John Stuart Mill in his essay *On Liberty*. They are appropriated and modified along lines of racialised ethnic differences, and as such they represent a process of political reformulation involving active reconstructions of 'majority' and 'minority'. We might say that there is an engagement here with the production itself of 'majoritarianism' and 'minoritisation'. Some form of ethnic erasure or ethnocide is in its very logic. The production of 'majority', and thus of 'minority', is both the means and end of this project. This takes me back to my earlier point that there is an active connection between ethnonationalism and the national demography, and that within this framework demography and democracy hold a contradictory relationship to each other. The more there is on one side, the less there is on the other.

So to recapitulate, an ethnic nationalist project is above all a demographic project. This is clear even to a *Globe and Mail* reporter, Paul Adams, who titles his column '"Baby Boom" May Affect Road to Peace' and begins his piece in the following way: 'Three-day-old Laif lay bawling on a bed in Ramallah hospital, wedged between his mother and grandmother. Although he has no way of knowing it, he may be part of the reason Israeli Prime Minister Ariel Sharon is getting serious about the u.s. backed "road map" peace plan'.[3] He also tells us that 'Although it has been hard to collect statistics during the current Palestinian uprising against Israeli rule – now three years old – there is a consensus that the Palestinian birth rate has risen yet further'.[4] As this article shows, the Israeli project is an illuminating example of the demographic thrust of ethnic nationalism, which calls for an actual numerical superiority of the ruling ethnicity. Otherwise there is trouble in the long run, as the South African case has shown. So this demographic imperative lies at the heart of Israel's settlement policies, even in the Zionist agencies' collection of Jewish orphans to settle them in Palestine long before the 1948 onslaught which resulted in massive expulsion of Palestinians from the land of their ancestors and birth. It also gave birth to the myth of Palestine as a land without people, a Zionist version of *terra nullius* practiced by white Australians regarding the aborigines. This national demographic imperative continues to function in the shape of expulsion or transfer and encirclement of Palestinians, and ultimately calls for the two nation/two state solution. It is manifest in preventing the Palestinian right of return and through the construction of an eight-metre-high wall sealing off Palestinians from Jews as well as in the creation of a collection of Bantustans in the name of Palestinian political autonomy. This demographic or ethnic nationalism accounts for the reason why any Jew born anywhere in the world has the right of 'return' and can become a citizen of Israel while exiled Palestinians have difficulty in obtaining a visitor's visa. They float around as the largest refugee group in the world, carrying the keys to their non-existent houses in villages either erased or renamed. Their homes and fields have become Israel's 'civilising' spaces or 'green' projects.

While Palestinians with historical residency of millennia cannot return to their own recent homes, mythic notions of origin, notions of Jews being god's

---

3   Adams 2003.
4   Ibid.

chosen people or divine promises of 'return' of the land to Jews guide policies of
Israeli occupation, colonisation and expulsion of Arabs. When considered from
the point of view of this ethnic demographic goal, the u.s. and self-advertised
reputation of Israel as a democracy explodes as a myth. The fear, as stated by
the *Globe and Mail* piece, is obvious. If the Palestinians are allowed the right of
return, as promised by the United Nations since 1948, they will outnumber the
Jews. Since the Zionist notion of 'democracy' is wholly encompassed within the
demographic boundary of ethnicity, with two tiers of political status consisting
of citizens (Jews) and subjects (Palestinians), Palestinian 'return' is unacceptable to the state of Israel. Thus, these notions of 'majority' and 'minority', as
ethnic citizens and subjects, are actually codes for relations of ruling within
Israel as a socio-cultural and economic-political entity. This illuminates the
reality that these ethnic ontologies of power are thus not as 'facts' or descriptive terms. I want to conclude this section on Israel/Palestine, which I use as
an archetype for ethnic nationalism, by pointing out the connection between
women, reproduction and the demography of democracy.

As Paul Adams' few lines show, little babies are deeply embedded in the
political relations of domination, resistance and survival. The wombs of Palestinian women become fertile fields for growing 'the enemy' for Zionists and the
state of Israel. They should, ideally, by the same logic of demographic imperative, not be allowed to have children. Not just suicide bombings of the Palestinians are moments of war, but also those at the checkpoints where women in
labour are left to perish with their new-borns. Social conditions of reproduction as a whole are systematically denied under conditions of besiegement.
Palestinian women as reproducers, the only challenges to denial of right of
return, are also targets of Israeli containment policies – in other words, of violence.

The political and ideological situation and specific demographic projects of
Zionists and Israeli state constitute a mirror in which we can best read the
situation of Muslim women in Gujarat and in India in general, particularly
if we live in the West. The earliest ideological development of Hindu fundamentalism dates back to the last quarter of the nineteenth century, when Zionism was also evolving as a political ideology. A 'national' cultural formulation
based on European orientalism slowly took a solid and clear shape proclaiming Hindu supremacy and constructing Hindus as victims of Muslims rather
than of the British colonial power. From the 1920s on there was much admiration expressed for the Nazis, for Hitler and a discourse of racial purity. In 1925
this Hindu right created a cultural and paramilitary organisation as groundwork for an eventual mono-ethnic high-caste Hindu state. Named Rashtriya
Swayamsevak Sangh (rss) or National Volunteers Association, the organisa-

tion saw itself as defining and diffusing a fundamental conception of Hinduism aiming first towards a 'cultural nationalism'. The second stage was to come after as 'political nationalism' when all Islamic traces, and perhaps of Muslims themselves, disappeared. As such, the RSS took no part in India's independence struggle, sometimes collaborated with the British, and its political ambitions of creating a monoethnic state went into abeyance after its associates assassinated Mahatma Gandhi in 1948. But with members, moles and friends in the high places of Indian politics, they regrouped through the 1960s, 1970s and 1980s and emerged with a strong bid for cultural hegemony and political/state power. Their ambition and ideological stance were helped by the partition of India into India and Pakistan, where the fact of ethnicity played a central role, especially manipulated by the departing British power. The two countries emerged with direct and indirect ethnic underpinnings. Though India did not have an ethnically identified constitution and national imaginary and functioned formally as a secular democracy within the juridical form of universal and individual citizenship and rights, there was the demographic fact of a Hindu 'majority' as cultural and political presence and agents. Pakistan was very directly ethnic and religious in its construction as not only a country of Muslims but also as an 'Islamic' republic, with Hindus, living mostly in East Pakistan (now Bangladesh), as a marginalised minority. In India there were 'riots', but it is since the destruction of the Babri mosque in 1992 that an aggressive moment of mono-ethnicism is emerging. The hitherto cumbrously functioning and covertly ethnicised secular democratic polity is now besieged by Hindu fundamentalists/supremacists, who would like to replace the present constitution with one of a Hindu state. Needless to say this has called forth much resistance not only from Indian Muslims, who form about 12.5 percent of the population, but much more actively and massively from India's left and democratic secular opposition, ranging from political parties to non-governmental organisations. But it is important to note that the Muslim population is in the vicious grip of the process of 'minoritisation' that I spoke to above.

The BJP and its civil society, so-called cultural organisations, are the instruments of these minoritising processes. They operationalise at everyday as well as at instituted political levels the concepts of *hindutva* and *hindu rashtra*. Through various myths of origin and racial purity reminiscent of the Nazi project and the even older anti-black racism, manipulation of high-caste Hinduism and long-standing Hindu-Muslim animosity or ethnic communalism which began one hundred years ago, and through the use of religious texts, history books, archaeology and so on, a violent Hindu ethnic nationalism has been clearly put in place. It functions through genocidal modalities of pogroms and massacres as well as the destruction of Muslim religious and cultural symbols, for example, of tombs of Muslim holy persons or musicians and poets. Slowly but surely these persistent activities have thoroughly ethnicised India's political culture. These groups and their sympathisers seek to define the notion and legalities of citizenship in wholly ethnic terms. They effectively manipulate both mechanisms of exclusion and inclusion to further their agenda of *hindutva* and to thus expand and define the Hindu demographic scope. Muslims and Christians are excluded as 'others', as alien or foreign, even though they originate in South Asia, on the ground that their religions do not. This exclusive defining move is complemented by an inclusive or expansionist one whereby Sikhs, Buddhists and Jains, as well as various animistic religious groups, are annexed into Hinduism. These moves for demographic realignment make Hindus into an overwhelming majority and, therefore, the Indian 'nation'. Through this construction of the Hindu as the hegemonic representative national category, the Hindu right wing cannibalises all substantiveness and differences of these non-Hindu religions that have evolved in the Indian subcontinent. By assimilating them into the Hindu demographic equation, they effectively exclude Muslims as Indian nationals.

This demographic nationalism actually plays within a bourgeois discourse of population, which is generally present in Indian or any other liberal democracy, and puts an added twist to an older class-based project of ruling and political entitlement. The usual contentious issue of population – of who can and should reproduce and how much, as well as who should not – already marked the Indian demographic project against the poor in the 1970s. This is what Sanjay Gandhi, aided and abetted by international organisations, once called 'something like a war' against poverty. It was a genocidal form of social engineering orchestrated from a class standpoint. This project of population control, regulation and anxiety regarding population 'explosion' of the minorities (especially Muslims), lower classes and lower castes came to a seething point with the new Hindu politics. As far as Muslims are concerned, the Hindu right proposes a direct reduction in numbers through intimidation, general marginalisation, physical elimination or expulsion (Muslims should go to Pakistan). Muslims are projected as an alien ethos to the Indian nation and, therefore, as undesirable as citizens. Under such circumstances the deep involvement in the 2002 carnage of the BJP-led state of Gujarat, dubbed a 'laboratory of *hindutva*' in 1998 when the BJP came to power there, should come as no surprise. The role of the chief minister, Narendra Modi, members of his cabinet, BJP MLAs, councillors and the police force in the violence is well known. This genocide cannot be laid at the door of civil society organisations such as the RSS or VHP alone, but shows itself to be the reason of state. At the level of the BJP-led central government in Delhi there is also an active complicity. And ethnocide works particularly well in a state where the Muslims are relatively prosperous and Hindu greed and envy strong. This is similar to the situation before the War of Jews in Germany and Austria, where they were relatively prosperous as well. In this political space where demography overrides democracy, there is no room for any rights-based discourse or citizenship, as citizenship within the state of ethno-nationalism is not a matter of rights but of birth or of various other culturally constructed forms of belonging.

This question of demography involving actualities of human reproduction entails in the issue of women's bodies as reproductive sites and, in relation to the Hindu right's agenda in India, that of Muslim women's bodies, especially of their reproductive parts. It is not surprising that violence against women qua women is an intrinsic moment of this demographic genocidal project. It has been generally acknowledged in all literature on women in conflict zones that these forms of violence are routine, even though the angle I emphasise is not available there. But it is documented by authors such as Susan Brownmiller or Cynthia Enloe that 'the enemy's women' are generally treated with a sexually nuanced violence. The u.s. army, states Brownmiller in *Against Our Will: Men, Women and Rape*, maintained a rape squad in Vietnam. The meaning of these actions is rightly read to be a militarised version of patriarchy/misogyny which mediates the relations of the (male) warring parties. This same misogyny and social militarism, mediated through a high caste/brahminical Hinduism, drives India's Hindu right as well. But violence against women in Gujarat, or elsewhere in times of war or 'ethnic cleansing', also involves a demographic project – producing 'majority' and 'minority' by securing and stopping population growth – both at an actual and a symbolic level. This calls for a reading of genocidal violence against women in a more complicated way than simply as inflicting 'dishonour' and humiliation upon the (male) enemy and violating their property. The demographic aspect of nation-making also emerges in the type of violence being inflicted. As we see in the case of Muslim women in Gujarat, horrible rapes, tearing open of genitalia and wombs, slashing wombs to pull out foetuses, charring them along with the bodies of women, and the slaughter of children – all signal complex levels of deterrence against Muslim reproduction. No ethnic cleansing is complete without that.

The hegemonic common sense of an ethnic nation, implying violent ethnic cleansing, is a part of political consciousness in the West as well. 'Race'-based stereotypes about non-white peoples are rampant in the West, which constructs them as animal-like and over-fecund. The fear of being outnumbered by black and Chicano/Hispanic peoples is a matter of common 'white' talk in the United States. In Canada the same fear, worked up by the media, dogs whites in major cities, where non-whites are seen as taking over both reproductively and culturally. Among the Hindus in India there also exists a long-standing stereotype, perhaps since the Partition riots of 1947 or even earlier, of Muslim 'over-reproduction'. When I conducted a CIDA-Shastri research project on perceptions of women's reproductive health in a Calcutta slum, our researchers had to contend with the view that Muslim women have too many children and resist all forms of birth control. Reality, of course, proved them to be remarkably similar to their Hindu sisters in their reproductive choices and number of children. But from the ethno-nationalist aspect of our independence struggles we, Hindus and Muslims, have both inherited a legacy of ethnic common senses with genocidal imperatives embedded in them. Among the Hindus it has spawned hegemonic communalist and racist stereotypes about the oversexed nature of Muslims in general, the rapacity of Muslim men, their ferocity and fanaticism and amoral worldview. The 'Muslim terrorist' is a composite of these stereotypes. The BJP or the Hindu right's popularity rests on this propaganda and ideology. We have heard in India the mythic demographic calculus of four wives permitted to Muslims. Narendra Modi gives voice to this pernicious myth when he says 'Our five, their twenty-five' regarding how fast Muslims reproduce. Therefore, in the Hindu right's demographic vision, Muslims are not a threatened minority but threatening bodies overwhelming the Hindu nation. They need to be exterminated, or at least physically disciplined, before they grow any further. With the logic of Belgians in the Congo as brought out in Conrad's *Heart of Darkness*, we are to fall on them with the cry of 'exterminate the vermin'. As the Hindu right's slogan goes, 'Stop Babur's children' (i.e., from growing in numbers). No cost, including the sacrifice of Hindu morality or humanity, is too high for that. Nor is it an aberration to take this stance, in spite of the prevalent human rights perspective. This cleansing reveals the real logic or normalcy of ethnic nationalism in its most brutal form. These cleansings are a means to a well-defined national goal. In every sense Muslims must disappear, become non-persons in India. This belief is so widely shared that some Gujarati Hindu women helped 'their' men to rape and perform other brutalities on Muslim women. They know what the southern U.S. whites know, that rape, castration and lynching are the most potent instruments for disciplining an undesirable population, of protecting their own 'purity of race'. So we can say that bodies of women and girls, of children born and unborn, are the war zones of genocide and ethnic cleansing. These reproductive deterrents are the physical equivalents at the human level of the use by the United States of scorched-earth agents and defoliants in Vietnam and other countries.

All genocides, including violence against women, need to be instrumentalised and orchestrated through culturally specific resources – through moralities and symbologies. It is here that genocide/ethnic cleansing takes on the culturally constructed characteristics of the organising aggressors. An eye on the symbolic forms and practices of high-caste Hinduism helps us to recognise the brahminical sacrificial character of these modes of cleansing. Though caste is claimed not to be material to the construction of the ideology of *hindutva*, declaring itself to be a pan-Indian or even a pan-Hindu consciousness, its caste elitism, that is, brahmanism, is constantly betrayed by its rituals and symbolism. They provide the discourse and basic legitimation of mosque breaking, temple-making and general Muslim persecution. Ignoring all social, cultural and religious diversities in India with their myriad contradictions and differences, the Hindu right synthesises its credo of *hindutva* from a unifying, erasing synthesis. This ideological bloc centralises Hindu religious epics from North India's Hindi-speaking region, the *Ramayana* in particular. These symbolisms and rituals are then deployed in 'cleansing' of the demographic barriers to the homogenisation of the Indian body politic.

Consistent with the brahminical/high caste obsession with purity and pollution at all levels, ranging from racial and physical to symbolic-cultural, the Hindu right is attempting to purify or sanskritise blood, creed and conduct. This has meant an abhorrence of physical/biological mixing of body fluids and a rejection of any hybridity between the separate 'races' of Hindus and Muslims. There are powerful taboos as well forbidding consumption of meat, and beef in particular as 'Muslim' food. Other 'cultural' mixings are also unacceptable, for example of languages, in spite of the fact that Urdu and Hindi are both saturated with vocabulary originating from Persian and Arabic, dubbed as Muslim languages. A steady discourse of inferiority, impurity and bastardisation haunts the Hindu right's general rhetoric, and as we have seen, this impelled it towards the appropriation of Nazi rhetoric from its very inception. The situation might become clearer to Westerners if the word 'Muslim' were to be substituted point for point for the word 'Jew'. A Hindu woman cohabiting with a Muslim would not be treated dissimilarly to a German woman in the 1930s considered to be a 'Jew's whore'. Mixed marriages between Hindus and Muslims could, therefore, run into grave danger and the children of these marriages face powerful hostilities.

There is a paranoiac anxiety in the Hindu right ideology and psyche regarding impurity and bastardisation. Muslims in general and Muslim women in particular are feared and blamed as sources for socio-cultural and physical pollution or impurity, as also are India's other 'others', such as dalits and Christians. As this population sullies the body politic and individual bodies of the nation, and are the identified sources of reproduction of impurity, a ritual of 'cleansing' or *shuddhi* is an imperative for the development of a desired 'Hindu nation' and its state. This ritual of purification has traditionally ranged from pogroms involving rapes and mutilation against Muslims, dalits or Christians, to penances imposed on Hindu violators of taboos, to ritual conversion of Christians, but not Muslims, into the lowest rung of Hinduism. These forced re-conversions have been in practice since 1929 and proliferate now in flagrant violation of the Indian constitution. As I have said above, this absorption/assimilation of 'others' into the Hindu fold – increasing demographic homogeneity – should be seen in a continuum with violence against women as a part of the majoritarianism of the ethnic nation's demographic rather than democratic polity. In the last few decades, Christians have been significantly added to these sacrifices to the demographic nation state. Raping of nuns, assaulting priests, charring the missionary Graham Staines and his two young sons, and ransacking convents are all the material aspects of the discourse of an ethnic nation, now comfortably hitched to a rhetoric of authenticity and anti-colonialism.

It can be seen from what I have said how violence against women, ranging from gender regulation to rape and mutilation, is integral to genocide. The fascism of this brahminical genocide calls for a brutal masculinisation of its cadres. Their bodies become weapons against the communities they target and are combined with ritual implements of iron and wood. Thus tridents and trishuls, the symbol of the god Shiva, along with feudal implements of swords and sticks, blend with the guns and penises. Altogether they proclaim an invincible Hindu male power – 'death to the muslims and long live hindus'.

To conclude, I want to point out that genocide has, and had, a global reach. The Hindu right or Hindu fascists are a part of this long tradition of colonising bodies, lands and cultures – where demography and ethnicity become the ground for state formation. My effort here was to prompt a wider and detailed discussion of where violence against women fits in this political equation. I also wanted to draw attention to the general and the particular nature of the phenomenon of genocide itself, to show how in different cultural and historical environments genocide/ethnocide or ethnic cleansing takes on a particular ideological and symbolic constitution. In India this high caste/brahminical version combines the features of modern nation-building and nation state with those of invention of tradition in order to construct an ethnic nation.

CHAPTER 23

Cultural Nationalism and Woman as the Subject of the Nation

There is no document of civilisation which is not at the same time a document of barbarism.[1]

∴

1   Introduction: A Few Reminders about Nationalism, Cultural Nationalism and Imperialism

The last few decades have again seen massive attempts at unravelling the fabric of social justice woven by the world at least since 1789 – the year of the French Revolution. As the globe spills over in outrage against globalisation of capitalism, old forces of domination masquerading as freedom, democracy and civilisation, or as anti-colonialism for the defence of culture, nation and religion, envelop the world in a gathering fascism with many faces. We need to recognise this fascism wherever we see it – in the West or in the East, in the North or in the South. This chapter is an attempt at that recognition. In the memory of the Italian communist Antonio Gramsci, languishing in Mussolini's prison, I want to speak to what Gramsci calls our 'good sense' as against this continuum of 'common sense' fascism that runs through our cultures and politics.[2]

When I say 'again' with regard to the rise of fascism, I am alluding to the 1920s and 1930s, when fascism officially announced itself as a viable political option, one that millions followed in Europe, and not just in Germany.[3] But then as now there were also forces fighting fascism. I want us to listen to two

---

1   Walter Benjamin, *Theses on Philosophy of History* (1969b), p. 256.
2   See Gramsci's 'The Study of Philosophy' (in 1971, especially pp. 323–33).
3   In these two decades, most European countries were either directly or indirectly in fascist/Nazi control. We need only to think of Germany under Hitler, Italy under Mussolini, Spain with Franco, Portugal with Salizar and the eventual triumph of the Vichy in France after 1940 to see what I mean.

such voices, from the West and the East, voices that rose from the limbos of the hells of Nazi and Japanese fascism, and take our cues from them. They belong to Walter Benjamin from Germany and Rabindranath Tagore from India. Writing in his 'Theses in the Philosophy of History', in the gloom of Nazi Germany's victory march, Benjamin told us:

> Whoever emerges victorious participates ... in the triumphal procession in which the present rulers step over those who are lying prostrate. They are called cultural treasures, and a historical materialist views them with cautious detachment. For without exception the cultural treasures he surveys have an origin which he can not contemplate without horror ... There is no document of civilisation which is not at the same time a document of barbarism.[4]

Rabindranath Tagore, in 1938, wrote to Yone Noguchi, the poet of imperial Japan – a fellow Easterner – about the perils of a certain type of nationalism. I quote him at greater length because his voice has rarely been heard in the West after the Second World War.

> Humanity, in spite of its many failures, has believed in a fundamental moral structure of society. When you speak, therefore, of the 'inevitable means, terrible it is though, for establishing a new great world in the Asiatic continent' – signifying, I suppose, the bombing of Chinese women and children and the desecration of ancient temples and universities as a means of saving China for Asia – you are ascribing to humanity a way of life which is not even inevitable among the animals and would certainly not apply to the East, in spite of her occasional aberrations. You are building your conception of an Asia which would be raised on a tower of skulls ... When I protested against 'Westernisation' in my lectures in Japan, I contrasted the rapacious imperialism which some of the nations of Europe were cultivating with the ideal of perfection preached by Buddha and Christ, with the great heritage of culture and good neighbourliness that went [in]to the making of Asiatic and other civilisations.[5]

Do Benjamin's and Tagore's summations of Western and Eastern nationalism and imperialism, expressed in wars of aggression in the name of civilisation

---

4   Benjamin 1969b, p. 256.
5   Tagore 1997, p. 497.

and nation, remind us of the ideological legitimations, the war cries of George W. Bush and Osama bin Laden? Is Operation Enduring Freedom, now spreading on its 'axis of evil' from Afghanistan outwards, not built on 'the bombing of women and children', on a 'tower of skulls'? Equally, does not the jihad of bin Laden, spuriously linking itself to the defeat of the Moors in fifteenth-century Spain, building itself on the bodies of women/girls, on those of secular forces and the poor, only recently fattening itself on U.S. funding and military support, also come to mind?[6] We need to realise that the U.S. foreign policy of George W. Bush and Osama bin Laden and right-wing religious groups are historically and ideologically joined at the hip and are the flip side of each other. God, discourse of evil, anti-communism/socialism, religious fundamentalist rhetoric and Samuel Huntington's warmed-up cliché of 'clash of civilisations' serve both equally.[7]

If nothing else, these warning voices from the past teach us to look behind aggressive and facile categorisations in civilisational and moral terms. How then can we begin to inquire into the colonial or imperialist cultural nationalism of the West, or into the semi-feudal capitalist cultural nationalisms of the East? How can we get a clear view of what Frantz Fanon, the Martiniquan and Algerian revolutionary, in *The Wretched of the Earth* called 'false decolonisation'?[8] It is here that we must turn to feminist critiques – rooted in the concept of patriarchy and analyses of gender – in relation to social and political organisations, relations and ideologies.[9] They provide us with a formidable analytical key into the door of oppression and injustice. It is our right and responsibility to use this key in the service of social justice and critical epistemology, of intellectual inquiry. I intend to do so by looking into, from a marxist-feminist perspective, different ways in which various forms of nationalism work, inclusive their cultural, economic and state dimensions. During the process of this assessment I intend to critique certain established perspectives on nationalism as well. The goal is to render visible the formative connections between these

---

6   For an interesting, though pro-American and modified islamist, account of U.S. involvement in Afghanistan in order to oust communists and pro-Soviet forces and gain control over oil resources, see Rashid 2000. See also Moghadam 1997.

7   Huntington 1966.

8   Fanon 1963.

9   Among many others, for feminists living in the West see the works of Floya Anthias, Deniz Kandiyoti, Valentine Moghadam, Nira Yuval-Davis. South Asia has also produced a large body of feminist critiques of nationalism, but they differ strongly from their Western counterparts. Among them works of Jasodhara Bagchi, Uma Chakravarty, Kumkum Sangari, Radha Kumar, Urvashi Butalia, Nighat S. Khan, and Naila Kabeer are highly interesting and well-developed in their critique.

different aspects that make up the social and political whole. As I have said elsewhere, we need to link moral regulations and cultural constructions, such as those of patriarchal proprieties, with existing class or property relations and ideologies of national culture and the state.[10]

2   A Supportive Critical Review and Corrections of Feminist Critiques of Nationalism

Feminists have long tried to meet the challenge of nationalism both intellectually and politically, particularly in relation to war and patriotism. Here is Virginia Woolf in *Three Guineas*:

> What does 'our country' mean to me, an outsider? To decide this she will analyse the meaning of patriotism in her own case. She will inform herself of the amount of land, wealth and property in the possession of her own sex and class in the present – how much of England belongs to her ... 'Our country', she will say, 'throughout the greater part of history has treated me as a slave; it has denied me education or any share of its possessions ... in fact, as a woman, I have no country. As a woman I want no country'.[11]

This moving pronouncement by Woolf has been expanded upon in various ways by feminist critics of nationalism through the last few decades. In the West we need only to mention Nira Yuval-Davis, Flora Anthias, Denis Kandyoti, Valentine Moghadam and Anne McClintock to see what I mean by this expansion. Out of a vast body of literature on the topic, two main strands of feminist criticism of nationalism may be said to have emerged so far. One strand considers *any* nationalism as inherently patriarchal and containing oppressive and exclusive moral constructions and regulations within its cultural, ideological and state apparatus. A patriarchally constructed icon of woman serves as the cultural/moral sign of the nation.[12] Any national project, it is contended, identifies itself through this sign. Along with this critique of an integrally patriarchal utterance of the nation, there is another critique which deduces their patriarchal nature not from any direct patriarchal content but from an ideologically driven absence of women and gender within their purview. Both of these criticisms are apt and deserved, particularly with reference to certain types of

---

10   Bannerji, Mojab and Whitehead 2001.
11   Woolf 1938, p. 107.
12   For a good conception of what 'sign' means, see Barthes 1973.

national projects and discourses. But there is more to nationalism than what we find in these two dominant formulations. My presentation, while it belongs to the larger genre of feminist critique of nationalism, also tries to make the situation more complex and points out, through a marxist framework, what a more considered critique might mean. As such, I attempt both an extension and a correction of the feminist tradition of criticism. The idea is to broaden the parameters of feminist critique, both as politics and an epistemology, by situating the issues of patriarchy and gender justice within a wider space of revolutionary social criticism rooted in a demand for social justice – for all and at all levels. My refusal to segregate women, gender or patriarchy into ideologically free-standing or superordinating categories joins hands with those who find a socially uncomplicated or undifferentiated presentation of patriarchy both theoretically and politically unacceptable. It indicates the refusal of a fragmented way of thinking about the complex integrity of the organisation and relations of social wholeness in which culture, politics and economy are separated and then conveniently added to each other when the need arises. I also reject the presentation of all notions and projects of nation and decolonisation in an undifferentiated, ahistorical and politically unspecified manner.

Let us begin with the last point first. That there is a problem with essentialising nationalism should be obvious – as though all projects of nation can mean one and the same thing irrespective of their sociohistorical context and content. There has to be a distinction made, in the first place, between an anti-colonial or decolonising nationalism and the bourgeois nationalism of European countries which went out to colonise. It is a mistake to eliminate this basic difference between an aggressive European nationalism, with its own colonial practices and discourses of moral/political self-identity and forms of legitimation, and defensive, reactive and resisting ideologies and practices with an anticolonial context, equipped also with their own nationalist discourses or content of ideology and identity.[13] In conflating them, feminist critics rest on the same theoretical premises and make the same mistake as those theorists of nation whom they criticise.[14] In not making this distinction masculinist mod-

---

13   In this context, political/ideological differences between theorists of nationalism, such as Ernest Gellner, Eric Hobsbawm and Anthony Smith, are largely immaterial, as they hold up European nationalism as the archetype of *all* nationalisms. Where they do speak to nationalism in the third world, they measure it up by this typology. When they recognise a difference they base it on the Western form of nationalism being modernist and the third world variety as primordialist. This can hardly be said to be an analytical understanding of the difference. See Gellner 1983; Hobsbawm 1990; Smith 1986.

14   This position is best illustrated by Nira Yuval-Davis in her *Gender and Nation* (1997). In this, she recapitulates in a concise fashion major feminist positions on nationalism, outlining

ernists, such as Gellner and Hobsbawm, primordialists, such as Kedourie and van den Bughe, or theorists of ethno-nationalism, such as Anthony Smith,[15] and their feminist critics all operate on similar premises. This is not to say that a patriarchal or gender agenda is not vital in different types of nationalism, or that there are some similarities between them, but they are not necessarily the same in their political stances or discourses. Shifting the ground of nation-making or the national imaginary from the aggression of colonialism to resistance against it does call for a premise of difference, however politically problematic that resistance or anti-colonial gesture may be.[16]

The next important lacuna in conventional feminist critique is the obliteration of distinctions between different types of decolonising nationalisms. As Aijaz Ahmad has reminded us, there are 'historic and diverse practices of nationalisms', and 'it might be better to speak in the plural or at least in terms of *typologies* of nationalisms'.[17] Speaking typologically, then, there are at least three basic decolonising or anti-colonial nationalist ideological stances and state forms which we have historically experienced. They are all 'nationalist' in that they all create or aspire to a sovereign national state, but they are also quite different from each other. Two among them share a common social project of capital, class and property, both in national and international economic terms, while erecting different political structures, institutions and ideologies. One form leads to that of a post-colonial liberal democracy with a constitution resting on the separation of church and state, notions of legal citizenship resting on the notion of a proprietorial contract making, individual, civil and political rights and liberties, and secularism, as for example in India, Egypt, Mexico, etc.[18] They may also contain varying degrees of provision for social welfare and economic planning. These constitutional measures of liberal democracy are

---

in various ways the absence of women from male theorists' understanding of nation making processes, and an overall lack of gender analysis. Among others whose viewpoints she mentions, Carol Pateman, Rebecca Grant, Sylvia Walby, and Flora Anthias feature prominently.

15   Kedourie 1993; van den Bughe 1979; Smith 1986.

16   I have considered this issue in terms of difference, identity and history at length in my book *Thinking Through: Essays on Feminism, Marxism and Anti-racism* in the chapter 'The Passion of Naming: Identity, Difference and Politics of Class'.

17   Ahmad 1996, p. 403.

18   Though neither male nationalism theorists nor feminist critics, such as N. Yuval-Davis, F. Anthias, D. Kandyoti, among others, see liberal democracy as a viable form of post-colonial state, it happens to have been the case in Egypt, Mexico and India. Of course, post-modernist, post-colonial theorists have considered this form to be an inauthentic form for the third world; see Chatterjee 1986a. For a discussion of possible kinds of secularism in the third world, especially India, see Gopal 1996.

intended to mitigate through formal, not fully social and economic, but cultural and political equality some of the negative effects of existing and accepted inequalities produced through capital, class and gender. This state form and its national imaginary can be contrasted with another type of national project which is equally strong in its reliance on the rule of capital, class, and private property, but lacks the mitigating political dimensions of a bourgeois/liberal democracy. Instances of this may be found in Iran, Pakistan and Saudi Arabia.

This is an anti-democratic illiberal nationalism and state which cannot countenance equality at any level, and thus cannot accommodate political equality even at a formal level. Thus it rejects a constitution based on the provision of a rights-bearing citizen-individual and dispenses with all provisions for civil liberty. This national polity is often a direct expression and extension of a reductive version of ethnic/cultural identity, of community understood through hierarchy, and often rests on a fundamentalist or supremacist religious basis. It veers towards theocracy and the practice of ethnic citizenship. No equality measure or redress is possible here, either for individuals or for groups, outside of the dominant community norms, since they are encoded as criteria for citizenship in the national ideology and the state apparatus. Sri Lanka or Bangladesh may be considered here. In my 'Pygmalion Nation: Towards a Critique of Subaltern Studies and the 'Resolution of the Women's Question'', these 'types' of nationalism are discussed at length (see Chapter 9, this volume). They are very different from those of Nira Yuval-Davis' more commonly used distinctions in feminist circles. My distinctions rely centrally on the connection between all aspects of propriety or culture in nationalist projects and property relations, in resources extending from land and other forms of capital to human labour and social and reproductive resources. Class, therefore, in a broad sociological sense is a key marker for me. But for Yuval-Davis the issues of property and class are not intrinsicaly material. She phrases her types thus:

> I would like to differentiate between three major dimensions of nationalist project ... In my view it is very important not to conflate concerns emanating from constructions of nations based on notions of origin and those on culture. Both of them need also to be analytically distinguished from constructions of nations based on citizenship of states. Different aspects of gender relations play an important role in each of these dimensions of nationalist projects and are crucial for any valid theorisation of them.[19]

---

19   Yuval-Davis 1997, p. 21.

Both these proprietorial nationalisms are *necessarily and logically* patriarchal and, as such, are administratively, legally and culturally gendered. They both imply proprietorial and hierarchical social relations, and express the patriarchal morality of a class society based on the ownership of bodies, embodied labour, commodities and capital produced through this labour. But even so one cannot afford to forget a basic difference between these two national and state projects. Ethnic/cultural nationalism specifically lacks the visible contradiction which liberal democratic nationalism overtly presents between the legal rights of the individual as citizen and the actual patriarchal or other social relations of daily inequality between political subjecthood and social subjection. Cultural nationalism, on the other hand, lacks this contradiction and translates into a totalitarian political culture and state in which appeals to tradition, religion and ethnicity provide both moral and legal grounds of entitlement or political subjecthood. Thus it is that Islamic *sharia* or *hudood* can become the law of the state. A state, such as Pakistan, which is otherwise ruled by current laws of property and contract, has a general penal code and is able to embrace laws of 'globalisation', relies on 'tradition' and religion when it comes to women's conduct or property rights.[20] In its totalitarian nature, in its overwhelmingly exclusive polity and symbolic apparatus, a certain type of use of culture in nationalism logically climaxes in fascism. As Aijaz Ahmad says in *Lineages of the Present*, 'As culture, fascism is not merely opposed to and by nationalism, it is a kind of nationalism, drawing upon, and interpreting in a *fascist* way, that same national tradition which other – secular and democratic – nationalisms also invoke'.[21] So it is not the mere use of culture in nationalist politics that makes it fascistic, but interpreting culture in a particular way that does so. Feminist critique properly speaking should be aimed at these forms.

The third type of decolonising, national project I call 'national liberation'. This requires us to remember Nicaragua, for example. It is my claim that the ideology of national liberation does not logically arise from or extend into patriarchy or misogyny. As a liberatory project of social and economic equality it can, at least in theory, elaborate itself upon women's liberation, and thus resist women's status as property of men, of the family, the church and the nation state. Its basic anti-private property thrust, its rejection of ownership or oppression of bodies and labour, can enable it to do so, even if that has not

---

20   See Patel 1991 and also Narain 2001. Narain speaks of the peculiar combination of religious personal law with modern law in the course of Indian state formation. A large admixture of cultural nationalism for a state otherwise liberal democratic can reveal the implications of these two forms; India offers an example of such a mixed state.

21   Ahmad 1996, p. 232.

yet happened in practice as fully as it should. It should stand to reason that
the social imaginary of national liberation can conceive subjecthood, freedom
and individuality in terms other than those of ownership, and unlike cultural
nationalism it can create national collectivities and identities irrespective of
blood, birth and an essentialised religio-cultural belonging.

In my opinion many feminist critiques of nationalism have failed to make
these important distinctions. They have not been able to do so because of their
own lack of an historical materialist perspective, the lack of a critique of capital
or of class analysis. They failed to notice or theorise formative links between
property and propriety, that is, between class, capital (local and foreign) and
ideologies and unequal social relations of gender/patriarchy. A whole issue of
Feminist Review (Autumn 1997) on radical democracy, women and citizenship,
has generally managed to skirt around the issues of class, capital and imperialism while speaking for women's and minority groups' political entitlement. A
parallel classless language of agency, citizenship, community and participation
has been put in place by feminists unstintingly using classic liberal theories of
citizenship, such as those of T.H. Marshall[22] or the social democratic proposals of Bryan Turner.[23] These attempts conjure up the possibility of a capitalism
with a human face, the possibility of a society of equal citizenship which does
not challenge class or imperialism. It would appear from reading such feminist
theorists that if poverty management programmes were well in place both locally and globally, particularly through the agency of international bodies and
NGOs (which for some reason are called 'autonomous') one could live in a capitalist world and yet have provision of a full and active citizenship for women
and various minorities. The absurdity of such a conceptual and political stance,
which should be apparent to common sense, is often missing from much of the
critical literature on women, citizenship and nationalism.

This type of feminist critique relies on the epistemology of liberalism, which
compartmentalises complex and formative moments of the social as separated,
self-regulating spheres such as the economic, cultural and political.[24] Hence
class, if it is noticed at all, is mainly understood in reductive economic terms,
in relation to the index of consumption, and not as a basic formative aspect of
social organisation which is mediated through patriarchal norms and practices.
Seen thus, patriarchy becomes separable from class, a cultural phenomenon, an
attitudinal problem or a structure solely rooted in the family and male-female
relations – to be rectified by consciousness-raising, legislative demands, better

22   Marshall 1950.
23   Turner 1990, pp. 189–218.
24   On this compartmentalisation of liberal thought, see Macpherson 1977.

education for women, and citizenship and welfare management. The solution to the absence or diminishment of women's social agency and political entitlement seems to hinge mainly on equitable gender representation in the context of a class society which makes such equality impossible to realise. This demand for gender equality cannot be met with notions such as social citizenship or a fuller form of legal personhood, as women are subject to class, imperialism and colonialism differentially. Thus the idea of a 'transversal' feminist organising, an adapted version of coalition politics, where women are assumed to be the same/similar in some ways, while differing in others, does not offer an effective option as these differences encode fundamental power relations between women. The idea of 'transversal feminism' is found in the work of Nira Yuval-Davis, who needs to be quoted here:

> [T]ransversal politics aims to be an alternative to the universalism/ relativism dichotomy which is at the heart of the modernist/postmodernist feminist debate. It aims at providing answers to the crucial/theoretical political questions of how and with whom we should work if/when we accept that we are all different as deconstructionist theorists argue.[25]

This fundamental theoretical proposal does not translate out to much more than the old coalition politics between disparate women's (or other) groups. We are recommended to be 'aware of continuous historical changes and [to] keep our perceptions of the boundaries between collectivities sufficiently flexible and open so that exclusionary politics are not permitted'.[26] This stance is so unaware or unable to cope with fundamental contradictions or social relations and so voluntaristic that it then blithely proceeds to offer a bland form of politics in which

> [a]ll feminist (and other forms of democratic) politics should be viewed as a form of coalition politics in which the differences among women are recognised and given a voice, in and outside the political 'units', and the boundaries of this coalition should be set not in terms of 'who' we are but in terms of what we want to achieve.[27]

Viewed thus, all *social*, structural relations of power, underwritten by political ideologies, are erased and empowerment amounts to mere 'giving voices',

---

25   Yuval-Davis 1997, p. 125.
26   Ibid., p. 126.
27   Ibid., p. 126.

'recognising differences'. Who is entitled by social relations and locations to accord this recognition? What is being recognised? Can 'class' as *habitus* be wiped away by good wishes and voluntarisms?[28] In fact this idea can only be forwarded by feminists, such as Nira Yuval-Davis, as a viable form of politics because the irreducibly power-organised nature of some of these differences and similarities is not comprehended or neglected.[29] A deeper exploration of the failures of these 'transversal' attempts is ignored by Yuval-Davis. Profound relations of contradiction in and through which men and women hold a systemic relation of antithesis of power and interest with respect to each other are pushed out of sight in favour of manipulating an unequal status quo for limited and transitory results. The social cohesion proposed through this transversal or coalition politics, if it works at all, is at best a liberal stop-gap solution and most often a middle-class liberal political fantasy. In spite of protestations, this feminist solution is similar to Michael Ignatieff's notion of 'civic nationalism',[30] where similarity between power-differentiated groups will be promulgated in the public spheres of the nation state and legal citizenship, while real differences will be contained within the private domain wherever that may be located. The feminist solution makes the difference between women theoretically visible and material, but only to see it diminishing in practical political contexts. The radical and democratic feminist solutions, then, both turn out to be a modified version of the classic liberal separation of the public and the private, in which the social relations of gender, 'race' and class are to be aggregated and disaggregated situationally.

The broadest demand of non-marxist Western feminist critique of nationalism lies in that of an expansion of the notion of citizenship to include more fully women and minorities and third world migrants into 'transnational citizenship' as members of a borderless nation. While this idea has a utopian dimension, invoking the old humanist ideal of 'world citizenship', or a new ideal of movement of labour paralleling that of capital, it cannot provide concretely critical and political bases for the realisation of this proposal. Instead it diminishes or side-lines the roles of international and national capital and

---

28   In this context of understanding difference, see also the chapter 'But Who Speaks for Us?' in Bannerji 1995.

29   In spite or because of her 'intersectionality' framework, which conceives of class, gender and 'race' as separate strands and trajectories imposed on the social graph, because they can 'intersect' only if they are separate and discreet, Nira Yuval-Davis cannot conceptualise the above coded social relations inter-constitutively.

30   Ignatieff 1993. Ignatieff's 'civic nationalism' does not seem to be much more than the old bourgeois liberal-democratic state's nationalism – which rests on and guarantees a severe public/private divide.

power relations between the G8 states and others and occludes, therefore, the imperialist potential for such nationlessness or statelessness. As nations which are homes of corporate capital are now more nationalist than ever, it does not help to use an anti-national or international language or the services of Western capital's domesticated arbitrating bodies such as the United Nations for breaking down the barriers put up by third world nations. This in fact is the proposal of capital's globalisation. This seemingly ideal 'transnational' perspective prevents us from seeing that 'international' organisations such as the various agencies of the United Nations, international justice and financial bodies are only nominally nation-transcendent. As they stand, they are largely the instruments of Western capitalist, mainly U.S. corporate, domination. No one who has watched the manoeuvres of the U.N. weapons inspectors in Iraq or the activities of a U.S.-led NATO in the former Yugoslavia can think otherwise. Matching transnational capital with transnational citizenship has its own logic, but it can only validate the rule of capital over the world, unless it is employed in breaking down fortress Europe or America and resisting neo-colonialism, which so far has not been the case.

These issues that I mention would have been of major concern for feminist critics if they had politically not given up on socialist projects or on national liberation and intellectually on historical materialism, which could have given them an integrated analysis of capital and imperialism involving class, culture and ideology. This stance is particularly disturbing now as most projects of national liberation have succumbed to U.S.-led onslaughts. Even the liberal democracies of post-colonial nation states are being replaced, with U.S. help, by cultural nationalist states which simultaneously court American and other foreign capital and military aid while creating an internal ruling apparatus based on religious-cultural identities and ethnic citizenships.[31] Replete with a jargon of origin, ancient lineage, tradition and cultural authenticity, they target all internal oppositions, ranging from feminist to progressive and secular movements. These states are not only or necessarily theocratic, as in Iran, Afghanistan or Pakistan, but can also promote unitary ethnic identities based on language and general symbolic-cultural constitutions, such as in Sri Lanka or Bangladesh, which blend and bend with religious fundamentalisms or supremacisms. India comes to mind as well, particularly due to the convulsions in the

---

31   U.S.-'liberated' Afghanistan is a good example of this – as sharia still continues to rule society, providing its only juridical framework in non-economic and social fields. India also serves as an example, where a hindu fundamentalist nationalist government organises pogroms against the muslim minority, as in Gujarat from 27 February 2002 to the present time.

polity over the last ten years as Hindu fundamentalist/supremacist political parties and their civil society groups have increasingly wrested control from secular and left political parties and progressive, secular civil society organisations, such as Indian women's movements and trade unions.[32]

For reasons of elaborating hegemony and establishing jurisdiction or mandate, these cultural nationalist states tend to slip into theocracy – into religious fundamentalism – and always introduce a sacrosanct tone to the very topic of culture by using the adjective 'national'. This tone of induced veneration tries to forestall criticality in all its forms by inventing traditions which are grossly hierarchical, invoking ancient lineages and speaking in the name of god. Adopting the old colonial cultural/civilisational discourse encoded in the binary paradigm of 'tradition versus modernity', this nationalism creates an homogenised 'us and them' as much within the nation as between nations. Ethnicity and gender, religion and caste, race and tribe, all become criteria for national and social belonging and sometimes even of legal citizenship. A particular interpretation of culture, which Aijaz Ahmad called fascist, valorising a majoritarian and hierarchical culture, becomes the ground for nation-making.[33] It renders women and other groups marginal with the ruse of tradition which is largely an internalised form of colonial discourse, such as that of the Aryan myth bandied by Hindu nationalists in India.[34] All the while the doors to local and Western capital are wide open. Surely feminists need to recognise the difference between this political project and those of post-colonial liberal secular democracies, while maintaining a strict critique of patriarchy in all cases.

Ethnic nationalism, always veering towards religious fundamentalism and theocratic or monocultural communities and states, offers a clear picture of dangers entailed for women in such national imaginaries and states. The centrality of patriarchy for the national project, which relies on the control of women's bodies, their sexual and social conduct, becomes painfully obvious. The glorification of motherhood as nurturers and transmitters of national culture and cause, injunctions of sexual purity as chastity and virginity, and legitimised violence against women for being initiatory and explicitly sexual, are all parts of this national cause.[35] In fact, women's inclusion in the nation, pre- and post-state, is based primarily on their motherhood – as 'mothers of the nation'. This aspect of women's participation in bourgeois or petty bourgeois cultural

32   See Basu et al. 1993; also Sarkar and Butalia 1995.

33   Ahmad 1996, pp. 221–66.

34   In the context of Indo-Aryan nationalism, see Savarkar 1967 or Golwalkar 1963. There is no difference between their use of Aryan myth and that of the Nazis.

35   See Maunaguru 1995 and de Silva 1995; see also Sangari and Vaid 1996.

nationalist movements has been exhaustively researched by South Asian feminist historians, cultural theorists and social scientists.[36] Topics ranging from *satidaha* or burning of women on their husband's funeral pyres, dowry, widow remarriage, the oppression of the girl child, female foeticide through amniocentesis and sex selection processes, have all drawn much anger and organisation – theoretically and politically.[37]

Parallel with this searching feminist critique of bourgeois or petty bourgeois cultural nationalism runs a strain of criticism regarding the solidly ethnic – read, racist – nationalism of Western colonial projects. Any reader familiar with the critical cultural and historical writings of Anne McClintock, Laura Ann Stoller, Mariana Valverde or Anna Davin can remember the stake of the colonial governments or white-settler colonies in the motherhood of white women. Bourgeois women had to hold up the empire by being the iconic mothers of the 'race', whom the working-class white women had to emulate, particularly when they migrated to the colonies.[38] Laws against mixed marriages or sexual contacts, termed 'miscegenation' laws, were uniformly present in the colonies and in slave societies such as the United State of America.[39] The weight of holding up the white 'race' and culture – that is, the physical and social reproduction of racism – fell with great pressure on white women. In this context the ethnic nationalism of the German Third Reich may also be mentioned, as German women had to uphold the honour of an Aryan nation and their Nazi politics. Feminist critiques of the above ideologies and practices are fairly straightforward, as are the fascist projects themselves, which leave nothing to the imagination and create no obfuscation. Their totalitarianism gives them a unified nature and clarity of purpose, and their feminist criticism can be direct and hard hitting.

Feminist critique of bourgeois/ liberal democracy, however, is a more complex and ambivalent matter. This complication derives from the fact that the political apparatus of liberal democracy rests on universal principles while in actual terms the apparatus rests on unequal relations, primarily of class, gender and 'race'. Thus, promises of universal rights and freedoms enshrined in the constitution are constantly compromised by the conditions which make their realisation or practice impossible. This holds not only for working-class (non-white or white) women and men, but for women of the middle or upper classes as well. Many years of painstaking analysis of political theorists from

36   See Bagchi 1993; see also Jayawardena 1986.
37   See Kumar 1993; see also Khan 1992; Zafar 1991.
38   See also in this context Ware 1992.
39   Davis 1983.

Mary Wollstonecraft to Carol Pateman have revealed this Janus face of liberal democracy, which turns out to be neither liberal nor democratic for women. Exploration of this double face of liberal democracy, its basic contradiction between political promises and social actualities, has made it evident that the democratic nation and its state hold a core of patriarchal and racist cultural nationalism and commensurate ascribed or stereotyped identities. The state apparatus, especially its ideological and administrative apparatus, what Althusser calls the ideological state apparatus (ISA), is enunciated upon a cultural nationalist vision with normative typologies of identities.[40] In the context of Canada, questioning what it means to be a Canadian, as opposed to being an immigrant or a visible or ethnic minority, a newcomer, brings attention to this ethnic/racist national imaginary.[41] This ethnic nationalism is not only racist, but centrally patriarchal. White middle-class women fall fully within its purview, and are only partially able to fulfil the requirement of being typologically 'Canadian'.

To validate this point we need only observe the fact of control of white women's bodies as spelt out by the years of struggle over the issue of choice regarding abortion. The fact that the state's agenda often blurs with that of the Christian right is not a matter of accident.[42] Francophone ethnic nationalism gives to white francophone women the responsibility of reproducing white francophone 'race' and culture. We need only to remember Lucien Bouchard's speech to Quebec's women in relation to the referendum on separation.[43] Furthermore, in examining the state's agenda we can see that pejorative and idealised visions of motherhood are embedded in welfare laws regarding single mothers and women needing social assistance. Even in the choice of economic cutbacks the patriarchal cultural vision is at work. Cutbacks in various childcare services or services for the elderly tell us to reinforce the bourgeois family, mandate women to refrain from working or working out of their homes and to fulfil their roles as mothers, wives and daughters. These norms, encoded in state policies, laws, and administration, are not substantially different from those of ethnic/theocratic nationalist states, or those of the Vatican with world outreach into Catholic communities. The only difference lies in the fact that an individual rights-based constitution of the liberal democratic state leaves some scope to push the envelope, to ask for redress on both individual and universal grounds, and if nothing else debates and desires prompted by notions of these

---

40   Althusser 1977a.
41   See Bannerji 1997b.
42   Backhouse 1999, speaks of this conflation.
43   See the chapter 'Geography Lessons' in Bannerji (2001b).

rights help to raise popular consciousness on issues of difference, such as those of 'race' or patriarchy. Liberal feminists rest their hopes in this, and pursue their activities within this parameter.

Thus it is important to remember that cultural nationalism and related politics of identity, ethnicity, community and 'race' are not the sole prerogatives of third world nationalism. There is in the West a hegemonic colonial/imperialist identity politics waiting to be recognised as such, both in terms of what has come to be called 'knowledge', culture or civilisation and social and cultural values and political aspirations normalised through the world, most of which had been colonised. This has been noted by some feminist critics, such as Anne McClintock in *Imperial Leather*.[44] Critical race theories and cultural studies as well as post-colonial studies have much to say about 'colonial discourse' and racist cultures. But there is a divide between conventional post-colonial critiques and feminist critiques on nationalism. The reason why their difference is not as generally noticed as is, for example, the patriarchy of the Nation of Islam or that of religious extremists in South or West Asia, is that both mainstream or even radical Western feminists and post-colonialists think within the same paradigm of modernity and tradition and subscribe in some form to colonial/cultural nationalist discourses. Thus, many post-colonial critics who critique racist cultures have not spoken to patriarchy or class, and many critics of patriarchy have ignored 'race', class and imperialism. They have both placed cultural nationalism within the realm of pre-modern or the so-called traditional societies, and thus accepted the hegemony of a Western colonial or imperialist interpretive framework. The notions of progress, rationality and science that informed these old and new forms of colonial cultural discourses obscured their nationalistic natures. Liberal discourses have, therefore, been spared from criticism, and only the explicitly Christian/missionary discourse has received some criticism from Western liberals and feminists. But the secular and seemingly humanist versions of this same missionary approach prevails in various transnational/international projects for women or tribal and rural peoples of the third world. They have not aroused much suspicion or criticism.

In languages extending from discourse of civilisation to that of development, a deeply cultural nationalism and identity politics are at work both in the West and the rest of the world. Like many aggressive cultural nationalisms the justification for these discourses is the betterment of women. The disguised Euro-American cultural nationalism of non-governmental organisations holds a Christian resonance of rescue and charity and, as we saw in Afgh-

---

44   McClintock 1995.

anistan, proclaims its superiority with arms if necessary.[45] Their function is producing 'otherness' of non-Europeans or non-Americans as difference from their self. All wars and invasions conducted by the u.s. since the Second World War have been couched in a discourse of modernity, benevolence and rescue – self-arrogating the right to define democracy, freedom and human rights. Their main purpose has been to shatter projects of socialist or popular resistance. In the last few decades this has often been done in the name of helping third world women, rescuing them from men of their societies. This has been a convenient alibi for aggression, annexation and exploitation. From the orientalist rule in India in the eighteenth century to George W. Bush's war against Afghanistan post-September 11, upliftment of women has been the standard legitimation for waging wars mainly against civilians for economic and political reasons.[46] From the days of Helen of Troy to now, women have been the excuse for conquering or holding countries in cultural and economic bondage. In modern-day wars, encompassing not only oil pipelines but hegemonic cultural identities coupled with cultural commodity markets, religious fundamentalists such as Osama bin Laden and George W. Bush employ similar legitimation strategies, namely the totalising moral discourse of good versus evil. This is exemplified by the equivalence between Islamic jihad and Bush's creation of 'the axis of evil' as a ruse for invading at will any country that displeases the United States by standing in the path of its interests and expansionism. The categorical option of 'you are either with us or against us' serves both.

Both Western and third world feminists have been often taken in by the ruse of the paradigm of tradition and modernity or the civilisational discourse of Western colonialism and imperialism. They have failed to distinguish between different kinds of modernity – between liberationist or critical modernity and oppressive colonial modernity as well as plural forms of tradition. As the fem-

---

45   In this regard, it is important to remember the newspaper reporting on women in Afghanistan post-September 11, 2001, as well as Canadian Broadcasting Corporation (CBC) and other television reporting. In the newspapers, such as *The Globe and Mail*, columnists such as Margaret Wente, John Ibbitson, Alan Freeman, and Stephanie Nolan come to mind. The ideological self-interested nature of this reporting is obvious from the fact that even this sexist-racist reporting has ceased now, though women in Afghanistan are still governed by sharia, and are still in veils, and the money promised for them by the West has not come through.

46   The importance of women in the imperialist projects in the past and the present are manifest by the way they become excuses for colonial conquests and rule, as well as in invasions mounted for current-day projects of 'civilising' 'barbarian' nations. This is obvious from the way George W. Bush, Tony Blair and other Western leaders used feminists in their war propaganda machinery. In the earlier context, this is well discussed by Mani 1998. See also Bannerji 1998c.

inisms of international/transnational/UN-based NGOs often show, feminists employed and funded by them are often implicated as both ideologues and administrators of imperialism in administering third world women 'for their own good' – a role the Western women were generally denied in the colonial era. If there is any doubt about this, we need only to read/hear what present and former U.S. and U.K. first ladies Cherie Blair, Laura Bush and Hilary Clinton, accompanied by many, perhaps well-meaning, Western feminists who hold international offices or are public intellectuals, have to say about women of Afghanistan or West, Central or South Asia. The Afghan women who have long fought and spoken about their plight many years earlier were not heeded.[47] And now they have little choice in this discourse of rescue except to play passive roles of objects and victims of the Taliban, the cultural nation, or be the objects and victims of American foreign policy and its puppet government. The same is true for women in what the Western media has come to call 'the Islamic/Muslim world'. Such rendition completely obscures the actual histories of these women, their socio-cultural movements and political participation in their countries. As for the discourse of rescue and the need for modernisation, one needs only to remember that the current Afghan government, after the fall of the Taliban still rules women with sharia and the Western media has ceased speaking of them – revealing their own shameless opportunism and complicity with imperialism.

'Women', represented as an essentialised cultural/moral category, then, are caught between the cultural nationalisms of colonialism and imperialism and those of the autocratic/theocratic third world nation states who are often put there by U.S. and other Western powers. In such a representation and political situation women are transformed from actual people into a sign of either the nation or of 'civilisation' – of contestation, of masculine rivalries between national and foreign interests.[48] Nowhere is this as clear as in the sign of the veil. We need in this context to remember what Frantz Fanon wrote about the French imperialist unveiling of Algeria.[49] In this unveiling, or in the British 'protective' legislation pertaining to the 'age of consent' involving women and girls for consensual sex and marriage in nineteenth-century India, there is

---

47   Complaints were constantly made by feminists internationally regarding the situation of women in Afghanistan under both the Northern Alliance Mujaheddin and the Taliban and were not heeded by the West, or by the United States in particular, which was in close alliance with the former and not overly critical of the Taliban until recently. The Revolutionary Afghan Women's Association (RAWA) spoke of this situation constantly and desperately. See Moghadam 1997.

48   See Enloe 1990.

49   See Fanon's 'Unveiling Algeria' (1967, pp. 35–63); see also Sekyi-Otu 1996.

no voice of the targeted women themselves. What we hear are voices of the male contestants, of patriarchal colonisers and elite patriarchal nationalists who speak of indigenous women as 'their women' or 'our women', to cover and uncover at their will. The game is that Indian or Algerian cultural nationalists, or Afghan fundamentalists, using the rhetoric of tradition and religious injunctions, speaking of women's purity and need for protection, impose on them the veil or other symbols of modesty, while the colonisers try to unveil them for the sake of civilisation. But these patriarchal signifying devices or symbolic forms, like all symbols and signs, go beyond themselves, as they actually spatialise society into public and private domains, and seek to control half the population in one way or another. These practices and ideologies simultaneously demonstrate and establish women's status as national or imperial property. In the colonial context they serve as the first subjects of 'the nation' even before the nation becomes the nation state, and express the mandate of the colonial rule prior to that. The significational form merely throws a veil of abstraction or extends an aura of a metaphor over actual social violence against women. For the colonisers or imperialists the signs proclaim in abstract terms rights of ownership and rule over the land and all its resources, including the people, moral domains and sexual and social division of labour. Their laws and bombs are equally intent on unveiling women. These violent tasks are performed within the discourse of modernity while cultural nationalists deploy protectionist and controlling rhetoric in the name of anti-colonialism, autonomy and god.

In this context we should remember Malek Alloula, in *The Colonial Harem*, who discusses this misogynist/patriarchal violence of 'the colonial gaze'.[50] He discusses postcard photographs that French colonial administrators and tourists sent 'home' from Algeria. This colonial gaze is the same one that Lutz and Herman discuss in their investigation of *National Geographic*, a visual violence which symbolises and promises more.[51] Alloula offers the anti-colonial, antiracist feminist critic the following task: 'To track ... through the colonial representations of Algerian women – the figures of a phantasm – is to attempt a double operation: first to uncover the nature and meaning of the colonial gaze; then, to subvert the stereotype that is so tenaciously attached to the bodies of the women'.[52] In different ways Anne McClintock, Edward Said, Vron Ware or Sander Gilman perform this task of uncovering the actual violence that lies under 'the gaze'. This is our task regarding the reporting about Afghan women in the Western media since September 11. We need to place the not-so-subtle

---

50   Alloula 1986.
51   Lutz and Collins 1993.
52   Alloula 1986, p. 5.

talk about veils and unveiling by reporters such as Margaret Wente and Alan Freeman, where 'unveiling' not only signifies freedom for the Afghan woman but also a victory for the civilising mission of the war, in the context of the need for Western journalists and feminists to feel that they can penetrate all social spaces of 'the East'.

Upon examination, this interest in Afghan women turns out to be merely symbolic and opportunistic in the face of the long silence maintained by the media regarding Afghan women's oppression since the late 1980s – about which groups such as the Revolutionary Afghan Women's Association (RAWA), South Asian feminists, and their Western counterparts have long been talking. Since it is the United States that substantially helped to destroy all Afghan attempts at liberal democracy and socialism, set up Saudi groups headed by CIA-connected operatives such as Osama bin Laden, it was not opportune for the Western media until recently to reveal the violence of the Mujaheddin, the Northern Alliance or even the Taliban. This was also spelt out in silence regarding the Islamic and military terror of Zia ul Haq in Pakistan or General Ershad in Bangladesh. Lives of women endangered by grotesque implementation of *sharia* or *hudood* or deaths by landmine explosions never drew the outcry that went up when the one-thousand-year-old Bamiyan buddhas were blown up. Regrettable as that is, it is worse that the blowing up of actual people was and can be successfully depersonalised as 'collateral damage'. An icon of this godly, U.S.-helped, anti-left/secular violence is the stoning to death in Karachi, Pakistan, of a blind beggar girl who was raped in order to monumentalise Islamic morality.

Now the same Northern Alliance is in power, with the Western guard at its side. The same group that murdered Najibulla, stuffed his testicles in his mouth and hung him from a lamppost to rid Afghanistan of the evil of socialism, and which had a free pass to rape and mutilate women as war booty. We only need to remember the writings of Susan Brownmiller or Cynthia Enloe to understand what that means. No trial similar to the one of Slobodan Milošević of the former Yugoslavia was contemplated in that context. The Taliban continued the same rampage with active Pakistani and tacit U.S. support until U.S. interest was hindered.

Afghan women, then, appeared and disappeared at the need of Western interest. The Canadian journalists provided the instruments for that. We need only to remember their obsessive interest in facing and defacing Afghan women. I just want to draw attention to the front-page picture in *The Globe and Mail* (14 November 2001) of the moment of liberation epitomised by the image of a middle-aged Afghan woman lifting her blue veil in a street in Kabul. She is looking angry, confused – behind her stands a phalanx of boys and men. Everyone looks sullen and they are looking at someone who is presumably taking the picture. Reports of Western male journalists, for example Alan Freeman, are charged with something akin to thwarted desire – a mystique of the veil, to penetrate a reality that they are barred from. Women reporters write with pity and a breath-taking condescension. We hear of Afghan women until the fall of Kabul, Kandahar and Kunduz. Then they are gone from the journalistic map. Brutal massacres continue. If we are to trust veteran journalists, such as Ahmad Rashid, there is no reason for the violence against women to cease. In the meanwhile, with two women tokens in the government with their tied and veiled voices, laws about women are not 'civilised'. *Sharia* continues with vague promises of a more humane implementation. So women once again serve as justification for both nationalism and imperialism. No doubt we will hear soon about women living in the 'axis of evil' – the stage, the discourse, has been already put in place. It is only a couple of hundred years old but is as potent now as then.

This struggle for signs and for manufacturing symbols clearly demonstrates the cultural revolution that Philip Corrigan and Derek Sayer see as embedded within state formation and general projects of hegemony. As they put it:

> But the relation between state formation and cultural revolution in the long making of bourgeois civilisation, whether for England or more generally, is less often marked. Neither the profoundly cultural content of state institutions and activities nor the nature and extent of state regulation of cultural forms are adequately addressed [in much of the literature]. Still less is state formation grasped as the cultural revolution [we shall argue] it centrally is.[53]

Domination and its legitimation, various ways of 'manufacturing consent'[54] or what Gramsci would call creating 'hegemony', are this chapter's starting point. It is for this purpose that it inquired so far into the construction and deployment of the ideological category called 'woman' or its unitary plural, 'women'. Since this ideological objectification happens in and through culture, we need to understand culture as what Gramsci calls 'the pill-box' or fortification which sustains political movements as they aspire to become state.[55] This approach to the relationship of culture and politics is not new. The formative relation-

---

53   Corrigan and Sayer 1985, p. 9.
54   Chomsky 1992.
55   For Gramsci on civil society as the 'pill box' behind the state, see his 'State and Civil Society' (1971, pp. 206–78).

ships between the state, ideologies of the nation or the empire, common sense and everyday life of the civil society and signs and symbols of politics – have all been discussed in different contexts. In this context we only need to remember the Birmingham School of Cultural Studies and the writings of Stuart Hall, Paul Gilroy, Errol Lawrence, and Hazel Carby, among others.

Corrigan and Sayer, in particular, draw our attention to the moral, constructive and regulatory 'cultural revolution' of all projects of power.[56] Drawing on Durkheim in conjunction with Marx's thought on state and ideology, and to a lesser extent on Weber, they provide a complex analytical tool for understanding how social power works. They help us to see that all attempted or effective projects of ruling, whether of domination or of resistance, rely on culture – on beliefs, norms and practices of social good and moral conduct. Hegemony, therefore, is a successful moral/ideological directive, which, to paraphrase Marx, demonstrates that the ruling ideas of the ruling classes or of those aspiring to rule or administer have become diffused into the greater society, providing a cultural common sense. There is a dynamic creative process at work in building hegemony, whereby political ideologies and practices are evolved from selected and collated aspects of divergent or even contradictory strands of culture, while culture itself is full of debris and rubble of ruling and resistance ideologies – both old and new.

Hegemony is, therefore, not merely a passive state of consciousness, but rather both social and practical in nature. If patriarchy, involving moral constructions and regulations pertaining to women, rooted in social reproduction, sexuality or gender is a basic ingredient of social and political hegemony, then we need to explore the social *habitus* of patriarchy. Only a lived-in and a complexly ordered social space can be the working ground of hegemony. Hence we look to the institution called the family, with its masculine/feminine sexual moralities and mores of social reproduction connected with vice and virtue. We also need to recognise the fundamentally proprietorial nature of hegemony as expressed through patriarchy both in pre-capitalist and capitalist formations.[57] The peculiar socio-ideological complex that the institution of the family rests on makes it the most potent social form for blending patriarchy with class organisation and class rule.[58] To begin with, the family is a composite form created by the state and the church using biological-social groupings. This form corresponds, though not exactly, to the social organisation of the public and the private spheres from the early bourgeois period. Marxist feminists have

56   Corrigan and Sayer 1985.
57   Engels 1972.
58   see Davidoff and Hall 1987.

long noted this feature in seeing the bourgeois family form as a transformative junction between exchange value and use value.[59] But in a wider sense the family is a substantive social form which is the junction between social production and social/biological reproduction and must be materialised or practised through specific symbolic, semantic or signifying practices as well as through economic and political relations. This makes the family into both a public and a private institution.

At the heart of this family form there is a proprietorial morality marked by hierarchy and patriarchy, which reflect or sustain each other. Age and kinship previously contributory to a directly patriarchal arrangement yield place to a general social materialism as direct participation of the family in social production becomes at once more indirect, ramified and subtle. In this context the conduct, image and ownership of women (both in terms of labour and belief) become key issues, leading to a different but profound patriarchal agenda of power and politics at all levels. It expands out into socio-cultural movements, into ideological and political projects, such as that of nationalism, and into the organisation of national states as well as the organisation of colonial states and imperialist expansions.

If we keep in sight this indispensable and formative relationship between hegemony and patriarchy we can see why cultural nationalism of both the third world and of the Western powers possess a patriarchal core, and why that is undergirded by the paradigm of tradition versus modernity. Feminist support for modernity as a stance of critical reason/rationality, for an emancipatory modernist project, must distance itself carefully from both bourgeois and colonial/imperialist modernity. Feminists must realise that there are multiple modernities. Equally, post-colonial critics need to have a multiple and non-essentialist conception of tradition and the emancipatory social dynamics within third world societies. They need to resist falling for tradition as enunciated by cultural nationalists in their inverted colonial and fascistic interpretation of culture. All forms of modernity are not ruses for a colonial civilising mission and not all forms of feminism are inimical to projects of an actual decolonisation. There is, after all, a difference between women 'of' the nation and women living 'in' the nation. The feminist proposal that proclaims that women can only be fully subjects or entitled citizens if they are outside of a national space is not necessarily true. The nation can also be their nation under certain historical and political junctures. Otherwise women are removed

---

59   Canadian marxist feminists have commented on this phenomenon in the essays in Fox 1980.

from histories and politics of the very societies that they come from, where they also may have engaged in decolonising socially and economically emancipatory struggles. The moot issue here is the kind of nationalism that we are talking about – one that addresses structural and social inequalities along with cultural inequalities, or one in which a specific interpretation of culture subdues and subsumes all forms of social inequalities. There nationalism becomes a machinery for internal subjection.

I would like us to consider seriously the option of national liberation, which is simultaneously anti-capitalist, anti-feudal as well as anti-imperialist, as a feminist option. From this stance we should be able to think beyond the essentialised binary of tradition and modernity, of the West and the rest. We need to see that the values and practices that we have packaged into the singular term and form of modernity are actually plural and contradictory and that versions of modernities have existed the world over, a particular one of which has served as a ruse for colonialism and imperialism. Apart from all acts of physical and cultural genocide (exterminations and native residential schools, for example), slavery and ethno-racism, we need to recognise that this colonial modernity has never espoused anything vaguely resembling emancipation anywhere it went. What are significantly missing from it are: a) the concept of a rights-owning autonomous individual; b) notions of citizenship and democracy allowing the colonised population any political, economic and cultural control, participation or identity. Britain, for example, ruled itself democratically while ruling India autocratically. In John Stuart Mill's essay on representative government we see a stubborn denial of self-determination and self-government for the colonised.[60] This colonial modernity found its expression in Western societies in the concept of 'race', racist interpretations of civilisation and culture, and practices of everyday life.

With regard to women, the colonial state and its cultural discourse is not actually employed in modernising their world through real acts of social reform. As any student of colonial history can tell, indigenous women provide the colonial state with an occasion for characterising their societies in racial/ethnocentric terms as barbaric, savage or traditional while actively inventing traditions for them or crushing pre-existing dynamics of resistance.[61] An example is that of *satidaha*, in which, contrary to popular mythology, *sati* is first legalised by the colonial state in the teeth of local opposition and then criminalised by Britain. Such opportunistic colonial ventures for both civilising and tradi-

---

60   Mill 1972.
61   On this theme of invention of tradition, see Mani 1998, Ch. 1; see also Sinha 1995.

tionalising colonised or 'other' societies are deeply inscribed in mainstream anthropology and sociology.[62]

What is also forgotten in the dualist schema of colonisation versus nationalism is that the discourse of tradition is at the same time, in the first instance, a part of colonial discourse. It has served colonialism well in its own time, and imperialism now in its fight against socialism, communism and democratic secularism. Most of the forces of South Asia and the Middle East that now pose a great threat to the ordinary people of the region had been actively developed by or received support from the United States and its client states. Often military dictatorships have been put in place. They were consciously set up and continuously funded to fight the threat of communism, any and all projects of social and economic equality however muted or modified. In fact, they were also encouraged to destabilise liberal democracies. From the 1980s, as with Pakistan's Zia ul Haq, military dictatorships survived by supporting holy wars against Afghan socialists and communists largely in the service of the United States cold war. The creation of people such as Osama bin Laden and his al-Qaeda, bands of Saudi and other Middle Eastern mercenaries in the name of god and Islam, served American and world capitalist interests well until the fall of the Soviet Union, or even after. The violence of right-wing political use of Islam against women from then to now involves u.s. policies in the region. Equally noticeable is American support of the current Hindu fundamentalist government in India, which government and its political allies are not only tainted with massive economic but also moral corruption and violence. In the course of its coming to and maintaining power, this Hindu chauvinist combine has been responsible for situations causing the death of thousands of Muslims, rapes of Muslim and other non-Hindu women including Christian nuns, murders of Christian missionaries, and other violence in the name of god and good society.[63] Using the orientalist rhetoric of tradition claiming a Hindu essence for the nation and *hindutva*, an essentialist version of Hinduism, this political combine has put in place a project similar to that of the Nazis. This includes the use of the swastika and the claiming of an Aryan origin. Its current strongest allies are the u.s. and Israel, and its rhetoric against Indian Muslims after September 11 is the language of Islamic 'terror'. The ethnic/cultural nationalism of this group has also used women as a sacrifice to build the moral plinth of its Hindu national edifice. And who are its enemies? All secular, progressive, 'modernist' political forces, all socio-cultural and economically egalitarian

---

62   See, for example, Max Weber on Islam in Turner 1978.
63   On god and good society, i.e., political use of religion and religious fundamentalism, see Sarkar and Butalia 1995.

projects, and Muslims of any persuasion. All have been branded sexually and socially immoral, inauthentic in their Indian identity, and unpatriotic in their international solidarities.

The bottom line of cultural nationalism, then, is not the preservation of either tradition or modernity whatever their contested meanings, but rather the legitimation of an imperialism and capitalism admixture with cultural nationalism – by any means necessary. In this dialectic of power, all contradictions of thesis and antithesis coalesce into a synthesis of national and international domination. This synthesis of power is achieved in each case on the same ideological bases, through the same epistemological sleights of hand, namely through de-historicisation, essentialisation or homogenisation. Social complexities and contradictions anywhere in the East or the West are hidden, erased and occluded. The sociological or cultural paradigm of a Weberian/colonial version of tradition/modernity is an intellectual academic refinement whose vulgar version is in the crudities of Bush's war speeches or in the CNN – dominated Western media's ideological onslaughts. What is missing from the simplistic critique of most feminists is this very realisation. They have sacrificed their critical insights for a formulaic perception of third world women and decolonisation when they substitute social and a historical analysis with the above ideological paradigmatic interpretation. As stated before, their rejection of historical materialism converts actual historical and social relations and spaces into a state of mind – into essentialised civilisational or cultural discursivities. This kind of reading of non-Western societies is the source or device of not only the construction of jargons of lineages and origins, of traditional and authentic cultural identities, but also their correlate – the essential patriarchy of non-Westerners. Liberal or mainstream – and even radical – feminists and Bush's rescue mission share this interpretive ground in common.

It is only by adopting a feminist historical materialist perspective that we can see the inextricable and constitutive relationship between social organisation, relations and values of property and propriety, between capital, class and patriarchy in any society. From this critical standpoint it becomes clear that all civilisational or developmental missions and cultural constructions, including that of the nation, conducted from the platform of property and propriety, are what Walter Benjamin called 'documents of barbarism'. It is glaringly evident that property worshipping, socially hierarchical capitalist cultural nationalisms of the third world, for example, are simply the turned-coats of colonialisms or imperialisms. Embracing from this stance wholeheartedly and proclaiming with pride that we are Hindus or Muslims, modernists or civilisers, authentic carriers of our cultures, whether modern or traditional, does not take away from the underlying project of domination. Within the purview of this reversible imperialism and nationalism, women can never be more than signs of the patriarchal and hierarchical nation or of capitalism and imperialism. They can never be citizens, but only subjects of nations and their states anywhere.

3   Conclusion

Feminists then must be disloyal to both imperialist modernism and traditional national cultures, and place their politics on the ground of social justice. No essentialist dehistoricising rhetoric will do. If we are going to use the discourse of modernity, of freedom and democracy, at all, we need to disarticulate our modernism from colonialism, imperialism/globalisation, and capital. Essentialism is bad social science and bad politics no matter who does it or for what. And history, contrary to the proclamation of Francis Fukuyama, has not come to an end. So one has to be mindful of the fact that as there are many modes of domination, so there are many modernities and many traditions, and they are no more than cultural code names for historical and material social relations, of forms of consciousness and their practices.[64] This awareness is what Karl Marx signalled to by his anti-ideological epistemology, the purpose of which is to reveal the organisation of the social and its cultural/political forms.

If feminists are drawn in by the simplistic notions of either modernity or tradition, they miss history as lived time with all its contradictions, and consequently the politics which could make women citizens, not subjects, of nations. If they do not work on an even-handed critique of all forms of domination, they become the instruments of imperialism or ethnic/cultural nationalism of the West or the East. The mainstream Western feminists in the context of Afghanistan or of Palestine provide, perhaps in all good faith, the shock troops of imperialism, while women in the service of traditional/cultural nationalism not only betray themselves and all other women, but all possibilities of social justice and political agencies. Both groups prop up ideologies, cultural practices and nation states that destroy their own and others' lives and liberties.

It is never to be forgotten that women of both the first and third world have not achieved their full citizenships. They serve as signs and subjects of the nations in which they live. As things stand, they are mere appendages to nationalist and capitalist/imperialist agendas. If they are to be fully entitled social

---

64   Fukuyama 1992.

and political beings their struggles against proprieties of patriarchy must rest on struggles against all relations of property, relations that extend from ownership of women – their reproducing and labouring bodies – to all the social relations that form class, capital and imperialism.

CHAPTER 24

Patriarchy in the Era of Neoliberalism: The Case of India

For some time now India has been much in the news due to the large number of reported (gang) rapes and other violences against women.[1] Especially after the horrific incident of the gang rape of a young woman (alias Nirbhaya – Fearless) in a Delhi bus, which made its way into the world media,[2] the scrutiny has intensified. There is a debate between those who think that incidents of rapes of different kinds and other social violences against women have actually increased in India in the last decades, and others who say that the perception of this increase is dependent upon detailed and frequent reporting. The media is blamed for confusing the viewers/readers and using a seemingly anti-patriarchal stance to both stimulate and appease a growing appetite for witnessing sexual and other violence in order to increase their ratings. These appetites are claimed to be mainly sourced through digital media, cinema as well as television – both news and entertainment. There is no doubt that these mediated forms of violence have accorded a public spectacular status to violence as such, including that against women. Both of these positions contain elements of truth and are not mutually exclusive. While representations of violence have increased and the bar regarding what can be shown in the media has been considerably lowered, the fact remains that violence of all kinds has increased substantially.[3] This is the case locally and globally, as situations of imperialist aggressions and internecine militarised conflicts in many parts of the world and predations of neoliberalism have rendered lives and livelihoods of masses of people in India and elsewhere precarious. These wars, the utter dispossession, flights of refugees, the degeneration of the general social environment, are connected to capitalism in its present phase in one way or another. Such violence, even if reported more circumspectly, would produce a similar spectacularisation and acculturation to it. For the purpose of this paper, while we signal to the general fact of violence, we will focus on violence against

---

1   For Ratnabali Chattopadhyay, retired Professor, Calcutta University, Department of Islamic History.
2   Leslie Woodwin's documentary, *Daughter of India*, was much debated by feminists in India, for example by Vrinda Grover, for neglecting their protests and reading of the event.
3   For statistics on rape in India see http://en.m.widipedia.org/wiki/Rape_in_India.

women, in particular against poor or socially marginalised women, especially in India in the context of capitalist development.

Patriarchy, a social organisation of violence against women, of course far pre-dates capitalism – neoliberal or any other kind. This is true for India and elsewhere. But the intensity and the volume of depiction, debates, etc. indicate an urgency, a sort of crisis in the life situation of Indian women, including minor girls and small children, at the moment. This forms a part of the sense of social crisis experienced overall. Violence against women/girls has indeed taken both a quantitative as well as a qualitative leap. It is not only a matter of numbers, but of the modalities of their accomplishment. This change involves the shift from a person to person rape to that of gang rape, and thus rapes morphing into public, collective, spectacular acts. Continuing and intensifying old caste practices of assertion of social (Hindu male) power, Dalit, tribal and low caste women have been increasingly victimised. Women of minority communities, Muslim and Christian, are primary and integral parts of this spectrum of victimhood. It is important to note that, generally, gang rapes are found in situations of civil wars and military invasions, but in India they have become 'peace time' phenomena.[4]

It makes sense to use the year 2002 as a key moment in the public deployment of violence against women and non-Hindu populations. The pogrom against Muslims in Gujarat that year provides an iconic marker for the display of an extreme masculinist sexual-social behaviour enjoying the religious identity of 'hindutva'.[5] The perpetrators of various kinds of violence were vastly emboldened by their 'success' during and after the Ramjanmabhumi agitation and the destruction of the Babri masjid in Ayodhya, and the 2002 pogrom as a sort of culmination. Declaring Muslims, Christians and 'other(ed)' socio-

---

4   The history of sexual violence against women can be traced to communal riots and pogroms in pre- and post-independence India. The protracted civil war in Sri Lanka offers numerous and serious examples, as does the liberation war of Bangladesh. In the case of India militarised zones have provided instances through the immunity granted by the Armed Forces (Special Powers) Act. As an instrument of social war, women of dalit and oppressed groups have been violated and humiliated to keep the entire social group in its oppressed and humiliated niche. Regarding war and militarisation and violence against women see Enloe 2014 and 2004. In the Indian context, see also Uma Chakravarty's writings on violence against women.

5   *Hindutva* (hinduness) is an essentialised version of a heterodox diverse set of ideas, gods and practices of Hindus. It is rather a mythic civilisational construct – it has elite intellectual adherents as well as adherents among 'the people'. This task of creating the Hindu subject of the nation is not a matter of ideas and proselytization alone, but of mass reconversion ceremonies which suck back those who once in history sought to escape the violence of the Hindu caste system. See Bannerji 2011, ch. 1.

religious groups as lesser inhabitants and citizens of India, as those who are inherently inferior to high and middle caste Hindus, the Hindu right acted out their hate-filled legacies dating back to the early twentieth century. The Sangh Parivar, rooted in the RSS (founded in 1925), was not alone in this victorious display of masculinity, nor was this a retreat into feudalism or 'medieval' barbarism. The pogrom of 2002 was a modern enterprise for the facilitation of 'development' that went hand in hand with the misogyny of invented 'hindutva' tradition which provided the ideological unifier of Indian neoliberalism. The combination of political/ideological Hinduism and capitalist economic violence powered the BJP's triumphant march to Delhi. The existing violence against women in different states of India spread forth and intensified as the years unrolled.

We know that capitalism and patriarchy have always gone hand in hand. We should note that just as capitalism is not a self-contained social formation, patriarchy also cannot function alone in its isolated social precinct. The constellation of socio-sexual relations coded as patriarchy is an aspect of social organisation as a whole which interweaves ways of social being, moral regulations and division of labour. Social existence of, and as, men and women is not self-enclosed and self-reproducing. Power relations of the entire social organisation imbue gender relations in production and reproduction involving both property and propriety. Thus patriarchy is modified and mutated by significant changes in the mode of production. As essential components of that overall mode patriarchal relations and moral imperatives provide the mode with its concrete form. As such in the capitalist mode of production patriarchy as a pre-existing constitutive and conjunctural social element develops and continues in the new social formation. It is inextricable from economic and cultural relations and ideas. This is to be expected, as every new social organisation relies on historical practices, on prevailing values and cultural identities. In Indian civil society, as in any other, the ideological apparatus of the state and economic structures develop dynamically in mutually formative relations. They express visions and political projects of the ruling classes and the ruling parties, as well as competing visions of resistance. These contradictory and conflicting imperatives are not abstractions but are modes of mediation which affect forms of ruling, modifying the state apparatus. These modalities shape the intellectual-moral or cultural life of a society, including the economic. They are deeply experiential realities impinging on subjectivities and agencies of all. At the present phase of capitalism, when neoliberalism can call to aid essentialist religious ideologies and organises the repression of a secularised national state, a dense web of violence seeks to take over the social space not only of India alone, but also of West Asia and elsewhere. Economic and social violence enable each other, and patriarchy provides a staple for global accumulation. Violence is endowed with both a general character as such, but also a specific one as particularly employed.

Thus there is an 'elective affinity' between capitalism and patriarchy. Patriarchy is a violent social form, as is its habitus of actually existing capitalism. The first violence of capital lies in its very inception. As described by Marx, it initiated primitive accumulation, and turned European societies upside-down and achieved its history through 'blood and fire'. This primitive accumulation still, and necessarily, continues. The neoliberal phase provides the richest fertilisation for elaborate and multi-level forms of primitive accumulation for 'growth' (for a few) and dispossession (for most). Mutations of patriarchal practices and ideologies consisting of typologies of masculinity and femininity are redirected towards labour, ethno-nationalistic politics and ideologies such as those of the BJP and the sangh parivar. Women in general in their bodies and labour power become objects of possession and consumption simultaneously, as well as objects of *hindutva* based moral regulation. The situation of dominance intensifies for minoritised and poor women. But this intensification was gradual until it reached the current phase. Developing capitalism with its virulent commodity fetishism has increased the fetishism of women's bodies as objects of consumption to the point of sexual cannibalisation, speaking not just metaphorically. Deepening alienation with its frightening disregard for human well-being provides both a continuity and new turn to patriarchy, amplifying the old patriarchal distinction between 'a woman' and 'human'. Tendentious use of state institutions and governance with the elimination of the state's welfare responsibilities ushers in patriarchal neoliberalism verging on fascism, de-basing through ideological and practical means the daily life of people. A toxic social environment generated through the mix of extreme poverty, profound dispossession and ethics of acquisition and consumption are enabling factors of all violence, including violence against women. An ideologically manipulated naturalisation of social and economic violence implemented with draconian state directives – a feature of fascism – is clearly present in the ruling project of the BJP, that is, the neoliberal Hindu right.

The reports excerpted below illustrate the insane brutality of rapes that are happening and endow them with a ritual and, as gang rapes, a public spectacular character. In Kambuni, West Bengal eight men raped a woman behind the wall of a factory site.

> The girl was dragged inside as she came in the front gate, she was taken
> inside [a] room and the rapists pressed their hands against her mouth so
> that she could not scream. The rapists brutally raped her ... [They] said

they had murdered the girl because she would have identified them and have handed them over to the police. So they killed her and exposed her naked body, mercilessly tore her legs apart up to her navel and threw her body in the dump of hay.[6]

Unidentified men raped and brutalised a 28 year old, mentally challenged woman before killing her at Bahu Akbarpur in Haryana's Rohtak district on Sunday last. The woman's body was found without three organs on Wednesday along with sticks and stones and condoms stuck into her private parts, three days after she went missing. According to the coroner two stones were inserted into the slain woman's anus. 'Her face was eaten by animals, her lungs and heart were found missing. Also, her skull had fractured and there were injury marks on both her thighs and chest'.[7]

The Hindu reported on the court verdict in a case involving the abduction and sexual exploitation of a minor girl of Suryanelli in Iduki district of Kerala by several persons in 1996. 'The schoolgirl was enticed, abducted and sexually exploited by a bus conductor ... Then she was handed over to two others. The girl was taken to several places and ... was raped 67 times by 37 different people during 40 days from 16 January 1996 to 26 February 1996'. The High Court has acquitted most of these people.[8]

Murders and mutilations often accompany these assaults, which sometimes, as above, take on a ritualistic character. It is truly amazing that the perpetrators are often known by others and abscond in plain sight with the collaboration of their relatives and acquaintances. Neither the police nor the victim's acquaintances bring them to justice, and the police are negligent both in taking the First Information Report (FIR) and in enforcing existing assault or rape laws. This violence against women is carried out by men of all classes, contrary to the assumption that they are chiefly crimes of the underclasses. But significantly, men supportive of the *hindutva* agenda or other right-wing extremism feel empowered to act in this fashion. Patriarchal moral high ground rooted in casteist Hinduism is advanced to punish women, sometimes through the very communities they belong to. Examples are supplied by the caste (*khap*) panchayat crucial role in organising communal sexual violence against 'erring'

---

6 http://en.wikipedia.org/wiki/2013_Kamduni_gang_rape_murder_case.
7 *Times of India*, 20 February 2015.
8 *The Hindu*, 14 October 2015.

women. The irony lies in the fact that this violence is practised by men who often preach both nationally and internationally the goddess-like stature of women in Indian (read 'Hindu') culture.

1   Methodology

I am searching for a method that will help to expose the connections between violence against women and capitalism in general. I know that I may be asked to 'prove' a causal or direct relation between these social relations and ideologies, and failing that, to continue using them as two distinct social systems which may at best be aggregated if needed. But what constitutes 'proof' in any social inquiry cannot be based on an objectivist positivist stance. The realm of the social, which is complex, dialectical and constantly dynamic, cannot be explored with an epistemology that is meant for another purpose, for example, the realm of nature or the properties of inert matter, in all of which conscious social relations and ideas are not involved and historically rooted. The constitution and working processes of the 'social', our 'object' of exploration, does not lend itself to positivism. This 'reality' is both palpable and subtle, dynamic though liable to reification, experiential and ideological, hegemonic and resisted. It is (hu)man made. The method of inquiry here must suit the historical and material/social nature of the phenomenon under investigation. Our social is the habitus of existing conscious subjects and agents. Using a positivist and a strictly causal method of inquiry will distort or even destroy the very 'social' nature of the reality we want to understand.[9] To say this is not to forfeit the truth claim of knowledge and submit to postmodernist indeterminacy.[10] The 'truth' here is not one of 'fact' but of an associative assertion which fully utilises Marx's method of historical materialism. This method underlies the social analysis and organisational recommendation of the *Communist Manifesto*. It is

---

9   This issue of the relationship between the structural and practical aspects of a mode of production and forms of consciousness found therein has given rise to unending and inconclusive debates. The conjectures and refutations regarding 'base and superstructure', corresponding relations between economy and culture, reflectionist relations between representation and reality, testify to this. Mediations and determinations of different constitutive moments of the social are so shadowy, so finely modulated, and in spite and because of their contradictions and multiplicities can only be directly 'proved' in a limited way. This is where social history, study of social and individual psychology or historical sociology can provide a helping hand.

10   Smith 1999. See in particular the essays in the sections 'Theory', 'The ruling relations' and 'Telling the truth after postmodernism'.

not an idle preoccupation of philosophers, but rather an epistemological basis of social analysis for revolutionary social transformation.

In view of the fact that the cultural moment with all its political force is so aggressively present in the Indian right wing governing agenda, the issue of ideology becomes very crucial. To demystify the ideological ensemble of hindutva politics which masks as well as expresses its fascist agenda, Marx's own critique of ideology is central. It helps to reveal that the present religious identitarian nationalism both deflects attention from and legitimises neoliberalism's complicity with imperialism. This is the core content of the BJP's 'development' agenda, which arrogates unto itself the definition of 'nation' and true patriotism while aggressively conducting mass immiseration. The phenomenon of increased violence against women provides a 'concrete' aspect of the social reality of capitalism in India. This concreteness demands attention to the convergence of many social and cultural determinations which involve history and diverse forms of consciousness.[11] In *The German Ideology* Marx presents us with a whole range of forms of consciousness, named as practical, 'scientific' (i.e. historical materialist) and ideological. A close reading of his critique shows the part and the whole, the ideational and the sociological, in their concrete formative conjuncture in real time and space. We could then speak adequately about 'capitalist patriarchy' and accumulation as well as other social and ideological relations which concretise capitalism, such as those of 'race' and caste.

Marx assigns the rise of ideology at the point of the highest and increasingly systematised bifurcation of manual and mental labour, at the moment when mental production with its own reproductive technology takes on an appearance of independence from all other forms of life and labour. This division of labour arises from and within an already developed sexual and social division, reaching its full articulation and sustenance in the maturation of European capitalism. The process ramifies and reifies in a corresponding social spatialisation of the public and the private and is, crucially, empowered by the commodity form. All this has a huge impact on social life and manifests in changes in the family form or labour. Male-female relations, child-raising, property relations, religious and moral injunctions, or propriety and what parts men and women play in the economy are all reshaped. The family in bourgeois social organisation is now excluded from spaces of labour. Production and reproduction

---

11   Marx 1973. Regarding a 'scientifically correct method', Marx draws on the notion of the concreteness of social reality: 'The concrete is concrete because it is the concentration of many determinations, hence unity of the diverse' (1973, p. 101).

are cut asunder. Daily life, commonsense, sense of normalities and moralities all affect what people do or think on an everyday basis. Thus we come to understand what Marx meant when he said that 'ruling ideas' of any age are the ideas of the ruling classes. The very processes and politics of accumulation generate 'ruling relations' and ideas, including ideas of patriarchy and other hegemonic imperatives. They are a form of production and a body of content, both of which are situated in historical evolving and social organisation.

Why then can we not speak of patriarchy and capitalism together without having to 'prove' their generative connection? Why can we not end the segregation between the cultural/social and class/economic moments of reality? It is evident that worldviews, common sense, conventions of normalcy turn out in this scrutiny to be the ideational expression of social relations of power, including of patriarchy in both practical as well as discursive terms. A whole host of other ideas and practices of perceiving and constructing difference are inherited, generated and disseminated in and through a concrete mode of production. Thus class, 'race', gender, caste and other concepts of difference cannot be segregatively formulated.

Are all ideas ideological in nature? Marx would say that some ideas are ideological while others are not,[12] but all come to life in the course of development of any mode of production involving specific political and cultural aspects. Social and physical similarities and differences are thus understood practically, directly, while others are particularly interpreted and constructed. Marx speaks of both non-ideological and anti-ideological knowledge production when he speaks to 'practical' and 'scientific' consciousness. Types of ideas which Marx calls 'ruling ideas' or ideology enjoy the highest currency and the hegemonic status of 'truth' and normalcy backed by capitalist institutions of knowledge production. This generates and stores a definite body of ideological content – stereotypes, norms and moral regulations seep through the structures of governance. Most studies in socio-cultural fields regarding 'race', patriarchy, gender, caste or communalism criticise these stereotypes or the body of ideological content. The most ideological aspect of ideology, however, is not this body of content, but rather its claim that ideas precede existence and that experience and truth are disconnected or incompatible with each other. But this formal or epistemological aspect of ideology is mostly neglected. The

---

12   Other uses of the notion of ideology are detailed by Raymond Williams in his *Marxism and Literature*. The uses range from a system of organisation of ideas, 'separated' theory, political ideas/beliefs to the use I make of it following *The German Ideology* and the sociological method of Dorothy E. Smith. Ideology thus understood is not a neutral interpretive knowledge device.

particular epistemology employed in the production of ideology, that is, its conceptual grammar or productive technology, must be exposed and discarded if anti-social ideas are to be challenged. In *The German Ideology* Marx explores three 'tricks' of producing ideology, or the method of degrounding knowledge or producing groundless concepts. These are empty abstractions, universals and particulars which are isolated from social organisation; they are reificatory empiricisms (as distinct from the empirical).[13]

Critique of ideology extends from a catalogue and criticism of 'ruling' or 'bad' ideas to exposing how they are actually produced, even from perfectly innocuous or even theoretical expressions. Notions such as 'class' or 'economy' can be over-generalised and over-particularised, becoming a homogenising or isolating category. 'Culturalism' and 'economism' thus share the same ideological epistemology – suppressing the social, with its complex formative relations. Ideological deployment, for example, of the idea of the nation, can exclude, occlude or erase actual subjects, historical-social relations, experiences and ideas. Ideology can equally make a gesture of false inclusivity by introducing discursivities which arise in other and ideological contexts. Ideological stances can also create hierarchies among the different social moments and thus create a second level theoretical knowledge which makes reality its own affirmation. In this way concrete (material and historical) social relations lived/experienced directly by social subjects are decontextualised, substituted and displaced.[14] This serves to create a false sense of oneness which hides the realities of power and exploitation. The more complex and fracturing the social relations of capitalism become, as now in the neoliberal and financialised phase, the more important becomes the necessity for ideology. The inherent violence of cap-

---

13   Marx and Engels 1970. In the section on 'Ruling Class and Ruling Ideas' Marx exposes how 'ideology' in his sense is produced epistemologically. He connects this to the Hegelian 'trick' of proving the hegemony of the spirit: 'No. 1. One must separate the ideas of those ruling for empirical reasons, under empirical conditions and as empirical individuals, from these actual rulers, and thus recognise the rule of ideas or illusions in history. No. 2. One must bring order into this rule of ideas ... which is managed by understanding them as "acts of self-determination on the part of the concepts" ... No. 3. To remove the mystical appearance of this 'self-determining concept' it is changed into a person ...', that is, one must connect them with other unrelated discourses or personalise them (p. 67).

14   See Bannerji 2015a. In this way 'women' become subjects of patriarchy, or even essentialised into 'woman', an empty ideological category to be filled in by those who can express their own social interests through it. Liberal feminism is marked by this usage which excludes other formative social relations, for example class or racialisation, from the purview of this homogenisation. The same can be said of the decontextualised, unspecified use of 'man', 'race', 'development' and so on. Any category that leads us away from history and social organisation would fit the bill. See Bannerji 1991.

italism and class, patriarchy, fundamentalist religion and social hierarchies of caste or 'race' are not only occluded or normalised, but also offer a promise of power to those who 'belong', that is, are ideologically interpellated.[15] This can only be effectively challenged by people being awakened from their ideological submergence. This would apply particularly well to the notion of a nation artic-ulated upon mono-ethnicity and essentialised identity – all of which implies violence. 'Violence' then serves as the entry point to all systems of power and exploitation and allows us to explore the constitution of social and political ethos as well as the organisation of an overall mode of production.

Marx's critique of ideology helps us to see that patriarchy is not a self-sustaining form, nor is capitalism an abstract one-dimensional phenomenon. As it is actually practiced, concretised and realised, it is not solely an asocial matter of economic construction. A mode of production is simultaneously a mode of reproduction, and the whole mode has to be reproduced constantly at the level of multiple social relations and forms of consciousness which are inseparably implicated – this is the existential condition of social being. Violence inherent in this reality is the life-blood of all societies of property relations of social inequality. The claim that patriarchy morphs with changes in the mode of production and enables this very change includes violence against women. These changes are constellations rather than discrete items. They occur simultaneously and are not subject to 'proof' in a positivist sense.[16]

---

15   Ideological construction or deployment of concepts/categories deflects critiques and enhances social relations of power. Ideology admits of no epistemological disclosure of its constitution; as such, all categorical usages, concepts and expressions must be re-contexted in social relations and history. This should challenge their arbitrary and reifying function. When juxtaposed against detailed social description the hegemonic power of ideology dissolves.

16   In spite of changes in law pertaining to this matter, we find strong adaptations of it both by the market in objectifying women and by politics of identity through myths of religion and tradition. Complete exposures of the female body marketed currently in the name of modernity and the total covering up of it by islamic fundamentalist injunctions are the flip sides of the same violence. We can see broad patterns if we take a longer, wider view of social in which the immediate present is situated. This trajectory is not linear, but rather a dynamic and dialectical unfolding which can be both understood and described. This method of realism does not rest on the paradigm of base and superstructure, but on that of creative expressionism. Thus the violence of property is also the violence of patriarchal propriety, in and through which social and sexual division of labour come into being and sustain the whole complex.

2   An Anti-ideological Understanding of Violence against Women

The newspapers and social media create a storm in our mind with daily reporting of rapes of adult women, girl children, female infants and also boys. We
hear of gang rapes, rapes in police custody, and rapes by the Indian army or
the paramilitary. They range from urban centres to villages, forests and hills.
They are rapes of dalits, peasants, tribals, poor and middle-class women or the
destitute – the list goes on and on. Everyday sexual harassment is frequently
perpetrated by men, including by those in the top levels of state bureaucracy,
corporations and other businesses, and by academics and others in positions
of responsibility. In some cases, the rapes are enjoined by the caste (*khap*) pan-
chayats, and also mark religious rituals and pilgrimages. These rapes are added
on to established violent and coercive practices of dowry, including dowry
murders, casting out, female foeticide and infanticide, and some instances of
satidaha. Then there are extreme violences against women of Muslim or Christian communities in individual instances and in concerted riots and pogroms.
We should also mention socially sanctioned marital rapes, whose sanitised
expression is 'domestic violence', ever present in family lives of Indian and all
patriarchal societies. The list of grotesque and destructive activities targeting
women is ever expanding, as are the innovative ways of being violent. The very
'sex' of these activities lies in the perpetration of the violence itself.

According to the anti-ideological method outlined above, we need to situate these events through a dense description of not only the events and the
particular situations and the people involved, but extend the focus to all of
what surrounds them to the extent that we can. It is a representative realism
that calls for capturing the simultaneity of socio-economic, cultural and political phenomena. We also need to historicise them. The result is a collage or
mosaic created with our seemingly diverse findings which brings in the past
as well as the present. Any social event including of violence against women is
situated in an axis of time and space. In the immensely long persistence of patriarchy we note the symbiosis between production and reproduction; in societies of private property violence works as the prime social mover. To explore
this symbiotic violence of capitalist patriarchy we can begin with primitive
accumulation – not as an 'event' in history but a continuing process. Primitive accumulation involves covert and overt violations of life resources, as of
land, lives and bodies of all the underclasses, especially of women belonging
to them. This onslaught was and continues to be positively sanctioned by the
church and the state under various guises. Social power combined with class
power gives rise to nearly hegemonic (or totalising) systems of ideas/ideologies
which define a proper family, male and female relations and morality, 'nor-

mal' sexuality, 'good' or 'bad' women, control of women's access to economic resources and religious institutions, and so on. The feudal or even earlier ideological tryptic of the virgin, the mother and the whore remains constant in capitalism with further mutations. While the above references are to the history of Christian Europe, India, as scholars have noted, had/has a very similar ethos, and not only due to the intrusion of colonial rule. In India matters are more complex, as capitalist colonialism particularly conditioned the type of primitive accumulation caused here. Also pre-existing or continuing patriarchy or even misogyny marks all practiced religions. Even religions which are otherwise antagonistic to each other subscribe to the same or similar norms regarding women, enunciating them from a hierarchical space. They also continue to be internally contradictory, according to women a divine/pure or a demonic character, whose secular versions are present everywhere from the media to the market. The violence of this lies in the fact that, the contradiction of these stereotypes notwithstanding, women are differentiated from 'human' and posed as the 'other' of 'man'. Though this 'difference' is not invented by capitalism or always expressed in such extremes, it is reworked, women being rewarded or punished accordingly. This is sometimes done through its legal apparatus of the bourgeois nation state and sometimes through the social 'common sense' that accrues in and organises everyday life.[17] In most countries the family as a legal institution is conceived possessively and the social space is under masculinist authority. It is never trite to remember that the sexuality, sociality, and bodies of women or of children (whether in marriage or not) have provided the ideological apparatus of the state with moral and administrative regulation. The patriarchal family is a major institution in legal and social administration, and the economy is fundamentally organised in and through gender organisation of labour and private and public spaces. With the waning of feudalism and the rise of capitalism societies changed, but gendered power relations prevailed and expanded beyond familial paternalism. As it elaborates it becomes materialised in and through degradation of women's labour and the tyranny of the market. There is/was no contradiction between capitalism and secular or religious authoritarianism, and patriarchy has a place in them all.

Many dehumanising practices, such as those of patriarchy, 'race' or caste and their legitimations, proliferated and are enshrined within the economy, the state, religion and social conventions. This normalisation of violence in protean forms of capitalism threatening life itself is brutally evident in various critiques

---

17   For 'common sense' as a basic element of politics of hegemonic and counter-hegemonic nature, see Gramsci 1971. See especially 'State and Civil Society', and the section on the southern question in 'Notes on Italian History'.

of 'so-called primitive accumulation'.[18] Primitive accumulation affects men and women, though differentially, and combines with the violence of commodity fetishism and alienation. Women's bodies are reified in and for the market and made into objects of consumption. The present-day onslaught of global neo-liberalism has vast constitutive power on lives of people.

While talking about violence against women we need to note that primitive accumulation is both prior and coterminous, external and internal to capitalist development. It infiltrates as well as directly invades and destroys lives, labours and societies which were pre-capitalist, and it cannot be relegated to a stage in history. The eviction and dispossession that happened in the earlier phases of capitalism also exist within the developing economic system with the help of the evolving and expanding state. Civil society too takes its part and moulds lives in sync with the state and the economy. This apparently socio-legal, yet brute and armed force, while not always directly within the circuit of capital, undergirds the whole mode of production. Thus 'primitive accumulation' should be seen both as the enabling factor of capital's birth and its constant mode of renewal. The 'annals of blood and fire' continue in the present. Wars, invasions, colonisation, slavery and bonded labour are all present, but are continually being rewritten to suit capital's changing needs. No sustained distinction can be maintained, therefore, between primitive accumulation of growth and dispossession, as some have done.[19] Territorial space is still vital for capital, thus land is a crucial element, but along with that, labour, capacities of human minds and bodies, natural and industrial resources, etc., are constantly annexed and re-colonised through implementing different social and productive organisations. The ideological use of the notion of 'development' as under-

---

18   The first exposure of this violence is provided by Marx's analysis and description of the birth and workings of capital. See Marx, *Capital*, Vol. I, Part VIII: 'In times long gone by there were two sorts of people; one, the diligent, intelligent and, above all, a frugal elite; the other, lazy rascals, spending their substance, and more, in riotous living ... Thus it came to pass that the former sort accumulated wealth and the latter sort had at last nothing to sell but their own skins. And from this original sin dates the poverty of the great majority that, despite all its labour, has up to now nothing to sell but itself, and the wealth of the few that increases constantly although they have long ceased to work. Such insipid childishness is everyday preached to us in the defence of property' (p. 667).

19   See Harvey 2005, for instance, the originator of the notion of 'accumulation by dispossession', taking his cue from Rosa Luxembourg. There have been debates on the difference between those who espouse primitive accumulation as understood (supposedly) by Marx, and Harvey's position. Dunn (2007) gives a rundown on these discussions/debates. Whitehead (2010) tries to mediate between these positions, and in my opinion succeeds, as she demonstrates through her study of eviction and resettlement of people victimised by the Narmada dam project in India.

taken from capital's standpoint covers this truth and obfuscates the violence of the accumulation project. Capital's expansion depends on the annexation of spaces and speeding up of time, but all of that would be useless without constantly subjecting human beings and converting them into mere labouring and reproductive bodies. Lives or aspects of lives hitherto outside capitalism steadily come into its grip and are constantly re-worked. Newer forms of capitalist spaces and time schemes re-settle the earlier ones, and thus re-invent spaces of capital along with obliterating people standing in its path. Capitalist growth and human dispossession are twins. Capital's intrusion and constant reworking of the same grounds can be metaphorically captured by the tropes of 'rape' or 'gang rape', where the same body of land, nature and people are repeatedly violated to the point of extinction. Capital's grab for natural resources, markets, human labour and bodies are composites of a total violence which has engrossed the world in the last some centuries and been experienced as such by its victims. Furthermore, this violence increasingly nourishes the symbiotic relations of the state, the civil society and the economy in their porousness and circulatory constitution. Spaces for expansion and reproduction of capital and entire populations are conquered and re-invented within a time frame of hyper-rationalised labour. The world resonates with this taking over, breaking down and re-construction of productive resources, spaces and mentalities that facilitate them.[20] I will return to this frenetic use of time and the resulting human experiences later.

We must, therefore, see both the continuity and the change in capital's development with violence as a constant factor. The territorial expropriation and devastation presently growing in India and elsewhere means also the eviction and life destruction of the inhabitants and the extreme exploitation and repression imposed on them. Not only cheap labour but sexual and biological bodies of India's or the world's majority who cannot find a space in the labour market are thrust through capital's workings and turnovers into homelessness and dangerous flights. This results in various kinds of 'slavery', including what one could call bio-slavery.[21] The quintessential violence of this phenomenon is both obvious and subtle and present locally and globally. It is not a surprise, there-

---

20   See 'creative destruction', a term coined by Joseph Schumpeter and later used with reference to neoliberalism by Harvey, Marshall Berman and others.

21   I use this term to express the near absolute dispossession and bondage of this evicted, 'surplus' labour, whose very bodies and body parts become commodities, rather than their embodied labour. 'Harvesting' organs to patenting genes, to the renting of wombs and producing of babies as commodities, are all part of this process. The notion of 'slavery' here is iconic in the sense in which the Nazi holocaust is the central representation for measuring extermination of 'others'. See also Sylvia Federici, *Caliban and the Witch*. Here

fore, that the violence of patriarchy, in conjunction with the penetration of the market, land grab, degradation of human life and commodity fetishism in every aspect of life, has been erupting so powerfully in India in its convulsions to birth neoliberal capitalism from an erstwhile colonial capitalism.

According to an Indian proverb, land and women are spoils of heroes. A crucial mode of entry into the Indian form of patriarchal neoliberalism is through the struggles waged over land and common natural resources, but not so much of struggles to find labour. Villages, water, forests and other resources which are basic life requirements are sought to be privatised, of which one method is encroachment and the other through amendments to the 2013 Land Acquisition Act now sought to be pushed through by the BJP government, while relying at present on the promulgation of ordinances.[22] Though a 'development' agenda has existed in India under the earlier phases of the Congress government and state sponsored industrial capitalism, there has been a redirection in the last few years from a modicum of concern for the rendered poor, especially in the countryside, to the present, when such people are not seen as deserving of life protection in any way. Even the middle classes are seriously under pressure. The Land Acquisition Act (2013), which was just passed prior to the BJP accession to state power under pressure from the left and progressive political sections, had tried to stem, if limitedly, the primitive accumulation through the devastation of agriculture, forest lands, rivers and water systems, and of the environment in general. It had clauses pertaining to impact assessment of land acquisition on the population, on their livelihood and the environment, compensation and rehabilitation for the evicted and the displaced. Though it has had no time to be actualised, this Act had offered a formal and minimal recognition of popular possession through prior occupation of land or use of resources. The ordinances brought in by the BJP government are bent on destroying that limited claim. This violence is done to 'open up' India for 'free trade', with no barriers for foreign as well as national corporate investments, freeing the investors to 'develop' at will with little or no liabilities or obligation for compensation. Privatising state based enterprises has virtually gouged out large holes in the economy. Instead the Indian government is offering to pay minimally for the harms inflicted by these measures from the public exchequer. Though slowed down somewhat by the regional and general socio-political complexities and resistances put up by a parliamentary system, as well as the resistance of the left parties, unions and popular social movements, primitive

---

she provides a history of capitalism in terms of extreme violence against women, robbing them not only of control over the economy but of their very bodies and life.

22   See Rajlakshmi 2015; also Dasi 2015.

accumulation of the neoliberal era in India is fast accelerating. In this attempt at invention of new spaces for 'growth', not only are the 'undeveloped' (forest, mountain terrain and other mineral rich) areas being annexed, but previously developed agricultural holdings of middle to better off farmers are also constantly preyed upon and their assets devalued and land used as real estate. The perils of loans taken to sustain competition with larger and foreign capital as well as great neglect of agriculture can be measured in the thousands of suicides in recent years by indebted farmers.

The ideological discourse of 'development' (*vikas*) with its feel good quality was the BJP's winning slogan for coming to power.[23] Narendra Modi's enormously funded election campaign was fought on this platform of promise of development for all expressed in slogans of *acche din sabkeliye* (good days for everyone), and *sabkesath, sabke pas* (with everyone, near everyone), spinning a rhetorical web of inclusivity. The newly independent Indian state's aspiration to take on the guardianship of the poor, at least to some extent, in their food security, livelihood, health and education, as well as to strengthen the national industrial bourgeoisie, declined, and is now being mowed down by a storm of structural adjustment imperatives resting on privatisation and foreign direct investment. The significant tense shift in Modi's governmental rhetoric to 'make in India' (becoming the outsourcing and investment site for foreign capital) from the earlier governments' 'made in India' (import substitution) marks the distance traversed by the Indian state between the much earlier and the current stages of capitalist development.[24] Vast numbers of people live in great poverty and die from malnutrition related illnesses. The country is constantly

---

23   On Modi's development agenda see Varghese George, 'A leader and his narrative' in *The Hindu*, Magazine Section. 'Modi's doctrine in civilizational terms has proposed a new social contract in which the minorities and Dalits have limited or no place in political power. In Parliament, State Assemblies and councils of ministers at the centre and states, the muslims' representation has become negligible; for the first time in India there is not a single Muslim MP in the leading party of the ruling coalition. This way the proposed social contract suggests development not as a participatory process' (p. 1).

24   In India, as elsewhere, 'development' through industrial enterprises by the state in tandem with private national capital is rapidly declining, but 'development' for profit is taking place in the countryside by predatory private capital in mining, lumber and agribusiness. This phenomenon has been discussed by social scientists and journalists from India and elsewhere, but not to much effect. Public sector enterprises are predominantly disaggregated and privatised now, and sold off as time passes. In the new scheme of affairs, the city eats up the countryside, which rapidly converts into real estate or becomes wasteland. Building construction for housing (for the rich/middle class), land deals of all kinds, corporate office towers, and sites of low cost production and call centres figure prominently

traversed by fleeing voluntary or involuntary internal migrants. They are people rejected by the volatile local labour market and denied a viable subsistence on agriculture or any other kind of minimally sustaining work. Many are living and dying on city sidewalks. Neoliberalism has forced the growth of 'cities of slums' and trafficking of women, children and men for domestic or other lowest paid, unaccounted for labour, including sexual.

Everything I have touched upon so far is a matter of inflicting a systemic violence upon people. As I remark above and feminist scholars have shown, capitalism's organisational necessity of patriarchy – both in production and reproduction – is also foundational. Cultural stereotypes leading to high profit margins are ever present in all phases of capitalism. The social relations and values of the state and civil society work together to subjugate women, who are marginalised and thus deprived of property, civic and political participation. In this era of super-mobile and hyper-technology primitive accumulation is now not only securing cheap but almost unpaid labour. Nationally/locally or internationally active smugglers' organisations are not only supplying bodies for underground labour but also for marketing fertility and 'harvesting' organs. In this sense the type of 'primitive accumulation' as found in *Capital* (Volume I) needs a stretch, because capital is no longer in crucial need of an older style of mass proletariat for creating industrial enterprises of scale or for populating or 'settling' the colonies. But of course the very cheapest labour is still needed and found in the formerly colonised countries. In the global south as well as in the north a precarious, semi-bonded form of labour is found in the special economic zones of Mexico, Bangladesh, Sri Lanka and the Philippines and in piece-work factories in and around California. The earlier eviction in seventeenth- to twentieth-century Britain, for example, led to the creation of a substantial working class for giant industries which were concentrated in specific locations. The colonial mercantile conduits and the army relocated Europeans at the cost of indigenous peoples of the Americas and elsewhere. The neoliberal form of commodity producing capital, thanks to hyper-technology, may not need such a huge, spatially concentrated and long term labour force. Through the manipulation of various combinations of trade laws and technology the poorest and migrant labour, many of them women, can be inserted in the labour process in different countries at will. People survive under strict conditions of others' mercy.[25]

---

on this list, as also do shopping malls, recreational and leisure facilities (resorts, spas, golf courses). The penetrations of agriculture by biotech, chemical and pharmaceutical companies have been attested by great destructive chaos.

25   See Sassen 2010.

For many in India, Africa and elsewhere, to be alive is a privilege. What has been called 'precarious' life or 'bare' life is their permanent mode of chance existence.[26]

Under these circumstances what was called 'formal', i.e. normal, labour with a degree of predictability in duration, physical concentration and living wages has been replaced by the new normalcy of what was once called 'informal', i.e. occasional, casual or flexible labour. This new normalcy involving intense violation and rapacity has resulted in a growing decline in the older forms of trade unions or labour organising, and in terms of their strategies of creation of class consciousness and class struggle they have lost their edge. As women are entering abysmal conditions of export production the older ideas and practices of labour organisations have seriously declined. Now there is a need for innovation and expansion of labour organisations. This is happening very slowly due to the now internationally normalised precarious and temporary practices of labour. For a substantial majority of Indians, both women and men, their living bodies and labour are *de facto* redundant; their life spaces and sustenance are out of their reach.[27] In India the privatisation mandate has forced an orgy of de-institutionalising of the state in its social welfare and democracy promoting functions. Has this anything to do with the inertia of the Indian state in dealing with violence against women shown, for example, through police negligence and contribution towards crimes against women and the poor?[28] Has it also

---

26   See Agamben 2004.

27   In earlier communist literature, for example in Marx, there was an expectation of 'withering away of the state' when communism would prevail as the core of the mode of production. The agents of this 'withering' were to be the class conscious proletariat and their growing participation in shaping all aspects of life into a genuine democracy. Before communism could assume its concrete existence it was caught in the stranglehold of world capitalism led by the u.s. or the trammels of capitalist development in their own countries. Instead the slogan of 'less state' ironically has been raised by parties to neoliberalism. Mutations of earlier 'free trade' stand for this mythic 'freedom' of the market. From the mid-1980s or so there has been a noticeable withdrawal of the state everywhere through the structural adjustment fiats aimed at the third world countries and in the name of releasing creative entrepreneurialism in the West. The state was pulled away from a protective or ameliorative role of social welfare into eventually wholly augmenting the rule of free enterprise. India from the 1980s onwards embarked on this venture also and submitted to conditionalities of 'austerity' or 'reform' forced for the submergence of or the integration between Indian (national) and global imperialist capital. Doing this required intense violence and continues to do so systematically. SAP devastated the global south – the current European 'austerity' measures faced by Greece and other countries are now devastating the north in a similar fashion, for similar reasons.

28   For an example of police contribution to violence against women in India see *Times of India*, 2 January 2014, p. 1, a news report under the headline: 'Cops tell gang-rape vic-

not exponentially increased a cynicism among people at large about 'law and order', so that we see a rise in mob justice and lynching and so-called 'private' conflict resolution bodies often involving *khap* and other forms of civil society organisations which also give verdicts against women?[29]

Global neoliberalism, the imperialism of our time, is a human, social and ecological disaster. Rife with wars and civilisational destruction, we see masses plunged into abysmal existence and death. The very content of the word 'human' is being emptied out and filled with screams of agony of those condemned to it. In this atmosphere of violence how can violence against women not intensify, as an excrescence of this ordered disorder? There are occurrences of gang rapes, rapes of children and the elderly routinely. Patriarchy has been violently activated through the loss of livelihood and the ferocity of the market. Violent masculinism pumps up the ethic of grabbing fast all 'goods', including bodies of women. The whole social scene is one of a display of masculine bodily and economic prowess. A proper understanding of violence against women, then, needs to be mapped within the polity and economy of neoliberalism that I have outlined so far.[30]

---

tim's family to go back to Bihar: forcibly try to cremate body at night'. The article begins: 'Gang-raped twice and dumped in government hospital for three days with fatal burns, the 16-year old victim had no peace even after death. Police hijacked the hearse carrying her body on Tuesday night and forcibly took it to Nimtolla Ghat for cremation, ignoring the family's request to wait until Wednesday'.

29   The states in the global south, with their colonial inheritance of loss and distorted development, often had an element of a comprador state and the have now matured into a great collusion with and submission to national and foreign capital. The corruptions and crimes that have been overwhelming India and other parts of the world are not exceptions, but a constructional norm of capital, among other reasons, of financialisation. The Indian state's withdrawal is nearing its completion in creating poverty and handing over the poorer segments bound hand and foot to the 'freedom' of the market and financialised capital. Thus for the poor an 'end' of the state as an enabler has been truly in sight. The state's due diligence for public good is ended by making the state an instrument of capitalism. In its capacity of a national state it has signed away the rights and resources of the majority of the people. The role of the state in neoliberalism needs to be understood not only in its withdrawal but in its instrumental crucial role as the host of neoliberalism, signing away to private corporations all of what belongs to the people of India. See Das Gupta 2014; also McNally 2011. In matters of financial liability, insurance, legalization of all forms of primitive accumulation, the Indian state has created a landing pad for invading armies of foreign and national private capital. This entails a derangement in Indian lives and societies. The situation is tantamount to a state of war which is both economic and military. The ordinary people, the rural and urban poor, experience the state primarily as a repressive apparatus.

30   See Butalia and Sarkar 1995.

The lethal combination of patriarchy and neoliberalism which structure social life in India comes as no surprise. But we do have a surprise at hand when we move on to discuss how 'violence against women' can be deployed both as a generally descriptive expression and as an ideological category to limit its explanatory power and efficacy. Talking about violence against women disconnected from the overall social organisation, as liberal feminists do, prevents us from seeing it as an essential component of capitalist social formation and class and 'race' domination. Achieving an ideological status through an epistemological grammar of linguistic and legal usage, 'violence against women' as a self-standing category cuts out of the frame a whole slew of social and economic realities. This practice converts a descriptive expression to the main path for redress. It obscures real connections of social relations with each other and how they are bound together, isolating this violence from other ruling and exploiting relations and intentions.[31] Thus what is happening to women in a particular conjuncture of socio-economic relations is abstracted, and there is no clue within this usage to link the notion back to the relevant ground. This is apparent if we juxtapose 'violence against women' as a bounded legal category, as a textually mediating term, with its descriptive use which situates it, rather than offering an ideological presentation. A dominantly ideological use can make the newly abstracted category into an instrument of legal manipulation. It can only provide a limited scope for creating a base for political and social struggles for women's real emancipatory subjectivities and agencies.[32]

So the anti-ideological notion of 'violence against women' needs to be used in the context of an overall social organisation of the capitalist mode of pro-

---

31   Here we can see how Marx's three tricks for producing ideology can be applied to the notion of violence against women. Rather than being an analytical category it serves as an interpretive one. Rather than describing social behavior of a particular social moment, this becomes a standardizing category relating to the current state and governance, mainly for sociological coding and legal reform.

32   A fertile ground for ideological categories is provided by the binary use of concepts such as the public and the private, social and sexual divisions of labour. Commoditisation and degradation of labour and human bodies, especially of women's bodies, can be accomplished through ideology and ideological practices. This normalises violence in the family and society at large. The normalisation is itself a violence and provides the ideological core of 'violence against women'. What has to be stressed is that without rendering capitalist patriarchy invisible as violence, without normalising the violence against humanity implied in capitalism, violence against women cannot arise, sustain or increase. The extreme violence of gang rapes, dowry murders, witch burning, *satidaha* (burning women on their husbands' pyre) and cruelties of caste or community organisations towards women could not happen without the 'normal' violence of capitalism's dehumanising ethos at different phases and spaces of its development.

duction. This is a descriptive and identifying use of the notion. Used thus it becomes a notion for demanding social justice in a holistic manner because capitalism is inherently patriarchal. We also need to stress that latent violence attains blatant forms under some circumstances more than others, so in certain circumstances patriarchy can become virulent. In the present neoliberal social condition in India, where religious ethnicity provides the national imaginary, the conjuncture of forces is set for this extreme blatancy of patriarchy while other aspects of society are also undergoing a massive upheaval. Legitimation mechanisms of moral and political ideologies of the Hindu right have come to depict violence or brute strength as the dominant mode of self constitution. Ruthless individualism has cast aside social bonds in favour of profit and consumption. In the neoliberal phase of capitalism the imperatives of the 'base' have themselves become the 'superstructure', popularising the social Darwinian ethics of the survival of the fittest.[33] As we have seen in the last decades riots, pogroms against Muslims and other minorities and militancy and police confrontations, including fake encounters, created a permissive atmosphere for violence. Violence itself has become a mobilising force. The political parties of the right resort to violence on a daily basis.[34]

We need to remember the importance of ideology in the present situation which fractures the globe. It is also true that violence becomes most extreme and permitted when legitimised by moral and religious justification. When violent imperatives are embedded in popular moral, emotional and imaginative lives they aim to take on an unconditional existence. This is where the extensive civil society based ideological fieldwork of the Hindu right or the Sangh Parivar since 1925 provides their deepest violent inputs. The ideal of *hindutva*, a distillation of casteist Hinduism with roots in the hatred of 'others', especially of Muslims, is a moral-political ideology meant to construct a nation and poison the entire society through the dissemination of this ideology. Presented as absolute moral imperatives in the name of the Hindu pantheon and a pure and exalted form of civilisation, this ethnic nationalism calls Hindus to social/political action against all their 'enemies', which also include the secular and left population. Armed with this moral and divine strength, wearing masks of gods and heroes, violence against women, Muslims or undesirable 'others' assumes a public and spectacular form. Spectacles of the forces of religion and the state are the order of the day, and gang rape is also such a spectacu-

---

33   See Harvey 2009, ch. 4. See also Sassen 1999.
34   On riot and pogroms as modes of mobilisation for the BJP and other Hindu right-wing parties, such as the Shiv Sena, Maharashtra Navanirman party, etc., see Bannerji 2000, and Basu et al. 1993.

lar display of masculine power, which invests its perpetrators with a more than life-size brute force – a full synthesis of embodied masculinity. The deathly acts of the cadres of Hindu supremacism are projected as social/collective punishment for 'erring' women and overreaching religious minorities. Muslim, other minority and Dalit women are specially targeted because Hindu brahmanical masculine virtue must undertake it as a duty to preserve social order. These punishing acts range from caste *panchayat* (council) fiats to honour killing to gang rapes, all under the rubric of preserving moral purity. Rape then branches out from within the marital and family fold and private actions of individuals to the status of social or civilisational corrective. In the age of neoliberalism, where the idea of the social and binding social relations are sought to be erased and deranged, we are left with a macabre collage of patriarchal neoliberal capitalism with its ethics of hyper-consumption, fundamentalist Hinduism and a nation state aspiring to ethnic supremacy.[35]

Neoliberalism's affinity with religious fundamentalism rather than secular modernity in India and parts of the middle east is a consciously undertaken ideological-political project. The moral appeal of this stance can be found the world over. The religio-ethnic/communalist Hindu supremacism is thus not different in essence from Islamic or Zionist fundamentalisms that become state ideologies, nor is their union with neoliberalism so exceptional. Christian civilisational supremacism and all these other national and imperial projects rely on the evocation of the religious past and invented cultures and traditions. Mythification of history and politicisation of myths to create ideological foundations for nation states are particularly important in an era that grows by fracturing the social space. These religio-ideological stances are loaded with hatred against the 'other', invented enemies such as women, ethnic and religious 'others' and poor labouring people. Members of these categories, especially women, are not attributed with reason but equated with nature. Women are seen as natural resources or objects of consumption. In the Hindu right ideology they are treated as plinths of the Hindu family edifice and as properties of the patriarchal family, masculinist society and nation. This owned and subordinate status of women in all patriarchal societies has given rise from

---

35   'Violence against women', taken, therefore, as a singular legal category, as a solely 'patriarchal' behavior rather than an expression of an overall constellation of violent social relations, deflects our scrutiny from this composite reality and encourages us to treat women's maltreatment as a single issue, that of male domination over women. Without an acknowledgement of the complexity of neoliberal social formation not even a hint of an answer can be provided to the question of violence against women in current day India or whether this violence is increasing.

times immemorial to the idea of shaming the male 'others' of another group by raping 'their' women, and India is no exception.

The pseudo-historical recuperation by mythic ethnic nationalisms such as that prevalent in sections of present-day India, the pageants of holy war and claims of being the chosen of god, nurture a cult of heroes with a violent dark side. In fact without having the power of inflicting arbitrary violence, no one can be a hero at all. *Purushatwa* (masculinity) is the vital force of this domination at all levels. The code of conduct for the heroic and holy nation is of a perpetual war and the need to treat society as a battlefield. This war is against those designated as both dangerous and inferior; in the case of India they consist of religious minorities, communists, feminists and secularists. But their war is also against the weak, the poor, the defenceless, who hold the nation 'back'. They are the 'inferior' people whose lives are solely meant to provide services for the upper classes and upper castes. Women, religious minorities and other 'others' must thus be held down in their place by the 'order' of this aggressive fundamentalist and capitalist masculinity in its most marketised and advertised form. There is an active and pre-emptive and unsuccessful war going on against popular democratic aspiration on the people's part. Citizenship is highly contested. Any desire on the part of women and 'others' to control their own bodies, livelihoods and rights to justice is wholly unacceptable to these holy-minded illiberal neoliberals. In the Indian instance the word *purush*, signifying a quintessential maleness, performs an ideological function for the recruits of the Hindu right.[36] This high caste or brahmanical male typology projects rectitude, valour and sternness, which conceal in an ideological cloak of austerity the reality of a rapacious mode of production and societal injunctions. This political vision is not so different from the social vision of Hobbes' *Leviathan*, in which society is a man-made jungle with its 'natural' laws of cannibalising and ruthlessly eliminating those who are weak and fall behind.

3   Conclusion

It should be clear by now that due to the frenetic speeding up of time in the rationalisation of labour in the present phase of capital, enabled by exponential growth in information technology and extreme financialisation, there is a constant undoing and resettling of the same social and productive spaces. The

---

36   On the dominant masculinity of the Hindu right see Anand Patwardhan's documentary film, Father, Son and Holy War (1995). See also *Communalism Combat*, the issue on 'genocide', and writings of Teesta Setalvad.

resulting constant fracturing calls for a unifying ideological device if it is not to spin out of control politically, with unpredictable results for capital. This makes neoliberalism an age of ideology, making working class consciousness, which needs a larger segment of maturing time, very difficult to emerge. Thus a clearly articulated class struggle on the part of the working class or the unemployed is more difficult to sustain, though revolts are occurring in many countries, while the bourgeoisie are replete with their own class power and self-validation, and have their victory for the time being. We can speculate as to how to theorise and analyse this rapidity of breakdown and the setting up of neoliberal capital, with its sandstorm of appearances, and what socio-political forms these frantic activities add up to. This makes it all the more urgent to explore and critique the emerging forms of consciousness, the outpourings of ideologies both religious and secular and their co-existence. To make matters worse, neoliberal Hindu fascism is loaded with imagistic and narrative forms. The myth-filled, ritualistic nature of Hinduism blends in with competitive consumerism and heroic conquest of 'others'. In the latest Republic Day parade attended by Barak Obama – the largest ever held in India – the Hindu civil society groups also celebrate hitherto unseen traditional Hindu rituals in a more than life-size manner. Processions of towering god figures and religious-patriotic ones, pageants based on the epic Ramayana, the use of caparisoned elephants and horses, hundreds of thousands of men with tridents and spears, marked the Republic Day, along with the state's military paraphernalia. These were accompanied by a dizzying assemblage of sounds, colours and light. The word 'overwhelming' is inadequate for a description of the spectacle. What is offered is a stimulus for vision and a synesthetic representational totality that *blocks* seeing itself.

I would like to return to the themes of class and class consciousness based on a Fordist model of capitalism – involving industries of scale, large shop floors, huge assemblages of workers and long durée business plans – and its contrast to neoliberal workplaces and working modes. The earlier industrial capitalism has needed a collectivist workplace organisation and a coordinated continuous labour process over a long period. Vast numbers of highly or relatively skilled workers then worked together for reliable periods of time, which created possibilities of seeing themselves as bound by the same conditions, employers and interests and, as such, as members of a 'class'. This gave scope both to forging labour unions and forming 'proletarian' consciousness. This type of organisation of production has been declining in India and other countries, instead falling back on earlier capitalist forms of home-work, putting-out, piece and temporary work, rendering gigantic overall workforces of free trade and export zones practically invisible as a proletarian labour force. These and other semi-slave labour modes found in India, Bangladesh, Mexico, etc., mostly using women's labour, have not yet created legal or substantial social possibilities for organising of unions or associations. As the former long-term workers are being substituted by 'informal', 'flexible', 'temporary', 'part-time', and 'seasonal' labourers spread across different production sites globally, they are presenting needs for innovation in class politics. It is not true that commodity production has disappeared or that value is not really dependent upon concrete labour. But where, how, by whom and for how long – this concrete labour with its massive alterations has rendered earlier theories and practices analytically and organisationally inadequate. A fissiparous, competitive, transient mode of social being has produced a new productive subject whose imagined self and agentic consciousness become those of a vendor.

The steadiest economic activities visible to people are those of corporate capital or micro business enterprises which are constantly proliferating and dying. The primary social continuity and identity lies in being a consumer. The businessman and the worker see themselves as actual and potential entrepreneurs and consumers. This makes sense as, despairing of proper employment or of any control over their life circumstances, the majority of the population are constantly veering towards small entrepreneurialisation. They have been offered a fiction of independence related to business. This petty entrepreneurial consciousness is aided by the training they have been long receiving through creeping neoliberalism, NGOs, the remedy of micro credit, all for their 'empowerment'. Women in particular have been the trainees of this empowerment, through projects of small loans and so on. As such, a petty-bourgeois consciousness has become normalised as everybody's subjective consciousness. This subjectivity and its agentic forms are ideological ones, moving from the perception of 'people as makers' and producers of value to 'people the sellers and consumers' of whatever is around. This situation fosters primordialist types of consciousness which evade rational understanding. Class consciousness of such socio-economic subjects becomes a prey to competition, envy, and possessive individualism and develops political allegiances which are anti-worker, thus self-destructive. The thugs who now prevent or destroy working-class organising and class struggle from developing were, after all, former or would-be workers, now transformed into market hangers-on. The shock troops of fascism, of right-wing political parties, often come from these groups. They are the economic clientele and patronage seekers of these parties, clearing for them in exchange the social undergrowth of left resistance. This makes the established types of democratic resistance increasingly difficult to mobilise.

It is not a surprise, therefore, to see the appeal of religious communalist ideology or the intensification of violence against women among these patriarchal neoliberal object-subjects. New and invented traditions and re-interpreted ethnicities have been poured into old right-wing ideological containers of religion, of nationalisms of blood and belonging and the ethic of ownership of women and land. These are the dangerous and self-destructive sources for group identification offered by the oppressor to pacify the oppressed. These invented and synthesised religions are deeply inegalitarian, but create an illusion of equality within the manufactured group. Through this process of identity politics of religion and ethnic nationalism the disempowered experience an illusory closure of the gap between themselves and their rulers, and differences between themselves and 'others'. This is the sop that the *hindutva* project of the Sangh Parivar offers to Hindus as they destroy life certainties of the 'others'. To create a Hindu nation they propose 're-conversion' to increase the national space, making actual social relations of class, caste and patriarchy invisible. This ideology embraces neoliberalism, seeking to conceal violent poverty and inhuman life conditions which spin out in random and frequent violence against women. Pragmatically speaking, there is also the seduction of the hope of getting closer to those in power who may provide even a meagre livelihood. These ideological expansions are not long sustaining. So they have to be sustained by frequent aggressive actions of superiority, hence the necessity of pogroms, of lynching and riots, and finally – of rape to keep the mothers of the nation in place. Religion and capitalism have now entered into a murderous union and we can see that modernity is not the intrinsic tool for capitalist development. A powerful symbology which cathects social deprivation, frustration and angers to anti-socialism is spreading rapidly. Thus, a popular anger is carefully cultivated and deflected towards the weak, towards women and people like themselves, rather than attacking the real merchants of misery.

PART 5

Class, Culture and Representation

••
•

The Mirror of Class: Class Subjectivity and Politics in Nineteenth Century Bengal

A view of class in objective and economic terms provides us the basis, or the general parameter, within which classes individuate themselves in social and political terms. It offers us a set of structural and economic givens, but cannot provide any real insight into how classes exist as concrete sociological existences or actualities or as particular political entities, nor into the relationship between cultural practices, such as those of gender, for example, and politics. To gain this insight and to make different kinds of constitutive connections among the social moments, we need to establish and emphasise the social and the mediatory rather than the solely economic nature of class. This can only be accomplished if we see class in terms of socially organising practices elaborated in the process of *conscious labour*, as understood by Marx, as 'sensuous human activity, practice'.[1] These are the practices of everyday life which are to be seen as organising and expressive of the overall social relations coded by the word 'class', rather than defining class as a set of self-regulatory economic and general structural processes. In short, we must see class as *social*, rather than economic (a sub-set of social) relations of production, as Marx repeatedly insisted,[2] and must see these relations as active 'practices' of conscious and intending social subjects. This is the historiography of E.P. Thompson, which enables him to depict the English working class as conscious intending agents, as its own 'maker'. According to Thompson, the emphasis is on the word 'making' '... because it is a study in an active process, which owes as much to agency as to conditioning. The [working] class did not rise like the sun at an appointed time. It was present at its own making'.[3]

---

1 Marx 1970, p. 121.
2 This is an extensive topic, but any careful reading of Marx's discussion of the mode of production and class brings this out clearly. See also Hobsbawm 1964, as well as Marx 1973. In Marx's introduction, production is considered as *a social organisation* mediated through consumption, exchange and distribution – all implying active subjects in social relations of voluntary and involuntary nature. See also 1971b, where Marx says: '... capital is not a thing, but rather a definite social production relation, belonging to a definite historical formation of society, which is manifested in a thing and lends this thing a specific social character' (p. 814).
3 Thompson 1974, p. 8.

It can, therefore, be claimed that specific classes have a consciousness of themselves as such, and this consciousness is an internal, insider's knowledge of appropriate values and practices. These values and practices are not systematic or fully coherent, nor homogeneous, nor directed primarily outwards towards other classes. This type of class consciousness is different from 'class-consciousness' as elaborated by theorists such as Lenin[4] or Lukács,[5] but more in the nature of what Gramsci meant by 'common sense',[6] an untheorised non-homogeneous set of practices and values or beliefs which are implicit or immanent in the everyday life of groups or social subjects, which contain complex alignments, coherences, conflicts and contradictions. E.P. Thompson in *The Making of the English Working Class* shows how this kind of class-consciousness or social subjectivity is an irreducible aspect of class formation and class politics, and latterly works produced on culture and politics by the Birmingham Centre for Cultural Studies, such as Stuart Hall's *Resistance Through Rituals*, or *The Empire Strikes Back*, make an effective demonstration of the role of common sense in constructing and organising 'class'. In this chapter I would like to explore the kind of common sense or class-consciousness that the Bengali middle classes produced for themselves through their socio-cultural practices and ideological formulations, and show how it is that their emerging common sense organised and expressed their social subjectivity, political and cultural potential and agency. Both this extension and re-definition of the concept of class and the actual content of its social subjectivity are important for developing an insight into the nature of politics from the nineteenth century to the present day. It is also an indispensable exercise for understanding class in terms of social reproduction in complement with economic production.

The truth about class common sense, and the role it plays, both consciously and spontaneously, in the hegemonic design of that class, is always complex and elusive. But it can at least be partially approximated by a historical materialist search through the prevalent socio-cultural and ideological practices. If we want to know how the Bengali middle classes became the prime political agents of the province, and also want to know the nature and evolution of the

---

4   See Lenin 1970.

5   Lukács 1971.

6   Gramsci 1971, espesically in 'Studies in philosophy', elaborates on the notion of 'common sense'. A much more flexible concept than that of ideology, in admitting a non-systematised body of ideas and a general sense-making nature of human beings, it is permissive of contradictions, confusions, of generally grey areas of unsorted states of mind – but a state which is 'conscious' nonetheless. It can be a key concept in the formulation of a political agency of a social group.

different aspects of this agency, we have to return to the setting up of an urban colonial society in Bengal, whose chief actors are the middle classes. We have to take into account their terms of reference, the submission-competition dialectic that characterised their relations with dominant anglicising discourse and ruling practices. We could then form a clearer notion of why and how they created their hegemony, or attempted the construction of a 'historic bloc'[7] with other and even subaltern classes.[8] In short we have to explore the mundane and seemingly un- or non-political realm of the social and intellectual space of nineteenth century colonial Bengal.

It is legitimate to assume that given the complexity on all levels of social and political life, the British colonial penetration and imposition had the simultaneous dimensions of an external and an internal invasion. It was not simply through the direct mercantilist extractions, or the various forms of pillages, that the colonisers were able to create this impact, but significantly through the process which constructed and diffused or extended their apparatus of legitimation, which deepened, expanded and stabilised the colonial exploitation. It is in relation to the formation of this legitimation aspect of the ruling apparatus, including the inroad of the colonial state into Bengali social life (e.g. legislation regarding life and property of women, pertaining to education, etc.) that we must explore the self-activity of the Bengali middle classes, naturally within the colonial determination. It is in this mediatory and creative area that we most clearly find the production of particular types or trends of subjectivities, both in the direction of being appropriated and appropriating.

To acknowledge the self-activity of a class is to go beneath or beyond the stage of seeing any social group as objects of a set of self-regulating, solely external, processes. Seen thus, even the dominated middle classes of Bengal cannot simply be perceived as passive objects of foreign capital. Even their domination cannot be properly understood outside the frame of their role in the legitimation process. Not an autonomous role obviously, but nonetheless an active one, sometimes involuntary and sometimes voluntary and spontaneous. It is also evident that the degree of relative autonomy and leading agency

---

7 Gramsci 1971, 'Notes on Italian History'. In this text, as a part of the process of developing the concept of hegemony, Gramsci speaks of the formation of a 'historic bloc'. Hegemony is achieved through being able to 'Jacobinise' the other social groups which the aspiring group must either lead – socially and morally, intellectually, and eventually, politically – or 'liquidate' if they are antagonistic. See especially pp. 52–75.

8 A situation that is generally recognised by any student of Indian politics. For an intensive exploration of this in terms of political history, see Sarkar 1988; the new school of historical writing published in Guha 1982–1986; Pandey 1978; or intellectual history of Bengal in Broomfield 1968.

was attempted and achieved in the socio-cultural and political realms, which agency is still with them – even today. It is to these particular contents and forms of their attempts that we must attend a set of particularities that mark class formation and class politics as concrete sociological and historical entities. It is to these specific details that Marx referred when he spoke of 'the dress' or 'costumes' of class in *The Eighteenth Brumaire*.[9] These particularities, or formational specificities, in all their cultural features, connote the subjectivities of classes, and, as he points out in this and other historical writings, they are indispensable for deciphering the political direction as well as the cultural politics of any society. The 'costumes' which a class designs and presents itself in on the battle ground for hegemony largely decide, for Marx, the political outcome of the class struggle. In *The Eighteenth Brumaire* he consistently uses this sartorial metaphor and dramatic organisation to characterise the contradictions of the French Revolution and its after stages. The 'costumes' and 'dresses' – forms of subjectivities actively fashioned by the social classes – are then not simply the outer trappings or a circumstantial matter, to be stripped at will to discover the rational kernel of truth about class formation or struggle. Being nothing other than the particular forms of the common sense or self-consciousness of classes, the 'dress' expresses and affects the social relationships within the hegemonic class itself, and with other classes as well. It is from this perspective that we will explore the self-activity of the middle classes of nineteenth-century Bengal, and use what Bertolt Brecht called our 'sixth sense of history' in order to understand the social drama of class.[10]

We will begin by reminding ourselves of the fact that the moment of any social formation is one of an incredible effervescence and unclarity. The project of the creation of a new social identity or a new common sense is only partially a planned one. Its complex nature is not accounted for by the correspondence theory of base and superstructure, but rather it is various, disparate and *ad hoc*, and often in the colonial case, one of an acute and quick response. Imitation, reaction, absorption and recreation were all ingredients in this social response. Enthusiastic imitation, Hindu reaction or revivalism, and attempts to synthesise a new bourgeois consciousness from local and new European features, were the three main strands. Since Hindu revivalism did not emerge as an effective

---

9   See Marx 1972d, p. 437. While talking about the Roman costume in which bourgeois politics dresses itself in the post-French revolution era, Marx uses this sartorial metaphor right through the text to indicate the specificity of political forms, and shows class struggle as a concrete process, understood and constructed by the agents, thus giving consciousness and its products a secure place in class politics.

10   Brecht 1974, p. 32.

force in the political and cultural scene until the end of the nineteenth century, it is the other two groups that we must now concentrate upon. These, in different stages and ways, shaped a theist, eventually a secular, liberal humanism, which together contributed to the tone of the Bengali political-cultural intelligentsia and lay at the basis of our so called 'modernity'.

There was an initial period of a crude though only partial imitation or anglicisation. This first stage in the formation of class-consciousness, of those who were organic to the foundation of the new rule, is perhaps the least substantially active and creative of the phases of the formation of class-consciousness or common sense in Bengal. It was limited to a small number of the *nouveau riche* in Calcutta. During the first two decades of the nineteenth century the Bengali ruling classes remained contented by making money and gaining a limited social power. Some among them responded more readily to the possibilities of a different lifestyle implied in the colonial process and emulated the British blindly. It is only a few members of Calcutta's emerging intelligentsia who sought to understand in any depth the new social, moral and intellectual order that they were being shaped by. And even though they were not numerically dominant, it is important to note that it is they who were the chief ideological designers, the dressmakers of the new ruling classes. Neither the imitators nor the new social thinkers held, at their inception, even a modicum of revolt against the British.[11] From the first decades of the nineteenth century more and more well-to-do Bengalis, both due to the external circumstances and to personal willingness, allowed themselves to be moulded by the foreign

---

11   They supported neither the attempts of military expulsion of the British in 1857 (the 'sepoy mutiny') nor the peasant rebellions which happened incessantly due to the joint oppression that the new local ruling classes and their British masters perpetrated in the countryside. The Sannyasi-Fakir movement during the late 18th century, the Faraji movement of the 1820s and 1830s, the indigo rebellions of the 1850s, the Santhal and Munda uprisings of the late nineteenth century and the turn of the century, never found any substantial ally or approval of armed militancy among them. The Pabna rent revolt (1872–3) terrified them, though both in the case of the indigo rebellions and the Pabna rent revolt they attempted to lobby the British government. For discussion of this see Sarkar 1985, Chapters 1 and 2, and Guha 1982–86, Vol. 1. Sarkar's chapters discuss the ideological, intellectual formation of the nineteenth century – with particular emphasis on the 'break' with the feudal past, and the concept of 'Bengal Renaissance', assessing the ideological absorption of the intellectual in colonial forms of thinking and the consequences of this for the Indian nationalist movement. See also Sarkar 1988. Sarkar here discusses the problem of middle-class control of the nationalist politics of the Indian independence movement, in terms of the hegemonisation of the subaltern classes by INC as a bourgeois middle-class party, and the 'passive revolution' (Gramsci) that results and the transformist character of the communist movement in India.

socio-cultural forces. This formative process included in itself clearly defined ideologies or fields of verbal discourse – but also non-verbal ways of being and doing, which extended into the physical and moral fashioning of the social space demanded by the new urban centre of Calcutta, the second city in the British empire.[12]

An early genuine attempt at creating a substantive ideology and morality for the new ruling classes came from the *Brahmo Samaj*. Its beginnings lay in the work of social reformers such as Raja Rammohan Roy (1774–1833), who inspired the movement, and even among the 'Young Bengal' atheists, radical liberal intelligentsia, in spite of Rammohan's dislike of them. The *Brahmo* attempt at redefining the Hindu spiritual life and combining it with liberal reformism eventually and logically gave place to a progressive secularisation, both of the Brahmos and the Hindus. This, over a period, generally set the attitudinal direction of the 'cultured' Bengali middle class. Though leaning heavily on the West, and shot through with economic and political acquiescence, there was a genuine quest at an ideological level of dignity and self-reliance (for example, in the principle of 'self-strengthening' advocated by Rammohan Roy) in the attempts of social reform. A powerful moral and intellectual endeavour was afoot. As Addy and Azad put it:

> The rapid social change, as well as the cosmopolitan and colonial experience of the *bhadralok*, began to register itself from about 1813 in a new intellectual awareness, which grew until the turn of the twentieth century. This period, called the Bengali [sic] Renaissance, is distinguished by the prodigious intellectual achievements of the *bhadralok* intelligentsia. Confronted with the overwhelming power of European domination they learnt English, French, Hebrew, Greek and Latin in search of the essence of the culture of the west.[13]

---

12   The city of Calcutta became an embodiment of both the subjective and the objective aspects of changes brought in by the new mode of production. It is also the world which surrounds, constructs and is represented on the stages of the new theatre that came to life in the 1830s. Everything that happened here emanated from the new capitalist colonial social order, constructed of new terms. Contemporary essayists, novelists and playwrights all expressed a concern about this heedless flight into British culture, the rootlessness and the excesses of an uncritical emulation. See Tekchand Thakur's *Alaler Charer Dulal* (The Spoilt Darling of the New-rich), Kaliprasanna Sinha's *Hutom Penchar Naksha* (The Owl Skit), Ishwar Gupta's satirical verses, and Michael Madhushudan Dutt's *Ekeyi Ki Bole Subhyata?* (Is This Called Civilisation?), among innumerable pieces of writings.

13   Azad and Addy 1973. See also Shastri 1972, Biswas 1983, among numerous other books.

Though the changes all bore marks of anglicisation or Europeanisation, this phenomenon was far deeper and more extensive than the formal teaching of the English language and curriculum. It is interesting to note, for instance, that all of the major social reformers and writers of Bengal, beginning with Rammohan Roy himself, wrote their major works in Bengali. They were also well-versed in Sanskrit, and some in Persian and even Arabic. An older tendency towards a more liberal and egalitarian social ethics, as found for example in the religious works of the great popular syncretists,[14] continued along with new articulation of British material. Islamic arguments and Sufi philosophy on the equality of all souls provided the basis for a liberal social reform for Rammohan Roy, for example in his pre-British writing phase – in the *Tuhfatul Muwahiddin* (A Gift to Deists) (1973) – or the later agitation against *sati* and for women's property rights.[15] It is not surprising, therefore, interested as he already was in human freedom and happiness, and negative to authoritarianism of tradition, that Rammohan Roy should have been drawn to the principle of utility of Bentham and his precept of 'the greatest happiness of the greatest number',[16] and knew how to shape his reform project along both social and spiritual lines.

Known on the one hand as the crusader against sati, Rammohan Roy also provided the main impetus for the religious-social institution of the Brahmo Samaj through his Brahmo Sabha (1928). In an attempt to purify Hinduism, to make it more suitable to the times as well as to his own liberal and rationalist ideas, Rammohan proposed monotheistic, non-idolatrous, ethico-philo-

---

14   See Sarkar 1973, especially Chapter 2. See also De 1961. For a discussion of syncretism in
      Rammohan Roy's precepts for the Brahmo Samaj, see Sumit Sarkar 1985, Chapter 1.

15   Here, in trying to get away from both doctrinaire and institutional Hinduism and Islam,
      he supported 'the natural inspiration from god, which consists in attending to social life
      with one's own fellow species and having an intuitive faculty of discriminating good from
      evil' (Roy 1973, p. 20). He quoted a verse which says 'so many hypocritical acts of Shaikh;
      i.e. Spiritual Leaders, not worth a mite, give comfort to the hearts of people, this is the only
      Divine Doctrine' (ibid., p. 21).

16   Rammohan Roy's closeness to Bentham, and partially through him the influence of utilit-
      arianism on certain Brahmo codes of conduct, is manifested also in a personal friendship
      he developed with Bentham. His biographer notes the culmination of this friendship
      through correspondence during his visit to England: 'When he had retired to rest, and
      it was nearly midnight, Bentham called at the hotel, and left a laconic and characteristic
      note for him – "Jeremy Bentham to his friend Rammohan Roy" ... They afterwards met
      each other, and it must have been a very interesting sight to have seen these two great
      men engaged in conversation on the greatest happiness principles, in reference to politics
      and morals, on the condition of the natives, and on the administration of the East India
      Company. "Rammohan Roy", said the venerable founder of the utilitarian school, "has cast
      off three hundred and thirty millions of gods and has learnt from us to embrace reason in
      the all-important field of religion"'. (Ibid., p. 82).

sophical, non-caste Hinduism modulated by both Islam and Christianity.[17] The Brahmo Samaj from its inception to its mature phase, i.e., through the nineteenth century, mainly attracted a particular section of the new urban middle class. It was mainly a religion of the rising professionals and of the liberal intelligentsia. In the beginning, however, it also attracted the new mercantile families, who rose as the middlemen of the British and had compromised their caste purity through the exigencies of serving them.[18] Since they were somewhat socially ostracised, for example in matters of matrimonial alliances, and seen as *patita* or the 'fallen' from crucial caste practices, they turned to a religion that allowed them to pursue their economic and social vocations as well as remain some kind of a Hindu.

Other than the direct and immediate social facilitation of upward mobility within a colonial economy, there were other social and ethical aspects to the Brahmo Samaj. Even though the huge Hindu festivities, the autumnal worship of the goddess Durga, etc. were generally proscribed for these reformed Hindus (though some, such as Debendranath Thakur, continued), there were days of celebration for the foundation of the Brahmo Samaj, the founder's day, etc., where there would be gatherings at the private homes of the wealthy, or in the Brahmo Samaj prayer halls, when they were established. Rabindranath Thakur's novel *Gora*, named after a white foundling from the 'sepoy mutiny' (1857) who is brought up by Hindus and finally finds his real place among the Brahmos, is highly revealing in terms of the middle space that Brahmo Samaj occupied between Calcutta and the West. As we see in this novel, an atmosphere of contemplation and music may have attracted many who went there for ethico-spiritual direction, but they were also attracted by the social activities and networking carried on, as in the churches, where people would catch up with news, gossip, look for an eligible son-in-law, or conduct business. It was a new social space for a section of the new classes.

---

17   For Rammohan Roy's synthesis, see biographer Kissory Chand Mitter: 'While some represented him to be a Hindu, others affirmed that he was a christian. The Church of England party said that he was attached to their church; while the Unitarians claimed him for their own. The Vedantists represented him as literally a believer in their professed revelation; while the Mussulmans contended that he was a follower of the son of Abdullah' (ibid. p. 83). Also see Chattopadhyay 1928; Biswas 1983.

18   In fact, it facilitated the socio-economic relations which promoted the British rule, for example, by negating caste practices or allowing eating with the English. The fact that the Brahmos could override the strict hindu injunction against crossing the *kalapani* (the black waters), i.e., taking an ocean voyage (that too in a British ship, eating food prepared by non-Brahmins), made it possible for them to travel abroad easily and make contacts in England and find important patrons at home.

The social life first promulgated by the Brahmos and their sympathisers, as well as by the atheistic Young Bengal, became the social life of many who belonged to the new 'enlightened' set. This socio-cultural change may also have forestalled any significant conversion into Christianity, even among those who fully sided with the British. The Bengali ruling classes, but particularly the urban upper and middle classes, had managed to evolve a social definition, a set of practical social forms, which enabled them to retain some aspects of their Hindu past which were reworked into a new spiritualism and ethics suited to the requirements of capitalism's administration even in the outposts of the empire. Punctuality, thrift, frugality, work-ethic were all in fact enjoined by the new social code, as well as a concern for the autonomy of conscience, women's education and public life for women in mixed company. Since one's spiritual life was abstracted away from daily caste and religious observances and made largely a personal and private matter, it was not hard to reconcile spirituality in personal life with pragmatism or utilitarianism in daily life.[19]

This blend of the spiritual with the practical, and the serious, solemn and influential nature of these attempts at creating a new morality, a new cultural and social life (the ascending ideological mode or discourse), becomes apparent from the biographies and work of the reformers and early nationalist thinkers.[20] The spirit of new liberalism, a religious or secular humanism as displayed in the life of Rabindranath Thakur, for example, cannot be trivialised into a simple tale of imitation or of greed and opportunism of the betraying collaborators. But nor can it be ever forgotten that this world-view belonged to classes elaborated on the terrain of colonialism. Along with its own substantiveness it could tolerate a considerable amount of collaboration with foreign capital and did not seek (as well as categorically rejected) an armed struggle against the colonial state, for example in 1857. In novels such as *Ghare Baire* (At Home and Outside), *Char Adhyay* (The Four Chapters), and in many eloquent essays, Rabindranath devoted himself to showing the ugly face of Bengali armed resistance to colonial power during the Swadeshi phase.

---

19   John Stuart Mill's *Autobiography*, or his two essays on *Bentham* and *Coleridge*, Matthew Arnold's attempt to infuse 'sweetness and light' into capitalism in *Culture and Anarchy* and Charles Dickens' attempt in reconciling utilitarianism with romanticism in *Hard Times*, all testify to similar attempts at a kind of aggregative exercise, or a syncretism of idealism with materialism. Pamela McCallum's work on the literary method and social criticism of the writers mentioned above, but extended to cover F.R. Leavis, Northrop Frye and T.S. Eliot, deals incisively with this topic. See *Literature and Method* (1983). What is more, these aggregative exercises hold more than hypocrisy and pragmatism to them.

20   For an excellent account of their intellectual development, politics and reform, see Shastri 1972.

It is indeed instructive to read his autobiographical pieces, for example *Jibans-mriti*[21] (Recollections of My Life), in order to understand this mentality of 'giving unto Caesar what is Caesar's and unto God what is God's' – this dignified compromise with being ruled while also ruling through the fiat of the Permanent Settlement. In *Jibansmriti* he traces his spiritual and practical formation to the guidance provided by his father, Debendranath Thakur, a major figure in the Brahmo movement, in childhood and youth. In Rabindranath's portrayal of his father and his own character and educational development we find the mode for the ideal Brahmo and liberated Hindu gentleman's conduct – it is a curious combination of submission and judicious rule modulated with a dignified and distant patriarchy within the context of massive property ownership. Without the slightest sense of contradiction it weaves into one many contradictory elements, for example, a profound spirituality with an astute worldliness. As will be evident to students of nineteenth-century English socio-literary history, it is not dissimilar to the upbringing of a Victorian gentleman:

> When father returned to Calcutta for a few days, after long periods of exile, our home resonated with his presence. We saw that our much respected older relatives would only venture into his presence in neat and restrained apparels, dressed formally in *jobbas* [long coats], and spit out the betel leaves and nuts before entering the room. Everyone moved carefully. My mother herself sat in the kitchen supervising the cooking, lest there should be something amiss. Old Kinu Harkara would don his turban with the brass buckle, get into his uniform and stand guard at the door. We were always warned not to run around in the verandah disturbing his rest, so we walked softly, spoke softly, and did not even have the courage to peep into the room.[22]

These lines give a sense of the immense authority that male heads of families commanded in the wealthy homes. This authority, naturally, went beyond itself – this immediate locus of power in one male figure – and diffused itself as a code of proper masculine conduct and social-familial expectation among other males of the household. It is also interesting that this authority of the male is not based on brute force, but is composed of several layers of mediations and distance, based on moral power and social wealth. Not direct fear, but its more elevated form, respect, marks this father-son relation, not unlike

---

21 Thakur 1961.
22 Ibid., p. 36. Translation mine.

the god-man relation that the Brahmo sermons and hymns portrayed. In feudalism there was a much greater role of physical force, which is absent here. The following quotation is about the child poet's education in financial and social class matters.

> My father, probably in order to make me frugal and careful, gave me a few annas and asked me to keep an account of the spending. He also gave me the responsibility of winding his expensive gold watch. He did not consider the possibility of damage [to the watch] in this, because his intention was to teach me responsibility. When he went for walks in the morning he took me with him. If we saw beggars on the road he instructed me to give them alms. When the time came to give my accounts and balance the books, the figures would never tally. One day our cash increased in amount. He said, 'I think I should hire you as my cashier, my money increases in our hands'.[23]

This quotation also displays a great change from the past practice among the well-to-do of no involvement of the father in a male child's upbringing in an everyday sense. Lacking the old reliable code of feudal upbringing, or the community involvement in a child's growth, including a longer youth of professional preparations, the father's involvement with the male child's moral (never physical) and educational development increased and became a common practice among the middle classes. In Rabindranath's case these times with Debendranath were steps in the ladder of property supervision and rent collection. When older, Debendranath entrusted him with the responsibility for the supervision of a massive landed property at Pabna and Rajshahi. And even at this stage he met his father, who then was failing in vision, with trepidation and offered his accounts.

This training of morality and prudence was matched by a Victorian education in English and in physical and sexual matters:

> After father came back there were English lessons for an hour, after that bath in ice-cold water. From this there was no escape and none of the servants dared to mix hot water against his wish. In order to give me encouragement he would tell stories about how he took baths in intolerably cold water in his youth.[24]

---

23   Ibid., p. 42.
24   Ibid., p. 42.

This physical training is closely complemented by spirituality of a social or a solitary nature:

> I remember the Gurudarbar of Amritsar like a dream. On many mornings I accompanied my revered father on foot to the Sikh temple in the middle of the lake. There was always worship in progress. My father would sit amidst the Sikh worshippers and then suddenly join their worship music. They would be very happy hearing a stranger sing their devotional songs, and treat him with respect and concern.[25]

> When the twilight deepened my father would come and sit in the terrace facing the garden. Then I was summoned to sing Brahma-Sangeet [devotional songs] for him. The moon had risen and the moonlight penetrated the shadows of the trees and fell on the verandah. I would sing in *behag*: 'Who but you Lord can help me overcome this danger? Who is my helper in the darkness of this world?' He would be sitting absolutely still, his palms lying in his lap in a gesture of prayer. I still remember that image and those evenings[26]

In order to explore the formation of class-consciousness among the emerging ruling classes of Bengal, we have to pursue this discussion on the social relations of the family and shaping of the moral character of a child a little further, with particular emphasis on the responsibilities assigned to women and the concept of the 'home'. As a great deal of work done on the reorganisation of the family in the context of capitalist development shows, capitalism (even where only indirectly and non-productively present, as in the colonies) has a way of organising itself through the organisation of social life into public and private realms.

This division between the private and the public, which seems to be routinely capital's way of setting up its terrain, in the context of colonial Bengal was both sudden and pronounced. The public world, the world of males holding public offices and engaging in business with the English and each other, was anglicised. The pre-existing world of feudal society, though continuing to exert pressures and being reworked and reinserted in the new context, however, could mostly continue in the world of the family. The interior of the household, also architecturally designed as such with rooms facing a closed courtyard,

---

25   Ibid., p. 43.
26   Ibid., p. 44.

which had existed as a realm apart, as an expression of a rigid, sexual division of labour, now took on an added significance of being and inviolate *core* of the family in the face of a colonial socio-cultural domination. The family life was to become that part of the Bengali middle-class society which lay outside the influence of all changes brought in by the new mode of production. It is not surprising, therefore, that for the new, anglicised gentry of Bengal, the expectations regarding women's responsibility in maintaining emotional and physical comforts increased astronomically during this era, when they came to themselves and jockeyed for more power, and both sought and resented the British rule. In fact the compromise they made with the new rulers consisted of a public alliance and a social boycott at the level of family and personal life. It is only rarely, and that too from the mid-twentieth century onwards, that white people were ever allowed an entry into a Bengali household. This, to a large extent, is still the case today.[27]

Women, ideally, were invested with a highly symbolic role; entrusted with the bound-to-fail task of preserving or retaining at the family and personal level an autonomy – customs and practices – of a social order which had lost out economically, and therefore was clung to and fetishised culturally. It is not difficult to guess that this equation of women with the home became the only kind of freedom – i.e., private – that even ruling class men could enjoy in a colonial society. This arrangement did not often work positively for women

---

27   The number of Anglo-Indians of mixed origin are so low as to indicate a minuscule amount of intermarriage. In the following quotation, one may observe the response of the Bengali community to the visit of the Prince of Wales into the household of a wealthy Bengali lawyer practicing at the Calcutta High Court. "The Prince of Wales was taken into the inner quarters of the household. He did not allow anyone [among the English] to accompany him – not even the ladies. The Viceroy and others were displeased at this. In the women's quarters the Prince of Wales was given a throne to sit on. He was decorated with sandalwood paste. He was greeted with grains of rice, sheaves of green grass – the sound of conchshell and ululations. All these created a wonderful atmosphere in the room. The smell of incense and other aromatic substances delighted the senses ... The Prince was charmed – nay, overwhelmed. Delighted at this reception given to him by Jagadananda Mukhopadhyay's wife and other Bengali ladies, the Prince said, 'I feel no difference between this home of yours and my Windsor Castle'. Jagadananda received enough rewards for this act, but his life was made intolerable by lashes of satire and ridicule" (Mukhopadhyaya 1952, p. 326) (my translation).

The following response of the *Amrita Bazar Patrika* captures the sentiment of most of the society, at least of its male members. Female response would often be similar: 'Hindu society can tolerate all other humiliations and tortures except the dishonour of its women. He who brings a foreigner, an outsider, into the women's quarters, is an enemy of the Hindu society' (quoted in Ibid., p. 326). Needless to say muslims, with their established positon of *purdah and khandan* (honor, high status tradition) would not disagree with either.

themselves. Not only did they have to preserve and retain feudal social forms, which in this enclosed social space ossified their own lives, but actually in the context of colonialism they became the captives of male fantasy – of their over-protectiveness, over-possessiveness – and compromised as full human beings by an insistence on their pristine and pure qualities. One might venture to say that what the peasants often became to the Indian Maoists, or the workers to the members of the Second or the Fourth International, women became to middle-class men at the rise of colonialism. A woman's purity, maintained by her seclusion and economic dependence, 'embodied' her husband's refuge from being an absolute servant of the British. She was not only the angel or the goddess of the hearth (*grihalaksmi*), but buried under the foundation itself and made to become a spirit (*jakh*) which supplies the home with the right kind of emotionality and stability.

These two worlds of home and the outside, and their correlation with women and men, become evident in most literary exercises of the time. Let us take a look at two autobiographical pieces by Rabindranath Thakur himself, *Jibansmriti and Chhelebela* (Childhood). *Jibansmriti* is actually divided into two parts, *Andare* (in the interior/in the women's quarters – the same word used to denote both) and *Bahire* (outside/in the open in the public domain, etc). A great description of this divided world, exorcised of all the claustrophobia it holds for women, is to be found in *Jibansmriti*:

> When I came back it was not simply an act of physically returning home from abroad. I also returned then to that inner part of the home from which I lived in exile all this time, even when I lived at home. The barrier guarding the inner part of our home was lowered – I could no longer be contained in the servants' quarters. I occupied an important position in my mother's court, and received much affection and indulgence from her, who was then the youngest bride.
>
> People generally receive women's love in childhood, without having to ask for it. A man needs this affection and pampering just as much as he needs sunlight or air. But just as one takes light and air for granted, so it is natural for children to take women's care for granted. But if, for some reason, he does not get the right thing at the right time, they become insistent and craven. And that is what happened to me. Since I was raised by male servants in great strictness, once I tasted this unconditional love, I could not put it out of my mind. When, in infancy, the interior of our home was at a great distance from me, I had projected into it all my fantasies. In that place, which in common parlance is a restricted area, I envisioned the end of all my servitude. There, I thought, are no schools, no tears, no

one forces one to do anything that one does not want to; there solitude and privacy are possible and filled with mystery; there no one keeps time, there things happen as one wishes.

Until then what I saw of it [the women's quarters] seemed to me like pictures. It is nine o'clock at night. I am on my way to bed in the inner part of the house, after finishing my studies with Aghor master. There are lanterns flickering along the long corridor, protected from the world by wooden slats. I walk through it, walk down four or five dark steps into a courtyard, and then step onto a verandah of the interior. Moonlight had fallen at an angle onto the western part of the verandah, and the rest of it was in the dark. In that little circle of moonlight, the maids are sitting next to each other. They are sitting with their legs stretched out in front of them, rolling wicks for lamps on their thighs, and speaking softly to each other about their homes in their villages. How many such images are still etched on my memory! Then after dinner, and after cleaning our feet, we would get into bed – Sundari, Pyari and Tinkari would come and tell us about the long wanderings of the prince across the field at the world's end. When the story finished the bed would be very quiet. Turning my face to the wall, in that dim light, I would stare at the black and white lines and splotches created by mortar crumbling from the lime-washed wall. From these dots and lines I would conjure up strange images and drift off to sleep.[28]

We must note that this description, which is full of the magic of childhood, is not only at the level of desire, lost or gained, but at the level of normativeness as well (see para 2). These norms, as further specified in two of Rabindranath's essays on male-female relationships, are not exceptional to the norms held by the progressive middle class in general. Without denying women an equality in terms of sexual division of labour, and in fact, idealising such labour, and granting them such intelligence as well, he saw in women two 'eternal' characteristics – which are essential for maintaining that inner sanctum of the home intact. He wanted to preserve these in the face of the threat posed by middle-class women's education and professionalisation. The need for the economic viability of women had become an important issue among the middle-class intelligentsia by the turn of the nineteenth century. To the attempts to create 'opportunities' for women, he offered the following rejoinder:

---

28   Rabindranath Thakur, *Jibansmriti*, p. 48 (my translation).

Creating opportunities through artificial efforts does not really create real opportunities [for women]. The strong emotionalism [impulses of the heart] of a woman's nature cannot be got rid of by external pressures. The natural direction of these traits of her heart is not towards a dynamism or movement of progress, but rather towards clinging or holding fast. This is why a woman's quest achieves its fulfilment if it aspires to the wealth [value] which lies in familial enterprise. Otherwise she is bound to come into conflict with her own nature, and suffering from that ceaseless conflict she will never be able to outshine the male in competition ...

Woman has two aspects to her, one is that of the mother, and the other, that of lover. I have already spoken about her attempts at perfection in this direction. Her desire is not only for an offspring, but for a worthy human being as well, who is not merely an addition to the number [of children] but one who will overcome the sins, the privations and the lack of fulfilment to be found in the world. In her aspect as a lover, she gives life to all of man's best efforts. The quality which helps her in realising this is a sweet gentleness ...[29]

The practice of the middle class and its ideology regarding women of course varied from the wealthy homes, like that of the Thakur's, to the homes of the professionals or the lower level administrative and clerical workers, who filled the city as the century progressed. But it is also true that slowly there came to be some things in common between these different levels of the non-manual workers of the city and the upper classes in the countryside.

Linking the private with the public, particularly for the male child, bonds of institutional education were forged through the century. Macaulay wrote an interesting and now often-quoted note to the British authorities in his anglicist plea for education in India:

In India, English is the language spoken by the ruling class. It is spoken by the higher class of natives at the Seats of Government. It is likely to become the language of commerce throughout the seas of the East. It is the language of two great European communities which are rising, the one in the south of Africa, the other in Australia, communities which are every year becoming more important and more closely connected with our Indian empire ... *We must do our best to form a class who may be inter-*

---

29   Thakur 1977, vol. 13, pp. 18–19 (my translation).

*preters between us and the millions whom we govern ... a class of persons,
Indian in blood and colour but English in taste, in opinions, in morals and
in intellect.*[30]

The idea in this paragraph obviously was not only to reorganise the economy
of India with the economic collaboration of the 'natives', but actually to shape
and direct this formation in social, political and cultural terms. That is, this was
an attempt to shape the consciousness of the local ruling classes in a much discussed, debated and planned move. The purpose of anglicism was much more
than merely functional, it was an attempt at supplying ingredients of the new
subjectivity. English then was not only a neutral vehicle of communication and
administration, but it brought in a world of ideas and associations that fitted
in with the gradually developing colonial mode of production.

Of all the conscious efforts that the Bengali middle classes made in order
to differentiate themselves from other non-middle class social groups, instituting a system of education was the most important one. Anglicised education
and a quite substantial knowledge of English became the designatory mark of
the middle classes – and of a gentility and 'culture' to which the rural wealthy
also aspired. As the possession of land distinguished the landlord, and capital
and commodities for sale the trader, so Western education was the identifying feature of those seeking cultural and social assertion and advancement
along with, or regardless of, their possession of land or capital. With the help
of Western education, they became *bhadralok*, or a 'cultured' people – and this
distinguished them from the poor urban and country folk, elevating them in
status not only above the level of the peasants, but even of the *jotedars*. The
absentee landlords themselves spent much time in Calcutta acquiring informal
anglicisation, but some formal as well. They and the *jotedars* sent their children to English model or anglicised schools, which until the last decades of the
nineteenth century existed only in Calcutta.[31] This new educational system dis-
organised and devalued the former schooling system and knowledge apparatus
of the Brahminical tradition. Even Bengal's Brahmins made the same journey to
Calcutta as did other castes in order to acquire a knowledge that would secure

---

30   Macaulay's speech to the British Parliament (1935), as quoted in Chatterjee 1976, p. 58.
      Emphasis mine.
31   Slowly, with the expansion of British administration, forming administrative zones such
      as districts or mahakumas, with their suburban towns or mufassil sahars, some state-
      organised primary and lower secondary schools were set up. But their number was not
      very high. See Seal 1968, for details on educational expansion. See also Sen 1977, chapters
      1–2.

a living. When the boy Ishwar Chandra Vidyasagar, during the 1830s, made his journey to Calcutta, walking all the way, a few hundred kilometres from Medinipur, counting the milestones to learn English numbers, Bengal was already aware of the connection between education and socio-economic mobility.[32]

This new knowledge, both in terms of process and context, formal and informal, in English or in Bengali with a European content, was not politically neutral – nor again simply an instrument of economic manipulation. In both its form and content it acted as ideology and helped to shape the world-view of Bengali non-menial classes. It provided the language, the organisation of discourse, and many of the terms of reference in which were encoded both the social practices and the world-view of these ruling classes. This was a part of their common sense, as well as of their hegemony, with all the contradictions warranted by their situation. The cultural and social penetration was even more profound in this sphere because it did not happen only, or mainly, in English. Adapted and translated European and English literature filled the Bengali book-world. Education, combined with intense activity of printing presses, thoroughly ideologised first the middle-class men, and then the women.

The informal aspect of education becomes evident in the general diffusion and absorption of English and European literature from the early nineteenth century. Shakespeare or Byron become household names by the 1880s. The following description of Akshay Kumar Choudhury, a lawyer of the 1870s, provides a picture of the intellectual preoccupation of the Bengali gentry of Calcutta at the time. Even though it is only 40 years or so since Macaulay triumphed with his anglicist pleas (1835), it is neither absurd to Akshay Kumar, nor to the narrator, that he should be so enraptured with English literature:

---

32   In the old Brahminism education was a vocation, rather than a means of mobility, but in the new system, the younger sons of the gentry, poor Brahmins, aspiring caste Hindus or lower caste *jotedars*, all hoped to benefit economically and socially from the new use of education. On the other hand, perhaps because of the older association of high status with education, compounded by even a greater gap introduced between mental and manual labour, the stamp of the *bhadralok* gave one prestige, even if one were poorer, over those who made a living by trade, industry or tilling the soil. See Sen 1977, pp. 19–50. Sen both remarks on the enlightenment content of some of this education for the 'unproductive few', and points out the functional use of it for creating administration of the colonial economy. He says: '... the new Bengali middle class, whether already affluent or aspiring to rise in wealth and respectability ... owned no role of advancing the productive economy ... There was acknowledgment of the merits of Baconian rationality and empirical knowledge, but not of its historical identity with the industry of its artificers which lay at the roots of Bacon's vision and Utopia' (Ibid., p. 37).

Akshay completed his MA, BL and became an attorney. This was like a joke of god. Could a man like him, as innocent as a child, trusting, imaginative and emotional, a real poet at heart, have ever prepared in the ways of this world? He was a great devotee of Shakespeare. He used to teach Shakespeare to a few boys at home.

As he taught, tears would soak the clothes on his chest. One could very easily make him into an April fool. Once Rabi [Rabindranath] got dressed up as a Parsi in a beard and a moustache and played a great trick on him. I said to him, 'A Parsi gentleman has come from Bombay and he wants to discuss English literature with you'. Akshay immediately agreed. Rabi showed up in his disguise and started to talk with him ...

Akshay immediately started to talk about Byron, Shelley and other poets in a highly serious manner. It went on for a long time in this way, and we could not hold back our laughter.[33]

The point of this quotation is not only to make fun of this eminent nineteenth-century social thinker's credulity but to show how simply and naturally Akshay Kumar devoted himself to English literature, even though he was a Bengali poet and a proficient writer of Bengali prose. European and English novels, lives of their great men, stories of explorers, social customs and practices, are read avidly and re-worked into suitable Bengali forms. Thus begins for instance the rise of the novel, or essay writing in Bengal, and plots, characters and world-view of two worlds are woven in a tension or synthesised in them. Since the world of our rulers was a far-away world, it was filled not only with the rumour of superior culture of a superior race, but also the magic of a distant land, like images projected by a magic lantern. Allusions and references to things and names European, adaptations/translations of poems, stories and novels, as well as norms of a bourgeois society, blended in with a depiction of Bengali society and social practices made over with British influence. Very soon a Bengali child would learn about the chimes of the Big Ben, or of the Thames River, or, if older, about the English courting customs, or the neo-medieval romances of Sir Walter Scott.

The formative influence of English bourgeois attitudes transmitted through the formal educational system, mainly through basic vernacular textbooks (meant for the youngest children), is strikingly apparent in Ishwar Chandra Vidyasagar's primer.[34] In Lesson 9 to Lesson 19, each based on the simplest possible combination of letters in the alphabet, beyond the basic spelling, the

---

33   Chattopadhyay 1982, p. 59.
34   *Varna-Parichay*. Written in the 1850s, this textbook is used even now at the basic primary

importance of formal and institutional education which is grounded in the ruling apparatus of the colonial administration is explicit. The importance of organised and supervised lessons, associated with written texts, classroom and teachers, is continuously emphasised. They serve as the first step to an introduction to the ruling apparatus:

> Lesson 9: Gopal does not have a book [to study from]. Madhab went to study a long time ago. Jadav is still in bed.
> Lesson 10: I will not go to study today.
> Lesson 11: When will you go to study? We did not go to study yesterday.
> Lesson 12: Don't make noise during study time.
> Lesson 13: Tarak can read well. Ishan cannot read at all. Kailash could not repeat his lessons yesterday. Today I am sick, so I will not go to my lessons.
> Lesson 14: It's no longer night, the dawn is here. I will not lie around anymore. Let me get up and wash my face. After washing my face I dress myself. After dressing I sit down to study. If I don't practice my lessons I won't be able to repeat my lessons well. If I cannot do my lessons well, the teacher will be angry. He will not give me new lessons [to learn].
> Lesson 15: It's getting late. Let's go to study. I have dressed. You should dress. I have my books. Where are your books? Come, let us go, let us not delay any longer. Yesterday we went after everyone else; we could not attend to all the lessons.
> Lesson 16: Listen Ram, yesterday you made a lot of noise while studying. If there is noise during the lessons no one can study well, no one can hear [anything]. I am forbidding you, don't ever make noise while studying.
> Lesson 18: Girish, why didn't you come to study yesterday? I heard that you had nothing important to do; you were absent for nothing. All day you played, ran around in the sun, made a lot of trouble at home. Today [this time] I am letting you go [not saying anything to you]. See to it that this never happens again ...[35]

Lesson 19 is a typology of the perfect child, to be emulated by all others:

------

level. The text I use is 'approved as a supplementary textbook by West Bengal Education Board for Grade I', (reprinted in 1978).

35   Ibid., pp. 9–16, 18. My translation.

Gopal is a good boy. He does everything that his parents tell him to do. He eats whatever he gets, wears whatever he is given. He does not create a disturbance by saying 'I want to eat well, or dress well'. Gopal loves his little brothers and sisters. He never fights with them, or beats them. For all these reasons his parents love him.

When Gopal goes to study, he does not play on the way. He is the first to reach the school. When he is in the class, he sits at his own seat, and opens his book and starts to study. When the teacher gives new lessons he listens attentively.

When playtime comes, and all the boys play, Gopal also plays. The other boys fight and hit each other during the games, but Gopal is not like that. He never, not even for a day, fights with anyone, or hits anyone.

When school is over Gopal goes home and right away puts away his reader in a safe place. Then he changes his clothes and washes his face, hands and feet. Gopal eats whatever food his mother gives him, having eaten, he plays for a while with his little brothers and sisters.

Gopal never neglects his lessons. He reads over carefully at home whatever he has read in school. He goes over all his old lessons twice a day. During the lessons he is able to repeat his lessons better than anyone else.

Anyone that meets Gopal loves him. Every boy should be like Gopal[36]

I have translated these lessons in full because for over one hundred years this text of Ishwar Chandra Vidyasagar, the fountainhead of Bengali universal education movement, scholar, essayist, school inspector, and the principal of Sanskrit College, has helped to shape the literate Bengali child's mind. For those who have gone on to higher education he has been the base; for those who did not go beyond the primary level, due to poverty (that is, most people in Bengal) this book presents an unrealisable ideal and an indictment. It is interesting to note that in a country with a strong tradition of oral culture and traditional schooling of madrasas, tols and chatuspathis, Vidyasagar (this honorific title means 'The Ocean of Knowledge') only legitimises as education that which is both written and conducted in a classroom under the supervision of a teacher. The absolute insistence on this reflects both an anxiety about it, as well as the prescriptions for being 'good' and leading a 'good' life. The other virtues that are stressed are work-ethic, obedience, an ability to repeat instructions and, possibly, in future, to give command. But surely it is really docility, obedience and

---

36   Ibid., p. 19.

memorisation that distinguish Gopal, and his ability to be comfortable with hierarchy. These are ideal traits for becoming the obedient servants of British capital and the colonial state. There is nothing in Gopal which will make him rebel, or be able to take any initiative. Knowing his place in the chain of command, he will be a good white-collar worker or a second-level administrator. But, of course, his approved existence, his education, will always mark him out as a gentleman, he will be superior to most people (who are pre-literate) in his society. He will fulfil the conditions of his double location, of being ruled and becoming a small part of the ruling apparatus, in the great scheme of colonial capitalism.

In this textbook and many others, there is a message that to be a gentleman one must have an institutional, formal education, and to be without that kind of education is to be nobody. Schools organised the lives of middle class children, and as Philip Aries points out in his *Centuries of Childhood*, a separate period of childhood, boyhood and youth came into being which was set apart solely for instruction for profession.[37] Among the middle classes children and grown-ups did not accomplish together the main business of making a living, or of taking instruction at home in parental occupations, nor learning mainly by listening and memorising rather than by reading. Discrediting the previous practices, there arose a new formal school system, the main purpose of which was to teach ideas which were in keeping with a bourgeois society, and a serviceable amount of English. Those who could not avail this were performing manual and menial tasks. Their world-view, social practices, learning methods and content of knowledge, the language and discourse were all very different from those of the formally instructed. Peasants and *bhadralok* stood for the country and the city, for lower and upper classes, the ruled and the ruler, and even when the former came to the city as workers, and after many years of slum-living their children picked up a little formal education, the gap did not close. This country-city gap, and class gap, in Bengal between the middle (and upper) class and the so-called 'people' – meaning the poor – is not only one of money, but of a different language, systems of meaning, of social practices. It started in the nineteenth century and continues to this day – and even though in Vidyasagar's textbook formal education is portrayed not blatantly as a tool for social mobility, the status implication of mental labour and the ethical content of the lessons both create and exacerbate the class gap and shape the common sense of the class.

It is not surprising that it is from among the children of the Permanent Settlement gentry, who could rely on vast amounts of unearned income through

---

37   Aries 1962.

rent, or even from indigo plantations, that the idea of a non-instrumentalist education arose. The idea of 'educating' the faculties, activating the whole soul of the child, indeed the romantic, Rousseauesque/Reynoldsian child (the age-of-innocence brand), also of European origin, was mainly the literary gift of the very rich and secure Tagore family in its third generation of mercantile and landed wealth. One turns for this to Rabindranath Thakur, who started a 'national' school with ancient Indian ideals on the one hand, and on the other, with the European sentimental notion of the child. Other than establishing his ashram and school, Shantiniketan or Visva-Bharati ('Abode of Peace' and 'The World University'), he wrote numerous poems and books of poems on childhood – for example, *Shishu* (The Child), *Shishu Bholanath* (The Child Bholanath). and for children, such as *Katha O Kahini* (Legends and Stories), etc. – and the primer *Sahaj Path* (Easy Reading) for his own students. In an extraordinarily beautiful language, with an uncanny simplicity, precision, yet imaginative evocation, Rabindranath wrote the texts for his little readers with respect and delicacy. The texts are beautifully illustrated by one of the most renowned artists of the Bengal nationalist school of art – Nandalal Bose. And yet many of these imaginative pieces of prose, and some of the poems, are so neatly contained within an upper-class perception of the world that the world of the everyday life or daily work, which is continuously illustrated and observed, becomes a wealthy child's reverie as he daydreams at the window watching the others at work. In fact the life of work or physical effort reaches this child only as a rumour or beautiful images of toil, or services that the servants immediately provide. Let us look at a few passages, which in Bengali are unsurpassed cameos of beauty for the simplest use of languages:

> The day lengthens. The sun is hot over open and wide fields. From time to time gusts of wind raise a dust curtain in the far distance. The gardener Chuni draws water from the well, and the dove coos – coo, coo.[38]

Or,

> It is morning. Here comes the washerman. That is Loka the washerman. He lives at Gorabazar. His little baby is very plump, with round cheeks.
> There is his pet donkey. He has a bundle on his back. Open it and see. There are dhotis, shirts, socks, saris and who knows what else!
> His uncle sells thread, sells wool. His uncle sells bouquets of flowers.

---

38   Thakur 1977, p. 36. My translation.

> Do you know where the washerman washes? There, in that shallow, small pond. The water there is very muddy.[39]

These pieces do draw the child's attention to the world of labour, but with a distinct assumption that the child is superior to it, in fact has never needed to know it as his/her own activity. It speaks of the washerman with a casualness and distance of a social observer. This washerman could never be the relative of that child, and what would be familiar to any Bengali speaker is that this washerman is mentioned only by his first name, without any surname or honorific appellative. He is also spoken of without an honorific pronoun. This is only done for social inferiors and children, and a child in a middle-class family, who cannot address a person even six months older than himself without an older kinship term, is here expected to show no such regard or respect for a much older man. The child is clearly the master, and in text after text, either she/he is being conformed in that role or being taught it. Sometimes the lesson is more effective because the child is outside the frame of the text, like in the first, so that there is a sense of timelessness and non-specificity about it, which legitimates it as simply 'the way things are'.

The purpose of analysing the primers is to point out the class upbringing of children through education and to point out that literacy, formalisation or institutionalisation of education, combined with the actual content of the lessons, create and re-affirm a perception that ineluctably helps a class to organise itself, and in inter-class terms. A Bengali middle class is a mere abstraction without these forms and contents of social relations, and they in turn distinguish them from those who are not constructed through these particular practices and ideas, and are in no position to perpetuate them. This fact has a very important bearing for the purpose of studying politics and cultural activities of Bengal in either the nineteenth century or now. The terms and forms of class and their relations which were put in place then, continue to operate even now.

We can see clearly from the above discussion that moral and ideological attempts, along with everyday social practices of the family, assumptions about gender, formal education, etc., can all be seen as a part of the social organisation of class. What we have seen so far is a process of self-formation among the middle classes of Bengal, who like the ruling classes anywhere, embark on a particular kind of bourgeois project. To label and dismiss it as comprador consciousness – a mixture of voluntarism, opportunism and greed – does not add

---

39   Ibid., p. 46.

much to our knowledge of class formation. As with the discussion on all other instances of class formation, so in the colonial-imperialist context, the social being and consciousness of a class must be analysed both from the point of view of its ontology (i.e., its formation or the objective moment) and epistemology (i.e., how it sees the world and itself, or the subjective moment). Then the structural determinations and subjective creativity both become irreducible terms in understanding class and class politics.

To speak in terms of self-activity or the creation of a social subjectivity by any colonial middle class is not a current practice. The concept of comprador bourgeoisie, which is far more prevalent, dismisses such an exploration as a useless exercise in a study of class politics. But this view of class formation anywhere confers upon a class the status of class objects rather than subjects. It is primarily a behaviourist rather than a formational and relational way of studying class, and obscures from us the fact that in the case of Bengal the middle classes worked up for themselves a bourgeois social and political project, with various components of consciousness. To see the local bourgeois classes solely as puppets of the foreign bourgeoisie might serve the purpose of a deserved condemnation, but it still does not answer questions regarding the nature of class-consciousness or those of political agency in class struggle. In fact we are robbed of the politically indispensable concept of people as the subject *in* (not only *of*) history. And yet, even in the context of revolutionary national movements, the concept of the comprador has put a tremendous emphasis on the will and formative power of the external agent of the imperialist power, and underestimated the social subjectivity of classes in the third world. In his essay on 'National Liberation and Culture' Amilcar Cabral, for example, offers us a corrective in a discussion regarding the formation of a collaborationist, 'comprador' population in the context of the struggle in Guinea-Bissau. According to him:

> The experience of colonial domination shows that, in the effort to perpetuate exploitation, the coloniser not only creates a system to repress the cultural life of the colonised people: he also provokes and develops the cultural alienation of a part of the population, either by so-called assimilation of indigenous people, or by creating a social gap between the indigenous elites and the popular masses. As a result of this process of dividing or of deepening the divisions in the society, it happens that a considerable part of the population, notably the urban or peasant *petite bourgeoise*, assimilates the coloniser's mentality, and ignores or looks down upon their cultural values. This situation, characteristic of the majority of colonised intellectuals, is consolidated by increases in the social priv-

ilege of the assimilated or alienated group, with direct implications for the behaviour of individuals in this group in relation to the liberation movement.[40]

The full value of this statement by Cabral is going to be lost on anyone who subscribes to an objectivist notion of class and to this shallow notion of the comprador, and who is also uninterested in exploring the formation of bourgeois consciousness in a colonial context. Cabral however, while he realises, as above, the tremendous power of the coloniser's mechanism for producing collaboration and consent, also sees the subject status of the colonised which makes any revolutionary change or intervention possible. This is why he can speak of 'a reconversion of minds',[41] of a process of 're-Africanisation',[42] by which he means the possibility and actuality of the colonial middle class's participation in the African workers' and peasants' struggle. This, he feels, is both possible and necessary, since the colonial bourgeoisie, or the middle classes, are a divided entity, caught between being ruled and, conditionally, ruling. Even before they become fully 're-Africanised' or a part of the popular struggle (and in the case of India, only marginally becoming so), they often begin the first stage of a struggle, which involves the subaltern classes, in order to vindicate and assert themselves. As Cabral puts it:

> Hence, arises the apparent paradox of colonial domination; it is from within the indigenous *petite bourgeoisie*, a social class that grows from colonialism itself, that arise the first important steps towards a mobilising and organising the masses for the struggle against the colonial power.[43]

Whether or not we agree with Cabral's view regarding the petty bourgeoisie, it can still stand to reason that to assert this subject status of the different social classes, within the colonial terrain, is not to deny or underestimate the external determinations which are, *at the first instance*, extra-local, and continue always in part to be so.

---

40   Cabral 1973, p. 45. For an exhaustive discussion on class struggle in the context of imperialism and the national liberation movement, particularly as regards the positive and negative potential of the national bourgeoisie, see Fanon 1963, 1994 and other texts. For the colonial impact in terms of cultural imperialism, see wa Thiong'O 1983 and Césaire 1972.
41   Cabral 1973, p. 45.
42   Ibid., p. 45.
43   Ibid., p. 69.

The content of the social subjectivity of the Bengali middle classes decides the terms of the struggle they put forward in the fight against foreign capital, first as bourgeois nationalists and later as communists and socialists. These terms are created by the local social subjects and are simultaneously and inescapably in relation to and modulated by the deep and pervasive influence of the system which is being challenged. Partha Chatterjee, in his article 'Transferring a Political Theory', phrases this formational problem mainly in terms of 'transferring' and thus 'transcreating' the ideologies of 'modern' forms of nationalism, since the 'transfer' consists of importing European theories of nationalism and anthropology to a non-European cultural domain.[44] Though the problem is much deeper than that of a mere 'transfer of ideas', and indicates an overall social and economic reorganisation, one might agree with his following statement regarding the fusion and contradiction present in a colonial bourgeois consciousness:

> There is (consequently) an inherent contradictoriness in the nationalist thinking, because it reasons within a framework of knowledge whose representation structure corresponds to the very structure of power nationalist thought seeks to repudiate. It is this contradictoriness in the domain of thought which creates the possibilities for several divergent solutions to be proposed for the nationalist problematic.[45]

Even outside of the 'nationalist problematic', i.e. organised bourgeois politics in the daily social practices and ideas or intellectual syntheses, we find the same 'contradictions', the same underlying phenomenon, which Frantz Fanon, in *The Wretched of the Earth*, shows as creating 'false de-colonisation',[46] which ends the colonial phase at the door of neo-colonialism. The bourgeoisification of a national movement is not only a matter of clearly identifiable intentions but also that of common sense and a direction of history which create a practical saturation of the daily life of the colonised. Sumit Sarkar also points out the deep contradiction embedded in Rammohan Roy's attempts in achieving a 'break with the past'. According to Sarkar:

> This break, however, was of a limited and deeply contradictory kind. It was achieved mainly on the intellectual plane and not at the level of

---

44   Chatterjee 1986b, p. 120.
45   Ibid., p. 121.
46   Fanon 1963.

basic social transformation; and the 'renaissance' culture which Rammohan inaugurated inevitably remained confined within a Hindu-elitist and
colonial (one might almost add comprador) framework. What may be
loosely described as the negative aspects of the break became increasingly prominent as the nineteenth century advanced.[47]

Rammohan, Keshab Sen, Vidyasagar, to name a notable few among the social
reformers, could not go beyond the contradictions of their class, society and
personal lives. As a result of which limitations they were prompted both to
compromise and to compete.[48]

Juggling with such inconsistencies and pressures it is only to be expected
that the intelligentsia was deeply self-divided. Every aspect of life seemed
bifurcated, every practice had its antithesis, every aspiration its frustration.
Along with extreme rationalism, utilitarianism and positivism there was a high
degree of a reactive Hindu caste-based social ethics as well as local and foreign
forms of spiritualism. In fact, the aggregation of two opposing epistemologies
of materialism and idealism became the goal of many of the creators of the new
synthesis. The 'reconciliation of opposites', the project of conservative English romantics such as Wordsworth or Coleridge, was also the project of many
notable thinkers of Bengal in the nineteenth century.[49] Belief in science, technology and progress, in social mobility, and insistence on the individual's rights,

---

47   Sarkar 1985, p. 1.

48   Again the situation has been pointed out clearly by Sumit Sarkar in his assessment of Ram-
     mohan Roy: 'In India, full-scale colonial rule lasted the longest, and there was ample time
     for the growth of dependent and vested interests, the elaboration of hegemonic infra-
     structure producing 'voluntary' consent side by side with more direct politico-military
     domination. The English educated intelligentsia in its origins was very much a part of this
     system, nowhere more so than in Bengal; that it later turned to nationalist and even some-
     times Marxian ways did not automatically imply that the old presuppositions had been
     entirely and consciously overcome' (Ibid., p. 17).

49   The group of young men, known as Young Bengal (students of David Hare and later of
     Hindu College), and their intellectual and moral mentor Henry Vivian Derozio, must also
     be mentioned as exemplifying the same spirit of contradiction between defiance or inde-
     pendence and imitation. As Addy and Azad put it: 'Within the short space of his twenty-
     three years, Derozio himself absorbed the works of such major figures such as Adam
     Smith, Bentham, Berkeley, Locke, Mill, Hume and Kant, as well as the ideas of the French
     Revolution, principally Rousseau. Derozio gathered around him a constellation of young
     intellectuals who quickly rejected the intellectual pablum of Rammohan's *Brahmo Samaj*'
     (Azad and Addy 1973, p. 80). These young men 'cut their own way through ham and beef
     and waded to liberalism through tumblers of beer', and Derozio as a 'corrupter of youth'
     was eventually dismissed from his teaching position. Though later they were to revert to
     the fold of hinduism and Brahmoism, or resort to christianity and less radical politics.

all developed along with different forms of spirituality. Theosophy and science existed in the same person, as in the case of Jagadish Chandra Bose, a most notable Indian scientist who worked with photosynthesis, who was also a follower and a friend of the theosophist Annie Besant.

We can conclude this study of the process of formation of class subjectivity and its double-edged content for the Bengali colonial bourgeoisie or middle classes with a brief look at an archetypical figure of the nineteenth century. The case of Madhusudan Dutt exemplifies both the double-bind and the double politico-cultural possibility of the Bengali middle class or its intelligentsia. Born in Jessore, Bengal (in 1820) to a wealthy landowner's family, and sent to Calcutta for higher education, Madhusudan Dutt was completely seduced by the colonial culture. Loosely associated with the Young Bengal group, an admirer of Byron, Shakespeare, Tom Payne etc., Madhusudan's early life is a study in imitative behavior. Less than a hundred years after the takeover by the East India Company, it is amazing to see the degree of absorption of Western culture and self and social denigration practised by people such as him or many of his companions. This self-denigration was frequently published in the coloniser's language, and often in the form of the glorification of English as the carrier of a perfect civilisation. Despite the brief lamentation for the glory that was India in poems such as *Porus and Alexander*,

> But where, oh! where is Porus now?
> And where the noble hearts that bled
> For freedom – with the heroic glow
> In patient bosoms nourished[50]

it is in the public lecture entitled 'The Anglo-Saxon and the Hindu' that we get a better idea of one aspect of the state of the anglicised Bengali male mind:

> Volumes could be written on the glories of old India – volumes could be written on achievements in love and war of her heroic sons and lotus-eyed daughters. She is indeed an exhaustless mine for the poet, the Romanticist, the Historian, the Philosopher. But let me pass on ... The Hindu, as he stands before you, is a fallen being – once a green, a beautiful, tall, a majestical, a flowering tree; now – blasted by lightning! Who can call him to life?[51]

---

50   Dutt 1977, p. 466. My translation.
51   Ibid., p. 630.

Influenced by the formulation of the German organicist and romantic writers like Herder, whose historiography had reached Bengal, Madhusudan had concluded that, 'A nation, like a man, has its infancy, its youth, its manhood, its age',[52] and the Hindu was definitely 'aged' and 'senile' now. What then must be done to bring this Hindu to life? Madhusudan has an answer learnt from the books of missionaries and colonial emissaries of civilisation, to which he lends full support at this point in his life: 'Why has Providence given this queenly, this majestic land for a prey and a spoil to the Anglo-Saxon? Why? I say – it is the mission of the Anglo-Saxon to Christianise the Hindu ...'[53]

Since it was not possible to Christianise a whole population, at least it was to give the Hindu the tool of progress, poetry, science and civilisation – namely, the English language. No less than the most ardent anglicist of Britain, Madhusudan loved the English language. 'I acknowledge to you, and I need not blush to do so, that I love the language of the Anglo-Saxon'.[54] Madhusudan's excessive, almost violent anglicism and Europeanisation led to his personal conversion into Christianity, marriage with a British and later a French woman, an epic in English called *The Captive Lady* and numerous other English poems and pieces of prose.

But the other pole of his consciousness, which developed after the first imitative phase – that of a man living first in colonial Bengal and Madras, and later for years in England studying for a law degree at the Inner Temple – was that of an anti-colonialist. Though he earlier ignored the advice of Drinkwater Bethune to write in Bengali, his later need was to express himself in Bengali. Initially he moved beyond English to other European languages. Reading first European literature through English, he went on to become fluent in French and Italian, and also read Hebrew and Latin, together with Sanskrit, and had some working knowledge of German. Along with this he developed an interest in European nationalism, such as in Garibaldi, and bourgeois revolution as manifested in the French Revolution. Giving up slavish imitation, he introduced into Bengali poetry and drama innovations which he synthesised from European and ancient Indian literature. In the sonnet form of Petrarch he proclaimed his return to his mother tongue.

O Bengal, your treasury holds innumerable jewels ignoring which, foolishly, besotted by others' wealth,
I wandered abroad, in exile, begging for a living, in an evil hour.

---

52   Ibid., p. 631.
53   Ibid., p. 637.
54   Ibid., p. 638.

> Spent many days, shunning joy.
> Surrendering body and soul to hunger and sleeplessness.
> Worshipped the unpardonable –
> Wallowed in algae, forgetting the lotus grove.
> In a dream at last she came, your muse and spoke: 'Dear Child, your
> mother's chest is full of riches. Why then are you today in this beggar's
> dress? Return, O foolish one, return then to your home'. Obeying her com-
> mand, I discovered in time, the mine of my mother tongue, jewel-filled.[55]

This sonnet and the vast body of poetry that he left behind in epic and epis-
tolary forms, quatrains, terza rima and blank verse, were all new attempts –
for the first time in the history of Bengali poetry and drama. They showed in
the later Madhusudan the obverse side of the man who wrote once – 'I love
the Anglo-Saxon language ...' In an epic called *The Death of Meghanada*, he
offered a reinterpretation of the ancient epic *Ramayana*, making it an epic of
invasion and reversing the general pattern of good and evil.[56] It is not surprising
then, that it should be this Madhusudan Dutt who would translate Dinabandhu
Mitra's play in support of the indigo rebels, *Nil Darpan* (The Indigo Mirror), and
leave behind a wealth of plays and farces that challenged the conventions and
norms of all kinds of oppression both foreign and local.

With the example of Madhusudan Dutt, with its mixture of local and European values, practices and literary forms and ideas, and its decisive turn to
the creation of a national culture, we can conclude this essay on class and
political implications of cultural and social practices. The political, social and
cultural understanding of the Bengali middle classes originating in the terrain
of colonial capital was shaped through practices and ideas that came from the
bourgeois world of the west. Though distinctly rooted in their indigenous history and social organisation, in short, a whole field of predispositions, they
distinctly operated within the zone of derivative discourses and social prac-

---

55   Ibid., p. 159.
56   In his hands the traditional epic's version of the evil demons of Lanka, dark and non-
     Aryan, became the dark heroes of a helpless island, fighting the fair-skinned, crafty and
     cunning Aryan invaders. But the craft of the white invader Rama, his corrupting influ-
     ence, creates collaborators among the demons and brings into Lanka's city gates the Trojan
     horse of destruction. It is a dark, 'uncivilised' demon, prince Meghanada, who is the hero
     of Madhusudan's epic, as opposed to Rama in the Ramayana. For the collaborator, who
     is someone he understands, he has only scorn, as young Meghanada says to his betraying
     relative Bibhishana: '... now I know how they entered the palace. So uncle, that is your
     doing, you show the thief the way into your home ...' (*The Death of Meghanada*, canto 7,
     in ibid., p. 87).

tices. And yet the incoming discourse and practices originated in a mode of production, languages and worldviews which were not only alien to Bengal, but also at odds with it both in terms of power of assertion and contradiction with the existing social and cultural life. The work of the new classes, which were not organic to the older mode and were yet a part of an indigenous culture and history and language, lay in coping creatively with the new determining forces that impacted upon them. And either negatively or positively, or even synthetically, they tried to create forms that were meaningful and serviceable to themselves. They were not simply overdetermined by their pre-colonial history and culture, but insofar as a social formation is continuous and not liable to amnesia, they developed a constitutive relationship to both these indigenous and foreign elements which helped to articulate themselves as new classes. They developed a mode of doing and being, as the colonial era evolved, which provided them with a social physiognomy quite specific to themselves and distinct from other classes – both in the city and the countryside. When we contrast the nineteenth-century Bengali upper class society with its counterpart in eighteenth-century Bengal, the rapidity in the reworking of the social and intellectual space seems astronomical. The difference is so huge that one wonders at the historical necessity, the pressure and the resourcefulness with which this was achieved. This was both a matter of choice and need – or a need produced within a compulsion of the actuality of colonialism – which was met both consciously and spontaneously. It illustrates the truth of Marx's statement that people make history, but not as they please. It would appear that the formational drive that had plunged the 18th century in various struggles at different levels, of which the tragedy of Plassey (1757) may be seen as an index, continued into the colonial era – though within conditions of subordination. But particularly at the socio-cultural level, being firmly suppressed at the level of economy and politics, there were relatively autonomous and energetic formations. By the time the nineteenth century ended a sop of a syncretism, if not a synthesis, amounting to a kind of common sense, was achieved, with its own fragmentation and contradictory diversities. Both ruled and ruling, a kind of a Janus at birth, the colonial middle classes through their reorganisation of cultural and intellectual life captured moments of class experiences and desires.

CHAPTER 26

Language and Liberation: A Study of Political Theatre in West Bengal

Thus we must detach the phenomena from the form in which they are immediately given and discover the intervening links which connect them to their core, their essence. In so doing, we shall arrive at an understanding of their apparent form and see it as the form in which the inner core necessarily appears. It is necessary because of the historical character of the facts, because they have grown in the soil of ... society. This twofold character, the simultaneous recognition and transcendence of immediate appearance is precisely the dialectical nexus.[1]

∙∙
∙

1 The Indian People's Theater Association

In 1944 a theatre movement called the Indian People's Theatre Association was born. It was a novel phenomenon because it was organised on a national scale, it was non-commercial and, most importantly, an attempt to use culture for political mobilisation and to raise consciousness about politics and society. Culture itself was seen as organisable and a site for class struggle rather than as a matter of individual creativity and spontaneity. Created under the auspices of the united Communist Party of India, carried forward by the massive participation of the urban intelligentsia, this movement largely shaped the course of modern Indian theatre. Today's 'group theatre movements' or progressive theatre all acknowledge its legacy. The birth was dramatic: in 1944 in a working-class district of Bombay, 'the red capital of India', the IPTA held its inaugural conference and announced its motto with a great flourish 'The People's Theatre Stars the People'.

With the arrival of this new protagonist, 'the people', onto the theatrical stage the IPTA also announced a change in the Indian political scene. The same prot-

---

1 Lukács 1971, p. 8.

agonist 'the people' had also become the new revolutionary agent under the name of the proletariat as a combination of the urban working class and the landless and land-poor peasantry. The so-called 'natural' leaders of the people – landlords, the national bourgeoisie, and even the middle-class intelligentsia – had to yield place to this class at a theoretical level. Communist theories learnt from Marx, Lenin and the Bolsheviks had no provision for any other revolutionary hero.

This new communist politics totally radicalised the theatre scene in undivided Bengal. The focus of theatre shifted from the commercial stage to the amateur political stage and for the first time since the inception of Bengali theatre in the 1860s peasants and workers walked the boards of the stage in non-menial roles, as the organisers of their own struggles. Stages no longer reverberated with the heroic rantings and tragic declamations of the last kings and princes of India. In plays such as Bijan Bhattacharya's *The New Harvest* (*Nabanna*) or *The Confession* (*Jabanbandi*) a definite attempt was made to show the peasant's progress from powerlessness to power. From being portrayed as victims of the 1943 famine they were transformed into the members of a peasant collective who promised a fair fight to their oppressors in the next round. The same spirit, sharpened through the struggles of the Telengana[2] and the Bengal share-croppers (*Tebhaga Andolan*), found its expression in songs such as:

> Watch out, take care,
> Sharpen your scythes,
> Brothers, guard your rice and pride,
> For
> We will never again give up
> This rice
> That we have sowed with our blood.

These were new songs and plays about new times and new politics. And they needed, and were couched in, a new language. The Bengali of the middle class – the gentlemen, the academics, and the litterateurs – no longer sufficed; a different Bengali was resorted to – a Bengali spoken by the millions in the countryside, in the city slums. The middle-class activist in search of a language to expose exploitation and to give a voice to the new hero, 'the people', turned to the 'dialects' of different areas and the languages of the streets, the slums and different occupations.

---

2   Telengana was a peasant movement (1948–51), involving two to three million people, organised mainly around demands for the redistribution of land.

Popular language became a matter of deep concern for the IPTA particularly as its mainstay were members of the urban intelligentsia who engaged in a representational and educative politics. After all, 'the people's theatre' which 'starred' the people did so with the help of those who were formally educated and Westernised, equally removed from the countryside and the city slums. What were presented as people's stories were in most cases neither created by the people nor narrated in their own voices. It was the middle-class playwrights, with sympathetic observations of the miseries of the people, who wrote the plays, and it was middle-class actors and actresses who put on tattered clothes, carried begging bowls or sticks and spears, and spoke in dialects carefully erasing the traces of the 'proper' or 'high' Bengali they had spoken all their lives. And yet given the time and the embryonic state of communist organisation, the situation was unavoidable. Consequently, the problem of the medium of communication assumed large proportions since the project of this new political theatre was to be easily understood by the people, to represent popular reality both to them and the middle class, and to legitimise popular-folk forms as culture. This project groped for a new aesthetic and voiced a demand for a 'realist' theatre; outside and unaware of the European marxist debate over 'realism' the term was used to indicate the creation of an 'authentic picture' of popular life and contemporary reality. Language was an indisputable element in this effort at 'authenticity'.

In conveying the popular reality this new theatre sought to bridge the gap between the rural and the urban worlds as well as that between the middle and working classes. It sought to convey to the middle class in particular some knowledge about how the subaltern classes lived and the severity of their day-to-day existence. The task of producing a realist art in this context often meant that of a faithful description of the surface of life rather than a dramatisation of social analysis. As such the new theatre dismantled the palatial settings of the old stage and put up tin-can huts and torn burlap backdrops, replaced their tin swords with hammers and sickles, and filled the soundtracks with beggars' cries, the sounds of whiplashes and slogans rather than songs of courtesans. The dialogue naturally followed suit and the declamatory, rhetorical prose or blank verse were substituted with rural speech, street or factory talk, or even broken sentences. The result seems to have been particularly convincing to the middle class. The newspaper reviewers of *The New Harvest*, for example, and the established commercial actors, were all equally struck by the novelty and the lifelikeness of this new 'beggars' opera. It was felt that the use of new types of language was the main graphic tool for bringing the people's reality into the middle-class world. The use of dialect in particular was the hallmark of authenticity of the 'real' portrayal of the life of the 'real' people of Bengal.

While this equation of realism with a 'slice-of-life' approach to reality provided the middle class with a sense of the other kinds of lives lived by the poor, it left unanswered and unposed some major questions regarding analytical and explorative ways of uncovering the social relations that structured those lives. It also took 'reality' for granted, blocked questions regarding the methods of this 'realism' and equated a 'real' portrayal with a naturalistic mode of depiction. It often diverted the cultural activists towards an empiricist rather than an analytical and historical-materialist approach. Preoccupied with an immediate event or an image, the playwrights often left no dramatic provision for the extra-local character of the social forces that informed them. *The New Harvest* (1944), for example, while providing a vivid portrayal of the sufferings of a famine-stricken, once well-to-do peasant household, gives us little or no indication of the social forces that structure and surround these lives.[3] Nor is the devastation produced by the famine of 1943 (one and a half to three million are estimated to have died in it) made comprehensible by the presence of a few hoarders, black marketers, and brothel keepers.

This uncontextualised famine assumes the character of natural cataclysm which a careful build-up of dialogue in dialect, capturing moments of suffering, rage, and despair, only enhances rather than historicises. The concentration of the playwrights and the production (with special light effects, a revolving stage, and naturalist makeup and acting techniques) is too much on the surface, on the empirical immediate, which, of course, makes the last scene about collectivisation and militancy seem empty and rhetorical. It lacks the dynamism of a social process and becomes iconic rather than political, since organisation cannot happen 'in general' but must be context-specific. And yet this play, produced out of a real sympathy for the plight of the people, and unique in attempting to assign to the people an initiator's role, with all its shortcomings was seen by the middle class as the people's own version of the 1943 famine. When we ponder over the reasons for such a belief we can only come to the conclusion that it was due to the creation of a stereotypical environment of poverty and a dialogue in dialect. The attention of the audience was also riveted to the high display of feelings, which could be recognised by the middle-class audience as being noble enough or 'pathetic' enough to be worth heightening. The naturalism of language completes the illusion of reality. A lifelike copy seemed to be the aim of the producers, and the audience responded to this by finding in the play the 'real thing'. But because questions regarding the social construction of reality, or the mode called 'realism', were yet to be asked, it remained

---

3   Bhattacharya 1943.

unnoticed that often what passed for the peasants' reality was the middle-class version of the rural world. These plays fulfilled certain norms or expectations of the middle-class audience, which is why perhaps the reviewers could talk about the lead actor as being 'more of a peasant than a peasant could be'. Through the naturalism of acting and language the issue shifted from politics not only to imitation, but often also to the imitation of an idealised or stereotypical version of popular reality.

While such idealisation came from the communist movement and its overall social impact, the stereotypes of class, gender, age, good and evil mostly came from the conventions of the bourgeois commercial stage and petty-bourgeois or middle-class social ethos. Large numbers of the audience and most of the cultural producers were brought up within these theatrical conventions and this ethos. The theatrical conventions had naturalised certain stereotypical forms of characterisation and emotions. Neither was the influence of the English stage and dramatic tradition negligible in the development of these stage conventions. Overall they encoded the morality and the world view of a semi-feudal, semi-bourgeois urban population, not that of the working class or the peasantry. This largely unconscious legacy of what was once 'the theatre', in conjunction with an imitative realism, generated a form and a content which exposed the new theatre to the danger of subordinating the culture and politics of the very people they wished to help or idealised by offering a decontextualised, embourgeoisified version of their story. Again we may look at Bhattacharya's *The New Harvest* for an example. Here, in the character of the old peasant 'patriarch' Pradhan, Shakespeare's King Lear receives his peasant incarnation. Put through the trials of famine, fire, and flood he rises to great sonorous declamations of rage and despair. His pathos and all that he declaims provide the audience more with echoes of Shakespeare than the voice of the Bengali peasantry. That it is in a dialect does not change this, though the dialect lends a touch of the authenticity of peasant life or character. Other examples of conventionalisation and nonpopular ethics and world view may be found in the portrayals of women and children: quaint scenes of domesticity and moments of pathos introduced through dying, lisping, precocious babes and frequent weeping. The repudiation of these conventions does not signify that the peasantry or the slum-dwellers have no personal lives, no hearts and minds; but rather indicates what moments of their lives are selected to be put on view, or what is projected into their lives by the middle class, and to what extent these are in tune with the middle class's experience and conception of theatre and morality. It would often seem that with other clothes, other settings, and in another language for dialogue, many of these scenes could fit into the genre of drawing-room comedies. It also seems as though the middle-class

progressives measured the 'humanity' of the poor in terms of their approximation to middle-class morality and emotional life. The idea seems to have been
to point out how much like 'us' they were; that they too laughed, cried, loved,
and lamented like 'us'. Without disputing a genuine claim for an emotional life
for the subaltern classes one could ask the question – 'But do they laugh, cry,
sigh, and lament about the same things or love or die in the same way?' And
if they did not, would they be any less 'human'? Must not one avoid the values
and practices of the middle class becoming universalised into the human practice? Is the creation of the 'other' simply a matter of likeness and imitation –
sounding something like the other? Dialect, occupational languages, broken
sentences, stage props, lighting, and naturalistic acting may all contrive to lull
our minds while satisfying our eyes and ears.

The minds of the colonial middle-class audiences can also be lulled, for
instance by the echoes of Shakespeare, by allusions to a knowledge of 'tragic' conventions; the echoes may divert the audience from the fact that this
is not a mythic, structural use of Shakespeare but a reduction of a dramatic
text to a story, a set of typical speeches and fixed theatrical devices. The plays
of Aeschylus or Sophocles, or of Shakespeare for that matter, have been often
reworked or re-elaborated as myths rather than as stories told through historically specific stage conventions. Sartre in *The Flies*, Brecht in the retelling
of *Timon of Athens*, Aimé Césaire in *The Tempest*, Athol Fugard in *The Island*,
to name a few playwrights, have reworked certain basic themes to represent
Nazism, capitalism, imperialism, and apartheid respectively. But *in The New
Harvest* the thematic inner core, the mythic element of *King Lear*, has been
bypassed in favour of a ranting, pathetic emotionalism. The aim here seems to
be a piece that rouses the audience's emotions, not a comprehensible presentation of the peasant's world.

2   Group Theater in Bengal

The tradition of IPTA continues in the cities of India. The Group Theatre Movement of Calcutta works within this tradition and abounds with plays about the
Bengali peasantry. As before, fewer plays are written or performed about the
urban working class, the slum or pavement dwellers than about the peasantry.
And in all this the same kind of problem that faced the IPTA nearly forty years
ago continues to haunt the world of theatre. Since the 1940s the urban progressive or left-wing culture milieu is that of middle-class performers and writers
trying to enlighten their own class, exposing horror stories from the countryside
or the slums. The practice of an imitative realism also continues in all good faith

and political intention. Plays abound with attempts to reproduce an immaculate surface of life which comes into direct conflict within the play with a kind of 'iconic realism', which presents us with the peasant or the woman of the people, the worker, etc. This characterisation is not so much a Lukácsian 'type', a representative class character as he actually exists in the present conjuncture of social relations in Bengal, but more a set of fixed, static, idealised images of who he should be, given an abstract formulation of revolutions. As imitative realism suffers from an empiricist approach so this icon-building of workers and peasants suffers from an idealism and a political prescriptiveness. In this, revolution is not seen as a developing social process produced by certain historical classes beginning from where they are, but as an event which could be approximated by only the perfect character types. Even though this idealisation came about as a result of a change in the political perspective it moved away from the ground of history, took on an ideological character, and complemented the empirical fixity of naturalist description. Since here as well a process-oriented view of society and revolution was lacking, and yet a revolution or resistance was integral to the plot, these iconic representations accomplished this as a part of the idealisation itself. They are revolutionary because they are who they are, not because of, and in the way of, who they can become. They 'embody' class-consciousness rather than 'become' class conscious, much in the manner in which icons embody holiness. Hence they accomplish the task of resistance, as indeed they must, since in terms of the narrative development the play begins from the last victorious scene.

The use of dialect or appropriate language, however, lends these iconic idealisations the touch of typicality, and often, as for instance in Utpal Dutt's play *Titu Mir*, serves as a substitute for class analysis. In this play the peasant hero Titu Mir (the term 'peasant' here includes rich farmers such as Titu) stages an idealised uprising against the foreign invaders and dies a martyr's death. The historical Titu Mir as a member of a landed class, the social relations of contemporary Bengal, and the colonialist penetration are nowhere to be found, but instead we have a play in universalist terms outside of the frame of 'mere' history. Titu Mir and his followers as well as the foreign invaders are inflated beyond life size. One set was born to make heroic sacrifices and the other to dominate; they embody the primal forces of good and evil. As is common with this kind of play, exploitation or domination remains utterly non-specified or undifferentiated, making it impossible to grasp the real political process. There is about as much real political dynamism in this play as quickly shuffling through a pack of heroic pictures! It is basically a series of static images gaining momentum through a successive placement. Here the role of language is not only important in masking an ideological approach to politics, but also in distancing it into patriotism. This play, because it is placed in a distant past, has less of a clash between mimetic and iconic types of realism.

But outside of the naturalist use of language and the political rhetoric of the prescriptive ideological mode there has also developed a use of language that displays and clarifies the social relations of domination. Instead of a sustained use of a dialect which has a greater chance of presenting a middle-class version of reality than that of the working class or the peasantry, the playwrights often combine different types of speech to encode the different class views and relations. This method, instead of drawing the audience into an illusion of reality, distances the viewer and facilitates a clearer observation and a critical perspective. On the one hand, the typicality of the speech with its particular use of idioms, images, and constructions gives a sense of the group in itself, its cohesive community consciousness; on the other hand, the presence of other types of speech makes of language an area of class struggles as well. A good example of this is the use of language in a play by Arun Mukherjee called *The Tale of Marich* (*Marich-samvad*). Here Marx's statement about history as being the history of class struggles is dramatised over a long span of time. The narrative time ranges from the epic days of the *Ramayana* to the present, moving from the legendary world of the man-god Rama and the demon king Ravana of Sri Lanka to the streets of contemporary Calcutta. In between Mukherjee provides a detour through the United States of America. At each phase he presents an individual's response to the pressures exerted by the state and the ideological hegemony of the ruling classes, until he reaches the possibility of class struggle through an individual's growing class-conscious response. In each phase the play emphasises the particularity of the situation while containing it within an overall framework of domination and response. In this way, each scene which would have been impossible out of its own historical setting is also dovetailed into the next one. Much of this dialectical complexity is realised through the use of different types of speech.

The play starts in a Calcutta street where a street entertainer – a juggler/ magician/ singer/player – is drumming up his audience with a high sales pitch. Like all conmen he promises the impossible. He claims to be able to resurrect the mythic figures of the *Ramayana*, but also, in attempting to please other tastes, he promises scenes that appeal to modern sensibilities. He promises scenes from America as well as from the low life of Bengal. The play moves through a hilarious mixture of these levels creating confusions and mix-ups, but also using these confusions to achieve a clarity and continuity. The confusion created by the frequent mistakes made by the ruling classes about their different parts (sliding mid-speech from the dialogue of the mythic tyrant Ravana to that of the state department or CIA official) also serves as a basis for political clarity. Similarities and dissimilarities in the historical particularities build towards a resolution where all the subordinated characters get out of the magician-dramatist's directorial control and refuse to die in the service of or at the hands of the ruling classes. The shift in the use of speech indicates alteration without the use of curtains, changes of scenes, or situations. The epic characters (who frequently feature in the popular theatrical form known as *jatra*) speak in a highly declamatory blank verse with which the audience is familiar from its experience at the *jatras* and the other Bengali plays. The exhortation by the demon king Ravana to Marich, the turncoat pacifist demon who is pining away for Rama the man-god, well known to all Bengalis from the *Ramayana*, now takes on the tone of political harangue by the Congress (nationalist) leaders as they preach patriotism to the poor. This is further emphasised by the litany of patriotism delivered by a priest figure in mock-Sanskrit (Bengali spoken with Sanskrit endings). The contemporary relevance of this scene is further emphasised as the actor in Ravana's part confuses his cue and immediately descends to dialect. Now transformed into the landlord's bailiff he browbeats the ex-retainer of the landlord, a landless peasant called Isvar, to break a few heads during the rent collection. For both Marich and Isvar individual indebtedness, gratefulness to a good patron, patriotism, or the good of the village (identified with the good of the landlord) are used to prod them to identify with their oppressors.

The scope extends even further, laterally to the United States, rather than into the past, where a lackey of the state department harasses a liberal upper-middle-class young man to go to Vietnam to fight for his president and his country. As the patriotic injunction of President Kennedy booms through the auditorium – 'Ask not what your country can do for you but what you can do for your country' – the reply comes from the young man Gregory in a monotonous, dead Bengali of the right-wing daily newspaper *Ananda Bazar Patrika*. More of the same is continued by the state department official. This is strongly contrasted by the peasant speech of Isvar and the half-gentrified dialect of the bailiff, whose speech betrays class origin and present political affiliations. The audience is further entertained by the lumpenised street Bengali of the magician. The issue of understanding reality is no longer posed in terms of imitation, or lifelikeness, but of an overall dynamic version of the social relations that structure domination of different kinds. This particular use of language as integral to the narrative breaks the bourgeois dichotomy between form and context. There is no attempt here to present the poor peasant's world or worldview by trying to step into his shoes through an act of empathy, but instead to display the relations of inequality that entangle the different classes. There is a clear shift here from aiming at portraying the authentic peasant experience (which the middle class is structurally, existentially barred from doing) to politicising a problem no matter where it is located.

Other than using language politically in some plays, Bengali theatre has a remarkable instance of dramatisation of the issue of the politics of language. *The Tin Sword (Tiner Talwar)* by Utpal Dutt is a play about the necessity of a new aesthetic. It includes in its purview the problem of language as a medium of representation and communication, not only with middle-class audiences but with the people themselves. The first scene centres on the encounter between Benimadhab Chatujye (a drunk director of a commercial theatre) and a street sweeper who is also a latrine cleaner. The drunk Benimadhab is accosted by this character from the lower depths, who sticks out his head from a manhole and throws some dirt at the brahmin to affront him and attract his attention. Benimadhab, however, takes no offence at this, and instead gets into a conversation with him, trying to convince the sweeper to visit the theatre. At this point the following interchange takes place:

> Beni: ... so you don't go to plays?
> Sweeper: Why should I? What's in it for the likes of us anyway? The babus (gentlemen) will live it up at the theatres, screw around with women from the market, and use language that we can't understand. (*Pours out some more dirt.*) Better to watch the dancing girls or ramlila in our slum. This peacock Mayur play or whatever that you mentioned – what's that about?
> Beni: Mayurbahan, you see, is the prince of Kashmir. The story ...
> Sweeper: Damn the prince! Why do you have to do this? Get all dressed up in your red and blue clothes and tinsels, paint your faces and play at kings and princes? After all this education why must you tie a tin sword around your waist and act childish?
> Beni: Tin sword? Childish?
> Sweeper: Why can't you dress as who you are? Can't you see that there is a lot of dirt on you?

Acknowledging that 'there's a lot of dirt' on the middle class as a party to class exploitation, Utpal Dutt attempted to transform this tin sword of theatre, a plaything of the middle class and the entrepreneur, into a real sword, a revolutionary weapon. The use of language in this play is astounding in grasping the complexity that structures the sociocultural reality of a colonised middle class. He captures some of the existing contradictions in terms of dialect vs 'high' Bengali, colloquial vs formal Bengali, occupational language of the street vs academic Bengali, and finally in terms of English used by the educated 'Young

Bengal' confronted by the anticolonial Bengali of the national liberation movement. The issue of realism has moved very far away from its first groping phase.

In problematising some of the 'givens' of the earlier IPTA organisers the
group theatre movement has moved a step ahead. But this has been possible
because the IPTA has had a real impact on Indian theatre, and, however unsat-
isfactorily, has made the demand for a new realist aesthetic. It is not surprising
that this most conscious, unique play about language, reality, and politics – *The
Tin Sword* – comes from a playwright, actor, and director whose beginnings lie
in the IPTA. He and others have often considered it a political problem that the
middle class often stood in for the people. Even as long ago as the thirties the
Bengali poet Jatindranath Sengupta remarked in a satirical poem on the populism of the middle class:

> Remember, brothers,
> We are not peasants.
> We are the peasants' barristers.

This substitution was and remains as problematic as if Harriet Beecher-Stowe
or some other white American writer (no matter how sympathetic) were to
write about the 'authentic' black experience, or their Uncle Toms or Elizas were
to be seen as 'types' of the black American, or all black people were to be
presented as undifferentiated, stereotypical characters. When the oppressed
fight against using the oppressor's language and establish the legitimacy of
their own speech, the politics this process involves is radically different from
the one where members of the oppressing classes use the oppressed's language
to sympathetically mimic them into respectability. At that point even idealisation does not compensate for the harm done through the process. Not only
are we in danger of an illusion or a standing-in effect, but also the politics this
implies is, at its best, not brought beyond the immediate level of depiction
of misery. With a middle-class audience it might have some effect of sensitisation to poverty, though mainly of evoking an empty emotionalism; should
there actually be a popular audience, it would merely replay for them what they
already know. Both the slice-of-life approach and making an icon of a peasant
or a working-class hero seem singularly devoid of organisational implications.
A great deal more can be done by the progressive left-wing theatre activists by
placing themselves (in class terms) and their language into the plays. This may
liberate the political forces of theatre itself and lift it from an empiricism and
idealism, from liberal guilt or politics of sympathy into a real politics of class
struggle. Then with or without the use of dialect we might still attain a realism.

Nation and Class in Communist Aesthetics and the Theatre of Utpal Dutt

Political subjects in themselves do not make political theatre ... you can have a play dealing with racism, or sexism, or fascism, and if the subject is dealt with in, let's say, an Ibsen-like way, then the audience is left with nothing to do in working on the problem, you might just as well read about the subject in a newspaper. That is not political theatre.[1]

∴

In *Towards a Revolutionary Theatre* (TART) Utpal Dutt tries to develop a theory of revolutionary politics and theatre along the line of a specifically Indian and armed revolution. This line is one of balancing the relationship between communism and nationalism and their accommodation within a narrative and theatre form. To create a theatre based on that is the hallmark of political and theatrical realism for Utpal Dutt. He feels that the specificity and complexity of the state of class struggle in India is such that a political project in general and a political theatre project for India lie in conceiving the agent 'the people' as both a class entity and a non-class national cultural entity. A correct national liberation movement, according to Utpal Dutt, would also have to combine both – simulating a general national cultural movement as well as a class movement. For him correct party politics and political theatre could only be fashioned along Stalin's prescription for nationalist politics and a revolutionary national culture – that they should be national in form and socialist in content. This phrase in fact functions as a motto for his theatre, and it is in Stalin's essay, 'Marxism and the National Question', that we find the conceptual basis for Dutt's epic historical theatre and his guiding principle for constructing a communist movement in India.

More directly influential than Lenin's writings and debates in the Comintern on the same issue, Stalin's position in this document allows us an insight

---

1   Edward Bond interview in *Plays and Players*.

into the formative moment of an Indian Communist cultural as well as organisational stance. We can see how, from the IPTA (Indian People's Theatre Association) to now, political theatre of Bengal contends with the same issues in almost the same way. We can also see how the aesthetics and politics of representation of communism, from the CPSU (including Lukács' theories) to Utpal Dutt's theatre, are deeply rooted in the definition of a nation and the political strategies and goals outlined in this text.

We should begin with Stalin's definition of a nation:

> A nation is a historically constituted, stable community of people, formed on the basis of a common language, territory, economic life and psychological makeup manifested in a common culture.[2]

We can see that while conceptualising a nation, Stalin's stress is on the elements of commonality, rather than that of division. A nation is seen to be homogeneous, built on the ground of 'common culture'. It is not seen as a conflicted political entity – riven with class struggle for example – but rather as a 'stable community' which has been 'historically constituted' through a shared 'culture'. So while history and culture are important aspects of a nationalist politics, class is not even mentioned. The bases of nationalist politics are cultural rather than economic, and not connected to class exploitation, repression and discontentment. Nationalities or nations as such are discontented when cultural self-determination becomes impossible, 'because it [the nation] does not enjoy liberty of conscience (religious liberty)', for instance.[3] Politics of nationalism is then a politics that strictly busies itself with rights to self-determination on these 'super-structural' grounds.

But in a non-democratic and colonial/imperialist context such 'regional autonomy' or 'equal rights of nations' is impossible. In this situation the structural question of class – of politics based on local and foreign capital – becomes paramount and has to be waged before this historical cultural community of a nation can find its own free and equal expression. So what is possible for the minorities or nationalities in the context of a socialist republic such as the USSR is not possible in a colonised India. In such a situation the cultural, historical commonality of a nation, which exists independently from class politics, becomes the agenda for the local aspiring classes which fight foreign occupa-

---

2 Franklin 1972, p. 60.
3 Ibid., p. 80.

tion. If the bourgeois/landlord classes – the ruling classes – are in ascendancy in national politics, they articulate the nationalist (cultural) issues to their cause. Demands for a political and cultural autonomy become a way to strengthen a bourgeois-landlord hegemony. Class struggle of the proletariat and the peasantry is subsumed within bourgeois nationalism. As Stalin puts it:

> The bourgeoisie of the oppressed nation, repressed on every hand, is naturally stirred into movement. It appeals to its 'native folk' and begins to shout about the 'fatherland', claiming that its own cause is the cause of the nation as a whole. It recruits itself an army from among its 'countrymen' in the interest of … the 'fatherland'. Nor do the 'folk' always remain unresponsive to its appeals; they rally around its banner, the repression from above affects them too and provokes their discontent.[4]

And also:

> The strength of the national movement is determined by the degree to which the larger strata of the nation, the proletariat and the peasantry, participate in it.[5]

Stalin also outlines the nation as the condition under which bourgeois hegemony develops.

> … under the conditions of rising capitalism there is a struggle of the bourgeois classes among themselves. Sometimes the bourgeoisie succeeds in drawing the proletariat into the national movement, and then the national struggle externally assumes a 'nationwide' character. But this is so externally. In its essence it is always a bourgeois struggle, one that is to the advantage and profit mainly of the bourgeoisie.[6]

Stalin's statements regarding the situation when other class struggles are hijacked by the bourgeoisie for their own class power actually speak to the state of affairs in India. In fact Utpal Dutt, and other Progressive Writers' and Artists' Association and IPTA activists during and after the Indian independence, saw a similar process in action as the Indian National Congress rose to power. They also saw the communist movement failing itself and the people of India. They

---

4   Ibid., pp. 67–8.
5   Ibid., p. 68.
6   Ibid.

could agree with Stalin's view that, depending on 'the degree of development of class-antagonism, on the class-consciousness and degree of organisation of the proletariat [their Party]', it 'rallies to the banner of bourgeois nationalism' or does not.[7] They saw the bourgeois takeover being facilitated by 'diversions' created by the political persecutions carried on by the English rulers, because the attention 'of a large strata' was drawn away from 'social questions', to the ones 'common' to the proletariat and the bourgeoisie. Then arose notions such as 'harmony of interests' across classes, 'glossing over the class interest of the proletariat', resulting in 'intellectual enslavement of workers'.[8]

But whereas Stalin's essays gave an idea as to how nationalist movements should have a class thrust in colonial situations, it kept national/cultural issues intrinsically and theoretically separated from, though added to, class issues. Nor did it spell out the particulars of creating a movement in colonised countries which would have a mass and class character simultaneously. In fact the detailed analysis that he does offer is in the context of the USSR, where the socially and the economically contradictory character of nationalism is actually sought to be diffused by separating out class questions from what he calls national/cultural ones. Commonality is the element that is stressed as a feature of national groups, and the analysis always veers towards a cultural rather than a structural question, thereby creating two related but separate spheres. Nor does Stalin offer an insight into the question of how to create a 'proletarian' struggle when the industrial working class is very small and the peasantry predominates. In this context too, the category 'the people' (a keyword in nationalist movements) continuously slips from a class connotation, which divides the national terrain, into one of cultural, linguistic, religious, creative-cultural commonness, and unites by over-riding or subsuming many of the class elements.

A communist programme that unites these two aspects of national/cultural and class politics is to be found in the Communist Party of India (Marxist)'s (CPI(M)) programme of People's Democratic Revolution (PDR), which finally rests upon the proletariat (in the shape of the Party) the task of completing the project of the bourgeois revolution and enlightenment, and sees the projects of class and nation as compatible. Utpal Dutt fully subscribes to the PDR. It is the key to his epic aesthetics. For this reason he has been accused of political opportunism. But if we look at the thrust of Utpal's work from its very first stage, we can see the coincidence of liberal democracy with class struggle, which is the

---

7 Ibid.
8 Ibid., p. 63.

CPI(M) project. The People's Democratic Revolution, as he understands it, clarifies for him as a cultural producer the task of a theatre activist in the present political situation. We should attend to two statements in which he accurately presents the basic politico-cultural projects of the PDR:

> ... but I doubt if revolutionary practices of the theatre have worked out what this [People's Democratic Revolution] implies in terms of a battle for people's minds. I doubt if many of us have realised that this means that many of the slogans in such a revolution will be inherited from the great bourgeois-democratic revolutions of Europe, but since the semi-colonial bourgeoisie is incapable of raising them, the proletariat must take up the task and with the help of other revolutionary classes, fulfill the democratisation of the country. And since the proletariat must exercise hegemony in this revolution, it is no longer a bourgeois democratic revolution, but rather part of the world-socialist revolution. But its content will be democratic and therefore related to, for example, the thoughts of the Great French Revolution of 1789.[9]

> Where a people's democratic revolution will differ from the revolutionary ideas of Diderot and Rousseau will precisely be where the revolutionary bourgeois thinkers halted in confusion, where they became scared by their own honest findings, and instead of pursuing their own logic, sought to find compromise within the framework of bourgeois society. The proletarian democratic revolution is aimed at finally smashing that framework, and therefore will not halt, but pass onto the next stage, a socialist revolution.[10]

We should carefully attend to the statement that the content of Indian communist revolution 'will be inherited from the great bourgeois democratic revolutions', realise the 'ideas of Diderot and Rousseau' and be 'related to the Great French Revolution of 1789'. However, it will be the task of 'the proletariat' to 'fulfill the democratisation of the country', though of course 'with the help of other revolutionary classes'. And in the next stage – after ushering in an era of enlightenment and establishing a parliamentary democratic framework – the proletariat 'will not halt, but pass onto the next stage, a socialist revolution'. PDR is meant as the culmination of the incomplete revolution – the genuine

---

9   Dutt 1982, p. 64.
10   Ibid.

independence that bypassed India. This position can be directly related to a sentence from Stalin, which featured on the walls of Calcutta during the Stalin centenary year: 'The banner of bourgeois democracy lies in the dust today, the proletariat must pick it up and carry it forward'. Under this banner proletarian and bourgeois theatre can surely coexist side by side, as can socialism and class harmony.

We should note how the PDR and a Stalinist or Second Internationalist politics allows for the possibility of retainment of bourgeois culture. This is the result of both considering the bourgeoisie, and in particular the European bourgeoisie, as a revolutionary class, and culture in a non-mediatory relationship with class. These views allow Utpal Dutt to hold an admiration for two strident extremes of theatre/literature and even find a reconciling principle among them. He can admire and emulate high bourgeois culture and speak of class struggle, or use agit-prop forms, all at once. He assumes that the bourgeois literature of one era can be the legacy of, serviceable to, the proletariat of the next. These positions are overtly demonstrated in plays such as *Daraon Pathikbar* (Stay Passerby), where these antagonistic classes can come to an easy, spontaneous collaboration with each other, in which 'the people' find a natural leader (not just an ally), for instance in Madhusudan or Vidyasagar, in the bourgeoisie, who leads them on to a national struggle – in this instance a cultural struggle against colonialism. The use of the two categories, 'the people' and class, in this play shows clearly the problems involved in synthesising a dual politics – where relations between class and culture, revolution and bourgeois democracy, remain unsettled but constant. Again in *Tiner Talwar* (The Tin Sword) we find a similar reworking of the concepts of the people and revolution. Whereas in most of his other plays the spectrum includes workers and peasants, here with the exception of the first five minutes of the play, where a sweeper is introduced to us, 'the people' are the theatre people of the nineteenth-century stage. This redefinition of 'the people' and the politics of cultural nationalism speaks more of a cultural revolution under the leadership of the petty bourgeois intelligentsia than an armed class struggle. If it results in an armed struggle at all, it is more likely to be annexed to a bourgeois national venture than one of a class struggle and the victory of the proletariat.

A bourgeois theatre and a revolutionary project can be claimed to go well together if culture can be abstracted from class. The coherence between a Stalinist political project which separates class from culture and a bourgeois nationalist theatre aesthetic will become evident as we discuss the epic historic theatre of Utpal Dutt, with its core of mythic realism. This aesthetic project can be directly traced to the socialist epic-myth project developed by

Maxim Gorky in the Stalinist era. We should take note of Gorky's statement at the very beginning of our discussion:

> Any myth is a piece of imagining. Imagining means abstracting the funda-
> mental idea underlying the sum of a given reality, and embodying it in an
> image; that gives us realism. But if the meaning of what has been abstrac-
> ted from reality is amplified through the addition of the desired and the
> possible – if we supplement it through the logic of hypothesis – all this
> rounding off the image – then we have the kind of romanticism which
> underlies the myth, and is most beneficial in its prompting a revolution-
> ary attitude toward reality, an attitude that in practice refashions the
> world.[11]

The inspiration for Utpal Dutt's serious political theatre lies in the Stalinist politics discussed in the previous part and statements such as these. In fact he is a self-confessed Stalinist. He wrote two plays in homage to Stalin, *Louha Manab* (The Man of Iron) and *Stalin 1934*. And also in *Stanislavsky Theke Brecht* (From Stanislavsky to Brecht) he discusses the Stalinist base of his own epic philosophy:

> In the question of form there is nothing that is the greatest or the ultimate.
> Formula is the death of drama. Moreover according to Stalin the form
> always has to be national, the content socialist. Every nation [*jati*] created
> its favorite forms for many centuries. It will want to see its revolutionary
> theatre in those very forms. Perhaps the revolutionary message will reach
> the Japanese quickest if put through kabuki, to the people of Bengal in
> *jatra*, and in South India through dance, in Maharashtra in *tamasha*, in
> Uttar Pradesh in *nautanki*, in Gujarat through *bhawai*. The main issue is
> the revolutionary content. The form is dependent on a country and time,
> content is eternal.[12]

We can see from the quotation how Utpal assumes, as did Stalin and others, a commonality of culture at the level of the nation (*jati*) – both in ideas and forms of art, as well as in the separation between form and content. In their view national culture is assumed to be homogeneous and can override divi-sions such as that of class and manifest in a body of unified, shared images,

---

11   Gorky 1982, p. 323.
12   Dutt 1982, p. 82.

forms and ideas. To create a theatre that can thus capture the so-called spirit of a nation and an age through its form, and direct it towards the content of a communist revolution, is the historical mission of Utpal Dutt's political theatre.

In order to create a theatre which projects a commonality and builds a national theatre, and fuses or overrides the divisions of a class society, and yet accommodate class struggle, Utpal Dutt resorts to the notion of epic. Its end is to produce both national and proletarian myths to further a communist revolution. It consists of mythicisation and apotheosis, i.e., the fixation and enlargement of particular historical individuals and events in history. In order to put together such a governing aesthetic and a representational apparatus Utpal Dutt draws upon various and disparate indigenous and foreign sources. His sources range from Indian epics to bourgeois Bengali and European literature and mythopoeic attempts by nationalist and revolutionary writers, especially from Germany and the USSR. Though following Brecht and Piscator, and probably in order to give it a socialist context and legitimacy, he also called it 'epic theatre', Utpal's epic theatre is not the epic theatre of either of these dramatists. His epic theatre typically suits his own formulation, a combination of an Indian and a Soviet style politics.

In order to get to the heart of Utpal Dutt's politics, and since the concept of epic theatre has become identified with the theatre of Brecht, it is important to differentiate his theatre project from Brecht's epic theatre. Utpal's discussion of it is far more revealing of his own epic aesthetic and practice than that of Brecht. Here is his version of Brecht's intentions for constructing the epic form.

> After much thinking Brecht came to this conclusion, that showing too many emotions all together creates too much complication in the play. It creates confusion in an ordinary audience in understanding the theory of revolution. On the other hand as a Marxist, as a dialectician, it was impossible for him to think of man as purely white or black. His epic convention was a discovery to create a solution to this problem or we might say that it was a rediscovery. As he took from the ancient epics an analytical and distancing perspective, he also supplied the answer to the question of 'how shall I show man?' from that very ancient epic. Shakespeare's characters become increasingly more complex from scene to scene, but that never happens in the ancient epics. Arjun or Kama are never mentally agitated, they are great and tranquil as stone sculptures. In each canto they show different emotions. Arjun is sometimes a lover, sometimes a great warrior, and sometimes adverse to war ... This does not wait for so-called logic. An epic, because it distances itself, is not locked within

an everyday life. As we don't need a worldly logic for legends, so for epics. Brecht has reestablished this form in the light of modem science, and conferred on theatre the greatness of legends and the nobility of the epic. Courage is sometimes a mother, sometimes a cunning trader, sometimes a satirist of the feudal warmonger, sometimes bewildered and stupid ... All these, all together, slowly create the whole human being. Courage is the audience's imagination.[13]

Dutt's version of Brecht is actually a mirror of his own work. Brecht himself was not interested in a display of emotions – neither in 'too many all at once' nor sequentially – nor in creating characters with depth – 'the whole human being', and certainly not in 'greatness' and 'nobility'. In fact Brecht's interest in the epic form had nothing to do with its content of stories of heroic deeds of heroic men and their battles or historic, imperial missions. Unlike Utpal, he did not believe that they form the content of the cultural unconscious of Europe or that there was such a homogeneous cultural unconscious. Brecht used the epic form for the exact opposite reason of Dutt. Namely, to create distance and alienation – as a narrative form – not content – with which the European audiences of his time had very little connection. It was a major device for the 'alienation effect'. This alienation effect gave the distance required by the audience and author alike for a critical and a 'logical' representation of contemporary reality. So it was the form – the nonlinear, but not illogical, narrative structure – and not the content that interested Brecht in epics. He saw the epic structure as choppy, with self-contained episodes, each with its own life and logic. Through the use of this device he sought to destroy what might be called a singular focus or a perspective view on reality of theatre. Decentred in this way the pieces of episodes, possible actions and options could only form a whole dramatic structure as a set of social and critical relations with each other. The text was held together by these relations, and not through an internal, cause-and-effect sequence of events or emotional connections, or through any primary episode governing the others. His interest was in actively critical and mediatory relations between the parts, as well as between the play and the audience. Meaning was gained from referring the episodes and their relations within the play to a social reality and a social analysis that lie outside the text. The socialist/communist politics of a play such as *Mother Courage and her Children* or *The Life of Galileo*, for example, cannot be found in its story or dialogue – in any of the characters, events, or decisions – but rather in a series of provocative tex-

---

13   Ibid., pp. 80–1.

tual disjunctures and in the audience-text conjunction, which prompts one to think exactly the very opposite of what is happening on the stage. The need for breaking the old Aristotelian unities of time, space and action, in short a political and formal opposition to hundreds of years of theatre of property and the bourgeoisie, made Brecht gravitate towards the epic form.

Utpal Dutt on the other hand does not want to operate within the Brechtian tradition of alienation and criticality. He has only a limited interest in the form of epics, and makes no use of their discursive episodic structure, which Brecht used in order to insert political comments and social analysis. Utpal's comments on Brecht's particular use of epics offer us a point of entry for discussing his own:

> The amazing thing is that Brecht held up to us arrogantly the reverse of what people always understood the epic-hero to be. Brecht is suspicious of an earth shaking under heroic tirade. Only unfortunate countries need heroes. *Courage* and *Galileo* both say this. Brecht's heroes are dwarfs in social life. Brecht has created the fantasy world of epic and unleashed in it a bunch of kicked-around selfish little creatures, who think it's heroic to cheat others and survive. Brecht's epic is also a cruel satire of the ancient epics. His plays are not epics – but at once the re-establishment of it.[14]

Utpal's interest in epics is in their content, in the masculine and the heroic, and in terms of exaggerated emotions, large-scale characterisation and scope of action. Unlike Brecht, with his interest in distancing and alienation, Utpal's intention is to create a theatre of absorption through what he considers to be a common national heritage. According to Dutt the ancient epics – the *Mahabharata* and the *Ramayana* – are a part of 'our national psyche'. Trapped in this notion of a common heritage, he sees no distinction between how they are understood or used by the different classes, or in the cities and the countryside of Bengal and India. In fact, it is the perception and use of the Indian epics by his nineteenth-century middle-class ancestors that provides him with the basis and the perspective for the project of a national, cultural united front for politics. Heroism of both action and character, multiple incidents and great battles are what he selects out of the epic's content. This use of epics is a characteristic of nineteenth- and twentieth-century history plays and urbanised commercial *jatra*.[15] These features are also coherent with Utpal's own interest

---

14   Ibid., p. 136.
15   An originally rural popular Bengali theatrical form using highly declamatory blank verse.

in Shakespeare and Elizabethan plays. Furthermore, unlike Brecht, emotional absorption and excitement rather than criticality lie at the heart of Utpal's epic-mythic project. The epic, for him, is a matter of grand passion.

Utpal Dutt reworks the epic form and scope into a feudally veneered bourgeois play, with plots and subplots, many scenes, heroic characters and incidents. He changes its episodic structure into a linear dramatic pattern by introducing a single overriding action and focus, mounting emotionality and an internal sequence of regulating causality in a manner resembling fate. The Aristotelian unities reappear in either a modified or a direct way and contribute to the tale and the fate of one hero. Unlike Brecht's, Utpal's epic hero is constructed without irony, and the play revolves on his 'action' – i.e., on his success or failure as the plot centres on some world-shattering event, rather than on the trivia of capitalism that occupies Brecht. It is in his own theatre that we get an insight into what he considers to be a 'hero' or 'characters' (in the sense of the word the 'individual' and 'a quest for a whole man') in either the ancient epics or Brecht's plays, and why he finds them compatible with Shakespearean inner conflicts. We can see why he can erroneously deduce that Brecht used the epics for a sequence of actions and emotions to create a 'rounded character' as A.C. Bradley said of Shakespeare, or that he sought 'to create a whole man' out of fragmentary experiences.[16] His own plays are created on such a totalist view of reality, as for instance prescribed by Lukács, with an intact and sequentially organised surface, rather than as a set of Brechtian intersecting social relations.

Utpal Dutt's epic theatre, unlike Brecht's epic theatre for class struggle, is first and foremost a nationalist theatre with an added on rather than an intrinsic socialist agenda. Its purpose, as he himself points out, is not mainly to teach a critical class perspective, but rather to incite the audience to emotions of class hatred and armed political actions, with an assumption that the audience knows all it needs to know about class and the appropriate emotions pertaining to 'class characters'. Though Bharucha sees the box-office as the sole motive behind the emotionalism of his plays,[17] there is actually a political reason which is far more relevant:

> It is a proven fact that if we want to explain the rules of social change Brecht's technique is the best. But for a Marxist, to explain is not the only task, but also to incite, to promote class-hatred, to 'instill in the

---

16   Ibid., p. 124.
17   Bharucha 1983.

audience's subconscious a lack of faith in the bourgeois social organisation'. (Lenin. 'What is to be Done?')[18]

For Utpal Dutt a revolutionary theatre can only be created through introducing great feelings which inspire the audience to look beyond its petty lives into heroic exploits and sentiments, which in turn move it beyond the so-called logic of our daily world and 'refashion', as Gorky said, 'our attitude to reality'. The path of this popular revolutionary theatre for Utpal lies through the land of history, as legends of the heroic:

> ... [T]he petty-bourgeois writers and directors will never find content in the *cul-de-sac* of their own class. If they wish to survive as artists, they must listen to the screams, howls and songs issuing from the new Elsinore, watch new *Hamlets* and *Lohengrins* set out on a mission of setting right a world out of joint, confront new tragedies, taking massive shape just outside the petty bourgeois hovels.
>
> To create new tragedies, new heroes and their violence against new villains, the artist must acquire by choice the standpoint of the class that is making new history – namely the proletariat.[19]

It is melodrama, with its steep ups and down of passion, rather than epic, that serves his theatre in its revelation of what he calls the 'mythic' or essential reality. He reads just such a melodrama into Goethe's *Faust* (Part I), and in his reading he finds a suitable form and vision. According to Dutt, while the story of Faust encases the *Zeitgeist* of a capitalist Germany, its significance becomes universal for all of capitalism by the use of the form of melodrama which surpasses the 'realistic' level 'with ghosts, witches, and black magic ... including ... horror'.[20]

The ultimate purpose of Utpal's epic theatre is to create myths, rather than question the ones which already exist. Myths for him are characterised and fictionalised 'essences' or 'truths' – they are the product of the highest kind of realism. The literary method of this mythic realism is obviously not naturalism, but even its epistemology is not concerned with the actually existing everyday life. It is through a transcendence of the particular, of daily life, and historical and social time and space that his epic-mythic theatre is sought to

---

18   Dutt 1976, p. 48.
19   Dutt 1982, pp. 104–5.
20   Ibid., p. 131.

be created. His epic-mythic ideals are worth recounting in this context. In his essay on 'Form of Theatre' in *TART*, he makes the following statements:

> A myth is a poetic summary of a people's collective experiences. It is the signature of a whole historical epoch ...
>   A myth transposes time because it has nothing to do with 'realism' in the vulgar sense. It aims at the super-real and therefore remains true in different contexts, in different versions.[21]

The mythic therefore has to be not only artistic and artificial but also idealist in its conception of a temporality. Neither the 'essential' truth about reality nor the creation of true art is possible for him by staying close to what he calls 'life'. It comes out most clearly in *Stanislavskir Path* (The Way of Stanislavsky) when, assessing his favorite actor and director, he states both his and Stanislavsky's theatre ideal: 'Art is not created through an imitation of life. Acting is not a parody of man seen on the street. Acting is life-transcending, a harmonious expression that rises above life'.[22] In this kind of statement we see the coming together of a purely idealist version of truth and art with a political aim that purports to be communist/socialist and thus effect historical social changes within a distinctly temporal dimension.

   The mythic-epic attempt is meant to capture a whole people's collective experience (it is the national ideal again) as though such an experience were possible in actuality, rather than those of certain classes. It is interesting that along with this atemporal, essentialist project Utpal Dutt can talk at once about the importance of history. He speaks of 'transcending time', of art being 'super-real' and 'true in different contexts' as well as of socialist/communist revolution in the same breath. In order to establish a baseline that holds for all, Utpal Dutt ends up by eradicating the very contemporaneity and specificity which he holds characteristic of a non-abstract, 'non-quixotic' political theatre. These totalist epic ventures lack as yet, for Utpal, a fully accomplished form or a model. In *Stanislavskir Path* he tells us that he has to break a new path:

> The proletarian myths have not been created. The proletarian revolution has not produced its Goethe and Schiller yet. There are historical reasons for it ... the proletariat [however] under the bourgeois, is reduced to the

---

21   Ibid., pp. 131–2.
22   Dutt 1976, p. 23.

level of a cretin, except for a handful of labour aristocrats, who, being puppets to be used against the proletariat, no longer remain proletarian.[23]

He turns for hints and models to the established European bourgeois or Bengali
nationalist (also bourgeois) theatre. He finds in Shakespeare the most relevant structure of characterisation for the mythic-epic. In *Shakespearer Samaj-
Chetana* (Shakespeare's Social Consciousness) he speaks of Shakespeare's dramatic structures and characters – heroes and villains – that can embody 'the
spirit of the age' in 'mythic' figures such as that of Hamlet. In *Hamlet* and
King Lear, for example, he finds a total embodiment, a complete man, not to
be found anywhere else except in the epics. But Utpal reserves his greatest
praise for Richard Wagner for creating 'a new myth, a revolutionary Holy Grail,
a poetic reinterpretation of the oldest ballads in North European memory'.[24]
After discussing the operas he says that Wagner's great achievement was 'to
marshal the knight, armour and all, to the service of revolutionary bourgeois
ideology'.[25]

Among the Bengali theatre producers and playwrights he credits Girish
Ghosh[26] for having tried a mythopoeic theatre. But compared to Shakespeare,
Goethe, Schiller and Wagner, he feels Girish's work is a failure – 'his outlook was
probably vitiated by an unwarranted veneration for his heroes'.[27] Utpal blames
a historical determination for this failure, since colonialism prevented India
from producing either a real bourgeois or a proletarian revolution. 'Naturally
no myth, proletarian or bourgeois, has been created in India in the field of art
and literature'.[28] He also relies on the dramatised versions of epical stories in
jatra and the nineteenth-century historical and mythological plays. These modified examples of early or pre-capitalist theatre are considered by him as India's
only valid and substantive sources of heroism and grand visions necessary for
constructing myths. They are the Indian counterparts of the bourgeois heroic
myths of Europe, and reconcilable within the same text.

It is interesting that whereas Utpal Dutt spends much time discussing bourgeois playwrights and directors, such as Wagner, who had a mythic project
without an interest in socialism and a 'folkism' without any class content, he

---

23   Dutt 1982, p. 133.
24   Ibid., p. 109.
25   Ibid., p. 106.
26   Girish Ghosh (1844–1912), a dramatist, a director and an actor, was the most important fig-
      ure in nineteenth-century Bengali theatre. He created a dramatic form by synthesising
      existing Bengali drama with European influences, primarily of Shakespeare.
27   Ibid., p. 140.
28   Ibid., p. 139.

spends less time on a socialist playwright who also wanted to create proletarian myths. Though he alludes to Maxim Gorky periodically, produced *The Lower Depths* and used Gorky's advocacy of imagination as the way to truth to legitimise his own mythic project, he discusses him only cursorily, and finally even negatively. After many pages on the successes of Richard Wagner as creator of a genuine popular revolutionary myth in the legends of Siegfried, Lohengrin, Parcifal, etc. (later providing the mythology of the German National Socialist Party), he mentions Gorky only to inform us that he had failed in his mythic project due to his 'revolutionary romanticism'. Gorky was, in contrast to Wagner, for example, 'too involved in his hero's fate, too sympathetic to the hero's goal'.[29]

This assessment of Gorky is very intriguing. The fact is that Utpal's own project to create a national and revolutionary theatre, at the service of contemporary communist politics in a classically romantic mode, was most clearly formulated by Maxim Gorky in an effort of socialist construction in the USSR. This becomes evident from the documents of the 1934 Writers Congress held in the USSR. And furthermore, a similar directive presence of Lenin's and Stalin's thought also shapes the course of Gorky's literary philosophy and forms of production. Gorky was well known in India and there were many translations of his novels, plays and stories. His literary theories were also well-known and much debated.

In *TART* it is actually in the few allusions to Gorky that we find the parallel of another literature and theatre that is both socialist and romantic. Put in another way, it is in the project of socialist realism, with its core of revolutionary romanticism, that we find a European version of the aesthetic of the mythic-epic theatre of Utpal Dutt. Socialist realism of this type allows a blend of revolutionary nationalist theatre of urban Bengal (from Girish Ghosh to Sachin Sengupta), urbanised *jatra* and the progressive bourgeois literature/theatre of the West. It is in Gorky that Utpal Dutt gets his theory of myth, of a romantic political theatre which captures truth through imagination and exaggeration, rather than in the critical realism of the older socialist project. Feelings and national cultural myth and symbols become the staple of this art. As he calls his theatre 'epic' to situate it in a genealogy of political theatre, so too he used Gorky's definition of myth to legitimise his own practice: 'As Maxim Gorky explained Myth, it is not idle imagination or pure fabrication but a glorified, exaggerated statement of a very real problem of the ancient world'.[30]

---

29   Ibid., p. 134.
30   Ibid., p. 113.

Gorky's mythic project was simple and grand. He talked of a mythic work as being 'a piece of imagining', 'abstracting the fundamental idea', and 'embodying it in an image'. Contrary to what had so far been claimed as realism, his active exercise of this imagination, he claims, 'gives us realism'. But it is not the realism of daily life that surrounds us, rather 'reality is amplified', 'supplemented' by 'the logic of hypothesis'. This excursion into what does not yet exist, hitherto negatively branded as 'escapist', fantastic and romantic by both positivist and critical communism, had now become important for the work of revolutionary construction of the USSR. Stalin himself had endorsed romanticism, as did cultural theorists such as Zhdanov, Radek and Bucharin, as indicated by the 1934 Congress. But, as pointed out by Gorky in his essay 'Advice to Young Writers', this romanticism was not considered 'bourgeois' – consisting of decadence, despair and degeneracy – but rather 'revolutionary'. 'The kind of romanticism which underlies the myth' is aimed towards 'promoting a revolutionary attitude towards reality'. 'In practice', it 'refashions the world'. 'Romanticism', for Gorky, 'is an active attitude towards life'.[31]

We have discussed so far how at the level of content and construction of his plays and theatre philosophy, Utpal Dutt tries to create a 'popular' and 'revolutionary' theatre in accordance with a Stalinist political programme of a People's Democratic Revolution. In this section we will examine his use of various theatre styles and forms in order to find a language for the full range of his political theatre. We must remember that he has to produce theatre for an immediate pragmatic and daily business of the Communist Party, trade unions and provincial politics – as much as for his epic-mythic history project. As the purpose and the content varies, so must the form. Since from our standpoint politics and theatre are irreducible mediating components of each other, we must explore the form-content relationship in his work. Though Utpal himself, in the following quotation for example, separates out 'the message' or 'the content' from the form, and feels that the content remains uncompromised in its dress of whatever form 'pleases' the audience, we ourselves cannot adopt this attitude:

> The director belched: 'No Sir, why? Why should I put cheap and reactionary material on my stage? Whoever told you that whatever is stageable and popular is cheap and vulgar?'
> The playwright was pacing in intolerable rage.
> Continuing his pacing he asked: 'So what does popular or stageable really mean?'

---

31   Gorky 1982, p. 41.

The director picked his teeth with a match stick and said: 'I don't know about other theatres; maybe there they do use the audience as an excuse for showing cheap things, like the Bombay movie directors do. But I have faith in myself. It's impossible to bring any reactionary material in my theatre while trying to make it stageable. And yet, the play must have such tension, such speed, such surprise that the audience must get real pleasure from it, so that they won't boycott my theatre. I don't compromise at all on the count of content. I maintain the playwright's progressive message absolutely intact, because I am also a progressive man. But that message, that content must appear in front of the audience, set up on the stage with such styles and techniques that the audience can understand, appreciate, be pleased with it. Otherwise what will happen – just this, that even a strong message will appear in a non-understandable form, and no one will get it. The message is then completely lost. Formal experiments can never discount the question of the audience.'[32]

Whether Utpal Dutt's theatre politics furthers a revolutionary goal or not must therefore be answered in the context of a taken-for-granted set of theatre mediations, which constitute a part of the common sense of the theatre-going and producing Bengali middle class. This element of class subjectivity, expressed through the form, is a vital one in any study of political art.

We already know that an interest in both a national culture and class politics governs Dutt's theatrical choice and experiments. He is simultaneously theatrically pragmatic and ideologically dogmatic. What his audience is familiar with – the national tradition of bourgeois theatre – becomes the vehicle of his politics. After all, as Utpal says, even 'a terribly strong message' could also be 'lost' if the audience could not read it in the theatre's text nor relate it to any of their previous theatre experiences. It is for this reason, not simply out of a commercial interest, that he says, 'Formal experiments can never discount the question of the audience'.[33] As this politics tries to combine divergent ideological strands into one, so it does with divergent theatre traditions. Hence his search through both national and international repertoire. His theatrical eclecticism is a practical dimension of his political necessity. His search for form, and his formal combinations, are devices for presenting his politics effectively. What he sees as the ideal marxist/communist stand in the matter of formal experimentation, we find in the following remark on Brecht:

---

32   Dutt 1979, pp. 25–6.
33   Dutt 1976, p. 95.

There should be no obligation to obey any convention because it is established, nor should there be a reluctance to use it because it is an old convention. After all Brecht's theatre is political theatre, its politics must reach the people. This is the only intention of his theatre. Those who sit in judgement on Brecht's theatre using the criteria of aesthetics are as though judging a 25-inch cannon as a thing of beauty. A political theatre cannot be encompassed within an aesthetics any more than armaments can be. Political theatre operates with only one condition – whether the politics is accurately reaching the audience. One must do whatever is necessary for that. Brechtian techniques – alienation and surprise – are the creation of a political necessity.[34]

What we want to do then is not to explain away the seemingly antithetical aspects of Utpal's theatre and politics, but put side by side the form and the politics, and we will see, as we did in the previous section, why it is that these bourgeois playwrights proved to be of such interest and a source of influence for him, or why antithetical forms and contents can cohabit without producing a sense of contradiction. We found that the epic-mythic quest is largely suited to a national and bourgeois cultural quest – and not a part and parcel of a proletarian theatre. Instead of positing an unqualified contradiction between the European bourgeois or older nationalist theatre of Bengal and Utpal's own theatre, it would perhaps be more fruitful to ask what they have in common politically, so that his formal affinity and attitude to those theatres may be better understood. And furthermore, we should remember that Utpal considers theatre to be an art and the purpose of art as being to produce pleasure, consisting of a small core of instruction and a great deal of passion. Unlike Brecht, who also brought pleasure into the theatre, but insisted that it be of learning, Dutt does not equate the two. For him the message can come dressed in many forms. He is not particularly concerned about the problems that the message can get into, or be transformed into, as a result of the dresses or the forms. We have to question, then, why or how he can afford to overlook theatrical mediation's ability to mediate the politics of theatre.

Utpal Dutt is not only convinced that theatre is an art, but he is also a proponent of an ostentatious, self-conscious theatre art, of what Grotowski calls a 'rich theatre',[35] meaning a theatre that uses a proscenium stage and draws upon many other arts, disciplines and technology to enrich itself. Multiple forms and

---

34   Ibid.
35   Grotowski 1968, p. 112.

techniques combine to create his language of theatre, the less austere the better. Utpal sees theatre as an art that is synthetic, polymorphic and synesthetic. Asking the question, 'But where are the rules for theatre? Where is its grammar, its lexicon?',[36] he proceeds to list the elements of theatre, namely the actor with his dialogue, gestures and movement, and the stage design, light and music. Theatre is 'promiscuous', an attempt to unite what we hear and see. 'Isn't there such a ground at all where visuals and music, dance and words, without losing their integrity, sit at the same table?' With the proper daring, daring to be both artificial and artistic, one could create 'a theatre which was the combined creation of many arts ... where sound can become colour, and colour sound'.[37] Needless to say, with such an opulent view of theatre as a 'total' art, whose 'muse' is 'proud, queenly and resplendent', Utpal Dutt is an enthusiast of the proscenium stage.[38]

The theatre taste that derives from the last one hundred years of Bengali urban, professional stage is the staple of Utpal Dutt's theatre. The world of professional and traditional stage becomes Utpal's natural habitat, and at no point in time could he conceive of politics in any other way except theatrically, but nor did he ever attempt a theatre from which he did not glean a political service of sorts. But Utpal Dutt's standard remained the old proscenium stage, which has become identified with theatre proper. An elevated box stage with curtains, with inner stages, wings, revolving sets, light and amplification – this is the stage of mainstream theatre in front of which generations of audiences have waited for the thrill of the curtain to rise since the beginning of the national theatre era in Bengal. With some variations in its internal organisation, Utpal Dutt has mounted all his full-length plays on this stage and written them with this stage in mind. The stage directions in his printed texts point to stage environment, devices of organising, varying and speeding up the action, all of which clearly show the centrality of the stage as an organising principle of dramatic representation. Not only are there frequent changes of scene through the use of curtains, but also the role of light (in spotlighting acting zones by using certain colours of light and darkening the other areas) is similar, and as well signifies levels of reality within the play.

Utpal Dutt's stage is a direct descendent of nineteenth-century colonial, and by extension, bourgeois commercial European stage. In fact in its fullness of decor, sound and light, and excessiveness of emotions, it has a Victorian touch to it. It lacks the severity of a modernist stage. It is not the sparse stage of Brecht,

---

36   Dutt 1976, p. 95.
37   Ibid.
38   Ibid., p. 54.

nor the denuded stage of the theatre of the absurd. Nor is it the naturalistic stage of the drawing-room theatre. It is a little too stuffed, too warm. Often it conjures up the aura of red velvet stage furniture, gilded mirrors, and epic battlefields – no matter where they are – be they in Vietnam or the plains of Hindustan. It is, however, productive of illusions which quite openly suggest its own theatricality and separate reality. The use of painted scenes, not just objects and platforms that constitute space-time relations within a play, is still prevalent, as are heavy and manifold props, and certainly used consciously by Utpal Dutt when producing plays on nineteenth-century Bengali theatre and life. This stage, in short, is a highly 'theatrical' stage – and is modified to suit different types of this theatre.

Utpal Dutt's contribution to this stage has been to raise its theatricality or artificiality higher than usual within the IPTA left theatre heritage. It is meant to create an environment for his mythic-epic theatre. The stage for epic theatre, with a high quantity of advanced theatre technology and techniques which elevate it to an 'epic' or grand scope level, could not have been possible in the days of Girish Ghosh. The productive forces of his day were far lower, but now it is entirely possible to create a theatre where one not only hears dialogue but sees spectacles and hears music and other sound effects all at once. With Utpal Dutt the element of the spectacular dominates as a part of the epic-mythic expression – though there are also productions where he uses some features of the epic style to be found in Brecht and Piscator. In those plays the stage-scope is used to supply information and suggest complexity of action – though the attempt remains mainly that of developing a story linearly.

Along with the influence of bourgeois theatre proper both from Europe and Bengal, Uptal Dutt uses the indigenous urbanised dramatic tradition of *jatra*, as well as forms such as street theatre and agit-prop. Utpal Dutt's use of *jatra* however has not moved him away from the use of the proscenium and its general format. After all, it is not the rural version of *jatra* with its open platform stage that he draws on. In terms of textual construction Utpal Dutt has been more interested in the traditional mythological *jatra* with its morality plot, great battles, gods and goddesses, kings and queens, than the austere non-mythological, social *jatras* of the nationalist Mukunda Das. Utpal Dutt's own *jatras* are not distinguishable from his historical plays.

Because 'epic' theatre has to juggle with such diverse elements, the question of balancing or synthesising them becomes an important one. The principle of balance or synthesis becomes evident in Utpal's work as a director, even more than as a playwright. The 'dramatic action' is not only the story which Utpal tells, but a plot, and its staged form, in which the representation takes its complete shape. The directorial work consists of what is called the 'composition' of a show – its technique of 'mounting'. The particulars of the composition come as much from the types of theatre the director prefers as from his politics. In fact the plays are written by many playwrights with the composition in mind. A mode for Utpal's theatre is to be found in his version of Kshirodprasad Vidyavinod's play *Alamgir*. It is here, in a nationalist, big stage production, that we discover the key to Utpal's technique of dramatising the epic. In his ideal model of composition of a play the following elements are essential:

1. The speed of the action, i.e., the organisation of the events should make the audience breathless. There should be parallel actions, which are exciting as well.
2. The events should be unusual and surprise the audience continually.
3. There should be rapid change of mood as well as events.
4. There should be liberal use of humour – to satirise as well as please.
5. There should be a 'dramatic' development of characters. Nothing is too dramatic for the purpose of the epic stage:

    > The expression 'over-dramatised' is meaningless. Dramas are meant to be dramatic – pitched at an octave higher than life. Where massive personalities are clashing with each other, empires are rising or falling, how can any incident seem 'over-dramatic?'[39]

How Utpal himself learnt from his predecessors becomes evident from the organisation of the play *Tiner Talwar*. Here we see perfection in split-second timing, rapid rise and fall in moods, flow of action, surprise and humour which have been the envy of other directors.

The acting styles of Utpal Dutt's theatre reflect the particular requirements of his theatre. Since in Bengal there are no drama schools that train actors in different styles and traditions, the training of actors happens on the job, as it were, mainly showing what the director wants and is able to train them into. Utpal Dutt's requirements from actors demand fluency of acting idioms and styles. They range from the heroic of the old historical school to the simple imitative acting for a representation of everyday reality, to comic styles. These three styles – natural, heroic-tragic, and comic – have been common in both theatre and films of Bengal. 'Character acting', which requires empathy in the actor for his role and in producing empathy in the audience, is much emphasised. Notions such as alienation-effect (A-effect) of Brecht are not of any importance. Only the comic actor, as in the comedy tradition in general, retains a distance, a critical view of his role. For stylistic resources Dutt turns his attention to *jatra* conventions and styles for his historical plays, involving loud, bold

---

39   Dutt 1977, p. 30.

projection and non-naturalist acting, as well as the training in Shakespeare acting he received early in life in the school of Geoffrey Kendal, and experiences
of attending performances in England by Laurence Olivier, Paul Scoffield, and
others.

The retention of melodrama-based, old-stage acting in Utpal Dutt's theatre
is particularly useful to his epic-mythic mode, where the hero and the villain are
established with a great moral clarity. The acting idiom, including the famous
laughter of the villain, is used for presenting us with a moral/political schema
which is integral to the heroic mode, as for instance are the idioms of light and
music. When the hero Shardul Singh appears on the deck of the rebel ship Khy-
ber, singled out by a spotlight, calling out his refusal to surrender, he functions
in the significational frame of *Kallol* in the same way as the communist flag
does at the beginning of the play – flying red and resplendent in the bright
light of the 'spot'. It is interesting to note that Utpal refers far more frequently
and reverentially to Stanislavsky's apolitical theatre and theories in the matter
of justifying his acting style, than the political stylistic of Brecht or Piscator. His
actors are required to lose themselves in the part, no matter how heroic, and
hold no sense of irony towards them. Not Brecht's *Mother Courage*, but Utpal
Dutt's version of Wagnerian heroes, with their nation-building, or the feudal-
ised *jatra* history play's heroic or villainous type characters, become the actor's
source of emulation.

From his own account in *TART* and *Stanislavskir Path* Utpal Dutt's actor-
training programme comes out as highly authoritarian and encourages little
or no individual initiative or criticality among members of the group. He justifies this by referring to the acting theories of Stanislavsky. In Utpal's hands
Stanislavsky's idea of submitting to the 'ruling idea' of the text and the role
transforms into an absolute submission to the director's dictates. Stanislavsky's
training of 'psycho-technique' for Utpal translates out into an imperative for
breaking the actor's ego and developing an obedience and continuous readiness to submit to the director's needs, rather than the internalisation of the
part and the personalised projection of it. The only liberating aspect of his
training programme consists of his demand that his actors become free from
religion and politically and historically informed about India, though this is
also partially undercut by his attempts to 'civilise' the actor by familiarising him
or her with European literature, music, etc. An acquaintance with Mozart and
Beethoven, for example, is considered by him to be the hallmark of an actor's
necessary personal development.

Utpal Dutt's eclectic theatre puzzles if we look into his work for what Brecht
or Piscator would have called a proletarian or a full-scale anti-imperialist
theatre. But as we have found by examining his political intentions and theatre

forms, his eclecticism, which is operative both in the area of content and form, politics and art, leads him into contradictory dimensions. We can simultaneously see both a fit and gap between these elements of his theatre. On the one hand we have a theatre surface, in the action and the message of the text, where the direct and intended politics of class struggle fight with the form of presentation. Where, instead of mediating each other, the content or intention and representation contradict. On the other hand there is a level which they create by working together. Together they constitute a final political text with a deeper coherence by means of a political and aesthetic symbiosis, and reproduce the unclarity of the Stalinist political position itself, with a distinct weight on the bourgeois nationalist component. These different levels of Utpal's theatre have served to confuse critics, who usually argue solely about the surface of the text. The fact that Utpal's contradiction is accounted for by the framework of a national bourgeois socialism is thus invisible to them. Though his intention was to complete an unfinished revolution, which of necessity had to have a national dimension *vis-a-vis* foreign capital and internally one of class, his political and aesthetic framework precipitated him into contradictions and ambiguities. Nationalism and anti-imperialism become confused, and bourgeois social relations are simultaneously questioned and affirmed.

Some of the basic reasons for the class and political character of Utpal Dutt's ambitious project of epic-mythic realism can be summed up in the following points. They follow from the same confusion that the IPTA and the communist movement in India as a whole suffers from, namely that of a communism which actively seeks to combine itself with a bourgeois component. From the point of view of constructing a political culture (or theatre), the most explicit factors are that:

a)   he maintains a separation between class and culture;
b)   he subscribes to a reflectionist view of culture and ultimately an instrumental relationship between culture and politics, thus also seeing culture in terms of discrete products rather than social processes;
c)   he equates national theatre and culture primarily with bourgeois or embourgeoisified popular culture and uses bourgeois theatre as the vehicle for political theatre;
d)   he subscribes to a two-stage theory of socialist revolution (which is deeply embedded in India's communist movement from its first phases) in spite of his and the CPI(M)'s profession to the contrary;
e)   for him, as for the communist movement in general, proletarian leadership means the leadership of the primarily middle-class led and organised Communist Party.

For these reasons various bourgeois cultural projects are unproblematic for Utpal. He finds acceptable, for example, Wagner's use of the concept of 'the folk' without any class connotation, as though all of German society was a homogeneous community. From the Bengali tradition, Girish Ghosh's nationalism and Madhusudan Dutt's[40] liberal humanism are also attractive for him. He hopes to expand the framework of the professional stage by injecting into it the category 'people'. He discovers in nationalist playwrights a revolutionary populism, which he outlines in his extensive book on Girish Ghosh, *Girish Manas*. In his plays on the progressive intelligentsia of the nineteenth century we see that a marginal, radical liberal segment of the middle class, together with their lumpenised peers from the stage, are considered as popular revolutionary forces and classes. Utpal Dutt can reconcile the Hindu nationalist politics of Girish Ghosh with the secular liberalism of Madhusudan. Nor does he, in search of a socially binding form, image or myth, ask himself whether or not this harmonious manifestation of the so-called social/cultural unconscious depends for its harmony on the imposition on the people of the cultural productions of the ruling and propertied classes. Until one places Utpal's communism in its own tradition of bourgeois enlightenment and liberal progressivism, his astounding concept for both the actual proletariat and the petty bourgeois seems puzzling. We unavoidably come to the conclusion that, given the 'cretinous' state of the proletariat, our political and aesthetic resource lies solely in the aesthetics of the bourgeoisie.

It is ironic that all the things Utpal Dutt supposedly wants to resist politically, from cultural imperialism to elitism, become the logical features of his own theatre theories and practices as a result of his secure belonging to a colonial middle class and its particular type of socialism. In terms of his embourgeoisified values and tastes we need to only remind ourselves of the continuous praise and normalisation of the European bourgeoisie and their art. The praise of Wagner and claims of affinity with him over the work of Brecht, for example, infused Utpal Dutt's own work with a deeply imperialist element. This becomes grossly evident as colonial bourgeois snobbery when he outlines his expectations from his actors and his notion of what it means to be a 'cultured' person.

In his discussion about the petty-bourgeois actor's shortcomings he lists predominantly, and on par with their lack of information about Indian politics,

---

40   Michael Madhusudan Dutt (1820–73) is acclaimed as the greatest nineteenth-century Bengali poet and an important figure in Bengali theatre. After living and travelling extensively in Europe he returned to Bengal to create anti-colonial poetry. He also synthesised European poetic forms, such as epic or blank verse, with existing forms of Bengali poetry. See also above in this reader the concluding pages of the chapter 'The Mirror of Class'.

their lack of knowledge of European literature and culture, their poor English and lack of high Bengali pronunciation. In *Daraon Pathikbar* there is a fetishisation of Madhusudan's Britishism, his knowledge of European classical and romantic literature and languages, with which he outsmarts the Europeans. The avid use of little French phrases, or Latin proverbs, does not do much to convince us of the supposed anti-colonialist politics embodied in the character, nor does the frequent laughter raised at the incorrect English of the *babus*. What is made fun of is not that they need to speak English, but that they do it badly. Madhusudan and his friends however are perfect Black British, and Madhusudan is even more than that in being one of the first Bengali renaissance men. Madhusudan's proficiency in European literature and languages has a peculiar comprador and bourgeois twist, in the snobbery of display of familiarity with things European which are only names to most lower middle-class people. Utpal Dutt's own writing is replete with the same ostentation of erudition – of untranslated quotes or phrases in German and French. These habits are not only redundant, but particularly offensive from somebody whose politics is intended to promote a 'national culture' and a socialist revolution. When pursued thus, culture and colonial/imperialist bourgeois culture become synonymous.

Further affirmation of Utpal Dutt's bourgeois affinities lies not only in the song of praise to the Europeans and a handful of Bengali intellectuals, but also in the patronage and condescension that he shows to 'the people' when speaking of peasants and other lower classes. In attempting to justify the anti-intellectual, anti-critical and feeling-orientation of his theatre he takes recourse to the excuse that 'the people' are passionate and uncritical, and thus unable to like critical/intellectual theatre. They embody for Utpal the collective unconscious of society at its most primitive. According to him they can accept violence, insanity and grand rash emotions because, unlike the middle class, they are still close to their instincts. The view of 'the people' as the 'other' of the rational intellectual contains in it a primitivism that with effort can become a part of a fascist ideological apparatus. It is in keeping with Utpal's admiration for Wagner and his use of the concept of 'the folk' for a purpose that he considers to be revolutionary.

In the perspective of this cultural politics we can see how the conventions of bourgeois theatre, its commonsense practices, both express and mould Utpal's politics. For Utpal to question these representational modes and apparatuses would be tantamount to questioning the validity of theatre itself as an activity. This is the message in his defensive attacks against those who dare to experiment with and question them. This formal conservatism is further facilitated by the fact that Utpal Dutt has an insider's, i.e., a professional attachment to the bourgeois theatre. This practitioner's know-how, of being able to produce effects with ready-made devices, is 'natural' to him, and he is delighted to increase his theatre repertoire. He advances therefore his theory of epic and total theatre, which allows him to mix and maximise all aspects of a high-technique, high-cost and full theatre. A complete formal arsenal is drawn upon for creating 'the world-historical', the intended mythic-epic.

The issue of aesthetic representation is more than a question of exterior mechanism of theatre. Lukács, in the debate on realism, points out the political stake of forms and styles. When he fights for the 'realism' of certain representational modes and conventions, he is arguing for the validity of a version of reality and a politics based on that. The conceptual and formal conventions of any work of art direct us towards particular epistemologies and politics. The politics of Utpal's 'mythic realism' cannot be understood apart from a fuller discussion of this context.

For Utpal Dutt, as for Gorky, myth means a fictional construct on an imaginative abstraction of the essential reality. Therefore a myth is not a lie, nor a piece of fantasy. 'Myth' signifies the creation of what is 'true' by using the imagination to get at the truth, rather than logical reasoning. It is the total result of the 'epic' process, which confers a lasting significance to the imaginative discovery by framing, elevating, and enlarging it. The 'epic' in this sense is not an oral accretional development through time – as with the ancient Indian epics – but individually existing mythic content. Unlike the traditional epics, whose ideological and social purpose remains general and unstated, this epic attempt is directed towards a particular and ideologically formulated political agenda. As Utpal states in *Towards a Revolutionary Theatre*, his mythic project has the ambition of demonstrating in symbolic and fictional form a dialectical and revolutionary view of the world which teaches us the 'truth' about reality, which must be distinguished from a 'fact'. Getting at this truth requires getting behind what exists in our everyday life, leaving behind the phenomenal.

If Utpal had stopped at this point he would have been a simple idealist with a matching aesthetic of symbolic realism. But his being a socialist/communist makes the issue more complicated. Though he avoids what he calls the bourgeois vice of empiricism and advocates the use of intuition, he does not want to be seen as an idealist. He feels that as an objective communist who believes in history he cannot advocate 'truth' in any universal sense or accommodate a subjectivist view of class and society. He therefore advances the notion of a universal yet essential and objective socialist truth as 'class truth', which is arrived at by using intuition and imagination to penetrate into the essential nature of an objective reality which is historical.

Yet this assurance of objectivity and reference to history, and using the word 'class' as an adjective to 'truth', does not help Utpal to escape the pitfalls of an objective idealism. It is similar, though far less refined, to the ideological formulation of Lukács et al., and appeals to the 'laws' of history as objective essences with their internal laws of causality, which regulate historical changes. It is still an idealist position, and not the 'social-scientific' method of Brecht for example, where the talk of 'laws' is discarded in favour of the social relations. Utpal's mythic world-view cannot accommodate experience, observation, comparison, historicisation or criticism. For Brecht class is visible at the surface of daily life in the daily social relations. The abstract dialectical 'laws' of history with their economic core do not substitute for the uncountable social interactions between people. In Utpal's case however, 'class truth' is discovered by a reverse process, by referring back to the 'law' of class struggle until the proletariat triumphs. Thus class becomes a settled issue, a given. There is a strong imperative in this position not to attend to the existing social relations, in the name of essentiality – the mythic or the quintessential. This 'law' of class struggle – as an uncluttered ideological category – forms the core of the mythic, and the epic provides its expressive, more-than-life-size form. This is stated quite explicitly by Utpal Dutt when, instead of locating any specific action in the existing social organisation, he wants the liberty to expunge what actually happens in favour of the historical 'laws' of class struggle.

When we search in Utpal's theatre and theatre criticism for the content of 'class truth', we come up again with a notion of class as an objective category with a reflectionist notion of culture. Class can be ascertained in terms of occupation and ownership. To this straightforward economic notion of class is added the notion of an invariant historical law which exists objectively as an inherent principle of dynamism. This provides the basis on which the typicality of action and characterisation of the play are structured. For any play to create myth, the degree of idealisation and the resulting typicality must be high. This creates a problem by setting up a tension between the scheme of ideal action and typical characters, and the semblance of daily life which fills out the play and provides a point of reference for the audience. This subordination of the social, the practical and the experiential to the ideal and the typical makes for great difficulties in constructing plays about actual class and class struggle.

We will examine some of the actual devices through which the mythic realism of Utpal Dutt represents class struggle. As we saw in the section on form, when mythic-realism has to be dramatised Utpal Dutt takes recourse to conventions of Bengali bourgeois theatre and a melodramatic version of Shakespeare. This version of Shakespeare, typified by the tradition of Henry Irving, reworked by directors such as Geoffrey Kendal, with its blend of melodrama and a maximum use of new stage technology, is his main source of inspiration. Discussed by Utpal in connection with Kshirodprasad Vidyavinod's *Alamgir*, it is a kind of speeded-up Elizabethan-Aristotelian structure, with emotional ups and downs, a plot and multiple subplots, which, however, hangs together by heroic and villainous actions of a few characters. The plenitude of emotions and incidents of such plays, their sheer quality, are supposed to represent an artistic version of the complexity of social reality. This is in keeping with the Aristotelian (or Elizabethan) bourgeois tradition, in which reality must be represented as so many stories rather than as problems. In this dramatic or narrative convention the dramatist must have a complete story to tell, and the text as a whole is conceived as an interweaving of stories which all enrich one central story. Reality, when represented in this mode, is not relational or organisational, but rather a closed unit of a story with a beginning, middle and an end.

This type of closed narrative or dramatic construction that Utpal uses to create a self-contained mythic structure has been resisted from the early part of this century. A look at the debate on realism conducted among Ernst Bloch, George Lukács and Bertolt Brecht, as outlined in *Aesthetics and Politics*, shows Bloch's and Brecht's objections to this type of representational form.[41] Their criticisms of Lukács help throw light on the general problem created by the use of Aristotelian and neoclassical forms by communist realists. According to Brecht, the display of social reality as a 'totality' betrays the nature of social reality, which for him is relational and not 'total' or apprehensible as such from any locational vantage point. For the purpose of artistic representation which aims for an actual intervention rather than a neat interpretive construction, Brecht devised the episodic cum narrative form of epic theatre. He chose from the whole array of expressionist method a dramatic equivalent of the technique of montage, that is, a set of episodes that are juxtaposed or joined by a narrative, commenting in choric voices. This not only provoked the audience to work out the textual puzzle, but also actually represented in formal terms the notion of class as social relations and surfaces, rather than self-contained prescribed essences that can be contained in fully rounded 'mythic' forms. This continuously interrupted, continuously relating, juxtaposing form of Brecht's epic theatre challenged both the content and the forms of bourgeois society. Brecht's theatre began and ended in the middle so as to leave the plays as open-ended as possible, because the resolution of the episodic actions does not belong inside but outside of the theatre – in the political arena of society. For him the point of theatre was not to create myths but to demythologise.

---

41   Bloch 1977.

Utpal Dutt's dramatic structure in general, and epic-mythic project in particular, contains all the representational devices that Brecht and recent dramaturgs such as Augusto Boal, for instance, find conservative and repressive. He has a causally organised 'plot', with a fully rounded story with its accomplished action; he obeys the unities, though at times loosely. The multiplicity of emotions and incidents are marshalled to a certain interpretation which is to be taken as the 'truth' about history. The action of the play demonstrates laws that work inwardly and inherently in history with their objective causality. There are no loose ends, no pieces. This accounts for the non-interrupted, non-interventionist structure of his plays, where the main theatrical device is dialogue. Therefore a chorus or a commentator, though sometimes used for formal richness, is not necessary. Where attempts are made at all to go beyond linearity, seriality and causality, to rework space-time relations or show a state of mind (for example in *Dusswapner Nagari* [Nightmare City], where Utpal uses poor poetry), it jars dreadfully with the rest of the play. It is the same in *Tiner Talwar*, with a fully conventional sequence of time, place, action and dialogue, where a few moments of fantasy are introduced to project the inner conflict of the director Benimadhab regarding the purpose of theatre. In fully linear plays, the jarring note of introduction of nonlinear conventions merely serves to highlight the conventional, i.e. bourgeois, aspects of Utpal Dutt's theatre, as for example in the two above plays, with psychologism and vision.

The hero of Utpal Dutt's epic mythic theatre is not so distantly related to the superman. The movement of the action is utterly dependent on special individuals. This becomes apparent in many ways. In plays such as *Stalin 1934*, *Tota* (The Bullet), *Daraon Pathikbar*, *Ajeya Vietnam* (Undefeatable Vietnam), and others, the heroic stature of the protagonists is created not only through their own heroic actions, sufferings, etc., but by creating a contrasting set – the ordinary people – whose adoration of these characters gives us a signal of how to view them. The protagonists are idealised and idolised simultaneously. This idolisation is in keeping with the Aristotelian conventions of a glorious flaw (*hamartia*) – a flaw that even a hero may have – or he may even be completely flawless, as in the case of Stalin in the play of the same name. We are prompted to believe that dramatising 'class truth' very nearly amounts to creating an action-packed story of extraordinary individuals who create through passionate and moral confrontations.

The characters in Utpal's plays are 'essential' – i.e., 'typical' representations. Thereby it is assumed that classes have fixed, objective essences which manifest as character traits in ideal or typical individuals. The character traits always pertain to the 'laws' of class conflicts. For this reason working-class, peasant, middle-class and military heroes are hard to differentiate and share the same characteristics. Stalin and the nineteenth-century peasant leader Titumir have essentially the same dialogue in the same language of heroism, courage and self-sacrifice. They speak as should all leaders of the people. Even the ruling class heroic figures transcend the interests and politics of their class and identify themselves with those below them, for a national cause. The heroes rising from within the lower classes, on the other hand, are some sort of 'nature's aristocrats' or born leaders. The politics of mythic-epic is one of following the leader, who, however, does not need to understand history but embodies its principle. This mythic heroic figure is marked by vast, sweeping passions commensurable to the status of a spirit of an age or class. These feelings are suitably displayed through patriotism and heroism in battles (*Tota*), through patriotism, poetry and excessive temperament (*Daraon Pathikbar*), or dedication to socialist revolution (*Stalin 1934* or *Ajeya Vietnam*). Empathy and admiration for a hero or a leader figure – both within and outside of the text – are the staples of Utpal's epic project. Feeling, not criticality, is here assumed as the agent of change, both for the characters and the audience.

This appeal to vast feelings or passions is meant to enliven the otherwise dull and abstract notion of the type, and excite the audience into anger against tyranny. Utpal is insistent on the claim that all theatre, by which he means European and Indian, from Shakespeare to Ibsen or Gorky, is a grand attempt to create deep feelings in the audience. He indulges in frequent invectives and denunciations against the Bengali middle classes, particularly the poor sectors, for their lack of passion. He thinks that the ability to feel has shrunk among the petty-bourgeois, thus deadening heroic impulses. This is the very '*cul-de-sac*' of the petty-bourgeois life that he speaks of. In his eyes the emotions to be found among his middle-class audience and actors provide no ground for political theatre.

On the other hand, he tells us that 'the people' of Bengal, the peasantry, do not suffer from the atrophy of feelings that characterises the middle classes. This is his view of the people or the 'folk' as the primitive. 'The people' inhabit the world of the 'folk', of legends, of religious superstition, and do not understand the restrictive standards of rationality, criticism and science. They are solely emotional. Utpal Dutt justifies the excessive emotionalism of his plays by saying that 'political theatre has to stand in front of those little or half-educated audiences who don't dissect madness (of Hamlet or Ophelia) under a bourgeois microscope'.[42] Providing them with feelings rather than critical-

---

42   Dutt 1977, p. 13.

ity is the only way to politically educate them. 'We will have to take theatre to those who are sunk in the tradition of *Ramayana* and *Mahabharata*'.[43] This sort of statement reads strangely in view of the fact that Utpal Dutt and the People's Little Theatre[44] actually perform the bulk of their shows through the year to petty-bourgeois middle-class audiences. 'The people' and their imputed theatre habits seem to be more than justification for Utpal's own theatre habits and needs.

The excessiveness of feelings to which the members of Utpal's audience are encouraged through his theatre is supposed to testify to their political involvement. The collective political impact of a play is measured on the strength of feelings that it is able to evoke in the audience. Though Utpal Dutt claims an affinity between his theatre and the 'total' and epic theatre of Irwin Piscator, with his stage of hundreds and all available productive forces, it is difficult not to point out that Piscator was critical, unheroic, and severe – and not a member of the cult of feelings. The stage animator of the *Good Soldier Schweik*, the teacher of Peter Weiss and Ralph Hochhuth, Piscator would have despised Utpal's glowing outbursts of patriotism, nationalism and folkism. It is interesting that in spite of the objectivity and economism of Utpal's concept of class, his ultimate reliance for political results of theatre is on something so subjective. It seems as though it is the motor of feelings that moves history rather than political organisations based on class. The objective laws and class essences cannot otherwise have any dynamism which can be transformed into theatre. The politics of Utpal Dutt's theatre feeling is finally attached to an idealist, petty-bourgeois morality which is activated by the way the story of class struggle is told. As Max Raphael put it in *Proudhon, Marx, Picasso*, the petty-bourgeois revolutionary work of art stands as the mediating conscience between science and politics. In the idealised scheme of class struggle, even when a story begins on the social terrain, an abstract and idealist formulation necessary for the mythic quickly moves it from the realm of the political to that of the moral and the emotional – where the social and organisational specificity of the situation is expunged in favour of constructing an allegory of good fighting evil. Each history play thus loses its historicity and becomes an extended allegory, each political story a moral tale.

The type of realism then that emerges from this mythopoeic aesthetic is allegorical and iconic. The types that are deduced from the ideal laws of social dialectic are really more like icons of class, rather than the individuals or

---

43   Ibid.
44   A theatre group set up by Utpal Dutt with a cultural political philosophy of IPTA.

characters in the bourgeois tradition. If anything they smack of feudalism, of medieval morality plays, where in the name of Shakespearean absolute and ideal moral categories (good or bad angel, mercy, seven deadly sins, etc.) they wrestled over the soul of Everyman, as in *Dusswapner Nagari*. The enactment of ideal action performed by idealised subjects or agents, imbued by moral conflicts, together form the core of Utpal Dutt's mythic-epic theatre. This idealised political scheme, which does not really leave much for the audience to do except to feel the right passions and adore the right hero and the leader, and follow him on his historical mission, is hardly the theatre which can stimulate and mobilise towards an active and popular class struggle. The bourgeois national element, both in content and form, and political intent, overdetermine class struggle. Utpal Dutt's eclectic and mainly bourgeois theatre, guided by socialist realism and revolutionary romanticism, parallels his eclectic and contradictory politics. Here we have a whole range of different politics within the parameters of bourgeois nationalism.

Ultimately we must remember that Utpal Dutt's purpose is to create myth by using an epic mode, as opposed to subjecting myths to the scrutiny of the epic form. We must also remember that he inherited this project of socialist myth-building from the tradition of socialist realism. It so happens that the Soviet agenda also sought to bring together socialism, patriotism and nationalism. And this could not be done by means of critical realism. In the Soviet Union, having a socialist government in place, bourgeois society and class struggle were considered things of the past, and certainly divisive in a situation where divisions existed not only between the left and the right but also among the ranks of the left itself. Soviet cultural policy from the mid-1920s onwards is fraught with stronger and stronger directives to the writers to engage in the project of nation-building, as well as to diffuse possibilities of class struggle at levels other than those which are explicitly economic and political. From Kollontai to *proletcult*, from Mayakovsky to Eisenstein, all were prevented from asking disturbing and divisive questions. What was required – and even Gorky tired of this after a short enthusiastic period – were forms which would be acceptable to bourgeois or semi-feudal tastes and distinctly carry on in a continuous tradition, but which would be instrumentally used to popularise a socialist economy and its state. The work of the myth-maker was to leave behind the grimy, sordid, immediate and the experiential – particularly at a social level – and project the view of a classless society, an ideal class struggle. The utopianism of this cultural enterprise, needless to say, actually leaves intact bourgeois social formations. Class struggle takes place primarily at the level of economic and political power. The conscious myth-building with a worker hero – whose visual equivalents are in the many community posters of the era –

becomes a normative fantasy. Though it is supposed to serve as an encourage-ment for 'the people', it can become a distant and unconnected image, if not at times a condemnation of what actually people are at any given point in time. It certainly does not tell one how to get to the ideal stage from the present one.

What seems to have been forgotten in this attempt to consciously create a national literature of socialism, both in India and the Soviet Union, is the fact that myths, even of proletarian revolution, cannot be created by an individual choice, either by a limited number of persons or even by a successful com-munist party. Even while disputing the notions of collective unconscious and primal archetypes as the ground for myth – it is easily admissible that myths hold in suspension a common but contradictory set of practices and beliefs of large numbers of people over a long period of time, and are not consciously advanced ideological tasks. Myths are not created for the purpose of creating myths, they develop out of existing histories and experiences. They are a com-bination of existing narratives, images, experiences and emotions – polyvalent significations – that have a patina of time and use on them. Myths in that con-text are not meant to be inflated artistic generalisations but highly nuanced particularities. To hide the specificity of the mundane and the everyday was never the purpose of myth, but to crystallise them in a revealing manner. Con-scious mythic projects are at best redundant, at worst, due to the formal and epistemological compromises that have political implications, pernicious to the cause of class struggle. A myth-building exercise is an ideological exercise and not a substitute for, or to be confused with, the culture of resistance which is thrown up in a popular process of class struggle, where grounds for myths happen. An artist can only produce his or her art, it becomes a myth by being inserted into a popular social and political process. If we keep this in mind then we can see how – for all of the reasons outlined so far – India's incomplete revolution could not be taken very much further by such cultural projects as that of Utpal Dutt. His scheme of mythic realism is an aesthetic manifestation of his nationalist bourgeois socialism, whose code name could be Stalinism.

PART 6

Decolonisation

..

Nostalgia for the Future: The Poetry of Ernesto Cardenal

In October 1983, in a packed auditorium at the Ontario Institute for Studies in Education (Toronto), Ernesto Cardenal, poet, priest and Nicaragua's minister of culture in the Sandinista government, spoke about his country's desperate and courageous attempts to hold on to the revolution of 19 July 1979 and nurture it to its fullest development. Speaking of Nicaragua as a country besieged by economic and military aggression of the United States, Cardenal also emphasised the country's role as an emblem of hope in the Latin American and Caribbean struggle against imperialism. 'Are we exporting revolution?' he asked with a smile. 'I don't know about that, but we are certainly exporting hope'. Cardenal took pains to explain the Nicaraguan path to revolution: 'In four years of revolution Nicaragua has experienced profound changes, material as well as spiritual. The Nicaraguan revolution is a new one, without models. It is an original Nicaraguan revolution'.

What, we might ask, is the originality of Nicaragua's revolution? Cardenal outlined its main features for us. It is characterised by a mixed economy, it is popular and humanistic. Speaking about humanism, he remarked that this was the 'most generous revolution in history ... the first without the death penalty'. As Sandinista leader Tomaso Borge put it, 'In Nicaragua what has been executed is the past'. This humanism is complemented by an all-pervasive presence of Christian ethics:

> It is the first to be achieved with the mass participation of Christians. The reason is that the revolution was of the majority and that majority are Christians. It's not only that there are many priests in the government, but that there are many active lay people who hold government and cabinet posts.[1]

The popular aspect of the revolution becomes evident when the massive participation of women as well as that of young people of both sexes is considered:

---

1 Randall 1983 p. 15.

Nicaragua's second largest city, Leon, was liberated by a twenty-three-year-old woman commander, as were other cities. Today's army and police are made up of Sandinistas, which is to say, of many young women members.[2]

And as for young people, suffice it to say that 'at one time the most wanted person by the guard was a twelve-year-old revolutionary. They found him one day and killed him'. And finally Cardenal spoke about the collective nature of the leadership in Nicaragua.

Another aspect of Nicaragua's revolution, although not mentioned initially, began to be highlighted as the evening wore on. In the middle of the talk and questions about the political situation in Nicaragua someone introduced words like 'culture' and 'poetry'. But Cardenal had not come to Canada this time in his capacity as a poet, and he declined to read or recite from any of his poems. He remarked good-humouredly that a poet must forget his old poems in order to write new ones. Instead he spoke about the importance of cultural work as a process of socialist reconstruction. When speaking of culture he extended the conventional use of this term to speak of a culture of political economy, a cultural dimension of health care and the people's militia, pointing out that every project of reconstruction includes a cultural wing, through which people problematise their needs and raise consciousness. New and old cultural forms, verbal and nonverbal, are used. While this was reminiscent of the theories and practices of the Brazilian educationist Paolo Freire, what was important and original about Cardenal's position was not that he expanded the use of a certain device, but that he actually created the possibility of rethinking a body of work, activities and values which we call culture.

1   Making a Cultural Revolution

With this definition of cultural work, Cardenal, like many other politically committed artists, shifts from a conventional way of thinking about creative work towards a new aesthetic. It is not only that art, or 'culture', may be used to serve the people in understanding and expressing something, but also that it must reformulate itself in terms of social relations. Our conventional use of this term has been largely a topographical one; we use it to mark out a certain realm of activities, a certain aspect of our social geography. Culture in that sense is like

---

2   Randall 1984, p. 177.

a fence, a boundary, outside of which lie our non-cultural activities, whatever they may be. But how do we know how to classify some activities as cultural and others as not? The conventional practice has gone to various formal traditions, types of media and mediations, in establishing what qualifies a culture and what does not. That is, we have a cultural product index. We don't see it so much as an activity in the context of ongoing social relations but as an end product of a certain type, constructed within certain 'genres' or traditions.

In Cardenal's terms, however, it is possible to see culture not only as a previously coded body of products but also as a set of expressive formalising activities in the context of an ongoing set of social relations. Any change in the social relations can and indeed must bring about major changes in our formalising expressive activities – in their location, use and form. Perhaps then it is possible to say about culture what once Marx said about capital: that it is not a thing but a set of social relations concretised within history and formal traditions. So when new social relations evolve, in the process of creating revolution or in the post-revolutionary era, they lead to a redefinition of culture both as a category and as activity. This way of seeing of course provides an activist role for a population of producers of their own culture rather than the passive one of consumers of 'art' turned out by the socially disengaged artist. Cardenal himself has written about this in many of his poems, particularly in the context of language and culture, in the collection *Zero Hour and Other Documentary Poems*:

> 'Revolutionary art without artistic value ...'
> And artistic art without revolutionary value? It seems to me
> that great bards of the twentieth century are in Publicity
> those Keatses and Shelleys singing the Colgate smile
> Cosmic Coca-Cola, the pause that refreshes
>
> ...
>
> language, also polluted.
> 'It appears that he (Johnson) never understood
> that words also have a real meaning
> besides serving for propaganda'
> *Time* said that he does understand it and he lies just the same.
> And the defoliation of Vietnam
> is a Resource Control Program
> it's also a defoliation of language.
> And language avenges itself refusing to communicate.
> Plunder: investments.
> There are also crimes of the CIA in the realm of semantics.

Here in Nicaragua, as you have said:
the language of the government and private enterprise
against the language of the Nicaraguan people.
        Epistle to Jose Coronel Urtecho[3]

This view of language and art, that is of culture, suggests the need for a new aesthetic. A revolutionary struggle is also a cultural one; that is, it is a struggle for the reclamation of our everyday lives, for our right to express and communicate in our own way. And this struggle which is cultural-political is also personal because it involves making a choice, deciding what kind of social relations one wishes to live with, and this means knowing which side one is on. It is at this level that Ernesto Cardenal's poetry addresses its readers, as a personal message outlining the task of a personal political choice – particularly about Nicaragua.

In fact, Cardenal's poems are a lot like letters to the individual reader. They are an invitation for participation, for making a choice, and they demand a clear yes or no about their content. There is no standing by in an objectivist pose and watching in an act of abstract contemplation. Of course the reader may delay for a while, wander about with the book in a handbag, defer coming to any conclusions because that involves so many confusions, doubts, indecisions – but position oneself one must, or the process of reading this poetry will not be concluded. Cardenal is not a liberal relativist saying 'This is only my version of Nicaragua; you may have one too. Both are equally tenable, or the truth lies in between'. His vision is totally integrated with the revolutionary efforts of the Sandinistas, and he speaks with the absolute moral imperative of the revolutionary, and this absolutism is compounded by the morality of 'liberation theology'. If this version of history and social change is not to any reader's liking, if that reader also rejects this absolute moral imperative, then Cardenal is not his or her poet. And today in North America and elsewhere the world is divided between people who say yes to this political stand of Ernesto Cardenal and those who do not.

Cardenal's version of the world in which we live – in which Nicaragua lived – is simply the world of industrial capitalism in its imperialist phase, it is not meant for the advancement of people but profit. A world of 'Texaco, Standard Oil ... the monopolies', a world evolved from a long history of class societies, of 'private property and the accumulation of capital'.

---

3   All quotations from Cardenal poems are from Cardenal 1980.

Later on better than raising sheep was stealing sheep.
War could be an industry.
To guard the wheat as important as sowing it.
War could be productive.
And after domesticating animals man invented a way
to domesticate man.
Not killing the enemy: making him work.
Slavery was the basis of industry and the accumulation of capital

...

The division of classes a product of progress? Yes
but it did not accelerate, it retards future progress.
Progress in neolithic times was in the production processes
and it was made by the producers
but now these – the inventors – become
the lower class.

A world of beauty, of 'Moon pottery / (white laquer and fine-lined motifs).
Charming / red jaguars with a white background, incense pots' had fallen prey
to imperialist enterprises. On top of the world of freshness and beauty lay:

bits of Coca-Cola bottles and Goodyear tires and chamber pots.
Acahualinca begins there, the houses of cardboard and cans
where the sewers empty ...
Streets that smell of jails,
that characteristic jail smell
of shit and rancid urine
houses of cement bags gasoline cans rubble old rags.
The sewers end there.

...

There the children with wary little eyes
the children weak sickly enormous beetles
their bellies swollen and their legs thin as toothpicks

...

Old women crouched over the guts that the slaughterhouse throws out
scaring off the buzzards.
The pig and the pot-bellied kid in the same puddle.

...

I saw a papaya tree in a street like a miracle in that horror.

Oracle over Managua

This is clearly a degraded and inverted world. The humans have been denied all conditions of being human. 'Man's greatest crime is to prevent men from being men'. And to be set back on its feet, to be the right way up it must be turned upside down, a complete reversal. Hence revolution. Cardenal's poetry is full of insurrectionary, resurrectionary (which for him is also revolutionary) signs. Revolution is to be seen as a communion at the end of a long chapter of exploitation.

> *kupia-kumi* = 'one-single-heart'
> One-single-heart: the military and money look like that
> today (but those two have no heart). No: the sole trae kumi
> is Love, namely the union of the people to achieve
> the Revolution. Only Love is truly single-heart.
> > Nicaraguan Canto

And so for Cardenal revolution is inscribed as the last stage in the book of nature, in the evolutionary process; a denial of the revolution is the denial of God's will as expressed through nature.

> I said the iguanas lay their eggs ... It is the process. They
> (or else the frogs) in the silence of the carboniferous age
> made the first sound
> sang the first love song here on earth
> sang the first love song here beneath the moon
> it is the process.
> The process started with the stars.
> New relations of production: that too
> is part of production: that too
> is part of the process. Oppression. After oppression, liberation.
> The Revolution started in the stars, millions
> of light years away.
> > Nicaraguan Canto

These lines are not simply a matter of metaphors, poetic license; Cardenal means what he says. He is rather a literal writer and for him the Bible, nature and the revolutionary process are inextricably intertwined, in that together they illuminate the truth. The belief that holds him in the position of the minister of culture in the face of Vatican opposition and away from a life of contemplation is also articulated in the lines that follow. They are not merely 'poetic' moments or biblical metaphors, but a guide to conduct.

Because at times a man is born in a land
and he *is* that land.
And the land in which that man is buried
is that man.
And the men who afterward are born in that land
are that man.
And Adolfo Baez Bone was that man.

Nicaraguan Canto

2   The Land, the Man

Ernesto Cardenal was born into a well-to-do family in Granada, Nicaragua, in
1925. He studied at the University of Mexico (1943–7) and Columbia University
in New York (1947–9). During 1957–9 he was a novice at the Trappist monastery in Gethsemany, Kentucky, where poet and priest Thomas Merton was his
spiritual director. Cardenal's ill-health, among other reasons, prevented him
from taking the vow and he studied instead for the priesthood during 1959–
65. In 1965 he returned to Nicaragua and established a church and a commune
which he named Nuestra Señora de Solentiname. This place is an archipelago
of thirty-eight islands on Lake Nicaragua, with a population of one thousand
campesinos (peasants) and fishermen. In 1970 he went to Cuba to be a judge
for a poetry competition organised by Casa de las Americas. In 1977 the Somoza
dictatorship ordered the destruction of the commune and Cardenal fled to
Costa Rica. Thereafter he became the roving ambassador for the liberation
movement (FSLN) which in 1979 toppled the Somoza dictatorship. Cardenal
was chosen to be the minister of culture in the new government.

A poet and writer for a long time, Cardenal is relatively unknown to English readers. His books of poems which have received some attention in the
English-speaking world are *Apocalypse and Other Poems* (English translation
1977) and *Zero Hour and Other Documentary Poems* (English translation 1981).
Another work, *In Cuba* (English translation 1974), is an account of socialist
reconstruction in Cuba and an assessment of Christianity's methods, goals
and morality in relation to those of communism. The trip to Cuba convinced
Cardenal of the compatibility of the two. *Homage to the American Indian* (English translation 1973) is virtually unknown among English readers and difficult
to come by. There are also two other volumes, which consider the relationship
of Christianity to revolutionary activities, and specifically ponder the question of armed struggle, namely *The Sanctity of Revolution* (1976) and *The Gospel in Solentiname*. There is also a small illustrated book, published after the

revolution, about Solentiname and Cardenal's own involvement there, called *Nostalgia del Futuro*.

These are the bare facts of Ernesto Cardenal's life, and they have to be supplemented by other facts, contextualised in relation to the Nicaraguan reality. We must move out of individual biography to the history of the country, of the region and the relations of the US to Central America. Questions as to Cardenal's involvements before he became a priest, why he set up the commune of Solentiname, why it was destroyed, why he went to Cuba, how he can be part of a political group that espouses armed struggle, or a member of the state, far away from his priestly duties – these questions can only be answered by introducing the historical element into his personal life. Cardenal himself is acutely aware of being rooted in the Nicaraguan reality. In the 'Nicaraguan Canto', comparing his poetry to the local birds' song, he expresses a complete identification with his country:

> I'd like to watch the lumberjacks at work.
> To talk to turtle-catchers on the cays.
> This is the land I sing. My poetry belongs here,
> like the trumpeting zanate, or the wine-producing palm.
> I feel a longing for those eastern swamps.

His poetry is an epic verse rendition of Nicaraguan history and struggles, and it is to this history that we must now turn.

The history of Nicaragua has been one of a continuous battle against the local tyrants set up and propped up by US military power and the ubiquitous presence of the US multinationals or its adventurist gangsters, such as William Walker, earlier in this century. The attitudes and activities of the gangsters were actually not very different from those of the businessmen and the government interventions that were to follow, for example Cornelius Vanderbilt, the American railroad magnate who built an extensive empire in Central America, later companies such as the United Fruit Company, and even the White House itself. Always with the so-called business came the army. All talk by modern political theorists of the major capitalist countries about the 'relative autonomy' of the state breaks down in the face of this hand in glove relationship. As Cardenal puts it.

> To invest capital in Nicaragua and then to protect
> US investments was the State Department's job.

And

the marines landed to 'reestablish order'
and they stayed in Nicaragua for 13 years. Control
over railroads customs banks was not enough.
Nicaragua sold her territory as well ...
       Nicaraguan Canto

The Monroe Doctrine of 1823, which, as George Black points out in his book *Triumph of the People: The Sandinista Revolution in Nicaragua*, 'claimed the Americas as an exclusive target for US expansionism in exchange for non-intervention in the colonial affairs of the European powers',[4] is still in operation today. Whenever there is any attempt to move out of the u.s. economic and military stranglehold, local and u.s. repression descends. One such attempt led to the emergence of the liberation fighter Augusto Cesar Sandino in 1927, when 'the us marines duly disembarked at Corinto in January. This time the force was a large one: 215 officers commanding 865 marines and 3900 soldiers, accompanied by arms supplies ...'[5] Sandino, whose memory lives in the revolution of Nicaragua today, was a thirty-one-year-old worker who had returned to the country after years of working for the u.s. companies. In his account of the development of the Nicaraguan revolution, George Black outlines the nature of the resistance put up by Sandino and his guerrillas from the mountains of Segovia:

> His experience as a worker was vital to the formation of his anti-imperialist and to an extent class consciousness. As a warehouseman in Montecristo sugar mill in Honduras owned by the Honduras Sugar and Distilling Company; as a banana plantation worker for the United Fruit Company in Guatemala; as an oilfield worker for the South Pennsylvania Oil Company and Huasteca Petroleum Company, he had learned his lessons in politics. It had given him a firsthand knowledge of the reality of American imperialism in Central America. Under Sandino's leadership, the war against US intervention was Nicaragua's first organised questioning of bourgeois and imperialist power structures, and gave shape for the first time to a long – if sporadic – tradition of spontaneous popular revolt.[6]

For this resistance Sandino was murdered by Anastasio Somoza, the head of the National Guard, created by the u.s. in 1934, and of course with the active

---

4   Black 1981, p. 6.
5   Black 1981, p. 12.
6   Black 1981, p. 13.

support of the White House. Before he had him killed in an ambush, Somoza invited Sandino to Managua for peace talks and embraced him publicly.

How much of these events influenced Emesto Cardenal? People make their own history, but they don't do it just as they please. The world into which we are born, its politics, history and culture, provides us with the stage on which we act, parts that we have to reconstruct for ourselves. Not even the strongest individual consciousness is solely self-determined and immune to history. The Nicaragua into which Cardenal was born echoed with the struggle and the betrayal of Sandino. For almost half a century thereafter Cardenal and Nicaragua lived through the dual realities of repression and resistance. His life coincides with the founding of the Somoza dynasty and goes beyond. Changing neither their master nor their economic and political practices, the Somozas continued to grow from 1934 until by the 1970s the state of Nicaragua had become the private estate of the family. To this the people offered their persistent resistance, so during his student days Cardenal, like other young people of the country, found himself joining in the resistance attempts, which culminated again in an armed struggle. People from all walks of life found themselves next to each other in this process. Cardenal's poetry is a tribute to such people, every line filled with a direct knowledge of their sacrifice, their torture and death.

> That same night a boy stripped to his shorts.
> Like one of those frightened puppies.
> 'Drink it up', said Colonel Somoza Debayl to me. 'Isn't it your own
> blood? It won't hurt you'.
> I began to confess lies my voice faltering, the stenographers
> getting it down on paper with their swift pencils ...
> Between one torture and the next he'd see a movie,
>> Oracle Over Managua

3   Countdown to the Revolution

In the poem 'Zero Hour', written before Cardenal went to the Trappist monastery, we find the history of Nicaragua paralleled by Cardenal's own development; it is the countdown to the revolutionary moment. The poem is in four sections. The first section is an overview of Central America as a whole, narrowing down to Nicaragua.

> Tropical nights in Central America,
> with moonlit lagoons and volcanoes

and lights from the presidential palaces,
barracks and sad curfew warnings ...

And Managua the target of machine guns
from the chocolate cookie palace
and steel helmets patrolling the streets

Watchman! What hour is it of the night?
> Zero Hour

In the next section the particularity of Nicaragua is further specified, a country rendered to a carrion by the Somozas and their u.s. allies, with the multinationals crawling in it like so many maggots, and terrible man-made famines stalking the land.

The banana is left to rot on the plantations,
or to rot in the cars along the railroad tracks
or it's cut overripe so it can be rejected
when it reaches the wharf to be thrown into the sea;
the bunches of banana declared bruised or too skinny,
or withered, or green, or overripe, or diseased
so there'll be no cheap bananas,
or so as to buy bananas cheap.
> Zero Hour

Having outlined the different stages and causes of oppression the poem introduces the theme of resistance. Augusto Cesar Sandino becomes the embodiment of Nicaragua's struggle against foreign and local dictatorships. Cardenal takes historical details of this struggle and its betrayal, and projects them until there is a fusion between the past resistance and that of the FSLN leading to a victory in 1979. It was also in these northern mountains, Sandino's Segovias, that the Sandinistas regrouped themselves for the final onslaught against the Somoza regime. There, beckoned by the light of revolution, which is also the light of Sandino,

What is that light way off there? Is it a star?
It is Sandino's light shining in the black mountains.
The old and the new Sandinistas fuse into one.
There they are, he and his men, beside the red bonfire
with rifles slung and wrapped in their blankets,

smoking or singing sad songs from the North,
the men motionless and their shadows in motion.
    Zero Hour

The following section about the failed uprising of 1954 moves closer to Cardenal's personal experience. It is about his friend Adolfo Baez Bone's death, but also about himself and all the others who fought. Sandino's death is repeated but this time not with a simple act of treachery, but through tanks and planes that raze the house that hid Bone and his companions.

But April in Nicaragua is the month of death.
They killed them in April.
I was with them in the April rebellion
and I learned to handle a Reising machine gun.
And Adolfo Baez Bone was my friend:
They hunted him with airplanes, with trucks,
with floodlights, with tear-gas bombs,
with radios, with dogs, with police;
and I remembered the red clouds over the Presidential Mansion
like blood-red swabs of cotton.
    Zero Hour

In 'Nicaraguan Canto' and 'Oracle Over Managua', Cardenal writes of these deaths again and again – the deaths of the poets Lionel Rugama, Ruben Dario, and all others who were part of the struggle – 'Selim Shible, Silvio, Casimiro, Julio, they had fallen'. And 'Glory isn't what the history books teach: / it's a flock of buzzards in a field and a great stink'. But the theme of the undying freedom fighter who rises up or returns because he died for his people, a common myth of many agrarian struggles, is also present in Cardenal's poetry. It keeps alive the hope, the continuity of the people's struggle. 'The underground radio kept saying he was alive. / The people didn't believe he had died. / (And he hasn't died.)'

It was at this time (around 1954) that Cardenal seems to have turned to the church. When he went to the Trappist monastery at Gethsemane he couldn't have been very optimistic about anything, let alone about a successful armed uprising against the organised us-backed brutality of the Somoza regime. In this state, suffering from excruciating headaches, Cardenal was particularly fortunate in his spiritual director. It is Thomas Merton who gave him his new direction. In an interview with Margaret Randall, Cardenal gives us a brief history of the foundation of his contemplative activist community, Solentiname:

It was Thomas Merton who gave me the idea. He had been a monk for twenty years and had written a great deal about that life but had been unhappy with monastic life ... And after twenty years Merton was wanting out ... He knew it was a medieval, anachronistic lifestyle. Ridiculous. So he wanted to found a different kind of contemplative community outside the US. Merton was an enemy of the US, of Yankee civilisation and everything it represented. He hated the bourgeois mentality most monks had ... He told me I was in my monastic honeymoon and that within a few years I too would find the life arid.[7]

So Cardenal returned to his country and slowly developed the community of Our Lady of Solentiname. It was a long process of involvement in the life of the local people, becoming a part of their everyday life, not only as the priest in residence, but as a teacher, a friend. Much went on in this little community. The gospels were read, interpreted, poetry written, paintings done, and all the while the situation in Nicaragua examined, understood, actions considered in the light of new interpretations of the Bible in a communitarian context. Cardenal had once more turned to the struggle for the liberation of Nicaragua. Abstract contemplation, far from the world of pain and misery, was not to be his path. He engaged in what could be called 'praxis' and combined the understanding of history with struggle for change. The people of this community had come to the same conclusions as he had. One of the older members of the community, Olivia, had this to say to Margaret Randall when questioned on how she felt about revolutionary militancy:

> Each day we would learn new things, and I tell you that this is the sort of thing where you couldn't take it in and just live in peace. You begin to feel more committed, more concerned about others. If, living the life we led, we were concerned about all our neighbors, now we had concern for everything in the country. And afterwards, for everything not only in the country but also in Central America. And for what was happening in the world.[8]

There was an active contact with the FSLN, and many of the young people of the community became guerrillas and joined the liberation movement. This brought down tremendous repression, and finally in 1977 Solentiname was des-

---

7 Randall 1983, p. 41.
8 Randall 1983, p. 75.

troyed by the National Guard. The physical destruction of the community could not break the spirit of the people however. Though Cardenal fled to Costa Rica, the members of the community who survived continued to fight along FSLN lines. Cardenal himself became a spokesman for the liberation movement and represented it at UN meetings and in various countries. On 18 July 1979 he clandestinely flew back into the country. The next day Nicaragua was reborn from the ashes and debris of the past. In the poem 'Lights' in *Zero Hour*, this moment of possibility finds its expression.

> It's the most dangerous moment, enemy aircraft
> may be waiting for us over the airport.
> And the airport lights at last.
> We've landed. From out of the dark come olive-green comrades
> to greet us with hugs.
> We feel their warm bodies, that also come from the sun,
> that are also light.
> This revolution is fighting the darkness.
> It was daybreak on July 18th. And the beginning
> of all that was about to come.
>> Lights

4   Christian Communism

The Nicaraguan revolution, said Cardenal, was a unique revolution. This would appear to be the case if in particular one were to consider the nature of its political mobilisation. It is not so much a classically marxist as a populist revolution. It realises the dreams of both Christians and communists, one could even say of Christians as communists. How, the world has been asking, is that possible? After all, Christianity has been very ready to be of service to colonialism, imperialism and local exploitation. The cultural and ideological subjugation of the peoples of the Third World in the name of God, Christ and the church has been well recorded and much discussed. The Andean Indians who were declared to have no soul, and therefore to be of no consequence as human beings, were eliminated with the church's approval and help. The Africans who exchanged their land for the Bible, as the saying goes, lost more than their worldly possessions in the process. It is perhaps more than a piece of trivia that the first slave ship was called *Jesus*. (The examples of dissident Jesuits and priests do more than anything else to prove the exceptional nature of their commitment, rather than Christianity's positive contribution to the people's cause. The unpopularity of such clerics with the Vatican is also well recorded.)

The struggles of the poor during the last few centuries have not been able to sway the Catholic church or Christianity in general to act for them in any significant way. If there was once a contradiction between the church and growing capitalism (which appears upon close inspection to be a conflict of interest – feudalism fighting capitalism) there is certainly no vestige of that now. Once the church, though itself the biggest European landlord in the middle ages, forbade usury; now the Vatican has its own bank. Cardenal mentions this bank in 'Zero Hour': 'The Bank of the Holy Spirit has been closed. / A kind of automatic fruition, as if / money laboured'.

But it seems that time and time again the misery of the people and their social discontent catch up with their religious beliefs, and with or without sanction from the church institutions and ecclesiastical bodies, they proceed to put up their version of what God meant against the version of those in power. They speak in the language of religion because that is the clearest ideology that they have. And here we might mention from Marx the expressive aspect of religious ideology – not just the pacificatory one – since so far we have only heard of a truncated quotation from Marx on religion as the opiate of the masses. The fuller version of what Marx actually said widens the social implications of religious expressions:

> Religious distress is at the same time the expression of real distress and also the protest against real distress. Religion is the sigh of the oppressed creature, the heart of a heartless world, just as it is the spirit of the spiritless condition. It is the opium of the people.[9]

By the 1960s a popular and militant version of Christianity seemed to be emerging in Latin America. There was of course the impact of the Columbian priest Camillo Torres, excommunicated and killed, whose Christianity prompted him to pick up a gun to fight the exploitation of the rural poor in Columbia. And also there was a general disgust at the traditional church for its hand-in-glove complicity with the dictators. As Cardenal puts it,

> the church goes to bed with anyone at all ...
> Monsignor Borgia all in red tassels and phylacteries
> presiding over the Bishop's conference
> 'And that prick from Nazareth, what's he saying'
> ... the apostasy of the Nicaraguan church ...

---

9 Marx 1972e, p. 12.

Fernando said: don't fuck around.
Tinita Salazar doesn't earn ten pesos a week.
Pijulito died because the hospital wouldn't let him in.
And then they talk to me about God. Don't be ridiculous!

Zero Hour

Clearly if religion were going to mean anything for the people it had to be different from what the monsignors of this world had preached as the word of God. It would have to be a church that would not excommunicate the Camillo Torreses of Latin America. And a possibility arose from within the church itself for some reinterpretation to occur.

> The second Vatican Council called by Pope John XXIII in 1962 prescribed a gospel-oriented content for Christianity and a more socially conscious doctrine than that of previous papal encyclicals. A general ecumenical opening-up allowed for dialogue with other denominations and non-Christians. Lay people were given responsibility in the pastoral work of the church. Liturgical reforms included the introduction of language, songs and instruments native to different cultures and an end to masses in which priests kept their back to the people.[10]

The Latin American Bishop's Conference in Medillin, Columbia, in 1968 concretised the radical implications of this new papal encyclical. 'Liberation theology' began to be theorised and acted upon. The Catholic Church in Latin America had entered a new era. The long existing demand for equality of all people and social justice was now firmly anchored in the idea of a just God who punished the wicked and legitimised popular militancy against all forms of oppression. The life of Christ was read more directly, from the vantage point of the oppressed rather than mediated through the 'institution'. In fact the story of Christ became the story of the poor people themselves. Christ was seen as a poor revolutionary who sought justice for the poor and died on the cross of the ruling class. There was sought a return to the early pre-Constantine non-imperial days of the religion, to the days of the catacombs. Christianity was again to be a religion created by and for the poor, not that which was later adopted and radically adapted by the ruling class. There was an identification of the Christian in the catacombs with the guerrilla going underground to avoid Somoza's National Guard. 'With no alternative to death / You went underground / or as you said entered the catacombs'. The mystical tradition re-read

---

10   Randall 1984, p. 19.

thus could have profoundly political and incendiary possibilities. What actions should follow from lines such as these:

> The solution is simple: to give to others in brotherhood.
> Capitalism impedes communion.
> ...
> Saint Ambrose thundered in his Milan cathedral, on the threshold of
>   feudalism ...
> THE EARTH BELONGS TO EVERYBODY, NOT THE RICH
> and Saint John Chrysostom in Byzantium with his Biblical Marxism
> 'the community of goods is more faithful to nature'.
>   Zero Hour

Both the priests and the lay Catholic community were aware of the radical and novel nature of this interpretation, but neither group considered it as heretical. In fact the traditional church's record of repression and class service had earned it the name of 'church of hierarchy'. Not only was Christianity reconcilable with militant class struggle, it also actually offered the imperative of militancy out of its own nature.

This particular way of reading Christianity provided the majority of the people with a worldview, a language, a systematic organisation of symbols and signs, a basis for the construction of the struggle. There was no need to learn a completely new way of conceptualising and expressing; they could begin from where they were, transforming the world they inhabited. Part of the real social transformation was that very transformation of Christianity itself. It was both a tool for change and the tool forged in the struggle. God was called to be on the side of the poor, and it was felt that he was.

5   Visionaries and Revolutionaries

Such a large-scale reinterpretation of the Bible and formulation of social movements in terms of religious ideology is relatively new in the Catholic tradition. But Christianity had already served this purpose in the Protestant tradition. The peasants' war in Germany was fought in the name of Martin Luther, though he wanted no part in it, and the civil war in England, also called the 'puritan revolution', activated large-scale religio-political movements. In the English case in particular, during the war and even through the period of restoration and the eighteenth century, religious ideas of different types served as the common people's ideology of social struggle.

Radical activist Christian sects such as Levellers, Diggers, Ranters, Shakers, Quakers and Muggletonians have mostly disappeared, leaving behind a luminous history of visions of social change. The influence of John Muggleton and other poor people's mystics – such as shoemaker Jacob Boehm – on William Blake's revolutionary poetry has been discussed at length by writers such as E.P. Thompson. John Bunyan's *Pilgrim's Progress* is another vision that has found its way into English literature. The work of Cohn, *The Pursuit of the Millennium*,[11] and that of Christopher Hill, *The World Turned Upside Down*,[12] document many of these revolutionary religious movements. Religion was such an integral force in the demand for social change that Christopher Hill made the remark that '[i]ndeed it is perhaps misleading to differentiate too sharply between politics, religion and general scepticism'.[13] What he says of the seventeenth and eighteenth centuries is equally applicable to the popular revolutionary ideology of Central America.

Of course this reinterpretation was not a scholarly exercise, a textual debate on the Bible, but rather a way of exploring and realising the ethical imperatives of a certain type of Christianity. People acted on the belief that it was 'easier for a camel to pass through the eye of a needle than for the rich man to enter the kingdom of heaven'. They also acted on the promise that 'the meek shall inherit the earth', and made distinct attempts to attain the reward here and now. The kingdom of heaven would at least find its earthly expression in a new social order brought about by the militancy of the poor. It is illuminating to read in this context what the seventeenth-century Christian activist Gerald Winstanley said to the people of London:

> Freedom is the man that will turn the world upside down, therefore no wonder he hath enemies ... True freedom lies in the community, in spirit and community in the earthly treasury, and this is Christ the true man-child spread abroad in the creation, restoring all things unto himself.[14]

The social project of the common people of Europe in the seventeenth and eighteenth centuries was not very dissimilar to that of the common people of Nicaragua in the 1970s. An echo of Winstanley's sentiment can be heard in the words of Olivia, a poor woman living in the community of Solentiname, whom I quoted earlier:

---

11   Cohn 1970.
12   Hill 1975.
13   Hill 1975, p. 14.
14   Winstanley 1649, p. 5.

Revolution and religion go together; they are two equal things, never unequal. That is why I say that revolutionaries can be Christian. There is no contradiction. I have heard some people say that a revolutionary can't be a Christian. In truth, is a revolutionary not a real Christian? If a revolutionary does not mention God perhaps it is because he or she doesn't want to. In fact he or she is more Christian than many who say they are ... And any person who says they're very religious but they don't like the revolution must not understand Jesus.[15]

But then again, this is not the seventeenth century and there are distinct aspects to the Nicaraguan religio-political ideology which are features of a post-marxian era, filled with global anti-imperialistic struggles. Liberation theology, therefore, not only speaks of the rich and the poor, the just and the unjust, but also about relations between classes, and socio-economic systems of exploitation and foreign domination called capitalism and imperialism. It is in this that they can supersede the older millenarian movements, build a movement oriented to class struggle, make alliances with non-Christians and marxists and participate in the revolutionary armed struggles and the Sandinista government. Neither in the lay Catholic population nor in its priests – such as Ernesto Cardenal, Fernando Cardenal, Miguel de Scoto, Uriel Molina and others – do we see any doubt about the values embodied in the Nicaraguan revolution.

Cardenal's visit to Cuba, recorded in his book *In Cuba*, was one of a series of assessments made by Catholics, particularly priests, of the goals of a socialist revolution in the light of Christianity. Cardenal, for instance, found that communists or socialists and Christians could make close alliances and aimed for the same type of social justice. He feels strongly that the ethical imperatives of communism and Christianity, based on basic human needs and against different types of alienation, overlap. Going by the doctrines and practices of liberation theology, one could say that a new brand of militancy has evolved in Central America, a militancy of 'communist Christianity', and I emphasise the word 'communist' since 'community' and 'communion' are at the root of this word.

---

15   Randall 1983, p. 112.

6   The Poetics of Documentation

This 'communist Christianity' constitutes not only the politics of Ernesto Cardenal, but his poetics as well. The documentary quality of his poetry combines with a contemplative tone like that of Thomas Merton in an epic form. These formal devices are as essential to Cardenal as documentary film or news formats are to other 'reporters' and documentarians. In Cardenal's case, as a partisan to the revolution, he must explain the revolution to us, show the justice of his cause and demand that we take sides too. For this he needs a type of realism in his poetry, a realism which is not just disjointed bits of the social surface, but is more in the nature of a set of transparencies showing what is going on underneath and around them – in fact, the social relations, the contexts that produce and texture the surface. Here the 'natural' is relieved of its work of being a substitute for life. Events, bits of history, details of landscape and businesses, are all slides inserted into an 'epic' version of history which provides a systematic view of exploitation and resistance.

Cardenal's poetry, then, records what exists, bears witness to what happened and is happening, but at the same time it captures the transformative forces. He must be 'documentary' and 'revelatory' at the same time. The technical or formal aspects of his poetry combine with the Bible and Marx's *Capital* or *The Communist Manifesto*, not in a bid for eclecticism, but in an attempt at creating a new epistemology, a new way of knowing reality. The vast sweep of Cardenal's historic vision from the pre-Columbian days to now is also set within the Biblical myth of the fall, of 'Paradise lost' through the conquest and regained through the revolution.

Because Cardenal is a Christian communist he can see the world as a set of signs from which a believer can read the will of God. This way of looking at the natural and social world presupposes of course a knowledge of, a commitment to, the Christian code, which confers significance to the world of appearances and events.

The elements of Cardenal's poetry include: descriptions, reports, allusions and certain types of juxtapositions where manmade horror, inflicted by imperialism, is juxtaposed with the beauty of nature. In fact, throughout his poetry the beauty of nature serves as a source of healing, a reminder of the possibility of regeneration. In poem after poem filled with stories of moral and economic bankruptcy, hunger and exploitation, death and torture of those who protest, there are also moments reflecting the serenity and innocence of Nicaragua's nature and her humble people. The early morning following Sandino's murder is an instance of this:

It's the hour when the corn-mush star of Chontales
gets the little Indian girls up to make com mush,
and out come the chicle-seller, the wood-seller, and the root-seller
with the banana groves still silvered by the moon

...

The ranch hands begin to herd their cows

...

the boatmen hoist the sails of their boats;
And the Tuca squaws keep coming down the Hidden River
with the ducks going quack-quack-quack, and the echoes,
the echoes, while the tugboat goes with the Tuca squaws
slithering over the green-glass river
toward the Atlantic ...

> Zero Hour

This beauty of the natural world, set in contrast to Sandino's death, does not indicate nature's indifference to the goings-on in society, but rather resonates with the beauty of the 'newly-created' earth. The beauty remains and the revolution's project is not only to reclaim the earth, but also to recreate a redemptive social order eliminating the contrast between the innocent beauty of nature and the socio-political world. 'With all things held in common / as they were before the Fall of our First Parents'.

7   Marxism or Christianity

In the preface to *Zero Hour and Other Documentary Poems*, D.D. Walsh calls Cardenal a marxist-Christian poet. In his talk in Toronto, Cardenal himself endorsed this opinion. This raises questions which the epithet 'Christian communist' does not. Whereas the communitarian roots of Christianity with an emphasis on social justice can have exactly the same immediate political projects as those of marxist revolutionaries, their epistemological implications are very different. They spell out antithetical relationships between consciousness and the material world. This becomes a problem if marxism is seen as a philosophy, a worldview, a method of investigation of reality rather than solely as a political project: that is, if while discussing marxism we talk not only of *The Communist Manifesto*, but also, for example, of *The German Ideology*, if we see *Capital* not only as an exposure of a particular type of exploitation, but as a method of exploring social formations. If such considerations are kept in mind one must come to a conclusion of an irreducible contradiction existing between materialist and idealist interpretations of the relations between the socio-historical world and forms of consciousness. One approaches reality radically differently depending on whether one believes that God created man or man created God.

Cardenal himself, neither in his talk in Toronto nor in his writing, seems to think there is any contradiction. While answering questions regarding his marxism he equated the biblical notion of the Kingdom of Heaven on earth with the marxist concept of the dictatorship of the proletariat. He also made statements such as 'He saw that matter was good (a materialistic God)' and 'Idols are idealism / While the prophets were professing dialectical materialism'. What could he have possibly meant by using such words as 'materialism' or 'dialectical materialism' in such ways and such contexts? This is not a usage that either materialists or idealists would accept because it robs words of their meaning in a consistent philosophical tradition.

It is politically and morally acceptable to say that marxist politics and Christian ethics move towards the same goal. It is also true that the Nicaraguan 'church of revolution' and the marxists conceptualise history in terms of struggles of classes, struggles between oppressors and oppressed. Both reject exploitation and alienation and seek to establish a society of just distribution and development of creativity. Both consider basic needs rather than merit and at least in theory reject the division between mental and manual labour. So far so good. But things begin to stick at the epistemological divide. The secularism of marxism and the spiritualism of Christianity make it impossible for idealism and materialism to stand in for each other or be aggregated in a total world view. If anyone sees God as a figment of imagination, a product of idealist thought, that God cannot be seen as 'a materialist God'. It does make all the difference in the world whether we say that consciousness is determined by existence or the reverse. It could be that if these two traditions of thought were spelled out and developed to their fullest ramifications they would actually have different practical or political implications, not just epistemological ones. It is my feeling that a 'materialist' reading of the Bible would disempower the Bible itself of the type of moral force and revelatory character that Cardenal finds in it.

The other problem that emerges out of this attempt at what seems to me to be an unworkable synthesis is that the source of one's political and moral actions remains unclear and undifferentiated. This could pose a real problem if, for instance, one lost one's religious (idealist) motivations and had no secular ethics on which to proceed. This dilemma was posed a long time ago by Dostoevsky in The *Brothers Karamazov*, in the question of Ivan – if God is dead, must not all things lose value and all actions including murder become permissible? One need not cite such extreme examples except perhaps to point out the degree of confusion that such aggregation leaves one open to. Also, there are other possibilities that one must guard against. If, for instance, the people of Nicaragua see their revolution as a 'Christian revolution', then a strongly divided pulpit, as suggested by the attitudes or dictates of the right-wing Cardenal Obando y Bravo of Managua, or of the Pope himself, could confuse the people and re-assert reactionary trends. This could of course also weaken the participation of the clergy in general, and pose the problem of secession from the Roman church.

But even with these questions and reservations, one must revert to the position that the only revolutionary project that succeeds in any fundamental way must begin where people are. It must be a process that reclaims. regenerates and reconstructs the overall terrain of popular consciousness. The goal of social justice and the defence of the revolution from reaction and u.s. imperialism have drawn the Nicaraguan people together, believers and non-believers alike; the coincidence of the will of the people has led to a convergence of political understanding and symbols. It is this great social movement that has spoken through the available ideology of Christianity. It is this that has radicalised Christianity.

CHAPTER 29

A Transformational Pedagogy: Reflections on Rabindranath's Project of Decolonisation

Swadeshi, Swarajism, ordinarily produce intense excitement in the minds of my countrymen, because they carry in them some fervor of passion generated by the exclusiveness of their range. It cannot be said that I am untouched by this heat and movement. But somehow, by my temperament as a poet, I am incapable of accepting these objects as final. They claim from us a great deal more than is their due. After a certain point is reached, I find myself obliged to separate myself from my own people, with whom I have been working, and my soul cries out: 'The complete man must never be sacrificed to the patriotic man, or even to the merely moral man'. To me humanity is rich and large and many-sided.[1]

∴

Anyone writing on Rabindranath Tagore is aware of how daunting such a task is because of his decades-long voluminous multi-genre creative, critical and philosophical opus as well as his practical educational projects ranging from humanist studies and arts to agricultural and craft teaching institutions. This essay is an attempt to explore some of Rabindranath's basic ideas on education in their holistic, extra-institutional and pedagogic sense. In other words, this essay seeks to interpret his idea of education in terms of his broader vision of social transformation in general, but for colonial India in particular. There are two key concepts that I use for my interpretational task, and their usage should be clarified at the outset. These concepts are 'pedagogy' and 'decolonisation'. Let us begin with 'pedagogy'.

Though the word 'pedagogy' is commonly associated with formal and institutional education, it is used here to expand and re-define the notion of education in our daily usage, especially as applied by Rabindranath in the perspective of colonialism. My reading of 'pedagogy' is derived from the works of Paolo

---

1 From Letter to C.F. Andrews, 14 January 1921, quoted in Gupta 2009, p. 202.

Freire, especially from *The Pedagogy of the Oppressed*,[2] to indicate the philo-sophical and socially participatory dimensions of education in the context of social relations of domination and resistance. Pedagogy, for Freire, is much bey-ond literacy and factual content and should be seen as a mode of consciousness raising. It is an active process during which education becomes a broad form of social 'conscientisation', simultaneously involving both human potentials for knowledge as well as power relations which inhibit them. This version of ped-agogy includes the content of what is taught but also focuses on the form – the very activities and social relations of teaching which extend beyond the institutional. Pedagogy, thus, is an active concept involving formative relations between the various subjects and agents. The connotations of these activit-ies are not conveyed effectively by 'education', which has served as a relatively passive expression in much of the literature on it. The broader consciousness-raising goal of pedagogy, the essential purpose of education for Rabindranath, lies not only in teaching literacy, facts and skills, thus preparing students for livelihoods, but primarily in enhancing social and self-awareness which help to link the self with the other, with the larger society and the individual with the world. He says:

> We cannot remove the causes of our suffering from the outside, they have to be eradicated from within. If we wish to do that there are two tasks. First, to educate the common people of the country and connect their consciousness with all peoples of the world – detachment from the world has made their consciousness rustic and insular. They have to be lifted into the proud sphere of the humanity as a whole ... The other [task] is in the area of livelihood. They will have to be united with the world's human-ity [in this] and their labour connected with that of others.[3]

This quotation captures Rabindranath's aspiration to bring about a deep-rooted change in the Indian individual's consciousness and of society at large, and suggests that his pedagogic ideas and practices should be considered as critical pedagogy viable beyond India and the colonial context. Though Rabindranath's idea of pedagogy is not 'political' in any obvious or direct sense, its transformational ambition and method of social critique have profound political implications. As such his pedagogic project, particularly as regards detecting and challenging existing power relations, may be compared to Ant-

2   Freire 1970.
3   Tagore 1961, vol. 13, p. 419. My translation.

onio Gramsci's notion of hegemony, coding the idea of a transformation of culture/consciousness at the basic level of everyday life – at the foundation of what Gramsci calls the 'civil society'.[4] Throughout the *Selections from the Prison Notebooks*, especially in essays on intellectuals and education and their functions in the state and civil society, as well as in the 'Notes on Italian History', Gramsci puts forward a complex notion of 'hegemony' by retooling its connection to coercion or direct force with modes of changing popular consciousness. Though coercion was present in his formulation, in the last instance the creation of consent was of prime importance. For any group to be in power in any sustaining and pervasive sense, Gramsci felt, it had to create and diffuse forms of consciousness which would become pervasive in society – that is, the ideas, images, symbols and practices of this group would need to assume the status of common sense or culture most broadly defined. The relevance of Gramsci's idea of hegemony for a proper grasp of what I mean by Rabindranath's pedagogy of decolonisation mounted against relations of power is essential, because Rabindranath also sought a foundational social and cultural transformation, an education of not only ideas but even of sensibilities, of altering the existing 'structures of feeling' and common sense.[5] According to Gramsci, any state formation should be preceded by hegemonic success of the aspiring group if that state is to be associated with a new era in history. He says: 'A social group can, and indeed must, already exercise "leadership" before winning governmental power (this indeed is one of the principal conditions for

---

4   'Civil society' is a concept foundational to Gramsci's social and political thought. See Gramsci 1971, in which the notion abounds in its visible and invisible presence. 'State and Civil Society' in the same volume also deals with the concept at some length.

5   Gramsci and Rabindranath arrive at similar notions, though Rabindranath is unconnected to political organisation and Gramsci is connected with the Italian Communist Party (PCI) and trade unions of his time. Perhaps because Gramsci is reflecting on the failure of the PCI and the rise of fascism his conclusions are less pragmatic and more philosophical. For 'structures of feelings' see Williams 1978, pp. 128–35. A few lines quoted from this section make clear the connection between social experiences and the structures of feeling which are developed in conjunction. 'The term is difficult, but 'feeling' is chosen to emphasise a distinction from more formal concepts of "world-view" or "ideology". It is that we are concerned with meanings and values as they are actively lived and felt ... We are talking about characteristic elements of impulse, restraint and tone, specifically affective elements of consciousness and relationships: not feelings against thought, but thought as felt and feeling as thought: practical consciousness of a present kind, in a living and interrelated continuity'. (p. 132) We have no room here to go into any detail, but we can see how 'pedagogy' in its deepest sense is compatible with what Williams speaks about, as well as how a real hegemonic project would be successful only if it achieves this state.

the winning of such power); it subsequently becomes dominant when it exercises power; but even if it holds it firmly in its grasp, it must continue to lead as well'.[6]

A Gramscian reading of pedagogy in terms of its practices, social relations and its content and mode of dissemination, makes it into a multidimensional affair. Throughout the *Selections from the Prison Notebook* and in his *Letters from the Prison*[7] Gramsci paid meticulous theoretical attention to the role played by consciousness in matters of politics, life and art. The concerted attempt at a pervasive change of consciousness in fashioning basic social/cultural norms and forms was of the essence. This cultural normative production involved not only intellectuals, writers, politicians and priests, but also and mainly ordinary people going about their daily life as producers and as carriers of complex worldviews, of interpretive philosophy and, thus, of hegemony.[8] The home of this hegemony lay in the liminal space between the state and the civil society – this is the space of life activity, experience and cultural expression which holds a constitutive relation with the state and the economy. We can see then that the concept of hegemony can be meaningfully associated with formal education as well as with other efforts of conscientisation, and this is where Rabindranath's pedagogy crosses paths with Gramscian common sense production. Gramsci's insistence, in the course of rising communism in Italy, on repudiating the old by creating new hegemonic forms or common sense coincides with Rabindranath's life long struggle to conceptualise and to practicalise an emancipatory humanist and universalist social transformation in a country in the grip of colonialism. In rejecting and re-forming our so-called 'normal' culture, our ways of being and seeing, Rabindranath's vision and practices of social education and culture become 'political' in that they challenge the existing hegemony. Our understanding of Rabindranath is thus enriched by introducing a Gramscian lens which helps to further expose the hegemony of feudal and capitalist colonialism embedded in Indian and Bengal's civil society. We can better appreciate the essays in *Kalantar* or a novel like *Gora*[9] which speak to the need for a new consciousness for India which will impel it beyond colonialism. It is to this end that throughout his life Rabindranath forges and refines in the discourse of a new society, a new age heralded by a new human subject.

---

6 Gramsci 1971, pp. 57–8.

7 Gramsci 1971.

8 See Gramsci 1971 on how everyone is a philosopher, in 'The study of philosophy'. See also Thomas 2009, pp. 27–36.

9 Tagore 1961, vol. 13 and 1987, vol, 3.

Rabindranath, Gramsci and Freire all concur that emancipatory pedagogy rests on processes and ideas which are at once social and subjective, and it is the common people themselves who should produce the personally and socially transformative knowledge. They should preside over the birth of their own social consciousness and fashion their own culture,[10] and, by implication, their politics. This pedagogic undertaking rejects any idea of a piecemeal transformation and of the division of the social whole into components or fragments, such as that of the public and the private social spheres and of education as a pragmatic moment of intersection between otherwise separately conceived social strands, thus making the social whole into a sum of artificially created spheres. All aspects of Rabindranath's work, from the foundation of Santiniketan or Sriniketan to his creative and critical writings and practices, deny this division and reject a mere aggregation of the home and the world, the individual and the social, the personal and the universal.[11] It is this project of a liberatory hegemonic transformation, situated in the colonial context, that provides the content and the form of Rabindranath's pedagogy of decolonisation.

Now we turn to the concept of decolonisation, both substantively and as used in assessing Rabindranath, otherwise there is a chance of misunderstanding the idea of the pedagogy of decolonisation as a more nuanced variant of nationalism. In fact there have been attempts in this direction of turning him into a better or a higher kind of nationalist than his contemporaries, or a cosmopolitanist.[12] With regard to Rabindranath as a 'better nationalist', a good example is found in Uma Dasgupta's introduction to *Tagore: Selected Writings on Education and Nationalism*. Here Das Gupta clearly situates Rabindranath within the Indian nationalist tradition, albeit a modernist, perhaps what Partha Chatterjee would call a Neruvian one.[13] Das Gupta insists:

---

10   Regarding people's participatory role in fashioning their own social consciousness, rather than their conventional portrayal as externally shaped masses, see the 'Preface' in Thompson 1974.

11   For ideas embedded in Rabindranath's educational institutions Santiniketan and Sriniketan, see chapters 22, 23 in Dutta, Krishna and Robinson, Andrew 1995.

12   Regarding discussions on Rabindranath's 'cosmopolitanism' and internationalism, see Collins 2012. But also on the difficulties involved in the issue of 'cosmopolitanism', see Brennan 1997. Brennan does discuss Rabindranath, especially in connection with Martha Nussbaum's use of Rabindranath in the defence of cosmopolitanism (see Nussbaum 1994). On Rabindranath's internationalism see Sehanabis 1983.

13   Authors such as Partha Chatterjee do not entirely let Rabindranath off the hook of 'nationalism', but rather place him in a 'modernist' camp of nationalist thought derived from European Enlightenment, i.e., place him with Jawaharlal Nehru *et. al* as a thinker in the tradition of colonial modernism. See Chatterjee 1986a. See also Muthu 2000, and Sarton 2008.

Tagore did not reject nationalism as is commonly said or assumed. It is that he formed his own understanding of it by studying what was 'authentic' in his country's history, and by applying it to an education that would relate to the past and be receptive of the present. That is how *his thought on nationalism and education became one* (my emphasis).[14]

Setting aside the red-herring issue of 'authenticity', we can claim that Das Gupta's opinion misrepresents Rabindranath's decolonising vision by converting it into a better nationalist as opposed to a narrow nationalist one. We might dub her interpretation of Rabindranath's decolonising vision as his contribution to a 'better' citizenship in a nationalist state, and his 'decolonisation' as a version of a modernist nationalism rather than a thorough and trenchant critique and ultimate rejection of it. What she says flies in the face of all those who claim otherwise, including Rabindranath himself. One need only read his lectures on 'Nationalism' delivered in 1917 and *Sabhyatar Sankat* (Crisis in Civilisation) in 1940 to see that he remained a life-long critic of nationalism.[15]

In his short but insightful introduction to *The English Writings of Rabindranath Tagore*, Volume 2, Sisir Kumar Das points out how Rabindranath was interested in politics in its deepest aspect of all relations of power without being a 'nationalist', and 'politics' in his case would demand the assertion of the universal and the human, and this is not a passive assertion. In fact he comments: '... the essays included here will come as a shock and embarrassment because of their unabashed political association'.[16] We do not have space here to discuss in detail what the idea of 'the political' meant for Rabindranath, but we must note that for him or some others, being an antagonist of colonial-

---

14 Das Gupta 2009, p. xxvi.

15 See, for example, 'Nationalism', in Das 1996: 'And the idea of the Nation is one of the most powerful anesthetics that man has invented. Under the influence of its fumes the whole people can carry out its systematic programme of the most virulent self-seeking without being in the least aware of its moral perversion – in fact feeling dangerously resentful if it is pointed out'. (p. 434) Also: 'This European war of Nations is the war of retribution ... The time has come when for the sake of the whole outraged world, Europe should fully know in her own person the terrible absurdity of the thing called Nation' (p. 434). In 1940 in the midst of the second world war he again said, in 'Crisis in Civilization' (Das 1996): 'In the meanwhile the demon of barbarity has given up all pretence and has emerged with unconcealed fangs, ready to tear up humanity in an orgy of devastation. From one end of the world to the other the poisonous fumes of hatred darken the atmosphere. The spirit of violence which perhaps lay dormant in the psychology of the West, has at last roused itself and desecrates the spirit of Man' (p. 726). For Rabindranath's other writings on nationalism see also 'India and Europe' (1930), Vol. 3, and 'East and West' (1935), Vol. 3.

16 Das 1996, p. 20.

ism does not automatically entail being a nationalist, nor does being 'political' only and necessarily lead to the creation of political parties or a nation state.[17] Rabindranath's project of decolonisation, if scrutinised, could give clues to alternative types of anti-colonial, anti-oppression politics which go beyond the scope of the nation. In fact Rabindranath framed his decolonising philosophy, his vision of an emancipatory pedagogy, with the very evils of nationalism in mind. This holds true in spite of the temptations that Rabindranath sometimes felt to belong to a larger group, to be immediately needed by the dominant nationalist trends of his time. To this end Professor Das quoted a few lines from Rabindranath to Rothenstein:

> I have nothing *directly* to do with politics: I am not a nationalist, moder-
> ate or immoderate in my political aspirations. But politics is not a mere
> abstraction. It has its personality and it does intrude into my life when
> I am human. It kills and maims individuals, it tells lies, it uses its sacred
> sword of justice for the purpose of massacre, it spreads misery broadcast
> over centuries of exploitation and I cannot say to myself 'poet, you have
> nothing to do with these facts for they belong to politics'.[18]

In fact it is because Rabindranath was a social and political *anti*-nationalist that he struggled life-long to maintain a praxis of decolonisation and did so at considerable cost to himself. Professor Das points out that he was '... often condemned as unpatriotic because of his uncompromising denouncement of nationalism, which he considered to be an instrument of political hegemony and an ideology to legitimise the oppression of one nation by another ...'[19] Becoming 'the sentinel', serving as the conscience of Indian nationalism,[20] extracted a heavy toll from him, and I suggest that for him the antidote to nationalism lay in the pedagogy of decolonisation.

The issue of Rabindranath's critique of nationalism needs a little more exploration. An important attempt at tracing its development is made by Tanika Sarkar in 'Questioning Nationalism: The Difficult Writings of Rabindra-nath Tagore'.[21] Drawing on the works of Susobhanchandra Sarkar, Sumit Sarkar and Chinmohan Sehanabis,[22] among others, she sees a break in Rabindranath's

---

17   Das 1996, p. 20.
18   Das 1996, p. 20.
19   Das 1996, p. 21.
20   See Bhattacharya 1997.
21   Sarkar 2009.
22   Sarkar 1970; Sarkar 1988; Sehanabis 1983. Also see Dutta 2003.

thought regarding nationalism and ways he proposed for overcoming colonialism from the cultural and mental points of view. Sarkar situates the turning point, as do others, in the period of 1905–8, but more importantly she introduces a new critical possibility by making a distinction between 'country' (*desh*) and 'nation' (*jati*). Loving one's country, she says, has an affective, concrete and non-ideological quality to it absent in 'nationalism'. When *desh* became the Motherland in the ideological articulation of nationalism in Bengal it also became more abstract, more tethered to the public sphere and political machinery. But still it did not lose all its concreteness or its emotional power. Says Sarkar:

> Rather the valences of intimate familiarity and concrete knowledge, as well as ties of inheritance, residence and familial connections that belonged to a personal birthplace were transposed onto the increasingly larger, mostly unseen and abstract, space of a province or subcontinent. The consequence of this was to cover over the distant and imagined with emotions that, in the first instance, derived from an active and sensuous relationship with an actual home. The affective power of the nation became all the stronger as a result.[23]

One might then see Rabindranath as a lover of the country stated above, rather than a devotee of the nation and its state. This approach may dispel some of the speculations regarding Rabindranath's views on colonialism. In any case, the idea of decolonisation remains a valid description of his efforts to create simultaneously an anti-colonial, non-colonial as well as an overall anti-oppression praxis.[24]

---

23   Sarkar 1973, pp. 230–1.
24   With respect to the debates/discussions about placing Rabindranath within a political spectrum on nationalism, about whether he is an 'internationalist', a 'cosmopolitanist', a critical point needs to be noted. Are they versions of the same 'better' nationalism that Uma Dasgupta attributes to him, and/or do they evoke comments regarding 'nationalism' and 'patriotism'? In this connection it would not be amiss to quote a few lines from Timothy Brennan's comments on Martha Nussbaum: 'Martha Nussbaum faced off against an impressive array of intellectuals by defending the cosmopolitan ethos against a contemporary American 'patriotism'. Dissenting from Richard Rorty's appeal to patriotism as 'shared national identity', she invokes Rabindranath Tagore's novel *The Home and the World*, endorsing the message of that novel's central drama that 'patriotic pride is morally dangerous'. Rorty, she charges, 'substitutes a colorful idol for the substantive universal values and rights', for the point is to find what we all 'share as both rational and mutually dependent human beings' rather than as citizens of the United States'. Brennan 1997, p. 24.

'Decolonisation' in the sense I use the term resonates with Frantz Fanon's use of this concept forged during his participation in the Algerian revolution (1954–62). In *The Wretched of the Earth*[25] Fanon spoke of the 'pitfalls of national consciousness' and warned the aspirants of other third world revolutions to watch against a 'false decolonisation' in which rulers are substituted, blacks for whites, new anthems are sung and flags flown, but socio-economic and other relations of power do not change for the majority of the people in the new nation or in the state practices of governing.[26] Economic injustices and all forms of social deprivations including educational ones emerge from the new state, and essentially the old system of exploitation continues with new masks of rule and ties with the former colonialists are ever tightened. Fanon, therefore, emphasises the creation of a new hegemony, of basic changes in the socio-cultural as well as political consciousness and practices of the independent state and society. They have to be such that the old colonial hegemony is truly replaced by new cultural and social relations which are humanist, that is, universalist, and without reference to the paradigm of the discourses of colonialism. Nor can the new praxis simply be spontaneous, defensive and inverted responses to colonisation. The epistemological and practical premises of this decolonisation process must thus be constructed outside the constellation of the totalising relations between the native and the master as prescribed by a narrow nationalist discourse. According to the Fanon scholar Ato Sekyi-Otu, this premise for a fundamental change consists of the colonial subject's movement from the status of the 'native' to that of 'man' or 'human', not as abstract categories, but as the articulation of the concrete, socio-historically situated and dynamic human consciousness.[27] It is possible to see, then, the concur-

---

25   Fanon 1961.

26   On the topic of decolonization, see especially Fanon 1961, the chapter on 'The pitfalls of national consciousness', pp. 148–205. Fanon makes a distinction between 'true' and 'false' decolonisation. In the context he offers a nuanced critique of nationalism in relation to class relations and class consciousness. This is an excellent caution to be heeded by anti-colonial nationalists, so they do not produce unintended negative consequences for newly liberated people, their state and society.

27   On Fanon's humanism and universalism, as well as the distinction between 'true' and 'false' decolonisation, see Sekyi-Otu 1996. Fanon's humanism as a practical decolonising concept is described in this way by Sekyi-Otu: '[This will be a] Fanon who did indeed frame his account of the colonial condition and its aftermath in the language of human possibilities; a Fanon in whom this humanist vocabulary was by no means an occasional lapse from the sturdy posture of a sophisticated nihilism; a Fanon for whom the *raison d'etre* of racial and national liberation was that it would give back their dignity to all citizens, fill their minds and feast their eyes with *human things*, and create a prospect that is human because conscious and sovereign persons dwell therein ...' (p. 46) These few

rence between Rabindranath's and Fanon's positions and why Fanon's idea of decolonisation is a better way of naming Rabindranath's social and universalist pedagogy. Though Rabindranath himself never used this expression precisely, it seems to capture most adequately his vision and intention, his constellation of expressive, theoretical, critical and practical works.

For both Fanon and Rabindranath decolonisation conceptualises independence or freedom in substantive terms, not as in 'free from' but rather as 'free to', and shifts the problematic and politics from fetishising state formation. Nationalism as understood by Rabindranath, at least, has no telos of gaining state power and ownership of economic resources while fostering unfettered capitalist relations, whereas Fanon would completely reject capitalism but not the nation state.[28] Nor is it the case that Rabindranath eschews 'political nationalism' but espouses instead 'cultural nationalism', which is nationalism all the same. By jettisoning the very paradigm of 'nation' and 'nationalism' to think through Indian and social reality in general, Rabindranath rejects anti-colonial epistemological premises that are particularist and chauvinist, unable to incorporate within its framework a universalist subject and forms of consciousness. Thus Rabindranath's life's work is to invent and invest in the making of a social philosophy and praxis which sustains a non-antagonistic notion of the 'other', which is ultimately agonistic with a dialectical relation to antagonism. He is, therefore, not content with just 'social reform' or 'legislative reform', as were some of his reformist predecessors. Such reforms, while generally beneficial, were not always even implicitly universalist in their premises or postulated

---

lines show why I use the expression 'decolonisation' for capturing Rabindranath's pedagogical philosophy with regard to decolonising India. This 'humanism' is not a derivative of 'nationalism' in its usual sense. In 'Concerning Violence', Fanon tells us: 'Decolonization, as we know, is *a historical process*, that is to say, that it cannot be comprehended, it cannot disclose its intelligibility nor become transparent to itself except in the exact measure that we discern *the movement of historical becoming* ... which gives it form and content'. Quoted by Sekyi-Otu 1996, pp. 103–4.

28   The similarity between Rabindranath and Fanon should be considered in the topic of the relationship between the 'self' and the 'other'. Both colonialism and nationalism see this relationship as a Manichean one in which nothing other than an antagonistic relation is possible. In Rabindranath's and Fanon's universalist humanist vision another possibility is presented – that of a relation based on identification and empathy. How this state is to be arrived at, whether it can be achieved through nationalist dynamics, are questions that need to be explored. And what is to be done about the history, the actuality of colonialism or the master-slave relations, in this journey from antagonism to agonism provides the core of the decolonisation project. But even in the dark days of 'Crisis of Civilization' Rabindranath invoked this redemptive possibility of history. Resisting homogenisation of the West, memories of friendship with Western intellectuals play some part in Rabindranath's humanistic, principled hope. See Das 1996, p. 725.

on the idea of the 'human' or human capacities. It should be noted that the basic premises of Rabindranath's decolonising project and practices could have been formulated beyond the context of colonialism, but from the inequalities and deformities existing in any society of property and power. In all cases Rabindranath pursues the formation of an emancipated social subjectivity, similar to Fanon's. This subjectivity evolves from the 'native' (a construct of colonial domination) to the 'human' (a free and universal self-subject) and from a faceless 'mass' to the personified 'people'. For Rabindranath the subject in or of nationalist ideology would still be in a state of unfreedom if the subject's humanity was not realised through the emancipatory project and as an integral part of it.

Rabindranath made a distinction between the state, the nation and society and between the European culture of the state and the Indian culture of social reciprocity and collectivity.[29] So it is the redemptive change of the civil society – the habitus of the people – that he concentrated on, because the nation state became a secondary formation the over-emphasising of which was a source of rigidification and dehumanisation of both the individual and the society. The state he at best tolerated as a necessary evil of administrative arrangement. By rejecting the idea that the state should be the source for all social needs and goods, Rabindranath indicates that the trouble with the contemporary Indian state is not only that it is 'colonial', but that it is also a variant of the modern national state whose very character it is to usurp all social functions. This he rightly saw as a relatively new European invention, and that nationalism in India or elsewhere in spite of its claim of difference served as its organising tool.[30] He felt that nationalism could not tran-

---

29   On numerous occasions Rabindranath spoke about the village-centred nature of Indian society, and this society's lack of orientation to a state. This he contrasts with the West, where for centuries a culture of state has flourished. See 'Samaj' (society) in *Kalantar* in Tagore 1961, pp. 31, 372. On the difference between 'nation' and 'society' see Das 1996, where Rabindranath says: 'A nation, in the sense of the political and economic union of a people, is that aspect which a whole population assumes when organised for a mechanical purpose. A society has no ulterior purpose. It is an end in itself. It is a spontaneous self-expression of man as a social being ...' (p. 426) When the society, '... with the help of science ...' and focusing '... on the side of power ...', he continues, grows into an organisation for domination it becomes a nation state. It becomes an instrument of power, competition and greed: 'The time comes when it can stop no longer, for the competition grows keener, organization grows vaster, and selfishness obtains supremacy. Trading upon the greed and fear of man, it occupies more and more space in society, and at last becomes its ruling force'. (p. 426).

30   As mentioned above, this state-centred approach is Rabindranath's major disagreement with nationalist politics. He points out that, unlike in the West, the Indian common people

scend its particularist ideology, based on a self-enclosed and reified notion of culture and identity which demanded a binary and inverted collective self-representation. Rabindranath's perception is shared by Fanon, who also spoke about 'true' and 'false' decolonisation, but without rejecting all forms of nationalism.[31] Behind the phenomenal forms of contemporary colonial hegemony, Rabindranath saw other abiding sources of social and moral deformation in India which lay in its own religious institutions, in its age-old feudal customs, ideas and repressions.[32] Thus both the sources of problems and the objectives of transformation he found in the Indian *samaj* itself as modified by colonial capitalism. As pointed out by Jasodhara Bagchi, the ideal of the novel *Gora* rests on the evolving realisation of the protagonist that the primary object of redemption should be the *samaj* or society, and this would entail the creation of a secular and empathetic worldview.[33] In this context Bagchi discusses Rabindranath's concept of identity as an evolving and situated sense of self in the world. She also notes that Gora's evolving maturity depends on his disarticulation of the notion of identity from nationalism, from a discourse on religion, ethnicity, birth, blood and belonging. He ultimately arrives at a sense of an identity which is not acquired by birth and a given ethnicity, but rather through a spiritually animated and secular fusion of reason and emotion connected with the local circumstances and a universalist ideal. She writes:

> The secular outlook that *Gora* regains at the end of the novel is not just a narrative ploy, a happy ending that rounds things up in a spirit of reconciliation. Taking *Gora* and his discursive prose written through the first and second decades of this century, we see Tagore fighting religion as a

---

were not used to expecting social goods from the state, nor should or could the state, a bureaucratic machinery, actually serve genuine human needs and aspirations. See Das 1996, pp. 372–4. On the state-centered vs. community-centred approach see also Nandy 1994, and 1983.

31 See Fanon 1961. For a considered critique of 'false deconolization', with a 'native' bourgeoisie at its helm and a parochial nationalism, see the chapter, 'The pitfalls of national consciousness', pp. 148–205. See also Gohain 2011. Gohain also brings in Fanon in the comparison and complicates the issues of nationalist and class struggles and state formation.

32 In *Gora, Ghare Baire, Kalantar*, among numerous other texts, Rabindranath described, lamented and excoriated the complex deformations to be found in the Indian society and its villages. See 'Palli Prakriti' in Tagore 1961, pp. 493–582, also *Kalantar* in the same text, p. 502. Rabindranath felt that India was imprisoned by its own history and then strangled by colonial rule. See Tagore 1961, pp. 37–9.

33 Bagchi 1996.

basis of political life. While not denying the search for self identity, he searches for a secularism that is inclusive and indigenous at the same time.[34]

The aim of Rabindranath's decolonising pedagogy is to be found in a search for this secular but emotionally charged identity. His creative, critical and educational writings all testify to this, and the creation of Santiniketan and Sriniketan are means to facilitate its empirical development. Institutional logic or instrumental rationality of schooling and preparation for securing careers do not form a part of this identity.

This emancipatory conscientisation project of Rabindranath is not a *sui generis* phenomenon. We see traces of its genealogy in the agitation for social reform in the nineteenth and early twentieth centuries of Bengal.[35] But to see Rabindranath's pedagogy of decolonisation as only an extension of these social reform movements would be misleading. This would amount to restricting their scope and to truncating his holistic vision. His transformational project is beyond 'reform' and is articulated through foundational changes in epistemology and premises as expressed by his writings on the self, the personality, creativity, the subject and identity, as well as that of *samaj* or civil society. To develop his pedagogy Rabindranath conducts in his critique a thorough exploration of country-city division and relations, thus, industry's relationship with agriculture, the capitalist profit motive and greed for wealth generalised through society. To accomplish this, a typological contrast is established between an actual existing India and an ideal or icon of India, between the existing power-riven and greedy social economy which has engrossed the cultural life and a dignified future one based on social cooperation, family farming and a sense of community where science and technology are neither rejected nor fetishised but used for the common good.

Rabindranath deepens his pedagogic praxis in increasing interaction with crises in India, Asia and Europe through travels, intellectual and creative interchanges, and he accumulates a first-hand and rapidly growing knowledge of international politics. His transformative pedagogic vision is still relevant for us as we continue to live in a world born of the same colonial capitalism now in its neo-liberal imperialist phase.[36] Our alienation from each other, the dehuman-

---

34   Ibid., p. 57.

35   There is a vast array of books on this subject, but especially helpful is Sarkar 1973. See also Sangari and Vaid 1990. See also Bannerji 2011, chapter 6.

36   For Rabindranath's relevance at present, see Collins 2012: 'Both despite and because of incursions of global capitalism in its accelerated financial and commercial phases, the

isation of people and social relations, the destruction of the earth we inhabit, only grows more intense, not less. So even if we do not always share all of Rabindranath's ideas, we gain by becoming better acquainted with his pedagogy of decolonisation. He provides us with resources for critical reflections from which resistant and socially redemptive praxis may follow. In the next, section I will examine a crucial example of Rabindranath's commitment to decolonising pedagogy, in the search of a model for which he went to the Soviet Union.

1 Pedagogy for a New Hegemony: Rabindranath and *Russiar Chithi* (Letters from Russia)

Rabindranath, in a letter to Dorothy Straight (Elmhirst), wrote a few lines about his trip to the USSR. He was particularly careful about what he wrote, as he had tried 'to persuade her to pay for one of his Indian staff at Sriniketan to visit the Soviet Union rather than the United States for agricultural training'.[37] He had not met with any help, but felt obliged to give his impression:

> ... I cannot give you the details of my adventure in Soviet Russia. It has been a most wonderful experience for me and I assure you those people have done miracles in the realm of education. I implore you, do not hesitate to send Leonard to that country which is the only place where all the numerous activities of people's life are comprehended in a most intensive and intelligent form of education. My mind is humming with a swarm of suggestions for my own work – but my time is short, my resources are meagre ... [T]he proper training needed for India can only be had in Russia, where the cultivation of people's education is being carried on not [in] the soil of unlimited wealth but [by] indomitable energy and resourceful intelligence. I feel proud of the fact that the ideal which is [at] the centre of their effort is very similar to mine, only they have a very vast instrument and unobstructed perspective for their work. The titanic forces that are tremendously active over this vast country at the creation of a new

---

politics of collective identity, group belonging and nationalism show no signs of abating. From India to Europe and beyond, the politics of nationalism is manifesting itself in complex ways. In this context, Tagore's marginalised legacy, both in terms of his thinking about identity and in terms of what I ultimately see as the failure of his "politics", seems more relevant today than ever before'. (p. 160).

37   Dutta and Robinson 1997 p. 386.

world have very deeply impressed me, for the background of the manifestation of this great dream is not the limited area of national interest but all humanity.[38]

The same sentiment is repeated in *Russiar Chithi*, emphasising the profound socio-cultural, what I would call the hegemonic, implication of the Soviet educational project: He writes:

> I went to Russia to have a look at their method of education. It surprised me utterly. Within eight years [they have] changed the state of popular consciousness. Those who were silent have found a language of expression, for those who were uneducated the curtain over their consciousness has been lifted, the powerless have awakened into self-empowerment, those who were sunk in contempt/disrespect have emerged from within the locked spaces of society and are entitled to take their seat with others in the world.[39]

If we want to gauge the depth of Rabindranath's commitment to pedagogy of decolonisation, we cannot do better than to examine his interest in the emerging project of social transformation in the new Soviet Union. Produced from the standpoint of a colonised subject of Britain, *Russiar Chithi* is an invaluable collection which provides us with insights which are relevant even today. To my knowledge these letters are probably the only extensive account of the early years of the Soviet Union provided by an intellectual from any colonised part of the world. The Soviet revolution's vision of social transformation, the hegemonic attempts through its pedagogic philosophy and implementation, remain the grandest aspirations of social change, only comparable with that of China. Whatever were the merits and demerits of Soviet hegemonic theories and practices, they amazed the contemporary world with their scale and audacity. Seeking to create a counter-feudal and counter-capitalist hegemony, a new cultural common sense among its citizens, aimed at a radically different society than anyone had so far lived, the new Soviet state was busy with projects of consciousness covering all social and cultural dimensions.[40] Rabindranath, in his reflections from the ship *ss Bremen*, said '... the entire country has woven all divisions of labour into a web of nerves which by cre-

---

38   Dutta and Robinson 1997 p. 387.

39   *Russiar Chithi* (Letters from Russia) in Tagore, 1961, Part 10, p. 693. This and all subsequent translations are mine, though another translation exists and is to be found in Das 1996.

40   See Fitzpatrick 1970.

ating a huge body has taken the form of an enormous individual'. They have combined '... everyone's work, everyone's heart, everyone's spirit and created an extraordinary essence [of being]'.[41] Impressed by the scale of the Soviet project, Rabindranath compared the decolonisation project of India with the Soviet Union since its size and diversity would require a similar gigantic scale. He saw a connection between his own vision of change and that of the Soviet revolution because truly decolonising a society needs a revolutionising of it. It was not surprising then that, against the advice of some, Rabindranath went to Russia.[42] As he puts it: 'I thought that at the entrance of western civilisation, rendered invisible by the power of wealth, Russia has set up a space of dedication in the pursuit of developing the power of the powerless, ignoring entirely the frowns of western continents. If I don't go to see that for myself, who will?'[43] The 'I' here is definitely more than a personal subject, rather it represents a denizen of a colonial space struggling against an ascribed and internalised colonial subjectivity.

Though Rabindranath was neither a marxist nor a supporter of communism, his critical reservations notwithstanding he brought his own open-minded decolonising pedagogical concerns to the Soviet project and learnt much from it of what to accept and to reject. It is fascinating to read now how the new educational conscientisation of Soviet communism appeared to a critical and creative colonial subject who wanted to overcome the double hegemony of western capitalist colonialism and of Indian feudalism mutating into this capitalism. Rabindranath brought to the Soviet Union an outlook of solidarity and provided a context for a better understanding of the 1917 revolution. He praised what he saw as its intention and success:

> For people like us who are British subjects, it is beyond the limits of our imagination to comprehend the great, all-pervasive, extraordinary, untir-

---

41 Tagore 1961, vol. 10, p. 699.

42 Dutta and Robinson 1995, discuss this issue. Their tone is rather patronising regarding both the trip and the letters, etc. that he sent back. They misunderstood both his reason for the visit and also his vision, not only regarding the Soviet state and its project of social and cultural transformation, but also his own vision and practices of the pedagogy of decolonisation. If they were attuned to his social and life philosophy, of his need to create a counterhegemony to the colonial one, they would not have needed to apologise for this one 'wrong' step that he took. They are relieved by his criticisms of the Soviet Union, but silent about his enthusiasm and admiration. It should be noted that as late as 1940 Rabindranath compares Britain and Soviet Russia and comes out for the latter. This trip and his responses to it cannot be viewed as an aberration and examples of his misjudgment.

43 Tagore 1961, vol. 10, p. 681.

ing efforts that are going into educating/enabling the nationalities and tribes of Russia. That it is possible to go so far I never thought [possible] before coming here. Because the atmosphere of 'law and order' in which we grow up since childhood makes it impossible to be cognizant of any attempt that can go anywhere near to this.[44]

Rabindranath also came to the conclusion that they '... have understood that education is the only way which provides strength to the weak – food, health, security all depend on this. Empty 'law and order' does not fill our bellies or our hearts, yet we have become bankrupt by paying for them'.[45]

Rabindranath's interest in the USSR was not based on any ideology, but on his motivation for creating a radically new liberationist philosophy and cultural practices against the grain of an oppressive feudal and religious India and the dire consequences of a European/English colonial and industrial capitalism. The Soviet experience helped to clarify his own ideas and practical pedagogic strategies for overcoming India's double burden of local and foreign hegemony of the Indian masses. His letters and reflections from the *ss Bremen* are rich sources for the reader's clarification. They present historical and experiential cameos of Indian colonial development as well as of encounters with the newly developing communist society and popular existence. The letters offer a critique and an Indian analysis of colonialism and semi-feudal capitalism in both the 'East' and the 'West'. His Russian experience disclosed the possibilities of seeing education as a terrain for a universal change in social consciousness. This idea of education included agricultural practices among the Soviet peasantry and other labouring and common people. In his earnestness to make the matter accessible to his readers he, uncharacteristically, provided short statistical accounts.

Although Rabindranath was interested in the emerging Soviet intellectuals and the wealth and proficiency of the new art and literary forms, such as the highly modernist theatre of Meyerhold, he was keener on the lives of the Russian peasantry and common people, the poor of Czarist Russia, and in the measures undertaken for their amelioration and upliftment. This indicates that though a great literary figure himself, Rabindranath prioritised social and public education anywhere over high culture which is the domain of an elite few. He compared the repression of the Russian common people by the Czar and his ally the orthodox Russian church with the feudal, religious and colonial capital-

---

44   Ibid., p. 691.
45   Ibid., p. 682.

ist repression and exploitation of the Indian masses, particularly in the village. He did not hesitate to expose religious tyrannies of Hinduism and village customs. Both in its support and disagreement *Russiar Chithi* provides a complex and nuanced assessment of what he thought were India's key problems which needed to be solved to end the colonial hegemony and its distorted forms of capitalism. Rabindranath's assessments were not merely academic, an exercise in a one-sided critique, but those of a practitioner who sought to bring about a fundamental social transformation. Throughout his life Rabindranath insisted on rural reconstruction as the vital force for a true Indian decolonisation and social regeneration, and it is not surprising that he was deeply interested in the Soviet attempt.

Along with his description of the Soviet experience these letters often conveyed Rabindranath's own pedagogical aims and frustrations. He provided urgent reasons for the lack of education in Bengal/India in terms of both literacy and outlook, including scientific intervention in production and reproduction of everyday life. He did not expect the colonial state to care for its subjects and to fulfil these urgent needs. The Indian middle-class youth and intelligentsia formed through the colonial educational apparatus, he felt, were of no help because they had internalised, or been incorporated into, colonial hegemony. The Indian nationalists with their chauvinism and distorted indigenism, he felt, could not envision the nature and the full scope of necessary changes due to their inability to grasp that the core of Indian society lay in village India. Their mentality of the colonial elite, with its fetishisation of cities, industries and a general urbanity obscured the common people from their vision. In spite of much profession to the contrary, they were actually self-interested and ignorant of the needs of all classes except their own.

Having rejected institutional colonial education on the grounds of its destructive influence on human creativity, due to the social principles he developed from his early years, which was possible because he had other means of income, Rabindranath had no respect for a career or job-oriented education. Indian colonial schools were for him '... factories for the production of clerks'.[46] In detailing the effects of colonial schooling Rabindranath noted not only the arrogance towards lower classes but also the unquestioning and obsequious mentality it produced among the Indian upper classes and castes towards their colonial rulers. Institutional learning, the main vector of colonial and elite hegemony, he stated, had produced two classes, one oriented towards ruling and the other forced to be ruled, thus creating power-based stratas of the 'edu-

---

46   Ibid., p. 685.

cated' and the 'uneducated' equivalent to haves and have-nots. This deeply inculcated colonial hegemony among the upper and middle classes of Bengal, Rabindranath felt, had deprived the entire society of self-respect and social empowerment. This cringing attitude, he said, only earned the 'native' the deep contempt of the colonial rulers:

> The biggest price we pay for our powerlessness comes from the lack of efforts to eradicate our own contemptibleness. They serve to prove that we deserve contempt. Good education lies at the root of solving problems for humanity. The road to that education is blocked in our country because 'law and order' leaves no space for any other recourse. The treasury is entirely empty.[47]

In considering the myopia created by the colonial hegemony, including a system of crime and punishment among Indian higher classes and castes, Rabindranath self-critically situated himself within this colonial mentality. He spoke of how he himself had once thought that it was impossible to educate India's thirty-three crores (330 million) of non-literate people, not only due to their extensive numbers but also for their innate incapacity. At most, he thought, a basic literacy was all that they could achieve, but the Soviet experience taught him otherwise because they had devised a colossal and multi-faceted education system which was both formal and non-formal. It was not just a system for acquiring degrees in order to function within a grid of repetitive and mindless jobs implicated in building and maintaining power relations. Rabindranath's critique of colonial education was perhaps the most insightful and the earliest version of the critique of colonial discourse or hegemony which was to come decades later after his death, launched from anti-colonial and anti-imperialist perspectives. He criticised all modes for creating colonial and disempowered subjects through education in the service of reproduction of social relations rooted in inequality nationally, internationally and at all levels.

Rabindranath's own pedagogic objectives both philosophically and in the workings of his schools inspired him to visit a young pioneers' school as well as popular museums for culture and natural sciences in the Soviet Union. He asked detailed questions about the daily functioning of the schools and was pleasantly surprised by the confident and questioning tone of his young audience. His curiosity ranged from their academic syllabus to classroom interactions to the students' participation in self-disciplining, and also in deciding on

---

47   Ibid., p. 682.

their daily diet. He was impressed by the young peoples' knowledge of society and politics as they enacted for him the 'living newspaper',[48] a device he considered using among Santiniketan students. He also made direct inquiries into the peasants' educational programmes. The 'holistic' nature of their educational development became evident to him in face-to-face interactions with them. He says:

> One evening I went to a house which is a peasants' residence. When they come to the city upon any occasion they can live cheaply in that residence. I had a discussion with them. When I can have such a discussion with peasants of our country that day I will be able to offer a proper retort to the Simon Commission.[49]

Rabindranath outlines three major objectives of the Soviet revolution, namely, education, agriculture, and production and technology, and showed them as integrally connected with each other. His own holistic pedagogic philosophy was naturally supportive of this. From the point of view of decolonisation, he offers us a measure of his own ideal together with his observations of the new educational venture. Noting the Soviet educational integration of everyday life with learning, he said: 'I have always said that education should be carried on with living'.[50] Rabindranath also supported the Soviet and other European modernist incorporation of science and technology in the economy and in social outlook as well, but he insisted on the need to maintain an overall universalist and humanist outlook. As he puts it himself: 'Mere technology cannot accomplish anything, if the machinist does not become human'. But he felt that '[t]heir [i.e. Soviet] cultivation of fields is keeping pace with mental cultivation'.[51] He continues by saying: '[After] coming here I saw that they have breathed life into education. The reason for it is that they have not set apart or created a boundary between everyday life and the school ... They [aim to] teach for a holistic humanisation'.[52]

Regarding the educational inclusion of the Indian peasantry in a decolonising endeavour, Rabindranath regretted that the Indian nationalist movement and politicians showed such indifference to the peasantry and did not offer them any real social agency: 'I remember that during the Pabna conference I

48   Ibid., p. 696.
49   Ibid., p. 687.
50   Ibid., p. 693.
51   Ibid., p. 693.
52   Ibid., p. 694.

told a politician who was a very important figure at that time that if we want to make real our national upliftment then we have to nurture and "humanise" those who live "below",[53] but the suggestion was ignored. Rabindranath, however, persisted and attempted to introduce self-empowerment schemes at different socio-economic levels among the peasantry, simultaneously targeting their sense of self and dignity and their economic viability. These efforts on his part resulted in two crucial and related realisations: 'From the point of view of justice the land should not be the possession of the landlord, it is the peasants'; secondly, if one could not consolidate the [scattered] plots for cultivation through a co-operative mode, agriculture could never be improved'.[54] Both these realisations seemed unimplementable under the existing circumstances in India. He saw the land always devolving into the hands of the landlord, the moneylender and the trader, all of whom were working in the interest of the colonial regime. When he spoke to peasants regarding land and agriculture they agreed with him, but said that they lacked the necessary leadership for actualising his proposal. Rabindranath himself did not feel fit to provide that leadership as he thought that it must come from within their own ranks. The upliftment of the Soviet peasants revived Rabindranath's indignation on behalf of the Bengal peasantry, and he saw a glimmer of hope in their altered condition. Reflecting on the peasantry and other Indian underclasses he said:

> I remembered the workers and peasants of my own country. It [the Soviet situation] seemed the achievement of the magicians of the Arabian Nights. Even ten or so years ago they were exactly like the labourers of our country – illiterate, helpless, starving, blinded by superstition and ignorant religiosity. In their sorrow and danger they banged their heads on the threshold of [their] God, their intelligence a pawn in the hands of priests and their touts, in fear for afterlife and fear in this world [which rested] in the hands of the aristocracy, moneylenders and landlords. They cleaned the shoes of those who beat them with those [very] shoes. Thousands of years did not change their customs and traditions, their modes of transportation, their mills and grinders were from the time of their ancestors, they stubbornly refused to handle any modern equipment ... How this mountain of ignorance, of incapacity has been shaken in just a few years has utterly astounded this luckless denizen of India – [but] who else would be so overwhelmed?[55]

---

53   Ibid., p. 682.
54   Ibid., p. 683.
55   Ibid., p. 685.

It is important to remember here what Rabindranath wrote in his novel *Gora* so many years earlier (1910), when the protagonist went to Bengal's villages, abandoning his shelter in an idealised and abstract India:

> For the very first time Gora saw what our country is like outside of the gen-teel and educated Calcutta society. How disconnected, how narrow, how weak was this village society – how unconscious of its own power, how ignorant and indifferent to its [own] well-being. A deeply ingrained social difference [lay] at the distance of every few miles, how incapable it was by its self-created imagined prohibitions to participate in the world's arena of action and how it had elevated the trivial and frozen hard its every cus-tom, how dormant was its consciousness and how feeble its efforts.[56]

Rabindranath measured the success of the Soviet pedagogy in terms of 'human-isation' of such suffering common people through the respect that this ped-agogy mandates towards them:

> Here common people are not obscured by the shadows of the genteel folks. Those who were out of sight for aeons are now fully revealed. It did not take time to correct the mistaken view that they have merely learnt to grope through the printed letters of their children's primers. They have become 'human' in these last few years.[57]

He also commented on the creation of public spheres that serve as residential teaching-cum-meeting places for peasants and workers. These public spaces, he felt, have 'created the foundation for a socially encompassing new life'.[58] Rabindranath supported the view that the Soviet revolution was based on demands of equality in class relations, and to that end wrote about the extreme exploitation of the productive classes obtaining in Russia before 1917. He iden-tified with their hitherto unfulfilled demands and sympathised with their griev-ances:

> When I got introduced to those classes of people who in our country are silent and ignorant, whose minds have been buried under piles of internal and external poverty, deprived of all life opportunities – it is then that I

---

56   Ibid., p. 481.
57   Ibid., p. 686.
58   Ibid., p. 688.

understood how the uncaringness of a society robs the wealth of peoples' hearts. What a great waste! How cruel the injustice![59]

Rabindranath dubbed the neglected part of the society as the 'candle-holders' who do not benefit from the very light they generate and hold up for others.[60] He referred to his own normative values as those of a feudal and colonial capitalist society as a member of the propertied elite. This gave rise to self-criticism and criticism of his own class. That he along with the members of his class had once thought that the deprived existence of the masses was a necessary and productive sacrifice for the higher cause of civilisation embarrassed him now:

> I have thought about them [the peasants] for a long time, and felt there was no other recourse or solution. One group cannot exist at a higher level if another does not stay below, but there is a social need for some to be above ... Because the richest harvest of a civilisation comes from leisure – there is a need to preserve this leisure for a section of the society ... [O]thers, not only due to circumstances, but also due to their physical and mental state must toil at a lower level.[61]

This elite class common sense was shaken through his increasing critical reflections on Indian and Western nationalisms, through the European and Asian experiences of violence of imperialism and war, and finally by his visit to the USSR. His own views on class, caste and 'civilisational' certainties were deeply shaken by the realisation that they were similar to those of the European or colonial elite, who looked upon Indians, irrespective of their class, caste and cultural productivity as 'hewers of wood and drawers of water'. Their lives were to be sacrificed for the civilisational needs of Europe. The highest classes of the colonial society thus became the serving classes in the colonial gaze. He expressed the Indian relationship of servitude to colonial Britain and the West thus:

> Just imagine that a sustenance-deprived India has nurtured England with food. Many in England think that India's very fulfillment lies in sustaining England forever. England has achieved fame by performing a great task for humanity – and to achieve this end there is no guilt felt in enslaving a whole nation forever. What difference does it make if in this process the

59   Ibid., p. 686.
60   Ibid., p. 675.
61   Ibid., p. 675.

people eat less or dress less well? ... All they can get is *charity* but the limits of this charity are exposed when the self-interest of the dominator is questioned.[62]

Rabindranath's description of his Soviet experience was created through a critical anti-colonial perspective, but also on something akin to class awareness, and thus an understanding of actions resembling class struggle emerged in these letters and other writings. He contextualised the 1917 revolution with great popular immiseration produced by the accumulation of excessive wealth by a few. In fact it is in this commonly shared misery of the masses in Russia or elsewhere that he discovered the basis for resistance, the motive force for fighting against the wealthy exploiter. The shared fight against shared misery would be the source of their impetus for unity, their mutual and group identification animated by a common resolve for a better life. He called the labouring classes, generally known in Bengali as *shramajibi*, as *dukkhajibi* – as those who subsist not only on their labour but on their suffering.[63] He outlined revolutionary possibilities inhering in the extreme popular sufferings, and in the following paragraph spoke at once to colonial and capitalist class power – interweaving one into the other:

> The powerful are arrogant, but an aspiration for power circulating among the sad and the poor is making them restless. The powerful are trying to stop them and not letting their messengers enter into their own space and silencing their voices. But what they should fear most is the very sorrow of the miserable ones – but that is precisely what they have always felt contemptuous about. They have no fear of aggravating this misery in favour of their own profit making. Their hearts do not tremble when they force the hapless peasants into the grip of famine in order to extract two to three hundred percent interest ... [But already] excessive power cannot keep increasing itself in the face of incrementally growing powerlessness. If the powerful were not so intoxicated by their own power they would have feared this boundless inequality – because ultimately the lack of equilibrium or balance is against the very laws of universal order.[64]

In these letters and reflections Rabindranath spelled out the implications of colonialism and the relationship of class exploitation between the rich and the

---

62   Ibid., p. 675.
63   Ibid., p. 688.
64   Ibid., p. 680.

wretched, between Europe and its colonies, and these served as the reasons for the Russian revolution. He contrasted the egalitarian revolutionary aspirations with capitalist possessive individualism and the sheer greed for wealth:

> All other European countries have dedicated their efforts to individual profit and enjoyment. A violent agitation results from this churning, and like the [Hindu] scriptural narrative of the churning of the ocean, this present one too has yielded both nectar and poison. But this nectar is in the possession of a group, while the majority get nothing of it. This has created an endless unhappiness and a lack of peace. Everyone considers this situation as 'inevitable'. They claim that greed lies in human nature itself and the very function of greed is to create unequal enjoyment. Competition, therefore, will continue and one must always be battle-ready. But what the Soviet people are saying is that the truth lies in human unity and social divisions are mere illusions. Through unifying social consciousness and pooling our efforts, we will reject the naturalisation of disunity and ultimately the disparities will disappear as a mere dream.[65]

Rabindranath simultaneously drew attention to the extremely unequal power relations between the colonised and the coloniser, the invisibility of the colonised's repressed existence from eyes of the world, and the deafening culture of silence enveloping the heartland of the colonial countries:

> All of the avenues through which our complaints could reach the world's ear are closed. On the contrary, things are said about us around the world, the mode of diffusion lies in Western hands. This is a matter of deep humiliation for the weak nations today … [T]he instruments of communication and information are kept by the powerful nations in their own control while they pull the cover of infamy and vilification to obliterate the powerless ones.[66]

Comparing the Indian condition with that of the Soviet Union, Rabindranath unhesitatingly pointed to the hatred of the capitalist West towards the young communist nation. He drew attention to the exclusion and isolation of the USSR produced by the capitalist West in order to break it down. He repeatedly noted the severe material constraints under which the new Soviet government laboured:

---

65   Ibid., p. 699.
66   Ibid., p. 681.

They have a paucity of funds, they lack credit at the seats of foreign capital, sufficient industries and factories ... they are powerless to generate capital. For these reasons they sell the very food meant for their [own] stomachs to finance their developmental projects. Furthermore, the most unproductive department of the state – the military – has to be inevitably kept highly skilled because all the state powers of the modern capitalist era are their enemies and their arsenals are filled to the brim.[67]

He added: 'Foreign engineers have destroyed many of their factories. The required enterprise is vast and complex, and the time at hand is very limited. They do not dare to take the time for food production because they stand or fall in the face of the entire wealthy world'.[68]

As with colonial stereotypes about India, Rabindranath was also cognisant of the falsehoods and negative stereotypes generated by the colonial capitalist states regarding the Soviet Union. He compared these infamies with the criticism of India by the Christian missionaries and Western intellectuals. About this constant barrage of propaganda against the Soviet Union he stated that the Western countries had developed a 'professional habit ... to find faults; and they cannot tolerate any gesture of enlightenment, especially on the part of those whom they dislike'.[69] India was vilified for trying to throw off the colonial yoke, thereby disturbing colonial super exploitation and profit and disrupting comfortable lives in the metropole, and the Soviet Union hated for challenging the very system and principles of capitalist wealth. They were also hated for generating a worldview, a philosophy and a praxis of equality by rejecting private property in natural resources, in social labour and the fruits of that labour.

Russiar Chithi is a complex text because it swings between a wholehearted admiration for the Soviet project and serious criticism of some of its central tenets and modes of their implementation. This contradictory attitude and the reasons for holding both positions are scattered throughout his opus. Our reading of the volume should not be influenced by our own opinions regarding the successes and failures of the Soviet Union. Rabindranath's own account and its standpoint of decolonisation must be kept in mind, which in the first place provided him with the motive for engaging with post-1917 Russia. One can well imagine how titanic this revolution appeared to both the West and colonised countries at the time. While the Western states became panicked at a successful

---

67   Ibid., p. 605.
68   Ibid., p. 867.
69   Ibid., p. 867.

assault against feudalism and capital from a relatively underdeveloped semi-Asian country, the colonised peoples of the world, irrespective of their political ideology, were fascinated by the sheer scale and audacity as well as possibilities disclosed by the event. As a colonial subject Rabindranath himself had thought that overturning India's colonial reality was impossible. India's colonised status seemed predestined: 'I had to accept that, otherwise why should this state of degradation be our lot?'[70] But the Soviet example showed him that fundamentally oppositional possibilities existed, and nor was such a challenge dependent on highly developed socio-economic conditions. After all, the Russian reality was no better than India before 1917: 'Every sin of poverty, servitude and deprivation, religious bigotry and anti-semitism attended them'.[71] Yet they attempted a radical change and succeeded.

Rabindranath worked out the lowest common denominators in the resemblance between the two countries: both Russia and India were village-based societies with primarily agricultural economies and, thus, societies with a limited urban and industrial development. Both had long existed in the throes of feudal oppression, though India was in a worse state because it was also a prey to British colonialism, and both suffered from religious oppression and tyranny of tradition. Rabindranath felt that attempts at Indian decolonisation, for that matter at nationalism, should begin with the peasantry as the basic social unit and agricultural labourers as the determining form of labour.

But there Rabindranath's desire to emulate the Soviet project ended – there was a dividing line between his and their as well as the Indian nationalist goal. For unlike the nationalists and the communists Rabindranath was not a state-centred thinker and did not primarily aim towards the formation of a powerful indigenous state. For him the state was not the major site for either resistance or liberation and, therefore, not the primary agent for social transformation. The liberationist solution and agency, he thought, must originate within the society itself, which should also be the beginning and the endpoint of decolonisation. Though Indian nationalists could learn from Russia about how to deal with the ignorance brought on by poverty, religious and traditional oppression, he felt they should refrain from an obsession with the state and politics. Yet he praised the Soviet Union when he thought praise was due: 'The old religious traditions and antiquated statecraft overwhelmed their intelligence and nearly drained their life-force for centuries. The Soviet revolutionaries have uprooted both of these, the heart rejoices by seeing that such a shackled nation has been

---

70   Ibid., p. 703.
71   Ibid., p. 703.

offered such a great liberation'.[72] How did ignorance and superstitions, such as witch-burning, torture of heretics and other violences come to an end in Europe or in the Soviet Union, he asked? His answer was: by means of education.[73] If Russians could achieve this much success in these areas, and if Japan or Turkey could also do more, why could India not go beyond a mere alphabetisation of its people to a higher level of knowledge, thus bringing about a deeper social conscientisation? In order to build his argument Rabindranath provided an idealised version of ancient Indian civilisation:

> Once the Indian society was primarily a village society. In this intimacy of the village society there was a balance between private and social property. The influence of social opinion was such that the wealthy felt the condemnation for using their entire wealth for their own enjoyment ... In that society in order to maintain their own social status the wealthy had to put forward a large amount in tribute to the society as a whole.[74]

Rabindranath's invention of an ideal type for the representation of India provides an idealised point of departure for measuring both the current actuality and movement towards the future. The main point, therefore, is not that of factuality but of inspiration. He thought '[i]n this situation the voluntary [individual] participation merged with the wishes of the society [as a whole]' and '... this exchange was not through the state machinery'.[75] This society of all, instead of a ruling and guiding state, is what he would have wanted for the India of the future – a redemptive society which is not politically driven or brought about through state intervention.

Rabindranath commented on the decline of Indian villages and the rise of the cities and urban societies in Europe. He thought that this development towards urbanisation happened in stages, starting with the emergence of 'the mercantile community' whose 'primary business is in putting their wealth to work'.[76] This, however, in its inception did not make the reign of the wealthy merchants legitimate, because they lacked a high intellectual and cultural status within the social hierarchy, 'they were the fallen ones ... For this reason the gap between wealth and non-wealth was not so big'.[77] Into this world of

---

72   Ibid., p. 702.
73   Ibid., p. 703.
74   Ibid., p. 730.
75   Ibid., p. 730.
76   Ibid., p. 730.
77   Ibid., p. 730.

merchants and landlords entered other economic and social forces and actors, but unlike in Europe the developmental changes wrought by them were not organic in the case of Indian society. In spite of the introduction of capitalism in India by Britain, it was not industrialised but rather remained agricultural, as science and technology were not an indigenous outgrowth. He compared the current reality of stagnating Indian villages which produced no organic urban or industrial development to the civilisational trajectory of Western Europe:

> European civilisation focused on emergence of cities. In cities people's opportunities expand and their social relationships contract. The city is very large, in them people are scattered everywhere, individual difference becomes of the essence and the churning or upheaval of competition dominates the space.[78]

Emphasising the dynamic economy and social alienation of European capitalism and life in its cities, in contrast to the stagnation and isolation of Indian villages and scarce presence of urban centres, Rabindranath sought a postcolonial future for India that could bypass the problems of industrial capitalist urbanism in Europe:

> [T]here appeared [in Europe] the age of machine and industry, profit rose to an unbelievable level. When this epidemic of profit[making] started to spread over the world, then those who lived afar, those who were not rich, had recourse to nothing. China had to swallow opium and India dispersed all she owned and ever-oppressed Africa had to cope with even greater oppression.[79]

Rabindranath's acute awareness of how colonialism and the greed of industrial capitalism were integrally linked gave him an insight into the rise of Bolshevism in Russia. He also felt that some of those conditions obtained in India, or for that matter in Europe itself:

> The main point is that the individual accumulation of wealth in modern times which has bestowed on the rich their enormous wealth cannot be the cause of joy or dignity for all. On the one side there is an infinite greed and, on the other, a deep envy. Between them lies an unbridgeable

---

78　　Ibid., p. 731.

79　　Ibid., p. 731.

gap. This facilitates competition far more than cooperation. The competition is between one class and another – internally within the country, and externally between them [the countries]. There is no way to reduce their intensity.[80]

For the relation of violence between the haves and the have-nots, where deprivation of the most creates the enrichment for a few, he used a metaphor of vampirism in describing the relations between the coloniser and the colonised: He wrote of '... foreigners who pacify the hunger of the demon of luxury whose anemic wasting away only increases through the ages'.[81] The Russian revolution and the Bolshevik ideology, Rabindranath said, were the 'natural' outcomes of an 'unnatural' imbalance:

> In this inhuman condition of the current civilisation arose the Bolshevik ideology ... Because the equilibrium of the human society had broken down this unnatural revolution arrived. Because individualism's contempt for the collective [spirit] was ever increasing there arose the suicidal idea of only appealing to the people [as an abstract collective subject].[82]

The agency for the 'this unnatural revolution' devolved upon the wretched of the earth, '... those who suffer ceaselessly, those unfortunate ones are the mainstay of the messengers of the god of suffering – the fire of apocalypse is smoldering in their starvation'.[83]

Rabindranath's ultimate and trenchant criticism of the Soviet philosophy and practices arose from the same interest in a pedagogy for a holistic social transformation which drew him to Russia. In the last analysis he found the Soviet project to be both rich but also wanting in its abstract and collectivist as well as state-centred social vision, and the modalities of its implementation. He did not hold back from expressing these disagreements with the same openness with which he praised Russia. Soviet agricultural policy of collectivisation and the scheme for the eradication of private property in land and industry drew much of Rabindranath's criticism.[84] Indeed, his criticism exten-

---

80   Ibid., pp. 731–2.
81   Ibid., p. 731.
82   Ibid., p. 732.
83   Ibid., pp. 731–2.
84   For Rabindranath's economic views and his idea of cooperatives, see Chakrabarti, and Dhar 2008.

ded to what he considered to be the overall communist approach to private property. As noted above, the Bolshevik revolution seemed to him to be an 'unnatural' phenomenon as it entailed the affective and material negation of all private property, the basic need for which he found in 'human nature': 'Love for one's property is a matter of affection and attachment, not a matter of argument. It is customary or traditional for us. We want to express ourselves, having property is one way of doing that'.[85] He expands this idea:

> For common people their ownership of property is the language of their individuality – if s/he loses that it is akin to becoming dumb. If property were only a means of livelihood, not a form of self-expression, then it would have been easy to convince through reason that only by forfeiting private property their lives and livelihood would improve. Higher modes of self-expression – for example – of intelligence, skill or expertise, cannot be robbed by force but private property can be. It is for this reason the division of and the threat to enjoyment of property can produce such cruelty, deceit and unending discord in society.[86]

For Rabindranath the policy makers and planners of the Soviet state had ignored this fundamental emotional and expressive aspect of the proprietorial human nature by reducing the issue into only a state initiated rational economic proposition. He advocated a compromise instead, suggesting that: '[t]he solution to this cannot be anything [categorically exclusive] but something that lies midway'.[87] Human nature, as Rabindranath understood it, consists of two parts – an introvertive one, involved with the self, and another which seeks an involvement with others and is extrovertive in its sociality. Emphasising any one aspect at the cost of the other would mean either a high degree of greed, self-interest and a subservience to particularity, as evident in Western colonial capitalism, or a coerced submission to an abstract and mechanical state as the representative of an artificial collective good. This schema would lack an experiencing human subject or agent at its core and, thus, of any voluntary will and a desiring participation by the self. As Rabindranath saw the state as a merely governing machinery, he rejected the top-down command relations between the state and society. He also questioned the pedagogic philosophy that would flow from this situation. As Russian economic and social planning emanated

---

85   Tagore, vol. 10, 1961, p. 690.
86   Ibid., p. 690.
87   Ibid., p. 690.

from the rationality of a totalising state apparatus and took a social engineering approach to the task of transformation, it lacked the sense of the cultivation of the individual self in harmony with universalist humanism. Rabindranath, therefore, could not wholeheartedly accept it as a model for his own task of conscientisation.

Rabindranath criticised the dictatorship of the state in Russia. Though this state was supposed to embody the dictatorship of the proletariat through their collective representation in the Soviet communist party (CPSU), he did not consider it to be a genuine people's state. But all his criticism notwithstanding, Rabindranath's critique of the Soviet state has to be distinguished from indictments of communism by the USA and Western Europe both then and in the cold war era. We should also remember that his own stance against awarding centrality to the state and the importance of the civil society far pre-dated his visit to Russia. They developed through the days of his participation in and quitting of the Indian nationalist movement. From that period onwards Rabindranath honed his critique of a state-centred approach to human development and of politics severed from experiencing subjects and their everyday life. Indeed, since then he posed and tried to answer the question of how a society could decolonise without nationalism and transform anew without the fetishisation of the state and seduction by power politics.[88]

Rabindranath achieved his position by shifting his vision from nationalist mobilisation aimed towards a state formation to one of the development of a holistic pedagogy meant for the invention and diffusion of ideas and practices for decolonisation. He wrote the novels *Gora, Ghare Baire* and *Charadhyay* in complex structuring of the problematic and wrote numerous essays on politics, society, culture and education. All this was mostly before he went to the Soviet Union. What he saw there only affirmed his criticism of the state and society and in particular regarding the nature and needs of Indian society. He insisted on keeping a social space between state and society – a liminal space that was necessary for evolving a pedagogy of transformation that would inform every aspect of people's lives. As a hegemonic reality the new and evolving consciousness would penetrate the state as well. It is to this space of social life and consciousness that he devoted his conscientising imagina-

---

88   A passage from Tagore's 'Samaj' (Society), Vol. 13, 1961, demonstrates Rabindranath's view of the state and society. 'I have stated before that ours is not a unity centred on the state. We did not experience an one-ness for any length of time by attacking [our] enemies or defending ourselves against them, or lived under the same state's rule protecting mutualities of interest or well-being or the lack of it. We were always fragmented into territories and societies bounded by narrow provincialism or chauvinism' (p. 31).

tion. The European modern state, he felt, had absorbed into itself the society and social care, including norms or values and general welfare. It routinely performed micro-management of everyday civil society – a managerial tactic similar to what came to be called 'governmentality' in more recent times. This he considered to be the exact opposite of what should happen, converting social participation into passive objects of the state's social engineering. Europeans from the seventeenth century onwards had morphed into a culture of the state, to be peoples of nationalism meant to be in thrall of the nation state. Rabindranath predicted the outcome of this situation and was proved right in the case of Europe, the Soviet Union and Japan. The dictatorship of the modern nation especially, he felt, had much in common, despite differences of appearance, to the collectivist dictatorship of the Soviet state. In spite of the veneer of bourgeois democracy in the so-called 'liberal' states, the reality was the inculcation of the society in the ideological apparatus of the state, resting on its consent-making function. The Soviet state combined this legitimation function with a direct instruction for obedience. The non-voluntary nature of popular participation vitiated the results of both the state and social formation, even if the intention of the state, such as the Soviet one, was good in the first place. The presence of instrumental rationality, of a mechanical materialism, fuelled Rabindranath's complaints. The dictatorship of the proletariat in Russia and the dictatorship of the industrial capitalist state in Europe he found to bear many resemblances: 'If the people's destinies are not created or nurtured by their combined will, then they create a cage. One might get fed well there, but it is not a home. Living long in it paralyses the wings'.[89] Though Rabindranath's criticism of any dictatorship is unqualified, it is important to note that he is also ambivalent about characterising the Soviet Union as dictatorial in its ultimate development. The reason for this positive qualification is his perception of a chink in the state armour, that is, the extensive pedagogic apparatus devised by the Soviet state, whose implementation willy nilly required popular participation that he thought would produce an unpredictable popular agency. He said: 'I accept that dictatorship is a great evil. I believe that much repression in Russia flows from that. The negative side of this coercion is a sin, but its positive side lies in education – the exact opposite of coercion'.[90] He continues by saying:

> [T]hose who wish to keep a dictatorship in place cannot afford to educate people. Neither the Czar's rule nor the orthodox faith tried to free people

---

89   Ibid., p. 727.
90   Ibid., p. 727.

from ignorance and superstition. This ignorance could be easily manipulated to serve the Czar's purpose – for example, to get the christians to
attack the jews or to set the muslims against the Armenians – these were
grotesque intrusions in the name of religion.[91]

These intrusions and distortions, Rabindranath felt, were not the final goals of
the contemporary Soviet state and its equalist ideology. The great rush towards
an immediate and total transformation, he felt, could produce counterproduct-
ive results. He also understood the overwhelming pressure that drove the new
state. But he believed, or hoped, this state of dictatorship would be a trans-
itional phase because new agents and ways of thinking had unleashed an irre-
versible educational campaign. 'Its generalisation of education is extraordinary
...' wrote Rabindranath, and also that '... this state does not have a lust for personal and factional power or greed for money. There is an unstoppable urge
to initiate common people into an economic view in order to nurture them
irrespective of their race, colour or class'.[92] Though Rabindranath complained
that '[i]n the Soviet Union there is an attempt to shape everybody's judgment
in the same mold of the Marxian economic system ... [and f]ree discussion has
been forcibly closed down in the face of this obdurateness',[93] he is still tentative
regarding the value of the communist economic plan. He stated that '[t]he time
has not yet come to say whether that economic view is wholly acceptable or not
because until now this economic approach was primarily wandering around
on pages of books, and had not been released so courageously in such a vast
arena'.[94]

It is best perhaps to see Rabindranath's views on the USSR as wisely contradictory. His feelings and judgments were in a state of fluidity, both admiring and
critical, congratulatory and ambivalent. This was in synch with the situation
in the Soviet Union. When he says that the 'normal' life of Russia is actually
in 'a state of war' against internal and external political forces he captures a
turmoil of an emerging reality, as yet to be shaped, and it is undeniable that
he expressed a degree of sympathy and concern for the new beleaguered and
besieged state as an object of intended destruction by the European colonial
capitalist states: 'The condition of Russia is that of a war time, with enemies
on the inside and outside. Much plotting and deception is happening to ruin
the experiments undertaken there. So they have to solidify the foundation of

---

91   Ibid., p. 727.
92   Ibid., p. 727.
93   Ibid., p. 727.
94   Ibid., p. 727.

their construction as fast as possible [and] for this they do not hesitate to use force'.[95] As noted above, Rabindranath admired the philosophy and the scale of the Soviet social pedagogy aimed beyond literacy and skills towards a philosophy of unity and altruism, but had profound questions on the methods of implementation. The use of state force, he thought, contradicted the universality of the intent or the content of an egalitarian education. Rabindranath also feared that real transformative and popular content of Soviet education was prematurely conclusive, hardening before having enough time to interact with necessary socio-historical corrective processes. He noticed the irony in the fact that those who denied the absolutism of any religion offered their own political ideology as a religious substitute: '[They] who do not obey the scriptures are resting implacably on their scriptural approach to an economic system'.[96]

The Soviet experience in its good and bad aspects held up a mirror to Rabindranath's own ideas and also gave him some hope. It affirmed his belief that education or methods of social transformation should not be aimed towards or dependent primarily on the creation of a state apparatus, nor mechanised into a political ideological programme. His decolonising philosophy judged the Soviet system positively for its intention of reinforcing peoples' sense of self, their subjective desire for knowledge and promoting innovations. But he found that the pedagogy had an element of cooperation mixed with coercion which he saw as a barrier to social transformation. The principle of social cooperation which he saw as the core of a redemptive social transformation needed a dialectical synthesis of the private and externally directed aspects of the mind. He concluded *Russiar Chithi* by saying:

> I desire the victory of the law of cooperation in the villages of our country to create wealth and conduct our affairs. Because the cooperation implied in this process does not reprimand the participant's desires, it thus accepts human nature. If there is coercion against this nature it will not work.[97]

And he added:

> I desire that the villages of our country should not live on the leftovers and wastes of the cities; they should enjoy their prosperity. It is my faith

---

95   Ibid., p. 727.
96   Ibid., pp. 728–9.
97   Ibid., p. 732.

that only through the processes of cooperation will the villages be able to retrieve [their] whole/full potential from [the present] sunken condition.[98]

2 Conclusion

Insofar as such a nuanced presentation to be found in *Russiar Chithi* can be reasonably assessed, I offer here a few tentative remarks. The feasibility and importance of comparing Rabindranath's social pedagogic praxis with those of Gramsci's on hegemony and common sense, Freire's on conscientisation and Fanon's on decolonisation should be evident by now. Gandhi's vast project of political change notwithstanding, Rabindranath's stance of transformation of an entire life-culture of colonised peoples was at the fullest and the first. Though Mahatma Gandhi was a great theorist of social and moral hegemony as well as of political mobilisation, his vision is less nuanced and less critically reflexive, and reliant on traditions in Indian society that Rabindranath found objectionable.[99] Gandhi's grasp of universal humanism and social imaginary were overdetermined by his intransigent nationalism implying glorification of religion and tradition. While Gandhi aimed towards a national imaginary or identity by balancing the existing social hierarchies and proposing a conscientisation consistent with that, Rabindranath's critique is premised on a humanist universal beyond the binary of colonial discourse. He stood for the

---

98 Ibid., p. 733.
99 This difference in the social vision is captured in the oft noted *charka* controversy. In a letter to Rani Mahalanobis dated 16 October 1929 Rabindranath expressed the following opinion while commenting on spinning one's way to freedom: 'The *charka* does not require anyone to think: one simply turns the wheel of the antiquated invention endlessly, using the minimum of judgement and stamina. In a more industrious, vital country than ours such a proposition would have stood no chance of acceptance – but in this country anything more strenuous than spinning would be rejected. Just think what would happen if instead of spinning Mahatma were to rule that each cultivator must grow at least two seers of produce per *bigha* of land; that such a target should be his sole aim and a mark of his piety; and that his patriotism would be judged by the extent to which he achieved this aim – then everyone would argue that such a programme would require intelligence, knowledge, drive and commitment to productive agricultural techniques. Indeed it would – and those are precisely the means whereby a country may be liberated; a country cannot be awakened by the inane enthusiasm of ignorant minds. That the cultivators who form three-quarters of this country's population should receive advice on how to spin with a *charka* like an imbecile rather than on how to become better farmers, is an insult to their humanity' (p. 365).

right and necessity of all to a full expressive selfhood. While Gandhi's trajectory consisted of a movement from the particularities of a nation and nation state to the rest of the world, Rabindranath began from the world – from ideas of world history, universalism, and the concept of the human – and arrived from there to the local. The exchange of their letters is evidence to this difference between them. Rabindranath, in spite of the criticism of the nationalists, remained firm as an educator of a philosophy of universal humanism associated with creative freedom.

Rabindranath helps us to see commonalities between anti-colonial struggle and class struggle. Though not a marxist and reliant upon a structural analysis of colonial capitalism, he also called for relatively equitable distribution of wealth. In his critique of techno-rationalist worldview, of greed for money and power, of commodity fetishism and the dehumanisation of the self and the destruction of nature produced by the normalisation of colonialism and capitalism, Rabindranath offers a social critique that runs parallel to Marx's critique of alienation. *The Philosophical Manuscripts of 1844* and Rabindranath's socio-political essays and literary opus have a shared linguistic resonance.[100] Rabindranath and Marx were both master readers of feudalism and the deformation of creative, critical and human capacities by institutional religion and capitalism. Both emphasised the distortion of people's 'natural' selves in the developmental process of industrialism and profit as well as the destruction of nature and society. If Rabindranath had read Marx's critique of alienation – of how through an exploiting and repressive socio-economic system based on maximisation of profit 'Man' is alienated from nature, from other 'men', his own creations and from himself, he would have agreed with Marx. It seems that, knowingly or unknowingly, theorists of radical social transformation motivated by a quest of justice and social creativity share critical epistemological premises and ethical imperatives, as with Rabindranath, Gramsci, Fanon or Freire. Frantz Fanon, with his trenchant critique of petty-bourgeois nationalism, shares with Rabindranath his liberationist views, which at their best align colonial, imperial and class oppressions in a complex figuration. A knowledge of Rabindranath's pedagogy of decolonisation would have helped the anti-colonial and anti-imperialist thinkers who followed him. But since the 1940s, and to a large extent even now, Rabindranath has been shrouded in either silence or hagiography that presents him through a veil of mysticism. The approach of the majority of Indians and of the Bengali intelligentsia, along with non-Indians who are generally orientalist, continues to eclipse him as a power-

---

100   Marx 1964b.

ful social critic and a thinker of liberationist social praxis, though the moment of a powerful change of perception seems to have been launched.

In conclusion, I will make a brief attempt to situate Rabindranath in his own time. Extraordinary as were his creative and critical abilities, Rabindranath was not alone in thinking as he did. He shared with many others a lineage of social transformation and change of consciousness descending as much from the Upanishads of India and Raja Rammohan Roy or the popular syncretic thought of India as from the European enlightenment. His life was lived at the centre of attempts mounted by the reformers and educationists of eighteenth- and nineteenth-century Bengal/India and elsewhere, including Europe. His aspirations for a holistic and aesthetically driven pedagogy – its content and methods – were not particular to him. As a study of enlightenment social and political thought as well as of social reform traditions will reveal, the idea of a pedagogy without borders was in the air. Even those who were engaged in institutional schooling, liberal thought or political organisation were deeply concerned with the coincidence of education or pedagogy with larger social, including revolutionary, transformation. This concern extended from the design of the classroom to modes and methods of augmenting class consciousness and conducting class struggle. The two centuries of Europe preceding Rabindranath, as well as the nineteenth century of Bengal, should be called 'centuries of pedagogy'. They were multifaceted in their outlooks and enlivened with a passion for creating a 'new man', a 'new society' and a 'new age'. The works of Rousseau, Locke, Helvetius, the encyclopaedists and philosophers of the French Revolution, John Stuart Mill, Fourier, St. Simone and Marx, among others, ideologically different from each other in many ways, testify to the large visions of change.

Rabindranath's pedagogy is as commensurate with the European enlightenment's idea that 'man' is endowed by the faculties of reason and imagination, is capable of social critique, creativity and a conscious social change, as it is with the Upanishad's ideas of knowledge. In Europe from Giambattista Vico onwards many philosophers had dared to think that human reason could and should help to refashion society on humanist grounds, and reason helped to create representative and governing apparatuses to reflect that new order. Thus conscious attempts to educe and enlighten went far beyond restricted and elite cultural and intellectual spheres, and included the philosophical propaganda of the liberation struggles in the Americas or in the French revolution. As such, Jacobinism was a large part of the radical transformational common sense of the time. Seen in this light, Marx's *The Communist Manifesto* or *The Poverty of Philosophy*, J.S. Mill's *On Liberty*, as much as Mary Shelley's *Frankenstein*, could be read as much more than political and literary texts but rather as multidimensional pedagogical texts. The nature and role of consciousness were emphasised everywhere in debates of the time, which ranged from women's and anti-slavery movements to the development of proletarian consciousness for a communist revolution. Obviously Rousseau's *Emile* and *Social Contract*, Hegel's *Phenomenology of Mind*, and the poetry of the Romantics ranging from Schiller and Goethe to Wordsworth, shared similar philosophical or pedagogic premises and their innate transformative impulses. To do justice to Rabindranath, his readers have to place him in this grand tradition of radical and visionary philosophers and educators whose projects of conscious social intervention and infusing a new universalist consciousness were based on 'humanity' and 'truth' (not quite the same as 'fact').

The central figure of Rabindranath's imaginary of a truly decolonised human being is that of a free and creative self who is neither oppressed nor oppressive. This is the personification whom he calls 'Man' or the *'Mahamanab'* (the Great Man), an ideal type of human possibility. This figure is not representative of an empirically fixed form with his face carved in stone for all times. This 'new man', rising from social history, is not a 'found', pre-given and prescribed figure, nor is he likely to finally arrive at a conclusively achieved form. This 'human' or 'Man' is familiar to us as an echo of our own humanity, but he is also a newborn – a *nabajatak*. This adventure of becoming 'human', from the state of a biological being and the degraded and fixed subject of colonial and other forms of domination, preoccupied Rabindranath life-long as an artist and a social thinker. This is perhaps why 'reason' for him is not an instrumental, fact manufacturing human capacity, but rather able to relate intimately with imagination.

As a resistant subject of British colonial rule Rabindranath tried to perform a near impossible and ideal task through his universalist, humanist stance. In this process he rejected both nationalism and a particularist cultural identity. Rejecting nationalism for its parochialism in spite of the passion it evoked in the exploited, Rabindranath tried to imagine a 'freedom' on non-nationalist or particularist premises which would eschew the same thirst for power over others and hateful self-other relation that colonialism drew its life and energy from. A social consciousness and praxis motivated by the same competitiveness and always on the brink of a war could not win him over. In his novel *Ghare Baire* he tore away the false sense of freedom which nationalism offered while neglecting the real needs of human dignity and creative capacities and desires for sociality. Once more in the name of the nation, he thought, the people of India or elsewhere would be isolated within its enclosed space, but this time voluntarily. They would relinquish their space in the larger humanity, waging a war of each against all.

The issue of identity central to nationalism presented Rabindranath with complications for a flexible negotiation of the self and personality with the social collectivity and history. He knew well that political struggles are waged under a banner of named identity which unites people. Thus the political agency of the colonised and classed subject is activated through this identity. The identity, therefore, must be constructed through discursive resources which are directive of the transformative theories and their implementing practices. The identity that Rabindranath selects on the ground of its inclusivity and flexibility is that of 'the human' rather than the 'nation', a category of desire and capacities. The approximation of this 'human' is incumbent upon forging ideas of commonality between diverse and dispersed peoples and a vision of a 'world-society', a 'world-home' or a 'world-university', and this gesture blurs the boundaries between the self and the world, the interior and the exterior. Of course the magnitude of the concept of 'the human' borders on the brink of the metaphysical and creates the opportunity for seeing Rabindranath as a merely spiritual or a mystical thinker, as a 'romantic', and there is undoubtedly some truth to this figuration. His vast construction of a universal Man waits like a great blank in history to be filled in with changing concrete social experience, emotions and creations, all placed within lived time. The more concrete the world of the human becomes the more well-defined becomes the face of his great poesis of the 'human', but in a fluid and changing manner. As the ensemble of human capacities are a complex of the biological, the social and the aesthetic, consciousness can achieve a concreteness, an embodiment which both captures a finite form and that forms impermanence. The key realisation for the reader lies in the fact that the self of any subject is a being always in the process of becoming through personal experiences and mediating socio-historical relations with which the self is always already interacting. Rabindranath's pedagogy of decolonisation nurtures this social process of being and provides the possibilities for the emergence of the truly 'human' in us and the creation of a 'humane' society. This pedagogy thus opens the door for an aesthetic, ethical and critical philosophy and method for the birth of such a new person and a new society.

Beyond the Binaries: Notes on Karl Marx's and Rabindranath Tagore's Ideas on Human Capacities and Alienation

The chief defect of all hitherto existing materialism (that of Feuerbach included) is that the thing, reality, sensuousness, is conceived only in the form of the *object or of contemplation*, but not as *sensuous human activity, practice*, not subjectively. Hence, in contradistinction to materialism, the *active* side was developed abstractly by idealism – which, of course, does not know real, sensuous activity as such.[1]

∵

1 Introduction

It has not been a common practice to place Karl Marx and Rabindranath Tagore side by side to draw out their commonalities in any sustained fashion. If anything, there has been an assumption of radical difference. But in the last two decades there have been some attempts to relate them positively, though much more work still needs to be done. This work must avoid oversimplification and reductionism and depict similarities without losing sight of their specificities in epistemologies and practices. Their similarities and differences are to be explored in their worldviews, social understanding, ideas of subjectivity and agency and of production and reproduction. Nor should we overlook their commitment to creative human capacity in relation to production and labour, and as such their general sense of aesthetics. These point to some common basic concerns shared by Marx and Rabindranath which, if lost sight of, does disservice to them and their readers.

Our turn to Marx and Rabindranath is linked to the crisis of socialism that we face. This crisis is both a problem and an opportunity as it impels us to

---

1 Marx and Engels 1970, p. 121. Original emphasis.

examine and renew our understanding of socialism and what it has to offer us. If we are to go beyond tinkering with liberalism towards a fundamental, that is, a revolutionary social transformation, we would do well to re-examine and bring together the philosophic, social and political thoughts of Marx and Rabindranath. Marx's idea of communist revolution and Rabindranath's idea of a foundational transformation of colonial social consciousness towards decolonisation cannot be sealed away in separate boxes. Without engaging in rigidly spatialising epistemologies, social and aesthetic devices productive of the reified and binary notions of the East and the West, of tradition and modernity, we need to situate both Marx's and Rabindranath's urgent calls for social and historical awakening in the parameters of enlightenment which preceded them. Certain aspects of the enlightenment, speaking in terms of universal humanity and rationalist critical modernity, called for conceptualising socio-political, moral and aesthetic outlooks in material and transformative terms, while others signalled to modernist notions of domination. Marx and Rabindranath both subscribed to the universalist and rationalist approach. There were others who did the same. The precise ideological content, practices and goals of these efforts for social transformation may have even opposed each other, but the environment that they created resonated with ideas and desires for the creation of a 'new man', a 'new society', 'new art forms' and 'new social pedagogies'.[2] The present essay attempts to capture this spirit of these modernist times, times of critiques and the demand for fundamental changes in consciousness and social relations. It offers reflections on some of Marx's and Rabindranath's key ideas in a comparative and complimentary rather than an antithetical manner. The point of entry for this essay lies in Marx's and Rabindranath's universalist ideas of the 'human' and their own specific uses of the notion of 'humanism'. While the notion of universalist humanism has been readily associated with Rabindranath both by himself and his readers, it has been intensely debated as an attribute of Marx.

The debate on Marx's humanism is old and continuing. But the most influential moment of dispute was introduced by Louis Althusser in 1965 in *For Marx*.[3] Emphasising an 'epistemological break' between the young 'philosophical' Marx and the older 'scientific' Marx, with a new 'theoretical' consciousness as opposed to the earlier metaphysical one carried over from Feuerbach, Althusser said:

---

2   See Bannerji 2011, pp. 194–213. See also Draper 1978, Vol. II, Part II.
3   Althusser 1977b.

> There is an unequivocal *'epistemological break'* in Marx's work ... which is a critique of his erstwhile philosophical (ideological) conscience ... This 'epistemological break' concerns conjointly *two distinct theoretical disciplines*. By founding the theory of history (historical materialism), Marx simultaneously broke with his erstwhile ideological philosophy and established a new philosophy (dialectical materialism).[4]

According to Althusser this new philosophy is 'scientific'. Pages 21 to 86 of *For Marx* capture the basic ideas of the debates on Marx's humanism which others have elaborated on. Important opposition to Althusser's view comes from many authors who work on the problematics of alienation and reification as well as on labour and aesthetics in Marx. Two most rewarding sources for understanding Marx's 'humanism' and the idea of a historicised 'universalism' are István Mészáros' *Marx's Theory of Alienation* and Bertel Ollman's *Alienation: Marx's Conception of Man in Capitalist Society*.[5] 'Scientific' marxism originating from a positivist perspective has been carried on in the Althusserian tradition. This approach may have more to do with Engels and Lenin, morphing itself as 'structuralist' marxism.[6] Positivists or rational choice marxists have further developed this non-agentic, subjectless base and superstructure approach to society and history.

In order to see Marx as a humanist the conventional uses of the concepts of the 'human' and 'humanism' have to be put aside and undergo an epistemological shift. It requires that we treat both notions, along with the idea of the universal, as conceptual constellations rather than single definitions, as critical and discursive assemblages. We can neither see them as signifying a 'human essence' or as a code for 'human nature', nor can the idea of the 'human' hold a pre-scribed, unchanging body of content. In our epistemological shift we need to engage the 'human' with a critical methodology which incorporates the actuality of physical and mental human capacities, which gain their substance in social interaction, through the mediating process necessary for actualisation. This implies the presence of conscious social subjects and their practices and needs. The point of departure lies, as Marx noted, in endurance of human lives and societies through history. The idea of creative/productive human capacity gets its evidence from existing peoples' sustenance of life at the physical, social, political and historical levels. Production and reproduc-

---

4   Ibid., p. 33, Althusser's emphases.
5   Mészáros 1970; Ollman 1971.
6   See Williams 1977, especially pp. 75–114.

tion of lives, basic or complex and developed needs or mores, social forms, norms and relations, are a continuum of expression and object-making which blend into each other through developing human capacities. This creative/productive human capacity is integrally connected to what lies outside of each person and is susceptible to and creative of all socio-historical phenomena, including the human influence on nature. As such it is as productive of alienation and reification as of revolution under circumstances impinging on our very ways of being 'human'. The 'human' conceived in these terms is not an empiricist entity but itself a creation, and becomes something to discover and actively aspire to.

This essay, therefore, is an effort to validate the notion of the 'human' and humanism as political and moral imperatives interpreted in ways that include Marx and Rabindranath in their general purview. My interpretation relies on the epistemological critique provided by Marx in his 'Theses on Feuerbach', the first of which is cited in the epigramme to this introduction. As stated there, neither an inert, object-dependent materialism nor a purely subjectivist idealism can provide us with a standpoint for a proper humanist critique. What we need is an epistemological method which encompasses the socio-historical and political moments of a conscious subject-agent through which we can think of manifold forms of production in terms of *'sensuous, human activity, practice'*. This comprehensive idea of 'real sensuous activity' allows us to see the social nature of consciousness and consciousness embedded in the social. This is the interconstitutive relation that Marx clarifies in *The German Ideology*. Adopting such an epistemological stance will allow us to be 'humanists' without any danger of erasing either the specificities or the similarities between Marx and Rabindranath. In the case of Marx the secularisation, socialisation and historicisation of the concept of the 'human' is accomplished through his implication of the 'human' in his concept of 'labour' involving all human senses and capacities – through which labour becomes a transformative notion.

It should be noted at the outset that in the present time the ideas of the 'human' and 'humanism' are deeply tarnished. Critiques of colonial discourse, of racist discourses arising through conquest, colonialism, slavery and indentured labour have rightly subjected the 'human' and humanism to searing condemnations and shame. We have seen how the idea of the human, attempts at a monogenesist approach to race notwithstanding, has served as the cause of negative stereotypes or construction of Europe's 'others'. The baggage of power relations and discourse of civilising missions and violent practices have been directly and indirectly deployed in relation to the 'human' and humanism. In the context of capitalism's patriarchal and racist world history, the universalist potentials of the human and humanism have mainly generalised power-laden discourses and administration of 'difference'. It is not the enriching plenitude of the human and humanism that the world has experienced in any effective sense so far, instead these notions have served as modes of erasing and marginalising those who cannot be and do not fit the European/Western typology of the 'self', of a properly evolved 'human'. It is not surprising that so many resistance critiques have proudly taken up the ideology of anti-humanism.[7]

Why then should this essay pick up these oft-hated notions of the human and humanism and bring them in to serve as positive and even liberatory notions? I have tried to answer this question below, suggesting their thorough rethinking. This essay makes an attempt to go beyond the limits of the colonial and racialising use of these notions and explore why, how or to what extent the 'human' and its profession in 'humanism' can serve us. Not that any concept or any 'ism' can serve us as a talisman against the violence that faces us in imperialist wars, genocides and ethnocides in the names of civilisation, democracy, human rights, nation or god. But it might still be worth testing and retooling these notions that allow us to think beyond the fragmented social, the atomistic and self-serving particularisms and seeing the 'other' solely as an enemy. Not denying that the 'human' can serve as an alibi for oppressing the 'other', we need to create different forms of identification which can be called 'universal' in a historical materialist sense. This becomes our challenge to the mutilation of the social subject and life-world as created and activated by fully encapacitated and expressive humans within history and social formation. The idea here is to resituate and rework these notions in such a way that instead of the violence of abstracting one big homogeneous 'us' without specificities we may create an 'us' forged in actual historic, socio-cultural, political struggles. It is my

---

7 The reason for this lies in the exposures made by critical studies of colonialism, racialisation, gender, sexuality and other forms of social oppression. It is not surprising that the portent of 'humanism' put at the service of domination, including of colonialism, has shown how the notion of 'human' becomes a category of 'power/knowledge' when appropriated in an act of self-appellation by the colonial European bourgeoisies. Ranging from debates about whether Africans were 'humans' or 'animals', whether women were 'soulless' creatures of 'natural' reproductive imperative, or the working classes and the poor were innately unintelligent and uneducable – the actually existing 'humanism' of the European elite has been a mode of exclusion and erasure of the exploited and marginalised. In this sense the 'human' is a category of difference, where 'difference' means the creation of an 'other' who is inferior, and often despicable and dangerous. There are innumerable sources to cite as evidence of what I am saying, so I will only name a few key ones: Fanon 1963 and 1967; Gilman 1985b; Stoler 1995. The most trenchant anti-humanist theoretical impulse came from the works of Michel Foucault, which pushed aside much of the 'humanist' tradition espoused by different disciplines. To name a few texts of his which point the path to critique and rejection of direct and indirect forms of 'dominating' humanism we can cite: Foucault 1980b, 2003a, 2003b.

belief that a nuanced exploration of Marx and Rabindranath may help us get a better grasp of the processes entailed in shaping composite subject-agents who are the actors in creating a better and an oppositional world to the one we inhabit.

In order to perform our task we will need to understand humanism in ways that will equally avoid empty/abstract universalism or romantic wish-images, though these utopian images have a value in inspiring the spirit of struggle. We have to start from the existing reality in which the idea of the human gains a concrete conscious body and a historically and socially shaped sense of self. Humanism will then be dislocated from its metaphysical/ideological space and shift from general pious platitudes presented in terms of ineluctable binaries of body and mind, emotion and reason, and the self and other and so on. This will mean establishing an honest internal connection between 'real, existing individuals' and their consciousness. The idea of the human will encompass their historical and social lives and commonalities in terms of their basic creative, receptive and productive capacities. This is the epistemological critique put forward by Marx and Engels in the following lines:

> We set out from real, active men, and on the basis of their real life-process we demonstrate the development of the ideological reflexes and echoes of this life-process ... Morality, religion, metaphysics, all the rest of ideology and their corresponding forms of consciousness, thus no longer retain the semblance of independence. They have no history, no developments, but men, developing their material production and their intercourse, alter, along with their real existence, their thinking and products of their thinking. Life is not determined by consciousness but consciousness by life.[8]

On this note we will begin our exploration by first addressing Marx, and then move on to a discussion of Rabindranath.

> Estrangement is manifested not only in the fact that *my* means of life belong to *someone else*, that *my* desire is the inaccessible possession of *another*, but also in the fact that everything is itself something *different* from itself ..., all is under the sway of *inhuman* power.[9]

---

8   Marx and Engels 1970, p. 47.
9   Marx 1964b, p. 156. Marx's emphases.

Marxists and anti-marxists have equally presented us an economistic Marx who places consciousness in a secondary position to economic structures. This is the Marx of 'the base and superstructure', of 'correspondence' and 'reflective' relation between consciousness and reality.[10] This dualist Marx is the Marx of the 'epistemological break', the scientist of ideology as presented by Louis Althusser in *For Marx* (see above). A non-economistic or a non-scientistic and structuralist reading, however, reveals a different Marx, who does not radically 'break' with either his past methods or with politically/socially transformative goals, but rather expands and deepens his theorisation and critique. The claim that 'we begin from real life', from actually existing activities and societies, is presented thus by Marx and Engels:

> The premises from which we begin are not arbitrary ones, not dogmas, but real premises from which abstraction can only be made in the imagination. They are the real individuals, their activity and the material conditions under which they live, both those they find already existing and those produced by their activity.[11]

This new method is constantly expanded and explained throughout all of Marx's opus and multiply explored, and *The Communist Manifesto* (1848) presents for the first time the political fusion of knowing and doing. In this communist revolutionary process consciousness and concerns for the human, the universal nature of human capacities for living a sensuous life of producing and consuming/enjoying, are not left behind but given an increasingly fuller articulation. From the *Economic and Philosophical Manuscripts of 1844* through *The Communist Manifesto* (1848) to *Capital*, Volume I (1867) and beyond Marx keeps intact his quest for an integral social and self-emancipation, for a human

---

10   See Williams 1977, pp. 55–71, and 75–82. Williams attempts to rectify the economistic and positivist interpretations advanced by marxists regarding the issues of human consciousness and ideology. He reconsiders the notions of 'base' and 'superstructure' by suggesting that the use of these terms in Marx's opus 'is not primarily conceptual, in any precise way, but metaphorical'. (p. 77). Instead he claims, I think rightly, that Marx repudiated any derivative relation between consciousness ('superstructure') and the historical-social ('base'). Williams says: 'It is then ironic to remember that the force of Marx's original criticism had been mainly directed against the separation of 'areas' of thought and activity (as in the separation of consciousness from material production) and against the related evacuation of specific content – real human activities – by the imposition of abstract categories. The common abstraction of 'the base' and 'the superstructure' is thus a radical persistence of the modes of thought which he attacked'. (p. 78).

11   Marx and Engels 1970, p. 42.

liberation, intact. This concern is expressed in Marx's famous statement in *The Eighteenth Brumaire of Louis Bonaparte* (1852), where he says: 'Men make their own history, but they do not make it just as they please; they do not make it under circumstances chosen by themselves, but under circumstances directly found, given and transmitted from the past'.[12] The call for ending the eternal return of the past at the cost of transformation of society and self is the core of the revolutionary process for Marx. Otherwise, as he says, we are doomed to a situation where

> [t]he tradition of all the dead generations weighs like a nightmare on the brain of the living. And just when they seem engaged in revolutionising themselves and things, in creating something entirely new, precisely in such epochs of revolutionary crisis they anxiously conjure up the spirits of the past to their service and borrow from them names, battle slogans and costumes in order to present the new scene of world history in this time-honoured disguise and this borrowed language.[13]

Marx's emphasis is always on the conscious active and creative subject, the agent who is in a transformative relation with society, nature and history and whose activities are characterised as practical and sensuous human activity. The communist revolution, as *The German Ideology* (1846) and *The Communist Manifesto* and other writings of Marx present, is, therefore, *not an event*, but rather a cumulative, expanding organisational process entailing growing critical awareness, social analysis and historical contextualisation. The 'science', 'logic' or 'laws' of historical materialism, however, cannot be grasped in positivist, reductionist and economistic manners. For Marx the communist revolution is centrally the transformation of society and forms of consciousness of all aspects of human productive/creative capacity, including that of the economic.

The communist revolution as Marx proposes is thus not the function of self-shifting economic structures which merely use human subjects to get to different economic stages. The human subject is the key actor in the process and to displace this subject with objective forces would be idealism by another name. It is explicitly stated, as in the quotation from *The Eighteenth Brumaire*, that people make their own history. A view of 'history' using 'ideology' or 'structures' instead of conscious human subjects to move forward, which implies that history happens behind their backs, as it were, would involve us in a long dis-

---

12   Marx 1972d, p. 437.
13   Marx 1972d, p. 437.

cussion on Hegel's philosophy of history, an antithetical approach to Marx's historical materialism. But suffice it here to say that the communist revolution as projected by Marx is a conscious self-emancipatory project and has an actively organising collective subject. It is not an instance of Hegel's 'ruse of reason'.[14] Lukács remarks in *History and Class Consciousness* that subjects act as classes both *in* and *for* themselves and are conscious subject-agents of class struggle, the basic force of history.[15] They are *embodied*, experiencing, real people living in history and society, not abstract collectivities of a structurally driven and externally possessed consciousness. Nor is the development of communist consciousness dependent on elite intellectuals who claim to occupy a superior vantage point, to 'know' the 'science' of revolution and teach the workers their 'true' proletarian consciousness, creating a hierarchic relationship between leaders and cadres. In 'The critique of the Gotha programme' and in the 'Circular Letter to Bebel, Liebknecht, Bracke, and Others' we find Marx's stern rejection of elite, bourgeois and petty bourgeois leadership in the task of revolution. He says, for example, in the latter:

> As for ourselves, in view of our whole past there is only one path open to us. For almost forty years we have stressed the class struggle as the immediate driving power of history and in particular the class struggle between the bourgeoisie and proletariat as the great lever of the modern social revolution ... When the International was formed we expressly formulated the battle cry: The emancipation of the working class must be the work of the working class itself.[16]

The project of social and self-emancipation as proposed by Marx involves a change 'inside' the revolutionary subject in their consciousness as well as in and of the objective socio-historical world 'outside'. Each moment of class and social struggle implies an interconstitutiveness and a conscious agency of existing subjects. Beyond the binaries of the private and the public formulated by bourgeois thought and of the atomised individual and his/her 'other' self and society, the individual who is individuated in and through society is immersed in constant sensuous and practical engagements. We need to remember what

---

14   See Karl Marx and Frederick Engel, *The Communist Manifesto*, in Tucker, *Marx-Engels Reader*, where they outline the different typologies of class politics attempting to change/ make history. See also Draper's explorations of different types of revolution as conceived by Marx and Engels in *Marx's Theory of Revolution*.

15   Lukács 1971.

16   Marx 1972d, pp. 382–98 and 399–405, respectively. Quotation p. 405.

Marx had to say about the distinction between the bourgeois and historical materialist notions of the individual. Here Marx debunks the myth of man alone, asocial, non-reliant on socio-historical development of his human capacities. Marx's own point of departure is of course 'socially determined individual production'. He goes on to say that

> [t]he individual and isolated hunter and fisherman, with whom Smith and Ricardo begin, belongs among the unimaginative conceits of the eighteenth century Robinsonades, which in no way express merely a reaction against over-sophistication and a return to a misunderstood natural life, as cultural historians imagine. As little as Rousseau's *contract social*, which brings naturally independent, autonomous subjects into relation and connection by contract, rests on such naturalism. This is the semblance, the merely aesthetic semblance, of the Robinsonades, great and small.[17]

Marx spent his entire life in solving the riddle of the processes of psycho-social formation and political organisation vital for both communist revolution and counter-revolution.[18] It is not difficult to understand why the notion of 'human capacities' occupies a central position in Marx's theory of communist revolution. The socially in-formed, creative and dynamic capacities of the human being, in short, the *social* ontology of consciousness and its creative abilities, provide the forces and the vehicle of social transformation and transcreation. The 'universality' of this human consciousness amounts to self-reflexive, relational and practical capacities which allow the subject to move from the local, from the past, to the present and to the extra-local, from the individual to the social. These bases in consciousness, its transformative and reflexive capacities, allow Marx to distinguish between animals and man and to identify what he calls man's 'species being' – an old concept that he reworks through the historical materialist method. The kind of 'species being' that Marx attributes to humankind is expressed in an excerpt from *The Economic and Philosophical Manuscripts of 1844*:

---

17   Marx 1973, p. 83.
18   For Marx's understanding of communist revolution and counter-revolution, see *The Eighteenth Brumaire*, which offers an exemplar of these phenomena. See also *Civil War in France*. Engels said that these texts show Marx's 'remarkable gift ... for grasping clearly the character, the import and the necessary consequences of great historical events, at a time when these events are still in progress before our eyes, or have only just taken place'. (Marx 1972e, p. 526).

In creating an *objective world* by his practical activity, in *working-up* inorganic nature, man proves himself a conscious species being, i.e. a being that treats the species as its own essential being, or that treats itself as a species being. Admittedly animals also produce. They build themselves nests and dwellings, like the bees, the beavers, ants, etc. But an animal only produces what it immediately needs for itself or its young. It produces one-sidedly, while man produces universally ... [M]an produces even when he is free from physical needs and only truly produces in freedom therefrom.[19]

As Marx sees the content and extent of human consciousness implicated in society and history, consciousness is necessarily susceptible to their shaping power. This is the mode of new and future forms of social consciousness, practice, history and political activities. Both reaction and revolution may result from this interactivity and susceptibility and, therefore, the work of transformation of both society and social consciousness become one. These mutually formative interactions simultaneously shape, externalise and are shaped by the content of consciousness. Regarding this phenomenon Marx says:

[M]an also possesses 'consciousness', but, even so, not inherent, not pure consciousness. From the start the 'spirit' is afflicted with the curse of being 'burdened' with matter, which here makes its appearance in the form of agitated layers of air, sounds, in short, of language. Language is as old as consciousness, language *is* practical consciousness that exists also for other men, and for that reason alone it really exists for me personally as well; language, like consciousness, only arises from the need, the necessity, of intercourse with other men.[20]

The politics of consciousness, the creative potentialities of human capacity for both expression and alienation, require a brief overview of Marx's ideas regarding the development of human consciousness *per se*. In *The German Ideology*,

---

19   Marx 1964b, pp. 108–109. For Marx the difference between animal and man lies in conscious making/productive and aesthetic capacities. See also Baxandall and Morawski 1974: 'The animal is immediately identical with its life-activity. It does not distinguish itself from it. It is *its life-activity*. Man makes his life-activity itself the object of his will and of his consciousness. He has conscious life-activity. It is not a determination with which he directly merges' (p. 51). Excerpted from Marx 1964b.

20   Marx and Engels 1970, pp. 50–1. In this text he also says: 'The production of ideas, of conceptions, of consciousness, is at first directly interwoven with the material activity and the material intercourse of men, the language of real life' (p. 47).

where Marx presents most explicitly his method of historical materialism, he offers a brief account of how growing populations, their needs and productive forces are dialectically and historically reproduced, mediated and expanded. He discerns three aspects of human consciousness, and we can paraphrase them thus:

1) The most basic aspect of consciousness is its implication in human survival and in the capacity of communication as the vector and mediator of basic needs, feelings and social relations. He calls this *practical consciousness*, the example being the development of language, which, he says, means something for him because it means the same or similar things for others. This reveals the inherently social nature of consciousness. At this stage the production of ideas as such is not the goal, nor are they above or apart from reality. Though they are crucially involved in object making, the object is visibly related to the basic and immediate needs of the producer and the consumer.

2) As time passes and societies grow more complex, production and consumption lose their direct relations. Consciousness is absorbed in the organisational processes of complicated social division of mental and manual labour. At this evolved stage of mental labour ideas gain a seemingly separate sphere of productive technology and their own mode of production and circulation. They are then *seen* as autonomous and unconnected to each other, rather than as they are, as fundamentally rooted in and connected by historical-social modes of social production. This occlusive situation creates the primacy and the myth of self-generation of ideas and the perception that *essence* or ideas precede social and objective existence. This distance which arises between ideas and reality is a vital source of alienation, such that the actual connection between the two not only is not recognised, but that non-recognition itself and its reasons are themselves obscured. This, says Marx, is the moment of the birth of ideology, which requires a special kind of epistemology, to be found in metaphysics and philosophy, for example, which naturalises the idea that theory is separate from, and superior to, the material reality.[21]

3) In *The German Ideology* Marx points out the existence of another type of consciousness which is neither wholly practical nor ideological or abstract. This consciousness is critical, reflexive and analytical, which

---

21   The crux of the method of historical materialism lies in the inter-constitutive connection Marx makes between theory, practice and social reality in a historical context. *The Holy Family* and *The German Ideology* present this method most explicitly. This anti-ideological critique is expanded and applied exhaustively in *Capital* (Vols. 1–3).

uncovers the mechanics of the production of ideology. This form of consciousness is the result of a materialist critique. It is a method for anti-ideological knowledge production which reveals and re-establishes the lost creative, mediative connections between ideas and social reality, between ideology and other forms of thought. This epistemology is an anti-Hegelian critique and challenges Hegel's (and Feuerbach's and others') belief in the autonomy of ideas, their primacy in the movement of history, the separation between life and knowledge. By exploding the myth of self-sustaining independence of ideas Marx destroys the mystification regarding the origin of ideas. This critical anti-ideological method he calls 'science', and endows it with the potential for developing a revolutionary consciousness.[22] This relational method of critique called 'historical materialism' is a concrete and revolutionary analytical method for challenging alienation and reification and the oppressive social relations which produce them.

2   Consciousness, Alienation and Labour

What, then, constitutes the alienation of labour? First, the fact that labour is *external* to the worker, i.e., it does not belong to his essential being; that in his work, therefore, he does not affirm himself but denies himself, does not feel content but unhappy, does not develop freely his physical and mental energy but mortifies his body and ruins his mind. The worker therefore only feels himself outside his work, and in work feels outside himself. He is at home when he is not working, and when he is working he is not at home.[23]

---

22   In *The German Ideology* Marx and Engels speak of historical materialism as the 'science' for communist revolution. This method of analysis is also called by Engels dialectical materialism. But 'science' here has no positivist connotation, instead this is 'human science' whose method is not a transposition of natural sciences into social analysis or historiography. This 'scientific' epistemology that enables one to see that '... the *sensuous world* ... is, *not a thing* given from all eternity, remaining ever the same, but the product of industry and of the state of society; and, indeed, in the sense that it is an historical product, the result of the activity of a whole succession of generations, each standing on the shoulder of the preceding one, developing its industry and its intercourse, modifying its social system according to the changed needs'. (Marx and Engels 1970, p. 62). My emphasis.

23   Marx 1964b, p. 110. Marx's emphasis.

Let us consider now Marx's ideas of involvement of consciousness with labour and read this through the notion of all human activities as being social and 'sensuous human activity, practice'. Seen thus, Marx's concept of labour has an expressive dimension involving the same human capacities for all forms of production, making no actual distinction between industry and art. Such integrity of labour and consciousness presents an internal and formative relationship between them no matter how labour is employed. The social relations of different historical stages or modes of production give rise to different types of alienation, and in fact a kind of alienation is involved in any object creation, as noted by István Mészáros. It is evident that if labour is equated with *any* or *all* conscious productive activity the very fact of creating objects will involve a form of *alienation*. In so far as any humanly produced object implies externalisation, it is alienated or separated from being submerged in the inner life of the producer. An object is thus necessarily an external entity, therefore a phenomenon of *alienation* in an ordinary and practical sense.[24] Marx points out that the larger the social scope, the more complicated and indirect are the relations between production and consumption. The unity found between them in the very early stages of society is ruptured through varied productive mediations, social relations and organisations. As production and consumption are also *subject to property relations*, with modes of appropriation changing, the objects now enter a labyrinth of a different kind of alienation, where they and the very labour of the producer are appropriated by the owners of the means of production. The social circumstances of this are elaborated in the *Economic and Philosophical Manuscripts of 1844* and through the explicitly materialist analysis of *Capital*, Vol. I, centred on the concept of 'commodity' and its role in the capitalist mode of production.

The other point to be noted is that any act of object making in any productive process involves a transformation of nature through labour – thus resulting in a certain kind of alienation or taking away from nature. But this transformative action does not necessarily entail a relationship of negative or exploitive alienation between the producer and nature. Natural resources, including human

---

24   To anyone acquainted with *The Economic and Philosophical Manuscripts of 1844* it will be clear that Marx's critique of alienation is not about the fact of object production. Human beings are necessarily object-making creatures for production and reproduction of life itself. Alienation becomes a reality as production enters into exploitive and oppressive social relations in and for which objects are made, when we reach the state of the capitalist mode of production of commodity *proper*, i.e., in the generalization of capitalism beyond economy to society at large. In István Mészáros' seminal work, *Marx's Theory of Alienation*, we get a historical overview and insightful exposition of this development from object to commodity. See Mészáros 1970, pp. 66–119. See also Lukács 1971.

capacities as natural/physical resources, enter into productive relations which are social and are transformed into objects and skills to meet human needs, including that for beauty, under egalitarian or exploitive circumstances. This confirms for humans the 'external' status of nature, of what lies outside of them and not just of the objects that they produce. Thus a conscious separation is made between humans and nature, with humans no longer seeing themselves as a part of nature or conceiving nature in reverential religious terms.[25] Over time these changes in the mode of production result in andro/anthropocentrism, an attitude which considers nature's main purpose is to serve 'man' and, thus, with the development of science and technology calling for domination of nature. As this process/relationship evolves, nature eventually becomes the 'other' of the human self, and people become 'others' of each other connected to and through production and accumulation of surplus, subject to the exploitation of labour and relations of property.[26]

By seeing labour as evolving 'conscious' labour and situating labour in a complex of history, social organisation and relations, in industry, skills and aesthetics, Marx challenges the prevalent dualisms, for example between body and mind, individual consciousness and society, and the public and the private. The critical method of historical materialism helps in resolving the binaries of thinking and doing, mind and body, form and content, and reason and emotion.

---

25   The difference Marx makes between humans and animals or insects lies in human capacity for production in which practice and ideas, including imagination, are indissolubly implicated As he says: 'We pre-suppose labour in a form that stamps it as exclusively human. A spider conducts operations that resemble those of a weaver, and a bee puts to shame many an architect in the construction of her cells. But what distinguishes the worst architect from the best of bees is this, that the architect raises his structure in imagination before he erects it in reality. At the end of every labour-process, we get a result that already existed in the imagination of the labourer at its commencement' (Marx 1974, p. 174).

26   As the idea of practical consciousness in *The German Ideology* shows, all forms of production involve *conscious* (not involuntary) labour, unleashing increasing productive forces, giving rise to complex cultures and social forms, to science and technology. Engels speaks to this developmental process in *Dialectics of Nature*. Labour, always already *conscious*, grows exponentially in ideas and practices, giving rise to ever finer divisions of labour and complex resulting objects, until the moment ideology arrives with a separation evolved between mental and manual labour at the highest stage of social relations of property. Alienation thus produced results in people becoming 'others' of themselves and of each other as well as being separated from objects they make and the nature that they transform. Marx's strongest condemnation of capitalism is directed at its capacity for dehumanisation. His idea of communist revolution has something in common with Walter Benjamin's idea of 'redemption' of the world insofar as they both address dehumanisation and the use of desire in the service of commoditisation. See Benjamin 1969a.

Dualist epistemology dating back to earlier than seventeenth-century Europe and identified with Descartes, though found in many others, is rendered obsolete and engenders a historical dialectical approach overcoming conceptual alienation between theory and practice, reworking Hegel's idealist dialectical method. Marx also reminds us that, though there are periods of civilisational recession, as for example during the medieval period of European history, there is no absolute break in larger productive modes. Thus subsequent complex forms and organisation of labour are built on the transmutation of past labour, though in their new incarnations they acquire new characteristics. For example, the earliest sexual division of labour found in the family, which rests on slavery, or the unfree labour of captives of war, are not fully erased or left behind. Though they are superseded by changes in the modes of production, moving from slavery to 'free' or wage labour, they are also dissolved in the organisation and relations of production in all propertied societies, where they provide a silent and shaping presence. Mental and manual divisions of labour fully elaborated in capitalism produce commoditised objects, both conceptual and physical. Seemingly originating from unconnected spheres, the differences in the appearance of the objects provide grounds for the occlusion of their real relation. This gives rise to a fetishistic attitude towards objects functioning as commodities. All the while however, conscious, mediative, collective and practical labour works towards a co-operation between producers and consumers and is advantageous to property owners.

For Marx the question of alienation is ultimately about production of objects as commodities in the capitalist mode. The relational and productive modalities that govern the capitalist mode of production specify a form of alienation which is characterised by the absence of self-expression of the worker. Production and consumption become subservient to the need for profit, which distorts the creative and aesthetic capacities of humans. Labour as creative and conscious labour is the crux of Marx's idea of what it means to be human. A system of production that undercuts or robs humans on these grounds is total alienation. Though the phenomenon of alienation appears to be natural or automatic, beyond systematically produced objectification and linked to commodity production, its actuality is entirely socially organised. Alienation can neither be created nor understood or demystified outside the ensemble of relations of power and exploitation which make for life in capitalism. Alienation in capitalism calls for specific property and proprietary relations in which the majority labour and a few appropriate the fruits of their labour, through both juridical and coercive forces. It implies both overt and covert violence. Within capital's regime the life-world is organised through social relations of commodities rather than those of people themselves, through the relational modes of the market and wage labour. It is in an inverted world where things become people, or active agents, and people become things. Alienation is thus the most crucial internal relation within the capitalist system and the organic life of the social environment.

Marx offers a most nuanced account of alienation in his description of *fetishism* of commodities. He says:

> A commodity appears, at first sight, a very trivial thing, and easily understood. Its analysis shows that it is, in reality, a very queer thing, abounding in metaphysical subtleties and theoretical niceties. So far as it is a value in use, there is nothing mysterious about it, whether we consider it from the point of view that by its properties it is capable of satisfying human wants, or from the point that these properties are the product of human labour. It is as clear as noon-day that man, by his industry, changes the forms of the materials furnished by Nature, in such a way as to make them useful to him. The form of wood, for instance, is altered, by making a table out of it. Yet, for all that, the table continues to be that common everyday thing, wood. But, so soon as it steps forth as a commodity, it is changed into something transcendent. It not only stands with its feet on the ground, but, in relation to all other commodities, it stands on its head and evolves out of its wooden brain grotesque ideas, far more wonderful than 'table-turning' ever was.[27]

At the very foundation of the capitalist mode of production are workers/labour deprived of their means to sustain life and for this reason inducted into the world of the market and money since no need can be met outside of it. The only means of survival for these dispossessed individuals is their own labour power, which is their body and being which they sell in order to live. Here 'alienation' achieves its perfection, since basic human capacities for sentient creation and their sense of self have to be reified and commoditised to earn survival. Life in the environment of this commodity regime is wholly one of subjection to capital, no other viable mode of existence can obtain for anyone outside of this system, neither for the worker nor for the capitalist. Yet it is the worker who is forced to reproduce this self-destructive system of exploitation. The labouring subject, who is a conscious human being, who is creative, experiencing and changing through this productive labour, is trapped in the mechanics of the capitalist system, its flow of technological and social dynamism – nothing is

---

27   Marx 1971a, p. 76.

within her/his control. This alienation constitutes our life forms and has both experiential and psycho-social, not just economic-structural, consequences.

As mentioned earlier, productive activity or the making capacity is foundational to being human in every sense. It meets the needs of daily life and creativity and is daily renewed from the beginning of human history. The creation of objects as such is inescapable in the human condition – activities ranging from art to industry share that in common. Conscious labour from times immemorial has created taste, skills and aesthetic forms. Need for beauty, intellection and functional use objects all mark our patterns of consumption. These productive activities, with their motive force and enjoyment, involve all our senses and capacities and even set in place our structures of feelings.[28]

Alienation takes a systemic and deadly turn in capitalism as the works of our own hands, our feelings, our 'others' and nature itself turn against us. As Marx says in his critique of the myth of the self-sufficient and self-enclosed individuals or Robinsonades,[29] the mode of production invades and shapes our very being, we carry it within us in terms of our creative/productive capacities, skills and tastes. Through its historical generalisation capitalism's modalities of doing and being have become *naturalised*. We can only with great effort capture in our dreams of an opposite world other ways of being and doing. The capitalist way of life has come to be global and seems to be as 'natural' as the sun rising in the east. This captivated mindset is the largest success of 'alienation', and we consequently consider those who still partly live outside of capital's sway with their own residual pre- or non-capitalist social practices and values as 'primitive', 'savage' and so on. We consider them in need of 'development', that is, of incorporation into the capitalist mode of production and society. Once the colonialists justified their ventures as 'civilising missions'. The first struggle against capitalism and alienation is to *de-naturalise* it, and to open the door of other social and conceptual possibilities. The knowledge of history becomes our help in this process of resistance by showing how other social and productive organisations declined and yielded to the bourgeois worldview.

Wage labour indicates self-alienation in that there is a price for everything, even for what resides in our bodies and minds, which includes our making and

---

28   See Marx 1964b, p. 156.

29   On Robinsonades, see Marx 1973, p. 83: 'Individuals producing in society – hence socially
      determined individual production – is, of course, the point of departure. The individual
      and isolated hunter and fisherman, with whom Smith and Ricardo begin, belongs among
      the unimaginative conceits of the eighteenth century Robinsonades [from Daniel Defoe's
      Robinson Crusoe], which in no way express merely a reaction against over-sophistication
      and a return to a misunderstood natural life, as cultural historians imagine'.

expressive abilities. All social relations are generally accomplished through the capitalist activities and conceptions, thus alienating us from others, from those among whom we live. The more we talk about being an individual, even a possessive individual, about the freedom of our 'personal' life, the less we have of them. We crave a simple personal life but our insistent desire only indicates an absence of it and creates an illusion of reality called the 'private', which in actuality turns out to be isolation – living as we do as a 'thing' among 'things'. Yet it is also true that the situation holds contradictory possibilities, our desires and human capacities produce imaginaries and objective practices, a craving for a sense of self and direct self-expression, which point a way out of alienation. Thus in art, for example, though we cannot have the 'whole', we can feel and imagine a state of non-alienation, a self-coherence which enlivens our way to another world, to the opposite of isolated and hostile lives. European art and philosophical worlds are replete with contradictory notions regarding the making, gaining and the loss of the self, as well as the loss of the 'other' and our antagonistic as well as desiring relations with this other. And of course there is the mourning for 'the death of God' (Nietzsche), and Durkheim gave a name to life among these faceless, nameless others – anomie.

3   Marx's Humanism and Alienation

Many marxists, for example Althusserians, and certainly anti-marxists, deny an ethical basis to Marx's ideas and politics, disputing the enduring presence in his works of the idea of the human. Of course to see Marx as a humanist would be, for marxists, to render him a Hegelian – a closet idealist in the last instance. In this context it is important to quote Althusser:

> In the text entitled 'Marxism and Humanism', dating from 1963 I have already interpreted the present inflation of the themes of Marxist/Socialist Humanism as an ideological phenomenon ... I criticised the *theoretical* effects of ideology which are always a threat or a hindrance to *scientific* knowledge. And I pointed out that the inflation of the themes of 'Marxist humanism' and their enchantment on Marxist theory should be interpreted as a possible historical symptom of a double inability and a double danger. An inability to read the specificity of Marxist theory, and, correlatively, a *revisionist* danger of conferring it with pre-Marxist ideological interpretation.[30]

---

30   Althusser 1977b, p. 12. My emphases.

Althusser makes the interventions which have dogged the development of marxist theories to this day. He drew a 'line of demarcation' between marxist theory and 'forms of philosophical subjectivism'[31] and created a confrontation between Marx's early works and *Capital*. This reading of Marx in dualist terms and so-called materialist interpretations have created a rift between the humanist and the communist Marx, thereby denying a motive for communist revolution. This split, upon scrutiny, seems to be a spurious one, an attribution of one-dimensionality to Marx's complex transformative project. A historical materialist understanding of the concepts 'the human', 'universal', 'man' as well as of 'science', 'humanism' and 'communism', would help us to get beyond this aporia. After all, the point of departure for Marx's historical materialist epistemology lies in the 11th thesis on Feuerbach – 'philosophers have so far merely interpreted the world, the point is to change it'.[32] Marx devoted himself to developing a kind of knowledge which does not 'merely' interpret but also roots this interpretation in actual people's lives, in the societies, cultures and economies they have inherited and created, and in the histories that texture their present. And he does this for a reason, because he is looking for the coincidence of self- and human emancipation which actualises the full potential of human capabilities. This certainly is 'humanistic'.

Marx insists that the communist revolution, at once human and self-emancipation, is the path to the end of alienation. In bringing it about lost and distorted human capacities are resuscitated. These human capacities are the *sine qua non* of human species nature and they are vitalised and refined by practice and interacting with others. This subject-agent of revolution is captured in *The Communist Manifesto*, and alienation becomes visible through and resisted by the emergence of proletarian consciousness and the critical method of historical materialism. Utopian imagination and liberationist desires are connected to existing circumstances which call for radical transformation, the realisation of which requires all the resources of human capacity. By bringing together social interactions, analytical/critical thinking and creative/imaginative capacities, Marx breaks through the solipsism or alienation inherent in the rigid division of labour. After all, what is the purpose of knowledge that cannot enlighten the creation of the social and its multiple contradictions, and if in the end the production of theories had nothing to do with a fuller life for people? Why would we need a revolution at all if not to resolve the ongoing open and hidden struggles of classes?[33] Disengagement of human capacities,

---

31   Ibid., p. 11.
32   Marx and Engels 1970, 11th thesis on Feuerbach.
33   Marx and Engels 1972a.

the erasure of the active subject-agent, would make the revolution an event occurring behind our back.[34]

In his concern about human self-emancipation Marx is in company with many thinkers dating back at least two centuries and remembering the political philosophy of Greek and Roman times. He could well discern the shortcomings, and ultimately the reversals, brought about by the failure of the French Revolution, but he never lost faith in people's needs for creating history for themselves, and with all the drawbacks he shared the spirit and ambitions of the French Revolution or the Paris Commune. In his appraisal of the Paris commune he saluted the Promethean spirit that emerged from the vortex of inchoate short-lived moments of class struggle.[35] He too, with other revolutionaries and romantics, awaited the dawn of a new age, the birth of a new society and the appearance of a new 'man' cleansed of the marks of centuries of different kinds of alienation. His revolutionary inspiration had a qualitative commonality with Walter Benjamin's messianic language of revolution, or with those who, in Christopher Hill's appraisal, wanted to turn the world upside down.[36] Himself a romantic poet, a lover of literature, Marx was not immune to the poetry of revolution. It is as though Aristotle's idea of the 'good life', of *eumeria*, materialised itself through the dialectical relation between individual consciousness, a sense of history and the creation of the *polis*. It needs to be emphasised that Marx's revolution against alienation and reification of creative life forces is not just for a 'better life', but for a qualitatively 'different' life which dares to demand radically oppositional premises different from all exploitive property relations in human interactions and labour.

The revolutionary epistemology and the organisational processes advanced by Marx aimed for what we would call a new hegemony, countering the dominant common-sense of capital. The naturalisation of capital as the only way to live, as our inescapable horizon, needs to be cast aside, which could only be possible by revitalising human creative capacities, the oppositional revolutionary imagination. This new revolutionary common sense, felt in organisational, critical and creative intimations and intuitions of human capacities,

---

34   See Marx and Engels 1970, Feuerbach, first thesis. In idealist, functionalist or structuralist perceptions of revolution the space and agency for socio-historical change seems to be uninhabited. Lacking a human subject-agent people become no more than the objects of capital – part of the syllogism of the 'logic' of capital. In ultra-scientificism or one-dimensional materialism the agentic power conferred to 'structures' amounts to an 'objective idealism' and a cognate category to Hegel's 'subjective idealism', as for example in Hegel's *Phenomenology of the Mind*.

35   See Marx 1972e.

36   Hill 1975.

would be expressed through new forms of human labour. This labour would not derive from an escapist philosophy of art, but here art would serve human needs, enhancing the ways in which people enjoy their productive life activities. Thus we see labour not only as mechanical, market-oriented productivity but as activities which are sensuous practical and human.

4 Enter Rabindranath

> For man, as well as for animals, it is necessary to give expression to feelings of pleasure and fear, anger and love. In animals, these emotional expressions have gone little beyond their bounds of usefulness. But in man, though they still have roots in their original purposes, they have spread their branches far and wide in the infinite sky above their soil. Man has a fund of emotional energy which is not all occupied with his self-preservation. This surplus seeks its outlet in the creation of Art.[37]

> Man's social world is like some nebulous system of stars, consisting largely of a mist of abstractions, with such names as society, state, nation commerce, politics and war. In their dense amorphousness man is hidden and truth is blurred. The one vague *idea of war* covers from our sight a multitude of miseries, and obscures our sense of reality. The *idea of the nation* has created forms of slavery without number, which we tolerate simply because it has deadened our consciousness of the reality of the personal man. In the name of religion deeds have been done that would exhaust all the resources of hell itself for punishment, because with its creeds and dogmas it has applied an extensive plaster of anaesthetic over a large surface of feeling humanity.[38]

Now we should affect our transition to Rabindranath. It is our claim that Marx and Rabindranath held common assumptions regarding the historical and social nature of the location and relations of individuals and their productive and creative capacities. In their view individuals everywhere have physical and mental capacities which are peculiar to the human species and they create, live in and express themselves through society. Their sociality manifests itself in increasingly multifaceted symbiotic relations which give rise to ramified and

---

37   Tagore 2005, p. 14.
38   Ibid., pp. 27–8.

contradictory socio-economic, political and cultural formations. For neither of them is 'nature' to be seen as an antithesis to the human, but rather included in the symbiosis of conscious, transformative labour/activity. The 'human' for both thinkers is situated *in* nature, but this form of nature is imbued with critical consciousness. These creative and reflexive and critical capacities are lacking in other species in any meaningful or mindful sense. Similar to Marx, in his essay 'What is Art?' Rabindranath makes a sustained comparison between human and animal capacities. His observations, like those of Marx, go beyond functionality to the pleasure of making and enjoying the made object. In this regard Rabindranath too subscribed to what Marx called the human 'species being', which consists of conscious, creative labouring/making capacities of humans as compared to those of insects and animals. In contrast to Marx's interest in labour and production, as a whole Rabindranath is focused on art. He says: '... I shall not define Art, but question myself about the reason of its existence, and try to find out whether it owes its origin to some social purpose, or the need of caring for our aesthetic enjoyment, or whether it has come through some impulse of expression, which is the impulse of our being itself'.[39] But they concur in the human need for making and aesthetic expression. Creativity has a primacy for both, and for both the human is an imaginative, inquiring and incrementally developing subject who creates art and is engaged in simultaneous self, social and aesthetic transformation. The same transformative and interconstitutive facility is formed in their interaction with nature. Though Rabindranath made a conceptual separation between 'labour' and creative production, as he saw labour in mainly economic terms and made a distinction between 'labour' and creative and philosophical activities and the objects they produced, he was sensitive to the creative, imaginative side of daily labour.[40] Even mundane domestic acts in the environment of homes and institutions, for example Santiniketan, had to eschew a minimalist austerity, but convey a sense of beauty which satisfied beyond functionality. Rabindranath demonstrated through his own immersion in aesthetic production what he meant by becoming 'human'. He, like Marx, noticed the tragedy of alienation inflicted upon the human subject, condemning basic deformations of human capacities and destruction of nature, and locating these in histories and experiences of power relations culminating in colonial capitalism. Mental and phys-

---

39   Ibid., p. 12.

40   This sensitivity comes out in Rabindranath's love for 'craft' production, where the utility of a functional object is only a partial aim and making it beautiful completes the task as a whole. This beauty he finds in the pleasure principle of excess.

ical deprivations brought on through systematic economic exploitation of 'free' and forced labour provided the central themes of his social thought.

Rabindranath's thoughts on alienation and dehumanisation of 'man' brought on by relations of exploitation and degradation are evident throughout his opus. Profit motive, greed, competition and reification are castigated as sources of human deformation in the death of the creative principle, and he does not shy away from identifying industrial capitalism as the most violently exploitive system to date. In this context he commented frequently on science as a project of knowledge and human welfare in contrast to its servitude to capitalism – for profit and greed – and the nation state, particularly in the development of militarisation, war and annexation. Rabindranath's letter to Elmhirst of 7 November 1926 is a case in point:

> This time I have been able to see the state of things in Europe that has filled my mind with misgivings ... But today all the big nations seem to have gone half seas over in their reckless career of political ambition and adventures of greed. None of them has the natural privilege today to stand for the right when any great wrong is done to humanity ... Europe has got her science not as complimentary to religion but as its substitute. Science is great, but it only affords us knowledge, power, efficiency, but not ideal of unity, no aspiration for the perfect – it is nonhuman, impersonal, and therefore is like things that are inorganic, useful in many ways but useless as our food of life. If it is allowed to go on extending its sole dominion in the human world then the living flesh of man will wither away and his skeleton will reign supreme in the midst of his dead wealth.[41]

This insight into the alienation introduced in Europe by a lethal combination of science with greed is made explicit in the same letter: 'The standard of life has become so complex and costly that these people cannot help thinking that righteousness is a luxury that can only be indulged in when all claims [by] their insatiable self [are] fairly satisfied. They are ashamed of the sentiments that keep life green and tender and in its place they cultivate the sneering spirit of cynicism brilliant and barren'.[42] In a later letter to Elmhurst (3 September 1932) Rabindranath offers another example of alienating use of science. He writes:

---

41   Tagore 1997, pp. 340–1.
42   Ibid., p. 340. On this deadening, violent and instrumental use of science, see also Tagore
      1930, p. 95.

The Ideal, which I cherish in my heart for the work I have been struggling to build up through the best portion of my life [does] need qualifications that are not divided into compartments. It was not the Kingdom of the Expert in the midst of the inept and ignorant which we wanted to establish – although the experts' advice [is] valuable. The villages are waiting for the living touch of creative faith and not for the cold aloofness of science which uses efficient machinery for extracting statistics, the statistics that deal with *fragments of dissected life*.[43]

Given what we know of him, we could assume that if Rabindranath had read Marx's *Economic and Philosophical Manuscripts of 1844* he would have agreed with the point that Marx makes in that text. The centrality of the notion of 'man' or the 'human' and the urgency in eliminating the suppression and distortion of human capacities, and the existential social relations of power and inequality found in Marx, are present in equal measure in Rabindranath's work. All his life he spoke to the destructive aspects of alienation that Marx outlined. In plays, novels short stories and poetry Rabindranath dramatised or narrated alienation. As for Marx, this alienation is from the products humans create, from the process of production itself, from nature, from other fellow beings, and even from one's own self.

In his condemnation of alienation Rabindranath showed no simple, one-sided rejection of science and technology. He concentrated instead on the social relations with which they developed, the uses they were put to when they served colonial capitalism rather than human welfare. Thus he shared Marx's interest in science and technology and approved of the use of machines for augmenting social well-being. The discerning attitude that Rabindranath had towards science contradicts the one-dimensional approach of Gandhi. Acceptance of non-instrumental use of science is evident in Rabindranath's rebuttal of Gandhi's advocacy for a national practice of spinning and rejecting textile mills in favour of the *charka* or spinning wheel. In a letter to Rani Mahalanobis (16 October 1929) he astutely comments on Gandhi's advocacy as an 'ideology', not just a practice: '... [W]e fail to rise above the ideology of the *charka*'. He continues:

The *charka* does not require anyone to think: one simply turns the wheel of antiquated invention endlessly, using the minimum of judgement and stamina. In a more industrious, vital country than ours such a proposition

---

43   Tagore 1997, p. 413. My emphasis.

would stand no chance of acceptance ... Just think what would happen if instead of spinning the Mahatma were to rule that each cultivator must grow at least two seers of produce per *bigha* of land ... then everyone would argue that such a programme would require intelligence, knowledge, drive and commitment to productive agricultural technique.[44]

While rejecting the mechanical, unnatural cultural institutions and environment connected with instrumental rationality of capitalism, nationalism and greed, Rabindranath appreciated the spirit of inquiry, adventure and human potential of science. Neither he nor Marx were moral and epistemological political relativists, who rejected the idea of 'truth' both in relation to social reality an in imaginative and personal terms. This 'truth', beyond its empirical dimension, included for both the reality of thought, of critical capacities of consciousness, though for Marx the emphasis was on a nuanced historical materialist critique, while Rabindranath awarded imagination and intuition central roles in apprehending the 'truth'. They derived their ethical imperatives from belief in 'truth'. But epistemologically speaking they differed as the philosopher of historical materialism and as a poet-philosopher, and Marx did not accept a spiritual and poetic metaphysics of truth. Rabindranath, on his part, believed that truth lies within, while for Marx 'truth' was arrived at through a secular method of inquiry which combines social ontology, anthropology and critical epistemology. But just as Rabindranath had a great regard for a scientific worldview and connected imagination and truth, Marx in reverse conferred the creative capacity a central role in all things people do. Both saw 'truth' historically gleaned from the evidence of our predecessors' legacy everywhere and the internalisation of their creative forms, technology or skills underpinning our own.

The idea that 'truth' is distinct from 'fact' or 'information' holds good for both Marx and Rabindranath. Marx's anti-positivist view of the ideas of 'use' or 'use value' is, therefore, radically different from that of Bentham and his empiricist followers. But there is a difference in Rabindranath's infusing the notion of 'knowledge' with scientificity, and he prioritises man as a seer, a creator, over man as a knower in the restricted sense of the word 'knower': '[M]an, as a knower, is not fully himself – his *mere information* does not reveal him'. He continues:

But we live in an age when our world is turned inside out and when whatever lies at the bottom is dragged to the surface. Our very process of

---

44   Ibid., p., 365.

living, which is an unconscious process, we must bring under the scrutiny of our knowledge – even though to know is to kill our object of research and to make it a museum specimen.[45]

Rabindranath felt that the joy of creation both in the process of making and its final product could not be kept alive by tearing the creations to pieces through analysis or by reducing them to a mere definition. The root and goal of art, he felt, is life itself, and a positivist factual truth was not an equivalent for 'truth' in the deeper/real sense.

Despite their differences Marx and Rabindranath coincide in their delight in their experience of art. A sensuous enjoyment, the development of taste through the creative process and fulfilment in 'consumption' in its refined sense is discussed by Marx in *Grundrisse*.[46] If we confuse Rabindranath's view of art with the aesthetic elitism of 'art for art's sake', we would be making a mistake. We need to realise that 'art' for Rabindranath was the very vitality and core of life, and the pursuit of art was to be for 'life's' sake. Neither Rabindranath nor Marx were advocates of 'puritanism' and 'austerity'. Enjoyment is essential in their worldviews and an important part of Marx's idea of consumption. The 'good' that creativity or art does for us is not a didactic precept, but an embodiment of the pleasure principle, or what Rabindranath calls joy, present in 'knowing' and being.[47] We must remember that Rabindranath was a poet, and when he saw the transformative, enjoying capacity of human beings stagnated or imprisoned by barriers of facts, social prohibition and physical and mental deprivation, the situation became intolerable for him. A world where such things happened he saw as devouring the human. Rabindranath saw this in the wars brought on by imperialisms and nationalisms of his time.

The necessity for a creative and dynamic life were the central concerns for both Marx and Rabindranath. Marx's poetry of revolution resonates with the passion of Rabindranath's poetry and his universal humanism. Rabindranath's universal humanism, the wholeness of his vision, his self-proclamation as a universal human subject, is a daring move. The context of colonialism redeems Rabindranath's claim of universal humanity from being a cliché of Enlightenment. Considered as a lesser human than Europeans, Rabindranath took upon himself the task of human liberation on behalf of the entire oppressed humanity. He articulated the necessity for all humans, not just the colonised, to participate in the project of overthrowing forces of alienation. Colonisation

---

45   Tagore 2005, p. 11 (my emphasis).
46   Marx 1973, p. 92.
47   Tagore 2005, p. 13.

here serves as a trope for all forms of domination or restraint imposed upon humanity, obstacles in the path of achieving full humanity. For this reason Rabindranath rejected the paradigm of the nation, feeling that nationalism would end up by re-inventing the relations and social ascriptions of colonialism and the substitution of a native ruler for a foreign one. His ambition was to fashion a really *new* human subject and a hitherto unforeseen world.[48]

Rabindranath fought alienation in the name and language of the human or 'man', leaning on Upanishadic philosophical usage of the idea of the self.[49] He especially rejected and replaced the rigidity of commodity fetishism by substituting it with the aesthetic ideal of a dynamic yet contained form. The fetishism embodied in capitalist fixation on machines, on the frozen, and lifeless form of the commodity shorn of creative spirit, was to be discarded by new embodiments of the universally human. Neither Marx's nor Rabindranath's idea of 'man' was a homogenising abstraction, but rather conceived as intrinsic capacities of the human species-nature – a figure of an emancipated and encapacitated human in creative harmony with the self and the other, enriched by similarity and difference. Seen in this way the notion of 'man' itself is a poetic creation, a core of all human potentials.[50]

When we step out of the binary mode in which the 'human' and the 'social', the human and the natural, are treated as segregated realities and concepts, and speak instead of self, social and human emancipation in the same breath, we challenge the established dualisms of the subject and the object, the body and the mind, emotion and reason, and so on. This integrative epistemology shared by Marx and Rabindranath alters the conventional rationalist position which presents the whole as a serialisation or aggregation of particulars. We shift to another way of confronting reality in the shape of the *wholeness* of our social being. In both authors we find a desire for wholeness, without which the first premise of the universal human cannot be articulated.

---

48   On the formation of the 'self' of the colonial subject as the site of compounded alienation numerous authors have written a wide genre of literature and political philosophy on the strategies of decolonization. Some notable examples are Frantz Fanon, Aimé Césaire, Achille Mbembe, Sembene Osmane, N'gugi Wa Thiongo, George Lamming among others.

49   Rabindranath wrote extensively on the Upanishads and the notion of the self they contain. See, for example, *Santiniketan*.

50   For a proper understanding of this we need to know Rabindranath's worldview and its creative connections with Bauls, Sufis and other popular saints and with the Upanishads, about all of which he wrote extensively.

5   Rabindranath and Alienation of the Colonial Capitalist Subject

The social and individually experienced alienation explored by Marx in the
context of capitalist development receives an extra dimension in the light of
colonial capitalism. The colonised society suffers the double burden of indigenous and foreign domination and exploitation. Forced surplus production
and appropriation, the violence of 'primitive accumulation', are intensified in
colonisation more than in the rise of wage labour.[51] In the colonies the individual and the society suffer from birth in the ethos of this power-ridden and
violent social formation, and the self of the colonial subject becomes the site
of compounded alienation of self-division and unhappy consciousness, phenomena that Marx does not consider.[52] In the narratives of his own childhood, in *My Boyhood* for example, Rabindranath presents this problem of identity or personality formation, reminiscing on how he suffered at school and
other institutions and at the hands of English language education, all of which
repressed the child's imagination and self-expression.[53] In short stories, novels
and essays he provides us with rich material for understanding of the self-
developmental process of a child in an elite household in colonial Bengal. He
recounts actual experiences and descriptions of distortions inflicted on the
growing self through powerful colonial and class-caste based social norms and
forms in keeping with remnants of feudal hierarchic social mores. He captures the explicit as well as subtle and extensive diffusion of colonial culture in
Bengal, including in his descriptions of the colonial state's hegemonic influence
through promulgation of laws and public administration. The colonial subject,
especially of the middle class, he shows as both ruled and ruling and smart-
ing from the insult of being forced into the shoes of labouring classes.[54] This
situation works to their advantage in so far as they feel that they represent the

---

51   On 'primitive accumulation' see Marx, *Capital* Volume I, Part 8. This theme has been
      widely taken up in recent decades by critical geographers such as David Harvey and polit-
      ical economists. An interesting use of this theme has been made in the context of the
      occupation of Palestine by authors such as Nahla Abdo and Uri Davis.
52   In the context of social and subject formation under colonialism Marx's formulation of the
      concept of class and his social analysis of capitalism have to be modified. This is apparent
      from the first chapter of Fanon's *Wretched of the Earth*, 'On Violence'.
53   See Tagore, *My Boyhood* and *Jiban Smriti*. In these memoirs and other texts Rabindranath
      recounts the formation of the colonised subject. It also returns as an issue in his writing
      on 'personality'.
54   See Partha Chatterjee, Dipesh Chakrabarty and other members of the subaltern studies
      collective. It is probably such a perception that directed them to include the colonial
      middle class in the category of the 'subaltern'. Rabindranath, however, had harsh words
      for the middle class, for example in his essays in *Kalantar* or his letters in *Russiar Chithi*.

colonised society as a whole, but for the colonised subjects of lesser status the oppression is doubled as they suffer under local and foreign masters.

What Marx does not either describe or theorise Rabindranath does. He particularly reflects upon the twice oppressed conditions of a poor and rent-dominated peasantry in Bengal: the process of continual alienation created by eviction from land, by taxation and rent, by the neglect of the landlords and traditional casteist indoctrination, all ultimately connected to the land tenure system of the Permanent Settlement (1793).[55] The peasantry and the poor, he argued as an exceptionally compassionate landlord in his essays on village life and communities, are often reduced to a sub-human existence.[56] He also mentioned that social mores of both kinds of domination – local and foreign – are internalised and legitimated. They rob and denigrate the colonial subjects' self-confidence, agency and self-image along with economic well-being and productivity. He ponders over the identity of middle-class colonial subjects caught in a space between submission and resistance. A real decolonisation would involve the emergence of a universal subject. The enclosed and stultified existence of the peasants and labourers, along with the middle and lower middle classes, needed new vitality and imaginative thought. Though industrialisation was not extensively generalised in India, Rabindranath offered a trenchant critique of both physical and mental alienation of industrial workers based on his readings of first-hand knowledge of Europe and North America. With respect to India he relied on his knowledge of jute mills, coal mining and other aspects of Indian capitalist ventures. He noted the prevalent alienation in the industrial societies and some instances of industrial workers' actions there. He also kept a sustained communication with critical and political European intellectuals, some of whom, for instance Romain Rolland, were involved in the antifascist movement and drew him into its orbit. Occasionally in his dialogue with his Western interlocutors he used an orientalist or essentialist rhetoric comparing the West with the East, but in the main kept away from these simple binary formulations.

Rabindranath throughout explores the effects of alienation on human beings beyond the economic regime. In this sense, psychological and cultural alienation are his chief topics. He narrates in various forms the prevailing physical, emotional and cultural effects of colonisation in Bengal. He notices

---

55   On the Permanent Settlement (1793) see Guha 1982a and Mukherjee 1957.

56   Rabindranath's concern for the plight of the Bengal peasantry is so all-pervasive that it exceeds the need of citations. But it is worthwhile to remember *Russiar Chithi, Palli Prakriti, Samaj, Gora* or *Ghare Baire*. Rural upliftment was his life's ambition and he gave this an institutional and practical dimension in establishing Sriniketan.

astutely the representation of the colonised subject, the ubiquitous presence of colonial discourse ranging from law and governance to art and social theorisations, and how the tropes of degradation, savagery and decayed civilisation were constantly reproduced. He was aware that the domination of nature and peoples of the colonies and the treatment of Blacks were connected through the same logic, joined at the root of capitalism. Colonising capitalist ventures incorporated slavery and other forms of unfree labour as well as territorial annexations. The consciousness of the Europeans, he knew, insisted on a physicalisation of its subject peoples and obscured their intellectual, creative and critical capacities. As nature in the environment of socio-biology was perceived in a negative sense, the subjectivity of the colonised was seen as immersed or *immanent* in nature and thus incapable of transcendent consciousness. This schema projected the humanity of the coloniser and the animality or the particularism, the narrowness, seen as inherent among the colonised. And so it was that the typology of the European Man of Reason, such as Prospero, was confronted with Caliban, the man and animal hybrid in Shakespeare's *The Tempest*. Such a worldview could not develop without colonial capitalism, and rested on a degraded view of the human body, and, relatedly, on a severe division of mental and manual labour.

Unlike in Rabindranath, who had a liberating and aesthetic view of nature, nature in colonial capitalist discourse is characterised through racialising ideologies, practices and philosophies. This degradation of the labouring and reproducing body was formulated with the help of pseudo-sciences, especially of biological and other natural sciences, and culminated in potent discourses of 'race' and the inferiority of underclasses and women. Rabindranath critiqued the concept and practices of 'race' and racialisation. Rabindranath's insight about 'race' and racialisation is ubiquitously present, even in children's stories and parables.[57] Interestingly Marx, in spite of his writings on colonialism and African slavery, is less interested in connecting the concept of 'race' with that of class. By Marx's time Europeans had systematically organised capitalism both at home and in the colonies through the discourse of 'race'. From Rabindranath's standpoint as a colonised subject, however, 'race' was only too

---

57   Rabindranath's insight on 'race' and on the 'whitening' of and by the colonised subject herself/himself is beautifully expressed in a parable in *Shey*, where there is a pathetic and futile effort made by a fox to become 'human' by cutting off his tail, shaving his fur and tottering on his hind legs and speaking in the human tongue. This transformation leads to the creation of a sad and hideous identity which is the inevitable result of the British colonial 'civilising' or 'humanising' project. The issues of racism and self-racialisation resonate in every aspect of his writings, extending from the essays, letters, children's writings and novels, from *Gora* to *Sesher Kabita*.

visible both in India and abroad. He repeatedly noted in his writings, especially on nationalism, how the ideology of 'race' organised the administrative apparatus and legitimation device for colonial capitalism. The violence of the ideology of 'race' and actuality of colonialism become a potent technology for producing alienation internal to the self as a colonised subject. He was aware of how the racist discourse served as an alibi for the conquest and oppression of non-European others. Even without the process of industrialised capitalism, colonial relations were fundamentally alienating. This added dimension of alienation goes further and organises power and exploitation relations between colonial capitalism and waged and unwaged labour. The question of eradicating alienation in the colonial context becomes much more difficult than that existing in the industrial capitalist societies. This context makes Rabindranath's assumption of and advocacy for universal subjecthood a matter of revolutionary demand, a practice and claim of equality.

Rabindranath shows how class, 'race' and economic subjection cannot be articulated in separation from each other. This is as true about the colonised's society as it is of the coloniser's. Decolonising social transformation, therefore, is also not only an economic but also an ideological and cultural transformation – a transformation at the level of everyday life. This is a challenge to alienation in all countries both colonising and colonised and ending the connection between both colonialism and science/industry and capital. But we need to note here how 'race' functions for the colonial subjects of all classes as well as in colonising countries. 'Race' signifies a dis-empowerment of all colonised subjects, while for the colonising subjects, including for the workers, 'race' creates an empowerment in material and psychological terms expressed by the ideas of 'whiteness' and 'blackness'.[58] The working classes of the West experience a curious form of alienation which is simultaneously colluding with the 'white' ruling classes while fighting against them in their main locales of production. Their absorption and participation in colonialist and imperialist ventures produces a most profound form of alienation at all levels. Their absorption in the colonising ethos draws them into imperialism and militaristic ventures. Rabindranath sees this racialising ideology also in the nationalism of

---

58 Rabindranath's letters from the United States on the condition of the Afro-Americans need to be remembered in this regard. On the issue of 'race', a phenomenon expressive of alienation in self-other relation, as a relation of dualist power and a mechanism for reproducing such power relations, see for example, Rabindranath's letter to C.F. Andrews, in which he shows how the European civilizing discourse of the West and the East are racialised categories. Tagore 1997, pp. 332–6. See also Tangore 1930, pp. 725–6, in which Rabindranath leaves us his last testament against racialised rule of British colonialism.

the colonised, serving a similar mobilising and legitimating function and drawing common people into war, conquest and sense of cultural superiority.

Rabindranath remarks on the constitutive relations between colonialism, nationalism, caste and race and modes of capitalist production. The idea of racial purity for him is quintessential alienation and inhumanity. A critical exploration and rejection of racialisation is explicit in his novel *Gora*, where the eponymous hero arrives by the end of the novel to a 'human' identity beyond the binaries of 'race' and ethnicity. In Gora's struggle for a universal humanist identity Rabindranath captures the process that the colonised subject must undergo to move beyond a binary of 'self' and 'other', 'us' and 'them'.[59] The Europeans too, he felt, must go through a similar 'humanising' process.

Overcoming alienation for Rabindranath was not only a matter of moral and aesthetic judgments but of consciousness and cultural practices. This idea was simultaneously explained in his philosophy of education and practices of pedagogy. He propounded what we would call a theory of hegemony when he said that a major mechanism for incorporating Indian subjects in the colonial project was education. The creation of formal schooling, the diffusion of English language, and practice of English in governance all comprised this hegemony and alienated Indians from their very selves, others and their experiential lives. Thus literacy in English, institutional forms of knowledge production, even liberal arts education and general cultural diffusion through the print and other media, became hegemonic devices. The colonial subject's mimicry of the European and self-immersion in the culture of colonial capitalism he treated as the most destructive form of alienation.

The colonial subject's lack of power of self-definition, of personality and identity formation, along with the loss of control over economic and cultural production, were the prime sites for Rabindranath's project of decolonisation. The state orientation of nationalist politics gave place to a development of autonomy of subjecthood and cultural creation. This reality of being subjects of colonial discourse extended across all colonial classes. While the upper/rentier classes were impacted by the British, the indigenous lower classes suffered

---

59   We cannot conduct this discussion on 'race' as alienation, between the self and the other, without reference to Edward Said's *Orientalism*, which points out how the 'orient' or the 'east' is a racialised discourse in which geographical spaces are reformulated as racialised cultural objects, enclosed in the binary paradigm of the orient and the occident, paralleled by the discourse of tradition and modernity and other epistemes of the civilisational ideology. A newer version of this view, which itself originates from patriarchal imperialist patronage, becomes the ideological justification in the u.s. led invasions of Iraq and Afghanistan.

under the colonial hegemony as well as under their native masters. Thus alienation under colonial capitalist circumstances was compounded and called for the overthrow of colonial and class rule. Rabindranath rejected the ability of various nationalist ideologies to challenge or end alienation since he considered them as lacking the potential for a 'true' and substantive subject formation. As previously noted, Rabindranath attributed the inauthenticity of nationalist discourses to its absorption and accommodation of colonial discursivities insofar as they were marked by self-racialisation and ethnicisation and relied on ethics created from ideological inversion of these colonial norms and forms. As he developed from a nineteenth-century Bengali poet to a twentieth-century international personality, a critic of politics and society, and a poet of universal humanism, Rabindranath became an unqualified protestor of forces of alienation born of nationalist and fascist capitalism and war. He arrogated to himself the right and the responsibility to speak as the harbinger of the universal subject who demands conditions suitable for the development of universal humanism. This is the challenge he offered to European colonial modernity's monopoly over the discourse and voice of enlightenment. This voice coming from the subject peoples was most often buried under the 'civilising' discourse of the West. Rabindranath wrote against various kinds of binary concepts and dualism, against alienating discourses of the 'civilised and the savage', racist notions of purity and impurity inhering, for example, in race and caste, and reificatory paradigmatic use of the notions of tradition and modernity. He challenged these dualist categories productive of alienation through an aesthetic and critical definition of the concept of the 'the human' as a discursive constellation with the connotation of a universalism which embraces the creative and intellectual capacities inherent in people. In this usage 'man' or 'human' ceases to be an empty abstraction because they are grounded in an empirical dimension of human capacities while leaving an ideal opening for what 'man' could become in the evolutionary process of these capacities. The ideas of 'the human' or 'man' thus served as devices for critical knowledge transcending the restrictive and distorting binary relations between the self and the other, 'man' and nature, individual and society. This mode of transcendence offered Rabindranath an identificational space beyond the local and extra-local, beyond the barriers of the particular and the general. In his hands this shift to a third space of universalist humanism opened the door to creative and ethical possibilities. He concentrated all his effort to hold 'is' and 'ought' in a constitutive relation and balance with each other, even when he could not provide the workings of the internal relationship between the two, but rather relied on a poet's intuition and imagination which captures in a poem the embodiment of the actual/concrete and the ideal.

Though successful at an aesthetic and ethical level, Rabindranath was unable to arrive at a concretely social 'is-ought' dialectical or internal resolution and relation because he did not extend to 'art' the idea of production. He had set 'labour' apart from 'art', and thus could not link labour or production to creativity and imagination in any sustained way. It is in this that one set of binaries persisted in his vision, as he could not overcome mental and manual division of labour. This indicates an unresolved body-mind relation in his philosophy and social vision. His transcendental philosophy entailed the problem of socially concrete embodiment, leaving little room for labour in the conventional sense to be infused with aesthetic consciousness. Unlike Marx, who considered all forms of labour in a holistic sense, as 'conscious, sensuous practical human activity', and could thus integrate all forms of object making with imagination and usefulness, including pleasure, Rabindranath, though he sometimes hinted at such a possibility, saw creativity as a qualitatively different mental capacity involving activities distinct from labour. While for Marx alienation meant a disembodiment of labour and the separation of consciousness from material, 'sensuous practical human' creativity, Rabindranath saw alienation primarily at the level of consciousness, as mainly a mental phenomenon, as the after-effects of power-based mercantile-industrial, profit-based social relations. While his essays, short stories on Bengal's villages and the peasantry, and his letters regarding the degradation of life in India and the greed of industrial capitalism depict reflective relations between art and society, his metaphysical standpoint does not sufficiently materialise or socialise creativity. Thus the actual interpenetration between idea and reality that is needed for overcoming alienation as an existential practice could not be fully envisioned by him. In his theoretical moment consciousness, the mind or the spirit absorbed into itself the material sensuous and practical aspects of individual lives and societies. As his novels show, for example, that embodiment presented him with a problem. Thus, Rabindranath's treatment of the human body in terms of sexuality, gender and labour, remains ambiguous and often unintegrated with a sensuous, socially and physically grounded consciousness.[60]

It seems at times that Rabindranath sees the body as a 'cage' for the soul – a nameless bird that flies in and out of the cage with the breezes of birth and death. The human body in his writings is often on the brink of vanishing or bringing to the fore romantic and transcendent emotions, with a body as

---

60   This is especially evident in his treatment of sexuality, as for example, in Sachish's uncanny
      sexual experience in the cave in *Chaturanga* or in the relationship between Atin and Ela
      in *Ghare Baire* or Bimala and Sandip in *Charadhyay*.

bondage while consciousness ranges freely. But it should be added that though he often spoke of the spirit being burdened by matter, he also showed us in his creative works how the spirit becomes life. His aesthetic vision, replete in expression with concretising resources of images, metaphors, similes, allegories and so on, thus offer both an embodiment and ambiguity. The positivity of difference or specificity necessary for embodiment is often found in his creative writings in the plenitude of nature and in the nuanced difference between man and woman. This difference takes on a physico-emotional struggle or fusion, presenting masculinity and femininity as reason and emotion, as consciousness and nature. Yet alienation residing in the division of the body and the mind also becomes the central problematic of some of his novels and short stories.[61] In some of the novels, such as *Chaturanga* or *Charadhyay*, the women are all-risking central characters who search their authentic, true identities and throw themselves headlong into the vortex of reality. Though this self-quest is usually a pre-occupation attributed to men, the women subjects reach out beyond the pseudo-authenticities of the domestic woman only to approximate the 'natural' woman. Their natural though signified woman's 'body' is left behind or sacrificed to reason. The established gender or sexual dualities persist and women's entry into the sphere of the 'human', unlike for men, demands a curtailment of their personality. We see, however, in these narratives a productive use of 'alienation' itself. What is worth noting is that Rabindranath does not succumb to any easy or stereotypical 'resolution' in dealing with these binaries. He shares with his readers his own awareness of the absence of a comfort zone of reconciliation.[62] Regarding these binary relations Rabindranath was unresolved, though he was never comfortable with dualism, with a split between theory and practice, physical nature and consciousness. He established two unconventional educational institutions – Santiniketan and Sriniketan – to combat some of the evils of duality. In them he sought to balance the interac-

---

61   See Himani Bannerji 2011, chapter 5. We see the quest for and glimpses of a missing third term. His narratives, novels and short stories are works of irresolution – presenting at times reversals of situations, for example in *Charadhyay*, in which the woman takes on the traditionally ascribed attributes of masculinity and ushers in the crisis.

62   Rabindranath's narratives are concretised through associating the theme of sexuality with the moral spatialization of the private and the public, providing details of the domains of men and women. Through exploring these domains with their specific moralities of gendered roles Rabindranath offers the reader the elements of a social critique but it is not premised upon any sustained sufficiently developed analysis. The novel *Jogajog*, for example, involves both the showing and critique of the fetishisation of commodities and property, displaying the numbing effects of wealth. These themes resonate with his rejection of the substitution of the human by greed and technologies of profit.

tion of nature with the cultivation of the mind, local cultures with international ones, and brought within the purview of knowledge modern agricultural science and craft training.

In the last decades of his life Rabindranath's vision of a fundamental social and cultural transformation, of decolonisation, was overcome by the tide of industrial capitalism with its power of alienation and fetishisation, but also by nationalist colonising impulses within Europe. He wrote insistently on the evils of market norms, against acquisitive morality and possessive individualism, and on the need for cooperation. The culmination of his critique and denunciation of imperialist aggression is his poignant and last public piece – *The Crisis in Civilisation*. A terrible profiteering destructiveness, with its technology for mass killing, was bringing civilisations down to rubbles. Maintaining his principle of hope in the face of the devastation of Europe by 1931 Nazi-fascist forces, he wrote:

> As I look around I see the crumbling ruins of a proud civilisation like a vast heap of futility. And yet I shall not commit the grievous sin of losing faith in man. I would rather look forward to the opening of a new chapter in his history after the cataclysm is over and the atmosphere rendered clean with the spirit of service and sacrifice. Perhaps that dawn will come from the East where the sun rises. A day will come when unvanquished man will retrace his path of conquest, despite all the barriers, to win back his lost human heritage.[63]

A madness of greed and war had gripped both Europe (aided by the U.S.) and Asia. He wrote to Japan's imperial poet, Noguchi, regarding Japan's invasion of China and its broader imperialist ambitions:

> Humanity, in spite of its many failures, has believed in a fundamental moral structure of society. When you speak, therefore, of 'the inevitable means, terrible it is though, for establishing a new great world in the Asiatic continent' – signifying, I suppose, the bombing of Chinese women and children and desecration of ancient temples and universities as a

---

63   Tagore, 'Crisis in civilization', 726. It should also be noted, as Dutta and Robinson mention: 'In 1937, in a public appeal for the republican side in the Spanish civil war, Rabindranath wrote that 'this devastating tide of International Fascism must be checked ... come in your millions to the aid of democracy to the succor of civilization and culture' – and earned a public rebuke from Joseph Goebbels, speaking at the Nazi Party's Nuremburg rally' (Tagore 1997, pp. 492–3).

means of saving China for Asia – you are ascribing to humanity a way of
life which is not even inevitable among the animals ... [Y]ou are building
your conception of Asia which would be raised on a tower of skulls.[64]

Alienation in its ultimate and maximum sense had reached its fullness. Europe's self-devouring annexations and wars caused a deep despair in Rabindranath. He questioned Europe's 'civilising' claims:

> Such is the tragic tale of the gradual loss of my faith in the claims of the
> European nations to civilisation. In India the misfortune of being gov-
> erned by a foreign race is daily brought home to us not only in the callous
> neglect of such minimum necessities of life as adequate provision for
> food, clothing, educational and medical facilities for the people but in
> an even unhappier form in the way the people have been divided among
> themselves. The pity of it is that the blame is laid at the door of our own
> society.[65]

The death camps for the enemies of the Nazis and fascists were run with
the most efficient technologies and their beginnings were already evident
by the late 1930s. As Europe moved closer into the vortex of World War II,
Rabindranath, who followed closely newspaper and other reports, became
increasingly angry and depressed. On 14 April 1938 he wrote to E.P. Thompson:
'It is a torture for me to have to witness, in the last chapter of my life, the naus-
eating sight of maniacs let loose making playthings of all safeguards of human
culture'.[66] In August of 1941 Rabindranath died – not a happy man. Alienation
surrounded him on all sides. On the brink of this destruction he gathered his
principle of hope from the idea and intuition of the universal human which had
been forged with his life experience and from the wish images of a redeemed
world. But he knew that this 'human' he affirmed was not yet an empirical existence but rather a creation of desire and the potential of human capacities, a
desire for what people would continue to become in their long unfolding history. He held onto his hope, which came from his faith in the human spirit of
oneness, in human sympathy and creative capacity. Thus he sought to transcend alienation, fragmentation and enslavement to any form of power by
engaging through the process of imagining the universal and iconic human.
He left his immense creative and social responses and a vision of the universal

---

64   Tagore 1997, p. 497.
65   Ibid., p. 725.
66   Ibid., p. 493.

human for others with which to combat alienation in its destructive perniciousness. He left behind a sense of oneness with all aspects of life and nature that had been alienated through the long hard centuries of greed and repression of colonialism and capitalism.

Marx, on his part, socialised and politicised the problems of alienation and commodity fetishism, though he could convey as well the poetry of its overcoming. He sought to resolve the problem of alienation through the call to communist revolution. Marx's concept of 'the human' escapes a trap of idealism to become a concrete category – its concreteness resulting from the convergence of many determinations of history, society, and everyday experiences of myriads of men and women.

6   Conclusion

> The development of intelligence and physical power is equally necessary in animals and men for their purpose of living; but what is unique in man is the development of his consciousness, which gradually deepens and widens the realisation of his immortal being, the perfect, the eternal. It inspires those creations of his that reveal *the divinity in him – which is his humanity* – in the varied manifestations of truth, goodness and beauty, in the freedom of activity which is not for his use, but for his ultimate expression.[67]

Rabindranath and Marx both spoke in the name of the human and endowed this 'human' with great creative, imaginative and critical capacities. This similarity between them is also accompanied by their absolute negativity towards the history and social conditions which destroy, deny and distort the humanity of people the world over. The goal of creating a society and forms of consciousness that eliminate alienation brings them together in spite of their epistemological differences. It is obvious that Marx's historical materialism and Rabindranath's radical idealism rely on different theoretical/philosophical premises. But this theoretical difference notwithstanding, they notice the same and similar things along the way in what they observe about human capacities and potentials, in their desire for a human world, where 'man' is the subject and not the object of external forces. In this their paths coincide. While Rabindranath is a keen and feeling observer of history and social rela-

---

67   Tagore 1930, 88. My emphasis.

tions of power, and thus shares some of Marx's social critique, Marx shares a utopian moment with Rabindranath. The quotation above from 'The Religion of Man', though phrased through a metaphysical language, could be interpreted to resonate with Marx's view that the human, as spoken of in *The Economic and Philosophical Manuscripts*, is the measure of all things. And Rabindranath too speaks of 'the divinity in him – which is his humanity'.

The ways to reach this revolutionary or visionary redemptive moment of Marx and Rabindranath may need different compasses, but it is true that their 'true North' lies in the same direction. While Rabindranath offered trenchant criticism of social injustice and degradation anywhere and denounced alienation, greed for commodities and wealth and stressed empathy, creativity and the aesthetic, Marx shared his criticism and distilled his critique in the context of human labour/productivity. Marx socialised and politicised the problems of alienation and commodity fetishism, but he could not do without the poetry that lay in the desire of its overcoming. Nor could Rabindranath speak for the 'human' without responding to, engaging with, conditions such as India under British rule, landlord-tenant relations, fascism and Nazism, or the dangers of nationalism, even of the colonised. Unless we are going to be theoretically dogmatic and fall into the schismatic view of idealism vs. materialism, we can see that for both Marx and Rabindranath the 'human' becomes a concrete, living, breathing, creative being – the best that human capacities can create. Without this belief all theory is lifeless and all creativity a fetishised aestheticism.

CHAPTER 31

Himani Bannerji in Conversation with Somdatta Mandal

SM: Welcome Prof. Bannerji for agreeing to give us an interview for *Asiatic*. As you already know this is a Special Issue on the South Asian Diaspora and though many of our questions will be geared in that direction, we would like our readers to be in fact acquainted with your oeuvre.

Let us begin with the first phase of your diasporic status when you were born in what is now Bangladesh and then migrated to India. What is your reaction to that exilic shift?

HB: Exilic shift is not exactly the word I would use about myself accompanying my parents to India at the age of 17. We did not migrate to India, but rather my father became ill and died in Kolkata after some time. It was not a planned departure, and under no harsh circumstances. Kolkata was actually a very nice experience for me, since the world that we inhabited in then East Pakistan, where my father was a high court judge, was a restrictive one. It was restrictive not because we were Hindus, but because as members of the highest echelons of bureaucracy and myself studying at a very expensive private school, I didn't have almost any access to a local middle class world. Our stay in Kolkata provided me with a path out of that highly classed world, where I had never used public transport and rarely went anywhere alone. After the death of my father, Pakistan came fully under martial law and my mother stayed on with us, myself and two younger brothers, under conditions of great privation. Financially things were very difficult, as India and Pakistan ceased to have any contact with each other, and my father's provident fund and future pension were blocked. This situation freed me and allowed me to become much more independent and to mix freely with the kind of people that I did not encounter in Dhaka. My entry into Lady Brabourne College and years of university education were very happy ones for me. The political outlook and the friendships I developed then continue up to this day.

SM: You moved to Canada in 1969. As an academic, a poet and short story writer how do you share your identity crisis with other diasporic writers from South Asia?

HB: Coming to Canada in 1969 as a graduate student, and not an immigrant, was still a very shocking affair. I was teaching at that time in Jadavpur University and had come on leave, joined by my (ex)husband and daughter within the year. Though I never thought of not returning to Kolkata, I was still shocked by various forms of racism that I encountered, and gradually began to understand their nature and origin. In this journey I met many writers and activists who taught me a great deal. They were mostly black and also South Asians from former colonies. I also met aboriginal activists. I shared my identity 'crisis' with many, many people I met who were facing the same problems that I was. I came as an academic and 27 years old, and gradually developed as a writer, critic and activist. I would consider this experience to be the most valuable one for the person that I have become, and what could become a 'crisis' became the point of departure for my deepening of consciousness about both Indian and Canadian societies and international politics. There was pain in my loss of previous status, the privilege of being an ordinary self, but this is a pain that taught me a lot, and I decided not to lose my world in Kolkata entirely, and to this day continue to live in both Toronto and Canada.

SM: A true 'crosser of borders' Canada is now your world. Physical geography of the place is probably no longer much important to you as you religiously return to Kolkata every year. Your comments please.

HB: What I have said above more or less answers this question. I have added to my lived experience the city of Istanbul for the last many years, where I also returned religiously on my journey back and forth, to be stopped now by the crisis faced by Turkey under the extreme right-wing government of Erdoğan.

SM: As a creative writer your volumes of poetry and short stories speak much about Himani, the diasporic Indian, sharing the same predicament as other writers living a hyphenated existence. Please tell us your views.

HB: The notion of 'Himani the diasporic writer' is not exactly accurate, as I have lived almost 50 years in Canada with deep engagement with my teaching, research and writing. When I write about racism in my creative writing I am talking more about the experiences of the racialized subject. It really is the pain that racism inflicts upon all non-white 'others' at various levels of governance, social relations and cultural impositions that I have spoken to. These are the themes I also explore and analyse in my non-fictional writing. I have never been able to live on nostalgia, but rather in the real present, imperfect as it is, both in India and Canada.

SM: In your writing too there is a state where the sense of nostalgia and the sense of assimilation are juxtaposed. Do you agree?

HB: No, these are not my terms, and I don't think and live in that binary paradigm. Being a marxist, anti-racist feminist is not only a theoretical stand on my part, and I have never thought that my return to India was a return to an idyllic space. Much of my critical writing has been on Indian patriarchal, casteist, capitalist politics in India itself. In the last few years I have been exclusively working on the rise of the Hindu right in India and the perils of cultural nationalism, the crisis faced by the communist parties in India and disastrous deprivations faced by large sections of the Indian population – in fact the majority. This is the framework within which I live and think. I have comrades and close friends in both parts of the world.

SM: According to several diasporic critics, 'home' is a mythic place of desire in the diasporic imagination. It is also a place of no return. Do you, like Uma Parameswaran propagate the myth of the Trishanku, who is suspended between two worlds but belong to none?

HB: With all respect to those who inhabit the empty space between two worlds, suspended in mid-air, I cannot join their company. For me it is indeed one world, which encompasses all the nation states of this world within the compass of capitalism. Capitalism is not just an abstract theory for me, but a concrete set of social relations which have pulled into themselves, though in very specific ways, the different countries of the world. So anywhere I may live at this point in time I see the enmeshing of different aspects of the capitalist system. It is inherently violent in its organization and tasks of expansion.

SM: As we are discussing this straddling between two worlds, I am reminded of your short story "The Colour of Freedom," where the unnamed protagonist does not want to die in Canada on a wintry day in a dim February afternoon but longs to die "in the sun – and in the freedom of colours, not in the stifling monotony and purity of snow." Your observations, please.

HB: From what I have said above it should be clear that the title of the short story, "The Colour of Freedom", is an ironic one. That world of the yellow thistle flower, which is a child's memory, is neither present in India nor in Canada. The sunny world of India has to be understood in the light of other things the woman remembers, the horrors of the Indian partition – fires, dead bodies, smoke and dust – which are deathly as is the snow. The woman longs for something that is not here with us – her mother's faith in Gandhi, the beautiful flowers in the train tracks, and the mellow sunlight are unrealized and perhaps unrealizable spaces.

SM: There is another young black protagonist in your story "The Other Family", who faces trouble when, unaware of colour consciousness, she draws a picture of an ideal family with Caucasian features, later told by her mother that it does not represent them, the 'others.' What provided you the inspiration for writing such a story?

HB: The immediate inspiration of the story was not any one event, but the experience of my daughter as a non-white child growing up in a highly racialized environment. Written almost 40 years ago, this story is not only about one family but countless others, as the story has been used in numerous anthologies, textbooks for schools, and translated into Chinese, Farsi, Portuguese and French. So it must have resonated with what many others know, think and feel.

SM: This phase of our interview will focus on Himani the critic and activist. You had once mentioned that "you cannot change the world with art alone, nor can you do without it." Is this because you are also a serious activist?

HB: see answer to question below

SM: A major segment of your writing is devoted to issues of culture and politics – away from the romanticized nostalgia of diasporic writing. We are amazed to read of your wide range and subject matter. Through critical discussions of Marxist theatre in Bengal, the anti-racist and feminist poetry of Dionne Brand in Canada, the revolutionary poetry of Ernesto Cardenal in Nicaragua, a recent popular trend in Bengali fiction, and the films of Andrei Tarkovsky, your essays provide acute yet dispassionate insights into politically committed cultural activity. Your opinion please.

HB: I have never been a fan of 'art for art's sake'. I'm not sure I even understand what it would mean to strip art of its social content, of its location in society or of its social intentions, directly articulated or not. It doesn't mean that we have to look at social reality from a clear ideological position, but accept the fact that all linguistic, artistic utterances are intrinsically aspects of the social and historical forms prevailing among us. It is true that cultural forms and traditions are specific, but at the same time their specificities arise from certain general ways of seeing, standpoints of knowing and experiences emanating from a certain social setup. This does not mean a chauvinistic approach to culture or art, or that we cannot use forms in particularly suitable ways to our own reality. As an example, we can mention Bankimchandra Chattopadhyay's adaptation of English novels into great Bengali novels. Similarly, Michael Madhusudan Dutt's adaptation of the sonnet forms from Petrarch and blank verse from Shakespeare and other writers. So the boundaries of literature are not rigidly laid down, and sensibilities of people are also dynamic and innovative. The question of influence, then, makes evident to us the two sides – that which is influenced, and the influences that come in – and altogether synthesizes a new form. All of this may be read in the context of class, colonialism and gender, for example – all social relations of power which are augmented or resisted by cultural production. So divorcing culture or art from social reality is neither possible nor desirable. It is undesirable to use culture as a veil that hides culture's own social existence. To do that would be an aestheticization which is fundamentally reactionary. I'll end by quoting Walter Benjamin, who said in his essay "The work of art in an age of mechanical reproduction", that fascists aestheticize the political, and communists politicize the aesthetic.

SM: Could you tell us how upon your arrival in Canada you encountered a new form of violence which, unlike patriarchy and class related violence in India, was 'racism'.

HB: In my specific situation in India as an upper class and upper caste woman I had not encountered exclusion and repression through caste. When I was growing up in Bengal caste and untouchability were relatively minor themes in the social analysis available to us. Sometimes caste became a part of consideration of class, but class was the sovereign category. Perhaps if I were a low caste or untouchable person, and grew up in a rural society, I would have understood caste better as a part of my existential condition. But as things stood I did not encounter it as an important aspect of my life, did not read much about caste as a way to understand class, or know much about the anti-caste movements of southern India. Even though I was not rich, and belonged to a professional middle class world, I enjoyed the quiet privilege of remaining unaware of certain forms of struggles either in my own life or of those surrounding me. Gender was more obvious in our personal lives – and class, from living among countless poor.

Caste is something that is similar to race. However, the impact of racialization, that is, of being rendered into a member of an inferiorised social group, was imposed on me with a violence that was sudden and previously unexperienced. I had never faced such exclusion on the ground of being who I am rather than what I do. I also did not know that the set of stereotypes that I had read about in relation to the South African apartheid system or of southern United States are regularly visited upon non-Europeans in the West. I felt the common bond that binds me to the people of African descent living in England, the U.S. and Canada – three countries of which I have personal experience. There was obviously a lot for me to learn, and instead of hiding from it I owned all these experiences, which extended my sense of identity from being Bengali or Indian to that of being 'black'. In my opinion, South Asians coming abroad still need to travel the path that I did.

SM: In most of your essays you transform how theory is written by seamlessly moving between subjective – a poet's language, passionate – and political and disciplined theoretical formulation. As a non-white woman in the postcolonial world what is your stance at present?

HB: What you say is right, about the way I connect theorization with experience. I'm not sure what you mean by the term 'subjective'. It's not so much about the personal 'I', but more about experience in/of everyday life that provides the entry point for my attempts to understand the world in terms of social organization, forms of consciousness and their relationships to economy. Experience therefore becomes the door through which I enter into social inquiry. This is not exactly a descriptive use of experience alone, but looking for the historical, social/material elements that go into the making of that experience. I consider my personal experiences to be social experiences, and the same goes for the experiences of others. In this approach there is a legitimate role of feelings, passions and responses of all kinds. Anger and resistance necessarily play a part, since the world we inhabit is created through relations of inequality, oppression and injustice. I believe that attempts to understand the world should not only consist of nuanced description, but that such descriptions must motivate questions and practices of transformation. Thus my commitment to social transformation and socialist revolution remains consistent throughout.

SM: You have drawn our attention to the fact that none of the works by the South Asian diaspora that have won acclaim actually challenge the Canadian establishment. Could you tell us why you think so?

HB: I will answer these two questions together. Much of the South Asian diaspora came to Canada as economic migrants in search of prosperity, and without knowing anything about the country they were coming to. In their 'home' countries they had no quarrel with caste, class or capital and when they came to Canada they did not identify with either the aboriginal people, from whom the country was taken, nor with the immigrants of African descent who came into Canada from the West Indies, the African continent and the United States. South Asians tend to identify with the white population and see the 'others' as socially inferior to themselves. They have a legacy of patriarchy that is all their own, which blends in well with the racist patriarchy that characterises Canada. So they have no problem with any of these aspects of political, cultural and economic marginalization of a large population of Canadians. For these reasons South Asians are exemplified by the Canadian state as model minorities. They tend to keep apart even from mainstream politics, though now that is less so, especially in relation to the Liberal Party of Canada. But certainly they do not see themselves in any sense involved with resistance politics. Of course some South Asians with left politics and with refugee backgrounds, fleeing from Sri Lanka for example, or dictatorships in Pakistan, have shown interest and initiative in challenging the Canadian status quo. But by and large, as the writers of these communities are themselves deeply middle class, some very religious, and refuse to speak critically about their lives in Canada, they love to tell stories of their past. Many of these novels are not even their personal memories, but rather second or third hand reported experiences of older generations become the content of their narratives. Some of the novels are not only acts of merchandising memories, but also have a touch of anthropology which dishes up the everyday life of the people of their countries as native informants are supposed to do. There is an insatiable search for this kind of literature in the West, which becomes a niche for South Asian diasporic writers.

Moas Vassanji's novel, *No New Land*, is no exception to this type of writing, but what is more, it makes fun of not just myself, but of the protests mounted by non-white anti-racist organizers. What is ironic is that his own market in Canada and the West largely depends on the cultural-political struggle of the very people whom he caricatures.

SM: In the introduction to your volume of essays entitled *Thinking Through: Essays on Feminism, Marxism and Anti-Racism* (1995), you mentioned that you have spent half of your life in Toronto, coming no nearer and going no further than you did in the first few years. You called your journey in Canada "like an arc, suspended, which has not found a ground yet ..." Now after more than two decades, has your point of view changed or do you still believe in a similar manner?

HB: After these two decades I to some extent resolved this existential crisis, partly because I have been coming to India almost every year, and as a result the reality of everyday life, the political struggles, changes in lifestyles of the middle class, as well as the fast rise of the Hindu right have helped to reduce the mythic quality that the notion of 'home' has for the migrant. My attachment to India and the problems that I research about, my associations with Jadavpur University's School of Women's Studies, Marxian Studies, and the fellowship that I held for so long at the Institute for Development Studies Kolkata all combined to provide me with a critical analysis and politics at an anti-imperialist level. The problems encountered in Canada and India are part of a massive global expansion of capital, and the huge degradation in lives and work of people is created by the same forces. In my immediate vicinity I might add the United States and Mexico. More than ever I am convinced that capitalism and forms of consciousness this system gives rise to, its ever expanding destructive potential ranging from slavery and colonialism to neoliberalism, has to be defeated and replaced by democratic socialism. So I suppose that arc has lost its suspension.

SM: When asked in an interview with Arun Mukherjee about what it meant to be ethnic and what ethnicity has to do with being a 'visible minority', you had responded that it meant that you all were not considered to be Canadians. You were 'immigrant women'. Could you elaborate on this issue a little more?

HB: In my interview with Arun we considered the political appellations offered by the Canadian capitalist settler colonial state and the political meanings and possibilities that they contained. Though formally invested with citizenship, which promised a universal equality among peoples living in Canada, we noticed the mechanism of disempowerment at work. This mechanism constructed with notions such as 'immigrant women', 'visible minorities', 'Canadians' and 'new Canadians'. Observing closely the populations who were drawn within these categories, I found that they excluded people with European backgrounds, no matter how recently arrived. I considered this to be a manipulation of citizenship into finely graded hierarchies, and found the terminology to be an avenue for disempowerment and creation of systemic racism. It was of great interest to me and others how the work of racialization could be done by the state – it's citizenship, migration and labour laws – by creating different political locales, by distinguishing between 'Canadians' and 'others'. While a 'white' person from Poland was unquestioningly 'Canadian' from the moment of arrival into the country, even as a permanent resident the third generation of South Asians living in Canada's west coast continued to be called immigrants. Smuggled within this categorization is the factor of "race", which tended to marginalize and dilute the quality of citizenship of non-white peoples arriving to or residing in Canada. Finally, the peoples who pre-dated the colonial incursion of the French and the British in this land mass they named Canada, ancient as their lineage was, figured nowhere within the map of Canadian citizenship. Another set of laws ruled their lives, laws promulgated by the British Crown culminating in the 1876 Indian Act. The genocide that followed (the United Nations accuses Canada of cultural genocide) was not only cultural, but physical, social and political. It is on this plinth of utterly racist settler colonialism that the liberal democratic Canada was established.

SM: When you went to Canada way back in 1969, there were terms like 'racism', 'decolonisation', and 'anti-imperialism' that were the most prevalent. What about 'multiculturalism'? Do you notice any difference after the state-induced policy of multiculturalism came into existence in Canada in the 1980s?

HB: The 1960s, '70s, up to the mid-80s were years of great anti-imperialist revolution and of radical social transformations in North America, when I arrived. The symbiotic relationship between anti-racist movements, feminist and gay movements were at their peak at that time. This radicalism was infused with desires for socialist revolution. Altogether the international and national environments of politics were very threatening for the bourgeois status quo, consisting in Canada of a settler colonial capitalism hard-wired by patriarchy and racism. The state of Canada, which recruits labour for Canadian industry through processes of immigration, had 'opened up' in the '60s and '70s, bringing very large numbers of people of African descent from former colonies, brought to the West in the context of slavery and plantation economies. Doors were also opened to South Asians who brought with them skilled labour to Canada. This labour import was closely connected with lack of a substantial working age and skill population poised for an industrial take-off. There were of course also pre-existing racialized minorities which included the aboriginal peoples, the Francophones, the Chinese and Indians brought in the late 19th and early 20th century, and numerous groups of 'white' migrants brought in to settle and cultivate the land. The Canada I encountered through the '70s was riven with national claims by the Francophones and aboriginal people, and socio-economic and cultural claims of others. This crisis in the legitimacy of the state as arbiter of diverse and contradictory claims was managed literally introducing a legislated form of multiculturalism. In my book on the character of Canadian nationalism and racialized citizenship, *The Dark Side of the Nation*, I speak about the problems of this multiculturalism policy and programme, which produced stereotypes of different groups in Canada, converting demands of political representation into trivial cultural recognition.

This move on the part of the state, which I call 'multiculturalism from above', was radically against kinds of meaningful social transformation nuanced with a sense of revolution, which were truncated and managed by the state's legislative manoeuvre. Political subjectivity based on feminism and anti-racist class oppression morphed into co-optative categories of 'visible minorities', 'immigrants' and 'new Canadians' and so on. This liberal discourse changed the political environment, creating 'communities' which were clients of the state. At the level of civil society, the solidarity and involvement of immigrants with each other and with the aboriginal peoples was deformed through community politics and state-prescribed cultural identities. In a classic manner of divide and rule, multiculturalism from above manipulated these groups, managing to substantially dissipate the fundamental transformational thrust of social movements rising from below.

SM: One last question. When you declare, "I am the diaspora" you feel that you are also an alien in India. The diaspora has in fact objectified you. Your comments please.

HB: I'm not aware of where and in what context I said that. I can only say that I don't feel objectified by living in different parts of the world, and that the experience of having lived in Bangladesh (formerly East Pakistan) until the end of my high school and the unplanned arrival in India for a holiday which turned out to be a stay of ten years in Kolkata and Santiniketan, and subsequent departure for Canada all contributed to my becoming the person that I am. Very personally speaking, this has entailed senses of both gain and loss. I have found ways of being in the world, cultures and social relations that are quite similar to each other though they present themselves in very specific forms. As such, I think I moved out of the tropes of 'home', blood and belonging, and now live in intimate relations, activities and politics which are very familiar to me. Perhaps the major difference I feel is that in India I'm not an overtly racialized subject, but I am a member of the dominant class and caste, and in some ways I become the subject which in the context of "race" is called 'white'. My unawareness of the oppressive social relations immediately impacting upon me are substituted by the privilege of not having to be sustainedly self-aware. So becoming the 'self' rather than the 'other' is indeed a place of power. Forty years or more of living between India and Canada primarily, and visiting many other countries, I am at 'home' in my worldview and politics. I don't think that I fully belonged when I lived in India or East Pakistan, and that anyone, anywhere, doesn't have a sense of non-belonging to many of the aspects of the societies they come from. Perhaps things would have been different if I had not lived, worked, researched and taught in both countries, and left India 'for good'. I have created a kind of a path by constantly walking on the space between the two countries, and found Kolkata and Toronto connected through multiple relations of capital, class, patriarchy, colonialism and other relations of oppression – for example, caste playing the role of race.

In conclusion, I guess what I am trying to say is that home and homelessness are modes of feeling that are experiences of traveling. My 'home' is perhaps in my politics now, which consists of an awareness of myself as a marxist and anti-oppression feminist. However, there is something culturally that I miss in Canada, which is Bangla, my mother tongue, my language of certain kinds of social involvement, the literature of which and whose images of landscape are rooted in me since early childhood. Though there are reified and commodified forms of 'Bengali culture' which are imported in the suburbia of North American cities, they arrive frozen and packaged, like *ilish machch* from Bangladesh. It's very hard to breathe any life into these imports. But as I return to India yearly I don't depend on this reified culture.

sm: Thank you very much for giving us this interview. Is there anything else that you would like to add for the benefit of the readers? If yes, please go ahead, if no, once again a thank you from our end.

Bibliography

Abrams, Philip 1982, *Historical Sociology*, Ithica: Cornell University Press.

Acton, Janice (ed.) 1974, *Women at Work*: Ontario, 1850–1930, Toronto: Women's Press.

Adams, Mary Louise 1989, 'There is No Place like Home: On the Place of Identity in Feminist Politics', *Feminist Review*, 31: 22–33.

Adams, Paul 2003, Palestinian 'Baby Boom' may affect road to peace, *The Globe and Mail*, (28 July): A8.

Adamson, Nancy, Linda Briskin and Margaret McPhail 1988, *Feminist Organising for Change*, Toronto: Oxford University Press.

Addy, Premen, and Ibne Azad 1973, 'Politics and culture in Bengal', *New Left Review* 79: 71–112.

Adorno, T.W. and Horkheimer, M. 2002 [1973], *Dialectic of Enlightenment*, trans. E. Jephcott, Stanford, CA: Stanford University Press.

Agamben, G. 1998, *Homo Sacer: Sovereign Power and Bare Life*, Stanford: Stanford University Press.

Agarwal, Puroshottam 1995, 'Surat, Savarkar and Draupadi: Legitimising Rape as a Political Weapon', in *Women and Right-Wing Movements: Indian Experiences*, edited by T. Sarkar and U. Butalia, London, New Jersey: Zed Books.

Aggarwal, Arjun 1972, 'Characteristics of Sexual Harassment', in *Sexual Harassment in the Workplace*, Toronto: Butterworths.

Aguilar, D.D. 2015 'Intersectionality', in *Marxism and Feminism*, edited by S. Mojab, London: Zed Books.

Ahmad, Aijaz 1992, *In Theory: Classes, Nations and Literatures*, London: Verso.

Ahmad, Aijaz 1996, *Lineages of the Present: Political Essays*, New Delhi: Tulika.

Ahmad, Aijaz 2002, *On Communalism and Globalisation: Offensives of the Far Right*, New Delhi: Three Essays.

Alam, Javed 1983, 'Peasantry, Politics and Historiography: Critique of New Trends in Relation to Marxism', *Social Scientist* 117: 43–54.

Alarcon, Norma 1996, 'Conjugating Subjects in the Age of Multiculturalism', in *Mapping Multiculturalism*, edited by Avery Gordon and Christopher Newfield, Minnesota: University of Minnesota Press.

Alcoff, Linda 1988, 'Cultural Feminism versus Post-structuralism: The Identity Crisis in Feminist Theory', *Signs* 13, 3: 405–36.

Alexander, Jacqui, and Chandra Mohanty (eds.) 1997, *Feminist Genealogies, Colonial Legacies, Democratic Futures*, London and New York: Routledge.

Allen, Theodor 1994, *The Invention of the White Race: Racial Oppression and Social Control*, London: Verso.

Alloula, Malek 1986, *The Colonial Harem*, Minneapolis: University of Minnesota Press.

Althusser, Louis 1970, 'Idéologie et appareils idéologiques d'État (Notes pour une recherche)', *La Pensée*, 151: 3–38.

Althusser, Louis 1971, *Lenin and Philosophy*, trans., Ben Brewster. London: Verso.

Althusser, Louis 1977a, 'Ideology and Ideological State Apparatuses (Notes towards an Investigation)', in *Lenin and Philosophy and Other Essays*, London: New Left Books.

Althusser, Louis 1977b [1969], *For Marx*, trans. Ben Brewster, London: Verso.

Althusser, Louis 1984, *Essays on Ideology*, London: Verso.

Althusser, Louis, and Etienne Balibar 1973, *Reading Capital*, trans. Ben Brewster, London: New Left Books.

Ambedkar, B.R. 1992, 'Speech at Mahad' in *Poisoned Bread: Translations from Modern Marathi Dalit Literature*, edited by Arjun Dangle, Bombay: Orient Longman.

Anderson, Benedict 1991, *Imagined Communities*, London: Verso.

Anderson, Perry 1974, *Lineages of the Absolutist State*, London: N.L.B.

Anonymous 1869, 'Sindur' [Vermillion], *Bamabodhini Patrika*, 4 (63), (B.S. Kartik 1275).

Anonymous 1872, 'Meyether Poshak' [Attire of Women of Bengal], *Bamabodhini*, 99 (8), (B.S. Kartik 1278).

Anthias, Floya, Nira Yuval-Davis, and Harriet Cain (eds.) 1992, *Racialised Boundaries*, London and New York: Routledge.

Anzaldua, Gloria (ed.) 1990, *Making Face, Making Soul/Haciendo Caras: Creative and Critical Perspectives by Women of Color*, San Francisco: an aunt lute foundations book.

Anzaldua, Gloria, and Cherrie Moraga (eds.) 1983, *This Bridge Called My Back: Writings by Radical Women of Color*, New York: Kitchen Table Women of Color Press.

Archer, Mildred and Toby Falk 1989, *India Revealed: The Art and Adventure of James and William Fraser, 1801–35*, London: Cassel.

Aries, Philip 1962, *Centuries of Childhood: A Social History of Family Life*, New York: Vintage Books.

Aries, P. and G. Duby (eds.) 1992 [1987], *A History of Private Life*, 4 vol, Cambridge: Harvard University Paperback Editions.

Armstrong, Elizabeth 2014, *Gender and Neoliberalism: The All India Democratic Women's Association and Globalisation Politics*, New York: Routledge.

Armstrong, Frederick 1987, 'Ethnicity and the Formation of the Ontario Establishment', in *Ethnic Canada: Identities and Inequalities*, edited by L. Driedger, Toronto: Copp Clark Pitman.

Armstrong, Pat and Hugh Armstrong 1978, *Double Ghetto*, Toronto: McClelland and Stewart.

Armstrong, Pat and Patricia M. Connelly 1989, 'Feminist Political Economy: An Introduction', *Studies in Political Economy*, 30–1: 5–12.

Arnold, David 1993, *Colonising the Body: State Medicine and Epidemic Disease in Nineteenth-century India*, Berkeley and Los Angeles, California: University of California Press.

Aronowitz, Stanley 1992, *The Politics of Identity*, New York: Routledge.

Atwood, Margaret 1972, *Survival: A Thematic Guide to Canadian Literature*, Toronto: House of Anansi Press.

Avery, Donald 1995, *Reluctant Host: Canada's Response to Immigrant Workers, 1896–1994*, Toronto: McClelland & Stewart.

Backhouse, Constance 1999, *Colour-coded: A Legal History of Racism in Canada, 1900–1950*, Toronto: University of Toronto Press.

Bagchi, Jasodhara 1985, 'Positivism and Nationalism: Womanhood and Crisis in Nationalist Fiction – Bankimchandra's *Anandamath*', *Economic and Political Weekly* 20, 43: 58–62.

Bagchi, Jasodhara 1990, 'Representing Nationalism: Ideology of Motherhood in Colonial Bengal' *Economic and Political Weekly*, 25, 43: 65–71.

Bagchi, Jasodhara 1993, 'Colonialism and Socialisation: The Girl Child in Colonial Bengal', *Resources for Feminist Research* 22, 3 and 4: 22–31.

Bagchi, Jasodhara (ed.) 1995, *Indian Women: Myth and Reality*, Calcutta: Sangam Books.

Bagchi, Jasodhara 1996, 'Secularism as identity: The case of Tagore's *Gora*', in *The Nation, the State and Indian Identity*, edited by Dutta, M., Agnes, F., and Adarkar, N., Calcutta: Samya.

Bakan, Abigail B. 2008, 'Marxism and Antiracism: Rethinking the Politics of Difference', *Rethinking Marxism*, 20, 2: 238–56.

Balibar, Etienne 1970, 'On the Basic Concepts of Historical Materialism', in *Reading Capital*, edited by L. Althusser and E. Balibar, London: Verso.

Ballhatchet, Kenneth 1980, *Race, sex and class under the Raj: Imperial Attitudes and Policies and their Critics, 1793–1905*, London: Weidenfeld and Nicolson.

Bandyopadhyay, Shibaji 1991, *Gopal-Rakhal Dwanda Samas: Upanibeshbad O Bangla Shishu Sahitya* [An Elision of Gopal-Rakhal: Colonialism and Bengali Children's Literature], Calcutta: Papyrus.

Bannerjee, Sumanta 1988, *Keyabat Meye* [Bravo woman!], Calcutta.

Bannerjee, Sumanta 1989, *The Parlour and the Streets: Elite and Popular Culture in Nineteenth Century Calcutta*, Calcutta: Seagull Books.

Bannerji, Himani 1982, *A Separate Sky*, Toronto: Domestic Bliss Press.

Bannerji, Himani 1986a, 'Popular Images of South Asian Women', *Parallelogram* 2, 4.

Bannerji, Himani 1986b, *Doing Time*, Toronto: Sister Vision Press.

Bannerji, Himani 1987, 'Introducing Racism: Notes towards an Anti-Racist Feminism', *Resources for Feminist Research*, 16,1: 10–12.

Bannerji, Himani 1989, 'The Mirror of Class: Subjectivity and Politics in Nineteenth Century Bengal', *Economic and Political Weekly*, 24, 19: 1041–51.

Bannerji, Himani 1991, 'But Who Speaks for Us?' in *Unsettling Relations: The University as a Site of Feminist Struggles*, by Himani Bannerji, Linda Carty, Kari Dehli, Susan Heald and Kate McKenna, Toronto: Women's Press.

Bannerji, Himani 1992, 'Mothers and Teachers: Gender and Class in Educational Proposals for and by Women in Colonial Bengal', *Journal of Historical Sociology* 5, 1: 1–30.

Bannerji, Himani (ed.) 1993, *Returning the Gaze: Essays on Racism, Feminism and Politics*. Toronto: Sister Vision Press.

Bannerji, Himani 1994a, 'Textile Prison: Discourse on Shame (*Lajja*) in the Attire of the Gentlewoman (*Bhadramahila*) in Colonial Bengal', *Canadian Journal of Sociology/Cahiers Canadiens de Sociologie*, pp. 169–93.

Bannerji, Himani 1994b, 'Writing "India," Doing Ideology: William Jones' Construction of India as an Ideological Category', *Left History* 2, 2: 5–36.

Bannerji, Himani 1995, *Thinking Through: Essays on Feminism, Marxism, and Antiracism*, Toronto: Women's Press.

Bannerji, Himani 1997a, 'Fashioning a Self: Gender, Class and Moral Education for and by Women in Colonial Bengal', in *Discipline, Moral Regulation and Schooling: A Social History*, edited by Kate Rousmarie, Kari Delhi, and Ning de Coninck-Smith, New York & London: Garland.

Bannerji, Himani 1997b, 'Geography Lessons: On Being an Insider/Outsider to the Canadian Nation', in *Dangerous Territories: Struggles for Difference and Equality in Education*, edited by Leslie Roman and Linda Eyre, New York and London: Routledge.

Bannerji, Himani 1998a, 'On the Dark Side of the Nation: Politics of Multiculturalism and the State of "Canada"', in *Literary Pluralities*, edited by Christl Verduyn, Peterborough: Broadview Press. Reprinted in H. Bannerji 2000, *The Dark Side of the Nation*, Toronto: Canadian Scholars Press.

Bannerji, Himani 1998b, *The Mirror of Class: Essays on Bengali Theatre*, Calcutta: Papyrus.

Bannerji, Himani 1998c, 'Age of Consent and Hegemonic Social Reform', in *Gender and Imperialism*, edited by Clare Midgley, Manchester: Manchester University Press.

Bannerji, Himani 1999, 'A Question of Silence: Reflections on Violence against Women in Communities of Colour', in *Scratching the Surface: Canadian Anti-racist Feminist Thought*, edited by Enakshi Dua and Angela Robertson, Toronto: Women's Press.

Bannerji, Himani 2001a, *Inventing Subjects: Studies in Hegemony, Patriarchy and Colonialism*, New Delhi: Tulika.

Bannerji, Himani 2001b, 'Pygmalion Nation: Towards a Critique of Subaltern Studies and the Resolution of the Women's Question', in *Of Property and Propriety: The Role of Gender and Class in Imperialism and Nationalism*, edited by H. Bannerji, S. Mojab and J. Whitehead, Toronto: University of Toronto Press.

Bannerji, Himani 2003, 'The Tradition of Sociology and the Sociology of Tradition', *Qualitative Studies in Education*, 16, 2: 157–73.

Bannerji, Himani 2011, *Demography and Democracy: Essays on Nationalism, Gender and Ideology*, Toronto: Canadian Scholars' Press.

Bannerji, Himani 2014, 'Notes on Karl Marx's and Rabindranath Tagore's ideas on human capacities and alienation', in *Marxism: With and beyond Marx*, edited by A.K. Bagchi and A. Chatterjee, New Delhi: Routledge.

Bannerji, Himani 2015a, 'Building from Marx: Reflections on "Race," Gender and Class', in *Educating from Marx: Race, Gender and Learning*, edited by S. Carpenter and S. Mojab, New York: Palgrave Macmillan.

Bannerji, Himani 2015b, 'Ideology', in *Educating from Marx: Race, Gender and Learning*, edited by S. Carpenter and S. Mojab, New York: Palgrave Macmillan.

Bannerji, Himani 2019, "Towards a Communist Revolution: Gender and Class in *Capital* Volume One". In Marcello Musto (ed), *Marx's Capital after 150 Years: Critique and Alternative to Capitalism*. New York: Routledge.

Bannerji, H., S. Mojab, and J. Whitehead 2001, 'Introduction', in *Of Property and Propriety: The Role of Gender and Class in Imperialism and Nationalism*, edited by H. Bannerji, S. Mojab, and J. Whitehead, Toronto: University of Toronto Press.

Bannerji, Kaushalya 1993, *A New Remembrance*, Toronto: TSAR Publications.

Bano, Saira 2002, Shah-e-Alam Relief Camp, Ahmedabad, Gujarat, Recorded 27 March 2002, 'Genocide, Gujarat 2002' in *Communalism Combat*, No. 77–8.

Barrett, Michele 1988, 'Ideology and the Cultural Production of Gender' in *Women's Oppression Today: The Marxist Feminist Encounter*, London: Verso.

Basu, Chandranath 1892, *Hindutwa* [Hinduism], Calcutta.

Basu, Chandranath 1901, *Stridiger Prati Upadesh* [Advice to Women], Calcutta.

Basu, Ishwarchandra 1884, *Nariniti* [Woman's Conduct], Calcutta.

Basu, Manomohan 1884, *Garhasthya* [Domesticity], Calcutta.

Basu, Manomohan 1887, *Hindur Achar Vyavahar* [Hindu Customs], Calcutta.

Barthes, Roland 1973, *Mythologies*, trans. A. Lavers, New York: Jonathan Cape.

Basu, Shamita 2003, *Religious Revivalism as Nationalist Discourse: Swami Vivekananda and New Hinduism in Nineteenth Century Bengal*, Delhi: Oxford University Press.

Basu, Tapan, Pradip Datta, Sumit Sarkar, Tanika Sarkar, and Sambuddha Sen 1993, *Khaki Shorts Saffron Flags*, Hyderabad: Orient Longman.

Baxandall, Lee and Stefan Morawski, (eds.) 1974, *Karl Marx and Frederick Engels on Literature and Art*, New York: International General.

Beauvoir, Simone de 1974, *The Second Sex*, trans. H.M. Parshley, New York: Vintage.

Benjamin, Walter 1969a, 'The Work of Art in the Age of Mechanical Reproduction', in *Illuminations*, trans. Harry Zohn, New York: Schocken Books.

Benjamin, Walter 1969b, 'Theses on Philosophy of History' in *Illuminations*, trans. Harry Zohn, New York: Schocken Books.

Bernal, Martin 1993, 'Black Athena: Hostilities to Egypt in the Eighteenth Century', in *The "Racial" Economy of Science: Toward a Democratic Future*, edited by Sandra Harding, Bloomington: Indiana University Press.

Berger, John 1972, *Ways of Seeing*, London: BBC.

Bethe, Bhimsen 1992, 'Song', in *Poisoned Bread: Translations from Modern Marathi Dalit Literature*, edited by Arjun Dangle, Bombay: Orient Longman.

Bhabnani, Kumkum and Ann Phoenix (eds.) 1994, *Shifting Identities, Shifting Racisms*, London: Sage.

Bhadra, Gautam 1989, 'The Mentality of Subalternity', in *Subaltern Studies* VI, edited by Ranajit Guha, Delhi: Oxford University Press.

Bharucha, Rustam 1983, *Rehearsals of Revolution*, Honolulu, University of Hawaii Press.

Bharucha, Rustam 1993, *The Question of Faith*, New Delhi: Orient Longman.

Bhattacharya, Sabyasachi (ed.) 1997, 'Introduction' in *The Mahatma and the Poet: Letters and Debates between Gandhi and Tagore, 1915–1941*, National Book Trust: New Delhi.

Birmingham Centre for Contemporary Cultural Studies 1982, *The Empire Strikes Back: Race and Racism in 70s Britain*, Birmingham: Hutchinson.

Biswas, D.K. 1983, *Rammohan Samiksha* [Reflections of Rammohan].

Biswas, Taraknath 1886, *Bangya Mahila* [The Bengali Woman], Calcutta.

Black, George 1981, *Triumph of the People: The Sandinista Revolution in Nicaragua*, London: Zed Books.

Bloch, Ernst, T. Adorno, W. Benjamin, B. Brecht, and G. Lukács 1977, afterword by Frederic Jameson, *Aesthetics and Politics*, London: New Left Books.

Bolaria, B. Singh and Peter S. Li (eds) 1988, *Racial Oppression in Canada*, Toronto: Garamond Press.

Borthwick, Meredith 1984, *The Changing Roles of Women in Bengal, 1849–1905*, Princeton: Princeton University Press.

Brah, Avtar 1996, *Cartographies of Diaspora: Contesting Identities*, London and New York: Routledge.

Brand, Dionne 1983, *Winter Epigrams*, Toronto: Williams-Wallace.

Brand, Dionne 1990, *No Language Is Neutral*, Toronto: McClelland and Stewart.

Brand, Dionne 1991, *No Burden to Carry: Narratives of Black Working Women in Ontario, 1920s to 1950s*, Toronto: Women's Press.

Brand, Dionne 1994, *Bread Out of Stone*, Toronto: Coach House Press.

Brand, Dionne, and Krisantha Sri Bhaggiyadatta (eds.) 1985, *Rivers Have Sources, Trees Have Roots: Speaking of Racism*, Toronto: Cross Cultural Communications Centre.

Brecht, Bertolt 1974, *The Messingkauf Dialogues*, trans. John Willett, London: Methuen.

Brecht, Bertolt 1979, *Diaries, 1920–1922*, New York: St. Martin's Press.

Brennan, Timothy 1997, *At Home in the World: Cosmopolitanism Now*, Cambridge, MA: Harvard University Press.

Briskin, Linda 1990, 'Identity Politics and the Hierarchy of Oppression: A Comment', *Feminist Review*, 35: 102–8.

Broomfield, J.H. 1968, *Elite Conflicts in a Plural Society: Twentieth Century Bengal*, Berkeley: University of California Press.

Brownmiller, Susan 1975, *Against Our Will: Men, Women and Rape*. New York: Simon & Chuster.

Burton, Antoinette M. 1994, *Burdens of History: British Feminists, Indian Women, and Imperial Culture, 1865–1915*, Chapel Hill and London: University of North Carolina Press.

Butalia, Urvashi, and Tanika Sarkar (eds.) 1995, *Women and Right-Wing Movements, Indian Experiences*, London: Zed.

Butalia, Urvashi and Tanika Sarkar (eds.) 1997, *Women of the Hindu Right*, New Delhi: Kali for Women.

Butler Judith 2004, *Precarious Life: The Powers of Mourning and Violence*, London: Verso.

Cabral, Amilcar 1973, *Return to the Source: Selected Speeches of Amilcar Cabral*, New York: Monthly Review Press.

Carby, Hazel 1986, "White woman listen! Black Feminism and the Boundaries of Sisterhood", in *Black British Cultural Studies: A Reader*, edited by H.A. Baker Jr. and M. Diawara, Chicago: University of Chicago Press.

Carby, Hazel 1998, *Race Men*, Cambridge: Harvard University Press.

Cardenal, Ernesto 1980, *Zero Hour and Other Documentary Poems*, trans. Paul Borgeson Jr., New York: New Directions Paperbook.

Carpenter, Mary 1868, *Six Months in India*, London: Longmans.

Carr, E.H. 1964, *What is History?*, Harmondsworth: Penguin Books.

Carroll, L. 1983, 'Law, Custom, and Statutory Social Reform: The Hindu Widows' Remarriage Act of 1856', *The Indian Economic & Social History Review*, 20, 4:363–88.

Carty, Linda, and Dionne Brand 1993, 'Visible Minority Women: A Creation of the Colonial State', in *Returning the Gaze: Essays on Racism, Feminism and Politics*, edited by Himani Bannerji, Toronto: Sister Vision Press.

Césaire, Aimé 1972, *Discourse on Colonialism*, New York: Monthly Review Press.

Chakrabarti, Anjan and Arup Kumar Dhar 2008, 'Development, Capitalism and Socialism: A Marxian Encounter with Rabindranath Tagore's Ideas on the Cooperative Principle', *Rethinking Marxism* 20, 3: 487–99.

Chakrabarty, Dipesh 1992, 'Postcoloniality and the Artifice of History: Who Speaks for Indian Pasts?', *Representations* 37:1–26.

Chakrabarty, Dipesh 1995, 'Radical Histories and Question of Enlightenment Rationalism: Some Recent Critiques of Subaltern Studies', *Economic and Political Weekly* April 8:751–9.

Chakrabarty, Dipesh 1998, 'The Difference-Deferral of (a) Colonial Modernity: Public Debates on Domesticity in British India', in *Subaltern Studies VIII* edited by David Arnold and David Hardiman, Delhi: Oxford University Press.

Chakravarty, Uma 1990, 'Whatever Happened to the Vedic Dasi? Orientalism, Nationalism and a Script for the Past', in *Recasting Women: Essays in Indian Colonial History*, edited by Kumkum Sangari and Sudesh Vaid, New Brunswick, New Jersey: Rutgers University Press.

Chakravarty, Uma 1995, 'Gender, Caste and Labour: Ideological and Material Structure of Widowhood'. *Economic and Political Weekly*: 30, 36: 2248–56.

Chakravarty, Uma 1996, 'The Myth of 'Patriots' & 'Traitors:' Pandita Ramabai, Brahmanical Patriarchy and Militant Hindu Nationalism', in *Embodied Violence: Communalising Women's Sexuality in South Asia*, edited by Kumari Jayawardena and Malathi di Alwis, London: Zed.

Chakravarty, Uma 1998, *Rewriting History: The Life and Times of Pandita Ramabai*, New Delhi: Kali for Women.

Chatterjee, K. Kumar 1976, *English Education in India*, Delhi: Macmillan Co. of India; Columbia, MO: South Asia Books.

Chatterjee, Partha 1982, 'Agrarian Relations and Communalism in Bengal, 1926–1935', in *Subaltern Studies I*, edited by Ranajit Guha, Delhi: Oxford University Press.

Chatterjee, Partha 1983, 'More on Modes of Power and the Peasantry', in *Subaltern Studies II*, edited by Ranajit Guha, Delhi: Oxford University Press.

Chatterjee, Partha 1984, 'Gandhi and the Critique of Civil Society', in *Subaltern Studies III*, edited by Ranajit Guha, Delhi: Oxford University Press.

Chatterjee, Partha 1986a, *Nationalist Thought and the Colonial World – A Derivative Discourse?* London: Zed.

Chatterjee, Partha 1986b, 'Transferring a Political Theory: Early Nationalist Thought in India', *Economic and Political Weekly*, 21, 3: 120–8.

Chatterjee, Partha 1989a, 'Colonialism, Nationalism, and Colonialised Women: The Contest in India', *American Ethnologist* 16, 4: 622–33.

Chatterjee, Partha 1989b, 'Caste and Subaltern Consciousness', in *Subaltern Studies VI*, edited by Ranajit Guha, Delhi: Oxford University Press.

Chatterjee, Partha 1990, 'The Nationalist Resolution of the Women's Question', in *Recasting Women: Essays in Colonial History*, edited by Kumkum Sangari and Sudesh Vaid, New Brunswick, New Jersey: Rutgers University Press.

Chatterjee, Partha 1993a, *The Nation and Its Fragments: Colonial and Postcolonial Histories*, Delhi: Oxford University Press.

Chatterjee, Partha 1993b, 'A Religion of Urban Domesticity: Sri Ramakrishna and the Calcutta Middle Class', in *Subaltern Studies VII*, edited by Partha Chatterjee and Gyanendra Pandey, Delhi: Oxford University Press.

Chatterjee, Partha 1994, 'Secularism and Toleration', *Economic and Political Weekly* 29, 28: 1768–77.

Chatterjee, Partha 1995, 'The Disciplines in Colonial Bengal', in *Texts of Power: Emerging Disciplines of Colonial Bengal*, edited by Partha Chatterjee, Minnesota: University of Minnesota Press.

Chattopadhyay, B.K. (ed.) 1982, *Jyotirindranather Jivansmriti* [Jyotirindranath's Reminiscences].

Chattopadhyay, Nagendranath 1928, *Mahatma Rammohan Rayer Jibansmriti* [Mahatma Rammohan Ray's Reminiscences].

Chattopadhyay, Ratnabali 1992, 'The Queen's Daughters: Prostitutes as Outcast Group in Colonial India', Occasional Paper, Christian Michelsen Institute, Bergen, Norway.

Chaudhuri, Nupur and Margaret Strobel (eds.) 1992, *Western Women and Imperialism: Complicity and Resistance*, Bloomington: Indiana University Press.

Chomsky, N. 1992, *Manufacturing Consent: Noam Chomsky and the Media*, video recording, Dir. M. Achbar and P. Wintonick, Montreal: Necessary Illusions and the National Film Board.

Choudhury, Hemantakumari 1901, 'Striloker Paricchad' [Women's Attire], *Antapur*, yr. 4 (6) (B.S. Ashad 1308): 137–40.

Choudhury, Tapan Ray 1988, *Europe Reconsidered: Perceptions of the West in Nineteenth Century Bengal*, Delhi: Oxford University Press.

Chowdhury, Indira 2001, *The Virile Hero and Virile History: Gender and the Politics of Culture in Colonial Bengal*, Delhi: Oxford University Press.

Cohn, Bernard 1983, 'Representing Authority in Victorian India' in *The Invention of Tradition*, edited by E. Hobsbawm and T. Ranger, Cambridge: Cambridge University Press.

Cohn, Bernard 1985, 'The Command of Language and The Language of Command' in *Subaltern Studies IV*, edited by Ranajit Guha, Delhi: Oxford University Press.

Cohn, Norman 1970, *The Pursuit of the Millennium*, New York: Oxford University Press.

Collins, Michael 2012, *Empire, Nationalism and the Post-colonial World: Rabindranath Tagore's Writings on History, Politics and Society*, New York: Routledge.

Collins, Patricia Hill 1990, *Black Feminist Thought: Knowledge, Consciousness, and the Politics of Empowerment*, London: Harper Collins.

Collins, Patricia Hill 1998, *Fighting Words: Black Women and the Search for Justice*, Minneapolis: University of Minnesota Press.

Collins, Winfield 1981, 'The Truth About Lynching and the Negro in the South', in *Women, Race and Class*, edited by A.Y. Davis, New York: Vintage.

Comaroff, Jean and John Comaroff 1991, *Of Revelation and Revolution*, Chicago: University of Chicago Press.

Connolly, William 1995, *The Ethos of Pluralisation*, Minneapolis: University of Minnesota Press.

Copely, A. 1989, *Sexual Moralities in France 1780–1980: New Ideas on the Family, Divorce and Homosexuality*, London: Routledge.

Corrigan, Philip 1981, 'On moral regulation: Some preliminary remarks', *The Sociological Review* 29, 2: 313–37.

Corrigan, P. and D. Sayer, 1985, *The Great Arch: English State Formation as Cultural Revolution*, Blackwell.

Crenshaw, Kimberlé 1989, 'Demarginalising the intersection of race and sex: A black feminist critique of antidiscrimination doctrine, feminist theory and anti-racist politics', *University of Chicago Legal Forum*, 139: 139–67.

Cruz, Jon 1996, 'From Farce to Tragedy: Reflections on the Reification of Race at Century's End', in *Mapping Multiculturalism*, edited by Avery Gordon and Christopher Newfield, Minneapolis: University of Minnesota Press.

Curtin, P.D. (ed.) 1971, *Imperialism*, New York: Harper and Row.

Das, Krishnabhabini 1888, 'Swadhin o Paradhin Nari Jiban' [Independent and Subjected Life of Woman], in *Pradip*.

Das, Krishnabhabini 1890a, 'Amader Hobe Ki?' [What Will Happen to Us?], in *Sahitya* (B.S. Kartik Chaitra 1296).

Das, Krishnabhabini 1890b, 'Samaj o Samaj Samskar' [Society and Social Reform], in *Bharati O Balak* (B.S. Poush, 1297, 14 yr.).

Das, Krishnabhabini 1891a, 'Ingraj Mahilar Shiksha O Swadhinatar Gati' [English Women's Progress in Education and Independence], in *Bharati O Balak* (BS Sraban 1297, 14 yr): 286–91.

Das, Krishnabhabini 1891b, 'Kindergarten', in *Bharati O Balak* (BS Sraban 1297).

Das, Krishnabhabini 1891c, 'Shikshita Nari' [The Educated Woman], in *Sahitya* (B.S. Sraban, 1298, 14 yr): 474–78.

Das, Krishnabhabini 1892, 'Striloker Kaj o Kajer Mahatya' [Women's Work and Its Value], in *Pradip*.

Das, Krishnabhabini 1893, 'Sansare Shishu' [Child in the Family], in *Sahitya* (B.S. Ashad, 1299, 3rd yr.).

Das, Sisir Kumar (ed.) 1996, *The English Writings of Rabindranath Tagore*, Volume 2, New Delhi: Sahitya Akademy.

Das Gupta, Tania 1989, 'Introducing Race, Class and Gender: Towards an Anti-Racist, Working Class Feminist Movement' in *Race, Class, Gender: Bonds and Barriers*, Winnipeg: Between the Lines.

Das Gupta, Anil Chandra (ed.) 1959, *The Days of John Company: Selections from Calcutta Gazette 1824–32*, Calcutta: Govt. Print.

Das Gupta, Uma (ed.) 2009, *The Oxford India Tagore: Selected Writings on Education and Nationalism*, New Delhi: Oxford University Press.

Dasi, Prafulla 2015, 'Hill of Resistance – Fight against bauxite mining in Niyamgiri', *Frontline*, 20 March 2015.

Dasi, Rasasundari 1868, *Amar Jiban* [My Life], reprint, Calcutta: Dey Bookstore, 1987.

Davidoff, Leonore and Catherine Hall 1987, *Family Fortunes: Men and Women of the English Middle Class, 1780–1850*, Chicago: University of Chicago Press.

Davis, Angela Y. 1983, *Women, Race and Class*, New York: Vintage.

Davis, Angela Y. 1996, 'Gender, Class and Multiculturalism: Rethinking "Race" Politics', in *Mapping Multiculturalism*, edited by Avery Gordon and Christopher Newfield, Minneapolis: University of Minnesota Press.

De, S.K. 1961, *Early History of the Vaisnava Faith and Movement in Bengal*, Calcutta: Firma KLM Private Ltd.

Debi, Gyanadanandini 1882, 'Stri Shiksha' [Women's Education], *Bharati* (BS Asvin 1288).

Debi, Gyanadanandini 1884, 'Samaj Samskar o Kusamskar' [Social Reform and Superstitions], *Bharati* (BS Asad, 1290, 7 yr).

Debi, Hiranmayee 1891a, 'Sutikagrihey Banaratwa' [Apishness in the Nursery], in *Bharatio Balak*, 483–91 (B.S. Poush 1298).

Debi, Hiranmayee 1891b, 'Newnham College', in *Bharati o Balak* (B.S. Chaitra 1298): 612–23.

Debi, Sarala 1906, 'Amar Balya Jiban' [My Childhood], in *Bharati* (B.S. Baisakh, 1312).

Debi, Sarojkumari 1923, 'Krishnabhabini Das' in *Bharati*, (B.S. Agrahayan 1329 yr. 46).

Debi, Swarnakumari 1888, 'Strishiksha o Bethune School' [Women's Education and Bethune School], in *Bharati o Balak* (B.S. 1294).

Debi, Swarnakumari 1916, 'Sekele Katha' [Story of Old Times], *Bharati*, (B.S. Chaitra 1322): 1124–24, reprint of 'Amader Griha Antahpur Shiksha O Tahar Samskar' [Domestic Education in Our Household and Its Tradition], *Pradip*, 1899.

Debi, Rasasundari 1987, *Amar Jibon*, Calcutta: College Street Prakashani.

Derrida, Jacques 1978, *Writing and Difference*, Chicago: The University of Chicago Press.

Desai, Radhika 2002, *Slouching Towards Ayodhya*, New Delhi: Three Essays.

Dirks, N.B. 1992, *Colonialism and Culture*, Ann Arbor: University of Michigan Press.

Dirks, N.B. 1993. 'The Home and the World: The Invention of Modernity in Colonial India', *Visual Anthropology Review*, 9, 2: 19–31.

Draper, Hal 1978, *Karl Marx's Theory of Revolution*, Volume 2: *The Politics of Social Classes*, New York: Monthly Review Press.

Du Bois, W.E.B. 1996 [1903], *The Souls of Black Folk*. New York: Penguin.

Dua, Enakshi, and Angela Robertson (eds.) 1999, *Scratching the Surface: Canadian Anti-Racist Feminist Thought*, Toronto: Women's Press.

Dumont, Louis 1970, *Homo Hierarchicus: An Essay on the Caste System*. Chicago: University of Chicago Press.

Dunn, Bill 2007, 'Accumulation by Dispossession or Accumulation by Capital? The Case of China', *Journal of Australian Political Economy* 60: 5–27.

Dutt, Bharka 2002, 'Nothing New? Women as Victims', in *Gujarat: The Making of Tragedy*, edited by S. Varadarajan, New Delhi: Penguin India.

Dutt, Madhusudan 1977, 'King Porus' in *Madhusudan Rachanabali*, edited by K. Gupta.

Dutt, Madhusudan 1977, *A Poem on the Death of Meghanada* in *Madhusudan Rachanabali*, edited by K. Gupta.

Dutt, Madhusudan 1977, 'The Anglo-Saxon and the Hindu' in *Madhusudan Rachanabali*, edited by K. Gupta.

Dutt, Madhusudan 1977 *Chaturdaspadi Kavya* (Sonnets) in *Madhusudan Rachanabali*, edited by K. Gupta.

Dutt, Utpal 1976, *Stanislavskir Path* [The Way of Stanislavski]. Calcutta.

Dutt, Utpal 1977, *Epic Theatre*. Calcutta.

Dutt, Utpal 1979 *Chaer Dhoan* [Steam of the Tea]. Calcutta.

Dutt, Utpal 1982, *Towards a Revolutionary Theatre*, Calcutta: Seagull Books.

Dutta, Krishna and Andrew Robinson (eds.) 1995, *Rabindranath Tagore: The Myriad Minded Man*, London: Bloomsbury.

Dutta, Krishna and Andrew Robinson (eds.) 1997, *Selected Letters of Rabindranath Tagore*, Cambridge: Cambridge University Press.

Dutta, Madhusree, Flavia Agnes, and Nira Adarkar (eds.) 1996, *The Nation, the State and Indian Identity*, Calcutta: Samya.

Dutta, P.K. (ed.) 2003, *Rabindranath Tagore's The Home and the World: A Critical Companion*, Delhi: Permanent Black.

Dworkin, Andrea 1980, *Pornography*, New York: William Morrow.

Eagleton, Terry, Fredric Jameson, and Edward Said 1990, *Nationalism, Colonialism and Literature*. Minneapolis: University of Minnesota Press.

Egan Carolyn, Linda L. Gardner and Judy V. Persad 1987, 'The Politics of Transformation: Struggles with Race, Class and Sexuality in the March 8th Coalition', in *Feminism and Political Economy: Women's Work, Women's Struggles*, edited by Heather J. Maroney and Meg Luxton, Toronto: Methuen.

Eisentein, Hester and Alice Jardine (eds.) 1985, *The Future of Difference*, New Brunswick: Rutgers University Press.

Eliott, Jean L. and Angie Fleras 1992, *Multiculturalism in Canada: The Challenge of Diversity*, Toronto: Nelson.

Emberly, Julia 1993 'Introduction: Articulating Difference(s)', in *Thresholds of Difference: Feminist Critique, Native Women's Writings, Postcolonial Theory*, Toronto: University of Toronto Press.

Engels, Dagmar 1996, *Beyond Purdah? Women in Bengal, 1890–1939*, Delhi: Oxford University Press.

Engels, Friedrich 1969 [1878], *Socialism: Utopian and Scientific*, trans. Edward Aveling, New York: International Publishers.

Engels, Friedrich 1972 [1884], 'The Origin of the Family, Private Property, and the State' (excerpts) in *The Marx-Engels Reader*, edited by Robert C. Tucker, New York: Norton.

Engineer, A. Ali 2003, *The Gujarat Carnage*, New Delhi: Orient Longman.

Enloe, C. 1990, 'Women and Children: Making Feminist Sense of the Persian Gulf Crisis'. *Village Voice*, 25 September.

Enloe, C. 2004, *'Gender' is not Enough: The Need for a Feminist Politics*. London: Wiley.

Enloe, C. 2014, *Bananas, Beaches and Bases: Making Feminist Sense of International Politics*, Berkeley: University of California Press.

Evans-Pritchard, Edward E. 1965, *Theories of Primitive Religion*, Oxford: Clarendon Press.

Fanon, Frantz 1963, *The Wretched of the Earth*, New York: Grove Press.

Fanon, Frantz 1967, *Black Skin, White Masks*, New York: Grove Press.

Fanon, Frantz 1990 [1952], 'The Fact of Blackness', in *Anatomy of Racism*, edited by D.T. Goldberg, Minneapolis: University of Minnesota Press.

Fanon, Frantz 1994 [1959], *A Dying Colonialism*, New York: Grove/Atlantic.

Firestone, Shulamith 1970, *The Dialectic of Sex*, New York: William Morrow and Company.

FitzGerald, Maureen (ed.) 1982, *Still Ain't Satisfied*, Toronto: Women's Press.

Fitzpatrick, Sheila 1970, *The Commissariat of Enlightenment: Soviet Organisation of Education and the Arts under Lunacharsky, October 1917–1921*, Cambridge: University Press.

Fleras, Angie, and Jean Leonard Elliot (eds.) 1992, *Multiculturalism in Canada: The Challenge of Diversity*, Scarborough ON: Nelson.

Forbes, G.H. 1975, *Positivism in Bengal: A Case Study in the Transmission and Assimilation of an Ideology*, Calcutta: Minerva Associates Publications.

Foucault, Michel 1979 [1975], *Discipline and Punish: The Birth of Prison*, New York: Vintage Books.

Foucault, Michel 1980a, *Power/Knowledge*, New York: Pantheon.

Foucault, Michel 1980b [1976], *The History of Sexuality*, Volume 1: *An Introduction*, New York: Vintage Books.

Foucault, Michel 2003a, *Abnormal: Lectures at the College de France 1974–1975*, New York: Picador.

Foucault, Michel 2003b, *'Society Must Be Defended': Lectures at the College de France 1975–1976*, New York: Picador.

Fox, Bonnie (ed.) 1980, *Hidden in the Household*, Toronto: Women's Press.

Frankenberg, Ruth 1993, *White Women, Race Matters: The Social Construction of Whiteness*, Minneapolis: University of Minnesota Press.

Franklin, Bruce 1972, *The Essential Stalin*, New York: Doubleday Anchor Paperback.

Fraser, Joyce 1980, *Cry of the Illegal Immigrant*, Toronto: Williams-Wallace.

Freire, Paulo 1970, *The Pedagogy of the Oppressed*, New York: Continuum.

Fukuyama, F. 1992, *End of History and the Last Man*, New York: Free Press.

Gangopadhyay, Jyotirmaree 1924, 'Gown o Sari' [Gown or Sari] in *Bharati*, (B.S. Aswin 1330).

Ganjavi, Mahdi (Interviewer) and Bannerji, Himani (interviewee) 2016, 'Ideology, Anti-colonialism and Marxism', in *The Bullet*, http://socialistproject.ca/bullet/1341.php.

Gates, Henry L. Jr. 1985, *'Race', Writing, and Difference*. Chicago: Chicago University Press.

Geertz, Clifford 1988, *Works and Lives: The Anthropologist as Author*, Stanford, CA: Stanford University Press.

Gellner, E. 1983, *Nations and Nationalism*, Oxford: Oxford University Press.

Gilman, Sander 1985a, 'Black Bodies, White Bodies: Toward an Iconography of Female Sexuality in Late Nineteenth Century Art, Medicine and Literature', in *'Race' Writing and Difference* edited by Henry Louis Gates Jr., Chicago: University of Chicago Press.

Gilman, Sander 1985b, *Difference and Pathology: Stereotypes of Sexuality, Race and Madness*, Ithaca: Cornell University Press.

Gilroy, Paul 1987, *Ain't No Black in the Union Jack: The Cultural Politics of Race and Nation*, London: Hutchinson.

Gilroy, Paul 1993, *Black Atlantic: Modernity's Double Consciousness*, London: Verso.

Gohain, Hiren 2011, 'Two Roads to Decolonisation: Tagore and Gandhi', *Economic and Political Weekly*, XLVI, 31: 23–6.

Goldberg, David T. 1993. *Racist Culture: Philosophy and the Politics of Meaning*, Oxford: Blackwell.

Goldberg, David T. (ed.) 1994, *Multiculturalism: A Critical Reader*, Oxford: Blackwell.

Gomez-Peña, Guillermo 1996, *The New World Border*, San Francisco: City Lights Books.

Gopal, S. 1996, 'Nehru, Religion and Secularism', in *Tradition, Dissent and Ideology: Essays in Honour of Romila Thapar*, edited by R. Champaka Lakshmi and S. Gopal, New Delhi: Oxford University Press.

Gordon, Avery and Christopher Newfield (eds.) 1996, *Mapping Multiculturalism*. Minneapolis: University of Minnesota Press.

Gorky, Maxim 1982, *Collected Works*, Volume 10, trans. Igor Kruvtson, Moscow: Progress Publishers.

Gould, Stephen J. 1981, *The Mismeasure of Man*. New York: Norton.

Government of Canada 1974, *A Report of the Canadian Immigration and Population Study: Immigration Policy Perspective*, Ottawa: Department of Manpower and Immigration and Information Canada.

Government of Canada 1984, *Royal Commission Report on Equality in Employment*, Ottawa: Ministry of Supply and Services.

Government of Canada 1986, *Equality Now: Report of the Special Committee on Visible Minorities*, Ottawa: House of Commons.

Government of India 1882, Legislative Department, *Papers (Nos. 4, 11, 12) Relative to The Bill to Amend the Indian Penal Code and the Code of Criminal Procedure* (Indian Office Library and Records [IOLR]).

Gowalkar, M.S. 1939, *We, or Our Nationhood Defined*, Nagpur: Bharat Publications.

Gowalkar, M.S. 1963, *Bunch of Thoughts*, Bangalore: Jagarana Prakashan.

Gramsci, Antonio 1971, *Selections from the Prison Notebooks*, trans. and edited by Q. Hoare and G. Smith, New York: International Publishers.

Grotowski, Jerzy 1968, *Towards a Poor Theatre*, New York: Simon and Shuster.

Guha, Ranajit 1982a, *A Rule of Property for Bengal: An Essay on the Idea of Permanent Settlement*, New Delhi: Oxford University Press.

Guha, Ranajit 1982b, 'On Some Aspects of the Historiography of Colonial India', in *Subaltern Studies I*, edited by Ranajit Guha, Delhi: Oxford University Press.

Guha, Ranajit 1983, *Elementary Aspects of Peasant Insurgency in Colonial India*. Delhi: Oxford University Press.

Guha, Ranajit 1985, 'Chandra's Death', in *Subaltern Studies V*, edited by Ranajit Guha, Delhi: Oxford University Press.

Habermas, Jurgen 1975, *Legitimation Crisis*, Boston: Beacon Press.

Hall, Catherine 1992, 'Feminism and Feminist History', in *White, Male and Middle Class: Explorations in Feminism and History*, New York: Routledge.

Hall, Stuart 1992, 'New Ethnicities', in *'Race' Culture and Difference*, edited by James Donald and Ali Ratansi, London: Sage.

Hamilton, Roberta, and Michele Barrett (eds.) 1986, *The Politics of Diversity: Feminism, Marxism and Nationalism*, London: Verso.

Harding, Sandra (eds.) 1993, *The 'Racial' Economy of Science: Toward a Democratic Future*, Bloomington: Indiana University Press.

Harding, Sandra and Merrill B. Hintikka (eds.) 1983, *Discovering Reality*, Dordrecht, Holland: D. Reidel.

Haris, Kathryn 1989, 'New Alliances: Socialist Feminism in the Eighties', *Feminist Review*, 31: 34–54.

Hartmann, Heidi I. 1979, 'The Unhappy Marriage of Marxism and Feminism: Towards a More Progressive Union', *Capital & Class* 3,2: 1–33.

Hartsock, Nancy 1984, *Money, Sex and Power: Toward a Feminist Historical Materialism*, Boston: Northeastern University Press.

Harvey, David 1989, *The Conditions of Post-Modernity: An Enquiry into the Origins of Cultural Change*, Oxford: Blackwell.

Harvey, David 2005, *The New Imperialism*, Oxford: Oxford University Press.

Hasan, Zoya (ed.) 1994, *Forging Identities: Gender, Communities and the State*, New Delhi: Kali for Women.

Hasan, Zoya (ed.) 2000, *Politics and the State in India*, New Delhi: Sage.

Hegel, G.W.F. 1956 [1805], *The Philosophy of History*, New York: Dover Publications.

Hendricks, Margo and Patricia Parker (eds.) 1994, *Women, 'Race' and Writing*, London: Routledge.

Herf, Jeffrey 1986, *Reactionary Modernism: Technology, Culture, and Politics in Weimar and the Third Reich*, Cambridge: Cambridge University Press.

Hill, Christopher 1975, *The World Turned Upside Down: Radical Ideas During the English Revolution*, London: Penguin.

Hobsbawm, Eric 1964, 'Introduction' in *Pre-capitalist Economic Formations*, London: Lawrence and Wishart.

Hobsbawm, Eric 1974, *Industry and Empire*, Harmondsworth: Penguin Books.

Hobsbawm, Eric 1979, *The Age of Capital, 1848–1875*, New York: Mentor Books.

Hobsbawm, Eric 1990, *Nations and Nationalism Since 1780: Programme, Myth, Reality*, Cambridge: Cambridge University Press.

Hobsbawm, Eric 1996, *The Age of Revolution*, New York: Mentor Books.

Hobsbawm, Eric and T. Ranger (eds.) 1984, *The Invention of Tradition*, Cambridge: Cambridge University Press.

hooks, bell 1981, *Ain't I a Woman? Black Women and Feminism*, Boston: South End Press.

hooks, bell 1991, 'Sisterhood: Political Solidarity between Women', in *A Reader in Feminist Knowledge*, edited by S. Gunew, London: Routledge.

Huntington, S. 1996, *The Clash of Civilisations and the Remaking of the New World Order*, New York: Simon and Shuster.

Hyam, Ronald 1992, *Empire and Sexuality: The British Experience*, Manchester: Manchester University Press.

Ignatieff, Michael 1993, *Blood and Belonging: Journeys into the New Nationalisms*, London: BBC Books and London: Chatto and Windus.

Iliah, Kancha 1998, *Why I am not a Hindu*, Kolkata: Stree Publications.

Inden, Ronald 1990, *Imagining India*, Oxford: Basil Blackwell.

Ismail, Qadri and Pradeep Jeganathan (eds.) 1995, *Unmaking the Nation: The Politics of Identity and History in Modern Sri Lanka*, Colombo: Social Scientists' Association.

Jayawardena, K. 1986, *Feminism and Nationalism in the Third World*, London: Zed.

Jayawardena, Kumari, and Malathi de Alwis (eds.) 1996, *Embodied Violence: Communalising Women's Sexuality in South Asia*, London: Zed.

Jones, William 1799, *The Works of Sir William Jones*, Vol. I, London: Printed for G.G. and J. Robinson.

Jones, William 1970, *The Letters from William Jones*, edited by Gerland Cannon, 2 Volumes, Oxford: Clarendon Press.

Jordan, June 1989, *Moving Towards Home: Political Essays*. London: Virago.

Joseph, Gloria 1981, 'The Incompatible Ménage à Trois: Marxism, Feminism and Racism', in *Women and Revolution*, Boston: South End Press.

Joshi, V.C. (ed.) 1975, *Rammohun Roy and the Process of Modernisation in India*, New Delhi: Vikas.

Karlekar, M. 1991, *Voices from Within: Early Personal Narratives of Bengali Women*, Delhi: Oxford University Press.

Kaviraj, Sudipta 1995, *The Unhappy Consciousness: Bankimchandra Chattopadhyay and the Formation of Nationalist Discourse in India*, Delhi: Oxford University Press.

Khan, N.S. (ed.) 1992, *Voices Within: Dialogues with Women on Islam*, Lahore: ASR.

Khastagiri, Shrimati Soudamini 1872, 'Strigoner Parichad' [Women's Clothes], in *Bamabodhini Patrika*, 97 (8), (B.S. Bhadra 1278).

Kline, M. 1989, 'Women's Oppression and Racism: A Critique of the "Feminist Standpoint"', in *Race, Class, Gender: Bonds and Barriers*, Toronto: Between the Lines.

Krishnaraj, Maithreyi 1995, 'Motherhood: Power and Powerlessness', in *Indian Women: Myth snd Reality*, edited by Jasodhara Bagchi, Hyderabad: Sangam.

Kosambi, Meera 1991, 'Girl-Brides and Socio-Legal Change: Age of Consent Bill (1891) Controversy', *Economic and Political Weekly* 26, 31 & 32: 1856–68.

Kuhn, Annette and Ann Marie Wolpe 1980, *Feminism and Materialism: Women and Modes of Production*, London: Routledge and Kegan Paul.

Kuhn, Thomas 1970, *The Structure of Scientific Revolution*, Chicago: University of Chicago Press.

Kulchyski, Peter (ed.) 1994, *Unjust Relations: Aboriginal Rights in Canadian Courts*. Toronto: University of Toronto Press.

Kumar, Radha 1993, *The History of Doing: An Illustrated Account of Movements for Women's Rights and Feminism in India, 1800–1990*, New Delhi: Kali for Women.

Kuznets, S. 1966. *Modern Economic Growth: Rate, Structure, and Spread* (Volume 2). New Haven: Yale University Press.

Kymlicka, Will 1995, *Multicultural Citizenship: A Liberal Theory of Minority Rights*, Oxford: Clarendon Press.

Lacqueur, T and C. Gallagher (eds.) 1987, *The Making of the Modern Body: Sexuality and Society in the Nineteenth Century*, Berkeley and Los Angeles: University of California Press.

Laclau, Ernesto 1979, *Politics and Ideology in Marxist Theory*, London: Verso.

Laclau, Ernesto, and Chantal Mouffe 2001, *Hegemony and Socialist Strategy: Towards a Radical Democratic Politics*. London: Verso.

Law Union of Ontario 1981, *The Immigrants Handbook*. Montreal: Black Rose Books.

Lawrence, Errol 1982, 'Just Plain Common Sense: The 'Roots' of Racism', in *The Empire Strikes Back: Race and Racism in 70s Britain*, London: Hutchinson, in association with the Centre for Cultural Studies, University of Birmingham.

Lele, Jayant 1995, *Hindutva: The Emergence of the Right*, Madras: Earthworm.

Lenin, Vladimir Ilich 1970 [1902], *What is To Be Done?*, London: Panther.

Levin, P. 1987, *Victorian Feminism: 1850–1900*, London: Hutchinson.

Levin, P. 1994, 'Veneral Disease, Prostitution, and the Politics of Empire: The Case of British India', *Journal of the History of Sexuality*, 4, 4: 579–602.

Li, Peter S. 1993, 'Chinese Investment and Business in Canada: Ethnic Entrepreneurship Reconsidered', *Pacific Affairs* 66, 2: 219–43.

Liddel, Joanna, and Rama Joshi (eds.) 1986, *Daughters of Independence: Gender, Caste and Class in India*, London and New Delhi: Kali for Women and Zed.

Lloyd, Genevieve 1984, *The Man of Reason: 'Male' and 'Female' in Western Philosophy*, London: Methuen.

Long, Rev. J. 1974, *Calcutta in the Olden Times*, reprinted in *Nineteenth Century Studies 5*.

Loomba, Ania 1998, *Colonialism/Postcolonialism*, London: Routledge.

Lukács, George 1971 [1923], *History and Class Consciousness*, London: The Merlin Press.

Lukács, George 1980, *The Ontology of Social Being (vol.3): Labour*, trans. by David Fernbach, London: Merlin Press.

Lutz, Catherine and Jane L. Collins 1993, *Reading National Geographic*, Chicago: University of Chicago Press.

Luxton, Meg 1980, *More Than a Labour of Love*, Toronto: Women's Press.

Lyall, A.C. 1884, *Asiatic Studies, Religious and Social*. London: J. Murray.

MacKinnon, Catherine 1982, 'Feminism, Marxism, Method, and the State: An Agenda for Theory', *Signs: Journal of Women in Culture and Society*, 7, 3: 516–44.

Macpherson, C.B. 1977, *The Life and Times of Liberal Democracy*, Oxford: Oxford University Press.

Madan, T.N. 1998, 'Secularism in its Place', in *Secularism and its Critics*, edited by Rajeev Bhargava, Delhi: Oxford University Press.

Maine, H.S., 1876. *Village-communities in the East and West*. London: John Murray.

Majeed, Javed 1992, *Ungoverned Imaginings: James Mill's The History of British India and Orientalism*, Oxford: Clarendon Press.

Mandal, D. 1993, *Ayodhya: Archeology after Demolition*, Hyderabad: Orient Longman.

Mani, Lata 1990, 'Contentious Traditions: The Debate on Sati in Colonial India', in Sangari and Vaid, *Recasting Women: Essays in Indian Colonial History*, New Brunswick, NJ: Rutgers University Press.

Mani, Lata 1992, 'Cultural Theory, Colonial Texts: Reading Eyewitness Accounts of Widow Burning', in *Cultural Studies*, edited by L. Grossberb et al, New York: Routledge.

Mani, Lata 1998, *Contentious Traditions: The Debate on Sati in Colonial India*. Berkeley: University of California Press.

Marcuse, H. 1970, *Reason and Revolution*, Boston: Beacon Press.

Maroney, Heather Jon and Meg Luxton (eds.) 1987, *Feminism and Political Economy: Women's Work, Women's Struggles*, Toronto: Methuen.

Marshall, T.H. 1950, *Citizenship and Social Class*, Cambridge: Cambridge University Press.

Marshman, J.C. 1864, *Life and Times of Carey, Marshman and Ward*, London: Strahan.

Martin, J.R. 1837, *Notes on the Medical Topography of Calcutta*, Calcutta: Huttman.

Marx, Karl 1964a, *Pre-Capitalist Economic Formations*, edited by Eric Hobsbawm, New York: International Publishers.

Marx, Karl 1964b, *The Economic and Philosophical Manuscripts of 1844*, edited by Dirk Struik, New York: International Publishers.

Marx, Karl 1971a [1867], *Capital*, Volume 1, Moscow: Progress Publishers.

Marx, Karl 1971b [1894], *Capital*, Volume 3, Moscow: Progress Publishers.

Marx, Karl 1972b [1844], 'On the Jewish Question' (excerpts) in *The Marx-Engels Reader*, edited by Robert C. Tucker, New York: Norton.

Marx, Karl 1972c [1852], 'The Eighteenth Brumaire of Louis Bonaparte' in *The Marx-Engels Reader*, edited by Robert C. Tucker, New York: Norton.

Marx, Karl 1972d [1871], 'Civil War in France' in *The Marx-Engels Reader*, edited by Robert C. Tucker, New York: Norton.

Marx, Karl 1972e [1844], 'Contribution to the Critique of Hegel's *Philosophy of Right*: Introduction', in *The Marx-Engels Reader*, edited by Robert C. Tucker, New York: Norton.

Marx, Karl 1973 [1939], *Grundrisse: Foundations of the Critique of Political Economy (Rough Draft)*, trans. by Martin Nicolaus, London: Penguin Books, New Left Review.

Marx, Karl, and Friedrich Engels 1970 [1932], *The German Ideology*, edited by C.J. Arthur, New York: International Publishers.

Marx, Karl, and Friedrich Engels 1970 [1888], 'Theses on Feuerbach' in *The German Ideology*, edited by C.J. Arthur, New York: International Publishers.

Marx, Karl, and Friedrich Engels 1972 [1848], 'The Manifesto of the Communist Party' in *The Marx-Engels Reader*, edited by Robert C. Tucker, New York: Norton.

Marx, Karl, and Friedrich Engels 1972a [1845], 'The Holy Family' (excerpts) in *The Marx-Engels Reader*, edited by Robert C. Tucker, New York: Norton.

Maunaguru, S. 1995, 'Gendering Tamil Nationalism', in *Unmaking the Nation: The Politics of Identity and History in Modern Sri Lanka*, edited by P. Jeganathan and Q. Ismail, Colombo: Social Scientists' Association.

McClintock, Anne 1995, *Imperial Leather: Race, Gender, and Sexuality in the Colonial Contest*, London: Routledge.

McCallum, Pamela 1985, 'Woman as Ecriture or Woman as Other', *Canadian Journal of Political and Social Theory* 9, 1–2: 127–32.

McGifford, Diane, and Judith Kearn (eds.) 1990, *Shakti's Words*, Toronto: TSAR.

McLaren, Peter (ed.) 1997, *Revolutionary Multiculturalism: Pedagogies of Dissent in the New Millennium*. Boulder, Colorado: Westview Press.

McNally, David 2011, *Global Slump: The Economics and Politics of Crisis and Resistance*, Blackpoint, N.S.: Fernwood.

Mészáros, I. 1970, *Marx's Theory of Alienation*, London: Merlin Press.

Midgley, Clare (ed.) 1998, *Gender and Imperialism*, Manchester: Manchester University Press.

Miles, Angela 1985, 'Feminist Radicalism in the 1980s', *Canadian Journal of Political and Social Theory: Feminism Now* 9, 1–2: 16–39.

Miliband, Ralph 1984, *The State in Capitalist Society*, London: Quartet Books.

Mill, James 1968 [1817], *The History of British India*, 2 Volumes, with notes by H.H. Wilson and Introduction by John K. Galbraith, New York: Chelsea House.

Mill, J. Stuart 1972 [1859], 'On Liberty', in *Utilitarianism, Liberty and Representative Government*, edited by H.B. Acton, London: J.M. Dent.

Millet, Kate 1971, *Sexual Politics*, London: Sphere.

Minh-ha, Trin 1989, *Woman Native Other*, Bloomington: Indiana University Press.

Mistry, Rohinton 1995, *A Fine Balance*. Toronto: McClelland & Stewart.

Mitchell, Juliet and Ann Oakley (eds.) 1976, *The Rights and Wrongs of Women*, Harmondswort: Penguin.

Mitchell, Juliet and Ann Oakley (eds.) 1986, *What is Feminism?* New York: Pantheon.

Mitter, Baboo Kissory Chand 1834, *Rammohan Roy*, reprinted in *Nineteenth Century Studies* (Jan 1973).

Mitter, Swasti 1986, *Common Fate, Common Bond: Women in the Global Economy*, London. Pluto.

Modood, Tariq 1990, 'Political Blackness and British Asians', *Sociology* 28, 3: 859–76.

Moghadam, V. 1997, 'Nationalist Agendas and Women's Rights: Conflicts in Afghanistan in the Twentieth Century', in *Feminist Nationalism*, edited by L.A. West, New York: Routledge.

Mohammad, Abdul Jan 1986, 'The Economy of Manichean Allegory: The Function of Racial Difference in Colonial Literature', in *'Race', Writing and Difference*, edited by Henry Louis Gates, Chicago: University of Chicago Press.

Mohanty, Chandra Talpade 1991a, 'Introduction: Cartographies of Struggle: Third World Women and the Politics of Feminism', in *Third World Women and the Politics of Feminism*, edited by C. Mohanty, Ann Russo, and Lourdes Torres, Bloomington: Indiana University Press.

Mohanty, Chandra Talpade 1991b, 'Under Western Eyes: Feminist Scholarship and Colonial Discourses', in *Third World Women and the Politics of Feminism*, edited by C. Mohanty, Ann Russo, and Lourdes Torres, Bloomington: Indiana University Press.

Mohanty, Chandra, Ann Russo, and Lourdes Torres (eds.) 1991, *Third World Women and the Politics of Feminism*, Bloomington, Indiana: Indiana University Press.

Moi, Toril 1985 'Who is Afraid of Virginia Woolf: Feminist Readings of Woolf', *Canadian Journal of Political and Social Theory* 9, 1–2: 134–47.

Monture-Angus, Patricia 1995, *Thunder in My Soul: A Mohawk Woman Speaks*, Halifax, Nova Scotia: Fernwood Press.

Moore, J. Barrington 1967, *Social Origins of Dictatorship and Democracy: Lord and Peasant in the Making of the Modern World*. Boston: Beacon Press.

Mueller, F. Max 2000 [1883], *India: What Can It Teach Us?* New Delhi: Penguin India.

Mukherjee, Ramkrishna 1957, *The Dynamics of a Rural Society: A Study of the Economic Structure in Bengal Villages*, Berlin: Akademie-Verlag.

Mukhopadhyaya, K. 1952 *Bangla Natyashalar Itihas* [The History of Bengali Stage].

Murshid, Ghulam 1983, *Reluctant Debutante: Response of Bengali Women to Modernisation, 1849–1905*, Rajshahi: Shahitya Samsad, Rajshahi University.

Mustafi, Nagendrabala 1896, *Bamabodhini* (B.S. Vaisakh 1302).

Muthu, Sankar 2000, *Enlightenment Against Empire*, Princeton: Princeton University Press.

Nair, Janak 1994. 'On the Question of Agency in Indian Feminist Historiography', *Gender and History* 6, 1: 82–100.

Nandy, Ashis 1983, *The Intimate Enemy: Loss and Recovery of Self under Colonialism*, Delhi: Oxford University Press.

Nandy, Ashis 1994, *The Illegitimacy of Nationalism: Rabindranath Tagore and the Politics of the Self*, Delhi: Oxford University Press.

Nandy, Ashis 1998, 'The Politics of Secularism and the Recovery of Religious Tolerance', in *Secularism and its Critics*, edited by Rajeev Bhargava, Delhi: Oxford University Press.

Narain, V. 2000, *Gender and Community: Muslim Women's Rights in India*, Toronto: University of Toronto Press.

Ng, Roxana 1989, 'Sexism, Racism, Nationalism' in *Race, Class, Gender: Bonds and Barriers*, edited by Jessie Vorst, et al. Winnipeg: Between the Lines.

Ng, Roxana 1993, 'Sexism, Racism, Canadian Nationalism'. in *Returning the Gaze: Essays on Racism, Feminism and Politics*, edited by Himani Bannerji, Toronto: Sister Vision Press.

Niranjana, Tejaswini 1990, 'Translation, Colonialism and the Rise of English', *Economic and Political Weekly*, 25, 15: 773–7.

Niranjana, Tejaswini 1992, *Siting Translation: History, Post-Structuralism, and the Colonial Context*. Berkeley: University of California Press.

Noorani, A.G. 2000, *The RSS and the BJP: A Division of Labour*, New Delhi: Leftword.

Norris, Christopher 1993, *The Truth about Post-Modernism*, Oxford: Blackwell.

Nussbaum, Martha 1994, 'Patriotism and Cosmopolitanism', *Boston Review* 19, 5.

O'Brien, Mary 1981, *The Politics of Reproduction*, Boston: Routledge.

O'Hanlon, Rosalind 1988, 'Recovering the Subject: Subaltern Studies and Histories of Resistance in Colonial South Asia', *Modern Asian Studies* 22,1: 189–224.

O'Hanlon, Rosalind, and David Washbrook 1992, 'After Orientalism: Culture, Criticism, and Politics in the Third World', *Comparative Studies in Society and History* 34, 1: 141–67.

Ollman, Bertell 1971, *Alienation: Marx's Conception of Man in Capitalist Society*, New York: Cambridge University Press.

Omvedt, Gail 1993, *Reinventing Revolution: New Social Movements and the Socialist Tradition in India*, New York: Eastgate.

Pandey, Gyanendra 1978, *The Ascendency of the Congress in Uttar Pradesh, 1926–34: A Study in Imperfect Mobilisation*, New York: Oxford University Press.

Pandey, Gyanendra 1990, *The Construction of Communalism in Colonial North India*, Delhi: Oxford University Press.

Pandey, Gyanendra 1991, 'In Defence of the Fragment: Writing about Hindu Muslim Riot in India Today'. *Economic and Political Weekly*, Annual Number.

Parenti, Michael 1996, *Dirty Truths*. San Francisco: City Lights Books.

Parmar, Pratibha 1982, 'Gender, Race and Class: Asian Women in Resistance', in Centre for Contemporary Cultural Studies, *The Empire Strikes Back: Race and Racism in 70s Britain*.

Parmar, Prathiba 1990, 'Black Feminism: The Politics of Articulation', in *Identity, Community, Culture, Difference*, edited by Jonathan Rutherford, London: Lawrence and Wishart.

Patel, R. 1991, *Socio-economic Political Status and Women and Law in Pakistan*, Karachi: Faiza.

Pateman, Carole, and Mary Lyndon Shanley 1991, 'Introduction' in *Feminist Interpretations and Political Theory*, University Park, PA: Penn State University Press.

Porter, John 1965, *The Vertical Mosaic*, Toronto: University of Toronto Press.

Pratt, Mary Louise 1992, *Imperial Eyes: Travel Writing and Transculturation*, London: Routledge.

Radcliffe-Brown, Alfred 1965, *Structure and Function in Primitive Society*, New York: The Free Press.

Rajlakshmi, K. 2015, 'Land Bill Hits a Wall' in *Frontline*, 20 March 2015.

Randall, Margaret 1983, *Christians in the Nicaraguan Revolution, Interviews with Margaret Randall*, trans. Mariana Valverde, Vancouver: New Star Books.

Raphael, Max 1980, *Proudhon, Marx, Picasso: Three Studies in the Sociology of Art*, New Jersey: Humanities Press.

Rashid, A. 2000, *Taliban: Militant Islam, Oil and Fundamentalism in Central Asia*, New Haven: Yale University Press.

Raychaudhuri, Tapan 1988, *Europe Reconsidered: Perceptions of the West in Nineteenth Century Bengal*, Delhi: Oxford University Press.

Raychoudhury, G.P. 1884, *Grihalakshmi* [The Goddess Laxmi of the Hearth], Calcutta.

Razack, Sherene 2002, *Race, Space, and the Law: Unmapping a White Settler Society*, Toronto: Between the Lines Press.

Riley, Denise 1988, *'Am I That Name?': Feminism and the Category of 'Women' in History*, Minneapolis: University of Minnesota Press.

Robb, Martin 1992, *Shades of Right: Nativist and Fascist Politics in Canada, 1920–1940*, Toronto: University of Toronto Press.

Robinson, Cedric 1996, 'Manichaeism and Multiculturalism', in *Mapping Multiculturalism*, edited by Avery Gordon and Christopher Newfield, Minneapolis: University of Minnesota Press.

Roediger, David R. 1992, *The Wages of Whiteness: Race and the Making of the American Working Class*, London: Verso.

Roman, Leslie 1993, 'White is a Color! White Defensiveness, Postmodernism and Anti-Racist Pedagogy', in *Race, Identity and Representation in Education* edited by Warren Crichlow and Cameron McCarthy, New York and London: Routledge, 1993.

Rostow, W.W. 1985, *The Stages of Economic Growth: A non-Communist Manifesto*, Cambridge: Cambridge University Press.

Rouse, Shahnaz 1996, 'Gender, Nationalism(s) and Cultural Identity', in *Embodied Violence: Communalising Women's Sexuality in South Asia*, edited by Kumari Jayawardena and Malathi di Alwis, London: Zed.

Rowbotham, Sheila 1973. *Hidden from History: Rediscovering Women in History from the 17th Century to the Present*, London: Pluto Press.

Rowbotham, Sheila 1974, *Women, Resistance and Revolution*, New York: Vintage Books.

Roy, Rammohan 1820, *A Second Conference between an Advocate for and an Opponent of the Practice of Burning Widows Alive*, Calcutta.

Roy, Rammohan 1973 [1802], *Tuhfatul Muwahiddin*, reprinted in *Nineteenth Century Studies* (Jan 1973).

Said, Edward 1981, *Covering Islam: How the Media and the Experts Determine How We See the Rest of the World*, New York: Pantheon Books.

Said, Edward 1979, *Orientalism*. New York: Vintage.

Said, Edward 1993, *Culture and Imperialism*, New York: Vintage Books.

Sahlins, Marshal 1968, *Tribesmen*, Englewood Cliffs, N.J.: Prentice Hall.

Sandoval, Chela 1991, 'U.S. Third World Feminism: The Theory and Method of Oppositional Consciousness in the Postmodern World', *Genders* 10: 1–24.

Sangari, Kumkum 1995, 'Politics of Diversity – Religious Communities and Multiple Patriarchies', *Economic and Political Weekly* 30, 51: 3287–310; 30, 52: 3381–9.

Sangari, Kumkum and Sudesh Vaid (eds.) 1990, *Recasting Women: Essays in Indian Colonial History*, New Brunswick, NJ: Rutgers University Press.

Sangari, Kumkum and Sudesh Vaid (eds.) 1996, 'Widow Immolation in Contemporary Rajasthan' in *Embodied Violence: Communalising Women's Sexuality in South Asia*, edited by K. Jayawardena and M. de Alwis, London: Zed Books.

Sargent, Lydia (ed.) 1981, *Women and Revolution: A Discussion of the Unhappy Marriage of Marxism and Feminism*, Boston: South End Press.

Sarkar, Sumit 1973, *The Swadeslii Movement in Bengal, 1903–1908*, Delhi: People's Publishing House.

Sarkar, Sumit 1983, *Popular Movements and Middle Class Leadership in Late Colonial India: Perspectives and Problems of a 'History from Below'*, Calcutta: K.P. Bagchi.

Sarkar, Sumit 1984, 'The Conditions and Nature of Subaltern Militancy: Bengal from Swadeshi to Non-Cooperation, c. 1905–22', In *Subaltern Studies III*, edited by Ranajit Guha, Delhi: Oxford University Press.

Sarkar, Sumit 1985, *A Critique of Colonial India*. Calcutta: Papyrus.

Sarkar, Sumit 1985, 'The 'Women's Question' in Nineteenth Century Bengal', in *A Critique of Colonial India*. Calcutta: Papyrus.

Sarkar, Sumit 1988, *Modern India 1885–1947*, New York: Saint Martin's Press.

Sarkar, Sumit 1990, *Marxian Approaches to the History of Indian Nationalism*, Calcutta: K.P. Bagchi.

Sarkar, Sumit 1993, 'The Fascism of the Sangh Parivar', *Economic and Political Weekly* 27, 5: 163–7.

Sarkar, Sumit 1994, 'Orientalism Revisited: Saidian Frameworks in the Writing of Modern Indian History', *Oxford Literary Review* 16, 1–2: 205–24.

Sarkar, Sumit 1997a, *Writing Social History*, Delhi: Oxford University Press.

Sarkar, Sumit 1997b, 'The Many Worlds of Indian History', in *Writing Social History*, Delhi: Oxford University Press.

Sarkar, Sumit 1997c, 'The Decline of the Subaltern in Subaltern Studies', in *Writing Social History*, Delhi: Oxford University Press.

Sarkar, Sumit 1997d, 'Kaliyuga, Chakri and Bhakti: Ramakrishna and His Time', in *Writing Social History*, Delhi: Oxford University Press.

Sarkar, Sumit 1997e, 'Vidyasagar and Brahmanical Society', in *Writing Social History*. Delhi: Oxford University Press.

Sarkar, Sumit 1997f, 'Renaissance and Kaliyuga: Myth, Time and History in Colonial Bengal', in *Writing Social History*, Delhi: Oxford University Press.

Sarkar, Sumit 2002, *Beyond Nationalist Frames: Relocating Postmodernism, Hindutva, History*, Delhi: Permanent Black.

Sarkar, Susobhan 1970, 'Rabindranath Tagore and the Renaissance in Bengal', in *Bengal Renaissance and Other Essays*, Delhi: People's Publishing House.

Sarkar, Susobhan 1985 [1946], *On the Bengal Renaissance*, Calcutta: Papyrus.

Sarkar, Tanika 1987, 'Nationalist Iconography: Image of Women in Nineteenth Century Bengali Literature', *Economic and Political Weekly*, 22, 47: 2011–15.

Sarkar, Tanika 1989, *Indian Woman: Myth and Reality*, National Seminar Papers, School of Women's Studies, Jadavpur University, Calcutta.

Sarkar, Tanika 1992a 'The Hindu Wife and the Hindu Nation: Domesticity and Nationalism in Nineteenth Century Bengal', *Studies in History* 8, 2: 213–35.

Sarkar, Tanika 1992b, 'Rhetoric against Age of Consent: Resisting Colonial Reason and Death of a Child Wife', *Economic and Political Weekly*, 28, 36: 1869–78.

Sarkar, Tanika 1993a, 'Women's Agency within Authoritarian Communalism: The Rashtrasevika Samiti and Ramjanmabhoomi', in *Hindus and Others: The Question of Identity in India Today*, edited by Gyanendra Pandey, New Delhi: Viking.

Sarkar, Tanika 1993b, 'A Book of Her Own, a Life of Her Own: Autobiography of a Nineteenth Century Woman', *History Workshop Journal* 36: 35–65.

Sarkar, Tanika 2001, *Hindu Wife, Hindu Nation: Community, Religion and Cultural Nationalism*, Bloomington: Indiana University Press.

Sarkar, T. and U. Butalia 1995, *Women and Right-Wing Movements: Indian Experiences*, London: Zed Books.

Sarton, Andrew 2008, *Bengal in Global Concept History: Culturalism in the Age of Capital*, Chicago: University of Chicago Press.

Sassen Saskia 1999, *Globalisation and its Discontents*, New York: New Press.

Sassen Saskia 2014, *Expulsions: Brutality and Complexity in the Gobal Economy*, Cambridge MA: Harvard University Press.

Savarkar, V.D. 1923, *Hindutva: Who is a Hindu?* Pune: (Publisher unknown).

Savarkar, V.D. 1967. *Historic Statements*, Bombay: (Publisher unknown).

Scott, J. Wallach 1988, 'Women in *The Making of the English Working Class*', in *Gender and the Politics of History*, New York: Columbia University Press.

Seagal, Lynne 1987, *Is the Future Female? Troubled Thoughts on Contemporary Feminism*, London: Virago.

Seal, Anil 1968, *The Emergence of Indian Nationalism – Competition and Collaboration in the Later Nineteenth Century*, Cambridge: Cambridge University Press.

Sehanabis, Chinmohan 1983, *Rabindranather Antarjatik Chinta* [Rabindranath's Thoughts on the Socially Marginalised], Calcutta: Nabhana.

Sekyi-Otu, Ato 1996, *Fanon's Dialectic of Experience*. Cambridge: Harvard University Press.

Sen, Asok 1977, *Ishwar Chandra Vidyasagar and the Elusive Milestones*, Calcutta: Riddhi-India.

Sen, Asok 1987, 'Subaltern Studies: Capital, Class and Community' in *Subaltern Studies V* edited by Ranajit Guha, Delhi: Oxford University Press.

Setalvad, Teesta 2002, 'When Guardians Betray: The Role of the Police', in *Gujarat: The Making of Tragedy*, edited by S. Varadarajan, New Delhi: Penguin India.

Seth, S.L. 2000, 'Changing Terms of Elite Discourse: The Case of Reservation for "Other" Backward Classes', in *Politics and the State in India*, edited by Zoya Hassan, New Delhi: Sage.

Shah, Ghanashyam 2002, *Caste and Democratic Politics in India*, Delhi: Permanent Black.

Shastri, Sibnath 1972, *A History of the Renaissance in Bengal: Ramtanu Lahiri, Brahman and Reformer*, Calcutta: Editions Indian.

Silva, P.L. de 1995, 'The Efficacy of the Combat Mode', in *Unmaking the Nation: The Politics of Identity and History in Modern Sri Lanka*, edited by P. Jeganathan and Q. Ismail, Colombo: Social Scientists' Association.

Silvera, Makeda 1983, *Silenced: Caribbean Domestic Workers Talk with Makeda Silvera*, Toronto: Williams-Wallace.

Silvera, Makeda 1989, *Silenced: Talks with Working Class Caribbean Women about Their Lives and Struggles as Domestic Workers in Canada*, 2nd edition, Toronto: Sister Vision.

Sinha, Kaliprasanna 1856, *Hutom Penchar Naksha* [The Owl's Skits], Calcuta, reprint, 1992.

Sinha, Mrinalini 1989, 'The Age of Consent Act: The Ideal of Masculinity and Colonial Ideology in Nineteenth Century Bengal', in *Shaping Bengali Worlds: Public and Private*, edited by Tony Stewart, East Lansing, MI: Asian Studies Center.

Sinha, Mrinalini 1995, *Colonial Masculinity: The 'Manly Englishman' and the 'Effeminate Bengali' in the Late Nineteenth Century*, Manchester: Manchester University Press.

Sivanandan, A. 1982, *A Different Hunger: Writings on Black Resistance*, London: Pluto Press.

Skeldon, Ronald (ed) 1995, *Emigration from Hong Kong: Tendencies and Impacts*, Hong Kong: Chinese University Press.

Smith, Barbara, Gloria T. Hull, and Patricia Bell-Scott (eds.) 1982, *All the Women are White, All the Blacks are Men, But Some of Us are Brave*, New York: The Feminist Press.

Smith, Dorothy E. 1987, *The Everyday World as Problematic*, Toronto: University of Toronto Press.

Smith, Dorothy E. 1989, 'Feminist Reflections on Political Economy', *Studies in Political Economy*, 30, 1: 37–59.

Smith, Dorothy E. 1990, *Conceptual Practices of Power: A Feminist Sociology of Knowledge*, Toronto: University of Toronto Press.

Smith, Dorothy E. 1999, *Writing the Social: Critique, Theory, and Investigations*, Toronto: University of Toronto Press.

Smith, Dorothy E. 2015, 'Ideology, Science, and Social Relations: A Reinterpretation of Marx's Epistemology', in *Educating from Marx: Race, Gender and Learning*, edited by S. Carpenter and S. Mojab, New York: Palgrave Macmillan.

Soudamini, Kumari 1872, 'Lajja' [Modesty], *Bamabodhini Patrika*, 95 (7) (B.S. Ashad 1278).

Spelman, Elizabeth 1988, *Inessential Woman: Problems of Exclusion in Feminist Thought*. Boston: Beacon Press.

Spivak, G. Chakravorty 1988a, 'Subaltern Studies: Deconstructing Historiography', in *Selected Subaltern Studies*, edited by Ranajit Guha and G. Chakravorty Spivak, New York: Oxford University Press.

Spivak, G. Chakravorty 1988b, 'Can the Subaltern Speak?' in *Marxism and the Interpretations of Culture*, edited by C. Nelson and L. Grossberg, Urbana: University of Illinois Press.

Sri Bhaggiyadatta, Krisantha 1981, *Domestic Bliss*, Toronto: Five Press.

Sri Bhaggiyadatta, Krisantha 1993, *The 52nd State of Amnesia*, Toronto: TSAR.

Steedman, C. 1996, *Childhood, Culture and Class in Britain: Margaret McMillan, 1860–1931*, New Brunswick, NJ: Rutgers University Press.

Stephens, Julie 1989, 'Feminist Fictions: A Critique of the Category of 'Non-Western Woman' in Feminist Writings in India', in *Subaltern Studies VI*, edited by Ranajit Guha, Delhi: Oxford University Press.

Stokes, Eric 1969, *The English Utilitarians and India*, Oxford: Oxford University Press.

Stoler, Ann Laura 1989 'Rethinking Colonial Categories: European Communities and the Boundaries of Rule', *Comparative Studies in Society and History*, 31,1: 134–61.

Stoler, Ann Laura 1995, *Race and the Education of Desire: Foucault's History of Sexuality and the Colonial Order of Things*, Durham: Duke University Press.

Submissions of the Claiment 'X', prepared by the office of Comish and Associates, on behalf of the worker, to the Workers' Compensation Board, Claim #B15878672T.

Sudbury, Julia 1998, *'Other Kinds of Dreams': Black Women's Organisations and the Politics of Transformation*. London and New York, Routledge.

Tagore, Rabindranath 1930, 'The Religion of Man', in *The English Writings of Rabindranath Tagore*, Oxford: Hibbert Lectures.

Tagore, Rabindranath 1961, *Samabayniti* [The ethics/laws of cooperation], in *Rabindra Rachanabali* [Collected works], Centenary Edition, Volume 13, Kolkata: West Bengal Government.

Tagore, Rabindranath 1961, *Kalantar* [Changing Times], Volume 13, in *Rabindra Rachanabali* [Collected works], Centenary Edition, Volume 13, Kolkata: West Bengal Government.

Tagore, Rabindranath 1987 [1910], *Gora* [Gora], Volume 3, in *Rabindra Rachanabali*, Kolkata: Visva-Bharati Sulabh Sanskaran (1393).

Tagore, Rabindranath 1997, *Selected Letters of Rabindranath Tagore (Bengali and English)*, edited by K. Dutta and A. Robinson, Forward by A. Sen, Cambridge: Cambridge University Press.

Tagore, Rabindranath 2005, 'What is Art?' in *Arts and Aesthetics: A Selection of Lectures, Essays and Letters*, edited by Pritish Neogy, Kolkata: Subarnarekha.

Taussig, Michael 1992, 'Culture of Terror – Space of Death: Roger Casement's Putamayo Report and the Explanation of Torture' in *Colonialism and Culture*, edited by Nicholas Dirks, Ann Arbor: University of Michigan Press.

Taylor, Charles 1992, *Multiculturalism and the Politics of Recognition*, Princeton: Princeton University Press.

Taylor, Charles 1993, *Reconciling the Solitudes: Essays on Canadian Federalism and Nationalism*, Montreal: McGill-Queen's University Press.

Terkel, Studs 1992, *Race: How Blacks and Whites Think and Feel about the American Obsession*. New York: New Press.

Tester, Frank and Peter Kulchyski 1994, *Relocation in the Eastern Arctic*, Vancouver: University of British Columbia Press.

Thakur, Rabindranath 1961, 'Jibansmriti' in *Rabindra Rachanabali* [Collected Works of Rabindranath], Volume 10.

Thakur, Rabindranath 1977, *Sahaj Path*, Part I, Volume 13.

Thakur, Tekshand 1841, *Alaler Gharer Dulal* [Spoilt Darling of the Worthless Rich], Calcutta.

Thapar, Ramila 1993a, *Interpreting Early India*. Delhi: Oxford University Press.

Thapar, Ramila 1993b, 'Durkheim and Weber on Theories of Society and Race Relating to Pre-Colonial India', in *Interpreting Early India*, Delhi: Oxford University Press.

Thapar, Ramila 1993c, 'Imagined Religious Communities? Ancient History and the Modern Search for a Hindu Identity', in *Interpreting Early India*. Delhi: Oxford University Press.

Thapar, Suruchi 1993, 'Women as Activists, Women as Symbols: A Study of the Indian Nationalist Movement', *Feminist Review* 44: 81.

Tharu, Susie, and K. Lalita. 1993. 'Introduction', in *Women Writing in India*, edited by Susie Tharu and K. Lalita, New York: The Feminist Press.

Thomas, Peter 2009, 'Gramsci and the Political: From the State as 'Metaphysical Event' to Hegemony as 'Philosophical Fact'', *Radical Philosophy*, 153: 27–36.

Thompson, Edward P. 1974, *The Making of the English Working Class*. Harmondsworth: Penguin Books.

Thompson, Edward P. 1978, *The Poverty of Theory and Other Essays*, New York and London: Monthly Review Press.

Trudeau, Pierre 1968, *Federalism and the French Canadians*, trans. Patricia Claxton, Toronto: MacMillan.

Turner, Bryan 1978, *Marx and the End of Orientalism*. London: Allen & Unwin.

Turner, Bryan 1990, 'Outline of a Theory on Citizenship', *Sociology* 24, 2: 189–218.

Vanaik, Achin 1997, *Communalism Contested: Religion, Modernity and Secularisation*, New Delhi: Vistar.

Viswesaran, Kamala 1996, 'Small Speeches, Subaltern Gender: Nationalist Ideology and Its Historiography'. In *Subaltern Studies IX*, edited by Shahid Amin and Dipesh Chakrabarty, Delhi: Oxford University Press.

Visvanathan, Gauri 1989, *The Masks of Conquest: Literary Study and British Rule*, New York: Columbia University Press.

Volpp, Leti 1994, 'Misidentifying Culture: Asian Women and the Cultural Defense', *Harvard Women's Law Journal* 17: 57–101.

wa Thiong'o, Ngugi 1983, *Homecoming: Essays on African and Caribbean Literature, Culture and Politics*. New York: Lawrence Hill Books.

Walkowitz, Judith R. 1980, *Prostitution in Victorian Society: Women, Class and the State*, Cambridge: Cambridge University Press.

Walkowitz, Judith R. 1992, *City of Dreadful Delight: Narratives of Sexual Danger in Late Victorian London*, Chicago: University of Chicago Press.

Wallace, Michelle 1994, 'The Search for the 'Good Enough' Mammy: Multiculturalism, Popular Culture and Psychoanalysis', in *Multiculturalism: A Critical Reader*, edited by Theo Goldberg, Oxford: Blackwell.

Ward, William Peter 1978, *White Canada Forever*, Montreal: McGill-Queen's University Press.

Ware, Vron 1992, *Beyond the Pale: White Women, Racism and History*. London: Verso.

Weber, Max 2002 [1905], *The Protestant Ethic and the Spirit of Capitalism*. Los Angeles: Roxbury Publishing.

Whitehead, Judith 1995, 'Modernising the motherhood archetype: Public health models and the Child Marriage Restraint Act of 1929', *Contributions to Indian Sociology* 29, 1–2: 187–209.

Whitehead, Judith 2010, *Development and Dispossession in the Narmada Valley*, Delhi: Longman.

Williams, Raymond 1977, *Marxism and Literature*, Oxford: Oxford University Press.

Williams, Raymond 1980, *Problems in Materialism and Culture*, London: Verso.

Williams, Raymond 1983, *Keywords*, London: Flamingo.

Wolf, Eric 1982, *Europe and the People Without History*, Berkeley: University of California Press.

Wong, Lloyd 1997, 'Globalisation and Transnational Migration: A Study of Recent Chinese Capitalist Migration from the Asian Pacific to Canada', *International Sociology* 12, 3: 329–51.

Wood, Ellen Meiksins 1986, *The Retreat from Class: A New True Socialism?* London: Verso.

Yuval-Davis, N. 1997, *Gender and Nation*, London: Sage.

Zafar, F. (ed) 1991, *Finding Our Way: Readings on Women in Pakistan*, Lahore: ASR.

Index